COST ACCOUNTING
A Managerial Emphasis

PRENTICE-HALL, INC., ENGLEWOOD CLIFFS, NEW JERSEY

COST
ACCOUNTING
A Managerial Emphasis

CHARLES T. HORNGREN
Ph.D., C.P.A.
Stanford University

THIRD EDITION

Library of Congress Cataloging in Publication Data

Horngren, Charles T
    Cost accounting.

    "List of N. A. A. [National Association of
Accountants] research publications": p.
    Includes bibliographical references.
    1. Cost accounting.   2. Costs, Industrial.
I. Title.
HF5686.C8H59 1972   658.1'51   78-37392
ISBN 0-13-180034-5

Printed in the United States of America

10 9 8 7 6 5 4 3

PRENTICE-HALL INTERNATIONAL, Inc., London
PRENTICE-HALL OF AUSTRALIA Pty. Ltd., Sydney
PRENTICE-HALL OF CANADA, Ltd., Toronto
PRENTICE-HALL OF INDIA (Private) Ltd., New Delhi
PRENTICE-HALL OF JAPAN, Inc., Tokyo

To Professor William J. Vatter

Contents

SECTION TWO
MULTIPLE PURPOSE SYSTEMS FOR MANAGEMENT CONTROL

gets; Human aspect. TYPES OF BUDGETS: Time coverage; Classification of budgets. ILLUSTRATION OF MASTER BUDGET: Basic data and requirements; Basic approach to formulating master budget. SALES FORECASTING—A DIFFI-CULT TASK: Factors in sales forecasting; Forcasting procedures. SUMMARY. SUGGESTED READINGS. PROBLEM FOR SELF-STUDY. APPENDIX: INSTALL-ING AND ADMINISTERING THE BUDGET: Budgeting and the accounting sys-tem; Budget director; Budget committee; Budget manual; Follow-up is impor-tant. QUESTIONS, PROBLEMS, AND CASES.

6   Systems Design, Responsibility Accounting, and Motivation   153

GOAL SETTING AND SYSTEMS DESIGN: Focus of design must be on objec-tives; Characteristics of management accounting systems; Goal congruence; The need for multiple goals; Human resources accounting. RESPONSIBILITY ACCOUNTING: Systems and organization changes; Definition of responsibility accounting; Illustration of responsibility accounting; Format of feedback reports; Cooperation versus competition. CONTROLLABLE AND UNCONTROLLABLE COSTS: Definition of controllable costs; Determining controllability or responsi-bility; Reporting controllable and uncontrollable items; The time period and con-trol. EFFECT OF SYSTEMS ON HUMAN BEHAVIOR: Administration of the sys-tem; Our knowledge of behavioral effects; Participation in budgeting; System goals and personal goals; Slack: a universal behavioral problem; Importance of formal systems; Accurate scorekeeping; Intelligent analysis of relevant data; SUMMARY. SUGGESTED READINGS. PROBLEM FOR SELF-STUDY. QUES-TIONS, PROBLEMS, AND CASES.

7   Standard Costs: Direct Material and Direct Labor   186

EFFECTIVENESS AND EFFICIENCY. STANDARD COSTS AS MANAGEMENT AIDS: Nature of standards; Types of standards; Distinction between budgets and standards; Responsibility for developing standards; Analysis of variances: general approach; How output is expressed; Pinpointing responsibility; Trade-offs among variances; Physical standards and improvement of operations; Converting physi-cal standards into dollars. MATERIAL-PRICE STANDARDS: Basis for material-price standards; Who sets material-price standards? MATERIAL-QUANTITY STANDARDS: Nature of quantity standards; Setting quantity standards; Control of usage. GENERAL-LEDGER ENTRIES FOR MATERIAL: Two ways of reflecting variances; Comparison of cases 1 and 2; Columnar format: an important analyt-ical technique. LABOR-RATE STANDARDS. LABOR-EFFICIENCY STANDARDS: General characteristics; Setup time. GENERAL-LEDGER ENTRIES FOR DIRECT LABOR: Example of analysis of direct labor variances. ANALYSIS OF VARIANCES: Types of variances; When to investigate variance; Timing and aggregation. LEARNING CURVES AND ACCOUNTING: Effects of learning on productivity; Setting budgets or standards. SUMMARY. PROBLEMS FOR SELF-STUDY. QUES-TIONS, PROBLEMS, AND CASES.

decision making; Relevance as defined here. ILLUSTRATION OF RELEVANCE: CHOOSING ACTIVITY LEVELS: The special order; Fixed expenses and unit costs; Short run and long run; Qualitative factors; Reports for decision making. CONTRIBUTION APPROACH TO PRICING: Superiority of the contribution approach; The contribution approach or absorption costing? Need for clear information; The Robinson-Patman Act. OTHER ILLUSTRATIONS OF RELEVANCE AND THE CONTRIBUTION APPROACH: Dropping a product line; Contribution per unit of constraining factor; Make or buy and idle facilities; Essence of make or buy: utilization of facilities; Policy making for make or buy; Beware of unit costs. IRRELEVANCE OF PAST COSTS: Obsolete inventory; Regular inventory; Opportunity cost; Book value of old equipment; Examining alternatives over the long run. THE PROBLEM OF UNCERTAINTY. SUMMARY. PROBLEM FOR SELF-STUDY. APPENDIX A: COST TERMS USED FOR DIFFERENT PURPOSES. APPENDIX B: COST-PLUS FOR SETTING PRICES: Major influences on pricing; Example of contribution approach to pricing. QUESTIONS, PROBLEMS, AND CASES.

SECTION THREE
SPECIAL TOPICS FOR FURTHER STUDY

THE INTERDEPENDENT ASPECTS OF COST ALLOCATION: Three facets to cost allocation; Direct and indirect costs; Practicability and the cost object; Search for relationships; Choices of cost objects. THE CONTRIBUTION APPROACH TO COST ALLOCATION: Stress on cost behavior patterns; Revenues, variable costs, and contribution margins; Unallocated costs; Contribution controllable by division managers; Contribution by segments and income before income taxes; Reports by product lines and territories; Relating fixed costs to pricing decisions. CHOOSING AMONG VARIOUS COST-ALLOCATION BASES: Physical identification; Services used and facilities provided: the case of service departments; Beware of full reallocation of actual costs; How to allocate for planning and control; Benefits received; Ability to bear; Fairness or equity. COST POOLS AND HOMOGENEITY: Nature of homogeneity; Plant-wide rate versus departmental rates; Factors affecting homogeneity; Intermediate aggregations; Different bases for different departments. DIFFERENT ALLOCATION BASES FOR OVERHEAD APPLICATION TO PRODUCT: Physical units produced; Direct-labor hours; Machine-hours; Direct-labor cost; Direct materials; Comparison of bases. SERVICE DEPARTMENTS AND PRODUCT COSTING: Dual rates for reallocation; Need for tracing service-department costs to products; Direct reallocation—Method 1; Step method—Method 2; Arbitrary rules; Further illustration of reallocation; Computation techniques; Setting department overhead rates for product costing. RECIPROCAL SERVICES: MOTIVATION AND PARTIAL OR FULL ALLOCATION. SUMMARY. PROBLEMS FOR SELF-STUDY. QUESTIONS, PROBLEMS, AND CASES.

order quantity; Production runs; Quantity discounts. SAFETY STOCKS: When to order? Minimum inventory: safety allowance for fluctuations in demand; Computation of safety stock; Constant order-cycle system; Inventory turnover. SUMMARY OF OPTIMUM INVESTMENT IN INVENTORIES. THE MECHANICS OF THE SYSTEM: Fixing responsibility; Internal check; Purchase records; Factory usage. INVENTORY-VALUATION METHODS: Purpose of discussion of inventory methods; The question of timing; LIFO versus FIFO. SUMMARY. PROBLEMS FOR SELF-STUDY. QUESTIONS, PROBLEMS, AND CASES.

16   Joint-Product Costs and By-Product Costs   569

METHODS OF ASSIGNING JOINT COSTS TO PRODUCTS: Nature of joint-product cost; Physical measures; Relative-sales-value approach; Costs beyond split-off; Costing joint products at realizable values. IRRELEVANCE OF JOINT COSTS IN DECISION MAKING. ACCOUNTING FOR BY-PRODUCTS: Problems of definition; Accounting methods for by-products; Comparison of methods. SUMMARY. PROBLEM FOR SELF-STUDY. QUESTIONS, PROBLEMS, AND CASES.

17   Process Costing: A Type of Product Costing   596

GENERAL CHARACTERISTICS OF PROCESS COSTING: All product costing is averaging; Equivalent units: the key; Five basic steps to solution; Using the five steps; Beginning inventories. WEIGHTED AVERAGE METHOD: Description; Interdepartmental transfers; Journal entries and transfers; Alternative formats and techniques. FIRST-IN, FIRST-OUT: Illustration of FIFO; Effect of transfers: modification of FIFO; Alternative formats and techniques; Comparison of weighted-average and FIFO; Pitfalls to avoid in working problems. STANDARD COSTS AND PROCESS COSTS: Standards are useful; Computations under standard costing. ADDITIONAL ASPECTS OF PROCESS COSTING: Estimating degree of completion; Overhead and predetermined rates; Overhead and cost flow. SUMMARY. PROBLEMS FOR SELF-STUDY. QUESTIONS, PROBLEMS, AND CASES.

18   Spoilage, Waste, Defective Units, and Scrap   620

TERMINOLOGY. SPOILAGE IN GENERAL: Management implications and factor combination; Normal spoilage; Abnormal spoilage; General accounting procedures for spoilage. JOB COSTING AND SPOILAGE: Spoiled units sold for salvage: treatment in practice. DEFECTIVE UNITS. ACCOUNTING FOR SCRAP. COMPARISON OF ACCOUNTING FOR SPOILAGE, DEFECTIVE WORK, AND SCRAP. SOME APPLICATIONS TO STANDARD COSTS: Shrinkage and waste; Scrap; Spoilage. PROCESS-COST ACCOUNTING PROCEDURES AND SPOILAGE: Distinguish between normal and abnormal spoilage; Base for computing normal spoilage; Weighted-average process costing and spoilage; FIFO PROCESS COSTING AND SPOILAGE: Interim fluctuations in spoilage rates. SUMMARY. PROBLEMS FOR SELF-STUDY. QUESTIONS, PROBLEMS, AND CASES.

OF CONTROL CHART: The basic data; Standard deviation and control limits; Plotting; Observations out of control. STATISTICAL MEAN AND STANDARDS. ENGINEERING TOLERANCE LIMITS. SETTING CONTROL LIMITS. SUMMARY. SUGGESTED READINGS. PROBLEMS FOR SELF-STUDY. QUESTIONS, PROBLEMS, AND CASES.

SECTION FOUR
APPENDIXES

Preface

Cost accounting provides data for three major objectives of the firm: (1) planning and controlling routine operations; (2) nonroutine decisions, policy making, and long-range planning; and (3) inventory valuation and income determination. This volume gives abundant consideration to all three of these, but emphasis is placed on the first two. In short, the major theme is "different costs for different purposes."

The topics emphasized from the outset are those that challenge the student and spur his curiosity. Because the emphasis is on costs for planning and control, the following topics of prime managerial significance are introduced early: the role of the accountant in the organization; cost behavior and volume-profit relationships; responsibility accounting; standard costs; flexible budgets; cost structures for control and motivation; and relevant costs of nonroutine decisions. The favorable reaction to the format of previous editions is evidence that cost accounting courses can be enriched, relieved of drudgery, and broadened from coverage of procedures alone to a full-fledged treatment of concepts, analyses, and procedures that pays more than lip-service to accounting as a managerial tool.

This flexible treatment of cost accounting and management accounting presupposes just a one-term introduction to basic accounting. Ample material is provided for a two-semester or two-quarter course, especially if it is supplemented with outside readings. The need for supplementation may be diminished with this edition because it has more substance (especially in the latter half) than previously. The first eleven chapters provide the essence of a one-term course. Because instructors may disagree about what constitutes a proper sequence, this book has been designed to permit a maximum degree of flexibility with a minimum of discontinuity.

Cost accounting courses now cover a wider range of topics than ever. Some instructors prefer to concentrate on developing a solid comprehension of the uses and limitations of formal cost accounting systems as they exist. Others prefer a normative approach, focusing on how cost systems should be designed —or on how cost information should be provided for various classes of decisions. This book attempts to satisfy both needs: the order of chapters provided is only one of many possible sequences.

A major objective of this revision has been to promote flexibility by using a modular approach. The material has been arranged to allow instructors—who are working with students having different backgrounds and within curricula having various overlaps—the greatest latitude in picking and choosing chapters. For example, if the courses in finance emphasize cash budgeting and capital budgeting, Chapters 5, 13, and 14 might be omitted. If the instructor wishes to cover product costing systems in depth, Chapters 17 and 18 on process costing (except for the portions on standard costing) and Chapter 19 on payroll accounting might be assigned immediately after Chapter 4 on job order costing. The standard costing in Chapters 17 and 18 might then be assigned immediately after Chapter 9.

As in previous editions, there is an abundant supply of assignment materials. The variety of problems provides a wide choice both in subject matter and range of difficulty. The need for pertinent, well-edited homework material has received extensive attention and continues to be a key element in this book's preparation.

CHANGES IN THIS EDITION

In this edition changes have been made in both content and organization. Most chapters have been thoroughly rewritten. In addition, many new problems and cases have been provided. Major changes include:

1. Cost-volume-profit analysis for multiple products has been added to Chapter 3.

2. Chapter 6 is a thoroughly revised version of former Chapter 9 (on responsibility accounting and motivation). As a result, Chapters 6, 7, 8 from the previous edition become Chapters 7, 8, 9 in this one.

3. The introduction to standard costs (Chapter 7) gives more attention to learning curves. The proration of variances is now in Chapter 10.

4. Chapter 8 on flexible budgets includes material on work measurement, which had been in Chapter 12 (nonmanufacturing costs).

5. Chapter 10, which formerly covered the contribution approach to performance measurement and inventory valuation (direct costing), now focuses

on the effects on income of alternative product costing methods: direct cost-ing, the choice of an activity base in absorption costing, and the proration of variances.

6. Chapter 11 is a revision of former Chapter 13 on relevant cost analy-sis. It includes pricing decisions, which had been in Chapter 10.

7. The cost allocation chapter (formerly Chapter 17) has been completely reworked and moved up to become Chapter 12. It includes the contribution approach, which had been in Chapter 10. The material previously covered in Chapter 12 (nonmanufacturing costs) has been incorporated in the new Chap-ter 12 and elsewhere. For example, the topic of work measurement is now in Chapter 8.

9. Chapters 15 (inventory control), 16 (joint costs), 17 and 18 (process costs), 19 (payroll), and 20 (internal control) are revisions of Chapters 16, 18, 19, 20, 24 and 22, respectively.

10. Chapters 21 and 22 are entirely new. They cover decentralization, divisional performance measurement, and transfer pricing. They replace the former Chapter 11.

11. Chapter 23 (formerly Chapter 26) is a thoroughly rewritten treatment of decision theory and uncertainty.

12. Chapter 24 is also entirely new. It examines the difficulties of esti-mating cost functions and covers regression analysis.

13. Chapter 25 is a revision of former Chapter 27 on statistical methods. It contains a new section on when to investigate variances.

14. Chapter 26 is a revision of former Chapter 21 (mix variances). It takes a different position on the issues than was contained in the previous edition.

15. Chapter 27 was previously Chapter 28 (operations research). It pro-vides many new problems that apply quantitative approaches to cost account-ing decisions.

16. Chapter 28 is former Chapter 25 (cost accounting in the CPA ex-amination). It has been updated to reflect the increasing coverage of quantita-tive methods in the examination.

17. As with previous editions the problems are designed to stress key points. Many new ones have been added; for instance consider problems 2-22, 3-22, 3-25, 3-26, 6-32 through 6-36, 7-29, 7-30, 8-19, 8-21, 8-27, 9-24, 10-26, 10-27, 11-23, 12-16, 12-24, 12-29, 14-16, 14-18, and 15-28. Others are apparent for each chapter.

The placement of Chapter 6 (responsibility accounting and motivation) was a particularly troublesome decision. This chapter provides a perspective on management control systems. It is debatable whether it is most advantageous to provide this perspective before the details in Chapter 7 through 9; therefore, the instructor may choose to cover Chapters 7, 8, and 9 before 6. Another alternative might be to cover the chapters in the order presented but assign one problem from Chapter 6 with each succeeding assignment from Chapter 7 through 9.

Another consideration in preparing this revision was the extent to which a quantitative approach should be included. If more quantitative material is added, should it be interwoven with appropriate topics or considered separately? The choice was to add more quantitative material but to confine it to Chapters 23–27, again because it allows maximum flexibility. Those instructors wanting to integrate such material with earlier chapters may do so; suggestions as to how are provided in the solutions manual. Those who prefer to concentrate on other matters will not be hampered by the necessity to omit portions of chapters.

ACKNOWLEDGMENTS

I am indebted to many for ideas and assistance. The acknowledgments in the two previous editions contain a long list of my creditors. My primary obligation is to Professor William J. Vatter (California, Berkeley) to whom this book is dedicated. For those who know him, no words are necessary; for those who do not know him, no words will suffice.

Professor Dudley W. Curry (Southern Methodist) has aided me immensely with his detailed review of the manuscript of this edition. Moreover, he has prepared the quiz and examination material included in the solutions and a student's study guide that is available as supplementary material. The reviews by Joel S. Demski (Stanford) and Joshua Ronen (Chicago) have also been significantly helpful.

The following professors made extensive comments about the previous edition that heavily influenced this one: James R. Adler (New York); Lawrence Benninger (Florida); William F. Crum (Southern California); David Green (Chicago); Robert E. Hamilton (Southern California); Robert W. Koehler (Pennsylvania State); George I. Prater (Washington); Louis I. Rosen (Maryland); E. J. Schmidlein, Jr. (Southern Illinois); Elliott Slocum (Georgia State); John B. Sperry (Virginia Commonwealth); Clyde P. Stickney, Jr. (Chicago); Richard Strayer (San Fernando Valley); Gary Sundem (Washington); and Cecilia Tierney (Washington State). In addition, I have received helpful suggestions by mail from many users, too numerous to mention here.

Many students have read the manuscript and worked the new problems to insure that they are as error free as possible. They have also contributed ideas and material for revising chapters and preparing new problems. Particular thanks go to Melvin Arditi, Warren O'Buch, Walden W. O'Dell, Larry Lookabill, and Robert McCaskill.

A special note of gratitude is extended to Cristina Faragher for her skillful typing of many chapters in syllabus form.

Also, I thank the people at Prentice-Hall: Frederic K. Easter, Garret White, Marvin Warshaw, Jim Bacci, and Barbara Cassel.

Appreciation also goes to the American Institute of Certified Public Accountants, The National Association of Accountants, the Society of Industrial Accountants of Canada, the Certified General Accountants' Association of Canada, the Financial Executives Institute of America, and to many other publishers and companies for their generous permission to quote from their publications. Problems from the Uniform CPA Examinations are designated (CPA); problems from the Canadian examinations administered by the Society of Industrial Accountants are designated (SIA); problems from the Certified General Accountants' Association are designated (CGAA). Many of these problems are adapted to highlight particular points.

Comments from users are welcome.

CHARLES T. HORNGREN

COST ACCOUNTING
A Managerial Emphasis

SECTION
ONE

COST ACCOUNTING
FUNDAMENTALS

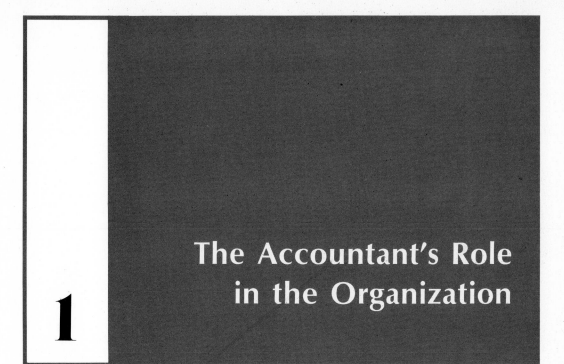

The Accountant's Role in the Organization

1

As this chapter is being written, former accountants are the top executives in many large companies, including Chrysler, International Telephone and Telegraph, and General Electric. Accounting duties played a key part in their rise to the management summit. Accounting cuts across all facets of the organization; the management accountant's duties are intertwined with executive planning and control.

The study of modern cost accounting yields insight and breadth regarding both the accountant's role and the manager's role in an organization. How are these two roles related? Where may they overlap? How can accounting help managers? This book tries to answer these questions. In this chapter, we[1] shall try to get some perspective on where the accountant should fit in the organization. Then we shall have a framework for studying the rest of the chapters.

PURPOSES OF MANAGEMENT ACCOUNTING, FINANCIAL ACCOUNTING, AND COST ACCOUNTING

The accounting system is the major quantitative information system in almost every organization. It should provide information for three broad purposes:

1. Internal reporting to managers, for use in planning and controlling routine operations

[1]Should an author use "I," "we," "the author," or "this writer" in contexts such as these? Each mode of expression has its weaknesses, but I prefer "we." As used in this book, "we" denotes a mutual exploration of the subject by the author and the readers.

2. Internal reporting to managers, for use in making nonroutine decisions and in formulating major plans and policies
3. External reporting to stockholders, government, and other outside parties

Both management and external parties share an interest in all three important purposes, but the emphases of financial accounting and management (internal) accounting differ. Financial accounting is mainly concerned with the historical, custodial, and stewardship aspects of external reporting. The distinguishing feature of management accounting—of accounting for planning and control—is its emphasis on the first and second purposes.

Where does "cost accounting" fit within the above framework? In its broadest sense, cost accounting has three major purposes, which parallel the three purposes above; in fact, its first and second purposes are identical to the first and second above. Its third purpose, costing products for inventory valuation and income determination, simultaneously fulfills the demands of outsiders and those of management for such information. So, when viewed in this way, cost accounting *is* management accounting, plus a small part of financial accounting—to the extent that its product-costing function satisfies the requisites of external reporting.

Originally, the label *cost accounting* referred to the ways of accumulating and assigning historical costs to units of product and departments, primarily for purposes of inventory valuation and income determination. Today, cost accounting is generally indistinguishable from so-called *management accounting* or *internal accounting,* because it serves multiple purposes. Most fundamentally, cost accounting now refers to the gathering and providing of information for decision needs of all sorts, ranging from the management of recurring operations to the making of nonrecurring strategic decisions and the formulation of major organizational policies. As in the past, cost accounting also helps fulfill the legal requirements of reporting to stockholders, creditors, government agencies, and other external parties.

We need not be greatly concerned with the boundaries of cost accounting. The major point is that the focus of a modern cost-accounting system is on helping managers deal with both the immediate and the distant future. Its concern with the past is justified only insofar as it helps prediction and satisfies external reporting requirements.

ACCOUNTING AND DECISIONS

the decision process Accounting information is supplied to assist the manager in his making of decisions. The essence of the management process is decision making, the purposeful choosing from among a set of alternative courses of action in light of some objective. These decisions range from the nonroutine (launching a new product line) to the routine (whether to schedule a job on machine number one or two).

The manager needs a method for choosing among different courses of action. This method is frequently called a *decision model,* and it provides a conceptual representation that enables the manager to measure the effects of alternative actions. As Chapter 23 explains in more detail, the particular objectives and decision models in use may have a dramatic effect on a manager's decision. For example, if a manager were told to maximize net income as measured by a typical accrual accounting model, his decisions might be quite different from those he would make if he were instructed to maximize net cash inflow as measured by a typical statement of cash receipts and disbursements.

mgmt control

planning
and control
defined

There are countless definitions of planning and control. For our purposes, we define *planning* as the selection of objectives and their means of attainment. Therefore, planning includes a delineation of goals and a choice of a decision model (decision method) for selecting means of achieving them. *Control* is the implementation of a decision model and the use of feedback so that objectives are optimally obtained. This definition of control is comprehensive and flexible. It is concerned with the successful *implementation* of a course of action as predetermined by a decision model; but it is also concerned with *feedback* that might (a) change the future plans given the model, and (b) possibly change the decision model itself or change the prediction method that provides input to the decision model.

For example, if a cost-budget model is used for making a production-scheduling decision, feedback might reveal a difference between the expected and the actual procedures used in a production operation. This information (a) may prompt a change in future plans to see that the given model, which incorporated a set of operating procedures, is better implemented; or (b) if the actual procedures represent improvements, may prompt a reformulation so that a different cost-budget model is constructed. Therefore, feedback can affect both the decision model and the implementation.

two important
phases:
decision
analysis and
implementation

Exhibit 1-1 shows how the prediction method and the decision model are used to help a manager analyze and make a choice. The management process has two important but interdependent phases:

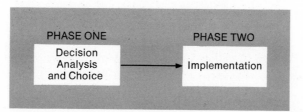

The first phase (steps 1 through 4 in Exhibit 1-1) is decision analysis and choice, which predominantly uses the tools and assumptions of economics to focus on the optimum allocation of the organization's scarce resources. The second phase is implementation of the solutions chosen in step 4, which uses a variety of human and other means to assure that the choices are achieved. If there are no particular difficulties apparent in implementation, the decision can be implemented easily. If there are serious difficulties in implementation, either the choice is altered or implementation is altered—via education of personnel, management persuasion, or other feasible means. In short, the feedback of the results may indicate that the assumptions of the prediction methods and decision models need correction for one or more of many reasons, including the difficulties of human motivation.

EXHIBIT 1-1
RELATIONSHIP OF ACCOUNTING INFORMATION
AND THE DECISION PROCESS

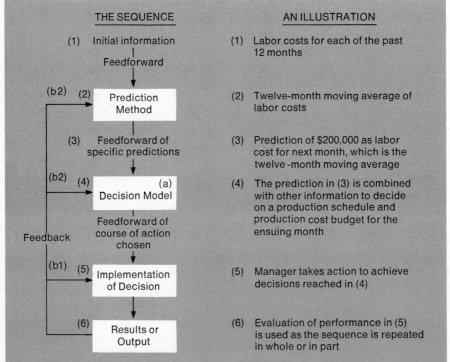

THE SEQUENCE	AN ILLUSTRATION
(1) Initial information Feedforward	(1) Labor costs for each of the past 12 months
(b2) (2) Prediction Method	(2) Twelve-month moving average of labor costs
(3) Feedforward of specific predictions	(3) Prediction of $200,000 as labor cost for next month, which is the twelve-month moving average
(b2) (4) (a) Decision Model	(4) The prediction in (3) is combined with other information to decide on a production schedule and production cost budget for the ensuing month
Feedforward of course of action chosen	
Feedback	
(b1) (5) Implementation of Decision	(5) Manager takes action to achieve decisions reached in (4)
(6) Results or Output	(6) Evaluation of performance in (5) is used as the sequence is repeated in whole or in part

(a) The decision model includes a specification of the objective function (e.g., maximize net income, minimize production costs) and of the interrelationships of the relevant variables. See Chapter 23 for an expanded discussion.
(b) Feedback might result in
  (1) Changes in implementation, given the models.
  (2) Changes in either the prediction method, the decision model, or both.
    For example, perhaps a twelve-month moving average is a poor prediction method that needs replacement.

cost and value of information

Although decision analysis and implementation may be separated for analytical purposes, in practice they are interwoven, so that managers often foresee behavioral implications and temper their choices beforehand to make them workable. The accountant and the manager must be concerned with both analysis and implementation as a unified whole. For example, a manager may wish to install an elaborate computerized inventory control system at the retail level. There may be no doubt in his mind that with the help of this system he could make more profitable decisions regarding the timing, variety, and amounts of inventory purchases. Nevertheless, he may reject the system because its prospective value (benefits) is exceeded by the measurable and unmeasurable costs of implementation, including the costs of educating personnel and of operating a more elaborate system. Sometimes these costs are hard to pinpoint; for instance, the extra time taken by clerks for record keeping may exceed the patience of customers and result in the loss of some sales.

Managers and accountants must repeatedly make decisions about whether a change in an accounting system is worth undertaking. They must compare the expected cost and expected value of information to see whether the change is economically feasible (justifiable). Often, the "value" of the information is measured by the expected savings or extra income that might be generated by using an improved accounting system or a more elaborate decision model (step 4 in Exhibit 1-1). But the cost of the information is usually measured in the implementation phase (step 5 in Exhibit 1-1). Again, this illustrates why decision analysis and implementation must be considered simultaneously. Unless implementation is explicitly considered, the accountant and the manager will have an incomplete picture of the scope of the management process and its accompanying accounting-information system.

accounting information and the decision process

To recapitulate, although at first glance it may appear awesome, Exhibit 1-1 is a simplified description of the role of information in the decision-making and implementation processes.[2] As viewed here, the control process monitors the implementation of decisions; in addition, the control process monitors the performance of the decision model and the prediction method chosen by the decision maker. The focus is on the total decision process and the identification of the points in the process that need monitoring.

The relationships in Exhibit 1-1 illustrate the interactive, interdependent nature of the decision-making and implementation processes. To reduce the likelihood of myopic blunders, these processes should be viewed in total and not as separable subparts.

---

[2] For a more rigorous conceptual analysis, see G. Feltham and J. Demski, "The Use of Models in Information Evaluation," *The Accounting Review,* XLV, No. 4.

Many of the ideas here and elsewhere in this text are studied in more theoretical depth in J. Demski, G. Feltham, C. Horngren, R. Jaedicke, and R. Sprouse, *Cost Concepts and Implementation Criteria,* tentatively scheduled for publication in 1973 by the American Institute of Certified Public Accountants.

DESIGNING ACCOUNTING SYSTEMS FOR DECISIONS

three types
of information
As a major provider of information for management decisions, the cost (management) accountant must focus on the decision-making process to determine what data are needed at various management levels. This approach was taken by a research team in a study of seven large companies.[3] The researchers identified three types of data, each serving a different purpose, often at various management levels. The data raise and help answer three basic questions:

1. *Scorecard questions:* Am I doing well or badly?
2. *Attention-directing questions:* What problems should I look into?
3. *Problem-solving questions:* Of the several ways of doing the job, which is the best?

The scorecard and attention-directing uses of data are closely related. The same data may serve a scorecard function for a foreman and an attention-directing function for his superior. For example, many accounting systems provide performance reports in which actual results are compared with previously determined budgets or standards. Such a performance report often helps to answer scorecard questions and attention-directing questions simultaneously. Furthermore, the actual results collected serve not only control purposes but also the traditional needs of financial accounting, which is chiefly concerned with the answering of scorecard questions. The collection, classification, and reporting of data are the tasks that dominate day-to-day accounting.

Problem-solving data may be used in long-range planning and in making special, nonrecurring decisions, such as whether to make or buy parts, replace equipment, add or drop a product, and so on. These decisions often require expert advice from specialists such as industrial engineers, budgetary accountants, and statisticians.

In sum, the accountant's task has three facets:

1. *Scorekeeping.* The accumulation of data. This aspect of accounting enables both internal and external parties to evaluate organizational performance and position.
2. *Attention directing.* The reporting and interpreting of information that helps managers to focus on operating problems, imperfections, inefficiencies, and opportunities. This aspect of accounting helps managers to concern themselves with important aspects of operations promptly enough for effective action, through either perceptive planning or astute day-to-day supervision. Attention directing is commonly associated with current planning and control and with the analysis and investigation of recurring, routine internal-accounting reports.
3. *Problem solving.* This aspect of accounting involves the concise quantification of the relative merits of possible courses of action, often with recommendations as to the best procedure. Problem solving is commonly associated with nonrecurring decisions—situations that require special accounting analyses or reports.

[3]H. A. Simon, H. Guetzkow, G. Kozmetsky, and G. Tyndall, *Centralization vs. Decentralization in Organizing the Controller's Department* (New York: Controllership Foundation, Inc., 1954). This perceptive study is much broader and more timeless than its title implies.

The distinctions above sometimes overlap or merge. Consequently, it is often difficult to pinpoint a particular accounting task as being scorekeeping, attention directing, or problem solving. Nevertheless, attempts to make these distinctions provide insight into the objectives and tasks of both accountants and managers.

goal congruence: the key to evaluating an accounting system The importance of the behavioral ramifications of accounting will be stressed throughout this book. Above all, management accounting systems and techniques should encourage managers to act in harmony with the overall objectives of the organization. This purpose has been called *goal congruence*, whereby goals and subgoals are specified to induce (or at least not discourage) decisions that will blend with top-management goals.

For example, four main functions of business—sales, production, purchasing, and finance—generate four views of inventories that are often in conflict. The sales manager has a natural desire to have plenty of everything on hand so that no customer is ever turned away or forced to wait because of lack of stock. The production manager likes to concentrate on continuous, single-product runs so as to spread such costs as setups, changeover, spoilage, and training over longer runs of product. The purchasing officer often prefers to buy in large quantities to take advantage of quantity discounts and lower freight costs. Sometimes he would like to outguess changing market prices and to postpone or accelerate purchases accordingly. The financial manager wants to pry loose as much inventory capital from inventory investment as is feasible so that it may be channeled into other profitable opportunities. Because of these conflicting functional objectives, any inventory-control policy must be carefully drawn if it is to benefit the business as a whole. Accounting information is essential in the formulation of such a policy.

In evaluating the accounting system for planning and control, the manager and the systems designer must begin by determining top management's objectives and model choice. Often, systems work quite well, but they induce managers toward the wrong goals. For example, many accounting systems may help overemphasize short-run profit maximization as an objective.

The point is that top management may choose wrong objective functions, such as "maximize reported earnings for next year regardless of other consequences." The systems designed to implement these objective functions should be judged in relation to how well any *given* objective function is achieved. For example, top managers may specify that earnings per share for the next year should be, say, $3, and they may use the accounting system to communicate and enforce this objective. Near the end of the year, if the earnings prospects are dim, top managers may exert immense pressure to reach the budgeted target. To reach the earnings goal, subordinates may be inclined to reduce current expenses by postponing outlays for maintenance, sales promotion, or research, even though such decisions could cripple future earning power. In short, some decisions may clearly benefit reported short-run performance but have a greater detrimental effect on future performance. We may deplore these decisions, but in this case we should deplore the choice of an objective function. Given the objective, the accounting system performed admirably as the helpmate of top management. Goal congruence was achieved; the trouble was that the goals may not have been appropriate.

THE PERVADING DUTIES OF THE MANAGEMENT ACCOUNTANT

line and staff relationships   Except for exerting line authority over his own department, the chief accounting executive generally fills a staff role in his company, as contrasted with the line roles of sales and production executives.

Most companies have the production and sale of goods as their basic objectives. Line managers are *directly* responsible for attaining these objectives as efficiently as possible. Staff elements of organizations exist because the scope of the line manager's responsibility and duties enlarges to such a degree that he needs specialized help to operate effectively. When a department's primary task is that of advice and service to other departments, it is a *staff* department.

However, because of the recent research in "organization theory," accentuated by the telling effects of digital computers on organization structures, many conflicting theories have arisen that blur the distinctions between "line" and "staff." But despite the whirling confusion, we shall find that line-staff distinctions are useful in evaluating the accountant's role in the organization.

The accounting function is usually "staff," with responsibility for providing line managers, and also other staff managers, with specialized service.[4] This includes advice and help in the areas of budgeting, controlling, pricing, and special decisions. The accounting department does not exercise direct authority over line departments. Uniformity of accounting and reporting is acquired through the delegation of authority on such matters to the controller by the top line management. Note carefully that when the controller prescribes the line department's role in supplying accounting information, he is speaking for top line management—not as the controller, a staff man. The uniform accounting procedure is authorized by the president and is installed for him by the controller.

Theoretically, the controller's decisions regarding the best accounting procedures to be followed by line people are transmitted to the president. In turn, the president communicates these procedures through a manual of instructions that comes down through the line chain of command to all people affected by the procedures.

Practically, the daily work of the controller is such that his face-to-face relationships with the production manager or foreman may call for his directing how production records should be kept or how work tickets should be com-

---

[4]Management literature is hazy on these distinctions, and we shall not belabor them here. For example, some writers distinguish among three types of authority: line, staff, and functional. Line authority is exerted downward over subordinates. Staff authority is the authority to *advise* but not command others; it is exercised laterally or upward. Functional authority is the right to *command* action laterally and downward with regard to a specific function or specialty.

pleted.[5] The controller usually holds delegated authority from top line management over such matters.

    Exhibit 1-2 shows the general organizational relationships described above. Note the distinction between producing departments and service departments. The primary purpose of a factory is to produce goods. Therefore, the production-line manufacturing departments are usually termed *producing* or *operating departments*. To facilitate production, most plants also have *service departments*, which exist to facilitate the tasks of the producing departments.

EXHIBIT 1-2

PARTIAL ORGANIZATION CHART OF A MANUFACTURING COMPANY

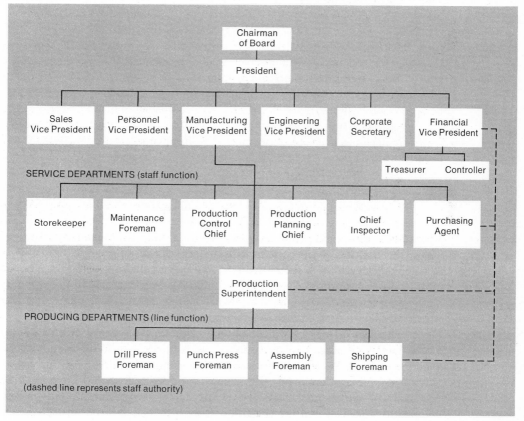

the controller: The word *controller* is applied to various accounting positions. The stature
the chief and duties of the controller vary from company to company. In some firms,
management he is little more than a glorified bookkeeper who compiles data primarily
accountant for conventional balance sheets and income statements. In other firms—for
example, General Electric—he is a key executive who aids management

[5]According to some writers, this would be exercising the *functional authority* described in the previous footnote.

planning and control in over 160 subdivisions. In most firms, he has a status somewhere between these two extremes. For example, his opinion on the tax implications of certain managerial decisions may be carefully weighed, yet his opinion on the other aspects of these decisions may not be sought. Whatever his title, he is viewed in this book as the chief management accounting executive. The point of terminology here is that the modern controller does not do any controlling in terms of line authority, except over his own department. Yet the modern concept of controllership maintains that the controller *does* control in a special sense. That is, by reporting and interpreting relevant data, the controller exerts a force or influence that impels management toward logical decisions consistent with objectives.

distinctions between controller and treasurer

Many people confuse the offices of controller and treasurer. The Financial Executives Institute, an association of corporate treasurers and controllers, distinguishes their functions as follows:

Controllership	Treasurership
1. Planning for control	1. Provision of capital
2. Reporting and interpreting	2. Investor relations
3. Evaluating and consulting	3. Short-term financing
4. Tax administration	4. Banking and custody
5. Government reporting	5. Credits and collections
6. Protection of assets	6. Investments
7. Economic appraisal	7. Insurance

Note how managerial cost accounting is the controller's primary *means* of implementing the first three functions of controllership.

We shall not dwell at length on the treasurer's functions. As the seven points indicate, he is concerned mainly with financial, as distinguished from operating, problems. The exact division of various accounting and financial duties obviously varies from company to company.

The controller has been compared to the ship's navigator. The navigator, with the help of his specialized training, assists the captain. Without the navigator, the ship may flounder on reefs or miss its destination entirely, but the captain exerts his right to command. The navigator guides and informs the captain as to how well the ship is being steered. This navigator role is especially evident in points 1 through 3 of the seven functions.

the division of accounting duties

Accountants are often placed in a dilemma because they attempt to fulfill conflicting duties simultaneously. On the one hand, they are supposed to be the helpers (interpreters and analysts) of various managers; on the other hand, they are supposed to be the policemen or watchdogs (cost accumulators and reporters) for top management. Because these roles clash, the controller's department should divorce attention directing from scorekeeping wherever feasible. Otherwise, the day-to-day routine, the unending deadlines, and the insidious pressures of cost accumulation will shunt interpretation (with the accompanying frequent contacts between accountants and operating managers) into the background and, most likely, into oblivion.

Exhibit 1-3 indicates how various duties might be divided. One effective way to improve mutual understanding is to have a member of the controller's staff personally explain and interpret reports as they are presented to line managers. This attention-directing role (for example, explaining the differences between budgeted and actual performance) should be manned by experienced accountants who, at least to some degree, can talk the line manager's language. Indeed, the interpreters are the individuals who will establish the status of the controller's department in the company. Close, direct contacts between accountants and operating managers usually instill confidence in the reliability of the financial reports, which are the measuring devices of performance.

Many companies deliberately rotate their young accountants through scorekeeping, attention-directing, and problem-solving posts. In this way, accountants are more likely to appreciate the decision maker's viewpoint and are thus more prone to keep the accounting system tuned to the needs of the users.

EXHIBIT 1-3

ORGANIZATION CHART OF A CONTROLLER'S DEPARTMENT

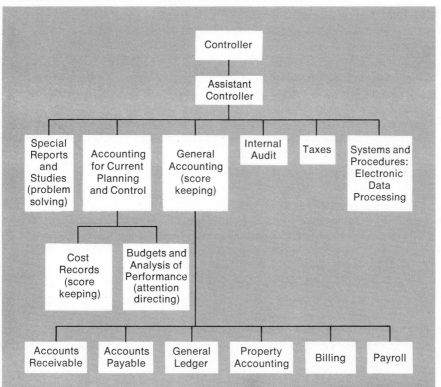

summary

Accounting's main purpose is to help managers make decisions. The accountant and the manager must be concerned with decision analysis and implementation as a unified whole. Unless implementation, with all its important human problems, is specifically considered, the accountant and the manager will have an incomplete picture of the breadth of the management process and its accompanying information system. Cost accounting is no longer a subject that concentrates on how to compute the costs of products for inventory valuation. Modern cost accounting now encompasses the gathering and reporting of information for decision needs of all kinds. The management accountant's task has three facets: scorekeeping, attention directing, and problem solving.

Goal congruence is the key to evaluating an accounting system. When managers and accountants are trying to decide among alternative management accounting techniques and systems, they should repeatedly ask, "Which alternative is most likely to motivate behavior that will harmonize with overall top-management objectives?"

Problems for Self-Study

(Try to solve these problems before examining the solutions that follow.)

PROBLEM 1   The accountant's usefulness to management is said to be directly affected by how good an attention director and problem solver he is. Assess this contention by specifically relating the accountant's duties to the duties of operating management.

SOLUTION 1   Depending on their responsibilities, operating managers may have to be good scorekeepers, but their chief duties are to make both routine and nonroutine decisions. Therefore, they need to concentrate on day-to-day problems that most need attention, to make longer-range plans and policies, and to arrive at special decisions. Accordingly, because the manager is concerned mainly with attention directing and problem solving, he will obtain the most benefit from the alert accountant who is a useful attention director and problem solver.

PROBLEM 2   Using the organization charts in this chapter (Exhibits 1-2 and 1-3), answer the following questions:
   a. Do the following have line or staff authority over the assembly foreman: maintenance foreman, manufacturing vice-president, production superintendent, purchasing agent, storekeeper, personnel vice-president, president, chief budgetary accountant, chief internal auditor?
   b. What is the general role of service departments in an organization? How are they distinguished from operating or producing departments?
   c. Does the controller have line or staff authority over the cost accountants? The accounts-receivable clerks?
   d. What is probably the *major duty* (scorekeeping, attention directing, or problem solving) of the following?

   Payroll clerk   Head of general accounting
   Accounts-receivable clerk   Head of taxes
   Cost-record clerk   Head of internal auditing

Budgetary accountant   Head of accounting for planning
Cost analyst   and control
Head of special reports and studies   Controller

A sad commentary on many existing accounting systems is that they fulfill their scorekeeping tasks admirably—but they stop there. With minimal additional cost, immense benefit could be generated if the attention-directing and problem-solving functions were also performed.

SOLUTION 2   a. The only executives having line authority over the assembly foreman are the president, the manufacturing vice-president, and the production superintendent.

b. A typical company's major purpose is to produce and sell goods or services. Unless a department is directly concerned with producing or selling, it is called a service or staff department. Service departments exist only to help the production and sales departments with their major tasks: the efficient production and sale of goods or services.

c. The controller has line authority over all members of his own department, all those shown in the controller's organization chart (Exhibit 1-3).

d. The major duty of the first five—through the head of taxes—is typically scorekeeping. Attention directing is probably the major duty of the next three. Problem solving is probably the primary duty of the head of special reports and studies. The head of accounting for planning and control and the controller should be concerned with all three duties: scorekeeping, attention directing, and problem solving. However, there is a perpetual danger that day-to-day pressures will emphasize scorekeeping. Therefore, accountants and managers should constantly see that attention directing and problem solving are also stressed. Otherwise, the major management benefits of an accounting system may be lost.

questions, problems, and cases

Special note about the assignment material: No attempt has been made to distinguish among questions, problems, and cases, because distinctions among them are so often artificial. Many problems are based on actual business situations. To aid selection, most problems have individual short titles that describe their subject matter.

1-1. Why do the controller and his staff have to understand the company organization structure?

1-2. As a new controller, answer this comment by a factory superintendent: "As I see it, our accountants may be needed to keep records for stockholders and Uncle Sam—but I don't want them sticking their noses in my day-to-day operations. I do the best I know how; no pencil-pusher knows enough about my responsibilities to be of any use to me."

1-3. "The way these modern controllers put themselves on a pedestal, you may as well give them the title of President and be done with it. Look at the first three points in their functions of controllership. With the change of a word or two, these points could be a job description for the company president." Discuss.

1-4. Define *decision* making.

1-5. Define *planning*. Distinguish it from control.

1-6. "Planning is really much more vital than control." Do you agree? Why?

1-7. Define *goal congruence*.

1-8. "The controller is both a line and a staff executive." Do you agree? Why?

1-9. "The modern concept of controllership maintains that the controller *does* control in a special sense." Explain.

1-10. What are some common causes of friction between line and staff executives?

1-11. How is cost accounting related to the concept of controllership?

1-12. Distinguish among line, staff, and functional authorities.

1-13. Role of the Accountant in the Organization: Line and Staff Functions.
1. Of the following, who have line authority over a cost-record clerk: budgetary accountant; head of accounting for current planning and control; head of general accounting; controller; storekeeper; production superintendent; manufacturing vice-president; president; production-control chief?
2. Of the following, who have line authority over an assembler: stamping foreman; assembly foreman; production superintendent; production-control chief; storekeeper; manufacturing vice-president; engineering vice-president; president; controller; budgetary accountant; cost-record clerk?

1-14. Scorekeeping, Attention Directing, and Problem Solving. For each of the following, identify the function the accountant is performing: i.e., scorekeeping, attention directing, or problem solving. *Also* state whether the departments mentioned are service or production departments.
1. Processing the weekly payroll for the maintenance department
2. Explaining the welding foreman's performance report
3. Analyzing the costs of several different ways to blend raw materials in the foundry
4. Tallying sales, by branches, for the sales vice-president
5. Analyzing, for the president, the impact on net income of a contemplated new product
6. Interpreting why a branch did not meet its sales quota
7. Interpreting variances on a machining foreman's performance report
8. Preparing the budget for research and development
9. Adjusting journal entries for depreciation on the personnel manager's office equipment
10. Preparing a customer's monthly statement

1-15. Draw an Organization Chart. Draw an organization chart for a company that has the following positions:

Vice-president, controller and treasurer
Chief designer
Receiving and stores superintendent
Branch A sales manager
Production superintendent
Chief of finished stockroom
Shipping-room head
Chief of cost accumulation
Maintenance superintendent
Employment manager
Building and grounds superintendent
Welding and assembly superintendent
Machining superintendent
Vice-president, manufacturing
Finishing-department superintendent

Vice-president, chief engineer
Foundry superintendent
Head of job evaluation
Vice-president, personnel
Head of general accounting
Budget director
Tool-room superintendent
Chief purchasing agent
Head of cost analysis
Inspection superintendent
Stamping superintendent
Head of research
President
Head of production control
Vice-president, sales

1-16. Responsibility for Analysis of Performance. John Phillipson is the new controller of a huge company that has just overhauled its organization structure.

The company is now decentralized. Each division is under an operating vice-president who, within wide limits, has responsibilities and authority to run his division like a separate company.

Phillipson has a number of bright staff members, one of whom, Bob Garrett, is in charge of a newly created performance-analysis staff. Garrett and his fellow staff members prepare monthly divisional performance reports for the company president. These reports are divisional income statements, showing budgeted performance and actual performance, and are accompanied by detailed written explanations and appraisals of variances. Each of Garrett's staff members had a major responsibility for analyzing one division; each consulted with divisional line and staff executives and became generally acquainted with the division's operations.

After a few months, Bill Whisler, vice-president in charge of Division C, has stormed into the controller's office. The gist of his complaint follows:

"Your staff is trying to take over part of my responsibilities. They come in, snoop around, ask hundreds of questions, and take up plenty of our time. It's up to me, not you and your detectives, to analyze and explain my division's performance to central headquarters. If you don't stop trying to grab my responsibilities, I'll raise the whole issue with the president."

required
1. What events or relationships may have led to Whisler's outburst?

2. As Phillipson, how would you answer Whisler's contentions?

3. What are some alternative actions that Phillipson can take to improve future relationships?

1-17. **Accountant's Role in Planning and Control.** Dick Victor has been president of Sampson Company, a multidivision textile company, for ten months. The company has an industry reputation as being conservative and having average profitability. Previously, Victor was associated with a very successful company that had a heavily formalized accounting system, with elaborate budgets and effective uses of performance reports.

Victor is contemplating the installation of a formal budgetary program. To signify its importance, he wants to hire a new vice-president for planning and control. This fellow would report directly to Victor and would have complete responsibility for implementing a system for budgeting and reporting performance.

If you were controller of Sampson Company, how would you react to Victor's proposed move? What alternatives are available to Victor for installing his budgetary program? In general, should figure specialists all report to one master figure expert, who in turn is responsible to the president?

1-18. **Organization of Accounting Department: Centralization or Decentralization.**[6] The following quotation is from an address made by an officer of the Ford Motor Company:

> We can all, I think, take pride in the way cost accounting has kept pace with industrial development in this country. Tremendous strides have been made during the last quarter of a century, and I'm sure that much more progress will be made in the future. In fact, progress will *have* to be made if we are to keep the science of cost accounting abreast of the times. The whole of industry is now operating on a different level than we have known before—a higher plateau, on which cost accounting appears in a new light, becomes more and more significant as a factor in business management.

[6]From the *N.A.C.A. Bulletin,* Vol. 29, No. 7, Sec. II.

It is my experience that the function of cost determination is basic to every other function of a modern business. Cost factors thread their way through every phase of a business and to a large extent influence the makeup of the entire enterprise—its products, its markets, and its methods of operation.

We must, of necessity, have rather complex and extensive costing organizations, but the principle according to which they work is the same—finding out what each of the operations costs before it is too late to avoid doing the wrong thing.

I am sure you would be interested in knowing that the accounting office at Ford was formerly almost completely centralized and that we have begun to install a decentralized system. . . .

It is planned that after the decentralized and the local organizations are prepared to assume the responsibilities involved, these accounting offices will be placed under the direct jurisdiction of the managers of the operations which they serve. . . .

Under the decentralized system, each division has its own complete accounting service. . . . Each separate activity, such as each assembly plant, has been provided with an accounting office to compile its own internal operating reports for its own use, and to forward the financial statements required by the central office.

required   1. Under the decentralized organization of the accounting work, would it be better for the controller of the Ford Motor Company to have direct authority or functional authority over the branch and divisional accounting offices? Discuss.

2. Will the decentralized system, in your opinion, make the cost accounting activities more significant in business management? In other words, is the change to a decentralized system in keeping with the trend that is outlined in the first three quoted paragraphs? Explain your answer, stating and illustrating advantages and disadvantages of the decentralized system in this case.

3. As a newly hired business school graduate in the plant controller's department, would you prefer that the plant controller's line responsibility be to the plant manager or to the company controller? Why?

1-19. **Scorekeeping, Attention Directing, and Problem Solving.**   Internal (management) accounting tends to emphasize the attention-directing and problem-solving functions of accounting. However, there are many companies with accounting systems that are oriented almost exclusively to scorekeeping. For example, one critic has stated:

Very few people in business have had the opportunity to reflect on the way in which the accounting model developed, particularly on how an instrument well adapted to detect fraud and measure tax liability has gradually been used as a general information source. Having become accustomed to information presented in this form, business people have adapted their concepts and patterns of thought and communication to it rather than adapting the information to the job or person. When one suggests the reverse process, as now seems not only logical but well within economic limits, he must expect a real reluctance to abandon a pattern of behavior that has a long history of working apparently quite well.[7]

[7]William R. Fair, "The Next Step in Management Controls," in Donald G. Malcom and Alan J. Rowe, eds., *Management Control Systems* (New York: John Wiley & Sons, Inc., 1960), pp. 229–30.

Considering the introductory material in this chapter, comment on this quotation, particularly on the meaning and implications for today's and tomorrow's controllers of the last sentence quoted.

1-20. **A Study in Anti-Paper Work.**   On January 13, 1961, *Time* magazine ran the following report concerning Marks & Spencer, Great Britain's most prosperous retail chain, with 237 stores and annual sales of $420 million:

> Marks & Spencer's vendetta against paper work started one Saturday early in 1957, when Sir Simon came across two salesgirls carefully filling out long inventory-replacement cards while customers fumed for service. "What are these cards for?" he asked. The girls did not know. Sir Simon found that they were to keep track of merchandise in the stockroom, to curb employee pilfering and to tell the store manager when to reorder. Sir Simon ordered them abolished and let the sales clerks go freely into the stockrooms to get whatever they needed to sell. Pilfering not only did not increase, but the clerks sold more because they knew exactly what was in stock. Furthermore, store managers found they could tell when to reorder simply by looking to see what shelves were getting bare.
>
> From then on, war was declared. Sir Simon found that his company was riddled with ponderous forms. "I didn't understand some of them. Why, I couldn't be a sales clerk in my own organization." He told his staff to examine every form and ask, "Would our entire business collapse if we dispensed with this form?"
>
> And so, while many businessmen are installing electronic gadgets to keep their records, 72-year-old Sir Simon is taking exactly the opposite approach. He has wiped out so much record keeping that he has junked 120 tons of paper forms, saved $14 million. He was able to cut prices 5% and was rewarded with an 18% sales increase from April through September 1960. Business in the second half of his fiscal year looks even better. Some 8,000 jobs out of 28,000 have been eliminated, but no one was fired, because Sir Simon promised when he began his Marksian revolution that he would absorb everyone either through expansion or simply not refilling a job when someone left.
>
> Sir Simon also gambled that customers are as trustworthy as sales clerks, and stopped giving out sales receipts, which most stores demand before they will take merchandise back from a customer. Now, as long as an article bears the M. & S. special St. Michael brand name (commemorating his father), it is easily exchanged at any branch. He threw out time clocks, reasoning that it was silly to keep tabs on employees who were only occasionally late, just to catch the few consistently late arrivers whose habits would be known to supervisors anyway. He silenced the jangling bell in employees' canteens that announced when lunch periods were over, letting clerks decide among themselves when to eat, thus checking on each other. Thick manuals that covered what to do in any situation were tossed out, replaced by one slim book. . . .
>
> Sir Simon still spends much of his time poking about his stores, chatting with clerks to see how much more paper work can be cut out. Any operation that has been in effect over six months—long enough for the paper work to sprout—is under suspicion.

Comment on the incidents. Do you agree with *Time*'s report?

An Introduction to Cost Terms and Purposes

2

In this chapter, we shall learn some basic terminology, the jargon that every technical subject seems to possess. And more important, we shall see quickly that there are different costs for different purposes and that cost-accounting systems should be designed to serve these multiple purposes.

Historically, many cost-accounting systems emphasized one cost objective—product costing for inventory valuation and income determination—as if it were an end in itself. Consequently, other uses were subordinated and many systems failed to adapt the data to the needs of the managers. However, modern systems have a more balanced approach; obtaining the cost of finished units is regarded as only one of the functions of the cost-accounting system.

We will frequently distinguish between the product-costing purpose of the system and all other purposes. For convenience, we will sometimes refer to the latter as the "control" purposes.

This chapter contains only a few widely recognized cost concepts and terms. These types are sufficient to demonstrate the multiple purposes that will be stressed throughout the book. There are many other types of costs, but you will not be swamped by them in this chapter. It will be more efficient if we ease into the subject matter of cost accounting, and so a discussion of many costs is being deliberately postponed. For example, the idea of controllable and uncontrollable costs is covered at length in Chapter 6, and opportunity cost is covered in Chapter 11.

In general, *cost* means sacrifice or foregoing, but there is no unique "correct" measure of cost that is applicable to all situations and pertinent for all purposes. For now, let us think of costs as being measured in the conventional accounting sense: dollars that must be paid for goods and services.

COSTS AND THE DECISION PROCESS

historical costs and predicted costs   The manager cannot change what has already happened. He is concerned about what to do next. Other than to satisfy legal requirements, the major justification for compiling historical costs is to help the manager predict what will occur. *Cost prediction* is an attempt to measure the expected, budgeted, or predetermined costs. Historical costs often provide the best basis for prediction, but they can rarely be used as measures of predicted costs without being altered in the light of other factors.

cost objects and decision alternatives   In choosing among his action alternatives, the decision maker (manager) inevitably wants to know what the total costs will be for each alternative. The basic objective is to predict the economic consequences for a host of decisions, including:

1. Which products should we produce?
2. What production schedules should we set?
3. What prices should we charge?
4. What plant and equipment should we buy?
5. Which managers should we praise or chastise?
6. Should we manufacture the subassembly or should we acquire it outside?
7. Which divisions are the most profitable? Should we increase or decrease our interests in this product line or that territory?
8. Which method of inventory valuation should we use?

Ideally, the manager would like to predict a cause-and-effect correspondence between a decision alternative and a cost incurrence. Failing this, he wants an idea of the relationships that seem to persist. These relationships may be clear or murky, and his confidence in his predictions varies accordingly.

Frequently, the cost objects and the decision alternatives are almost indistinguishable. For example, the manager may have to decide whether to produce and sell one unit of Product A or one unit of Product B. Having identified the manager's decision alternatives, the accountant should then focus on finding the cost of one unit of A and one unit of B. Note the crucial point: Conceptually, the specified decision alternatives determine what costs should be gathered. That is, the management accountant's primary focus should constantly be on decision needs; only in this way can he service managers with the costs that may form a basis for predictions for each alternative. This often means that historical data on Products A and B (or perhaps closely related products) might be gathered and used as a basis for predicting the total costs of a unit of A and a unit of B:

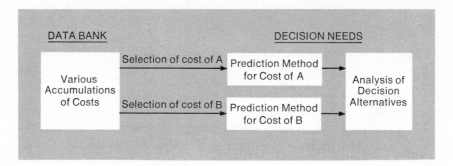

cost objects To guide his decisions, the manager needs data pertaining to a variety of
and accounting objectives. He needs the cost *of something.* It may be a product, a group
systems of products, a plant, a territory, a machine-hour, a labor-hour, an operating
division, a customer, an order, or a project. We shall call this something
a *cost object,* and define it as any alternative, activity, or part of an organization
for which a separate determination of costs is wanted.

As we saw in the preceding section, the manager's ultimate aim is to
associate costs with decision alternatives. Therefore, the accountant might want
to compile a massive bank of elementary data. Then, as each decision need arises,
the data bank can be directly tapped by determining costs on a special-study
basis. There would be no need for separate cost objects that exist independently
of the prediction methods. Such tailor-made service is impossible or infeasible
in nearly all organizations. The point is that an elementary data bank may require
too much analysis to fulfill a particular decision need in timely fashion.

The most economically feasible approach to the design of a management
accounting system is typically to assume some common needs for a variety of
decisions and choose cost objects for routine data accumulation in the light of
these needs. Some generalization about costs may be widely applicable to many
specific decisions, particularly repetitive decisions. Consequently, cost objects
(such as products and departments) are chosen as a focus for an accounting system
because they partially fulfill a variety of routine decision needs without necessi-
tating special studies at the time of decision.

Exhibit 2-1 highlights the strengths and weaknesses of most systems. Cost
objects are chosen for routine data accumulation, not for their own sake but
to facilitate decision needs. However, the trouble is that the relevant cost
assignment cannot be decided in a vacuum, apart from *specific* decision needs.
For example, the amount of factory heat properly assignable to a cost object
may be affected by the choice of a cost object, by the planning horizon, by the
nature of the decision (make or buy, pricing, product combination), and by the
objectives of the decision maker.

EXHIBIT 2-1

COST OBJECTS AND DECISION NEEDS

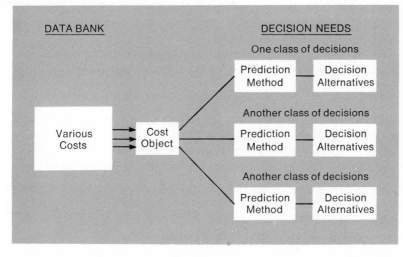

Example of the problem of systems design. The foregoing ideas may be clarified if we consider further the oversimplified example of deciding whether to produce and sell one unit of Product A or one unit of Product B. Suppose that the expected selling prices were identical and that the expected times required to make each unit were also identical. A special analysis might be made of the comparative effects on material, labor, and other costs of producing one unit of A or of B. More likely, the system was designed to anticipate such decisions, and historical or budgeted costs per unit are readily available to the decision maker. The manager may accept these costs as his best prediction without question; or, starting with these costs, the manager may then perform some specific adjustments to form his own prediction method. For instance, the unit costs provided by the system may require adjustment for this decision because they are based on production runs of one hundred units rather than one unit. The point is that, as we study cost-accounting procedures, methods, and systems, we should be on guard to ask what assumptions underlie the data and whether the data are relevant for the particular decision at hand. Different costs for different purposes is not just an empty phrase; it is a fundamental approach to the providing of data to management.

VARIABLE COSTS AND FIXED COSTS

costs and changes in activity Variable and fixed costs are usually defined in terms of how a total cost changes in relation to fluctuations in the activity (quantity) of a chosen cost object or cost allocation base. Activity bases are diverse. They may be units of product manufactured or sold, man-hours worked, miles driven, gallons consumed, patients seen, payroll checks processed, lines typed, or some other index of volume. If a total cost changes directly in proportion to changes in activity, it is variable; if a cost remains unchanged in total for a given time period despite wide fluctuations in activity, it is fixed. Consider two examples:

1. If Massive Motors Company buys one type of battery at $5 each for its M-1 model car, then the total cost of batteries should be $5 times the the number of cars produced. This is an example of a variable cost, a cost that is uniform *per unit* but that fluctuates in total in direct proportion to changes in the total activity (volume). Examples include most materials and parts, many types of assembly labor, sales commissions, and certain supplies.

    Variable cost behavior may be plotted graphically. Exhibit 2-2 shows the relationship between total commissions and dollar sales, whereas Exhibit 2-3 shows the relationship between raw material costs and units produced.

2. Massive Motors may incur $100 million in a given year for property taxes, executive salaries, rent, insurance, and depreciation. These are examples of fixed costs, costs that do not fluctuate in total over a wide range of volume during a given time span, but that become progressively smaller on a *per unit* basis as production increases.

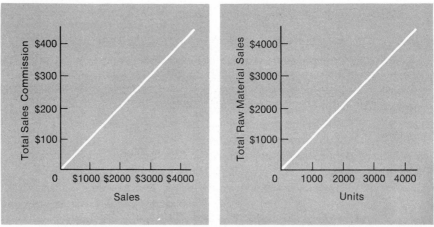

EXHIBIT 2-2

SALES COMMISSIONS—
10% OF SALES

EXHIBIT 2-3

RAW-MATERIAL COSTS—
$1.00 PER UNIT

fixed costs and shutdown costs   A fixed cost is fixed only in relationship to a given period of time and a given, though wide, range of activity, called the "relevant range." Thus, a company's fixed costs may be unchanged for a given year, although property-tax rates and executive salaries may be higher the next year. In addition, the fixed-cost level may be applicable to, say, a range of 30,000 to 95,000 hours of activity per month. But a prolonged strike or economic recession may cause executive salary cuts, layoffs, or shutdowns. Therefore, fixed costs may be reduced substantially if activity levels fall drastically. In some cases, an entire plant may be shut down, virtually eliminating the need for executive and service personnel.

These relationships are shown in Exhibit 2-4. The likelihood of activities being outside the relevant range is usually slight, so $50,000 becomes the fixed-cost level. The three-level refinement in Exhibit 2-4 is not usually required,

EXHIBIT 2-4

TOTAL MONTHLY FIXED COSTS—CONCEPTUAL ANALYSIS

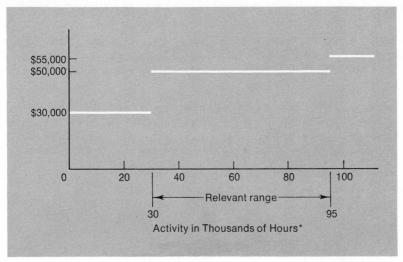

*$50,000 level between 30,000 and 95,000 hours.
$55,000 level in excess of 95,000 hours: hiring of additional supervision.
$30,000 level from shutdown (zero hours) to 30,000 hours: laying-off of supervision.

because the chances are very remote that activity will be less than 30,000 hours or more than 95,000 hours. Exhibit 2-5 shows how this $50,000 figure is usually plotted in practice.

cost functions   Nearly every business has costs that may be classified as either variable or fixed. Throughout this book we shall see why the accountant and the manager find this distinction helpful. For now, the major point is that managers

EXHIBIT 2-5

TOTAL MONTHLY FIXED COSTS AS PLOTTED IN PRACTICE

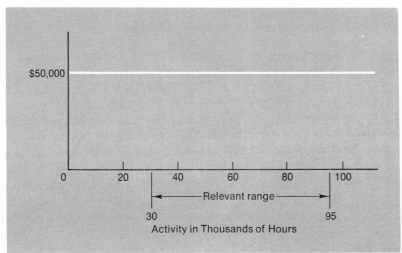

must have knowledge of their firm's cost behavior patterns (cost functions) in order to predict the impact of their decisions on profits and in order to formulate means for controlling cost incurrence.

Such costs behavior is not confined solely to manufacturing costs; selling and administrative costs also have fixed and variable components. Some costs are difficult to categorize as being either strictly variable or strictly fixed. Few costs fit neatly into one or the other category. The distinction between variable and fixed is dependent on what activity base is chosen. An automobile leasing company might regard insurance and licenses as variable costs if the activity base is the number of cars leased. However, such costs are fixed for a car owner who chooses miles driven as an activity base.

An identification of cost behavior patterns (cost functions) helps describe the types of direct and indirect relationships that exist between total costs and cost objects. Variable and fixed costs are just two of an assortment of cost functions that might portray such relationships. For the time being, we shall assume that costs may be placed in one of these two classifications. In practice, of course, the task of classification is exceedingly difficult and nearly always necessitates some simplifying assumptions.

An additional simplification is the widespread assumption that cost functions are linear rather than curvilinear. Moreover, in practice, activity is inevitably assumed to be unidimensional: units of product, or labor-hours, or machine-hours, or sales dollars, and so on. The relationships between a given cost incurrence and changes in related activity levels may be vastly oversimplified and misleading because many costs are clearly affected by more than one factor. These ideas are explored more fully in Chapters 7 and 8.

UNIT COSTS AND TOTAL COSTS

The preceding section concentrated on the behavior patterns of total costs in relation to chosen activity levels. Generally, the decision maker should take a straightforward analytical approach by thinking in terms of total costs rather than unit costs. As we shall see momentarily, unit costs must be interpreted carefully. Nevertheless, the use of unit costs is essential in many decision contexts. For example, the chairman of the social committee of a fraternity or a senior class may be trying to decide whether to hire a prominent musical group for a forthcoming party. The total fee may be predicted with certainty at $1,000. This knowledge is essential for the decision, but it may not be enough.

Before a decision can be reached, the decision maker must predict both the total cost and the probable number of persons who will attend. Without knowledge of both, he cannot decide intelligently on a possible admission price or even on whether to have a party at all. So he computes a unit cost by dividing the total cost by the expected number of persons who will attend. If 1,000 people attend, the unit cost is $1; if 100 attend, the unit cost soars to $10 per person. Unless the total cost is "unitized," the $1,000 cost is difficult to interpret; so the unit cost combines the total cost and the number of persons in a handy communicative way.

In management accounting, different measurement bases (denominators) may be used as units, depending on the circumstances. Generally, *unit costs should be expressed in terms most meaningful to the people who are responsible for incurring the costs.* The unit in question is not always a physical product; the unit (base) should be that objectively definable statistic of activity that is most closely correlated with cost incurrence. Thus, the base may differ between departments; it may be machine-hours in a factory department, pounds handled in the shipping department, and number of invoices processed or lines billed in the billing department.

The unit cost of making a finished good is sometimes computed by accumulating manufacturing costs and then dividing the total by the number of units produced. For example:

Total costs of manufacturing 1,000 units	$3,800
Divided by the number of units produced	÷ 1,000
Equals a cost per unit	= $3.80

Suppose that 800 units are sold and 200 units remain in ending inventory. The unit-cost idea facilitates the assignment of a total cost to various accounts:

Cost of goods sold, 800 units × $3.80	= $3,040
Ending inventory of finished goods, 200 units × $3.80 =	760

Unit costs are averages, and they must be interpreted with caution. For example, what does it mean to say that the unit cost for the musicians is $1 if 1,000 persons attend? A $1 unit cost would be valid for predicting total costs if the musicians indeed charged a fee at the rate of $1 per person, so that the total cost would be $800 if only 800 persons actually attended. However, the total cost is a lump sum, $1,000, and in this instance the unit cost is strictly dependent on the size of the denominator. As we shall discuss more fully in Chapters 9 and 11, unit costs often represent the averaging of a lump-sum total, a fixed cost (the musicians' fee). Such unit costs must be interpreted quite differently from variable costs, where the unit costs are indeed valid indicators of how a total cost fluctuates in relation to the denominator (a fuel pump for automobiles). One of the most common mistakes in cost analysis is to regard all unit costs indiscriminately—as if all the total costs to which they are related are variable costs. Changes in activity (the denominator) will affect total variable costs, but not total fixed costs.

PRODUCT COSTS AND PERIOD COSTS

distinctions between manufacturing and non- manufacturing activities

Some form of cost accounting is applicable to manufacturing companies, retail stores, insurance companies, advertising agencies, and nearly all organizations. We shall consider both manufacturing and nonmanufacturing companies throughout this book, but we shall begin with the manufacturing company because it provides the most general case—embracing production, marketing, and general administration functions. This will develop a completely general understanding of cost accounting that you can readily apply to any organization.

Historically, accounting techniques for planning and control arose in conjunction with manufacturing rather than nonmanufacturing because the measurement problems were less imposing and external factors such as economic conditions, customer reactions, and competitor activity were generally less influential. However, the basic concepts of planning and control are equally applicable to both manufacturing and nonmanufacturing activities. At the moment, we will examine manufacturing and nonmanufacturing from the viewpoint of inventory costing and income determination—the product-costing purpose, when the cost object is the unit of product.

Manufacturing is the transformation of materials into other goods through the use of labor and factory facilities. Merchandising is the selling of goods without changing their basic form. For example, assume that Jack Nentlaw wants to make hairdressing and sell it directly to retailers. He may buy certain oils and fancy containers, purchase a factory and equipment, hire some workers, and manufacture thousands of units of finished product. This is his manufacturing function. But in order to persuade retailers to buy his hairdressing, Nentlaw will have to convince the ultimate consumer that this product is desirable. This means advertising, including the development of a sales appeal, the selection of a brand name, the choice of media, and so forth. To maximize his success, Nentlaw must effectively manage both manufacturing and merchandizing functions.

three
manufacturing
cost elements

Notice the basic difference between the conventional income statements of Nentlaw's business and Crump's Department Store in Exhibit 2-6. In the cost-of-goods-sold section, the Nentlaw statement has a "cost of goods manufactured" line instead of the "purchases" line found in the Crump statement. The details of the cost of goods manufactured appear in a separate supporting schedule.

There are three major elements in the cost of a manufactured product:

1. *Direct materials.* All materials that are an integral part of the finished good and that may be conveniently assigned to specific physical units; for example, sheet steel and subassemblies. Certain minor materials, such as glue or nails, may be considered either *supplies* or *indirect materials* rather than direct materials, because of the impracticality of tracing these items to specific physical units of product.
2. *Direct labor.* All labor obviously related to and expediently traceable to specific products; for example, labor of machine operators and assemblers. Much labor, such as that of material handlers, janitors, and plant guards, is considered *indirect labor* because of the difficulty or impracticality of tracing such items to specific physical units.
3. *Factory overhead.* All factory costs other than direct materials and direct labor. Other terms to describe this category include *indirect manufacturing costs, factory burden, manufacturing overhead,* and *manufacturing expenses.* There are two major types of factory overhead:
   a. *Variable factory overhead.* The two main examples are supplies and most

EXHIBIT 2-6

COMPARISON OF INCOME STATEMENTS

NENTLAW (*A manufacturer*)			CRUMP'S (*A retailer*)		
Income Statement			*Income Statement*		
For the Year Ended December 31, 19_2			*For the Year Ended December 31, 19_2*		
Sales		$210,000	Sales		$1,500,000
Less cost of goods sold:			Less cost of goods sold:		
Finished goods, December 31, 19_1	$ 22,000		Merchandise inventory, December 31, 19_1	$ 95,000	
Cost of goods manufactured (see schedule)	104,000		Purchases	1,100,000	
Cost of goods available for sale	$126,000		Cost of goods available for sale	$1,195,000	
Finished goods, December 31, 19_2	18,000		Merchandise inventory, December 31,	130,000	
Cost of goods sold			sold		1,065,000
Gross margin					$ 435,000
Less selling and administrative expenses (detailed)			ministrative d)		315,000
Net income					$ 120,000

Sche...

Direct materials:			
Inventory, December 31, 19_1		$11,000	
Purchases of direct materials		73,000	
Cost of direct materials available for use		$84,000	
Inventory, December 31, 19_2		8,000	
Direct materials used			$ 76,000
Direct labor			18,000
Factory overhead:			
Indirect labor		$ 4,000	
Supplies		1,000	
Heat, light and power		1,500	
Depreciation—Plant building		1,500	
Depreciation—Equipment		2,500	
Miscellaneous		500	11,000
Manufacturing costs incurred during 19_2			$105,000
Add work-in-process inventory, December 31, 19_1			6,000
Manufacturing costs to account for			$111,000
Less work-in-process inventory, December 31, 19_2			7,000
Cost of goods manufactured* (to Income Statement)			$104,000

*Note that the term *cost of goods manufactured* refers to the cost of goods brought to completion (finished) during the year, whether they were started before or during the current year. Some of the manufacturing costs incurred are held back as costs of the ending work in process; similarly, the costs of the beginning work in process become a part of the cost of goods manufactured for 19_2. Note too that this schedule can become a Schedule of Cost of Goods Manufactured and Sold simply by including the opening and closing finished-goods inventory figures in the supporting schedule rather than directly in the body of the income statement.

indirect labor. Whether the cost of a specific subcategory of indirect labor is variable or fixed depends on its behavior pattern in a given company. In this book, unless we specify otherwise, indirect labor will be considered a variable rather than a fixed cost.

b. *Fixed factory overhead.* Examples are rent, insurance, property taxes, depreciation, and supervisory salaries.

Two of the three major elements are sometimes combined in cost terminology as follows: *Prime cost* consists of (1) + (2), direct materials plus direct labor. *Conversion cost* consists of (2) + (3), direct labor plus factory overhead.

Indirect manufacturing costs is a more accurate descriptive term than *factory overhead,* but the latter will be used throughout this book because it is briefer. The term *overhead* is peculiar; its origins are unclear. Some accountants have wondered why such costs are not called "underfoot" rather than "overhead" costs.

direct and indirect costs The terms *direct* and *indirect* have no meaning unless they are related to an object of costing. Traceability is the essence of the distinction. The word *direct* refers to the practicable, obvious, physical tracing of cost as incurred to a given cost object. A cost may be direct with respect to an activity but indirect with respect to a product. For example, the salary cost of a foreman may be ·a direct charge to a department but an indirect charge to a variety of products being manufactured in that department.

The distinction between direct and indirect costs can be illustrated as follows:

	OBJECTS OF COSTING	
NATURE OF CLASSIFICATION	PRODUCING DEPARTMENT OR FUNCTION	PRODUCTS
Materials used	D	D
Supplies used	D	D or I*
Assembly labor	D	D
Material-handling labor	D	D or I*
Depreciation—building	I	I
Assembly foreman's salary	D	D or I*
Building and grounds supervisor's salary	I	I

D = direct   I = indirect
*Whether such costs are direct or indirect depends on the types of products in question.

In product costing, the distinction between direct and indirect costs is evidenced by the procedures used for the allocation. For direct cost:

1. There is almost always some sort of observable *physical identification* with the cost object that is explicitly measured in terms of the quantity of the input used.
2. There is *no intervening basis* for allocation.

For example, direct materials and direct labor are allocated on the basis of the physical quantities of inputs consumed. However, indirect materials and indirect labor, even though they may be highly related to output to the extent that such a relationship is physically observable, are allocated to the product via some intervening base such as direct-labor hours.

These two characteristics help support the basic implication of the direct-cost classification. The accountant might say, "The cause and effect relation between the cost and the cost object is obvious, so our record-keeping procedures should preserve this clarity wherever economically feasible." If the cost is direct, there is virtual certainty (allowing, of course, for random variation in efficiency) that y amount of output will cause x amount of cost.

The direct/indirect distinction is along a continuum:

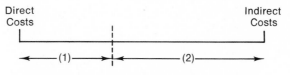

Direct
Costs

Indirect
Costs

(1) Associated with cost object by physical observation that is explicitly measured in terms of the quantity of input used.
(2) Associated with cost object by using an intervening basis for allocation.

product costs (inventoriable costs) and income measurement The scope of the term *cost* is extremely broad and general. When used, the word *cost* is usually linked with some adjective in order to avoid ambiguity. For example, costs may be *unexpired* or *expired*. Unexpired costs are carried forward to future periods as assets. Expired costs are those that should be released to the current period as *expenses* or *losses* (sometimes called *period costs*); they are costs that cannot be justifiably carried forward to future periods either because they do not represent future benefits or because the future benefits are so uncertain as to defy measurement.

A major objective of accounting is income measurement. In their efforts to refine the measure of income, accountants have developed certain practical classification techniques for distinguishing between assets and expenses. This distinction is accomplished to a large extent by viewing manufacturing costs as inventoriable costs.

If costs can be looked upon as "attaching" or "clinging" to units produced, they are classified as *inventoriable costs*, also commonly called *product costs*. These costs are assets until the goods to which they relate are sold; then the costs are released as expenses and matched against sales. All costs in the schedule of cost of goods manufactured in Exhibit 2-6 are called product costs. Direct-material, direct-labor, and factory-overhead items are inventoriable costs because they are costs of services utilized in forming the product. In general, the costs of operating the factory—the manufacturing costs—are classified as product costs.

Two decisions are made about costs with regard to income determination. Decision 1: Which costs apply to the current accounting period? Decision 2: Which of those under Decision 1 are inventoriable? For example, a three-year $300 insurance premium may be charged originally to an asset account, *unexpired insurance.* The subsequent accounting for this cost will hinge on (a) the amount applicable to the current period—say, $100 for the first year—and (b) the purpose of the insurance coverage. Insurance on factory machinery is inventoriable and is therefore transferred from unexpired insurance to an inventory account. Insurance on a sales office is not inventoriable and is therefore transferred from unexpired insurance to an outright expense account.

Let us review the terminology. In manufacturing accounting, many unexpired costs (assets) are transferred from one classification of unexpired costs to another before becoming expired costs (expense). Examples are factory insurance, depreciation on plant, and wages of production workers. These items are held back as product costs (inventory costs); they are released later to expense as part of cost of goods sold (an expense). The reader should distinguish sharply between the merchandising accounting and the manufacturing accounting for such costs as insurance, depreciation, and wages. In merchandising accounting, such items are generally treated as expired costs (expenses); whereas in manufacturing accounting, most of such items are related to production activities and thus are inventoriable costs—costs that do not expire (become expense) until the goods to which they relate are sold. These relationships are depicted in Exhibit 2–7.

troublesome   There are many terms that have very special meanings in accounting. The
terminology   meanings often differ from company to company; each organization seems to develop its own distinctive and extensive accounting language. This is why you will save much confusion and wasted time if you always find out the exact meanings of any strange jargon that you encounter.

For example, the term *manufacturing expenses,* which is often used to describe factory overhead, is a misnomer. Factory overhead is not an expense. It is a part of product cost and will funnel into the expense stream only when the product costs are released as cost of goods sold.

Also, *cost of goods sold* is a widely used term that is somewhat misleading when you try to pin down the meaning of *cost.* Cost of goods sold is an *expense* because it is an expired cost; it is every bit as much an expense as are salesmen's commissions. Cost of goods sold is also often called *cost of sales.*

subdivisions   The terminology for labor costs is usually the most confusing, because each
of labor costs   organization has seemingly developed its own interpretation of various labor-cost classifications. Let us consider some commonly encountered labor terminology.

All factory-labor costs other than direct labor are usually classified as *indirect labor,* a major component of indirect manufacturing costs. The term has many subsidiary classifications to facilitate appraisal of these costs. Thus, wages of fork-lift truck operators are generally not commingled with janitors' salaries, although both are regarded as indirect labor.

EXHIBIT 2-7

RELATIONSHIPS OF PRODUCT AND PERIOD COSTS

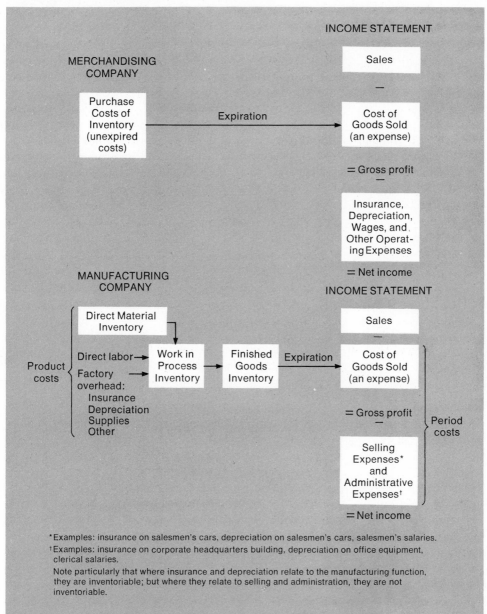

*Examples: insurance on salesmen's cars, depreciation on salesmen's cars, salesmen's salaries.

†Examples: insurance on corporate headquarters building, depreciation on office equipment, clerical salaries.

Note particularly that where insurance and depreciation relate to the manufacturing function, they are inventoriable; but where they relate to selling and administration, they are not inventoriable.

Costs are classified in a detailed fashion primarily in the attempt to associate a specific cost with its specific cause or reason for incurrence. Two classes of indirect labor need special mention. *Overtime premium* paid to factory workers is usually considered a part of overhead. If a lathe operator gets $3.00 per hour for straight time and time and one-half for overtime, his *premium* would be $1.50 per overtime hour. If he works forty-four hours, including four overtime hours, in one week, his gross earnings would be classified as follows:

Direct labor:	44 hours × $3.00	$132.00
Overtime premium (factory overhead):		
	4 hours × $1.50	6.00
	Total earnings	$138.00

Another subsidiary classification of indirect labor is *idle time*. This typically represents wages paid for unproductive time caused by machine breakdowns, material shortages, sloppy production scheduling, and the like. For example, if the lathe operator's machine broke down for three hours, his earnings would be classified as follows:

Direct labor:	41 hours × $3.00	$123.00
Overtime premium (factory overhead):		
	4 hours × $1.50	6.00
Idle time (factory overhead):		
	3 hours × $3.00	9.00
	Total earnings	$138.00

Why is overtime premium usually considered an indirect cost rather than direct? After all, it can usually be traced to specific batches of work. It is usually not considered a direct charge because the scheduling of production jobs is generally random. For example, assume that Jobs 1 through 5 are scheduled for a specific workday of ten hours, including two overtime hours. Each job requires two hours. Should the job scheduled during hours 9 and 10 be assigned the overtime premium? Or should the premium be prorated over all the jobs? The latter approach does not penalize a particular batch of work solely because it happened to be worked on during the overtime hours. Instead, the overtime premium is considered to be attributable to the heavy overall volume of work, and its cost is thus regarded as factory overhead, which is borne by all units produced.

payroll fringe costs The classification of factory-payroll fringe costs, such as employer contributions to Social Security, life insurance, health, pension, and miscellaneous other employee benefits, differs from company to company. In most companies, these are classified as factory overhead. For instance, a direct laborer such as a lathe operator, whose gross paycheck is computed on the basis of a $3.00 straight-time hourly rate, may enjoy payroll fringe benefits totaling, say, $.75 per hour. Most companies tend to classify the $3.00 as direct labor and the $.75 as factory overhead. In some companies, however, the fringe benefits related to direct labor are charged as an additional direct-labor cost; these companies would classify the entire $3.75 as direct labor. The latter approach is preferable because most of these costs are also a fundamental part of acquiring labor services.

balance sheet   Balance sheets of manufacturers and merchandisers differ with respect to inventories. The merchandise inventory account is supplanted in a manufacturing concern by three inventory classes: *materials and supplies inventory; work-in-process inventory* (cost of uncompleted goods still on the production line containing appropriate amounts of the three major manufacturing costs: direct material, direct labor, and factory overhead); and *finished goods* (fully completed goods). The only essential difference between the structure of the balance sheet of a manufacturer and that of the balance sheet of a retailer would appear in their respective current-asset sections:

CURRENT-ASSET SECTIONS OF BALANCE SHEETS

MANUFACTURER			RETAILER	
Cash		$ 4,000	Cash	$ 30,000
Receivables		5,000	Receivables	70,000
Finished goods	$12,000			
Work in process	2,000			
Materials and supplies	3,000			
Total inventories		17,000	Merchandise inventories	100,000
Prepaid expenses		1,000	Prepaid expenses	3,000
Total current assets		$27,000	Total current assets	$203,000

perpetual and periodic inventories   There are two fundamental ways of accounting for inventories: perpetual and periodic. The *perpetual inventory method* keeps a continuous record of additions to or reductions of materials, work in process, and cost of goods sold on a day-to-day basis. Such a record facilitates managerial control and preparation of interim financial statements. Physical inventory counts are usually taken at least once a year in order to check on the validity of the clerical records.

The *periodic inventory method* does not keep a day-to-day record of inventories. Instead, costs are recorded by natural classifications, such as Material Purchases, Freight In, and Purchase Discounts. Costs of materials used or costs of goods sold cannot be computed accurately until ending inventories, determined by physical count, are subtracted from the sum of the opening inventory, purchases, and other operating costs. See Exhibit 2–8 for a comparison of perpetual and periodic inventory methods.

EXHIBIT 2-8

SUMMARY COMPARISON OF PERIODIC AND
PERPETUAL INVENTORY METHODS
(*Figures from Exhibit 2-6*)

PERIODIC METHOD		PERPETUAL METHOD	
Beginning inventories (by physical count)	$ 22,000	Cost of goods sold (kept on a day-to-day basis rather than being determined periodically)*	$108,000
Add: Manufacturing costs (direct materials used, direct labor, factory overhead)	104,000		
Cost of goods available for sale	126,000		
Less ending inventories (by physical count)	18,000		
Cost of goods sold	$108,000		

*Such a condensed figure does not preclude the presentation of a supplementary schedule showing details of production costs similar to that in Exhibit 2-6.

CLASSIFICATIONS OF COST

This chapter has merely hinted at the vast number of classifications of cost that have proven useful for various purposes. Among other categories, classifications can be made by:

1. Time when computed
   a. Historical costs
   b. Budgeted or predetermined costs (via cost "prediction")
2. Behavior in relation to fluctuations in activity
   a. Variable-cost function
   b. Fixed-cost function
   c. Other cost function
3. Degree of averaging
   a. Total costs
   b. Unit costs
4. Management function
   a. Manufacturing costs
   b. Selling costs
   c. Administrative costs
5. Ease of traceability
   a. Direct costs
   b. Indirect costs
6. Timing of charges against revenue
   a. Product costs
   b. Period costs

summary

Accounting systems should serve multiple decision purposes, and there are different measures of cost for different purposes. Cost estimation is an attempt to measure historical costs for the ultimate purpose of facilitating the prediction of expected costs for decision purposes. A frequent distinction that is made concerning cost-accounting systems is between the purpose of providing costs for inventory valuation and that of providing costs for other purposes. These purposes are sometimes called (a) product costing and (b) control.

The most economically feasible approach to designing a management accounting system is to assume some common needs for a variety of decisions and choose cost objects for routine data accumulation in light of these needs.

The mass of cost terms covered in this chapter provides just a tiny glimpse of a vast number of cost concepts that we will study in future chapters.

Problem for Self-Study

(Try to solve this problem before examining the solution that follows.)

PROBLEM   Consider the following data of the Laimon Company for the year 19_1:

Sandpaper	$ 2,000	Depreciation—Equipment	$ 40,000
Material handling	40,000	Factory rent	50,000
Lubricants and coolants	5,000	Property taxes on equipment	4,000
Overtime premium	20,000	Fire insurance on equipment	3,000
Idle time	10,000	Direct materials purchased	400,000
Miscellaneous indirect labor	40,000	Direct materials, 12/31/_1	50,000
Direct labor	300,000	Sales	1,200,000
Direct materials, 12/31/_0	40,000	Sales commissions	60,000
Finished goods, 12/31/_1	150,000	Sales salaries	100,000
Finished goods, 12/31/_0	100,000	Shipping expenses	70,000
Work in process, 12/31/_0	10,000	Administrative expenses	100,000
Work in process, 12/31/_1	14,000		

required
1. Prepare an income statement with a separate supporting schedule of cost of goods manufactured. For all items except sales, purchases of direct materials, and inventories, indicate by "V" or "F" whether each is basically a variable or a fixed cost. If in doubt, decide on the basis of whether the total cost will fluctuate substantially over a wide range of volume.

2. Suppose that both the direct-material and rent costs were related to the manufacturing of the equivalent of 900,000 units. What is the unit cost for the direct materials assigned to those units? What is the unit cost of the factory rent? Assume that the rent is a fixed cost.

3. Repeat the computation in part 2 for direct materials and factory rent, assuming that the costs are being predicted for the manufacturing of the equivalent of 1,000,000 units next year. Assume that the implied cost behavior patterns persist.

4. As a management consultant, explain concisely to the president why the unit costs for materials and rent differed in parts 2 and 3.

SOLUTION   1.

LAIMON COMPANY

Income Statement

For the Year Ended December 31, 19_1

Sales		$1,200,000
Less cost of goods sold:		
Finished goods, December 31, 19_0	$ 100,000	
Cost of goods manufactured (see schedule below)	900,000	
Cost of goods available for sale	$1,000,000	
Finished goods, December 31, 19_1	150,000	
Cost of goods sold		850,000
Gross margin		$ 350,000
Less selling and administrative expenses:		
Sales commissions	$ 60,000 (V)	
Sales salaries	100,000 (F)	
Shipping expenses	70,000 (V)	
Administrative expenses	100,000*	330,000
Net income		$ 20,000

*Probably a mixture of fixed and variable items.

LAIMON COMPANY

Schedule of Cost of Goods Manufactured

For the Year Ended December 31, 19_1

Direct materials:		
Inventory, December 31, 19_0	$ 40,000	
Purchases of direct materials	400,000	
Cost of direct materials available for use	$440,000	
Inventory, December 31, 19_1	50,000	
Direct materials used	$390,000 (V)	
Direct labor	300,000 (V)	
Indirect manufacturing costs:		
Sandpaper	$ 2,000 (V)	
Lubricants and coolants	5,000 (V)	
Material handling (Example: wages of fork-lift truck operators)	40,000 (V)	
Overtime premium	20,000 (V)	
Idle time	10,000 (V)	
Miscellaneous indirect labor	40,000 (V)	
Factory rent	50,000 (F)	
Depreciation—Equipment	40,000 (F)	
Property taxes on equipment	4,000 (F)	
Fire insurance on equipment	3,000 (F)	214,000
Manufacturing costs incurred during 19_1		$904,000
Add work in process, December 31, 19_0		10,000
Manufacturing costs to account for		$914,000
Less work in process, December 31, 19_1		14,000
Cost of goods manufactured (to Income Statement)		$900,000

2. Direct-material unit cost = Direct materials used ÷ Units produced
     = $390,000 ÷ 900,000 = $.4333
   Factory-rent unit cost   = Factory rent ÷ Units produced
     = $50,000 ÷ 900,000 = $.0556

3. The material costs are variable, so they would increase in total. However, their unit costs would be unaffected:

   Direct materials = $433,333 ÷ 1,000,000 units = $.4333

   In contrast, the factory rent is fixed, so it would not increase in total. However, if the rent is assigned to units produced, the unit costs would decline from $.0556 to $.05:

   Factory-rent unit cost = $50,000 ÷ 1,000,000 = $.05

4. The explanation would begin with the answer to part 3. The accountant should stress that the unitization of costs having different behavior patterns can be misleading. A common error is to assume that a total unit cost, which is often a sum of some variable unit costs and some fixed unit costs, is an indicator that *total* costs change in a wholly variable way as activity fluctuates. The next chapter demonstrates the necessity for distinguishing between cost behavior patterns.

As already mentioned, in information gathering the elementary need is for a set of signals that will facilitate the prediction of how the costs of the total organization will be affected under each decision alternative. The total costs assigned to a cost object are essentially an estimate of how the total costs of the organization have been affected by a particular action. That is, if the cost object (e.g., unit of product) had not been present, the total costs assigned thereto would not have been incurred. In practice, this ideal is rarely attainable. Above all, the user must be wary about unit fixed costs. Too often, unit fixed costs are erroneously regarded as indistinguishable from variable costs.

questions, problems, and cases

2-1. What two major purposes of cost accounting were stressed in this chapter?

2-2. Distinguish between *manufacturing* and *merchandising*.

2-3. What are the three major elements in the cost of a manufactured product?

2-4. Define the following: *direct materials, direct labor, indirect materials, indirect labor, factory overhead, prime cost, conversion cost.*

2-5. Give at least four terms that may be substituted for the term *factory overhead.*

2-6. Distinguish among *direct labor, indirect labor, overtime premium,* and *idle time.*

2-7. What is the major difference between the balance sheets of manufacturers and merchandisers?

2-8. Distinguish between *unexpired costs* and *expired costs.* How are manufacturing costs classified in relation to the problem of income measurement?

2-9. "For purposes of income determination, insurance, depreciation, and wages should always be treated alike." Comment.

2-10. Why is the term *manufacturing expenses* a misnomer?

2-11. "Cost of goods sold is an expense." Do you agree? Explain.

2-12. Why is the unit-cost concept helpful in accounting?

2-13. Define: *variable cost, fixed cost, relevant range.*

2-14. Give three examples of variable factory overhead.

2-15. Distinguish between *costing for control* and *product costing.*

2-16. Give three examples of fixed factory overhead.

2-17. "Fixed costs are really variable. The more you produce, the less they become." Do you agree? Explain.

2-18. "An action once taken cannot be changed by subsequent events." What implications does this have for the cost accountant?

2-19. Why is overtime premium usually considered an indirect cost rather than direct?

2-20. Periodic or Perpetual Inventory Methods [SIA]. The terms *periodic* and *perpetual inventories* are referred to frequently in presenting the accounting procedures that are followed by businesses in recording their business transactions in any given period of their operations. Discuss the difference between periodic and perpetual inventory procedures and indicate the advantages and disadvantages of each method.

2-21. Statement of Cost of Goods Manufactured [SIA, adapted]. M-P Company Limited manufactures a single product. The treasurer has asked you to help him prepare a manufacturing statement for the month ended March 31, 19_0. He gives you the following information:

Sales = 10,000 units at $20.00 per unit

Production = 12,000 units

Finished-goods inventory, March 1, 19_0 = 3,000 units valued at $16.00 each

Raw-materials inventory, March 1, 19_0 = 1,000 units valued at $5.00 each

Purchases of raw materials, March 4 = 8,000 units at $6.00 each
  March 20 = 5,000 units at $5.00 each

The company uses the first-in, first-out method of determining raw-materials inventories.

In-process inventory, March, 1, 19_0 = 2,000 units valued at $16,000
  March 31, 19_0 = 2,000 units valued at $21,000

Fixed assets—machinery $240,000 original cost
      —office equipment   6,000 original cost

Depreciation is determined on a straight-line basis at the rate of 10% per annum.

Other information:

Sales returns and allowances	$ 3,500
Salesmen's salaries	2,500
Freight out	4,000
Direct labor	100,000
Indirect labor	45,000
Office salaries	7,000
Heat, light, and power	2,000
Factory rent	8,000
Interest expense	2,000
Miscellaneous factory overhead	10,000

required   Prepare a statement of cost of goods manufactured for the month ended March 31, 19_1. One unit of raw material is used for each unit of finished goods. There is no spoilage.

2-22. Statement of Cost of Goods Manufactured and Sold. The following items pertain to the Engle Corporation:

			FOR YEAR 19_2
Work in process, Dec. 31, 19_2	$ 2,000	Selling and administrative	
Finished goods, Dec. 31, 19_1	40,000	expenses (total)	$70,000
Accounts receivable, Dec. 31,		Direct materials purchased	80,000
19_2	30,000	Direct labor	70,000
Accounts payable, Dec. 31,		Factory supplies	6,000
19_1	40,000	Property taxes on factory	1,000
Direct materials, Dec. 31, 19_1	30,000	Factory utilities	5,000
Work in process, Dec. 31, 19_1	10,000	Indirect labor	20,000
Direct materials, Dec. 31, 19_2	5,000	Depreciation—Plant and	
Finished goods, Dec. 31, 19_2	12,000	equipment	21,000
Accounts payable, Dec. 31,		Sales	350,000
19_2	20,000	Miscellaneous factory overhead	10,000
Accounts receivable, Dec. 31,			
19_1	50,000		

required   1. Prepare an income statement and a supporting schedule of cost of goods manufactured.

2. Suppose that both the direct materials and the depreciation were related to the manufacturing of the equivalent of 105,000 units. What is the unit cost for the direct materials assigned to those units? What is the unit cost of the depreciation? Assume that depreciation is a straight-line fixed cost.

3. Repeat the computations in part 2 for direct materials and depreciation, assuming that the costs are being predicted for the manufacture of the equivalent of 126,000 units next year. Assume the implied cost behavior patterns persist.

4. As a management accountant, explain concisely to Mr. Engle why the unit costs differed in parts 2 and 3.

2-23. Answers from Incomplete Data. The following accounts of a manufacturing company appeared in the balance sheets of December 31, 19_1 and December 31, 19_2:

	DEC. 31, 19_1	DEC. 31, 19_2
Raw-materials inventory	$30,000	$48,000
Goods-in-process inventory	17,500	19,000
Finished-goods inventory	23,000	20,000
Accrued factory payroll	3,400	2,400
Accrued interest on notes receivable	120	80

The following amounts appeared in the income statement for 19_2:

Raw materials used	$300,000
Cost of goods sold	920,000
Factory labor	275,000
Interest income	500

required

1. Raw materials purchased in 19_2
2. Cost of goods manufactured for 19_2
3. Factory labor paid in 19_2
4. Interest received on notes in 19_2

2-24. **Statement of Cost of Goods Manufactured and Sold.** From the Younger Manufacturing Company's adjusted trial balance of December 31, 19_1, the following account balances have been obtained:

Raw materials, January 1, 19_1	$ 75,000
Work in process, Janaury 1, 19_1	21,200
Finished goods, January 1, 19_1	50,000
Purchases	198,000
Purchase returns and allowances	3,000
Direct labor	125,000
Indirect labor	40,000
Heat, light, and power	35,000
Insurance (75% of which is apportioned to factory)	8,000
Factory and machine maintenance	8,000
Factory supplies	6,000
Depreciation—Factory building	9,000
Depreciation—Equipment	39,000
Property taxes (90% of which are apportioned to factory)	4,000

In addition, raw materials costing $187,000 were used, the cost of goods manufactured for the year 19_1 was $440,000, and the cost of goods sold was $430,000.

required

1. A statement of cost of goods manufactured and sold for the year 19_1.

2. Suppose that both the direct materials and the depreciation were related to the production of the equivalent of 200,000 units. What is the unit cost for the direct materials assigned to those units? What is the unit cost of the depreciation on the factory building and on the machinery? Assume that depreciation is a straight-line, fixed cost.

3. Repeat the computations in part 2 for direct materials and depreciation, assuming that costs are being predicted for the manufacture of 160,000 units next year. Assume that the implied cost behavior patterns persist.

4. As the controller, explain concisely to the president why the unit costs differed in parts 2 and 3.

2-25. **Finding Unknown Balances.** For each of the cases in the list at the top of page 43, find the unknowns designated by letters.

2-26. **Fire Loss; Computing Inventory Costs.** A distraught employee, Fang W. Arson, put a torch to a factory on a blustery February 26. The resulting blaze

	CASE 1	CASE 2	CASE 3	CASE 4
Finished-goods inventory, 1/1	$ 5,000	$ 4,000	$ 7,800	$ G
Direct materials used	8,000	6,000	3,600	5,000
Direct labor	13,000	12,000	8,000	6,000
Factory overhead	7,000	D	13,000	7,000
Purchases of direct materials	9,000	7,000	8,000	8,000
Sales	44,000	33,800	E	41,000
Accounts receivable, 1/1	2,000	1,400	3,000	400
Accounts receivable, 12/31	6,000	2,100	3,000	2,800
Cost of goods sold	A	22,000	33,000	16,000
Accounts payable, 1/1	3,000	1,700	1,600	300
Accounts payable, 12/31	1,800	1,500	1,800	1,200
Finished-goods inventory, 12/31	B	5,300	F	7,600
Gross profit	11,300	C	12,000	25,000
Work in process, 1/1	–0–	800	1,300	2,000
Work in process, 12/31	–0–	3,000	300	2,500

completely destroyed the plant and its contents. Fortunately, certain accounting records were kept in another building. They revealed the following for the period December 31, 19_1–February 26, 19_2:

> Prime costs average 70 percent of goods manufactured.
> Gross profit percentage based on net sales, 20 percent.
> Cost of goods available for sale, $460,000.
> Direct materials purchased, $170,000.
> Work in process, 12/31/_1, $34,000.
> Direct materials, 12/31/_1, $16,000.
> Finished goods, 12/31/_1, $30,000.
> Factory overhead, 40 percent of conversion costs.
> Sales, $500,000.
> Direct labor, $180,000.

The loss was fully covered by insurance. The insurance company wants to know the approximate cost of the inventories as a basis for negotiating a settlement, which is really to be based on replacement costs, not historical cost.

required   Calculate the cost of:

1. Finished-goods inventory, 2/26/_2
2. Work-in-process inventory, 2/26/_2
3. Direct-material inventory, 2/26/_2

2-27. Classification of Costs.   Classify each of the following as direct or indirect (D or I) with respect to product, and as variable or fixed (V or F) with respect to whether the cost fluctuates in total as activity or volume changes. You will have two answers, D or I and V or F, for *each* of the ten items:

1. Cutting bits in a machinery department
2. Workmen's compensation insurance in a factory
3. Cement for a roadbuilder
4. Steel scrap for a blast furnace
5. Paper towels for a factory washroom

6. Food for a factory cafeteria
7. Factory rent
8. Salary of a factory storeroom clerk
9. Foreman training program
10. Abrasives (sandpaper, etc.)

2-28. Different Cost Classifications for Different Purposes. A machining department has a number of cost accounts. Some accounts selected at random are reproduced below.

Use two columns to classify each account in two ways: direct or indirect product costs (D or I), and variable or fixed costs (V or F). If in doubt about the latter, select on the basis of whether the item will vary over wide ranges of activity.

example   Foreman's salary I, F.

1. Cutting tools
2. Lubricants
3. Patterns
4. Nails, rivets, etc.
5. Factory rent
6. Repairs
7. Castings
8. Freight in on castings
9. Material handling
10. 25 percent of superintendent's salary
11. Direct labor
12. Idle time
13. Overtime premium
14. Employer payroll taxes
15. Compensation insurance
16. Fire insurance on equipment
17. Depreciation—Equipment
18. Property taxes on equipment
19. Blueprints prepared by drafting department

2-29. Classification of Costs; Objective Answers. The following example is a guide for solving this problem. Five columns are to be used as choices for possible classification (see table at the top of page 45).

On a separate sheet, do the same for the following accounts, all of which are not necessarily for a single company. You may use numbers to list the accounts instead of recopying the account descriptions.

1. Salesmen's entertainment costs
2. Public-accounting fees
3. Salary of factory stores clerk
4. Overtime premium—Punch press
5. Idle time—Assembly
6. Rework—Machining
7. Salaries—Engineering department

example

	SELLING COST	GENERAL ADMINIS-TRATIVE COST	MANUFACTURING COST DIRECT OR INDIRECT	VARIABLE OR FIXED*	OTHER (SPECIFY)
Direct materials	___	___	D	V	___
Bond interest expense	___	___	___	F	Financial expense
Fire loss	___	___	___	___	Non-recurring loss
President's salary	___	✔	___	F	___
Insurance on factory equipment	___	___	I	F	___

*If in doubt, decide on the basis of whether the total cost will fluctuate substantially over a wide range of volume.

8. Sandpaper purchases for a furniture manufacturer
9. Cost estimator's salary for a missile manufacturer
10. Cleanup labor—Machining
11. Material-handling labor—Machining
12. Factory power
13. Shop patterns and forge dies
14. Property taxes
15. Freight in on materials used
16. Shipping supplies
17. Heat of factory
18. Costs of developing patents—Factory engineering department
19. Amortization of patents
20. Freight out
21. Salesmen's commissions
22. Salesmen's salaries
23. Fire insurance—Factory
24. Executive training program—General
25. Company picnic costs
26. Salesmen's samples
27. Bribes paid to public officials
28. Perfume bottles of a perfume manufacturer
29. Individual boxes for perfume
30. Glue for labels on perfume bottles
31. Packing cartons of various sizes used by shipping department
32. Salaries—Production control

2-30. **Comprehensive Problem on Unit Costs, Product Costs, Variable and Fixed Costs.** The Morrow Company makes a single product. Costs are as follows (V stands for variable, F for fixed):

Production in units	100,000
Costs incurred:	
Direct materials used	$100,000 V
Direct labor	70,000 V
Power	5,000 V
Indirect labor	10,000 V
Indirect labor	20,000 F
Other factory overhead	8,000 V

Other factory overhead	20,000 F
Selling expenses	30,000 V
Selling expenses	20,000 F
Administrative expenses	50,000 F
Work-in-process inventory, December 31, 19_1	—
Direct-materials inventory, December 31, 19_1	2,000 lbs.
Finished-goods inventory, December 31, 19_1	$ 20,970

Dollar sales were $364,000 in 19_1. There were no beginning inventories in 19_1. The company's ending inventory of finished goods was carried at the average unit cost of production for 19_1. Direct-material prices have been stable throughout the year. Two pounds of direct materials are used to make a unit of finished product.

required

1. Direct-material inventory, total cost, December 31, 19_1.

2. Finished-goods inventory, total units, December 31, 19_1.

3. Unit sales price, 19_1.

4. Net income, 19_1. Show computations.

2-31. Budgeted Income Statement.   This problem is more difficult than previous problems. Refer to Problem 2-30.

Management has asked that you prepare a budgeted income statement for 19_2, assuming that all unit prices for sales and variable costs will not change. Assume that sales will be 102,000 units and that ending inventory of finished goods, December 31, 19_2, will be 12,000 units. Assume that fixed costs will remain the same. Show supporting computations, and include a schedule of cost of goods manufactured. The ending inventory of finished goods is to be carried at the average unit cost of production for 19_2.

Cost-Volume-Profit Relationships

3

The previous chapter distinguished sharply between two major purposes of cost accounting: (a) decision making for planning and control, and (b) product costing for inventory valuation and income determination. This chapter and the next will examine these two purposes in more depth. Cost–volume–profit analysis is a subject inherently appealing to most students of business, because it gives a sweeping overview of the planning process and because it provides a concrete example of why an understanding of cost behavior is important. That is why we consider this subject now, even though it could just as easily be studied later.

Managers are constantly faced with decisions about selling prices, variable costs, and fixed costs. Basically, managers must decide how to acquire and utilize economic resources in light of some objective. Unless they can make reasonably accurate predictions about cost and revenue levels, their decisions may yield undesirable or even disastrous results. These decisions are usually short run: How many units should we manufacture? Should we change our price? Should we spend more on advertising? However, decisions such as buying plant and equipment also hinge on predictions of the resulting cost–volume–profit relationships.

At the outset, remember that we will be considering simplified versions of the real world. Are these simplifications justifiable? The answer depends on the facts in a particular case. The simplifications are warranted if they lead to the same or better decisions than might be provided by more realistic, complex, and costly models.

THE BREAKEVEN POINT

We learn quickly that knowledge of cost behavior patterns—the response of costs to a variety of influences—is invaluable in guiding management decisions. First, we obtain an overview by examining the interrelationships of changes in costs, volume, and profits—sometimes too narrowly described as breakeven analysis. The breakeven point is often only incidental in these studies. Instead, the focus is on the impact upon net income of various decisions that affect sales and costs. The breakeven point is that point of activity (sales volume) where total revenues and total expenses are equal; it is the point of zero profits and zero loss.

basic technique

example

A person plans to sell a toy rocket at the state fair. He may purchase these rockets at 50¢ each with the privilege of returning all unsold rockets. The booth rental is $200, payable in advance. The rockets will be sold at 90¢ each. How many rockets must be sold to break even?

Equation technique.   The first approach to a solution may be called the *equation technique.* Every income statement may be expressed in equation form, as follows:

Sales = Variable Expenses + Fixed Expenses + Net Income

This equation may be adapted to any breakeven or profit-estimate situation. For the example above:

Let X = Number of units to be sold to break even

$$\$.90\,X = \$.50\,X + \$200 + 0$$
$$\$.40\,X = \$200 + 0$$
$$X = \frac{\$200 + 0}{\$.40}$$
$$X = 500 \text{ units}$$

Contribution margin technique.   A second solution method is the *contribution margin* or *marginal income* technique. *Contribution margin* is the excess of sales over *variable* expenses. Sales and expenses are analyzed as follows:

1. *Unit contribution margin* to coverage of fixed expenses and desired net income

= Unit sales price − Unit variable expense = $.90 − $.50 = $.40

2. *Breakeven point* in terms of units sold

$$= \frac{\text{Fixed Expenses} + \text{Desired Net Income}}{\text{Unit Contribution Margin}} = \frac{\$200 + 0}{\$.40} = 500 \text{ units}$$

Stop a moment and relate this contribution margin technique to the equation technique. The key calculation was dividing $200 by $.40. Look at the third line in the equation solution. It reads:

$$\$.40\,X = \$200 + 0$$

$$X = \frac{\$200 + 0}{\$.40}, \text{ giving us a general formula:}$$

$$\text{Breakeven in Units} = \frac{\text{Fixed Expenses} + \text{Desired Net Income}}{\text{Contribution Margin per Unit}}$$

The *contribution margin* technique is merely a restatement of the *equation* in different form. Use either technique; the choice is a matter of personal preference.

The term *contribution margin* will be used frequently in this book. It may be expressed as a total, as an amount per unit, or as a percentage. In our example, the *total contribution margin* is 500 units $\times$ $.40, or $200; the *unit contribution margin* is $.40; and the *contribution margin percentage or ratio* is $.40 $\div$ $.90, or 44.44 percent.

The contribution margin ratio is necessary for cost–volume–profit analysis where the information is expressed in terms of dollars instead of units. Most companies have more than one product, and the overall breakeven point is often expressed in sales dollars because of the variety of product lines. For instance, although apples and oranges cannot be meaningfully added, their sales values provide a useful common denominator. In the example, the breakeven point in dollars may be computed most easily by merely multiplying the 500 units by $.90 to obtain $450. However, the breakeven point may also be obtained by the following version of the contribution margin approach:

$$\text{Breakeven Point in Dollars} = \frac{\text{Fixed Expenses} + \text{Desired Net Income}}{\text{Contribution Margin Ratio}}$$

$$= \frac{\$200 + 0}{.4444} = \$450$$

The first problem for self-study in this chapter elaborates on the uses of the contribution margin ratio.

graphic *approach*   The relationships in the example given may be graphed as shown in Exhibit 3-1.

EXHIBIT 3-1

COST-VOLUME-PROFIT CHART

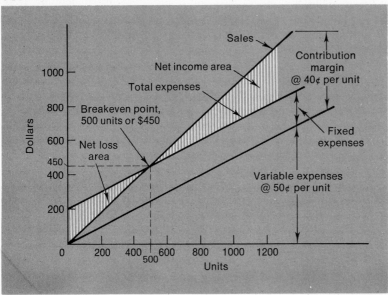

The graph in Exhibit 3-1 used the following building blocks:

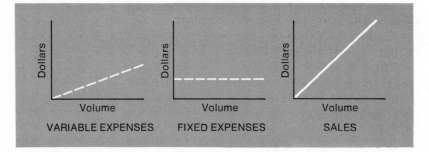

Note that total sales and total variable expenses fluctuate in direct proportion to changes in physical volume, whereas fixed expenses are the same in total over the entire volume range.

Now combine the fixed and variable expenses in a single graph:

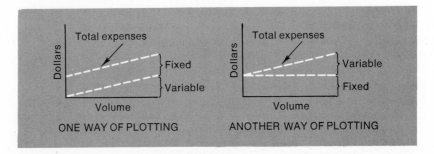

Note that the "total expenses" line is the same under either method. The graph that plots fixed expenses above the variable expenses is preferred by many accountants because it emphasizes the contribution margin notion. (See Exhibit 3-1.) When operations are below the breakeven point, the vertical distance between the sales line and the variable-cost line measures the "contribution" that sales volume is making to fixed expenses.

Finally, introduce the sales line:

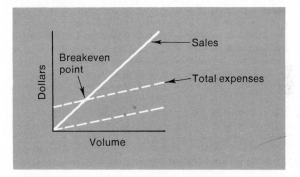

Exhibit 3-1 shows the complete breakeven chart. The *breakeven point* is the point where the total-sales line and total-expense line intersect. But note further that this graph shows the profit or loss outlook for a wide range of volume. The confidence we place in any particular breakeven chart is naturally a consequence of the relative accuracy of the cost–volume–profit relationships depicted.[1]

target net income   Let us introduce a profit element by asking, *How many rockets must be sold to yield a net income of 20 percent of sales?* The same basic approach may be used:

Equation technique

Let X = Number of units to be sold to yield desired net income.
Sales = Variable Expenses + Fixed Expenses + Desired Net Income
$$\$.90\,X = \$.50\,X + \$200 + .20(\$.90\,X)$$
$$\$.90\,X = \$.50\,X + \$200 + \$.18\,X$$
$$\$.22\,X = \$200$$
$$X = 910 \text{ units}$$

Proof:			
	Sales = 910 × $.90	$819	100.00%
	Variable expenses = 910 × $.50	455	55.56
	Contribution margin	$364	44.44%
	Fixed expenses	200	24.42
	Net income	$164	20.02%

[1]For an exploration of the role of uncertainty in cost–volume–profit analysis, see Problems 23-31 and 23-32.

Find the 910-unit volume on the graph in Exhibit 3-1. The difference between sales and total expenses at that volume is the $164 net income.

Contribution margin technique

$$X = \frac{\text{Fixed Expenses} + \text{Desired Net Income}}{\text{Unit Contribution Margin}}$$

$$X = \frac{\$200 + .20(\$.90\,X)}{\$.40}$$

$$\$.40\,X = \$200 + \$.18\,X$$
$$\$.22\,X = \$200$$
$$X = 910 \text{ units}$$

cost–volume– profit assumptions

The following assumptions usually underlie a given breakeven analysis:

1. The behavior of costs and revenues has been reliably determined and is linear over the relevant range.
2. All costs may be resolved into fixed and variable elements.
3. Fixed costs remain constant over the volume range on the breakeven chart.
4. Variable costs fluctuate proportionally with volume.
5. Selling prices are to be unchanged.
6. Prices of cost factors are to be unchanged.
7. Efficiency and productivity are to be unchanged.
8. The analysis either covers a single product or it assumes that a given sales mix will be maintained as volume changes. *Sales mix* may be defined as the relative combination of quantities of a variety of company products that compose total sales. If the mix changes, overall sales targets may be achieved, but the effects on profits depend on whether low-margin or high-margin goods predominate in the sales mix.
9. Revenue and costs are being compared on a common activity base (for example, sales value of production or units produced).
10. Perhaps the most basic assumption of all is that volume is the only relevant factor affecting cost. Of course, other factors also affect costs and sales. Ordinary cost–volume–profit analysis is a crude oversimplification when these factors are unjustifiably ignored.
11. Changes in beginning and ending inventory levels are insignificant in amount. (The impact of inventory changes on cost–volume–profit analysis is discussed in Chapter 10.)

The reliability of cost–volume–profit analysis is dependent upon reasonably accurate portrayals of cost behavior. The first step in analyzing costs is to divide them into fixed and variable categories. The objective is to determine total fixed costs and the rate at which variable costs change with volume.

Cost behavior is affected by the interplay of a number of factors. Volume is only one of these factors; others include unit prices, sales mix, efficiency, changes in production methodology, wars, strikes, legislation, and so forth. Any breakeven analysis is based on assumptions made about the behavior of revenue, costs, and volume. A change in expected behavior will alter the breakeven point;

in other words, profits are affected by changes in other factors besides volume. A breakeven chart must be interpreted in the light of the limitations of its underlying assumptions, especially with respect to the price and sales-mix factors. *The real benefit of preparing breakeven charts is in the enrichment of under-standing of the interrelationships of all factors affecting profits, especially cost behavior patterns over ranges of volume.*

the economist's breakeven chart   Two principal differences between the accountant's and the economist's breakeven charts are:

1. The accountant usually assumes a constant unit variable cost instead of a unit variable cost that changes with the rate production. The accountant assumes linearity, but the economist does not.
2. The accountant's sales line is drawn under the assumption that price does not change with the rate of production or sale, but the economist assumes that price changes may be needed to spur sales volume. Therefore, the economist's chart is nonlinear.

The differences can be graphed as follows:

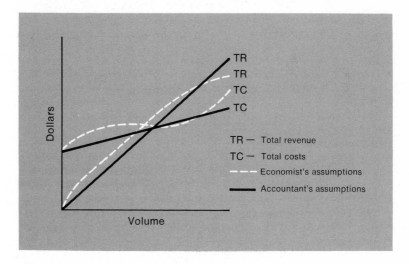

The economist's assumptions are undoubtedly more valid; the accountant's simplifications may or may not lead to less profitable decisions. The point is that obtaining more accurate cost functions is often difficult and expensive. Managers and accountants are aware of the simplifications introduced by the assumptions of linearity, but generally they have decided that the value of any additional information that might be gained from more accurate data would not exceed the additional costs of obtaining the data. They also take comfort in knowing that most of their decisions are made within the relevant range of volume, where the linearity assumption is likely to be more accurate.

relevant range   In a real-life company situation, the breakeven point may be drawn as shown in Exhibit 3-1. However, the many assumptions that underlie the chart are subject to change if actual volume falls outside the relevant range that was the basis for drawing the chart. It would be more realistic if the lines on these charts were not extended back to the origin, as follows:

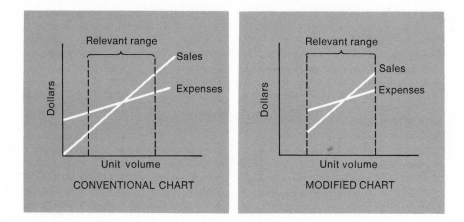

The modified chart highlights the fact that tenuous, static assumptions underlie a graph of cost–volume–profit relationships. The sales and expense relationships may be valid within a band of activity called the *relevant range.* The relevant range is usually a range in which the firm has had some recent experience. But the same relationships are unlikely to persist if volume falls outside the limits of the relevant range. For example, as shown in the previous chapter, some fixed costs may be avoided at low volume levels.

Business is dynamic, not static. The user of cost–volume–profit analysis must constantly challenge and reexamine his assumptions in the light of changes in business conditions, prices, cost factors, sales mixes, cost mixes, and the like. Moreover, cost–volume–profit analysis need not adhere rigidly to the traditional assumptions of linearity.

INTERRELATIONSHIPS OF COST, VOLUME, AND PROFITS

variable cost   In breakeven analysis, variable cost is generally expressed either as a
and   percentage of the sales dollar, as an amount per unit, or as an absolute
contribution   amount at a specified level of activity. When the variable cost ratio—the
margin   total variable costs divided by total sales—is known, the total variable costs at any level of activity are easily computed. But the variable cost ratio may be altered by changes in material prices, wage rates, efficiency, and selling price.

The *contribution margin ratio* is the complement of the *variable cost ratio.* It is the proportion of the sales dollar available for coverage of fixed costs and attainment of profit. It is computed by subtracting the variable cost ratio from

100 percent. This relationship may be expressed in dollars as the *contribution margin*—the difference between total revenue and total variable costs at any volume.

If the contribution margin ratio is known, the change in profits forthcoming from a contemplated change in sales may be easily calculated. For example:

	GIVEN VOLUME	PERCENT	INCREASE IN VOLUME	DECREASE IN VOLUME
Sales	$1,000	100	$200	$300
Variable costs	700	70	140	210
Contribution margin	$ 300	30	$ 60	$ 90
Fixed costs	300		(Unchanged)	(Unchanged)
Net income	$ 0		$ 60	$ 90

The application of the contribution margin ratio, 30 percent, to the sales increment, $200, or the sales decline, $300, will easily yield the given answers of $60 and $90—*the changes* that would result. Because total fixed costs do not change over the contemplated volume range, they are not relevant in the computation of any change in profit arising from changes in volume.

The contribution margin ratio may provide management with some useful information. If a firm is operating at a loss, the contribution margin ratio indicates how much the net loss will either diminish or increase with each dollar change in sales. A high contribution margin ratio will cause greater profits than a smaller contribution margin ratio as volume in dollars increases above the breakeven point. The opposite holds when sales volume is below the breakeven point: the higher the contribution margin ratio, the greater the loss as the dollar volume of sales decreases. A low contribution margin ratio necessitates great increases in volume to obtain noticeable increases in profits. The larger the ratio, the larger the change in profit for a given change in volume (*N.A.A. Research Series No. 17*, p. 533):

> . . . For example, a high marginal income ratio [contribution margin ratio] indicates that comparatively large additional expenditures for advertising and selling directed toward obtaining added sales volume may be profitable because the margin available from such sales is adequate to absorb the expenditures and still leave a contribution to profits. However, it should be recognized that additional expenditures for sales promotion may partly or wholly cancel the advantage gained. As an alternative, price reductions might be used if sales volume responds readily to price changes, although here again action should not be taken without considering the probable action of competitors. Reductions in price required by competition can also be absorbed more readily by a company having a high marginal income ratio. Since changes in variable cost also affect the marginal income ratio, this ratio indicates how readily the business can absorb cost increases without serious loss of profit.

Both the contribution margin and the breakeven point are altered by changes in unit variable costs. Thus, in the toy-rocket example, if the cost of a toy rocket is raised from 50¢ to 70¢ and the sales price is unchanged, the unit contribution falls from 40¢ to 20¢, and the breakeven point increases from 500 to 1,000 units. A decrease in rocket cost from 50¢ to 30¢ would change the unit contribution from 40¢ to 60¢. The new breakeven point would become 334 units ($200 fixed expenses divided by $.60).

Variable costs are subject to various degrees of control at different volumes because of psychological as well as other factors. When business is booming, management tends to be preoccupied with the generation of volume "at all costs." When business is slack, management tends to ride herd on costs. Decreases in volume are often accompanied by increases in selling expenses and lower selling prices; but at the same time labor turnover falls, labor productivity tends to increase, and raw-material prices may drift down. This is another illustration of the limitations of a breakeven chart; conventional breakeven charts assume proportional fluctuations of variable costs with volume. This implies adequate and uniform control over costs. In practice, such control is often erratic.

changes in fixed costs   Fixed costs are not static year after year. They may be deliberately increased in order to obtain more profitable combinations of production and distribution; these affect the three major profit determinants: revenue, variable costs, and fixed expenses. For example, a sales force may be established to reach markets directly instead of through wholesalers, thereby obtaining increased unit sales prices. More complicated machinery may be bought so as to reduce unit variable costs. Increases in labor rates are likely to make it desirable for a firm to invest in labor-saving equipment. In some cases, on the other hand, it may be wise to reduce fixed costs in order to obtain a more favorable combination. Thus, direct selling may be supplanted by the use of manufacturers' agents. A company producing stoves may find it desirable to dispose of its foundry if the resulting reduction in fixed costs would more than counterbalance increases in the variable costs of purchased castings over the expected volume range.

When a major change in fixed costs is proposed, management needs forecasts of the effect on the breakeven point and the contribution margin as a guide toward a wise decision. The management accountant makes continuing analyses of cost behavior and redetermines breakeven points periodically. He keeps management informed for the cumulative effect of major and minor changes in the company's cost and revenue patterns.

Fixed costs are constant only over contemplated ranges of activity. The volume range rarely extends from shutdown levels to 100 percent capacity. Thus, when a radical reduction in volume is foreseen, many fixed costs are "jarred loose" by managerial action. The slashing of fixed costs lowers the breakeven point and enables the firm to endure a greater decrease in volume before losses appear.

example of importance of fixed costs   In November 1950, some months after the Korean outbreak, a major automobile company applied to the federal price-control agency for permission to raise car prices. A frequent reason for price increases is the increased cost of labor and materials. But this case was different; the company wanted to increase prices because of the fixed-cost–volume relationship. The government's drastic curtailment of output for the consumer markets had resulted in the halving of the company's production. Although variable costs had remained fairly steady per car, the fixed costs had to be spread over 50 percent fewer units. Thus, a price increase was granted in order that an equitable return on investment might be earned. For example (totals are in millions):

BEFORE KOREAN WAR			DURING KOREAN WAR		
Sales, 100,000 units @ $2,000		$200	Sales, 50,000 units @ $2,000		$100
Variable expenses, 100,000 units @ $900	$90		Variable expenses, 50,000 units @ $900	$45	
Fixed expenses	30	120	Fixed expenses	30	75
Gross profit, 40% of sales		$ 80	Gross profit, 25% of sales		$ 25

The spreading of $30 million of fixed costs over 50,000 units instead of 100,000 units resulted in the application of $600 to each car instead of the former $300 amount. Note that the basis for the price increase was the mere drop in production, not an increase in unit prices of variable-cost factors. Fixed costs remained the same—$30 million; the reduced number of units sold had to carry higher price tags in order to get a large enough contribution margin per unit to recover the fixed costs and provide the same percentage of gross profit on sales.

margin of safety The *margin of safety* is the excess of budgeted or actual sales over the breakeven sales volume. It shows the amount by which sales may decrease before losses occur. This concept may be expressed as a percentage through dividing the dollar margin of safety by budgeted or actual sales (M/S). The validity of such a margin depends on the accuracy of cost estimates at the contemplated breakeven point. Often any drastic decrease in sales is accompanied by severe slashes in costs; the margin of safety is an approximation that presupposes given cost relationships.

The combination of high fixed costs, a high contribution margin ratio, and a low margin of safety usually calls for managerial action to get reductions in fixed costs or to stimulate sales volume.

If both the margin of safety and the contribution margin ratio are low, management would tend to concentrate on possible upward revisions in selling prices or on ways and means of reducing variable expenses.

APPLICATIONS OF COST–VOLUME–PROFIT ANALYSIS

Breakeven analysis has wide applicability for managerial decision making. Cost–volume–profit analysis provides helpful information for decisions as to pricing, cost alternatives, sales mix, channels of distribution, possible sales promotion, addition or deletion of product lines, acceptance of special orders, entering foreign markets, and changing plant layout.

cost–volume–profit analysis and budgets   The derivation of cost–volume–profit relationships, whether in connection with breakeven charts or with budgets, permits a quick preview of potential profits over a wide range of volume. Many firms use preliminary budget figures as a basis for a breakeven chart. If the forecast does not satisfy management, changes are made before a final budget is drawn.

The breakeven chart is a convenient way of reporting on the overall business plan (the budget). The chart often has educational advantages, in that it conveys the story to line executives more easily than do numerical exhibits. Thus, it creates a greater awareness of these relationships on the part of line executives.

In long-run capital budget situations, breakeven charts may be helpful in showing future operating conditions if certain expenditures are to be made. A form of breakeven chart is also helpful in showing the relative costs of borrowing versus obtaining additional ownership capital.

contribution margin and the short run   In the short run it is often helpful to offer numerical income statements that highlight the contribution margins of various products. As compared with the conventional income statement, where no sharp distinctions are made between fixed costs and variable costs, the contribution margin statement explains better the basic cost–revenue–profit behavior. This type of statement reflects a useful management approach to decisions with respect to hiring a salesman, conducting a special advertising campaign, making or buying a part, bidding on a special order, and so on. The differences in costs are compared with the differences in revenue in order to obtain an accurate basis for decision. Further, this type of statement helps to direct management attention toward the high- or low-margin-producing power of its various products.

The decisions mentioned in the previous paragraph will be given more attention in later chapters, but an illustration may clarify the importance of volume in relation to total contribution margin and net profit.

A large brewery circulated a written explanation of breakeven analysis to its wholesalers. The explanation contained the following assumptions for a typical wholesaler:

		PER UNIT
Sales price		$2.60
Variable expenses:		
Cost of beer	$2.00	
Variable selling expenses	.15	2.15
Contribution margin		$ .45
Fixed expenses, $30,000 per year.		

The brewery used breakeven analysis to point out the sizable impact on profits of high-volume operations. In this situation, if a wholesaler could increase his volume by 25,000 cases, his income would rise by $11,250 (a change in revenue of $2.60 × 25,000 cases, or $65,000, minus change in expenses of

	BREAKEVEN VOLUME	PRESENT VOLUME	POSSIBLE CHANGES	POSSIBLE VOLUME
Cases per year	66,667	100,000	25,000	125,000
Sales @ $2.60	$173,333	$260,000	$65,000	$325,000
Variable expenses @ $2.15	143,333	215,000	53,750	268,750
Contribution margin @ $.45	$ 30,000	$ 45,000	$11,250	$ 56,250
Fixed expenses	30,000	30,000	—	30,000
Net income	$ 0	$ 15,000	$11,250	$ 26,250

$2.15 × 25,000 cases, or $53,750). Fixed expenses have already been recovered and are not affected by the volume change. The only additional outlays are the variable expenses. The brewery suggested that the wholesaler could achieve a dramatic change in net income (a 75 percent change) with a mere 25 percent increase in volume. The brewery also suggested that the wholesaler could easily take on a special promotional expense—say, $5,000—because the increase in volume would still leave a $6,250 increase in income for the wholesaler.

The validity of this approach to a specific decision again depends on the facts in a case. If the wholesaler described above was working at peak capacity at a 100,000-case level, in order to increase volume he would have to buy more trucks, rent more storage space, raise more capital, and so forth. Then the facts change, and the analysis would depend not only on the extra contribution margin to be gained. but also on the additional fixed costs to be incurred.

The size of the contribution margin would also influence the decision. If the margin were only 12¢ a case instead of 45¢, the 25,000-case extra volume would not increase the total contribution margin enough (25,000 × $.12, or $3,000) to warrant the risk of a large promotional outlay.

A word of caution is needed here. Costs must be related to time; that is, a cost that is fixed over a short period is variable over a longer period. Profits may increase momentarily by applying the contribution margin approach to decisions; but over the long run, profits may suffer by inordinate use of such an approach. For example (*N.A.A. Research Series No. 17*, p. 552):

> One company stated that it solicits subcontract work for other manufacturers during periods when sales of its own products do not fully utilize the plant, but that such work cannot be carried on regularly without expansion of its plant. The profit margin on subcontracts is not sufficiently large to cover these additional costs and hence work is accepted only when other business is lacking. The same company sometimes meets a period of high volume by purchasing parts or having them made by subcontractors. While the cost of such parts is usually higher than the cost to make them in the company's own plant, the additional cost is less than it would be if they were made on equipment which could be used only part of the time.

long-range planning   Knowledge of cost behavior patterns is helpful for long-run planning. The following description illustrates how a five-year plan is formulated by studying fixed costs and variable costs, relating costs to target sales, and then revising the plan as needed (*N.A.A. Accounting Practice Report No. 10*, p. 32):

> We have established a five-year planned profit goal based on an equitable return on investment from a five-day, two-shift operation. With this as a starting point, we have planned our fixed charge budgets. The profit goal, plus fixed cost, equals the total contribution margin which must be generated to cover the fixed cost and the desired profit return. We compute our two-shift, five-day volume and arrive at the gross profit per unit. Since we then have only variable costs to consider, we use our experienced standard variables by product line and, adding this to the gross profit, we arrive at a net sales figure which must be attained if we are to meet our profit objective.
>
> If the sales figure so reached is not competitive, we reverse the procedure by starting with competitive prices and determining the number of units we would sell on a two-shift, five-day basis. From this, we deduct our variable costs and then fixed expense and compare the operating profit result with our goal. If we find our expected profit is less than the goal, we know that we must: (1) review and reduce fixed charges, (2) reduce variable cost, (3) increase the sales volume and extend operations above the normal level, and/or (4) develop new or improved products commanding a higher price in relation to variable costs.

Other instances of cost–volume–profit analysis and long-range planning are examined in Chapter 13.

the P/V chart   Exhibit 3-1 can be recast in simpler form as a so-called P/V chart (a profit–volume graph). This form is preferred by many managers who are interested mainly in the impact of changes in volume on net income. The first graph in Exhibit 3-2 illustrates the chart, using the data in our example. The chart is constructed as follows:

1. The vertical axis is net income in dollars. The horizontal axis is volume in units (or in sales dollars, in many cases).
2. At zero volume, the net loss would be approximated by the total fixed costs—$200 in this example.
3. A contribution margin line will slope upward from the −$200 intercept at the rate of the unit contribution margin of 40¢. The line will intersect the volume axis at the breakeven point of 500 units. Each unit sold beyond the breakeven point will add 40¢ to net income.

The P/V chart provides a quick condensed comparison of how alternatives on pricing, variable costs, or fixed costs may affect net income as volume changes. For example, the second graph in Exhibit 3-2 shows how net income and the breakeven point would be affected by a decrease in rocket cost from 50¢ to 30¢ and an increase in rent from $200 to $240. The unit contribution would become 60¢, and the breakeven point would fall from 500 units to 400 units:

$$\text{New breakeven point} = \$240 \div \$.60$$
$$= 400 \text{ units}$$

Note also that the net income will increase at a much faster rate as volume increases.

EXHIBIT 3-2

P/V CHART

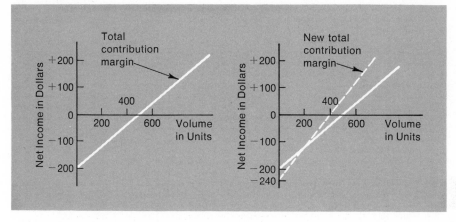

effects of The cost–volume–profit analysis in this chapter has focused on single
sales mix products. In multiproduct firms, sales mix is an important factor in calculating an overall company breakeven point. If the proportions of the mix
change, the cost–volume–profit relationships also change. When managers choose
a sales mix, it can be depicted on a breakeven chart or P/V chart by assuming
average revenues and costs for a given mix.

For example, suppose that a two-product company has a unit contribution
margin of $1 for Product A and $2 for Product B, and that fixed costs are
$100,000. The breakeven point would be 100,000 units if only A were sold and
50,000 units if only B were sold. Suppose the planned mix is three units of A
for each unit of B. The contribution margin for each "package" of products would
be 3 × $1 plus 1 × $2, or $5. The average contribution margin per unit of
product would be $5 ÷ 4 units in each package = $1.25. The breakeven point,
assuming that the mix is maintained, would be:

$$\$100{,}000 \div \$1.25 = 80{,}000 \text{ units (consisting of } 60{,}000 \text{ units of A}$$
$$\text{and } 20{,}000 \text{ of B)}$$

These relationships are shown in Exhibit 3-3. The slopes of the solid lines
depict the unit contribution margins of each product. The slope of the broken
line depicts the average contribution per unit. Suppose the total planned sales
are 160,000 units, consisting of 120,000 units of A and 40,000 of B. Exhibit 3-3
shows that if overall unit sales and mix targets are achieved, net income would
be $100,000. However, if the mix changes, net income may be much greater
because the proportion of sales of B might be higher than anticipated. The
opposite effect would occur if A sold in a higher proportion than expected. When
the sales mix changes, the breakeven point and the expected net income at various
sales levels are altered. Chapter 26 investigates the problem of sales mix in more
detail.

61

EXHIBIT 3-3

P/V CHART AND SALES MIX

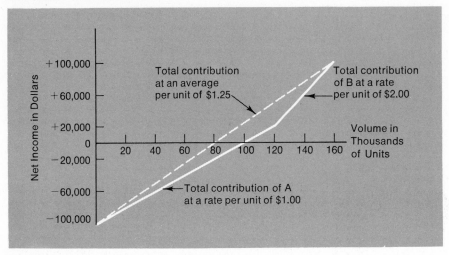

summary

The modern multiproduct company's performance is influenced by so many factors that the attempt to portray all of them on a breakeven chart by making assumptions is an ambitious one. The breakeven chart may be compared to the use of a meat-ax, not a scalpel. The chart is useful as a frame of reference for analysis, as a vehicle for expressing overall performance, and as a planning device.

The following points highlight the analytical usefulness of cost–volume–profit analysis as a tool for profit planning:

1. A change in either the selling price or the variable cost rates alters the breakeven point and the contribution margin ratio (marginal income ratio).
2. As sales exceed the breakeven point, a high contribution margin ratio will result in greater profits than a small contribution margin ratio.
3. A low contribution margin ratio necessitates great increases in volume to obtain noticeable increases in profits.
4. If other factors do not change, a percentage change in fixed costs alters the breakeven point by the same percentage and alters the net profit by the amount of the change.
5. A large margin of safety means that a large decrease in sales can occur before losses are suffered.

Whenever the underlying assumptions of cost–volume–profit analysis do not correspond to a given situation, the limitations of the analysis must be clearly recognized. A single breakeven graph is static, because it is a picture of relationships that prevail under only one set of assumptions. If conditions change, a different set of cost–volume–profit relationships is likely to appear. The fluid nature of these relationships must be kept uppermost in the minds of executives and accountants if the breakeven tool is to be useful and educational.

Properly used, cost–volume–profit analysis offers essential background for important management decisions regarding distribution channels, outside contracting, sales-promotion expenditures, and pricing strategies. It offers an overall view of costs and sales in relation to profit planning, and it provides clues to possible changes in management strategy. It is also the springboard for a different type of income statement, which emphasizes cost behavior patterns. This is often called the "contribution" income statement; it is contrasted with the traditional income statement in Problem 2 of the Problems for Self-Study in this chapter.

suggested readings

The National Association of Accountants (N.A.A.) has published a vast number of research reports throughout the years. A complete list will be found in the appendix of this book. The following reports are especially pertinent to cost–volume–profit analysis: Nos. 16, 17, 18, 23, and 37.

In subsequent chapters, additional references will be made to pertinent N.A.A. reports, not only for their own sake, but also because they usually contain helpful references to applicable literature.

Problems for Self-Study

Problem 1 Here is the income statement of C Company:

Net sales		$500,000
Less expenses:		
Variable	$350,000	
Fixed	250,000	600,000
Net loss		($100,000)

Assume that variable expenses will always remain the same percentage of sales.
  a. If fixed expenses are increased by $100,000, what amount of sales will cause the firm to break even?
  b. With the proposed increase in fixed expenses, what amount of sales will yield a net income of $50,000?

Solution 1 This problem differs from the example in the text because all data are expressed in dollars; no information is given on the number of units:
  a. Let S = Breakeven sales in dollars

$$S = \text{Variable Expenses} + \text{Fixed Expenses} + \text{Desired Net Income}$$

$$S = \frac{\$350,000}{\$500,000} S + (\$250,000 + \$100,000)$$

$$S = .70\,S + \$350,000$$

$$.30\,S = \$350,000$$

$$S = \$1,166,667$$

b. Let S = Sales needed to earn \$50,000

$$S = .70\,S + \$350,000 + \$50,000$$

$$.30\,S = \$400,000$$

$$S = \$1,333,333$$

Note that 30 percent of each sales dollar is available for the coverage of fixed expenses and the making of *net income*. This *contribution margin ratio* (*variable income ratio* or *contribution percentage*) is computed by subtracting the variable expense percentage, 70 percent, from 100 percent. This relationship is the foundation for the following commonly used formulas:

a. $\text{B.E.} = \dfrac{\text{Fixed Expenses} + \text{Desired Net Income}}{1 - \dfrac{\text{Variable Expenses}}{\text{Sales}}}$

or $\dfrac{\text{Fixed Expenses} + \text{Desired Net Income}}{\text{Contribution Margin Ratio}}$

$\text{B.E.} = \dfrac{\$350,000}{1 - \dfrac{\$350,000}{\$500,000}}$ or $\dfrac{\$350,000}{.30}$

$\text{B.E.} = \$1,166,667$

b. $\text{Required Sales } (RS) = \dfrac{\text{Fixed Expenses} + \text{Desired Net Income}}{\text{Contribution Margin Ratio}}$

$$RS = \dfrac{\$400,000}{.30}$$

$$RS = \$1,333,333$$

These examples demonstrate some very fundamental points about breakeven analysis. The most important point is the contribution margin notion, the idea that every dollar of sales contains the same contribution toward the coverage of fixed costs and the earning of net income.

Problem 2   Costing for planning and control emphasizes variable- and fixed-cost behavior patterns. In contrast, product costing emphasizes functional cost classifications. When cost behavior is the focus, financial statements are often based on a contribution approach rather than on the traditional functional approach that you learned in Chapter 2. Exhibit 3-4 shows the difference in outline form:

EXHIBIT 3-4

CONTRIBUTION APPROACH		TRADITIONAL (FUNCTIONAL) APPROACH	
Sales	XXX	Sales	XXX
Less all variable expenses	XXX	Less manufacturing cost of	
Contribution margin	XXX	goods sold	XXX
Less fixed expenses	XXX	Gross profit	XXX
Operating income	XXX	Less selling and administrative	
		expenses	XXX
		Operating income	XXX

Using the following data (in millions) for 19_3 for the Sprouse Company, prepare a contribution income statement and a traditional income statement. Assume that there are no beginning or ending inventories. (The problem of changes in inventory levels and how they affect these statements is discussed in Chapter 10.)

Sales	$150	Variable factory overhead	$ 5
Variable selling expenses*	15	Direct labor	20
Variable administrative expenses	12	Direct materials used	50
Fixed selling expenses	20	Fixed administrative expenses	5
Fixed factory overhead	10		

* These and other expenses would be detailed.

Solution 2

SPROUSE CO.		SPROUSE CO.	
Contribution Income Statement For the Year Ending Dec. 31, 19_3 (In millions of dollars)		Traditional (Functional) Income Statement For the Year Ending Dec. 31, 19_3 (In millions of dollars)	

SPROUSE CO.

Contribution Income Statement
For the Year Ending Dec. 31, 19_3
(In millions of dollars)

Sales		$150
Less variable expenses:		
Direct materials used	$50	
Direct labor	20	
Variable factory over-head	5	
Total variable manu-facturing costs	$75	
Variable selling expenses	15	
Variable administrative expenses	12	
Total variable expenses		102
Contribution margin		$ 48
Less fixed expenses:		
Fixed factory overhead	$10	
Fixed selling expenses	20	
Fixed administrative expenses	5	
Total fixed expenses		35
Operating income		$ 13

SPROUSE CO.

Traditional (Functional) Income Statement
For the Year Ending Dec. 31, 19_3
(In millions of dollars)

Sales			$150
Less manufacturing cost of goods sold:			
Direct material used	$50		
Direct labor	20		
Variable factory over-head	5		
Fixed factory overhead	10	85	
Gross profit			$ 65
Selling expenses:			
Variable	$15		
Fixed	20	$35	
Administrative expenses:			
Variable	$12		
Fixed	5	17	
Total selling and ad-ministrative expenses			52
Operating income			$ 13

---

questions, problems, and cases

3-1. Why is it more accurate to describe the subject matter of this chapter as *cost–volume–profit relationships* rather than as *breakeven analysis?*

3-2. Why is it often more desirable to plot fixed costs above the variable costs on a breakeven chart?

3-3. What are the principal differences between the accountant's and the economist's breakeven charts?

3-4. Define: *contribution margin, variable cost ratio, contribution margin ratio,* and *margin of safety.*

3-5. "This breakeven approach is great stuff. All you need to do is worry about variable costs. The fixed costs will take care of themselves." Discuss.

3-6 A lithographic company follows a policy of high pricing each month until it reaches its monthly breakeven point. After this point is reached, the company tends to quote low prices on jobs for the rest of the month. What is your opinion of this policy? As a regular customer, and suspecting this policy, what would you do?

3-7. Define *sales mix*. What relation does sales mix have to cost–volume–profit analysis?

3-8. Cost–Volume–Profits and Shoe Stores.   The Walk Rite Shoe Company operates a chain of rented shoe stores. The stores sell ten different styles of men's shoes with identical purchase costs and selling prices. Walk Rite is trying to determine the desirability of opening another store, which would have the following expense and revenue relationships:

	Per Pair
Variable data:	
Selling price	$ 30.00
Cost of shoes	$ 19.50
Salesmen's commissions	1.50
Total variable expenses	$ 21.00
Annual fixed expenses:	
Rent	$ 60,000
Salaries	$200,000
Advertising	80,000
Other fixed expenses	20,000
	$360,000

required   (Consider each question independently.)

1. What is the annual breakeven point in dollar sales and in unit sales?
2. If 35,000 pairs of shoes are sold, what would be the store's net income (loss)?
3. If the store manager were paid 30¢ per pair as commission, what would be the annual breakeven point in dollar sales and in unit sales?
4. Refer to the original data. If sales commissions were discontinued in favor of an $81,000 increase in fixed salaries, what would be the annual breakeven point in dollars and in unit sales?
5. Refer to the original data. If the store manager were paid 30¢ per pair as commission on each pair sold in excess of the breakeven point, what would be the store's net income if 50,000 pairs were sold?

3-9. Exercises in Cost–Volume–Profit Relationships.   The Fresh Buy Grocers Corporation owns and operates twelve supermarkets in and around Chicago. You are given the following corporate budget data for next year:

Sales	$10,000,000
Fixed expenses	1,650,000
Variable expenses	8,200,000

required   Compute expected profit for each of the following deviations from budgeted data. (Consider each case independently.)

A. 10 percent increase in total contribution margin
B. 10 percent decrease in total contribution margin
C. 5 percent increase in fixed costs

D. 5 percent decrease in fixed costs

E. 8 percent increase in sales volume

F. 8 percent decrease in sales volume

G. 10 percent increase in fixed costs and 10 percent increase in sales volume

H. 5 percent increase in fixed costs and 5 percent decrease in variable costs

3-10. **Effects of Price Changes.**

1. The Charta Company has just been formed. The owners have a patented process that will make them the sole distributors of Product Y. Their first year, the capacity of their plant will be 9,000 units, and this is the amount they feel they will be able to sell.

   Their costs are:

   Direct labor, $1.50 per unit
   Raw materials, $0.50 per unit
   Other variable costs, $1.00 per unit
   Fixed costs, $24,000

   If the company wishes to make a profit of $30,000 the first year, what should their selling price be? What is the contribution margin?

2. At the end of the first year, they wish to increase their volume. An increase of $10,000 in annual fixed costs will increase their capacity to 50,000 units. They now want a profit of $76,000, and to achieve this end they also invest $50,000 in advertising. No other costs change. Under these new conditions, how many units will they have to sell to realize this profit, if their new selling price will be $7 per unit?

3-11. **Effects of Size of Machines.** The Dore Foods Company is planning to manufacture doughnuts for its chain of coffee shops throughout the city. Two alternatives have been proposed for the production of the doughnuts—use of a semiautomatic machine, or a fully automatic machine.

The shops now purchase their doughnuts from an outside supplier at a cost of 5¢ per doughnut.

	SEMIAUTOMATIC	AUTOMATIC
Annual fixed cost	$3,000	$5,000
Variable cost per doughnut	$ .02	$ .015

required The president has asked for the following information:

1. For each machine, the minimum annual number of doughnuts that must be sold in order to have the total annual costs equal to outside purchase costs

2. The most profitable alternative for 300,000 doughnuts annually

3. The most profitable alternative for 600,000 doughnuts annually

4. The volume level that would produce the same net income regardless of the type of machine owned

3-12. **Effects of Sales Forecast.** The Fragile Company has just been incorporated and plans to produce a product that will sell for $10 per unit. Preliminary market surveys show that demand will be less than 10,000 units per year, but it is not as yet clear how much less.

The company has the choice of buying one of two machines, each of which has a capacity of 10,000 units per year. Machine A would have fixed costs of $30,000 per year and would yield a profit of $30,000 per year if sales were 10,000 units. Machine B has a fixed cost per year of $16,000 and would yield a profit of $24,000 per year with sales of 10,000 units. Variable costs behave linearly for both machines.

required

1. Breakeven sales for each machine

2. The sales level where both machines are equally profitable

3. The range of sales where one machine is more profitable than the other

3-13. Fill In Blanks.   In the data presented below, fill in the information that belongs in the blank spaces.

SALES	VARIABLE EXPENSES	FIXED EXPENSES	TOTAL COSTS	NET PROFIT	CONTRIBUTION MARGIN RATIO
$1,000	$700	$___	$1,000	$___	___
1,500	___	300	___	___	.30
___	500	___	800	1,200	___
2,000	___	300	___	200	___

3-14. Cost–Volume–Profit Relationships.   The Dowell Company makes and sells pens. Some pertinent facts follow:

Present sales volume, 500,000 units per year at a selling price of 50¢ per unit. Fixed expenses, $80,000 per year. Variable expenses are 30¢ per unit.

required

(Consider each case separately.)

1. a. What is the present total profit for a year?
   b. What is the present breakeven point in dollars?

Compute the new profit for each of the following changes:

2. A 4¢-per-unit increase in variable expenses

3. A 10 percent increase in fixed expenses and a 10 percent increase in sales volume

4. A 20 percent decrease in fixed expenses, a 20 percent decrease in selling price, a 10 percent decrease in variable expenses per unit, and a 40 percent increase in units sold

Compute the new breakeven point in units for each of the following changes:

5. A 10 percent increase in fixed expenses

6. A 10 percent increase in selling price and a $20,000 increase in fixed expenses

3-15. Choosing Most Profitable Volume Level.

1. Company B manufactures and sells dresses at a variable cost of $3 each and a fixed cost of x. It can sell 6,000 dresses at $5 and net $2,000 profit, or it can sell 3,500 at $6 and another 2,000 at $4 each. Which alternative should Company B choose?

2. Company C manufactures and sells a consumer item. It can produce and sell up to 3,000 units at a variable cost of $1.50 per unit and fixed costs of $5,000; from 3,001 to 6,000 units at a variable cost of $1 per unit and fixed costs of $7,000; and from 6,001 to 10,000 units at a variable cost of $.50 per unit and fixed costs of $15,000. The president of Company C has discovered that 2,500 units can be sold at a price of $6 each, or 5,000 at a price of $4 each. 8,000 units probably could be sold at $3.50 per unit if advertising were increased by $1,000 and selling costs by $.10 per unit. The latter costs are in addition to those already stated for the 6,001-to-10,000-unit range. How many units should Company C plan to produce and sell—2,500, 5,000, or 8,000?

3-16. **Target Net Incomes and Contribution Margins.** The Blair Company has a maximum capacity of 200,000 units per year. Variable manufacturing costs are $12 per unit. Fixed factory overhead is $600,000 per year. Variable selling and administrative costs are $5 per unit, whereas fixed selling and administrative costs are $300,000 per year. Current sales price is $23 per unit.

required (Consider each situation independently.)

1. What is the breakeven point in (a) units? (b) dollar sales?
2. How many *units* must be sold to earn a target net income of $240,000 per year?
3. Assume that the company's sales for the year just ended totaled 185,000 units. A strike at a major supplier has caused a materials shortage, so that the current year's sales will reach only 160,000 units. Top management is planning to slash fixed costs so that the total for the current year will be $59,000 less than last year. Management is also thinking of either increasing the selling price or reducing variable costs, or both, in order to earn a target net income that will be the same dollar amount as last year's. The company has already sold 30,000 units this year at a sales price of $23 per unit with variable costs per unit unchanged. What contribution margin per unit is needed on the remaining 130,000 units in order to reach the target net income?

3-17. **Effect on Profits of Change in Price [SIA].** The Canadian Zinc Diecasting Company is one of several suppliers of part X to an automobile manufacturing firm. Orders are distributed to the various diecasting companies on a fairly even basis; however, the sales manager of Canadian Zinc believes that with a reduction in price he could secure another 30 percent increase in units sold.

The general manager has asked you to analyze the sales manager's proposal and submit your recommendation.

The following data are available:

	PRESENT	PROPOSED
Unit price	$2.50	$2.00
Unit sales volume	200,000 units	Plus 30%
Variable cost (total)	$350,000	Same unit variable cost
Fixed cost	$120,000	$120,000
Profit	$ 30,000	?

required
1. Net profit or loss based on the sales manager's proposal
2. Unit sales required under the proposed price to make the original $30,000 profit

3-18. **Effect of Cost Behavior on Profits; Changing Channels of Distribution.** Eastinghouse Co., an appliance manufacturer, has always sold its products through wholesalers. Last year its sales were $2,000,000 and its net profit 10 percent of sales.

As a result of the increase in appliance sales in department stores and discount houses, Eastinghouse is considering eliminating its wholesalers and selling directly to retailers. It is estimated that this would result in a 40 percent drop in sales, but net profit would be $180,000 as a result of elimination of the middleman. Fixed expenses would increase from the present figure of $200,000 to $300,000, owing to the additional warehouses and distribution facilities required.

required
1. Would the proposed change raise or lower the breakeven point in dollars? By how much?

2. What dollar sales volume must Eastinghouse obtain under the proposed plan to make as much profit as it made last year?

3-19. Influence of Relevant Range on Cost Behavior. The Charne Company's cost behavior is as follows:

PRODUCTION RANGE IN UNITS	FIXED COSTS
0– 20,000	$160,000
20,001– 65,000	190,000
65,001– 90,000	210,000
90,001–100,000	250,000

At an activity of 70,000 units per year, variable costs total $280,000. Full capacity is 100,000 units per year.

required
(Each case given below is independent of any other and should be considered individually.)

1. Production is now set at 50,000 units per year with a sales price of $7.50 per unit. What is the minimum number of additional units needed to be sold in an unrelated market at $5.50 per unit to show a total net profit of $3,000 per year?

2. Production is now set at 60,000 units per year. By how much may sales-promotion costs be increased to bring production up to 80,000 units and still earn a net profit of 5 percent of total sales if the selling price is held at $7.50?

3. If net profit is currently $10,000, with fixed costs at $160,000, and a 2 percent increase in price will leave units sold unchanged but increase profits by $5,000, what is the present volume in units?

3-20. Comparison of Two Companies [SIA, adapted]. Black and White are the owners of the Modern Processing Company and the Oldway Manufacturing Company, respectively. These companies manufacture and sell the same product, and competition between the two owners has always been friendly. Cost and profit data have been freely exchanged. Uniform selling prices have been set by market conditions.

Black and White differ markedly in their management thinking. Operations at Modern are highly mechanized and the direct labor force is paid on a fixed-salary basis. Oldway uses manual hourly paid labor for the most part and pays incentive bonuses. Modern's salesmen are paid a fixed salary, whereas Oldway's salesmen are paid small salaries plus commissions. Mr. White takes pride in his ability to adapt his costs to fluctuations in sales volume and has frequently chided Mr. Black on Modern's "inflexible overhead."

During 19_2, both firms reported the same profit on sales of $100,000. However, when comparing results at the end of 19_3, Mr. White was startled by the following results:

	MODERN		OLDWAY	
	19_2	*19_3*	*19_2*	*19_3*
Sales revenue	$100,000	$120,000	$100,000	$150,000
Costs and expenses	90,000	94,000	90,000	130,000
Net income	$ 10,000	$ 26,000	$ 10,000	$ 20,000
Percent on sales	10%	21⅔%	10%	13⅓%

On the assumption that operating inefficiencies must have existed, White and his accountant made a thorough investigation of costs but could not uncover any evidence of costs that were out of line. At a loss to explain the lower increase in profits on a much higher increase in sales volume, they have asked you to prepare an explanation.

You find that fixed costs and expenses recorded over the two-year period were as follows:

Modern	$70,000 each year
Oldway	$10,000 each year

required

1. Prepare an explanation for Mr. White showing why Oldway's profits for 19_3 were lower than those reported by Modern despite the fact that Oldway's sales had been higher. Show relevant calculations to clarify the issue.

2. Indicate the volume of sales Oldway would have to have had in 19_3 to achieve the profit of $26,000 realized by Modern in 19_3.

3. Comment on the relative future positions of the two companies when there are reductions in sales volume.

3-21. **Comparison of Two Businesses.** Consider two businesses with the following unit prices and fixed and variable costs:

Business A:
Selling price per unit	$1.00
Variable cost per unit	$ .20
Fixed cost of operations per year	$5,000

Business B:
Selling price per unit	$1.00
Variable cost per unit	$ .60
Fixed cost of operations per year	$2,500

required

1. Calculate the breakeven point of each business in units.

2. Compute the profits of each business if sales in units are 10 percent above the breakeven point.

3. Which business would fare better if sales dropped to 5,000 units? Why?

4. Which business would fare better if the market collapsed and the price per unit fell to 50¢? Why?

3-22. **Promotion of Entertainment.** George Florene, a theatrical promoter, is trying to decide whether to engage The Bugs, a very popular singing group, for a one-night appearance at the local arena, which has a salable capacity of 5,000 seats. He has gathered the following data:

Rental, including ushering and cleanup service	$ 4,000
Advertising	3,000
Ticket service and ticket printing	1,000
Miscellaneous expenses	2,000
Entertainers' fee	10,000
Total	$20,000

Sales and entertainment taxes are 10 percent of the price (excluding the tax) on each ticket, and ticket prices include this tax. That is, if the price of the ticket is $5 (excluding taxes), the total price is $5.50. Therefore, the tax is one-eleventh of the total price of the ticket.

required All prices include the sales and entertainment taxes.

1. What is the average price for each ticket that is needed for Florene to break even, assuming that the arena can be filled to capacity?

2. Suppose Florene thinks that he can maximize his return by pricing as follows: 1,000 seats @ $10; 1,000 @ $8; 1,000 @ $6; and 2,000 @ $4. If the house were sold out, how much net income would be produced for Florene at such prices?

3. Suppose that The Bugs appeal mainly to young people who are unlikely to pay high prices. Suppose 300 seats are sold @ $10; 700 @ $8; 900 @ $6; and 2,000 @ $4. (a) How much net income would Florene make? (b) What is the average price of the sold tickets? How does it compare with your answer in part 1? In your own words, explain the difference.

4. a. The Bugs' agent phoned Florene and offered an alternate arrangement for compensation: $5,000 plus $1 per ticket sold, regardless of the ticket price. How would this arrangement affect your answers to parts 1, 2, and 3a? Show computations.
   b. If you were Florene, which arrangement would you prefer? Why?
   c. Would your answer to part 4b change if the compensation were based on $1.20 per ticket rather than $1.00? Why?

3-23. **Cost–Volume–Profit Relationships.** The McCovey Company has a maximum production capacity of 20,000 units per year. At that level, fixed costs are $280,000 annually. Variable costs per unit are $30 at all production levels.

For the ensuing year, the company has orders of 24,000 units at $50. If the company desires to make a minimum overall net income of $148,000 on these 24,000 units, what maximum unit purchase price would it be willing to pay to a subcontractor for 4,000 units? Assume that the subcontractor would act as McCovey's agent and deliver the units to customers directly and bear all related costs of manufacture, delivery, and so on. The customers, however, would pay McCovey directly as goods are delivered.

3-24. **Miscellaneous Alternatives; Contribution Income Statement.** The income statement of the Hall Company appears on the next page. Commissions are based on sales dollars; all other variable expenses vary in terms of units sold.

The factory has a capacity of 150,000 units per year. The results for 19_1 have been disappointing. Top management is sifting a number of possible ways to make operations profitable in 19_2.

required (Consider each situation independently.)

1. Recast the income statement into a contribution format. There will be three major sections: sales, variable expenses, and fixed expenses. Show costs per unit in an adjacent column. Allow adjacent space for entering your answers to part 2.

2. The sales manager is torn between two courses of action.
   a. He has studied the market potential and believes that a 15 percent slash in price would fill the plant to capacity
   b. He wants to increase prices by 25 percent, to increase advertising by $150,000, and to boost commissions to 10 percent of sales. Under these circumstances, he thinks that unit volume will increase by 50 percent. Prepare the budgeted income statements, using a contribution margin format and two columns. What would be the new net income or loss under each alternative? Assume that there are no changes in fixed costs other than advertising.

HALL COMPANY

Income Statement
For the Year Ended December 31, 19_1

Sales (90,000 units @ $4.00)			$360,000
Cost of goods sold:			
Direct materials		$90,000	
Direct labor		90,000	
Factory overhead:			
Variable	$18,000		
Fixed	80,000	98,000	278,000
Gross margin			$ 82,000
Selling expenses:			
Variable:			
Sales commissions*	$18,000		
Shipping	3,600	$21,600	
Fixed:			
Advertising, salaries, etc.		40,000	$61,600
Administrative expenses:			
Variable		$ 4,500	
Fixed		20,400	24,900	86,500
Net loss			$ (4,500)

*Based on sales dollars, not physical units.

3. The president does not want to tinker with the price. How much may advertising be increased to bring production and sales up to 130,000 units and still earn a target profit of 5 percent of sales?

4. A mail-order firm is willing to buy 60,000 units of product "if the price is right." Assume that the present market of 90,000 units at $4 each will not be disturbed. Hall Company will not pay any sales commission. The mail-order firm will pick up the units directly at the Hall factory. However, Hall must refund $24,000 of the total sales price as a promotional and advertising allowance for the mail-order firm. In addition, special packaging will increase manufacturing costs on these 60,000 units by 10¢ per unit. At what unit price must the mail-order chain business be quoted for Hall to break even in 19_2?

5. The president's mother-in-law thinks that a fancy new package will aid consumer sales and ultimately Hall's sales. Present packaging costs per unit are all variable and consist of 5¢ direct materials and 4¢ direct labor; new packaging costs will be 30¢ and 13¢, respectively. Assuming no other changes in cost behavior, how many units must be sold to earn a net profit of $20,000?

3-25. **P/V Chart and Sales Mix.** The Bannister Company has three products—A, B, and C—having contribution margins of $3, $2, and $1, respectively. The president is planning to sell 200,000 units in the forthcoming period, consisting of 20,000 A, 100,000 B, and 80,000 C. The company's fixed costs for the period are $255,000.

required

1. What is the company breakeven point in units, assuming that the given sales mix is maintained?

2. Prepare a P/V chart for a volume of 200,000 units. Have a broken line represent the average contribution margin per unit and have a solid line

represent the contribution margins of each product. What is the total contribution margin at a volume of 200,000 units? Net income?

3. What would net income become if 20,000 units of A, 80,000 units of B, and 100,000 units of C were sold?

3-26. Breakeven Analysis and the Product Mix Assumption. Suppose that a company has the following budget data for 19_1 for the Blanton Company:

	PRODUCT		TOTAL
	X	Y	
Selling price	$3	$6	
Variable expenses	1	2	
Contribution margin	$2	$4	
Total fixed expenses	$100,000	$120,000	
Number of units to be sold to break even	?	?	?
Number of units expected to be sold	30,000	50,000	80,000

required

1. Compute the breakeven point for each product.

2. Suppose that Products X and Y were made in the same plant. Assume that a prolonged strike at the factory of the sole supplier of raw materials prevented the production of X for all of 19_1. Suppose also that the Blanton fixed costs were unaffected.
   a. What is the breakeven point for the company as a whole, assuming that no X is produced?
   b. Suppose instead that the shortage applied so that only X and no Y could be produced. Then what is the breakeven point for the company as a whole?

3. Draw a breakeven chart for the company as a whole, using an average selling price and an average variable expense per unit. What is the breakeven point under this aggregate approach? What is the breakeven point if you add together the individual breakeven points that you computed in requirement 1? Why is the aggregate breakeven point different from the sum of the individual breakeven points?

3-27. Product Mix and Breakeven Computations [SIA]. The Diogo Co., Ltd., manufactures and sells three products—A, B, and C. The following data apply to these products:

	PRODUCT A	PRODUCT B	PRODUCT C
Units sold during the year just ended	10,000	5,000	25,000
Selling price per unit	$ 10.00	$ 10.00	$ 20.00
Variable costs per unit	7.50	5.00	12.00
Allocated fixed costs (annual)	50,000.00	25,000.00	25,000.00

The controller calculates the company's breakeven point on the foregoing data to be 16,000 units. At a meeting of the budget committee, he gave to each member of the committee a copy of the breakeven chart.

The sales manager asked the controller to state what he expected the company to make next year, assuming the following sales:

Product A	10,000 units
Product B	10,000 units
Product C	20,000 units
	40,000 units

The controller answered, "As you can see by the breakeven chart, our profit will be $150,000 for 40,000 units."

required

1. Do you agree with an estimated profit of $150,000 for the next year? Why?

2. Based on the sales manager's expectations of sales, calculate the breakeven point in units for next year and give the product mix in units.

3. On which basis might the fixed costs be allocated to the three types of products so that the total of the breakeven points specific to each type of product equals the company's breakeven point? Submit data as proof.

3-28. **Review of Chapters 2 and 3.** For each of the following independent cases, find the unknowns designated by letters.

	CASE 1	CASE 2	CASE 3	CASE 4
Sales	$100,000	$100,000	$ M	$100,000
Direct materials used	29,000	H	55,000	40,000
Direct labor	10,000	30,000	25,000	15,000
Variable selling and administrative expenses	16,000	K	70,000	T
Fixed manufacturing overhead	30,000	I	Q	20,000
Fixed selling and administrative expenses	9,000	J	R	10,000
Gross profit	A	25,000	P	20,000
Finished-goods inventory, 1/1	0	0	0	5,000
Finished-goods inventory, 12/31	0	0	0	5,000
Contribution margin (dollars)	E	30,000	40,000	V
Direct-material inventory, 1/1	3,000	12,000	N	20,000
Direct-material inventory, 12/31	10,000	5,000	20,000	W
Variable manufacturing overhead	C	5,000	10,000	X
Work in process, 1/1	0	0	0	9,000
Work in process, 12/31	0	0	0	9,000
Purchases of direct materials	D	15,000	60,000	50,000
Breakeven point (in dollars)	F	66,667	S	Y
Cost of goods manufactured	B	G	110,000	U
Net income (loss)	1,000	L	5,000	(5,000)

Cost Accumulation for Product Costing: Job-Order Accounting

4

This chapter examines the general approach to accounting for costs in a multiple-purpose accounting system. Two major cost objects are discussed: departments and units of product. The former illustrates the control purpose of the system; the latter illustrates the inventory-valuation purpose.

Here we must dwell heavily on techniques, because they are an essential part of the accounting function. Equally important, there is an opportunity to become familiar with many terms and fundamental ledger relationships that will aid visualization and comprehension of the key subjects covered in Chapters 5 through 11.

If you have never worked in a factory, you will need to study this chapter and its appendix with care. The chapter was written to be understood by the student with little business background. If you have had some business experience, you will probably be able to skip the appendix to this chapter. If you want a more complete study of the bookkeeping aspects of cost accounting, refer to Chapter 19 and the appendix to Chapter 20.

In any event, all students should study the section on overhead accounting very carefully.

JOB-ORDER APPROACH TO COSTING PRODUCTS

departments or cost centers   Management accounting concentrates on departments as the locus of cost planning, cost accumulation, and cost control. These departments are often called *cost centers*. A cost center is the smallest segment of activity or area of responsibility for which costs are accumulated. Typically, cost centers are departments, but in some instances a department may contain several cost centers. For example, although a machining department may be under one foreman, it may contain various groups of machines, such as lathes, punch presses, and milling machines. Each group of machines is sometimes regarded as a separate cost center with its own assistant foreman.

The individuals in charge of departments or cost centers should have the authority and the responsibility for efficient performance. An accounting system may accumulate costs by departments or cost centers, to assist planning and control by pinpointing responsibility as much as possible.

A second major objective of the accounting system is product costing for purposes of inventory valuation and income determination. This product-costing purpose means that department costs must be applied (assigned) to the physical units that pass through the departments. Therefore, the accountant must satisfy two purposes: control and product costing.

Traditionally, accounting systems have been oriented toward product costing rather than planning and control. This chapter will examine the job-order costing method as an example of a traditional and widespread accounting system that emphasizes product costing.

distinction between job costing and process costing: a matter of averaging   The two polar extremes of product costing are usually labeled as *job-order costing* and *process costing*. *Job-order* (or *job-cost* or *production-order*) accounting methods are used by companies whose products are readily identified by individual units or batches, each of which receives varying degrees of attention and skill. Industries that commonly use job-order methods include construction, printing, aircraft, furniture, and machinery.

Process costing is most often found in such industries as chemicals, oil, textiles, plastics, paints, flour, canneries, rubber, lumber, food processing, glass, mining, cement, and meat packing. In these there is mass production of like units, which usually pass in continuous fashion through a series of uniform production steps called *operations* or *processes*. This is in contrast to the production of tailor-made or unique goods, such as special-purpose machinery or printing.

Where manufacturing is conducted by continuous operations, costs are accumulated by departments (sometimes also called *operations* or *processes*). The center of attention is the total department costs for a given time period in relation to the units processed. Accumulated department costs are divided by quantities produced during a given period in order to get broad, average unit costs. Then unit costs are multiplied by units transferred to obtain total costs applied to those units. These details of *process costing* are discussed in Chapter 17, which may be studied immediately after Chapter 4, if preferred.

The distinction between the job-cost and the process-cost methods centers largely around how product costing is accomplished. Unlike process costing, which deals with broad averages and great masses of like units, the essential feature of the job-cost method is the attempt to apply costs to specific jobs, which may consist of either a single physical unit (like a custom sofa) or a few like units (such as a dozen tables) in a distinct batch or job lot.

The most important point is that product costing under both cost methods is an averaging process. The unit cost used for inventory purposes is the result of taking some accumulated cost and dividing it by some measure of production.

EXHIBIT 4-1

JOB-COST SHEET

SAMPLE COMPANY   Job Order No._____

For stock _____ Customer_____

Product _____ Date started _____ Date completed _____

Department A

Direct Material			Direct Labor			Overhead	
Date	Reference	Amount	Date	Reference	Amount	Date	Amount
	(stores requisition number)			(work ticket number)			(based on predetermined overhead rate)

Department B

Direct Material			Direct Labor			Overhead	
Date	Reference	Amount	Date	Reference	Amount	Date	Amount

Summary

Selling Price   xxx

		Dept. A	Dept. B	Total
Costs:	Direct material	xx	xx	xxx
	Direct labor	xx	xx	xxx
	Factory overhead applied	xx	xx	xxx
		xxx	xxx	
				xxx
Gross Profit				xx

The basic distinction between job-order costing and process costing is the breadth of the denominator: In job-order costing, it is small (for example, one painting, 100 advertising circulars, or one special packaging machine); but in process costing, it is large (for example, thousands of pounds, gallons, or board feet).

Again one must distinguish between costs for control and product costs. Whether a process-cost or a job-cost approach is used, costs must be accumulated by cost centers or departments for control purposes. The typical job-order approach uses one account for tracing product cost and another account or accounts for accumulating department costs.

The basic document used to accumulate product costs is called the *job-order* or *job-cost sheet*. The file of uncompleted job orders makes up the subsidiary ledger for Work-in-Process Control. Exhibit 4-1 illustrates a job-cost sheet.

Job shops usually have several jobs passing through the plant simultaneously. Each job typically requires different kinds of materials and department effort. Thus, jobs may have different routings, different operations, and different times required for completion. *Stores requisitions* (Exhibit 4-2) are used to charge job-cost sheets for direct materials used. *Work tickets* (Exhibit 4-3) are used to charge jobs for direct labor used. This work ticket (sometimes called *time ticket* or *time card*) indicates the time spent on a specific job. An employee who is paid an hourly wage and who operates a lathe will have one *clock card* (Exhibit 4-4), which is used as a basis for determining his individual earnings; but he will also fill out or punch several *work tickets* each day as he starts and stops work on particular jobs or operations.

EXHIBIT 4-2

STORES REQUISITION

Job No.———————————————
Department———————— .   .   Date————————————
Debit Account——————————————
Authorized by———————————— .

Description	Quantity	Unit Cost	Amount

EXHIBIT 4-3

WORK TICKET

Employee No. _741_	Date _2/22_	Job No. _41_
Operation _drill_	Account _Work in Process_	Dept. _A_
		Pieces:
Stop _4:45 P.M._	Rate _$6.00_	Worked _15_
		Rejected _—_
Start _4:00 P.M._	Amount _$4.50_	Completed _15_

responsibility and control   The department responsibility for usage of direct materials and direct labor is clearly drawn. Copies of direct-material requisitions and direct-labor work tickets are used for two purposes. One copy is used to post to job-cost sheets; another copy is used for fixing responsibility by departments. The department heads are usually kept informed of their direct-material and direct-labor performance by daily or weekly classified summaries of requisitions and work tickets charged to their departments.

In addition, the job-cost sheets serve a control function. Comparisons are made between predictions of job costs and the costs finally applied to the job. Deviations are investigated so that their underlying causes may be discovered.

EXHIBIT 4-4

CLOCK CARD

Name_____   Employee Number_____

Department_____   Week ending_____

Date	AM		PM		Excess Hours		Total Hours
	In	Out	In	Out	In	Out	

Regular Time_____ hrs. @ _____ _____

Overtime Premium_____ hrs. @ _____ _____

Gross Earnings _____

ILLUSTRATION OF JOB-ORDER ACCOUNTING

Because each job order often contains different materials from the others and gets a different routing through departments, the time, costs, and attention devoted by departments to any given job may vary considerably. It is desirable, therefore, to keep a separate account for inventory purposes and another account, or other accounts, for department responsibility purposes. In practice, a Work-in-Process account, supported by a subsidiary ledger of individual job orders, is widely used for product-costing purposes. However, practice differs greatly as to the general-ledger accumulation of costs for department responsibility purposes.

Now let us turn to a specific example. Assume that a factory has two departments and uses the job-cost system. Department A is the machining department; Department B is the assembly department. Exhibit 4-5 shows T-account relationships. Typical general-journal entries for a job-cost system follow. (It is helpful to trace each entry to the accounts in Exhibit 4-5.) Special points are included in the explanation for each entry.

1. Stores control*	60,000	
Accounts (or vouchers) payable		60,000
To record purchases of materials and supplies.		

* The word "control," as used in journal entries and general-ledger accounts, has a narrow bookkeeping meaning. As contrasted with "control" in the management sense, "control" here means that the control account in question is supported by an underlying subsidiary ledger. To illustrate: In financial accounting, Accounts Receivable–Control is supported by a subsidiary customers' ledger. The same meaning applies here.

All purchases of materials and supplies are charged to Stores as purchased because the storekeeper is accountable for them. The subsidiary records for Stores Control would be perpetual-inventory records called *stores cards*. As a minimum, these cards would contain quantity columns for receipts, issues, and balance. Exhibit 4-6 is an illustration of a stores card.

2. Work-in-process control	48,000	
Factory department overhead control (supplies)	4,000	
Stores control		52,000
To record materials and supplies issued.		

Responsibility is fixed by using *stores requisitions* (sometimes called *material requisitions*) as a basis for charging departments. A stores requisition was shown in Exhibit 4-2.

Direct materials are charged to job orders; indirect materials (supplies) are charged to individual department-overhead cost sheets, which form a subsidiary ledger for Factory Department Overhead Control. In job-cost accounting, a single Factory Department Overhead Control account may be kept in the general ledger. The detail of factory overhead is charged to departments and recorded in subsidiary department-overhead ledgers (department-overhead cost sheets). (See Exhibit 4-7.) In turn, the overhead is applied to jobs, as will be described later.

EXHIBIT 4-5

JOB-COST SYSTEM, DIAGRAM OF LEDGER RELATIONSHIPS

(Circled numbers refer to journal entries described more thoroughly in text.)

① Purchases

② Usage of direct materials ($48,000) and supplies ($4,000)

③ Incurrence of direct labor ($39,000) and indirect labor ($5,000)

④ Payment of payroll liability

⑤ Incurrence of other factory overhead

⑥ Application of factory overhead

⑦ Completion of goods

⑧ Cost of goods sold

General Ledger

STORES CONTROL

| ① 60,000 | ② 52,000 |

WORK-IN-PROCESS CONTROL

② 48,000	⑦ 108,800
③ 39,000	
⑥ 26,460	

FINISHED-GOODS CONTROL

| ⑦ 108,800 | ⑧ 102,000 |

COST OF SALES

| ⑧ 102,000 | |

FACTORY DEPARTMENT OVERHEAD CONTROL

② 4,000	
③ 5,000	
⑤ 18,000	

FACTORY OVERHEAD APPLIED

| | ⑥ 26,460 |

ACCRUED PAYROLL

| ④ 44,000 | ③ 44,000 |

ACCOUNTS PAYABLE

| | ① 60,000 |
| | ⑤ 11,000 |

UNEXPIRED INSURANCE

| | ⑤ 1,000 |

ALLOWANCE FOR DEPRECIATION

| | ⑤ 6,000 |

CASH

| | ④ 44,000 |

EXHIBIT 4-5 *(Cont.)*

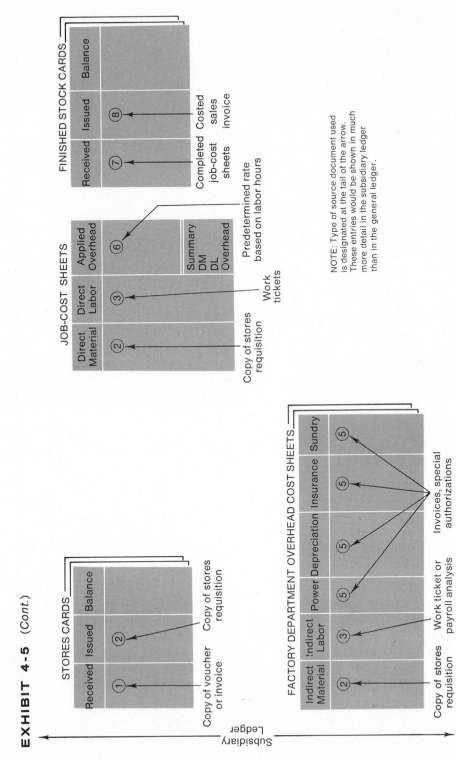

STORES CARDS

Received	Issued	Balance
①	②	

Copy of voucher or invoice
Copy of stores requisition

JOB-COST SHEETS

Direct Material	Direct Labor	Applied Overhead
②	③	⑥
		Summary DM DL Overhead

Copy of stores requisition
Work tickets
Predetermined rate based on labor hours

FINISHED STOCK CARDS

Received	Issued	Balance
⑦	⑧	

Completed job-cost sheets
Costed sales invoice

FACTORY DEPARTMENT OVERHEAD COST SHEETS

Indirect Material	Indirect Labor	Power	Depreciation	Insurance	Sundry
②	③	⑤	⑤	⑤	⑤

Copy of stores requisition
Work ticket or payroll analysis
Invoices, special authorizations

NOTE: Type of source document used is designated at the tail of the arrow. These entries would be shown in much more detail in the subsidiary ledger than in the general ledger.

Subsidiary Ledger

83

EXHIBIT 4-6

STORES CARD

		Received			Issued			Balance		
Date	Reference	Quantity	Unit Cost	Total Cost	Quantity	Unit Cost	Total Cost	Quantity	Unit Cost	Total Cost

3. Work-in-process control (direct labor)	39,000	
Factory department overhead control (indirect labor)	5,000	
Accrued payroll		44,000
To record incurrence of factory payroll costs.		

Payroll withholdings from employees are ignored in this example. Responsibility is fixed by using work tickets (Exhibit 4-3) or individual time summaries as a basis for tracing direct labor to jobs and direct and indirect labor to departments. Clock cards (Exhibit 4-4) are widely used as attendance records and as the basis for computation of payroll.

4. Accrued payroll	44,000	
Cash		44,000
To record payment of payroll.		

Actual payments and entries may be made weekly, even though entry 3 is made monthly. The reason for this is that paydays seldom coincide with the

EXHIBIT 4-7

FACTORY DEPARTMENT OVERHEAD COST SHEET

Date	Source Document	Lubricants	Other Supplies	Material Handling	Idle Time	Overtime Premium	Other Labor	Utilities	Insurance	Depr.
	Requisitions	xx	xx							
	Labor recap.			xx	xx	xx	xx			
	Invoices							xx		
	Special memos from chief accountant on accruals, prepayments, etc.							xx	xx	xx

84

conventional accounting period (the month) for which costs are accumulated in the general ledger.[1] Thus, the Accrued Payroll account appears as follows:

ACCRUED PAYROLL

PAYMENTS	GROSS EARNINGS
	Balance represents wages earned but unpaid.

5. Factory department overhead control	18,000	
Accounts payable		11,000
Unexpired insurance		1,000
Allowance for depreciation—Equipment		6,000
To record incurrence of other factory-overhead costs:		
Utilities, repairs, etc.	$11,000	
Depreciation	6,000	
Insurance	1,000	
	$18,000	

The detail of these costs is distributed to the appropriate columns of the individual department-overhead cost sheets that make up the subsidiary ledger for Factory Department Overhead Control. The basic documents for these distributions may be vouchers, invoices, or special memos from the responsible accounting officer.

6. Work-in-process control	26,460	
Factory overhead applied		26,460
To record application of factory overhead to job orders.		

The predetermined overhead rate used here is $2.70 per direct-labor hour. Thus, the amount of overhead applied to a particular job is dependent on the amount of direct-labor hours used on that job. It is assumed here that 9,800 direct-labor hours were used for all jobs, resulting in a total overhead application of $26,460. This entry is explained further in a subsequent section of this chapter.

7. Finished-goods control	108,800	
Work-in-process control		108,800
To record completion of Job Nos. 101–108.		

As job orders are completed, the job-cost sheets are totaled. Some companies use the competed job-cost sheets as their subsidiary ledger for finished goods. Other companies use separate finished-stock cards to form a subsidiary ledger.

8. Cost of sales	102,000	
Finished-goods control		102,000
To record cost of goods sold.		

[1] For a detailed treatment of the mechanics of payroll accounting, see Chapter 19.

The eight summary entries are usually made monthly. The biggest share of clerical time is devoted to compiling the day-to-day details that are recorded in subsidiary ledgers. There is a mass of daily detail that finds its way to subsidiary ledgers, in contrast to the summaries of the detail that are posted monthly to the general ledger. Incidentally, these "ledgers" are increasingly being kept on magnetic tape rather than on loose-leaf pages.

THE CONCEPTUAL APPROACH
TO ACCOUNTING FOR PRIME COSTS

The general-ledger treatment of prime costs—direct materials and direct labor—differs extensively among companies. The method illustrated in our example is probably the easiest to learn because it uses the fewest journal entries and accounts. However, the conceptual treatment ought to be examined so that the short-cut treatment may be viewed as a practical expedient rather than as the best theoretical design. See Exhibit 4-8 for a comparison of the conceptual notion with a treatment common in practice.

Exhibit 4-8 shows that direct materials and direct labor conceptually are (a) charged to departments and (b) then applied to jobs. But note that the department account becomes a clearing account for direct materials and direct labor. For example, the debit to Department Responsibility Cost Control in 2(a) is immediately offset by the credit in 2(b). A common practical treatment is to charge these items directly to the Work-in-Process account and not use the Department Responsibility account for either direct materials or direct labor. This simplifies the general ledger and, as we shall see, highlights the intricate problem of overhead accounting. Make no mistake—accounting records are kept of department responsibility for direct materials and direct labor, but they are material- and labor-usage summaries and reports, which are kept outside the general ledger itself.

These reports, plus the report on department-overhead costs, may easily have different timing. Depending on their relative importance, direct-material usage may be reported daily; direct-labor usage, weekly; and department-overhead incurrence, monthly. In such cases, there is little need for keeping a subsidiary multicolumn department-cost sheet for direct-material, direct-labor, and overhead items. *Instead, the department cost sheet is usually kept only for overhead items, whereas direct-material-usage and direct-labor-usage reports are automatically produced in summaries of requisitions and work tickets. Thus, source documents for direct materials and direct labor are used directly as a basis for control without necessarily having them formally summarized by department in either the subsidiary ledgers or the general ledger.*

LIMITATIONS OF GENERAL LEDGER

We cannot overemphasize the fact that many appropriate accumulations of costs for planning and control are too broad and too deep to be fitted into a general ledger. The scope of management accounting extends far beyond ledger bookkeeping. Because most general ledgers are traditionally oriented toward

EXHIBIT 4-8

JOURNAL ENTRIES FOR DIRECT MATERIALS AND
DIRECT LABOR—JOB-ORDER SYSTEM

CONCEPTUAL TREATMENT	*PRACTICAL TREATMENT*
Direct materials and direct labor are (a) charged to the department and (b) applied to product.	Direct materials and direct labor are charged directly to product. Accounting records are kept outside the general ledger to fix department responsibility for material and labor usage. Analysis sheets that summarize material usage and labor usage by departments are used for performance reports. These reports may be made weekly, daily, or sometimes even hourly. Furthermore, the direct-material usage and labor usage may be reported separately.

DIRECT-MATERIAL USAGE

2(a). Department-responsibility cost control	xx		2. Work-in-process control	xx
Stores control		xx	Stores control	xx
2(b). Work-in-process control	xx			
Department-responsibility cost control		xx		

DIRECT-LABOR USAGE

3(a). Department-responsibility cost control	xx		3. Work-in-process control	xx
Accrued payroll		xx	Accrued payroll	xx
3(b). Work-in-process control	xx			
Department-responsibility cost control		xx		

product costing, especially in accounting for materials and labor, the reader must be on guard to avoid being preoccupied with the product-costing purpose while losing sight of the major purpose of management accounting: that of aiding decisions for planning and control. A practical compromise that we shall take is to have the general ledger emphasize the responsibility approach to cost accounting without allowing the entries to become impossibly voluminous. Put another way, the position here is that costing for control is a day-to-day task that is primarily accomplished by source documents and daily or weekly summaries. Although the control devices may be fully integrated into the general ledger, its resulting complexities are more cumbersome than the benefits derived.

OVERHEAD APPLICATION

tracing overhead to product Entry 6 (see page 82) in our master illustration used a predetermined overhead rate to apply factory overhead to product. Direct materials and direct labor may be traced to physical units worked on with the help of requisitions and work tickets. But, by its very nature, factory overhead cannot be specifically identified with physical units. Yet the making of goods would be impossible without the incurrence of such overhead costs as depreciation, material handling, janitorial services, repairs, property taxes, heat, light, and so on.

Overhead is applied to products because of the managerial need for a close approximation of costs of different products. Essentially, this need is for pricing, income determination, and inventory valuation. If such product costs are to be helpful to management, they must be timely as well as accurate.

If the objective were to apply all actual overhead to actual production for the year, the most accurate application of overhead could be made only at the end of the year, after actual results were determined. However, this would be too late. Managers need product-cost information throughout the year. Therefore, overhead application rates are computed in advance of production.

Accountants have chosen an averaging process for identifying overhead with product. Overhead items are carefully classified into variable and fixed categories. The behavior of individual overhead items is forecast for the forthcoming year. The total forecast overhead is related to some common denominator or base, such as expected total machine-hours, direct-labor hours, or direct-labor dollars for the ensuing year. A predetermined overhead rate is obtained by dividing the expected overhead costs by the chosen base. This rate is used to apply overhead to specific jobs as they are manufactured.

To illustrate, a company may budget its factory overhead for a forthcoming year as shown in Exhibit 4-9. Assume that the forecast is based on a volume of activity expressed in direct-labor hours. Then, if detailed forecasts result in a prediction of total overhead of $324,000 for the forthcoming year at an anticipated 120,000-direct-labor-hour level of activity, the predetermined overhead rate would be:

$$\frac{\text{Total budgeted overhead}}{\text{Total budgeted volume expressed in direct labor hours}} = \frac{\$324,000}{120,000}$$

$$= \$2.70 \text{ per hour}$$

(This example assumes that the same overhead rate is appropriate for Departments A and B. This is an oversimplification. There are usually different overhead rates for different departments. These are illustrated and explained in Chapter 12, which can just as easily be studied now if desired.)

The $2.70 rate would be used for costing job orders. For example, during 19_1, a job-cost sheet for Job 323 included the following information:

Direct-material cost $100
Direct-labor cost $280
Direct-labor hours   40

The overhead to be applied to Job 323 would be: 40 hours times $2.70, or $108. The total cost of Job 323 would be: $100 plus $280 plus $108, or $488.

If actual results for the year conform to the prediction of the $324,000 overhead cost and the 120,000-direct-labor-hour level of activity, total overhead

EXHIBIT 4-9

BUDGET OF FACTORY OVERHEAD FOR THE YEAR ENDING 19_1

	DEPARTMENT A	DEPARTMENT B	TOTAL
Overhead expected:			
Variable items:			
Lubricants	$ 5,000	$ 3,000	$ 8,000
Other supplies	19,000	21,000	40,000
Material handling[a]	9,000	12,000	21,000
Idle time[b]	2,000	2,000	4,000
Overtime premium	3,000	5,000	8,000
Other labor	30,000	35,000	65,000
Utilities and other variable overhead	34,000	24,000	58,000
Total variable overhead	$102,000	$102,000	$204,000
Fixed items:			
Insurance	$ 2,000	$ 3,000	$ 5,000
Depreciation	30,000	35,000	65,000
Supervision	16,000	15,000	31,000
Other fixed overhead	12,000	7,000	19,000
Total fixed overhead	$ 60,000	$ 60,000	$120,000
Total budgeted overhead	$162,000	$162,000	$324,000
Divided by:			
Expected direct-labor hours	60,000	60,000	120,000
Predetermined overhead rate per hour	$ 2.70	$ 2.70	$ 2.70

[a]Labor costs of moving materials and supplies.
[b]Labor costs incurred for employee time not devoted to production. Causes include equipment failure, poor scheduling, material shortages, and the like.

costs will be exactly applied to products worked on during the year. The basic idea of this approach is to use an annual average overhead cost per hour without changing this annual overhead rate in costing jobs from day to day and from month to month. The resultant product costs are more properly called *normal costs* rather than *actual costs*, because they include an average or normalized chunk of overhead.

annualized rates
Should overhead rates be set on the basis of weekly, or monthly, or yearly activity? There are two major conditions that have prompted the use of an annualized basis for predetermined rates:

1. To overcome distortions in computed unit costs that would result because of fluctuations in the volume of activity (the denominator reason) from month to month. This is the dominant reason.

2. To overcome the distortion in computed unit costs that would result because of seasonal, calendar, and other peculiar variations in the total level of overhead costs (the numerator reason) incurred each month.

The denominator reason: fluctuations in monthly activity. Some overhead costs are variable (for example, supplies and indirect labor), whereas others are fixed (for example, property taxes, rent, and depreciation). If production fluctuates from month to month, variable overhead cost incurrence will change in close proportion to variations in production, whereas total fixed overhead will remain unchanged. This means that overhead rates based on monthly activity may differ greatly from month to month because of fluctuations in the volume of activity over which fixed overhead is spread.

Exhibit 4-10 gives an example of a company that gears production of its single product to a highly seasonal sales pattern. Few people support the contention that an identical product should be inventoried with an $11.00 or $51.00 overhead rate at the end of July or August and only a $2.25 or $2.00 overhead rate at the end of March or April. These different overhead rates are not representative of typical, normal production conditions. Management has committed itself to a certain level of fixed costs in the light of foreseeable needs far beyond a mere thirty days. Thus, where production fluctuates, monthly overhead rates may be volatile. An average, annualized rate based on the relationship of total annual overhead to total annual activity is more representative than a monthly rate.

EXHIBIT 4-10

MONTHLY VERSUS ANNUAL OVERHEAD RATES

MONTH	TOTAL FACTORY OVERHEAD BUDGETED ($50,000 PER MONTH PLUS $1 PER HOUR)	DIRECT LABOR HOURS	MONTHLY RATE PER HOUR	ANNUAL RATE PER HOUR*
January	$ 70,000	20,000	$ 3.50	$3.715
February	80,000	30,000	2.67	3.715
March	90,000	40,000	2.25	3.715
April	100,000	50,000	2.00	3.715
May	65,000	15,000	4.33	3.715
June	60,000	10,000	6.00	3.715
July	55,000	5,000	11.00	3.715
August	51,000	1,000	51.00	3.715
September	55,000	5,000	11.00	3.715
October	60,000	10,000	6.00	3.715
November	65,000	15,000	4.33	3.715
December	70,000	20,000	3.50	3.715
	$821,000	221,000	—	3.715

*Can be subdivided as follows:

$$\text{Variable-overhead portion} = \frac{\$821,000 - (\$50,000 \times 12)}{221,000} = \$1.000$$

$$\text{Fixed-overhead portion} = \frac{\$600,000}{221,000} = 2.715$$

$$\text{Combined-overhead rate} = \$3.715$$

The numerator reason: peculiarities of specific overhead items. Fluctuation in monthly volume rather than fluctuation in monthly costs incurred is the dominant reason for using an annualized overhead rate. Still, certain costs are incurred in different amounts at various times of the year. If a month's costs alone were considered, the heating cost, for example, would be charged only to winter production and the air-conditioning cost only to summer production.

Typical examples of erratic behavior include repairs, maintenance, and certain supplies requisitioned in one month that will last two or more months. These items may be charged to a department on the basis of monthly repair orders or requisitions. Yet the benefits of such charges may easily extend over a number of months' production. It would be illogical to load any single month with costs that are caused by several months' operations.

The calendar itself has an unbusinesslike design; some months have twenty workdays while others have twenty-four or more. Is it sensible to say that a product made in February should bear a greater share of overhead like depreciation and property taxes than it would if it were produced in March?

Other erratic items that distort monthly overhead rates are vacation and holiday pay, professional fees, subscriptions that may fall due in one month, extra costs of learning, idle time connected with the installation of a new machine or product line, and the employer's share of Social Security taxes—which is lightest late in the year, after employee wages exceed the taxable maximum.

All the costs and peculiarities mentioned above are collected in the annual-overhead pool along with the kinds of overhead that do have uniform behavior patterns (for example, many supplies and indirect labor). In other words, the accountant throws up his hands and says, "We have to start somewhere, so let's pool the year's overhead and develop an annual overhead rate regardless of month-to-month peculiarities of specific overhead costs." Such an approach provides a *normal* product cost that is based on an annual average instead of a so-called "actual" product cost that is affected by month-to-month fluctuations in production volume and by erratic or seasonal behavior of many overhead costs.

ledger Let us see how the notions above affect general-ledger procedure. For some
procedure reason, students have great trouble in understanding this phase of product
for overhead costing; therefore, special study of this section is warranted.

As overhead costs are incurred by departments from month to month, these "actual" costs are charged in detail to department-overhead cost sheets (the subsidiary ledger) and in summary to Factory Department Overhead Control. These costs are accumulated weekly or monthly without regard to how factory overhead is applied to specific jobs. This ledger procedure serves the purpose of managerial control of overhead. These actual costs are compared with budgeted amounts in performance reports.

Because a predetermined overhead rate (at $2.70 per direct-labor hour) is an average used to apply costs to products, the daily, weekly, or monthly costing of *inventory* is independent of the incurrence of overhead costs by *departments.* For this reason, at any given time during the year, the balance in Factory Department Overhead Control is unlikely to coincide with the amount applied to product. In other words, managerial control is exercised by comparing, say, actual lubricants used with the budget for lubricants. The actual lubricants used are accumulated on the department-overhead cost sheet. For product costing, all overhead items are lumped together, a predetermined overhead rate is computed, and this average rate is used on job orders for costing Work in Process. The use of an annual average results in inventories bearing a normalized share of factory overhead.

Most accountants stress this peculiarity of overhead accounting by confining Factory Department Overhead Control to the accumulation of "actual" overhead charges incurred and by setting up the credit side in a separate account called *Factory Overhead Applied* (sometimes called Factory Overhead *Absorbed*), much as Allowance for Depreciation is the separate credit side of, say, a Machinery account. To illustrate:

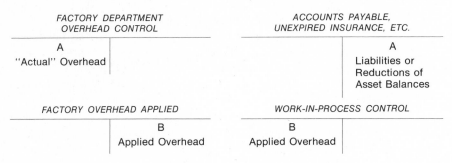

FACTORY DEPARTMENT OVERHEAD CONTROL		ACCOUNTS PAYABLE, UNEXPIRED INSURANCE, ETC.	
A "Actual" Overhead			A Liabilities or Reductions of Asset Balances

FACTORY OVERHEAD APPLIED		WORK-IN-PROCESS CONTROL	
	B Applied Overhead	B Applied Overhead	

underapplied or overapplied overhead The workings of the ledger accounts for overhead may be more clearly understood if we pursue our master illustration. Let us assume that the month's entries are for January, the first month of the company's year. Postings would appear as follows:

FACTORY DEPARTMENT OVERHEAD CONTROL		FACTORY OVERHEAD APPLIED	
Jan. 31(2) 4,000			Jan. 31(6) 26,460
Jan. 31(3) 5,000			
Jan. 31(5) 18,000			
Jan. 31 Balance 27,000			

The monthly debits to Factory Department Overhead will never equal the monthly credits to Factory Overhead Applied except by coincidence. In January, for example, there is a $540 difference between the two balances. This $540 amount is commonly referred to as *underapplied* (or *underabsorbed*) *overhead.* Overhead is underapplied when the applied balance is less than the incurred (actual) balance; it is overapplied when the applied balance exceeds the incurred balance.

Although the month-end balances may not coincide, the final year-end balances should be nearly equal. Experienced budgetary accountants can pre-determine rates with astounding accuracy (with 1 percent error). Of course, the accuracy of predetermined overhead rates depends largely on the skill of those who do the predicting and on the nature of the business. Assume that the year's overhead costs incurred are $326,000, while only $324,000 has been applied to product. The year-end balances are closed out against one another; any insignificant difference between the final balances is generally carried to Cost of Sales as an adjustment of that figure. Several bookkeeping techniques may be used. One simple way is:

Cost of sales	2,000	
Factory overhead applied	324,000	
Factory department overhead control		326,000

To close and to charge underapplied overhead to
Cost of Sales. If overhead is overapplied, the
overapplication would be credited to Cost of Sales.

Conceptually, the disposition of under- or overapplied overhead should entail correction of the costs of jobs worked on during the year. These jobs were costed by using a predetermined overhead rate instead of the actual overhead rate, which can be determined only at year-end. Ideally, a clerk would get all the job orders worked on during the year and would adjust their final costs. Thus, the most defensible way to convert job orders to "actual" costs would appear as in Exhibit 4-11.

Assume that the year-end analysis is as shown in Exhibit 4-11. Ideally, the $2,000 underapplied overhead should be spread over the three accounts that

EXHIBIT 4-11

ANALYSIS FOR PRORATION OF UNDERAPPLIED OVERHEAD

		Ending Balance in Accounts				Correction for Under-Applied Overhead	
		Overhead	%	Total Product Cost	%	Account	Based on Overhead Applied (first choice)	Based on Total Costs in Accounts (second choice)
Jobs worked on: 101 — 150								
Sold:	101 — 140	$275,400	85	$900,000	90	Cost of sales	$1,700	$1,800
Finished:	141 — 146	32,400	10	70,000	7	Finished goods	200	140
In process:	147 — 150	16,200	5	30,000	3	Work in process	100	60
		$324,000	100%	$1,000,000	100%		$2,000	$2,000

contain the job costs. This proration should theoretically be in proportion to the unadjusted overhead component in each account. The journal entry would appear as follows:

Cost of sales	1,700	
Finished goods	200	
Work in process	100	
Factory overhead applied	324,000	
Factory department overhead control		326,000

To close and to prorate underapplied overhead among the three relevant accounts.

Some companies will prorate in proportion to total product costs. This method is theoretically valid only when the proportions of direct material, direct labor, and overhead costs are constant among jobs. To illustrate, if alligator leather is used for making 100 purses (Job A) and imitation alligator is used for making 100 identical purses (Job B), the respective total job costs will differ markedly; yet their overhead components are unlikely to differ, because the labor-hours on each job should be about the same. In this case, to adjust for underapplied overhead on the basis of total product costs would be misleading, because conceptually a different base is used for year-end adjustments from what was used for overhead application during the year. Despite these objections, many companies will prorate on the basis of total product costs because the increase in accuracy is not significant enough to warrant the additional effort. For example, examine the small difference in the results of the two methods as shown in Exhibit 4-11.

Despite the theoretical superiority of the foregoing kinds of adjustments, *adjusting Cost of Sales for all the under- or overapplied overhead is the most widely practiced treatment.* It is valid as long as final results are not misleading. Exhibit 4-11 shows that more refined calculations that result in proration may not affect final costs enough to be significant. However, if under- or overapplied overhead is large enough to indicate some significant error in the overhead rate, the under- or overapplied overhead should be spread over the three accounts that contain the jobs bearing the faulty rate.

interim financial statements   The closing process for under- and overapplied overhead ordinarily takes place only at the end of the year. But what happens from month to month when interim financial statements must be prepared?[2]

We have already seen that month-to-month balances in the incurred and applied accounts do not agree. Look at these two accounts again:

[2]For a thorough, provocative discussion of these problems, see David Green, Jr., "Towards a Theory of Interim Reports," *Journal of Accounting Research,* Spring 1964, pp. 35–49. Also see Alfred Rappaport, "Towards a Theory of Interim Reports: A Modification and an Extension," *Journal of Accounting Research,* Spring 1966, pp. 121–26.

FACTORY DEPARTMENT OVERHEAD CONTROL			FACTORY OVERHEAD APPLIED	
Jan.	$27,000		Jan.	$26,460
Feb.	26,000		Feb.	26,810
Together	$53,000		Together	$53,270

Statements for January (not for the two months together) may be prepared on one of two options:

OPTION ONE
Partial Income Statement

Sales (assumed)		$150,000
Cost of sales (per account)	$102,000	
Add:		
Underapplied factory overhead*	540	
Adjusted cost of sales		102,540
Gross margin		$ 47,460

*Difference between January 31 balances in Factory Department Overhead Control and Factory Overhead Applied.

Balance Sheet

(Prepared on usual basis)

OPTION TWO
Partial Income Statement

Sales	$150,000	
Cost of sales	102,000	
Gross margin	$ 48,000	

Balance Sheet

ASSETS			EQUITIES	
Current assets:				
Cash	$ xx		Liabilities	$ xx
Receivables	xx		Ownership equity	xx
Inventories	xx			
Underapplied overhead	540	$ xx		
Other assets		xx		
Total		$ xx	Total	$ xx

Option One treats underapplied overhead as if it were immediately chargeable to the period. Option Two treats underapplied overhead as a cost that will benefit the rest of the year's production. Top-management preference would dictate which of the two options is to be used for reporting purposes.

This author prefers Option Two because it allows Cost of Sales to be stated at average or representative amounts; it also recognizes the fact that overhead cost incurrence does not necessarily mean such cost should be immediately written off to expense. For example, a repair will benefit the entire year's production, not just one month's. Further, the central idea of overhead application is the use of a predetermined annual average rate. There are bound to be random month-to-month under- or overapplications that should come near to offsetting one another by the end of the year. The most frequent causes of these month-to-month deviations are (a) operations at different levels of activity; and (b) the presence of seasonal costs, such as heating, that are averaged in with other overhead items in setting an annual overhead rate.

January and February results taken together show a net overapplied balance of $270. Option One's approach would deduct this amount from Cost of Sales on the income statement for the two months ending February 28, 19_1. Option Two's approach would show the $270 either as a deferred credit on the right-hand side of the balance sheet or as an offset to inventory.

There can be a variety of reasons and explanations for the existence of under- or overapplied overhead. This complex subject is discussed fully in Chapters 9 and 12. At this stage, the reader should concentrate on terminology and ledger relationships.

summary

Scorekeeping for the purpose of planning and control consists largely of *accumulating* costs by departments; for the product-costing purpose, it consists largely of *applying* costs to products in order to obtain a representative indication of the relative costs of resources devoted to various physical units of product. As in most phases of accounting, the bulk of clerical time is spent on basic source documents and subsidiary ledgers rather than on the general ledger itself. However, the general-ledger relationships of job costing offer a bird's-eye view of an entire system.

Industry uses a variety of general-ledger designs, but nearly all general ledgers are concerned primarily with product costs rather than cost control. This does not necessarily mean that cost control is neglected. It is doubtful that the general ledger itself, with its emphasis on historical summaries, yields much insight into the problem of cost control. Control is an hour-to-hour, day-to-day task that is accomplished mainly via source documents and prompt summaries.

There are two widely used approaches to assigning costs to manufactured goods: job-order costing and process costing. In practice, each company's approach is tailored to its needs and is usually some sort of hybrid. Job-order costing was discussed at length in this chapter. Chapter 17, which can be studied now if desired, discusses process costing and compares it with job-order costing.

Many companies apply overhead with predetermined rates. The resultant product cost consists of "actual" direct materials, "actual" direct labor, and "predetermined" overhead. Thus, this total product cost should be called a *normal* cost rather than an *actual* cost. Therefore, a given product-costing system can properly be called an *actual-cost* system (where no costs are predetermined), a *normal-cost* system (where predetermined rates are used to apply overhead), or a *standard-cost* system (where, as discussed in Chapters 7, 8, and 9, predetermined rates are used to apply material and labor as well as overhead). Within a given system, either a job-order-costing approach or a process-costing approach or some hybrid approach is tailored to needs.

Some thoughtful solving of homework at this stage will strengthen your understanding of basic relationships and terminology.

Problem for Self-Study

Restudy the illustration of job-order accounting in this chapter. Then try to solve one or two straightforward job-order problems such as Problems 4-8 and 4-11. Then try to solve the following problem, which requires consideration of most of this chapter's important points.

PROBLEM   You are asked to bring the following incomplete accounts of a plant in a foreign country up to date through January 31, 19_2. Also consider the data that appear after the T-accounts.

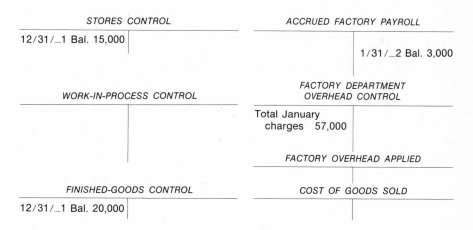

Additional Information

1. The overhead is applied using a predetermined rate that is set every December by forecasting the following year's overhead and relating it to forecast direct-labor costs. The budget for 19_2 called for $400,000 of direct labor and $600,000 of factory overhead.

2. The only job unfinished on January 31, 19_2, was No. 419, on which total labor charges were $2,000 (1,000 direct-labor hours) and total direct-material charges were $8,000.

3. Total materials placed into production during January totaled $90,000.

4. Cost of goods completed during January was $180,000.

5. January 31 balances on stores cards totaled $20,000.

6. Finished-goods inventory as of January 31 was $15,000.

7. All factory workers earn the same rate of pay. Direct man-hours for January totaled 20,000. Indirect labor and supervision totaled $10,000.

8. The gross factory payroll paid on January paydays totaled $52,000. Ignore withholdings.

9. All "actual" factory overhead incurred during January has already been posted.

required
a. Materials purchased during January
b. Cost of goods sold during January
c. Direct-labor costs incurred during January
d. Overhead applied during January
e. Balance, Accrued Factory Payroll, December 31, 19_1
f. Balance, Work in Process, December 31, 19_1
g. Balance, Work in Process, January 31, 19_2
h. Over- or underapplied overhead for January

SOLUTION
a. $95,000   c. $40,000   e. $5,000   g. $13,000
b. $185,000 d. $60,000   f. $3,000   h. $ 3,000 overapplied

Entries in T-accounts are numbered in accordance with the "additional information" in the problem and lettered in accordance with the amounts required to be determined.

STORES CONTROL

(given) 12/31/_1 Bal.		15,000		
	(a)	95,000*	(3)	90,000
1/31/_2 Bal.	(5)	20,000		

WORK-IN-PROCESS CONTROL

12/31/_1 Bal.	(f)		3,000*	(4)	180,000
Direct materials	(3)		90,000		
Direct labor	(2) (7)	(c)	40,000		
Overhead	(7) (1)	(d)	60,000		
1/31/_2 Bal.	(2) (g)		13,000		

FINISHED-GOODS CONTROL

(given) 12/31/_1 Bal.		20,000		
(4)		180,000	(6)	(b) 185,000
1/31/_2 Bal.	(6)	15,000		

ACCRUED FACTORY PAYROLL

(8)	52,000	12/31-1 (e)	5,000*
		(7)	{ 40,000 { 10,000
		1/31/_2 Bal. (given)	3,000

*Can be computed only after all other postings in the account have been found, so (g) must be computed before (f).

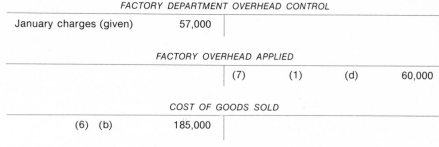

FACTORY DEPARTMENT OVERHEAD CONTROL

January charges (given)	57,000	

FACTORY OVERHEAD APPLIED

		(7)	(1)	(d)	60,000

COST OF GOODS SOLD

(6) (b)	185,000	

Notes: (1) Overhead rate is $600,000 ÷ $400,000, or 150% of direct labor cost.
(2) Ending work in process is $8,000 + $2,000 + 150% of $2,000.

APPENDIX: SUPPLEMENTARY DESCRIPTION OF LEDGER RELATIONSHIPS

This appendix explains some of the paper work that underlies the general-ledger relationships described in this chapter. It also contains an exhibit that summarizes sample accounting entries for job costing.

subsidiary ledgers and general ledger   The general ledger is a summary device. Postings are made to it from totals and subtotals of underlying transactions. For example, the balance of the Stores Control may be supported by a voluminous file of stores cards. Postings to the debit side of the Stores Control may be made from the Stores column in a special journal, such as a purchases journal or a voucher register. But the specific stores card in the subsidiary ledger is posted from a copy of a voucher or an invoice.

The general ledger gives a bird's-eye view of cost-accounting relationships; the subsidiary ledgers contain the underlying details—the worm's-eye view. In turn, source documents, such as voucher copies, stores requisitions, work tickets, clock cards, and other memoranda, are the primary means of recording business events. In a sense, the source documents are the everyday tools for systematically recording operating activities. They are vital because all subsequent accounting classifications and reports are dependent on source documents.

direct-material-usage reports   A multicopy stores requisition may be made out by a foreman. For example, separate copies may serve as follows:

Copy 1—Kept by storekeeper
Copy 2—Used by job-order cost clerk to post to job-cost sheet
Copy 3—Used by accounting department as a basis for a summary of requisitions

This summary is the support for the general-ledger entry;

Work-in-process control	xx	
Stores control		xx

This entry is usually made monthly, although it can be made more frequently if desired.

Copy 4—Used by department cost clerk as a basis for material-usage reports to departments. If these reports are to prove useful for control, they must typically be prepared more often than once a month. Stale, month-old reports concerning major costs are not helpful. Daily or weekly reports are common. This is another reason why the general ledger is oriented toward product costing rather than toward costing for control. The reports for control are needed before formal postings can be made.

Copy 5—Retained by foreman. He can use these as a cross-check against the usage reports sent to him by the accounting department.

The accounting department may use punched cards as requisitions. These may be sorted in many ways. For example:

DIRECT MATERIAL REQUISITION SUMMARY					
Requisition Number	Job Order	Department	Amount	Job Order Subtotals	Department Subtotals
501	1415	26	$ 32.00		
502	1415	27	51.00	$83.00	
503	1408	26	204.00		
504	1414	26	19.00		$255.00
505	1409	28	101.00		

Machine accounting facilitates the accumulation and tabulation of data so that they may be classified, reclassified, summarized, and resummarized to provide the specific information needed by management. Thus, a material-usage report like the following may be submitted to the foreman of Department 26 on a daily, weekly, or monthly basis:

Department 26		
DIRECT MATERIAL USAGE		
For the week ending _____		
Requisition Number	Job Order	Amount
501	1415	$ 32.00
503	1408	204.00
504	1414	19.00
510	1408	55.00
511	1412	122.00

direct-labor-cost recapitulation   Similar analysis can be applied to the sorting of direct-labor costs, using the work ticket as the source document. Producing departments may have their labor classified by operations as well as by jobs. For example, the machining department may perform one or more of the following operations: milling, cleaning, grinding, and facing. Thus, work tickets may be recapitulated as follows:

				DIRECT LABOR COST RECAPITULATION					
Work Ticket Number	Employee Identification Number	Job Number	Department Number	Operation Number	Amount	Job Subtotals	Operation Subtotals	Department Subtotals
14	49	1410	26	6500	$20.00		$20.00	
15	49	1410	26	6501	6.00		6.00	$26.00
16	52	1410	27	7520	19.00		19.00	
17	53	1410	27	7522	16.00	$61.00		
18	30	1411	25	5298	30.00	30.00	30.00	30.00
19	61	1409	28	8414	24.60		24.60	24.60
20	52	1409	27	7522	9.75	34.35	25.75	44.75

This labor recapitulation can be used as a basis for the general-ledger entry that charges direct labor to product:

Work in process   xx

    Accrued payroll   xx

This entry is usually made monthly, although it can be made more frequently if desired.

The recapitulation also supplies the information for daily, weekly, or monthly usage reports to the department foreman. These reports may be broken down by jobs or operations to suit the wants and needs of the foreman.

Work tickets may also be used for idle time (for example, caused by machine breakdowns or shortages of material), overtime premium, material handling, and so forth. A clerk or timekeeper may have the duty of preparing a daily reconciliation of employee clock cards with individual work tickets to see that all clock-card time is accounted for as direct labor, idle time, overtime premium, and so forth.

sample entries   Exhibit 4-12 summarizes the accounting entries for job costing.

questions, problems, and cases

4-1. Distinguish between producing departments and service departments.

4-2. Give two definitions of *control* as the word may be used by an accountant.

4-3. What is the purpose of a *department cost sheet?*

EXHIBIT 4-12

JOB-ORDER-SYSTEM SAMPLE ENTRIES

Transaction	General Ledger Effects	Subsidiary Ledgers	Source Documents	Explanatory Comments
1. Purchases of materials or supplies	Stores control Accounts payable	Dr. Stores card, "Received" column	Approved invoice	
2. Issuance of direct materials	Work in process control Stores control	Dr. Job order Cr. Stores card, "Issued" column	Stores requisition	Requisitions are summarized and classified by department for hourly, daily, weekly, or monthly direct material usage reports
3. Issuance of supplies	Factory department overhead control Stores control	Dr. Department overhead cost sheets, appropriate columns Cr. Stores card, "Issued" column	Stores requisition	
4. Distribution of labor costs	Work in process control Factory department overhead control Accrued payroll	Dr. Job orders Dr. Department overhead cost sheets, appropriate columns for various classes of indirect labor	Summary of work tickets or daily time analyses. This summary is sometimes called a labor cost distribution summary or a payroll recapitulation	
5. Payment of payroll (for a complete description, see Chapter 19)	Accrued payroll Withholdings payable Cash		Summary of clock cards and individual withholdings as shown on payroll sheets	This entry is usually made weekly, while the cost distribution (the prior entry) is not necessarily made at the same time
6. Payment of withholdings	Withholdings payable Cash			Withholdings are usually broken down by type rather than lumped in one account
7. Employer payroll taxes	Factory department overhead control Employer payroll taxes payable	Dr. Department overhead cost sheets, appropriate columns	Accrual memoranda from accounting officer	

EXHIBIT 4-12 (*Cont.*)

Transaction	General Ledger Effects	Subsidiary Ledgers	Source Documents	Explanatory Comments
8. Utilities	Factory department overhead control Accounts payable or Accrued utilities	Dr. Department overhead cost sheets, appropriate columns	Approved invoices or accrual memoranda	
9. Depreciation on factory equipment	Factory department overhead control Allowance for depreciation-Equipment	Dr. Department overhead cost sheets, appropriate columns	Depreciation schedule	
10. Factory insurance write-off	Factory department overhead control Unexpired insurance	Dr. Department overhead cost sheets, appropriate columns	Insurance register or memoranda from accounting officer	
11. Application of overhead to product	Work in process control Factory overhead applied	Dr. Job order	Predetermined overhead rate computed by using overhead budget	
12. Transfer completed goods to finished stock	Finished goods control Work in process control	Dr. Finished stock card, "Received" column Cr. Job order	Production report	Sometimes the completed job order serves as a finished stock card.
13. Sales	Accounts receivable control Sales	Dr. Customers' accounts	Copy of sales invoice	
14. Cost of sales	Cost of sales Finished goods control	Dr. Cost of sales record (optional) Cr. Finished stock cards	Copy of sales invoice plus costs as shown on finished stock cards	
15. Yearly closing of overhead accounts	Factory overhead applied Factory department overhead control Cost of sales (cr. if overhead is overapplied; dr. if overhead is under-applied)		General ledger balances	

103

4-4. What is the principal difference between job-cost and process-cost accounting systems?

4-5. Distinguish between a *clock card* and a *work ticket.*

4-6. What are the limitations of the general ledger as a cost-accounting device?

4-7. What is a *normal product cost?*

4-8. Journal Entries. The following data relate to operations of the Himer Manufacturing Co. for the year 19_4, its first year of operations:

Materials and supplies purchased on account	$150,000
Materials issued to the producing departments for production	120,000
Supplies issued to the producing departments	10,000
Materials returned to the storeroom from the factory	5,000
Labor used directly on production	100,000
Indirect labor incurred	30,000
Depreciation—Plant and equipment	10,000
Miscellaneous factory overhead incurred (ordinarily would be detailed)	23,000
Overhead applied at a rate of 60 percent of direct-labor cost	?
Cost of production completed	260,000
Sales	200,000
Cost of goods sold	180,000
Returned sales—at selling prices, $5,000; at factory cost, $4,500.	

required

1. General-journal entries. Number your entries.

2. Show the T-account for Factory Department Overhead Control. Sketch how this account's subsidiary ledger would appear, assuming that there are four factory departments. You need not show any numbers in the subsidiary ledger.

3. Show T-accounts and the closing balances for all inventories. Assume that over- or underapplied overhead is closed directly to cost of goods sold (show the journal entry).

4-9. Source Documents. Refer to Problem 4-8. For each entry, (a) indicate the most likely name of the source documents that would authorize the entry, and (b) give a description of the entry into the subsidiary ledgers affected, if any.

4-10. Journal Entries. The H Company uses a job-order cost system. The following relate to the month of March:

1. Raw materials issued to production, $96,000
2. Direct-labor analysis, $78,000
3. Manufacturing overhead is applied to production on the basis of $4.00 per direct-labor hour. There were 13,000 direct-labor hours incurred.
4. Total manufacturing overhead for the month was $54,000.
5. Production orders that cost $200,000 were completed during the month.
6. Production orders that cost $190,000 were shipped and invoiced to customers during the month at a profit of 20 percent based on cost.

required

The beginning inventory of work in process was $20,000. Prepare the general-journal entries required to record this information. What is the ending balance of work in process?

4-11. **Accounting for Overhead; Predetermined Rates.** The Aaron Company uses a predetermined overhead rate in applying overhead to production orders on a *labor-cost* basis for Department A and on a machine-hour basis for Department B. At the beginning of 19_1, the company made the following predictions:

	Dept. A	Dept. B
Direct-labor cost	$128,000	$ 35,000
Factory overhead	144,000	150,000
Direct-labor hours	16,000	5,000
Machine-hours	1,000	20,000

required

1. What is the predetermined overhead *rate* that should be used in Department A? In Department B?

   During the month of January, the cost sheet for production order No. 200 shows the following:

	Dept. A	Dept. B
Materials requisitioned	$20.00	$40.00
Direct-labor cost	$32.00	$21.00
Direct-labor hours	4	3
Machine-hours	1	13

2. What is the *total overhead* cost of production order No. 200?

3. Assuming that Job No. 200 consisted of 20 units of product, what is the *unit cost* of Job No. 200?

4. At the *end* of 19_1, it was found that *actual* factory-overhead costs amounted to $160,000 in Department A and $138,000 in Department B.

required

Give the over- or underapplied overhead amount for each department and for the factory as a whole. Assume that total actual direct-labor costs and machine-hours conformed with the original predictions.

4-12. **Incomplete Data; Journal Entries.** The following account balances were selected from the general ledger of the Cepeda Manufacturing Company at the start of business on January 1, 19_1, and the close of business on December 31, 19_1. The company uses perpetual inventories.

	BALANCES, JANUARY 1, 19_1	BALANCES, DECEMBER 31, 19_1
Stores	$ 5,000	$ 20,000
Manufacturing overhead	—	22,000
Manufacturing overhead applied (at a rate of ⅔ of the direct-labor cost)	—	20,000
Work in process	35,000	15,000
Finished goods	20,000	30,000
Cost of goods sold	—	100,000

required

Entries in general-journal form summarizing the operating activities of the year 19_1, which were recorded in the above accounts. Present T-accounts also.

4-13. Incomplete Data; Find Unknowns. The Torre Company uses perpetual inventories. Following are selected balances taken from certain accounts:

	BALANCES DECEMBER 31, 19_1	BALANCES DECEMBER 31, 19_2
Stores	$10,000	$ 22,000
Cost of goods sold	—	130,000
Factory overhead applied (at 50% of direct-labor cost)	—	30,000
Work in process	14,000	10,000
Factory-overhead control	—	32,000
Finished goods	30,000	50,000

required   Before considering any year-end adjustments for over- or underapplied overhead:

1. What was the cost of goods completed during 19_2?

2. What was the cost of materials purchased during 19_2?

4-14. Overview of General-Ledger Relationships. The Blakely Company uses a job-order cost system. The total debits and credits in certain accounts at year-end are:

	DECEMBER 31, 19_6	
	TOTAL DEBITS	TOTAL CREDITS
Direct-material control	$100,000	$ 70,000
Work-in-process control	320,000	305,000
Factory department overhead control	85,000	—
Finished-goods control	327,000	300,000
Cost of goods sold	300,000	—
Factory department overhead applied	—	90,000

Note that "total debits" in the inventory accounts would include beginning inventory balances, if any.

The above accounts *do not* include the following:

a. The labor-cost recapitulation for the December 31 working day: direct labor, $5,000, and indirect labor, $1,000.

b. Miscellaneous factory overhead incurred on December 30 and December 31: $1,000.

Additional Information

a. Factory overhead is applied as a percentage of direct labor.

b. Direct-material purchases during 19_6 were $90,000.

c. There were no returns to suppliers.

d. Direct-labor costs during 19_6 totaled $150,000, not including the December 31 working day described above.

required   1. Beginning inventories of direct materials, work in process, and finished goods. Show T-accounts.

2. Prepare all adjusting and closing journal entries for these accounts. Assume

that all under- or overapplied overhead is closed directly to Cost of Goods Sold.

3. Ending inventories, after adjustments and closing, of direct materials, work in process, and finished goods.

4-15. Meaning of Overapplied Overhead. The Walgenbach Company had budgeted the following performance for 19_3:

Units	100,000
Sales	$110,000
Total variable expenses	65,000
Total fixed expenses	40,000
Net income	5,000
Factory overhead:	
Variable	5,000
Fixed	30,000
Beginning inventories	None

It is now the end of 19_3. A factory-overhead rate of 35¢ per unit was used throughout the year for costing product. Total factory overhead incurred was $35,000. Overapplied factory overhead was $2,100. There is no work in process. How many units were produced during 19_3?

4-16. Year-End Disposition of Overhead. The Bower Company's overhead is applied to products using a predetermined rate that is set every December by forecasting the following year's overhead and relating it to forecast direct-labor *dollars*. The budget for 19_2 was $500,000 for direct labor and $250,000 for factory overhead.

The only job unfinished on December 31, 19_2, was No. 485, on which total direct-labor charges were $50,000 (10,000 direct-labor hours). Machine-hours were 5,000, and total direct-material charges were $25,000.

The total charges to Factory Department Overhead Control through December 31 were $270,000. Total direct-labor costs for the year were $480,000, representing 96,000 direct-labor hours.

There were no beginning inventories. In addition to the ending work in process described above, the ending finished goods showed a balance of $400,000. Cost of goods for the year totaled $500,000. These figures are *normal* costs; that is, no year-end adjustments have been made for under- or overapplied overhead.

required

1. Balance, Work in Process, December 31, 19_2 (at *normal cost*).

2. Over- or Underapplied Overhead for 19_2. Be certain to designate whether the dollar amount you show represents over- or underapplied overhead.

3. For this part, assume (ignore your answer to part 2) that overhead for 19_2 was underapplied by $50,000. The company usually charges or credits over- or underapplied overhead to Cost of Goods Sold at year-end. If instead the company followed the alternative practice of prorating over- or underapplied overhead over the ending balances (at normal cost) of Work in Process, Finished Goods, and Cost of Goods Sold, by what amount would net income differ?

4-17. Journal Entries, Year-End Disposition of Overhead. Tuttle Company uses a job-order cost system. Factory overhead is applied at a rate of $2.50 per direct-labor hour. Both beginning and closing balances in work in process and finished goods are zero. You are given the following data for 19_4, and the fact that all goods manufactured are sold.

Direct-labor hours used	50,000
Direct materials used	$ 50,000
Direct labor used	100,000
Indirect labor used	25,000
Indirect supplies used	10,000
Rent—Plant and equipment	50,000
Miscellaneous overhead	50,000
Cost of goods sold	275,000

All under- or overapplied overhead is allocated wholly to cost of goods sold at the end of the year.

required

1. Factory overhead applied.
2. Factory overhead incurred.
3. Prepare journal entries to record all the facts above, including all necessary entries to adjust for over- or underapplied overhead.

4-18. Multiple Choice; Incomplete Data. Some of the general-ledger accounts of the Sharman Manufacturing Company appear as follows on January 31, 19_1.

The accounts are incomplete because the accountant had an emergency operation for ulcers after he ate lunch in the company cafeteria on January 31. The treasurer, an old friend of yours, supplied you with the following incomplete accounts and three bits of additional information.

DIRECT-MATERIAL STORES CONTROL

Bal. Jan. 1 15,000	
35,000	

WORK-IN-PROCESS CONTROL

Bal. Jan. 1 1,000	40,000
Direct mate-	
rials requi-	
sitioned 20,000	

FINISHED-GOODS CONTROL

Bal. Jan. 1 10,000	20,000

COST OF GOODS SOLD

ACCRUED FACTORY PAYROLL

	Bal. Jan. 1 1,000
	Gross earnings
	of all factory
	workers 40,000

Additional Information

a. Factory Overhead Applied is credited for all indirect costs that are applied to production orders.
b. Work tickets for the month totaled 5,500 direct man-hours. All factory workers received $6.00 per hour.
c. Indirect costs are applied at a rate of $4.00 per direct man-hour.

After giving you a few minutes to look over the data given, your old friend asks you the following (place all answers on an answer sheet; indicate your answer by letter):

required

1. The January 31 balance of Direct-Material Stores Control should be:

   a. $50,000
   b. $25,000
   c. $30,000

   d. $20,000
   e. $35,000
   f. None of these

2. The amount of total direct-labor cost that should have been charged to all the individual production orders worked on during January should be:

   a. $40,000
   b. $41,000
   c. $55,000

   d. $30,000
   e. $33,000
   f. None of the these

3. The *total* factory-labor cost for the month of January (ignoring employer's Social Security contributions) is:

   a. $41,000
   b. $40,000
   c. $55,000

   d. $33,000
   e. $56,000
   f. None of these

4. The total *indirect* cost that should have been applied to production is:

   a. $17,000
   b. $75,000
   c. $40,000

   d. $33,000
   e. $24,000
   f. None of these

5. The January 31 balance of Work-in-Process Control should be:

   a. $75,000
   b. $77,000
   c. $76,000

   d. $36,000
   e. $35,000
   f. None of these

6. The January 31 balance of Finished-Goods Control should be:

   a. $ 5,000
   b. $10,000
   c. $20,000

   d. $25,000
   e. $30,000
   f. None of these

7. *Total* indirect costs actually incurred during the month amount to $24,000. The balance in Factory-Overhead Control at the end of January should be:

   a. $24,000
   b. $17,000
   c. $26,000
   d. $41,000

   e. $22,000
   f. $ 2,000
   g. None of these

8. The Cost of Goods Sold during January was:

   a. $40,000
   b. $10,000
   c. $20,000

   d. $30,000
   e. $50,000
   f. None of these

9. The Janaury 31 balance of Factory Overhead Applied should be:

   a. $33,000
   b. $40,000
   c. $24,000
   d. $22,000

   e. $26,000
   f. $30,000
   g. None of these

10. The amount of underapplied (or overapplied) costs for January is:

(a) Underapplied by $1,000
(b) Underapplied by $2,000
(c) Overapplied by $1,000
(d) Overapplied by $2,000
(e) Overapplied by $3,000
(f) Neither overapplied nor underapplied
(g) None of these

4-19.   **General-Ledger Relationships; Incomplete Data.**   You are asked to bring the following incomplete accounts up to date through May 19_1. Also consider the additional information that follows the T-accounts.

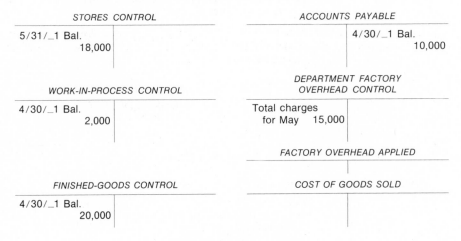

STORES CONTROL		ACCOUNTS PAYABLE	
5/31/_1 Bal. 18,000			4/30/_1 Bal. 10,000

WORK-IN-PROCESS CONTROL		DEPARTMENT FACTORY OVERHEAD CONTROL	
4/30/_1 Bal. 2,000		Total charges for May 15,000	

FACTORY OVERHEAD APPLIED

FINISHED-GOODS CONTROL		COST OF GOODS SOLD	
4/30/_1 Bal. 20,000			

Additional Information

a. The overhead is applied by using a predetermined rate that is set at the beginning of each year by forecasting the year's overhead and relating it to forecast direct-labor hours. The budget for 19_1 called for a total of 150,000 hours of direct labor and $225,000 of factory overhead.

b. The accounts payable are for direct materials only. The balance on May 31 was $5,000. Payments of $35,000 were made during May.

c. The finished-goods inventory as of May 31 was $22,000.

d. The cost of goods sold during the month was $60,000.

e. On May 31, there was only one unfinished job in the factory. Cost records show that $1,000 (400 hours) of direct labor and $2,000 of direct materials had been charged to the job.

f. A total of 9,400 direct man-hours were worked during the month of May. All factory workers earn the same rate of pay.

g. All "actual" factory overhead incurred during May has already been posted.

required

1. Materials purchased during May

2. Cost of goods completed during May

3. Overhead applied during May

4. Balance, Work in Process, May 31, 19_1

5. Materials used during May

6. Balance, Stores Control, April 30, 19_1

7. Over- or underapplied overhead for May

4-20. Underapplied Overhead on Interim Income Statements. The following data are available for ABC Company covering the month of January 19_4.

Sales	$100,000
Cost of sales (per account)	75,000
Factory overhead incurred	25,500
Factory overhead applied	22,100
Selling and administrative expenses	10,000

required You are to prepare interim income statements for the month of January:

1. Assuming underapplied overhead is immediately chargeable to the period
2. Assuming underapplied overhead as a cost that will benefit the rest of the year's production

4-21. Analysis of General-Ledger Accounts; Multiple Choice. Following is a partial list of the accounts appearing on the trial balance of the Clancy Manufacturing Company.

CLANCY MANUFACTURING COMPANY
Partial General-Ledger Trial Balance (Adjusted)
September 30, 19_0

	DR.	CR.
Materials and supplies stores control	$ 17,500	
Work-in-process control	21,000	
Finished-goods stock control	39,400	
Sales, net after discounts		$275,000
Factory costs of goods shipped	155,000	
Selling cost control	14,000	
Manufacturing-overhead control	95,000	
Manufacturing overhead applied to product		98,000
Administrative and general cost control	11,500	

required For the following statements, in terms of inferences to be made from the partial data, indicate:

    a. If the statement is a likely inference to be made
    b. If the statement is *not* a likely inference to be made
    c. If the statement is such that no reasonable inference can be made

1. The company owns its factory building.
2. Indirect Labor would be a debit in the completed trial balance.
3. Factory Cost of Goods Shipped is debited with the actual costs incurred.
4. Officers' Salaries would be a debit in the completed general-ledger trial balance.
5. A perpetual-inventory record is maintained, at least for materials and supplies.
6. Manufacturing-Overhead Control is an expense account.
7. There have been no losses on uncollectible accounts this period.
8. The difference between the Manufacturing-Overhead Control account and the Manufacturing Overhead Applied to Product account is the amount by which the computation of "normal" product cost for the year to date differs from the actual costs of running the factory for the same period.

9. There is, at the time of this trial balance, an overabsorption of factory cost.

10. Selling-Cost Control is an expense account.

11. The Board of Directors should be able to declare a dividend when they meet on October 15.

12. The Manufacturing Overhead Applied to Product records total normal costs applicable to units of product worked upon, as determined by cost accountant's computations.

4-22. **Comprehensive Review Problem—Job-Order Costs.** This problem is intended to provide a summary of general-ledger and subsidiary-ledger relationships for factory costs under a job-order cost system. The facts are unrealistic because, to save student time, the tremendous detail and number of accounts in a real situation are not reproduced here. But the solving of this problem should provide the student with a comprehensive view of the basic ledger framework.

Assume that the Mafco Company has been in business in Hong Kong for many years. It rents its factory building. Mafco uses a job-order cost system because it has a wide variety of products that receive varying attention and effort in the two factory departments, Machining and Assembly.

Mafco has the following trial balance as of December 31, 19_0.

Cash	$ 15,000	
Accounts receivable	40,000	
Stores control	29,600	
Work-in-process control	4,000	
Finished-goods control	20,000	
Unexpired insurance	12,000	
Office equipment	15,000	
Accumulated depreciation—Office equipment		$ 5,000
Factory equipment	950,000	
Accumulated depreciation—Factory equipment		220,000
Accounts payable		23,000
Accrued payroll		1,000
Accrued utilities		2,000
Accrued property taxes		3,000
Capital stock		100,000
Retained earnings		731,600
	$1,085,600	$1,085,600

DETAIL ON SUBSIDIARY RECORDS AS OF DECEMBER 31, 19_0

Stores:

CODE	QUANTITY	UNIT COST	AMOUNT
A	5,000	$2.00	$10,000
B	10,000	1.50	15,000
C	400	8.00	3,200
Supplies	Various	—	1,400
			$29,600

Work in process:

JOB-ORDER NUMBER	DEPARTMENT	DIRECT MATERIALS	DIRECT LABOR	FACTORY OVERHEAD	TOTAL
100	Machining	$1,800	$800	$900	$3,500
	Assembly	200	200	100	500
					$4,000

Finished goods:

STOCK NO.	REFERENCE	QUANTITY	UNIT COST	AMOUNT
X-1	Job 97	100	$80	$ 8,000
X-2	Job 99	1,000	12	12,000
				$20,000

The following factory-overhead budget has been prepared for the coming year, 19_1:

	FACTORY OVERHEAD BUDGET FOR YEAR ENDING DECEMBER 31, 19_1		
	MACHINING	ASSEMBLY	TOTAL
Factory overhead:			
Controllable:			
Supplies	$ 14,400	$ 5,400	$ 19,800
Indirect labor	22,800	16,800	39,600
Utilities	30,000	9,000	39,000
Repairs	24,000	6,000	30,000
Miscellaneous	22,800	12,000	34,800
	$114,000	$ 49,200	$163,200
Uncontrollable:			
Insurance	$ 7,200	$ 2,400	$ 9,600
Depreciation	114,000	14,400	128,400
Rent	24,000	16,800	40,800
Property taxes	4,200	1,200	5,400
Supervision	14,400	19,200	33,600
	$163,800	$ 54,000	$217,800
Total factory overhead	$277,800	$103,200	$381,000

This budget has been prepared after careful consideration of the sales outlook for the coming year. The production schedules are geared to the forecast sales pattern.

In order to cost jobs as they are worked on, a predetermined overhead rate is computed as follows:

	YEAR 19_1	
	MACHINING	ASSEMBLY
Factory overhead	$277,800	$103,200
Machine-hours	69,450	
Direct-labor cost		$206,400
Rate per machine-hour	$ 4.00	
Rate per direct-labor dollar		50%

These overhead rates will be used throughout the year to cost various jobs as they are worked on by each department. All overhead will be applied to all jobs worked on during the year in proportion to the machine-hour or direct-labor cost factor devoted to each job. If management predictions are accurate, total overhead applied to the year's jobs through the use of predetermined rates should be equal to the total overhead costs actually incurred.

January data:

1. Purchases for stores (credit Accounts Payable):

	QUANTITY	UNIT COST	JANUARY
A	7,500	$2.00	$15,000
B	14,000	1.50	21,000
C	2,125	8.00	17,000
Supplies			2,000
			$55,000

2. Returns (debit Accounts Payable): 50 units of Material B.
3. The direct-material requisitions were summarized, and the following data were shown on a material-usage report. These reports were submitted weekly to department foremen, although monthly data are shown here.

MACHINING DEPARTMENT
Direct-Material Usage
For the Month ending January 31, 19_1

REQUISITION	TYPE	JOB ORDER	QUANTITY	UNIT COST	AMOUNT
M89	B	101	1,500	$1.50	$ 2,250
M90	A	102	3,000	2.00	6,000
M91	A	103	1,000	2.00	2,000
M92	B	103	1,000	1.50	1,500
M93	B	102	3,000	1.50	4,500
M94	B	101	200	1.50	300
M95	A	104	2,000	2.00	4,000
					$20,550

ASSEMBLY DEPARTMENT
Direct-Material Usage
For the Month ending January 31, 19_1

REQUISITION	TYPE	JOB ORDER	QUANTITY	UNIT COST	AMOUNT
A301	C	100	5	$8.00	$ 40
A302	C	103	200	8.00	1,600
A303	C	101	800	8.00	6,400
A304	C	102	1,500	8.00	12,000
A305	C	103	20	8.00	160
					$20,200

4. A summary of payroll costs incurred follows. Compare with item (g) below. Payments (settlements) are independent of recognition of cost incurrence. In other words, costs may be summarized monthly while settlements are made weekly.

WORK TICKET*	JOB ORDER	LABOR HOURS		COST		TOTAL
		MACHINING	ASSEMBLY	MACHINING	ASSEMBLY	
ML480	101	20		$ 50	$	$ 50
ML481	101	1,500		3,750		3,750
ML482	103	1,000		2,500		2,500
ML483	102	1,200		3,000		3,000
ML484	104	500		1,250		1,250
ML485	103	100		250		250
AL 60	100		20		40	40
AL 61	102		7,000		14,000	14,000
AL 62	101		500		1,000	1,000
AL 63	103		1,000		2,000	2,000
AL 64	102		200		400	400
Total direct labor		4,320	8,720	$10,800	$17,440	$28,240
Indirect labor				2,000	1,500	3,500
Supervision				1,200	1,600	2,800
Total factory labor				$14,000	$20,540	$34,540
Selling and administrative wages						6,000
Total payroll costs						$40,540

*In practice, there would be many more of these. Often they are recapitulated daily and posted to each job in groups rather than as individual tickets.

5. Apply overhead to jobs. Rates as calculated when overhead budget was prepared: Machining, $4.00 per machine-hour; Assembly, 50 percent of direct-labor cost. See data for entry 6 to obtain machine-hours worked.
6. Production and sales data:*

JOB	UNITS COMPLETED	FINISHED	FINISHED STOCK NO.	UNITS SOLD	SOLD FOR	JANUARY MACHINE-HOURS WORKED IN MACHINING DEPT.
97	100	19_0	X-1	100	$ 9,000	
98	—	—	—	—	—	
99	1000	19_0	X-2	1000	16,000	
100	50	Jan. 5, 19_1	X-1	20	1,800	
101	1750	Jan. 12, 19_1	X-2	900	14,400	3,000
102	1000	Jan. 19, 19_1	X-3	950	55,000	2,000
103	100	Jan. 30, 19_1	X-4	50	6,500	150
104	Unfinished					800
					$102,700	5,950

7. Gross payroll paid in cash during month, $39,000.
8. The following additional overhead costs were incurred during January:

| ITEM | TOTAL | DEPARTMENT | | SELLING AND ADMINISTRATIVE | GENERAL-LEDGER ACCOUNT TO BE CREDITED |
		MACHINING	ASSEMBLY		
Supplies requisitioned	$ 2,000	$ 1,500	$ 400	$ 100	?
Utilities (cost recognized on basis of usage estimates for month rather than on basis of invoices, which may cover other dates than a current calendar month)	4,000	2,700	800	500	Accrued Utilities Payable
Repairs by outsiders (parts and labor)	3,000	2,350	600	50	Accounts Payable
Miscellaneous	3,000	2,000	900	100	Accounts Payable
Insurance	1,000	600	200	200	?
Depreciation on equipment	11,000	9,500	1,200	300	?
Rent	4,000	2,000	1,400	600	Accounts Payable
Property taxes	500	350	100	50	Accrued Property Taxes
	$28,500	$21,000	$5,600	$1,900	

9. Utility bills received, $2,900 (dr. Accrued Utilities).
10. Utility bills paid, $2,525 (dr. Accounts Payable).
11. Other selling and administrative expenses, $15,000 (cr. Accounts Payable).
12. Payments on accounts payable, other than the $2,525 in (10), $65,300.
13. Collections on accounts receivable, $99,000.

required

1. Enter beginning balances in general-ledger T-accounts.
2. Draw up stores cards, job-cost sheets, and finished-goods stock cards. Be sure to put in "reference" columns so that appropriate requisitions and work tickets, as well as dollar amounts, may be entered in the subsidiary ledger. A sample stores card and job-cost sheet appear on page 117.

   Finished-stock cards would be similar in design to stores cards.

   The factory-overhead cost sheets have columns for: date, reference, supplies, indirect labor, utilities, repairs, miscellaneous, insurance, depreciation on equipment, rent, property taxes, and supervision.

   Post beginning balances to subsidiary records.
3. Journalize and post entries for January.
4. Prepare a trial balance as of January 31, 19_1. Also prepare schedules of subsidiary-ledger balances.
5. Prepare an income statement for January and a balance sheet as of January 31, 19_1. Underapplied overhead is treated as a balance-sheet item on interim financial statements.

STORES CARD

Material A

Reference	Received			Issued			Balance			
	Quantity	Unit Cost	Amount	Quantity	Unit Cost	Amount	Date	Quantity	Unit Cost	Amount
Vouchers, Invoices or Requisitions							$^{12}/31/_{x0}$	5,000	$2.00	$10,000

Job Order No. __100__

MACHINING DEPARTMENT

Direct Material				Direct Labor				Overhead	
Reference	Quantity	Unit Cost	Amount	Reference	Quantity	Unit Cost	Amount	Machine Hours Worked	Amount
Req. #A88	900	$2.00	$1800	Work tickets	320 hrs	$2.50	$800	225	$900

ASSEMBLY DEPARTMENT

Direct Material				Direct Labor				Overhead	
Reference	Quantity	Unit Cost	Amount	Reference	Quantity	Unit Cost	Amount	Reference	Amount
Req. #A300	25	$8.00	$200	Work tickets	100 hrs	$2.00	$200	50% of direct labor	$100

Summary		Machining	Assembly	Total
Direct material		$_____	$_____	$_____
Direct labor		_____	_____	_____
Factory overhead applied		_____	_____	_____
Total cost		$_____	$_____	$_____

117

6. Prepare factory-overhead performance reports for January, one for Machining and one for Assembly. Show actual overhead, budgeted overhead, and variances. Assume arbitrarily that budget figures for January are $\frac{1}{12}$ of those shown in the annual overhead budget.

7. Assume that operations continue for the remainder of 19_1. Certain balances at December 31, 19_1 follow:

Stores	$ 30,000	
Work in process	10,000	
Finished goods	30,000	
Cost of sales	960,000	
Factory-overhead control	400,000	
Factory overhead applied		$385,000

Prepare journal entries to close the factory-overhead accounts, assuming that:

a. Underapplied overhead is treated as a direct adjustment of Cost of Sales.

b. Underapplied overhead is spread over appropriate accounts in proportion to their unadjusted ending balances.

SECTION TWO

MULTIPLE-PURPOSE
SYSTEMS FOR
MANAGEMENT CONTROL

5

Budgeting in General: Profit Planning

Previous chapters have stressed the point that the essence of management is decision making and that the methods for making decisions are increasingly being called *decision models*. For example, Chapter 3 introduced cost–volume–profit analysis, which provides models for making decisions on prices, quantities, mix, and so on. Now we take an overview of the entire network of these decisions. This comprehensive view is expressed in the form of a master budget that encompasses and summarizes the expected impact of all the operating and financing decisions on income, financial position, and cash flows.

This chapter examines the master budget as a planning and coordinating device. The succeeding three chapters examine some detailed aspects of the budgeting decisions and their implementation.

MAJOR FEATURES OF BUDGETS

definition and role of budgets A budget is a quantitative expression of a plan of action and an aid to coordination and implementation. Budgets may be formulated for the organization as a whole or for any subunit. The master budget summarizes the objectives of all subunits of an organization—sales, production, distribution, and finance. It quantifies the expectations regarding future income, cash flows, financial status, and supporting plans. These are the culmination of a series of decisions resulting from a careful look at the organization's future. In most cases, the master budget is the best practical approximation to a formal model of the total organization: its objectives, its inputs, and its outputs.

Budgets are designed to carry out a variety of functions: planning, evaluating performance, coordinating activities, implementing plans, communicating, motivating, and authorizing actions. The last-named role seems to predominate in government budgeting and not-for-profit budgeting, where budget appropriations serve as authorizations and ceilings for management actions.

This book emphasizes how accounting helps the manager make *operating decisions,* those concerning the acquisition and utilization of scarce resources. However, we cannot ignore the importance of *financing decisions,* which concern the obtaining of funds for acquisition of resources. The master budget embraces the impact of both kinds of decisions; that is why this chapter examines cash budgets as well as operating budgets. Incidentally, the leading organizations are usually marked by both impressive operating management and excellent financial management. Business failures are often attributable to weaknesses in one or the other of these responsibilities.

financial-planning models and simulation
If the master budget serves as a "total decision model" for top management, then decisions about strategies for the forthcoming period may be formulated and altered during the budgetary process. Traditionally, this has been a step-by-step process whereby tentative plans are gradually changed as executives exchange views on various aspects of expected activities.

In the future, much of the interaction and interdependence of the decisions will probably be formalized in mathematical simulation models—"total models" that are sometimes called *corporate financial-planning models.* These models are mathematical statements of the relationships in the organization among all the operating and financial activities, as well as other major internal and external factors that may affect decisions.[1]

Some companies have prepared computerized versions of the manual budget. For example, the Sun Oil Company[2] has expressed its processes and accounting as a series of equations that can be manipulated by the computer. The working version required thirteen man-years to complete: ten man-years of analytical time and three of computer coding. An additional ten man-years were devoted to educating management at many levels regarding how to use the model.

The Sun model is constructed and working. It is used for budgeting, for revising budgets with little incremental effort, and for comparing a variety of decision alternatives as they affect the entire firm. The model speeds the budgetary process because the sensitivity of income and cash flows to various decisions

---

[1] See Thomas J. Gorman, "Corporate Financial Models in Planning and Control," *The Price Waterhouse Review,* XV, No. 2, 41–53. Another provocative approach is to look upon the budgetary process as a linear programming model. One experimental model has an objective of maximizing net additions to retained earnings subject to a host of constraints, including limits on cash balances and production capacity. See Y. Ijiri, F. K. Levy, and R. C. Lyon, "A Linear Programming Model for Budgeting and Financial Planning," *Journal of Accounting Research,* Vol. I, No. 2, 198–212.

[2] George W. Gershefski, "Building a Corporate Financial Model," *Harvard Business Review,* Vol. 47, No. 4, 61–72.

can be tested promptly via a simulation. Management can react quickly to events and to revisions in predictions of various aspects of operations. Moreover, mathematical probabilities can be incorporated in these models, so that uncertainty can be dealt with explicitly rather than informally.

The point is that the master budget should be a powerful aid to the most crucial decisions of top management. Often, it falls far short of that role because its potential is misunderstood. Instead of being regarded as a management tool, in many cases the budget is unfortunately looked upon as a necessary evil.

applicability Budgetary systems are more common in larger companies, where for-
of budgets malized and sophisticated techniques are developed to serve management.

Still, the usefulness of budgeting to very small concerns should not be overlooked. Many deaths (and unwarranted creations) of small businesses could have been circumvented by an early attempt to quantify the dreams of headstrong but sloppy-thinking entrepreneurs who never directly faced the uncertainties of their venture.

For example, a small business moved into a lush market for school equipment with lofty hopes. However, failure to quantify the long collection periods, to forecast a maximum sales potential, and to control costs from the outset resulted in disaster within a year. Budgets for small businesses need not be as elaborate as those outlined in budgeting textbooks, but some budgeting is useful to an enterprise of any size. In fact, many companies have implicit budgets without even realizing their existence; that is, every businessman considers the future as he makes decisions.

Many businessmen claim that the uncertainties peculiar to their business make budgets impractical for them. Yet one can nearly always find at least some companies in the same industry that use budgets. Such companies are usually among the industry leaders, and they regard budgets as indispensable aids. The point is that managers must grapple with uncertainties, either with a budget or without one. The advocates of budgeting maintain that the benefits from budgeting nearly always exceed the costs. Some budget program, at least, will be helpful in almost every organization.

advantages When administered wisely, budgets (a) compel management planning, (b)
of budgets provide definite expectations that are the best framework for judging
subsequent performance, and (c) promote communication and coordination among the various segments of the business.

Compelled planning. "Plan ahead" is a redundant watchword for business managers and for any individual as well. Yet too often, everyday problems interfere with such planning; operations drift along until the passage of time catches the firms or individuals in undesirable situations that should have been anticipated and avoided.

Budgets formulate expected performance; they express managerial targets. Without such targets, operations lack direction, problems are not foreseen, results lack meaning, and the implications for future policies are dwarfed by the pressure of the present. The planning role of all levels of management should be accentuated and enlarged by a budgetary system. Managers will be compelled to look ahead and will be ready for changing conditions. This forced planning is by far the greatest contribution of budgeting to management.

Budgets have direct or indirect influence on business policies. Policies are relatively general and permanent plans that change as conditions or objectives change—for example, when new products are added, old products are dropped, organizations are revamped, or production methods are changed. Budgets definitely affect the formulation of overall company policies and then help to implement such policies. These policy changes are often affected either directly by budgetary information or indirectly by the thinking that evolved from dealing with budgets.

Expectations as a framework for judging performance.   Despite the existence of complex computers and automation, individuals still run businesses, from the president down to the foreman of the smallest department. Employees do not like to fumble along not really knowing what their superiors anticipate or to see such expectations vary depending upon, for example, the condition of the superior's sinus trouble. The budget helps meet this difficulty by letting employees know what is expected of them.

As a basis for judging actual results, budgeted performance is generally viewed as being a better index than past performance. The fact that sales are better than last year's, or that direct-labor costs are lower than last year's, may be encouraging—but it is by no means conclusive as a measure of success. For example, the news that a company sold 100,000 units this year as compared with 90,000 units in the previous year may not necessarily by greeted with joy. Perhaps sales should have been 112,000 units this year. The major weakness of using historical data for judging performance is that inefficiencies may be buried in the past performance. Furthermore, the usefulness of comparisons with the past may be hampered by intervening changes in technology, personnel, products, competition, and general economic conditions.

Communication and coordination.   Coordination is the meshing and balancing of all the factors of production and of all the departments and functions of the business so that the joint objectives are obtained—so that the interests of the individual managers are subordinated for the benefit of the business as a whole.

The concept of coordination implies, for example, that purchasing officers integrate their plans with production requirements, and that production officers use the sales budget as a basis for planning manpower needs and utilization of machinery.

Budgets help management in several ways to coordinate:

1. The existence of a well-laid plan is the major step toward achieving coordination. Executives are forced to think of the relationship of individual operations, other operations, and the company as a whole.

2. Budgets help to restrain the empire-building efforts of executives. Budgets broaden individual thinking by helping to remove unconscious biases on the part of engineering, sales, and production officers.

3. Budgets help to search out weaknesses in the organizational structure. The administration of budgets isolates problems of communication, of fixing responsibility, and of working relationships.

The idea that budgets improve coordination and communication may look promising on paper, but it takes plenty of intelligent administration to achieve in practice. For instance, the use of budgets to judge performance may cause managers to wear blinders and concentrate more than ever on their individual worlds. We shall examine this problem in more detail in the next chapter.

The cost-conscious, cooperative attitudes toward budgetary control must permeate all levels of management. A skeptical top-management attitude will trickle down to the detriment of the entire company. *Top management must understand and enthusiastically support the budget.*

Administration of budgets must not be rigid. Changed conditions call for changes in plans. The budget must receive respect, but it does not have to be so revered that it prevents a manager from taking prudent action. A department head prepares and accepts his budget; he commits himself to the outlined performance. But if matters develop so that some special repairs or a special advertising outlay will best serve the interests of the firm, the manager should feel free to request permission for such outlays. Or the budget itself can provide enough flexibility to permit a manager reasonable discretion in deciding how best to get his job done.

human aspect   Budgeting is too often looked upon from a purely mechanistic viewpoint.

The human factors in budgeting are more important than the accounting techniques. The success of a budgetary system depends upon its acceptance by the company members who are affected by the budgets. Attitudes ideally are sympathetic, cooperative, and cost-conscious.

Budgets place managers in the spotlight. The natural reaction to restriction, to criticism, and to control is resistance and self-defense. *The job of education and selling is overwhelmingly important here.* Too many department heads think that budgets represent a penny-pinching, negative brand of managerial pressure.[3] To them, the word *budget* is about as popular as, say, *layoff, strike,* or *pay decrease.* Ideally, company personnel should understand and accept the role of budgets as positive vehicles for company improvement, department improvement, and individual improvement. The budget is not a heinous means of

---

[3] Pressure, in varying amounts, is a part of almost every job responsibility. Used with care, pressure motivates toward goals and is thus desirable. However, the word *pressure* has unappealing connotations and usually indicates unreasonable, unbearable stress.

squeezing the last drop of sweat out of employees. Properly used, it is simply a systematic tool for establishing standards of performance, for providing motivation, for gauging results, and for helping management advance toward its objectives. The budget technique in itself is free of emotion; its administration, however, is often packed with trouble. The budget's major role is to communicate the various motivations that basically already exist among the management personnel, so that everybody sees, understands, and coordinates the goals, means, and drives of the organization.

The importance of these human aspects cannot be overemphasized. Without a thoroughly educated and cooperative management group at all levels of responsibility, budgets are a drain on the funds of the business and are a hindrance instead of a help to efficient operations. A budgetary program per se is not a remedy for weak managerial talent, faulty organization, or a poor information system. This subject is explored more fully in Chapter 6.

TYPES OF BUDGETS

time coverage　Budgets may span a period of one year or less—or, in cases of capital budgeting for plant and product changes, up to ten or more years. More and more companies are using budgets as essential tools for long-range planning. The usual planning-and-control budget period is one year. The annual budget is often broken down by months for the first quarter and by quarters for the remainder of the year. *Continuous budgets* are increasingly used, whereby a twelve-month forecast is always available by adding a month or quarter in the future as the month or quarter just ended is dropped. Continuous budgets are desirable because they force management constantly to think concretely about the forthcoming twelve months, irrespective of whether the month at hand is May or October. The choice of budget periods largely flows from the objectives, uses, and dependability of the budget data.

classification　Budgets are basically forecasted financial statements. They are sometimes *of budgets*　called *pro forma* statements. Various descriptive terms for budgets have arisen. The difficulties of terminology are not insurmountable, but the reader should remember that terms vary among firms.

There are countless forms of budgets. Many special budgets are prepared.

SPECIAL BUDGET REPORTS

Comparisons of planning budgets with actual performance (performance reports)
Reports for specific managerial needs—for example, breakeven projections
Long-term budgets, often called "capital" or "facilities" budgets (see Chapter 13)
Flexible overhead budget (see Chapter 8)

The following is a simplified sub-classification of the master budget, the comprehensive plan. Many subsidiary budget schedules are necessary in actual practice.

MASTER BUDGET, CONSISTING OF:

OPERATING BUDGET, CONSISTING OF:	FINANCIAL BUDGET, CONSISTING OF:
Budgeted income statement	Cash budget
Sales budget	Receipts
Production budget	Disbursements
Materials	Budgeted balance sheet
Direct labor	Budgeted statement of sources and
Factory overhead	applications of funds
Inventory levels	
Cost-of-goods-sold budget	
Selling-expense budget	
Administrative-expense budget	

ILLUSTRATION OF MASTER BUDGET

Try to take the following basic data and prepare the required budgets before glancing at the solution. A step-by-step approach to formulating a master budget is described after the basic data are given. This illustration is largely mechanical, but remember that the master-budget process generates key top-management decisions regarding pricing, product lines, production scheduling, capital expenditures, research and development, management assignments, and so on. For instance, the first draft of the budget almost always leads to decisions that prompt further drafts before a final budget is chosen.

basic data and requirements

The M Company uses a normal cost system. The company is ready to prepare its master budget for the year 19B. Having carefully examined all relevant factors, the executives expect the following for 19B:

Materials:
Material 111	$1.20 per unit
Material 112	$2.60 per unit
Direct labor	$2.05 per hour

Overhead is applied on the basis of direct-labor hours.

	Product F, Special Widgets	Product G, De Luxe Widgets
Finished products (content of each unit):		
Material 111	12 units	12 units
Material 112	6 units	8 units
Direct labor	14 hours	20 hours

The balance sheet for the year just ended is given below:

M COMPANY

Balance Sheet

December 31, 19A

ASSETS

Current assets:		
Cash	$ 10,000	
Accounts receivable	25,000	
Materials	19,000	
Finished goods	14,480	
		$ 68,480
Fixed assets:		
Land	$ 50,000	
Building and equipment	380,000	
Accumulated depreciation	(75,000)	355,000
Total assets		$423,480

EQUITIES

Current liabilities:		
Accounts payable	$ 8,200	
Income taxes payable	5,000	$ 13,200
Stockholders' equity:		
Common stock, no-par—25,000 shares outstanding	$350,000	
Retained income	60,280	410,280
Total equities		$423,480

Additional information regarding the year 19B:

	FINISHED PRODUCT	
	F	G
Expected sales in units	5,000	1,000
Selling price per unit	$ 105.40	$ 164.00
Desired ending inventory in units	1,100	50
Beginning inventory in units	100	50

	DIRECT MATERIALS	
	111	112
Beginning inventory in units	5,000	5,000
Desired ending inventory in units	6,000	1,000

(Work in process is negligible and may be ignored.)

At anticipated volume levels, the following costs will be incurred:

Factory overhead:

Supplies	$ 30,000
Indirect labor	70,000
Payroll fringe costs	25,000
Power—variable portion	8,000
Maintenance—variable portion	20,000
Depreciation	25,000
Property taxes	4,000
Property insurance	500
Supervision	20,000
Power—fixed portion	1,000
Maintenance—fixed portion	4,500
	$208,000

Selling and administrative expenses:

Sales commissions	$ 20,000
Advertising	3,000
Sales salaries	10,000
Travel	5,000
Clerical wages	10,000
Supplies	1,000
Executive salaries	21,000
Miscellaneous	5,000
	$ 75,000

Budgeted cash flows are:

	QUARTERS			
	1	2	3	4
Collections from customers	$125,000	$150,000	$160,000	$221,000
Disbursements:				
For materials	20,000	35,000	35,000	44,200
For other costs and expenses	25,000	20,000	20,000	27,000
For payroll	90,000	95,000	95,000	109,200
For income taxes	5,000	—	—	—
For machinery purchase	—	—	—	20,000

(The quarterly data are given for your convenience. The figures are based on the cash effects of the operations formulated in Schedules 1 through 8 in the solution.)

The company desires to maintain a $15,000 minimum cash balance at the end of each of the first three quarters, but increased working-capital requirements at the end of the year 19B will necessitate a minimum ending cash balance of $40,000. Money can be borrowed or repaid in multiples of $500 at an interest rate of 6 percent per annum. Management does not want to borrow any more cash than is necessary and wants to repay as promptly as possible. In any event, loans may not extend beyond four quarters. Interest is computed and paid when the principal is repaid. Assume that borrowings take place at the beginning and repayments at the end of the quarters in question. Compute interest to the nearest dollar.

required

Prepare a master budget for the year 19B. Include the following detailed schedules:

1. Sales budget
2. Production budget
3. Direct-material-purchases budget
4. Direct-labor budget
5. Factory-overhead budget
6. Ending-inventory budget
7. Cost-of-goods-sold budget
8. Selling and administrative expense budget

and

I. Budgeted income statement (Assume income taxes for 19B to be $20,000.)
II. Budgeted statement of cash receipts and disbursements by quarters, including details of borrowings, repayments, and interest
III. Budgeted balance sheet

basic approach to formulating master budget

This chapter provides a review of the technical material covered in the previous chapters, because the master budget (the overall business plan) is basically nothing more than the preparation of the familiar financial statements. The major technical difference is that the accountant is dealing with expected future data rather than with historical data.

The following techniques are basic to the study of budgeting. First, the steps in preparation are presented. Second, some condensed, illustrative budget reports are shown in the solution to the problem.

The basic steps in preparing budgeted financial statements follow:

1. *The sales forecast is the starting point for budgeting,* because inventory levels and production (and hence costs) are generally geared to the rate of sales activity.[4] The sales budget (Schedule 1 in the solution) is the result of a series of management decisions reached through a process that is described more fully in a separate section near the end of this chapter.

2. After sales are budgeted, the production budget (Schedule 2) may be prepared. The total units needed will be the sum of the desired ending inventory plus the amount needed to fulfill budgeted sales. The total need will be partially met by the beginning inventory; the remainder must come from planned production. Therefore, production is computed as follows:

---

[4]Occasionally, limits to productive capacity result in sales being geared to production rather than vice versa. Examples are shortages of machinery, manpower, or materials because of wars, strikes, or other imbalances in supply and demand.

Units to be Produced = Desired Ending Inventory of Finished Goods
+ Budgeted Sales — Beginning Inventory of Finished Goods

Note that the production budget is stated in physical units. As the calculation indicates, production is affected by both inventory levels and the sales budget. Frequently, production is stabilized throughout the year despite seasonal fluctuations in sales. Therefore, inventory serves as a coordinating link between manufacturing and sales by providing a cushion that satisfies the marketing need for goods when demand is unusually heavy and that also satisfies a production aim of stable utilization of manpower and facilities.

    3. When the level of production activity has been determined, the following budget schedules may be constructed:

    a. Material usage and purchases (Schedule 3). Usage will depend upon the level of production activity determined in step 2 above (Note A to Schedule 3). The purchases are influenced by both expected usage and inventory levels. The computation is Purchases in Units = Desired Ending Material Inventory Quantities + Usage — Beginning Inventory Quantities.

    b. Direct-labor costs (Schedule 4). These depend upon the type of products produced and the labor rates and methods that must be used to obtain desired production.

    c. Factory-overhead costs (Schedule 5). These depend upon the behavior of costs of the individual overhead items in relation to the anticipated level of production.

    d. Inventory levels (Schedule 6). These are the desired ending inventories. This information is required for the construction of budgeted financial statements.

    4. Cost-of-goods-sold budget (Schedule 7). This budget depends upon the information gathered in step 3.

    5. Budget of selling, administrative, and other expenses (Schedule 8).

    6. Budgeted income statement (Exhibit I). Steps 1 through 5 will provide enough information for this statement.

    7. Cash budget (Exhibit II), predicting effects on cash position of the levels of operation above. The illustrative cash budget is presented by quarters to show the impact of cash-flow timing on bank loan schedules. In practice, monthly—and sometimes weekly—cash budgets are very helpful for cash planning and control. Cash budgets aid in avoiding unnecessary idle cash and unnecessary cash deficiencies. The astute mapping of a financing program keeps cash balances in reasonable relation to needs. Ordinarily, the cash budget (Budgeted Statement of Cash Receipts and Disbursements) has the following main sections:

    a. The beginning cash balance plus cash receipts yield the total cash available for needs, before financing. Cash receipts depend on collections of accounts receivable, cash sales, and miscellaneous recurring sources such as rental or royalty receipts. Studies of the prospective collectibility of accounts receivable are needed for accurate predictions. Key factors include bad-debt experience and average time lag between sales and collections.

    b. Cash disbursements:

        (1) Material purchases—depends on credit terms extended by suppliers and bill-paying habits of the buyer.

        (2) Direct labor and other wage outlays—depends on payroll dates.

(3) Other costs and expenses—depends on timing and credit terms. Note that depreciation does not entail a cash outlay.

(4) Other disbursements—purchases of fixed assets, long-term investments.

c. Financing requirements depend on how the total cash available for needs, keyed as (a) in Exhibit II, compares with the total cash needed. Needs include disbursements, keyed as (b), plus the ending cash balance desired, keyed as (d). The financing plans will depend on the relationship of cash available to cash sought. If there is an excess, loans may be repaid or temporary investments made. The pertinent outlays for interest expenses are usually shown in this section of the cash budget.

d. The ending cash balance. The effect of the financing decisions on the cash budget, keyed as (c) in Exhibit II, may be positive (borrowing) or negative (repayment), and the ending cash balance, (d), equals (a) + (c) − (b).

The cash budget in Exhibit II shows the pattern of short-term "self-liquidating cash loans." Seasonal peaks of production or sales often result in heavy cash disbursements for purchases, payroll, and other operating outlays as the products are produced and sold. Cash receipts from customers typically lag behind sales. The loan is self-liquidating in the sense that the borrowed money is used to acquire resources that are combined for sale, and the proceeds from the sale are used to repay the loan. This cycle (sometimes called the *working-capital, cash,* or *operating cycle*) moves from cash to inventories to receivables and back to cash.

Cash budgets help managers avoid having unnecessary idle cash, on the one hand, and unnecessary nerve-racking cash deficiencies on the other.

8. Budgeted balance sheet (Exhibit III). Each item is projected in the light of the details of the business plan as expressed in the previous schedules. For example, the ending balance of Accounts Receivable would be computed by adding the budgeted sales (from Schedule 1) to the beginning balance (given) and subtracting cash receipts (given and in Exhibit II).

SOLUTION

M COMPANY

Sales Budget
For the Year Ending December 31, 19B

SCHEDULE 1

	UNITS	SELLING PRICE	TOTAL SALES
Product F (deluxe)	5,000	$105.40	$527,000
Product G (super deluxe)	1,000	164.00	164,000
			$691,000

M COMPANY

Production Budget,* in Units
For the Year Ending December 31, 19B

SCHEDULE 2

	PRODUCTS	
	F	G
Planned sales (Schedule 1)	5,000	1,000
Desired ending finished-goods inventory	1,100	50
Total needs	6,100	1,050
Less beginning finished-goods inventory	100	50
Units to be produced	6,000	1,000

*Work in process is negligible and is ignored.

M COMPANY

Direct-Material-Purchases Budget
For the Year Ending December 31, 19B

SCHEDULE 3

	MATERIAL 111	MATERIAL 112	TOTAL
Desired ending direct-material inventory in units	6,000	1,000	
Units needed for production (Note A)	84,000	44,000	
Total needs	90,000	45,000	
Less beginning direct-material inventory in units	5,000	5,000	
Units to be purchased	85,000	40,000	
Unit price	$ 1.20	$ 2.60	
Purchase cost	$102,000	$104,000	$206,000

NOTE A TO SCHEDULE 3—USAGE OF DIRECT MATERIALS IN UNITS AND DOLLARS

DIRECT MATERIALS	PRODUCTION		TOTAL DIRECT-MATERIAL USAGE	MATERIAL UNIT COST	COST OF MATERIALS USED
	PRODUCT F (6,000 UNITS)	PRODUCT G (1,000 UNITS)			
111 (12 units per finished product)	72,000	12,000	84,000	$1.20	$100,800
112 (6 units per Product F, 8 units per Product G)	36,000	8,000	44,000	2.60	114,400
					$215,200

M COMPANY

Direct-Labor Budget
For the Year Ending December 31, 19B

SCHEDULE 4

	UNITS PRODUCED	DIRECT-LABOR HOURS PER UNIT	TOTAL HOURS	TOTAL BUDGET @ $2.05 PER HOUR
Product F	6,000	14	84,000	$172,200
Product G	1,000	20	20,000	41,000
			104,000	$213,200

M COMPANY

Factory-Overhead Budget
For the Year Ending December 31, 19B

SCHEDULE 5

At anticipated activity of 104,000 direct labor hours:

Supplies	$30,000	
Indirect labor	70,000	
Payroll fringe costs	25,000	
Power—variable portion	8,000	
Maintenance—variable portion	20,000	
Total variable overhead		$153,000
Depreciation	$25,000	
Property taxes	4,000	
Property insurance	500	
Supervision	20,000	
Power—fixed portion	1,000	
Maintenance—fixed portion	4,500	
Total fixed overhead		55,000
Total factory overhead:		
($208,000 ÷ 104,000 is $2.00 per direct-labor hour)		$208,000

M COMPANY

Ending-Inventory Budget
December 31, 19B

SCHEDULE 6

	UNITS	UNIT COST	TOTAL AMOUNT	
Direct materials:				
111	6,000*	$ 1.20	$ 7,200	
112	1,000*	2.60	2,600	$ 9,800
Finished goods:				
F	1,100**	$ 86.70***	95,370	
G	50**	116.20***	5,810	101,180
Total				$110,980

*From top line in Schedule 3
**From second line in Schedule 2
***Computation of unit costs:

		PRODUCT F		PRODUCT G	
	UNIT COST	UNITS	AMOUNT	UNITS	AMOUNT
Material 111	$1.20	12	$14.40	12	$ 14.40
Material 112	2.60	6	15.60	8	20.80
Direct labor	2.05	14	28.70	20	41.00
Factory overhead	2.00	14	28.00	20	40.00
			$86.70		$116.20

M COMPANY

Cost-of-Goods-Sold Budget
For the Year Ending December 31, 19B

SCHEDULE 7

	FROM SCHEDULE		
Direct materials used	3		$215,200
Direct labor	4		213,200
Factory overhead	5		208,000
Total manufacturing costs			$636,400
Add finished goods, December 31, 19A	Given	$ 14,480	
Less finished goods, December 31, 19B	6	101,180	
Inventory increase for year			(86,700)
			$549,700

M COMPANY

Selling and Administrative Expense Budget
For the Year Ending December 31, 19B

SCHEDULE 8

Sales commissions	$20,000	
Advertising	3,000	
Sales salaries	10,000	
Travel	5,000	
Total selling expenses		$38,000
Clerical wages	$10,000	
Supplies	1,000	
Executive salaries	21,000	
Miscellaneous	5,000	
Total administrative expenses		37,000
Total selling and administrative expenses		$75,000

M COMPANY

Budgeted Income Statement
For the Year Ending December 31, 19B

EXHIBIT I

	FROM SCHEDULE		
Sales	1		$691,000
Cost of goods sold	7		549,700
Gross margin			$141,300
Selling and administrative expenses	8	$75,000	
Interest expense ($1,058 + $233)	Exhibits II and III	1,291	76,291
Net income before income taxes			$ 65,009
Income taxes	Assumed		20,000
Net income after income taxes			$ 45,009

M COMPANY
Budgeted Statement of Cash Receipts and Disbursements
For the Year Ending December 31, 19B

EXHIBIT II

		QUARTERS			FOR THE YEAR AS A WHOLE
	1	2	3	4	
Cash balance, beginning	$ 10,000	$ 15,000	$ 15,000	$ 15,072	$ 10,000
Add receipts:					
Collections from customers	125,000	150,000	160,000	221,000	656,000
(a) Total available before current financing	$135,000	$165,000	$175,000	$236,072	$666,000
Less disbursements:					
For materials	$ 20,000	$ 35,000	$ 35,000	$ 44,200	$134,200
For other costs and expenses	25,000	20,000	20,000	27,000	92,000
For payroll	90,000	95,000	95,000	109,200	389,200
For income tax	5,000	—	—	—	5,000
For machinery purchase	—	—	—	20,000	20,000
(b) Total disbursements	$140,000	$150,000	$150,000	$200,400	$640,400
Minimum cash balance desired	15,000	15,000	15,000	40,000	40,000
Total cash needed	$155,000	$165,000	$165,000	$240,400	$680,400
Excess of total cash available over total cash needed before current financing (deficiency)	$ (20,000)	$ —	$ 10,000	$ (4,328)**	$ (14,400)
Financing:					
Borrowings (at beginning)	$ 20,000	$ —	$ —	$ 15,500	$ 35,500
Repayments (at end)	—	—	(9,500)	(10,500)	(20,000)
*Interest (at 6% per annum)	—	—	(428)	(630)	(1,058)
(c) Total effects of financing	$ 20,000	$ —	$ (9,928)	$ 4,370	$ 14,442
(d) Cash balance, end (a + c − b)	$ 15,000	$ 15,000	$ 15,072	$ 40,042	$ 40,042

*The interest payments pertain only to the amount of principal being repaid at the end of a given quarter. Note that the $20,000 loan must be repaid by the end of the fourth quarter. Also note that depreciation does not necessitate a cash outlay.

**Note that the financing must also provide the repayment of the initial loan. Therefore, the total borrowing of $15,500 provides for $4,328 deficiency plus the $10,500 repayment of principal and $630 interest on the initial loan.

M COMPANY
Budgeted Balance Sheet
December 31, 19B

EXHIBIT III

ASSETS

Current assets:			
Cash		$ 40,042	
Accounts receivable (1)		60,000	
Materials (2)		9,800	
Finished goods (2)		101,180	$211,022
Fixed assets:			
Land (3)		$ 50,000	
Building and equipment (4)	$400,000		
Accumulated depreciation (5)	100,000	300,000	350,000
Total assets			$561,022

EQUITIES

Current liabilities:			
Accounts payable (6)		$ 70,000	
Income taxes payable (7)		20,000	
Notes payable (8)		15,500	
Accrued interest payable (9)		233	$105,733
Stockholders' equity:			
Common stock, no-par, 25,000 shares outstanding (10)		$350,000	
Retained income (11)		105,289	455,289
Total equities			$561,022

Notes:
Beginning balances are used as a start for most of the following computations:
(1) $25,000 + $691,000 sales − $656,000 receipts = $60,000.
(2) From Schedule 6.
(3) From beginning balance sheet.
(4) $380,000 + $20,000 purchases.
(5) $75,000 + $25,000 depreciation.
(6) $8,200 + ($206,000 purchases, $213,200 direct labor, $183,000 factory overhead,* $75,000 selling and administrative expenses) − ($134,200 materials, $92,000 other costs and expenses, and $389,200 payroll) = $70,000.
(7) $5,000 + $20,000 current year − $5,000 payment.
(8) From Exhibit II, fourth quarter.
(9) $15,500 × .06 × ¼ = $233.
(10) From beginning balance sheet.
(11) $60,280 + $45,009 net income.
* $208,000 from Schedule 5 minus depreciation of $25,000.

SALES FORECASTING—A DIFFICULT TASK

factors
in sales
forecasting
Incurrence of cost is necessarily keyed to production activity. Activity, in turn, depends on predicted sales. The sales prediction is the foundation for the quantification of the entire business plan.[5]

The chief sales officer has direct responsibility for the preparation of the sales budget. The task of preparation forces him to crystallize his plans. The sales forecast is made after consideration of the following factors:

1. Past sales volume
2. General economic and industry conditions
3. Relationship of sales to economic indicators such as gross national product, personal income, employment, prices, and industrial production
4. Relative product profitability
5. Market research studies
6. Pricing policies
7. Advertising and other promotion
8. Quality of sales force
9. Competition
10. Seasonal variations
11. Production capacity
12. Long-term sales trends for various products

forecasting
procedures
An effective aid to accurate forecasting is to approach the same goal by several methods; each forecast acts as a check on the others. The three methods described below are usually combined in some fashion that is suitable for a specific company.

Sales staff procedure.   As is the case for all budgets, those responsible should have an active role in sales-budget formulation. If possible, the budget data should flow from individual salesmen or district sales managers upward to the chief sales officer. A valuable benefit from the budgeting process is the holding of discussions, which generally result in adjustments and which tend to broaden participants' thinking.

Previous sales volumes are usually the springboard for sales predictions. Sales executives examine historical sales behavior and relate it to other historical data such as economic indicators, advertising, pricing policies, and competitive conditions. Current information is assembled, production capacity is considered, and then the outlook is derived for the ensuing months (years, in long-run sales budgets).

One of the common difficulties in budgeting sales is the widespread aversion of sales executives to figures. The usefulness of budgeting must be sold to salesmen. The best sales executives may not particularly enjoy working with figures,

---

[5] The term *sales forecast* is sometimes distinguished from *sales budget* as follows: The forecast is the estimate—the prediction—that may or may not become the sales budget. The forecast becomes the budget only if management accepts it as an objective. Often, the forecast leads to adjustments of managerial plans, so that the final sales budget differs from the original sales forecast.

but they realize that intelligent decisions cannot be made without concrete information. Market research is a sales executive's tool that helps to eliminate hunches and guessing. The market research group is a major staff department in many corporations.

Statistical Approaches. Trend, cycle projection, and correlation analysis are useful supplementary techniques. Correlations between sales and economic indicators help make sales forecasts more reliable, especially if fluctuations in certain economic indicators precede fluctuations in company sales. However, no firm should rely entirely on this approach. Too much reliance on statistical evidence is dangerous, because chance variations in statistical data may completely upset a program. As always, statistical analysis can provide help but not outright answers.

Group Executive Judgment. All top officers, including production, purchasing, finance, and administrative officers, may use their experience and knowledge to project sales on the basis of group opinion. This quick method dispenses with intricate statistical accumulations; however, it muddles responsibility for sales predictions and ignores the need for a tough-minded approach to this important task.

It is beyond the scope of this book to give a detailed description of all phases of sales-budget preparation, but its key importance should be kept in mind. The Suggested Readings at the end of this chapter list some references on sales forecasting.

summary

Comprehensive budgeting is the expression of management's master operating and financing plan—the formalized outlining of company objectives and their means of attainment. When administered wisely, budgets (a) compel management planning, (b) provide definite expectations that are the best framework for judging subsequent performance, and (c) promote communication and coordination among the various segments of the business.

The human factors in budgeting are more important than the technical intricacies. The job of education and selling is crucial. Otherwise, employees will resist and thwart the effectiveness of budgets as a helpful planning and control tool.

The foundation for budgeting is the sales forecast. Inventory, production, and cost incurrence are generally geared to the rate of sales activity.

suggested readings

Knight, D., and E. Weinwurm, *Managerial Budgeting*. New York: The Macmillan Company, 1964.

Welsch, G., *Budgeting: Profit Planning and Control*, 3rd ed. Englewood Cliffs, N.J.: Prentice-Hall, Inc., 1971.

The following references pertain especially to the difficult problem of sales forecasting:

Green, Paul E., and Donald S. Tull, *Research for Marketing Decisions*, 2nd ed. Englewood Cliffs, N.J.: Prentice-Hall, Inc., 1970. Chapter 16 covers sales forecasting.

Wolfe, Harry D., *Business Forecasting Methods*. New York: Holt, Rinehart & Winston, Inc., 1966.

Problem for Self-Study

Before trying to solve the homework problems, review the illustration in this chapter.

APPENDIX: INSTALLING AND ADMINISTERING THE BUDGET

budgeting and the accounting system The accounting system and the budgetary system should be synchronized with the organizational structure. Although budgets may be used for *planning* without being integrated with the accounting system, they may rarely be used for comprehensive *control* without being so integrated. Progressive firms link a budget with an accounting system that accumulates homogeneous information from the lowest levels of responsibility to the highest.

budget director Although line management has the ultimate responsibility for the preparation of individual budgets, there is also an evident need for technical, unbiased help and overall responsibility for the budget program. This need is usually satisfied by assigning responsibility to a budget director for establishing preparatory procedures, designing forms, *effective educating and selling*, collecting and coordinating data, verifying information, and reporting performance. The budget director is usually the controller or somebody who is responsible to the controller. He serves as the staff expert, the person upon whom line management depends for technical guidance. He may also be a valuable communications official between line and staff departments.

The able budget director typically has warm rapport with line management. He particularly avoids grabbing line authority—an easy trap to fall into because of his position as the company expert on budgetary matters.

budget committee A budget committee usually serves as a consulting body to the budget officer. Members generally include the budget director and the top-level line executives. However, very large businesses often exclude line executives other than the president from their budget committees; membership is confined to the budget director, the treasurer, the economist, and the president. Special budget committees are formed also—for example, a sales-budget committee and a production-budget committee.

The budget committee is concerned with developing and scrutinizing long-term operating and financial plans, offering advice, reconciling divergent views, and coordinating budgetary activities. The committee's very existence lends an aura of formality and prestige to the budget program.

The budget committee generally has an advisory role only; yet its advice is usually very influential. Initially, the committee usually assembles, reviews, and transmits underlying economic conditions and assumptions in relation to the ensuing budget period. It reviews departmental budgets and makes recommendations. It scrutinizes periodic reports comparing actual performance with the budget. As a result, it submits a variety of recommendations for top-management decision making.

budget manual It is usually desirable to have policies, organizational structure, and designations of responsibility and authority expressed in writing. The budget manual is a written set of instructions and pertinent information that serves as a rule book and a reference for the implementation of a budget program. It tells what to do, how to do it, when to do it, and which form to do it on. The effort and time needed for the manual's preparation are justified by its long-run usefulness, its tendency to crystallize all aspects of a budget program, and its documentation of procedures that otherwise are carried around in the heads of individuals who will not have the same job forever.

follow-up is important The investigation of budget deviations is the line manager's responsibility. The controller may assist to a very great extent, but the actual preparation of individual department budgets and decisions on deviations should be the responsibility of line management.

Ineffective budgetary systems are marked by failure to develop and use budgets to their fullest potential. That is, budgets are often used as tools for *planning* only. Great benefits from budgeting lie in the quick investigation of deviations and in the subsequent corrective action. Budgets should not be prepared in the first place if they are ignored, buried in files, or improperly interpreted. Abuses in this area of control probably outnumber the good uses. Again this points up the dire need for the education of company personnel.

questions, problems, and cases

5-1. What are the two major features of a budgetary program? Which feature is more important? Why?

5-2. What are the elements of the budgetary cycle?

5-3. Define: *continuous budget, pro forma statements.*

5-4. "The sales forecast is the cornerstone for budgeting." Why?

5-5. Enumerate four common duties of a budget director.

5-6. What is the function of a *budget committee?* A *budget manual?*

5-7. "Budgets are half-used if they serve only as a planning device." Explain.

5-8. Budgeting Material Purchases. The X Company has prepared a sales budget of 42,000 finished units for a three-month period. The company has an inventory of finished goods on hand at December 31 and desires a finished-goods inventory at the end of the succeeding quarter as follows:

	UNITS	
	DEC. 31	MARCH 31
Finished product	22,000	24,000

It takes three units of direct materials to make one unit of finished product. The company has an inventory of units of raw material at December 31 and desires an ending raw-material inventory as follows:

	UNITS	
	DEC. 31	MARCH 31
Direct materials	100,000	110,000

How many units of direct materials should be purchased during the three months ending March 31?

5-9. Budgeting Material Costs. The Maxwell Company uses a single raw material to make its product; for each unit of product, three pounds of this material are required. The price of this material is $10 per pound. The company follows a purchasing policy of placing orders on or before the fifth of each month to cover that month's requirements. It plans its inventory position in advance, to cover expected situations.

> The inventory of material at June 30, 19_1 was   9,000 pounds
> The inventory level planned for July 31 was   15,000 pounds
> The inventory level planned for August 31 was   35,000 pounds
> The inventory level planned for September 30 was   20,000 pounds

Production scheduled for the three-month period was:

> During July,   10,000 units of product
> During August,   12,000 units of product
> During September,   15,000 units of product

Suppose that this set of plans is carried out. What will be the total cost of materials purchased for the month of July? August? September?

5-10. Budgeted Manufacturing Costs. The Bridget Company has budgeted sales for 100,000 units of its product for 19_1. Expected unit costs, based on past experience, should be $60 for direct materials, $40 for direct labor, and $30 for manufacturing overhead. Assume no beginning or ending inventory in process. Bridget begins the year with 40,000 finished units on hand but budgets the ending finished-goods inventory at only 10,000 units. Compute the budgeted costs of production for 19_1.

5-11. Cash Budget. Using the information below, prepare a cash budget showing expected cash receipts and disbursements for the month of May, and balance expected at May 31, 19_1.

> Planned cash balance, May 1, 19_1: $60,000.
> Sales for May: $800,000, half collected in month of sale, 40 percent in next month, 10 percent in third month.
> Customer receivables as of May 1: $70,000 from March sales; $450,000 from April sales.
> Merchandise purchases for May: $500,000, 40 percent paid in month of purchase, 60 percent paid in next month.
> Payrolls due in May, $88,000.
> Three-year insurance policy due in May for renewal: $2,000, to be paid in cash.
> Other expenses for May, payable in May: $41,000.
> Depreciation for month of May: $2,000.
> Accrued taxes for May, payable in December: $6,000.
> Bank note due May 15: $175,000, plus $10,000 interest.

5-12. Cash Budget [SIA, adapted]. The directors of the TUV Company Limited, of which you are accountant, decide that in the future a short-term cash budget should be prepared for each quarter. Your company sells directly to the public for cash and through trade outlets on credit terms of 2/10, n/30. The accounts receivable have been analyzed and show the following record of collection:

> 70 percent of credit sales collected within the discount period
> 20 percent paid at the end of the 30-day period
> Balance paid at the end of a 60-day period

At the end of any month, 25 percent of sales on which the cash discounts will be taken are on the books as unpaid accounts receivable. Estimated sales for your first quarterly cash budget are as follows:

	19_1		
	JANUARY	FEBRUARY	MARCH
Cash sales	$30,000	$38,000	$45,500
Credit sales	74,000	79,000	85,000

TUV Company Limited makes purchases of goods for resale by paying for goods as delivered. By so doing they obtain a cash discount of 3 percent.

The markup on sales presently in effect provides a gross margin of 50 percent on gross cost (before cash discounts).

The minimum inventory required for efficient operation is $100,000 at retail prices.

Expenses are estimated as follows:

	SELLING	GENERAL
Fixed expenses	$6,000 per month	$10,000 per month
Variable expenses	10% of sales	5% of sales

Expenses are paid monthly as they arise.

Ten percent of fixed expenses represents depreciation and amortization of deferred charges.

A piece of land priced at $30,000 is under option. Your cash budget will indicate to the directors whether or not they can purchase the land for cash on March 31, 19_1. Cash must be available to pay a quarterly dividend of $7,500 on preferred shares on March 31. The purchase of land must not affect the general current position of the company.

The following information is taken from the December 31, 19_0, Balance Sheet:

Cash	$29,000
Accounts receivable	20,000*
Inventory at gross cost	70,000

*Credit sales for December were $31,580, of which $15,000 is still outstanding. November sales still outstanding are $4,000. $1,000 is uncollectible.

1. Schedule of collections on accounts for each month of January, February, and March.

2. Schedule of cash required for purchases for each month of January, February, and March.

3. Cash budget for each of the three months ended January 31, February 28, and March 31, 19_1.

4. Brief comments for directors on the significance of the cash budget.

5-13. **Budget of Cash Requirements [C.G.A., adapted].** Based on a sales forecast for the season, the planning department of a manufacturing company has prepared the following production schedule for the coming month: 30,000 units of Product A and 20,000 units of Product B. The manufacturing specifications for the products are as follows:

PRODUCT A	PRODUCT B
2 lbs. material X @ $.30	3 lbs. material W @ $.80
1/2 lb. material Y @ $.20	3/4 lb. material Y @ $.20
2 hours direct labor @ $2.00	1.5 hours direct labor @ $2.00

To the direct-labor hours, a 5 percent allowance for idleness (accounted for as overhead) should be added. Indirect-labor time is estimated to be 5 percent of direct-labor hours (excluding idleness), and the wage rate for indirect labor is $1.50. The overhead estimate (not shown above) is as follows:

FIXED COSTS PER MONTH		VARIABLE COSTS
Depreciation	$ 6,900	$.80 per direct-labor hour.
Expired insurance	800	NOTE: This rate includes the
Superintendence	3,000	costs of idle time and
	$10,700	indirect labor.

It is planned to increase the inventory of raw material X by 4,000 lbs. and to decrease the inventory of raw material W by 2,000 lbs. as of the beginning of the next month.

required Prepare a prediction of the amount of cash necessary for the manufacturing operations of the coming month. Assume that materials and payroll costs are paid for in the month of purchase.

5-14. **Comprehensive Budget; Fill in Schedules.** Following is certain information relative to the position and business of the Newport Store:

Current assets as of Sept. 30:	
Cash on deposit	$12,000
Inventory	63,600
Accounts receivable	10,000
Fixed assets—net	100,000
Current liabilities as of Sept. 30:	None
Recent and anticipated sales:	
September	$ 40,000
October	48,000
November	60,000
December	80,000
January	36,000

Credit sales: Sales are 75 percent for cash, and 25 percent on credit. Assume that credit accounts are all collected within 30 days from sale. The accounts receivable on Sept. 30 are the result of the credit sales for September (25 percent of $40,000).

Gross profit averages 30 percent of sales. Purchase discounts are treated on the income statement as "other income" by this company.

Expenses: Salaries and wages average 15 percent of sales; rent 5 percent; all other expenses, excluding depreciation, 4 percent. Assume that these expenses are disbursed each month. Depreciation is $750 per month.

Purchases: There is a basic inventory of $30,000. The policy is to purchase each month additional inventory in the amount necessary to provide for the following month's sales. Terms on purchases are 2/10, n/30. Assume that payments are made in the month of purchase, and that all discounts are taken.

Fixtures: In October, $600 is spent for fixtures, and in November, $400 is to be expended for this purpose.

Assume that a minimum cash balance of $8,000 is to be maintained. Assume that all borrowings are effective at the beginning of the month and all repayments are made at the end of the month of repayment. Interest is paid only at the time of repaying principal. Interest rate is 6 percent per annum.

required   On the basis of the facts as given above:

1. Complete Schedule A.

SCHEDULE A—BUDGETED MONTHLY DOLLAR RECEIPTS

ITEM	SEPTEMBER	OCTOBER	NOVEMBER	DECEMBER
Total sales	$40,000	$48,000	$60,000	$80,000
Credit sales	10,000	12,000	_____	_____
	_____	_____	_____	_____
Receipts:				
Cash sales		$36,000		
Collections on accounts receivable		10,000	_____	_____
Total		$46,000	_____	_____

2. Complete Schedule B. Note that purchases are 70 percent of next month's sales.

SCHEDULE B—BUDGETED MONTHLY CASH DISBURSEMENTS FOR PURCHASES

ITEM	OCTOBER	NOVEMBER	DECEMBER	TOTAL
Purchases	$42,000			
Less 2% cash discount	840			
Disbursements	$41,160			

3. Complete Schedule C.

SCHEDULE C—BUDGETED MONTHLY CASH DISBURSEMENTS FOR OPERATING EXPENSES

ITEM	OCTOBER	NOVEMBER	DECEMBER	TOTAL
Salaries and wages	$ 7,200			
Rent	2,400			
Other expenses	1,920			
Total	$11,520			

4. Complete Schedule D.

SCHEDULE D—BUDGETED TOTAL MONTHLY DISBURSEMENTS

ITEM	OCTOBER	NOVEMBER	DECEMBER	TOTAL
Purchases	$41,160			
Operating expenses	11,520			
Fixtures	600			
Total	$53,280			

5. Complete Schedule E.

SCHEDULE E—BUDGETED CASH RECEIPTS AND DISBURSEMENTS

ITEM	OCTOBER	NOVEMBER	DECEMBER	TOTAL
Receipts	$46,000			
Disbursements	53,280			
Net cash increase				
Net cash decrease	$ 7,280			

6. Complete Schedule F (assume that borrowings must be made in multiples of $1,000). Schedule F is on the next page.

7. What do you think is the most logical means of arranging the financing needed by Newport Store? Explain.

8. Prepare a pro forma income statement for the fourth quarter and a balance sheet as of December 31.

9. Certain simplifications have been introduced in this problem. What complicating factors would be met in a typical business situation?

SCHEDULE F—FINANCING REQUIRED BY NEWPORT STORE

ITEM	OCTOBER	NOVEMBER	DECEMBER	TOTAL
Opening cash	$12,000	$ 8,720		
Net cash increase				
Net cash decrease	7,280			
Cash position before financing	4,720			
Financing required	4,000			
Interest payments				
Financing retired				
Closing balance	$ 8,720			

5-15. Cash Budget [SIA]. The XY Trading Company follows the practice of preparing a sales forecast annually. The forecast for the company's fiscal year ending June 30, 19_1, was that the company would sell 160,000 units, distributed monthly as follows:

July	9%	November	10%	March	6%
August	10%	December	15%	April	7%
September	12%	January	3%	May	6%
October	9%	February	5%	June	8%

The company's average rate of gross profit on gross costs is $33\frac{1}{3}$ percent (before considering cash discounts). Its terms for sales are 2 percent 10 days, net 30 days, and it has been its experience that discounts on 80 percent of billings have been allowed and that, of the remainder, one-half have been paid during the month following the billing and the balance in the succeeding month.

Regarding its purchases of merchandise, the company receives the terms of 2 percent 10 days, net 60 days. However, it regularly takes discount on the tenth day after the invoice date.

The company stresses promptness of delivery in its advertising, so to ensure the immediate filling of orders, the inventories at December 31 and January 31 are maintained at 6 percent of the number of units estimated to be sold throughout the year; during the rest of the year, the inventories are maintained at 10 percent of that number.

Total budgeted selling, administrative, and general expenses for the fiscal year ended June 30, 19_1, are estimated at $624,000, of which $240,000 are fixed expenses (inclusive of $48,000 annual depreciation). These fixed expenses are incurred uniformly throughout the year. The other selling, administrative, and general expenses, which amount to $384,000, or 12 percent of total sales, vary proportionately with sales. Expenses are paid as incurred, without discounts.

Assume:

a. That one-third of the purchases of any month are due for discount and are paid for in the following month.

b. That the cash balance at January 1, 19_1, is $224,000.

c. That all discounted items are collected during the month of sale.

required   A budget of the cash receipts, disbursements, and balance for the three months ending March 31, 19_1.

5-16. Cash Budget [CPA, adapted]. The Standard Mercantile Corporation is a wholesaler and ends its fiscal year on December 31. You have been requested, in early January 19_4, to assist in the preparation of a cash forecast. The following information is available regarding the company's operations:

1. Management believes the 19_3 sales pattern is a reasonable estimate of 19_4 sales. Sales in 19_3 were as follows:

January	$ 360,000
February	420,000
March	600,000
April	540,000
May	480,000
June	400,000
July	350,000
August	550,000
September	500,000
October	400,000
November	600,000
December	800,000
Total	$6,000,000

2. The accounts receivable at December 31 total $380,000. Sales collections are generally made as follows:

During month of sale	60%
In first subsequent month	30%
In second subsequent month	9%
Uncollectible	1%

3. The purchase cost of goods averages 60 percent of selling price. The cost of the inventory on hand at December 31 is $840,000, of which $30,000 is obsolete. Arrangements have been made to sell the obsolete inventory in January at half the normal selling price on a C.O.D. basis.

   The company wishes to maintain the inventory as of the first of each month at a level of three months' sales as determined by the sales forecast for the next three months. All purchases are paid for on the tenth of the following month. Accounts payable for purchases at December 31 total $370,000.

4. Recurring fixed expenses amount to $120,000 per month, including depreciation of $20,000. For accounting purposes, the company apportions the recurring fixed expenses to the various months in the same proportion as that month's estimated sales figure bears to the estimated total annual sales. Variable expenses amount to 10 percent of sales.

   Payments for expenses are made as follows:

	DURING MONTH INCURRED	DURING FOLLOWING MONTH
Fixed expenses	55%	45%
Variable expenses	70%	30%

5. Annual property taxes amount to $50,000 and are paid in equal installments on December 31 and March 31. The property taxes are in addition to the expenses in item 4 above.

6. It is anticipated that cash dividends of $20,000 will be paid each quarter on the fifteenth day of the third month of the quarter.
7. During the winter, unusual advertising costs will be incurred that will require cash payments of $10,000 in February and $15,000 in March. The advertising costs are in addition to the expenses in item 4 above.
8. Equipment replacements are made at the rate of $3,000 per month. The equipment has an average estimated life of six years.
9. A $60,000 installment of the company's income tax for 19_3 is due on March 15, 19_4.
10. At December 31, 19_3, the company had a bank loan with an unpaid balance of $280,000. The loan requires a principal payment of $20,000 on the last day of each month plus interest at $\frac{1}{2}$ percent per month on the unpaid balance at the first of the month. The entire balance is due on March 31, 19_4.
11. The cash balance at December 31, 19_3, is $100,000.

required   Prepare a cash forecast statement by months for the first three months of 19_4 for the Standard Mercantile Corporation. The statement should show the amount of cash on hand (or deficiency of cash) at the end of each month. All computations and supporting schedules should be presented in good form.

5-17. Inventory Budgets and Cash Budgets [CPA, adapted].   The Modern Products Corporation, a manufacturer of molded plastic containers, determined in October 19_8 that it needed cash to continue operations. The corporation began negotiating for a one-month bank loan of $100,000 that would be discounted at 6 percent per annum on November 1. In considering the loan, the bank requested a cash budget for the month of November.

The following information is available:
a. Sales were budgeted at 120,000 units per month in October 19_8, December 19_8, and January 19_9, and at 90,000 units in November 19_8.

The selling price is $2 per unit. Sales are billed on the fifteenth and the last day of each month on terms of 2/10, net 30. Past experience indicates sales are even throughout the month and 50 percent of the customers pay the billed amount within the discount period. The remainder pay at the end of 30 days, except for bad debts, which average $\frac{1}{2}$ percent of gross sales. On its income statement, the corporation deducts directly from gross sales the estimated amounts for cash discounts on sales and losses on bad debts.

b. The inventory of finished goods on October 1 was 24,000 units. The finished-goods inventory at the end of each month is to be maintained at 20 percent of sales anticipated for the following month. There is no work in process.

c. The inventory of raw materials on October 1 was 22,800 pounds. At the end of each month, the raw-material inventory is to be maintained at not less than 40 percent of production requirements for the following month. Materials are purchased as needed in minimum quantities of 25,000 pounds per shipment. Raw-material purchases of each month are paid in the next succeeding month on terms of net 30 days.

d. All salaries and wages are paid on the fifteenth and the last day of each month for the period ending on the date of payment.

e. All manufacturing overhead and selling and administrative expenses are paid on the tenth of the month following the month in which incurred. Selling expenses are 10 percent of gross sales. Administrative expenses, which include depreciation of $500 per month on office furniture and fixtures, total $33,000 per month.

f. The budgeted cost of a molded plastic container, based on "normal" production of 100,000 units per month, is as follows:

Materials—½ pound	$ .50
Labor	.40
Variable overhead	.20
Fixed overhead	.10
Total	$1.20

Fixed overhead includes depreciation on factory equipment of $4,000 per month.

g. The cash balance on November 1 is expected to be $10,000.

required   Prepare the following for the Modern Products Corporation, assuming the bank loan is granted. (Do not consider income taxes.)

1. Schedules computing inventory budgets by months for:
   a. Finished-goods production in units for October, November, and December.
   b. Raw-material purchases in pounds for October and November.

2. A cash forecast for the month of November, showing the opening balance, receipts (itemized by dates of collection), disbursements, and balance at end of month.

5-18. Cash Budgeting. On Dec. 1, 19_1, the XYZ Wholesale Co. is attempting to project cash receipts and disbursements through Jan. 31, 19_2. On this latter date, a note will be payable in the amount of $10,000. This amount was borrowed in September to carry the company through the seasonal peak in November and December.

The trial balance on Dec. 1 shows in part:

Cash	$ 1,000	
Accounts receivable	28,000	
Allowance for bad debts		$1,580
Inventory	8,750	
Accounts payable		9,200

Sales terms call for a 2 percent discount if paid within the first ten days of the month after purchase, with the balance due by the end of the month after purchase. Experience has shown that 70 percent of the billings will be collected within the discount period, 20 percent by the end of the month after purchase, and 8 percent in the following month, and that 2 percent will be uncollectible.

The unit sales price of the company's one product is $10. Actual and projected sales are:

October actual	$ 18,000
November actual	25,000
December estimated	30,000
January estimated	15,000
February estimated	12,000
Total estimated for year ending June 30	150,000

All purchases are payable within fifteen days. Thus, approximately 50 percent of the purchases in a month are due and payable in the next month.

The unit purchase cost is $7. Target ending inventories are 500 units plus 25 percent of the next month's unit sales.

Total budgeted selling and administrative expenses for the year are $40,000. Of this amount, $15,000 is considered fixed (includes depreciation of $3,000). The remainder varies with sales. Both fixed and variable selling and administrative expenses are paid as incurred.

required   Prepare a columnar statement of budgeted cash receipts and disbursements for December and January.

6

Systems Design, Responsibility Accounting, and Motivation

Accounting systems for helping decision making must be designed in relation to management objectives. In this chapter, we obtain perspective on the critical factors that deserve attention when managers and accountants evaluate or choose an accounting system.

We consider goal congruence, responsibility accounting, controllable costs, and the effect of systems on human motivation. The human aspects of management accounting cannot be overemphasized.

GOAL SETTING AND SYSTEMS DESIGN

focus of design must be on objectives Ideally, an accounting system is the major information system of any organization. It is the formal communications network that supplies data to help executives strive toward a mass of predetermined top-management objectives and subobjectives. Because modern organizations seem to be in an almost constant state of change, the expert designer of accounting systems is perpetually concerned with shifts in objectives, in behavior, in available resources, and in organizational structures. Only in this way can an accounting system be designed to accumulate, classify, measure, and report the types of data that management objectives require.

characteristics of management accounting systems
The management *process* is a series of decisions aimed at some objective or set of objectives. Accounting *systems* for management decision making and implementation (hereafter often called *planning and control systems, control systems, management accounting systems* or *information systems*) are the means for data accumulation, interpretation, and reporting that are tailored to aid management processes.

Even though systems may be designed to fulfill multiple purposes, the economics of the cost and value of information tends to gear systems for the management processes that are repeated in a routine fashion. For instance, most accounting systems are designed to facilitate the economical recording of frequently encountered transactions. This feature leads to having special journals or "canned" computer programs for high-volume tasks. Hence, the isolated nonrecurring transaction is often jammed into the system in a seemingly inefficient way. In these cases, the system dominates an activity that by itself might be handled more directly. For example, a cash purchase under a voucher system is recorded in a voucher register and a check register, even though simpler techniques can be conceived.

The management process in its entirety varies from very complex top-level decisions regarding objectives and policies to fairly simple day-to-day supervisory decisions. The complex decisions are relatively unstructured, nonrepetitive, often long range, and often dependent on expert advice from "staff." There is little that is systematic about this activity, which has often been called *strategic planning.*[1] The provision of data for special decisions will always entail preparing much data that will not lie within the system.

Systems design is a very practical task. The criterion of "those data would be nice to have" is not enough. A major question that must eventually be asked is whether the extra costs of accumulating the data exceed the expected value of the data in question. Special decisions often require data that are not routinely accumulated because they are not routinely needed.

Systems are especially helpful for the simpler or the more highly structured decisions. That is, many decisions can be "engineered" or "programmed" so that predetermined rules can closely govern day-to-day or second-to-second performance. The accomplishments in the exploration of outer space are probably the best example of how systems can facilitate decision making and implementation. In all types of organizations, there are many basic decisions that are now being implemented by computers. For example, elaborate mathematical models have been formulated for calculating production mixes, determining when to reorder inventories, processing oil company credit cards, and auditing income tax returns. The models are designed and the computers are programmed by humans, but the implementation is by machine instead of by man.

Most of these subparts of control systems are concerned with physical or technical matters. Dehumanization of specific decisions occurs when mathe-

[1] Robert N. Anthony, *Planning and Control Systems: A Framework for Analysis* (Boston: Harvard Business School, 1965), p. 5.

matical models and computers are used. Therefore, at least for particular decisions, the human problem disappears as activities are finely programmed and
computerized. But there are still many behavioral ramifications. How do more
rules and models affect the organization as a whole and the managers who
determine the inputs to the models?[2]

To be complete, a managerial accounting system for decision making and
implementation must provide feedback, so that results are available for evaluation
and the improvement of future decisions. For example, the ritual of compiling
budgets will not bear much fruit if no comparison is made of the actual results
with the predictions.

The future will see increasing attempts to formalize management decision
making via mathematical models and computers. Still, when management accounting systems are viewed in their entirety, the problems of their effects on
human motivation and decisions are critical. That is why the task of the accountant is more complex, more ill-structured, and more affected by the human
aspects than many people believe at first glance.

goal
congruence
How should accountants and managers judge a given management accounting system? We need some criteria, some benchmarks, to gauge the
quality of a system. Present criteria tend to concentrate on physical or
data-processing aspects, such as the routing of multiple copies of source documents or the cost of processing a payroll check. A system may earn the highest
ratings under these criteria. Nevertheless, such criteria are incomplete, and the
system may be weak because it is hindering rather than helping the attainment
of top-management objectives.

Above all, as Chapter 1 stressed, the aim of a system is to get management
goals in congruence. The first question to ask is: *Does the system provide a global
emphasis, so that all major goals and their interrelationships are considered as
far as possible when managers act? Expressed another way, does the system
specify goals and subgoals to encourage behavior that blends with top-
management goals?*

the need for
multiple goals
The aim of a system is to get subgoals in congruence, and this requires
direction and balance. It is fairly easy to assess the direction of each subgoal
by itself; the trouble is that they are interdependent. Moreover, the selection of subgoals is essentially based on a series of assumptions regarding optimization that must be made at the strategic-planning level. For example, the
General Electric Company[3] has stressed multiple goals by stating that orga-

[2] See "American Accounting Association Report of Committee on Managerial Decision Models,"
Accounting Review Supplement, Vol. XLIV, especially pp. 43–46.

[3] See E. Kirby Warren, *Long-Range Planning: The Executive Viewpoint* (Englewood Cliffs, N.J.:
Prentice-Hall, Inc., 1966), Chapter 5.

nizational performance will be measured in the following eight areas:

1. Profitability
2. Market position
3. Productivity
4. Product leadership
5. Personnel development
6. Employee attitudes
7. Public responsibility
8. Balance between short-range and long-range goals

General Electric's efforts basically try to juggle two conflicting tendencies in goal setting. First, the overemphasis on multiple goals may lead to diffusion of efforts and the failure to perform as well as expected in any one area. Second, the overemphasis on a single goal may lead to success in one area but failure to attain other goals.

example   The Soviet Union provides many cases where overstress on one or two aspects of the measurement system may lead to uneconomic behavior that focuses on a subgoal without considering overall organizational goals. To illustrate, taxi drivers were put on a bonus system based on mileage. Soon the Moscow suburbs were full of empty taxis barreling down the boulevards to fatten their bonuses. In response to bonuses based on tonnage norms, a Moscow chandelier factory produced heavier and heavier chandeliers, until they started pulling ceilings down.

The most common instance is the short-run maximization of net income or sales that hurts long-run results. There are many questionable ways to improve short-run performance—stinting, for example, on repairs, quality control, advertising, research, or training. A manager may successfully exert pressure on employees for more productivity for short spurts of time. This may have some unfavorable long-run overtones.

As we explore various facets of systems design and techniques, we will see the importance of goal congruence in example after example. Top management must explicitly face the job of goal setting and coordination; it should not be a product of chance or a by-product of the day-to-day extinguishing of business brush fires. Financial-planning models and master budgets plus feedback reporting are probably the most widely used techniques for coordinating goals.

human resources accounting   Despite the efforts of some top managements to have systems designed to stress other goals in addition to the goal of profitability, the accounting system remains the most pervasive formal device for measuring performance. In the eyes of many, this has led to a short-run bias on the part of many managers, because accounting conventions (a) lead to immediate write-offs as expenses of outlays that should really be carried forward as assets, and (b) adhere to historical costs and ignore changes in the "real values" of many assets.

A notable example of this criticism is the research conducted by Rensis Likert, a social psychologist, and his colleagues. For many years, Likert has stressed that accounting systems encourage the misuse of human resources; that managers tend to ignore the need for more employee participation in decision making and for more training of subordinates; and moreover, that pressures for short-run profits lead to unnecessary and uneconomical layoffs and discharges. According to Likert, the short-run increases in profit are illusory, because increases in turnover and later additional spending for hiring and training more than offset the immediate savings. Likert advocates incorporating "human resource" accounting as part of the formal accounting system. As a minimum measure, this would entail recording as assets the outlays for recruiting and training managers. These costs would be amortized over the expected useful lives of the employees.

Regardless of your reaction to Likert's ideas, you should recognize that—after decades of research on the utilization of human resources—Likert apparently feels that the major formal performance-measurement system (the accounting system) is the best way to accomplish his ends. Other means, such as reporting measures of employee turnover and conducting attitude surveys, have generally been unsatisfactory because they have been regarded as supplementary and secondary in importance to accounting measures of income or costs. Consequently, to avoid its being given little attention, some kind of accounting for human resources must be incorporated within the accounting system. Likert is intrigued by human-asset accounting because he wants to repair what he perceives to be the motivational errors of existing formal control systems. He wants the system to change so that managers will make different decisions.[4]

Similarly, General Electric, despite citing eight separate goals, has found managers stressing one goal above all others: profitability. When several executives of General Electric were cited by the Justice Department for price fixing, one of the strongest arguments mustered in their defense was that a sense of internal pressure for profits had led toward this action, even though, in addition to being illegal, it was clearly opposed to the company's longer-run interests.[5]

The lesson is that the accounting system is still dominant as a means for setting goals and influencing management behavior in most organizations. Goals outside the accounting system, even though meritorious, are regarded as supplementary unless top management follows through and acts as if they are indeed as important as short-run financial performance.

RESPONSIBILITY ACCOUNTING

systems and organization changes   Ideally, the organization itself and its processes must be thoroughly appraised, understood, and altered, if necessary, before a system is constructed. That is, the design of a system and the design of an organizational structure are really inseparable and interdependent. The point is that the most

---

[4] See Rensis Likert, *The Human Organization, Its Management and Value* (New York: McGraw-Hill Book Company, 1967). Also see "Participative Management: Time for a Second Look," *Fortune*, May 1967, p. 167. In addition, several articles were published in 1969, 1970, and 1971 by R. Lee Brummet, Eric G. Flamholtz, and William C. Pyle on the implementation of a human-resource accounting system at the R. G. Barry Corporation of Columbus, Ohio. For example, see their co-authored article in *Management Accounting*, August 1969, and the articles by Pyle in the *Financial Analysts Journal*, September–October 1970 and January–February 1971.

[5] For this and other examples, see E. Kirby Warren, *op. cit.*, Chapter 5.

streamlined system is not a cure-all or a substitute for basic organizational ills or management ineptitude. On a practical level, there may be a powerful temptation to separate the design of system from the design of organizational processes by assuming that the organizational structure is given and therefore not subject to change. But some sad experiences with the hasty installation of computers demonstrate the weakness of such an approach.

To work optimally, top managers subdivide processes and stipulate an organizational hierarchy of managers, each of whom is expected to oversee a sphere of responsibility and ordinarily has some degree of latitude to make decisions within that sphere. The sphere of responsibility may be called a cost center; or, if the manager must also make decisions about sales or investments, the responsibility sphere may be called a profit center or investment center. Some form of responsibility accounting system usually accompanies this subdivision of decision making.

definition of responsibility accounting   *Responsibility accounting, profitability accounting,* or *activity accounting* systems recognize various decision centers throughout an organization and trace costs (and revenues, assets, and liabilities, where pertinent) to the individual managers who are primarily responsible for making decisions about the costs in question.

The impact of the responsibility accounting approach is described in the following:

> The sales department requests a rush production. The plant scheduler argues that it will disrupt his production and cost a substantial though not clearly determined amount of money. The answer coming from sales is: "Do you want to take the responsibility of losing the X Company as a customer?" Of course the production scheduler does not want to take such a responsibility, and he gives up, but not before a heavy exchange of arguments and the accumulation of a substantial backlog of ill feeling. Analysis of the payroll in the assembly department, determining the costs involved in getting out rush orders, eliminated the cause for argument. Henceforth, any rush order was accepted with a smile by the production scheduler, who made sure that the extra cost would be duly recorded and charged to the sales department—"no questions asked." As a result, the tension created by rush orders disappeared completely; and, somehow, the number of rush orders requested by the sales department was progressively reduced to an insignificant level.[6]

Ideally, revenues and costs are recorded and automatically traced to the one individual in the organization who shoulders primary decision responsibility for the item. He is in the best position to evaluate and to influence a situation—to implement decisions. In practice, the diffusion of control throughout the organization complicates the task of collecting relevant data by responsibility centers. The organizational networks, the communication patterns, and the decision-

---

[6]Raymond Villers, "Control and Freedom in a Decentralized Company," *Harvard Business Review,* XXXII, No. 2, 95.

making processes are complex—far too complex to yield either pat answers or an ideal management accounting system.

illustration of The simplified organization chart in Exhibit 6-1 will be the basis for our
responsibility illustration. We will concentrate on the manufacturing phase of the business.
accounting The lines of responsibility are easily seen in Exhibit 6-2, which is an overall view of responsibility reporting. Starting with the supervisor of the machining department and working toward the top, we shall see how these reports may be integrated through three levels of responsibility.

In Exhibit 6-3, all direct material is charged at budgeted unit prices to the machining department only. The other producing departments do not include the same direct materials in their budgets. In this way, the Curry Co. incorporates direct materials and direct labor, as well as the controllable overhead items, in

EXHIBIT 6-1

CURRY CO.: SIMPLIFIED ORGANIZATION CHART

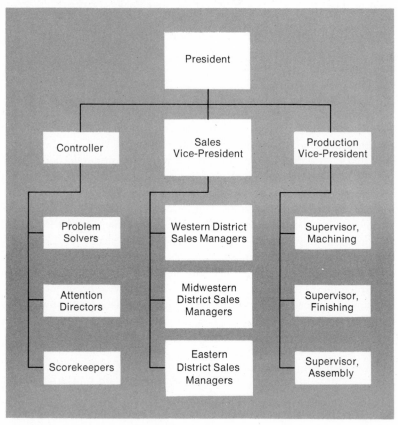

EXHIBIT 6-2

RESPONSIBILITY REPORTING AT VARIOUS MANAGEMENT LEVELS

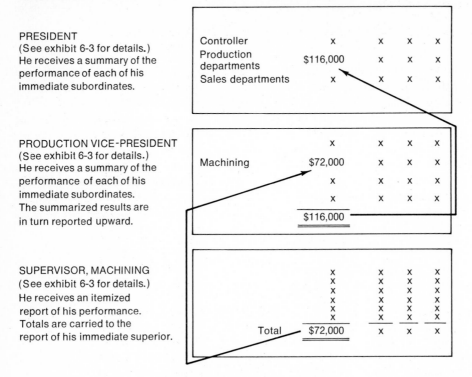

PRESIDENT
(See exhibit 6-3 for details.)
He receives a summary of the
performance of each of his
immediate subordinates.

Controller	x	x	x	x
Production departments	$116,000	x	x	x
Sales departments	x	x	x	x

PRODUCTION VICE-PRESIDENT
(See exhibit 6-3 for details.)
He receives a summary of the
performance of each of his
immediate subordinates.
The summarized results are
in turn reported upward.

	x	x	x	x
Machining	$72,000	x	x	x
	x	x	x	x
	x	x	x	x
	$116,000			

SUPERVISOR, MACHINING
(See exhibit 6-3 for details.)
He receives an itemized
report of his performance.
Totals are carried to the
report of his immediate superior.

	x	x	x	x
	x	x	x	x
	x	x	x	x
	x	x	x	x
	x	x	x	x
	x	x	x	x
Total	$72,000	x	x	x

its departmental budgets. All the variances shown may be subdivided for further analysis, either in these reports or in subsidiary reports.

Note that each of these three responsibility reports furnishes the department head with figures on only those items subject to his control. Items not subject to his control are removed from these performance reports; he should not receive data that may clutter and confuse his decision making.

Trace the $72,000 total from the machining department report in Exhibit 6-3 to the production vice-president's report. The vice-president's report merely summarizes the reports of the three individuals under his jurisdiction. He may also want copies of the detailed statements of each supervisor responsible to him.

Also trace the $116,000 total from the production vice-president's report to the president's report. His summary report includes data for his own office plus a summarization of the entire company's current cost-control performance.

format of feedback reports   This set of illustrative reports shows only the budgeted amount and the variance, which is defined as the difference between the budgeted and the actual amounts. This places the focus on the variances and illustrates *management by exception,* which means that the executive's attention is concentrated on the important deviations from budgeted items. In this way,

EXHIBIT 6-3

CURRY CO.

*President's Monthly Responsibility
Performance Report*

	BUDGET		VARIANCE: FAVORABLE, (UNFAVORABLE)	
	THIS MONTH	YEAR TO DATE	THIS MONTH	YEAR TO DATE
President's office	$ 6,000	$ 20,000	$ 100	$ 400
Controller	4,000	13,000	(200)	(1,000)
Production vice-president	116,000	377,000	(8,950)	(20,600)
Sales vice-president	40,000	130,000	(1,000)	(4,000)
Total controllable costs	$166,000	$540,000	$(10,050)	$(25,200)

*Production Vice-President's
Monthly Responsibility
Performance Report*

	BUDGET		VARIANCE: FAVORABLE, (UNFAVORABLE)	
	THIS MONTH	YEAR TO DATE	THIS MONTH	YEAR TO DATE
Vice-president's office	$ 9,000	$ 29,000	$ (1,000)	$ (1,000)
Machining department	72,000	236,000	(2,950)	(11,600)
Finishing department	15,000	50,000	(2,000)	(3,000)
Assembly department	20,000	62,000	(3,000)	(5,000)
Total controllable costs	$116,000	$377,000	$ (8,950)	$(20,600)

*Machining Department
Supervisor's Monthly Responsibility
Performance Report*

	BUDGET		VARIANCE: FAVORABLE, (UNFAVORABLE)	
	THIS MONTH	YEAR TO DATE	THIS MONTH	YEAR TO DATE
Direct materials	$ 40,000	$140,000	$ (1,000)	$ (4,000)
Direct labor	25,000	75,000	(2,000)	(7,000)
Setup	4,000	12,000	400	100
Rework	2,000	6,000	(200)	(300)
Supplies	200	600	(40)	(100)
Small tools	300	900	(50)	(100)
Other	500	1,500	(60)	(200)
Total controllable costs	$ 72,000	$236,000	$ (2,950)	$(11,600)

managers do not waste time on those parts of the reports that reflect the smoothly running phases of operations.

Of course, this illustration is only one possible means of presenting a report of performance. Another common reporting method shows three sets of dollar figures instead of two sets. Moreover, the variances could also be expressed in terms of percentages of budgeted amounts. For example, direct labor in the machining department could appear as follows:

	BUDGET		ACTUAL RESULTS		VARIANCE: FAVORABLE, (UNFAVORABLE)		VARIANCE: PERCENT OF BUDGETED AMOUNT	
	THIS MONTH	YEAR TO DATE	THIS MONTH	YEAR TO DATE	THIS MONTH	YEAR TO DATE	THIS MONTH	YEAR TO DATE
Direct labor	$25,000	$75,000	$27,000	$82,000	$(2,000)	$(7,000)	(8.0%)	(9.4%)

The full performance report would contain a similar line-by-line analysis of all items. The exact format adopted in a particular organization depends heavily on user preferences.

cooperation versus competition A fragile balance must be struck between careful delineation of responsibility, on the one hand, and a too-rigid separation of responsibility, on the other hand. Buck passing is a pervasive tendency that is supposedly minimized when responsibility is fixed unequivocally.

example A large utility used to hire college graduates and rotate them among all departments in the company during a two-year training program. Their salaries were not assigned to the departments, and individual managers took little interest in the trainees. But now it assigns the trainee to a definite department that fits his primary interest, where he is given direct responsibility as soon as possible. Both the trainees and the managers are much more satisfied with the new responsibility arrangement.

But often the motivational impact boomerangs; too much falls between the chairs. Managers often wear blinders and concentrate more than ever on their individual worlds. Family cooperation is replaced by intracompany competition.

example Two departments performed successive operations in a line-production process making automobile frames. The frames were transferred from the first to the second department via an overhead conveyor system. Because of machine breakdowns in his department, the Department 2 manager requested the Department 1 manager to slow down production. He refused, and the frames had to be removed from the conveyor and stacked to await further processing. A bitter squabble ensued regarding which department should bear the extra labor cost of stacking the frames.

CONTROLLABLE AND UNCONTROLLABLE COSTS

definition of
controllable
costs
Responsibility accounting has a natural appeal because it specifies a boundary of operations and distinguishes between controllable and uncontrollable costs. It is easy to say that a manager's performance should be judged on the basis of only those items subject to his control. But experienced cost accountants and managers will testify that it is far from easy to decide whether an item is controllable or uncontrollable. Moreover, there are shades of influence—an item may be controllable in whole or in part. Therefore, do not expect to get a crystal-clear, practical concept of a controllable cost. It does not exist. Still, accountants must grapple with this problem, even though their approaches are often coarse.

The concept of a controllable cost is associated with the implementation of decisions. It is a critical underpinning of the ideas of responsibility accounting. The basic idea is that only humans can influence the level of cost incurrence. The focus is on the activity or organization unit under the supervision of an individual. Controllable costs are those that may be directly regulated at a given level of management authority. Put another way, controllable costs are those that are directly influenced by a *manager* within a *given time span.*

The definition has two important ingredients. First, we cannot distinguish controllable from uncontrollable costs without specifying a level and scope of management authority. That is, we must circumscribe the activity or organizational unit that is under the direction of the manager. For example, insurance costs on machinery may not be controllable by the manager of a producing department. However, such costs may indeed be controllable by the manager of the insurance department.

Second, the time-period assumption is important. If the time period were long enough, virtually all costs would be controllable by somebody in the organization. On the other hand, as the time period shortens, very few costs may be controllable. In the insurance example, note that the cost of a one-year insurance policy might not be controllable, even by the insurance manager, if the time period for evaluation were a week or a month instead of a year. In contrast, the rent on a building having a thirty-year lease could be viewed as controllable by the building and facilities manager if the time period used for evaluation were thirty years.

determining
controllability
or responsibility
The main trouble for the designer of a responsibility accounting system is that controllability is a matter of degree: (a) There are usually few costs that are clearly the *sole* responsibility of one person; and (b) the time-period problem is almost impossible to solve for many costs. Although controllability may often be difficult to pinpoint, responsibility accounting nevertheless clings to a tough-minded approach. It asks, Who is the one person in the organization with the most decision-making power over the item in question? This is usually the executive who most closely supervises the day-to-day ac-

tivities that influence that cost. He typically has the authority to accept or reject the material or service in question. Therefore, he must bear the responsibility, and so must his superiors.

If the manager is responsible for both the acquisition and the use of the service, the cost should be deemed as controllable by him. However, the diffusion of control throughout the organization complicates the task of collecting data by responsibility centers. For example, raw-material *prices* may be most affected by the decisions of the purchasing officer, whereas raw-material *usage* may be most strongly influenced by the production supervisor.

As the next chapter will show in detail, the management accountant approaches this problem by charging the production department for raw materials at predetermined unit prices rather than actual unit prices. In this way, month-to-month price fluctuations do not affect the performance of the production supervisor. Predetermined prices (most often called *budgeted* or *standard* prices) are frequently utilized so that performance measures may exclude the possible misleading effects of changes in unit prices.

The whole complex problem of allocating indirect costs to departments, territories, products, and other cost objects, as we shall see in Chapter 12, illustrates how messy the idea of fixing responsibility or controllability can become. There are many instances where a manager can indirectly influence the amount of cost incurred. For instance, if a repair and maintenance department renders service to many departments, the level of repair costs borne by any production supervisor for nonroutine repairs can be affected by the wage rates in the repair department, the efficiency of the repair work force, the supervisory skills of the repair foreman, the efficiency of the production workers, the timing and care of the ordinary repairs done by regular production personnel, and so on.

reporting
controllable
and
uncontrollable
items

In a given situation, therefore, some costs may be regarded as controllable with various degrees of influence and others as uncontrollable. Most advocates of responsibility accounting favor excluding the uncontrollable items from a performance report. For example, the report for a shop foreman's department would contain only his controllable costs. Such items as property taxes and rent would not appear on his report; from his standpoint, these are uncontrollable costs.

The countervailing view is that uncontrollable items that are indirectly caused by the existence of the foreman's department should be included in his report. In this way, managers become aware of the whole organization and its costs. The behavioral implication of this idea is that some managers in the organization influence almost every cost; by also assigning that cost to some other executives in the organization, these executives will be more inclined to influence the manager who has primary control over the cost.

example

A president of a large corporation insists that central basic research costs be fully allocated to all divisions despite objections about uncontrollability. His goal is to force division managers' interests toward such research activity. The basic question is whether the accounting system is the best vehicle for reaching such an objective. Indiscriminate cost allocations may undermine the confidence of the managers in the entire accounting system.

But there is also a pitfall here. There can be overdependence on an accounting system as being the prime means of motivation and the final word on the appraisal of performance. Although the system may play a necessary role in coordination and motivation, its many limitations deserve recognition, too, particularly in matters of cost allocations. A common complaint of managers, often marked by tones of discouragement, is that they are being unfairly charged with uncontrollable costs. In any event, if management insists that both controllable and uncontrollable costs appear on the same report, these costs should not be mingled indiscriminately.

the time period and control   The influence of the time period on determining whether a cost is controllable is a vexing problem. Too often, managers are inclined to oversimplify by assuming that variable costs are controllable and fixed costs are uncontrollable. Such thinking may lead to erroneous conclusions. For example, rent is uncontrollable by the assembly foreman, but it may be controllable by, say, the executive vice-president, who is assigned the responsibility of choosing plant facilities and of deciding whether to own or rent. Moreover, managers frequently have the option of trading off variable for fixed costs—for example, by purchasing labor-saving devices.

Some of the most severe analytical difficulties arise because of the existence of long-run costs like depreciation. How, for example, should depreciation be regarded in a situation where (a) a department already has all its needed equipment, (b) the current department manager has inherited the equipment from his predecessor, and (c) the life of the equipment is long? In such a situation, the main control must be exerted at the time of acquisition of the equipment; once incurred, the level of cost may be hard to influence for many years. Chapter 12 shows a possible way to report costs so that these long-run committed costs are sharply differentiated from other fixed and variable costs that are subject to short-run decisions.

EFFECT OF SYSTEMS ON HUMAN BEHAVIOR

administration of the system   We all know that top managers achieve objectives through human beings with the help of inanimate resources like machines, computers, buildings, materials, and accounting techniques. To do a good job, the laborer must use the machines and materials skillfully. And so it is with accounting techniques and systems; they must be administered astutely to obtain management objectives in an optimal fashion.

In many cases of weak systems, the technical aspects of the system are not the culprits. The weaknesses are inept administration, the neglect of education and communication, ignorance of the motivational impact of the system, and, probably most important, lack of active top-management support. For example, unless the top managers take budgets seriously and use feedback reports to make decisions, the likelihood is remote that their subordinates will view the system as a key to their success. The uses of a management control system can be affected both by its technical perfection and by other nontechnical factors that influence management behavior.

our knowledge of behavioral effects The data produced by decision models and accounting systems are supposed to have actual or potential influence on designated decisions. Little systematic evidence is available concerning the complicated effects of systems on user behavior. Instead, either the relationship is overlooked or it is propounded by flat assertions. Although useful generalizations are often suggested, they must be regarded as tentative hypotheses rather than as universal truths. Our knowledge about human behavior in organizational settings is still too fragmented to warrant much guidance beyond the "each case is different" caveat.

A simple awareness of the importance of goal congruence and the motivational impact of systems is at least a first step toward obtaining an informative perspective on the design of systems and the selection of accounting techniques. The point is that the same questions are applicable to a wide variety of organizations, even though the answers may differ in kind or degree.

participation in budgeting The budgeting process provides communications devices in the form of conferences and copies of budgets or other plans. The polar types of budget processes have been characterized as *authoritative* and *participative*. Authoritative processes impose budget goals on management. There is a minimal voice from subordinates, and budgetary accountants often prepare the budgets after little consultation with the line executives who are responsible for achieving the specified goals. On the other hand, participative budgets are a team effort. The executives with line responsibility hammer out the budget goals, and the budgetary accountants provide advice and technical help. However, participation is not always easy to achieve:

> One weakness noted in some interviews concerned the inability of the budget staff to obtain line participation in developing budgets. There was a noticeable tendency in some cases on the part of line people to relinquish line budget responsibilities to the budget staff. Line personnel simply did not wish to be bothered with it. In most of these cases the budget staff have no desire to prepare budgets, and for them to do so was contrary to the intent of top management.
>
> This condition seems to be one of the major weaknesses existing in profit planning. Correction . . . involves education of management, especially at lower management levels. . . .[7]

[7] Burnard H. Sord and Glenn A. Welsch, *Business Budgeting* (New York: Controllership Foundation, Inc., 1958), p. 102.

As you might suspect, behavioral scientists tend to favor participative rather than authoritative budget processes because participation is more likely to have a favorable motivational impact. *Motivation* is the need to achieve some selected goal and the resulting drive that influences action toward the chosen goal. Therefore, motivation may be judged, as Professor R. N. Anthony has said, by its *direction* and its *strength*.

system goals and personal goals   It is not enough for the control system simply to specify subgoals so that they harmonize with top-management goals. Ideally, management should also design the system to lead the individual managers toward *acceptance* of those subgoals as their own personal goals. In this way, managers, working in their best self-interest as they perceive it, will make decisions that are congruent with top-management goals. For example, how important is conformity to a budget prediction? If conformity is accepted by the manager as being important, and the accounting feedback is regarded as the most important source of information regarding his own appraisal of self-worth (for example, it tells him, "I am competent"), then the budget will be a crucial part of the control system.

Of course, the accounting system is only one of many control systems that influence an individual's behavior. Society as a whole can be viewed as a control system, and various institutions can impinge on an individual's values and reactions. For example, a person can be affected by his family, religion, profession, company, department, and so forth. This point may be obvious, but it is not trivial.

The budgetary accountant may try to influence the individual's acceptance of goals. However, his influence may be overwhelmed by the values of society and the feedback information from other sources. Furthermore, in practice it is very hard to detect and allow for the variations in perceived individual self-worths. For example, the design of budget systems for professional personnel, such as research scientists, is often particularly difficult. This is undoubtedly partially attributable to the phenomenon that perceived self-worth may be little affected by the formal control system per se. In short, propositions such as "It's important to adhere to budget" may be relatively unimportant to a researcher. Moreover, his feedback sources are more likely to be informal than formal. The opinions of co-workers and external critics may count heavily.

The point is that the motivational effects of accounting systems are often weighty; however, in some parts of the organization they may simply be unimportant. Personal goals, to the extent that acceptance of goals (such as budget goals) can be affected by formal systems within the organization, are likely to be heavily influenced by how higher executives support the system. Without massive top-management backing, the goals specified by the system, which should aim at goal congruence, are less likely to gain acceptance as personal goals. Note too that acceptance is the key; acceptance may be best achieved in some cases by participatory processes and in other cases by authoritative processes.

slack: The budgetary process entails the setting of goals. If the budget is over-
a universal emphasized or viewed as a rigid monitor of performance, managers and
behavioral employees are induced toward behavior that is not usually consonant with
problem the typical goals of the organization as a whole. For example, budgets in
not-for-profit organizations usually stipulate a top spending limit. This
creates a philosophy of "We'd better spend it or we'll lose it," which does not
lead to long-range cost reduction. Similarly, managers in industry are often
disinclined to reduce costs because this leads to cuts in budget allowances for
future periods. In other words, cost-cutting performance now may generate
temporary praise or rewards but will make the job tougher later because the
future budget will not be as easy to attain.

The personal goals of managers (personal income, size of staff, esteem,
power) will often lead to a "bargained" budget, whereby managers intentionally
create *slack* as a protective device.[8] Slack can be defined in a cost context as
the difference between the minimum necessary costs and the actual costs of the
firm. (Slack may be called *padding* in some organizations.) This seeking of slack
permeates all budgeting in every conceivable sort of organization. Little has been
done to counteract it.

An example of the attempt to reduce slack is the widespread use of lump-
sum rewards to managers and other employees for "permanent" cost-savings.
Another example is allowing the manager to "keep" the saving, in the form of
not tightening the budget for a specified subsequent span of one to three years.
Therefore, even though the old cost budget of $100,000 should be decreased
to $90,000 because of the discovery of a new production method, the cut may
be postponed for a year or more. Despite these attempts at counteraction, slack
remains as one of the major unsolved problems in budgetary control.

importance of   In countless organizations, informal information systems are dominant in
formal systems decision making. There is widespread use of little black books and special
memorandums. In addition, many executives, including top managers, rely
on rules of thumb and accumulated experience rather than on the output of
formal systems like accounting reports. This method often proves satisfactory
because such executives are evaluating the information wisely and making
decisions that keep their companies competitive.

As companies grow, managers become more dependent on formal rather
than informal information systems. Professor Richard Vancil has observed that
the formal system provides a crutch for the orderly succession of management.
Large companies, with mobile executives who typically move frequently, must
have such a system; after all, most managers do not have thirty years of experience on which to base their decisions. The introduction of formal decision models
in business is an example of the response to the need for more crutches. For

---

[8]M. Schiff and A. Lewin, "Where Traditional Budgeting Fails," *Financial Executive*, XXXVI,
No. 5, 51–62; and "The Impact of People on Budgets," *The Accounting Review*, XLV, No. 2 (April
1970), 259–69.

instance, the blending of various ingredients in sausage was once the task of some wise individual with a good feel for the critical variables. Now the blending decision is made by a computer program that resulted from the formalization of a previously informal process.

A prime challenge for systems designers is to discover whether some or all of the informal information system is leading to successful decisions. If so, the designer should attempt to formalize those parts of the informal system. For example, the formal system should aim at incorporating the key numbers or events that a manager may be keeping informally. Consider the pricing decision. The formal system may compile data so that they are ignored by the manager when he is setting prices because his experience and readings of industry or economic data are the keys to his decisions. The designer should then try to crystallize the manager's decision model explicitly, so that the critical data may be supplied by the formal system. In this way, the formal system can become the key information system, can engender sincere management support, and can ease the tasks of management succession.

accurate Textbooks do not devote much space to the problems of obtaining accurate
scorekeeping source documents. Yet this is easily one of the most pervasive, everlasting problems in collecting information. An accounting system cannot help managers predict and make decisions if its scorekeeping is haphazard.

Pressures may spur managers to encourage their subordinates to record time erroneously or to tinker with scrap or usage reports.

example The maintenance crews of one telephone company regularly performed recurring short-term maintenance and repair work on various projects. At other times, the same crews would be concerned with huge construction projects—installing or building plant and equipment. The company had weekly reports on performance of the regular maintenance work, but had only loose control over the construction projects. An investigation disclosed that the foremen were encouraging the workmen to boost the time on the construction projects and to understate the time on the regular maintenance projects. Thus the foremen's performance on the latter always looked good. The situation was corrected when the emphases on maintenance and on construction were balanced so that both were currently budgeted and controlled.

Accurate record keeping is essentially a problem of motivation. The accountant and manager should be more sensitive to possible errors, more aware of the futility of trying to get usage of time and materials reported accurately in small increments, and more conscious of the natural tendency of individuals to report their activities so as to minimize their personal bother and maximize their own showing.[9] The hazard of trying to get extremely detailed reports extends not only to lack of confidence in individual reports themselves but to the likelihood of generating monumental contempt for the entire system.

[9] Also see Sam E. Scharff, "The Industrial Engineer and the Cost Accountant," *N.A.A. Bulletin,* XLII, No. 7, Section 1, for more examples.

Top managers can induce accurate scorekeeping if they can persuade subordinates that the documents are important for decision making. Again we see the need for active management support:

example   A firm of civil engineers has surveying jobs throughout California that are largely obtained by firm price quotations. A key to profitability is the ability to predict how much time will be required for the various subtasks on the job. The president of the firm feels so strongly about the need for feedback that his field crew managers must mail daily time reports to the central office. If they are not received on the day expected, the president immediately phones to find out why.

intelligent   The accounting system should produce information that leads managers
analysis of   toward correct decisions regarding either evaluation of performance or
relevant data   selection among courses of action. Intelligent analysis of costs is often
dependent on explicit distinctions between cost behavior patterns, which is more likely to be achieved via the contribution approach than via traditional methods. The general tendency toward indiscriminate full-cost allocations raises analytical dangers.

example   A bakery distributed its products through route salesmen, each of whom loaded a truck with an assortment of products in the morning and spent the day calling on customers in an assigned territory. Believing that some items were more profitable than others, management asked for an analysis of product costs and sales. The accountants to whom the task was assigned allocated all manufacturing and marketing costs to products to obtain a net profit for each product. The resulting figures indicated that some of the products were being sold at a loss, and management discontinued these products. However, when this change was put into effect, the company's overall profit declined. It was then seen that, by dropping some products, sales revenues had been reduced without commensurate reduction in costs because the joint manufacturing costs and route sales costs had to be continued in order to make and sell remaining products.[10]

summary

When systems design is viewed as a whole, the importance of top-management goal setting and support becomes apparent. To insure goal congruence, managers must accept the goals specified by the system as their own personal goals.

Responsibility accounting accumulates and reports items in accordance with the structure of the organization. It focuses on the manager's area of control—such as a department, territory, or division. Attempts are made to distinguish between controllable and uncontrollable costs.

[10]Walter B. McFarland, "The Field of Management Accounting," *N.A.A. Bulletin,* XLV, No. 10, Sec. 3, 19.

The human aspects of management accounting systems are much more troublesome in practice than the technical factors. Budgets and standards will be helpful tools if managers and accountants use them adroitly. A superior tool in the hands of a clumsy oaf may do more harm than good; in the hands of a skillful artisan, it becomes an important instrument that helps toward pleasing results.

Motivation is the overriding consideration that should influence management in formulating and using performance measures and in designing management control systems. Above all, the system and techniques should impel managers toward management objectives. If this supposition is valid, any system's rules, criteria, checklists, or questionnaires should explicitly include an appraisal of the motivational influences of the system under review. Among the questions that seem especially crucial are:

1. Does the system specify its goals and subgoals to encourage behavior that blends with top-management goals?
2. Is the accounting system tailored to the organization structure to strengthen motivation?
3. Are the goals as specified by the top management and through the system accepted by managers as their personal goals?
4. Does the system properly guide managers in the acquisition and utilization of resources by providing accurate, timely, relevant data?

Subquestions deserving consideration would cover such commonly encountered difficulties as the overemphasis on a subgoal; the overemphasis on short-run performance; failure to pinpoint responsibility; cooperation versus competition; the lack of distinction between controllable and uncontrollable costs; limitations of records as motivation devices; inaccurate source documents; and faulty cost analysis.

suggested readings

American Accounting Association, "Report of Committee on Managerial Decision Models," *Accounting Review Supplement*, Vol. XLIV, pp. 43–78.

Anthony, Robert N., *Planning and Control Systems: A Framework for Analysis*. Boston: Harvard Business School, 1965. Anthony's writings are always worth reading because he has a special knack for focusing on central issues.

Becker, Selwyn, and David Green, Jr., "Budgeting and Employee Behavior," *Journal of Business*, October 1962, pp. 392–403. Also see the *Journal of Business*, April 1964, for a reply by Andrew C. Stedry to the Becker and Green article, plus a rejoinder to that reply.

Beyer, Robert, *Profitability Accounting*. New York: The Ronald Press Company, 1963. This book offers practical coverage of responsibility accounting.

Bruns, William J., Jr., and Don T. DeCoster, eds., *Accounting and its Behavioral Implications*. New York: McGraw-Hill Book Company, 1969. This is an edited and abridged collection of forty articles on behavioral accounting.

Burns, Thomas J., ed., *The Behavioral Aspects of Accounting Data for Performance Evaluation.* Columbus, O.: College of Administrative Science, Ohio State University, 1970. This is a collection of six papers, seven critiques, and proceedings of an accounting symposium.

Hofstede, G. H., *The Game of Budget Control.* New York: D. Van Nostrand and Company, 1967.

Likert, Rensis, *The Human Organization, Its Management and Value.* New York: McGraw-Hill Book Company, 1967.

Simon, H. A., H. Guetzkow, G. Kosmetsky, and G. Tyndall, *Centralization vs. Decentralization in Organizing the Controller's Department.* New York: The Controllership Foundation, Inc., 1954. This book is incisive and readable. Its title is deceiving because the book covers the entire range of management accounting. Unfortunately, the book is out of print, so you may have difficulty in getting a copy.

Sord, Burnard H., and Glenn A. Welsch, *Business Budgeting.* New York: Controllership Foundation, Inc., 1958.

Stedry, Andrew C., *Budget Control and Cost Behavior.* Englewood Cliffs, N.J.: Prentice-Hall, Inc., 1960.

Sord, Welsch, and Stedry discuss the role of motivation in budgeting. The study by Stedry is controversial.

Problem for Self-Study

PROBLEM   Construct a chart with the following headings:

| | | | CONTROLLABLE COST | | |
	PRODUCT COST	VARIABLE COST	BY SALES VICE-PRESIDENT	BY ASSEMBLY SUPERVISOR	BY PRODUCTION VICE-PRESIDENT
Salesmen's commissions					
Direct materials					
Machining department— direct labor					
Finishing department— supplies					
Sales vice-president's salary					
Straight-line depreciation—equipment in assembly department					
Management consulting fee for improving labor methods in assembly department					

Assume the same organization chart as shown in Exhibit 6-1. For each account, answer "yes" or "no" as to whether the cost is a product cost, a variable cost, and a cost controllable by the four officers indicated. Thus, you will have five answers, entered horizontally, for each account.

SOLUTION Note particularly how the concepts of variable/fixed and controllable/uncontrollable costs differ. A variable cost is not necessarily a controllable cost. Controllability is dependent on a manager's responsibility within a given time period. Note, too, that all costs that are controllable by a manager are also regarded as being controllable by his superior line executive.

			CONTROLLABLE COST		
	PRODUCT COST	VARIABLE COST	BY SALES VICE-PRESIDENT	BY ASSEMBLY SUPERVISOR	BY PRODUCTION VICE-PRESIDENT
Salesmen's commissions	No	Yes	Yes	No	No
Direct materials	Yes	Yes	No	Yes	Yes
Machining department— direct labor	Yes	Yes	No	No	Yes
Finishing department— supplies	Yes	Yes	No	No	Yes
Sales vice-president's salary	No	No	No	No	No
Straight-line depreciation—equipment in assembly department	Yes	No	No	No	No*
Management consulting fee for assembly dept.	Yes	No	No	Yes**	Yes

*Note that the time element is important here. Although depreciation may not be controllable in the short run, the production vice-president's policies on selection and timing of equipment purchases influence depreciation costs.
**Note that this is a fixed cost because it will be unaffected by fluctuations in production activity. Still, it is a controllable cost because either the assembly supervisor or one of his superiors decided to incur the cost in order to reduce labor costs. This is an example of a cost that is fixed but that may be controllable by the assembly supervisor. Of course, if he has no voice in the decision, the cost may be uncontrollable by him but controllable by one of his superiors.

questions, problems, and cases

6-1. Define *responsibility accounting*.

6-2. Define *controllable cost*. What two major factors help an evaluation of whether a given cost is controllable?

6-3. What guides are available in deciding the appropriate costs to be charged to a person?

6-4. "An action once taken cannot be changed by subsequent events." What implications does this have for the cost accountant?

6-5. List five common complaints about control budgets.

6-6. "Budgets are wonderful vehicles for communication." Comment.

6-7. Define *motivation*. How does it differ from *need*?

6-8. Give an example of how a control system can motivate a manager to behave against the best interests of the company as a whole.

6-9. "I'm majoring in accounting. This study of human relations is fruitless. You've got to be born with a flair for getting along with others. You can't learn it!" Do you agree? Why?

6-10. "Interpretation is essential for understanding accounting reports." Suggest how the accounting function may be organized to emphasize interpretation.

6-11. Budgets as Motivators. "Budgets and responsibility accounting and other modern accounting techniques foster a policed, departmental orientation rather than a positive, overall organizational orientation." Do you agree? Explain.

6-12. Budgets as Pressure Devices. Sord and Welsch have stated: "It should be recognized that pressure on supervisors need not come from control techniques, assuming that standards of performance are not unfair or too high. Pressure on supervisors comes from the responsibilities inherent in the supervisor's job." Do you agree? Why?

6-13. Budgets as Motivators. "To accept budgets as motivators is to imply that supervisors do not have adequate interest in their job. This is seen as an insult to a man's integrity, and the factory supervisors resent it strongly." Do you agree? Why?

6-14. Attitudes Toward the Accountant. A prominent financial analyst, who became very successful with his Wall Street investments, once commented:

"My experience with the accountant is that for him everything has equal importance. He is like the Lord in the Bible, where it is written that 'a thousand years are in His sight as yesterday' when it is past—except that it is just the other way around with the accountant: 10 cents in the balance sheet is just as important as a million dollars. The main thing for him is that every figure should be correct."

Elbert Hubbard, a philosopher popular early in the twentieth century, made the following remarks:

"The typical auditor is a man past middle age, spare, wrinkled, intelligent, cold, passive, non-committal, with eyes like a codfish, polite in contact, but at the same time unresponsive, cold; calm and damnably composed as a concrete post or a plaster-of-paris cast; a human petrification with a heart of feldspar and without charm of the friendly germ, minus bowels, passion, or a sense of humour. Happily, they never reproduce and all of them finally go to Hell."

In general, do you agree with the remarks above? Why?

6-15. Interdepartmental Conflict and Budgets. Professor Argyris and others have pointed out that budgets help foster a *departmental* orientation rather than a *plant-wide* orientation. This causes trouble because departmental executives concentrate on the correct functioning of their individual departments but pay no attention to the functioning of individual departments in relation to one another.

For example, Argyris cites the example of the plant in which a mistake was made on a customer order. The goods were returned and a correction was made at a cost of $3,000, a large amount. Some department had to be charged with the error. But which department?

After two months of battling among the supervisors as to who was guilty, emotions became so heated that two supervisors stopped talking to each other.

The plant manager finally gave up; he decided to charge the error to no department. He explained, "I thought it might be best to put the whole thing under general factory loss. Or else someone would be hurt."

required Do you agree that budgets foster too narrow an orientation? Do you agree with the action of the plant manager? Did the budget and departmental accounting system cause the trouble? Explain fully.

6-16. Inaccuracies in Source Documents. Interdepartmental confusion in a printing company was described by Professor George Shultz.[11] A producing department's production committee complained vigorously about the planning done by the scheduling department. Workmen objected that frequently they set up a job only to discover that the specific paper needed was unavailable. Although paper for other jobs was available, a switch was not desirable because setup time was too great. This complaint involved other departments, so that the production committee could not correct the situation themselves. They passed it upward to a top committee, which included the president.

The head of the scheduling department was naturally upset by this complaint, so he investigated the matter thoroughly in preparation for the meeting. The worker prepares a time slip for each job, showing the total elapsed time in terms of running time, delays, and so on. The scheduling department uses this information for production planning. The scheduling department head examined the file of these slips and found that there was really extremely little delay due to "insufficient paper."

At the meeting he triumphantly provided these "facts" and maintained that the complaint was insignificant. Shultz reports that this disclosure was greeted with embarrassed silence. After a long half-minute, a worker said: "Those time slips are way off. We fill them out. We were told by the foreman that he would get in trouble if we showed that delay time, so we usually added it to the running time. We've been doing it that way for years. We had no idea that you were using the slips as a basis for planning."

required   Why are accurate source documents important? What are the practical problems of getting accurate source documents?

6-17.   **Inaccuracies in Source Documents.**[12]   A study was made of time reporting in the shops of a large steel and alloy plate fabricator to determine to what degree the time reporting was accurate, what kind of errors were being made, and the probable cause of these errors. In this company's time-reporting system, each workman reported his own time. The findings revealed that the time reported against any job could vary as much as 15 to 20 percent from actual time without the discrepancy's being detected by the foreman's checking of time cards at the end of the day or by other checks, such as comparing estimated with actual hours, and so forth.

The two most glaring sources of variances were, first, inadvertently charging time to the wrong job, and second, willfully charging time to the wrong job when it was obvious that a given job was running over the estimated hours. There were numerous reasons for this being so, from improper identification of the material being worked on to workmen covering up excessive personal time. In all, some twenty-five sources of error were identified.

List four common reasons for inaccuracies in timekeeping by foremen and workmen. What should the accountant learn from the above example?

6-18.   **Auto Dealership Profit Centers.**   Many automobile dealers divide their businesses into two major divisions: (a) parts and service and (b) vehicle sales. The gross profit of the parts and service activity is looked upon as the amount that is supposed to "cover" all parts and service overhead plus all general overhead of the dealership. If this goal can be achieved, the gross profit of the vehicle division can be regarded as "gravy"—as net profit. In other words,

[11]G. P. Shultz, "Worker Participation on Production Problems," *Personnel,* Vol. 28, No. 3, pp. 209–10.

[12]Adapted from Sam E. Scharff, "The Industrial Engineer and the Cost Accountant," *N.A.A. Bulletin,* XLII, No. 7, 17.

the contribution margin of the parts and service activity is looked upon as a cost recovery, whereas the vehicle sales are regarded as the profit-making mechanism.

required   Evaluate the merits of this approach. If you were managing an automobile dealership, would you view your operations any differently? How?

6-19. Computation of Gross Profits on Car Sales.   Many auto dealers use the "washout" concept. *Washout* is the method for computing gross profits on a series of deals starting with the sale of a new unit and ending with the straight (no trade-in) sale of the last vehicle in the series. The gross profit on the sale of the new unit and used units is totaled and stated in terms of gross profit per new unit retailed.

required   Evaluate the washout concept in terms of assigning responsibility to profit centers. How else could gross profit be computed?

6-20. Possible Causes of Variations.   Hower, Inc., determines that the Variable Factory Overhead for the period was as follows:

	DEPT. A		DEPT. B	
	ACTUAL	BUDGET	ACTUAL	BUDGET
Material handling	$5,000	$5,000	$3,000	$3,100
Idle time	510	500	1,510	500
Rework	1,300	900	130	100
Supplies	2,800	3,200	5,000	5,900
	$9,610	$9,600	$9,640	$9,600

In the period, one of the machines in Dept. A developed a twisted cutting tool that was not noted until the machine had been used for some time. This product follows an assembly-line pattern, moving from Dept. A to Dept. B.

required   Explain the possible causes of variations noted above in the light of information given here. Comment on the controllability of the cost elements noted.

6-21. Coordination and Accountants' Attitudes.   The problem of coordination is directly affected by the accountants' attitudes. Frederick G. Lesieur, an authority on the Scanlon Plan for labor compensation, has observed:

> . . . In my work, during the past eight years, I've been amazed to find how many accounting groups in companies have become so inflexible that they make very little constructive contribution. Rather than accounting servicing the company, it is often true that the company is servicing the accounting group. Why, even in some of these situations it seems to make little difference to the accounting people whether the company was losing or making money. This may seem a little harsh, but what I am driving at is that sometimes when suggestions are made to the accounting people that a change in their system or procedure might help the company, you run into a great deal of resistance. The accountants answer: "We've got a perfect accounting system here, and under no conditions do we want to alter it." The fact that making even minor changes in procedures might help the plant was not important. The thing that seemed most important to these accounting people was "don't disturb our setup."

I share Joe Scanlon's conviction that this particular group can make a contribution that is probably unparalleled in the firm. This is the group that has the records for what is taking place in the firm. But, too often, trying to translate that record into something meaningful, which can be understood by the men and women in the plant, seems to be considered almost impossible.[13]

required Is Lesieur justified in making these comments? Should the accountant bear all the blame? Why?

6-22. Nature of Controllable Costs and Responsibility Accounting.

1. Define *controllable cost*. What two major factors help decide whether a given cost is controllable?
2. Briefly describe responsibility accounting.
3. What guides are available to decide what costs may be appropriately charged to a person?

6-23. Controllable or Uncontrollable Costs.   Refer to Problem 2-28. Indicate by "C" or "U" whether each item is controllable or uncontrollable by a machinery department foreman.

6-24. Controllable-Cost Concepts; Fill in Blanks.   Assume the same organization chart as shown in Exhibit 1-2. For each item listed, indicate by "Yes" or "No" whether it would be classified as a product cost, variable cost, and controllable cost. If you are in doubt about whether an item has strictly variable or strictly fixed cost behavior, decide on the basis of whether the total cost will fluctuate substantially over a wide range of volume.

			CONTROLLABLE COST			
	PRODUCT COST	VARIABLE COST	BY SALES VICE-PRESIDENT	BY DRILL-PRESS FOREMAN	BY PRODUCTION SUPERIN-TENDENT	BY MANU-FACTURING VICE-PRESIDENT
Assembly department— Polishing material	————	————	————	————	————	————
Secretary-Treasurer's salary	————	————	————	————	————	————
Chief inspector's department—Supplies	————	————	————	————	————	————
Straight-line depreciation—Equipment in drill-press department	————	————	————	————	————	————
Salesmen's travel expenses	————	————	————	————	————	————
Drill-press department— Direct materials	————	————	————	————	————	————

6-25. Application of Responsibility Accounting.   In early 19_2 the volume of errors submitted to the Mammoth Corporation electronic data-processing center at Center, Illinois, had grown to such a degree that the one employee whose task it was to correct the information and follow through on resubmittal to the computer was hard pressed to keep current with his work. Frequently

[13]Frederick G. Lesieur, "What the Plant Isn't and What It Is," *Scanlon Plan . . . A Frontier in Labor–Management Cooperation* (New York: The Technology Press of Massachusetts Institute of Technology and John Wiley & Sons, Inc., 1958), p. 39.

overtime was necessary, and if the volume of errors persisted, an additional employee would be needed.

It was believed that the volume of errors could be reduced but that the gravity of the matter had not been successfully communicated to the office managers at the various parts depots. A series of letters had been sent attempting to communicate this concern. Also, an attempt at education was made in a letter explaining the probable cause of each of the most frequently occurring errors.

All these attempts were unsuccessful; errors continued to persist in approximately the same volume as before.

What could be done? (a) The errors could be sent back to the submitting parts depots for correction and resubmittal; (b) efforts could be continued to gain cooperation from the office managers to reduce the number of errors; or (c) an additional employee could be hired to cope with the increased volume of errors. Because (a) and (c) were unattractive, efforts had to be restricted to gaining help from the submitting depots.

required   1. Could responsibility accounting help in solving this difficulty?

2. Explain briefly how this might be done.

6-26. **Responsibility of Purchasing Agent.**[14]   Richards had just taken a new job as purchasing agent for The Hart Manufacturing Company. Sampson is head of the production planning and control department. Every six months, Sampson gives Richards a general purchasing program. Richards gets specifications from the engineering department. He then selects suppliers and negotiates prices.

When he took this job, Richards was informed very clearly that he bore responsibility for meeting the general purchasing program once he accepted it from Sampson.

During Week No. 24, Richards was advised that Part No. 1234—a critical part—would be needed for assembly on Tuesday morning, Week No. 32. He found that the regular supplier could not deliver. He called everywhere, finally found a supplier in the Middle West, and accepted the commitment.

He followed up by mail. Yes, the supplier assured him, the part would be ready. The matter was so important that on Thursday of Week No. 31, Richards checked by phone. Yes, the shipment had left in time. Richards was reassured and did not check further. But on Tuesday of Week No. 32, the part was not in the warehouse. Inquiry revealed that the shipment had been misdirected by the railroad company and was still in Chicago.

required   What department should bear the costs of time lost in the plant? Why? As purchasing agent, do you think it fair that such costs be charged to your department?

6-27. **A Study in Responsibility Accounting.**   The David Machine Tool Company is in the doldrums. Production volume has fallen to a ten-year low. The company has a nucleus of skilled tool-and-die men who could find employment elsewhere if they were laid off. Three of these men have been transferred temporarily to the building and grounds department, where they have been doing menial tasks like sweeping, washing walls, and so on, for the past month. These men have earned their regular rate of $8 per hour. Their wages have been charged to the building and grounds department. The supervisor of building and grounds has just confronted the controller as follows: "Look at

---

[14] Adapted from Raymond Villers, "Control and Freedom in a Decentralized Company," *Harvard Business Review*, Vol. XXXII, No. 2, 89–96.

the cockeyed performance report you pencil pushers have given me. The helpers' line reads:

	BUDGET	ACTUAL	DEVIATION	
Wages of helpers	$1,764	$4,704	$2,940	Unfavorable

"This is just another example of how unrealistic you bookkeepers are! Those tool-and-die guys are loafing on the job because they know we won't lay them off. The regular hourly rate for my three helpers is $3. Now that my regular helpers are laid off, my work is piling up, so that when they return they'll either have to put in overtime or I'll have to get part-time help to catch up with things. Instead of charging me at $8 per hour, you should charge about $2—that's all those tool-and-die slobs are worth at their best."

required As the controller, what would you do *now*? Would you handle the accounting for these wages any differently?

6-28. **Budgets and Incentives.** You are working as a supervisor in a manufacturing department that has substantial amounts of men and equipment. You are paid a "base" salary that is actually low for this type of work. The firm has a very liberal bonus plan, which pays you another $1,000 each time you "make the budget" and 2 percent of the amount you are able to save.

Your past experiences have been as follows:

PERIOD	1	2	3	4	5	6
Budget	$40,000	$40,000	$39,000	$36,000	$36,000	$36,250
Actual	41,000	39,500	37,000	37,000	36,500	36,000
Variance	$ 1,000 U	$ 500 F	$ 2,000 F	$ 1,000 U	$ 500 U	$ 250 F

required 1. What would you do as a "rational man" if you were starting the job all over again from period 1 with the above information?

2. What would you recommend, if anything, be done to the system if you are now promoted to a higher job in management and required to handle the "bonus system" in this department?

6-29. **Cost Savings and Compensation Plans.** Amy Deere operates a reducing salon, The Gym Dandy. She used the services of three maintenance men, Sam, Jim, and Bob. Each had charge of a group of exercise and apparatus rooms similar in all regards. Miss Deere offered three methods of payment to the men:

Method A. A flat wage of $3.75 per hour.
Method B. A base rate of $3.50 per hour and 20 percent of all reduction in expenses below a "norm" of $500 per week.
Method C. No base rate, but a bonus of $160 for meeting the "norm," plus 10 percent of all reductions in expense below the norm.

Assume a 40-hour week. The men selected their method of compensation before commencing work.

The record for the past six weeks for the three areas follows (all figures are in dollars):

	WEEKS					
	1	*2*	*3*	*4*	*5*	*6*
Sam:						
Heat and light	150	150	150	150	150	150
Supplies	100	100	100	100	100	100
Repairs and miscellaneous	250	200	265	220	260	305
Total	500	450	515	470	510	555
Jim:						
Heat and light	150	150	150	150	150	150
Supplies	100	100	100	100	100	100
Repairs and miscellaneous	250	250	250	250	250	250
Total	500	500	500	500	500	500
Bob:						
Heat and light	150	150	150	150	150	150
Supplies	180	20	20	260	100	20
Repairs and miscellaneous	305	250	220	265	260	200
Total	635	420	390	675	510	370

required

1. Which payment methods were chosen by Sam, Jim, and Bob? Base your answer on an analysis of cost behavior patterns. Assume that each man chose a different plan.

2. Which method would have been most profitable for a conniving man?

3. If you bought the salon from Miss Deere, what changes would you make in the payment plan? Discuss.

6-30. Objectives of Public Accounting Firm. All personnel, including partners, of public accounting firms must usually turn in biweekly time reports, showing how many hours were devoted to their various duties. These firms have traditionally looked unfavorably on idle or unassigned staff time. They have looked favorably on heavy percentages of chargeable (billable) time because this maximizes revenue. What effect is such a policy likely to have on the behavior of the firm's personnel? Can you relate this practice to the problem of harmony of goals that was discussed in the chapter? How?

6-31. Choosing Budget Goals. A news item stated: "Top executives of Crown Cork & Seal Co. receive blocks of heavy transparent plastic to set on their desks. The blocks have the executives' names engraved on them. They also have four quarters and four dimes imbedded inside, a constant reminder that President John Connelly is counting on the company to earn $1.40 a share this year."

required

What are the strengths and weaknesses of choosing a specific target of $1.40 per share and of emphasizing the target as Mr. Connelly has done?

6-32. Multiple Goals and Profitability.[15] The following are the multiple goals of the General Electric Company:

[15] Adapted from a problem originally appearing in R. H. Hassler and Neil E. Harlan, *Cases in Controllership* (Englewood Cliffs, N.J.: Prentice-Hall, Inc., 1958).

1. Profitability
2. Market position
3. Productivity
4. Product leadership
5. Personnel development
6. Employee attitudes
7. Public responsibility
8. Balance between short-range and long-range goals

General Electric is a Goliath corporation with sales of about $9 billion and assets of $6 billion in 1970. It had approximately 170 responsibility centers called "departments," but that is a deceiving term. In most other companies, these departments would be called divisions. For example, some GE departments have sales of over $300 million.

Each department manager's performance is evaluated annually in relation to the specified multiple goals. A special measurements group was set up in 1952 to devise ways of quantifying accomplishments in each of the areas. In this way, the evaluation of performance would become more objective as the various measures were developed and improved.

required

1. How would you measure performance in each of these areas? Be specific.

2. Can the other goals be encompassed as ingredients of a formal measure of profitability? In other words, can profitability per se be defined to include the other goals?

6-33. Commission Plan for New-Car Salesmen. As an automobile dealer, you are faced with the problem of formulating a commission plan for new-car salesmen. You have listed the following alternatives:

(a) Commissions based on a flat percentage of dollar sales.

(b) Commissions based on varying percentages of dollar sales. The higher the sales price of a deal, the higher the commission rate. Also, commissions will vary depending on the accessories sold.

(c) Commissions based on net profit after allocation of a fair share of all operating expenses.

required

Evaluate these alternatives. Are there other methods that deserve consideration?

6-34. Budgeting Time and Judging Performance for Professional Services. Henry Johnson, an affable young accounting major, went to work for White, Green, Black & Co., a large CPA firm, shortly after graduation from college. He became an assistant to Fritz Wilcox, an auditing "senior" who was twenty-six years old and had just become a CPA. Henry had had no auditing courses in college, so he spent the first two weeks of work reading auditing textbooks and doing menial tasks around the office. He finally got his first assignment during the third week. Fritz Wilcox and he went to the office of a client and started to trace paid checks to their invoices. Although the work was tedious, Henry was pleased because he could now start to "earn his pay" by doing actual work instead of studying.

Fritz told Henry that the job had been budgeted for thirty-two hours (two days' work for the two men) by the partner in charge of the engagement. Early in the afternoon of the second day, however, it became obvious that the job would be completed sooner than expected. They finished at 4:00 P.M., an hour early, so the actual time spent was thirty hours instead of the budgeted thirty-two. Henry, very conscientious about his new job, quickly gathered his papers together in order to return to the office. Fritz said, "Whoa, Henry. There's no need to hurry. The job was supposed to take us two days, so the boss won't be expecting us back at the office this afternoon. We might as well just leave early and charge the whole two days to the client on our time sheets. Anyway, if we go back to the office, by the time we get there, we won't have time left to get any work done."

That evening Henry was puzzled over the statement Fritz had made. Henry was glad to charge the whole two days to the client because it gave his firm more revenue. But on the other hand, Henry remembered that when he had been going through orientation, one of the partners had instructed him never to charge time to a client unless the time so charged was actually spent on the client's audit. This made sense to Henry; he realized that the firm might lose clients if billings were too high. The partner had also said that time not spent on a client's audit should be allocated to "available time" (nonchargeable time) on Henry's time sheet.

Henry finally decided that the idea Fritz had had to charge the thirty-first and thirty-second hours to the client was really the best course because it increased Henry's chargeable-time-to-total-time ratio on his time sheet. He felt this would please the partners, because he had learned through the grapevine that the partners had complimented employees in the past who had high chargeable-time-to-total-time ratios. This last point was crucial to Henry, since he was anxious to log as much chargeable time as possible so that the firm could recover the wages it had paid him for the first two weeks of his employ.

required Is it "healthy," from the viewpoint of White, Green, Black & Co., for Henry to be puzzled about this? Why?

6-35. **Responsibility Accounting and Control of Costs.** The Sharp Company develops, manufactures, and markets several product lines of low-cost consumer goods. Top management of the company is attempting to evaluate the present method and a new method of charging the different production departments for the services they receive from one of the engineering departments, which is called Manufacturing Engineering Services (MES).

The function of MES, which consists of about thirty engineers and ten draftsmen, is to reduce the costs of producing the different products of the company by improving machine and manufacturing process design, while maintaining the required level of quality. The MES manager reports to the engineering supervisor, who reports to the vice-president, manufacturing. The MES manager may increase or decrease the number of engineers under him. He is evaluated on the basis of several variables, one of which is the annual incremental savings to the company brought about by his department in excess of the costs of operating his department. These costs consist of actual salaries, a share of corporate overhead, the cost of office supplies used by his department, and a cost of capital charge. An individual engineer is evaluated on the basis of the ratio of the annual savings he effects to his annual salary. The salary range of an engineer is defined by his personnel classification; there are four classifications, and promotion from one classification to another depends on the approval of a panel that includes both production and engineering personnel.

Production department managers report to a production supervisor, who reports to the vice-president, manufacturing. The production department for each product line is treated as a profit center, and engineering services are provided at a cost, according to the following plan. When a production department manager and an engineer agree on a possible project to improve production efficiency, they sign a contract that specifies the scope of the project, the estimated savings to be realized, the probability of success, and the number of engineering man-hours of each personnel classification required. The charge to the particular production department is determined by the product of the number of man-hours required times the "classification rate" for each personnel classification. This rate depends on the average salary for the classification involved and a share of the engineering department's other costs. An engineer is expected to spend at least 85 percent of his time on specific, contracted projects; the remainder may be used for preliminary investigations of potential cost-saving projects or self-improving study. A recent survey showed that production managers have a high degree of confidence in the MES engineers.

A new plan has been proposed to top management, in which no charge will be made to production departments for engineering services. In all other respects the new system will be identical to the present. Production managers will continue to request engineering services as under the present plan. Proponents of the new plan say that under it, production managers will take a greater advantage of existing engineering talent. Regardless of how engineering services are accounted for, the company is committed to the idea of production departments being profit centers.

required   Evaluate the strong and weak points of the present and proposed plans. Will the company tend to hire the optimal quantity of engineering talent? Will this engineering talent be used as effectively as possible?

6-36. **Human Resource Accounting.**   The body of the chapter referred to experimentation with human-resource accounting. Exhibit 6-4 is an excerpt from the Barry Corporation's annual report for 1969. The Barry Corporation is a manufacturer of leisure footwear in Columbus, Ohio. William C. Pyle has commented on Barry's experience as follows:

Managers are preparing capital budgets for human resources. For example, on an individual basis, the firm invests approximately $3,000 in replacing a first-line supervisor, $15,000 for a middle manager, and upwards of $30,000 in hiring and developing a top-level executive. Appropriate personnel costs are now formally recognized as long-lived assets which need not be justified as operating expenses, hence make it easier for a manager to secure funds for hiring, transferring and developing human resources.

Under the human-resource accounting system, turnover information is presented both as a rate and in terms of its monetary impact. As previously noted, if human assets expire before the end of the expected service life period, through premature separations or skill obsolescence, the remaining net-asset value is charged off against current earnings. The conventional practice of reporting turnover merely as a rate obscures its true significance because employee separations represent a greater financial loss if they occur among employees in whom the firm has invested either more recently or more heavily.

For example, during 1969, the Barry Corporation's net investment in human resources increased by approximately $174,000, reflecting the fact that new investments were being undertaken more rapidly than they were being consumed. If the manager of one division had increased conventional profits at the expense of improper maintenance or utilization of employees, the profit figure incorporating human resource accounting would have been reduced in amount of any abnormal separation losses. It should be emphasized, however, that at this point financial statements are being adjusted only for *internal management* purposes.

EXHIBIT 6-4

R. G. BARRY CORPORATION AND SUBSIDIARIES
(Financial and Human-Resource Accounting)

Balance Sheet	1969 FINANCIAL AND HUMAN RESOURCE	1969 FINANCIAL ONLY
Assets:		
Total current assets	$10,003,628	$10,003,628
Net property, plant, and equipment	1,770,717	1,770,717
Excess of purchase price of subsidiaries over net assets acquired	1,188,704	1,188,704
Net investments in human resources	986,094	—
Other assets	106,783	106,783
	$14,055,926	$13,069,832
Liabilities and stockholders' equity:		
Total current liabilities	$ 5,715,708	$ 5,715,708
Long-term debt, excluding current installments	1,935,500	1,935,500
Deferred compensation	62,380	62,380
Deferred federal income taxes as a result of appropriation for human resources	493,047	—
Stockholders' equity:		
Capital stock	879,116	879,116
Additional capital in excess of par value	1,736,253	1,736,253
Retained earnings:		
Financial	2,740,875	2,740,875
Appropriation for human resources	493,047	—
Total stockholders' equity	5,849,291	5,356,244
	$14,055,926	$13,069,832

Statement of Income	1969 FINANCIAL AND HUMAN RESOURCE	1969 FINANCIAL ONLY
Net sales	$25,310,588	$25,310,588
Cost of sales	16,275,876	16,275,876
Gross profit	9,034,712	9,034,712
Selling, general, and administrative expenses	6,737,313	6,737,313
Operating income	2,297,399	2,297,399
Other deductions, net	953,177	953,177
Income before federal income taxes	1,344,222	1,344,222
Human-resource expenses applicable to future periods	173,569	—
Adjusted income before federal income taxes	1,517,791	1,344,222
Federal income taxes	730,785	644,000
Net income	$ 787,006	$ 700,222

Although the primary reason for adoption of human-resource accounting has been to improve the management of the business, the Barry Corporation's treasurer, Edward Stan, reports that these data also have important implications for interested outsiders:

"A review of our past balance sheets indicates that we have always been able to attract more borrowing power than our 'cold figures' would justify on the surface. In making lending-limit determinations, representatives of financial institutions have made trips to our facilities, have analyzed our financial statements, and have talked to our people.

In making these assessments, the human-resource factor was surely considered. With our human-resource accounting system, we are now able to provide them with more precise information to consider in their evaluations.

"The use of human-resource accounting in acquisitions is also very important. In the process of evaluating different candidates, we have to make human-asset appraisals—just like the banks do on us. Human-resource accounting makes the process easier, and, after the acquisition, gives us a base for a continued surveillance and measurement of the human-asset gains or losses."

Data from the firm's human-resource accounting system have *not* yet been incorporated into the company's audited financial statements. Nevertheless, as seen in [Exhibit 6-4], the Barry Corporation's 1969 Annual Report contained a balance sheet and income statement that reflect human assets and changes in those assets during the period. This information is contrasted with their conventional financial statements in a special section of the report dealing with human resources. Net investments in managerial personnel of approximately one million dollars are recognized. The liabilities and stockholders' equity side of the balance sheet indicates approximately $500,000 for "Deferred Federal Income Taxes as a Result of Appropriation for Human Resources" and an equal amount for an "Appropriation for Human Resources" under retained earnings.

Turning to the income statement, a net change of $173,569 in human-resource investments during 1969 is applied as a positive adjustment to income before taxes. After making a provision for deferred federal income tax, this change results in an upward adjustment of about $87,000 to conventionally determined net income of about $700,000. This adjustment reflects the fact that during 1969, new investments in human resources were undertaken more rapidly than they were written off. The firm's Vice-President of Human Resources, Robert L. Woodruff, Jr., explained that these data were included in the Annual Report to provide their stockholders with an example of the type of information executives are using to improve the management of human resources.[16]

required Do you favor implementing human-resource accounting for internal-reporting purposes? Why do you think human-resource accounting is preferred by Pyle, Likert, and others to the use of less formal measures, such as employee-attitude surveys, absenteeism, turnover rates, and so on? Be specific.

[16]William C. Pyle, "Human Resource Accounting, *Financial Analysts Journal,* September–October 1970.

7

Standard Costs: Direct Materials and Direct Labor

Standard costs are the building blocks of a budgeting and feedback system. The cost-accounting literature often mistakenly divides product cost-accounting systems into three systems, as if they were mutually exclusive: job costing, process costing, and standard costing. Such a three-way classification is erroneous, because standard costs can be used in a wide variety of organizations and in conjunction with any kind of product costing, whether it be job-order costing, process costing or some hybrid product costing.

EFFECTIVENESS AND EFFICIENCY

Managers make two major types of decisions in the planning and controlling of costs: *price* decisions and *quantity* decisions. That is, materials and human resources are supposed to be obtained at the lowest possible price consistent with quality and other long-run objectives. These resources are *inputs;* they should be used efficiently to produce the maximum possible good *output*.

Distinctions between effectiveness and efficiency[1] are frequently very helpful in discussing planning and controlling. *Effectiveness* is the accomplishment of a desired objective. *Efficiency* is an optimum relationship between input and output. As a colleague has pointed out, the killing of a housefly with a sledge hammer may be effective, but it is not efficient.

---

[1]For good discussions, see David Novick, ed., *Program Budgeting,* 2nd ed. (New York: Holt, Rinehart & Winston, Inc., 1969), pp. 48–51; and Robert N. Anthony, *Planning and Control Systems: A Framework for Analysis* (Boston: Harvard Business School, 1965), pp. 27–28.

Performance may be both effective and efficient, but either condition can occur without the other. For example, a company may set 200,000 units as a production objective. Subsequently, because of material shortages or other reasons, only 150,000 units may be produced with 100 percent efficiency. Performance would be efficient but not effective. In contrast, 200,000 units may be produced on schedule with horrible waste of labor and materials. Performance would be effective but inefficient.

In short, two major questions about performance are: (a) Is the manager effective? and (b) Is he efficient? Question (a) often deals with attaining a revenue or volume target. Question (b) is an input–output engineering question; that is, given a particular level of revenue or volume (output), did the manager control his inputs as he should have?

STANDARD COSTS AS MANAGEMENT AIDS

nature of standards Standard costs are carefully predetermined costs; they are target costs, costs that should be attained. Standard costs help to build budgets, gauge performance, obtain product costs, and save bookkeeping costs.

A set of standards outlines how a task should be accomplished and how much it should cost. As work is done, actual costs incurred are compared with standard costs to reveal variances. The variances are investigated to discover better ways of adhering to standards, of altering standards, or of accomplishing objectives.

Consider the following example. If the standard cost of material for a garden tool is 50¢ per unit, then superior or inferior performance may be judged by comparing incurred costs with standard costs. If the incurred cost happens to be 60¢, then the 10¢ variance may be analyzed and investigated to discover reasons for the variation. As will be seen later, the difference may be due to price changes, shoddy materials, faulty workmanship, and so forth. The important point at this stage is that an evaluation of performance depends on a comparison of actual costs with some stable goal. Merely to compare this month's costs with last month's or with those of the corresponding month of last year is likely to cloud the *inefficiencies that may already be reflected in prior costs.* Moreover, changes in technology, equipment, and methods limit the validity of comparisons with the past.

types of standards How demanding should standards be? Should they express perfection, or should they allow for the various factors that prevent perfect performance?

Accounting writers have coined a variety of names for different kinds of standards. Standards are often classified into three types:

1. *Basic cost standards* are unchanging standards. They provide the base for comparing actual costs through the years with the same standard. Thus the accounting reports spotlight trends. Price effects and changes in efficiency are

gauged by comparison with the prices and efficiency that prevailed when standards were determined. Basic standard costs are seldom used because frequent changes in products and methods necessitate changes in standards. Thus, the trends lose their significance because of the short time that elapses between changes in products and methods.

2. *Perfection, ideal, maximum efficiency, or theoretical standard costs* reflect industrial engineers' dreams of a "factory heaven." Perfection standard costs are the absolute minimum costs that are possible under the best conceivable operating conditions, using existing specifications and equipment. Ideal standards, like other standards, are used where the management feels that they provide the best type of standard for motivation and cost control. Ideal standards, as Professor Sidney Davidson tells his students, are like a dream of Sophia Loren—distant, desirable, and rarely attainable. But their use is preferred where management believes them to be psychologically productive.

3. *Currently attainable standard costs* are the costs that should be incurred under forthcoming efficient operating conditions. They are difficult but possible to achieve. Attainable standards are looser than ideal standards because of allowance for normal spoilage, ordinary machine breakdowns, and lost time. However, attainable standards are usually set tight enough so that the operating people will consider the achievement of standard performance to be a satisfying accomplishment. In other words, variances are more likely to be slightly unfavorable than favorable—but favorable variances may be attained by a little more than expected efficiency.

In sum, most accountants and executives would probably agree with the following observations:

> Interview results show that a particular figure does not operate as a norm in either a score-card or attention-directing sense simply because the controller's department calls it a standard. It operates as a norm only to the extent that the executives and supervisors whose activity it measures accept it as a fair and attainable yardstick of their performance. Generally, operating executives were inclined to accept a standard to the extent that they were satisfied that the data were accurately recorded, that the standard level was reasonably attainable, and that the variables it measured were controllable by them.[2]

A major benefit from using *currently attainable standards* is the multipurpose use of the resultant standard costs. They may be used simultaneously for product costing, master budgets, and motivation. Throughout the illustrations and problems in this book, unless otherwise stated, currently attainable standards are assumed to be in use.

Terminology difficulties should also be kept in mind. Thus, *perfection standard* may be a *currently attainable standard* in some cases. For example, the outside purchases of expensive subassemblies such as tires or picture tubes

---

[2] H. A. Simon, H. Guetzkow, G. Kozmetsky, and G. Tyndall, *Centralization vs. Decentralization in Organizing the Controller's Department* (New York: The Controllership Foundation, Inc., 1954), p. 29. But for an opposite view, see Andrew Stedry, *Budget Control and Cost Behavior* (Englewood Cliffs, N.J.: Prentice-Hall, Inc., 1960).

should result in no waste in the assembly of a finished product. The standard here would be both *ideal* and *currently attainable*. As you might imagine, ideal or perfection standards are more likely to be used for material specifications than for labor control.

distinction between budgets and standards   What is the difference between a standard amount and a budget amount? If standards are currently attainable, there is no conceptual difference. The term *standard cost*, as it is most widely used, is a unit concept; that is, the standard cost of material per unit is, say, $1. The term *budgeted cost*, as it is most widely used, is a total concept; that is, the budgeted cost of material is $10,000 if 10,000 units are to be produced at a standard cost of $1 per unit. It may be helpful to think of a standard as a budget for the production of a single unit. However, in many companies, the terms *budgeted performance* and *standard performance* are used interchangeably.

In practice, direct materials and direct labor are said to be controlled with the help of *standard costs*, whereas all other costs are usually said to be controlled with the help of *department overhead budgets*. This distinction probably arose because of different timing and control techniques for various costs. Direct materials and direct labor are generally relatively costly, and are easily identifiable for decision purposes. Therefore, techniques for planning and controlling these costs are relatively refined. Overhead costs are combinations of many individual items, none of which justifies an elaborate control system. In consequence, use of direct materials may be closely watched on an hourly basis; direct labor, on a daily basis; and factory overhead, on a weekly or monthly basis.

All this leads to the following straightforward approach (using assumed figures), which we will pursue throughout the remainder of this book. The *standard* is a *unit* idea; the *budget* is a *total* idea:

	STANDARDS	BUDGET FOR 40,000 UNITS AND 10,000 HOURS
Direct materials	$.25 per unit	$10,000
Direct labor	$4 per hour or $1 per unit	40,000
Factory overhead (detailed)*	$2 per hour or $.50 per unit	20,000
Selling expenses (detailed)*		15,000
Administrative expenses (detailed)*		5,000

*For planning and control, these individual detailed costs are not usually expressed as a standard cost per unit, although there are exceptions. On the other hand, for product-costing purposes, total factory overhead is often expressed as a standard cost per unit.

If standards are not currently attainable because they are perfection standards, the amount budgeted for financial (cash) planning purposes has to differ from the standard. Otherwise, projected income and cash disbursements will be forecast incorrectly. In such cases, perfection standards may be used for compiling performance reports, but expected variances are stipulated in the master budget for financial planning. For example, if unusually strict labor standards are used, the standard cost per finished unit may be $1 despite the fact that top management anticipates an unfavorable performance variance of $.10 per unit. In the master budget, the total labor costs would be $1.10 per unit: $1 plus an expected variance of $.10. In our example, a master budget could conceivably include the following item:

Direct labor:

Budget allowance shown on departmental performance report	$40,000
Expected variance that will appear on departmental performance report	4,000
Total budget allowance for cash planning	$44,000

responsibility for developing standards   The standard-setting and budget-setting process in an organization should be primarily the responsibility of the line personnel directly involved. The relative tightness of the budget should be the result of face-to-face discussion and bargaining between the manager and his immediate superior. The budgetary accountants, the industrial engineers, and the market researchers should extend all desired technical assistance and advice, but the final decisions should not be theirs. The line manager is the person who is supposed to accept and live with the budget or standard.

The job of the accounting department is (a) to price the physical standards—that is, to express the physical standards in the form of dollars and cents; and (b) to report operating performance in comparison with standards.

analysis of variances: general approach   All variance analysis includes a general approach wherein a total variance should be computed first. In turn, the total variance is subdivided into two component variances: (a) price or rate, and (b) usage or efficiency, as shown below.

(1) Inputs at Actual Prices	(2) Inputs at Standard Prices	(3) Outputs at Standard Prices
Actual Inputs	Actual Inputs	Good Outputs
×	×	×
Actual Price:	Standard Price:	Standard Price:
XXX	XXX	XXX

(a) Price or Rate Variance (Difference in Price × Actual Quantity)	(b) Quantity or Usage or Efficiency Variance (Difference in Quantity × Standard Price)

Total variance to be explained

Essentially, efficient operating control means getting the maximum possible good outputs for a given quantity of inputs; or, expressed another way, it means utilizing the minimum possible inputs for a given quantity of good outputs. The input-output distinction is helpful in retaining perspective on the analysis of variances.

Assume that a table manufacturer uses formica tops. Formica is purchased in large sizes, cut down as needed, and then glued to the tables. A given-sized table will require a specified amount of formica. If the amount of formica needed per Type-F TV table is 4 square feet and cost per square foot is 65¢, then the standard cost of formica for a single TV table would be $2.60. But a certain production run of 1,000 tables results in usage of 4,300 square feet at 70¢ per square foot, a total cost of $3,010. Total standard cost would be $2,600 (1,000 units @ $2.60, or 4,000 square feet @ 65¢). The total variance of $410 would be analyzed as follows:

(1) Inputs at Actual Prices	(2) Inputs at Standard Prices	(3) Outputs at Standard Prices
Actual Inputs	Actual Inputs	Good Outputs
×	×	×
Actual Price:	Standard Price	Standard Price
(4,300 sq. ft. × $.70)	(4,300 sq. ft. × $.65)	(4,000 sq. ft. × $.65)
$3,010	$2,795	$2,600

Component analysis of variances

(a) Price Variance   (b) Quantity Variance

(4,300 × $.05) or $215 U   (4,300 − 4,000) × $.65, or $195 U

Total Variance

Total variance to be explained $410 U

U = Unfavorable (price exceeds standard price, or usage exceeds standard usage allowed).

A short-cut approach follows:

(a) *Price variances:*
  (Difference in unit price) times (actual inputs used)
  (70¢ − 65¢)   ×   4,300 square feet is $215 U

(b) *Quantity or usage variance:*
  (Difference in inputs and outputs) times (standard unit price)
  (4,300 − 4,000)   ×   65¢ is   195 U
  Total variance $410 U

how output is expressed   The most difficult concept to grasp at this stage is how outputs are measured and expressed. Note under column (3) in our example that the outputs are measured and expressed, not as 1,000 tables, but as 4,000 square feet—the standard quantity of formica allowed to produce 1,000 tables. The point is that, to ease the input–output analysis, production is often expressed in terms of what inputs *should* have been utilized rather than what inputs actually were utilized. For instance, if it takes one quarter-hour to assemble a table, the analysis of direct-labor input–output will be facilitated by expressing the output of 1,000 tables in terms of the standard number of hours allowed to produce the tables, $\frac{1}{4} \times 1,000$ or 250 hours. In this situation, output may be expressed as *250 standard hours allowed* (also called *standard hours allowed for work done* or *standard hours worked* or *standard hours earned*). This is a key concept in standard costs. Standard hours allowed is the number of hours that *should* have been used to produce a given output. This way of expressing output is particularly helpful when a factory produces a variety of products, each having a different standard time allowance. *Standard hours allowed* becomes the common denominator and the best way to express overall production. (An example of the analysis of direct labor appears later in this chapter.)

pinpointing   Cost control is aided by measuring variances in terms of responsibilities.
responsibility   Typically, usage is the major responsibility of one department head (a foreman), whereas price may be the major responsibility of a different department head (a purchasing officer). Therefore, the dollar measure of the quantity variance should not be influenced by changes in unit prices. Price is held constant at standard, and the resultant quantity variance is attributable solely to off-standard usage by the foreman's department. In the case of the price variance, because the purchasing office does not influence the quantity used, the difference in unit price is said to be applicable to all quantities used.

A chart of the relationship of price and quantity variances may be helpful. Exhibit 7-1 shows a graphic analysis that demonstrates variance computations in rectangular terms. Theoretically, as shown in the graph, the price variance should be subdivided into two variances:

1. Pure Price Variance = Difference in Price × Standard Quantity
(instead of Actual Quantity)
2. Combined or Joint Price–Quantity Variance = Difference in
Price × Difference in Quantity

The importance of this refinement depends on the significance and usefulness of isolating the joint variance. Where executive bonuses depend on variances, this refinement may be necessary. For example, an unfavorable total-price variance, as ordinarily computed, could be partially attributable to inefficient usage. Thus, $15 ($.05 × 300 sq. ft.) of the $215 price variance in our example would not have arisen if the quantities used did not exceed standard. In this book, we shall not refine our analysis this far; all of the $215 is called a price variance. That is, we shall consider the price variance to be the sum of the pure price variance and the combined price–quantity variance.

Analysis of variances may be further subdivided beyond price and quantity variances. For example, the quantity variance may be partially explained by inferior quality; by faulty workmanship, such as sloppy trimming or careless

EXHIBIT 7-1

GRAPHIC ANALYSIS OF VARIANCES

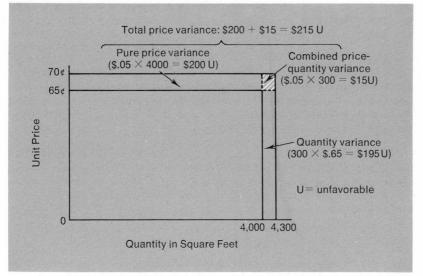

glueing; by substitute materials; by improper mix of materials; or for some other reason. The specific reasons are sought to pin down responsibility for control purposes.

The key questions in deciding how variances should be collected and analyzed are: *Why* do we wish to identify this particular variance? What will we *do* with it? If we cannot make practical use of the variance, then we should not bother to compute it.

trade-offs among variances Elaborate standard-cost accounting systems and fancy reports of variance analysis will be of little benefit if the managers responsible do not use the reports as clues for investigation of off-standard performance. The real benefits become evident when managers seize the system and the reports as the starting points for improving operations.

Managers often have opportunities to take advantage of bargain purchases or to combine available resources in a way that will save overall costs. For example, a quantity of a raw material having a few inferior characteristics (perhaps a different grade of lumber or shade of color) might be consciously acquired at an unusually low price. This material might lead to unusually heavy spoilage or excessive labor times in order to produce a finished product that will meet the standard quality specifications. Nevertheless, the manager may have enough discretion to proceed. His aim would be to reduce the total costs of manufacturing by trading off favorable price variances against expected unfavorable usage variances.

A standard-cost system should not be a straitjacket that prevents the manager from looking at the overall company objectives. Too often, each un-

193

favorable variance is regarded as, ipso facto, bad; and each favorable variance is regarded as, ipso facto, good. If the manager guesses wrong, and the unfavorable usage variances exceed the favorable price variance, the decision to make the bargain purchase was unfavorable despite the favorable label pinned on the price variance. Similarly, if the manager guesses correctly, so that the favorable price variance exceeds the unfavorable usage variances, the decision was favorable despite the unfavorable label pinned on the usage variances. The point is that there are too many interdependencies among activities; an "unfavorable" or a "favorable" label should not lead the manager to jump to conclusions about what happened. By themselves, such labels merely raise questions and provide clues. They are attention directors, not answer givers.

physical standards and improvement of operations

Physical standards are the foundation of a standard-cost system. Ideally, they should represent reliable engineering or physical estimates, which are expressed in tons or gallons produced; in operation methods; and in minutes or hours of labor. These standards are often constructed from systematic observation, measurement, and controlled experiment. Analyses of the kinds and amounts of materials, labor time and methods, and necessary overhead items lead to these so-called engineered standards. The entire productive process is divided into various operations or activities, and the proper material and labor usage is rigorously estimated.

Textbooks generally give the impression that standard costs are always based on technical engineering studies and rigorous specifications. Accurate measurement is indeed the foundation for control. However, although a rigorous approach is desirable, it should be remembered that even less scientific standards provide a forceful way of presenting information in order to stimulate corrective action.

converting physical standards into dollars

Standard costs are developed by multiplying the physical standards by appropriate price factors. In other words, physical usage and prices are combined to obtain standard costs. In the formica example cited previously, the physical standard was 4 square feet per Type-F table. The standard cost per table was secured by multiplying the standard square footage by the unit price of 65¢ to obtain $2.60 per table.

The use of price factors allows all standards in the company to be expressed in a common denominator—dollars. Furthermore, the pricing of physical standards calls attention to the expensive items that tend to deserve more managerial attention.

In many instances, the building of standard costs is not extraordinarily difficult, especially where operations are repetitive and extensive quantities of similar products are produced. But in other cases, the technical complexities are imposing because of the nonuniformity of products. In the latter cases, labor operations must be dissected into individual steps as far as possible. Then the individual steps, with their specific costs, may be regrouped to build standard costs for a variety of products that may require different sequences of labor operations. For example, a table manufacturer may apply formica tops to some types of tables and not to others. The standard labor cost of formica tables would naturally include the costs of applying formica, whereas such costs would be excluded from costing other types of tables. Note that costing for control concentrates on the *operation* in a *cost center*, whereas costing for inventory concentrates on the physical unit as the costing objective.

Costing for control requires breaking down manufacturing elements so that they may be regulated at the source (the cost center) on an individual basis. Thus, the standards for usage of material *elements* and labor *elements* are more significant than overall product-cost standards.

For example, the standard cost of making a kitchen table may be $18. For control purposes, this cost is not as significant as its component parts because control must be exercised by regulating usage of the separate elements that make up the cost.

MATERIAL-PRICE STANDARDS

basis for material-price standards In most companies, the acquisition and the usage of raw materials require different decisions. The purchasing officer worries about getting the specified materials in the correct quantities at the right time and at the right price. The production officer concentrates on using the materials efficiently. The assessment of a manager's performance is facilitated by separating the factors that are directly subject to his decisions from those that are not. A popular way to achieve this separation is to isolate price variances so that they do not affect the performance of the production manager. That is, the production departments are charged for materials at standard prices instead of actual prices. For example, a production department that is scheduled to produce 10,000 finished units may be allowed 10,000 pounds of a raw material at a standard price of $1.00 per pound. Suppose that the production manager has no responsibility or influence over the price of the material. If the price increases to $1.20, the price variance of 20¢ per pound should not affect the performance of the production manager. Therefore, materials would be charged to the production department at the actual quantity used, multiplied by the standard price. Efficiency can then be judged without being mingled with unit-price effects that may be confusing.

Our formica illustration showed how the price and usage variances for materials were computed simultaneously as production took place. This approach is adequate where material prices are not too volatile, or where heavy raw-material inventories are not carried, or where the purpose is solely to remove influences of price from usage reports. However, when current control of purchasing activities is also a major objective of isolating price variances, the approach should be modified, as we shall see.

Material-price standards are usually based either on expected prices for the period in question (usually a year) or on prices prevailing at the time that standards are set. Price variances for purposes of *control* are computed at the time of *purchase* by taking the difference beween actual and standard unit price times the actual quantity acquired. To delay the computation of the price variance until the time the quantity is *issued* usually defeats the usefulness of the information for control, because corrective action is then seldom possible.

Ideally, where price variances are used for *control* purposes, they should be computed when the original purchase order is sent to the supplier. Practically, such variances are usually not computed until the invoice is received, because the latter event triggers entry into the formal accounting records, whereas the sending of the purchase order does not.

who sets material-price standards? If any one person is responsible for material-price variances, it is probably the purchasing officer. Therefore, he should have a strong role in setting price standards. Nevertheless, many companies have the accounting department and the purchasing department work out the task jointly. Responsibility as to price standards is twofold:

1. Because prices are often set by external influences, setting price standards is mostly a task of accurate prediction. Thus, price variances are probably more a measure of forecasting ability than of failure to buy at predetermined standard prices.

2. Some control may be exerted over prices by getting numerous quotations, purchasing in optimum lots, hunting for bargains, selecting the most economical means of transportation, and taking advantage of cash discounts. Effective price standards help reduce the tendency of many purchasing people to play favorites among suppliers. Some check is desirable on the purchasing officer's setting of price standards. He should have to submit evidence in support of his standards to a standards committee or to the accounting department.

Failure to meet price standards may often be due to external factors mentioned previously or to departments other than the purchasing department. For example, sudden rush orders or unexpected volume changes in production may upset material price standards. In such cases, the major responsibility for variances may rest with the sales manager because of his faulty forecasting or with the head of production planning because of his sloppy production scheduling. The intelligent analysis of variances will help pinpoint responsibility in these situations. The reports of price variances are often the starting point for management's finding substitute materials, changing methods or specifications, and altering selling prices.

MATERIAL-QUANTITY STANDARDS

nature of quantity standards Although material prices are frequently difficult to control, the quantity of direct materials used is subject to closer regulation.

Most companies rely on engineering studies as a basis for determining quantity standards for material. Blueprints, product specifications, normal spoilage, unavoidable waste, and production methods are considered in preparing the *standard bill of materials* (Exhibit 7-2), which is the formal expression of material-quantity standards. Note that we are considering physical standards; price factors are not relevant from a quantity-control standpoint, once the types and quantities of materials are determined. A quantity variance may be expressed in dollars by merely multiplying the standard unit price by the physical quantity variance.

In addition to formal engineering studies, sample runs under regulated conditions or historical studies of material usage in a specific product may be used in setting material-quantity standards. Of course, care must be exercised when relying on past performance because it may have been off-standard. Depending on specific materials or plant conditions, companies may use engineering studies, sample runs, historical studies, or some combination thereof.

setting quantity standards Quantity standards are usually set by the engineering department with the aid of the production department and the cost-accounting department. Although the production executive responsible for meeting the standards should participate, he should not have the final authority in setting the standards. But at least he should understand the standards and accept them as his targets.

control of usage Control over usage of material is best exerted when the foreman has timely comparisons of actual results with standards. When they are very important, these comparisons may be made continuously, or at least hourly. The exact control procedure depends on several factors, such as the following (*N.A.A. Research Series No. 12*, p. 908):

1. The nature and value of the materials
2. The type of accounting plan used
3. The methods used for detecting and measuring losses of material in production

EXHIBIT 7-2

STANDARD BILL OF MATERIALS

Assembly No. ____b____   Description ___TV Table___

Part Number		Number Required	Description
A	1426	4 sq. ft.	Formica — Pearl grey
	455	1/8 lb.	Adhesive
	642	1	Table top
	714	4	Steel legs
	961	1	Nut and bolt kit

The nature and value of the materials.   Usage of subassemblies and expensive parts can be predicted easily and can be accurately accounted for. Predictions of usage of bulk materials such as iron ore, alcohol, and coal are based on average consumption. Variances for these materials are aggregated as totals for given periods.

The type of accounting plan used.   Where process costing is used, quantity variances are often determined periodically. Where job-order costing is used, quantity variances may be determined for each order if desired.

The methods used for detecting and measuring losses of material in production.   When a department is expected to turn out a given job, batch, or specified number of product units, a standard bill of materials or stores requisition may be submitted to stores for withdrawal of the standard amount of direct materials needed. *As production takes place, any additional materials needed may be obtained from stores only by submitting an excess-materials requisition, which is usually of a distinct color.* Thus, the foreman is immediately informed of off-standard performance because he must sign the excess-materials requisition. A periodic summary of these requisitions provides the total unfavorable quantity variance. If performance is better than standard, special returned-materials forms are used to compute favorable quantity variances.

Other control methods are necessary when there is a varying amount of output from a given amount of input. A comparison of good production with input of direct materials is needed in order to judge performance, the key question being whether the standard amount of materials was used to obtain the given output. The difficulty here is that computation of variances is delayed until production is completed. To better achieve control in these cases, procedures have been developed to detect some variances prior to completion of work. These procedures include inspection at key operation points while work is in process, so that spoilage and other losses may be measured before full completion of the product.

Daily and weekly reports of variances are often expressed in physical terms only—gallons used, pounds consumed, and so on. The bases for these reports are usually the original source documents, such as excess-materials requisitions, scrap reports, inspection reports, and the like.

GENERAL-LEDGER ENTRIES FOR MATERIALS

two ways of reflecting variances   There is a wide variety of general-ledger treatments of accounting for direct materials in standard-cost accounting. Just because standards are used for control does not necessarily mean that they have to be integrated into the general ledger. However, most standard-cost systems are reflected in the general ledger. Usually, the general-ledger relationships follow the timing of the isolation of detailed variances in day-to-day cost control. Keep in mind, however, that general-ledger entries are usually monthly summaries of detailed variances that were isolated from day to day. Thus, the general-ledger accounts do not provide any particular help for cost-control purposes.

Consider the following data:

Standard price per square foot	$.65
Actual price per square foot	$.62*
Standard quantity allowed	4,000 square feet
Actual quantity used	4,300 square feet
Actual quantity purchased	5,000 square feet

* This actual price differs from the actual price used in the example earlier in the chapter.

Case 1. Our formica example demonstrated the simultaneous isolation of price and usage variances. This approach is easiest to see, but as was pointed out, its delay in segregating price variances is unsuitable if current control of *purchasing* activities is a major objective of the price-variance computation. From this point on, then, we shall stress this control feature, which simply calls for the isolation of variances just as early as is feasible. When price variances are isolated as materials are purchased, the following general-ledger entry is made:

1. Stores (5,000 sq. ft. @ 65¢)	$3,250	
Material-price variance (5,000 sq. ft. @ 3¢) (F)		$ 150
Accounts payable (5,000 sq. ft. @ 62¢)		3,100
To record direct-material purchases. The variance would be posted as a debit if unfavorable (U), as a credit if favorable (F).		

If quantity variances are isolated by use of excess-materials requisitions, the following general-ledger entry is made:

2. Work in process (4,000 sq. ft. @ 65¢)	$2,600	
Material-quantity variance (300 sq. ft. @ 65¢) (U)	195	
Stores (4,300 sq. ft. @ 65¢)		$2,795
To record direct materials used.		

T-accounts would appear as follows:

STORES		MATERIAL PRICE VARIANCE	
1. Actual quantity purchased × standard price, $3,250.	2. Actual quantity requisitioned × standard price, $2,795.		1. Actual quantity purchased × difference in price, $150.

WORK IN PROCESS		MATERIAL QUANTITY VARIANCE	
2. Standard quantity requisitioned × standard price, $2,600.		2. Difference in quantity used × standard price, $195.	

Case 2. (This is the method featured earlier, in our formica example. It is less desirable for current control of purchasing activities, but it is often found in

practice. The reader should concentrate on Case 1.) Some companies prefer to carry materials in Stores at actual prices. The typical entry for a purchase would be:

1. Stores	$3,100	
Accounts payable		$3,100

Entry upon issuance:

2. Work in process (4,300 × 65¢)	$2,795	
Material-price variance (4,300 × 3¢) (F)		$ 129
Stores (4,300 × 62¢)		2,666

As mentioned previously, because of continuous processing, some companies do not discover the material-quantity variances until goods are completed. A typical entry for completion would be:

3. Finished goods (4,000 × 65¢)	$2,600	
Material-quantity variance (300 × 65¢) (U)	195	
Work in process (4,300 × 65¢)		$2,795
To transfer material cost of completed goods and isolate quantity variance.		

or the above entry may be divided into two parts, each part perhaps being entered at different times:

3(a) Finished goods	$2,600	
Work in process		$2,600
To transfer.		

and

3(b) Material-quantity variance (U)	$ 195	
Work in process		$ 195
To isolate material-quantity variances, which are not discovered until physical inventories of work in process are taken or approximated.		

T-accounts would appear as follows:

STORES		MATERIAL PRICE VARIANCE	
1. Actual quantity purchased × actual price, $3,100.	2. Actual quantity requisitioned × actual price, $2,666.		2. Actual quantity requisitioned × difference in price, $129.

WORK IN PROCESS		MATERIAL QUANTITY VARIANCE	
2. Actual quantity requisitioned × standard price, $2,795.	3(a) Standard quantity finished × standard price, $2,600. 3(b) Difference in quantity needed to complete × standard price, $195.	3(b) Difference in quantity used × standard price, $195.	

comparison of *The author favors the Case 1 approach where practical, because it stresses*
cases 1 and 2 the control aspects of standard costs; that is, timeliness of information is
needed for control, and Case 1 isolates variances more quickly. For example,
price variances are isolated when *purchases* are made rather than when materials
are issued. Quantity variances are isolated as excess-materials requisitions are
prepared while goods are in process, rather than being isolated *after* goods are
completed.

The Case 1 approach will be used in this book, *but the reader should be
aware of other possible general-ledger treatments.* Note, for example, that Work
in Process is always carried at *standard* quantities and standard prices in the
Case 1 approach, whereas Case 2 shows Work in Process being carried at *actual*
quantities and standard prices until the variance is removed.

Carefully compare the approaches for Case 1 and Case 2. Note that they
basically try to obtain two major types of variances: price and usage. Although
everything dovetails neatly in Case 2, the approach in Case 1 is more useful
for purposes of controlling purchasing activities, because it isolates price variances at the point of purchase rather than at the point of usage. Which approach
to measuring material-price variance, Case 1 or Case 2, is better? There is no
pat answer. Again and again we shall see that the "best" methods in cost analysis
depend heavily on the purpose sought. In this instance, the Case 1 approach
is better if a serious attempt is made to use the resulting price variances for
purposes of current control of purchasing activities. If, instead, the price variance
is being computed primarily to remove the influences of price from usage reports,
then the Case 2 approach is adequate *for that purpose.*

Another advantage of the Case 1 approach is that many managers prefer
the simplicity of carrying inventories at standard prices. It avoids the problems
and extra bookkeeping costs of making cost-flow assumptions such as first-in,
first-out, or last-in, first-out.

Note further that there is no difference in the usage variances between
Cases 1 and 2. (The usage variance measures, for any given output, the difference
between the actual input and the standard input allowed, multiplied by a standard
price.) The difference in price variance between Cases 1 and 2 is explained by
the delay in isolating such variances until the material is used. Therefore, the
price variance in Case 2 is associated with the 4,300 square feet used instead
of the 5,000 square feet purchased.

columnar Although many short-cut techniques are available for analyzing variances,
format: an you will find the following columnar technique extremely valuable:
important
analytical For Case 1 (the approach that will be used almost exclusively
technique throughout this book):

(1)	(2)	(3)
Inputs at Actual Prices	Inputs at Standard Prices	Outputs at Standard Prices
Actual	Actual Quantity	Units Produced
×	×	×
Actual:	Standard Price:	Standard Price:
(Purchases)	(Purchases) | (Usage)	(Usage)
(5,000 × 62¢)	(5,000 × 65¢) | (4,300 × 65¢)	(4,000 × 65¢)
$3,100	$3,250 | $2,795	$2,600

↑⎯⎯ (5,000 × 3¢) ⎯⎯↑ ⎯⎯⎯ ↑⎯⎯ (300 × 65¢) ⎯⎯↑

Purchase-Price Variance, $150 F   Usage Variance, $195 U

For Case 2 (where the price variance refers only to the material used in production):

(1)	(2)	(3)
Inputs at Actual Prices	Inputs at Standard Prices	Outputs at Standard Prices
Actual	Actual Inputs	Units Produced
×	×	×
Actual:	Standard Price:	Standard Price:
(4,300 × 62¢)	(4,300 × 65¢)	(4,000 × 65¢)
$2,666	$2,795	$2,600

↑⎯⎯ (4,300 × 3¢) ⎯⎯↑ ⎯⎯ (300 × 65¢) ⎯⎯↑

Price Variance, $129 F   Usage Variance, $195 U

↑⎯⎯⎯⎯⎯⎯⎯⎯⎯⎯⎯⎯⎯⎯⎯⎯⎯⎯⎯⎯⎯⎯⎯⎯⎯↑

Total variance explained, $66 U

LABOR-RATE STANDARDS

Price factors are usually not subject to as much control as are quantity factors. Department heads' control of labor rates is usually limited, because the rates are the result of union negotiations or local conditions of labor supply and demand. The cost department computes standard costs by applying the rates to the physical labor standards. Most companies change labor-rate standards as rates change. Therefore, the timing often follows labor contract changes.

If rate standards are kept up to date, the variances should be relatively small. Such variances are regarded as the responsibility of the foreman. He must match the men and the machines to the tasks at hand by using the proper grade of labor. Variances usually arise from (a) the use of a man with a wrong rate for a specific operation, (b) use of excess men per machine, or (c) paying expensive day rates instead of prescribed piece rates because of low productivity.

If rate standards are not kept in line with changes in actual labor rates, the resulting variances cannot be considered the foreman's responsibility.

To develop standard unit costs, a single average labor rate may be used for a given operation. The rates of individual workers performing this operation may vary slightly from the average rate because of seniority or inexperience.

Rate variances generally are not large and consequently do not get the managerial attention that efficiency variances get. In companies where rate variances are small, little formal reporting of variances takes place. In companies where rate variances are important, variance reports are submitted to the executives responsible for the controllable variances.

LABOR-EFFICIENCY STANDARDS

general characteristics The human element makes the setting of labor-quantity (also called *labor-performance, labor-time,* and *labor-efficiency*) standards a complicated task.

As may be expected, disputes over proper standards are much more likely to arise over labor-efficiency standards than over material-quantity standards.

Time and motion study is the most widely used method of setting operation-time standards. To be effective, it must consider the conditions prevailing around the labor operation as well as the operation itself. This means thorough consideration of such factors as equipment, material handling and availability, routing, and instructions for the worker. Properly trained and experienced methods engineers, acting in a staff capacity, usually set labor-time standards. Time standards are typically set for each individual operation. In turn, *master operations lists,* such as the one in Exhibit 7-3, may be compiled for scheduling and routing a variety of individual products.

What factors are usually considered in setting time standards? Some allowance is usually made for fatigue, rest time, and faulty material. Because the purpose of time standards is to measure efficiency, factors not caused by variations in individual efficiency are isolated and often are treated as part of factory overhead. Examples are machine breakdowns, idle time spent awaiting materials, rework, and vacation time.

Time standards are usually set tight enough to provide incentives and yet not so tight as to be unattainable. Thus, time variances generally are unfavorable. Favorable variances are usually caused by exceptionally efficient performance or loose standards. The latter exist because of failure to have standards reflect changes in operating methods or failure to have uniform working conditions. For cost-control purposes, time standards should be reviewed for change whenever operation methods have changed.

Foremen are held responsible for time variances under their control. Variance reports are regularly submitted to foremen, often on a daily or weekly basis. The source documents for such reports are usually some type of work ticket. These work tickets are analyzed and variances are coded and classified. The classifications are almost always by responsibility (that is, by cost center), and often by operations, products, orders, and causes. Thus, a work ticket may have a number designating departmental responsibility and another number designating the cause of the variance. Causes may include machinery breakdowns, rework, faulty material, use of nonpreferred equipment, and so forth.

EXHIBIT 7-3

OPERATIONS ROUTING SHEET

				MASTER OPERATIONS LIST

Part Name ___Fuel pump body with bushings___ Part Number ___B-489___

Stock Specifications ___Grey iron casting___ Standard Quantity ___200___

Operation Number	Department Number	Standard Time Allowed in Minutes		Description of Operation
		Setup	Operation Per Unit	
20	27	90	10.2	Drill, bore, face, chamfer and ream
25	29	18	.7	Face and chamfer hub
30	29	12	1.5	Mill eng. fit pad
35	31	18	8.0	Drill and tap complete
40	29	12	1.5	Mill clearance
45	29	—	1.8	Clean and grind hose connection
50	29	12	2.3	Press in 2 bushings G-98 and face flange on mandrel
	13			Inspect
	21			To stockroom

When variance reports are submitted, major variances are discussed by the interested executives. Investigations of possible operating improvements may be conducted by either line executives or staff experts on standards, or both. Foremen generally have to explain off-standard performance to their superiors.

setup time Machines and accessory equipment often must be adjusted and "made ready" before a particular operation or job can commence. This setup time is easily traceable to an operation or a job, yet its total cost is seldom affected by whether 100 pieces or 2,000 pieces are subsequently processed. The question then is whether setup costs should be treated as direct labor or as a part of factory overhead. No categorical answer can be given. It seems clear that if production runs fluctuate wildly, setup costs should not ordinarily be regarded as direct labor, because the cost *per unit* of product would fluctuate solely because of the length of production run.

For analytical purposes and for cost-control follow-up, setup costs should not be commingled and averaged with the regular direct-labor costs even if it seems desirable to trace setup costs to specific jobs or operations. Most standard-cost systems have standard lot sizes for production runs. Often setup costs are allowed for in the standard direct-labor cost per unit by allocating the setup labor for each operation over the quantity in the standard lot. This practice may be suitable for product-costing purposes; but it has drawbacks for cost-control purposes, especially where standard lot sizes are seldom adhered to, because it mixes together two dissimilar elements that are subject to different control features. As a minimum, then, setup costs should always be coded so that they may be sharply distinguished from operating-labor costs. In this book, we shall assume that setup costs are classified as a part of overhead.

GENERAL-LEDGER ENTRIES FOR DIRECT LABOR

The handling of direct-labor costs in the general ledger varies considerably. The objective is to charge products at standard cost (standard usage × standard rate) but to recognize actual liabilities as incurred.

Case 1.   The basic treatment is as follows:

Facts:

Standard hours	20,000
Standard rate	$8.00 per hour
Actual hours	20,526
Actual rate	$7.90 per hour

Entry:

Work in process (20,000 × $8.00)	$160,000.00	
Direct-labor efficiency variance (526 × $8.00)	4,208.00	
Direct-labor rate variance (20,526 × $.10)		$ 2,052.60
Accrued payroll (20,526 × $7.90)		162,155.40

To record liability for and distribution of direct-labor costs. Note again that unfavorable variances are debits and favorable variances are credits.

Note again that Work in Process is carried at *standard* hours allowed times standard rates. The basic format for analysis of labor variances follows:

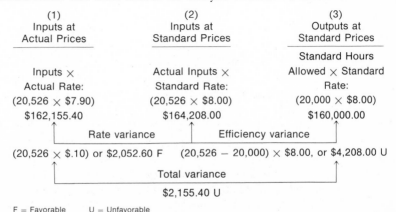

(1) Inputs at Actual Prices	(2) Inputs at Standard Prices	(3) Outputs at Standard Prices
		Standard Hours
Inputs × Actual Rate: (20,526 × $7.90) $162,155.40	Actual Inputs × Standard Rate: (20,526 × $8.00) $164,208.00	Allowed × Standard Rate: (20,000 × $8.00) $160,000.00

Rate variance   Efficiency variance

(20,526 × $.10) or $2,052.60 F   (20,526 − 20,000) × $8.00, or $4,208.00 U

Total variance

$2,155.40 U

F = Favorable   U = Unfavorable

Case 2. There are many other ways of handling direct labor. One method is to isolate (a) rate variances as payrolls are accrued or paid, and (b) time variances as units are transferred from Work in Process to Finished Goods. Appropriate entries follow:

1. Work in process (actual quantity × standard rate) $164,208.00
       Direct-labor rate variance (F) $ 2,052.60
       Accrued payroll   162,155.40
     To record payroll liability for and distribution
       of direct-labor costs.
2. (a) Finished goods   160,000.00
         Work in process   160,000.00
       To transfer.
   (b) Direct labor efficiency variance (U)   4,208.00
         Work in process   4,208.00
       To isolate efficiency variance.

Note here that Work in Process is carried at *actual* hours times standard rate.

The timing of labor entries, number of labor accounts used, and isolation of labor variances depend on management preference and the feasibility of collecting time variances prior to completion of goods.

example of   N.A.A. *Research Series No. 22*, p. 1561, reports:

analysis of
direct-labor This company's operations consist of machining and assembly on a job-order basis.
variances The number of employees in all operations is approximately 3,800. Labor variances, expressed in man-hours only, are analyzed according to a predetermined list of causes.

    On completion of each operation, the foreman indicates the reason for labor hours over or under standard, using the code shown in [Exhibit 7-4]. Timekeepers record the information on time cards and summaries are produced by mechanical tabulation.

    When the variance is less than 10% of standard time, no explanation is required. If a given variance is due to two or more causes, the foreman apportions the variance hours between the causes. Variance data recorded by the timekeepers are summarized monthly by the accounting department to produce the report shown in Exhibit 7-4. In the report, individual variance causes are designated as controllable or noncontrollable according to whether or not the cause is controllable by the foremen. This classification of variances was developed jointly by accounting and top factory management. While the position of some items may be questionable, the classification is sufficiently reliable to have practical usefulness. Supervision over foremen is relied upon to overcome any tendency to designate controllable causes as noncontrollable.

    It was stated that supplementary explanations are seldom needed, since the reports have been designed to answer most of the questions which arise in connection with labor-variance causes.

A careful study of this example demonstrates how management uses a standard-cost system to control by the principle of exception. The system supplies variances, but the total variances are not enough. It is through detailed analysis of the variances that better ways of getting things done are found. Exhibit 7-4 readily shows a *partial* list of the great variety of causes of direct-labor efficiency variances.

ANALYSIS OF VARIANCES

types of When there are many resources being used to manufacture a product, *variances* trade-offs may be deliberately encouraged, within limits. For example, different choices of materials may affect the usage of labor. Therefore, the amount of one variance may be affected by some other variance. If simultaneous variances occur, they must be evaluated as a set.

Variances help the feedback processes by directing attention to the areas most in need of investigation. Managers conduct variance analysis to (a) decide on any necessary actions to improve the implementation of a given decision model, or (b) decide on whether to change the model itself or the prediction method itself.

For example, a decision may have specified a standard cost of $3 for the use of one gallon of a chemical needed for one unit of output. A variance might reveal excess usage that upon investigation is traceable to faulty pouring equip-

EXHIBIT 7-4

DEPARTMENTAL MANUFACTURING EFFICIENCY IN COMPLETED OPERATIONS

Dept. No. _____   Month of _____

CODE	REASON FOR VARIANCE (C MEANS CONTROLLABLE, N NONCONTROLLABLE)		ACTUAL HOURS	VARIANCE HOURS	COST
0	No reason, variances less than 10 percent.	C			
1	Estimated running time too high. Reported to Standards Dept.	N			
2	Estimated setup time too high. Reported to Standards Dept.	N			
3	Men's effort and/or ability above average.	C			
4	New machine, standard has not been changed.	N			
5	Change in methods, standard has not been changed.	N			
6	New or improved tools, standard has not been changed.	N			
7	Used setup from previous job.	C			
8	Time set for man operating one machine, ran two.	C			
9	Time clock registers to 0.1 hour only.	N			
10	Work done under special supervision.	C			

Total Gains

EXHIBIT 7-4 *(Cont.)*

CODE	REASON FOR VARIANCE (C MEANS CONTROLLABLE, N NONCONTROLLABLE)		ACTUAL HOURS	VARIANCE HOURS	COST
0	No reason, variances less than 10 percent.	C			
51	Standard too low. Reported to Standards Dept.	N			
52	First time job was made.	C			
53	Slow or obsolete machine used.	N			
54	Planning not correct. Was changed. Standards Dept. notified.	N			
55	Could not follow operation as planned. Delivery requirements.	N			
56	Operations in previous departments not performed as planned.	N			
57	Time set for man operating two machines. One available.	N			
58	Quantity too small.	N			
59	Extra setup result of machine breakdown.	N			
60	Extra work.	N			
61	Two men had to be assigned to job due to nature of job.	N			
62	Learner, apprentice, or student.	N			
63	Man inexperienced. Undergoing instruct.	N			
67	Operation not performed correctly. Added time required.	C			
68	Parts spoiled. Had to make more parts.	C			
72	Broke tool. Time lost redressing and sharpening.	C			
73	Oversized material used.	N			
	Total Losses				
	Total				
Efficiency % Controllable by Foreman		C			
Efficiency % Noncontrollable		N			
Efficiency % Overall					

ment. The correction of the equipment illustrates how action can be taken to improve the implementation of a given decision model.

Sometimes the variance may point toward the need for changing the decision model or the prediction method. For example, if it represents a permanent change, a price variance for the chemical may prompt a complete revision in raw-material specifications, which would be a change in the model. An example of a variance that might prompt a change in a prediction method would be the discovery that the standard usage was incorrectly specified.

when to investigate variances   When should variances be investigated? Frequently the answer to such a question is based on subjective judgments, hunches, guesses, and rules of thumb. The most troublesome aspect of feedback is deciding when a variance is significant enough to warrant management's attention. For some items, a small deviation may prompt follow-up. For other items, a minimum dollar amount or 5, 10, or 25 percent deviations from budget may be necessary before investigations commence. Of course, a 4 percent variance in a $1 million material cost may deserve more attention than a 20 percent variance in a $10,000 repair cost. Therefore, rules such as "Investigate all variances exceeding $5,000, or 25 percent of standard cost, whichever is lower" are common.

Variance analysis is subject to the same cost–benefit test as other phases of an information system. The trouble with the foregoing rules of thumb is that they are too frequently based on subjective assessments, guesses, or hunches. The field of statistics offers tools to help reduce these subjective features of variance analysis. These tools help answer the cost–benefit question, and they help separate variances caused by random events from variances that are controllable.

Accounting systems have traditionally implied that a standard is a single acceptable measure. Practically, the accountant (and everybody else) realizes that the standard is a *band* or *range* of possible acceptable outcomes. Consequently, he expects variances to fluctuate randomly within some normal limits.

By definition, a random variance per se calls for no corrective action to an existing process. In short, random variances are attributable to chance rather than to management's implementation decisions. For a further discussion, see Chapter 25.

timing and aggregation Another difficulty is that the accounting system often compiles variances for a period of time. A cost-conscious management will follow up variances quickly—sometimes daily, or even hourly. But delayed reports and everyday work often allow variances to accumulate, so that it becomes too late to find out what caused them. Further, favorable and unfavorable variances are frequently combined, so that significant variances may be offset in accounts and in management reports. Each overtime authorization, for example, is an incremental decision and should not be related to average rates of overtime allowances. This combination of delayed reporting and of cost accumulations that represent a conglomeration of different operations makes it difficult to find causes for variances and to trace causes for them below the foreman level to individual machines, men, and materials.

LEARNING CURVES AND ACCOUNTING

effects of learning on productivity When new products or processes are initiated, a learning or familiarity phenomenon occurs. As experience is gained, productivity heightens. The effect of learning on output per labor-hour or machine-hour is usually depicted by a learning curve, which helps managers to predict how costs will change as the process matures. Case studies have shown that the time needed per unit of product should be progressively smaller at some constant percentage rate as experience is gained. The applicable percentage rate varies from 60 to 85 percent or more, but 80 percent is common. For example, as cumulative quantities double, average time per unit may fall 20 percent. Exhibit 7-5 demonstrates an 80 percent learning curve, using the following data:

| QUANTITY | | TIME IN MINUTES | |
PER LOT	CUMULATIVE	CUMULATIVE	CUMULATIVE AVERAGE PER UNIT
10	10	300	30.0
10	20	480	24.0 (30.0 × 80%)
20	40	768	19.2 (24.0 × 80%)
40	80	1,232	15.4 (19.2 × 80%)
80	160	1,968	12.3 (15.4 × 80%)

As Exhibit 7-5 indicates, as production quantities increase, the average time per unit starts to level off; so if total production were large enough, the time per unit would become quite stable.

EXHIBIT 7-5

EIGHTY PERCENT LEARNING CURVE*

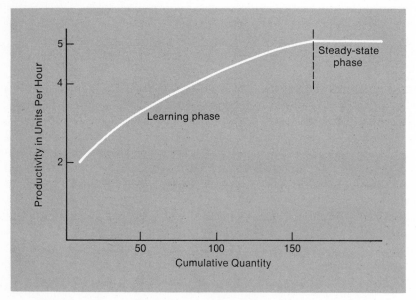

*In practice, these curves are plotted on log-log graph paper, so that they appear as straight lines for ease of use. Also, some learning curves express productivity in terms of average time or average cost per unit, which would be expected to fall as learning increases.

The learning curve is applicable only with respect to setting standards during the learning or start-up phases of production.[3] If production life is

[3] For an expanded discussion, see E. L. Summers and G. A. Welsch, "How Learning Curve Models Can be Applied to Profit Planning," *Management Services*, Vol. 7, No. 2, 45–50; and N. Baloff and J. W. Kennelly, "Accounting Implications of Product and Process Startups," *Journal of Accounting*

sufficiently long, or if the operations are relatively routine, a steady-state phase eventually occurs whereby no increases in productivity are predicted. Exhibit 7-5 shows the learning phase and the steady-state phase. Indices of productivity may be expressed, depending on the industry, as tons per machine-hour or finished units per labor-hour, or some other measure.

setting budgets Predictions of costs should allow for the effects of learning. The costs most
or standards likely to be affected include labor, material usage, power, and other related
overhead. Some costs may be unaffected. These typically include some materials, supplies, packing, selling, and nearly all fixed costs.

Standards during the learning phase are often erroneously based on stable or steady-state conditions. Using these standards to plan and to judge performance may have undesirable consequences. Among the dangers are faulty cash planning and production scheduling because of failure to allow for the unusually high costs and time consumption of start-ups.

In addition, the inapplicable standards may have an unfavorable motivational impact. If the unfavorable discrepancy between the steady-state standard and actual performance is large and persistent, the goal may be rejected as unattainable. For example, in the steel industry, workers have aborted start-ups at artificially low productivity levels.[4]

summary

Standard costs are used for building a budgeting and feedback system. They aid management predictions and provide a framework for judging performance. Actual costs are compared with standard costs to obtain variances. Variances raise questions; they do not provide answers. The variances are investigated to decide (a) how to improve the implementation of a given decision model or set of plans, or (b) how to change objectives, methods, or standards.

Currently attainable standards are the most widely used because they usually have the most desirable motivational impact and because they may be

---

Research, Vol. 5, No. 2, 131–43. The learning-curve model is a power function:

$$y = ax^b$$

where y = productivity
x = cumulative output
a = parameter value, the productivity during the first unit of output
b = parameter value, the index of the rate of increase in productivity during learning

[4] See N. Baloff and R. B. McKersie, "Motivating Startups," *Journal of Business,* Vol. 39, No. 4, 473–84.

used for a variety of accounting purposes, including financial planning, as well as for monitoring departmental performance.

When standards are currently attainable, there is no logical difference between standards and budgets. A standard is a *unit* concept, whereas a budget is a *total* concept. In a sense, the standard is the budget for one unit.

Material and labor variances are primarily divided into two categories: (a) price or rate, and (b) usage or efficiency. Price or rate variances are computed by multiplying differences in price by actual quantities. Usage or efficiency variances remove influences of price changes; they are computed by multiplying differences in quantities by a standard price.

General-ledger treatments for standard costs vary considerably. The method advocated in this book stresses isolation of variances as quickly as possible.

It is extremely important to personalize variances so that each variance is assignable to the person primarily responsible. Otherwise, the investigative follow-ups of reported variances—where the real payoff lies—will be fruitless. There is also a need to have some objective way to decide when a given variance is significant enough to warrant investigation.

Problems for Self-Study

PROBLEM 1   The Chester Company uses standard costs. The purchasing manager is responsible for material-price variances, and the production manager is responsible for material-usage variances and direct-labor rate and efficiency variances.

The standard price for metal used as a principal raw material was $2 per pound. The standard allowance was six pounds per finished unit of product.

The standard rate for direct labor was $7 per hour. The standard allowance was one hour per finished unit of product.

During the past week, 10,000 good finished units were produced. However, labor trouble caused the production manager to use much nonpreferred personnel. Actual labor costs were $78,000 for 13,000 actual hours. 80,000 pounds of metal were acquired for $1.80 per pound. 71,000 pounds of metal were consumed during production.

required   1. Material purchase-price variance, material-quantity variance, direct-labor rate variance, and direct-labor efficiency variance.

2. As a supervisor of both the purchasing manager and the production manager, how would you interpret the feedback provided by the computed variances?

3. What are the budget allowances for the production manager for direct materials and direct labor? Would they be different if production were 7,000 good finished units?

4. Prepare a condensed responsibility performance report for the production manager for the 10,000 units produced. Show three columns: budget, actual, and variance.

SOLUTION 1   1. The format for the solution (Exhibit 7-6) may seem awkward at first, but upon review you will discover that it provides perspective and insight.

2. The variances direct attention and prompt investigation about the following possibilities at first glance. The purchasing manager made an advantageous purchase, but the favorable variance may be attributable to a number of causes. The manager may have predicted prices incorrectly so that the standard of $2 is inaccurate, or he may have made a bargain purchase through his own

EXHIBIT 7-6

FRAMEWORK FOR ANALYSIS OF VARIANCES

Control Point	Cost Incurred: Actual Quantity × Actual Rate	Actual Quantity × Standard Price	Total Standard Quantity Allowed for Good Units Produced × Standard Price
Purchasing	(80,000 lbs. × $1.80) $144,000	(80,000 lbs. × $2.00) $160,000	
	↑ (80,000 lbs. × $.20) ↑		
	Price variance, $16,000 F		
Production (Direct materials)		(71,000 lbs. × $2.00) $142,000	(60,000 lbs. × $2.00) $120,000
		↑ (11,000 lbs. × $2.00) ↑	
		Quantity variance, $22,000 U	
Production (Direct labor)	(13,000 hrs. × $6.00) $78,000	(13,000 hrs. × $7.00) $91,000	(10,000 hrs. × $7.00) $70,000
	↑ (13,000 hrs. × $1.00) ↑	(3,000 hrs. × $7.00)	
	Rate variance, $13,000 F	Efficiency variance, $21,000 U	
	↑ Total direct-labor variance, $8,000 U ↑		

F = Favorable   U = Unfavorable

special skills, or some combination thereof. Moreover, if the quality were less than normal, the savings in unit purchase cost may be more than offset by excessive usage or may have contributed to excessive usage. (Note too that the facts are unclear as to whether the material used came from the units purchased currently or from previous stockpiles, or both.)

The production manager probably had abnormal troubles. Among the possible causes are the use of inferior materials or of nonpreferred workmen, or some combination of both. Assume that the materials were of normal quality. The trade-off of lower-rate labor for more inefficiency apparently led to net higher costs of direct-labor and direct-material usage. In short, less-skilled workers probably used too much time and too much materials to produce the 10,000 units of output.

3. The chapter made the point that standard costs can be thought of as the budget allowance for one unit of output. That is, the standard is a *unit* concept and the budget is a *total* concept. Viewed in this way, the budget allowances for the production manager would be:

Direct materials, 60,000 lbs. × $2.00	$120,000
Direct labor, 10,000 hrs. × $7.00	70,000

Note that the budget allowance is the same as (is equal to) the total standard quantity allowed for the good units produced times the standard price.

If 7,000 units were produced, the budget allowance would be lowered accordingly:

Direct materials, 7,000 × 6 lbs. × $2.00	$84,000
Direct labor, 7,000 × 1 hr. × $7.00	49,000

213

4.

	BUDGET	ACTUAL	VARIANCE
Direct materials (at standard unit prices)	$120,000	$142,000*	$22,000 U
Direct labor	70,000	78,000	8,000 U

* This "actual" charge of $142,000 illustrates the basic nature of responsibility accounting. The $142,000 is not an actual cost in the usual sense, because materials are charged to the production manager at a predetermined standard unit price. In this way, fluctuations in material *prices,* which are supposed to be the primary responsibility of the purchasing manager, do not affect the production manager's performance report. In contrast, because the production manager is deemed to be responsible for both labor rates and labor efficiency, actual labor cost is assigned in full to him.

PROBLEM 2   Consider the following for April, when 2,000 finished units were produced: Direct materials used, 4,400 pounds. The standard allowance per finished unit is two pounds at $5 per pound. Six thousand pounds were purchased at $5.50 per pound, a total of $33,000.

Actual direct-labor hours were 6,500 at a total cost of $40,300. The standard labor cost per finished unit was $18. Standard labor time allowed is three hours per unit.

required   *1.* Journal entries for a "normal" cost system as described in Chapter 4. That is, "actual" charges for direct materials and direct labor are charged to Work in Process.

2. Journal entries for a "standard cost" system.

3. Show an alternate approach, including journal entries, to the way you quantified the material-price variance in requirement 2. Which way is better? Explain.

SOLUTION 2   1.   NORMAL COST SYSTEM

Stores or Direct-material inventory	$33,000	
Accounts payable		$33,000
Work in process (4,400 @ $5.50)	24,200	
Stores		24,200
Work in process (6,500 @ $6.20)	40,300	
Accrued payroll		40,300

2.   STANDARD COST SYSTEM

Stores or Direct-material inventory	$30,000	
Direct-material purchase price variance	3,000	
Accounts payable		$33,000
Work in process (4,000 @ $5.00)	20,000	
Direct-material quantity variance	2,000	
Stores (4,400 @ $5.00)		22,000
Work in process	36,000	
Direct-labor rate variance	1,300	
Direct-labor efficiency variance	3,000	
Accrued payroll		40,300

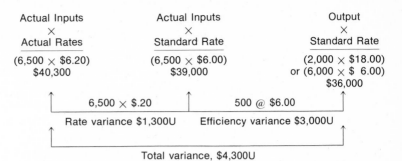

Actual Inputs	Actual Inputs	Output
×	×	×
Actual Rates	Standard Rate	Standard Rate
(6,500 × $6.20)	(6,500 × $6.00)	(2,000 × $18.00)
$40,300	$39,000	or (6,000 × $ 6.00)
		$36,000

6,500 @ $.20   500 @ $6.00

Rate variance $1,300U   Efficiency variance $3,000U

Total variance, $4,300U

3. An alternate standard-cost approach to that shown in 2 (Approach in 2 is better because it isolates variances earlier, when something is more likely to be done about the variances):

Stores	$33,000	
Accounts payable		$33,000
Work in process (4,400 @ $5.00)	22,000	
Direct-material price variance (4,400 @ $.50)	2,200	
Stores (4,400 @ $5.50)		24,200
Finished goods	20,000	
Direct-material quantity variance	2,000	
Work in process		22,000

questions, problems, and cases

7-1. What are standard costs? Why is their use superior to comparisons of actual data with past data?

7-2. What are the key questions in deciding how variances should be collected and analyzed?

7-3. List and briefly describe three different types of standards.

7-4. "Cost control means cost reduction." Do you agree? Why?

7-5. List four common causes of material-price variances.

7-6. List the major factors that affect control procedures for material quantities.

7-7. Define: *standard bill of materials, excess materials, requisition, operations list.*

7-8. "Setup costs are easily traceable to specific jobs. Therefore, they should be classified as direct-labor costs." Do you agree? Why?

7-9. "Standard costing is O.K. for big companies that can afford such an elaborate system. But our company relies on an 'actual' system because it saves clerical costs." Comment.

7-10. How does management decide when a variance is large enough to warrant investigation?

7-11. List five purposes of standard costs.

7-12. Who should ordinarily be responsible for the extra costs arising from rush sales orders? Why?

7-13. Define *learning curve*. Name four of its uses.

7-14. Who is responsible for developing standards?

7-15. Why do budgeted variances arise?

7-16. When will budgets differ from standards? When will they be the same?

7-17. **Inefficiency and Product Costing.** [CPA] Discuss the following quotation from the standpoint of:

1. The places in the accounting procedure at which wastes may be most readily recognized, measured, and analyzed
2. The accounting techniques available to aid in isolating these wastes

> Gradually, the older belief that every expense incurred in the factory must be considered a cost of the products of the factory is giving way to the more logical one that recognizes that some of the expenditures . . . are costs of goods and some are costs of idleness, of wasted time and materials, and of general inefficiency. . . .

7-18. **Choice of Material Specifications [SIA, adapted].** Your company is in the furniture manufacturing business. It follows the policy, whenever possible, of using the lowest-grade lumber consistent with costs. The particular order under review involves a cutting of the following range of sizes: 35″, 27″, 21″, and 15″, the grade of the finished piece to be clear on one side.

Two grades of lumber are suitable for this order. If the cutting is made from No. 1 common lumber, the wastage is 34 percent; if it is made from No. 2 common lumber, the wastage is 42 percent. Percentages are based on input, not net yield.

required   The cost of lumber and of the direct labor involved in its conversion are as follows:

LUMBER

$165 per thousand feet kiln-dried for No. 1 common
$115 per thousand feet kiln-dried for No. 2 common
Lumber cut (before allowing for wastage) in an 8-hour day:
   either 5,000 No. 1 common
   or   4,000 No. 2 common

LABOR

Labor cost per hour on the basis of an 8-hour day: $13
Labor overtime cost per hour: time and a half

Assuming that there are sufficient orders to keep production running at full activity (no overtime) if the most efficient grade (minimum total cost) is always used, compute the saving on this particular order per thousand feet of net yield when the more efficient grade is used.

7-19. **Analysis of Variances.** Chemical, Inc., has set up the following standards for materials and direct labor:

	PER FINISHED BATCH
Materials: 10 lbs. @ $3.00	$30.00
Direct labor: 4 hours @ $2.50	10.00

The number of finished units budgeted for the period was 10,000; 9,810 units were actually produced.

Actual results were:

> Materials: 98,073 lbs. used
> Direct labor: 39,300 hrs. $98,240

required   During the month, purchases amounted to 100,000 lbs. at a total cost of $301,193.

1. Give journal entries to record the data above.

2. Show computations of all material and labor variances.

3. Comment on each of the variances.

7-20. **Budgets and Expected Variances.** The Werelius Manufacturing Company uses standard costs and budgets for planning and controlling current production of its two products, F and G. Schedules for the year ending December, 19_1, call for the production of 6,000 units of F and 1,000 units of G.

The standards set for direct labor call for 14 direct-labor hours per unit for F and 20 direct-labor hours for G. However, these standards have been deliberately made tight so as to encourage better performance. Management expects that direct-labor performance will fall short of these goals by one direct-labor hour per unit for each product.

The standard rate for direct labor is $6 per hour. However, negotiations are under way with the union for a new contract. Although the results of these negotiations are uncertain, management expects the rate for direct labor to rise to $6.30 per hour.

Develop the budget for direct labor, showing both standard cost and expected cost, and show any expected or budgeted variances.

7-21. **Learning Curve and Cost Estimation.** The Smyth Company, a subcontractor for the aircraft and missile industry, has been asked to bid on a prospective contract for 900 units of a precision missile part. Two months ago, the Smyth Company had produced 300 of these parts at the following total costs:

Direct materials	$12,000
Direct labor (6,000 hours @ $4.00)	24,000
Tooling cost[a]	3,000
Variable overhead[b]	3,000
Other overhead[c]	6,000
Total costs	$48,000

[a]Tooling can be reused, even though all of its cost was assigned to the original order of 300 parts.
[b]Variable-overhead incurrence is directly affected by direct-labor hours.
[c]Other overhead is assigned at a flat rate of 25 percent of direct-labor cost for purposes of bidding on contracts.

The Smyth Company has used an 80 percent learning curve as a basis for forecasting what pertinent costs should be.

required   Prepare a prediction of the total expected costs for bidding on a contract of 900 units.

7-22. **Comparison of General-Ledger Entries for Direct Materials and Direct**

Labor. The Sweeney Co. has the following data for the month of March, when 1,100 finished units were produced:

Direct materials used, 3,600 pounds. The standard allowance per finished unit is 3 pounds at $3.00 per pound. Five thousand pounds were purchased at $3.25 per pound, a total of $16,250.

Direct labor, actual hours, was 2,450 hours at a total cost of $9,800. The standard labor cost per finished unit was $7.60. Standard time allowed is 2 hours per unit.

required

1. Prepare journal entries for a "normal" cost system.

2. Prepare journal entries for a "standard" cost system. Support your entries with a detailed variance analysis, using the columnar analytical format illustrated in the chapter.

3. Show an alternate approach, including journal entries, to the way you quantified the material price variance in 2. Which way is better, and why?

7-23. **Journal Entries for Standard Costs.** A machining department works on three varieties of a basic product. The product contains two raw materials and entails a sequence of from two to four operations, depending on the model type.

STANDARD USAGE PER FINISHED UNIT

FINISHED PRODUCT	UNITS OF RAW MATERIALS		STANDARD TIME PER LABOR OPERATION IN HOURS			
	A	B	1	2	3	4
X	3	1	1	2	–	–
Y	3	2	1	–	3	–
Z	3	3	1	2	3	1

STANDARD PRICES AND LABOR RATES

Raw material A, $5 per unit
Raw material B, $1 per unit
Labor rates:

OPERATION	PER HOUR
1	$2.40
2	3.00
3	3.20
4	4.00

OPERATING DATA

Purchases:		
Material A	120,000 units	$612,000
Material B	65,000 units	61,750

Material requisitions:

Issued from stores:	A	B
Standard quantity	105,000	61,000
Over standard	5,000	3,000
Returned to stores		400

Direct labor:

OPERATION	ACTUAL HOURS	TOTAL ACTUAL COST
1	36,000	$ 90,000
2	48,000	144,960
3	58,000	174,000
4	6,900	28,980
		$437,940

There are no beginning or ending work-in-process inventories. Units produced:

X	16,000
Y	12,000
Z	7,000

required

1. Journal entries, assuming that material-price variances are isolated upon purchase. Accompany each journal entry with a detailed analysis of variances as far as the data permit.

2. Prime standard costs per unit for Products X, Y, and Z. Show computations.

3. What are some of the frequent causes for the variances computed in 1?

4. What is the merit of isolating price variances as materials are purchased rather than as they are issued?

7-24. Journal Entries for Standard Costs.   Here is a summary of certain September data for a job shop that uses standard costs for direct materials and direct labor.

MATERIALS	PURCHASES	PURCHASE COST	STANDARD PRICE PER POUND	USAGE
A	2,000 lbs.	$10,200	$5.00	1,800 lbs.
B	4,000 lbs.	26,800	7.00	3,500 lbs.

The company produced a wide variety of job orders, two of which required all the A and B materials used above. The standard quantities allowed for the output on which A and B were used were:

		PER UNIT OF FINISHED PRODUCT	
FINISHED PRODUCT	JOB NOS.	MATERIAL A	MATERIAL B
800 widgets	101, 104, 109	1.1 lbs.	3 lbs.
200 gidgets	103, 105	5.0 lbs.	6 lbs.

Four basic operations were used in the shop, but not all operations are used uniformly on all jobs.

	OPERATIONS				FINISHED UNITS
	1	2	3	4	
Standard hours per unit	1	2	4	3	
Standard labor rate per hour	$5.50	$2	$4	$3	
Operations performed:					
Job No. 101	√	√	√	√	400
103	√		√	√	150
104			√	√ √	200
105	√	√	√		50
109	√	√		√	200

Summary of actual direct-labor usage on the jobs above:

	HOURS	ACTUAL DIRECT-LABOR COSTS INCURRED
Operation 1	850	$ 4,590
Operation 2	1,670	3,340
Operation 3	3,300	13,860
Operation 4	2,800	8,540
		$30,330

required

1. Journal entries, assuming that material-price variances are isolated upon purchase. Also assume that Stores Control is the general-ledger account for all materials. Support all journal entries with detailed analyses of variance computations.

2. What are the relative merits of isolating material-price variances upon purchase rather than upon withdrawal from the storeroom?

3. In terms of clerical costs, compare a standard-cost system with a regular job-order cost system.

7-25. Analysis of Variances [SIA, adapted].   The Alpha Co. Ltd. produces toys for national distribution. The management has recently established a standard-cost system to control costs. Established standard costs are:

(a) Materials: 12 pieces per unit at 56¢ per piece
(b) Labor: 2 hours per unit at $2.75 per hour

During the month of December 1966, the company produced 1,000 units of finished goods. Production information for December is as follows:

(a) Materials: 14,000 pieces at a total cost of $7,140
(b) Labor costs: $8,000
(c) Direct-labor hours worked were 2,500
(e) Inventories: December 1, nil
    December 31, nil

required

1. Computation of material price and quantity variances and labor-rate and efficiency variances.

2. A brief explanation to management giving the significance of each variance.

7-26. Analysis of Variances [CPA, adapted].   Ross Shirts, Inc., manufactures short- and long-sleeve men's shirts for large stores. Ross produces a single-quality shirt in lots to each customer's order and attaches the store's label to each. The standard costs for a dozen long-sleeve shirts include:

Direct materials	24 yards @ $ .55	$13.20
Direct labor	3 hours @ 2.45	7.35

During October 19_9, Ross worked on three orders for long-sleeve shirts. Job-cost records for the month disclose the following:

LOT	UNITS IN LOT	MATERIALS USED	HOURS WORKED
30	1,000 dozen	24,100 yards	2,980
31	1,700 dozen	40,440 yards	5,130
32	1,200 dozen	28,825 yards	2,890

The following information is also available:

(a) Ross purchased 95,000 yards of material during the month at a cost of $53,200. The material-price variance is recorded when goods are purchased, and all inventories are carried at standard cost.

(b) Direct labor incurred amounted to $27,500 during October. According to payroll records, production employees were paid $2.50 per hour.

(c) There was no work in process at October 1. During October, lots 30 and 31 were completed, and all material was issued for lot 32, which was 80 percent completed as to labor.

required

1. Prepare a schedule computing the material-price variance for October 19_9 and indicate whether the variance is favorable or unfavorable.

2. Prepare schedules computing, and indicating whether favorable or unfavorable, for each lot produced during October 19_9:
   a. Material-quantity variance in yards
   b. Labor-efficiency variance in hours
   c. Labor-rate variance in dollars

7-27. Analysis of Variances [CPA, adapted]. The Conti Pharmaceutical Company processes a single compound-product known as NLAX and uses a standard-cost accounting system. The process requires preparation and blending of three materials in large batches with a variation from the standard mixture sometimes necessary to maintain quality. Conti's cost accountant became ill at the end of October, and you were engaged to determine standard costs of October production and explain any differences between actual and standard costs for the month. The following information is available from the blending department:

(a) The standard-cost card for a 500-pound batch included the following standard costs:

	QUANTITY	PRICE	TOTAL COST
Materials:			
Mucilloid	250 pounds	$.14	$35
Dextrose	200 pounds	.09	18
Other ingredients	50 pounds	.08	4
Total per batch	500 pounds		$57
Labor:			
Preparation and blending	10 hours	$3.00	$30

(b) During October, 410 batches of 500 pounds each of the finished compound were completed and transferred to the packaging department.

(c) Blending-department inventories totaled 6,000 pounds at the beginning of the month and 9,000 pounds at the end of the month (assume both inventories were completely processed but not transferred and consisted of materials in their standard proportions). Inventories are carried in the accounts at standard-cost prices.

(d) During the month of October, the following materials were purchased and put into production:

	POUNDS	PRICE	TOTAL COST
Mucilloid	114,400	$.17	$19,448
Dextrose	85,800	.11	9,438
Other ingredients	19,800	.07	1,386
Totals	220,000		$30,272

(e) Wages paid for 4,212 hours of direct labor at $3.25 per hour amounted to $13,689.

1. Prepare a schedule presenting the computation for the blending department of:
   a. October production in both pounds and batches
   b. The prime cost of October production itemized by components of materials and labor

2. Prepare schedules computing the differences between actual and standard costs and analyzing the differences as:
   a. Material variances (for each material) caused by
      (1) Price differences
      (2) Usage differences
   b. Labor variances caused by
      (1) Rate difference
      (2) Efficiency difference

3. Explain how the material variances arising from usage differences could be further analyzed (no computations are necessary).

7-28. Learning Curve, Cost Predictions, and Pricing. The Boeheed Corporation is a large, multidivision company with annual sales in excess of one billion dollars. One of Boeheed's divisions, the Spriggs Division, manufactures aircraft. The division is currently developing a new type of aircraft that will determine the success of the division for the next few years.

Spriggs has already spent $200 million on developing and testing the new technology that the aircraft will utilize. It is also constructing a new $20 million specialized-production facility, which would become totally obsolete after production of the planes was completed. The engineering department has predicted that an additional $20 million will have to be spent on further development and testing before the aircraft is ready for production. Boeheed's accounting policy was to capitalize all development and equipment costs until production actually started.

The division is presently attempting to determine a price for the aircraft. A price is necessary now because of the long production-schedule lead time of about twelve months, which results from the limited production capacity of ten aircraft per month.

Orders will be made on the basis of this established price even though deliveries will not be made for one or two years.

The marketing department has forecast that demand for the aircraft will range between 200 and 300 units. The actual demand will be determined by both the ultimate aircraft characteristics and, more important, the aircraft price.

The division has made detailed predictions of the aircraft's production costs. These predictions have proven to be extremely accurate on previous projects of this type. All the aircraft parts requirements are subcontracted for fabrication. Spriggs has already contracted for parts for 200 aircraft, which will cost $3 million per aircraft. These contracts have a provision for parts for an additional 100 aircraft but at a 10 percent decrease in cost per aircraft.

Direct labor is the most significant element of the production costs. Labor costs are substantial in an absolute sense, but large reductions are possible because of the "learning curve" that affects the labor costs during the production period. The learning curve applicable to the new aircraft is based on ten-unit production lots, with the following cost-reduction schedule based on an initial Lot 1 having labor costs of $8 million:

LOT NO.	LEARNING CURVE (% OF INITIAL COSTS)	COST PER AIRCRAFT (MILLIONS)
1	100%	$8.0
2	80	6.4
4	64	5.1
8	51	4.0
12	44	3.5
16	41	3.2
24	35	2.8
32	32	2.5

For example, the overall direct-labor cost per plane for the seventy-first through the eightieth planes produced should be $4 million per plane, or a total direct-labor cost for Lot No. 8 of $40 million.

The general manager and the controller, naturally concerned about setting a unit price for the aircraft, decided to view the new aircraft program as a single job order. They prepared a graph of the predicted direct-labor costs (see Exhibit 7-7). They segmented the graph to develop total direct-labor costs for each segment. They analyzed segments as follows:

SEGMENTS IN EXHIBIT 7–7	AVERAGE DIRECT-LABOR COST PER UNIT IN SEGMENT
0–40	82% of initial unit cost
41–100	55%
101–200	42%
201–300	34%

Combined applicable general, administrative, and indirect production costs are estimated at $50 million annually. Historically, these costs have been applied on the basis of direct-labor costs.

They decided that the fixed costs applicable to the program that must be recovered included $240 million plus whatever indirect production costs and general and administrative costs were incurred. Their prediction of the latter

EXHIBIT 7-7

EFFECT OF "LEARNING CURVE" ON DIRECT-LABOR COST

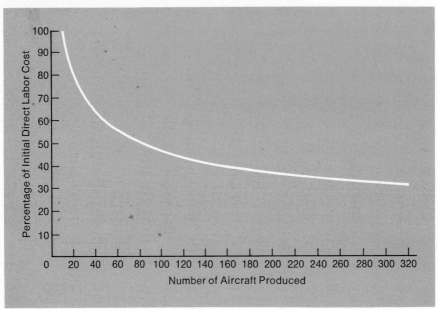

was $100 million if 200 units were produced and sold (2 years × $50 million) and $150 million if 300 units were produced and sold (3 years × $50 million).

required

1. What price must be set to break even, assuming 200 units are sold? Assuming 300 units are sold?

2. Suppose that Spriggs sets a price of $8.6 million. This price has produced orders for 250 planes. The marketing department now reports that a potential new customer will purchase 50 planes, but only if the price is $8.1 million or less. This price reduction would have to be made retroactive and applied to all customers. Should Spriggs accept the new order?

7-29. Combined or Joint Price–Quantity Variance and Incentives. The Van Aucklen Company had an incentive system that each Christmas rewarded managers for cost savings on materials. The manager of purchasing received 10 percent of any favorable price variance accumulated for the fiscal year ending November 30. Similarly, the production manager received 10 percent of the favorable quantity variances. In addition, each manager received 10 percent of the favorable net material variances. Note, however, that all variances were included in the computations. That is, an unfavorable variance in one month would offset a favorable variance in another month.

In the opinion of the company president, this system had worked reasonably well in past years. Of course, because of the sensitivity of the incentive system, the standards were carefully specified and adjusted each quarter. Only minimal inventories were kept at any time. Bonuses had varied from zero to 20 percent of the managers' base salaries. The purchasing manager's base salary for a recent fiscal year ending November 30 was $24,000; the production manager's was $30,000.

The operating results on Material A for a recent month were:

Purchase-price variance	$ 72,000 unfavorable
Quantity variance	36,000 unfavorable
Net material variance	$108,000 unfavorable

Two pounds of Material A was the standard quantity allowed for every unit of a particular finished product, a chemical used in petroleum refining. One hundred thousand units of the chemical had been manufactured. The average price actually paid for Material A was 30¢ per pound in excess of the standard price.

required

1. Number of pounds of Material A purchased.

2. Standard cost per pound of Material A.

3. Total standard cost allowed for material component of the finished product manufactured.

4. As the purchasing manager, what is your opinion of the bonus system? Would your answer be the same if the actual raw-material price paid had been 70¢ per pound? Explain fully.

5. As the production manager, what is your opinion of the bonus system? Why?

6. Why is part of the bonus dependent on the net material variance?

7. Assume that some bonus system tied to variance analysis is maintained. What changes would you recommend?

7-30. **Control of Direct Materials and Direct Labor.** Early in 19_5, the following major costs of the cabinet department were reported to George Jaedicke, president of the Jaedicke Manufacturing Company:

	19_4	19_3	DIFFERENCE
Direct materials	$2,123,000	$2,060,000	$63,000 Unfavorable
Direct labor	798,000	801,000	3,000 Favorable
Prime costs	$2,921,000	$2,861,000	$60,000 Unfavorable

Mr. Jaedicke was unhappy about the increase in costs because he had thought control was better in 19_4 than in 19_3.

The department made two types of office cabinets, A and B, using the same materials. The A cabinet required twice as much material as the B cabinet. However, twice as much direct-labor time was needed for B as for A because of special hand finishing applied to B. Ordinarily, B cabinets were produced at a rate of two per man-hour. When efficiently produced, B cabinets required three units of raw materials.

About 965,000 units of raw materials had been acquired and used in 19_4, whereas 1,030,000 units had been acquired and used in 19_3. A unit of raw materials cost $2 in 19_3, but increases in the purchase price during 19_4 averaged 10 percent.

The average wage rate in the department was about $8 per hour in both 19_3 and 19_4. Failure to schedule work correctly and unexpected absenteeism caused the use of overtime upon occasion. Overtime was discouraged as being too expensive because of its 50 percent extra cost. No budgetary allowance was provided for overtime, and all direct-labor costs, including overtime premiums, were charged to a single direct-labor account. To cope with absenteeism, workers from the other departments were sometimes used. When skilled tradesmen from the custom-furniture department were utilized, the wage rate was $9.50 per hour. Payroll records showed that 89,000 direct-labor hours were actually paid for in 19_3, and 95,000 direct-labor hours were actually paid for in 19_4.

Production was:

	19_4	19_3
A Cabinets	100,000	100,000
B Cabinets	120,000	110,000

required

1. Analyze the differences in costs between 19_3 and 19_4. Present a report to Mr. Jaedicke explaining as clearly as possible the details of the net difference of $60,000.

2. Was the cabinet department efficient in 19_4? Why? Describe a way to report costs in the future that is better than the condensed summary given above.

8

Flexible Budgets and Various Cost Behavior Patterns

This chapter concentrates on the flexible budget and work measurement as tools for management decisions and feedback. Various cost behavior patterns are also described, and the problems of estimating costs are delineated.

FLEXIBLE BUDGETS

the variety of control techniques As you saw in Chapter 5, budgets may be developed on a company-wide basis to cover all activities, from sales to direct materials to sweeping compound, and from spending on new plant to expected drains on petty cash. A budget may be expressed on the accrual basis or on a cash-flow basis; it may be highly condensed or exceedingly detailed. All the budgets discussed in Chapter 5 are *static* (inflexible). That is, a typical master planning budget is a plan tailored to a single target volume level of, say, 100,000 units. All results would be compared with the original plan, regardless of changes in ensuing conditions—even though, for example, volume turns out to be 90,000 units instead of the original 100,000.

In contrast, *flexible* budgets, also called *variable* budgets, have the following distinguishing features: (a) They are prepared for a range of activity instead of a single level. (b) They supply a dynamic basis for comparison because they are automatically geared to changes in volume. The flexible-budget approach says, "You tell me what your activity level was during the past week or month, and I'll provide a budget that specifies what costs *should have been.* I'll tailor a budget to the particular volume—*after the fact.*"

Every organization has individual items of cost that are relatively huge. In a wholesaling or retailing business, the purchase cost of merchandise is usually the most significant item. In a manufacturing business, the costs of direct materials and direct labor are usually both important. The distinct significance of such individual items generates elaborate formal techniques for decisions and feedback regarding them.

Total factory overhead, as well as selling and administrative overhead, is usually a major part of total costs. Yet individual overhead items generally are not large in comparison with direct materials and direct labor. Therefore, although the ideas underlying the control of overhead are basically the same, the techniques differ because the size of individual overhead costs often does not justify elaborate control systems that routinely produce exhaustive analyses of variances in individual items.

In practice, direct materials and direct labor are said to be controlled with the help of *standard costs*, whereas factory overhead is usually said to be controlled with the help of *department-overhead budgets*. This distinction probably arises because the timing and the techniques for controlling direct materials, direct labor, and overhead differ. For example, in a paper mill, direct-material usage may be closely watched on an hour-to-hour basis; direct-labor efficiency may be followed on a day-to-day basis; and department overhead may be scrutinized on a month-to-month basis. Conceptually, however, *all* factory costs—direct materials, direct labor, and overhead—can properly be included in a single factory-department budget. The notion of a flexible budget may also be applied to administrative and selling functions. The key point is not what items are in a particular flexible budget; it is rather the flexibility that is incorporated in the technique.

comparison of static and flexible budgets Consider the following condensed example. The planned level of activity for a machining department, expressed in finished units of production, is 5,000 for the next month. Exhibit 8-1 is the budget for the variable overhead items. (Although other items having various cost behavior patterns could be included, this example is confined to variable overhead in order to highlight the basic idea of a flexible budget.)

EXHIBIT 8-1

MACHINING DEPARTMENT
STATIC BUDGET, VARIABLE OVERHEAD
For the Month of June 19_1

Units to be produced	5,000
Variable overhead:	
Indirect labor	$2,100
Supplies	500
Repairs	400
Total	$3,000

EXHIBIT 8-2

VARIABLE-OVERHEAD PERFORMANCE REPORT

	ACTUAL	BUDGET	VARIANCE
Units produced	4,700	5,000	300 U
Indirect labor	$2,080	$2,100	$ 20 F
Supplies	480	500	20 F
Repairs	400	400	—
Total	$2,960	$3,000	$ 40 F

Assume that June has ended. The units produced were only 4,700, principally because of a work stoppage caused by a storm. Exhibit 8-2 is the performance report that would be prepared under a static-budget approach.

In addition to meeting quality specifications for the product, the foreman of this department has two major obligations: (a) to be effective—that is, to attain his scheduled production volume; and (b) to produce any given output efficiently. These two obligations can and should be separated in judging his total performance. The trouble with the static budget is that it fails to distinguish between these two facets of a manager's performance.

The idea of comparing performance at one activity level with a plan that was developed at some other activity level is nonsense from the viewpoint of judging how *efficiently* a manager has produced any given output. However, such a comparison may be pertinent in judging his *effectiveness*. It shows how well a manager has adhered to a single objective, the meeting of a target production schedule. The foreman and his superiors may wish to know about the top line in Exhibit 8-2, which contains the information that production was only 4,700, rather than 5,000 units. The use of a static budget for this purpose provides helpful information. However, the use of a 5,000-unit budget for judging how efficiently (on the next three lines of the report) the given output of 4,700 units was produced is an example of using a good tool for the wrong purpose.

basic approach of the flexible budget The flexible-budget approach is based on an adequate knowledge of cost behavior patterns. It is essentially a means for constructing a budget tailored to *any* level of activity. In some companies using a flexible-budget technique, the budget for variable overhead would resemble Exhibit 8-3.

Note that the budget would not necessarily have to be shown for the 4,600 to 5,200 activity levels. The essential ingredient is the budget formula, which may be used in constructing a total budget for any given activity level. For example, the performance report prepared at the *end* of June (Exhibit 8-4) shows the application of the budget formula to the 4,700-unit level of activity.

This report shows unfavorable variances, in contrast to the favorable variances in the performance report prepared under the static budget (Exhibit 8-2). Unfavorable variances do not always indicate inefficiency. In this case, the unfavorable performance is largely traceable to outside influences—the storm. Random influences will always affect variances to some extent. However, it should

EXHIBIT 8-3

MACHINING DEPARTMENT
FLEXIBLE BUDGET, VARIABLE OVERHEAD

For the Month of June 19_1

	BUDGET FORMULA*	VARIOUS LEVELS OF ACTIVITY			
Units produced		4,600	4,800	5,000	5,200
Indirect labor	42¢ per unit	$1,932	$2,016	$2,100	$2,184
Supplies	10¢ per unit	460	480	500	520
Repairs	8¢ per unit	368	384	400	416
Total variable overhead	60¢ per unit	$2,760	$2,880	$3,000	$3,120

*The budget formulas used here assume strictly variable behavior. Flexible budgets can often encompass other costs also.

be evident that the flexible budget presents a more meaningful comparison of the foreman's day-to-day overhead-cost control, because the level of activity underlying the comparison is the same. On the other hand, the flexible budget does not directly report the foreman's deviation from his scheduled production volume. The ideal combination, therefore, is a flexible budget for measuring efficient use of input factors, accompanied by information, perhaps expressed in units only, such as that shown at the top of Exhibit 8-4, about the manager's ability to meet any single production schedule (or, in the case of a sales manager, any single sales target).

how should activity be measured? Our example measured activity or volume in terms of units of product. In practice, the measurement of volume is not so easy, except in the rare instance of a department that produces only one uniform product. When there is a variety of products or operations, the following criteria should be of help in selecting a measure of volume.

1. *Cause of Cost Fluctuation.* An individual cost should be related to some activity that causes that cost to vary. Common measures include hours of labor,

EXHIBIT 8-4

MACHINING DEPARTMENT
VARIABLE OVERHEAD PERFORMANCE REPORT

For the Month of June 19_1

Units originally scheduled	5,000			
Units produced	4,700			
	ACTUAL	BUDGET*	VARIANCE	EXPLANATION
Indirect labor	$2,080	$1,974	$106 U	Idle time due to storm
Supplies	480	470	10 U	None offered
Repairs	400	376	24 U	Extra repairs due to storm
Total variable overhead	$2,960	$2,820	$140 U	

*For 4,700 units produced.

machine-hours, weight of materials handled, miles traveled, number of calls made by salesmen, number of beds in a hospital, number of lines billed, number of credit investigations, and so forth.

2. *Independence of Activity Unit.* The activity unit should not be greatly affected by variable factors other than volume. For example, the use of total direct-labor dollars or total dollar sales as a measure of volume is subject to the basic weakness of being changeable by labor-rate or price fluctuations. The use of machine-hours or labor-hours eliminates the unwanted influence of fluctuations in the purchasing power of the dollar. Then, if physical volume does not change, a change in wage rates does not necessarily mean a change in other costs. The effects of price changes should not affect the unit with which activity is measured; this is usually accomplished by using standard wage rates or uniform sales prices.

3. *Ease of Understanding.* Units for the measurement of activity should be easily understandable and should be obtainable at a minimum clerical expense. Complicated indexes are undesirable.

4. *Adequacy of Control over Base.* The common denominator that serves as a measure of activity must be under adequate control. *Because it is not affected by variations in performance, the standard direct-labor hours allowed (or machine-hours allowed) for units produced is a better measure of volume than actual direct-labor hours.* A department head should not enjoy a more generous budget allowance because of his inefficiency, which would increase both the actual hours and his budget—if the budget were based on actual hours instead of standard hours allowed.

If standard allowances are developed for all the factors of production, one factor may be tied to the other so that all factors may be related to a common base. For example, if it takes one pound of direct materials, one grinding wheel, one machine-hour, and one direct-labor hour to produce one finished unit, usage may be related to the standard direct-labor hour as follows: If 1,000 standard direct-labor hours are used, the use of 1,000 units of each of the other factors may be anticipated. These relationships may be expedient and meaningful even though use of grinding wheels, repairs, and the like is most closely related to finished units produced or to an assortment of causal factors. It is because of the latter phenomenon that we have stressed the need for an item-by-item analysis of variances.

To summarize, an index of activity based on actual hours fluctuates with efficiency; it is not a uniform common denominator. The use of standard hours or of some base built on standard hours (for example, standard direct-labor dollars) causes the cost variations due to inefficient usage of the budget-base factor to appear as variances.

spending and efficiency variances   The preceding section stressed the point that volume should be measured in terms of outputs, rather than inputs, for determining flexible-budget allowances. Consider an example where activity is measured in standard direct-labor hours; this is simply a way of expressing *output*. Unless the units of output are known, the standard hours allowed to produce that output cannot be calculated. In contrast, the actual direct labor hours utilized is an *input* concept.

Assume that a department is scheduled to produce 10,000 units of product in 10,000 standard direct-labor hours. However, it has taken 12,000 actual direct-labor hours to produce the 10,000 units. The variable overhead items are as follows:

	BUDGET FORMULA PER STANDARD DIRECT-LABOR HOUR	ACTUAL COSTS INCURRED
Indirect	$1.00	$11,700
Maintenance	.10	1,150
Lubricants	.05	600
Cutting tools	.08	1,500
	$1.23	$14,950

The actual direct-labor rate is $8.10 per hour; the standard rate is $8.00. You are asked to:

1. Prepare a detailed performance report, with two major sections: direct labor and variable overhead.
2. Explain the similarities and differences between the direct-labor and the variable-overhead variances.

One version of a performance report would be highly condensed, as shown at the top of Exhibit 8-5. The budget column is based on the standard hours allowed for the given output. The budget variance is merely the difference between the numbers in the first two columns.

Another version is shown at the bottom of Exhibit 8-5. It begins with an analysis of the direct-labor variance, which is divided between a rate variance and an efficiency variance in the identical way described in the preceding chapter. The subdivision (see Exhibit 8-5) of the budget variance for variable overhead into *spending variance* and *efficiency variance* is similar to the split of the total direct-labor variance into *rate variance* and *efficiency variance*.

The fundamental assumption underlying the usual efficiency-variance computation for variable overhead is simple but fragile: Variable-overhead costs should fluctuate in direct proportion to changes in standard direct-labor hours. Therefore, the efficiency variance for variable overhead is a measure of the extra overhead (or savings) incurred solely because direct-labor usage exceeded (or was less than) the standard direct-labor hours allowed:

Overhead efficiency variance = (Actual hours − Standard hours allowed)
$$\times \text{ Standard overhead rate}$$

Note the similarity between the efficiency variances for direct labor and for variable overhead. Both are differences between actual hours and standard hours allowed, multiplied by a standard rate. For instance, the budget variance

EXHIBIT 8-5

TWO VERSIONS OF A DEPARTMENT PERFORMANCE REPORT
DIRECT LABOR AND VARIABLE OVERHEAD

For the Month of October 19_1

Actual hours, 12,000   Standard hours allowed, 10,000   Excess hours, 2,000

CONDENSED VERSION

	INCURRED	BUDGET	BUDGET VARIANCE
Direct labor	$ 97,200*	$80,000	$17,200 U
Indirect labor	11,700	10,000	1,700 U
Maintenance	1,150	1,000	150 U
Lubricants	600	500	100 U
Cutting tools	1,500	800	700 U
Total	$112,150	$92,300	$19,850 U

DETAILED VERSION

	(1) INPUTS: ACTUAL COSTS INCURRED	(2) INPUTS: BUDGET BASED ON 12,000 ACTUAL DIRECT HOURS	(3) OUTPUTS: BUDGET BASED ON 10,000 STANDARD DIRECT HOURS OF WORK ALLOWED FOR UNITS PRODUCED	(4) (1) – (3) BUDGET VARIANCE TO BE ANALYZED	ANALYSIS OF (4) (1) – (2) SPENDING VARIANCE	(2) – (3) EFFICIENCY VARIANCE
Direct labor	$97,200	$96,000	$80,000	$17,200 U	$1,200 U**	$16,000 U
Variable overhead:						
Indirect labor	$11,700	$12,000	$10,000	$ 1,700 U	$ 300 F	$ 2,000 U
Maintenance	1,150	1,200	1,000	150 U	50 F	200 U
Lubricants	600	600	500	100 U	—	100 U
Cutting tools	1,500	960	800	700 U	540 U	160 U
Total variable overhead	$14,950	$14,760	$12,300	$ 2,650 U	$ 190 U	$ 2,460 U

*12,000 hours @ $8.10

**This $1,200 variance is a direct-labor *rate* variance. The term *spending* variance pertains to overhead items only.

for lubricants in Exhibit 8-5 was $100, unfavorable. Under this approach, the entire variance is attributed to the inefficiency of a related factor, direct labor. That is, because direct labor was inefficiently used by 2,000 hours, or 20 percent of the 10,000 standard hours allowed, we would expect the related usage of lubricants to be proportionately excessive solely because of *labor* inefficiency.

The spending variance is similar to the labor-rate variance, but its causal factors encompass more than price changes alone. Other causes include poor budget estimates for one or more individual overhead items; variation in attention to and control of individual costs; and erratic behavior of individual overhead items that have been squeezed for convenience into a budget formula with only one base (that is, hours of labor). The cost of indirect labor for handling materials, for example, may be closely related to the number of units started during a period and have nothing directly to do with the standard direct-labor hours worked. Also, the usage of cutting tools may be more closely related to machine-hours than to labor-hours. In these days of automation, one laborer may operate several machines simultaneously.

To recapitulate, suppose you investigate why there was a $700 unfavorable variance in Exhibit 8-5 for cutting tools. The performance report implies:

Actual costs		$1,500
Efficiency variance—This is the amount that would be expected to be incurred *because of the inefficient use of direct labor.* Since variable-overhead costs generally fluctuate in relation to corresponding fluctuations in direct-labor costs, the excess use of direct labor would be expected to cause a corresponding increase in the cost of cutting tools of 2,000 × $.08 =	$160	
Spending variance—This is the amount unexplained by the efficiency-variance analysis above. It could arise, say, from a unit *price* change for cutting tools. But it could also arise simply from general waste and inefficient use of such materials. In short, this too could be partially or solely traceable to *more inefficiency,* even though it is labeled as a spending variance.	540	
Total variance		700
Budgeted amount		$ 800

Above all, the limitation of the analyses of variances should be underscored. The *only* way to discover why variable-overhead performance did not agree with the budget is to investigate possible causes, item by item, from Indirect Labor to Maintenance to Lubricants to Cutting Tools. However, the summary analysis yields an overall view that may be used as a springboard for a more rigorous analysis.

use of Note that the budget in Exhibit 8-5 is based on standard hours (output)
standard hours rather than actual hours (input). If it were based on actual hours, the *only*
as a variance that would be produced would be the spending variance, column
budget base (1) minus column (2). There would be no efficiency variances. The manager would get only a partial size-up of performance; he would have a focus

only on input relationships (given the inputs, how much cost should I have incurred?). By basing the budget on standard hours, he focuses on input *and* output relationships (given the outputs, how many inputs should I have incurred?). The standard-hour budget base generates both spending and efficiency variances.

the scope of flexible budgets Earlier in this chapter, the point was made that the term *flexible budget* is often used to describe a department-overhead budget. Moreover, the earlier exhibits were confined to only a few overhead items to illustrate the essential idea that flexible budgets are tailored to cover a relevant range rather than merely one level of activity.

Flexible budgets may be broadened to include all cost (and revenue) items if desired. For example, Exhibit 8-5 showed a first step in that direction by including direct labor as well as variable overhead. Consider Exhibit 8-6. It differs from Exhibit 8-5 in only one respect. It shows how a performance report might appear when fixed costs are included. The portion of the budget attributable to fixed costs will remain constant regardless of fluctuations in production volume, but the variable costs will be affected. Therefore, the budget in such cases could be expressed by the following overall formula: a static portion of $35,000 per month plus variable portions of $8.00 per hour for direct labor and $1.23 per hour for variable overhead. Note that it is the variable-cost portion of the formula that injects the flex into the flexible budget.

EXHIBIT 8-6

CONDENSED DEPARTMENT-PERFORMANCE REPORT
CONVERSION COSTS
For the Month of October 19_1

Actual hours, 12,000   Standard hours allowed, 10,000   Excess hours, 2,000

	INCURRED	BUDGET	BUDGET VARIANCE
Direct labor	$ 97,200	$ 80,000	$17,200 U
Indirect labor	11,700	10,000	1,700 U
Maintenance	1,150	1,000	150 U
Lubricants	600	500	100 U
Cutting tools	1,500	800	700 U
Total variable costs	$112,150	$ 92,300	$19,850 U
Fixed Costs:			
Supervision	$ 14,400	$ 14,000	$ 400 U
Rent	5,000	5,000	—
Depreciation	15,000	15,000	—
Property taxes	1,000	1,000	—
Total fixed costs	$ 35,400	$ 35,000	$ 400 U
Total manufacturing costs	$147,550	$127,300	$20,250 U

Unfortunately for cost analysts, the world cannot be neatly divided between variable and fixed costs. In most organizations, the behavior of each cost item is predicted on a line-by-line basis. Sometimes this is an easy chore, but often careful studies are needed. Therefore, the budget formulas for some individual costs will not be flatly stated as $.80 per hour or as $1,000 per month. Instead, a variety of prediction equations might be utilized.

TYPES OF VARIABLE COSTS

Variable and fixed costs must be viewed as generic terms. In their purest sense, they represent polar ends of a spectrum of various existing cost behavior patterns (cost functions). We now refine our distinctions between costs to include proportionately variable, step, discretionary fixed, committed fixed, and mixed costs.

***assumption of
strict linearity***
Economists tend to draw curved lines for variable costs; accountants tend to draw straight lines for costs. Economists correctly view variable costs as behaving differently at low and high volumes. The accountant usually takes a straight-line approach because he can generally assume that the curve is *straight within the relevant range of activity* (see Exhibit 8-7) with only a small error.

When flexible budgets are prepared, any known curvilinear costs can be included either by formula or by obtaining the appropriate total from a graph of the cost.

EXHIBIT 8-7

VARIABLE COST BEHAVIOR, CURVILINEAR

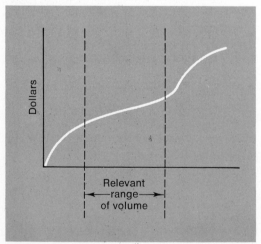

EXHIBIT 8-8

VARIABLE COST BEHAVIOR

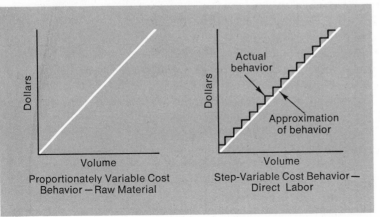

Proportionately Variable Cost
Behavior — Raw Material

Step-Variable Cost Behavior —
Direct Labor

step-like Variable costs are those that are expected to fluctuate, in total, directly
behavior in proportion to sales, production volume, or some other *measure of
activity.* The last is stressed because some items may be variable but may
lead or lag in relation to production or sales. For example, the number of service
calls on product warranties in a given period may have no relation to the sales
or production of that period. Still, the cost of service calls is regarded as variable.

Raw materials are examples of *proportionately variable* costs. These items
may be acquired in the exact quantities needed. Moreover, they may be stored
for future use. They are proportionately variable because they should fluctuate
directly in proportion to changes in activity or volume.

Labor costs of all sorts—direct or indirect, manufacturing or administrative—often represent step-variable costs. These increase or decrease abruptly
at intervals of activity because their acquisition comes in indivisible chunks.
Labor services cannot be stored for future use and are either utilized or lost
as the workday ebbs away. They cannot be turned on or off like a faucet.

The graphs in Exhibit 8-8 show the difference between strict linear variability and step variability of costs. The ideal objective in the planning and
control of step costs is to attain activity or utilization at the highest volume for
any given step. This will maximize returns for each dollar spent, because the
services involved will be fully utilized and their unit cost will be least.

Width of steps. The problems of measurement are much more difficult for
step-variable costs than for proportionately variable costs. The need for a unit
of raw material is easy to determine, but the measurement of direct labor, indirect
labor, administrative labor, and selling labor becomes progressively more difficult.
In practice, secretaries, stockboys, file clerks, and others are frequently subject
to uneven work pressures. They may be able to work intensively or leisurely
for various spurts of time.

237

The width and height of the steps may vary among the types of labor services. For instance, the number of hours worked by each direct laborer may be closely geared to production. The use of overtime, part-time help, or short workweeks may cause the direct-labor-cost steps to be very narrow and very small so that they approximate a strictly variable cost behavior pattern. On the other hand, failures to use part-time help, to gear the workweek to current needs, and to use overtime tend to widen and heighten the labor-cost steps.

Of course, as the steps widen, a so-called step-variable cost may become a "step-fixed" or even a "fixed" cost. Exhibit 8-8 shows how direct labor may be regarded as a variable cost because only a small error is caused by using a straight line instead of a step function. On the other hand, Exhibit 8-9 demonstrates how supervision costs may have wider steps, so that a fixed-cost approximation would be more accurate than a variable-cost approximation for the bulk of the relevant range under consideration.

MIXED COSTS

nature of
mixed costs
As the name implies, a mixed cost has both fixed and variable elements (see Exhibit 8-10). The fixed element represents the minimum cost of supplying a service. The variable element is that portion of the mixed cost that is influenced by changes in activity. An example of a mixed cost is the rental of a delivery truck for a fixed cost per month plus a variable cost based on mileage.

Ideally, there should be no accounts for mixed costs. All such costs should be subdivided into two accounts, one for the variable portion and one for the fixed portion. In practice, these distinctions are rarely made in the recording

EXHIBIT 8-9

STEP-FIXED COST BEHAVIOR
SUPERVISION COSTS

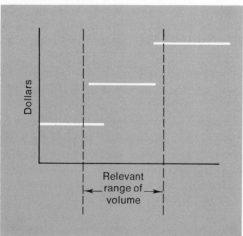

EXHIBIT 8-10

MIXED COST

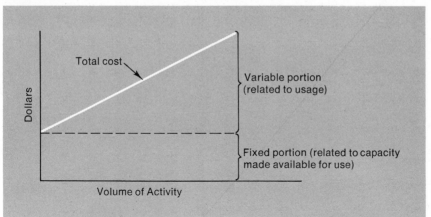

process because of the difficulty of analyzing day-to-day cost data into variable and fixed sections. Costs like power, indirect labor, repairs, and maintenance are generally accounted for in total. It is generally very difficult to decide, as such costs are incurred, whether a particular invoice or work ticket represents a variable or fixed item. Moreover, even if it were possible to make such distinctions, the advantages might not be worth the additional clerical effort and costs. Whenever cost classifications are too refined, the perpetual problem of getting accurate source documents is intensified.

In sum, mixed costs are merely a blend of two unlike cost behavior patterns; they do not entail new conceptual approaches. Anybody who obtains a working knowledge of the planning and controlling of variable and fixed costs, separately, can adapt to a mixed-cost situation when necessary.

***budgeting
mixed costs***   How should mixed costs be budgeted? Ideally, of course, their variable and fixed elements should be isolated and budgeted separately. One widely practiced method is a budget formula that contains both a fixed and a variable element. For example, repairs for delivery trucks might be budgeted at $15 per month plus 1¢ per mile.

The estimation of mixed-cost behavior patterns should preferably begin with a scatter chart of past cost levels, a graph on which dots are plotted to show various historical costs. A line is fitted to the points, either visually or by the statistical method of least squares (described in Chapter 24). The intersection of the line with the vertical axis indicates the amount of the fixed-cost component.

A simplified version of the scatter chart is the *high-low two-point method.* Although this method is not sufficiently accurate for wide use, it illustrates the utility of studying past cost behavior patterns. The high-low two-point method of estimating mixed costs (Exhibit 8-11) requires the plotting of two points, representing the highest cost and the lowest cost, respectively, *over the contemplated relevant range.* A solid line is used to connect the high point and the low

EXHIBIT 8-11

HIGH-LOW TWO-POINT METHOD OF ESTIMATING MIXED COSTS

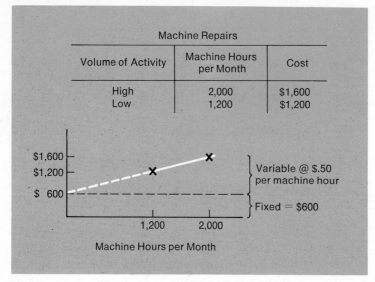

point. This line is extended back to intersect the vertical axis at the height at which the fixed portion of the cost has been plotted ($600 in Exhibit 8-11). The slope, or rate of change, of the line (50¢ per machine-hour) represents the variable portion of the mixed cost. Thus, the formula that depicts the behavior of this mixed cost is $600 per month plus 50¢ per machine-hour.

The same results could be computed by using the following algebraic technique:

$$\text{Variable rate} = \frac{\text{Change in mixed cost}}{\text{Change in machine-hours}}$$

$$= \frac{\$1,600 - \$1,200}{2,000 - 1,200} = \frac{\$400}{800} = \$.50 \text{ per machine-hour}$$

Fixed-overhead component

= Total mixed cost less variable component

At 1,200-hour level of activity:

$$= \$1,200 - \$.50(1,200) = \$1,200 - \$600 = \$600$$

At 2,000-hour level of activity:

$$= \$1,600 - \$.50(2,000) = \$1,600 - \$1,000 = \$600$$

Cost formula = $600 per month plus $.50 per machine-hour

Such cost formulas are only the first step in the budgetary process. The budgeted figures are expected *future* data, so cost formulas must be altered to reflect anticipated changes in prices, efficiency, technology, and other influential factors.

TYPES OF FIXED COSTS

fixed costs provide capacity   Fixed costs are those that are not expected to change in total within the current budget year, regardless of fluctuations in the volume of activity. As companies become more obligated to stabilize employment, and as industry becomes more automated, the likelihood is great that most companies will contend with a higher proportion of fixed costs as compared with variable costs. Because all costs vary in the long run, fixed costs must always be analyzed in relation to given conditions or plans. In general, few day-to-day or month-to-month decisions affect fixed costs, so a company's performance is somewhat locked in by far-reaching decisions concerning fixed costs. That is why the *planning* process is crucial.

Fixed costs, also called *capacity costs*, measure capacity for manufacturing, sales, administration, and research. They reflect the capability for sustaining a planned volume of activity. Once acquired, the capacity should be *utilized* as much as possible—provided, of course, that the increase in revenue exceeds the increase in variable costs as volume increases.

In short, fixed costs have two major implications for management: First, planning is crucial. Second, full utilization of capacity is often desirable.

The size of fixed costs is influenced by long-run marketing conditions, by technology, and by the methods and strategies of management. Examples of the last include sales salaries versus sales commissions and one-shift versus two-shift operations. Fixed costs are often the result of a trade-off decision whereby lower variable costs are attained in exchange for higher fixed costs. For example, automatic equipment may be acquired to reduce labor costs.

Generally, a heavier proportion of fixed to variable costs lessens management's ability to respond to short-run changes in economic conditions and opportunities. Still, unwillingness to incur fixed costs reveals an aversion to risk that may exclude a company from profitable ventures. For instance, the launching of new products often requires very large fixed costs for research, advertising, equipment, and working capital.

committed fixed costs   For planning and control, fixed costs may be usefully subdivided into committed and discretionary costs. *Committed fixed costs* consist largely of those fixed costs that arise from the possession of plant, of equipment, and of a basic organization. Examples are depreciation, property taxes, rent, insurance, and the salaries of key personnel. These costs are affected primarily by long-run sales forecasts that, in turn, indicate the long-run capacity needs.

The behavior of committed fixed costs may best be viewed by assuming a zero volume of activity in an enterprise that fully expects to resume normal activity (for example, during a strike or a shortage of materials that forces a complete shutdown of activity). The committed fixed costs are all those organization and plant costs that continue to be incurred and that cannot be reduced without injuring the organization's competence to meet long-range goals. Committed fixed costs are the least responsive of the fixed costs, because they tend to be less affected by month-to-month and year-to-year decisions.

In planning, the focus is on the impact of these costs over a number of years. Such planning usually requires tailoring the capacity to future demand for the organization's products in the most economical manner. For example, should the store size be 50,000 square feet, or 80,000, or 100,000? Should the gasoline station have one, or two, or more stalls for servicing automobiles? Such decisions usually involve selecting the point of optimal trade-off between present and future operating costs. That is, constructing excess capacity now may save costs in the long run, because construction costs per square foot may be much higher later. On the other hand, if the forecast demand never develops, the organization may own facilities that are unnecessarily idle.

These decisions regarding capital expenditures are generally shown in an annual budget called the *capital budget* or *capital-spending budget.* As you recall, the *master budget* is based primarily on the annual sales forecast, the cornerstone of budgeting. Similarly, all capital-spending decisions are ultimately based on long-range sales forecasts. Capital budgeting is discussed in Chapter 13.

Once buildings are erected and equipment is installed, little can be done in day-to-day operations to affect the *total level* of committed costs. From a control standpoint, the objective is usually to increase current utilization of facilities, because this will ordinarily increase net income.

There is another aspect to the control problem, however. A follow-up, or audit, is needed to find out how well the ensuing utilization harmonizes with the decision that authorized the facilities in the first place. The latter approach helps management to evaluate the wisdom of its past long-range decisions and, in turn, should improve the quality of future decisions.

discretionary fixed costs

Discretionary fixed costs (sometimes called *managed* or *programmed costs*) are fixed costs that arise from periodic (usually yearly) appropriation decisions that directly reflect top-management policies. Discretionary costs may have no particular relation to volume of activity. Examples are research and development, advertising, sales promotion, donations, management consulting fees, and many employee training programs. Conceivably, these costs could be reduced almost entirely for a given year in dire times, whereas the committed costs would be much more difficult to reduce.

Discretionary fixed costs are decided upon by management at the start of the budget period. Goals are selected, the means for their attainment are chosen, the maximum expense to be incurred is specified, and the total amount to be spent is appropriated. For example, a company may appropriate $5 million for an advertising campaign. The company's advertising agency is unlikely to exceed that amount, nor is it likely to spend much less than $5 million in trying to attain the company goals. In the give-and-take of the process of preparing the master budget, the discretionary costs are the most likely to be revised.

Discretionary fixed costs represent an assortment of manufacturing, selling, administrative, and research items. As in the case of committed costs, the resources acquired should be carefully planned and fully utilized if net income is to be maximized. Unlike committed costs, discretionary costs can be influenced more easily from period to period. It is also harder to measure the utilization of resources acquired via discretionary costs, principally because the results of services like creative personnel, advertising, research, and training programs are much more difficult to isolate and quantify than the results of utilizing plant and equipment to make products.

The behavior of some discretionary fixed costs is easy to delineate. Advertising, research, donations, and training programs, for example, are usually formulated with certain objectives in mind. The execution of such projects is measured by comparing total expenditures with the appropriation. Because the tendency is to spend the entire appropriation, the resulting dollar variances are generally trivial. But planning is far more important than this kind of day-to-day control. The perfect execution of an advertising program—in the sense that the full amount authorized was spent in the specified media at the predetermined times—will be fruitless if the advertisements are unimaginative and lifeless and if they reach the wrong audience.

The most noteworthy aspect of discretionary fixed costs is that, unlike most other costs, they are not subject to ordinary engineering input–output analysis. For example, an optimum relationship between inputs and outputs can be specified for direct materials because it takes three pounds or five gallons or two square feet to make a finished product. In contrast, we are usually unsure of the "correct" amount of advertising, research, management training, donations, and management consulting costs.

discretionary costs may not be fixed   Costs are frequently classified into variable, discretionary fixed, and committed fixed categories. The term "discretionary" is usually linked with a class of fixed costs because their behavior falls into that category. However, sometimes a few discretionary costs take on a variable-cost behavior pattern. Therefore, although it is rarely done, the variable costs could be divided into "engineered" and "discretionary" categories. Most types of variable costs have an explicit "engineered" or physical relationship with volume. An "engineered" variable cost exists when an optimum relationship between inputs and outputs is closely specified. For example, an automobile may have exact specifications: one battery, one radiator, two fan belts, and so forth. In short, there is a clear-cut interdependence between sales (or production) levels and many variable costs. However, depending on management policy, there may be other costs that will go up and down with sales (or production) merely because management has predetermined that the organization can afford to spend a certain percentage of the sales dollar for items like research, donations, and advertising. These costs would have a graphical pattern of variability, but not for the same reasons as direct materials or direct labor. An increase in such costs may be due to management's authorization to spend "because we can afford it" rather than because there is an obvious cause-and-effect relationship between such costs and sales.

WORK MEASUREMENT

measurement
is needed
for control

There are two management approaches to cost control. The first, most widespread approach is informal and is heavily dependent on human supervision for successful control. The second approach is more formal and is dependent on work measurement as well as on human supervision for successful control; it is getting more attention from organizations as they seek to improve their efficiency. This approach is based on a fundamental premise: Permanent improvement in any performance is impossible unless the work is measured.

To portray cost behavior as it responds to volume, we need to measure volume (the horizontal axis) as well as cost (the vertical axis). Industrial engineers and others concerned with cost control stoutly maintain that control is impossible without careful measures of work loads and capability. Work measurement began in the factory but has extended into selling and administrative clerical areas in recent years.

Work measurement is the careful analysis of a task, its size, the methods used in its performance, and its efficiency. Its objective is to determine the work load in an operation and the number of workers needed to perform that work efficiently. The techniques used include time and motion study, observation of a random sample of the work (that is, work sampling), and the estimation, by a work-measurement analyst and a line supervisor, of the amount of time required for the work (that is, time analysis). The work load is expressed in *control-factor units*, which are used in formulating the budget.

For example, the control-factor units in a payroll department might include operations performed on time cards, on notices of change in the labor rate, on notices of employee promotion, on new employment and termination reports, and on routine weekly and monthly reports. All of these would be weighed. The estimated work load would then be used for determining the required labor force and budgetary allowance.

Another example of work measurement would be the physical handling of goods in warehousing, shipping, receiving, or shelving. In these instances, a *standard handling unit* may be formulated. The standard handling unit may be a case of goods; then barrels, packages, sacks, and other items "may be expressed as multiple or fractional handling units according to their time-of-handling relationship to that of the case of goods (the standard unit)." [1]

The activity measure used as a budget base may be sales dollars, product units, cases, tons, or some other unit that best reflects cost influence:

[1] Charles H. Sevin, *Marketing Productivity Analysis* (New York: McGraw-Hill Book Company, Inc., 1965), p. 21.

Operation	*Unit of Measure (Control-Factor Unit)*
Billing	Lines per hour
Warehouse labor	Pounds or cases handled per day
Packing	Pieces packed per hour
Posting accounts receivable	Postings per hour
Mailing	Pieces mailed per hour

Standards for certain order-filling activities, such as packing or driving a truck, may necessarily be less refined than for such manufacturing activities as assembly work, but they still provide the best available formal tool for planning and control. For example, short-interval scheduling has been attempted; this technique routes all work through a supervisor, who batches the work in hourly lots. This develops standards, controls backlogs, and provides close follow-up.[2]

The measurement of work often spurs controversy, because employees do not usually welcome more stringent monitoring of their productivity. Despite some delicate problems of human relations, there is an increasing tendency for work measurement to be applied in office, transportation, and other nonmanufacturing activities.

budgeting of order-filling and administrative costs: two approaches

There is much disagreement about how order-filling and administrative costs should be controlled. Advocates of work measurement favor a more rigorous approach, which essentially regards these costs as variable. In contrast, a discretionary-cost approach, which basically regards these costs as fixed, is more often found in practice.

Assume that ten payroll clerks are employed, and that each clerk's operating efficiency *should be* the processing of the pay records of 500 employees per month. In the month of June, 4,700 individuals' pay records were processed by these ten clerks. Each clerk earns $600 per month. The variances shown by the variable-cost approach and the discretionary fixed-cost approach are tabulated below and graphed in Exhibit 8-12.

The engineered variable-cost approach: perfection standards. The engineered variable-cost approach to this situation is to base the budget formula on the unit cost of the individual pay record processed—$600 ÷ 500 records, or $1.20. Therefore, the budget allowance for payroll-clerk labor would be $1.20 × 4,700, or $5,640. Assume that the ten employees worked throughout the month. The following performance report would be prepared:

	ACTUAL COST	FLEXIBLE BUDGET: TOTAL STANDARD QUANTITY ALLOWED FOR GOOD UNITS PRODUCED	BUDGET VARIANCE
Payroll clerk labor	$6,000	$5,640	$360 U
	(10 × $600)	(4,700 × $1.20)	

[2]Vincent Melore, "Cutting Payroll Costs in Manufacturing Staffs," *Management Services,* Vol. 1, No. 3, 24.

EXHIBIT 8-12

	Budget as a Variable Cost (ideal)	Budget as a Discretionary Cost (currently attainable)
Actual cost incurred	$6,000	$6,000
Budget allowance	5,640*	6,000
Variance	360 *U*	0

*Rate = $6,000 ÷ 5,000 records or $1.20 per record; total = 4,700 records @ $1.20 = $5,640.

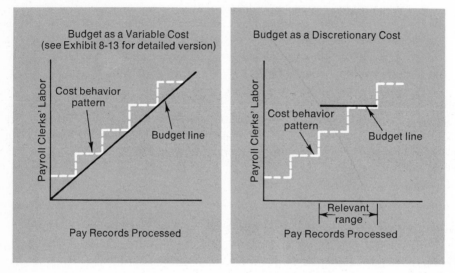

A graphic representation of what has occurred (Exhibit 8-13) may yield insight.

Essentially, two decisions must be made in this operation. The first is a policy decision. How many clerks do we need? How flexible should we be? How divisible is the task? Should we use part-time help? Should we hire and fire as the volume of work fluctuates? The implication of these questions is that once the hiring decision is made, the total costs incurred can be predicted easily— $6,000 in our example.

The second decision concentrates on day-to-day control, on how efficiently and effectively the given resources are being utilized. The work-measurement approach is an explicit and formal attempt to measure the utilization of resources by:

1. Assuming a proportionately variable budget and the complete divisibility of the work load into small units. Note that the budget line on the graph in Exhibit 8-13 is proportionately variable, despite the fact that the costs are really incurred in steps.
2. Generating a budget variance that assumes a comparison of actual costs with a perfection standard—the cost that would be incurred if payroll-clerk labor could be turned on and off like a faucet. In this case, the variance of $360 informs management that there was overstaffing (that is, the tenth step was only partially utilized). The work-load capability was 5,000 pay records, not the 4,700 actually processed. $360 is the extra cost that resulted from operating in a way that does not attain the lowest possible cost, even though

this may not be the result of a conscious decision but merely the effect of producing the volume that satisfies the monthly changes in demand. Robert Beyer writes that such a variance points out "an area in which the managers should be alert for cost reduction opportunities, since alternatives may be available." [3] Such an approach provides a measure ($360) of the amount that management is currently investing to provide stability in the work force.

Advocates of work measurement maintain that such an approach is the only reliable way to satisfy management's desire to plan and control such costs. The use of a tight budget based on ideal standards generates variances that upon investigation will reveal either or both of the following: (a) inefficient use or underutilization of available personnel (for instance, perhaps 5,000 individual payroll records had to be processed, and other clerks or supervisors had to pitch in to get all the work done); (b) the cost of a management policy of deliberately retaining personnel to service long-run needs even though the volume of the current work load is insufficient (for instance, the maximum work available for

[3] *Profitability Accounting for Planning and Control* (New York: The Ronald Press Company, 1963), p. 162.

EXHIBIT 8-13

STEP-VARIABLE COSTS AND VARIANCES

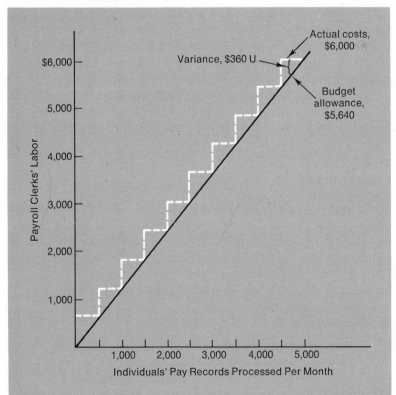

payroll clerical labor may be 4,700 individual payroll records and the individual work may have been performed with complete efficiency).

The discretionary fixed-cost approach: currently attainable standards. Work-measurement techniques are not used in the vast majority of organizations. Consequently, the tendency is to rely on the experience of the department head and his superior for judging the size of the work force needed to carry out the department's functions. There is a genuine reluctance to overhire because there is a corresponding slowness in discharging or laying off people when volume slackens. As a result, temporary peak loads are often met by hiring temporary workers or by having the regular employees work overtime.

In most cases, the relevant range of activity during the budget period can be predicted with assurance, and the work force needed for the marketing and administrative functions can be readily determined. If management refuses, consciously or unconsciously, to rigidly control costs in accordance with short-run fluctuations in activity, these costs become discretionary. That is, their total amount is relatively fixed and unresponsive to short-run variations in volume.

Hence, there is a conflict between common practice and the objective of work measurement, which is to treat most costs as variable and so subject them to short-range management control. *The moral is that management's attitudes and its planning and controlling decisions often determine whether a cost is fixed or variable. A change in policy can transform a fixed cost into a variable cost, and vice versa.*

Moreover, management may regard a cost as a discretionary fixed cost for *cash-planning purposes* in the preparation of the master budget but may use the variable-cost approach for *control purposes* in the preparation of flexible budgets for performance evaluation. These two views may be reconciled within the same overall system. In our example, a master budget conceivably could include the following item:

Payroll-clerk labor:	
Flexible-budget allowance for control	$5,640
Expected flexible-budget variance (due to deliberate overstaffing)	360
Total budget allowance for cash planning	$6,000

The common impression, which is reinforced by work-measurement approaches, is that control should be constantly exerted to be effective. However, the National Association of Accountants comments:

> In one company, where considerable study had been devoted to determining how costs ought to be affected by volume changes, it was concluded that certain costs (e.g., maintenance) which management had attempted to control with current volume could better be controlled as managed [i.e., discretionary] capacity costs. While this conclusion was contrary to management's impression that it was desirable to control costs with current volume wherever possible, trials showed savings when all relevant factors including quality and reliability of services were included in the comparison.[4]

[4] *Accounting for Costs of Capacity, N.A.A. Research Report No. 39* (New York, 1963), p. 13.

Follow-up of discretionary fixed costs.   Thus, we see that control may be exercised (a) in the commonly accepted sense of the day-to-day follow-up that is associated with variable costs; and (b) in the special sense of periodically evaluating an expenditure, relating it to the objectives sought, and carefully planning the total amount of the cost for the ensuing period. The latter approach does not mean that day-to-day follow-up is neglected; follow-up is necessary to see that the resources made available are being used fully and efficiently. It does mean that perceptive planning is stressed and that daily control is de-emphasized. Reliance is placed more on hiring capable people and less on frequent checking up.

The practical effects of the discretionary fixed-cost approach are that the budgeted costs and the actual costs tend to be very close, so that resulting budget variances are small. Follow-ups to see that the available resources are being fully and efficiently utilized are regarded as the managers' responsibility, a duty that can be achieved by face-to-face control and by records of physical quantities (for example, pounds handled per day in a warehouse, pieces mailed per hour in a mailing room) that do not have to be formally integrated into the accounting records in dollar terms.

difficulties in   The success of the work-measurement, engineered variable-cost approach
applying work   to order-filling and administrative costs is limited by the nature of the work
measurement   being performed. Attempts have been made to measure the work of legal personnel and claims adjusters in insurance companies, of economists in a Federal Reserve Bank, and of stockboys in retail stores. Such attempts have achieved only limited success because of either (a) the inability to develop a satisfactory control-factor unit, (b) the diversity of tasks and objectives of such personnel, or (c) the difficulty of measuring the output of lawyers or economists.

For example, consider the attempt to measure the work of clerks and stockboys in a food store. Their tasks are routine and repetitive, but they are often splintered. Attempts at measuring employee work have shown volatile results. Such results indicate that there are opportunities for better utilization of personnel. The trouble is that each employee usually performs a variety of tasks on a variety of items. He may unpack, price-mark, stock shelves, operate a cash register, bag groceries, cart groceries to automobiles, sweep floors, and watch for shoplifters.

Control-factor units may be satisfactorily established for each individual task, but the comparison of results must be made with care. For instance, a comparison showed that in one store, productivity was 14 cases of frozen food per man-hour for receiving, price-marking, and displaying; in another, the productivity was 22 cases per hour.[5] These results may prompt investigation in the low-productivity store, but other factors may narrow the apparent difference in productivity. Such overstaffing may occur because, after experimentation, the store manager has decided that his local competitive situation requires a

---

[5] *The Economics of Frozen Foods,* McKinsey-Birds Eye Study, General Foods Corporation (White Plains, N.Y.: 1964), p. 37.

certain number of clerks and stockboys to service customers. Merchandise characteristics are secondary, and the "case per hour" figure may reflect a more leisurely work pace simply because the alternative is idle time during a certain span of the day. The point is that an able store manager, one who can see the jointness of the problem and who is willing to experiment and to compare his practices with those of other stores, is still the key to successful operations. Work measurement is helpful, because measurement is a first step toward control. But it is only a step.

DETERMINING COST FUNCTIONS

The process of determining cost behavior patterns (cost functions) can become complex. It is described in more detail in Chapter 24; however, some major points are summarized here. Except when they are unavailable, historical costs often provide the starting point for determining cost functions. The term *cost estimation*[6] is often used to describe the attempt to measure historical costs for the ultimate purpose of facilitating the prediction of expected costs for decision purposes.

industrial-engineering approach   The engineering approach involves a study to find the most efficient means of achieving wanted production. It entails a systematic review of materials, labor, services, and facilities needed to accomplish objectives. Time and motion studies and evaluation of men and materials are essentials. The industrial-engineering staff works in conjunction with those people responsible for budgets. Engineers express requirements in terms of physical measures—hours of labor, tons of material, number of supervisors, and so forth. Then the physical measures are transformed into dollar budgets by the application of appropriate unit prices.

Standard costs are usually determined for direct materials and direct labor. If they reflect current price levels, these standard costs are usually used in building the budget for materials and labor. Other costs are studied separately. To illustrate, indirect labor is usually divided into its components, such as janitorial, clerical, supervisory, inspection, and so forth. Each individual labor duty is reviewed in the setting of the budget. The duty is examined with respect to its characteristics and objectives. The number of employees needed for each duty at two or more volumes is then determined. When converted into dollar cost, these data compose the basis for the flexible budget. Similar procedures are used in budgeting other costs.

---

[6] Many accountants and managers tend to regard historical costs as "actual" or "true" costs. This is misleading, because the accountant's measures of costs are heavily affected by many assumptions and averages. Consequently, some accountants and statisticians distinguish between *cost estimation*, which in their minds is an attempt to measure historical costs, and *cost prediction*. Unfortunately, that distinction is not universal. As you know, the accountant and the layman often use *estimated cost* and *cost estimation* to describe forecasts or predictions. Consequently, be on guard when you encounter the term, to make sure of its meaning in a particular situation.

direct   A frequently used but crude way to classify costs into variable and fixed
estimate   categories is to inspect the chart of accounts. Sometimes historical data
are unavailable for use in projecting future costs, management decisions
cause historical cost patterns to change, or specific cost predictions, such as new
supervision and terminal wage payments, are nearly impossible to approach by
other methods. In these cases, predictions are usually prepared for each mixed
cost at several volume levels within the anticipated activity range. The executives
concerned usually agree on amounts after discussion and the use of analytical
studies made by the industrial-engineering and budget staffs.

past   Past experience is used as a guide for predicting the future. Simple statistical
experience and   or mathematical techniques are usually adequate analytical tools.
statistical   The scatter chart is often used to analyze cost variation. As Exhibit 8-14
tools   shows, past monthly behavior of individual costs at different volumes is
plotted on separate charts. Scrutiny of the scatter of points will indicate the
degree of correlation between cost and volume. A clear pattern of behavior of the
points is indicative of a high degree of correlation. A widely dispersed arrangement
of points is indicative of low correlation.

       If the position of the plotted points indicates that cost follows volume, a
line is either visually located or is fitted to the points by the method of least
squares, or multiple regression may be used in complex cases. This line indicates
the specific dollar cost to be budgeted at different volumes. The slope of the
line reflects the rate at which the particular cost has fluctuated with each unit
change in volume. If cost behavior is irregular, so that it is difficult to fit the
data to a formula, the graph is used as a basis for assigning costs at different
activity levels directly to a department budget.

       One of the dangers in overreliance on the statistical analysis of past cost
behavior is the tendency to ignore other important factors. *Concern with the
past is justified only insofar as it helps prediction.* Management wants to plan
what costs should be, not what costs have been.

EXHIBIT 8-14

SCATTER CHARTS

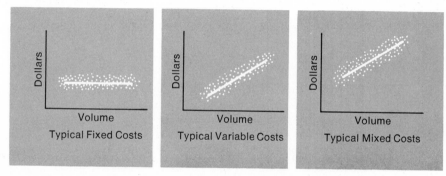

Typical Fixed Costs   Typical Variable Costs   Typical Mixed Costs

The scatter chart is probably the most important single tool available for estimating the past behavior of costs. A careful scrutiny of such a chart by knowledgeable managers will yield many insights about cost behavior that cannot be obtained by using statistical formulas. The indiscriminate use of data without such scrutiny will tend to overlook the past quirks in behavior that are obvious to the observer of a scatter chart. These quirks, such as strikes, material shortages, inclement weather, and clerical errors in accruals or classifications, must be eliminated or adjusted before a useful estimate of behavior can be formulated. Moreover, seeming inconsistencies in the data on a scatter chart may indicate that factors other than volume or activity have also significantly affected cost behavior. This may necessitate the use of more sophisticated techniques.

In industry, a crucial assumption is commonly made when cost behavior is estimated—that costs go up and down solely because of fluctuations in the volume of one causative factor. Such an assumption may be practical and adequate in many cases, but it is a simplification that may prove dangerous. *There is frequently more than one causative factor:* for example, product mix, material yield, weather, sizes of production runs, number of setups, weight, time, and so forth. The costs of a shipping department may be affected not only by the numbers of orders processed; other influences may be weather and the weight of the units. If these factors are important, even the simple least-squares method would be inadequate. Multiple regression should then be used, because it measures the influence of more than one factor on costs. Computers have made multiple-regression analysis economically feasible, so we can expect to see such analysis used more widely. Although regression analysis is a valuable tool for management, it has many pitfalls and should be conducted only by analysts who have adequate statistical skills.[7]

For our purposes, we can get an introductory grasp of the overall problems without using such advanced statistical techniques.

nonvolume influences   Many factors besides volume cause costs to vary. *N.A.A. Research Series No. 16*, p. 1229, points out that when costs show a poor correlation with volume, "it is necessary to assume that these nonvolume factors affecting costs will remain constant for the period during which the conclusions are to be applied." The combined effect on costs of the factors discussed below tend to becloud the fluctuations due to volume alone. Some adjustment or selection of data is usually needed before the rate at which cost should vary with volume can be formulated.

Nonvolume factors include:

1. *Changes in Plant and Equipment.* Mechanization or reshuffling of plant and equipment may make it necessary to ignore certain prior cost behavior.

2. *Changes in Products Made, Materials Used, or Methods of Manufacture.*

---

[7] For elaboration, see George J. Benston, "Multiple Regression Analysis of Cost Behavior," *Accounting Review,* October 1966, pp. 657–72.

Where such changes alter cost behavior, experience with prior changes and the probable effect of the current changes must be used as a basis for forecasting.

3. *Changes in Organization, Personnel, Working Hours or Conditions, and Efficiency.* In particular, where variable costs have not been effectively controlled in relation to volume, a scatter chart is likely to show a poor correlation between cost and volume.

4. *Changes in Prices Paid for Cost Factors.* Projected costs should reflect the expected price level of various factors for both variable and fixed costs.

5. *Changes in Managerial Policy Toward Costs.* Changes in policy such as the following affect costs: layoffs, voluntary labor turnover, purchasing policies, research, and advertising.

6. *Lag Between Cost Incurrence and Measurement of Volume.* When costs are incurred long before production emerges, great care must be taken in the selection of the measure of volume. It is best to measure volume in these cases by input (labor hours), not output (finished units).

7. *Random Fluctuation of Costs.* Costs sometimes deviate from their regular pattern during certain periods, owing to wars, strikes, labor slowdowns, changes in supervisors, and so forth. (See *N.A.A. Research Series No. 16*, pp. 1230–33.)

8. *Seasonal Costs.* Costs such as heating and air conditioning are often more closely related to the weather than to any other factor. Furthermore, efficiency may be influenced by general weather conditions, such as prolonged hot spells.

summary

A flexible budget is a budget that may be tailored to any level of activity, so that the evaluation of efficiency (the relation of inputs to outputs) is not contaminated by comparing a budget for one level of activity with results for another level of activity. Although they are most often associated with the control of overhead, flexible budgets may also include direct materials and direct labor. Flexible budgets are based on careful studies of cost behavior patterns; therefore, they may be fitted to a particular volume—before or after the fact.

Flexible budgets tell how much cost should be incurred for any level of *output*, which is usually expressed in product units or standard direct-labor hours. Because it is not affected by variations in performance, the standard direct-labor hours allowed is a better yardstick than actual direct-labor hours for measuring volume or activity.

When variable overhead is closely associated with direct-labor costs, the efficiency variance for variable-overhead items might be better labeled as a "labor efficiency" variance. This is because the efficiency variance is an estimation of how much more (or less) variable overhead would be expected solely because of the inefficiency (or extra efficiency) of direct labor.

The most important aspect of intelligent cost planning is an understanding of cost behavior patterns and influences. The behavior patterns may be roughly divided between variable and fixed. However, there are proportionately variable, step-variable, step-fixed, mixed, committed fixed, and discretionary fixed costs. Moreover, there are curvilinear as well as linear behavior patterns. The accountant tends to oversimplify these behavior patterns. Whether this simplification is justified depends on how sensitive the manager's decisions are to the errors that the simplifications might generate. In some cases, additional accuracy may not make any difference; in other cases, it may be significant.

The job of cost analysis is quickly complicated in the real world by a variety of causal factors that underlie any particular result. Modern cost accounting offers useful techniques, although they sometimes seem too crude for the task at hand. Measurement frequently seems to be performed with a yardstick rather than with a micrometer. But a yardstick is sufficient for many measurement problems for which a micrometer is either unnecessary or impractical.

suggested readings

Beyer, Robert, *Profitability Accounting for Planning and Control.* New York: The Ronald Press Company, 1963. Beyer's book is particularly strong in the area of flexible budgeting.

N.A.A. Research Reports No. 16–18 and *N.A.A. Practice Report No. 10* explore the subject of flexible budgeting and estimating cost behavior patterns thoroughly.

Problems for Self-Study

PROBLEM 1   The Rank Company had scheduled production of 1,000 units of product in 1,000 hours. However, it has taken 1,100 hours to manufacture the 1,000 units. The variable-overhead items are:

	EXPECTED COST BEHAVIOR PER STANDARD DIRECT-LABOR HOUR	COSTS INCURRED
Rework and inspection	$ .60	$ 720
Cleanup time	.20	250
Oilers and cleaners	.10	120
Maintenance	.10	130
	$1.00	$1,220

required   1. Prepare a detailed performance report for the foreman, showing:

(1) INCURRED	(2) BUDGET BASED ON 1,100 ACTUAL HOURS	(3) BUDGET BASED ON 1,000 STANDARD HOURS ALLOWED	(4) (1) – (3) TOTAL BUDGET VARIANCE	ANALYSIS OF (4)	
				(1) – (2) SPENDING VARIANCE	(2) – (3) EFFICIENCY VARIANCE

2. The analysis in part 1 basically assumed that the budget allowances were based on the standard hours allowed for good *output*. Repeat part 1, but assume that budget allowances are based solely on actual hours worked (inputs). What would be the total budget variance? Could it be subdivided for further analysis?

SOLUTION 1 1.

	(1) INPUTS: INCURRED	(2) INPUTS: BUDGET BASED ON 1,100 ACTUAL HOURS OF WORK DONE	(3) OUTPUTS: BUDGET BASED ON 1,000 STANDARD HOURS OF WORK ALLOWED FOR UNITS PRODUCED	(4) (1) – (3) TOTAL BUDGET VARIANCE	ANALYSIS OF (4)	
					(1) – (2) SPENDING VARIANCE	(2) – (3) EFFICIENCY VARIANCE
Rework and inspection	$ 720	$ 660	$ 600	$120 U	$ 60 U	$ 60 U
Cleanup time	250	220	200	50	30	20
Oilers and cleaners	120	110	100	20	10	10
Maintenance	130	110	100	30	20	10
Total variable overhead	$1,220	$1,100	$1,000	$220 U	$120 U	$100 U

2. A performance report based solely on actual hours worked would have three columns. The first two would coincide with columns (1) and (2) in requirement 1. The third would coincide with the Spending Variance column in requirement 1, but now it would be labeled as the Total Budget Variance, $120. As a total budget variance, this variance could not be subdivided for further analysis in a manner similar to requirements 1 and 2.

Think carefully about the differences in approach. Ideally, a performance report based on *both* bases, such as the one in requirement 1, would be most informative. If one base is to be used, standard hours is the better base because the overhead budget will not be influenced by the variations in usage of the labor hours (inputs) that formulate the base. In other words, an unchanging yardstick based on good output is used to judge cost incurrence. The amount of overhead that a department head should incur is not increased because the usage (input) of direct labor has been excessive. Furthermore, the use of standard hours (*output-oriented*) as a budget base generates two subvariances, *efficiency* and *spending*, whereas the use of actual hours as the budget base generates only the *spending* variance.

PROBLEM 2 The Alic Co. has many small accounts receivable. Work measurement of billing labor has shown that a billing clerk can process 2,000 customers' accounts per month. The company employs 30 billing clerks at an annual salary of $4,800 each. The outlook for next year is for a decline in the number of customers, from 59,900 to 56,300 per month.

required 1. Assume that management has decided to continue to employ the 30 clerks despite the expected drop in billings. Show two approaches, the variable-cost approach and the discretionary fixed-cost approach, to the budgeting of billing labor. Show how the *performance report* for the year would appear under each approach.

2. Some managers favor using tight budgets as motivating devices for controlling operations. In these cases, the managers really expect an unfavorable

variance and must allow, in financial planning, for such a variance so that adequate cash will be available as needed. What would be the budgeted variance, also sometimes called expected variance, in this instance?

3. Assume that the workers are reasonably efficient. (a) Interpret the budget variances under the variable-cost approach and the discretionary fixed-cost approach. (b) What should management do to exert better control over clerical costs?

SOLUTION 2   1. Variable-cost approach:

Standard Unit Rate = $4,800 ÷ 2,000 = $2.40 per customer per year
or = $ .20 per customer per month

	ACTUAL COST	FLEXIBLE BUDGET: TOTAL STANDARD QUANTITY ALLOWED FOR GOOD UNITS PRODUCED × STANDARD UNIT RATE	BUDGET VARIANCE
Billing-clerk labor	(30 × $4,800)	(56,300 × $.20 × 12 months)	
	$144,000	$135,120	$8,800 U

Discretionary fixed-cost approach:

	ACTUAL COST	BUDGET	BUDGET VARIANCE
Billing-clerk labor	$144,000	$144,000	—

2. The budgeted variance would be $8,880 unfavorable. The master budget for financial planning must provide for labor costs of $144,000; therefore, if the variable-cost approach were being used for control, the master budget might specify:

Billing-clerk labor:	
Control-budget allowance	$135,120
Expected control-budget variance	8,880
Total budget allowance for financial planning	$144,000

3. As the chapter explains, management decisions and policies are often of determining importance in categorizing a cost as fixed or variable. If management refuses, as in this case, to control costs rigidly in accordance with short-run fluctuations in activity, these costs are discretionary. The $8,880 variance represents the price that management, consciously or unconsciously, is willing to pay currently in order to maintain a stable work force geared to management's ideas of "normal needs."

Management should be given an approximation of such an extra cost. There is no single "right way" to keep management informed on such matters. Two approaches were demonstrated in the previous parts of this problem. The important point is that clerical work loads and capability must be measured before effective control may be exerted. Such measures may be formal or informal. The latter is often achieved through a supervisor's regular observation, so that he knows how efficiently work is being performed.

questions, problems, and cases

8-1. Why do techniques for overhead control differ from techniques for control of direct materials and direct labor?

8-2. When can't the terms *budgeted performance* and *standard performance* be used interchangeably?

8-3. What two basic questions must be asked in approaching the control of overhead?

8-4. Define: *step cost, mixed cost.*

8-5. "For practical purposes, curvilinear variable costs almost always may be treated as if they had straight-line behavior." Why?

8-6. What factors must management consider in the year-to-year planning of fixed costs?

8-7. "There are different types of fixed costs." Explain.

8-8. "The idea of comparing performance at one activity level with a plan that was developed at some other activity level must be pertinent in judging the effectiveness of planning and control." Comment.

8-9. Why is the title "flexible budget" a misnomer?

8-10. "If only one budget base is to be used for appraising performance, *standard* direct-labor hours is a better base than *actual* direct-labor hours." Do you agree? Why?

8-11. List four criteria for selecting a volume base.

8-12. List six factors besides volume that cause costs to vary.

8-13. Flexible and Static Budgets. Torrance Transportation Company executives have had trouble interpreting operating performance for a number of years. The company has used a budget based on detailed expectations for the forthcoming quarter. For example, the condensed performance report for a recent quarter for a midwestern branch was (in dollars):

	BUDGET	ACTUAL	VARIANCE
Net revenue	10,000,000	9,500,000	500,000 U
Fuel	200,000	196,000	4,000 F
Repairs and maintenance	100,000	98,000	2,000 F
Supplies and miscellaneous	1,000,000	985,000	15,000 F
Variable payroll	6,700,000	6,500,000	200,000 F
Total variable costs*	8,000,000	7,779,000	221,000 F
Supervision	200,000	200,000	—
Rent	200,000	200,000	—
Depreciation	600,000	600,000	—
Other fixed costs	200,000	200,000	—
Total fixed costs	1,200,000	1,200,000	—
Total costs charged against revenue	9,200,000	8,979,000	221,000 F
Net operating income	800,000	521,000	279,000 U

*For purposes of this analysis, assume that all these costs are totally variable. In practice, many are mixed and have to be subdivided into variable and fixed components before a meaningful analysis can be made.

Although the branch manager was upset about not obtaining enough revenue, he was happy that his control performance was favorable; otherwise his net operating income would be even worse.

His immediate superior, the vice-president for operations, was totally unhappy and remarked, "I can see some merit in comparing actual performance with budgeted performance in the sense that we can see whether actual revenue coincided with our best guess for budget purposes. But I can't see how this performance report helps me evaluate the cost-control performance of the department head."

required

1. (a) As vice-president, what two major questions about the branch manager's performance would you want answered? (b) Prepare a performance report that might provide the vice-president with better insight into the branch manager's performance in relation to the questions.

2. Prepare a columnar flexible budget for expected costs at $9-, $10-, and $11-million levels of revenue. Include both variable and fixed costs in your budget.

3. Express requirement 2 in formula form.

4. In light of requirements 1 through 3, evaluate the contention that performance reports should exclude fixed costs.

8-14. **Fundamentals of Flexible Budgets.** The Barry Company produces one uniform product. The assembly department encounters wide fluctuations in activity levels from month to month. However, the following department-overhead budget depicts expectations of currently attainable efficiency for an "average" or "normal" level of activity of 20,000 units of production per month:

	BUDGET— NORMAL MONTH	INCURRED "ACTUAL" COSTS IN JUNE
Indirect labor—variable	$20,000	$19,540
Supplies—variable	1,000	1,000
Power—variable	1,000	980
Repairs—variable	1,000	880
Other variable overhead	2,000	1,800
Depreciation—fixed	10,000	10,000
Other fixed overhead	5,000	5,000
	$40,000	$39,200

required

1. Prepare a columnar flexible budget at 16,000-, 20,000-, and 24,000-unit levels of activity.

2. Express requirement 1 in formula form.

3. In June, the department operated at a 17,600-unit level of activity. Prepare two performance reports, comparing actual performance with (a) budget at normal activity and (b) budget at a 17,600-unit level of activity.

4. Which comparison, 3(a) or 3(b), would be more helpful in judging the foreman's efficiency? Why?

5. Sketch a graph (not necessarily to exact scale) of how the flexible-budget total behaves over the 16,000- to 24,000-unit range of activity. Sketch a

graph of how the variable-overhead items behave and of how the fixed-overhead items behave. Why is the "flex" in the flexible budget confined to variable overhead?

8-15. Fundamentals of Flexible Budgets.   John Harrow, the manager of a finishing department for the Maddick Manufacturing Company, was very pleased with his performance report for the past week. Some selected indirect-cost items included:

	BUDGETED COST BEHAVIOR PATTERN PER DIRECT-LABOR HOUR	BUDGET BASED ON 40,000 ACTUAL LABOR HOURS	ACTUAL	VARIANCE AMOUNT	VARIANCE PERCENTAGE OF BUDGET
Repairs	$1.00	$40,000	$36,000	$4,000 F	10%
Rework	.50	20,000	20,000	—	—
Material handling	.90	36,000	33,000	3,000 F	8%
Grinding and polishing wheels	.60	24,000	22,000	2,000 F	8%

The new production manager, Charles Bohane, examined the report and found it unrevealing. He asked you, because you had moved with Bohane to the Maddick Company from a management consulting firm, to reconstruct the performance report. Bohane said, "I want a report that is more analytical, one that will really give me a monitoring of efficiency in that department."

Your investigation showed that 33,000 standard direct-labor hours should have been allowed for the finished output of the department.

required

1. For the four selected items, prepare a performance report that will probably be more revealing to Mr. Bohane.

2. Why is your report in requirement 1 better than the one that had been used? Be specific.

3. How can such indirect-cost items as repairs, rework, material handling, and grinding wheels be related to direct-labor hours as an activity base? Would you prefer other activity bases? Explain.

8-16. Flexible Budget, Selection of Appropriate Activity Base, and Analysis of Variable-Overhead Variances.   The Selkirk Company has produced 10,000 units of product. The *standard direct-labor hours allowed* (also called *standard hours earned* or *standard hours worked*) were 2 hours per unit, or a total of 20,000 hours. The actual direct-labor hours worked were 21,000. The standard direct-labor rate is $3 per hour. Actual direct-labor costs totaled $65,100. Variable overhead was divided into the following categories:

INCURRED	TYPE OF OVERHEAD ITEM	STANDARD COST BEHAVIOR PATTERN*
$14,700	Indirect labor—variable	$ .70
2,000	Supplies—variable	.10
2,200	Repairs—variable	.10
2,100	Power—variable	.10
$21,000	Total variable overhead	$1.00

*Per standard direct-labor hour.

required

1. Standard costs applied to production have sometimes been referred to as a function of *outputs*, whereas actual costs incurred have sometimes been called a function of *inputs*. Analyze the variances for direct labor and then comment on your analysis in relation to the outputs–inputs distinction and to the terminology distinction between *standard hours worked* and *actual hours worked*.

2. Prepare a detailed performance report for the foreman, showing:

(1) INCURRED	(2) BUDGET BASED ON 21,000 HOURS	(3) BUDGET BASED ON 20,000 HOURS	(4) (1) – (3) TOTAL BUDGET VARIANCE	ANALYSIS OF (4)	
				(1) – (2) SPENDING VARIANCE	(2) – (3) EFFICIENCY VARIANCE

3. Prepare a summary analysis of the total variance for total variable overhead.

4. The analysis in parts 2 and 3 basically assumed that the budget allowances were based on the standard hours allowed for good *output*. Repeat parts 2 and 3, but assume that budget allowances are based solely on actual hours worked (inputs). What would be the total budget variance? Could it be subdivided for further analysis?

5. Compare and contrast the rate and efficiency variances of direct labor with the spending and efficiency variances of variable overhead.

8-17. **Flexible Budget; Selection of Volume Base.**   The variable-overhead components of a machining cost center include:

COSTS INCURRED THIS WEEK		COST BEHAVIOR PATTERN FOR WEEKLY BUDGET PER DIRECT-LABOR HOUR
	Indirect labor:	
$ 225	Inspectors	$ .15
30	Rework	.05
175	Idle time	None allowed for
425	Material handling	.30
340	Setup time	.20
90	Oilers and cleaners	.05
	Overtime premium	.10
	Supplies:	
200	Grinding and polishing wheels	.15
70	Paints and lubricants	.05
90	Miscellaneous	.05
420	Maintenance and repairs	.20
165	Power	.10
$2,230	Total per direct-labor hour	$1.40

The cost center was scheduled to work 2,000 standard direct-labor hours for a given week.

A severe thunderstorm in midweek forced a temporary curtailment of power and cut production to 1,500 standard hours of work done.[8] Actual time devoted to the work accomplished was 1,600 hours.

required   1. Prepare a performance report for the foreman, showing:

(1) INCURRED	(2) BUDGET BASED ON 1,600 HOURS	(1) − (2) VARIANCE	(3) BUDGET BASED ON 1,500 HOURS	(1) − (3) VARIANCE

2. From the point of view of control budgets, should management base budget allowances on actual hours worked or on standard hours worked? Why?

3. How can such overhead items as inspection labor, setup time, and grinding wheels be related to direct-labor hours as an activity base? What other possible bases seem more sensible?

8-18. **Control of Discretionary Costs.**   The manager of a regional warehouse for a mail-order firm is concerned with the control of his fixed costs. He has recently applied work-measurement techniques and a variable-cost approach to the staff of order clerks and is wondering if a similar technique could be applied to the workers who collect merchandise in the warehouse and bring it to the area where orders are assembled for shipment.

The warehouse foreman contends that this should not be done, because the present work force of twenty men should be viewed as a fixed cost necessary to handle the normal volume of orders with a minimum of delay. These men work a forty-hour week at $2.50 per hour.

Preliminary studies show that it takes an average of twelve minutes for a worker to locate an article and take it to the order-assembly area, and that the average order is for two different articles. At present the volume of orders to be processed is 1,800 per week.

required   1. For the present volume of orders, develop a discretionary-cost and a variable-cost approach for the weekly performance report.

2. Repeat 1 for volume levels of 1,600 and 1,400 orders per week.

3. What other factors should be compared with the budget variances found in 1 and 2 in order to make a decision on the size of the work force?

8-19. **Work Measurement.**   The Hayward Company has installed a work-measurement program for its billing operations. A standard billing cost of $.50 per bill has been used, based on hourly labor rates of $4.00 and an average processing rate of 8 bills of 10 lines each per hour. Each clerk has a $7\frac{1}{2}$-hour workday and a 5-day workweek.

The supervisor has received the following report of performance from his superior—the office manager, Mr. Davis—for a recent 4-week period regarding his clerks:

	ACTUAL	BUDGET	VARIANCE AMOUNT	VARIANCE EQUIVALENT PERSONS
Billing labor (5 clerks)	$3,000	$1,850 (3,700 bills × $.50)	$1,150 U	1.9

---

[8] An example of the distinction between actual hours worked and standard hours worked is as follows: A lathe operation may require a standard of 10 pieces to be turned per hour. If the necessary operation is performed on 100 pieces in 11 hours, the actual hours worked would be 11 but the standard hours worked (sometimes called *standard hours earned* or *standard hours allowed*) would be 100 ÷ 10, or only 10 hours.

The supervisor knows that he must explain the unfavorable variance and offer suggestions regarding how to avoid such an unfavorable variance in the future. Because of a recession, the office manager is under severe pressure to cut staff. In fact, he had penciled a question on the report: "Looks as if we can get along with two less clerks?"

Anticipating the pressures, the supervisor had taken a random sample of 400 of the 3,700 bills that were prepared during the period under review. His count of the lines in the sample totaled 5,200.

required   As the supervisor, prepare a one-page explanation of the $1,150 unfavorable variance, together with your remedial suggestions.

8-20. **Ford Motor Company's Flexible-Budget Control over Clerical Costs Through Work Measurement.**   This case illustrates a method by which flexible-budget controls have been adapted to a nonmanufacturing operation to control costs that might normally be classed as fixed labor and operating expense. It is possible and practical to control many expenses of this nature by the use of "standard" processing rates for work performed.

The following information is presented as background material to outline the control approach followed by this company:

The parts and accessories division of the Ford Motor Company controls and evaluates the performance of its branch-warehouse operations by the use of "flexible labor and expense budgets." These budgetary controls are in use in both the warehousing and the accounting activities of these operations and are used for both weekly and monthly analysis.

Primarily, variable-labor functions and controllable-expense classifications are supervised in this manner. Fixed costs that are not controllable by local management, such as supervision, taxes, and depreciation, are administered by the use of fixed (static) budget allowances.

All variable functions of the warehousing and accounting activities have been analyzed and standardized and related to some measurable work output. By maintaining daily control of these functional productivities and related daily labor charges, the required operating reports are prepared and submitted to the general office for analysis, consolidation, and comparison to national operating-budget levels.

A primary source of output statistics is obtained from a record of actual daily shipments made by the warehouse, as many accounting-function productivities are based on this measurement. The determinable output measurements are compared to the predetermined functional-budget rate to calculate "budget hours generated" during the budget period under review. The operating variances are determined by comparing generated budget hours to actual functional-labor charges during the same period. These variances are expressed both in hours of variance and equivalent-persons variance. The latter variance is calculated by comparing the hourly variance amounts to the forty shift-hours available in the budget period under review.

For a recent normal workweek of five operating days, the following output information and labor-distribution detail have been accumulated for certain selected accounting-department functions. The complete budget review is actually applied to approximately fifty separate and distinct activities in this operation.

required   1. Determine labor variance by function. Express variance in both hours and equivalent persons.

2. Calculate total labor variance in dollars.

3. Analyze the total dollar variance as determined in part 2. What portion

OUTPUT STATISTICS

1. Number of orders shipped	8,640
2. Number of line items* shipped	99,280
3. Number of line items backordered in warehouse	2,720
4. Number of checks written for merchandise received	3,290
5. Number of line items on shipments received	4,960
6. Number of credit adjustments approved	975

*Represents a single part number shipped or received, regardless of quantity.

FUNCTIONAL BUDGET RATES AND LABOR DISTRIBUTION

FUNCTION	BUDGET RATE PER HOUR	ACTUAL HOURS WORKED
Invoice scheduling	135 orders shipped	68.0
Keypunch†	680 line items processed	142.0
Keyverification†	1360 line items processed	71.0
IBM machine operator†	1020 line items printed	108.0
Proofreading†	510 line items proofread	208.0
Accounts payable:		
Invoice matching	80 line items received	
Check auditing	70 payments made	125.0
Credit adjustments	15 adjustments issued	69.0
Budgeted hourly labor rate—$5.00 per hour		
Actual payroll costs —$2,256.00		

† To determine the output allowance, the 2,720 line items backordered should be added to the 99,280 items shipped.

of this variance was attributable to a labor-rate variance and a labor-efficiency variance?

8-21. Guaranteed Minimum Wages and Cost Behavior Patterns. [Prepared by the author and adapted for use in a CPA examination] The Lavin Company had a contract with a labor union that guaranteed a minimum wage of $500 payable monthly to direct laborers with at least 12 years service. One hundred workers currently qualified for such coverage. All direct-labor employees are paid $5 per hour.

The budget for 19_1 was based on the usage of 400,000 hours of direct labor, a total of $2,000,000. Of this amount, $600,000 (100 men × $500 × 12 months) was regarded as fixed.

Data on performance for the first three months of 19_1 follow:

	JANUARY	FEBRUARY	MARCH
Direct-labor hours actually worked	22,000	32,000	42,000
Standard direct-labor hours allowed*	22,000	32,000	42,000
Direct-labor costs budgeted	$127,000	$162,000	$197,000
Direct-labor costs incurred	110,000	160,000	210,000
Variance (U = unfavorable; F = favorable)	17,000 F	2,000 F	13,000 U

*Note that perfect efficiency is being assumed.

The factory manager was perplexed by the results, which showed favorable variances when production was low and unfavorable variances when production was high. He felt that his control over labor costs was consistently good.

required

1. Why did the variances arise? Explain, using amounts and diagrams as necessary.

2. Does this direct-labor budget provide a basis for evaluating direct-labor performance? Explain, assuming that only 5,000 standard and actual hours were utilized in a given month. What variances would arise under the approach used in 1? Under the approach you recommend?

3. Suppose that 5,500 actual hours were used, but that only 5,000 standard hours were allowed for the work accomplished. What variances would arise under the approach used in 1? Under the approach you recommend?

8-22. Division of Mixed Costs Into Variable and Fixed Components. The controller of the Ijiri Co. wants you to approximate the fundamental variable- and fixed-cost behavior of an account called Maintenance from the following:

MONTHLY ACTIVITY IN MACHINE-HOURS	MONTHLY MAINTENANCE COSTS INCURRED
4,000	$3,000
7,000	3,900

8-23. Flexible Budget and the Special Order. Although the company had planned for production and sales of 60,000 units per month, results for the first month of this fiscal year showed production of 50,000 units and sales of only 40,000 units. The outlook for the near future makes it doubtful whether additional sales can be made at present prices; indeed, the level of 40,000 units per month seems to be a maximum at the present price of $3.50 per unit. Operating charges for the first month (which agree precisely with the flexible-budget figures) and the budget for 60,000 units of production and sales are given below:

	MANUFACTURING COSTS LAST MONTH	ORIGINAL BUDGET
Units produced	50,000	60,000
Costs of manufacturing:		
Direct materials	$60,000	$72,000
Direct labor	45,000	54,000
Other payroll costs (indirect labor, supervision, payroll taxes, etc.)	12,000	13,200
Power	8,000	9,600
Depreciation and maintenance	2,000	2,000
Miscellaneous	5,000	5,000

	SELLING AND OTHER COSTS LAST MONTH	ORIGINAL BUDGET
Units sold	40,000	60,000
Costs of selling and administration:		
Salesmen's commissions	$ 6,000	$ 9,000
Packing costs	9,000	12,000
Shipping costs	4,000	6,000
Advertising	1,000	1,200
Miscellaneous payrolls (office)	2,000	2,400
Other miscellaneous costs	3,000	3,000

The management of this company is considering an offer from a well-known chain to contract for 10,000 units of this product per month at a price of $3.00 each, terms net. f.o.b. the company's plant. This contract would have no effect upon the company's other sales, although commissions will have to be paid at regular rates (percent of sales dollar) to the company's salesmen on deliveries to the chain. The firm's policy is to carry no finished-goods inventory beyond the 10,000 units now on hand; it schedules its production to fit customer demand. All cost behaviors are continuous and linear.

required   From the data given, show your calculations to support or refute the desirability of accepting the offer.

8-24. **Various Cost Behavior Patterns [CPA, adapted].** Select the graph below that matches the numbered factory-cost or expense data. You are to indicate by letter which of the graphs best fits each of the situations or items described.

The vertical axes of the graphs represent *total* dollars of expense and the horizontal axes represent production. In each case the zero point is at the intersection of the two axes. The graphs may be used more than once.

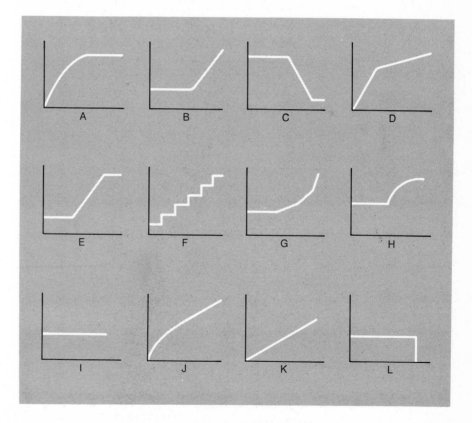

1. Depreciation of equipment, where the amount of depreciation charged is computed by the machine-hours method.
2. Electricity bill—a flat fixed charge, plus a variable cost after a certain number of kilowatt hours are used.

3. City water bill, which is computed as follows:

First 1,000,000 gallons or less	$1,000 flat fee
Next 10,000 gallons	.003 per gallon used
Next 10,000 gallons	.006 per gallon used
Next 10,000 gallons	.009 per gallon used
etc.	etc.

4. Cost of lubricant for machines, where cost per unit decreases with each pound of lubricant used (for example, if one pound is used, the cost is $10; if two pounds are used, the cost is $19.98; if three pounds are used, the cost is $29.94) with a minimum cost per pound of $9.25.

5. Depreciation of equipment, where the amount is computed by the straight-line method. When the depreciation rate was established, it was anticipated that the obsolescence factor would be greater than the wear-and-tear factor.

6. Rent on a factory building donated by the city, where the agreement calls for a fixed-fee payment unless 200,000 man-hours are worked, in which case no rent need be paid.

7. Salaries of repairmen, where one repairman is needed for every 1,000 machine-hours or less (that is, 0 to 1,000 hours requires one repairman, 1,001 to 2,000 hours requires two repairmen, and so forth).

8. Federal unemployment compensation taxes for the year, where labor force is constant in number throughout the year (average annual salary is $6,000 per worker). Maximum salary subject to tax is $3,000 per employee.

9. Cost of raw materials used.

10. Rent on a factory building donated by county, where agreement calls for rent of $100,000 less $1 for each direct-labor hour worked in excess of 200,000 hours, but minimum rental payment of $20,000 must be paid.

8-25. **Matching Graphs with Descriptions of Cost Behavior.** [Prepared by Professor David Green, Jr.] Given below are a number of charts, each indicating some relationship between cost and another variable. No attempt has been made to draw these charts to any particular scale; the absolute numbers on each axis may be closely or widely spaced.

You are to indicate by number which of the charts best fits each of the situations or items described. Each situation or item is independent of all the others; all factors not stated are assumed to be irrelevant. Only one answer will be counted for any item. Some charts will be used more than once; some may not apply to any of the situations. Note that category 14, "No relationship," is not the same as 15, "Some other pattern."

A. Taking the horizontal axis as rate of activity over the year and the vertical axis as *total cost* or *revenue*, indicate the pattern or relationship for each of the following items:

1. Direct-material cost.
2. Federal Social Security tax, as legally assessed, per worker, with workers earning over $9,000 per year, which is the maximum subject to tax.
3. Foremen's salaries.
4. A breakeven chart.
5. Total average unit cost.
6. Mixed costs—for example, electric power *demand charge* plus usage rate.
7. Average versus marginal cost.

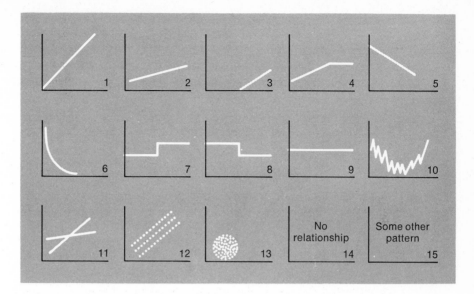

8. Depreciation of plant, computed on a straight-line, time basis.
9. Data supporting the use of a variable-cost rate, such as $2 per direct man-hour.
10. Vacation pay accrued for all workers in a department or plant.
11. Data indicating that an indirect-cost rate based on the given activity measure is spurious.
12. Variable costs *per unit* of output.
13. Incentive bonus plan, operating only above some level of activity.
14. Interest charges on money borrowed to finance acquisition of plant, before any payments on principal.

B. Taking the horizontal axis to represent a time series of weeks during a year and the vertical axis as representing *total cost per week*, match the following items with the relationship shown by the charts:
15. Direct-labor cost under stable production.
16. Direct materials purchased in small quantities during a period of widely fluctuating prices (inventory held at zero).
17. Effect of declining production volume over the year.
18. Result of a shutdown because of vacations, a serious casualty, or complete failure of demand. The shutdown continues to the end of the year.
19. Under- or overabsorbed factory overhead, taken weekly over the year, when volume varies widely and the cost rate is assumed to be correct.
20. Seasonal fluctuation in the use of fuel for heating the plant building over the year.

C. Taking the horizontal axis to represent a time series of weeks or months during a year, but the vertical axis to represent *unit-product cost* as determined by conventional methods, that is, by using indirect-cost rates, match the charts with each of the following items:
21. Upward revision during the year of the variable indirect-cost rate, because of changes in price, or other factors, expected to be permanent.
22. Indirect materials acquired for immediate use in small quantities at fluctuating prices.

23. Unusual repair charges caused by careless operation of the machinery.
24. A downward revision of the fixed indirect-cost rate because of greater volume than was anticipated; the higher volume is expected to continue over the rest of the year.

8-26. Budgeting Indirect Labor; Mixed Cost. A certain foreign unionized company hires indirect laborers to support direct laborers by performing a variety of unskilled tasks, such as machine cleanup and material handling and trucking. The direct laborers usually run two machines simultaneously. The relationships that have prevailed in the past three years are as follows:

	19_6			*19_7*		
	DIRECT LABOR	*MACHINE-HOURS*	*AUXILIARY LABOR*	*DIRECT LABOR*	*MACHINE-HOURS*	*AUXILIARY LABOR*
First quarter	$150,000	100,000	$20,000	$162,000	90,000	$22,800
Second quarter	182,000	120,000	22,000	183,000	100,000	24,000
Third quarter	163,000	110,000	21,000	200,000	110,000	25,200
Fourth quarter	158,000	105,000	20,500	205,000	115,000	25,800

	19_8		
	DIRECT LABOR	*MACHINE-HOURS*	*AUXILIARY LABOR*
First quarter	$238,000	120,000	$29,040
Second quarter	199,000	100,000	26,400
Third quarter	206,000	105,000	27,060
Fourth quarter	189,000	95,000	25,740

The company is installing a budgetary system. You have been asked to prepare an estimate of the quarterly costs of auxiliary labor for 19_9, given the data above and the following. The union contract for auxiliary labor has not been negotiated for 19_9 as yet.

	19_9	
	DIRECT LABOR	*MACHINE-HOURS*
First quarter	$231,000	110,000
Second quarter	189,000	90,000
Third quarter	199,500	95,000
Fourth quarter	210,000	100,000

Thoroughly justify your estimate with computations and words that can be understood by the president, a nasty sort who despises technical jargon but admires clear reasoning.

8-27. Reformulating a Performance Report. The Touche Manufacturing Company produces and sells instruments for the aircraft industry. Material and labor standards and overhead budgets have been developed for each of the departments. The assembly department budget for 19_4 appears in Exhibit 8-15.

Monthly reports are prepared comparing actual department costs with budgeted department costs. The June report for the assembly department is shown in Exhibit 8-16.

EXHIBIT 8-15

TOUCHE MANUFACTURING COMPANY
ASSEMBLY DEPARTMENT
19_4 CONVERSION-COST BUDGET

Expected Volume—40,000 Direct-Labor Hours

	FIXED COSTS	VARIABLE COSTS	TOTAL COSTS	VARIABLE RATE PER STANDARD DIRECT-LABOR DOLLAR
Standard direct-labor cost	$ —	$200,000	$200,000	—
Overhead:				
Indirect labor	$24,000	$ 32,000	$ 56,000	.160
Supplies	1,800	6,000	7,800	.030
Tools	5,400	5,200	10,600	.026
Power	4,800	8,000	12,800	.040
Maintenance	13,200	15,000	28,200	.075
Fringe benefits	12,000	32,000	44,000	.160
Scrap	—	24,000	24,000	.120
Depreciation and taxes	36,000	—	36,000	—
Total overhead	$97,200	$122,200	$219,400	.611
Total conversion costs	$97,200	$322,200	$419,400	

EXHIBIT 8-16

TOUCHE MANUFACTURING COMPANY
ASSEMBLY DEPARTMENT
PERFORMANCE

June, 19_4

	BUDGET	ACTUAL	VARIANCE: FAVORABLE (UNFAVORABLE)
Standard direct-labor cost	$15,500	$17,800[a]	$(2,300)
Overhead:			
Indirect labor	$ 4,480[b]	$ 4,735	$ (255)
Supplies	615	660	(45)
Tools	853	904	(51)
Power	1,020	1,087	(67)
Maintenance	2,263	2,382	(119)
Fringe benefits	3,480	3,848	(368)
Scrap	1,860	2,042	(182)
Depreciation and taxes	3,000	3,000	—
Total overhead	$17,571	$18,658	$(1,087)
Total conversion costs	$33,071	$36,458	$(3,387)

[a] There were no deviations from standard labor rates.
[b] The basic cost behavior pattern is revealed in Exhibit 8-15: $2,000 per month + .16($15,500) = $4,480.

269

"You're trying to tell me I spent too much," the department foreman shouted when he saw the report, "and I deny it! I've got control over my costs. Look at Fringe Benefits. How can I spend too much? It's a fixed percent of the wages. And direct-labor wages are set by the union contract, so the only way I can spend too much is to work overtime. There were 320 hours of overtime, but that only cost $800, not $2,300."

"I'm being charged for costs I can't control," he complained again. "You know those rush orders Sales keeps bringing us? When we complain we don't have time to do them, they argue that we will be responsible for losing business. So we do them. And they run up the costs.

"There were two special orders this month. One was for #720 thermostats, and the other for #4 altimeters. We usually do up to 1,000 thermostats at a time, and we're allowed 1,100 hours. That 1,100 includes 20 hours of setup time and 20 hours of tear-down time. We need that much time no matter how many we do. They wanted only 500 thermostats. I had to spend 590 hours to complete it and only 50 hours were overtime.

"We usually do 1,000 altimeters and have 1,500 hours[9] to complete them, including 30 hours each of setup time and tear-down time. They wanted 400 altimeters, and it took us 636 hours to do them. We had to work 40 hours overtime on that one. Then, we wasted another 40 hours sitting around waiting for materials that Purchasing should have had in the plant. And that preventive maintenance didn't prevent one of the machines from breaking down. We sat around for 100 hours waiting for that to be fixed.

"How do you expect me to keep my costs down when all of this is going on? Just tell me that!"

The production manager told the controller about the foreman's complaint and asked for a different report, which would be more meaningful to the foreman.

required

1. Prepare the revised report to show how the foreman is really doing. Use the June 19_4 data. (*Hint:* One way to approach a solution to part 1 would be to expand Exhibit 8-16 by adding two rows. Insert a row at the top for "Direct-labor hours." Change the line "Standard direct-labor cost" to "Standard direct-labor cost of hours above." Add another row after "Standard direct-labor cost" labeled "Overtime premium," removing that amount from the total now in the "Standard direct-labor cost" row. Then add seven columns with the overall label "Analysis of Variances," including two columns for special orders, two for unavoidable wait time, one for "Balance to be explained," one for spending and one for efficiency. This problem is more detailed than any in this chapter, but careful study will pay off in added understanding of standards and budgets.)

2. For which of these costs can the foreman really be held accountable? Comment.

[9] Therefore, apparently the original allowed hours included in the budget in Exhibit 8-16 for the smaller runs were 110% × 500 and 150% × 400, respectively.

Standard Costs and Product Costing: Analysis of Overhead Variances

This chapter is very important, because it integrates, contrasts, and compares the control and product-costing purposes of cost accounting. It also gives you a chance to consolidate and crystallize your study of the previous two chapters. You will then have a solid grasp of flexible budgets and standard costs.

The objective of this chapter is to examine the relationships of overhead control and overhead application, with particular emphasis on the variances between incurrence and application. Although the ideas presented here are simple, the analysis of overhead variances becomes confusing if the two purposes of overhead accounting—control and product costing—are overlooked or misunderstood.

Chapter 4 contained a discussion of the necessity for using predetermined overhead rates in applying overhead to products.[1] Now we shall consider this problem in more detail.

Because of the differences in behavior and controllability of costs, management has found that the distinction between variable costs and fixed costs is useful in budgeting and in product costing. Where feasible, it is desirable to classify overhead items into variable and fixed categories, even though the danger of oversimplification exists. The variable–fixed distinction should probably improve the comprehension of the decision maker concerning the uses and limitations of the cost measures.

---

[1] Several important intricacies of overhead accounting are being skipped temporarily. They include (a) factors to be considered in selecting the appropriate base for product costing, (b) department versus plant-wide overhead rates, and (c) reapportionment of service-department costs to producing departments before setting rates. These issues are discussed in Chapters 10 and 12.

Two overhead rates are established: a variable-overhead rate and a fixed-overhead rate. First, we shall consider the variable-overhead rate.

VARIABLE-OVERHEAD RATE

developing   As we saw in Chapter 8, the budget usually covers a range of anticipated
the rate   activity expressed in terms of the base for overhead allocation. On a
monthly basis, the flexible budget may appear as in Exhibit 9-1.

For purposes of computing standard unit costs of products, detailed studies
of usage of direct materials and direct labor are made in order to trace these
costs to the physical units produced. If overhead costs have been properly
classified, variable overhead may be assigned to products with assurance, because
the hourly or product rate used is valid at any level of production over wide
ranges. Thus, a standard-cost sheet may contain the following:

M COMPANY

Standard-Cost Sheet
Product X (Per Unit)

Direct materials, 40 pounds @ 50¢	$20.00
Direct labor, 3 hours @ $7.00	21.00
Variable overhead, 3 hours @ $1.70	5.10
Fixed overhead, 3 hours @ ? (to be discussed later)	?
Total standard cost per unit	$?

By definition, total variable-overhead costs fluctuate in proportion to
changes in activity levels. A variable-overhead rate is often developed with labor
hours as the base. This rate is merely multiplied by the number of standard hours

EXHIBIT 9-1

M COMPANY
MACHINING DEPARTMENT

Simplified Flexible Factory-Overhead Budget
For Anticipated Monthly Activity Range

Standard direct-labor hours allowed	8,000	9,000	10,000	11,000
Variable factory overhead:				
Material handling	$ 8,000	$ 9,000	$10,000	$11,000
Idle time	800	900	1,000	1,100
Rework	800	900	1,000	1,100
Overtime premium	400	450	500	550
Supplies	3,600	4,050	4,500	4,950
Total	$13,600	$15,300	$17,000	$18,700

Variable-overhead rate, $1.70 per DLH.

Fixed factory overhead: (To be considered in Exhibit 9–4)

necessary to produce a product; the result is the variable-overhead component of the total standard cost per unit of product (3 hours × $1.70, in the example).

Consider these additional facts concerning one month's operations (Variable-overhead rate, $1.70 per hour or $5.10 per unit of product):

Variable overhead incurred for 7,900 actual direct labor hours worked	$14,250
Variable overhead applied to product: Standard hours allowed, 8,000 × $1.70 (or may be computed as units produced, 2,666-2/3 × $5.10)	13,600
Variable-overhead variance	$ 650 Unfavorable

general-ledger entries   The summary general-ledger treatment of the facts above would be:

Variable factory-overhead control	14,250	
Accounts payable, Accrued Payroll, etc.		14,250

To record actual variable overhead incurred. Detailed postings of variable-overhead items, such as material handling, supplies, and idle time, would be made to the department-overhead sheets in the subsidiary ledger for Variable Factory-Overhead Control.

Work in process (at standard)	13,600	
Variable factory overhead applied		13,600

To apply overhead at the predetermined rate times work done as expressed in *standard hours allowed* (often called *standard hours worked* or *standard hours earned*). This would be $1.70 × 8,000 standard hours. Note that this calculation coincides with the flexible-budget total for this level of activity expressed in standard hours. The budget total would be $1.70 × 8,000 hours, or $13,600.

The only change in general-ledger procedure in this chapter is the replacement of a single Department Factory Overhead Control account with two new accounts, one for variable overhead and another for fixed overhead. Also, there will be two Applied accounts instead of the single Applied account used previously.

At this point, note that the total variable-overhead variance is not in a separate variance account, whereas direct-material and direct-labor variances are commonly isolated in separate accounts as general-ledger entries are made. However, the total variable-overhead variance may be readily computed by taking the difference between the Variable Factory Overhead Control balance and the Variable Factory Overhead Applied balance.

The general-ledger treatment practiced in standard-cost systems is not at all uniform. The reader who really understands the features of standard costs can easily adapt himself to any given bookkeeping system. Differences in general-ledger treatment usually center around (a) the number of detailed variance accounts desired, and (b) the timing of isolation of variances in the ledger.

analysis of
variable-
overhead
variances

The previous chapter (specifically, Exhibit 8-5) demonstrated how variances in variable overhead were analyzed, so there is no need for repetition here. However, there are a few points that deserve emphasis:

EXHIBIT 9-2

M COMPANY
MACHINING DEPARTMENT

Summary Analysis of Variable Overhead
For the Month Ending March 31, 19_1

(1) Inputs × Actual Rate	(2) Inputs × Standard Rate*	(3) Outputs × Standard Rate
	(7,900 × $1.70)	(8,000 × $1.70)
$14,250	$13,430	$13,600

Spending variance, $820 U   Efficiency variance, $170 F

(8,000 − 7,900 hours) × $1.70 = $170

Total (budget) variance, $650 U

*This is akin to preparing a flexible budget based on actual hours of input rather than on standard hours allowed. Also see Exhibit 8-5 in the preceding chapter.

1. As Exhibit 9-2 shows, the variable overhead applied to product in the general ledger ($13,600) coincides *exactly* with the amount provided in the flexible budget. Therefore, there is no conflict between the information generated for product-costing purposes and that developed for control purposes.

2. The total variance to be explained, $650, is often called the *budget* variance, because it is the difference between the amount incurred and the amount of variable cost provided for in the flexible budget.

3. Many companies refrain from subdividing the variable-overhead variance beyond the *budget variance* stage. This simplifies reports, but it does not yield as much information. Such an approach, which was originally illustrated at the top of Exhibit 8-5 in the preceding chapter, would yield an itemized report as follows:

DETAILED ANALYSIS	ACTUAL	BUDGET— 8,000 STANDARD HOURS ALLOWED	VARIANCE	EXPLANATION
Variable factory overhead:				
Material handling	$ 8,325	$ 8,000	$325 U	High-rate workers used
Idle time	850	800	50 U	Machine #1 breakdown
⋮	⋮	⋮	⋮	
Total variable overhead	$14,250	$13,600	$650 U	

FIXED OVERHEAD AND STANDARD COSTS OF PRODUCT

selecting a level of activity By definition, *total* fixed-overhead costs do not change over wide ranges of activity. However, unit costs do change; the higher the level of activity, the lower the unit cost. A costing difficulty arises here, because management desires a single representative standard cost for a *product* despite month-to-month changes in production volume. What level of activity should be used in developing a single application rate for applying fixed overhead to product? Consider this illustration:

M COMPANY

Standard Cost Sheet
Product X (Per Unit)

Direct materials, 40 pounds @ 50¢	$20.00
Direct labor, 3 hours @ $7.00	21.00
Variable overhead, 3 hours @ $1.70	5.10
Fixed overhead, 3 hours @?	?
Total standard cost per unit	$?

Now consider the budget for fixed overhead (the bottom half of the flexible budget in Exhibit 9-3).

Total fixed overhead is $10,000. Although Exhibit 9-3 indicates an 8,000- to 11,000-hour range, monthly volume expressed in standard labor hours might

EXHIBIT 9-3

M COMPANY
MACHINING DEPARTMENT

Simplified Flexible Factory-Overhead Budget
For Anticipated Monthly Activity Range

Standard direct-labor hours allowed	8,000	9,000	10,000	11,000
Variable factory overhead:				
Material handling	$ 8,000	$ 9,000	$10,000	$11,000
Idle time	800	900	1,000	1,100
Rework	800	900	1,000	1,100
Overtime premium	400	450	500	550
Supplies	3,600	4,050	4,500	4,950
Total	$13,600	$15,300	$17,000	$18,700
Variable-overhead rate, $1.70 per DLH				
Fixed factory overhead:				
Supervision	$ 1,700	$ 1,700	$ 1,700	$ 1,700
Depreciation—Plant	2,000	2,000	2,000	2,000
Depreciation—Equipment	5,000	5,000	5,000	5,000
Property taxes	1,000	1,000	1,000	1,000
Insurance—Factory	300	300	300	300
Total	$10,000	$10,000	$10,000	$10,000

Fixed-overhead rate based on denominator application level of 10,000 hours, $1.00 per DLH gyrate even more widely, from 5,000 up to a maximum of 15,000. Thus, the hourly cost of fixed overhead could fluctuate from $2.00 down to 66⅔¢, with a consequent effect on standard product costs. This problem does not arise with variable overhead, because by definition, anticipated total variable overhead would be $8,500 at a 5,000-hour level of activity and $25,500 at a 15,000-hour level of activity—a constant hourly rate of $1.70 no matter what the volume.

fixed-overhead application and the denominator
To obtain a single standard product cost for pricing and inventory uses, a selection of an appropriate activity (often called *volume*) level is necessary. A predetermined rate for applying fixed overhead is computed as follows:

$$\text{Predetermined fixed factory-overhead rate for applying costs to product} = \frac{\text{Budgeted fixed factory overhead}}{\text{Some preselected activity level for the year}}$$

In Exhibit 9-3, the 10,000-hour level is merely an expression in monthly terms of the following plans for the year:

$$\text{Fixed overhead rate} = \frac{\$120,000 \text{ (the budget for the year)}}{120,000 \text{ hours (the chosen denominator level of activity for the year}}$$

Fixed overhead rate = $1.00

Note that Exhibit 9-3 expresses expectations in monthly terms, but that the predetermination and choice of overhead rate is usually done annually. Therefore, the preselected activity level may be expressed as either 120,000 hours for the year or as an average of 10,000 hours per month. This preselected activity level will be referred to as the *denominator level*.

If fixed costs are important, the denominator level can have a significant effect on standard unit costs. For example, consider the data in Exhibit 9-3. Note how unit costs would change if a different denominator level were chosen:

(1) VARIOUS MONTHLY LEVELS OF ACTIVITY	(2) TOTAL BUDGETED FIXED OVERHEAD FOR THE YEAR ($10,000 × 12 MONTHS)	(3) TOTAL ACTIVITY FOR THE YEAR (MONTHLY LEVEL × 12)	(2) ÷ (3) PREDETERMINED FIXED-OVERHEAD RATE FOR PRODUCT COSTING
8,000	$120,000	96,000	$1.25
9,000	120,000	108,000	1.11+
10,000	120,000	120,000	1.00
11,000	120,000	132,000	.91−

selecting the denominator level
The selection of an appropriate denominator level for the predetermination of fixed-overhead rates is a matter of judgment; a dozen independent accountants or engineers would probably decide on a dozen different denominator levels based on the same set of available facts. Thus, the standard product cost would differ, depending on who sets the rate for fixed

overhead. The problem of choosing the "best" denominator level is discussed more fully in the next chapter.

Exhibit 9-3 also indicates that the applications to product of both variable and fixed overhead are based on standard direct-labor hours. Ideally, separate criteria may be used in selecting a base for a variable-overhead rate, as opposed to those used in selecting a different base for a fixed-overhead rate. The variable-overhead rate would be related to the activity base that is most logically linked to fluctuations in variable-overhead costs. On the other hand, fixed overhead does not vary in relation to any base; therefore, the preferred base for applying fixed overhead is one that best expresses the production capability of the plant. One of the purposes of fixed-overhead application is to obtain some measurement of the utilization of capacity. Where there are a variety of products, this capacity measure is often fundamentally expressed as labor-hours or machine-hours.

Although fixed-overhead rates are important for product costing and long-run pricing, such rates *have limited significance for control purposes.* At the lower levels of supervision, almost no fixed costs are under direct control; even at higher levels of supervision, few fixed costs are controllable within wide ranges of anticipated activity.

general-ledger entries   Consider the following facts as an example of the monthly treatment of fixed overhead in the general ledger:

Fixed overhead budgeted (this total is the same over wide ranges of activity)	$10,000
Denominator level, expressed in standard hours allowed for good output	10,000
Predetermined overhead rate per hour	$ 1.00
Fixed overhead incurred	$10,200
Fixed overhead applied (computed by multiplying $1.00 × 8,000, the good output expressed in standard hours allowed)	$ 8,000
Total fixed-overhead variance, $10,200 − $8,000	$ 2,200
Actual hours of input	7,900

The summary general-ledger treatment of the facts above would be:

Fixed factory-overhead control	10,200	
Accrued payroll, Allowance for depreciation, etc.		10,200

To record actual fixed overhead incurred. Detailed postings of fixed-overhead items, such as salaries, depreciation, property taxes, and insurance, would be made to the department-overhead sheets in the subsidiary ledger for Fixed Factory-Overhead Control.

Work in process (at standard)	8,000	
Fixed factory overhead applied		8,000

To apply overhead at the predetermined rate times work done as expressed in standard hours allowed. Note that this total differs from the fixed-overhead budget for this level of activity. The budget total for fixed overhead is $10,000 at any level of activity.

analysis of fixed-overhead variance   The first step in analyzing overhead is to calculate the total variance. In this example, the total variance is $2,200, the difference between $10,200 incurred and $8,000 applied. This $2,200 may be broken down into two

EXHIBIT 9-4

M COMPANY
MACHINING DEPARTMENT

Analysis of Variance in Fixed Overhead
For the Month Ending March 31, 19_1

ITEM*	ACTUAL	BUDGET	VARIANCE	EXPLANATION
Supervision	$ 1,700	$ 1,700	$ —	
Depreciation—Plant	2,000	2,000	—	
Depreciation—Equipment	5,000	5,000	—	
Property taxes	1,150	1,000	150 U	Increased assessment
Insurance—Factory	350	300	50 U	Increased coverage
	$10,200*	$10,000	$200 U	

Summary analysis. The denominator activity for setting the rate is 10,000 standard hours. Standard hours allowed for output were 8,000.

(1)	(2)	(3)
	Budget:	
	Same Regardless	
Actual	of Activity Level	Outputs × Standard Rate
		(8,000 × $1.00)
$10,200	$10,000	$8,000

Budget variance, $200 U† | Activity or Volume variance, $2,000 U‡

(10,000 − 8,000 hours) × $1.00 = $2,000

Total variance, $2,200 U

*To simplify the example, not all possible fixed-overhead items are included here.
†The *budget variance* for fixed overhead is the difference between the amount incurred and the budget figure. Keep in mind that the budget figure would be the same regardless of the actual level of activity.
‡The *activity variance* is also called the *volume variance,* the *utilization variance,* and the *capacity variance.* It *is the difference between fixed overhead applied and budgeted. It can also be expressed as the fixed-overhead rate times the difference between the denominator hours used for determining the rate and standard hours allowed:*

subvariances, the *budget variance* and the *volume variance.* A variance report may take the form of Exhibit 9-4.

nature of fixed-overhead variances   The major difficulty in analyzing fixed-overhead variances arises from the fundamental behavior of fixed costs in relation to the dual purposes (control and product costing) of cost accounting. For control purposes, each overhead item is studied in relation to changes in activity. Budgets are devised, and results are compared with the budget. The deviations from budget are known as *budget variances.* Although these fixed-overhead variances are often beyond immediate managerial control, this information at least calls attention to changes in price factors.

Think about the flexible budget once again. How flexible is it, really? The flex in the flexible budget is confined to the variable overhead. The fixed-overhead component is really static for a vast range of anticipated activity. Thus, the conventional flexible budget is really composed of two separate budgets: a really flexible budget for variable overhead plus a static budget for fixed overhead. This point is important. The analysis of fixed-overhead variance differs from the analysis of variable-overhead variance *because fixed costs do not behave in the same way, nor do they have the same control features.*

Let us compare the general behavior patterns of variable and fixed overhead. Exhibit 9-5 offers the appropriate comparison. Costs are plotted on the vertical axis (the *y*-axis) while volume is plotted on the horizontal axis (the *x*-axis). First, concentrate on the budget lines. Note that the budget line for variable overhead extends diagonally upward, although the budget line for fixed overhead is horizontal.

Now concentrate on the graph for variable overhead. At zero volume, no variable overhead is incurred, nor is any variable overhead applied to production—there is no production. The cost line slopes upward at the rate of $1.70 per standard direct-labor hour. Slope is the amount by which *y* increases when *x* increases by one unit, or the variable-overhead cost per unit of product. The equation for this budget is $y = bx$ ($y = \$1.70\,x$); the same equation holds for overhead application, so a single line portrays *both* budgeted amounts for control and overhead application for product costing. Conceptually, there are really two lines on the graph, but the budget line and the applied line are superimposed on one another.

If incurred costs lie above the budget and overhead-applied line, the budget variance is unfavorable, and vice versa.

EXHIBIT 9-5

COMPARISON OF CONTROL AND PRODUCT-COSTING PURPOSES,
VARIABLE OVERHEAD AND FIXED OVERHEAD

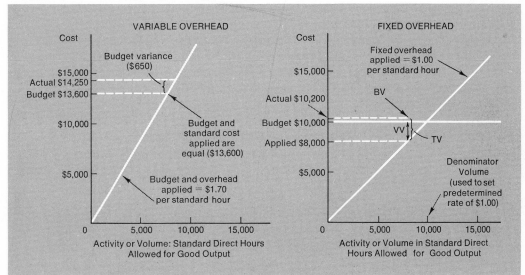

Note that the total variance is always the difference between actual costs incurred and costs applied. An analysis of this variance may then be made:

Total variance = Budget variance + Volume variance
TV = BV ($200) + VV ($2,000)

Now examine fixed overhead. For product-costing purposes, it is necessary to apply fixed overhead by using a predetermined rate that is usually based on standard hours allowed at some denominator level of activity. This predetermined rate is used to cost production regardless of the activity levels encountered. An activity variance ($2,000, in the example above) arises whenever production expressed in standard hours worked deviates from the activity level selected as the denominator for computing the product-costing rate. Because the term *volume variance* is used so widely to describe the activity variance, either term will be used here to denote this variance. *The volume variance is a conventional measure of the cost of failure to operate at the denominator activity (or the benefit of operating at above the denominator activity).*

Most companies consider volume variances to be beyond immediate control—although sometimes the top sales executive has to do some explaining or investigating, because denominator volume is often geared to anticipated sales. Sometimes, failure to reach denominator volume is caused by idleness due to poor production scheduling, unusual machine breakdowns, shortages of skilled workers, strikes, storms, and the like.

There is no volume variance for variable overhead. The concept of volume variance arises for fixed overhead because of the conflict between accounting for control (by budgets) and accounting for product costing (by application rates). Note carefully that the fixed-overhead budget serves the control purpose, whereas the development of a product-costing rate results in the treatment of fixed overhead *as if it were* a variable cost. In other words, the applied line in Exhibit 9-5 is artificial in the sense that, for product-costing purposes, it seemingly transforms a fixed cost into a variable cost. This bit of magic forcefully illustrates the distinction between accounting for control and accounting for product costing.

To summarize, volume variance arises because the activity level encountered (expressed as *standard hours allowed*) frequently does not coincide with the activity level used as a basis for selecting a predetermined product-costing rate for fixed factory overhead.

1. When denominator activity and standard hours allowed are identical, there is no volume variance.
2. When standard hours allowed are less than denominator activity, the volume variance is unfavorable. It is measured in Exhibit 9-5 as follows:

(Denominator Activity minus Standard Hours Allowed)
$\times$ Predetermined Fixed Overhead Rate = Volume Variance
(10,000 hours − 8,000 hours) $\times$ $1.00 = $2,000

or

Budget minus Applied = Volume Variance
$10,000 − $8,000 = $2,000

3. When standard hours allowed exceed denominator activity, the volume variance is favorable, because it is an index of better-than-average utilization of facilities.

weaknesses and dangers in fixed-overhead analysis

Above all, we should recognize that fixed costs are simply not divisible like variable costs; they come in big chunks and they are related to the provision of big chunks of production or sales capability rather than to the production or sale of a single unit of product.

There are conflicting views on how fixed-overhead variances are best analyzed. These views are discussed in Chapter 28. Obviously, the "best" way is the one that provides management in a particular company with the most insight. Consequently, overhead analysis varies from company to company. In many companies, variances are most usefully expressed in physical terms only. For instance, an activity variance could be expressed in machine-hours or kilowatt-hours.

The position in this chapter has been to distinguish between fixed and variable overhead as being separate management problems. This contrasts with the tendency among many accountants to analyze variable costs and fixed costs in a parallel manner. For instance, an efficiency variance for fixed overhead is often computed, just as it is for other variable costs:

Efficiency variance[2] = (Actual hours − Standard hours allowed)

$$× \text{ Hourly fixed-overhead rate}$$

However, the resulting variance is very different from the efficiency variances for materials, labor, and variable overhead. Efficient usage of these three factors can affect actual cost, but short-run fixed-overhead cost is not affected by efficiency. Furthermore, the managers responsible for inefficiency will be aware of its existence through reports on variable-cost control, so there is little to gain from expressing ineffective utilization of facilities in historical dollar terms.

Finally, what is the economic significance of unit fixed costs? Unlike variable costs, total fixed costs do not change in the short run as production or sales fluctuate. Management would obtain a better measure of the cost of underutilization of physical facilities by trying to approximate the related lost-contribution margins instead of the related historical fixed costs. Fixed-cost incurrence often involves lump-sum outlays based on a pattern of expected recoupment. But ineffective utilization of existing facilities has no bearing on the amount of fixed costs currently incurred. The economic effects of the inability to reach target volume levels are often directly measured by lost-contribution margins, even if these have to be approximated. The historical-cost approach fails to emphasize the distinction between *fixed-cost incurrence*, on the one hand, and the objective

---

[2]Some accountants favor computing volume variance on the basis of the difference between the fixed-overhead budget ($10,000) and (actual hours worked × fixed-overhead rate). In this example, the volume variance would then become $10,000 − (7,900 × $1), or $2,100 unfavorable. The remaining variance of $100 favorable [(actual hours − standard hours) × $1 overhead rate] is sometimes called the fixed-overhead *efficiency* or *effectiveness* variance—the measure of the ineffective use or waste of facilities because of off-standard labor performance. This breakdown of the volume variance really attempts to separate the cost of *misused* facilities from the cost of *unused* facilities.

The author thinks this refinement is unnecessary in most cases, because (a) in the short run, total fixed costs incurred are *not* changed by efficiency changes, and (b) if the budget uses standard hours as a base, the *volume* variance is more logically calculated by comparing standard hours worked with the denominator volume that was used as a basis for setting the predetermined overhead rate. For an elaboration, see Chapter 28.

of *maximizing the total contribution margin,* on the other hand. These are separable management problems, and the utilization of existing capacity is more closely related to the latter.[3]

For instance, in our example the activity variance was computed at $2,000 by multiplying a unit fixed cost of $1.00 by the 2,000-hour difference between the 10,000 hours of normal activity and 8,000 standard hours earned. This $2,000 figure may be helpful in the sense that management is alerted in some crude way to the probable costs of failure to use 10,000 hours. But the more relevant information is the lost-contribution margins that pertain to the 2,000 hours. This information may not be so easy to obtain. The lost-contribution margins may be zero in those cases where there are no opportunities to obtain any contribution margin from alternative uses of available capacity; in other cases, however, the lost-contribution margins may be substantial. For example, if demand is high, the breakdown of key equipment may cost a company many thousands of dollars in lost-contribution margins. Unfortunately, in these cases, existing accounting systems would show volume variances based on the unitized fixed costs and entirely ignore any lost-contribution margins.

summary

Thorough study of the contents of this chapter should be rewarding, because analysis of overhead variances must consider two major frames of reference: the flexible budget for control and the use of predetermined overhead rates for product costing. The budget variance is considered to be controllable, at least to some degree. The volume variance is considered uncontrollable in most instances. Thus, this chapter has highlighted and contrasted the many purposes that must be served in accounting for overhead. The general ledger is designed mainly to serve purposes of product costing. Yet management's major purpose, that of control, is aided by using flexible budget figures, which are not highlighted in general-ledger balances. As is often the case, conventional general-ledger bookkeeping for overhead often provides only a minimum of the information needed for control.

This chapter covered only some of the many methods of budgeting overhead, applying overhead, and analyzing overhead variances. How overhead is budgeted, applied, analyzed, and reported is really determined by the individual managements concerned. For further consideration of alternative versions of overhead analysis, see Chapter 28.

Note that the general-ledger entries in this chapter sharply distinguish between fixed and variable overhead. This treatment is more effective for management than combining the two because it emphasizes the basic differences in cost behavior of these two kinds of overhead. Such basic differences are often important in influencing managerial decisions. The appendix demonstrates that

---

[3]For an elaboration of these ideas, see Charles T. Horngren, "A Contribution Margin Approach to the Analysis of Capacity Utilization," *The Accounting Review,* XLII, No. 2, 254–64.

these distinctions can be maintained even if a combined overhead rate is used for product costing.

The worksheet analysis illustrated in Exhibit 9-6, page 284, provides a useful approach to the analysis of overhead variances. The first step is to obtain the total variance—the difference between overhead incurred and overhead applied. Then any further variance breakdowns can be added algebraically and checked against the total variance.

suggested readings

N.A.A. Research Series Nos. 11, 15, 17, 22, and *28* contain much discussion of the analysis of variances.

Problem for Self-Study

PROBLEM The McDermott Furniture Company has established standard costs for the cabinet department, in which one size of a single four-drawer style of dresser is produced. The standard costs are used in evaluating actual performance. The standard costs of producing one of these dressers are shown below:

STANDARD-COST CARD

DRESSER, STYLE AAA

Materials: Lumber—50 board feet @ $.20	$10.00
Direct labor: 3 hours @ $6.00	18.00
Indirect costs:	
Variable charges—3 hours @ $1.00	3.00
Fixed charges—3 hours @ $.50	1.50
Total per dresser	$32.50

The costs of operations to produce 400 of these dressers during January are stated below (there were no initial inventories):

Materials purchased:	25,000 board feet @ $.21	$5,250.00
Materials used:	19,000 board feet	
Direct labor:	1,100 hours at $5.90	6,490.00
Indirect costs:		
Variable charges		1,300.00
Fixed charges		710.00

The flexible budget for this department at the monthly activity level used to set the fixed-overhead rate called for 1,400 direct-labor hours of operation. At this level, the variable indirect cost was budgeted at $1,400, and the fixed indirect cost at $700.

required All journal entries. Compute the following variations from standard cost. Label your answers as *favorable* (F) or *unfavorable* (U).

1. Material purchase price.
2. Material usage.

EXHIBIT 9-6

McDermott Furniture Company

Analysis of Manufacturing Costs

Direct Materials

(1) Inputs Actual × Actual Rate	(2) Inputs Actual × Standard		(3) Outputs Flexible Budget* and Applied: Standard Hours Allowed for Actual Units Produced × Standard Rate
	Purchases	Usage	
(25,000 @ $.21) $5,250	(25,000 @ $.20) $5,000	(19,000 @ $.20) $3,800	(20,000 @ $.20) $4,000

(25,000 × $.01)
Price variance, $250 U

(1,000 × $.20)
Usage variance, $200 F

Direct Labor

Actual Usage × Standard Rate

(1,100 × $5.90) $6,490	(1,100 × $6.00) $6,600	(400 × 3) × $6.00 $7,200

(1,100 × $.10)
Rate variance, $110 F

(100 × $6.00)
Efficiency variance, $600 F

Total (budget) variance, $710 F

Variable Overhead

(1,100 × $1.1818) $1,300	(1,100 × $1.00) $1,100	(1,200 × $1.00) $1,200

(1,100 × $.1818)
Spending variance, $200 U

(100 × $1.00)
Efficiency variance, $100 F

Total (budget) variance, $100 U

Fixed Overhead

(1) Incurred	(2) Not Applicable to Analysis of Fixed Costs	(3) Flexible Budget:† Same Regardless of Activity Level	(4) Outputs Applied: Standard Hours Allowed for Actual Units Produced × Standard Rate
$710		$700	1,200 × $.50 $600

Budget variance, $10 U

(1,400 − 1,200) × $.50
Volume variance, $100 U

Total variance, $110 U

U = Unfavorable   F = Favorable   *See next page.   †See next page.

284

3. (a) Direct-labor rate;
   (b) Direct-labor efficiency.
4. (a) Variable-overhead budget variance;
   (b) Fixed-overhead budget variance;
   (c) Fixed-overhead volume variance.
5. (a) Variable-overhead spending variance;
   (b) Variable-overhead efficiency variance.

SOLUTION Journal entries are supported by pertinent variance analysis.

1. Stores control (25,000 @ $.20)	5,000	
Material purchase-price variance (25,000 @ $.01)	250	
Accounts payable (25,000 @ $.21)		5,250

---

*Graphically, the flexible budget line for variable costs and the applied line for variable costs are identical. For example, for variable overhead:

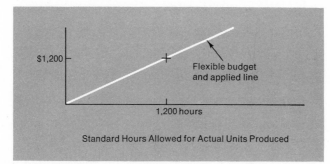

†Graphically, the flexible budget line for fixed costs is not really flexible because it is horizontal (the total budgeted fixed overhead is the same over a wide range of volume). Hence the budget amount will differ from the applied amount when activity is not at the level (here called denominator activity) used to set the fixed overhead rate for product costing.

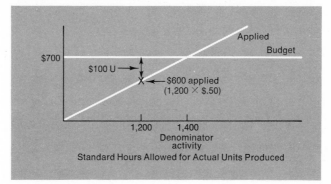

In sum, the acccuntant is faced with a special problem with regard to fixed overhead, which has very different cost behavior characteristics and cost control features than variable overhead. In trying to assign fixed overhead to product, he must develop a predetermined costing rate. In so doing, he has to select a level of activity as the denominator in his formula:

$$\text{Fixed Overhead Rate} = \frac{\text{Budget}}{\text{Denominator activity}} = \frac{\$700}{1,400 \text{ hours}} = \$.50 \text{ per hour}$$

Therefore, a volume variance will arise when ensuing activity differs from denominator activity.

Volume variance arises only in connection with fixed overhead. There is no volume variance for variable overhead. That is why column (4) in the exhibit is extended to the right to stand alone — to highlight the fact that the budget and the applied amounts for fixed overhead will usually not be equal, in contrast to the equality of the budget and applied amounts for variable costs.

2. Work-in-process control (400 units × 50 board feet × $.20)   4,000
    Material-usage variance (1,000 × $.20)   200
    Stores control (19,000 × $.20)   3,800
3. Work-in-process control (400 units × $18.00)   7,200
    Direct-labor rate variance (1,100 hrs. × $.10)   110
    Direct-labor efficiency variance (100 hrs. × $6.00)   600
    Accrued payroll (1,100 hrs. × $5.90)   6,490
    For analysis of variances, see Exhibit 9-6.
4. Variable-overhead control   1,300
    Accounts payable and other accounts   1,300
  Work-in-process control   1,200
    Variable overhead applied (400 × 3 × $1.00)   1,200
5. Fixed-overhead control   710
    Accounts payable and other accounts   710
  Work-in-process control   600
    Fixed overhead applied (400 × 3 × $.50)   600

The analysis of variances in Exhibit 9-6 summarizes the characteristics of different cost behavior patterns. The approaches to direct labor and variable overhead are basically the same. Furthermore, there is no fundamental conflict between the budgetary and product-costing purposes; that is, the applied amounts in column (3) would also be the flexible-budget allowances. In contrast, the behavior patterns and control features of fixed overhead require a different analytical approach. The budget is static, not flexible. There is no efficiency variance for fixed factory overhead because short-run performance cannot ordinarily affect incurrence of fixed factory overhead. Finally, there will nearly always be a conflict between the budgetary and product-costing purposes because the applied amount in column (3) for fixed overhead will differ from the static budget allowance. The latter conflict is highlighted by the volume variance, which measures the effects of working at other than the volume used to set the product-costing rate.

The following is a summary of variances:

1. Material purchase price $250 U
2. Material usage   200 F
3. (a) Direct-labor rate   110 F
   (b) Direct-labor efficiency   600 F
4. (a) Variable-overhead budget variance   100 U
   (b) Fixed-overhead budget variance   10 U
   (c) Fixed-overhead volume variance   100 U
5. (a) Variable-overhead spending variance   200 U
   (b) Variable-overhead efficiency variance   100 F

OVERHEAD VARIANCES IN THE LEDGER

There are several ways of accounting for overhead variances. The easiest way is probably to allow the department-overhead control accounts and applied accounts to cumulate month-to-month postings until the end of the year. Monthly variances would not be isolated formally in the accounts, although monthly variance reports would be prepared. Assume that the data in the review problem are for the *year* rather than for the *month*. At the year-end, isolating and closing entries could be made as follows:

Variable factory overhead applied	$1,200	
Variable-overhead spending variance	200	
Variable-overhead efficiency variance		$ 100
Variable factory overhead control		1,300
To isolate variances for the year.		
Fixed factory overhead applied	600	
Fixed-overhead budget (or spending) variance	10	
Fixed-overhead volume variance	100	
Fixed factory overhead control		710
To isolate variances for the year.		
Income summary (or Cost of goods sold)	100	
Variable-overhead efficiency variance	100	
Variable-overhead spending variance		200
To close.		
Income summary (or Cost of goods sold)	110	
Fixed-overhead budget variance		10
Fixed-overhead volume variance		100
To close.		

If desired, the isolation entries for monthly variances could be made monthly, although the closing entries are usually confined to the year-end.

Of course, rather than being closed directly to the Income Summary or Cost of Goods Sold, in certain cases the overhead variances may be prorated at year end, as is shown in the next chapter.

APPENDIX: COMBINED-OVERHEAD RATE AND TWO-WAY AND THREE-WAY ANALYSIS

combined rate   Many companies, while separating variable overhead and fixed overhead for control purposes, combine them for product-costing purposes and use a single predetermined overhead rate. In the example in this chapter, such a rate would be $2.70—the variable-overhead rate of $1.70 plus the fixed-overhead rate of $1.00. (See Exhibit 9-3.) In such cases, the overhead-variance analysis would be basically the same. Therefore, this discussion appears in an appendix rather than in the body of the chapter. The study of the many varieties of overhead analysis can easily bewilder the student who is exposed to this material for the first time. The body of this chapter presents a sufficient fundamental background about overhead analysis. Do not attempt the study of this appendix until you are thoroughly familiar with the material in the body of the chapter.

The easiest way to grasp these relationships is to examine Exhibit 9-7, which is really a combination of the two graphs in Exhibit 9-5. You can readily see that what we are about to study is nothing more than a simultaneous consideration of the variable and fixed components, where the flexible-budget formula is expressed as $10,000 per month plus $1.70 per hour.

EXHIBIT 9-7

COMBINED VARIABLE- AND FIXED-OVERHEAD BUDGET AND APPLICATION OF
VARIOUS MONTHLY PRODUCTION VOLUMES

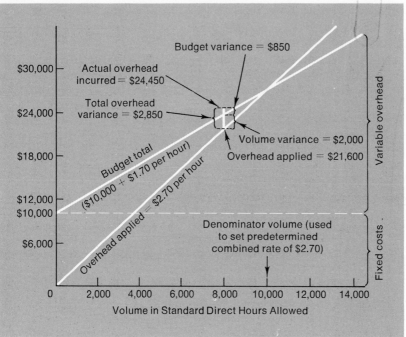

Exhibit 9-8 provides a comprehensive analysis of all relationships among the combined-overhead analysis and its variable and fixed parts.

Even when the actual overhead costs cannot be separated into variable and fixed components, it is still possible to generate almost all of the flexible-budget analysis illustrated in the chapter. The only variances that could not be derived are the separate variable-overhead spending variance and the separate fixed-overhead budget variance.

two-way and three-way analysis Note that Exhibit 9-8 distinguishes between the so-called two-way and three-way overhead analysis. The three-way analysis is the method that was used in the body of the chapter, where three different variances were computed: spending, efficiency, and volume. The two-way analysis computes only two variances: budget (sometimes called the *controllable variance*) and volume. The budget variance, as is clear in Exhibit 9-8, is simply the difference between actual costs and the budget allowance based on standard hours allowed. The two-way analysis stops there; it does not subdivide the budget variance into spending and efficiency variances.

overhead analysis in nonstandard-cost systems Overhead variance analysis is possible and beneficial in both standard cost systems and the normal cost systems that were introduced in Chapter 4. Analysis in the latter situations is restricted to a two-way analysis, because the budgeted and applied amounts would be expressed in actual hours only.

EXHIBIT 9-8

WORKSHEET SUMMARY OF RELATIONSHIPS OF COMBINED-OVERHEAD ANALYSIS AND ITS VARIABLE AND FIXED PARTS

	(1) Inputs: Incurred	(2) Inputs: Budget* Based on 7,900 Actual Hours Worked	(3) Outputs: Budget* Based on 8,000 Standard Hours of Work Allowed	(4) Outputs: Applied
V	14,250	13,430	13,600	$(8,000 \times \$1.70) = 13,600$
F	10,200	10,000	10,000	$(8,000 \times \$1.00) = 8,000$
Combined	24,450	23,430	23,600	$(8,000 \times \$2.70) = 21,600$

3-way Analysis

Total Spending Variance (1) − (2)
- V 820 U
- F 200 U
- Combined 1,020 U

Total Efficiency Variance (2) − (3)
- V 170 Fav.
- F (not applicable)
- Combined 170 Fav.

Total Volume Variance (3) − (4)
- V (not applicable)
- F 2,000 U
- Combined 2,000 U

2-way Analysis

Total Budget Variance (1) − (3)
- V 650 U
- F 200 U
- Combined 850 U

Total Volume Variance (3) − (4)
- V (not applicable)
- F 2,000 U
- Combined 2,000 U

Total Variance

Total Overhead Variance (1) − (4)
- V 650 U
- F 2,200 U
- Combined 2,850 U

U = Unfavorable   Fav. = Favorable   V = Variable   F = Fixed
* Budget Formula: $10,000 per month + $1.70 per hour.
Note: See footnote 2 in this chapter for a discussion of an alternative way to compute the volume variance.

No information on standard hours is available. Therefore, the following analysis is applicable:

(1)	(2)	(3)
Incurred	Budget	Applied
xxx	xxx	xxx

Budget Variance   Volume Variance
(1) − (2)   (2) − (3)

For a numerical exercise, see Problem 9-13.

questions, problems, and cases

9-1. What is the essential difficulty in applying fixed overhead to product?

9-2. "There should be an efficiency variance for fixed overhead. A foreman can inefficiently use his fixed resources." Comment.

9-3. Fundamentals of Overhead Variances. The Breen Company in installing a standard-cost system and a flexible-overhead budget. Standard costs have been recently developed for its only product and are as follows:

Direct materials, 2 pounds @ $15	$30.00
Direct labor, 6 hours @ $8.00	48.00
Variable overhead, 6 hours @ $1.00	6.00
Fixed overhead	?
Standard cost per unit of finished product	$?

Denominator activity is expressed as 12,000 standard direct-labor hours per month. Fixed overhead is expected to be $18,000 per month.

required

1. Calculate the proper fixed-overhead rate per standard direct-labor hour and per unit.

2. Graph the following for activity from zero to 15,000 hours:
   (a) Budgeted variable overhead
   (b) Variable overhead applied

3. Graph the following for activity from zero to 15,000 hours:
   (a) Budgeted fixed overhead
   (b) Fixed overhead applied

4. Assume that 10,000 standard direct-labor hours are allowed for the output during a given month. Input was 10,800 actual hours. Actual variable overhead incurred was $11,100. Actual fixed overhead was $18,500. What are the variable-overhead spending and efficiency variances? Fixed-overhead budget and volume variances?

5. Assume that 12,500 standard direct-labor hours are allowed for the output during a given month. Input was 12,200 actual hours. Actual overhead incurred was $30,500, $18,000 of which was fixed. What are the variable-

overhead spending and efficiency variances? Fixed-overhead budget and volume variances? In words rather than figures, explain the meaning of each variance.

6. Prepare the necessary journal entries to record the overhead in requirement 4.

9-4. Variance Analysis and Journal Entries for Overhead.　The Starr Company uses a standard-cost system. Denominator output per month is 5,000 units.

Standard Costs:	
Direct labor, 3 hrs. @ $5.00	$15.00
Direct materials, 20 lbs. @ $.30	6.00
Overhead, 20% of direct labor	3.00
Total cost per finished unit	$24.00

The following production data are for the month of July 19_0:

Work in process, July 1	–0–
Units completed by July 31	4,500
Work in process, July 31	–0–
Materials purchased, 120,000 lbs. @ $.31	$ 37,200
Materials used	105,000 lbs.
Variable overhead incurred	$ 8,500
Direct-labor use, 13,750 hrs. @ $5.10 per hr.	$ 70,125
Fixed overhead incurred	$ 6,000

The overhead flexible-budget formula has a variable cost component of 60¢ per standard direct-labor hour.

required

1. Prepare complete analyses of variances for materials, labor, variable overhead, and fixed overhead.

2. Prepare journal entries for the overhead incurrence and application. You may omit the entries for materials and labor.

9-5. Comprehensive, Straightforward Problem on Standard-Cost System. The Brandon Company uses a standard-cost system. The month's data regarding its lone product follow:

Fixed-overhead costs incurred, $6,150
Variable overhead applied at $.90 per hour
Standard direct-labor cost, $4.00 per hour
Standard material cost, $1.00 per pound
Standard pounds of material in a finished unit, 3
Denominator production per month, 2,500 units
Standard direct-labor hours per finished unit, 5
Materials purchased, 10,000 lbs., $9,500
Materials used, 6,700 lbs.
Direct-labor costs incurred, 11,000 hours, $41,800
Variable-overhead costs incurred, $9,500
Fixed overhead budget variance, $100, favorable
Finished units produced, 2,000

required

Prepare journal entries. Prepare schedules of all variances, using the worksheet approach described in this chapter.

9-6. Analysis of Fixed Overhead; Choice of Denominator. The fixed overhead items of the lathe department of The Clancy Company include, for the month of January, 19_4:

ITEM	ACTUAL	BUDGET
Supervision	$ 900	$ 800
Depreciation—Plant	750	750
Depreciation—Equipment	1,750	1,750
Property taxes	350	400
Insurance—Factory	400	300
	$4,150	$4,000

Expected activity for the lathe department is 1,000 standard hours per month. Practical capacity is 1,600 standard hours per month. Standard hours allowed for work done (good units actually produced) were 1,250.

required

1. Prepare a summary analysis of fixed-overhead variances, using expected activity as the denominator base.

2. Prepare a summary analysis of fixed overhead variances, using practical capacity as the denominator base.

3. Explain why the budget variances in parts 1 and 2 are identical whereas the volume variances are different.

9-7. Characteristics of Fixed-Overhead Variances. Fox Company executives have studied their operations carefully and have been using a standard-cost system for years. They are now formulating currently attainable standards for 19_1. They agree that the standards for direct materials will amount to $10 per finished unit produced and that the standards for direct labor and variable overhead are to be $9 and $1 per direct-labor hour, respectively. Total fixed overhead is expected to be $600,000. Two hours of direct labor is the standard time for finishing one unit of finished product.

required

1. Graph the budgeted fixed overhead for 400,000 to 800,000 standard allowed direct-labor hours of activity, assuming that the total budget will not change over that activity level. What would be the appropriate product-costing rate per standard direct-labor hour for fixed overhead if denominator activity is 500,000 hours? Graph the applied fixed-overhead line.

2. Assume that 250,000 units of product were produced. How much fixed overhead would be applied to product? Would there be a volume variance? Why? Assume that 200,000 units were produced. Would there be a volume variance? Why? Show the latter volume variance on a graph. In your own words, define volume variance. Why does it arise? Can a volume variance exist for variable overhead? Why?

3. Assume that 220,000 units are produced. Fixed-overhead costs incurred were $617,000. What is the total fixed-overhead variance? Budget variance? Volume variance? Use the analytical technique illustrated in the chapter.

4. In part 1 (ignoring parts 2 and 3), what would be the appropriate product-costing rate per standard direct-labor hour for fixed overhead if denominator activity is estimated at 400,000 hours? At 600,000 hours? At 800,000 hours? Draw a graph showing budgeted fixed overhead and three "applied" lines, using the three rates just calculated. If 200,000 units are produced, and the denominator activity is 600,000 standard direct-labor hours, what is the

volume variance? Now compare this with the volume variance in your answer to part 2; explain the difference.

5. Specifically, what are the implications in parts 1 and 4 regarding (a) the setting of product-costing rates for fixed overhead, (b) the meaning of budget and volume variances, and (c) the major differences in planning and control techniques for variable and fixed costs?

9-8. Find the Unknowns. Consider each of the following situations independently. Data refer to operations for a week in April. For each situation assume a standard product-cost system. Also assume the use of a flexible budget for control of variable and fixed overhead based on standard direct-labor hours.

	A	B	C	D	E	F
			CASES			
(1) Actual fixed overhead	—	$ 9,900	$12,550	—	$12,000	$10,600
(2) Actual variable overhead	$ 7,500	12,000	9,500	—	—	7,000
(3) Denominator activity in hours	10,000	—	6,000	—	11,000	5,000
(4) Standard hours allowed for good output	11,000	12,000	—	6,500	—	—
Flexible-budget data:						
(5) Fixed factory overhead	5,000	—	—	—	—	—
(6) Variable factory overhead (per standard hour)	70¢	—	75¢	85¢	50¢	—
(7) Budgeted fixed factory overhead	5,000	—	—	—	11,000	10,000
(8) Budgeted variable factory overhead*	—	—	—.	—	—	—
(9) Total budgeted factory overhead*	—	a	21,000	12,525	—	—
(10) Standard variable overhead applied	—	—	9,000	—	—	7,500
(11) Standard fixed overhead applied	—	—	—	—	—	10,000
(12) Activity or volume variance	—	600F	—	500U	500F	—
(13) Variable-overhead spending variance	—	—	100F	-0-	250U	950F
(14) Variable-overhead efficiency variance	—	—	—	-0-	100U	—
(15) Fixed-overhead budget variance	300U	—	—	300F	—	—
(16) Actual hours of input	11,200	11,700	—	—	—	—

ᵃ$21,200 at 10,000 hours; $27,800 at 16,000 hours.
* For standard hours allowed for work done.

required   Fill in the blanks under each case. Prepare your answer by (a) listing the numbers that are blank for each case and (b) putting the final answers next to the numbers. Prepare supporting computations on a separate sheet. For example, your answer to Case A would contain a vertical listing of the numbers 1, 8, 9, 10, 11, 12, 13, and 14, with answers next to the appropriate numbers.

9-9. Variance Analysis [CPA]. The H. G. Company uses a standard-cost system in accounting for the cost of one of its products, which is produced in a foreign country (to take advantage of lower labor costs).

The standard is based on a budgeted monthly production of 100 units per day for the usual 22 workdays per month. Standard cost per unit for direct labor is 16 hours at $1.50 per hour. Standard cost for overhead was set as follows:

Fixed overhead per month	$29,040
Variable overhead per month	39,600
Total budgeted overhead	$68,640
Expected direct-labor cost	$52,800
Overhead rate per dollar of labor	$ 1.30
Standard overhead per unit	$ 31.20

During the month of September, the plant operated only 20 days. Cost for the 2,080 units produced were:

Direct labor, 32,860 hours @ $1.52	$49,947.20
Fixed overhead	29,300.00
Variable overhead	39,065.00

required

1. Compute the variance from standard in September for (a) direct labor cost, and (b) overhead.

2. Analyze the variances from standard into identifiable causes for (a) direct labor, and (b) for fixed and variable overhead.

9-10. Compute Standard Cost Per Unit; Variance Analysis. X department uses a standard-cost system and a flexible budget.

Denominator activity is:	
Machine-hours	140
Finished pieces produced	2,800

The standard costs in connection with this production are:

Direct materials	$3,360
Direct labor	315
Factory overhead (includes an allowance for variable overhead at the rate of 30¢ per piece)	1,400
	$5,075

The actual production for a month was:

Machine-hours	130
Finished pieces produced	2,860

The actual cost of this production was:

Direct materials	$3,575
Direct labor	286
Factory overhead, including $573 of fixed overhead	1,573
	$5,434

Direct-labor hours and machine-hours are proportional.

required

Answer the following questions. Be certain of the given facts and relationships before going ahead.

1. What was the standard cost per finished piece?

For questions 2-8, use *F* or *U* to indicate whether the variance is favorable or unfavorable. Give the dollar amounts.

2. What is total material variance?

3. Direct-labor rate variance?

4. Direct-labor efficiency variance?

5. Variable-overhead spending variance?

6. Variable-overhead efficiency variance?

7. Fixed-overhead budget variance?

8. Fixed-overhead volume variance?

9-11. Standard Costs; Journal Entries; Analysis of Variances; Combined-Overhead Analysis; Income Statement [CPA, adapted]. The Smith Company uses a standard-cost system. The standards are based on a budget for operations at the rate of production anticipated for the current period. In its general ledger, the company records variations in material prices and usage, wage rates, and labor efficiency. Two accounts for manufacturing overhead are kept in the general ledger: Manufacturing Overhead Control and Manufacturing Overhead Applied; the month-end differences in their balances are analyzed in a supporting schedule. Three summary overhead variances are shown: spending variance, efficiency variance, and volume variance.

Current standards are as follows:

Materials:

Material A	$1.20 per unit
Material B	2.60 per unit
Direct labor	$2.05 per hour

	SPECIAL WIDGETS	DE LUXE WIDGETS
Finished products (content of each unit):		
Material A	12 units	12 units
Material B	6 units	8 units
Direct labor	14 hours	20 hours

The general ledger does not include a finished-goods inventory account; costs are transferred directly from Work in Process to Cost of Sales at the time finished products are sold.

The budget and operating data for the month of August 19_7 are summarized as follows:

Budget for 9,000 projected direct-labor hours:	
Fixed manufacturing overhead	$ 4,500
Variable manufacturing overhead	13,500
Selling expenses	4,000
Administrative expenses	7,500
Operating data:	
Sales:	
500 special widgets	$52,700
100 de luxe widgets	16,400
Purchases:	
Material A	8,500 units, $ 9,725
Material B	1,800 units, 5,635

Material requisitions:

	MATERIAL A	MATERIAL B
Issued from stores:		
Standard quantity	8,400 units	3,200 units
Over standard	400 units	150 units
Returned to stores	75 units	

Direct-labor hours:

Standard (including those still in Work in Process)		9,600 hours
Actual		10,000 hours

Wages paid:

500 hours at	$2.10
8,000 hours at	2.00
1,500 hours at	1.90

Other costs:

Manufacturing overhead	$20,125, including $4,625 of fixed overhead
Selling	3,250
Administrative	6,460

required

1. Prepare journal entries to record operations for the month of August 19_7. Show computations of the amounts used in each journal entry. Raw-material purchases are recorded at standard. (Note that there is work in process at the end of the month. Because the problem does not disclose how many units are still in process, it is impossible to reconcile standard hours worked with goods completed. This will not prevent solution of the problem, however.)

2. Prepare a statement of income for the month supported by an analysis of variations. (Treat all variations as if they were adjustments of standard cost of sales.)

9-12. **Variance Analysis; Combined Overhead Rate.** The Trowbridge Trinket Corporation makes various small novelty gifts and seasonal decorations. The chief cost accountant has developed standards for usage of materials and for the various direct-labor operations. The company uses a flexible budget as an aid in overhead control. Budgeted *total* overhead at a 40,000-standard-direct-labor-hour level is $85,500. Budgeted *variable* overhead at a 30,000-standard-direct-labor-hour level is $27,000.

The following data were available for analysis at the end of the month of June:

Volume variance	$ 3,300 (Unfavorable)
Material purchases	100,000
Direct-labor costs incurred	104,400
Direct-labor rate variance	4,350 (Favorable)
Total direct-labor variance	600 (Favorable)
Average wage rate (10¢ less than the average standard rate)	$2.40 per hour
Total actual overhead for month	$ 88,750
Fixed overhead for the month	$ 50,000

The company uses a combined-overhead rate of 80 percent of standard direct-labor cost.

required

Analyze all variances as far as the data permit, showing all supporting work, including amounts for costs incurred and costs applied for direct labor, variable overhead, and fixed overhead. Be sure to give a complete analysis of variable and fixed components of overhead.

9-13. **Normal Costing and Overhead Analysis.** The Blaney Company had *budgeted* the following performance for 19_4:

Units	10,000
Sales	$120,000
Total variable production costs, including variable factory overhead of $5,000	60,000
Total fixed production costs	25,000
Gross margin	35,000
Beginning inventories	None

It is now December 31, 19_4. The factory-overhead rate that was used throughout the year was $3 per unit. Total factory overhead incurred was $30,000. Underapplied factory overhead was $900. There is no work in process.

required

1. How many units were produced during 19_4?

2. Nine thousand units were sold at regular prices during 19_4. Assuming that the predicted cost behavior patterns implicit in the budget above have conformed to the plan (except for variable factory overhead), and that underapplied factory overhead is written off directly as an adjustment of cost of goods sold, what is the gross margin for 19_4? How much factory overhead should be assigned to the ending inventory if it is to be carried at "normal" cost?

3. Explain *why* overhead was underapplied by $900. In other words, analyze the variable- and fixed-overhead variances as far as the data permit.

9-14. Variance Analysis; Find Standard Time Per Unit.   The Mahon Electrical Company manufactures special electrical equipment. The management has established standard costs for many of its operations and uses a flexible budget. Overhead is applied on a basis of standard labor hours. The Transformer Assembly Department operates at the following standard rates:

STANDARD COSTS
One Multiplex Transformer TR-906

Materials:
    4 sheets soft iron, 9 × 16 in. @ $1.12 ea.
    2 spools copper wire   @ $2.39 ea.
Direct-labor rate $2.50 per hour
Combined-overhead rate $2.10 per direct-labor hour

The flexible budget indicates that total overhead would amount to $4,489 and $4,989 at production levels of 500 and 600 units, respectively. The production budget for the past month called for 2,340 direct-labor hours, $2,925 variable-overhead costs, and $1,989 fixed-overhead costs. Only 550 transformers were produced, at the costs listed below:

Materials purchased:
    3,000 sheets soft iron, $3,300
    1,500 spools copper wire, $3,600
Materials used:
    2,215 sheets soft iron
    1,106 spools copper wire
Direct labor:
    2,113 hours, $5,409.28
Overhead:
   Variable costs, $2,769
   Fixed costs, $2,110

required

1. What is the standard time for assembling a transformer?
2. What is the standard unit cost?
3. What was the material-price variance during the past month?
4. The material-quantity variance?
5. The direct-labor rate variance?
6. The direct-labor efficiency variance?
7. Variable-overhead spending variance?
8. Variable-overhead efficiency variance?
9. Fixed-overhead budget variance?
10. Fixed-overhead volume variance?

9-15. Multiple Choice; Working Backward from Given Variances. [Adapted from a problem prepared by Walter Kennon and David Green, Jr.] The Kengreen Manufacturing Company produces only one product. Indirect costs are assigned on the basis of direct-labor hours.

At denominator activity, the standard cost per unit is as follows:

COST STANDARD

	MOLDING DEPARTMENT	PAINTING DEPARTMENT	TOTAL
Direct materials:			
Molding powder, 3 lbs. @ $6 per lb.	$18.00		
Paint, 1 gallon, @ $4.00		$4.00	$22.00
Direct labor:			
4 hours, @ $2.50	10.00		
½ hour, @ $2.00		1.00	11.00
Variable indirect costs:			
4 hours, @ $1.50	6.00		
½ hour, @ $3.00		1.50	7.50
Fixed indirect costs:			
4 hours, @ 50¢	2.00		
½ hour, @ $1.00		.50	2.50
Total	$36.00	$7.00	$43.00

For the month of February 19_1, the following statement presents the comparison of actual costs with standard costs.

COMPARISON OF ACTUAL AND STANDARD COSTS

	STANDARD*	ACTUAL	TOTAL VARIANCE†
Molding Department			
Direct materials	$ 7,560	$ 7,869	$309
Direct labor	4,200	4,125	75 F
Variable indirect costs	2,520	2,640	120
Fixed indirect costs	840	1,200	360
Total Molding Dept. costs	$15,120	$15,834	$714

Painting Department

Direct materials	$ 1,680	$ 1,350	$330 F
Direct labor	420	500	80
Variable indirect costs	630	550	80 F
Fixed indirect costs	210	375	165
Total Painting Dept. costs	$ 2,940	$ 2,775	$165
Total	$18,060	$18,609	$549

* Represents standard costs applied to product.
† Favorable variances are indicated by F. Unfavorable variances are unmarked.

VARIANCE ANALYSIS

	MOLDING DEPT.	PAINTING DEPT.	TOTAL
Direct Materials:			
Usage	$180	$120	$300
Price	129	450 F	321 F
Total direct-material variance	$309	$330 F	$ 21 F
Direct Labor:			
Efficiency	$ 75 F	$ 20 F	$ 95 F
Wage rate		100	100
Total direct-labor variance	$ 75 F	$ 80	$ 5
Variable Indirect Costs:			
Efficiency	$ 45 F	$ 30 F	$ 75 F
Spending	165	50 F	115
Total variable indirect costs	$120	$ 80 F	$ 40
Fixed Indirect Costs:			
Budget	$	$ 75	$ 75
Volume	360	90	450
Total fixed indirect costs	$360	$165	$525
Total variance	$714	$165 F	$549

There are no inventories of work in process at the beginning or at the end of February.

Labor wage-rate standards are set according to the union contract, but new employees have to be paid a premium because of a shortage of workers.

Material-price standards are set according to the company budget as to estimated material prices from regular suppliers. Prices are accepted as external to the company and not under company control.

required   (Support your answers with computations.)

1. The number of units produced during February were:
   a. 420
   b. 423
   c. 370
   d. None of these, but can be determined from the data given
   e. Cannot be determined from the information given

2. The number of pounds of molding powder used during February were:
   a. 1,260
   b. 1,282
   c. 1,305
   d. 1,290
   e. None of these

3. The average actual wage rate for direct labor in the painting department during February was:
   a. $2.00 per hour
   b. $2.50 per hour
   c. $1.93 per hour
   d. $2.27 per hour
   e. None of these

4. The unfavorable material-price variance of $129 in the molding department is the responsibility of:
   a. The molding department foreman and workers
   b. The engineer who designed the product
   c. The president of the company
   d. The controller and head accountant of the company
   e. No one in the company organization

5. The denominator operating activity of the painting department is:
   a. 200 direct-labor hours
   b. 300 direct-labor hours
   c. 210 direct-labor hours
   d. 310 direct-labor hours
   e. Cannot be determined from the data given

6. The $75 unfavorable budget variance for fixed costs in the painting department represents:
   a. The actual total fixed costs in excess of the fixed cost applied to product at the rate of $1.00 per direct-labor hour
   b. The actual total fixed costs in excess of the budget
   c. The actual direct-labor hours in excess of the standard hours allowed costed at the rate of $1.00 per hour
   d. Denominator activity less actual hours costed at the rate of $1.00 per hour
   e. Cost over- or underapplied

7. The $45 favorable efficiency variance for Variable Indirect Costs in the molding department represents:
   a. The amount the molding department was able to save by reducing variable costs when the department did not produce at full capacity
   b. The standard time required at full capacity less the actual hours operated costed at the standard variable indirect-cost rate of $1.50 per hour
   c. An amount the molding department was able to save by producing in less time than the standard allowed
   d. Actual variable indirect cost less the actual hours operated costed at the standard rate of $1.50 per hour
   e. Actual variable indirect cost less standard indirect cost

8. The flexible *budget for actual hours of input* worked for Variable Indirect Costs in the molding department was:
   a. $2,400
   b. $2,520
   c. $2,475

    d. $2,565

    e. None of these

9. The budget for total fixed indirect costs in the molding department was:

    a. $1,000

    b. $1,560

    c. $840

    d. $1,200

    e. None of these

9-16. Variance Analysis from Fragmentary Evidence.   Being a bright young man, you have just landed a wonderful job as assistant controller of Gyp-Clip, a new and promising division of Croding Metals Corporation. The Gyp-Clip Division has been formed to produce a single product, a new-model paper clip. Croding Laboratories has developed an extremely springy and lightweight new alloy, Clypton, which is expected to revolutionize the paper-clip industry.

    Gyp-Clip has been in business one month; it is your first day on the job. The controller takes you on a tour of the plant and explains the operation in detail: Clypton wire is received on two-mile spools from the Croding mill at a fixed price of $40 a spool, which is not subject to change. Clips are bent, cut, and shipped in bulk to the Croding packaging plant. Factory rent, depreciation, and all other items of fixed factory overhead are handled by the home office at a set rate of $100,000 per month. Ten thousand tons of paper clips have been produced, but this is only 75 percent of denominator activity, since demand for the product must be built up.

    The controller has just figured out the month's variances; he is looking for a method of presenting them in clear, logical form to top management at the home office. You say that you know of just the method, and promise to have the analysis ready the next morning.

    Filled with zeal and enthusiasm, feeling that your future as a rising star in this growing company is secure, you decide to take your wife out to dinner to celebrate the trust and confidence that your superior has placed in you.

    Upon returning home, with the flush of four martinis still upon you, you are horrified to discover your dog happily devouring the controller's figure sheet. You manage to salvage only the following fragments:

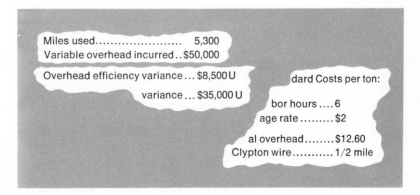

Miles used...................... 5,300
Variable overhead incurred.. $50,000

Overhead efficiency variance ... $8,500 U

           variance ... $35,000 U

dard Costs per ton:

bor hours 6

age rate $2

al overhead........ $12.60

Clypton wire........... 1/2 mile

    You remembered that the $35,000 variance did not represent the grand total of all variances. You also recalled that variance analysis was easier to tackle by expressing items in terms of hours rather than units.

required   Don't let the controller think you're a knucklehead; go ahead and make up your analysis of all variances.

9-17. **Combined-Overhead Rate; Determine Denominator Volume.** Department 385 has an overhead rate of 80 percent of direct-labor dollars for product-costing purposes. Its budgeted overhead at $25,000 of direct-labor cost is $22,400; at $40,000 of direct-labor cost, $27,200. What is denominator volume?

9-18. **Combined-Overhead Rate; Determine Overhead Behavior.**   A machining department has a flexible-overhead budget based on direct-labor cost. At direct-labor-cost levels of $3,500 and $4,000, budgeted overhead is $6,820 and $7,170, respectively. Factory overhead is applied to product at a rate of 165 percent of direct-labor cost.

required   1. Variable-overhead rate per direct-labor dollar

2. Fixed-overhead budget

3. Denominator activity expressed in direct-labor dollars

9-19. **Analysis of Variances; Combined-Overhead Rate [CPA].**   The Jones Furniture Company uses a standard-cost system in accounting for its production costs.

The standard cost of a unit of furniture follows:

Lumber, 100 feet @ $150 per 1,000 feet		$15.00
Direct labor, 4 hours @ $2.50 per hour		10.00
Manufacturing overhead:		
Fixed (30% of direct labor)	$3.00	
Variable (60% of direct labor)	6.00	9.00
Total unit cost		$34.00

The following monthly flexible overhead budget is in effect:

DIRECT-LABOR HOURS	ESTIMATED OVERHEAD
5,200	$10,800
4,800	10,200
4,400	9,600
4,000 (denominator activity)	9,000
3,600	8,400

The actual unit costs for the month of December were as follows:

Lumber used (110 feet @ $120 per 1,000 feet)	$13.20
Direct labor (4¼ hours @ $2.60 per hour)	11.05
Manufacturing overhead ($10,560 ÷ 1,200 units)	8.80
Total actual unit cost	$33.05

required   Prepare a schedule that shows an analysis of each element of the total variance from standard cost for the month of December.

9-20. **Working Backward from Given Variances.**   The Vanguard Company manufactures one product. Its standard-cost system incorporates flexible budgets and assigns indirect costs on the basis of standard direct-labor hours.

At denominator activity, the standard cost per unit is as follows:

Direct materials, 3 lbs. @ $5.00	$15.00
Direct labor, 2 hrs. @ $4.00	8.00
Variable indirect costs, 2 hrs. @ $1.20	2.40
Fixed indirect costs, 2 hrs. @ $.80	1.60
Total	$27.00

For the month of October 19_2, the performance report included the following information (in dollars):

	INCURRED AT ACTUAL PRICE	STANDARD COSTS APPLIED	TOTAL VARIANCE	VARIANCE ANALYSIS PRICE OR RATE	USAGE OR EFFICIENCY	VOLUME
Direct materials used	$134,400	$135,000	$ 600 F	$5,600 F	$ 5,000 U	—
Direct labor	77,900	72,000	5,900 U	1,900 U	4,000 U	—
Variable indirect costs	21,500	21,600	100 F	1,300 F	1,200 U	—
Fixed indirect costs	15,800	14,400	1,400 U	200 F*	—	$1,600 U
	$249,600	$243,000	$6,600 U	$5,200 F	$10,200 U	$1,600 U

* Budget variance.

Direct materials were quoted at $5.50 per pound throughout September and October by all suppliers. There was no purchase-price variance for materials in October; the price variance shown relates solely to the materials used during October.

Wage standards were set in accordance with an annual union contract, but a shortage of workers in the local area has resulted in rates higher than standard.

There were no beginning or ending inventories of work in process.

required   For the month of October:

1. Number of units produced. Triple-check your computations here before proceeding.

2. Actual number of direct-labor hours.

3. Actual wage rate.

4. Budget for fixed indirect costs.

5. Denominator activity expressed in direct-labor hours.

6. Pounds of direct materials purchased.

7. Pounds of direct materials used.

9-21. Standard Costing and Net Income.   The Dreb Company had net income for the first ten months of 19_1 of $100,000. There were absolutely no cost variances of any kind through October 31. One hundred thousand units were produced and sold during the ten-month period. Fixed manufacturing overhead was $1,000,000 through October 31. The company uses a standard-costing system. All variances are disposed of at year-end as an adjustment to Standard Cost of Goods Sold. There are no ending inventories.

required   If a total of 25,000 units are produced and sold during the remainder of the year, what is the net income for the year likely to be?

9-22. **Variable- and Fixed-Overhead Variances.** George Hallway has asked you to prepare an analysis of the overhead costs of his department. As a first step, you decide to prepare a summary of the events that bear on overhead for the most recent period. The variable-overhead budget variance was $1,000, unfavorable. The volume variance was $5,000, favorable. Budgeted fixed factory overhead was $110,000; the variable-overhead rate per hour was $.50. The denominator activity in hours was 110,000. Actual fixed overhead was $120,000. The variable-overhead spending variance was $2,000, favorable.

required

1. Actual variable overhead

2. Variable-overhead efficiency variance

3. Fixed-overhead budget variance

4. Fixed overhead applied to product

5. Variable overhead applied to product

6. Standard hours allowed for work done

7. Actual hours of input

9-23. **Working Backward from Given Variances.** The Brile Company uses a flexible budget and standard costs to aid planning and control. At a 60,000-direct-labor-hour level, budgeted variable overhead is $30,000 and budgeted direct labor is $240,000.

The following are some results for August:

Variable-overhead budget variance	$ 10,500 U
Variable-overhead efficiency variance	9,500 U
Actual direct-labor costs incurred	294,000
Material purchase-price variance (based on goods purchased)	16,000 F
Material-usage variance	9,000 U
Fixed overhead incurred	50,000
Fixed-overhead spending variance	2,000 U

The standard cost per pound of direct materials is $1.50. The standard allowance is one pound of direct materials for each unit of finished product. Ninety thousand units of product were made during August. There was no beginning or ending work in process. In July, the material-usage variance was $1,000, favorable, and the purchase-price variance was $.20 per pound, unfavorable. In August, the purchase-price variance was $.10 per pound.

In July, labor troubles caused an immense slowdown in the pace of production. There had been an unfavorable direct-labor efficiency variance of $60,000; there was no labor-rate variance. These troubles had persisted in August. Some workers quit. Their replacements had to be hired at higher rates, which had to be extended to all workers. The actual average wage rate in August exceeded the standard average wage rate by $.20 per hour.

required

For August:

1. Total pounds of direct materials purchased during August

2. Total number of pounds of excess material usage

3. Variable-overhead spending variance

4. Total number of actual hours worked

5. Total number of standard hours allowed for the finished units produced

9-24. **Two Plants and Standard Costs.** The Orose Glass Company is organized into three divisions. The Industrial Glass Division, headed by Bill Carder, general manager, has seven plants, located in various parts of the United States.

The plants are located near the ultimate customers, because competition is very intense. A manufacturer that has to add long-haul freight costs into a bid stands little chance of getting profitable business.

On this particular morning, Bill was talking to two of his plant managers, who supplied adjacent geographical locations in the western part of the country. "A new technique has been developed that will impregnate glass with a special material, Al_1N_2. Glass impregnated with this material effectively filters 99.9 percent of harmful rays from the sun, at the same time allowing an observer to determine the color and quantity of the material in the bottle.

"Market research on the product indicates that Orose Glass will not be able to pass on any added cost of this product to the industrial consumer. However, the research did show that if containers made of the new material are sold at the same price as present containers ($295 per batch), the demand would be heavy. The market forecast is 500 batches. [A batch is 10,000 bottles.]

"We want to convert a part of one plant to the new process. We would like it to be one of your plants because of the similarity of your activities. Since you share a common sales force, your sales are just about equal. The operating costs for this product for your two plants are very similar." (Exhibit 9-9.)

EXHIBIT 9-9

(Because of the similarities of the two plants, one operating statement for this product is applicable to both plants.)

Sales: 350 batches			
Total revenue (350 × $295)		$103,250.00	
Cost of sales:			
Direct labor at standard	$ 8,575.00		
Direct materials at standard	61,250.00		
Total prime costs		$69,825.00	
Overhead costs at flexible budgeted amounts:			
Indirect labor	$ 4,700.00		
Power	2,375.00		
Maintenance and repair	1,605.00		
Supplies	387.50		
Supervision	4,000.00		
Division administrative expense	2,500.00		
Home-office burden	3,500.00		
Depreciation*	13,000.00		
Total overhead costs		32,067.50	
Total cost		$101,892.50	
Plant profit before variances		$ 1,357.50	
Spending and rate variances	$ 1,000 F		
Efficiency variances	1,000 U	0	
Plant profit		$ 1,357.50	

*Does not include allowance for new equipment.

Bill went on to say, "Because of the density of the liquid glass when it contains Al_1N_2, a new glass-blowing machine will have to be purchased. However, the rest of the production process can use existing equipment. The cost of the new machine is $50,000, and it has an expected life of 20 years. Straight-line depreciation will be used for internal control and evaluation. The cost of the Al_1N_2 will be $15 a batch.

"Well, boys, that's the story," said Bill. "Why don't you take a look at the figures and let me know which of you thinks he can make a profit on the new process."

Jim Cline took one look at the numbers and said, "This baby will cost me a lot of money. Take a look. The full cost to produce a batch is $280.30 [Exhibit 9-10]. If we add $15 to that, I am going to lose 30¢ a batch plus the added cost of depreciation. Besides, my volume variance was unfavorable by $3,787.50 last year, which means my batch cost must be more than $280.30. No thanks; I don't want that new process."

EXHIBIT 9-10

Denominator volume:		400 batches (4,000,000 units)
Practical capacity:		600 batches (6,000,000 units)
Average volume last three years:		350 batches (3,500,000 units)

Standard costs based on denominator volume of 400 batches:

	TOTAL COST (400 BATCHES)	STANDARD COST PER BATCH
Direct labor	$ 9,800	$ 24.50
Direct materials	70,000	175.00
Indirect labor	4,800	12.00
Power	2,500	6.25
Maintenance and repair	1,620	4.05
Supplies	400	1.00
Supervision	4,000	10.00
Division administrative expense	2,500	6.25
Home-office burden	3,500	8.75
Depreciation	13,000	32.50
Total cost at standard	$112,120	$280.30

Standard cost per batch = $280.30

George Atkins pondered the numbers a little longer and said, "I haven't had time to check all the numbers, but I think this might be a money maker. Let me work on this a while, Bill, and I'll let you know if I want to use it."

required

1. Who is right, Jim or George?

2. If the process is used, how much will profits increase or decrease?

3. Explain the $3,787.50 variance that Jim mentioned. Why is it not in Exhibit 9-9?

4. Given your answer to 2, assume that the material Al_1N_2 could go up or down in price over the next few months. At what price level would the new

process be exactly as profitable as the old (given that sales would be at 500 batches a year)?

Note 1: Old glass-blowing machines are fully depreciated and have no salvage value. The cost of removal is very small.

Note 2: Inventories of products are not maintained. Production is done on a job-order basis in batches of 10,000. Standard costs are determined for batches of 10,000.

10

Income Effects
of Alternative
Product-Costing
Methods

When an accounting system is designed, managers and accountants must choose an inventory-valuation method. This decision is vital for many reasons, including its effects on reported income in any given year, on the evaluation of a manager's performance, and on pricing decisions. We will now explore the impact of various alternatives on income and on some operating decisions.

The major purpose of this chapter is to examine and compare the effects of various alternatives on product costs and income. Other decision implications of these alternatives are also mentioned, but they are discussed more fully in subsequent chapters.

We consider three major topics: (a) the contribution approach to income measurement, often called direct costing; (b) the role of various activity levels in absorption costing; and (c) standard-cost variances and the income statement. These topics are related sufficiently to warrant their being considered in a single chapter. However, they may be studied independently. Consequently, each of the three Problems for Self-Study in this chapter is placed at the end of the appropriate major section. If you cover all topics, you will benefit by pausing at the end of each section and solving the pertinent Problem for Self-Study.

CONTRIBUTION APPROACH TO INVENTORY VALUATION: DIRECT COSTING

contribution approach versus traditional approach

As the Problem for Self-Study in Chapter 3 showed, the major difference between the traditional and the contribution approaches is the tendency of the traditional approach to emphasize a functional-cost classification as opposed to a classification by cost behaviors. Hence, the traditional income statement would have the following pattern:

Sales	xx
Less manufacturing cost of goods sold (including fixed manufacturing overhead)	xx
Gross profit	xx
Less selling and administrative expenses	xx
Operating income	xx

In contrast, the contribution approach stresses cost behavior as the primary classification scheme:

Sales		xx
Less variable costs:		
Manufacturing	xx	
Selling	xx	
Administrative	xx	xx
Contribution margin		xx
Less fixed costs:		
Manufacturing	xx	
Selling	xx	
Administrative	xx	xx
Operating income		xx

Note that the traditional statement does not show any contribution margin. This raises analytical difficulties in the computation of the impact on net income of changes in sales. Fixed manufacturing overhead, under traditional procedures, is unitized and assigned to products. Hence, unit costs and gross-profit figures include fixed overhead that must be removed for a short-run cost–volume–profit analysis.

The contribution approach stresses the lump-sum amount of fixed costs to be recouped before net income emerges. This highlighting of total fixed costs helps to attract management attention to fixed-cost behavior and control when both short-run and long-run plans are being made. Keep in mind that advocates of this contribution approach *do not maintain that fixed costs are unimportant or irrelevant;* but they do stress that the distinctions between behaviors of variable and fixed costs are crucial for certain decisions.

advantages of
contribution
margins
and ratios

The advantages of knowing the contribution margins and ratios of divisions and product lines may be summarized as follows:

1. *Contribution-margin ratios* often help management decide on which products to push and which to de-emphasize or to tolerate only because of the sales benefits that relate to other products.

2. *Contribution margins* are essential for helping management to decide whether a product line should be dropped. In the short run, if a product recovers more than its variable costs, it is making a contribution to overall profits. This information is provided promptly by the contribution approach. Under the traditional approach, the relevant information is not only difficult to gather, but there is a danger that management may be misled by reliance on unit costs that contain an element of fixed overhead.

3. Contribution margins may be used to appraise alternatives that arise with respect to price reductions, special discounts, special advertising campaigns, and the use of premiums to spur sales volume. Decisions such as these are really determined by a comparison of the added costs with the prospective additions in sales revenue. Ordinarily, the higher the contribution-margin ratio, the better the opportunity for sales promotion; the lower the ratio, the greater the increase in volume that is necessary to recover additional sales-promotion commitments.

4. When desired profits are agreed upon, their attainability may be quickly appraised by computing the number of units that must be sold to secure the wanted profits. The computation is easily made by dividing the fixed costs plus desired profits by the contribution margin per unit.

5. Decisions must often be made as to how to utilize a given set of resources (for example, machines or materials) most profitably. The contribution approach furnishes the data for a proper decision, because the latter is determined by the product that makes the largest total contribution to profits. (However, the solution to the problem of calculating the maximum contribution is not always intuitively obvious. This point is amplified in Chapters 11 and 27.)

6. The contribution approach is helpful where selling prices are firmly established in the industry, because the principal problem for the individual company is how much variable cost is allowable (a matter most heavily affected in many companies by design of products) and how much volume can be obtained.

7. Pricing will be discussed at greater length in the next chapter. Ultimately, maximum prices are set by customer demand. Minimum short-run prices are sometimes determined by the variable costs of producing and selling. Advocates of a contribution approach maintain that the compilation of unit costs for products on a contribution basis helps managers understand the relationship among costs, volume, prices, and profits and hence leads to wiser pricing decisions.

absorption
costing and
direct costing

The contribution approach to inventory valuation differs from the traditional approach in only one conceptual respect: Fixed manufacturing overhead is excluded from the inventory cost of manufactured products.

Chapter 9 demonstrated the traditional approach, whereby fixed manufacturing overhead was unitized and became absorbed as a cost of product along with the variable manufacturing overhead.

Before continuing, let us consider some new terminology. There are two opposing ideas, commonly labeled as *absorption costing* and *direct costing*. Absorption costing (the traditional approach) signifies that fixed factory overhead is inventoried. In contrast, direct costing signifies that fixed factory overhead is not inventoried. These terms may be coupled with either of the two product-costing systems you have learned in this book—normal costing and standard costing—depending solely on whether a particular system inventories fixed overhead:

1. *Normal absorption costing.* Includes actual prime costs (direct materials and direct labor) plus predetermined variable and fixed manufacturing overhead.
2. *Standard absorption costing.* Includes predetermined prime costs plus predetermined variable and fixed overhead.
3. *Normal direct costing.* Includes actual prime costs plus predetermined variable manufacturing overhead; excludes fixed manufacturing overhead.
4. *Standard direct costing.* Includes predetermined prime costs plus predetermined variable manufacturing overhead; excludes fixed manufacturing overhead.

Absorption costing is much more widely used than direct costing, although the growing use of the contribution approach in performance measurement and cost analysis has led to increasing use of direct costing.

Direct costing is more accurately called *variable* or *marginal* costing, because in substance it applies only the *variable* production costs to the cost of the product. Direct costing has an impact on net income different from that of absorption costing because fixed manufacturing is regarded as a period cost (charged against revenue immediately) rather than as a product cost (assigned to units produced).

Direct costing has been a controversial subject among accountants—not so much because there is disagreement about the need for delineating between variable- and fixed-cost behavior patterns for management planning and control, but because there is a question about its theoretical propriety for *external* reporting. Proponents of direct costing maintain that the fixed part of factory overhead is more closely related to the *capacity* to produce than to the production of specific units. Opponents of direct costing maintain that inventories should carry a fixed-cost component, because both variable and fixed costs are necessary to produce goods; both these costs should be inventoriable, regardless of their differences in behavior patterns. Neither the public accounting profession nor the Internal Revenue Service has approved of direct costing as a generally acceptable method of inventory valuation.

The notion of direct costing blends easily with the contribution-margin approach advocated in this text. Exhibit 10-1 illustrates the principal differences between direct costing and absorption costing. Note the following points about the exhibit:

1. Under absorption costing, fixed production costs are applied to the product, to be subsequently released to expense as a part of Cost of Goods Sold. Under

EXHIBIT 10-1

COMPARISON OF ABSORPTION AND DIRECT COSTING

B Company
Income Statements
For the Year Ending Dec. 31, 19_1

(Date assumed; there is no beginning inventory; the unit variable manufacturing cost is $6.00.)

ABSORPTION COSTING

	UNIT COST		
Sales, 1,000 units @ $10.00			$10,000
Cost of goods sold:			
Variable manufacturing costs:			
1,100 units	$6.00	$6,600	
Fixed manufacturing costs	2.00	2,200	
Cost of goods available for sale	$8.00	$8,800	
Less ending inventory:			
(100 units)	8.00	800	
			8,000
Gross margin			$ 2,000
Less total selling and administrative expenses, including $400 of variable expenses			900
Net income			$ 1,100*

DIRECT COSTING

Sales		$10,000
Variable manufacturing costs of goods produced	$6,600	
Less ending inventory: 100 units @ $6.00	600	
Variable manufacturing cost of goods sold	$6,000	
Add variable selling and administrative expenses	400	
Total variable costs charged against sales		6,400
Contribution margin		$ 3,600
Less fixed costs:		
Fixed manufacturing costs	$2,200	
Fixed selling and administrative expenses	500	
		2,700
Net income		$ 900*

*The $200 difference in net income is caused by the $200 ($800 − $600) difference in ending inventories. Under absorption costing, $200 of the $2,200 fixed manufacturing costs is held back in inventory; whereas under direct costing, the $200 is released immediately as a charge against sales.

direct costing, fixed production costs are regarded as period costs and are immediately released to expense along with the selling and administrative expenses.

2. Under direct costing, only the variable manufacturing costs are regarded as product costs. Variability with manufacturing volume is the criterion used for the classification of costs into product or period categories.

3. In direct costing, the *contribution margin*—the excess of sales over variable costs—is a highlight of the income statement. Other terms for *contribution margin* include *marginal income, marginal balance, profit contribution,* and *contribution to fixed costs.*

4. The absorption-costing statement in Exhibit 10-1 differentiates between the variable and fixed costs only to aid your comparison. Costs are seldom classified as fixed or variable in absorption-costing statements, although such a classification is possible. Managers who are accustomed to looking at operations from a breakeven-analysis and flexible-budget viewpoint find that the absorption income statement fails to dovetail with cost–volume–profit relationships. They are then forced to take time for an attempt to reconcile and interpret two or more sets of figures that portray a single operating situation. Direct-costing proponents say that it is more efficient to present important cost–volume–profit relationships as integral parts of the major financial statements.

5. If inventories increase during a period, the direct-costing method will generally report less net income than absorption costing; when inventories decrease, direct costing will report more net income than absorption costing. The differences in net income, as the note at the bottom of Exhibit 10-1 indicates, are due *solely* to the difference in accounting for *fixed* manufacturing costs.

Whether direct costing should be acceptable for external reporting need not be of paramount importance to accountants or managers. Company systems can accommodate either method; the important point is that the internal reports should use the contribution approach as a technique for evaluation and control.

the central issue: a question of timing

Nearly all accountants agree that distinctions between variable and fixed costs are helpful for a wide variety of managerial decisions. The traditional view recognizes this need, but takes the position that such information may be supplied without changing the conventional methods of income determination. Adherents of direct costing maintain that the importance of variable- and fixed-cost behavior should be spotlighted not only by changing the format of the financial statements but also by changing the basic principles or concepts whereby fixed factory overhead is written off in the period incurred rather than funneled into inventory as an integral part of inventory costs. Thus, the central question becomes, What is the proper *timing* for release of fixed factory overhead as expense: at the time of incurrence, or at the time that the finished units to which the fixed overhead relates are sold? The focus must be upon relating fixed overhead to the definition of an asset.[1]

---

[1] See G. H. Sorter and C. T. Horngren, "Asset Recognition and Economic Attributes—The Relevant Costing Approach," *The Accounting Review,* XXXVII, No. 3, for a discussion of the role of fixed overhead in the valuation of inventory.

EXHIBIT 10-2

COMPARISON OF DIRECT COSTING AND ABSORPTION COSTING—
ANNUAL STATEMENTS

Basic production data at standard cost:

Direct materials	$1.30	
Direct labor	1.50	
Variable overhead	.20	$3.00
Fixed overhead ($150,000 ÷ 150,000 unit denominator volume)		1.00
Total		$4.00

Sales price, $5.00 per unit.

Selling and administrative expense, assumed for simplicity as being all fixed, $100,000 per year.

	FIRST YEAR	SECOND YEAR	THIRD YEAR	FOURTH YEAR	FOUR YEARS TOGETHER
Opening inventory in units	—	—	30,000	10,000	—
Production	150,000	170,000	140,000	150,000	610,000
Sales	150,000	140,000	160,000	160,000	610,000
Closing inventory in units	—	30,000	10,000	—	—
Direct costing:					
Sales	$750,000	$700,000	$800,000	$800,000	$3,050,000
Cost of goods manufactured	$450,000	$510,000	$420,000	$450,000	$1,830,000
Add opening inventory @ $3	—	—	90,000	30,000	—
Available for sale	$450,000	$510,000	$510,000	$480,000	$1,830,000
Deduct ending inventory @ $3	—	90,000	30,000	—	—
Cost of goods sold	$450,000	$420,000	$480,000	$480,000	$1,830,000
Contribution margin	$300,000	$280,000	$320,000	$320,000	$1,220,000
Fixed factory overhead	150,000	150,000	150,000	150,000	600,000
Selling and administrative expense	100,000	100,000	100,000	100,000	400,000
Net operating income	$ 50,000	$ 30,000	$ 70,000	$ 70,000	$ 220,000
Absorption costing:					
Sales	$750,000	$700,000	$800,000	$800,000	$3,050,000
Cost of goods manufactured	$600,000	$680,000	$560,000	$600,000	$2,440,000
Add opening inventory @ $4	—	—	120,000	40,000	—
Available for sale	$600,000	$680,000	$680,000	$640,000	$2,440,000
Deduct ending inventory @ $4	—	120,000	40,000	—	—
Cost of goods sold	$600,000	$560,000	$640,000	$640,000	$2,440,000
Volume variance*	—	(20,000)**	10,000	—	(10,000)
Adjusted cost of goods sold	$600,000	$540,000	$650,000	$640,000	$2,430,000
Gross margin	$150,000	$160,000	$150,000	$160,000	$ 620,000
Selling and administrative expense	100,000	100,000	100,000	100,000	400,000
Net operating income	$ 50,000	$ 60,000	$ 50,000	$ 60,000	$ 220,000

*Computation of volume variance based on denominator volume of 150,000 units:

Second year	$20,000 overapplied: (170,000 − 150,000) × $1.00
Third year	10,000 underapplied: (150,000 − 140,000) × $1.00
Four years together	$10,000 overapplied: (610,000 − 600,000) × $1.00

** As explained later in this chapter, some accountants favor prorating this variance between inventory and cost of goods sold.

comparison of
income figures

Exhibit 10-2 leads to the following generalizations about the comparative effects on net income of direct costing and absorption costing.[2]

1. When sales and production are in balance, direct- and absorption-costing methods yield the same profit. Under both methods, the amount of fixed cost incurred during the period is charged against revenue of the period. (See the first year in Exhibit 10-2.)

2. When production exceeds sales (that is, when in-process and finished inventories are increasing), absorption costing shows a higher profit than does direct costing. The reason is that, in absorption costing, a portion of the fixed manufacturing cost of the period is charged to inventory and thereby deferred to future periods. The total fixed cost charged against revenue of the period, therefore, is less than the amount of fixed cost incurred during the period. (See the second year in Exhibit 10-2.)

3. When sales exceed production (that is, when in-process and finished inventories are decreasing), absorption costing shows a lower profit than does direct costing. Under absorption costing, fixed costs previously deferred in inventory are charged against revenue in the period in which the goods are sold. Total fixed costs charged against revenue, therefore, exceed the amount of fixed cost incurred during the period. (See the third and fourth years in Exhibit 10-2.)

4. When sales volume is constant but production volume fluctuates, direct costing yields a constant profit figure, because profit is not affected by inventory changes. Under the same circumstances, absorption costing yields a fluctuating profit figure, which will be directly affected by the direction and amount of the *changes* in inventories. (See the third and fourth years in Exhibit 10-2.)

5. If production volume is constant, profit moves in harmony with sales under either direct or absorption costing. The profit figures will move in the same direction but will not necessarily be the same in amount, because inventory costs that are carried over from period to period will be greater under absorption costing. (See the first and fourth years in Exhibit 10-2.)

6. The divergence between periodic profit figures computed by direct- and absorption-costing methods tends to be smaller for long periods than for short periods, because production and sales volume tend to approach equality over a long period. Thus, the difference between total profit figures computed by the two methods is usually smaller for a few years (taken together) than the difference between year-to-year profit figures. Over a period of years, the methods should give substantially the same result, because sales cannot continuously exceed production, nor can production continuously exceed sales.

Direct costing excludes fixed factory overhead from inventory. In formula form, the difference between net incomes of absorption and direct costing may

---

[2]"Direct Costing," *N.A.A. Research Report No. 23*, pp. 38–39, adapted. Also see Yuji Ijiri, Robert K. Jaedicke, and John L. Livingstone, "The Effect of Inventory Costing Methods on Full and Direct Costing," *Journal of Accounting Research*, Vol. III, No. 1, 63–74.

be shown as follows:

$$\begin{matrix} \text{Profit Computed} \\ \text{by Absorption} \\ \text{Costing} \end{matrix} - \begin{matrix} \text{Profit Computed} \\ \text{by Direct Costing} \end{matrix} = \frac{\begin{matrix} \text{Total Fixed} \\ \text{Factory Overhead} \end{matrix}}{\begin{matrix} \text{Volume Used} \\ \text{for Unitizing} \\ \text{Fixed Overhead} \end{matrix}} \times \begin{matrix} \text{(Volume} \\ \text{Produced minus} \\ \text{Volume Sold)} \end{matrix}$$

or

$$\text{Difference in Profits} = \frac{\text{Fixed Factory Overhead}}{\text{per Unit}} \times \begin{matrix} \text{Change in} \\ \text{Inventory Units} \end{matrix}$$

Application of the formula above to Exhibit 10-2 is shown as follows:

	YEARS				FOUR YEARS TOGETHER
	1	2	3	4	
Absorption-cost profit	$50,000	$60,000	$50,000	$60,000	$220,000
Direct-cost profit	50,000	30,000	70,000	70,000	220,000
Difference	—	$30,000	$ (20,000)	$ (10,000)	—
Change in inventory in units (increase)	—	30,000	(20,000)	(10,000)	—
Multiply by $1.00					
Change in amount of fixed cost in inventory*	—	$30,000	$(20,000)	$(10,000)	—

* Change in units × fixed overhead rate of $1.00.

Note carefully that the difference in profits does not consist merely of the volume variance computed under absorption costing. This difference is related to the change in inventory position; and this change is independent of a given volume variance.

Absorption costing is far from being uniform in its application. There are different inventory methods, such as first-in, first-out; last-in, first-out; and weighted average.[3] There are different assumptions as to overhead application, such as the inclusion of some administrative costs in inventory and the classification of packaging costs. These problems remain, whether direct costing or absorption costing is used. The issue thus narrows to the propriety of excluding fixed costs from inventory.

Problem for Self-Study

PROBLEM   The Blazek Company had the following operating characteristics in 19_4 and 19_5:

Basic production data at standard cost:

Direct materials	$1.30	
Direct labor	1.50	
Variable overhead	.20	$3.00
Fixed overhead ($150,000 ÷ 150,000 units of denominator volume)		1.00
Total factory cost at standard		$4.00

[3] For a discussion, see Chapter 15.

Sales price, $5.00 per unit.

Selling and administrative expense is assumed for simplicity as being all fixed at $65,000 yearly, except for sales commissions at 5% of dollar sales.

	19_4	19_5
In units:		
Opening inventory	—	30,000
Production	170,000	140,000
Sales	140,000	160,000
Closing inventory	30,000	10,000

There were no variances from the standard variable costs, and fixed overhead incurred was exactly $150,000 per year. Any volume variance (under- or overapplied overhead) is written off directly at year-end as an adjustment to Cost of Goods Sold.

required

1. Income statements for 19_4 and 19_5 under direct costing and absorption costing.

2. A reconciliation of the difference in net income for 19_4, 19_5, and the two years as a whole.

SOLUTION 1.

BLAZEK COMPANY

Comparative Income Statements (in thousands of dollars)
For the Years 19_4 and 19_5

		19_4	19_5
Direct Costing:			
Sales	(1)	700	800
Opening inventory—at variable standard cost		—	90
Add variable cost of goods manufactured		510	420
Available for sale		510	510
Deduct ending inventory—at variable standard cost		90	30
Variable cost of goods sold		420	480
Variable selling expenses—at 5% of dollar sales		35	40
Total variable expenses	(2)	455	520
Contribution margin	(3) = (1) − (2)	245	280
Fixed factory overhead		150	150
Fixed selling and administrative expenses		65	65
Total fixed expenses	(4)	215	215
Net income	(3) − (4)	30	65

Absorption Costing:

Sales	700	800
Opening inventory—at standard absorption cost	—	120
Cost of goods manufactured	680	560
Available for sale	680	680
Deduct ending inventory	120	40
Cost of goods sold—at standard	560	640
Volume variance*	(20)	10
Adjusted cost of goods sold	540	650
Gross margin or gross profit—at "actual"	160	150
Selling and administrative expenses	100	105
Net income	60	45

* Computation of volume variance based on denominator volume of 150,000 units:

19_4	$20,000 overapplied (170,000 − 150,000) × $1.00
19_5	10,000 underapplied (150,000 − 140,000) × $1.00
Two years together	$10,000 overapplied (310,000 − 300,000) × $1.00

2. Reconciliation of differences in net income:

	19_4	19_5	TOGETHER
Net income under:			
Apsorption costing	$60,000	$45,000	$105,000
Direct costing	30,000	65,000	95,000
Difference to be explained	$30,000	$−20,000	$ 10,000
The difference can be reconciled by multiplying the fixed-overhead rate by the *change* in the total inventory units:			
Fixed-overhead rate	$1.00	$1.00	$1.00
Change in inventory units:			
Beginning inventory	—	30,000	—
Ending inventory	30,000	10,000	10,000
Change	30,000	20,000	10,000
Difference in net income explained	$30,000	$−20,000	$ 10,000

ROLE OF VARIOUS ACTIVITY LEVELS IN ABSORPTION COSTING

Chapter 9 pointed out that product costs and income can be significantly affected by the choice of a particular activity level as a denominator in the computation of fixed-overhead rates. We now study how various alternative levels of activity can affect operating income under absorption costing. As fixed costs become a more prominent part of an organization's total costs, the importance of this choice becomes greater.

characteristics
of capacity The choice of a capacity size is usually the result of capital-budgeting decisions, which are reached after studying the expected impact of these capital outlays on operations over a number of years. The choice may be influenced by a combination of two major factors, each involving trade-off decisions and each heavily depending on long-range forecasts of demand, material costs, and labor costs.

1. Provision for seasonal and cyclical *fluctuations* in demand. The trade-off is between (a) additional costs of physical capacity and (b) the costs of inventory stockouts and/or the carrying costs of inventory safety stocks of such magnitude to compensate for seasonal and cyclical variations, the costs of overtime premium, subcontracting, and so on.

2. Provision for upward *trends* in demand. The trade-off is between (a) the costs of constructing too much capacity for initial needs and (b) the later extra costs of satisfying demand by alternative means. For example, should a factory designed to make color television tubes have an area of 100,000, 150,000, or 200,000 square feet?

Although it can be defined and measured in a particular situation, capacity is an illusive concept. Consider, for example, the following:

> Capacity planning requires definition and measurement of capacity in a manner relevant to questions which arise in the planning process. This problem has two aspects. First, it is necessary to specify capacity in terms of how much the company should be prepared to make and to sell. Second, the capacity of specific facilities available or to be acquired must be determined. . . . A variety of alternative combinations of capacity and operating patterns is usually possible.[4]

There is much fluidity in the quotation above. To most people, the term *capacity* implies a constraint, an upper limit. We sometimes hear, "I'm working to capacity now. I simply can't do more." This same notion of capacity as a constraint is commonly held in industry.

Although the term *capacity* is usually applied to plant and equipment, it is equally applicable to other resources, such as men and materials. A shortage of direct labor, executive time, or raw materials may be determinative in limiting company production or sales.

The upper limit of capacity is seldom absolutely rigid, at least from an engineering viewpoint. That is, ways—such as overtime, subcontracting, or premium prices for raw materials—can usually be found to expand production. But these ways may be totally unattractive from an economic viewpoint. Hence, the upper limit of capacity is *specified* by management for current planning and control purposes after considering engineering and economic factors. The upper limit is usually *imposed* by management, not by external forces.

In our subsequent discussion, let us consider the word *capacity* as representing *practical capacity* (sometimes called *practical attainable capacity*), the

---

[4]"Accounting for Costs of Capacity," *N.A.A. Research Series Report No. 39* (New York: National Association of Accountants, 1963), p. 10.

maximum level at which the plant or department can operate most efficiently. Practical capacity allows for unavoidable operating interruptions such as repair time or waiting time (downtime).

Two commonly used[5] levels of capacity utilization are:

1. *Normal activity,* which is the level of capacity utilization that will satisfy average consumer demand over a span of time (often five years) that includes seasonal, cyclical, and trend factors; and
2. *Expected annual activity,* which is the anticipated level of capacity utilization for the coming year.

There are apt to be differences in terminology between companies, so be sure to obtain an understanding of terms in a given situation.

normal activity
versus
expected
annual activity

Expected annual activity, which may also be called *master-budgeted activity,* is the basis for applying all fixed overhead to products in any given year, while the overhead rate based on *normal activity* attempts to apply fixed overhead by using a *longer-run* average expected activity. Conceptually, the *normal rate* results in overapplications in some years that are offset by underapplications in other years.

We shall deal with fixed overhead only, because variable overhead fluctuates with changes in activity, and fixed overhead does not. *Thus, the entire problem of using expected annual activity or normal activity is raised by the presence of fixed overhead.* (If you will recall, the volume variance in Chapter 9 was confined to fixed overhead.) Consider the following data:

Fixed factory overhead	$500,000
Practical capacity per year	100,000 standard direct-labor hours
Normal activity	90,000 standard direct-labor hours
Expected annual activity for specific year	(Fluctuates from year to year)
Normal overhead rate, $500,000 ÷ 90,000 hours	$5.55
Expected annual overhead rate	(Varies from year to year)

Exhibit 10-3 shows that if normal activity is the base, the overhead rate of $5.55 would be used for costing inventory. In the second year, there would be an underapplied fixed-overhead balance of $5.55 times 20,000 hours, or $111,000. This unfavorable volume variance would be considered the measure of the cost of *not* producing—the loss from idle capacity. Inventories would be costed with a $5.55 rate instead of a $7.15 rate. Under the expected-annual-activity method, if volume fluctuates from year to year, product and

---

[5] It is difficult to make sweeping generalizations about how companies apply overhead to product. Studies of practice show conflicting results about whether actual or predetermined rates are used. In the latter cases, there are no clear patterns as to how normal activity, expected annual activity, or some other basis for application is selected in a particular company. See Charles R. Purdy, "Industry Patterns of Capacity or Volume Choice: Their Existence and Rationale," *Journal of Accounting Research,* Vol. III, No. 2, 228–41.

EXHIBIT 10-3

COMPARISON OF EXPECTED ANNUAL AND NORMAL ACTIVITY
FOR OVERHEAD APPLICATION

YEAR	STANDARD LABOR-HOURS WORKED*	EXPECTED ANNUAL ACTIVITY BASIS			NORMAL ACTIVITY BASIS		
		OVER-HEAD RATE	TOTAL APPLIED	UNDER-(OVER-) APPLIED	OVER-HEAD RATE	TOTAL APPLIED	UNDER-(OVER-) APPLIED†
1	90,000	$5.55	$500,000	$ —	$5.55	$500,000	$ —
2	70,000	7.15	500,000	—	5.55	389,000	111,000
3	100,000	5.00	500,000	—	5.55	555,000	(55,000)
4	80,000	6.33	500,000	—	5.55	445,000	55,000
5	100,000	5.00	500,000	—	5.55	555,000	(55,000)
6	100,000	5.00	500,000	—	5.55	555,000	(55,000)
				$ —			$ -0-‡

* For illustrative purposes, we assume that expected annual activity and standard labor-hours worked are equal.
† Debit underapplied or credit overapplied overhead directly to Income Summary as a measure of gain or loss from under- or overutilization of capacity. Note that this is simply the volume variance.
‡ Rounded

inventory costs will vary solely because of differences in utilization of facilities. Using a normal rate will avoid capricious changes in unit costs and will also provide a yearly and monthly measure of the cost of idle capacity.

Note carefully that Exhibit 10-3 is designed to stress only the computation of overhead rates under different activity bases. It deliberately avoids introducing changes in budgeted fixed-overhead costs; instead, it assumes that total fixed costs are constant from year to year. Actually, year-to-year changes in the prices paid for fixed-overhead items and services can affect the overhead rate, regardless of whether expected annual activity, normal activity, or some other activity base is used to set the rate.

selection of activity base The activity base to be used depends largely on the nature of the business. Fixed costs measure the capacity to make and sell. They usually include at least depreciation and a core of salaried payroll costs. The total fixed-cost commitment is influenced by the long-run sales outlook. The conventional view is that all products should receive some "equitable" portion of fixed overhead.

If the total sales volume does not change greatly from year to year, *expected annual activity* for each year is a rational base, because expected annual activity and normal activity coincide. In these cases, even if the companies have seasonal sales patterns, all fixed factory overhead is exactly applied to product by the end of the year. See Exhibit 10-3.

Many accountants reject the normal-activity notion and maintain that each year must stand by itself; that is, each year's overhead must be applied to each year's production, written off as a loss, or both. This attitude arises from (a) the widespread conviction that the year is the key time period, and (b) adherence to the idea that overhead costs for a given year generally must cling or attach to the units produced during that year regardless of the relationship of that year's activity to average long-run activity.

A more convincing reason for using expected annual activity as a base is the overwhelming measurement problem that accompanies the determination of normal activity. Sales not only fluctuate cyclically, but they have trends over the long run. In effect, the use of normal activity implies an unusual talent for accurate long-run forecasting. Many accountants and executives who reject the normal-activity idea as a base claim that the nature of their company's business precludes accurate forecasts beyond one year.

Where companies use normal activity, the objective is to choose a period long enough to average out sizable fluctuations in volume and to allow for trends in sales. The uniform rate for applying fixed overhead supposedly provides for "recovery" of fixed costs over the long run. General Motors' pricing policy uses this approach. Companies expect that overapplications in some years will be offset by underapplications in other years.

Conceptually, when *normal activity* is the base, the yearly over- or under-applied overhead should be carried forward on the balance sheet. Practically, however, year-end balances are closed directly to Income Summary, because the accounting profession (and the Internal Revenue Service) generally views the year as being the terminal time span for allocation of under- or overapplied overhead. In year 2 in Exhibit 10-3, the year-end journal entry for closing the fixed Factory Overhead accounts may appear as follows:

Fixed factory overhead applied	389,000	
Volume variance, unfavorable (to income summary)	111,000	
Fixed factory overhead control		500,000

The journal entry for the end of year 3 would appear as follows:

Fixed factory overhead applied	555,000	
Volume variance, favorable		55,000
Fixed factory overhead control		500,000

The logical question that should arise at this point is: Why use normal activity at all if the yearly over- or underapplications are written off at year-end anyway? Are the yearly results not the same, whether expected annual activity or normal activity are used? The Problem for Self-Study shows the fundamental answer: "There is still a difference, because inventory costs are different."

practical capacity   Many managements want to keep running at full capacity, which really means practical capacity. Their "normal activity" for applying fixed costs is "practical capacity"; anything less reduces profits and is undesirable. Therefore, the overhead-costing rates are relatively lower than if lesser activity levels were used as a base. Where product costs are used as guides for pricing, some managers say that this policy results in more competitive pricing, which maximizes both volume and profits in good times and bad. The accounting effects of such a policy are lower unit costs for inventory purposes and the almost perpetual appearance of an unfavorable volume variance (loss from idle capacity) on the income statements.

significance of activity base for product costing and control We can conclude from the discussion above that the proper activity base for product costing is largely a matter of opinion. The selection of a base probably becomes crucial where product costs heavily influence managerial decisions, particularly pricing decisions. For example, in a cyclical industry, the use of expected annual activity rather than normal activity as a base would tend to cause a company to quote low prices in boom years and high prices in depression years—in obvious conflict with good business judgment. That is why normal activity makes more sense as an overhead base when there are wide swings in business volume through the years, even though the yearly over- and underapplied overhead is not carried forward in the balance sheet from year to year.

In the realm of current planning and control, however, normal activity is an empty concept. Normal activity is used as a basis for long-range plans. It depends on the time span selected, the forecasts made for each year, and the weighting of these forecasts. In Exhibit 10-3, a comparison in year 2 of the 70,000-hour expected annual activity with the 90,000-hour normal activity might be suggested as the best basis for auditing long-range planning. However, normal activity is an average that has no particular significance with respect to a follow-up for a particular year. The pertinent comparison is a particular year's expected annual activity with that year's activity level used in the authorization for the acquisition of facilities. This comparison may be done project by project. It need not be integrated in the accounting system on a routine basis. Furthermore, attempting to use normal activity as a reference point for judging current performance is an example of misusing a long-range measure for a short-range purpose.

The expected annual activity, rather than normal activity or practical capacity, is more germane to the evaluation of current results. Expected annual activity is the basis for the year's master budget—the principal short-run planning and control tool. Managers feel much more obligated to reach the levels stipulated in the master budget, which should have been carefully set in relation to the maximum opportunities for sales in the current period. In contrast, normal activity and practical capacity are not so pertinent to current operating problems, because they are not usually incorporated in the comprehensive or master budget—the focus of attention.

Problem for Self-Study

PROBLEM The Shane Co. incurs fixed manufacturing overhead of $500,000 annually. Practical capacity is 100,000 standard direct-labor hours; normal activity, 90,000 hours; and expected annual activity, 70,000 hours. In 19_1, 70,000 units were produced (in 70,000 standard hours) and 60,000 units were sold. Standard hours worked were 70,000. There was no beginning inventory.

required

1. Prepare a three-column comparison of the various methods of applying fixed overhead to product. Designate which methods would result in the highest and the lowest net income. For each method, show the amounts that would be charged to:

Cost of sales (expense)
Loss from idle capacity, volume variance (loss)
Ending inventory

2. Why is expected annual activity better than either practical capacity or normal activity for judging current operating performance?

SOLUTION

1. Exhibit 10-4 shows that the use of different activity bases for developing product-costing overhead rates results in different *inventory valuations* and different net incomes. Further, the measure of utilization of facilities, the volume variance, will differ markedly. In Exhibit 10-4, income is lowest where practical capacity is the overhead base and highest when expected annual activity is the overhead base, because a smaller portion of overhead is held back as an asset in inventory when a lower overhead rate is used.

The exhibit also indicates that the accounting effects of using practical capacity are lower unit costs for inventory purposes and the steady appearance of "Loss from idle capacity" on the income statement.

2. As is explained more fully in the chapter, expected annual activity is more pertinent to current operating problems because it is usually the notion of activity that is incorporated in the master budget. Therefore, it has more current meaning to the department managers who must live with the budget.

STANDARD-COST VARIANCES AND THE INCOME STATEMENT

proration of variances

The advocates of currently attainable standard costs for product costing maintain that the results are conceptually superior to the results under "actual" or "normal" product-costing systems. They contend that variances are measures of inefficiency or abnormal efficiency. Therefore, variances are not inventoriable and should be completely charged or credited against revenue of the period instead of being prorated among inventories and cost of sales. In this way, inventory valuations will be more representative of desirable and attainable costs.

STIN COMPANY PROBLEM

An example of the effects of these conflicting viewpoints follows:

Stin Company has the following results for the year:

Purchases of direct materials (charged to Stores at standard prices)	$100,000
Purchase-price variance	10,000
Direct labor—applied at standard rate	40,000
Direct-labor rate variance	1,000
Direct-labor efficiency variance	4,000
Direct-material usage variance	4,000
Direct-materials—applied at standard prices	80,000

EXHIBIT 10-4

SOLUTION TO SELF-STUDY PROBLEM, PART 1

Income-Statement Effects of Using Various Activity Bases for Overhead Application

	EXPECTED ANNUAL ACTIVITY[a] USING A $7.15 OVERHEAD RATE	NORMAL ACTIVITY[b] USING A $5.55 OVERHEAD RATE	PRACTICAL CAPACITY[c] USING A $5.00 OVERHEAD RATE
Sales	$ xxx	$ xxx	$ xxx
Production costs:			
Direct materials, direct labor, variable overhead	$ xxx	$ xxx	$ xxx
Fixed overhead applied to product	500,000	389,000	350,000
Total production costs—70,000 units	$ xxx	$ xxx	$ xxx
Ending inventory—fixed-overhead component—10,000 units	71,500	55,555	50,000
Total fixed-overhead component of cost of sales	428,500	333,445	300,000
Loss from idle capacity (shown separately on income statements)—the volume variance, unfavorable	None	111,000	150,000
Total fixed overhead charged to the period's sales	$428,500	$444,445	$450,000
Net income	Highest	Middle	Lowest
Recapitulation:			
Total overhead to account for	$500,000	$500,000	$500,000
Accounted for as follows:			
Charged to Cost of Sales (expense)	$428,500	$333,445	$300,000
Charged to Loss from Idle Capacity, volume variance (loss)	None	111,000	150,000
Charged to Ending Inventory (asset)	71,500	55,555	50,000
Overhead accounted for	$500,000	$500,000	$500,000

[a] $500,000 ÷ 70,000 hours worked = $7.15 (rounded)
[b] $500,000 ÷ 90,000 hours normal activity = $5.55
[c] $500,000 ÷ 100,000 hours practical capacity = $5.00

Manufacturing overhead applied—at standard rate	$ 40,000
Manufacturing overhead incurred	45,000
Sales	135,000
Selling and administrative expenses	20,000

Assume that there is no ending work in process. Assume that one uniform product is made and that 60 percent of the production has been sold. There were no beginning inventories.

required   A comparative analysis of the effects on net income of the following assumptions:

1. Actual historical costing. That is, no predetermined costs are used.
2. Normal costing[6] with proration of underapplied overhead.
3. Normal costing without proration of underapplied overhead.
4. Standard costing with proration of all variances.
5. Standard costing without proration of any variances.

Try to solve this example before examining the solution that is in Exhibit 10-5. The answers show that differences could become significant, particularly where inventories have increased or decreased substantially or where the variances are relatively large.

In practice, the charging or crediting of variances directly to Cost of Sales or treating them as separate income additions or deductions from income would be considered acceptable as long as the standards are deemed to be currently attainable or as long as the net income and inventory figures are not greatly distorted; otherwise, the complete proration of variances is desirable and necessary. Many accountants favor showing the variances as completely separate deductions after the gross margin on sales. The latter approach helps distinguish between product costing (Cost of Sales at Standard) and loss recognition (unfavorable variances are lost costs because inefficiencies are not inventoriable).

The most accurate proration of material-price variances would be over five accounts—Direct-Material Usage Variance, Stores, Work in Process, Finished Goods, and Cost of Sales—in proportion to the standard material charges in each account. As the next step, the adjusted Material-Usage Variance should be prorated to Work in Process, Finished Goods, and Cost of Sales. Labor variances and overhead variances are usually prorated in the same manner as the material-usage variance. Variations of these proration methods may be desirable under certain conditions. For instance, efficiency variances may be viewed as being currently avoidable and price variances as being unavoidable and therefore proratable. Conceptually, this is superior to the other methods because the costs of avoidable inefficiency are written off, whereas unavoidable costs are not. This is correct because the costs of avoidable inefficiency do not qualify as assets under any economic test.

The author believes that unfavorable variances do not have to be inventoried as long as standards are currently attainable. However, if standards are not up to date, or if they reflect ideal performance rather than expected per-

---

[6]Chapter 4 explained that *normal costing* applies to units produced—the actual direct materials consumed, the actual direct labor used, and a predetermined overhead rate.

formance under reasonably efficient conditions, then conceptually the variances should be split between the portion that reflects departures from currently attainable standards and the portion that does not. The former should be written off as period charges; the latter should be prorated to inventories and cost of sales. For example, assume that an operation has an ideal standard time allowed of 50 minutes, which is reflected in a formal standard-cost system. The currently attainable standard is 60 minutes. Now if it takes, say, 75 actual minutes to perform the operation, the conceptual adjustment would call for writing off 15 minutes of the 25-minute variance as a period cost and for treating the remaining 10-minute variance as a product cost.

Problem for Self-Study

PROBLEM   The Bridget Company began operations on January 2, 19_4. Results for 19_4 are:

Direct labor incurred, 85,000 hours @ $6.05 per hour	$514,250
Sales	$660,000
Factory overhead incurred	$161,000
Selling and administrative expenses	$ 70,000
Purchase of direct materials, 100,000 lbs. @ $1.10. Standard price is $1.00. Purchases are charged to Stores at standard prices. The standard allowance per unit of finished output is one pound.	
Pounds of material consumed	90,000
Production in units	80,000
Sales in units	60,000

Direct-labor standards are one hour per unit at $6 per hour. Factory overhead is applied at a rate of $2 per standard hour.

required
1. Using standard absorption costing, prepare an income statement. Assume that all variances, including under- or overapplied overhead, are written off at year-end as separate deductions after the gross profit (at standard) is computed.

2. Prepare an income statement based on a proration of all variances. Include a schedule showing the proration to Direct-Material Usage Variance, Finished Goods, Cost of Goods Sold, and Stores.

3. Explain why operating income in requirement 2 differs from that in 1.

SOLUTION   1.

BRIDGET COMPANY

Income Statement
For the Year Ending December 31, 19_4

Sales	$660,000
Cost of goods sold—at standard cost of $9 per unit*	540,000
Gross profit—at standard	$120,000
Deduct unfavorable variances (see schedule)	55,250
Gross profit—at actual	$ 64,750
Selling and administrative expenses	70,000
Operating income (loss)	$ (5,250)

*$1 + $6 + $2 = $9 per unit

EXHIBIT 10-5

SOLUTION TO STIN COMPANY PROBLEM

		COMPARATIVE INCOME STATEMENTS			
ASSUMPTION	(1)	(2)	(3)	(4)	(5)
Sales	$135,000	$135,000	$135,000	$135,000	$135,000
Less cost of goods sold—at standard, .60 × ($80,000 + $40,000 + $40,000), or .60 × $160,000	96,000	96,000	96,000	96,000	96,000
Add proration of variances (see schedule):					
(1)	13,440				
(2)		13,440			
(3) $13,440 + $2,000 (see schedule)			15,440		
(4)				13,440	
(5)					24,000
Cost of goods sold—adjusted for variances	109,440	109,440	111,440	109,440	120,000
Selling and administrative expenses	20,000	20,000	20,000	20,000	20,000
Total charges to revenue	129,440	129,440	131,440	129,440	140,000
Net income (loss)	$ 5,560	$ 5,560	$ 3,560	$ 5,560	$ (5,000)

328

GENERAL SCHEDULE OF PRORATION OF VARIANCES (IN DOLLARS, ALL UNFAVORABLE)

	TOTAL	DIRECT-MATERIAL USAGE	TO STORES	TO FINISHED GOODS	TO COST OF GOODS SOLD
Standard costs of materials	100,000	4,000	16,000	32,000	48,000
Prorations of variances:					
Purchase price	10,000	400	1,600	3,200	4,800
Direct-material usage:					
Unadjusted balance	4,000	4,000			
Adjusted balance		4,400	—	1,760	2,640
Direct-labor rate	1,000			400	600
Direct-labor efficiency	4,000			1,600	2,400
Manufacturing overhead	5,000			2,000	3,000
	24,000		1,600	8,960	13,440

(1) Actual historical costing. Except for the purchase-price variance, the schedule prorates 40 percent of all variances to Finished Goods and 60 percent to Cost of Goods Sold.

(2) Normal costing with proration of underapplied overhead. Final result is the same as under (1).

(3) Normal costing without proration of underapplied overhead. The $2,000 charged to Finished Goods under (1) and (2) would be charged to Cost of Goods Sold.

(4) Standard costing with proration of all variances. Final result is the same as under (1) and (2).

(5) Standard costing without proration of any variances. All variances are charged to Cost of Goods Sold.

Note: For simplicity, the manufacturing-overhead variance has not been broken down into components such as spending, efficiency, or volume variances.

329

SCHEDULE OF VARIANCES

Direct-material purchase price, 100,000 lbs. @ $.10	$ 10,000
Direct-material usage, 10,000 lbs. @ $1.00	10,000
Direct-labor rate, 85,000 hrs. @ $.05	4,250
Direct-labor efficiency, 5,000 hrs. @ $6.00	30,000
Total overhead variance	1,000
Total variances (to income statement)	$ 55,250

2.

BRIDGET COMPANY

Income Statement
For the Year Ending December 31, 19_4

Sales	$660,000
Cost of goods sold (see schedule)	580,688
Gross profit	$ 79,312
Selling and administrative expenses	70,000
Operating income	$ 9,312

SCHEDULE OF PRORATION OF VARIANCES

	TOTAL	DIRECT-MATERIAL USAGE	TO STORES	TO FINISHED GOODS	TO COST OF GOODS SOLD
Standard costs of materials	$100,000	$10,000	$10,000	$20,000	$ 60,000
Prorations of variances:					
Purchase price	$ 10,000	$ 1,000	$ 1,000	$ 2,000	$ 6,000
Direct-material usage:					
Unadjusted balance	10,000	10,000			
Adjusted balance		$11,000		2,750	8,250
Direct-labor rate	4,250			1,062	3,188
Direct-labor efficiency	30,000			7,500	22,500
Total overhead variance	1,000			250	750
	$ 55,250		$ 1,000	$13,562	$ 40,688
Standard cost of goods sold					540,000
"Actual" cost of goods sold					$580,688

Note: The material-purchase price variance was prorated in proportion to the standard costs of materials in each account. The remaining variances should also be allocated in proportion to the related standard costs in each account. For example, direct labor would be prorated in proportion to the standard direct-labor components of Work in Process, Finished Goods, and Cost of Goods Sold. Because we are dealing with a uniform product here, we merely allocate $20/80$, or $1/4$, to Finished Goods and $60/80$, or $3/4$, to Cost of Goods Sold.

3. The $14,562 difference, $9,312 − ($−5,250), in operating income is explained by the holding back of variances of $14,562 as inventory ($13,562 in Finished Goods and $1,000 in Raw-Material Stores). Note that even though variances may be small in relation to total standard costs incurred, they may be large in relation to operating income.

summary

Many varieties of product costing are in use. For years, manufacturing companies have regularly used absorption costing, which includes fixed factory overhead as a part of the cost of product. In contrast, direct costing, which is more accurately called *variable costing*, charges fixed factory overhead to the period immediately; that is, fixed overhead is excluded from inventories. Absorption costing continues to be much more widely used than direct costing, although the growing use of the contribution approach in performance measurement has led to increasing use of direct costing.

Three commonly used activity bases for developing product-costing overhead rates are (a) expected annual activity, (b) normal activity over three to five years, and (c) practical capacity. The selection is essentially a matter of opinion. The choice will influence inventory valuations and resultant timing of income recognition.

The advocates of currently attainable standard costs for product costing maintain that the results are conceptually superior to the results under "actual" or "normal" product-costing systems. They contend that the costs of inefficiency are not inventoriable.

suggested readings

Various issues of *Management Accounting* (formerly called the *N.A.A. Bulletin*) are permeated with articles on direct costing and the contribution approach. *N.A.A. Research Reports Nos. 23, 24,* and *37* are informative.

questions, problems, and cases

10-1. Why is *direct costing* a misnomer?

10-2. List four alternate terms for *contribution margin.*

10-3. "The central issue in direct costing is *timing.*" Explain.

10-4. "The main trouble with direct costing is that it ignores the increasing importance of fixed costs in modern business." Do you agree? Why?

10-5. "The depreciation on the paper machine is every bit as much a part of the cost of the manufactured paper as the cost of the raw pulp." Do you agree? Why?

10-6. Comparison of Direct Costing and Absorption Costing.   From the following information (dollars are in thousands) pertaining to a year's operations, answer the questions below:

Units sold	1,000
Units produced	1,100
Fixed manufacturing overhead	$2,200
Variable manufacturing overhead	500
Selling and administrative expenses (all fixed)	900
Direct labor	4,000
Direct materials used	2,100
Beginning inventories	–0–
Contribution margin	4,000
Direct material inventory, end	1,000

There are no work-in-process inventories.

1. What is the ending finished-goods inventory cost under absorption costing procedures?

2. What is the ending finished-goods inventory cost under variable costing procedures (direct costing)?

10-7. Comparison of Direct Costing and Absorption Costing. The Blazek Company had the following operating characteristics in 19_4 and 19_5:

Basic production data at standard cost:

Direct materials	$1.30
Direct labor	1.50
Variable overhead	.20
Fixed overhead ($150,000 ÷ 150,000 units of normal volume)	1.00
Total factory cost at standard	$4.00

Sales price, $5.00 per unit.

Selling and administrative expense is assumed for simplicity as being all fixed at $65,000 yearly, except for sales commissions at 5% of dollar sales.

	19_4	19_5
In units:		
Opening inventory	—	30,000
Production	170,000	140,000
Sales	140,000	160,000
Closing inventory	30,000	10,000

There were no variances from the standard variable costs. Any under- or overapplied overhead is written off directly at year-end as an adjustment to Cost of Goods Sold.

required

1. Income statements for 19_4 and 19_5 under direct costing and absorption costing.

2. A reconciliation of the difference in net income for 19_4, 19_5, and the two years as a whole.

10-8. Direct Costing and Cost–Volume–Profit Relationships.   [Prepared by the author and adapted for use in a CPA examination] The Fleer Company has a maximum capacity of 210,000 units per year. Normal activity is regarded as 180,000 units per year. Standard variable manufacturing costs are $11 per unit. Fixed factory overhead is $540,000 per year. Variable selling costs are $2 per unit, while fixed selling costs are $252,000 per year. Sales price is $20 per unit.

required   (Assume no variances from standard variable manufacturing costs in parts 1 through 3)

1. What is the breakeven point expressed in *dollar* sales?

2. How many *units* must be sold to earn a target net income of $60,000 per year?

3. How many units must be sold to earn a net income of 10 percent of sales?

4. Assume the following results for a given year:

   Sales, 150,000 units. Net variance for standard variable manufacturing costs, $40,000, unfavorable. Production, 160,000 units. Beginning inventory, 10,000 units.

   All variances are written off as additions to (or deductions from) Standard Cost of Sales.
   a. Prepare income statements for the year under:
      (1) Absorption
      (2) Direct costing
   b. In fifty words or less, explain the difference in net income between the two statements.

10-9. **The All-Fixed Company in 1996.** [Adapted from an article by Raymond P. Marple, "Try This on Your Class, Professor," *Accounting Review*, XXXI, No. 3.] It is the end of 1996. The All-Fixed Company began operations in January 1995. The company is so named because it has no variable costs. All its costs are fixed; they do not vary with output.

The All-Fixed Company is located on the bank of a river and has its own hydroelectric plant to supply power, light, and heat. The company manufactures a synthetic fertilizer from air and river water, and sells its product at a price that is not expected to change. It has a small staff of employees, all hired on an annual-salary basis. The output of the plant can be increased or decreased by adjusting a few dials on a control panel.

The following are data regarding the operations by the All-Fixed Company:

	1995	1996*
Sales	10,000 tons	10,000 tons
Production	20,000 tons	—
Selling price	$30 per ton	$30 per ton
Costs (all fixed):		
Production	$280,000	$280,000
General and administrative	$ 40,000	$ 40,000

*Management adopted the policy, effective January 1, 1996, of producing only as the product was needed to fill sales. During 1996, sales were the same as for 1995 and were filled entirely from inventory. There was no beginning inventory at the start of 1995.

required   1. Prepare three-column income statements for 1995, 1996, and the two years together, using
   a. Absorption costing
   b. Direct (variable) costing

2. What is the breakeven point under (a) absorption costing and (b) variable costing?

3. What inventory costs would be carried on the balance sheets at December 31, 1995 and 1996, under each method?

4. Comment on the results in 1 and 2. Which costing method appears more useful?

10-10. **The Semi-Fixed Company in 1996.** [Adapted from Marple, "Try This on Your Class."] The Semi-Fixed Company began operations in 1995 and differs from The All-Fixed Company (described in Problem 10-9) in only one respect: It has both fixed and variable production costs. Its variable costs are $7 per ton and its fixed production costs $140,000 a year. Normal activity is 20,000 tons per year.

required

1. Using the same data as in Problem 10-9, except for the change in production-cost behavior, prepare three-column income statements for 1995, 1996, and the two years together, under
   a. Absorption costing
   b. Variable costing

2. Why did the Semi-Fixed Company earn a profit for the two-year period while the All-Fixed Company in Problem 10-9 suffered a loss?

3. What inventory costs would be carried on the balance sheets at December 31, 1995 and 1996, under each method?

4. How may the variable-costing approach be reconciled with the definition of an asset as being "economic service potential"?

10-11. **Direct and Absorption Costing.** The Mears Company had net income for the first ten months of 19_2 of $200,000. There were no variances of any kind through October 31. One hundred thousand units were manufactured and sold during the ten-month period. Fixed manufacturing overhead was $2,000,000 through October 31. The company uses a standard-costing system. All variances are disposed of at year-end as an adjustment to Standard Cost of Goods Sold. Both variable and fixed costs are expected to continue at the same rates for the balance of the year.

There were 10,000 units in the beginning inventory. During the remainder of the year, 13,000 units are to be produced and 14,000 units are to be sold.

required

If operations proceed as described, what is the net income for 19_2 likely to be under (a) direct costing; (b) absorption costing?

10-12. **Comparison of Direct Costing and Absorption Costing; Volume Variance.** The Davis Company uses a standard absorption-costing system. Standard variable manufacturing costs are $3.00 per unit. Standard fixed factory overhead is $.50 per unit ($300,000 ÷ 600,000 units of normal activity). Sales price is $5.00 per unit. Variable selling and administrative costs are $1.00 per unit. Fixed selling and administrative costs are $120,000. Beginning inventory in 19_1 was 30,000 units; ending inventory was 40,000 units. Variances from standard variable manufacturing costs in 19_1 totaled $110,000, unfavorable. Sales in 19_1 were 540,000 units.

required

1. Income statement for 19_1, assuming that all variances are written off directly at year-end as an adjustment to Cost of Goods Sold.
2. The president has heard about direct costing. He asks you to recast the 19_1 statement as it should appear under direct costing.
3. Explain the difference in net income as calculated in parts 1 and 2.

10-13. Inventory Techniques and Management Planning. It is November 30, 19_4. Given the following for a company division's operations for January through November, 19_4:

DIVISION G

Income Statement

For Eleven Months Ending November 30, 19_4

	UNITS	DOLLARS	
Sales @ $1,000	1,000		1,000,000
Less cost of goods sold:			
Beginning inventory, December 31, 19_3, @ $800	50	40,000	
Manufacturing costs @ $800, including $600 per unit for fixed overhead	1,100	880,000	
Total standard cost of goods available for sale	1,150	920,000	
Ending inventory, November 30, 19_4, @ $800	150	120,000	
Standard cost of goods sold*	1,000		800,000
Gross margin			200,000
Other expenses:			
Variable, 1,000 units @ $50		50,000	
Fixed, @ $10,000 monthly		110,000	160,000
Net operating income			40,000

*There are absolutely no variances for the eleven-month period considered as a whole.

Production in the past three months has been 100 units monthly. Practical capacity is 125 units monthly. In order to retain a stable nucleus of key employees, monthly production is never scheduled at less than 40 units.

Maximum available storage space for inventory is regarded as 200 units. The sales outlook for the next four months is 70 units monthly. Inventory is never to be less than 50 units.

The company uses a standard absorption-costing system. Denominator production activity is 1,200 units annually. All variances are disposed of at year-end as an adjustment to Standard Cost of Goods Sold.

required

1. The division manager is given an annual bonus that is geared to net operating income. Given the data above, assume that the manager wants to maximize the company's net income for 19_4. How many units should he schedule for production in December? Note carefully that you do not have to (*nor should you*) compute the exact net income for 19_4 in this or in subsequent parts of this question.

2. Assume that standard direct costing is in use rather than standard absorption costing. Would direct-costing net income for 19_4 be higher, lower, or the same as standard absorption-costing net income, assuming that production for December is 80 units and sales are 70 units? Why?

3. If standard direct costing were used, what production schedule should the division manager set? Why?

4. Assume that the manager is interested in maximizing his performance over the long run, and that his performance is being judged on an after-income-tax basis. Given the data in the beginning of the problem, assume that income tax rates will be halved in 19_5, and assume that the year-end write-offs of variances are acceptable for income tax purposes. Assume that standard absorption costing is used. How many units should be scheduled for production in December? Why?

10-14. Some Additional Requirements to Problem 10-13; Absorption Costing and Volume Variances. Refer to Problem 10-13.

1. What net operating income will be reported for 19_4 as a whole, assuming that the implied cost behavior patterns will continue in December as they did in January through November, and assuming—without regard to your answer to requirement 1 in Problem 10-13—that production for December is 80 units and sales are 70 units?

2. Assume the same conditions as in requirement 1, except that practical capacity was used in setting fixed-overhead rates for product costing throughout 19_4. What volume variance would be reported for 19_4?

10-15. Prepare Income Statement on Direct-Costing Basis. A fire partially destroyed the records of the McBee Manufacturing Company on December 31, 19_1. You have been asked to prepare a comparative statement of the original budgeted income statement for the year and the actual results. Even though the company has kept records on an absorption-costing basis, you have decided to prepare a statement on the direct-costing basis.

On an absorption-costing basis, the unfavorable volume variance for fixed factory overhead was $13,650. 52,000 units were produced and sold at an average selling price of $20 per unit. The standard contribution margin was $5 per unit. Budgeted and actual fixed costs were the same for both manufacturing ($122,850) and nonmanufacturing ($80,000). The total rate and efficiency variances were $36,000, unfavorable. On an absorption-costing basis, fixed factory overhead had been applied on the basis of the expected volume level used in the original budget.

10-16. Different Activity Bases [SICA, adapted]. The production manager of a small company realizes that although various bases (such as direct-labor hours or machine-hours) can be used to apply factory overhead to product costs, another problem of fundamental importance is the way in which each of these bases will be expressed. That is, should the base decided upon be expressed in terms of "expected annual activity," "average or normal activity," or "practical capacity"? The manager is uncertain, however, how the use of overhead rates based on each of these capacity-utilization concepts may give different results.

The following information related to the planned operations of the company during 19_4:

	HOURS
Maximum capacity utilization, based on absolute physical potential	100,000
Practical capacity utilization, after allowance for normal breakdowns, maintenance lost time, etc.	95,000
Average or normal activity, based on the average production requirements for 5 years	75,000
Expected activity, based on the 19_4 production requirements	85,000

required   Explain fully why the use of each of the three capacity-utilization concepts referred to in the first paragraph above will cause different total variances between actual and applied overhead for the year 19_4.

10-17. Overhead Rates and Cyclical Business. It is a time of severe business depression throughout the capital-goods industries. A division manager for a large corporation in a heavy-machinery industry is confused and unhappy. He is distressed with the controller, whose cost department keeps feeding the manager costs that are of little use because they are higher than ever before. At the same time, the manager has to quote lower prices than before in order to get any business.

required

1. What activity base is probably being used for application of overhead?

2. How might the overhead be applied in order to make the cost data more useful in making price quotations?

3. Would the product costs furnished by the cost department be satisfactory for the costing of the annual inventory?

10-18. Argument About Proper Activity Base. The president, the controller, and the assistant controller have studied possible alternative activity bases for overhead application to products. Until now, the company has applied all actual overhead to products on a month-to-month basis. The three executives have different views as to the most appropriate base. They briefly summarized their thinking as follows:

President: "The only time I'm satisfied is when we are operating at peak capacity. If we're not, our profits are less than what they should be. As I understand it, the use of practical capacity as a base will result in lower product costs. This will allow us to price more competitively, and at the same time we'll have some idea of the loss from our inability to utilize full capacity."

Controller: "The only proper base for overhead application is expected activity for the year. Each year's costs are borne to benefit each year's production. The only sensible way to track yearly overhead costs is to pool them and then use an annual average rate to funnel them to products as they are manufactured. Any major year-end over- or underabsorbed overhead should be prorated over the year's production by an adjusting entry."

Assistant Controller (who plans to resign next week): "You're both wrong! Anybody who thinks this matter through realizes that the core of the question is the sticky, almost unalterable behavior of fixed overhead. Commitments like fixed assets, research costs, and executive salaries not only do not change from month to month; they do not even change materially from year to year. These commitments are made to sustain a level of operations for three or four years ahead. We should use normal activity as a base. Furthermore, major year-end under- or overabsorbed overhead should be carried forward on the balance sheet from year to year. Over a three- or four-year period, such overhead will be largely counterbalanced."

Pertinent data on factory overhead for this company follow:

	YEAR	VARIABLE OVERHEAD	FIXED OVERHEAD	TOTAL OVERHEAD	STANDARD DIRECT-LABOR HOURS
Past data:					
	1	$ 500,000	$1,000,000	$1,500,000	500,000
	2	1,000,000	1,100,000	2,100,000	1,000,000
	3	800,000	1,200,000	2,000,000	800,000
Future estimates:					
	4	880,000	1,300,000	2,180,000	800,000
	5	1,100,000	1,300,000	2,400,000	1,000,000
	6	1,320,000	1,400,000	2,720,000	1,200,000

required   As a management consultant who specializes in cost-accounting difficulties, write a concise report supporting the most proper overhead activity base to be used in this case. As an appendix, write a brief answer to each of the contentions of the president, controller, and assistant controller. Assume that practical capacity is 1,300,000 hours.

10-19. **Choice of Activity Base and Proration of Variances [CPA, adapted].** Last year, the Crowley Corporation adopted a standard-cost system. Labor standards were set on the basis of time studies and prevailing wage rates. Material standards were determined from material specifications and prices then in effect. In determining its standard for overhead, Crowley estimated that a total of 6,000,000 finished units would be produced during the next five years to satisfy demand for its product. The five-year period was selected to average out seasonal and cyclical fluctuations and allow for sales trends. By dividing the annual average of 1,200,000 units into the total annual budgeted overhead, a standard cost was developed for manufacturing overhead.

At June 30, 19_9, the end of the current fiscal year, a partial trial balance revealed the following:

	DEBITS	CREDITS
Material-price variance		$25,000
Material-quantity variance	$ 9,000	
Labor-rate variance	30,000	
Labor-efficiency variance	7,500	
Controllable-overhead variance	2,000	
Noncontrollable (capacity) overhead variance	75,000	

Standards were set at the beginning of the year and have remained unchanged. All inventories are priced at standard cost.

required   1. What conclusions can be drawn from each of the six variances shown in Crowley's trial balance?

2. The amount of nonvariable manufacturing-overhead cost to be included in product cost depends on whether or not the allocation is based on: (a) ideal (or theoretical) capacity, (b) practical capacity, (c) normal activity, or (d) expected annual activity. Describe each of these allocation bases and give a theoretical principal argument for each.

3. Give the theoretical justification for each of the following methods of accounting for the net amount of all standard-cost variances for year-end financial reporting:
   a. Presenting the net variance as an income or expense on the income statement
   b. Allocating the net variance among Inventories and Cost of Goods Sold
   c. Presenting the net variance as an adjustment to Cost of Goods Sold

10-20. **Revision of Standards [CPA].** Following is the previously computed standard prime cost of Product X, manufactured by the XYZ Manufacturing Company:

	PRIME COST
Material A	$10.00
Material B	5.00
Material C	2.00
Direct labor—Cutting	8.00
Direct labor—Shaping	4.00
Direct labor—Assembling	2.00
Direct labor—Boxing	1.00
Total	$32.00

The budget called for the manufacture of 10,000 units of Product X at a total prime cost of $320,000 for the period under review.

The following variance accounts relating to Product X appear on the books for the period:

	DEBIT	CREDIT
Material-price variance:		
Due to a favorable purchase of total requirements of Material A		$19,500
Material-usage variance:		
Excessive waste during period	$ 3,000	
Labor-rate variance:		
5% wage increase to direct workers	7,500	
Labor-productivity variance:		
Due to shutdown caused by strike	15,000	

The inventory at the end of the period is as follows:

100 units Material A	@ $10.00	$ 1,000
100 units Material B	@ 5.00	500
100 units Material C	@ 2.00	200
200 units Product X in process— cut	@ 25.00	5,000
200 units Product X in process— shaped	@ 29.00	5,800
200 units Product X in process— assembled	@ 31.00	6,200
200 units Product X finished and boxed	@ 32.00	6,400
Total		$25,100

required
1. A schedule of revised standard prime cost that will clearly indicate the cumulative standard for each successive operation.

2. A schedule applying the revised standard to the ending inventory.

10-21. Proration of Variances [CPA, adapted]. The Du-Rite Corporation was established in 19_3 and manufactures a single product that passes through several departments. The company has a standard-cost system.

The company's inventories at standard cost are as follows:

	DECEMBER 31, 19_3
Raw materials	-0-
Work in process:	
Materials	$ 75,000
Labor	7,500
Overhead	15,000
Total	97,500
Finished goods:	
Materials	60,000
Labor	20,000
Overhead	40,000
Total	120,000
Total inventories	$217,500

The company's preliminary income statement for the year ended December 31, 19_3, prior to any year-end inventory adjustments, follows:

Sales			$900,000
Cost of goods sold:			
Standard cost of goods sold:			
Materials	$300,000		
Labor	100,000		
Overhead	200,000		
Total	600,000		
Variances:			
Materials	25,400		
Labor	25,500		
Overabsorbed overhead	(16,500)		
Total	34,400	634,400	
Gross profit		265,600	
Selling expenses:			
Salaries	28,000		
Commissions	72,000		
Shipping expense	18,000		
Other	7,000		
Total	125,000		
General and administrative expenses	50,000	175,000	
Profit from operations		90,600	
Other income:			
Purchases discount	8,000		
Scrap sales	9,000	17,000	
Net income before taxes		$107,600	

All purchase discounts were earned on the purchase of raw materials. The company has included a scrap allowance in the overhead-cost standards; the scrap sold cannot be traced to any particular operation or department.

required

1. Prepare a schedule computing the "actual" cost of goods manufactured. The schedule should provide for a separation of costs into material, labor, and overhead costs.

2. Prepare a schedule comparing the computation of ending inventories at standard cost and at actual cost. The schedule should provide for a separation of costs into material, labor, and overhead costs.

10-22. Income Effects of Standard Costs and Normal Costs.   The Drake Company began business on January 1, 19_1. A standard absorption-costing system has been in use. Balances in certain accounts at December 31, 19_1, are as follows:

At standard unit prices:	
Stores	$ 20,000
Work in process	10,000
Finished goods	30,000
Cost of goods sold	60,000
	$120,000

Variances (unfavorable):	
Direct-material usage	$ 10,000
Direct-material purchase price	12,000
Direct-labor rate	2,000
Direct-labor efficiency	10,000
Underapplied overhead	5,000
	$ 39,000
Sales	$150,000

required

1. The executives have asked you to compute the gross margin (after deductions for variances, if any) had the company followed these assumptions:
   a. Actual historical costing—that is, no predetermined costs used
   b. Normal costing with proration of underapplied overhead
   c. Normal costing without proration of underapplied overhead
   d. Standard costing with proration of all variances
   e. Standard costing without proration of variances
   Assume that all variances that are not prorated are considered direct adjustments of standard cost of goods sold. Assume that prorations are based on the ending balances of the applicable accounts affected, even though more refined methods would be possible if additional data were available. There are not enough data about the direct-material components in the various accounts to warrant the proration of some of the direct-material purchase-price variance to the direct-material usage variance; therefore, prorate the price variance directly to Stores, Work in Process, Finished Goods, and Cost of Goods Sold.

2. Analyze the results in requirement 1. Which assumption writes costs off to expense most quickly? What other generalizations about the five assumptions can be made? Do you think Drake's standards were currently attainable? Why, or why not?

3. What approach would you take if you had more data and wanted to obtain a more accurate proration of variances?

10-23. Comprehensive Review of Normal Costs and Standard Costs, Including Proration of Variances.   The Scarni Company uses a standard-costing system.

Operations began on January 2, 19_1. A summary of results for the year follows:

Direct materials purchased, 100,000 lbs. @ $1.10
Production units, 80,000
Sales in units, 60,000
Pounds of direct materials consumed, 90,000
Standard allowances per unit of finished output:

Direct materials, 1 lb. @ $1.00	=	$1.00
Direct labor, 1 hour @ $3.00	=	3.00
Factory overhead, 1 hour @ $2.00	=	2.00
Total standard cost per unit		$6.00

Direct labor incurred, 85,000 hours @ $3.05, or $259,250
Factory overhead incurred, $161,000

required

1. In adjoining columns, prepare journal entries to record the information above under (a) standard costing, using the Case 1 approaches to isolating variances that were described in Chapter 7; and (b) normal costing, as described in Chapter 4. Note that Work in Process is charged on the basis of standard allowances under standard costing, in contrast to the basis of *inputs* under normal costing. In a sense, standard-cost systems can be thought of as being *output*-oriented, whereas normal costing systems are *input*-oriented. For example, the factors of production are charged and credited to Work in Process at what they *should* cost for good output, not at what they actually cost in terms of inputs.

2. Assume that sales were $500,000 and that selling and administrative expenses were $90,000. Prepare a comparative schedule showing net income computations under standard costing and normal costing. Assume that all variances, including under- or overapplied overhead, are written off at year-end as adjustments to Cost of Goods Sold.

3. Prepare a detailed reconciliation explaining the difference between the net incomes computed in requirement 2. You will be aided if you set up a supporting schedule of all variances, as follows:

		APPLICABLE TO			
	TOTAL VARIANCE	DIRECT-MATERIAL USAGE	FINISHED GOODS	COST OF GOODS SOLD	STORES
Example, direct-labor efficiency, etc.	$15,000	—	$3,750	$11,250	—

10-24. **Computation of Net Income Under Nine Different Costing Assumptions.** The Wixkell Company began operations a year ago. There was no beginning inventory. The company has produced 100,000 units; it has sold 80,000 units for a total revenue of $680,000. Experienced executives initiated a carefully planned standard-cost system at the outset. Cost data for the year follow:

Standard costs of production:

Direct materials	$300,000
Direct labor	200,000
Variable indirect manufacturing costs	40,000
Fixed indirect manufacturing costs	100,000
	$640,000

Variances (all unfavorable):

Direct materials	$ 30,000
Direct labor	25,000
Variable indirect manufacturing costs	10,000
Fixed indirect manufacturing costs	5,000
	$ 70,000

Selling and administrative expenses incurred:

Variable	$ 40,000
Fixed	60,000
	$100,000
Total of the three categories	$810,000

The top officers are anxious to know what the net income is for 19_1, because they know this will influence their immediate plans for seeking more capital. They have asked you to compute the company net income. You have explored various costing methods or assumptions as a part of your task. You have pinpointed the following:

a. Actual historical costs; that is, no predetermined costs are used
b. Standard absorption costing—proration of variances
c. Standard absorption costing—without proration of variances
d. Normal[7] absorption costing—proration of variances
e. Normal absorption costing—without proration of variances
f. Standard variable costing—proration of variances
g. Standard variable costing—without proration of variances
h. Normal variable costing—proration of variances
i. Normal variable costing—without proration of variances

required What net income (loss) would be shown under the various costing methods? Arrange your answer so that comparisons of the alternatives may be made easily.

Special Review Material for Chapters 7 through 10

10-25. Comparison of Alternative Income Statements. [Prepared by James H. March and adapted for use in SICA examination] By applying a variety of cost-accounting methods to the operating data of a given year, the controller of a manufacturing company prepares the following alternative income statements:

	A	B	C	D
Sales	$1,000,000	$1,000,000	$1,000,000	$1,000,000
Cost of goods sold	$ 375,000	$ 250,000	$ 420,000	$ 395,000
Variances:				
Direct materials	15,000	15,000	—	—
Direct labor	5,000	5,000	—	—
Manufacturing overhead	25,000	—	—	25,000
Other expenses (all fixed)	350,000	475,000	350,000	350,000
	$ 770,000	$ 745,000	$ 770,000	$ 770,000
Net income before tax	$ 230,000	$ 255,000	$ 230,000	$ 230,000

[7] "Normal" costing is historical costing using predetermined overhead rates.

required   1. The controller used the following costing methods: (a) actual cost, (b) actual materials and labor, predetermined overhead, (c) standard absorption costing, and (d) standard variable costing. Match each of these methods with the appropriate income statement, A, B, C, or D above, and briefly explain the basis of your selection.

2. During the year, did inventory quantities increase, decrease, or remain the same? Explain briefly.

3. During the year, was the volume of production higher than, lower than, or equal to the company's denominator level of volume? Explain briefly.

4. During the year, was the variable manufacturing overhead incurred more than, less than, or equal to the budget? Explain briefly.

10-26. **Review of Absorption Costing, Direct Costing, and Analysis of Variances.** On December 30, 19_1, a bomb blast destroyed the bulk of the accounting records of the Horne Division, a small one-product manufacturing division that uses standard costs, flexible budgets, and rate-of-return computations. All variances are written off as additions to (or deductions from) income; none are prorated to inventories. In addition, the chief accountant mysteriously disappeared. You have the task of reconstructing the records for the year 19_1. The general manager has said that the accountant had been experimenting with both absorption costing and direct costing.

The records are a mess, but you have gathered the following data for 19_1:

a. Cash on hand, December 31, 19_1	$ 10
b. Sales	128,000
c. Actual fixed indirect manufacturing costs	21,000
d. Accounts receivable, December 31, 19_1	20,000
e. Standard variable manufacturing costs per unit	1
f. Variances from standard of all variable manufacturing costs	5,000 U
g. Operating income, absorption-costing basis	14,400
h. Accounts payable, December 31, 19_1	18,000
i. Gross profit, absorption costing at standard (before deducting variances)	22,400
j. Total liabilities	100,000
k. Unfavorable budget variance, fixed manufacturing costs	1,000
l. Notes receivable from chief accountant	4,000
m. Contribution margin, at standard (before deducting variances)	48,000
n. Direct-material purchases, at standard prices	50,000
o. Actual selling and administrative costs (all fixed)	6,000

required   These do not necessarily have to be solved in any particular order. Ignore income taxes.

1. Operating income on a direct-costing basis.

2. Number of units sold.

3. Number of units produced.

4. Number of units used as the denominator to obtain fixed indirect cost rate application rate per unit on absorption-costing basis.

5. Did inventory (in units) increase or decrease? Explain.

6. By how much in dollars did the inventory level change (a) under absorption costing; (b) under direct costing?

7. Variable manufacturing cost of goods sold, at standard prices.

8. Manufacturing cost of goods sold at standard prices, absorption costing.

10-27. **Comprehensive Review of Flexible Budgets and Standard Product Costs.** [Prepared by Walter Warrick] "It's darn tough for an old dog like me to have to keep learning new tricks!" exclaimed Mr. Walter Warrick in some exasperation. Mr. Warrick, president of the PH Manufacturing Co., explained that he had given his son full responsibility for the operations of one branch of the business a few months previously. "Since then," he said, "it's been one dad-blamed thing after another!"

The most recent cause for complaint was the latest monthly income statement received from the plant run by his son:

INCOME FOR MONTH ENDING APRIL, 30, 19_1

Sales:		
14,000 X frames @ $7.50	$105,000	
12,000 H frames @ $8.00	96,000	$201,000
Standard cost of goods sold:		
26,000 × $4.50		117,000
Standard gross profit		$ 84,000

	LOSS	GAIN	
Material variance		$1,500	
Labor variance	$3,100		
Burden and overhead variance		3,700	
	$3,100	$5,200	2,100
Gross profit			$ 86,100
Selling and administrative expenses			40,000
Income before income tax			$ 46,100

Mr. Warrick explained that at the beginning of the year his son had prepared a "Profit-Graph" (Exhibit 10-6), which showed for various levels of volume what his plant sales, various categories of expense, and profit should be. "As nearly as I can figure out that thing, he should have showed a profit of just under $50,000 even at our regular price of $7.50 per frame. Since it looks as if he got a better rate on his H frames this month, doesn't it look to you as if he should have cleared almost $56,000?" demanded Mr. Warrick.

Further investigation disclosed that the plant under consideration made two types of metal frames that were used in the construction industry. The X frame, although larger than the H frame, was less complex and required less welding than did the H frame. At the beginning of the year when standards were set, it so happened that the extra material cost of the X frame was exactly offset by the extra labor cost of the H frame, so that the prime cost (direct labor plus materials) of each frame was $3.00. This greatly facilitated the preparation of volume–cost–profit estimates such as the Profit-Graph.

At that time, it was estimated that each X frame required two units of metal stripping and one unit of welding supplies. The H frame, on the other hand, required one unit of metal stripping and two units of welding supplies. Metal stripping normally cost $1.00 per unit and the welding supplies cost 60¢ per unit.

The direct-labor requirement was the opposite of that for the raw materials. The X frame required approximately half the time to fabricate than the H frame did. It was estimated that under normal working conditions, five H frames per man-hour could be assembled and one welder could keep up with two assemblers. That is, H frames could be welded at the rate of ten per welder-hour. Assemblers normally received $2.50 per hour and welders $3.00 per hour. Failure to schedule work properly and failure to provide adequately for absenteeism sometimes resulted in overtime or night work, which, of course, was paid for at premium rates. For purposes of variance computation, such extra pay was shown as a labor cost, not a burden cost, since it was felt that this placed the responsibility more nearly where it belonged.

The term "plant overhead" was used to describe a series of costs actually incurred at the plant where the frames were manufactured. Indirect labor consisted mainly of the wages paid to several material handlers employed at the plant. At the time the standards were set, power was purchased at the rate of $0.008 per kwh. Since that time, the rate had gone up to $0.009, although no change had been made in the standards. For control purposes it was assumed that the power requirements would vary directly with the total number of frames produced. Supervision and inspection made up a fairly expensive item that tended to be reasonably constant over quite a wide range of output. Depreciation was computed on a straight-line basis and naturally depended upon the cost of the production facilities of the part of the firm under consideration.

An examination of the general burden revealed that this cost was an assigned cost. It was the practice of the PH Manufacturing Co. to assign the general administration burden (the cost of such departments as accounting, engineering, etc., which were grouped at a central location) to the various operating branches of the firm. It was the policy of the company to anticipate this category of expense and assign a fixed sum monthly to each of the operating plants. However, when, as occasionally happened, the expenses of these central departments exceeded the amount anticipated, larger sums were assigned to the operating branches in order that such costs might be fully allocated by the end of the year.

Selling and administrative expense was budgeted at a fixed sum per month, since this expense was regarded as a direct result of management decision making and did not vary in direct relation with any of the standard parameters by which business activity might be judged.

Mr. Warrick pointed out that in general, apart from the change in power rate noted above, only one change from standard had been made in the base rate paid for any input to the plant. He explained that the plant was now paying less than formerly for their supply of welding rod. "I'm really tickled at the interest the boy has taken in every part of the operation," he confided. "As you can see, he has managed to raise the price we are getting for H frames. Not only that, he looked around until he found a fellow who would sell us welding rod at a lower price. Rod that used to cost us sixty cents we are now getting for only fifty. I guess we have to burn a little more, but you can see from that material variance that we are money ahead in the long run."

"Not only that," he continued, "a couple of months ago he talked me into buying some portable conveyors, which he put in the plant and which cut the cost of material handling quite a bit. They were not cheap, but they will last ten years and I expect they will pay for themselves several times over before that."

"Still and all," Mr. Warrick grumbled, resuming the earlier trend of his

EXHIBIT 10-6

MONTHLY "PROFIT-GRAPH"

(*Based on January 19_1 estimates*)

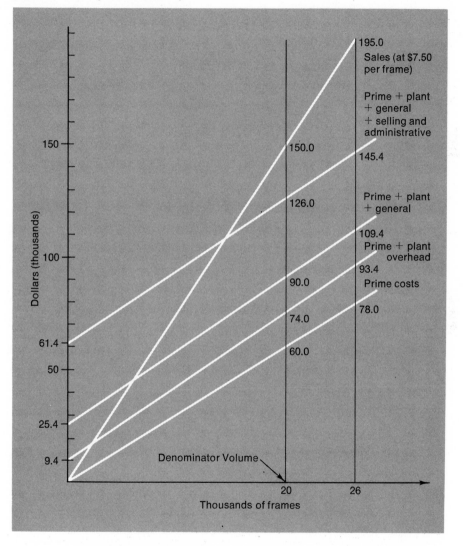

STANDARD COSTS AT DENOMINATOR VOLUME OF 10,000 UNITS OF EACH FRAME:

Prime costs at standard		$3.00
Plant overhead:		
Indirect labor	$ .20	
Power	.03	
Supervision and inspection	.27	
Depreciation	.20	
Sub-total plant overhead		.70
General burden:		.80
Total standard cost per frame		$4.50

conversation, "I wish I could get a little more accurate estimate of how well he is doing. When I got lost on that income statement, I asked for a little more dope; here are the actual figures for his April Operations."

Raw materials consumed:		
Metal stripping	36,300 units	$ 36,300
Welding supplies	39,600 units	19,800
Direct labor:		
Assemblers	3,450 hours	9,000
Welders	2,160 hours	8,500
Plant overhead:		
Supervision and inspection		5,400
Power		900
Depreciation		7,000
Indirect labor		1,000
General burden		18,000
Total		$105,900

Production: 12,000 X frames;   12,000 H frames

"In spite of the fact that his income statement does not show him making as much as he ought to from the Profit-Graph, it looks to me as if the actual cost for the average frame he has turned out this month is only $4.41—almost a dime less than standard. It is all pretty confusing," concluded Mr. Warrick. "I would like you to explain a few things to me in plain English. First of all, how come the income statement does not agree with the Profit-Graph? Is it only because of the rate changes from standard? Is there some less confusing (and not too expensive) way of reporting on how well he's making out? Second, how well is he doing? Is he making progress or is he just making changes? Third, he says because of the changes he has made, some of our standards should be changed. What does he mean by that?"

required   Answer Mr. Warrick's questions as completely and simply as possible. Include your supporting computations.

11

Relevant Costs and the Contribution Approach to Decisions

We have already seen how the contribution approach, with its emphasis on cost behavior patterns, helps cost analysis and the evaluation of performance. Our study has had two purposes: product costing and costing for routine control of operations. In this chapter we turn to a third purpose: costing for special non-recurring decisions, such as the addition or deletion of a product line, the manufacture or purchase of direct materials (make or buy), the acceptance or rejection of a special order, the replacement of equipment, and countless others. Teamwork among executives is commonly used in reaching these decisions, which are often fusions of the thinking of engineers, economists, production managers, sales managers, mathematicians, and accountants. Cost analysis is nearly always needed, and that is why the cost accountant plays an important role in these special decisions.

Before the mid-1960's, the word "relevant" was not overused. Now it seems to be applied in every context imaginable. Nevertheless, "relevant" is particularly apt for our purposes, so we will stress the word in this chapter. When is an item relevant? When is it irrelevant? These distinctions are crucial to the making of intelligent decisions. The contribution approach, combined with the ability to distinguish relevance from irrelevance, will enable the accountant to reach correct conclusions in this challenging area.

349

THE ACCOUNTANT'S ROLE IN SPECIAL DECISIONS

relevance and accuracy Accountants have an important role in the decision-making process, not as the decision makers themselves, but as collectors and reporters of relevant information. Many managers want the accountant to offer recommendations about a decision, even though the final choice always rests with the operating executive.

Relevance and accuracy are not identical concepts. *Relevance* means pertinence to the decision at hand. Figures are relevant if they guide the manager toward the decision that harmonizes with top-management objectives. Ideally, the information should be *relevant* (valid or pertinent) and *accurate* (precise). However, figures may be accurate but irrelevant, or inaccurate but relevant. For example, the advertising manager's salary may be exactly $45,500 per year, but this fact may have no bearing on whether to add or drop a product line.

qualitative and quantitative factors The consequences of each alternative may be divided into two broad categories, *qualitative* and *quantitative*. Qualitative factors are those whose measurement in dollars and cents is difficult and imprecise; yet a qualitative factor may easily be given more weight than the measurable cost savings.

For example, a militant union that opposes the introduction of some labor-saving machinery may cause an executive to defer or to reject completely the contemplated installation. Or the chance to manufacture some product components at a saving below supplier quotations may be rejected because of a long-run dependency on the supplier for other important subassemblies. Quantitative factors are those that may more easily be reduced to terms of dollars and cents, such as projected alternative costs of materials, direct labor, and overhead. The accountant, statistician, and mathematician increasingly try to express as many decision factors as possible in quantitative terms. This approach tends to reduce the number of qualitative factors to be judged.

MEANING OF RELEVANCE

the nature of decision making Because the nature and method of decision making are examined in depth elsewhere, we will not dwell on them here. Nevertheless, decision making deserves scrutiny because it should be the fundamental focus of cost accounting. Decision making is a goal-seeking process; to decide is to choose from among a set of alternative courses of action in light of some objective. The decision maker must (a) recognize why a choice is necessary; (b) delineate the set of alternative courses of action; (c) evaluate the alternatives; and (d) pick a course of action.

Every decision deals with the future—whether it be ten seconds ahead (the decision to adjust a dial) or eighty years ahead (the decision of where to locate a factory). A decision always involves a prediction. Therefore, the function of decision making is to select courses of action for the future. There is no opportunity to alter the past.

Note too that the set of alternative actions and the objective of the decision are also predictions. In selecting a set of alternatives, the decision maker (hereafter often referred to as a manager) must predict that the set contains the best of the possible alternatives. That is, the manager may choose the best alternative in a given set, but he might have come closer to his objective had he picked an alternative that was overlooked and was excluded from the set he considered. For example, a manager may choose between Machines A and B and completely overlook the availability of Machine C, which may be the best alternative.

Moreover, the manager may have chosen the wrong objective. For example, the basic goal may be to maximize the market value of the common shares. The manager may think that the best way to accomplish this is to maximize earnings per share, so he uses this yardstick as his objective. But perhaps in this case a better way to maximize market value is to maximize the net cash flow available for dividends. Hence, he may err in a decision because he predicted incorrectly by selecting an inferior objective.

The manager needs a method for making a choice among different courses of action. This method is frequently called a *decision model*. A *model* is an abstraction and depiction of the relationships among the recognized objects in a particular concrete situation; it emphasizes the key interrelationships and often excludes some unimportant factors. Models have many forms and purposes: They may be descriptive or predictive; verbal, physical, or mathematical; dynamic or static; and so on. For instance, accounting systems and financial reports are financial models of an organization's operations. A *decision model* provides a conceptual representation that enables the manager to measure the effects of alternative actions.

relevance as defined here The words *information* and *data* have a variety of meanings in both the popular and the technical literature. For our purposes, information is that subset of data that is likely to alter a decision maker's prediction. Exhibit 11-1 sketches the decision process and uses an illustration of a decision to rearrange plant facilities. Accounting records show that past direct-labor costs were $2 per unit. No wage-rate changes are anticipated, but the rearrangement is expected to reduce direct-labor usage by 25 percent. Direct-material costs of $5 per unit will not change under either alternative.

The somewhat elaborate mechanism shown in Exhibit 11-1 seems unnecessary for this decision. After all, the analysis in a nutshell is:

	RELEVANT COSTS PER UNIT	
	DO NOT REARRANGE	REARRANGE
Direct labor	$2.00	$1.50

EXHIBIT 11-1

DECISION PROCESS AND ROLE OF INFORMATION

The decision is whether to invest in the rearrangement of plant facilities.
The objective is to minimize costs.

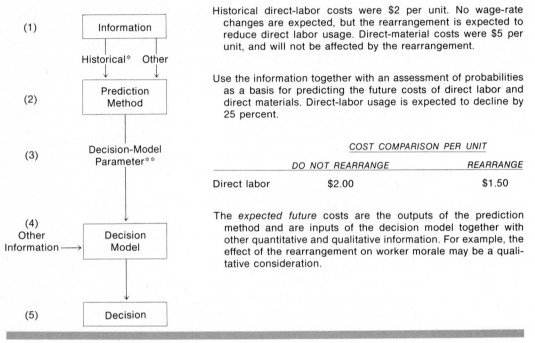

(1) Information

Historical*   Other

(2) Prediction Method

(3) Decision-Model Parameter**

(4) Other Information ⟶ Decision Model

(5) Decision

Historical direct-labor costs were $2 per unit. No wage-rate changes are expected, but the rearrangement is expected to reduce direct labor usage. Direct-material costs were $5 per unit, and will not be affected by the rearrangement.

Use the information together with an assessment of probabilities as a basis for predicting the future costs of direct labor and direct materials. Direct-labor usage is expected to decline by 25 percent.

COST COMPARISON PER UNIT

	DO NOT REARRANGE	REARRANGE
Direct labor	$2.00	$1.50

The *expected future* costs are the outputs of the prediction method and are inputs of the decision model together with other quantitative and qualitative information. For example, the effect of the rearrangement on worker morale may be a qualitative consideration.

* Note that historical data may be relevant for prediction methods.
** Historical data are never relevant per se for decision models. Only those expected future data that are different are really relevant. For instance, in this example, direct labor makes a difference and direct material does not. Therefore, *under our definition here*, direct material is irrelevant.

If all other considerations are a standoff, and the objective is to minimize costs, then rearrangement is the more desirable alternative.

Note that the method used for making the decision per se (the decision model) necessitated a comparison of *expected future costs* that will *differ* under alternatives. The $2 direct-labor charge may be the same as in the past, and the past records may have been extremely helpful in preparing the $2 forecast. The trouble is that most accountants and managers view the $2 past cost as the future cost. But the crucial point is that the $2 is an expected future cost, not a past cost. *Historical costs in themselves are irrelevant to the decision per se, even though they may be the best available basis for predicting future costs.*

The direct-material costs of $5 per unit are expected future costs, not historical costs. Yet these future costs are irrelevant because they will not differ under alternatives. There may be no harm in preparing a comparative analysis that includes both the relevant direct-labor-cost forecast and the irrelevant direct-material-cost forecast:

	COST COMPARISON PER UNIT	
	DO NOT REARRANGE	REARRANGE
Direct materials	$5.00	$5.00
Direct labor	2.00	1.50

However, note that we can safely ignore the direct-material cost, because it is not an element of difference between the alternatives. The point is that irrelevant costs may be included in cost comparisons for decisions, provided that they are included properly and do not mislead the decision maker. A corollary point is that concentrating solely on relevant costs may eliminate bothersome irrelevancies and may sharpen both the accountant's and the manager's thinking regarding costs for decision making. A key question in determining relevance is, "What difference will it make?"

In summary, the chart below shows that relevant costs for decisions are expected future costs that will differ under alternatives. Historical costs, although helpful in predicting relevant costs, are always irrelevant costs per se:

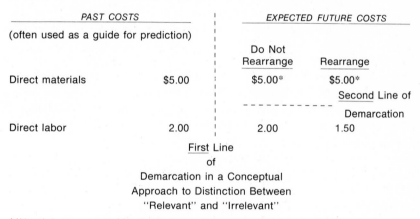

PAST COSTS		EXPECTED FUTURE COSTS	
(often used as a guide for prediction)		Do Not Rearrange	Rearrange
Direct materials	$5.00	$5.00*	$5.00*
			Second Line of Demarcation
Direct labor	2.00	2.00	1.50

First Line
of
Demarcation in a Conceptual
Approach to Distinction Between
"Relevant" and "Irrelevant"

*Although these are expected future costs, they are irrelevant because they are the same for both alternatives. Thus, the second line of demarcation is drawn between those costs that are the same for the alternatives under consideration and those that differ; *only* the latter are relevant costs *as we define them.*

The definition of relevance is the major conceptual lesson in this chapter. This idea of relevance, coupled with the contribution approach, arms the manager and the accountant with a powerful general weapon for making special decisions. The rest of this chapter will show how to apply these notions to some commonly encountered decisions. Note particularly that the analytical approach is consistent regardless of the particular decision encountered.

ILLUSTRATION OF RELEVANCE: CHOOSING ACTIVITY LEVELS

Decisions that affect activity levels are made under a given set of conditions, including existing plant capacity, equipment, and basic operating conditions.

Such decisions are essentially short-run in nature; but they have long-run overtones that should never be overlooked.

the special order

Management is sometimes faced with the problem of price quotations on special orders when there is idle capacity.

example

X Company manufactures overshoes. The current operating level, which is below full capacity of 110,000 pairs per year, will probably show the results for the year as contained in Exhibit 11-2. (Note that these are predictions.)

A mail-order chain offers to buy 20,000 pairs at $7.50, for a total of $150,000. The buyer will pay for the shipping expenses. The acceptance of this special order will not affect regular sales. The president is reluctant to accept that order because the $7.50 price is below the $8.125 factory unit cost. Should the offer be accepted?

Exhibit 11-3 shows a report based on the contribution approach that might be presented as a guide for decision making. The relevant costs are those that will be affected by taking the special order—the variable *manufacturing* costs. The fixed manufacturing costs and all of the selling expenses are irrelevant. The only relevant items are sales and variable manufacturing costs.

fixed expenses and unit costs

Exhibit 11-3 also illustrates the frequent irrelevance of fixed costs in a decision of this kind. If the fixed costs remain the same under both alternatives (acceptance or rejection), then the $330,000 is irrelevant. You may substitute $1 or $1,000,000 wherever the $330,000 fixed-cost amount is shown without changing the net difference in result.

Note also that the full factory unit cost at the 80,000-unit activity level was $8.125. If such a cost were used as a guide in deciding, the offer might be

EXHIBIT 11-2

PREDICTED INCOME STATEMENT FOR THE YEAR

Absorption Format

		PER UNIT
Sales—80,000 pairs @ $10.00	$800,000	$10.000
Manufacturing cost of goods sold*	650,000	8.125
Gross profit or gross margin	$150,000	$ 1.875
Selling expenses**	120,000	1.500
Operating income	$ 30,000	$ .375

*Includes fixed costs of $250,000.

**Includes fixed costs of $80,000. The remaining $40,000 consists only of shipping expenses of $.50 per pair.

To obtain a target operating income of $30,000, note that the normal or target markup percentage per pair based on absorption cost (total variable and fixed manufacturing cost) must be $1.875 ÷ $8.125 = 23.1% of such cost.

EXHIBIT 11-3

COMPARATIVE PREDICTED INCOME STATEMENTS FOR THE YEAR

Contribution Format, Two Decision Alternatives

	WITHOUT SPECIAL ORDER, 80,000 UNITS		WITH SPECIAL ORDER, 100,000 UNITS	
	PER UNIT	TOTAL	TOTAL	DIFFERENCE
Sales	$10.000	$800,000	$950,000	$150,000*
Variable costs:				
Manufacturing	$ 5.000	$400,000	$500,000	$100,000**
Selling	.500	40,000	40,000	—
Total variable costs	$ 5.500	$440,000	$540,000	$100,000
Contribution margin	$ 4.500	$360,000	$410,000	$ 50,000
Fixed costs:				
Manufacturing	$ 3.125	$250,000	$250,000	—
Selling	1.000	80,000	80,000	—
Total fixed costs	$ 4.125	$330,000	$330,000	—
Operating income	$ .375	$ 30,000	$ 80,000	$ 50,000

* 20,000 @ $7.50
** 20,000 @ $5.00

To obtain a target operating income of $30,000 (without the special order), the normal or target markup percentage per pair based on total variable costs must be $4.50 ÷ $5.50 = 81.8% of total variable costs.

unwisely rejected, on the grounds that the $7.50 prospective selling price is well below the $8.125 unit cost. In most cases it is safer to compare *total* costs rather than *unit* costs. Thus, fixed costs must be analyzed carefully, because their behavior is unique. The spreading of the $250,000 fixed manufacturing cost over 100,000 units instead of 80,000 units will lower the unit cost for all units produced. But how fixed costs are attached to units of product has no bearing on this decision because the total fixed costs are unaffected.

short run and long run Do not jump to the conclusion that all variable costs are relevant and all fixed costs are irrelevant. This preconceived attack may be handy, but it is far from being foolproof. For instance, in this special-order example, although the selling costs are variable, they are irrelevant because they are not affected by this special order.

Economists and accountants agree that if the length of time under consideration becomes long enough, no type of cost is fixed. Yet management is faced with the task of making decisions when the length of time under consideration is short enough so that many conditions and costs are fixed. What role should fixed costs play in decision making? No categorical answer may be given to this question. About the most useful generalization is that fixed costs should be considered when they are expected to be altered, either immediately or in the future, by the decision at hand. If activity levels change so that additional supervision, plant, equipment, insurance, and property taxes are needed, these

355

new fixed costs are relevant. For example, sales or production may expand to the point where a new delivery truck may be bought.

qualitative factors   The problem of tracing or allocating the effects of various decisions on total costs is a major difficulty facing managers and accountants. Many managers believe intuitively that variable costs or some other obvious approximation of additional costs yields understatements of the "real" additions to costs caused by a decision alternative in question. That is why they feel that perhaps absorption cost or some other version of "full" cost may be a better approximation of the unknown "real" additions to costs.

reports for decision making   Frequently, the decision alternatives are compared as in Exhibit 11-3 by preparing a separate income statement for each alternative, as well as by showing the differences. But shortcut reports may emphasize *differences* in order to spotlight only the relevant factors that influence the final results. A shortcut analysis would be confined to the "difference" column in Exhibit 11-3.

The point here is that concentration on the revenues and costs that make a difference in analyzing data does not necessarily mean that the final reports submitted to the decision-making executives should contain only these differential items. The final reports should be tailored to managerial quirks and wants. There is no single way to present reports. However, the contribution approach tends to facilitate understanding.

CONTRIBUTION APPROACH TO PRICING

The special-order decision is merely one example of a pervasive difficulty that confronts managers: the pricing decision. This decision is the subject of an extensive literature in economics, so we will concentrate on only a few aspects here. The major purpose is to put the role of costs in perspective with regard to the pricing decision.

superiority of the contribution approach   When used intelligently, the contribution approach has distinct advantages over the absorption-costing approach to guiding a pricing decision.

First, the contribution approach offers more detailed information than the absorption-costing approach, because variable- and fixed-cost behavior patterns are delineated. Because the contribution approach is sensitive to cost–volume–profit relationships, it is a better, easier basis for developing pricing formulas.

Second, a "normal" or "target" pricing formula can be as easily developed under the contribution approach as under absorption costing. Consider the facts in Exhibit 11-2. Note that the target markup percentage (23.1 percent) is often expressed as a percentage of absorption cost. In contrast, as Exhibit 11-3 demonstrates, the target markup percentage might be expressed as 81.8 percent of total variable costs. Under *either* approach, the pricing-decision maker will have a formula that will lead him toward the *same* target price. If he is unable to obtain such a price consistently, the company will not achieve its $30,000 income objective or its desired operating-income percentage of sales.

Third, as the preceding example shows, the contribution approach offers insight into short-run versus long-run effects of cutting prices on special orders. Generally, a manager can weigh such decisions by asking whether the expected long-run benefits of not cutting the price are worth a present "investment" equal to the immediate contribution to operating income ($50,000 in Exhibit 11-3). Under absorption costing, he must ordinarily conduct a special study to find the immediate effects; under the contribution approach, he has a system that will routinely provide such information.

the contribution approach or absorption costing?   A major criticism leveled at the contribution approach is that it will result in underpricing and ultimate company disaster. Such a criticism implies that full manufacturing cost is a safer guide because it does not ignore fixed factory overhead and will therefore lead to better long-run pricing decisions.

There are at least four basic weaknesses in that argument. First, full manufacturing cost also ignores some costs—the selling and administrative costs, which are often substantial. Under absorption costing, pricing decisions are often guided by unit gross profit rather than by unit net profit.[1] Second, even when absorption costing is used, there is no single unit cost that may be used as a guide as long as volume is a variable. Third, cost accountants and businessmen give excessive emphasis to costs as a guide to pricing. That is, they say and perhaps think that costs influence pricing decisions, but their actions show that *customer demand* and *competitor behavior* greatly overshadow costs as price-influencing factors.[2] Fourth, an N.A.A. survey (*Report No. 37*, p. 55) of 38 companies that use direct costing reported:

> No instance of unprofitable pricing attributable to direct costing was reported, but, on the contrary, opinion was frequently expressed to the effect that direct costing had contributed to better pricing decisions. However, companies restrict product cost and margin data to individuals qualified to interpret such data and responsible for pricing policy decisions.

Our general theme of different costs for different purposes also extends into the area of pricing. To say that the contribution approach or absorption costing provides the best guide to pricing decisions is a dangerous oversimplification of one of the most perplexing problems in business. Lack of understanding and judgment can lead to unprofitable pricing regardless of the kind of cost data available or cost-accounting system used.

need for clear information   Pricing decisions almost inevitably have long-run implications and thus require acute ability for proper weighting of short-run and long-run impacts. Because of the bewildering number of influencing factors, many

---

[1] *Current Application of Direct Costing, N.A.A. Research Report No. 37* (January 1961), p. 43.
[2] For an expanded discussion, see the second appendix to this chapter.

managers are content with "satisfactory" returns rather than "maximum" returns—primarily because they are rarely sure of what the latter amounts may be. The contribution-margin approach will help clarify some factors that are not easily brought out by the conventional approach. *N.A.A. Research Report No. 37* (page 55) cited the following cases, which took place before the contribution approach was adopted:

> Instances were cited in which management had unknowingly continued selling products below out-of-pocket cost or had decided to withdraw from the market when a substantial portion of the [fixed] costs could have been recovered . . . .
>
> In one interview . . . when direct costing was introduced, analysis demonstrated that contracts which would have contributed to [fixed] costs had often been refused at times when the company had a large amount of idle capacity.

the robinson-patman act Another major factor that influences pricing decisions is the Robinson-Patman Act. This legislation forbids quoting different prices to competing customers unless such price discrimination is justified by differences in costs of manufacturing, sale, or delivery. Decisions of courts and the Federal Trade Commission have been based on full-costing allocations rather than on direct or differential costing.

Most of these price differentials are justified by differences in distribution costs like advertising, warehousing, and freight, rather than in manufacturing costs. That is why companies with flexible pricing policies need to keep careful records of distribution costs to answer any government inquiries. However, cost justification is only one aspect of these cases. In most instances, it has been overshadowed by the issues of lessening competition and price cutting in good faith.[3]

OTHER ILLUSTRATIONS OF RELEVANCE AND THE CONTRIBUTION APPROACH

dropping a product line Assume that a company has three product lines, all produced in one factory. Management is considering dropping Product C, which has consistently shown a net loss. The predicted income statements follow:

| | PRODUCT | | | |
	A	B	C	TOTAL
Sales	$500,000	$400,000	$100,000	$1,000,000
Variable expenses	295,000	280,000	75,000	650,000
Contribution margin	$205,000(41%)	$120,000(30%)	$ 25,000(25%)	$ 350,000(35%)
Fixed expenses (salaries, depreciation, property taxes, insurance)	165,000	90,000	45,000*	300,000
Operating income	$ 40,000	$ 30,000	$(20,000)	$ 50,000

*Includes product-line supervisor's salary of $20,000.

[3] For an expanded discussion, see Herbert Taggert, *Cost Justification* (Ann Arbor, Mich.: Bureau of Business Research, University of Michigan, 1959).

Assume that the only available alternatives are to drop Product C or to continue with Product C. Assume further that the total assets invested will not be affected by the decision. Thus, the issue becomes one of selecting the production combination that will provide maximum profits. Comparisons follow:

INCOME STATEMENTS	KEEP PRODUCT C	DROP PRODUCT C	DIFFERENCE
Sales	$1,000,000	$900,000	−$100,000
Variable expenses	$ 650,000	$575,000	−$ 75,000
Fixed expenses	300,000	280,000	− 20,000
Total expenses	$ 950,000	$855,000	−$ 95,000
Operating income	$ 50,000	$ 45,000	−$ 5,000

The data above reveal that dropping unprofitable Product C would make matters worse instead of better. Why? Because all the fixed expenses would continue except for the $20,000 that would be jarred loose through discharging supervisory help. Product C now contributes $25,000 toward the coverage of fixed overhead; thus, the net effect of dropping Product C would be to forego the $25,000 contribution in order to save the $20,000 salaries. The result would be a $5,000 drop in overall profit, from $50,000 to $45,000.

Another important alternative besides the two discussed above is the possibility of dropping Product C, keeping the supervisor, and using the vacant facilities to produce, say, Product A to satisfy its expanding demand. If this happened, and if sales of Product A are expanded by $100,000, income would increase by $16,000, as follows:

	TOTAL, KEEP PRODUCT C	TOTAL, DROP C, PRODUCE MORE A	DIFFERENCE DROP C	MORE A
Sales	$1,000,000	$1,000,000	−$100,000	+$100,000
Variable expenses	$ 650,000	$ 634,000	−$ 75,000	+$ 59,000
Fixed expenses	300,000	300,000		
Total expenses	$ 950,000	$ 934,000	−$ 75,000	+$ 59,000
Operating income	$ 50,000	$ 66,000	−$ 25,000	+$ 41,000

Note that a shortcut solution to this problem could be found by concentrating on the differences shown in the two right-hand columns of the tabulation. These make up the final $16,000 difference in net income.

Note further that, with given facilities and given fixed expenses, the emphasis on products with higher contribution margins apparently maximizes operating income. Although this may be true in many instances, the matter is not quite that simple, as our next section demonstrates.

contribution per unit of constraining factor When a multiproduct plant is being operated at capacity, decisions must often be made as to which orders to accept. The contribution approach supplies the data for a proper decision, because the latter is determined by the product that makes the largest *total* contribution to profits. This does not necessarily mean that the products to be pushed are those with the biggest contribution-margin ratios per unit of product or per sales dollar. The objective is to maximize total profits, which depend on getting the highest contribution margin per unit of the *constraining (scarce, limiting,* or *critical) factor.* The following example may clarify the point. Assume that a company has two products:

	PRODUCT (PER UNIT)	
	A	B
Selling price	$10	$15
Variable expenses	7	9
Contribution margin	$ 3	$ 6
Contribution-margin ratio	30%	40%

At first glance, B looks more profitable than A. However, if you were the division manager, had 1,000 hours of capacity available, and knew that you could turn out 3 units of A per hour and only 1 unit of B per hour, your choice would be A, because it contributes the most margin *per hour,* the constraining factor in this example:

	A	B
Contribution margin per hour	$ 9	$ 6
Total contribution for 1,000 hours	$9,000	$6,000

The constraining factor is the item that restricts or limits the production or sale of a given product. Thus, *the criterion for maximum profits, for a given capacity, is the greatest possible contribution to profit per unit of the constraining factor.* The constraining factor in the example above may be machine-hours or labor-hours. It may be cubic feet of display space; in such cases, a ratio such as the contribution-margin ratio is an insufficient clue to profitability. The ratio must be multiplied by the stock turnover (number of times the average inventory is sold per year) in order to obtain comparable measures of product profitability.

The success of the suburban discount department stores illustrates the concept of the contribution to profit per unit of constraining factor. These stores have been satisfied with subnormal markups because they have been able to increase turnover and thus increase the contribution to profit per unit of space. Exhibit 11-4 demonstrates this point and assumes that the same total selling space is used in each store.

As you can imagine, there may be many constraining factors that must be utilized by each of a variety of products. The problem of formulating the most profitable production schedules and the mixes of raw materials is essentially that of maximizing the contribution in the face of many constraints. These complications are solved by linear programming techniques, which are discussed in Chapter 27.

EXHIBIT 11-4

	REGULAR DEPARTMENT STORE	DISCOUNT DEPARTMENT STORE
Retail price	$4.00	$3.50
Cost of merchandise	3.00	3.00
Contribution to profit per unit	$1.00(25%)	$ .50(14 + %)
Units sold per year	20,000	44,000
Total contribution to profit	$20,000	$22,000

***make or buy,
and idle
facilities***
Manufacturers are often confronted with the question of whether to make or buy a product—whether, for example, to manufacture their own parts and subassemblies or to buy them from vendors. The qualitative factors may be of paramount importance. Sometimes the manufacture of parts requires special know-how, unusually skilled labor, rare materials, and the like. The desire to control the quality of parts is often the determining factor in the decision to make them. On the other hand, companies hesitate to destroy mutually advantageous long-run relationships by the erratic order-giving that results from making parts during slack times and buying them during prosperous times. They may have difficulty in obtaining any parts during boom times, when there are shortages of materials and workers and no shortage of sales orders.

What are the quantitative factors relevant to the decision of whether to make or buy? The answer, again, depends on the context. A key factor is whether there are idle facilities. Many companies make parts only when their facilities cannot be used to better advantage.

Assume that the following costs are reported:

	COST OF MAKING PART NO. 300	
	PER UNIT	10,000 UNITS
Direct materials	$ 1	$ 10,000
Direct labor	8	80,000
Variable overhead	4	40,000
Fixed overhead applied	5	50,000
Total costs	$18	$180,000

Another manufacturer offers to sell B Company the same part for $16. Should B Company make or buy the part?

Although the figures above seemingly indicate that the company should buy, the answer is rarely obvious. The key question is the difference in future costs between the alternatives. Consider the fixed overhead. The total applied to the part is $50,000. Perhaps $30,000 of this fixed overhead represents those costs (for example, depreciation, property taxes, insurance, and allocated executive salaries) that will continue regardless of the decision. If so, the entire $30,000 becomes irrelevant.

Again it is risky to say categorically that only the variable costs are relevant. Perhaps, as we assume here, $20,000 of the fixed costs will be saved if the parts are bought instead of made. In other words, fixed costs that may be avoided in the future are relevant.

For the moment, let us assume that the capacity now used to make parts will become idle if the parts are purchased. The relevant computations follow:

	PER UNIT		TOTALS	
	MAKE	BUY	MAKE	BUY
Direct materials	$ 1		$ 10,000	
Direct labor	8		80,000	
Variable overhead	4		40,000	
Fixed overhead that can be avoided by not making	2		20,000	
Total relevant costs	$15	$16	$150,000	$160,000
Difference in favor of making		$1	$10,000	

essence of make or buy: utilization of facilities The choice in our example is not really whether to make or buy; it is how best to utilize available facilities. Although the data above indicate that making the part is the better choice, the figures are not conclusive—primarily because we have no idea of what can be done with the manufacturing facilities if the component is bought. Only if the released facilities are to remain idle are the figures above valid.

If the released facilities can be used advantageously in some other manufacturing activity or can be rented out, these alternatives also may merit consideration. The two courses of action have become four (figures are in thousands):

	MAKE	BUY AND LEAVE FACILITIES IDLE	BUY AND RENT	BUY AND USE FACILITIES FOR OTHER PRODUCTS
Rent revenue	$ —	$ —	$ 5	$ —
Contribution from other products	—	—	—	19
Obtaining of parts	(150)	(160)	(160)	(160)
Net relevant costs	$(150)	$(160)	$(155)	$(141)

The analysis indicates that buying the parts and using the vacated facilities for the production of other products should yield best results.

policy making for make or buy Costs must be related to time. A cost that is fixed over a short period may be variable over a longer period. Profits may increase momentarily by applying the contribution-margin approach to decisions, but, over the long run, profits may suffer by inordinate use of such an approach. Thus, companies develop long-run policies for the use of capacity:

One company stated that it solicits subcontract work for other manufacturers during periods when sales of its own products do not fully utilize the plant, but that such work cannot be carried on regularly without expansion of its plant. The profit margin on subcontracts is not sufficiently large to cover these additional costs, and hence work is accepted only when other business is lacking. The same company sometimes meets a period of high volume by purchasing parts or having them made by subcontractors. While the cost of such parts is usually higher than the cost to make them in the company's own plant, the additional cost is less than it would be if they were made on equipment which could be used only part of the time.[4]

beware of unit costs Unit costs should be analyzed with care in decision making. There are two major ways to go wrong: (a) the inclusion of irrelevant costs, such as the $3 allocation of fixed costs in the make-or-buy comparison, which would result in a unit cost of $18 instead of the relevant unit cost of $15; and (b) comparisons of unit costs not computed on the same basis. Generally, it is advisable to use total costs rather than unit costs. Then, if desired, the total may be unitized. Machinery salesmen, for example, often brag about the low unit costs of using their new machines. Sometimes they neglect to point out that the unit costs are based on outputs far in excess of the volume of activity of their prospective customer. The unitization of fixed costs in this manner can be particularly misleading. The lesson here is to use total costs, not unit costs, in relevant cost analysis when possible.

IRRELEVANCE OF PAST COSTS

As defined earlier, a relevant cost is (a) an expected future cost that will (b) differ between alternatives. The contribution aspect of relevant-cost analysis has shown that those expected future costs that will not differ among alternatives are irrelevant. Now we return to the idea that all past costs are also irrelevant.

obsolete inventory A company has 100 obsolete missile parts that are carried in inventory at a manufacturing cost of $100,000. The parts can be: (a) remachined for $30,000, and then sold for $50,000; or (b) scrapped for $5,000. Which should be done?

This is an unfortunate situation; yet the $100,000 cost is irrelevant to the decision to remachine or scrap. The only relevant factors are the expected future revenue and costs:

	REMACHINE	SCRAP	DIFFERENCE
Expected future revenue	$ 50,000	$ 5,000	$45,000
Expected future costs	30,000	–	30,000
Relevant excess of revenue over costs	$ 20,000	$ 5,000	$15,000
Accumulated historical inventory costs*	100,000	100,000	–
Net overall loss on project	$ (80,000)	$ (95,000)	$15,000

* Irrelevant because it is not an element of difference as between the alternatives.

[4] *The Analysis of Cost–Volume–Profit Relationships,* N.A.A. Research Series No. 17, p. 552.

We could completely ignore the historical cost and still arrive at the $15,000 difference, the key figure in the analysis.

regular inventory Note another important point. Although this example dealt with obsolete parts, the idea that past costs are irrelevant per se applies to the historical cost of *any* inventory, whether obsolete or fully merchantable. The replacement cost of additional units of inventory is a future cash outflow that is likely to be common to nearly all alternatives under consideration. However, it is a separate outflow; it should not be confused with the question of what to do with the units on hand. This point may be clarified by an example.

Suppose a company uses copper as an input. At the beginning of the period, there are 1,000 units in copper inventory that were acquired for $110 per unit. Assume further that if the company decides not to use the 1,000 units on hand, it is possible to sell them to a salvage yard for $95 per unit. Another salvage yard has offered $90. There are many alternative end-product uses for the copper. Another alternative would be to throw the units in the city dump. A "total-alternatives" approach to the analysis follows (in thousands of dollars):

| | CHOICES | | | | | | |
| | USE COPPER IN PRODUCT | | | | SALVAGE | | THROW AWAY |
	A	B	C	D	1	2	
Expected future revenue	220	204	186	170	95	90	–
Expected future costs:							
Labor and overhead	90	70	60	100	–	–	–
Excess of revenue over costs	130	134	126	70	95	90	–
		Best					

opportunity cost Note that all alternatives are listed and analyzed in the same systematic way under the total-alternatives approach. Ideally, the decision maker should be able to list an exhaustive number of alternatives and then compute the expected results under each, giving full consideration to interdependent and long-run effects. Practically, the decision maker sifts among the possible alternatives, discards many out of hand as being obviously unattractive, undoubtedly overlooks some attractive possibilities, and concentrates on a limited number.

The idea of an opportunity cost has arisen because some alternatives are excluded from formal consideration. An *opportunity cost* is defined as the maximum contribution that is foregone by using limited resources for a particular purpose. For example, suppose that the total alternatives under formal consideration are described by choices A through D above but that the salvage and throw-away alternatives will not be analyzed in the same format. Then an opportunity approach is needed.

The opportunity-cost approach may take many forms. A common way to analyze the alternatives above would be to assign a $95 opportunity cost to the inventory. The decision maker would then organize his analysis of the remaining alternatives as follows (in thousands of dollars):

	CHOICES			
	USE COPPER IN PRODUCT			
	A	B	C	D
Revenue	220	204	186	170
Relevant costs:				
Opportunity cost of copper	95	95	95	95
Labor and overhead	90	70	60	100
Total relevant costs	185	165	155	195
Net advantage	35	39	31	(25)

Note that the *best* of the excluded alternatives is included in the formal comparison as an opportunity cost. The other two (or more) excluded alternatives are not in this analysis. The possible uses of the copper in Products A, C, and D may also eventually become excluded alternatives, but they are excluded after formal consideration in the decision model used.

Suppose the copper could be sold for a scrap price of $195 instead of $95. Then all the results for the alternatives formally included above would be negative. This would indicate that the best excluded alternative, the scrap sale at $195, is in fact optimum.

Note that an opportunity cost is not ordinarily incorporated in formal accounting systems. Such a cost represents income foregone by receipts or outlays. Accountants usually confine their recording to those events that ultimately involve exchanges of assets. Accountants confine their history to alternatives selected rather than those rejected, primarily because of their impracticality or impossibility of accumulating meaningful data on what might have been.

book value of old equipment   Assume that there is a machine, with a cost of $120,000, two-thirds depreciated on a straight-line basis, with a book value of $40,000, and with a remaining useful life of four years. The old machine has a $4,000 disposal value now; in four years, its disposal value will be zero. A new machine is available that will dramatically reduce operating costs. Annual revenue of $100,000 will not change regardless of the decision. The new machine will cost $60,000 and have zero disposal value at the end of its four-year life. The new machine promises to slash variable operating costs from $80,000 per year to $56,000 per year. Many managers and accountants would not replace the old machine because it would entail recognizing a $36,000 "loss on disposal," whereas retention would allow spreading the $40,000 over four years in the form of "depreciation expense" (a more appealing term than "loss on disposal").

Under our definition of relevant costs, book value of old fixed assets is always irrelevant in making decisions. This proposition is by far the most difficult for managers and accountants alike to accept. The real concept of importance here is that *all* historical costs are irrelevant. At one time or another, we all like to think that we can soothe our wounded pride arising from having made a bad purchase decision by using the item instead of replacing it. The fallacy here is in erroneously thinking that a current or future action can influence the long-run impact of a past outlay. All past costs are down the drain. *Nothing* can change what has already happened.

We can apply our definition of relevance to four commonly encountered items:

1. *Book value of old equipment.* Irrelevant, because it is a past (historical) cost.
2. *Disposal value of old equipment.* Relevant (ordinarily), because it is an expected future inflow that usually differs between alternatives.
3. *Gain or loss on disposal.* This is the algebraic difference between 1 and 2. It is therefore a meaningless combination of book value, which is always irrelevant, and disposal value, which is usually relevant. The combination form, *loss* (or *gain) on disposal,* blurs the distinction between the irrelevant book value and the relevant disposal value. Consequently, it is best to think of each separately.[5]
4. *Cost of new equipment.* Relevant, because it is an expected future outflow that will differ between alternatives.

Exhibit 11-5 should clarify the above assertions. Book value of old equipment is irrelevant regardless of the decision-making technique used. The Difference columns in Exhibit 11-5 show that book value of old equipment is not an element of difference between alternatives and could be completely ignored without changing the $10,000 difference in average annual net income. No matter what the *timing* of the charge against revenue, the *amount* charged is still $40,000 regardless of any available alternative. In either event, the undepreciated cost will be written off with the same ultimate effect on profit.[6] The $40,000 creeps into the income statement either as a $40,000 offset against the $4,000 proceeds to obtain the $36,000 *loss on disposal* in one year or as $10,000 depreciation in each of four years. But how it appears is irrelevant to the replacement decision. In contrast, the $15,000 annual depreciation on the new equipment *is* relevant because the total $60,000 depreciation may be avoided by not replacing.

Note the motivational factors here. A manager may be reluctant to replace simply because the large loss on disposal will severely harm his profit performance in the first year. This demonstrates how overemphasis on short-run income may conflict with the objective of maximizing income over the long run.

---

[5] For simplicity, we ignore income tax considerations and the effects of the interest value of money in this chapter. But book value is irrelevant even if income taxes are considered, because the relevant item is then the tax cash flow, not the book value. Using the approach in Exhibit 11-1, the book value is essential information for the *prediction method,* but the expected future income tax cash outflows are the relevant information for the *decision model.* The prediction method would be: Disposal value, $4,000 − Book value, $40,000 = Loss on disposal, $36,000. If the income tax rate is 50 percent, the income tax cash saving would be $18,000. This $18,000 would be the expected future cash flow that is relevant input to the decision model. For elaboration, see Chapter 23.

[6] We are deliberately ignoring income tax factors for the time being. If income taxes are considered, the *timing* of the writing off of fixed-asset costs may influence income tax payments. In this example, there will be a small real difference: the present value of $40,000 as a tax deduction now versus the present value of a $10,000 tax deduction each year for four years. But this difference in *future* income tax flows is the *relevant* item—not the book value of the old fixed asset per se. See Chapter 14.

EXHIBIT 11-5

COST COMPARISON—REPLACEMENT OF MACHINE,
INCLUDING RELEVANT AND IRRELEVANT ITEMS

(*In Thousands of Dollars*)

	FOUR YEARS TOGETHER			ANNUALIZED (DIVIDED BY 4)		
	KEEP	REPLACE	DIFFERENCE	KEEP	REPLACE	DIFFERENCE
Sales	$400	$400	$—	$100	$100	$—
Expenses:						
Variable	320	224	96	80	56	24
Old machine (book value):						
Periodic write-off	40		—	10		—
or						
Lump-sum write-off		40*			10	
Disposal value		−4*	4	—	−1	1
New machine, written off periodically as depreciation	—	60	−60	—	15	−15
Total expenses	$360	$320	$ 40	$ 90	$ 80	$ 10
Operating income	$ 40	$ 80	$ 40	$ 10	$ 20	$ 10

The advantage of replacement is $40,000 for the four years together; the *average* annual advantage is $10,000.

* In a formal income statement, these two items would be combined as "loss on disposal" of $36,000.

***examining
alternatives
over the
long run***   The foregoing is the first example that has looked beyond one year. A useful technique is to view the alternatives over their entire lives and then to compute annual average results. In this way, peculiar nonrecurring items (such as loss on disposal) will not obstruct the long-run view that must necessarily be taken in almost all special managerial decisions.

Exhibit 11-6 concentrates on relevant items only. Note that the same answer (the $40,000 net difference) will be produced even though the book value is completely omitted from the calculations. The only relevant items are the variable operating costs, the disposal value of the old equipment, and the depreciation on the new equipment.

EXHIBIT 11-6

COST COMPARISON—REPLACEMENT OF MACHINE: RELEVANT ITEMS ONLY

(*In Thousands of Dollars*)

	FOUR YEARS TOGETHER			ANNUALIZED (DIVIDED BY 4)		
	KEEP	REPLACE	DIFFERENCE	KEEP	REPLACE	DIFFERENCE
Variable expenses	$320	$224	$ 96	$ 80	$ 56	$ 24
Disposal value of old equipment	—	−4	4		−1	1
Depreciation—new equipment	—	60	−60		15	−15
Total relevant expenses	$320	$280	$ 40	$ 80	$ 70	$ 10

THE PROBLEM OF UNCERTAINTY

It is vitally important to recognize that throughout this chapter and the next, dollar amounts of future sales and operating costs are assumed in order to highlight and to simplify various important points. In practice, the forecasting of these key figures is generally the most difficult aspect of decision analysis. For elaboration, see Chapter 23.

summary

The accountant's role in special decisions is basically that of a technical expert on cost analysis. His responsibility is to see that the manager is supplied with relevant data for guiding decisions.

To be relevant to a particular decision, a cost must meet two criteria: (a) it must be an expected *future* cost; and (b) it must be an element of *difference* between alternatives. The key question is, "What difference does it make?" If the objective of the decision maker is to maximize long-run net income, all *past* (*historical*) costs are irrelevant to any *decision* about the future.

The role that past costs play in decision making is an auxiliary one; the distinction here should be definitive, not fuzzy. Past (irrelevant) costs are useful because they provide empirical evidence that often helps sharpen *predictions* of future relevant costs. But the expected future costs are the *only* cost ingredients in any decision model per se.

The ability to distinguish relevant from irrelevant items and the use of the contribution approach to cost analysis are twin foundations for tackling many decisions.

In decisions about activity levels (the special order, make or buy, and adding or dropping a product line), there may be a temptation to say that variable costs are always relevant and that fixed costs are always irrelevant. This is a dangerous generalization, because fixed costs are often affected by a decision. For example, plans to buy a second car for family use should be most heavily influenced by the new set of fixed costs that would be encountered. Conceivably, if the total family mileage were unaffected, the variable costs could be wholly irrelevant.

For a given set of facilities or resources, the key to maximizing net income is to obtain the largest possible contribution per unit of constraining factor.

Generally, in cost analysis it is advisable to use total costs, not unit costs, because unitized fixed costs are often erroneously interpreted as if they behaved like variable costs. A common activity or volume level must underlie the comparison of equipment.

The book value of old equipment is always irrelevant in replacement decisions. Disposal value, however, is usually relevant.

Incremental or differential costs are the differences in total costs under each alternative.

Opportunity cost is the maximum contribution that is foregone by using limited resources for a particular purpose. The use of opportunity cost is a practical means of reducing the alternatives under consideration; the solution reached is still the same as that given by a more complete "total-alternatives" approach. The decision maker says, "There are many alternatives that I want to reject without conducting a thorough analysis. Therefore, I shall take the best of these, compute its contribution, and use that as the cost of the scarce resource [copper in the example] when I explicitly analyze the remaining alternatives."

Cost reports for special decisions may concentrate on relevant items only (Exhibit 11-5), or they may encompass both relevant and irrelevant items (Exhibit 11-6). The best format depends on individual preferences. The shortcut approach concentrates only on the Difference column, because it summarizes the relevant items. The problem of uncertainty, which is discussed in Chapter 23, complicates prediction and is easily the gravest practical difficulty.

Problem for Self-Study

PROBLEM   The San Carlos Company is an electronics company having eight product lines. Income data for one of the products for the year just ended follow (in millions):

Sales—200,000 units @ average price of $100		$20
Variable costs:		
Direct materials @ $35	$7	
Direct labor @ $10	2	
Variable factory overhead @ $5	1	
Sales commissions @ 15 percent of selling price	3	
Other variable costs @ $5	1	
Total variable costs @ $70		14
Contribution margin		$ 6
Fixed costs:		
Discretionary (See Chapter 8)	$3	
Committed (See Chapter 8)	2	
Total fixed costs		5
Operating income		$ 1

required   1. The electronics industry had severe price competition throughout the year. Near the end of the year, Abrams Co., which was experimenting with various components in its regular product line, offered $80 each for 3,000 units. The latter would have been in addition to the 200,000 units actually sold. The acceptance of this special order by San Carlos would not affect regular sales. The salesman hoped that the order might provide entrance into a new application, so he told George Holtz, the product manager, that he would accept half his regular commission rate if the order were accepted. Holtz pondered for a day, but he was afraid of the precedent that might be set by cutting the price. He said, "The price is below our full costs of $95 per unit. I think we should quote a full price, or Abrams Co. will expect favored treatment again and again if we continue to do business with them." If Holtz had accepted the offer, what would operating income have been?

2. The Gregorio Company had offered to supply a key part (M-I-A) for $20 each. One M-I-A is used in every finished unit. The San Carlos Company

had made these parts for variable costs of $18 plus some additional fixed costs of $200,000 for supervision and other items. What would operating income have been if San Carlos purchased rather than made the parts? Assume that the discretionary costs for supervision and other items would have been avoided if the parts were purchased.

3. The company could have purchased the M-I-A parts for $20 each and used the vacated space for the manufacture of a different electronics component on a subcontracting basis for Hewlett-Packard, a much larger company. Assume that 40,000 special components could have been made for Hewlett-Packard (and sold in addition to the 200,000 regular units through regular channels) at a unit variable cost of $150, exclusive of parts. Part M-I-A would be needed for these components as well as for the regular production. No sales commission would have to be paid. All the fixed costs pertaining to the M-I-A parts would have continued, including the supervisory costs, because they related mainly to the facilities used. What would operating income have been if San Carlos had made and sold the components to Hewlett-Packard for $170 per unit and bought the M-I-A parts?

SOLUTION 1. Analysis of special order:

Additional sales of 3,000 units @ $80		$240,000
Direct materials—3,000 units @ $35	$105,000	
Direct labor—3,000 units @ $10	30,000	
Variable factory overhead—3,000 units @ $5	15,000	
Other variable costs—3,000 units @ $5	15,000	
Sales commission—(15% of $80,000) × .5	6,000	
Total variable costs		171,000
Contribution margin		$ 69,000

Note that the variable costs, except for commissions, are affected by physical units of volume, not dollar revenue.

Operating income would have been $1,000,000 plus $69,000, or $1,069,000, if the order had been accepted. In a sense, the decision to reject the offer means that San Carlos is willing to invest $69,000 in immediate gains foregone (an opportunity cost) to preserve the long-run selling-price structure.

2.

	MAKE	PURCHASE
Purchase cost @ $20		$4,000,000
Variable costs @ $18	$3,600,000	
Avoidable discretionary costs	200,000	
Total relevant costs	$3,800,000	$4,000,000

Operating income would have fallen by $200,000, or from $1,000,000 to $800,000, if San Carlos had purchased the parts.

3.

Sales would increase by 40,000 units @ $170	$6,800,000
Additional costs to the company as a whole:	
Variable costs exclusive of M-I-A parts would increase by 40,000 units @ $150	$6,000,000

Effects on overall costs
of M-I-A parts:

Cost of 240,000 parts purchased @ $20	$4,800,000		
Less savings from not making 200,000 parts @ $18 (only the variable costs are relevant because fixed costs continue)	3,600,000		
Additional cost of parts		1,200,000	7,200,000
Disadvantage of making components			$ (400,000)

Operating income would decline by $400,000, from $1,000,000 to $600,000.

APPENDIX A: COST TERMS USED FOR DIFFERENT PURPOSES

Because costs must be tailored to the decision at hand, many terms (too many!) have arisen to describe different types of cost. The author believes that the variety of terms is more confusing than illuminating; yet the varying usage of such terms necessitates a familiarity with them. Whenever you are confronted by these terms in practice, you will save much confusion and wasted time if you find out their exact meaning in the given case. For that matter, this word of caution applies to all the weird accounting terms used from company to company. Individual companies frequently develop their own extensive and distinctive accounting language. This language is not readily understood by accountants outside the company. The following terms will be related to other terms used previously in this book.

Imputed cost is a cost that does not appear in conventional accounting records and does not entail dollar outlays. A common example is the inclusion of "interest" on ownership equity as a part of operating expenses.

The terms *opportunity costs* (described in this chapter) and *imputed costs*[7] are used interchangeably in many other situations (for example, charging operations with rent or interest that could be gained from alternate uses of resources). However, there is a distinction in some cases. The opportunity-cost notion is demand-oriented; it is the measure of profits foregone. Sometimes the imputed-cost notion is the same as the opportunity-cost idea. At other times, however, it is cost-oriented, closer to the internal situation rather than the external situation. For example, transfer prices between departments or divisions of the same company could be imputed in a number of ways. Assume that an iron-ore mining division produces ore for a steel-producing division of Ford Motor Company. There are at least three ways of charging the steel-producing division for iron ore: (a) at cost in the conventional sense, (b) at imputed cost based on the lowest alternative supplier price (opportunity-cost idea), and (c) at imputed cost based on some arbitrary markup over mining cost (arbitrary imputed-cost idea).

---

[7] Some accountants may say that *imputed cost* is a narrow term because it refers only to "interest" charges that do not involve out-of-pocket expenditures.

Out-of-pocket costs, a short-run concept, are those costs that entail current or near-future outlays for the decision at hand. For example, the acceptance of an order so that otherwise idle facilities may be used would entail a compilation of the out-of-pocket costs that otherwise could be avoided by not accepting the order; the depreciation on the machinery and equipment used for production would be irrelevant, because it does not entail out-of-pocket outlays as a result of the decision.

Joint cost is that term most often applied to the costs of manufactured goods that are produced by a single process and that are not identifiable as individual types of products until a certain stage of production known as the *split-off point* (point of separation) is reached. Examples of such products are soap and glycerin, kerosene and gasoline, chemicals, and lumber. Joint costs are total costs incurred up to the point of separation. Inasmuch as joint costs by their very nature cannot be directly traced to units worked on, any method of apportioning such costs to various units produced is essentially arbitrary. The usefulness of joint-cost apportionment is limited to purposes of inventory costing. Such apportionment is useless for cost-planning and control purposes.

Viewed broadly, joint costs plague the accountant throughout his work. Few costs are not joint in relation to some other factor, such as time or facilities. The entire problem of allocating the costs of fixed assets to months, years, departments, and products is essentially that of joint costing. Sometimes the term *common cost* is used instead of *joint cost* to describe another aspect of joint costing, such as the problem of determining unit cost of such services as bank accounts. Any allocation method is arbitrary, because many facilities and services are shared by many revenue-producing activities. The entire problem of re-apportioning service-department costs among producing departments is really one of joint cost.

Postponable costs are those that may be shifted to the future with little or no effect on the efficiency of current operations. The best example of these is maintenance and repairs. Railroads sometimes go on an economy binge and cut their sizable maintenance budgets. But it is really a matter of deferral and not avoidance. Eventually some overhauls must be made and tracks must be repaired.

Avoidable costs are those that may be saved by not adopting a given alternative. For example, by not adopting a new product line, the appropriate direct-material, direct-labor, and variable-overhead costs could be avoided. The criterion here is the question: Which costs can be saved by not adopting a given alternative?

Sunk cost is another term for a past cost that is unavoidable because it cannot be changed no matter what action is taken. The author dislikes this term because it often beclouds the distinction between historical and future costs. However, *sunk cost* is discussed here because it is one of the most widely used terms in special-decision making.

To illustrate, if old equipment has book value of $600,000 and scrap value of $70,000, what is the sunk cost? There are two ways of looking at the $600,000 book value of old equipment. This author agrees with a minority view maintaining that the entire $600,000 is sunk because it represents an outlay made in the past that cannot be changed; the $70,000 scrap value is a future factor, to be considered apart from the $600,000 sunk cost. The majority view maintains that $530,000 of the $600,000 is sunk, whereas $70,000 is not sunk because it is immediately recoverable through scrapping. Thus, the sunk part of a historical cost is what is irrecoverable in a given situation. The latter view is that the two factors (book value and present scrap value) are complementary in replacement decisions; that is, book value minus scrap value equals sunk cost.

In the author's opinion, the term *sunk cost* should not be used at all. It muddles the task of collecting proper costs for decision making. Because all past costs are irrelevant, it is fruitless to introduce unnecessary terms to describe past costs. The issue of what part of a past cost is sunk need not arise. The essence of the distinction between costs, past and future, irrelevant and relevant, was described earlier in this chapter. These distinctions are all that are needed for approaching special decisions. The term *sunk cost* is often more befuddling than enlightening. If it is going to be used, *sunk cost* should have the same meaning as *past cost*.

APPENDIX B: COST-PLUS FOR SETTING PRICES

major influences on pricing Professional economists, self-styled economists, and businessmen have been arguing for centuries about the cause-and-effect relationships between costs and prices. The problems here are intricate because of the interplay of long-run and short-run factors.

Many businessmen maintain that they use cost-plus pricing. They say that they figure their average unit costs and tack on a "fair" margin that will yield an adequate return on investment. This entails circular reasoning, because price, which influences sales, depends upon full cost, which in turn is partly determined by the *volume* of sales. Also, this "plus" in cost-plus is bothersome. It is rarely a rigid "plus." Instead, it is flexible, depending on the behavior of competitors and customers. There are at least three major influences on pricing decisions: customers, competitors, and costs.

Customers. The businessman must always examine his pricing problems through the eyes of his customers. He cannot level a shotgun at his customers and say, "Buy, or else!" Customers can reject a company's product and turn to competitors' products or, perhaps, to a completely different industry for a substitute product. When coffee prices are high, many people drink one cup instead of two; others switch to tea. If a company's prices get too high, the immediate reaction of the customer is to check with competitors, who welcome such inquiries. Perhaps the customer makes its own product or tries to find whether a different product will serve just as well (aluminum instead of copper). For example, buyers of welding equipment are often most heavily influenced by the way the product affects their costs. The buyer not only has alternate sources of supply within the welding equipment industry; he may not buy at all, but may keep using his existing equipment. He may substitute some other kind of equipment to accomplish his tasks; or he may manufacture the needed equipment himself.

Competitors. Rivals' reactions or lack of reactions will influence pricing decisions. In guessing a competitor's reactions, one must speculate on what the competitor's costs are, rather than be concerned with his own costs. Of course, one's own costs may be helpful in guessing, but it is the rival's costs that are relevant. Knowledge of the rival's technology, plant size, and operating policies help sharpen estimates of his costs. Companies within industries that loathe price competition have been known to swap detailed cost information for mutual benefit. Where there is no collusion, rivals' reactions and price quotations must be guessed when pricing decisions are made.

Costs. The maximum price that may be charged is the one that does not drive the customer away. The minimum price is zero. Companies occasionally will give or virtually give their products away in order to get entrenched in a market or to obtain a profitable long-run relationship with a customer. A more practical guide is gleaned from our study of cost–volume–profit relationships. In the short run, the minimum price to be quoted should be the additional costs from accepting the order or segment of available business. Any amount in excess of those additional costs directly increases income.

Where a company has some discretion in price setting, customer demand at various price levels determines the sales volume. In these situations, study must be given to differential cost–volume–profit relationships; in turn, these relationships are dependent on market conditions, elasticity of industry demand, concentration of capacity, and rivals' reactions.

Where a company has little discretion, it accepts the price that competition has set. Then, under given economic conditions, the company ordinarily selects the level of production and sales that maximizes profits.

example of contribution approach to pricing Exhibit 11-7 shows an actual price-quote format used by the president and sales manager of a small job shop that bids on special machinery orders under highly competitive conditions. This approach is a tool for flexible pricing. Note that the maximum price is not a matter of cost at all; the minimum price is set by the total variable costs.

Note also, in Exhibit 11-7, that the costs are classified and tailored especially for the pricing task. Pricing duties may be in the hands of a number of different executives. Often it is a joint effort on the part of the sales manager, production manager, and general manager, with the last-named having the final authority. The accountant's task is to supply a format that is understandable and that involves a minimum of computations. That is why direct labor and variable overhead are lumped together in one overall rate; all fixed costs, whether factory, engineering, selling, or administrative, are lumped together for the same reason.

EXHIBIT 11-7

QUOTE SHEET

(*Data Assumed*)

Direct materials (materials only, at cost)	$25,000
Direct labor and variable overhead (direct-labor hours × $3.50)	
3,000 hrs × $3.50 =	10,500
Commission (varies with job)	3,000
Total variable costs—Minimum price	$38,500
Add fixed costs applied (direct-labor hours × $4.75)	
3,000 hrs × $4.75 =	14,250
Total costs (including share of fixed costs)	$52,750
Add desired profit	9,250
Selling price (What you think you can get—Maximum price)	$62,000

The quote sheet above shows two prices, maximum and minimum. Any amount you can get over the minimum price is a contribution margin.

questions, problems, and cases

11-1. Distinguish briefly between *quantitative* and *qualitative* factors in decision making.

11-2. Define *relevant cost* as the term is used in this chapter. Why are historical costs irrelevant?

11-3. What is a *differential cost?* Distinguish it from a relevant cost.

11-4. "All future costs are relevant." Do you agree? Why?

11-5. Theater prices are usually lower for matinees than for evening performances. Why? As a movie-theater manager, what factors would influence your decision as to conducting matinees? To what degree are operating costs affected by the size of the audience?

11-6. Questions on Disposal of Assets.

1. A company has an inventory of 1,000 assorted missile parts for a line of missiles that has been junked. The inventory cost $100,000. The parts can be either (a) remachined at total additional costs of $30,000 and then sold for a total of $35,000, or (b) scrapped for $2,000. What should be done?

2. A truck, costing $10,000 and uninsured, is wrecked the first day in use. It can be either (a) disposed of for $1,000 cash and replaced with a similar truck costing $10,200, or (b) rebuilt for $8,500 and be brand-new as far as operating characteristics and looks are concerned. What should be done?

11-7. The Careening Bookkeeping Machine. [From W. A. Paton, "Restoration of Fixed Asset Values to the Balance Sheet," *Accounting Review* XXII, No. 2, 194–210.] A young lady in the accounting department of a certain business was moving a bookkeeping machine from one room to another. As she came alongside an open stairway, she carelessly slipped and let the machine get away from her. It went careening down the stairs with a great racket and wound up at the bottom in some thousands of pieces, completely wrecked. Hearing the crash, the office manager came rushing out, and turned rather white when he saw what had happened. "Someone tell me quickly," he yelled, "if that is one of our fully amortized units." A check of the equipment cards showed that the smashed machine was, indeed, one of those which had been written off. "Thank God!" said the manager.

required   Explain and comment on the point of Professor Paton's anecdote.

11-8. **Determination of Relevant Costs.** The Frel Company makes a standard line of gauges. A large aircraft company has asked for competitive bids on an order of 10,000 special gauges for use in the manufacture of aircraft parts. Frel Company wants to know the minimum price to bid that will insure at least a $5,000 increase in net income.

The operating picture, as it will appear for the year if the extra order is not landed, is as follows:

FREL COMPANY

Income Statement
For the Year Ending December 31, 19–1

Sales (40,000 gauges)		$600,000
Cost of sales:		
Direct materials	$100,000	
Direct labor	200,000	
Variable overhead (varies with direct-labor hours)	50,000	
Fixed overhead	100,000	450,000
Gross margin		$150,000
Selling and administrative expenses:		
Variable (including shipping costs of 40¢ per unit)	$ 30,000	
Fixed	80,000	110,000
Net income		$ 40,000

Assume that the cost behavior patterns will not be changed by the additional order, except as follows:

a. Shipping costs, which are ordinarily borne by the Frel Company, will be paid for and borne by the aircraft company.

b. Special setup costs and the cost of special tools (that will not be reusable) will total $5,000.

c. Direct-labor charges on these gauges will be 20 percent higher because of more time needed per unit.

required   1. Prepare a new income statement, assuming that the order is landed after the minimum price has been quoted. Set up your solution in the following manner:

	COLUMN		
	(A) OLD INCOME STATEMENT	*(B)* CHANGE	*(C)* NEW INCOME STATEMENT
Sales			
Cost of sales:			
Direct materials			
Direct labor			
(and so forth)			

2. Examine the format of your answer to requirement 1. How else could the information be presented?

11-9. Relevance of Equipment Costs. The Auto Wash Company has just installed a special machine for washing cars. The machine cost $20,000. Its operating costs, based on a yearly volume of 100,000 cars, total $15,000, exclusive of depreciation. The machine will have a four-year useful life and no residual value.

After the machine has been used one day, a machine salesman offers a different machine that promises to do the same job at a yearly operating cost of $9,000, exclusive of depreciation. The new machine will cost $24,000 cash, installed. The "old" machine is unique and can be sold outright for only $10,000, less $2,000 removal cost. The new machine, like the old one, will have a four-year useful life and no residual value.

Sales, all in cash, will be $150,000 per year and other cash expenses will be $110,000 annually, regardless of this decision.

required

1. Prepare income statements as they would appear for each of the next four years under both alternatives. What is the net difference in income for the four years taken together?

2. Prepare cash-flow (cash receipts and disbursements) statements as they would appear for each of the next four years under both alternatives. What is the net difference in cash flow for the four years taken together?

3. What are the irrelevant items in each of your presentations in parts 1 and 2? Why are they irrelevant?

4. Describe your thoughts on the role of book value in replacement of equipment.

5. Should the new equipment be bought if the difference in its favor is $2,400 for the four years taken together? Why?

11-10. Costs of Operating an Automobile. Here are typical costs of operating a salesman's car for 30,000 miles in a year:

Gasoline—2,000 gallons @ 40¢	$ 800
Oil changes and lubrication—5 @ $10	50
Tire wear (based on life of 20,000 miles; a new set of 4 costs $100)	150
Regular maintenance and repair	210
Auto insurance	290
Washing and waxing	100
Licenses	100
Garage rent and parking fees	300
Depreciation—($3,800 − $1,800) ÷ 2-year life	1,000
	$3,000

Unit cost is $3,000 ÷ 30,000 miles, or 10¢ per mile.

required

1. If the salesman drives 20,000 miles per year, what would be the average unit cost per mile? If he drives 40,000 miles?

2. He takes his car on a 200-mile journey with a friend who agrees to share the cost of the trip. How much should the friend pay?

3. The salesman's wife wants a similar car for shopping and other errands that the husband now performs. If he buys the second car, it will be driven 4,000

miles per year; but suppose the total mileage of the two cars taken together will still be 30,000 miles. What will the annual cost of operating the second car be? The average unit cost? What costs are relevant? Why?

4. List other possible costs of car ownership that are not included in the tabulation above.

5. What costs are relevant to the question of selling the car at the end of one year (market value, $2,500) and using other means of transportation?

6. Assume that the salesman has no car. What costs are relevant to the question of buying the car described versus using other means of transportation?

11-11. **Relevance of Inventory Costs to a Business Investment Decision.** Assume that a wealthy investor is contemplating buying a paper-manufacturing company. Certain inventory of the paper company is carried at $100,000, including $40,000 of variable production costs and $60,000 of fixed factory overhead.

required   How much should the investor pay for the inventory? Why?

11-12. **An Argument About Pricing.** A column in a newspaper contained the following:

Dear Miss Lovelorn: My husband and I are in constant disagreement because he drives 10 miles to work every day, and drives a mile in the opposite direction to pick up and deliver the man who rides with him. For this service the man pays $2 every other week toward gas. Bus fare would cost $5 each week, as two bus lines are involved. I say this fellow should pay at least $3 each week, which would be one-half the cost for the week's gas. But my husband says he can't just ask him for the money, so he settles for this arrangement month after month. We have three children and are in debt for several hundred dollars, and even this $3 a week would really help, as we live on a very tight budget. Am I reasonable to think the gas expense should be split 50-50?

required   As Miss Lovelorn, write a reply.

11-13. **Contribution Approach to Pricing.** A company has a budget for 19_2; the absorption-costing approach follows (figures assumed):

Sales	$100,000	100%
Factory cost of goods sold, including $20,000 fixed costs	60,000	60
Gross profit	$ 40,000	40%
Operating expenses, including $20,000 fixed costs	30,000	30
Net income target	$ 10,000	10%

Normal or target markup percentage:
$40,000 ÷ $60,000 = 66.7% of absorption cost

required   1. Recast the income statement in a contribution format. Indicate the normal or target markup percentage based on total variable costs.

2. Assume the same cost behavior patterns as above. Assume further that a customer offers $540 for some units that have a factory cost of goods manufactured of $600 and total variable costs of $500. Should the offer be accepted? Explain.

11-14. **Contribution Approach to Pricing.** The Dill Company had the following operating characteristics in 19_4:

Basic production data at standard cost:

Direct materials	$1.30
Direct labor	1.50
Variable overhead	.20
Fixed overhead ($150,000 ÷ 150,000 units of denominator volume)	1.00
Total factory cost at standard	$4.00

Sales price, $5.00 per unit.

Selling and administrative expense is assumed for simplicity as being all fixed at $65,000 yearly, except for sales commissions at 5% of dollar sales.

In 19_4, a Dill Company salesman had asked the president for permission to sell 1,000 units to a particular customer for $3.80 per unit. The president refused, stating that the price was below factory cost. Based solely on the information given, compute the effect of the president's decision on 19_4 net income. Specifically, what would be the reasoning of the contribution approach to such a decision?

11-15. Costs and Formulas for Pricing. A contractor has prepared the following budgeted figures for the current year:

Sales		$148,230
Direct-material costs, including sales taxes	$40,000	
Direct labor	75,000	
Payroll taxes, insurance, and welfare contributions related to direct labor	7,500	
Other "job" overhead (variable)	2,500	
General overhead (fixed)	9,750	134,750
Target net income		$ 13,480

The contractor has followed general industry practice in his approach to pricing. He estimates the amount of materials and direct labor and then adds a markup for overhead and another markup for desired net income. For example, suppose that a representative job is estimated to cost $400 for direct materials and $750 for direct labor. He would prepare the following analysis for pricing:

Direct materials	$ 400.00
Direct labor	750.00
Add 10% for fringe benefits	75.00
Subtotal	$1,225.00
Add 10% for overhead	122.50
Subtotal	$1,347.50
Add 10% for net profit	134.75
Target selling price	$1,482.25

Note how the costs of this job parallel the cost relationships in the budget. Assume that operations were exactly in accordance with the budget. Target selling prices were achieved on every order.

required

1. Prepare two budgeted income statements for the year, one with a traditional format and a second with a contribution format.

2. The contractor asks you to demonstrate at least three other ways to analyze the costs of the representative job and yet yield the same target price of $1,482.25. Include a demonstration of the so-called contribution approach in two of your analyses. Briefly explain why all the different methods yield the same price; indicate which method you prefer and why.

   You analyze the data above and determine that the overall overhead rate is 26.3 percent of direct labor; the variable-overhead rate is 13.3 percent of direct labor; the fixed-overhead rate is 13.0 percent of direct labor; the contribution-margin percentage based on variable costs is 18.5 percent; and the net-income percentage based on total costs is 10.0 percent.

   As long as the overall target net income is known, all the possible markup formulas can be structured to yield the same target price. For example, a straightforward contribution approach would be to compile the total variable costs and then add a target markup of 18.5 percent of variable costs.

3. Late in the year, the contractor bid $1,482.25 for a subcontracting job. He was told by the general contractor, "Your price is too high. If you want the work, you'll have to do the job for $1,340." He refused to accept the $1,340 price. His refusal affected his net income for the year. By how much? Should he have accepted the $1,340 price? Why?

4. "The contribution approach to pricing is extremely dangerous, because it deludes the salesmen into thinking that costs are low and it leads to suicidal price cutting." Do you agree? Why?

11-16. Costs and Pricing. Specialty Oils, Inc., is a small producer of specialized oils and related products for industrial use. Its primary manufacturing process consists of blending raw materials—various types of basic petroleum and animal oils, industrial acids, water, etc.—in steel tanks designed for this purpose. The blending process is of two types: (a) simple blending of basic materials in an open tank, and (b) complex manufacturing in which materials are combined under heat and/or pressure in a closed tank. The tanks in the process all have some sort of blending mechanism. They range in capacity from 300 to 5,000 gallons. Some blending is even done in small casks or drums with a 45-gallon capacity. The tanks themselves have a working life of forty years or more and show little, if any, deterioration over time.

The production process is relatively simple. A product's ingredients are injected into a tank and blended according to the manufacturing specifications of mix, timing, heat, and pressure. The finished product is then drawn off into casks, which are weighed (the products are sold by weight) before storing or shipping. Handling the individual casks of raw materials or finished products, each of which weighs over 400 pounds, is a difficult and time-consuming task. Therefore, the cost of labor for handling is a constant source of management concern. Some economies can be effected in storing and handling by using large storage tanks for storing raw materials and pumping these materials directly into the blending tanks when needed. Similar economies can be obtained by pumping the finished product directly into a tank carrier for shipment. The difficulty is that many of the raw materials and finished products are used in such small quantities that bulk handling is not possible.

Specialty Oils takes particular pride in its service to industry. To provide that service, Specialty offers a line of over 1,000 products, for which it receives orders ranging from half-gallon tins to 1,500-gallon-tank loads. Company policy is to fill all orders as rapidly as possible in the order in which they are received, either from the small finished-product inventory kept on hand, or by immediately scheduling the production required. The prices for its products are based on the standard costs of these products as computed by the accounting department. These costs are computed on a per-gallon basis by the following formula:

Raw Material Cost (revised for ingredient price or mix changes)

+

Blending Charge (fixed by type of blending, rarely changed)

+

Labor Charge (varies with changes in wage rates)

+

Overhead Allowance (a fixed percentage of the previous total, rarely changed)

+

Profit (a fixed percentage of the previous total, rarely changed)

+

Shipping Charge (a fixed rate, varies with changes in shipping rates)

The resulting figure guides the final pricing decision. It is modified only slightly up or down, if at all, by one of the top executives according to his subjective feel for conditions in the market for the product. The final per-gallon figure can be further modified by per-gallon price increases if an order is for ten gallons or less, or by per-gallon price decreases if an order is for 500 gallons or more.

The president of Specialty Oils explains his company's pricing policy in this way: "We are under a constant cost–price squeeze. We have to maintain our margin of profit. As long as we maintain our margins, I know we're all right." His philosophy extends throughout the organization. The treasurer has instituted a system that calculates the per-gallon differential, either favorable or unfavorable, between the price set in the office and the price actually obtained for each product sale. This differential is multiplied by the total quantity purchased to get the total differential for the sale. Each month the treasurer examines the total differential for the entire month's sales and uses this figure as his primary gauge by which to judge that month's results. The sales force is motivated to maintain a favorable differential by receiving its commissions as a sliding percentage of the sale obtained. The higher the price on the sale, the higher the rate of commission.

required

1. How does management's pricing policy contribute to the goals of the company?

2. What problems can you see arising from this policy?

3. What alternative pricing policy would you suggest for the company?

11-17. Make or Buy [SIA]. The Wise Company, Ltd., uses machine tools that it has been manufacturing for its own use. The company currently has excess capacity, and the tools are being manufactured in a part of the plant that would otherwise lie idle.

A salesman of machine tools, who has been attempting to sell to the Wise Company, has prepared the following analysis in cooperation with company personnel:

	COST OF MANUFACTURING THE NEXT YEAR'S SUPPLY OF TOOLS	COST OF BUYING THE NEXT YEAR'S SUPPLY OF TOOLS
Cost of purchasing tools		$210,000
Cost of parts and materials	$100,000	
Labor (especially hired for this type of work)	40,000	
Labor (distribution of labor costs of regular hourly workers based on hours of actual labor)	30,000	
Labor (allocation of labor costs of salaried employees)	20,000	
Variable overhead	10,000	
Fixed overhead (includes $20,000 of depreciation of equipment especially purchased for this purpose in the past)	40,000	
	$240,000	$210,000

The purchased machine tools will have no operating advantage over the tools made by the plant itself.

required

1. Prepare an analysis showing whether the Wise Company should purchase or make its own machine tools to fill its needs. State your assumptions with respect to behavior of costs. Ignore income tax implications.

2. State the qualitative (nonquantitative) factors that must be considered in reaching the decision.

11-18. Discontinuing a Department; Make or Buy [CPA]. The Ace Publishing Company in Hong Kong is in the business of publishing and printing guidebooks and directories. The board of directors has engaged you to make a cost study to determine whether the company is economically justified in continuing to print, as well as publish, its books and directories. You obtain the following information from the company's cost-accounting records for the preceding fiscal year:

	DEPARTMENTS			
	PUBLISHING	PRINTING	SHIPPING	TOTAL
Salaries and wages	$275,000	$150,000	$25,000	$ 450,000
Telephone and telegraph	12,000	3,700	300	16,000
Materials and supplies	50,000	250,000	10,000	310,000
Occupancy costs	75,000	80,000	10,000	165,000
General and administrative	40,000	30,000	4,000	74,000
Depreciation	5,000	40,000	5,000	50,000
	$457,000	$553,700	$54,300	$1,065,000

Additional Data

1. A review of personnel requirements indicates that if printing is discontinued, the publishing department will need one additional clerk at $4,000 per year

to handle correspondence with the printer. Two layout men and a proof-reader will be required, at an aggregate annual cost of $17,000; other personnel in the printing department can be released. One mailing clerk, at $3,000, will be retained; others in the shipping department can be released. Employees whose employment was being terminated would immediately receive, on the average, three months' termination pay. The termination pay would be amortized over a five-year period.

2. Long-distance telephone and telegraph charges are identified and distributed to the responsible department. The remainder of the telephone bill, representing basic service at a cost of $4,000, was allocated in the ratio of 10 to publishing, 5 to printing, and 1 to shipping. The discontinuance of printing is not expected to have a material effect on the basic service cost.

3. Shipping supplies consist of cartons, envelopes, and stamps. It is estimated that the cost of envelopes and stamps for mailing material to an outside printer would be $5,000 per year.

4. If printing were discontinued, the company would retain its present building but would sublet a portion of the space at an annual rental of $50,000. Taxes, insurance, heat, light, and other occupancy costs would not be significantly affected.

5. One cost clerk would not be required ($5,000 per year) if printing is discontinued. Other general and administrative personnel would be retained.

6. Included in administrative expenses is interest expense on a 5 percent mortgage loan of $500,000.

7. Printing and shipping-room machinery and equipment having a net book value of $300,000 can be sold without gain or loss. These funds in excess of termination pay would be invested in marketable securities earning 5 percent.

8. The company has received a proposal for a five-year contract from an outside printer, under which the volume of work done last year would be printed at a cost of $550,000 per year.

9. Assume continued volume and prices at last year's level.

required Prepare a statement setting forth in comparative form the costs of operation of the printing and shipping departments under the present arrangement and under an arrangement in which inside printing is discontinued. Summarize the net saving or extra cost in case printing is discontinued.

11-19. Order-Filling Costs and Minimum Order Size. The Independent Wholesale Drug Co. has made a time study of the cost of filling orders, with the following results:

SIZE OF ORDERS IN DOLLARS	AVERAGE TIME REQUIRED
$ 0.00 to $ 2.00	0.10 hours
$ 2.01 to $ 5.00	0.12 hours
$ 5.01 to $15.00	0.16 hours
$15.01 to $25.00	0.20 hours
Over $25.00	0.25 hours

Order-filling costs totaled $4,480 for the month in which the study was made, and 1,600 man-hours were worked in the Order-Filling Department. During the same period, the costs of receiving orders and of billing and posting the customers' accounts were calculated at a minimum of 16¢ per order. Gross margin (profit) on the company's merchandise averages 20 percent.

Ignoring all considerations other than these cost data, should the company adopt a rule that it will accept orders only above some minimum size? If so, what minimum order size would you recommend?

11-20. Different Cost Terms [CPA]. *Instructions:* You are to match each of the nine numbered "items" that follow with the *one* term listed immediately below (A through R) that *most specifically* identifies the cost concept indicated parenthetically. (*Caution:* An item of cost may be classified in several ways, depending on the purpose of the classification. For example, the commissions on sales of a proposed new product line might be classified as *direct, variable,* and *marginal,* among others. However, if such costs are being considered specifically as to the amount of *cash outlay* required in making a decision concerning adoption of the new line, the commissions are *out-of-pocket costs.* That would be the *most* appropriate answer in the context.) The same term may be used more than once.

Indicate your choice of answer for each item by printing beside the item numbers the capital letter that identifies the term you select.

Terms

A. By-product cost	J. Indirect cost
B. Common or joint cost	K. Opportunity cost
C. Controllable cost	L. Original cost
D. Direct cost	M. Out-of-pocket cost
E. Estimated cost	N. Prime cost
F. Fixed cost	O. Replacement cost
G. Historical cost	P. Standard cost
H. Imputed cost	Q. Sunk cost
I. Differential cost	R. Variable cost

Items

1. The management of a corporation is considering replacing a machine that is operating satisfactorily with a more efficient new model. Depreciation on the cost of the existing machine is omitted from the data used in judging the proposal, because it has little or no significance with respect to such a decision. (*The omitted cost.*)
2. One of the problems encountered by a bank in attempting to establish the cost of a commercial-deposit account is the fact that many facilities and services are shared by many revenue-producing activities. (*Costs of the shared facilities and services.*)
3. A company declined an offer received to rent one of its warehouses and elected to use the warehouse for storage of extra raw materials to insure uninterrupted production. Storage cost has been charged with *the monthly amount of the rental offered.* (*This cost is known as?*)
4. A manufacturing company excludes all "fixed" costs from its valuation of inventories, assigning to inventory only *applicable portions of costs that vary with changes in volume of product.* (*The term employed for the variable costs in this context by advocates of this costing procedure.*)
5. The sales department urges an increase in production of a product and, as part of the data presented in support of its proposal, indicates the total additional cost involved for the volume level it proposes. (*The increase in total cost.*)
6. A CPA takes exception to his client's inclusion, in the cost of a fixed asset, of an "interest" charge based on the client's own funds invested in the asset.

The client states that the charge was intended to obtain a cost comparable to what would have been the case if funds had been borrowed to finance the acquisition. (*The term that describes such interest charges.*)

7. The "direct" production cost of a unit includes those portions of factory overhead, *labor*, and *materials* that are obviously traceable directly to the unit. (*The term used to specify the last two of the named components.*)

8. Calling upon the special facilities of the production, planning, personnel, and other departments, a firm estimated its future unit cost of production and used this cost (analyzed by cost elements) in its accounts. (*The term used to specify this scientifically predetermined estimate.*)

9. A chemical-manufacturing company produces three products originating in a common initial material mix. Each product gains a separate identity partway through processing and requires additional processing after the "split." Each contributes a significant share of revenue. The company plans to spread the costs up to the "split" among the three products by the use of relative market values. (*The term used to specify the costs accumulated up to the point of the split.*)

11-21. **Best Production and Sales Mix [CPA, adapted].** The Marcia Company has asked your assistance in determining an economical sales and production mix of their products for 19_4. The company manufactures a line of dolls and a doll-dress sewing kit.

The company's sales department provides the following data:

ITEM	ESTIMATED DEMAND FOR 19_4 (UNITS)	ESTABLISHED NET PRICE (UNITS)
Laurie	50,000	$5.20
Debbie	42,000	2.40
Sarah	35,000	8.50
Kathy	40,000	4.00
Sewing kit	325,000	3.00

To promote sales of the sewing kit, there is a 15 percent reduction in the established net price for a kit purchased at the same time that a Marcia Company doll is purchased.

From accounting records, you develop the following data:

a. The production standards per unit:

ITEM	MATERIALS	LABOR
Laurie	$1.40	$ .80
Debbie	.70	.50
Sarah	2.69	1.40
Kathy	1.00	1.00
Sewing kit	.60	.40

b. The labor rate of $2 per hour is expected to continue without change in 19_4. The plant has an effective capacity of 130,000 labor-hours per year on a single-shift basis. Present equipment can produce all the products.

c. The total fixed costs for 19_4 will be $100,000. Variable costs will be equivalent to 50 percent of direct-labor cost.

d. The company has a small inventory of its products that can be ignored.

required
1. Prepare a schedule computing the contribution to profit of a unit of each product.
2. Prepare a schedule computing the contribution to profit of a unit of each product per labor-dollar expended on the product.
3. Prepare a schedule computing the total labor-hours required to produce the estimated sales units for 19_4. Indicate the item and number of units that you would recommend be increased (or decreased) in production to attain the company's effective productive capacity.
4. Without regard to your answer in part c, assume that the estimated sales units for 19_4 would require 12,000 labor-hours in excess of the company's effective productive capacity. Discuss the possible methods of providing the missing capacity. Include in your discussion all factors that must be taken into consideration in evaluating the methods of providing the missing capacity.

11-22. Selection of Most Profitable Product. The Flabbo Co. produces two basic types of reducing equipment, G and H. Pertinent data follow:

	PER UNIT	
	G	H
Sales price	$100.00	$70.00
Expenses:		
Direct materials	$ 28.00	$13.00
Direct labor	15.00	25.00
Variable factory overhead*	25.00	12.50
Fixed factory overhead*	10.00	5.00
Selling expenses (all variable)	14.00	10.00
	$ 92.00	$65.50
Net margin	$ 8.00	$ 4.50

* Applied on the basis of machine-hours.

The reducing craze is such that enough of either G or H can be sold to keep the plant operating at full capacity. Both products are processed through the same production centers.

required
Which product should be produced? If more than one should be produced, indicate the proportions of each. Briefly explain your answer.

11-23. Choosing Profitable Products. The subsidiary of a multinational drug company was the largest firm in a developing nation's pharmaceutical industry (comprising some 30 manufacturers), with sales in the vicinity of $20 million. The manufacturing operation consisted primarily of processing and packing imported bulk materials into finished products. The 98 finished products were made from some 50 different kinds of raw (bulk) materials, almost all of which were imported. The firm had its own well-trained "detail" sales force and distribution network.

The subsidiary had grown rapidly after commencing operations in the mid-1950's and became the largest company in terms of sales in 1966 after overtaking its British rival. Although sales had grown phenomenally, the profit performance of the subsidiary had been relatively poor as measured by profits as a percentage of sales. The first president of the company had stressed sales and volume and had provided the sales force with all the financial benefits and assistance possible. His successor, in an effort to improve profitability, had concentrated on reducing costs.

The country in which the subsidiary was located was typical of many developing nations, in that it suffered from severe foreign-exchange problems. Some 80 percent of the foreign exchange available was devoted to the import of food and defense equipment, the remainder being made available for all other imports, including drugs. The amount of foreign exchange available was rationed by industry and by company on a six-month basis. Firms then received permits of $X of foreign exchange, which they could use to import materials not available in the country in any quantities and in any combination. The permitted amount for each company could vary by significant amounts, but planning beyond a six-month period was almost impossible.

The foreign-exchange limitation made the market for drugs in the country a seller's market. The government kept a close watch on prices, and the pharmaceutical industry was extremely sensitive to arousing public hostility due to pricing as had been the case in some other developing countries. The task, therefore, was to find a straightforward technique—not requiring sophisticated quantitative skills—that could be used as a guide to maximizing profits.

There are practically no constraints in manufacturing, and a wide range in production quantities of the 98 different products is possible. For the purpose of this problem, assume that any product can be dropped if necessary.

required   The following information was chosen at random. Rank the products in order of desired production and sales effort. Explain your ranking.

	PER UNIT OF PRODUCT		
	A	B	C
Selling price (in dollar equivalents)	$10.50	$12.00	$8.00
Cost of imported materials	2.00	1.00	1.00
Variable costs of production and selling*	2.50	5.00	2.00

*Excluding imported materials.

11-24. **Disposal Value, Book Value, Loss on Old Equipment.**   A toy manufacturer specializes in making fad items. He has just acquired a special-purpose molding machine for $50,000 cash. It automatically produces a special toy. The machine will be useless after the 100,000-unit total market potential, spread evenly over four years, is exhausted.

Expected annual operating data are as follows (in thousands):

Sales		$90.0
Direct materials	$10.0	
Direct labor	20.0	
Variable manufacturing overhead (75% of direct labor)	15.0	
Fixed manufacturing overhead*	7.5	
Depreciation, straight-line	11.9	
Selling and administrative expenses:		
Variable	4.0	
Fixed	8.0	76.4
Net income		$13.6

*Exclusive of depreciation on machine.

The disposal value of the machine is $6,000 now and will be $2,400 four years from now. The machine has been used to produce one unit. Suddenly a machine salesman appears. He says, "I have a new machine that is ideally suited for this production problem. My machine will be useless after your 100,000-unit total market potential is exhausted. But it has distinct operating superiority over your 'old' machine. It will reduce material usage by 10 percent, produce twice as many units per hour, cost $44,000, and have zero disposal value at the end of four years."

The toy manufacturer responds, "I don't want your new machine. I must retain the $50,000 machine because we've got to keep using it to recover our investment."

required

1. How will net income be affected if the "old" machine is scrapped and the new machine is purchased? Show computations for the four years taken together and on an average annual basis.

2. Evaluate the toy manufacturer's reaction to the proposal.

11-25. Relationship of Disposal Value, Book Value, and Net Loss on Old Equipment. Scott Harshaw is the president of a small plastics company. He wants to replace an old special-purpose molding machine (original cost, $18,700; eight years old; book value, $9,100; straight-line depreciation, $1,200 per year; residual value at end of useful life, $700) with a new, more efficient machine. The new machine has an expected useful life of only seven years, but it promises savings in cash operating costs of $2,257 per year. Operating costs with the new machine are $30,000; with the old machine, $32,257. The cost of the new machine is $8,800. The old machine can be sold outright for $2,300, less $200 removal cost. It is estimated that the old machine would have a net disposal value of $700 seven years from now; the new machine, a value of $750 seven years from now.

Vladimar Galoot, controller, opposes replacement because no advantage is apparent. His analysis shows:

Cost of new investment:

Outlay	$ 8,800
Loss on old machine ($9,100 minus $2,100)	7,000
Total cost	$15,800
Savings: $2,257 per year × 7 years	15,800 (rounded)
Net advantage of replacement	$ 0

He also adds, "I can't ever see disposing of fixed assets at a loss before their useful life expires. Plant and equipment are bought and depreciated with some useful life in mind. We are in business to maximize income (or minimize loss). It seems to me that the alternatives are clear: (a) disposal of a fixed asset before it diminishes to zero or residual book value often results in a loss; (b) keeping and *using* the same fixed asset avoids such a loss. Now, any sensible person will have brains enough to avoid a loss when his other alternative is recognizing a loss. It makes sense to use a fixed asset till you get your money out of it."

Yearly sales are $90,000, and cash expenses, excluding the data given above, are $50,000.

required

(Ignore income tax effects.)

1. How will net income be affected if the old machine is scrapped and the new machine is purchased? Show computations for the seven years taken together and on an average annual basis.

2. Prepare columnar income statements for years 1 through 7 under both alternatives, as follows:

	EACH YEAR,	7 YEARS
YEAR 1	2–7	TOGETHER

3. Generalize as to the role of disposal value on old equipment in these decisions.

4. Generalize as to the role of (a) book value in these decisions and (b) net loss on disposal of old fixed assets.

5. Criticize Galoot's schedule and his comments.

6. What important cost factor has been ignored in your answers to 1 and 2?

11-26. **Multiple Choice; Comprehensive Problem on Relevant Costs.** The following are the Class Company's *unit* costs of making and selling a given item at a level of 20,000 units per month:

Manufacturing:	
Direct materials	$1.00
Direct labor	1.20
Variable indirect cost	.80
Fixed indirect cost	.50
Selling and other:	
Variable	1.50
Fixed	.90

The following situations refer only to the data given above—there is *no connection* between the situations. Unless stated otherwise, assume a regular selling price of $6 per unit.

Choose the answer corresponding to the most nearly acceptable or correct answer in each of the nine items. Support each answer with summarized computations.

1. In presenting an inventory of 10,000 items on the balance sheet, the unit cost conventionally to be used is:
   a. $3.00
   b. $3.50
   c. $5.00
   d. $5.90
   e. $2.20

2. The unit cost relevant to setting a *normal* price for this product, assuming that the implied level of operations is to be maintained, is:
   a. $5.00
   b. $4.50
   c. $3.50
   d. $3.00
   e. $5.90

3. This product is usually sold at the rate of 240,000 units per year (an average of 20,000 per month). At a sales price of $6.00 per unit, this yields total sales of $1,440,000, total costs of $1,416,000, and a net margin of $24,000, or 10¢ per unit. It is estimated by market research that volume could be increased by 10 percent if prices were cut to $5.80. Assuming the implied cost behavior patterns to be correct, this action, if taken, would:
   a. Decrease profits by a net of $7,200.

    b. Decrease profits by 20¢ per unit, $48,000, but increase profits by 10 percent of sales, $144,000; net, $86,000 increase.

    c. Decrease unit fixed costs by 10 percent or 14¢ per unit and thus decrease profits by 20¢ − 14¢, or 6¢ per unit.

    d. Increase sales volume to 264,000 units, which at the $5.80 price would give total sales of $1,531,200; costs of $5.90 per unit for 264,000 units would be $1,557,600, and a loss of $26,400 would result.

    e. None of these.

4. A cost contract with the government (for 5,000 units of product) calls for the reimbursement of all costs of production plus a fixed fee of $1,000. This production is part of the regular 20,000 units of production per month. The delivery of these 5,000 units of product increases profits from what they would have been, were these units not sold, by:

    a. $1,000

    b. $2,500

    c. $3,500

    d. $300

    e. None of these

5. Assume the same data as in 4 above, except that the 5,000 units will displace 5,000 other units from production. The latter 5,000 units would have been sold through regular channels for $30,000 had they been made. The delivery to the government increases (or decreases) net profits from what they would have been, were the other 5,000 units sold, by:

    a. $4,000 decrease

    b. $3,000 increase

    c. $6,500 decrease

    d. $500 increase

    e. None of these

6. The company desires to enter a foreign market, in which price competition is keen. An order for 10,000 units of this product is being sought on a minimum unit-price basis. It is expected that shipping costs for this order will amount to only 75¢ per unit but that fixed costs of obtaining the contract will be $4,000. Domestic business will be unaffected. The minimum basis for breakeven price is:

    a. $3.50

    b. $4.15

    c. $4.25

    d. $5.00

    e. $3.00

7. The company has an inventory of 1,000 units of this item left over from last year's model. These must be sold through regular channels at reduced prices. The inventory will be valueless unless sold this way. The unit cost that is relevant for establishing the minimum selling price would be:

    a. $4.50

    b. $4.00

    c. $3.00

    d. $1.50

    e. $5.90

8. A proposal is received from an outside supplier who will make and ship this item directly to the Class Company's customers as sales orders are forwarded from Class's sales staff. Class's fixed selling costs will be unaffected, but its variable selling costs will be slashed 20 percent. Class's plant will be idle, but its fixed factory overhead would continue at 50 percent

of present levels. To compare with the quotation received from the supplier, the company should use a unit cost of:

a. $4.75
b. $3.95
c. $2.95
d. $5.35
e. None of these

9. Assume the same facts as in 8 above, except that if the supplier's offer is accepted, the present plant facilities will be used to make a product whose unit costs will be:

Variable manufacturing costs	$5.00
Fixed manufacturing costs	1.00
Variable selling costs	2.00
Fixed selling costs	.50

Total fixed factory overhead will be unchanged, while fixed selling costs will increase as indicated. The new product will sell for $9. This minimum desired net profit on the two products taken together is $50,000 per year. What is the maximum purchase cost per unit that the Class Company should be willing to pay for subcontracting the old production?

SECTION THREE

SPECIAL TOPICS
FOR FURTHER STUDY

Cost Allocation for Various Purposes

12

The late 1960's and early 1970's have been marked by many widely publicized disputes about the supposedly high costs of various defense contracts. In 1971, a Cost Accounting Standards Board was formed to establish uniform cost-accounting standards, which will be used by defense contractors and federal agencies in the pricing of negotiated contracts. One of the problems that led to the formation of this board was that of how costs should be allocated among contracts and among commercial and defense products.

Cost allocation is an inescapable problem in nearly every organization. How should university costs be split among undergraduate programs, graduate programs, and research? How should the costs of expensive medical equipment, facilities, and staff be allocated in a hospital? How should computer costs be allocated to various departments? Advertising? Central corporate staff? Personnel-department costs? These are inevitably tough questions, so the answers often are not clearly right or clearly wrong. Nevertheless, we shall try to obtain some insights into the pervasive problem of cost allocation—at least to understand the dimensions of the problem, even if the answers seem illusory. The chances are overwhelming that you will be directly faced with this problem sometime during your career, regardless of whether you become a professional accountant or hold some other position.

Before studying this chapter, you will benefit from rereading the first part of Chapter 2, on costs and the decision process.

We shall now examine the pervasive problems of tracing costs to cost objects. Various books and organizations use diverse terminology to describe this tracing procedure: cost allocation, cost assignment, cost apportionment, cost reapportionment, and cost distribution. We use the term *cost allocation* here, but be on the alert to pinpoint the exact meaning of such terms in a particular organization.

By the way, note that the terms *cost application* and *cost absorption* tend to have a fairly uniform usage. They are confined to a special type of cost allocation, the tracing of costs to *products*, as distinguished from departments or divisions or cost centers.

THE INTERDEPENDENT ASPECTS OF COST ALLOCATION

three facets of cost allocation

There are essentially three facets of cost allocation:

1. Choosing the cost object, which is essentially an *action*[1] (the independent variable). Examples are products, processes, or departments, which are basically abbreviations for various actions.

2. Choosing and accumulating the costs that relate to the cost object (the dependent variable). Examples are material, labor, and overhead.

3. Choosing a method for specifically identifying 2 with 1. This usually entails choosing an allocation base. (The cost function can then be determined.) An example is the use of direct-labor hours as an allocation base to apply various overhead costs to product.

The choice of an allocation base is often necessary because there is no obvious or convenient direct link between a cost and the cost object. The choice of the base is dependent on the total cost in question, the cost object, and the purpose of the allocation.

direct and indirect costs

The section on direct and indirect costs in Chapter 2, which you may wish to review now, stressed that the terms *direct* and *indirect* have no meaning unless they are related to the object of costing. In product costing, a cost is direct if (a) it can be physically identified with the cost object and measured in terms of the quantity of input used, and (b) there is no intervening basis for allocation. For example, direct materials and direct labor are allocated on the basis of the physical quantities of the input that is consumed or that should be consumed. In contrast, indirect materials and indirect labor are allocated on the basis of some intervening base—not indirect materials or indirect labor consumed, but perhaps direct labor or machine-hours consumed.

[1]George J. Staubus, *Activity Costing and Input-Output Accounting* (Homewood, Ill.: Richard D. Irwin, Inc., 1971), p. 1, stresses that we must recognize that in essence we are determining the cost of an activity or action:

"Costing is the process of determining the cost of doing something, e.g., the cost of manufacturing an article, rendering a service, or performing a function. The article manufactured, service rendered, or function performed is known as the object of costing. . . . Objects of costing are always activities. We want to know the cost of doing something. We may, however, find ourselves speaking of the cost of a product as an abbreviation for the cost of acquiring or manufacturing that product . . . ."

When lump sums of materials or labor or other resources can be assigned *in toto* to a particular object of costing, the precision of the charge is almost indisputable. However, the charge becomes less precise when averages are used. The necessity for detailed source documents and the accumulation of direct costs via unit rates for materials and labor is the first example of the use of averages.

practicability and the cost object

An implicit cost and value of information model heavily affects how a given cost is assigned to a cost object. Whether a cost is direct or indirect often depends upon the ease of linking such costs as power, supplies, material handling, and supervision with particular product runs, lots, or contracts. For example, many such costs are regarded as direct costs in process-cost industries. On the other hand, when many different jobs are manufactured, the extra record-keeping costs seem to exceed any apparent benefits from tracing such individual costs to batches of product. So only major individual material and labor costs are typically regarded as direct costs of product batches in job-order industries.

Note that the selection of the cost object affects the classification of the cost as direct or indirect. Product costing is an averaging process. The basic distinction between job-order costing and process costing is the breadth of the denominator. It is small in job-order costing but large in process costing. This is another example of how the choice of the cost object interacts with the cost-allocation process and the classification of direct and indirect costs.

search for relationships

The collection of total costs is often referred to as an *aggregating* or *pooling* of costs. Given a total-cost pool and a cost object, the most important criterion for selecting a cost allocation base is to relate the total cost to its most causal factor.[2] Unfortunately, specific causes and effects are frequently difficult to pinpoint with assurance. As a practical matter, *relationships* are sought between the cost object and the cost incurred. The preferable cost-allocation base is one that facilitates the prediction of changes in total costs, that accurately depicts persistent relationships, regardless of whether we view either the cost object or the cost incurrence as the cause or the effect.

Physical observation is probably the best evidence of a cause-and-effect relationship. That is why the distinction between direct and indirect costs is important. Direct costs are the obvious effects of the choice of a particular action; the indirect costs are not so obviously affected. For example, the production of more television sets will have an obvious impact on the total costs of purchased picture tubes utilized. Not many troubles arise in cost analysis under such

---

[2] It is an oversimplification to say that there is a single cause-and-effect relationship between cost incurrence and the application base used. William J. Vatter, in "Limitations of Overhead Allocation," *Accounting Review*, Vol. XX, No. 2, 164–65, observed: "Every cause has a number of effects; every event arises from many causes; all incidents and observations are bound together by many ties. All costs are more or less interwoven in a complex fabric; in large measure, costs are joint as to their incurrence, as well as to their associations with various costing units."

circumstances. The troubles arise where there is no convincing relationship, or where the association is indirect and unclear, or where perhaps the relation is multiple and, worse still, often impossible to measure. Examples include advertising, research, sales promotion, and public relations.

If the decision maker cannot resort to physical identification to establish cause and effect, he may use regression analysis to help identify a causal relationship. But first he uses his prior knowledge of operations to choose a particular relationship that may be so intuitively satisfying that formal regression is unnecessary (for example, allocating power on the basis of related machine-hours). Of course, where applicable and feasible, such intuition should be buttressed by regression analysis.

Note that knowledge of operations is needed for intelligent regression analysis. For example:

> . . . repairs to equipment in a machine shop is a cost-causing activity that often is not specified because of the quantification difficulties. However, these repairs may be made when output is low because the machines can be taken out of service at these times. Thus repair costs will be negatively correlated with output. If these costs are not separated from other costs, the estimated coefficient of output will be biased downward, so that the true extent of variableness of cost with output will be masked.[3]

Ideally, qualitative correlation, which is in our minds and discerns causality in a logical sense, should be coupled with quantitative correlation, which uses formal statistical means to determine the extent to which a change in one factor is accompanied by a change in another factor. Regression analysis is a valuable tool, but it must be used skillfully and cautiously. The clumsy use of regression analysis may produce deceptive results.

In summary, the following guides should help obtain cost allocations that reflect underlying causal relationships as closely as possible:

1. To the extent that physical relationships are observable, use them.

2. To the extent that relationships can be implicitly established via logic and knowledge of operations, use them—preferably in conjunction with 3.

3. To the extent that relationships can be explicitly established via regression analysis, use them. The use of 3 is a check on 2.

4. To the extent that an allocation base is no more logically or empirically defensible than some other base, either do not allocate or allocate via preestablished agreement. When such allocations are made, all interested parties should understand their arbitrary nature.

choices of cost objects Earlier we saw that an allocation base is usually used to assign costs to a cost object. In some instances, particularly where the cost object is large, no base is needed. For example, where the cost object is a building or a government contract, many costs may be assigned directly thereto in lump sums.

[3]G. Benston, "Multiple Regression Analysis of Cost Behavior," *Accounting Review*, XLI, No. 4, 668.

But usually the cost object in product costing is small enough to require using an allocation base. Moreover, departments are also cost objects, and many individual costs must be charged to departments via allocation bases.

In most instances, the costs are initially traced to responsibility centers or departments, which are the cost objects at the point of origin of the cost. But allocation rarely stops at the point of individual responsibility. This is merely a first step toward the ultimate linking of costs with other cost objects—for example, units of product. The point is that the use of the criterion of human responsibility, point of origin, or control by itself helps identify costs with one set of cost objects (the responsibility centers) but falls short of identifying costs with another set of cost objects (products) needed for many decision alternatives.

The steps taken are often complex, entailing many cost reallocations and involving many intermediate decision makers and cost objects. For example, the manager in a repair department may originate costs via the acquisition of parts and services, but the responsibility for the bulk of those costs typically rests with the producing departments that have requisitioned the repair services. In turn, the operating of machinery and the manufacturing of various products by that machinery justify the eventual allocation of such costs to those products.

THE CONTRIBUTION APPROACH TO COST ALLOCATION

stress on cost behavior patterns
The most frequently encountered cost objects are responsibility centers or products. Cost objects can be any *segment* (a line of activity or part of an organization) for which a separate computation of costs is sought. The contribution approach provides a valuable general framework for cost allocation because it is applicable to all types of cost objects and because it spotlights the cost behavior patterns that are nearly always essential for evaluating performance and making decisions.

Exhibit 12-1 illustrates the contribution approach to cost allocation. This is an unusually important exhibit because it provides a sweeping glimpse of how accounting information may be organized to facilitate decisions and their implementation. The stress is on cost behavior patterns. Failure to distinguish cost behavior patterns is a big roadblock to clarity in cost analysis.

revenues, variable costs, and contribution margins
The allocation of revenue and of variable costs is usually straightforward, because each item is directly and specifically identifiable with a given segment of activity. The Contribution Margin, Line (1) in Exhibit 12-1, is particularly helpful for predicting the impact on income of short-run changes in volume. Changes in income may be quickly calculated by multiplying the change in units by the unit contribution margin or by multiplying the increment in dollar sales by the contribution-margin ratio. For example, the contribution-margin ratio of Product 1 is $120 \div $300 = 40$ percent. The increase in net income resulting from a $20 increase in sales can be readily computed as $.40 \times 20, or $8.

EXHIBIT 12-1

THE CONTRIBUTION APPROACH: MODEL INCOME STATEMENT BY SEGMENTS*

(In Thousands of Dollars)

	COMPANY AS A WHOLE	COMPANY BREAK-DOWN INTO TWO DIVISIONS		POSSIBLE BREAKDOWN OF DIVISION B ONLY				
		DIVISION A	DIVISION B	NOT ALLOCATED	PRODUCT 1	PRODUCT 2	PRODUCT 3	PRODUCT 4
Net sales	1,500	500	1,000		300	200	100	400
Variable manufacturing cost of sales	780	200	580		120	155	45	260
Manufacturing contribution margin	720	300	420		180	45	55	140
Variable selling and administrative costs	220	100	120		60	15	25	20
(1) Contribution margin	500	200	300		120	30	30	120
Fixed costs controllable by division managers (certain advertising, sales promotion, salesmen's salaries, engineering, research, management consulting, and supervision costs)	190	110	80	45†	10	6	4	15
(2) Contribution controllable by division managers	310	90	220	(45)	110	24	26	105
Fixed costs controllable by others (such as depreciation, property taxes, insurance, and perhaps the division manager's salary)	70	20	50	20	3	15	4	8
(3) Contribution by segments	240	70	170	(65)	107	9	22	97
Unallocated costs (not clearly or practically allocable to any segment except by some questionable allocation base)	135							
(4) Income before income taxes	105							

*There are two different types of segments illustrated here: divisions and products. As you read across, note that the focus becomes narrower: from the company as a whole, to Divisions A and B, to Division B only.

† Only those costs clearly identifiable to a product line should be allocated.

unallocated costs   An unallocated cost is common to all the segments in question and is not clearly or practically assignable except on some questionable basis. Examples of unallocated costs may be the salaries of the president and other top officers, basic research and development, and some central corporate costs like public relations or corporate-image advertising.

Discretionary and committed costs may or may not be allocated, *depending on the segments in question.* For example, a salesman's salary may be easily identified with a particular territory. However, if he is selling a vast number of products, the allocation of his salary among such products is questionable. Consequently, there may be a limit to the allocation of a given cost in a given income statement. For instance, the Divisions in Exhibit 12-1 could be territorial. The salary of the salesman just described could be readily allocated to Division A or B (a territory), but it could not be allocated convincingly among the products. The point is that a given cost may be allocated with respect to one segment of the organization and unallocated with respect to another.

contribution controllable by division managers   As Chapter 25 explains more fully, a distinction should be made between the performance of the segment manager and the performance of the segment as an economic investment. That distinction is keyed in the form of subtotals (2) and (3) in Exhibit 12-1. Our discussion of controllability and uncontrollability in Chapter 6 stressed how performance may be affected by factors that are subject to varying degrees of influence by a particular manager.

The reason for this distinction comes sharply into focus if you consider that many companies deliberately assign their best manager to their least-profitable divisions with the hope that improvements will be forthcoming. Unless some discrimination is made between the manager and the responsibility center as an economic entity, the skillful manager will be reluctant to accept assignments to troublesome responsibilities. Sometimes it takes a miracle worker to get a limping segment up to a minimally acceptable level of income.

What version of income is most appropriate for judging performance by division managers or product managers? The controllable contribution, keyed as item (2) in Exhibit 12-1, should be helpful, especially when it is interpreted in conjunction with the contribution margin. This is because most top managers can influence many fixed costs, particularly *discretionary fixed costs.* (Examples of these costs are given in Exhibit 12-1.) The incurrence of discretionary costs may have interacting effects on variable costs. For example, heavier outlays for maintenance, engineering, or management consulting may reduce repairs, increase machine speeds, heighten labor productivity, and so forth. Also, decisions on advertising, research, and sales-promotion budgets are necessarily related to expected impacts on sales volumes.

Note at this stage that, although many discretionary costs may be easily traced to divisions, they may not all be directly traceable to products. Some advertising expenses for Division B may be common to all products. For example,

Products 1, 2, and 3 may be consumer items to which common costs apply, while Product 4 may be an item sold to manufacturers by a separate sales organization with its own fixed costs.

The line between controllable and uncontrollable costs must be drawn on a company-by-company basis. For example, some managements may prefer to have depreciation on some classes of plant and equipment deducted when item (2), the controllable contribution, is computed. Getting agreement as to these classifications may be bothersome, but it is not a Herculean task.

The income statement in Exhibit 12-1 has four measures of performance, ranging from contribution margin through income before income taxes. There is nothing hallowed about these four illustrative measures; some organizations may want to use only two or three such measures.

contribution by segments and income before income taxes   Contribution by segments, item (3) in Exhibit 12-1, is computed after deducting the fixed cost classified as uncontrollable by the managers in the short run. Although this figure may be helpful as a crude indicator of long-run segment profitability as an economic investment, it should definitely not influence appraisals of current performance of managers.

Income before taxes, item (4) in Exhibit 12-1, may sometimes be a helpful gauge of the long-run earning power of a whole company. However, it may be misleading to refine this ultimate measure by breaking it into segments (and still have the whole equal the sum of the parts).

It is difficult to see how segment performance can be judged on the basis of income after deductions for a "fair" share of general company costs over which the segment manager exerts no influence. Examples of such costs would be central-research and central-headquarters costs, including salaries of the president and other high officers. Unless the general company costs are clearly traceable to segments, allocation serves no useful purpose and should not be made. Therefore, income is not computed by segments in Exhibit 12-1.

This refusal to allocate some costs is the most controversial aspect of the contribution approach to the income statement. Accountants and managers are used to the whole being completely broken down into neat parts that can be added up again to equal the whole. In traditional segment income statements, all costs are fully allocated, so that the segments show final net incomes that can be summed to equal the net income for the company as a whole.

Of course, if for some reason management prefers a whole-equals-the-sum-of-its-parts net-income statement, the unallocated costs may be allocated so that the segments show income figures that will cross-add to equal the income for the company as a whole. The important point is that the contribution approach distinguishes between various degrees of objectivity in cost allocations. As you read downward in Exhibit 12-1, you become less and less confident about the validity and accuracy of the cost allocations. A dozen independent accountants will be most likely to agree on how the variable costs should be allocated and least likely to agree on whether and how the unallocated costs should be accounted for.

reports by product lines and territories The most widely used detailed operating statements are tabulated by product lines and by sales territories. The emphasis depends on the organization of the marketing function. Some companies have distinct product lines with separate sales forces and separate advertising programs, and their operating reports emphasize contributions by products. Other companies make a multitude of products that are promoted by brand-name advertising and that are all sold by the same salesmen. Their operating reports emphasize territorial or district sales and contributions to profit.

relating fixed costs to pricing decisions The contribution approach to cost allocation has many uses. For example, consider the pricing decision. The general relationship of prices to fixed (period) costs is complicated because many of these costs have only obscure relationships to various segments. In pricing, it is useful to view the ability of individual divisions, products, departments, and so forth, to contribute to the common pools of fixed costs. *N.A.A. Research Report No. 37* pointed out (pp. 42–43):

> The ability to contribute on the part of individual segments is determined by market demand and does not necessarily correspond with the benefits received from common cost factors as measured by the bases which the accountant uses to allocate period costs . . . .
>
> The characteristics of period [fixed] costs . . . make it particularly important for management to have cost and income margin data which show clearly the consequences of proposed pricing decisions. Regardless of the plan of accounting used, there seems to be need for distinction between direct and period costs wherever pricing alternatives . . . involve differing volumes of production and sales.

To summarize, the data organized in the manner shown in Exhibit 12-1 will be more informative and useful for pricing than the conventional data that commonly fail to distinguish between variable and fixed costs. Where feasible, there is much merit in dividing fixed costs between those clearly applicable to the segment (say, a product) and those whose application base has low reliability.

CHOOSING AMONG VARIOUS COST-ALLOCATION BASES

Exhibit 12-2 illustrates that there is wide variety of bases for allocating and reallocating costs. The literature is replete with conflicting and not mutually exclusive criteria for choosing a cost-allocation base. Among the possible criteria are physical identification, services used, facilities provided, benefits received, ability to bear, and fairness or equity.[4]

These terms have been used too loosely. We will now sift among these criteria to see how they may be related. We will also develop some guides as to how to choose among them.

The accountant looks for evidence that provides a likely trail between cause and effect. That is, the cost object (which, you will recall, is essentially an *action*)

---

[4] William J. Vatter, "Limitations of Overhead Allocation," pp. 165ff.

EXHIBIT 12-2

TYPICAL BASES FOR REALLOCATION OF SERVICE-DEPARTMENT
COSTS TO PRODUCTION DEPARTMENTS

SERVICE DEPARTMENT	BASE FOR REALLOCATION OF COSTS
Building and Grounds	Square footage or cubic footage
Cafeteria	Number of workers
Cost Accounting	Labor hours
Engineering	*Analysis of services rendered each department; labor hours
Maintenance	Direct charges on basis of materials used plus hours worked for each department
Material Handling	Units carried; tonnage; hours of service rendered
Medical	Number of employees; labor hours; number of cases
Personnel or Employment	Number of workers; rate of labor turnover; number of workers hired; *analysis of time spent for each department
Production Planning and Control	Machine-hours; labor-hours; analysis of services rendered
Power	Metered usage; capacity of equipment; machine-hours; formula weighting capacity and machine-hours
Receiving, Shipping, and Stores	Pounds handled; requisitions; receiving slips; issues
Tool Room	Requisitions

*Sometimes detailed analyses or surveys are made of services rendered over two, six, or twelve months; the results of the "sample" are used as a basis for reallocation until conditions warrant another sample survey.

is viewed as the "cause" of the cost in question. For example, if ten more units of Product A are manufactured, the costs allocated to Product A supposedly represent the increase in total costs caused by that production. Elaborate cost-reallocation schemes have been developed in an attempt to trace cause-and-effect relationships. In this sense, even though specified actions cause the costs to be incurred, the inanimate cost objects are viewed as being the cause of cost incurrence, just as an automobile is viewed as causing various cost incurrences.

physical identification In a decision-making context, costs are usually incurred because of the desire for the cost object. Hence, the base itself should preferably be physically associated with the cost object. For example, direct-labor hours are incurred because of the desire for the product and are physically related to the product. Consequently, the use of direct-labor hours as an allocation base for direct-labor cost is usually a logical choice because the criterion of physical identification is satisfied. Physical linkage usually provides overwhelming evidence of cause-and-effect relationships.

As already mentioned, the primary aim should be to associate the cost in question with its fundamental causal factor. Evidence is sought to establish these cause-and-effect relationships. Sometimes, as in the case of many materials and classes of labor, the physical evidence is straightforward. As the relationship becomes hazier, the accountant nevertheless often insists that the intervening allocation base be somehow physically associated with the cost object. He probably insists on some physical association because at least he knows that the incurrence of the base itself is due to the desire for the cost object. For example, man-hours and number of employees are frequently used as allocation bases. Of course, even though the denominator (cost-allocation base) can be physically associated with the cost object, the relationship between the numerator (the total cost in question) and the denominator is inevitably not as convincing when indirect costs are allocated.

services used and facilities provided: the case of service departments

Services used is usually a clear-cut cause of cost incurrence: power, repairs, computers, and so on. But too often, no distinction is made between the variable costs and the fixed costs of such services. This lumping may result in allocations that portray inaccurate cause-and-effect relationships, particularly where fixed costs are significant. Although variable costs of such services may fluctuate in proportion to fluctuations in the services used during a given period, the fixed costs are more likely to be affected by long-range decisions.

The use of separate cost-allocation rates for variable and fixed costs is an attempt to recognize some differences in cause-and-effect relationships. Variable costs might be allocated on the basis of *services utilized*. Fixed costs might be allocated via a predetermined periodic lump sum for providing a fundamental *capacity to serve* based on the needs of the operating departments that justified the incurring of the fixed costs initially. This may be practical capacity or perhaps some "normal" percentage of practical capacity.

The fixed costs of service departments usually arise because service departments must have a basic capability to provide for the fundamental demands of consuming departments. Therefore, to the extent feasible, such costs might be reallocated in accordance with the plans that generated such fixed commitments. Again, the reallocation depends on decision needs. For example, what factors influence the equipping of power service departments or maintenance departments? If they are equipped with key men and machinery so that they may meet the peak needs of production departments, then the peak activity levels of the production departments should be the basis for reallocations of costs. If, on the other hand, they are equipped to meet the long-run average needs, then the "normal" level of activity in each production department should be the basis for reallocations of costs. Finally, if they are equipped because of the whims of the president's wife, there is no preferable base for allocation.

beware of full reallocation of actual costs

Many companies fully reallocate all service-department costs monthly on the basis of actual hours used in servicing the needs of the operating departments. The rate used is obtained by dividing the total actual costs of the service department by the total hours actually used by the operating departments.

EXHIBIT 12-3

REALLOCATIONS OF SERVICE-DEPARTMENT COSTS

*AT A 10,000-MACHINE-HOUR LEVEL
OF THE PRODUCTION DEPARTMENTS:*

Actual costs = $6,000 + $.40 (10,000 hours)	= $10,000
Rate per hour = $10,000 ÷ 10,000 = $1.00	
To Department 1: 5,000 hrs. × $1.00	= $ 5,000
To Department 2: 5,000 hrs. × $1.00	= 5,000
Total reallocated	$10,000

AT AN 8.000-MACHINE-HOUR LEVEL:

Actual costs = $6,000 + $.40 (8,000 hours)	= $ 9,200
Rate per hour = $9,200 ÷ 8,000 hours = $1.15	
To Department 1: 5,000 hrs. × $1.15	= $ 5,750
To Department 2: 3,000 hrs. × $1.15	= 3,450
Total reallocated	$ 9,200

Consider the following example. There are two operating departments and one service department. The actual monthly costs of the service department are reallocated on the basis of the total machine-hours actually worked by the operating departments as shown at the top of Exhibit 12-3 for a 10,000-hour level. Note that the basic cost behavior pattern of the service department is $6,000 monthly plus 40¢ per machine-hour used in the operating departments.

But suppose one of the operating departments worked only 3,000 hours instead of 5,000 hours. The next section of Exhibit 12-3 shows the new results.

Note that there are two basic faults in fully reallocating actual costs. First, a specific period's charges to an operating department depended on how much of the service was being consumed by the *other* operating department(s). In this example, given the same utilization of services as measured by the total labor-hours it incurred, Department 1 had 15 percent more costs (an increase from $5,000 to $5,750) solely because Department 2's volume declined.

Second, the amount charged is dependent on factors not directly subject to the control of the operating managers: the unit price and the efficiency of the services rendered. Frequently, operating managers do not complain so much about the allocation base used as they do about the total costs incurred by the service departments. If this service-department manager does not properly control his costs, his inefficiencies or high rates are routinely passed along to the producing departments.

***how to
allocate for
planning and
control***

The following guidance should help in deciding on what procedures to use for reallocating service-department or -division costs:

1. Plan and control the costs of service departments or divisions just like those of operating departments or divisions. The fundamental distinc-

tions between variable- and fixed-cost behavior patterns should be preserved. Flexible budgets and standards should be used wherever feasible.

2. Use predetermined or budgeted unit prices or rates, not actual unit prices or rates, to charge departments.

3. Do not allow charges to a specific department to depend on how much of the service is being consumed by other departments.

4. Where feasible, use a dual system that distinguishes between variable and fixed costs.

5. Where feasible, charge on the basis of predetermined standard or budgeted times allowed for services rendered. This is especially applicable to routine service. In this way, the operating department is responsible for the overall quantity of services consumed, but not directly for fluctuations in unit prices or efficiency.

These points are illustrated in the second Problem for Self-Study at the end of this chapter.

benefits received   Much literature on cost accounting has maintained that indirect costs should be assigned to operations and products according to the relative benefits received by each. Under this view, the notion of a cause-and-effect criterion is rejected, because no particular job can be cited as being responsible for property taxes, depreciation on buildings, and similar items. In effect, however, the benefits-received criterion is indeed fundamentally a long-run cause-and-effect criterion. It can be interpreted as follows: "The manufacture of the product causes these costs to exist, not in an hour-to-hour or day-to-day sense, but in a cumulative sense."

However, in product costing, the benefits-received criterion also often implies that the incurrence of the cost has not only helped the production of the goods but it has also helped their revenue-producing power. This is a much stronger implication than the causal criterion advocated above. It introduces a value-added test that sometimes makes a benefits-received criterion indistinguishable from an ability-to-bear criterion. If the benefits-received criterion is used to justify allocations that are proportional to values added (such as sales dollars), it becomes a second-best approach that is likely to mask underlying relationships. For example, if the sales price is raised on a particular product line, there is no fundamental relationship that justifies the soaking of that product line with a higher dose of some cost that is being allocated to products on the basis of sales dollars.

The benefits-received criterion tends to be cited when other criteria are lacking, when no other logical or empirical basis can be found for allocation. Examples are allocations of corporate administrative costs and public-image advertising. Consider whether the costs of a corporate executive-training program are allocable to a particular government contract. The benefits-received argument is: "The contract obviously benefits from better-trained executives, so a portion of such costs should be allocated thereto." The causal argument is: "The existence of the contract causes a need for better-trained executives and therefore results in increased costs for executive-training programs." The latter argument is based on the idea that somehow in the long run, the magnitude of such costs is affected by the presence of the cost object.

The arguments may be unimpressive because the relationship between the cost object and cost is so obscure that any means for allocation is unconvincing. If so, either no allocation should be made or all interested parties should agree on some method in advance.

ability to bear   When cause-and-effect relationships are impossible to establish, accountants and managers often resort to arbitrary bases. An often misused base is actual sales dollars or gross margins or some other "ability-to-bear" base that often has a most tenuous causal relationship to the costs being allocated. The costs of administrative and central corporate effort are frequently independent of the results obtained, in the sense that the costs are budgeted by management discretion or in relation to sales *targets*. The point is that sales dollars may be a good surrogate for establishing cause-and-effect relationships, but there should always be a serious examination of whether a better base is available or whether any allocation is indeed warranted.

The use of revenue or sales as a base is a clear example of an "ability-to-bear" philosophy as contrasted with a services-rendered or benefits-received approach. A survey by the National Industrial Conference Board showed that 41 of 109 companies surveyed used actual sales as the sole base for allocating central expenses to divisions.[5] Sales is frequently a last resort in the search for a common denominator. The costs of efforts are independent of the results actually obtained, in the sense that the costs are programmed by management, not determined by sales. Moreover, the allocation of costs on the basis of dollar sales entails circular reasoning. That is, the costs per segment are determined by relative sales per segment. For example, examine the effects in the following situation (figures are in millions of dollars):

YEAR 1	PRODUCT			TOTAL	
	A	B	C		
Sales	$100	$100	$100	$300	(100%)
Costs allocated by dollar sales	$ 10	$ 10	$ 10	$ 30	(10%)

Assume that the dollar volume of A and B rises considerably. However, the direct costs and sales of Product C are not changed. The total costs to be allocated on the basis of dollar sales are also unchanged.

---

[5] *Allocating Corporate Expenses,* Studies in Business Policy, No. 108 (New York: National Industrial Conference Board), 13. This book has a good overall discussion of this topic.

YEAR 2	PRODUCT			TOTAL	
	A	B	C		
Sales	$137.5	$137.5	$100.0	$375.0	(100%)
Costs allocated by dollar sales	$ 11.0	$ 11.0	$ 8.0	$ 30.0	(8%)

The ratio between the costs allocated on the basis of dollar sales and total sales was reduced, in the second year, to 8 percent ($30 ÷ $375), as compared with 10 percent ($30 ÷ $300) in the first year. This resulted in less cost being allocated to Product C, despite the fact that its unit volume and directly attributable costs were the same as for the first year. So the product that did the worst is relieved of costs without any reference to underlying causal relationships.

Advertising is a prime example of a cost that is typically allocated on the basis of dollar sales. Basing allocation on dollar sales *achieved* may be questionable, because the unsuccessful product or territory may be unjustifiably relieved of costs. However, there is some merit in basing allocation on *potential* sales or purchasing power available in a particular territory or for a particular product. For example, there would be a consistent relationship between the advertising costs and sales volume in each territory, if all territories were equally efficient. If, however, a manager has poor outlets or a weak sales staff, one of the indicators would be a high ratio of advertising to sales.

fairness or equity Of particular note is the frequency with which fairness or equity is cited as a basis for choice. For example:

> In ascertaining what constitutes cost, any generally accepted method of determining or estimating cost that is *equitable* under the circumstances may be used.[6]
>
> A cost is allowable if it is assignable to a particular cost objective . . . in accordance with the relative *benefits received* or other *equitable* relationships.[7]
>
> Any base that is chosen for proration purposes should meet two tests; it should be *equitable* and it should be *practicable*. Thus it should result in charges to each department that will be reasonable in view of the benefit the department receives, and it should not be too costly to use.[8]

The trouble with fairness or equity as a possible criterion is that it is so broad that other criteria must be devised to assure the existence of fairness. Equity and fairness are ethical standards that should be avoided in the building of concepts for a measurement system. In short, they are lofty objectives rather than criteria. To say that cost allocations must be fair or equitable is not an operational statement. Without specific criteria, we cannot judge how fairness conforms to overall tests of truth, justice, equity and candor.

[6]*Armed Services Procurement Regulations*, Section XV. [Emphasis added.]

[7]*Ibid.* [Emphasis added.]

[8]Robert Dickey (ed.), *Cost Accountants' Handbook* (New York: The Ronald Press Company, 1960), Section 8, p. 7. [Emphasis in original.]

COST POOLS AND HOMOGENEITY

nature of The idea of aggregating or pooling costs is the result of abandoning ideal
homogeneity cost-allocation schemes for practical reasons. That is, instead of taking
detailed costs in their most elemental form, one at a time, and deciding
how they should be allocated, we aggregate them; we almost always choose one
base for allocating the group (whereas individually we might choose more than
one). This averaging process inevitably results in a loss of accuracy. The justification for using one or two cost pools and one or two cost-allocation bases is that
the added cost of a more detailed cost-allocation scheme exceeds the expected
benefits from getting more precise information.

This could be a testable proposition in some cases. For example, if costs
directly influence pricing decisions, the effects on decisions of various cost-
aggregation schemes (such as absorption and direct costing) and allocation bases
could be predicted. The sensitivity and payoffs of the decisions would then
determine the degree of cost aggregation that would be optimal.

The literature contains numerous exhortations about the desirability of
achieving homogeneity in the averaging process. However, homogeneity has not
been sharply defined. We define it as a characteristic of any aggregated cost-
allocation rate. It is measured by comparing the costs assigned to the various
cost objects of interest, using an aggregated cost-allocation rate, with what the
costs assigned would have been if disaggregated rates had been used. If there
are no differences, the rate is perfectly homogeneous. Note that the concept of
homogeneity springs from the aggregation process. If elemental individual rates
were used, no test for homogeneity would be needed. This implies that the choice
of a base may still be a problem at the individual level, but it is not a problem
of homogeneity.

plant-wide The problem of homogeneity is widespread because most factories produce
rate versus more than one product. The variety of products commands varying atten-
departmental tion and effort, different material usages, and different production routings.
rates These situations call for refinement of overhead application by departments
or cost centers so that different products may bear their related share of
factory overhead.

Assume that one job is routed through two departments: machining and
finishing. The machining department is heavily mechanized with costly semiautomatic and automatic equipment. The finishing department contains a few
simple tools and is dependent on painstaking skilled workmanship. Overhead
costs would be relatively large in machining and small in finishing.

Now consider two jobs. The first requires one hour of machining time and
ten hours of finishing time. The second requires nine hours of machining time
and two hours of finishing time. If a single, plant-wide, blanket overhead rate
based on labor-hours is used, each job would receive the same total-overhead
application. But this probably would not be a sufficiently accurate measurement

EXHIBIT 12-4

PLANT-WIDE OVERHEAD RATE VERSUS DEPARTMENTAL OVERHEAD RATES

	PLANT-WIDE RATE		DEPARTMENTAL RATES		
	MACHINING	FINISHING	MACHINING	FINISHING	
Budgeted annual overhead	$100,000	$ 8,000	$100,000	$ 8,000	—
Direct-labor hours	10,000	10,000	10,000	10,000	
Blanket rate per DLH:					
$108,000 ÷ 20,000		$ 5.40			
Departmental rates per DLH			$ 10.00	$ .80	
Overhead application:					
Job No. 1					
Labor time, 11 hours @ $5.40		$59.40			
or					
Labor time:					
Machining, 1 hour @ $10.00			$ 10.00		*TOTAL*
Finishing, 10 hours @ $.80				$ 8.00	$18.00
Job No. 2					
Labor time, 11 hours @ $5.40		$59.40			
or					
Labor time:					
Machining, 9 hours @ $10.00			$ 90.00		
Finishing, 2 hours @ $.80				$ 1.60	$91.60

of the underlying relationship, because Job No. 1 made light use of overhead-incurring factors while Job No. 2 made heavy use of such services. Departmental rates, as shown in Exhibit 12-4, result in a more accurate linking of overhead with specific jobs when products do not move uniformly through the plant.

To summarize, when products are heterogeneous, receiving uneven attention and effort as they move through various departments or cost centers, departmental or cost-center overhead rates are necessary to achieve more accurate product costs. In these situations, the departmental rates are frequently described as being more homogeneous than the plant-wide rates.

factors
affecting
homogeneity

Homogeneity refers to all ingredients of the cost-allocation rate, both within and between the numerator and denominator. That is, defects in either the numerator or the denominator can result in a nonhomogeneous average cost rate. For example, the summing of recruiting costs and data-processing costs and dividing by machine-hours is likely to be nonhomogeneous because (a) the costs in the numerator have little commonality of purpose, and (b) the allocation base has no direct causal relationship to these costs.

Note especially the interdependent effects of the cost objects, the allocation base, and cost pools. For example, the testing for homogeneity might lead to:

1. Redefining the cost objects, because there may be no need to discriminate among them. Perhaps no distinction is needed between, say, Plane 1 and Plane 2; the cost object should be both Planes 1 and 2 together.

411

2. Choosing a different allocation base, because in testing we discover another base (say, number of employees instead of direct-labor hours) that will yield a more acceptable[9] level of homogeneity.
3. Choosing different cost pools. There may be too much aggregation of, say, different classes of labor with different rates.

An advantage of testing for homogeneity is that it forces a simultaneous consideration of all three crucial factors in cost allocation: the object, the base, and the cost aggregations. Accuracy cannot be judged by looking at one or two factors at a time.

Homogeneity is a matter of degree. At one extreme, all costs for all departments would be pooled and allocated, using a single allocation base. At the other extreme, each cost would be allocated, using individual allocation bases. In concept, the latter method is the ideal. In practice, a system approaching the former method is favored. The tendency toward the simpler, cruder methods is the result of an implicit or explicit cost and value of information decision. As already mentioned, the prevailing attitude seems to be that the additional accuracy provided by increased homogeneity will not make much difference in management decisions. Of course, this is a testable proposition that should be examined periodically in every organization—particularly those where costs directly influence pricing or product-combination decisions.

intermediate aggregations

The complete testing of homogeneity may be regarded as infeasible because of the difficulties of linking unaggregated costs[10] to cost objects on a one-by-one basis. If this is the case, there may be some intermediate aggregations that can be used as a guide for tests. These intermediate aggregations take three forms that are not necessarily mutually exclusive nor ranked in order of importance: responsibility center, cost behavior pattern, and functional orientation.

The conglomeration of various costs in massive plant-wide cost pools is likely to be the antithesis of homogeneity. The first intermediate aggregation that can test the plant-wide rate is that of responsibility centers (departments) and the use of departmental allocation rates. Because the costs attributable to responsibility centers are routinely accumulated anyway, the use of departmental rates should not overburden the cost-accounting system.

The second intermediate aggregation that can test any given rate or rates is based on the distinction between variable and fixed costs. Separate bases can be developed for each, and the resulting cost applications can be compared with those obtained via a more highly aggregated rate. Note that department costs

---

[9] The magnitude of an "acceptable" level would depend on the cost and value of the additional information that might be supplied by more disaggregation. Also see Yuji Ijiri, *Foundations of Accounting Measurement* (Englewood Cliffs, N. J.: Prentice-Hall, Inc., 1967), pp. 117–31.

[10] Technically, in most accounting systems it is indeed difficult to find unaggregated costs in their purest form. For example, consider the travel costs that might be recorded. Usually some aggregation occurs even before recording on the source documents. Breakfasts, lunches, and dinners become "meals"; each taxi fare becomes "local transportation"; and so on.

(a cost pool) may be subdivided into two pools by using separate departmental rates for variable and fixed costs.

The third intermediate aggregation that can test any given rate is based on a functional orientation. Vatter[11] illustrates this idea with a classification that includes the following:

TYPES OF COSTS	EXAMPLES	SUGGESTED USUAL ALLOCATION BASE
People-oriented	Personnel department	Number of employees
Payroll-oriented	Vacation pay, payroll taxes	Payroll dollars
Materials-oriented	Storeroom costs, internal transport	Units of material, weight, size
Machine-oriented	Variable costs of power, supplies, routine maintenance	Machine-hours

Conceivably, any given aggregated allocation rate could be compared against less aggregated intermediate rates based on both variable-fixed and functional subclassifications within departments.

different bases for different departments Some companies use different overhead bases for different departments. Exhibit 12-4 used direct-labor hours as the base for the machining department because it was assumed that direct-labor time was proportionate to machine time. In Exhibit 12-4, if labor time was not proportionate to machine time, machine-hours would be the overhead base in the machining department whereas labor hours would continue to be the base in the finishing department. Some machines may be almost entirely automatic; or an operator may be able to run two or three machines simultaneously on some jobs but only one machine at a time on other jobs.

DIFFERENT ALLOCATION BASES FOR OVERHEAD APPLICATION TO PRODUCT

There is a tendency in practice to aggregate overhead costs in pools and use one allocation base for each pool as a denominator for applying those costs to product.

The most widely used bases are selected after considering (a) the factors already associated with the individual products or jobs (for example, direct materials and direct labor), (b) necessary clerical costs and effort in application,

[11] *Standards for Cost Analysis,* a research report prepared by William J. Vatter for the comptroller general of the United States, August 1969, pp. 56–59. Vatter's report had great influence on many parts of this chapter. Early drafts of material on cost allocation by J. Demski, G. Feltham, C. Horngren, R. Jaedicke, and R. Sprouse, which will probably be published in 1973 by the American Institute of CPAs, have also heavily influenced parts of this chapter.

and (c) differences in final results. Where results do not differ significantly, the easier method is used.

The following bases are widely used. Two or more bases may be used by a company for applying different classes of overhead.

physical units produced   The formula used is as follows: Total Overhead ÷ Total Units Produced = Overhead Rate. This base is valid only when the units produced are alike and receive nearly identical attention and effort.

direct-labor hours   Most overhead costs are more closely related to time expiration than to any other factor. Fixed costs such as depreciation, rent, taxes, and insurance relate to a given time period. Indirect labor and supply usage are most closely related to the input of hours of effort. That is why time devoted to specific products is often used for correlating overhead with products. Time is traced to specific products by using work tickets for direct labor. Predetermined overhead rates are developed by dividing predicted total overhead by predicted total direct hours. Thus, the amount of overhead applied to any given product is dependent on the amount of time devoted to an operation or product.

machine-hours   In these days of mechanized production, machine time is often a better predictor of overhead-cost incurrence than direct-labor time. Depreciation, property taxes, supply usage, and indirect labor are frequently more closely related to machinery utilization than to direct-labor usage. In theory, then, machine time may be the most accurate base for overhead application.

In practice, however, machine time is not used as often as labor time because of the added clerical cost and the difficulty of computing machine time on individual jobs. Machine time may be ignored where the relationship of labor time or labor costs to machine time is unchanging between jobs; that is, the final overhead application to a given type of job would not differ (for example, one direct laborer runs two similar machines). This neglect of machine time as a base is acceptable only as long as the final job costs are not greatly inaccurate.

direct-labor cost   If labor rates are nearly uniform for every operation, the use of a labor-*dollar* base for overhead application yields the same results as using direct-labor *hours*. Otherwise, direct-labor *hours* is the better base in most instances, particularly where the senior and junior workers are equally efficient and therefore use the same amounts of overhead services per hour. For example, a senior worker may earn $8 per hour while a junior worker may earn $7.50 per hour. If a 200-percent-of-direct-labor-cost rate is in effect, the overhead cost of a given job requiring one hour of direct labor would be $16 if the senior worker were used and $15 if the junior worker were used. Standard or average labor rates generally prevent such ridiculous results.

Direct-labor *dollars* as an overhead base may be conceptually better than labor *hours* where many overhead items represent fringe labor costs, which are primarily tied to direct-labor *cost* or where high-cost direct laborers make the greatest use of high-cost facilities and complex machinery.

direct Unless the labor and equipment needed for material handling are a major
material part of overhead, the use of direct-material dollars or weights is not a valid basis for overhead application. Again, materials may be used as a base where the final results are the same regardless of the overhead base adopted. Sometimes storeroom and material-handling overhead is separated from other factory overhead and is applied to jobs on the basis of direct-material weight or bulk. The remaining overhead items would be applied by using some other base.

comparison If all data are accurate and denominator activity is achieved, the annual
of bases overhead will be fully applied to jobs regardless of the base selected. The major problem in choosing a proper base is to relate overhead to its most closely related causal factor. (Avoid the misconception that it is correct to use the number of tranquilizer tablets consumed by the president as a base if it best correlates with overhead behavior. Such coincidences may lead to misleading overhead rates, because the apparent relationship is mere happenstance and not a continuing one. Apparent correlation is only part of the check.)

As long as all the possible causal factors are used proportionately on individual jobs, each job will get the same amount of overhead.

Exhibit 12-5 illustrates the following important points:

1. Either direct-labor dollars or direct-labor time may be used as a basis for overhead application to product, as long as the direct-labor dollars and hours vary in direct proportion; that is, as long as labor rates are uniform on similar jobs.

2. Where costs related to machines are the predominant overhead factor, machine-hours should be used instead of labor-hours if both do not fluctuate in proportion. In other words, if one operator runs one machine for a certain job and three similar machines for another job, other things being equal, the machine-hour base is more rational than a labor base.

3. If labor time has a proportionate relationship to machine time, it is unnecessary to use machine-hours because the final costs of a job will not differ.

4. The base factor that is easiest and cheapest to apply should be selected, as long as individual job costs are not significantly affected. Note in Exhibit 12-5 that the final results are the same on a specific job because all base factors are used proportionately. But if the possible bases are not used proportionately on individual jobs, certain jobs may receive relatively inaccurate amounts of over-

EXHIBIT 12-5

COMPARISON OF OVERHEAD APPLICATION TO PRODUCT WHEN BASES ARE USED PROPORTIONATELY

ANNUAL OVERHEAD BUDGET DATA:

	TOTAL	*POSSIBLE RATES*
Total overhead	$100,000	
Direct-labor cost	$200,000	50% of direct-labor cost
Direct-labor hours	100,000	$1.00 per DLH
Direct-material usage	$400,000	25% of direct materials
Machine-hours	20,000	$5.00 per machine-hour

Job data:

Job No. 1

Direct-labor hours	5
Machine-hours	1
Direct materials	$ 20
Direct-labor cost	10
Prime cost	$ 30

POSSIBLE OVERHEAD APPLICATION USING FOLLOWING BASES:

	DIRECT MATERIALS	*DIRECT-LABOR HOURS*	*DIRECT LABOR*	*MACHINE-HOURS*
Overhead	.25($20) = $5	$1.00(5 hr.) = $5	.50($10) = $5	1 hr.($5) = $5
Total job cost	$ 35			

Job No. 2

Direct-labor hours	25
Machine-hours	5
Direct materials	$100
Direct-labor cost	50
Prime cost	$150

	DIRECT MATERIALS	*DIRECT-LABOR HOURS*	*DIRECT LABOR*	*MACHINE-HOURS*
Overhead	.25($100) = $25	$1.00(25 hr.) = $25	.50($50) = $25	.5 hr.($5) = $25
Total job cost	$175			

head. This latter point is not illustrated specifically in the exhibit. However, the point can be readily seen by changing the number of machine-hours on Job No. 2 from five to six. This would change the overhead application, using a machine-hour rate, from $25 to $30.

SERVICE DEPARTMENTS AND PRODUCT COSTING

dual rates for reallocation   Earlier in this chapter, some suggestions were given for planning and controlling service-department costs, including the suggestion that variable and fixed costs be reallocated separately to other departments. Many companies find it useful to have two overhead rates for product costing: one for variable and one for fixed overhead. These rates are not difficult to develop for companies that use flexible-overhead budgets. They supply more useful data, because product costs may be broken down more minutely for a variety of decision-making purposes—especially for decisions on regulating volume. In addition, dual rates permit closer dovetailing of cost accounting for product-costing purposes and for budgetary-control purposes.

In practice, dual overhead rates are not found very often; instead, all overhead items are pooled together regardless of individual behavior and applied to products via a single overhead rate. This method is often adequate for the determination of product costs for inventory and ordinary pricing purposes.

The following section uses single reallocation rates rather than dual rates in order to simplify the illustrations. However, keep in mind that this approach may not be warranted in some instances. Again, in specific cases the question that must be answered is whether the additional costs of a more refined information system are exceeded by the expected additional benefits.

need for tracing service- department costs to products   Service departments benefit the manufacture of products, even though goods do not physically flow through any service departments. Therefore, predetermined overhead-application rates are based not only on producing-department costs per se, but also on the service-department costs reallocated to producing departments. The justification for this inclusion is that the service-department cost is every bit as much a product cost as are the lubricants used by the machining department.

The relationships of various overhead items to physical products are not all alike. It is fairly easy to see a relationship between a product and the salaries of material handlers, the power costs of running equipment, and the consumption of small cutting tools. Relationships between product and overhead costs become more hazy and tenuous when one tries to link the factory nurse's salary, the costs of personnel testing, the loss from the factory cafeteria, and the cost of the factory picnic to specific products. Still, the general opinion prevails that service departments facilitate production and that no product cost should be relieved of an "equitable" share of these auxiliary costs.

The general idea is to somehow funnel all factory costs, whether they originate in service departments or production departments, to the *production departments.* In turn, these costs are applied to *products*, using overhead rates that encompass both production and service department costs:

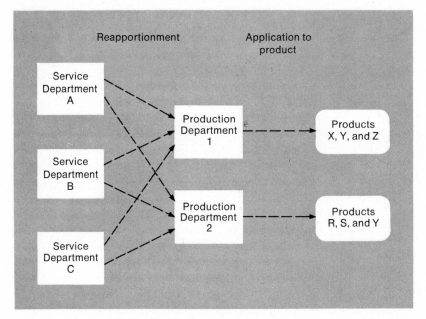

Assume that a company has four departments. The two service departments are general factory administration and engineering. The two production departments are machining and assembly. Overhead costs are budgeted on a flexible basis and are accumulated by department responsibility for control purposes. For product-costing purposes, the service department costs at levels that support "normal" production activity are reallocated to other departments. The base for reallocation is the common denominator that best measures the services rendered to the other service and producing departments. The data for our example follow:

| | SERVICE DEPARTMENTS | | PRODUCING DEPARTMENTS | | |
	GENERAL FACTORY ADMINISTRATION	ENGINEERING	MACHINING	ASSEMBLY	TOTALS
	1	*2*	*A*	*B*	
Overhead costs before reallocation of service-department costs	$600,000	$116,000	$400,000	$200,000	$1,316,000
Proportions of service furnished: By Department 1 (based on total man-hours):					
Total man-hours		24,000	12,000	36,000	72,000
Proportion		$2/6$	$1/6$	$3/6$	$6/6$

By Department
2 (based on engi-
neering hours
worked for each
department):
Engineering

hours	2,000	16,000	2,000	20,000
Proportion	10%	80%	10%	100%

direct
reallocation—
method 1

Direct reallocation, or some similar method, is the most widely used method for reallocation of service-department costs. This method ignores any service rendered by one service department to another; it reallocates each service department's total costs directly to the producing departments. Note in Exhibit 12-6 that this method ignores the service rendered by the general factory administration department to the engineering department and also the service rendered by engineering to general factory administration. The base used for reapportionment of general factory administration costs is the 48,000 man-hours worked in the producing departments. Distinguish between *total* labor-hours (which includes indirect hours) and *direct*-labor hours. Total labor-hours are often used as bases for reallocations, whereas direct-labor hours are often used as bases for developing predetermined overhead rates in producing departments for product-costing purposes.

EXHIBIT 12-6

DIRECT METHOD OF REALLOCATION

	DEPARTMENT				
	1	2	A	B	TOTAL
Overhead costs before reallocation	$600,000	$116,000	$400,000	$200,000	$1,316,000
Reallocation:					
Department 1 ($\frac{1}{4}$, $\frac{3}{4}$)*	($600,000)		150,000	450,000	
Department 2 ($\frac{8}{9}$, $\frac{1}{9}$)†		($116,000)	103,111	12,889	
Total overhead of producing departments			$653,111	$662,889	$1,316,000
Computation of predetermined overhead rates for product-costing purposes:					
Divide by machine-hours			40,000		
Divide by direct-labor hours				30,000	
Rate			$ 16.328	$ 22.096	

*Base is (12,000 + 36,000), or 48,000 hours.
† Base is (16,000 + 2,000), or 18,000 hours.

**step method—
method 2**   Many companies use the *step method* of reallocation, which recognizes services rendered by service departments to other service departments. This method is more complicated, because a sequence of reallocations must be chosen. The sequence typically begins with the department that renders service to the greatest number of other service departments; the sequence continues in step-by-step fashion and ends with the reallocation of costs of the service department that renders service to the least number of other departments. Thus, departments like building and grounds or personnel would be reallocated earlier than would production control or product engineering.

Exhibit 12-7 shows the step method. Note that Department 1 costs are reallocated to another service department as well as to the producing departments. Note also that, once Department 1 costs are reallocated, Department 2 costs include a share of Department 1 costs. The new total for Department 2 is then reallocated to *subsequent* departments only. *Once a service department's costs have been reallocated, no subsequent service-department costs are recirculated back to it.*

Note further that *in this case* the overhead rates for product-costing purposes are significantly different under the two methods. For example, the machine-hour rate is $16.33 under the direct method and $19.522 under the step method. Note also that Department A's rate is higher under the step method while Department B's rate is lower. The step method would be preferable because it recognizes the service rendered to engineering by general factory administration, whereas the direct method ignores this relationship.

EXHIBIT 12-7

STEP METHOD OF REALLOCATION

	1	2	A	B	TOTAL
Overhead costs before reallocation	$600,000	$116,000	$400,000	$200,000	$1,316,000
Reallocation:					
Department 1 ($\frac{2}{6}, \frac{1}{6}, \frac{3}{6}$)	(600,000)	200,000	100,000	300,000	
Department 2 ($\frac{8}{9}, \frac{1}{9}$)		($316,000)	280,889	35,111	
Total overhead of producing departments			$780,889	$535,111	$1,316,000
Computation of predetermined overhead rates for product-costing purposes:					
Divide by machine-hours			40,000		
Divide by direct-labor hours				30,000	
Rate			$ 19.522	$ 17.837	

arbitrary
rules
The entire methodology of reallocation of service-department costs is plagued by the frequent reliance on some arbitrary rules that are designed to charge producing departments in some "equitable" manner. Some common denominator is sought that will provide for acceptable parceling of service-department costs. Thus, personnel-department costs are usually reallocated on the basis of the number of employees in each of the other departments. The underlying assumption here would be that each employee receives his pro rata share of the personnel department's attention. Of course, this is rarely realistic, because labor turnover and types of skilled and unskilled employees may heavily influence the personnel department's efforts and time. Yet it is an expedient oversimplification to use number of employees as a base. The additional refinement of the measuring stick is seldom viewed as being worthwhile in terms of expected additional benefits.

further
illustration of
reallocation
Now we turn to a more complicated illustration, shown in Exhibit 12-8. Observe that costs are first accumulated by departmental responsibility; then the service-department costs are reapportioned first because it renders more service to building and grounds than the latter renders to repair and maintenance.[12] Exhibit 12-8 also shows that the basis for reallocation differs, depending on the service department in question.

computation
techniques
Lines 20–22 of Exhibit 12-8 show the two computation techniques for re-apportionment. Building and grounds is reallocated on the basis of the departmental percentage of total square footage. An alternate method would be to develop a rate per square foot—$5,592 divided by 100,000 square feet, or $.05592 per square foot. Then the square footage in each department would be multiplied by the rate. The two calculations are logically identical, and they give the same results. Personal preference determines the arithmetical method used in a specific case.

setting
department-
overhead rates
for product
costing
Besides demonstrating how service-department costs are reapportioned, Exhibit 12-8 also illustrates how overhead rates for the producing departments are developed. The bases used in this illustration are standard direct-labor hours in each department. Note that product-costing rates are used only for producing departments, because products flow only through producing departments.

[12] Difficulties arise when there are two or more service departments that serve the same number of other departments. Which department's costs are to be reallocated first? Generally, when two or more departments serve the same number of other departments, the one with the biggest total cost is reapportioned first, because the costliest department supposedly provides the largest amount of service.
    This criterion has been criticized as follows: "It is not the absolute size of the balance in any service department which is of consequence; it is the relative importance of the service balance due *from* other service departments in excess of the amount due *to* others which minimizes the error." See Carl Thomas Devine, *Cost Accounting and Analysis* (New York: The Macmillan Company, 1950), Chapter III, for a thorough discussion.

EXHIBIT 12-8

SAMPLE COMPANY

Factory Overhead Budget—Step Method of Reallocation
(Normal Month)

LINE	(ALLOCATION BASIS)	SERVICE DEPARTMENTS			PRODUCTION DEPARTMENTS			TOTAL
		REPAIR AND MAINTENANCE	BUILDINGS AND GROUNDS	FACTORY ADMINIS-TRATION	MACHINING	ASSEMBLY	FINISHING	
1	Indirect labor [Direct to departments (payroll analysis or work tickets)]	$ 400	$ 960	$2,200	$ 4,900	$ 1,000	$ 360	$ 9,820
2	Supplies [Direct to departments (requisitions)]	640	700	240	3,500	400	1,400	6,880
3	Power (Meters or horsepower ratings)	130	1,600	25	1,800	200	500	4,255
4	Payroll taxes (Department payrolls)	200	50	200	1,300	300	100	2,150
5	Overtime premium (Department payrolls)	100	—	60	600	140	50	950
6	Rework (Direct to responsible department)	—	—	—	300	150	40	490
7	Fuel	—	100	—	—	—	—	100
8	Total variable overhead	$1,470	$3,410	$2,725	$12,400	$ 2,190	$ 2,450	$24,645
9	Property taxes and insurance	140	770	760	600	100	100	2,470
10	Depreciation	150	700	300	2,300	400	300	4,150
11	Supervisor	700	220	4,015	1,800	1,010	550	8,295
12	Total department overhead before reallocation	$2,460	$5,100	$7,800	$17,100	$ 3,700	$ 3,400	$39,560

Reallocation of service-department costs (See Note A):

13	Repair and maintenance (Maintenance service, current month)	$2,460	492	25	1,476	246	221	$39,560
14	Building and grounds (Square footage occupied)		$5,592	559	3,355	1,119	559	
15	Factory administration (Direct-labor hours)*			$8,384	6,708	838	838	
16	Total production-department overhead				$28,639	$5,903	$5,018	
17	Application bases—budgeted standard direct-labor hours				24,000	3,000	3,000	
18	Overhead rate per standard direct-labor hour				$1.1933	$1.9677	$1.6727	

Note A: Percentage used for reallocation:

19	Repair and maintenance, based on specific maintenance service	100%	20%	1%	60%	10%	9%	
20	Building and grounds, based on square footage in each department			10,000	60,000	20,000	10,000	100,000
21	Using rate method, $5,592 ÷ 100,000 sq. feet = $.05592 per sq. ft. or (.05592 × 10,000),(.05592 × 60,000), (.05592 × 20,000),(.05592 × 10,000)							
22	Percentages based on square footage		100%	10%	60%	20%	10%	
23	Factory administration, based on direct-labor hours			100%	80%	10%	10%	

*Other possible bases might be number of employees or total labor-hours.

RECIPROCAL SERVICES

The step method is not theoretically accurate if service departments render services to one another reciprocally. For example, the factory administration department serves the employees of the building and grounds department, while the factory administration department occupies some floor space and has janitorial attention. If reciprocal services between service departments are significant, elaborate schemes of reallocation involving simultaneous equations may be adopted. Ordinarily, however, the step method (a simpler model) will yield final charges to the producing departments that are acceptable approximations of the results that would come from a more complex model requiring simultaneous equations. Consequently, the use of simultaneous equations or linear algebra is rare in practice. But digital computers now facilitate the computations, so we may expect an increasing use of linear algebra.

The use of linear algebra may make a difference in decisions upon occasion. For example, suppose that the conditions in Exhibit 12-9 exist. The repair department serves the power department and vice versa. Note that a step method of reallocation may produce significantly different answers from those by the linear algebra method, using the simultaneous equations at the bottom of the exhibit. Linear algebra is the most theoretically defensible method. For example, suppose the company had the opportunity to buy its power outside for $16,500. The step method used in Exhibit 12-9 shows a power cost of $16,000, but the linear algebra method shows a power cost of $17,391. In decisions like these, the cost-reallocation method may indeed have an influential difference.

The example in Exhibit 12-9 used only two service departments and two production departments. This required the use of two simultaneous equations. Of course, in practice, many more simultaneous equations may be required. A generalized approach for solving large systems of equations is provided by matrix algebra.[13]

When should linear algebra be used? If management is using the results of reallocations to make decisions on pricing products, on internal or external purchasing of services, on setting levels of output, and on related activities, the results of step-method reallocations should be periodically tested against the results obtained by the algebraic method. If the decisions are not sensitive to the results of the algebraic computations, then the simpler methods are adequate.

MOTIVATION AND PARTIAL OR FULL ALLOCATION

The point has been made that motivation should be a major criterion in the allocation of costs. Anthony (*Accounting Review,* Vol. XXXII, No. 2) has indicated the key question: "What cost constructions are most likely to induce

---

[13]See Chapter 27, Problem 27-21 for an example. Also see Thomas H. Williams and Charles H. Griffin, "Matrix Theory and Cost Allocation," *Accounting Review,* XXXIX, No. 3, 671–78; Neil C. Churchill, "Linear Algebra and Cost Allocations: Some Examples," *Accounting Review,* XXXIV, No. 4, 894–904, and Rene P. Manes, "Comment on Matrix Theory and Cost Allocation," *Accounting Review,* XL, No. 3, 640–43.

EXHIBIT 12-9

COMPARISON OF STEP METHOD AND METHOD USING LINEAR ALGEBRA

(*Data Assumed*)

	SERVICE DEPARTMENTS		PRODUCTION DEPARTMENTS	
	REPAIR	*POWER*	*MACHINING*	*ASSEMBLY**
Man-hours of repair service used		1,000	3,000	1,000
Percentage of service to other departments		20%	60%	20%
Units of power consumed	4,000		2,000	4,000
Percentage of service to other departments	40%		20%	40%
Reallocation using step method:				
Total relevant department costs before reallocation	$ 30,000	$ 10,000	$ —	$ —
Repairs (allocated first†)	(30,000)	6,000	18,000	6,000
Power department		(16,000)	5,333	10,667
Relevant costs after reallocation	$ 0	$ 0	$23,333	$16,667
Reallocation using linear algebra‡:				
Relevant costs before reallocation	$ 30,000	$ 10,000	$ —	$ —
Repairs	(36,957)	7,391	22,174	7,392
Power	6,957	(17,391)	3,477	6,957
Relevant costs after reallocation	$ 0	$ 0	$25,651	$14,349

* Heavily automated with modern equipment.

† Some companies might prefer to allocate power first. You may wish on your own to allocate power first to see how the results compare to the "ideal" results under the reciprocal method.

‡ The following equations represent the essence of the linear algebra method. In this case, two simultaneous equations are used to find the value of two unknowns:

Let R = total costs of repair department
P = total costs of power department

(1) $R = \$30,000 + .4P$
(2) $P = \$10,000 + .2R$

Substituting in (1): $R = \$30,000 + .4\ (\$10,000 + .2R)$
$R = \$30,000 + \$4,000 + .08R$
$.92R = \$34,000$
$R = \$36,957$[a]

Substituting in (2): $P = \$10,000 + .2\ (\$36,957) = \$17,391$[a]

[a] Instead of using equations, we could obtain the same results by using successive rounds of reducing-amount computations:

Amounts before reallocation	$30,000.00	$10,000.00
20% of $30,000		6,000.00
Total		$16,000.00
40% of $16,000	6,400.00	
20% of $6,400		1,280.00
40% of $1,280	512.00	
20% of $512		102.40
40% of $102.40	40.96	
20% of $40.96		8.19
40% of $8.19	3.28	
20% of $3.28		.66
Totals as above	$36,956.24	$17,391.25

people to take the action that management desires?" A general answer could be: "The cost construction that best measures cause-and-effect relationships is most likely to provide information that will lead to optimum decisions."

The fully allocated versus partially allocated cost-allocation controversy illustrates the point. Some accountants favor the full allocation of costs because it makes the managers aware that the support of much of the entire organization is necessary for an individual responsibility center to run smoothly. On the other hand, some accountants maintain that some costs, such as central corporate costs, should never be allocated because no cause-and-effect relationships can be established. There can be no right answer here without knowing what decisions, if any, are affected by the cost allocations and what their differences in payoff would be.

In any event, little is known empirically about the effects on decisions of alternative cost-allocation bases. By implication, those who favor an arbitrary allocation of costs regardless of the lack of verifiable cause-and-effect relationships are saying that the danger of overstatement of costs is less than that of under-statement. For example, if costs are fully allocated, managers are less likely to cut prices, to underbid, to be inefficient, to overexpand, and so on. The widespread advocacy of full cost allocations is indicative that such assertions are widely believed. But we have no evidence to support either side of the argument.

Many managers insist that all costs should be fully allocated and reallocated to all departments, regardless of their controllability. Such a practice is supposed to make all managers more aware of the cost incurred and benefits offered by other parts of the organization. This practice may be desirable to the extent that this objective is reached without causing confusion in cost analysis and resentment about the methods of cost allocation.

Whether to include uncontrollable or indirect costs is a difficult question, which must ultimately be resolved in terms of how the given alternatives *influence management behavior* in a particular organization. In one organization, allocation may be desirable because it induces the desired behavior. In another organization, the same allocation procedure may cause an opposite behavioral effect. In any event, the current literature maintains that controllable and uncontrollable costs, when included in the same report, should not be commingled indiscriminately.

Are there any service departments whose costs should not be allocated even though they are clearly necessitated by the other parts of the organization? Consider the internal-auditing department or the legal department as examples. Ordinarily, where the other department managers have no discretion over their consumption of such services, the argument in favor of reallocation rests on the idea that the costs should be allocated anyway, and that managers generally do not get too concerned about such allocations as long as all departments are subject to a uniform cost-reallocation procedure. The argument against the reallocation of such costs rests on the idea that no costs should be reallocated to a manager unless he has some direct influence over their amount.

In some organizations, however, operating managers may have much leeway over their usage of such services. Charging for the auditing or legal services on the basis of the amount provided may discourage their use, even though such use may be very desirable from the standpoint of the organization as a whole. In such instances, either no charge may be made, or a flat annual fee may be charged regardless of the quantity of services consumed. For instance, a large automobile-manufacturing company does not charge for its internal-auditing services because it wants to encourage its managers to utilize such services.

As a general rule, the same objective will be attained by allocating a flat sum to the various departments regardless of actual use. A possible advantage of this procedure is its retainer-fee effect, where the user feels that he is paying for the service in any event, so he had better take advantage of its availability. Of course, there is always the danger that a few managers may demand too much of what they would then regard as a "free" service. Then some priority system must be instituted, and a method of charging on the basis of services consumed may be finally adopted.

Some managers maintain that the morale effects of allocation procedures on the operating departments are given too much attention. There are also important effects on the morale of the service-department employees. That is, if the other departments are not charged with service-department costs, the service-department staff is likely to feel that it lacks the status of first-class citizenship as an integral part of the organization.

summary

Costs are allocated ultimately for the purpose of decision making. There are three aspects to the cost allocation problem: the choice of a cost object (some action or activity), the pooling of costs, and the choice of an allocation base. These must be considered simultaneously because they are interdependent.

The cause-and-effect objective should be used as a frame of reference for judging various criteria for cost allocation. Wanting to know the impact of decision alternatives on costs, and faced with few instances of obvious cause-and-effect relationships, the manager is forced to rely on surrogates as approximations of these causal relationships. Without such surrogates, he rightfully fears that he will overlook some costs that are only circuitously affected by a given change in inputs or outputs. Hence, the fully allocated cost rather than a variable cost is often used as an approximation of "the real long-run" incremental cost.

The whole matter of reallocation is complicated by many computations. There is a misleading aura of precision, which is heightened by elaborate working papers and several decimal places. The complexity of the particular reallocation method chosen should be influenced by how sensitive the decisions are to the results of alternative reallocation methods. Again, the key question is, What difference does it make?

The crudity of existing cost systems may be appalling. Nevertheless, the heavy use of averages and the universal tendency toward full allocations of costs are the practical means of seeking optimization. A decision to produce a given batch of product may not, by itself, be causing an increase in a particular cost at its given moment of production. But its cumulative, indirect effects do indeed cause increases in costs. These cumulative effects are approximated by applying average unit costs to products. The unanswered question is, How accurate are such approximations?—that is, do they provide reasonable predictions of the cumulative changes in total costs? Only specific empirical research can answer such a question.

The contribution approach to the income statement and to the problems of cost allocation is accounting's most effective method for helping management to evaluate performance and make decisions. Allocations are made with thoughtful regard for the purpose of the information being compiled. Various subdivisions of net income are drawn for different purposes. The contribution approach distinguishes sharply between various degrees of objectivity in cost allocations.

Where feasible, fixed costs of service departments should be reallocated by using predetermined monthly lump sums for providing a basic capacity to serve. Variable costs should be reallocated by using a predetermined standard unit rate for the services utilized.

Problems for Self-Study

PROBLEM 1　Review the section on the contribution approach to cost allocation, especially Exhibit 12-1.

SOLUTION 1　See Exhibit 12-1.

PROBLEM 2　Examine Exhibit 12-3 and the accompanying text. Suppose that the service department's fundamental readiness to serve was based on long-run expected activity of 4,000 machine-hours per month in Department 1 and 6,000 hours in Department 2. The company decided to reallocate fixed costs on a predetermined lump-sum basis and variable costs on a predetermined standard cost-per-hour basis.
a. Show the reallocations to both departments at a 10,000-hour level and an 8,000-hour level as indicated in Exhibit 12-3. Compare the results with those in Exhibit 12-3. Explain the differences.
b. Suppose the service department had inefficiencies and price and rate changes at a 10,000-hour level. The service department incurred costs of $11,000 instead of the $10,000 originally budgeted. How would this change the cost reallocations under the method in Exhibit 12-3 and under the alternative method? Be specific.

SOLUTION 2　a. Fixed costs allocated on a 4/10 and 6/10 basis, or $(.4 \times \$6,000)$ and $(.6 \times \$6,000)$ respectively. Variable costs allocated at 40¢ per machine-hour.

At a 10,000-hour level:

To Department 1: $2,400 + ($.40 \times 5,000) =$	$ 4,400
To Department 2: $3,600 + ($.40 \times 5,000) =$	5,600
Total reallocated	$10,000

At an 8,000-hour level:

To Department 1: $2,400 + ($.40 × 5,000) = $ 4,400

To Department 2: $3,600 + ($.40 × 3,000) =   4,800

Total reallocated $ 9,200

The rates used in Exhibit 12-3 were combined and not predetermined. That is, no distinction was made between variable and fixed costs, and the single combined unit rate was computed after the fact—after the actual hours used were tallied.

In contrast, a flexible budget was used in this recommended alternative analysis. Note that the charges to Department 1 do not depend on how much service is being consumed by Department 2. The $4,400 charge to Department 1 depends solely on the 5,000 hours consumed by Department 1, whereas in Exhibit 12-3, Department 1's charges went up from $5,000 to $5,750 solely because of a decrease in usage by Department 2.

    b. In Exhibit 12-3, costs would go up by 10 percent for both Departments 1 and 2. Under the alternative method, the extra $1,000 would not be reallocated. The amount would remain charged to the service department as a $1,000 variance to be explained by the manager who had the most direct influence over such cost incurrence.

PROBLEM 3   Consider the following case, adapted from a CPA examination:

You have been engaged to install a cost system for the Martin Company. Your investigation of the manufacturing operations of the business discloses these facts:

1. The company makes a line of lighting fixtures and lamps. The material cost of any particular item ranges from 15 percent to 60 percent of total factory cost, depending on the kind of metal and fabric used in making it.
2. The business is subject to wide cyclical fluctuations, for the sales volume follows new-housing construction.
3. About 60 percent of the manufacturing is normally done in the first quarter of the year.
4. For the whole plant, the wage rates range from $4.25 to $8.75 an hour. However, within each of the eight individual departments, the spread between the high and low wage rates is less than 5 percent.
5. Each of the products made uses all eight of the manufacturing departments but not proportionately.
6. Within the individual manufacturing departments, factory overhead ranges from 30 percent to 80 percent of conversion cost.

Based on the information above, you are to prepare a statement or letter for the president of the company, explaining whether in its cost system Martin Company should use:

    a. A normal overhead rate or an expected-actual-capacity annual overhead rate;

    b. An overall overhead rate or a departmental overhead rate;

    c. A method of factory-overhead application based on direct-labor hours, direct-labor cost, or prime cost.

Include the reasons supporting *each* of your three recommendations.

SOLUTION 3

Dear Sir:

From a study of the manufacturing operations of the Martin Company, it is my recommendation that, in applying its manufacturing overhead, the company use normal departmental overhead rates applied as percentages of the *direct-labor cost*.

The company should use normal rather than expected actual overhead rates because of the wide seasonal and cyclical fluctuations in its business. Expected actual rates would, owing to the large fixed-overhead expenses, make the per-unit overhead costs high in the low-production periods and low in the high-production periods. The use of normal rates would apply the same per-unit overhead costs regardless of month-to-month and year-to-year fluctuations. Both for quoting prices and for pricing inventories, it is best to use per-unit costs neither inflated by the costs of available but unused factory facilities nor deflated by the gains of better-than-normal use of the factory facilities.

The company should use departmental overhead rates because the rates obviously vary so markedly among the departments. If a blanket rate were used as an average rate, it would not be correct for any department. Because the company's overhead is a large part of factory cost, the inaccuracy in the per-unit costs caused by the use of a blanket rate would be substantial. If all the products made used all the departments proportionately, a blanket rate would result in substantially accurate total (but not departmental) unit-overhead costs. However, in the Martin Company, the products do not use all the departments proportionately.

As the wage rates are substantially uniform within the separate departments, the labor costs in each department are closely proportionate to the labor time. Therefore, the percent-of-direct-labor-cost method of applying the factory overhead would in this case effect about as accurate an application as would the rate-per-direct-labor-hour method. The clerical expense of the percent-of-direct-labor-cost method would be low, because the method does not require accumulation of the number of direct-labor hours applicable to each job.

The percent-of-prime-cost method of overhead application is not recommended because of the wide differences in the costs of the materials that may be used to make a given lamp or fixture. Factory overhead is primarily the cost of using factory facilities. The factory facilities applied to make a lamp of silver are not more than those used to make the same lamp of copper. For this reason, the use of prime cost (because it includes material cost) would result in an excessive charge to lamps using expensive materials.

Very truly yours,

questions, problems, and cases

12-1. What is the most important criterion for selecting an overhead base?

12-2. Why are departmental overhead rates generally preferable to plant-wide rates?

12-3. "Service-department costs shouldn't be reapportioned." Do you agree? Why?

12-4. What are the criteria for selecting reapportionment bases for service-department costs?

12-5. "In order to save time and effort, we use a single reapportionment plan to fulfill both product-costing and control purposes." Discuss.

12-6. A prominent economist once said, "Not even Almighty God can tell a railroad the cost of moving a hundred tons of freight from Boston to New York." Do you agree? Why?

12-7. Indirect Costs and Government Contracts.   The president of a large university commented on the previous year's operations as follows:

"I should point out that, if the Congress had not recently reduced the ceiling on indirect-cost recovery in connection with research grants by the Department of Defense and the independent agencies from 25 percent, as it now is for the National Science Foundation and the National Aeronautics and Space Administration, to 20 percent, income for the next academic year would have come close to cancelling the anticipated deficit. This is another way of saying that government research grants require some sharing of the cost from general university funds, for our calculated indirect costs are about 32 percent. In other words, we recover only 63 percent of the true indirect costs."

"How do we obtain these funds? The answer is, through careful planning and hard work on the part of many people, including trustees, officers, deans, chairmen, faculty, the Development Office, the Alumni Fund, and friends of the university."

For example, a research contract that formerly called for $100,000 direct costs plus $25,000, or $125,000, would now be $100,000 plus $20,000, or $120,000.

required Evaluate the president's comments. Do you agree with his analysis? Why, or why not?

12-8. Selection of Most Suitable Application Base. [Prepared by William J. Vatter] The manufacturing operations of this Hong Kong company are highly seasonal; production reaches a peak in April, May, and June of each year. The following are typical data concerning production activities over a year:

	INDIRECT COSTS INCURRED	DIRECT-LABOR COST	DIRECT MAN-HOURS	MACHINE HOURS
January	$ 8,800	$ 8,000	6,500	3,600
February	8,400	7,600	6,200	3,200
March	9,600	8,600	7,400	3,800
April	11,200	10,000	7,800	4,600
May	12,000	11,600	8,100	6,000
June	11,600	12,000	8,500	7,800
July	10,000	9,000	7,500	5,600
August	9,200	8,200	6,800	4,200
September	9,400	8,600	7,200	5,000
October	8,600	7,200	6,300	3,400
November	8,000	6,000	6,000	3,300
December	7,200	4,000	5,000	2,500
	$114,000	$100,800	83,300	53,000

required
1. Prepare predetermined overhead-application rates, using three different bases or methods.

2. For a given batch of product involving direct materials costing $84, direct-labor cost of $72, 40 direct-labor man-hours, and 20 machine-hours, what would be the total cost as assigned by the use of each of the rates computed in requirement 1?

3. Which of these three rates is in your opinion most suitable for establishing the cost of product for purposes of determining income, assuming a constant price level for all cost factors? Why?

12-9. **Cost-Allocation Base and Divisional Performance.** The Foster Company is a large, diversified manufacturer of capital equipment for industry. Its products are sold all over the world.

Two of the divisions of the Foster Company, Divisions A and B, have their manufacturing facilities on the same plant site in a small eastern community. These two divisions are operated on a profit-center basis and make essentially dissimilar products. All the products made by the two divisions are custom-made. They are priced on a cost-plus basis. The desired profit before taxes is 20 percent. The markets for the products of these two divisions are very competitive.

A substantial part of the finished product of Division B consists of a casting manufactured in Division A's foundry. All castings are transferred from Division A to Division B at cost plus the desired margin. The breakdown of costs in the foundry for a job sold to B is as follows:

Direct materials, 20,000 lbs. @ 50¢/lb.	$10,000
Direct labor, 2,500 hours @ $4.00/hour	10,000
Overhead, $4.00 per direct-labor hour	10,000
Total costs	$30,000
Profit (20%)	6,000
Price to Division B	$36,000

Division A also uses castings from its foundry in making other products that are sold directly in other markets. The costs of foundry products incorporated in Division A products are:

Direct materials, 5,000 lbs. @ 50¢/lb.	$ 2,500
Direct labor, 1,000 hours @ $4.00/hour	4,000
Overhead, $4.00 per direct-labor hour	4,000
Total costs	$10,500

Production of these products in the foundry is ten per year of Division B's, and 200 per year of Division A's.

These foundry products are then finished in the separate divisions and sold. The costs for the two divisions beyond the foundry are:

	A	B
Foundry materials	$10,500	$36,000
Additional direct materials	3,500	24,000
Additional labor	3,000	20,000
Division overhead	8,000	10,000
Total costs	$25,000	$90,000
Add: Profit (20%)	5,000	18,000
Selling price	$30,000	$108,000

At these rates all costs are applied; that is, there are no unplanned variances at the end of the year.

The group vice-president called the general managers from Divisions A and B into his office for a review of their operations. During the review, he chided the manager of A for consistently failing to meet the desired profit margins;

as a result, the entire company was failing to meet its goal. The division manager of A explained that it was almost impossible to meet the going market price on most jobs without cutting the price a little.

The division manager of B was praised for consistently being able to generate maximum volume without having to resort to price cutting or any other questionable technique.

When the general manager of A returned to his office, he immediately asked his newly hired assistant to investigate the matter. "Tom," he said, "Our profits aren't high enough. I think it's our costs. I want you to find out what the trouble is."

After reviewing the finishing operations with great care, Tom proceeded to the foundry operations. He discovered something peculiar. The foundry accountant was still charging cast iron at 50¢ a pound, even though the actual cost of iron is 87½¢ a pound. The remaining 37½¢ he includes in overhead, to be applied with the indirect items on a direct-labor-hour basis.

The foundry accountant said, "We set up the 50¢ standard twenty years ago. When the price of iron started to go up, it seemed like too much trouble to change the standard; we just charge the excess off to overhead. I don't see what difference it makes—It all comes out of the same pocket!"

required   Does Tom's discovery help to explain the problem? If so, recast the figures to show what the problem is and what changes should be made in the pricing system.

12-10. **Divisional Contribution, Performance, and Segment Margins.** The president of the Midwestern Railroad wants to obtain an overview of his operations, particularly with respect to comparing freight and passenger business. He has heard about some new "contribution" approaches to cost allocations that emphasize cost behavior patterns and so-called *contribution margins*, contribution controllable by division managers, and contribution by segments. Pertinent data for the year ended December 31, 19_2, follow:

Total revenue was $100 million, of which $90 million was freight traffic and $10 million was passenger traffic. Half the latter was generated by Division 1; 40 percent by Division 2; and 10 percent by Division 3.

Total variable costs were $56 million, of which $44 million was freight traffic. Of the $12 million allocable to passenger traffic, $4.4, $3.7, and $3.9 million could be allocated to Divisions 1, 2, and 3, respectively.

Total separable discretionary fixed costs were $10 million, of which $9.5 million applied to freight traffic. Of the remainder, $100,000 could not be allocated to specific divisions, although it was clearly traceable to passenger traffic in general. Divisions 1, 2, and 3 should be allocated $300,000, $70,000, and $30,000, respectively.

Total separable committed costs were $30 million, of which 90 percent was allocable to freight traffic. Of the 10 percent traceable to passenger traffic, Divisions 1, 2, and 3 should be allocated $1,800,000, $420,000, and $180,000, respectively; the balance was unallocable to a specific division.

The joint fixed costs not clearly allocable to any part of the company amounted to $1,000,000.

required   1. The president asks you to prepare statements, dividing the data for the company as a whole between the freight and passenger traffic and then subdividing the passenger traffic into three divisions.

2. Some competing railroads actively promote a series of one-day sightseeing tours on summer weekends. Most often, these tours are timed so that the

cars with the tourists are hitched on with regularly scheduled passenger trains.

What costs are relevant for making decisions to run such tours? Other railroads, facing the same general cost picture, refuse to conduct such sightseeing tours. Why?

3. For purposes of this analysis, even though the numbers may be unrealistic, suppose that Division No. 2's figures represented a specific run for a train instead of a division. Suppose further that the railroad has petitioned government authorities for permission to drop No. 2. What would be the effect on overall company net income for 19_3, assuming that the figures are accurate and that 19_3 operations are in all other respects a duplication of 19_2 operations?

12-11. **Contribution Approach to Cost Allocation: Income Statement by Segments.** Stuart Philatelic Sales, Inc., is engaged in the business of selling postage stamps and supplies to collectors on a retail basis. Stuart also makes up packets of inexpensive stamps that it sells on a wholesale basis to stamp departments of five-and-ten-cent stores.

Stuart's retail division has two stores, A and B, each of which has a stamp department and an albums and supplies department. Stuart had total net sales in 19_4 of $960,000; cost of merchandise sold was $490,000; and variable operating expenses were $120,000. The company's nonvariable costs, which it fully allocated to its two divisions, were $105,000 of advertising expense and $120,000 of various commented costs. Stuart's joint discretionary and committed costs were $35,000.

The costs of merchandise sold and variable operating expenses allocated to the retail division were $190,000 and $50,000, respectively. Net sales of Retail were $390,000, two-thirds of which were Store A's net sales. Sixty percent of Retail's merchandise costs and 54 percent of its variable operating expenses were allocated to Store A. Advertising costs of $40,000 were allocated to Retail, which in turn allocated 45 percent directly to Store A and 5 percent to Store B; the rest of the $40,000 was unallocated. Of the $120,000 separable committed costs, 50 percent were allocated to Retail, which in turn allocated 50 percent of its committed costs to Store A, had $25,000 of unallocated costs, and allocated the rest to Store B.

Other information:

(1) Allocations to Store B—stamp department:

Net sales	$100,000
Cost of merchandise sold	$ 58,000
Variable operating expenses	$ 17,000

Allocations to Store B—Albums and Supplies Department:

Net sales	$ 30,000
Cost of merchandise sold	$ 18,000
Variable operating expenses	$ 6,000

(2) One-half of Store B's allocated advertising expenses could not be further allocated either to Stamps or to Albums and Supplies; the other half of B's allocated advertising expenses was equally divided between the two departments.

(3) Sixty percent of Store B's committed costs were unallocated; three-fourths of the rest was allocated to the stamp department and one-fourth to the albums and supplies department.

required

1. What was operating income before taxes for the company as a whole?

2. Determine the contribution margin, contribution controllable by division managers and contribution by segments for each of the following:
   a. Company as a whole
   b. Wholesale division
   c. Retail division
   d. Store A of the retail division
   e. Store B of the retail division
   f. Stamps department of Store B
   g. Albums and supplies department of Store B

12-12. Cost Allocation and Choosing the Most Profitable Product.   The Poesch Company produces a range of products in its decentralized divisions. All these products utilize a special fireproofing agent patented by the company.

William Poesch, the president, and Ralph Morton, the controller, helped start PC twenty-two years ago. One day, they were deeply engrossed in discussion about several papers on Poesch's desk. Among the papers were a budgeted income statement (Exhibit 12-10) and some supporting calculations showing manufacturing-overhead allocations (Exhibit 12-11).

"Ralph, I just don't see how we can be in such bad shape in Division B! That dry wall is selling beyond expectations, but we still project a loss for the year. . . . It's shattering!" said Poesch in dismay.

Morton replied, "I thought it might be the overhead allocations, but I've checked them a half-dozen times. I just can't see anything wrong. It's the same basic formula we have used for seventeen years. Because our manufacturing overhead is related to sales volume and space for manufacturing and storage, I certainly think we are getting a fair measure of relative profitability. I admit

EXHIBIT 12-10

POESCH COMPANY

Budgeted Income Statement for Next Fiscal Year
(*In Thousands of Dollars*)

		DIVISION				
	A	B	C	D	E	TOTAL COMPANY
Net sales	2,050	4,500	5,200	2,250	4,500	18,500
Less manufacturing cost of goods sold*	1,700	4,400	4,950	1,800	4,000	16,850
Gross profit	350	100	250	450	500	1,650
Less selling, administration, and corporate research expenses*	62	159	111	159	109	600
Operating income	288	(59)	139	291	391	1,050

*For details of these costs and expenses, see Exhibit 12-11.

DIVISION CODE	PRODUCT
A	Fire rated wallpaper
B	Four hour rated dry wall
C	"Fireguard" business forms
D	"Safelon" paper garment fabric
E	"Safetrim" Christmas trees

EXHIBIT 12-11

ANALYSIS OF COSTS AND EXPENSES

A. Manufacturing Cost of Goods (in thousands of dollars):

	DIVISION					TOTAL COMPANY
	A	B	C	D	E	
Direct materials and direct labor	1,050	3,150	4,250	1,500	3,750	13,700
Fixed overhead*	650	1,250	700	300	250	3,150
Total cost of goods sold	1,700	4,400	4,950	1,800	4,000	16,850

*Fixed overhead is allocated on the basis of sales revenue as well as that of manufacturing and storage space. An estimate is made of the overhead items most closely associated with either of these parameters, and they are allocated in proportion to the relative sales revenues and space requirements per division. The formula used for these distributions was as follows:

Fixed-Overhead Allocation = $.05 per dollar of sales revenue + $.06 per square-foot-day of storage and manufacturing-space usage

Fixed-overhead costs associated primarily with usage of space: $2,224,000
Total square-foot-day usage: 102,772 sq. ft. × 365 days = 37,083,333 sq. ft. days
  Allocation rate = $2,224,000 ÷ 37,083,333 = $.06 per sq. ft. day
Fixed-overhead costs associated primarily with sales revenue: $926,000
Total anticipated sales revenue: $18,500,000
  Allocation rate = $926,000 ÷ $18,500,000 = $.05 per dollar of sales

Summary of allocation of fixed manufacturing overhead (some figures are rounded):

	DIVISION					TOTAL COMPANY
	A	B	C	D	E	
1. Expected sales*	$ 2,050	$ 4,500	$ 5,200	$2,250	$4,500	$ 18,500
2. Space required (in sq. ft.)	25,000	46,804	20,091	8,562	2,315	102,772
3. Days used per year	365	365	365	365	180	—
4. Space-days used (line 2 × line 3)*	9,125	17,083	7,333	3,124	422	37,083
5. Overhead based on space ($.06 × line 4)*	$ 547	$ 1,025	$ 440	$ 187	$ 25	$ 2,224
6. Overhead based on sales ($.05 × line 1)*	103	225	260	113	225	926
Total fixed manufacturing overhead	$ 650	$ 1,250	$ 700	$ 300	$ 250	$ 3,150

*000's omitted.

B. Allocation of Administrative, Selling, and Corporate Research Expenses (in thousands of dollars):

	DIVISION					TOTAL COMPANY
	A	B	C	D	E	
Variable costs	30	90	30	120	40	310
Fixed costs**	32	69	81	39	69	290
Total	62	159	111	159	109	600

**Fixed costs are allocated in proportion to anticipated sales revenue for each division. The allocation rate is $290,000 ÷ $18,500,000 = $.01567 per dollar of sales.

that it's difficult to make allocations because we are all in the same building and use certain facilities in common."

Poesch asked, "Have you been able to use that new business-school graduate who is supposed to get a better handle on costs attributable specifically to each of the divisions?"

Morton exclaimed, "He's trying, but it's a messy problem! I have one of his working papers here [Exhibit 12-12]. He has $1,180,000 of fixed costs that he doesn't know what to do with. He has manufacturing, selling and administration, and research all mixed up. Bill, I know he is trying, but I guess these management schools just don't train them to do a decent job of cost allocation."

At that moment there was an impatient knock on the door. The corporate marketing manager and the central purchasing agent burst into the room. The purchasing agent said, "Chambers Chemical just went on strike! The trade says that it's likely to last for three or four months. We don't have a second source for our fireproofing agent, and our inventories just won't carry us at full production volume on all our lines. We're going to have to ration materials to our divisions."

Poesch examined the budgeted income statement on his desk. He looked up and said, "It looks as though we'll have to start cutting back on the dry-wall production in Division B."

required

Do you agree with Mr. Poesch? Support your conclusion with any necessary calculations. Assume that the data in Exhibit 12-12 are correct. Identify any other major factors related to the economics of this decision that should be considered. How would you include them in the analysis?

EXHIBIT 12-12

PRELIMINARY ANALYSIS OF FIXED COSTS

Following is a preliminary analysis of the fixed costs incurred by the Poesch Company as projected for the next fiscal year. It was found that some of the costs could be directly assigned to various divisions. Others could not be directly identified with the activities of any given division and these are simply aggregated.

A. Costs associated with designated division (in thousands of dollars):

	DIVISION					TOTAL COMPANY
	A	B	C	D	E	
Discretionary fixed costs (Promotion, advertising, research, engineering, supervisory salaries)	325	240	340	175	265	1,345
Other fixed costs (Depreciation on equipment, insurance, division manager's salary)	175	425	215	75	25	915

B. Costs that could not be clearly assigned to any one of the divisions. Examples include general corporate advertising (image-type), which has been maintained at the same general level for several years; long-range corporate research; salaries of corporate management; central accounting activities; and legal services to corporate management.   1,180

    Total fixed costs for the company   3,440

12-13. Reapportion Service-Department Costs. The X Company has prepared departmental overhead budgets for normal activity levels before reapportionments, as follows:

Building and grounds	$ 10,000
Personnel	1,000
General factory administration*	26,090
Cafeteria—operating loss	1,640
Storeroom	2,670
Machining	34,700
Assembly	48,900
	$125,000

* To be reapportioned before cafeteria.

Management has decided that the most sensible product costs are achieved by using departmental overhead rates. These rates are developed after appropriate service-department costs are reapportioned to production departments. Bases for reapportionment are to be selected from the following:

DEPARTMENT	DIRECT-LABOR HOURS	NUMBER OF EMPLOYEES	SQUARE FEET OF FLOOR SPACE OCCUPIED	TOTAL LABOR-HOURS	NUMBER OF REQUISITIONS
Building & grounds	—	—	—		
Personnel*	—	—	2,000	—	
General factory administration		35	7,000	—	
Cafeteria— operating loss		10	4,000	1,000	
Storeroom		5	7,000	1,000	
Machining	5,000	50	30,000	8,000	2,000
Assembly	15,000	100	50,000	17,000	1,000
	20,000	200	100,000	27,000	3,000

* Basis used is number of employees.

required

1. Using a worksheet, reapportion service-department costs by the step method. Develop overhead rates per direct-labor hour for machining and assembly.
2. Same as in 1, using the direct method.
3. What would be the blanket plant-wide factory-overhead application rate, assuming that direct-labor hours are used as a base?
4. Using the following information about two jobs, prepare three different total-overhead costs for each job, using rates developed in 1, 2, and 3 above.

	DIRECT-LABOR HOURS	
	MACHINING	ASSEMBLY
Job 88	18	2
Job 89	3	17

12-14. Comparison of Departmental and Plant-wide Overhead Rates [CGAA]. The Sayther Company manufactured two products, A and B, during the first year of its operations. For purposes of product costing, an overhead rate of application of $1.70 per direct-labor hour was used, based on budgeted factory overhead of $340,000 and 200,000 budgeted direct-labor hours, as shown below:

	BUDGETED OVERHEAD	BUDGETED HOURS
Department 1	$240,000	100,000
Department 2	100,000	100,000
Total	$340,000	200,000

The number of labor hours required to manufacture each of these products was:

	PRODUCT A	PRODUCT B
In Department 1	4	1
In Department 2	1	4
Total	5	5

At the end of the year, there was no work in process and there were 2,000 and 6,000 finished units, respectively, of products A and B on hand. Assume that budgeted activity was attained.

required

1. What was the effect on the company's income of using a plant-wide overhead rate instead of departmental overhead rates?

2. Assume that material and labor costs per unit of Product A are $10 and that the selling price is established by adding 40 percent to factory-overhead costs to cover profit and selling and administrative expenses. What difference in selling price would result from the use of departmental overhead rates?

3. Explain briefly but clearly why departmental overhead rates are generally preferable to plant-wide rates.

12-15. Reapportionment; Departmental versus Plant-wide Applications. The following are pertinent data for the Alou Company:

BUDGET DATA FOR 19_7	(S1) FACTORY PERSONNEL	(S2) PRODUCTION PLANNING AND CONTROL	(P1) MACHINING	(P2) ASSEMBLY
Estimated overhead	$51,000	$198,500	$2,235,500	$755,000
Machine-hours			300,000	—
Direct-labor hours			40,000	500,000
Orders to be processed			8,000	2,000
Number of employees		10	30	300

Factory personnel-department costs are to be reapportioned on the basis of number of employees; production planning and control, on the basis of orders processed. The step basis is used for reapportionment.

This company produces a wide variety of products on a job-order basis. Management has always used a single, plant-wide overhead application rate based on direct-labor hours.

Recently, however, customer complaints on price quotations, plus the outside auditor's criticism of the plant-wide rate, has prompted management to ask you, the controller, to restudy the situation before setting rates for 19_7.

You decide that departmental overhead rates should be developed, at least as a method of attack. You think that a machine-hour rate should be used for the machining department, which contains costly automatic and semiautomatic equipment manned by a few workers who tend and control many machines simultaneously.

The workers may operate a couple of machines at a time on certain jobs, and as many as six machines or more on other jobs. Because the assembly department requires painstaking workmanship but little equipment, you think that direct-labor hours is the most proper overhead base there.

The budget data for 19_7 are little different from those for 19_6, so you pick five representative jobs worked on during December 19_6 as a basis for comparing the blanket rate with departmental rates. You keep careful records of machine-hours as well as of the direct-labor hours. The results follow:

	MACHINING		ASSEMBLY
JOB NUMBER	MACHINE-HOURS	DLH	DLH
300	5	2	10
301	40	4	40
302	10	2	30
303	7	1	5
304	15	11	30

required

(Show and label computations)

1. Departmental overhead rates.

2. Plant-wide rate.

3. A detailed summary by jobs of (a) total overhead applied, using departmental rates; (b) total overhead applied, using a plant-wide rate; (c) difference between (a) and (b).

4. What is the total difference for the jobs taken together?

5. What overhead application base would you recommend? Why?

12-16. Allocation of Travel Costs.   Joseph Lowell, a graduating senior at a university near San Francisco, received an invitation to visit a prospective employer in Lansing, Michigan. A few days later, he received a second invitation to visit another prospective employer in New York. The following day he received a similar invitation to visit Chicago. He decided to combine the visits, traveling from San Francisco to Chicago to Lansing to New York to San Francisco.

He received job offers from all three locations. Upon his return, he decided to accept the Chicago offer. Joseph was puzzled about how to allocate his travel costs among the three prospective employers. He gathered the following information:

Round-trip sedan service, Menlo Park to San Francisco airport	$ 18
Regular round-trip fares from San Francisco to:	
Lansing	270
New York	326
Chicago	246
Actual airfare paid	340

required

How much should each employer pay for Lowell's travel costs? Why? Explain. Show computations.

12-17. **Cost Allocation Among Stores [CPA].** Thrift-Shops, Inc., operates a chain of three food stores in a state that recently enacted legislation permitting municipalities within the state to levy an income tax on corporations operating within their respective municipalities. The legislation establishes a uniform tax rate that the municipalities may levy, and regulations that provide that the tax is to be computed on income derived within the taxing municipality after a reasonable and consistent allocation of general-overhead expenses. General-overhead expenses have not been allocated to individual stores previously and include warehouse, general office, advertising, and delivery expenses.

Each of the municipalities in which Thrift-Shops, Inc., operates a store has levied the corporate income tax as provided by state legislation, and management is considering two plans for allocating general-overhead expenses to the stores. The 19_9 operating results before general overhead and taxes for each store were:

	STORE			
	ASHVILLE	BURNS	CLINTON	TOTAL
Sales, net	$416,000	$353,600	$270,400	$1,040,000
Less cost of sales	215,700	183,300	140,200	539,200
Gross margin	200,300	170,300	130,200	500,800
Less local operating expenses:				
Fixed	60,800	48,750	50,200	159,750
Variable	54,700	64,220	27,448	146,368
Total	115,500	112,970	77,648	306,118
Income before general overhead and taxes	$ 84,800	$ 57,330	$ 52,552	$ 194,682

General-overhead expenses in 19_9 were as follows:

Warehousing and delivery expenses:		
Warehouse depreciation	$20,000	
Warehouse operations	30,000	
Delivery expenses	40,000	$ 90,000
Central-office expenses:		
Advertising	18,000	
Central-office salaries	37,000	
Other central-office expenses	28,000	83,000
Total general overhead		$173,000

Additional information includes the following:

a. One-fifth of the warehouse space is used to house the central office, and depreciation on this space is included in Other Central-Office Expenses. Warehouse operating expenses vary with quantity of merchandise sold.

b. Delivery expenses vary with distance and number of deliveries. The distances from the warehouse to each store and the number of deliveries made in 19_9 were as follows:

STORE	MILES	NUMBER OF DELIVERIES
Ashville	120	140
Burns	200	64
Clinton	100	104

c. All advertising is prepared by the central office and is distributed in the areas in which stores are located.

d. As each store was opened, the fixed portion of central-office salaries increased by $7,000 and other central-office expenses increased by $2,500. Basic fixed central-office salaries amount to $10,000, and basic fixed other central-office expenses amount to $12,000. The remainder of central-office salaries and the remainder of other central-office expenses vary with sales.

required

1. For each of the following plans for allocating general-overhead expenses, compute the income of each store that would be subject to the municipal levy on corporation income:

Plan 1. Allocate all general-overhead expenses on the basis of sales volume.

Plan 2. First, allocate central-office salaries and other central-office expenses evenly to warehouse operations and each store. Second, allocate the resulting warehouse-operations expenses, warehouse depreciation, and advertising to each store on the basis of sales volume. Third, allocate delivery expenses to each store on the basis of delivery miles times number of deliveries.

2. Management has decided to expand one of the three stores to increase sales by $50,000. The expansion will increase local fixed operating expenses by $7,500 and require ten additional deliveries from the warehouse. Determine which store management should select for expansion to maximize corporate profits.

12-18. Allocation of Advertising [SIA].   The H Company allocates national magazine advertising cost to territories on the basis of circulation, weighted by an index that measures relative buying power in the territories. Does this method give cost and profit figures appropriate for the following decisions? Indicate clearly why or why not.

1. For deciding whether or not to close an unprofitable territory
2. For deciding whether or not a territorial manager has obtained sufficient sales volume
3. For determining how efficiently the territorial manager has operated his territory
4. For determining whether or not advertising costs are being satisfactorily controlled

12-19. Retailing and Costs for Decision Making [CPA].   You have a client who operates a large retail self-service grocery store that has a full range of departments. The management has encountered difficulty in using accounting data as a basis for decisions as to possible changes in departments operated, products, marketing methods, and so forth. List several overhead costs, or costs not applicable to a particular department, and explain how the existence of such costs (sometimes called *common costs* or *joint costs*) complicates and limits the use of accounting data in making decisions in such a store.

12-20. Cost of Servicing a Bank Account [CPA].   A bank stated that the service charge it makes on accounts is based upon the cost of handling each account. A customer states that he does not see how it is possible to determine the cost of handling his account. Do you agree?

Discuss fully the problems involved in determining cost for such a service, including the limitations of the cost figures obtained.

12-21. Analysis of Channels of Distribution and Territories.   The Manning Co. has three sales territories that sell a single product. Its income statement for 19_2 contained the following data:

	TOTAL	A	B	C
			TERRITORY	
Sales: 100,000 units, @ $11	$1,100,000	$550,000	$330,000	$220,000
Cost of goods sold, including $100,000 of fixed factory overhead	500,000	250,000	150,000	100,000
Gross margin	$ 600,000	$300,000	$180,000	$120,000
Order-filling costs:				
Freight out	$ 68,000	$ 34,000	$ 20,400	$ 13,600
Shipping supplies	50,000	25,000	15,000	10,000
Packing and shipping labor	50,000	25,000	15,000	10,000
Total	$ 168,000	$ 84,000	$ 50,400	$ 33,600
Order-getting costs:				
Salesmen's salaries	$ 50,000	$ 50,000		
Salesmen's commissions	26,400		$ 26,400	
Agents' commissions	11,000			$ 11,000
Sales manager's salary	30,000	15,000	9,000	6,000
Advertising, local	80,000	40,000	24,000	16,000
Advertising, national	100,000	50,000	30,000	20,000
Total	$ 297,400	$155,000	$ 89,400	$ 53,000
Total marketing costs	$ 465,400	$239,000	$139,800	$ 86,600
Administrative expenses:				
Variable	$ 50,000	$ 25,000	$ 15,000	$ 10,000
Nonvariable	100,000	50,000	30,000	20,000
Total administrative expense	$ 150,000	$ 75,000	$ 45,000	$ 30,000
Total expenses	$ 615,400	$314,000	$184,800	$116,600
Net operating income	$ (15,400)	$(14,000)	$ (4,800)	$ 3,400

Territory A contains the company's only factory and central headquarters. This district employs five salaried salesmen.

Territory B is 200 to 400 miles from the factory. The district employs three salesmen on a commission basis and advertises weekly, locally.

Territory C is 400 to 600 miles from the factory. The district employs three manufacturers' agents. Local advertising costs are split fifty-fifty between the agents and the company. Cost per unit of advertising space is the same as in Territory A.

The following variable unit costs have been computed:

Freight out, per unit	$.50, $.70, and $1.10, for Territories A, B, and C, respectively
Shipping supplies, per unit	.50
Packing and shipping labor, per unit	.50
Variable administrative cost, per sales order	2.00

Territory A had 17,000 orders; Territory B, 6,000; and Territory C, 2,000. Local advertising costs were $60,000, $15,000, and $5,000, for Territories A, B, and C, respectively.

required

1. Mr. Manning asks you to recast the income statement in accordance with the contribution approach that he heard described at a recent sales conven-

tion. Assume that fixed manufacturing overhead, national advertising, the sales manager's salary, and nonvariable administrative expense are not allocated?

2. What is the contribution by territory per order in each territory? What clues for management investigation are generated by such a computation?

3. The salesmen in Territory B have suggested a saturation campaign in local newspaper advertising, to cost $30,000. How much must the sales volume in Territory B increase to justify such an additional investment?

4. Why does Territory A have the highest contribution-margin percentage but the lowest territorial-margin percentage?

5. On the basis of the given data, what courses of action seem most likely to improve profits? Should Territory A be dropped? Why?

12-22. Control of Service-Department Costs. The Hotpoint Company, a division of General Electric, is operated on a "departmental" basis. The principal departments involved in this accounting situation are:

Plant 1, Production of washers and dryers
Plant 2, Production of ranges, ovens, etc.
Plant 3, Production of component parts
Plant 6, Relations and Utilities Department
Plant 8, Production of refrigerators

The production departments are self-explanatory. The purpose of the R&U department centers around ownership of office building, maintenance of buildings and machines, and production of steam. When employees of R&U perform work for a productive department, R&U bills the productive department. Against these billings, R&U incurs costs for plumbers, electricians, carpenters, and so forth.

Being a service department as opposed to a productive department, R&U does not generate income as ordinarily conceived. The book profit or loss remaining at the end of the year is reapportioned to the production departments.

The relations and utilities department usually presented a problem to the production departments. In some instances, similar work could be contracted for with outside vendors for less cost. The executives of the R&U department maintained that they were required to have a standby maintenance crew for emergencies. They also maintained that, if their charges were slightly high, any book profits were redistributed to the production departments.

Against this background, the accounting problems that arose concerned the production of steam. R&U accumulated all the costs relative to steam in one account. The credits to this account arose when the production departments were billed for the steam.

The production of steam presented a slightly unique problem. A group of men were assigned to the steam facilities. A few men were "floaters." These men worked at various boiler rooms during the course of the week. In summer, when less steam was required, these men supposedly maintained the equipment, although the maintenance work was never recorded.

The production departments had the following accounting procedure for all utility expenses. The utility expenses *including steam* were accumulated in a clearing account. This account was credited and manufacturing operations were charged during the year based on units produced or budgeted.

The R&U department had a similar accounting procedure for accumulating steam costs. All steam costs incurred were also accumulated in a clearing account. The R&U clearing account was credited when the production departments were billed for their steam usage. At year-end, the R&U clearing-account balance was apportioned to the production departments.

The problem encountered with the present accounting procedure was control. Steam costs, which included labor (firemen), gas, oil, water, depreciation, maintenance, and so forth, amounted to one million dollars a year.

The R&U department constructed a very general budget or schedule of steam costs to be incurred during the coming year. The amount of steam to be produced was estimated based on prior years. The production departments followed the same pattern. Utility costs in their budget were based on prior years.

At year-end, the manufacturing operations absorbed the over- or under-absorbed utility and steam expenses. If the clearing account was overabsorbed, everyone was happy and no questions were asked. If the clearing account was underabsorbed, it was chalked up to experience.

required How do you control such costs? Is a nonprofit service department desirable? Would you make any organizational or accounting changes in the current setup?

12-23. Using revenue as a basis for allocating costs.   The Mideastern Transportation Company has had a long-standing policy of fully allocating all costs to its various divisions. Among the costs allocated were general and administrative costs in central headquarters, consisting of office salaries, executive salaries, travel expense, accounting costs, office supplies, donations, rents, depreciation, postage, and similar items.

All these costs were difficult to trace directly to the individual divisions benefited, so they were allocated on the basis of the total revenue of each of the divisions. The same basis was used for allocating general advertising and miscellaneous selling costs. For example, in 19_3 the following allocations were made:

	DIVISIONS			
	A	B	C	TOTAL
Revenue (in millions)	$50.0	$40.0	$10.0	$100.0
Costs allocated on the basis of revenue	6.0	4.8	1.2	12.0

In 19_4, Division A's revenue was expected to rise. But the division encountered severe competitive conditions; its revenue remained at $50 million. In contrast, Division C enjoyed explosive growth in traffic because of the completion of several huge factories in its area; its revenue rose to $30 million. Division B's revenue remained unchanged. Careful supervision kept the total costs allocated on the basis of revenue at $12 million.

required 1. What costs will be allocated to each division in 19_4?

2. Using the results in part 1, comment on the limitations of using revenue as a basis for cost allocation.

12-24. Reallocation of costs.   The Trans Company has two operating departments (A and B) and one service department. The actual monthly costs of the service department are reallocated on the basis of the net ton-miles operated. The budgeted cost behavior pattern of the service department is $200,000 monthly plus $.50 per 1,000 ton-miles operated in Departments A and B.

1. In May, the Trans Company handled 300 million ton-miles of traffic, half in each operating department. The actual costs of the service department were precisely as budgeted. How much cost would be reallocated to each department?

2. Suppose that in part 1, Department B handled only 90 million ton-miles instead of 150 million. Department A handled 150 million ton-miles. Also suppose that the actual costs of the service department were precisely as budgeted for this lower level of activity. How much cost would be reallocated to each department?

3. Suppose that in part 1, the actual costs of the service department were $420,000 because of various inefficiencies and unfavorable but controllable rate or price changes in various items. How much cost would be reallocated to each department? Does such reallocation seem justified? If not, what improvement in the reallocation procedure would you suggest?

4. Suppose that various investment outlays for space and equipment in the service department were made to provide a basic maximum capacity to serve other departments, under the assumption that Department A would operate at a maximum monthly level of 160 million ton-miles and Department B at a level of 200 million ton-miles. In part 2, suppose fixed costs are reallocated via a predetermined monthly lump sum for providing a basic maximum capacity to serve; variable costs are reallocated via a predetermined standard unit rate per 1,000 ton-miles. How much cost would be reallocated to each department? What are the advantages of this method over other methods?

12-25. Dual reallocation. The power plant that services all factory departments has a budget for the forthcoming year. This budget has been expressed in the following terms, for a normal month:

	KILOWATT HOURS	
FACTORY DEPARTMENTS	NEEDED AT PRACTICAL CAPACITY PRODUCTION VOLUME*	AVERAGE EXPECTED MONTHLY USAGE
A	10,000	8,000
B	20,000	9,000
X	12,000	7,000
Y	8,000	6,000
Totals	50,000	30,000

*This was the most influential factor in planning the size of the power plant.

The expected monthly costs for operating the department during the budget year are $15,000—$6,000 variable and $9,000 fixed.

What dollar amounts should be reapportioned to each department? Show three different sets of answers. Which method do you prefer? Why?

12-26. Evaluating a reallocation method. The Daden Company has a service department that provides production departments with power. The budget for the power department was based on its normal anticipated monthly activity of providing power for 17,000 machine-hours at a total cost of $8,500, or $.50 per hour. The consuming departments had the following characteristics:

	PRODUCTION DEPARTMENT			
	A	B	C	TOTAL
Practical capacity in machine-hours	7,000	10,000	3,000	20,000
Normal activity in machine-hours	6,000	8,500	2,500	17,000
Actual activity in October— machine-hours actually used	6,000	5,000	2,700	13,700
Standard machine-hours allowed for the output produced in October	5,500	5,000	2,800	13,300

The *budget* allowance for the production departments was based on the 50-cent rate times the standard machine-hours allowed for the output produced. However, the *actual* costs incurred by the service department were fully allocated monthly to each production department on the basis of the actual hours consumed by the production departments.

The service department incurred actual costs of $8,220 in October.

required

1. Using the company's method of cost allocation, prepare a performance report for each production department, showing the amounts budgeted, the actual amounts incurred, and the variances. Use *U* or *F* to indicate whether each variance is unfavorable or favorable. Explain the meaning of the variance as reported by dividing each variance into two or more subparts in columnar fashion and commenting on the significance of your variance analysis.

2. This information should *not* be used in answering the previous part. A study of the power costs showed that efficient operation of the service department should result in total costs of $8,900 at a level of 19,000 machine-hours. Using this as well as the previous information, show how you would improve on the way the Daden Company allocates its power costs to its production departments. Give a complete illustration of how the allocations would be made for October, including a presentation of budgeted costs, actual costs, and variances by department. Explain fully why your suggested method is better.

12-27. Reciprocal Cost Allocations and Sensitivity of Results. The Manes Company has two main products, X and Y, each of which is produced in a separate department. In order to produce X and Y, the Manes Company has two major service departments, A and B (for the sake of discussion, a material-handling department and a power-generating department, respectively).

An analysis of the work done by Departments A and B in a typical period follows:

SOURCE	USER				TOTAL UNITS OF WORK DONE
	A	B	X	Y	
Material handling (Dept. A)	0	20	50	30	100
Power (Dept. B)	50	0	10	40	100

The costs of departments during this typical period are stated below:

	A	B
Variable labor and material costs	$ 7,000	$1,000
Supervision	1,000	1,000
Depreciation	2,000	2,000
	$10,000	$4,000
	+ Power costs	+ Material-handling costs

Supervisory costs represent salary costs. Depreciation in B represents the straight-line depreciation of power-generation equipment in its nineteenth year of an estimated 25-year life; it is old but well-maintained equipment.

required

1. What are the allocations of costs of Departments A and B to X and Y using the direct method, two different sequences of the step method, and the reciprocal method of reallocation?

2. The power company has offered to supply all the power needed by the Manes Company and to provide all the services of the present power department. The cost of this will be $40 per unit. Should Manes accept?

12-28. Reciprocal Cost Allocations.   [Prepared by David Green, Jr.] The Prairie State Paper Company located a plant near one of its forests. At the time of construction, there were no utility companies equipped to provide this plant with water, power, or fuel. Therefore, included in the original facilities were (1) a water plant, which pumped water from a nearby lake and filtered it; (2) a coal-fired boiler room that produced steam, part of which was used for the manufacturing process and the balance for producing electricity; and (3) an electric plant.

An analysis of these activities has revealed that 60 percent of the water is used for the production of steam and 40 percent is used in manufacturing. Half of the steam produced is used for the production of electric power and half for manufacturing. Twenty percent of the electric power is used by the water plant and 80 percent goes to manufacturing.

For the year 19_9, the costs charged to these departments were:

	VARIABLE	FIXED	TOTAL
Water plant	$ 2,000	$ 8,000	$10,000
Steam room	18,000	12,000	30,000
Electric plant	6,000	9,000	15,000
			$55,000

required

1. How would you allocate these costs in a typical product-cost determination situation?

2. A new power company has offered to sell electricity to Prairie State for two cents a kilowatt-hour. In 19_9, the electric plant generated 600,000 kilowatt-hours. The manager of the electric plant has advised that the offer be rejected, since (he says) "our variable costs were only one cent per kilowatt-hour in 19_9." Was this the right answer? Show computations.

12-29. Allocation of Computer Costs.   Salquist, Inc., is an international ethical pharmaceutical manufacturer that specializes in hormone research and the development and marketing of hormone-base products. The 22 different wholly owned subsidiaries and separate divisions that comprise the organization are highly decentralized, but they receive overall direction from a small corporate staff at parent-corporation headquarters in Palo Alto. The laboratories division, research division, and all corporate offices are located at the home-office site. Each of the divisional functional areas operates as a cost center. That is, labs accounting, labs production, labs sales, research accounting, and research operations are separate cost centers. Corporate purchasing, employee relations, office services, and computer (EDP) systems also function as individual cost centers, and they provide their services to Research, Labs, and the other divisions as necessary.

Until recently, no costs of the corporate service cost centers were allocated to the divisional cost centers; they were simply lumped together as central corporate overhead. Recently, however, it was decided to start charging the operating units (that is, the cost centers) for their EDP usage. Prior to this time, EDP services were simply requested as desired by the cost centers; priorities were determined by negotiations, with ultimate recourse to an EDP control committee (each cost center was represented); and all charges were absorbed as corporate overhead.

EDP systems comprise both systems programming services and computer operations. In the current "charge-back" system, the EDP director prepares a budget at the start of each quarter based upon his estimates of user demand. Using full absorption costing, he then computes an hourly charge rate, which he promulgates to the user cost centers. The users prepare their budgets utilizing his charge rate and their estimates of the services they think they will be needing. When a user desires to undertake any specific project or use EDP services, he negotiates an agreement with EDP on the hours (thus cost) that he will be charged. The user is free to reject the EDP "bid" and obtain outside services if he does not feel the EDP job estimates are reasonable. Also, since many projects last a year or more but service agreements are arranged on a quarterly basis, the user can drop a project in midstream at the end of a quarter if his overall budget should become too tight. If the actual hours needed to complete a given job exceed those contracted for, the EDP center must absorb the extra cost as an unfavorable overhead variance.

The performance of all cost centers is evaluated on the basis of how closely their actual results match budget. Thus the EDP director must not only assure that his actual expenditures coincide with those that were budgeted, but that he is able to bill other centers for all his actual charges. He must be sure that he contracts for enough projects from the users to absorb his budget.

The shift to the charge-back method was imposed by the corporate financial vice-president for the "purpose of putting control and responsibility for expenditures where the benefits are received." The VP also felt the move was necessary to avoid a "mushrooming of the EDP group" and to make users more aware of the costs they were incurring. An additional factor mentioned was an almost irresistible tide of "allocationism" prevalent in local industry because of the overpowering influence of government contracting there. He does feel he will resist allocating the other services, however, with the possible exception of printing and reproduction, which has grown to be quite costly in the last few years. The major rationale for not allocating the other services is that they are all uniform, predictable functions, whereas the EDP services are more spasmodic and project-oriented.

The head of the EDP group is strongly opposed to the new system. He believes that there is "too much lip service paid to the specialized nature of computers" and that the new system is reducing the effectiveness of the EDP group to the corporation as a whole. He and several of the user–directors believe the shift was simply a political maneuver on the part of the VP to consolidate the EDP empire under the aegis of the corporate staff. The head of the EDP group believes a nonchargeable system administered by the EDP control committee would yield better results.

required

1. What are the motivational and operational effects of this change on users, EDP group, and corporation?

2. Evaluate the impact of having coexistence of allocated and nonallocated services.

3. Evaluate the operation of this particular allocation system.

13

Cost Analysis and Capital Budgeting

Should we add a product? Should we buy the new equipment? Should we delete a division? Managers often use information provided by accountants to guide nonrecurring decisions having a long-range impact on the organization. These are frequently called capital-budgeting decisions. In recent years, new decision models have been used for capital budgeting. These models have incorporated the time value of money; they represent a sharp departure from the conventional accounting models so widely used previously.

The manager and the accountant should understand the uses and limitations of the various decision models for capital budgeting. Most important, managers should particularly recognize the basic incompatibility between the discounted cash-flow models for decisions and the conventional accounting models so often used for the evaluation of the results of those decisions. Let us examine and compare these models.

CONTRASTS IN PURPOSES OF COST ANALYSIS

At this stage, we again focus on purpose. Income determination and the planning and controlling of operations primarily have a *current time-period* orientation. Special decisions and long-range planning primarily have a *project* orientation with a far-reaching time span.

The project and time-period orientations of Exhibit 13-1 represent two distinct cross sections of the total corporate assets. The vertical dimension signifies the total investment (assets) of the company, which may be subdivided into

EXHIBIT 13-1

THE PROJECT ORIENTATION OF CAPITAL BUDGETING

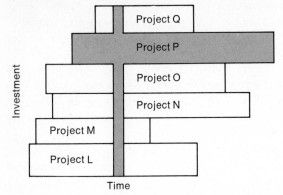

divisions, product lines, departments, buildings, a fleet of trucks, or machines. These parts of an organization's resources are individual *projects*, or investment decisions. The horizontal dimension represents successive years in a company's life.

The black horizontal rectangle shows that many projects entail commitments over a prolonged span of time, not just one year. The focus is on a single cross section, a lone investment venture, throughout its life. The interest income that can be earned over a period of time (that is, the time value of money) often looms large in special decisions and in long-range planning.

The black vertical rectangle illustrates the focus of income determination and current planning and control. The cross-sectional emphasis is upon the company's overall performance and status for a year or less. The time period is relatively short, and the interest value of money is usually not directly involved.

The point of all this is that our ordinary accounting systems and techniques have been designed to determine the cost and income of products for current planning and control. There is a great danger of using the existing general-purpose accounting system incorrectly—that is, of using data indiscriminately for solving special problems.

So in this chapter, we shift gears. We shall take a fresh look at the purpose of the special decision, and then we shall decide what models seem best for achieving that purpose.

DEFINITION OF CAPITAL BUDGETING

Capital budgeting is the making of long-term planning decisions for investments and their financing. Most expenditures for plant, equipment, and other long-lived assets affect operations over a series of years. They are large, permanent commitments that influence long-run flexibility and earning power. Decisions in this area are among the most difficult, primarily because the future to be foreseen is distant and hard to perceive. Because the unknowable factors are many, it is imperative that all the knowable factors be collected and properly measured before a decision is reached.

The profitability of a business decision depends on two vital factors: (a) future net increases in cash inflows or net savings in cash outflows; and (b) required investment. Thus, a chance to receive an annual return of $5,000 on a bond or stock can be judged only in relationship to how much money need be committed to obtain the $5,000. If the required capital is $10,000, the $5,000 (50 percent) return may be extremely appealing. If the required investment is $1 million, the $5,000 ($\frac{1}{2}$ percent) return will probably be unappealing. Depending on risk and available alternatives, individuals and corporate investors usually have some notion of a minimum rate of return that would make various projects desirable investments.

The quantitative approach to the selection of projects generally compares predicted cash flows to the required investments. Thus, all projects whose rate of return exceeds the minimum rate of return would be desirable, and vice versa. A project that is expected to produce a return of 25 percent would ordinarily be more desirable than one with a return of 12 percent. The problem of choosing the minimum acceptable rate of return (more a problem of finance than of accounting) is extremely complex. In this chapter, we shall assume that the minimum acceptable rate of return is given to the accountant by management. The next chapter explores this question in more detail.

There are several different models for the capital-budgeting decision. Although we shall discuss (a) urgency and persuasion, (b) discounted cash flow, (c) payback, and (d) the accounting method, we shall concentrate on discounted cash flow because it is conceptually superior to the others.

URGENCY AND PERSUASION

Many phases of business operations are managed in the same manner that many individuals care for their cars. How many of us keep cars going until that bald tire becomes suddenly useless, the old battery refuses to perform, or the sticky valves keep the car from starting in cold weather? Then what happens? Stop-gap action may be taken so that the car can be back in service quickly. When a machine part fails, a belt breaks, or a generator wears out, routine replacements are made to avoid disruption in production. If the old machine on the assembly line suddenly disintegrates, there may be a fast but uneconomic replacement so that down time is minimized. All repairs, maintenance, and replacements should be implementations of an overall equipment policy that considers future-cost comparisons and timing. The repair of the moment is only one of a series that are upcoming. All these outlays should be considered together and matched against future benefits and alternatives. Because of widespread ignorance and faulty criteria for replacement decisions, many businesses keep equipment far longer than they should.

Often the urgent action taken is correct on logical grounds. But it is correct by coincidence rather than by methodical analysis. The pressures of the moment lead to quick remedial action. Then too, commonsense action, such as replacing worn gaskets to prevent oil leakage, is too obvious to warrant formal pro-and-con analysis. However, when a contemplated outlay is large and far-reaching in its effects, urgency should not be a convincing influence.

The individual manager's power of persuasion is a key factor where urgency or postponability is paramount in influencing the spending decisions of top management. The managers who are best at selling their own projects to the decision maker get the lion's portion of the available money, whereas the rest of the managers either get nothing or wait, and then wait some more. Economic considerations become secondary as individual managers war with words and with impressive operating performance that may or may not be relevant to the capital-budgeting problem at hand.

DISCOUNTED CASH FLOW

time value
of money
The discounted cash-flow model for capital-budgeting decisions recognizes that the use of money has a cost (interest), just as the use of a building or an automobile may have a cost (rent). A dollar in the hand today is worth more than a dollar to be received (or spent) five years from today. For instance, in the interim a dollar can be invested in a savings institution; the dollar would grow markedly during a five-year span because of the interest it would earn. *Because the discounted cash-flow method explicitly and routinely weighs the time value of money, it is the best method to use for long-range decisions.*

Another major aspect of the cash-flow method is its focus on *cash* inflows and outflows rather than on *net income* as computed in the conventional accounting sense. Cash is invested now with the hope of receiving cash in a greater amount in the future. As we shall see, the student without a strong accounting background has an advantage here. He does not have to unlearn the accrual concepts of accounting, which the accounting student often wrongly tries to inject into discounted cash-flow analysis.

There are two main variations of the discounted cash-flow method: (a) time-adjusted rate of return (also often called *internal rate of return*); and (b) net present value. A brief summary of the tables and formulas used is included in Appendix B at the end of this book; *before reading on, be sure you understand this appendix.*

time-adjusted
rate of return
The time-adjusted rate of return may be defined as "the maximum rate of interest that could be paid for the capital employed over the life of an investment without loss on the project."[1] This rate corresponds to the effective rate of interest so widely computed for bonds purchased or sold at discounts or premiums.

example a
A manager is considering buying a new special-purpose machine, which is expected to have a five-year useful life, have zero disposal value, and result in cash operating savings of $1,000 annually. If the machine will cost $3,791 now, what is the time-adjusted rate of return on this project?

[1] *Research Report 35, Return on Capital as a Guide to Managerial Decisions,* National Association of Accountants (December 1959), p. 57. *Rate of return* may alternatively be defined as the discounting rate that makes the present value of a project equal to the cost of the project.

EXHIBIT 13-2

TWO PROOFS OF TIME-ADJUSTED RATE OF RETURN

Original investment	$3,791
Useful life	5 years
Annual cash inflow from operations	$1,000
Rate of return	10%[a]

Proof 1: Discounting Each Year's Cash Inflow Separately[b]

	PRESENT VALUE OF $1, DISCOUNTED AT 10%	TOTAL PRESENT VALUE	SKETCH OF CASH FLOWS					
End of Year			0	1	2	3	4	5
Cash flows:								
Annual cash savings	.909	$ 909		$1,000				
	.826	826			$1,000			
	.751	751				$1,000		
	.683	683					$1,000	
	.621	621						$1,000
Present value of future inflows		$3,791[c]						
Initial outlay	1.000	(3,791)	$(3,791)					
Net present value (the zero difference proves that the rate of return is 10%)		$ 0						

Proof 2: Using Annuity Table[d]

Annual cash savings	3.791	$3,791		$1,000	$1,000	$1,000	$1,000	$1,000
Initial outlay	1.000	(3,791)	$(3,791)					
Net present value		$ 0						

[a] The rate of return would be computed by trial-and-error methods; this is explained later in the chapter.
[b] Present values from Table 2, Appendix B at the end of the book.
[c] Sum is really $3,790, but is rounded.
[d] Present values of annuity from Table 4, Appendix B.

Note in Exhibit 13-2 that $3,791 is the present value, at a rate of return of 10 percent, of a five-year stream of inflows of $1,000 in cash per year. Ten percent is the rate that equates the amount invested ($3,791) with the present value of the cash inflows ($1,000 per year for five years). In other words, *if* money were borrowed at an effective interest rate of 10 percent, the cash inflow produced by the project would exactly repay the hypothetical loan plus interest over the five years. If the minimum desired rate of return[2] is less than 10 percent,

---

[2] Minimum desired rate of return (cost of capital) is discussed in Chapter 14. For now, we assume the cost of capital as given; it is the minimum desired rate of return. Any project whose rate of return exceeds the cost of capital is desirable. Cost of capital is usually a long-run weighted average based on both debt and equity. Cost of capital is *not* typically a piecemeal computation based on the market rate of interest; that is, cost of capital is not "interest expense" on borrowed money as the accountant usually conceives it to be. For example, a mortgage-free house still has a cost of capital—the amount that could be earned with the proceeds if the house were sold.

EXHIBIT 13-3

RATIONALE UNDERLYING TIME-ADJUSTED RATE OF RETURN

(*Same data as in Exhibit 13-2*)

	Original investment	$3,791
	Annual cash inflow from operations	1,000
	Useful life	5 years
	Rate of return	10%

	(1)	(2)	(3)	(4)	(5)
YEAR	UNRECOVERED INVESTMENT AT BEGINNING OF YEAR	ANNUAL CASH INFLOW	RETURN AT 10% PER YEAR (1) × 10%	AMOUNT OF INVESTMENT RECOVERED AT END OF YEAR (2) − (3)	UNRECOVERED INVESTMENT AT END OF YEAR (1) − (4)
1	$3,791	$1,000	$ 379	$ 621	$3,170
2	3,170	1,000	317	683	2,487
3	2,487	1,000	249	751	1,736
4	1,736	1,000	173	827	909
5	909	1,000	91	909	0
		$5,000	$1,209	$3,791	

Assumptions: Unrecovered investment at beginning of each year earns interest for whole year. Annual cash inflows are received at the end of each year. For simplicity in the use of tables, all operating cash inflows or outflows are assumed to take place at the *end* of the years in question. This is unrealistic because such cash flows ordinarily occur uniformly throughout the given year, rather than in lump sums at the end of the year. Compound-interest tables especially tailored for these more stringent conditions are available, but we shall not consider them here.

the project will be profitable. If the cost of capital exceeds 10 percent, the cash inflow will be insufficient to pay interest and repay the principal of the hypothetical loan. Therefore, 10 percent is the time-adjusted rate of return for this project.

explanation of compound interest The time-adjusted rate of return is computed on the basis of the funds in use from period to period instead of on the original investment. See Exhibit 13-3. The return in that exhibit is 10 percent of the capital invested during each year. The cash flows in excess of the 10 percent "rent" on the invested capital are regarded as recoveries of the original investment. In this example, the five-year cash inflow recovers the original investment plus annual interest at a rate of 10 percent on the as yet unrecovered capital.

depreciation and discounted cash flow Students are often perplexed by the seeming exclusion of depreciation from discounted cash-flow computations. A common homework error is to discount cash flows less depreciation. This tendency betrays a lack of understanding of a basic idea of the time-adjusted rate of return. Discounted cash-flow techniques and tables *automatically* provide for recoupment of principal in computing time-adjusted rates of return. Consequently, *it is unnecessary to deduct depreciation charges from cash inflows before consulting* *present-value tables.* For example, reexamine Exhibit 13-3. Note that at the end of year 1, the $1,000 cash inflow represents a 10 percent ($379) return on the $3,791 unrecovered investment at the beginning of year 1 *plus* a $621 recovery of principal. (The latter is akin to the depreciation provision in conventional accounting.)

This difficult point warrants another illustration. Assume that a company is considering investing in a project with a two-year life and no residual value. Cash flow is to be received in equal payments of $3,000 at the end of each of the two years. How much would the company be willing to invest in order to earn a time-adjusted rate of return of 6 percent? A quick look at the table for either the present value of $1 (Appendix B at end of book, Table 2) or the present value of an ordinary annuity of $1 (Table 4) will show:

P.V. of annuity of $3,000 for 2 years at 6% is: $3,000 × 1.833 = $5,499
  or
P.V. of $3,000 at end of year 1: $3,000 × .943 = $2,829
P.V. of $3,000 at end of year 2: $3,000 × .890 = $\underline{2,670}$
$\overline{\$5,499}$

Following is an analysis of computations that are automatically considered when present-value tables are used:

YEAR	INVESTMENT AT BEGINNING OF YEAR	OPERATING CASH INFLOW	RETURN AT 6% PER YEAR	AMOUNT OF INVESTMENT RECEIVED AT END OF YEAR	UNRECOVERED INVESTMENT AT END OF YEAR
1	$5,499	$3,000	.06 × $5,499 = $330	$3,000 − $330 = $2,670	$5,499 − $2,670 = $2,829
2	$2,829	$3,000	.06 × $2,829 = $170	$3,000 − $170 = $2,830	$2,829 − $2,830 = −$1*

*Discrepancy due to rounding.

A study of these computations will show that discounted cash-flow techniques do consider recovery of investment in rate-of-return computations and that the discount tables have built-in provisions for recovery of investment.

net present-value method Another type of discounted cash-flow approach may be called the net present-value method. Computing the exact time-adjusted rate of return entails trial and error and, sometimes, cumbersome hand calculations and interpolations within a compound-interest table. In contrast, the net present-value method assumes some minimum desired rate of return. All expected cash flows are discounted to the present, using this minimum desired rate. If the result is positive, the project is desirable because its return exceeds the desired minimum. If the result is negative, the project is undesirable.

Example A will also be used to demonstrate the net present-value approach. The new machine will cost $3,791. Exhibit 13-4 indicates a net present value of $202; therefore, the investment is desirable. The manager would be able to invest $202 more, or a total of $3,993 (that is, $3,791 + $202), and still earn 8 percent on the project.

EXHIBIT 13-4

NET PRESENT-VALUE TECHNIQUE

Original investment	$3,791	
Useful life	5 years	
Annual cash inflow from operations	$1,000	
Minimum desired rate of return	8%	

Approach 1: Discounting Each Year's Cash Inflow Separately*

	PRESENT VALUE OF $1, DISCOUNTED @ 8%	TOTAL PRESENT VALUE	SKETCH OF CASH FLOWS					
End of Year			0	1	2	3	4	5
Cash flows:								
Annual cash savings	.926	926		$1,000				
	.857	857			$1,000			
	.794	794				$1,000		
	.735	735					$1,000	
	.681	681						$1,000
Present value of future inflows		$3,993						
Initial outlay	1.000	(3,791)	$(3,791)					
Net present value		$ 202						

Approach 2: Using Annuity Table†

Annual cash savings	3.993	$3,993		$1,000	$1,000	$1,000	$1,000	$1,000
Initial outlay	1.000	(3,791)	$(3,791)					
Net present value		$ 202‡						

* Present values from Table 2, Appendix B.
† Present annuity values from Table 4.
‡ Rounded.

The higher the minimum desired rate of return, the less the manager would be willing to invest in this project. At a rate of 12 percent, the net present value would be $−185 (that is, $1,000 × 3.605, the present value factor from Table 4, = $3,605, which is $185 less than the required investment of $3,791). When the desired rate of return is 12 percent, rather than 8 percent, the machine is undesirable at its selling price of $3,791.

COMPARISON OF NET PRESENT-VALUE AND TIME-ADJUSTED METHODS

As we have seen, there are two discounted cash-flow methods: time-adjusted rate of return and net present value. Now we shall compare them and also review what this chapter has covered so far.

example b   The Block Company is thinking of buying, at a cost of $22,000, some new material-handling equipment that is expected to save $5,000 in cash operating costs per year. Its estimated useful life is ten years, and it will have zero disposal value.

required   1. Time-adjusted rate of return.

2. Net present value if the minimum desired rate of return is 16 percent.

SOLUTION   1. Time-adjusted rate of return: $22,000 = P.V. of annuity of $5,000 at X percent for 10 years, or what factor (F) in the table of present values of an annuity (Table 4) will satisfy the following equation:

$$\$22,000 = \$5,000 \ (F)$$
$$F = \$22,000/\$5,000 = 4.400$$

Now, on the ten-year line in the table for the present value of an annuity (Table 4), find the column that is closest to 4.400. You will find that 4.400 lies somewhere between a rate of return of 18 percent and one of 20 percent. Interpolate as follows:

18%		4.494	4.494
True rate ⟶			4.400
20%		4.192	
Difference		.302	.094

True rate: 18% plus (.094/.302)(2%)
18% plus .31 (2%)
18% plus .62%, or   18.62%

The time-adjusted rate (18.62 percent) is the rate that equates the amount invested ($22,000) with the present value of the cash inflows ($5,000 per year for ten years). In other words, if money were borrowed at an effective interest rate of 18.62 percent, the cash inflow (or savings) produced by the project would exactly repay the loan and interest over the ten years. If the cost of capital is less than 18.62 percent, the project will be profitable at a rate measured by the difference between the cost of capital and the rate earned by the investment (18.62 percent). If the cost of capital exceeds 18.62 percent, the cash inflow (or savings) will not be enough to pay interest and repay the principal of the hypothetical loan. Therefore, 18.62 percent is the rate of return in this instance.

2. Net present value:
This method takes the same basic equation used in 1:

$$\$22,000 = \text{P.V. of annuity of } \$5,000 \text{ at } X \text{ percent for 10 years}$$

However, this time we shall replace the $22,000 with an unknown and replace X percent with the minimum desired rate of return (assumed to be 16 percent):

$$X = \text{P.V. of annuity of } \$5,000 \text{ at 16 percent for 10 years}$$

Consult the table for the present worth of an annuity. Find the 16-percent column and the 10-year row. The factor is 4.833. Substitute in the equation:

$$X = \$5,000 \ (4.833)$$
$$X = \$24,165$$

Net present value = $24,165 minus $22,000 = $2,165

The computed present value is compared to the required investment. If the present value exceeds the required investment, the project is desirable, and vice versa.

We can summarize the decision rules offered by these two methods as follows:

Time-Adjusted Rate of Return	Net Present Value
1. Using present value tables, compute the time-adjusted rate of return by trial-and-error interpolation.	1. Calculate the net present value, using the minimum desired rate of return as the discount rate.
2. If this rate equals or exceeds the minimum desired rate of return, accept the project; if not, reject the project.	2. If the net present value is zero or positive, accept the project; if negative, reject the project.

We emphasize the net present-value method in this text because it has distinct advantages over the time-adjusted rate of return. The net present-value approach does not entail scouring tables and solving for the "true" rate of return by trial and error. It can be applied to any situation, regardless of whether there is uniform cash flow (present value of annuity) or some uneven cash flows. The latter is more tedious, as Example C will demonstrate, because it calls for taking the future cash flows for *each* year in the contemplated project and discounting them to the present. (See the next chapter for a more detailed comparison.)

In practice, the time-adjusted rate of return is used more widely than the net present-value measure. Most accountants and managers seem to be able to interpret the time-adjusted rate more easily; moreover, with this method they are not forced to specify a minimum desired rate as a prerequisite to discounted cash-flow computations. Awkward trial-and-error calculations of the time-adjusted rate, which students must frequently perform by hand, can be performed swiftly by electronic computers. Canned computer programs are commonly available for such computations.

DEALING WITH UNCERTAINTY

expected values and probability distributions
In this and other chapters, we almost always work with the expected values (single dollar amounts) of cash flows in order to emphasize and simplify various important points. These cash flows are subject to varying degrees of risk or uncertainty; risk or uncertainty is defined here as the possibility that the actual cash flow will deviate from the expected cash flow. Nevertheless, as a minimum, a manager must make some prediction of the probable outcome of various alternative projects. These expected values really should be analyzed in conjunction with probability distributions, as we see in Chapter 23. However, to stress the fundamental differences among various decision models, in this chapter we deal only with the expected values.

sensitivity analysis
Sensitivity analysis is a widely used approach to the problem of uncertainty. Sensitivity analysis is a technique that measures how the basic forecast results in a decision model will be affected by changes in the critical

data inputs that influence those results. In the context of capital budgeting, sensitivity analysis answers the question, "How will my rate of return or net present value be changed if the useful life or the cash flows that I used for its computation are inaccurate?"

Sensitivity analysis is best understood by example. Suppose that in Exhibit 13-4, the cash inflows were $800 annually instead of $1,000. What would be the net present value? The annuity factor of 3.993 would be multiplied by $800, producing a gross present value of $3,194 and a negative net present value of $3,194 − $3,791, or $−597. Alternatively, management may want to know how far cash inflows will have to fall to break even on the investment. In this context, "break even" means arrive at the point of indifference, the point where the net present value is zero:

Let X = annual cash inflows and let net present value = 0
Then $0 = 3.933(X) − \$3,791$
$X = \$950$

Thus, cash inflows can drop only $50 ($1,000 − $950) annually to reach the point of indifference regarding the investment.

Another critical factor is useful life. If useful life were only four years, the gross present value would be $1,000 times 3.312 (from the period 4 row in Table 4), or $3,312, again producing a negative net present value, $3,312 − $3,791, or $−479.

These calculations are also applicable to testing the sensitivity of rates of return. A fall in the annual cash inflow from $1,000 to $900 reduces the rate of return from 10 percent (which was proven in Exhibit 13-3) to 6 percent:

Investment = P.V. of annuity of $900 at X percent for 5 years, or what factor (F) in Table 4 will satisfy the following equation:
$\$3,791 = \$900(F)$
$F = 4.212$

Examine the five-year line in Table 4. Find the column closest to 4.212. In this instance, you do not have to interpolate; the rate is exactly 6 percent.

Of course, sensitivity analysis works both ways. It can measure the potential increases in net present value or rate of return as well as the decreases. The major contribution of sensitivity analysis is that it provides an immediate financial measure of the possible errors in forecasting. Therefore, it can be very useful because it helps focus on those decisions that may be very sensitive indeed, and it eases the manager's mind about those decisions that are not so sensitive.[3]

In addition, sensitivity analysis is applicable to the comparison of various capital-budgeting decision models. That is, as Appendix B at the end of this chapter explores in more detail, the results under the discounted cash-flow model may be compared to the results, using the same basic data, generated under simpler models like payback and accounting rate of return.

[3] For a fuller discussion, see Alfred Rappaport, "Sensitivity Analysis in Decision Making," *The Accounting Review*, XLII, No. 3, 441–56.

NET PRESENT-VALUE COMPARISON OF TWO PROJECTS

incremental
versus total
project
approach

The mechanics of compound interest may appear formidable to those readers who are encountering them for the first time. However, a little practice with the interest tables should easily clarify the mechanical aspect. More important, we shall now blend some relevant cost analysis with the discounted cash-flow approach.

example c

A company owns a packaging machine, which was purchased three years ago for $56,000. The machine has a remaining useful life of five years, but will require a major overhaul at the end of two more years of life, at a cost of $10,000. Its disposal value now is $20,000; in five years its disposal value is expected to be $8,000, assuming that the $10,000 major overhaul will be done on schedule. The cash operating costs of this machine are expected to be $40,000 annually.

A salesman has offered a substitute machine for $51,000, or for $31,000 plus the old machine. The new machine will slash annual cash operating costs by $10,000, will not require any overhauls, will have a useful life of five years, and will have a disposal value of $3,000.

required

Assume that the minimum desired rate of return is 14 percent. Using the net present-value technique, show whether the new machine should be purchased, using (a) a total-project approach; (b) an incremental approach. Try to solve before examining the solution.

SOLUTION

A difficult part of long-range decision making is the structuring of the data. We want to see the effects of each alternative on future cash flows. The focus here is on bona fide *cash* transactions, not on opportunity costs. Using an opportunity-cost approach may yield the same answers, but repeated classroom experimentation with various analytical methods has convinced the author that the following steps are likely to be the clearest:

Step 1. Arrange the relevant cash flows by project, so that a sharp distinction is made between total-project flows and incremental flows. The incremental flows are merely algebraic differences between two alternatives. (There are *always* at least two alternatives. One is the status quo, the alternative of doing nothing.) Exhibit 13-5 shows how the cash flows for *each* alternative are sketched.

Step 2. Discount the expected cash flows and choose the project with the least cost or the greatest benefit. Both the total-project approach and the incremental approach are illustrated in Exhibit 13-5. Which approach you use is a matter of preference. However, to develop confidence in this area, you should work with both at the start. In this example, the $8,425 net difference in favor of replacement is the ultimate result under either approach.[4]

analysis of
typical items
under
discounted
cash flow

1. Future disposal values.   The disposal value at the date of termination of a project is an increase in the cash inflow in the year of disposal. Errors in forecasting disposal value are usually not crucial because the present value is usually small.

2. Current disposal values and required investment.   In a replacement decision, how should the current disposal value affect the computations? For

---

[4] The time-adjusted rate of return on the investment of $31,000 is 26 percent. See Appendix C to this chapter for the computations, using trial-and-error methods.

EXHIBIT 13-5

TOTAL PROJECT VERSUS INCREMENTAL APPROACH TO NET PRESENT VALUE

(Data from Example C)

End of Year	PRESENT-VALUE DISCOUNT FACTOR, @ 14%	TOTAL PRESENT VALUE	0	1	2	3	4	5
					SKETCH OF CASH FLOWS			
TOTAL PROJECT APPROACH								
A. *Replace*								
Recurring cash operating costs, using an annuity table*	3.433	$(102,990)		($30,000)	($30,000)	($30,000)	($30,000)	($30,000)
Disposal value, end of Year 5	.519	1,557						3,000
Initial required investment	1.000	(31,000)	($31,000)					
Present value of net cash outflows		$(132,433)						
B. *Keep*								
Recurring cash operating costs, using an annuity table*	3.433	$(137,320)		($40,000)	($40,000)	($40,000)	($40,000)	($40,000)
Overhaul, end of Year 2	.769	(7,690)			(10,000)			
Disposal value, end of Year 5	.519	4,152						8,000
Present value of net cash outflows		$(140,858)						
Difference in favor of replacement		$ 8,425						
INCREMENTAL APPROACH								
A–B *Analysis Confined to Differences*								
Recurring cash operating savings, using an annuity table*	3.433	$ 34,330		$10,000	$10,000	$10,000	$10,000	$10,000
Overhaul avoided, end of Year 2	.769	7,690			10,000			
Difference in disposal values, end of Year 5	.519	(2,595)						(5,000)
Incremental initial investment	1.000	(31,000)	($31,000)					
Net present value of replacement		$ 8,425						

* Table 4, Appendix B, at the end of the book.

example, suppose that the current disposal value of old equipment is $5,000 and that new equipment is available at $40,000. There are a number of correct ways to analyze these items, all of which will have the same ultimate effect on the decision. Generally, the required investment is most easily measured by offsetting the disposal value of the old assets against the gross cost of the new assets ($40,000) and by showing the net cash outgo at $35,000.

3. Book value and depreciation. Depreciation is a phenomenon of accrual accounting that entails an allocation of cost, not a specific cash outlay. Depreciation and book value are ignored in discounted cash-flow approaches for the reasons mentioned earlier in this chapter.

4. Income taxes. In practice, comparison between alternatives is best made after considering tax effects, because the tax impact may alter the picture. (The effects of income taxes are considered in Chapter 14 and may be studied now if desired.)

5. Overhead analysis. In the relevant cost analysis of overhead, only the overhead that will differ between alternatives is pertinent. There is need for careful study of the fixed overhead under the available alternatives. In practice, this is an extremely difficult phase of cost analysis, because it is difficult to relate the individual costs to any single project.

6. Unequal lives. Where projects have unequal lives, comparisons may be made either over the useful life of the longer-lived project or over the useful life of the shorter-lived project. For our purposes, let us predict what the residual values will be at the end of the longer-lived project. We must also assume a reinvestment at the end of the shorter-lived project. This makes sense primarily because the decision maker should extend his time horizon as far as possible. If he is considering a longer-lived project, he should give serious consideration to what actually could be done in the time interval between the termination dates of the shorter-lived and longer-lived projects.

7. Mutually exclusive projects. When the projects are mutually exclusive, so that the acceptance of one automatically entails the rejection of the other (for example, buying Dodge or Ford trucks), the project that maximizes wealth measured in net present value in dollars should be undertaken.

8. A word of caution. The foregoing material has been an *introduction* to the area of capital budgeting, which is, in practice, complicated by a variety of factors: unequal lives; mutually exclusive investments; major differences in the size of alternative investments; peculiarities in time-adjusted rate-of-return computations; various ways of allowing for uncertainty (see Chapter 23); changes, over time, in desired rates of return; the indivisibility of projects in relation to a fixed overall capital-budget appropriation; and more. These niceties are beyond the scope of this introductory chapter, but the next chapter will help you pursue the subject in more depth.

PAYBACK

uniform   *Payback*, sometimes called *payout* or *payoff*, is a rough-and-ready model
cash inflows   that is looked upon with disdain by many academic theorists. Yet payback is the most widely used decision model, and it certainly is an improvement over the criterion of urgency or postponability. Furthermore, it is a handy device (a) where precision in estimates of profitability is not crucial and preliminary screening of a rash of proposals is necessary; (b) where a weak cash-and-credit position has a heavy bearing on the selection of investment possibilities; and (c) where the contemplated project is extremely risky.

Assume that $4,500 is spent for a machine that has an estimated useful life of ten years. It promises cost savings of $1,000 a year in *cash flow from operations* (depreciation is ignored). The payback calculations follow:

$$P = I/O_c$$
$$P = \$4,500/\$1,000 = 4.5 \text{ years}$$

P is the payback time, I is the initial incremental amount invested; and O_c is the uniform annual incremental cash inflow from operations.

Essentially, payback is a measure of the *time* it will take to recoup in the form of cash from operations only the original dollars invested. Given the useful life of an asset and uniform cash flows, the less the payout period, the greater the profitability; or, given the payback period, the greater the useful life of the asset, the greater the profitability.

Although the payback method may often yield clues to profitability, it should not be used blindly. Note that payback does *not* measure profitability; it does measure how quickly investment dollars may be recouped. An investment's main objective is profitability, not recapturing the original outlay. If a company wants to recover its investment outlay rapidly, it need not bother spending in the first place. Then the payback time is zero; no waiting time is needed.

The major weakness of the payback model is its neglect of profitability. The mere fact that a project has a satisfactory payback does not mean that it should be selected in preference to an alternative project with a longer payback time. To illustrate, consider an alternative to the $4,500 machine mentioned earlier. Assume that this other machine requires only a $3,000 investment and will also result in gross earnings of $1,000 per year before depreciation. Compare the two payback periods:

$$P_1 = \$4,500/\$1,000 = 4.5 \text{ years}$$
$$P_2 = \$3,000/\$1,000 = 3.0 \text{ years}$$

The payback criterion would favor buying the $3,000 machine. However, one fact about this machine has been purposely withheld. Its useful life is only three years. Ignoring the complexities of compound interest for the moment, one finds that the $3,000 machine results in zero profits, whereas the $4,500 machine yields profits for five and one-half years beyond its payback period. Despite these criticisms, a form of the payback method, called the *payback reciprocal*, discussed in Appendix B to this chapter, is useful in many situations.[5]

ACCOUNTING RATE OF RETURN: CONFLICT OF MODELS

the basic   The *accounting rate of return* is also known as the *unadjusted rate of return*,
computation   the *book-value rate of return*, and the *approximate rate of return*. In its simplest form, the accounting rate of return is the following fraction:

$$\frac{\text{Increase in expected future average annual net income}}{\text{Initial increase in required investment}}$$

Sometimes the denominator is the average increase in investment, rather than the initial increase.

The facts in our payback illustration would yield the following accounting rate of return ($4,500 cost, 10-year life, $1,000 cash inflow from operations):

$$R = \frac{\$1,000 - \$450 \text{ average depreciation}}{\$4,500} = 12.2\%$$

If the denominator is the "average" investment ($4,500 ÷ 2) instead of the initial investment, the rate would be doubled.

Note that the accounting rate of return is based on the familiar financial statements prepared under accrual accounting. Unlike the payback model, the accounting-rate-of-return model at least has profitability as an objective. However, its most serious drawback is its ignoring of the time value of money. Appendix A to this chapter explores the accounting method in more detail.

evaluation   The use of the conventional accrual accounting methods for evaluating
of performance   performance is a stumbling block to the implementation of present-value models for capital-bugeting decisions. To illustrate, the manager of a division of a huge company took a course in management accounting in an executive program. He learned about discounted cash flow. He was convinced that such a method would lead to decisions that would better achieve the long-range profit goals of the company.

When he returned to his company, he was more frustrated than ever. Top management used the overall rate of return of his division to judge his performance. That is, each year divisional net income was divided by average divisional assets to obtain his rate of return (ROI). Such a measure usually inhibits invest-

---

[5] Also see Alfred Rappaport, "The Discounted Payback Period," *Management Services*, Volume 2, No. 4, 30–35.

ments in plant and equipment that might be clearly attractive using the present-value models. Why? Because a huge investment often boosts depreciation inordinately in the early years under accelerated-depreciation methods, thus reducing the numerator in the ROI computation. Also, the denominator is increased substantially by the initial cost of the new assets. As one manager said, "Top management is always giving me hell about my new flour mill, even though I know it is the most efficient we've got regardless of what the figures say."

Obviously, there is an inconsistency between citing present-value models as being best for capital-budgeting decisions and then using quite different concepts for monitoring subsequent performance. As long as such practices continue, managers will frequently be tempted to make decisions that may be nonoptimal under the present-value criterion but optimal, at least over short or intermediate spans of time, under conventional methods of evaluating operating performance. Such temptations become more pronounced when managers are subject to regular transfers and promotions. For a deeper explanation of this issue, see Chapter 21.

ADMINISTRATION OF CAPITAL BUDGETS

Although ordinary budget procedures are well entrenched in many companies, formal capital budgeting is still quite undeveloped, largely because it has flowered fairly recently.

The first feature of effective capital-budgeting administration is the awareness on the part of all managers that long-run expenditures are generators of long-run profits. This engenders a constant search for new methods, processes, and products.

Approval of overall capital budgets is usually the responsibility of the board of directors. Depending on the amounts involved, individual projects receive approval at various managerial levels. Requests are usually made semiannually or annually. They are reviewed as they pass upward through managerial levels until they reach a committee that examines capital-budget requests and submits recommendations to the president. In turn, the president submits final recommendations to the board of directors.

Of course, most companies will have a set of forms and a timetabled, uniform routine for processing capital budgets.

When projects are authorized, there is a need for follow-up on two counts. First, control is needed to see that spending and specifications conform to the plan as approved. Second, the very existence of such follow-up will cause capital-spending requests to be sharply conceived and honestly estimated.

Systematic procedures are needed not only to implement capital budgets but to appraise (audit) the profitability performance of projects. This is *vital* to a successful capital budgeting program. The follow-up comparison of performance with original estimates not only better insures careful forecasts but also helps sharpen the tools for improving future forecasts.

summary

Product costing, income determination, and the planning and controlling of operations have a current time-period orientation. Special decisions and long-range planning have primarily a project orientation. There is a danger in using ordinary accounting data for special purposes. Discounted cash-flow techniques have been developed for the making of special decisions and for long-range planning, because the time value of money becomes extremely important when projects extend beyond one year.

The field of capital budgeting is important because lump-sum expenditures on long-life projects have far-reaching effects on profitability and flexibility. It is imperative that management develop carefully laid plans based on reliable forecasting procedures.

Urgency, favoritism, and subjectivity should be minor criteria in the selection of capital projects.

Capital budgeting is long-term planning for proposed capital outlays and their financing. Projects are accepted if their rate of return exceeds a minimum desired rate of return.

Because the discounted cash-flow method explicitly and automatically weighs the time value of money, it is the best method to use for long-range decisions. The overriding goal is maximum long-run net cash inflows.

The discounted cash-flow approach has two variations; time-adjusted rate of return and net present value. Both approaches take into account the timing of cash flows and are thus superior to other methods.

The payback method is the most widely used approach to capital-spending decisions. It is simple and easily understood, but it neglects profitability.

The accounting rate of return (discussed more fully in Appendix A to this chapter) is widely used, although it is much cruder than discounted cash-flow methods. It fails to recognize explicitly the time value of money. Instead, the accounting method depends on averaging techniques that may yield inaccurate answers, particularly when cash flows are not uniform through the life of a project. The accounting method is adequate where the return plainly far exceeds the minimum desired rate or where projects are not subject to close competition from other projects.

The prediction of cost savings (different cash flows) is the key measurement for capital budgeting. Factors that must be considered in these calculations include income taxes and different capacities of plant and equipment, as well as the usual recurring operating costs. The use of sensitivity analysis and probability theory can help approach and measure the uncertainty that plagues this work.

A serious practical impediment to the adoption of discounted cash-flow models is the widespread use of conventional accrual models for evaluating performance. Frequently, the optimal decision under discounted cash flow will not produce a good showing in the early years, when performance is computed under conventional accounting methods. For example, heavy depreciation charges and the expensing rather than capitalizing of initial development costs will hurt reported income for the first year.

The difficult forecasting problem makes capital budgeting one of the most imposing tasks of management. Although judgment and attitudes are important ingredients of capital budgeting, the correct application of the techniques described here should crystallize the relevant factors and help management toward intelligent decision making.

Problem for Self-Study

Special problems in relevant costs and capital budgeting, including income tax factors, are discussed in Chapter 14. A suggested reading list appears at the end of Chapter 14.

PROBLEM   A toy manufacturer who specializes in making fad items has just developed a $50,000 molding machine for automatically producing a special toy. The machine has been used to produce only one unit so far. It is planned to depreciate the $50,000 original cost evenly over four years, after which time production of the toy will be stopped.

Suddenly a machine salesman appears. He has a new machine that is ideally suited for producing this toy. His automatic machine is distinctly superior. It reduces the cost of materials by 10 percent and produces twice as many units per hour. It will cost $44,000 and will have zero disposal value at the end of four years.

Production and sales would continue to be at a rate of 25,000 per year for four years; annual sales will be $90,000. The scrap value of the toy company's machine is now $5,000 and will be $2,600 four years from now. Both machines will be useless after the 100,000-unit total market potential is exhausted.

With its present equipment, the company's annual expenses will be: direct materials, $10,000; direct labor, $20,000; and variable factory overhead, $15,000. Fixed factory overhead, exclusive of depreciation, is $7,500 annually, and fixed selling and administrative expenses are $12,000 annually.

required   1. Assume that the minimum rate of return desired is 18 percent. Using discounted cash-flow techniques, show whether the new equipment should be purchased. Use a total-project approach and an incremental approach. What is the role of the book value of the old equipment in the analysis?

2. What is the payback period for the new equipment?

3. As the manager who developed the $50,000 molding machine, you are trying to justify not buying the new $44,000 machine. You question the accuracy of the expected cash operating savings. By how much must these cash savings fall before the point of indifference, the point where net present value of the project is zero, is reached?

SOLUTION   1. The first step is to analyze all relevant operating cash flows and align them with the appropriate alternative. This analysis is shown at the top of page 470.

The next step is to sketch the *other* relevant cash flows, as shown in Exhibit 13-6. Either the total-project approach or the incremental approach results in the same $9,423 net present value in favor of replacement.

Note that the book value of the old machine is irrelevant, and so is completely ignored. In the light of subsequent events, nobody will deny that the original $50,000 investment could have been avoided, with a little luck or foresight. But nothing can be done to alter the past. The next question is

	(1) PRESENT SITUATION	(2) NEW SITUATION	(3) INCREMENT
Sales (irrelevant)			
Expenses:			
Direct materials	$10,000	$ 9,000	$ 1,000
Direct labor	20,000	10,000	10,000
Variable overhead	15,000	7,500	7,500
Fixed overhead (irrelevant)			
Selling and administrative expenses (irrelevant)			
Total relevant operating cash outflows	$45,000	$26,500	$18,500

whether the company will nevertheless be better off by buying the new machine. Management would have been much happier had the $50,000 never been spent in the first place, but the original mistake should not be compounded by keeping the old machine.

2. The payback formula can be used because the operating savings are uniform:

$$P = \frac{I}{O} = \frac{\$44,000 - \$5,000}{\$18,500} = 2.1 \text{ years}$$

3. This is an example of sensitivity analysis:

Let X = annual cash savings and let net present value = O
Then $O = 2.690\ (X) + \$5,000 - \$44,000 - \$1,342$

(Note that the $5,000, $44,000, and $1,342 are at the bottom of Exhibit 13-6.)

$$2.690\ X = \$40,342$$

$$X = \$14,997$$

If the annual savings fall $3,503, from the estimated $18,500 to $14,997, the point of indifference will be reached. Rounding errors may affect the computation slightly.

An alternative way to get the same answer would be to divide the net present value of $9,423 (see bottom of Exhibit 13-6) by 2.690, obtaining $3,503, the amount of the annual difference in savings that will eliminate the $9,423 of net present value.

APPENDIX A: ACCOUNTING METHOD OF RATE OF RETURN

fundamental   Although discounted cash-flow approaches to business decisions are being
model   increasingly used, they are still relatively new. There are other techniques with which the accountant and manager should be at least somewhat familiar, because they are entrenched in many businesses.

The technique we are about to discuss is conceptually inferior to discounted cash-flow approaches. Then why do we bother studying it? First, changes in business practice occur slowly. If older methods, such as payback or the accounting method, are used despite the availability of better tools, they should be used

EXHIBIT 13-6
SOLUTION TO REQUIREMENT 1 OF PROBLEM FOR SELF-STUDY

End of Year	PRESENT-VALUE DISCOUNT FACTOR, @ 18%	TOTAL PRESENT VALUE	SKETCH OF CASH FLOWS				
			0	1	2	3	4
TOTAL-PROJECT APPROACH							
A. *New Situation*							
Recurring cash operating costs, using an annuity table*	2.690	$ (71,285)		($26,500)	($26,500)	($26,500)	($26,500)
Disposal value of old equipment now	1.000	5,000	$ 5,000				
Cost of new equipment	1.000	(44,000)	($44,000)				
Present value of net cash outflows		$(110,285)					
B. *Present Situation*							
Recurring cash operating costs, using an annuity table*	2.690	$(121,050)		($45,000)	($45,000)	($45,000)	($45,000)
Disposal value of old equipment four years hence	.516	1,342					$ 2,600
Present value of net cash outflows		$(119,708)					
Difference in favor of replacement		$ 9,423					
INCREMENTAL APPROACH							
A–B *Analysis Confined to Differences*							
Recurring cash operating savings, using an annuity table*	2.690	$ 49,765		$18,500	$18,500	$18,500	$18,500
Disposal value of old equipment now	1.000	5,000	$ 5,000				
Cost of new equipment	1.000	(44,000)	($44,000)				
Disposal value of old equipment foregone four years hence	.516	(1,342)					$ 2,600
Net present value of replacement		$ 9,423					

*From Table 2, Appendix B at the end of this book.

properly. Many managers use the accounting method because they regard it as satisfactory for their particular needs. In other words, they feel that the use of this tool is adequate for guiding their decisions even though the more refined discounted cash-flow tools are available. In such cases, care should be taken so that the cruder tool is used properly. The situation is similar to using a pocket knife instead of a scalpel for removing a person's appendix. If the pocket knife is used by a knowledgeable and skilled surgeon, the chances for success are much better than if it is used by a bungling layman.

The label for the *accounting method* is not uniform. It is also known as the *financial-statement method*, the *book-value method*, the *rate-of-return on assets method*, the *approximate rate-of-return method*, and the *unadjusted rate-of-return method*. Its computations supposedly dovetail most closely with conventional accounting methods of calculating income and required investment. However, the dovetailing objective is not easily attained, because the purposes of the computations differ. The most troublesome aspects are depreciation and decisions concerning capitalization versus expense. For example, advertising and research are usually expensed, even though they may often be viewed as long-range investments.

The equations for the accounting rate of return are:

$$\text{Accounting rate of return} = \frac{\text{Increase in future average annual net income}}{\text{Initial increase in required investment}} \quad (1)$$

$$R = \frac{O_c - W - S}{I} \quad (2)$$

where R = Average annual rate of return on initial incremental investment

O_c = Average annual incremental cash inflow from operations

W = Average annual write-off of incremental investment (akin to depreciation except that salvage value is handled separately)

S = Average annual incremental effects of salvage values

I = Initial increase in required investment

Assume the same facts as in our payback illustrations: cost of machine, $4,500; useful life, ten years; estimated disposal value, zero; and expected annual cash inflow from operations, $1,000. Substitute these amounts into Eq. (2):

$$R = \frac{\$1,000 - \$450 - 0}{\$4,500} = 12.2\%$$

the Many advocates of the accounting method would not use $4,500 in the
denominator: denominator. Instead, they would halve the original investment, because
investment only about half the $4,500, or $2,250, is the average amount invested in
base the machine over its ten-year life. Their reasoning is that depreciable assets do not require a permanent investment of the original amount. The funds

are gradually recovered as the earnings are realized.[6] Under this approach, the rate of return would obviously be doubled, as follows:

$$R = \frac{\$1,000 - \$450 - 0}{\$2,250} = 24.4\%$$

initial Although our examples in this appendix will use the initial-investment base,
investment practice is not uniform as to whether initial investment or average invest-
as a base ment in fixed assets should be used in the denominator. Companies defend
the use of the initial-investment base because it does not change over the
life of the investment; therefore, follow-up and comparison of actual rate of
return against predicted rate of return is facilitated. This follow-up is crucial for
control and for improving future capital planning and comparison on a year-
to-year, plant-to-plant, and division-to-division basis. The initial base is not
affected by depreciation methods.

In most cases, the rankings of competing projects will not differ regardless
of whether the gross or average investment base is used. Of course, using the
average base will show substantially higher rates of return; however, the desirable
rate of return used as a cut-off for accepting projects is also higher.

current assets Current assets, such as cash, receivables, and inventories, often are expanded
as a part of in order to sustain higher activity levels. In our example, if a $1,000 increase
investment in current assets is required, the denominator will be $4,500 plus $1,000,
base or $5,500. This $1,000 increase in current assets will be fully committed
for the life of the project; so, under the average-investment method, the
average base would be $3,250 ($2,250 average investment in equipment plus
$1,000 average investment in current assets).

danger of The gross or initial investment in the project should include the following:
understating all additional required current assets, fixed assets, research costs, engineering
investment costs, market-testing costs, start-up costs, initial costs of sales promotion,
and so forth. The omission of any of these items from the base can give
misleading results.

Although the *accounting-method* approach to investment decisions tries to
approximate the figures as they will eventually appear in financial statements,
there is not always an exact agreement between figures on conventional statements and figures used for decision making. The tendency in accounting practice
is to write costs off to expense quickly. Thus, the assembly of figures for special
decisions requires care to see that investment is not understated. Often the
investment base for decision making should include items, such as research and

---

[6] The measure of funds recovered in the example above is $450 a year, the amount of the annual depreciation. Consequently, the average funds committed to the project would decline at a rate of $450 per year from $4,500 to zero; hence, the average investment would be the beginning balance plus the ending balance ($4,500 + 0) divided by 2, or $2,250.

sales-promotion costs, that the accountant ordinarily writes off immediately as expenses.

accounting The unadjusted method ignores the time value of money. Expected future
method is an dollars are unrealistically and erroneously regarded as equal to present
averaging dollars. The discounted cash-flow method explicitly allows for the force
technique of interest and the exact timing of cash flows. In contrast, the unadjusted
method is based on *annual averages*.

Compare the time-adjusted rate of return in Example B, 18.62 percent, with the accounting rate of return:

Based on initial investment:

$$R = \frac{O_c - W - S}{\text{Initial } I} = \frac{\$5,000 - \$2,200 - 0}{\$22,000} = 12.727\%$$

Based on average investment:

$$R = \frac{O_c - W - S}{\text{Average } I} = \frac{\$5,000 - \$2,200 - 0}{.5(\$22,000)} = 25.455\%$$

Note how the accounting rate of return, however calculated, can produce results that differ markedly from the time-adjusted rate of return.

To demonstrate how the accounting method is basically an averaging technique that ignores the time value of money, reexamine Example C:

INCREMENTAL EFFECTS	FIVE YEARS TOGETHER	ANNUAL AVERAGE
Recurring cash operating savings	$50,000	$10,000
Overhaul avoided, end of year 2	10,000	2,000
Average annual incremental cash inflow from operations		$12,000 = O_c
Incremental initial investment ($51,000 − $20,000)	31,000	= I
Average annual write-off of incremental investment		6,200 = W
Difference in disposal values: new equipment, $3,000; old equipment, $8,000	5,000	
Average annual incremental effects of disposal values		1,000 = S

$$R = \frac{O_c - W - S}{I} = \frac{\$12,000 - \$6,200 - \$1,000}{\$31,000} = \frac{\$4,800}{\$31,000} = 15.48\% \text{ or } 15\%^*$$

*Because we deal with uncertainty about expected future data, computations to the nearest whole percent should be satisfactory.

Note in the illustration that net disposal value of old assets should be offset against the gross cost of new assets in computing the *incremental* (additional) initial-investment base. *One of the most frequent mistakes in the accounting method is to fail to relate the proper investment base to the proper operating figures.* The $4,800 net annual advantage should be related to the $31,000 *additional* investment, not the $51,000 total investment.

conflict of concepts and purposes The discounted cash-flow method is more objective because its answer is not directly influenced by decisions as to depreciation methods, capitalization-versus-expense decisions, and conservatism. (These decisions do influence income tax cash flows, however.) Erratic flows of revenue and expense over the project's life are directly considered under discounted cash flow but are "averaged" under the accounting method. "The [accounting method] utilizes concepts of capital and income which were originally designed for the quite different purpose of accounting for periodic income and financial position."[7] Thus, in the accounting method, the initial capital may be computed differently, the force of interest may be ignored, and the approximation of the average rate of return may be far from the real mark. The degree of error often becomes larger where the cash inflows do not have a uniform pattern. Equipment becomes much more desirable where cash savings are bigger in early years than where they are spread evenly throughout the useful life. Yet the accounting method would not make this distinction in computing average annual effects.

uneven cash flows Discounted cash-flow techniques can more readily compare projects having different lives and having different timings of cash inflows because discounting allows comparisons to be made at the same point in time. See Exhibit 13-7 for an illustration of the effect of different timings of cash flows. Some projects, such as mines and oil wells, have heavy earnings in early years. Other projects, like new product lines and new stores, take more time to produce maximum earnings.

postaudit The accounting method usually facilitates follow-up, because the same approach is used in the forecast as is used in the accounts. Yet exceptions to this ideal situation often occur. The most common exceptions arise from the inclusion in the forecast of some initial-investment items that are not handled in the same manner in the subsequent accounting records. For example, the accounting for trade-ins and disposal values varies considerably. In practice, test checks are frequently used on key items. An interesting suggestion on the problem of postaudit follows:

> When a major project is undertaken, it seems desirable to prepare project cost and income budgets employing the usual accounting classifications, so that subsequent actual figures drawn from the accounts can be compared directly with estimates. Rates of return can also be computed by the [accounting method], using the budgeted and actual data. Thus . . . the discounted cash-flow method would

[7] *N.A.A. Research Report 35, Return on Capital as a Guide to Managerial Decisions*, p. 64.

EXHIBIT 13-7

COMPARISON OF RATES OF RETURN BY
ACCOUNTING METHOD AND DISCOUNTED CASH-FLOW METHOD*

	PROJECT A	PROJECT B	PROJECT C
Amount invested	$ 75,000	$ 75,000	$ 75,000
Cumulative† cash inflow from operations:			
Years 1–5	$160,000	$ 80,000	$ 40,000
6–10	100,000	80,000	80,000
11–15	80,000	80,000	120,000
16–20	40,000	80,000	100,000
21–25	20,000	80,000	60,000
Totals	$400,000	$400,000	$400,000
Average annual cash flow	$ 16,000	$ 16,000	$ 16,000
Less depreciation ($75,000 ÷ 25)	3,000	3,000	3,000
Average annual net income	$ 13,000	$ 13,000	$ 13,000
Rate of return on original investment ($13,000 ÷ $75,000)	17.3%	17.3%	17.3%
Rate of return on average investment ($13,000 ÷ $37,500)	34.7%	34.7%	34.7%
Rate of return by discounted cash-flow method‡	40.5%	21.4%	16.6%

* Source: *N.A.A. Research Report 35, Return on Capital as a Guide to Managerial Decisions*, p. 67.
† For example, Project A's cash inflow is $32,000 annually for the first five years, $20,000 annually for the next five years, and so forth.
‡ These time-adjusted rates could be computed by trial-and-error methods. As you can imagine, this is a tedious process if you use hand calculations. In this case, the N.A.A. used tables that assumed cash inflows to be forthcoming *throughout* the year rather than at the *end* of the year. Table 4 in Appendix B at the end of this book assumes the latter; this would produce slightly lower rates. (Why?)

be used as a basis for project selection, and rate of return based upon a financial budget for the project would be used as a goal against which to compare subsequent performance.[8]

understand-   There is general agreement that the accounting method is easier to under-
ability   stand and apply than the discounted cash-flow method. Yet proponents of discounted cash flow maintain that its difficulty is overestimated, that reluctance to use it is based more on unfamiliarity than on inherent complexity. (Experience in the author's classes indicates that the student has far more difficulty understanding the accounting method than the discounted cash-flow method.) Tables and shortcuts are available to reduce the pencil pushing. Also, the prediction of cash flows does not require a knowledge of the intricacies of accounting concepts and conventions.

    The choice of method is ultimately dependent on personal preference and on the danger of making wrong decisions by using the less precise accounting method. *In any event, the isolation and prediction of relevant revenue and cost*

[8] *N.A.A. Research Report 35, op cit.*, pp. 72–73.

factors are usually more important than which evaluation technique is used. Because we are dealing only with future costs, all the compiled figures are necessarily clouded by varying degrees of uncertainty;[9] any intricate compound-interest techniques applied to these estimates are useful only insofar as the basic data are reliable.

APPENDIX B: COMPARISON OF DECISION MODELS

The sensitivity analysis described in the chapter is also applicable to a comparison of various capital-budgeting decision models. This appendix will discuss some additional aspects of the payback model; it will then show how the results of the payback model and the accounting rate-of-return models compare with the results of the time-adjusted rate-of-return model.

nonuniform   The payback formula is designed for uniform cash inflows. When cash
cash inflows   inflows are not uniform, the payback computation takes a cumulative form. That is, each year's net cash inflows are accumulated until the initial investment is recovered. For example, assume that the $4,500 machine produces a total cash savings of $10,000 over ten years, but not at a rate of $1,000 annually. Instead, the inflows are as follows:

YEAR	CASH SAVINGS	ACCUMULATED	YEAR	CASH SAVINGS	ACCUMULATED
1	$2,000	$2,000	6	$800	$ 8,300
2	1,800	3,800	7	600	8,900
3	1,500	5,300	8	400	9,300
4	1,200	6,500	9	400	9,700
5	1,000	7,500	10	300	10,000

The payback time is slightly beyond the second year. Straight-line interpolation within the third year reveals that the final $700 (that is, $4,500 − $3,800) needed to recover the investment would be forthcoming in 2.47 years—that is,

$$\frac{\$700}{\$1,500} \times 1 \text{ year} = .47 \text{ years}$$

the bail-out   The typical payback computation tries to answer the question, "How soon
factor: will it be before I can recoup my investment *if operations proceed as*
a better   *planned?*" However, a more fundamental question is, "Which of the
approach   competing projects has the best bail-out protection if things go wrong?
to payback   In other words, which has the least risk?" To answer such a question, we

[9]See Chapter 23 for an extended discussion of how to deal with uncertainty. Also see the suggested readings in Chapter 14, particularly the Hertz articles. Hertz uses a simulation approach that yields an expected value together with a range of minimum and maximum probable values.

must consider the salvage value of the equipment throughout its life, an item that is ignored in the usual payback computations.

For instance, salvage values of general-purpose equipment far exceed those of special-purpose equipment. These salvage values can be incorporated in a bail-out approach to payback as follows:

Assume that Equipment A (general-purpose) costs $100,000 and that Equipment B (special-purpose) costs $150,000. Each has a ten-year life. A is expected to produce uniform annual cash savings of $20,000; B, of $40,000. A's salvage value is expected to be $70,000 at the end of year 1; it is expected to decline at a rate of $10,000 annually thereafter. B's salvage value is expected to be $80,000 at the end of year 1; it is expected to decline at a rate of $20,000 annually. Note the difference in results under the traditional payback and the bail-out payback methods. The "bail-out payback time" is reached when the cumulative cash operating savings plus the salvage value at the end of a particular year equals the original investment:

TRADITIONAL PAYBACK		*BAIL-OUT PAYBACK*		
If operations go as expected:	If the project fails to meet expectations:			
	AT END OF	*CUMULATIVE CASH OPERATING SAVINGS*	*SALVAGE VALUE*	*CUMULATIVE TOTAL*
A: $P = \dfrac{I}{O_c} = \dfrac{\$100,000}{20,000} = 5$ years	A: Year 1	$ 20,000 +	$70,000 =	$ 90,000
	Year 2	40,000 +	60,000 =	100,000
	Therefore, payback is 2 years.			
B: $P = \dfrac{I}{O_c} = \dfrac{\$150,000}{40,000} = 3.75$ years	B: Year 1	$ 40,000 +	$80,000 =	$120,000
	Year 2	80,000 +	60,000 =	140,000
	Year 3	120,000 +	40,000 =	160,000
	Therefore, payback is 2.75 years, assuming that the salvage value would also be $40,000 at the end of that time.			

The analysis above demonstrates how different interpretations of the payback method can produce different results. If the objective is to measure risk (in the sense of how to avoid loss), the bail-out method is better than the traditional method.

annuity formula and payback reciprocal The much-maligned traditional payback method has received increasing attention[10] and approval as being useful for a wide number of situations.

The major argument in favor of payback is based on the equation for the present value of an annuity.

General formula for present value of annuity:

$$P_N = O_c \left(\frac{1 - \dfrac{1}{(1 + R)^N}}{R} \right) \qquad (1)$$

[10] Myron Gordon, "Payoff Period and Rate of Profit," *Journal of Business*, XXVIII, No. 4, 253–60.

Restated:

$$P_N = \frac{O_c}{R} - \frac{O_c}{R}\left(\frac{1}{(1 + R)^N}\right) \tag{2}$$

Multiply by R:

$$RP_N = O_c - O_c\left(\frac{1}{(1 + R)^N}\right) \tag{3}$$

Solve for R:

$$R = \frac{O_c}{P_N} - \frac{O_c}{P_N}\left(\frac{1}{(1 + R)^N}\right) \tag{4}$$

P_N = investment; O_c = annual *cash* savings or cash inflow from operations; R = rate of return; N = life of investment in years.

Note in equation (4) that the first right-hand term is the reciprocal of the payback period. The second right-hand term is the same reciprocal multiplied by $1/(1 + R)^N$. Now, if either R or N is large, this second term becomes small; therefore, *in these cases,* the rate of return will be closely approximated by the payback reciprocal. (Will the payout reciprocal be larger or smaller than the true rate of return?)

limitations of payback reciprocal   A project with an infinite life would have a rate of return exactly equal to its payback reciprocal, because the second right-hand term, in equation (4), becomes zero. Thus, in practice, the payback reciprocal is a helpful tool in quickly estimating the true rate of return where the project life is *at least twice the payback period.*

The payback reciprocal has wide applicability as a meaningful though rough tool. But its major limitations should be kept in mind:

1. It is valid only when the useful life of the project is at least twice the payback period. In any event, the payback reciprocal will always exceed the true rate of return.
2. It assumes that earnings or savings are constant over the investment's life.

relationships of payback reciprocal to rate of return   Exhibit 13-8 shows the relationships of the payback reciprocal to the rate of return for a project with a five-year payback period (payback reciprocal is 20 percent) and various useful lives. Note that the payback reciprocal gives a reasonable approximation of the time-adjusted rate of return only if the useful life of the project is at least ten years—twice the payback period. Otherwise, the regular time-adjusted computations must be made.

The table in Exhibit 13–9 shows various combinations of payback periods and time-adjusted rates of return. The table is based on one used by a company that uses the payback period in approximating the rate of return. Examples of how to use the table are included in Exhibit 13-9.

Returning to Example B, discussed earlier in this chapter:

$$\text{Payback reciprocal} = O_c/I = \frac{\$5,000}{\$22,000} = \underline{\underline{22.73\%}}$$

EXHIBIT 13-8

RECIPROCAL OF PAYBACK PERIOD COMPARED WITH RATE OF RETURN

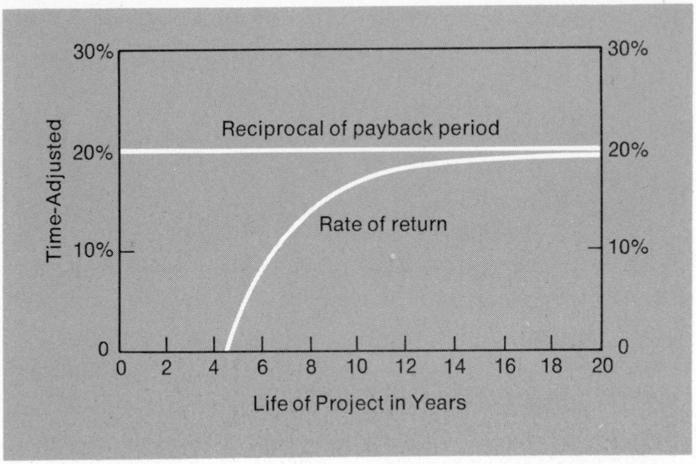

Source: N.A.A. Research Report 35, *Return on Capital as a Guide to Managerial Decisions*, p. 78.

Note that this rate is closer to the time-adjusted rate (18.62 percent) of return than is either answer provided by the accounting method, discussed in Appendix A.

Note also that the table in Exhibit 13-9 would be used as follows:

$$\text{Payback period} = \frac{\$22,000}{\$5,000} = 4.400 \text{ or } 4\frac{1}{2} \text{ years}$$

The useful life is ten years. The table's ten-year row and 4½-year column indicate a time-adjusted rate of return of 19 percent, a very accurate approximation.

Payback is widely used in industry. Prudent use of the device shows that it may be very helpful:

> This company uses the rate of return on "book investment" [i.e., the accounting method], exclusively for projects costing over $25,000. For smaller projects, it uses the payback period. The controller stated that, as a general guide, the company "should get its money back in no more than half the expected life of the project" and that furthermore this payback period should be a relatively short period of years. Apparently he realized that, where the life of the project is substantially in excess of the payback period, the payback period varies inversely with rate of return and, by keeping the payback period short, the company insures a fairly high rate of return.[11]

accounting rates and time-adjusted rates As the payback reciprocal demonstrated, the accuracy of a shortcut model as an approximation of the time-adjusted rate of return is a function of two variables: the economic life of the investment proposal (N) and the time-adjusted rate (R). As Exhibit 13-10 shows, the payback reciprocal is a better approximator than the accounting methods when the economic

[11] For this and other examples of company uses of payback methods, see *N.A.A. Research Report 35, op. cit.*, pp. 80–81.

EXHIBIT 13-9

TABLE FOR APPROXIMATING RATE OF RETURN

Useful life in years	Time-Adjusted Rate of Return (per cent)										
3	0										
4	15	11	7	3	0						
5	23	19	15	12	9	6	4	2	0		
6	27	23	20	17	15	12	10	8	6	3	0
7	29	26	23	20	18	15	13	11	10	7	4
8	30	27	25	22	20	18	16	14	12	10	8
9	31	28	26	23	21	19	18	16	15	12	10
10	32	29	27	24	22	21	19	18	16	14	11
15	33	30	28	25	25	23	22	20	19	16	15
20	33	30	28	26	25	23	22	20	19	18	16
Over 20	33	31	29	27	25	24	23	21	20	19	17
Payback period in years	3	$3\frac{1}{4}$	$3\frac{1}{2}$	$3\frac{3}{4}$	4	$4\frac{1}{4}$	$4\frac{1}{2}$	$4\frac{3}{4}$	5	$5\frac{1}{2}$	6

Source: Adapted from N.A.A. Research Report 35, *Return on Capital as a Guide to Managerial Decisions*, p. 76.

Example 1.(Same facts as plotted in graph in Exhibit 13-8.) Project savings expected to last ten years; computed payback period is five years (a payback reciprocal of 20%). Enter table at ten-year row and five-year column. Table shows 16% time-adjusted rate of return. (The relationships on the graph in Exhibit 13-8 can also be found in the five-year column of this table.)

Example 2. Project savings expected to last 12 years. Computed payback period is 4.7 years. Enter table using nearest values; that is, use 10 years for savings and 4¾ years for payback period. Table shows 18% time-adjusted rate of return. For more accurate computations, interpolation may be used.

life is long and the time-adjusted rate is large. The comparisons for the earlier illustration (investment, $4,500; life, 10 years; annual operating inflow, $1,000) follow:

Time-adjusted rate of return:

$$\$4,500 = \$1,000(F)$$

$$F = 4.500$$

Therefore, 10-year line in Table 4 indicates time-adjusted rate is 18.0%.

Payback reciprocal = $1,000 ÷ $4,500 = 22.2%

Accounting rate based on total investment $= \dfrac{\$1,000 - \$450}{\$4,500} = 12.2\%$

Accounting rate based on average investment $= \dfrac{\$1,000 - \$450}{.5(\$4,500)} = 24.4\%$

EXHIBIT 13-10

SETS *R* AND *N* FOR WHICH EACH ALTERNATIVE MODEL PROVIDES THE
CLOSEST APPROXIMATION TO THE TIME-ADJUSTED RATE OF RETURN

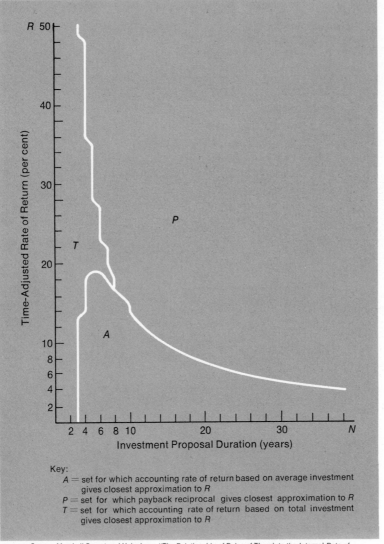

Key:
A = set for which accounting rate of return based on average investment
    gives closest approximation to *R*
P = set for which payback reciprocal gives closest approximation to *R*
T = set for which accounting rate of return based on total investment
    gives closest approximation to *R*

Source: Marshall Sarnat and Haim Levy, "The Relationship of Rules of Thumb to the Internal Rate of
Return: A Restatement and Generalization," *Journal of Finance*, XXIV, No. 3 (June 1969), 486.

Note that the *P* set in Exhibit 13-10 gives a more accurate approximation
than the two variants of the accounting rate of return for an investment with
a life of ten years and a time-adjusted rate above 14 percent.

Now suppose that the investment is $6,710 instead of $4,500:

Time-adjusted rate of return:

$$\$6,710 = \$1,000(F)$$
$$F = 6.710$$

Therefore, 10-year line in Table 4 indicates time-adjusted rate is 8.0%.

Payback reciprocal = $1,000 ÷ $6,710 = 14.9%

$$\text{Accounting rate based on total investment} = \frac{\$1,000 - \$671}{\$6,710} = 4.9\%$$

$$\text{Accounting rate based on average investment} = \frac{\$1,000 - \$671}{.5(\$6,710)} = 9.8\%$$

Note that the A set in Exhibit 13-10 gives a more accurate approximation than the other two sets for investment proposals with economic lives longer than three years and with time-adjusted rates of 19 percent and lower as the life lengthens.[12]

This comparison of models illustrates how managers and accountants often may intuitively use simple models (rules of thumb, shortcuts, or crude approximations) that they perceive as "good enough" in particular circumstances. The point is that our increasing knowledge of decision models now often permits us to use sensitivity analysis to test whether the simpler models are indeed leading to optimal decisions.

APPENDIX C: TIME-ADJUSTED RATE OF RETURN USING TRIAL-AND-ERROR METHODS

The data are from Exhibit 13-5, the incremental approach. Trial-and-error methods must be used to calculate the rate of return that will equate future cash flows with the incremental initial investment of $31,000. If there were only an annuity of $10,000 per year, the factor for the true rate would be $31,000 ÷ 10,000 = 3.100, which is between 18 and 20 percent on the 5-year line of Table 4 in Appendix B at the end of the book. Because there is an additional benefit at the end of year 2, you may want to try a higher rate, say 20 percent. Apply this rate to all flows, year by year; use Table 2, because the flows are not uniform:

YEAR	NET CASH INFLOWS	FIRST TRIAL: 20 PERCENT PRESENT-VALUE FACTOR	TOTAL PRESENT VALUE	SECOND TRIAL: 22 PERCENT PRESENT-VALUE FACTOR	TOTAL PRESENT VALUE
1	$10,000	.833	$ 8,330	.820	$ 8,220
2	20,000	.694	13,880	.672	13,440
3	10,000	.579	5,790	.551	5,551
4	10,000	.482	4,820	.451	4,510
5	5,000	.402	2,010	.370	1,850
			$34,830		$33,571

At 20 percent, the total present value of the future cash flows *exceeds* the initial investment. This means that the "true" rate must be higher than 20

[12] The Sarnat and Levy article cited in Exhibit 13-10 stresses that the relationships among the alternative models shown in the exhibit remain invariant for any level of taxation. Thus, all the general properties of the relationships hold for both the before-tax and after-tax cases.

percent. You are trying to find a rate that will make the total present value exactly *equal* to $31,000. A second trial shows that 22 percent is also too low. The third trial, at 26 percent, produces an answer so close that interpolation is not needed. The time-adjusted rate is 26 percent:

| | | THIRD TRIAL: 26 PERCENT | |
YEAR	NET CASH INFLOWS	PRESENT-VALUE FACTOR	TOTAL PRESENT VALUE
1	$10,000	.794	$ 7,940
2	20,000	.630	12,600
3	10,000	.500	5,000
4	10,000	.397	3,970
5	5,000	.315	1,575
			$31,085

Note that a much cruder approach might be used. For example, we may think with some assurance that the rate is surely above 14 percent and below 30 percent. We compute, using these widely different rates, and interpolate:

| | | TRIAL: 14 PERCENT | | TRIAL: 30 PERCENT | |
YEAR	NET CASH INFLOWS	PRESENT-VALUE FACTOR	TOTAL PRESENT VALUE	PRESENT-VALUE FACTOR	TOTAL PRESENT VALUE
1	$10,000	.877	$ 8,770	.769	$ 7,690
2	20,000	.769	15,380	.592	11,840
3	10,000	.675	6,750	.455	4,550
4	10,000	.592	5,920	.350	3,500
5	5,000	.519	2,538	.269	1,345
			$39,358		$28,925

The true rate is somewhere between 14 and 30 percent. It can be crudely approximated by straight-line interpolation even though the present-value tables are not based on linear relationships:

	TOTAL PRESENT VALUES	
14%	$39,358	$39,358
True rate		31,000
30%	28,925	
Difference	$10,433	$ 8,358

Therefore: True rate $= 14\% + \dfrac{\$ 8,358}{\$10,433}\ (30\% - 14\%)$

$= 14\% + .8(16\%)$

$= 14\% + 12.8\%$

$= 26.8\%$

Note that 26.8 percent is a fairly good approximation of the true rate, even though straight-line interpolation was used between widely separated trial rates.

questions, problems, and cases

Special note: For all problems, ignore income taxes. The effects of income taxes are considered in Chapter 14.

13-1. Define *capital budgeting.*

13-2. What is the payback method? What is its main weakness?

13-3. Define *time-adjusted rate of return.*

13-4. "The payback reciprocal has wide applicability as a meaningful approximation of the time-adjusted rate of return. But it has two major limitations." What are the two limitations?

13-5. "The trouble with discounted cash-flow techniques is that their use ignores depreciation costs." Do you agree? Why?

13-6. "Accelerated depreciation provides higher cash flows in early years." Do you agree? Why?

13-7. "A project with a useful life of sixty years would have a time-adjusted rate of return practically exactly equal to its payback reciprocal." Why?

13-8. Exercises in Compound Interest. To be sure that you understand how to use the tables in Appendix B to this book, solve the following exercises. Do the exercises on your own before checking your answers. The correct answers rounded to the nearest dollar are printed after Problem 13-33.

1. You have just won $5,000. How much money will you have at the end of ten years if you invest it at 6 percent compounded annually? Ignore income taxes in this and other parts of this problem.

2. Ten years from now, the unpaid principal of the mortgage on your house will be $8,955. How much do you have to invest today at 6 percent interest compounded annually just to accumulate the $8,955 in ten years?

3. You plan to save $500 of your earnings each year for the next ten years. How much money will you have at the end of the tenth year if you invest your savings compounded at 6 percent per year?

4. If the unpaid mortgage on your house in ten years will be $8,955, how much money do you have to invest annually at 6 percent to have just this amount on hand at the end of the tenth year?

5. You hold an endowment insurance policy that will pay you a lump sum of $20,000 at age 65. If you invest the sum at 6 percent, how much money can you withdraw from your account in equal amounts each year so that at the end of ten years there will be nothing left?

6. You have estimated that for the first ten years after you retire, you will need an annual income of $2,720. How much money must you invest at 6 percent at age 65 to just realize this annual income?

7. The table below shows two schedules of prospective operating cash inflows, each of which requires the same initial investment:

| YEAR | ANNUAL CASH INFLOWS | |
	PLAN A	PLAN B
0	$ 1,000	$ 5,000
1	2,000	4,000
2	3,000	3,000
3	4,000	2,000
4	5,000	1,000
Total	$15,000	$15,000

The minimum desired rate of return is 6 percent compounded annually. In terms of present values, which plan is more desirable? Show computations.

13-9. Compare Two Projects [SIA, adapted]. The management of Dilex Diversified must decide between two proposals. The following information is available:

| | INVESTMENT NOW | NET CASH INFLOWS | | |
PROPOSAL		PERIOD 1	PERIOD 2	PERIOD 3
A	$ 80,000	$95,400	$39,000	$12,000
B	100,000	35,000	57,500	80,000

required   Assuming that the company can earn 12 percent on projects of this type and that the cash inflows are received at the end of each period, advise management regarding the proposal that should be selected. Submit computations of net present values. Ignore income tax considerations.

13-10. Payback Period. A manager is considering three mutually exclusive investment projects, A, B, and C, each promising a cash flow of $20,000 per year for an initial investment of $100,000. Useful lives are as follows:

PROJECT	YEARS
A	5
B	6
C	7

required   1. Compute the payback period for each project. If payback time is the sole criterion for the decision, which project is most desirable?

2. Which project offers the highest rate of return?

13-11. Comparison of Approaches to Capital Budgeting. Refer to Problem 11-9. Using all data given there, compute:
1. Payback period
2. Time-adjusted rate of return by trial and error
3. Net present value of future savings discounted at a 10 percent minimum desired rate of return.

13-12. Comparison of Approaches to Capital Budgeting. The Gehrig Company estimates that it can save $2,800 a year in cash operating costs for the next ten years if it buys a special-purpose machine at a cost of $11,000. No residual value is expected. The company's minimum desired rate of return is 14 percent.

required   (Round all computations to the nearest dollar. Ignore income taxes.)
1. Payback period
2. Using discounted cash flow:
    a. Time-adjusted rate of return
    b. Net present value
3. Payback reciprocal

13-13. Sensitivity Analysis, Payback Reciprocal. The All Directions Railroad is considering the replacement of an old power jack tamper used in the maintenance of track with a new improved version that should save $5,000 per year in net cash operating costs.

The old equipment has zero disposal value, but it could be used indefinitely. The estimated useful life of the new equipment is 12 years and it will cost $20,000.

required

1. Payback time.

2. Time-adjusted rate of return.

3. Management is unsure about the useful life. What would be the rate of return if the useful life were (a) 6 years instead of 12, and (b) 20 years instead of 12?

4. Suppose the life will be 12 years, but the savings will be $3,000 per year instead of $5,000. What would be the rate of return?

5. Suppose the annual savings will be $4,000 for 6 years. What would be the rate of return?

6. Professor Myron Gordon has pointed out that the payback reciprocal can be a crude approximation of the true rate of return where (a) the project life is at least twice the payback period, and (b) the cash earnings or savings are uniformly received in equal amounts throughout the investment's life. The payback reciprocal, using the original data, will be $5,000 ÷ $20,000, or 25 percent.
   a. How close is this to the time-adjusted rate of return?
   b. Compute the payback reciprocals for 3(a) and 3(b). How close are they to the time-adjusted rates of return?
   c. Compute the payback reciprocals for (4) and (5). How close are they to the time-adjusted rates of return?

13-14. **Replacement of Machine and Uncertainty.** The Field Co. manufactures a basic auto part, which it markets together with several related parts. Each year the basic part is adapted or a new one produced to meet market trends. The following alternatives are being considered.

First, modify an existing machine at a cost of $12,000. This machine was bought a year ago for $45,000. It could be used for another two years and would then be worthless. The contribution margin of 40 percent will not be affected if this machine is modified.

Second, buy a new machine for $50,000 and sell the old one for $4,000 cash. The new machine could be used for two years and would then have a scrap value of $4,000. The contribution margin will be raised to 60 percent if this machine is used.

It is fairly certain that revenue for the first year will be $200,000. A foreign manufacturer, who has not yet entered the domestic market, is expected to be in competition within a year. The outlook for the second year is uncertain. The feeling of the planning committee is that demand may decline by 25 percent in the second year.

Under either alternative and given either outcome, $100,000 is expected to be tied up in working capital over the two years. The required rate of return is about 30 percent before taxes. Ignore the calculation of tax liability arising from this project. For simplicity, assume that the present value of $1 payable at the end of one and two years, respectively, is 0.80 and 0.60.

required

The net present value of each alternative for both the best and worst outcomes, treating cash inflows as being received at the end of each year.

13-15. **Different Approaches to Capital Budgeting; Proper Investment Base.** The Ruth Company has been operating a small lunch counter for the convenience of employees. The counter occupies space that is not needed for any other business purpose. The lunch counter has been managed by a part-time employee whose annual salary is $3,000. Yearly operations have consistently shown a loss as follows:

Receipts		$20,000
Expenses for food, supplies (in cash)	$19,000	
Salary	3,000	22,000
Net loss		$(2,000)

A company has offered to sell Ruth automatic vending machines for a total cost of $13,000, less $1,000 trade-in allowance on old equipment (which was carried at zero book value and which could be sold outright for $1,000 cash) now used in the lunch-counter operation. Sales terms are cash on delivery. The old equipment will have zero disposal value ten years from now.

The predicted useful life of the equipment is ten years, with zero scrap value. The equipment will easily serve the same volume that the lunch counter handled. A catering company will completely service and supply the machines. Prices and variety of food and drink will be the same as those that prevailed for the lunch counter. The catering company will pay 5 percent of gross receipts to the Ruth Company and will bear all costs of foods, repairs, and so forth. The part-time employee will be discharged. Thus, Ruth's only cost will be the initial outlay for the machines.

required   Consider only the two alternatives mentioned.

1. Prospective annual income statement under new plan. What is the annual income difference between alternatives?

2. Compute the payback period.

3. Compute:
   a. Present value under discounted cash-flow method if relevant cost of company capital is 20 percent.
   b. Rate of return under discounted cash-flow method.

4. Compute the payback reciprocal. Compare your answer with the result in 3(b).

5. Management is very uncertain about the prospective revenue from the vending equipment. Suppose that the gross receipts amounted to $14,000 instead of $20,000. Repeat the computation in part 3(a).

6. What would be the minimum amount of annual gross receipts from the vending equipment that would justify making the investment? Show computations.

7. What other considerations may influence the decision?

13-16. Choosing an Automobile. Having given the matter some thought, you decide that you would be equally happy buying:
a. A Cadillac and trading every sixth year.
b. A Pontiac and trading every third year.
c. A Pinto and trading every second year.

You have decided to base your decision on the present value of the expected future costs. You have predicted your costs as follows:

	CADILLAC	PONTIAC	PINTO
Original cost	$6,500	$4,500	$3,000
Market value at trade-in time	1,000	2,000	1,500
Annual operating costs, excluding depreciation	600	700	500
Overhaul, fourth year	500		
Overhaul, second year		150	
Minimum desired rate of return is 6%.			

required   Select the alternative that promises the greatest financial advantage. Show computations.

13-17. Replacement of Machine.   The Maris Company is considering the purchase of a vertical milling machine to replace an obsolete milling machine. The machine currently being used for the operation is in good working order and will last, physically, for at least ten years. However, the proposed machine will perform the operations so much more efficiently that Maris Company engineers predict that labor, materials, and other direct costs of the operation will be reduced $2,000 a year if the proposed machine is installed. The proposed milling machine costs $10,000 delivered and installed. The company requires a minimum of 20 percent on all investments. Taxes are to be disregarded. The new machine's useful life is ten years.

Note: The present value of $1 received annually for ten years at various interest rates is:

15%	16%	18%	20%	22%	25%
5.019	4.833	4.494	4.192	3.923	3.571

required

1. Assuming that the present machine is being depreciated at a rate of $800 per year, that it has a book value of $8,000 (cost, $18,000; accumulated depreciation, $10,000), and that it has zero net salvage value today, what action should be taken? What time-adjusted rate of return would be earned on the investment in the new machine?
2. Data of part 1, except that the net salvage value of the old machine today is $2,000, and if retained for ten years its salvage value will be zero. How is your answer to part 1 altered?

13-18. Two Sizes of Machines; Uneven Revenue Stream; Price-Level Change.   The Kubek Company has developed a new product for which a growing demand is anticipated. During the first year, sales are expected to be 20,000 units; the second year, 30,000 units; the third year, 50,000 units; the fourth year and each year thereafter, 80,000 units.

The Kubek Company must choose between two alternative production arrangements:
1. Buy a big, heavy-duty machine with a capacity of 90,000 units and an estimated useful life of six years. This machine costs $250,000.
2. Buy a smaller machine with a capacity of 50,000 units and an estimated useful life of three years. Three years from today buy two such machines to replace the one that will be worn out. The smaller machines now cost $100,000 each.

Property taxes and insurance per year are expected to be $8,000 on the big machine and 4 percent of original cost of equipment in use on the small machines. Maintenance cost is expected to be $2,000 per year on the big machine and $1,200 per year on each of the smaller machines. Variable production costs per unit will be $3.00 with the big machine and $3.10 with the smaller machines. Both machines will have zero disposal values at the end of their respective useful lives.

Prices on this type of machinery have been increasing at the rate of 4 percent compounded annually. Which alternative is more attractive? Show all computations clearly, using the total present values of all outlays for each alternative. The minimum desired rate of return is 10 percent. Assume that all outlays take place at the end of the accounting periods. Round off present value factors to two decimal places.

13-19. Elimination of Department. The Howard Pharmacy is considering eliminating its soda fountain. The proprietor feels that the space can be devoted to more profitable use if he expands his displays of over-the-counter pharmaceuticals. The income statement is presented below:

	PRESCRIPTIONS	OVER-THE-COUNTER PHARMACEUTICALS	FOUNTAIN	TOTAL
Sales	$50,000	$70,000	$40,000	$160,000
Less: Cost of sales	28,000	56,000	20,000	104,000
Gross profit	$22,000	$14,000	$20,000	$ 56,000
Variable expenses	$11,000	$ 8,000	$16,000	$ 35,000
Fixed expenses*	3,000	2,000	5,000	10,000
Depreciation	500	1,000	1,800	3,300
Total expenses	$14,500	$11,000	$22,800	$ 48,300
Net profit	$ 7,500	$ 3,000	$(2,800)	$ 7,700

*Exclusive of depreciation.

From past experience, the proprietor feels that he can increase his sales of over-the-counter pharmaceuticals by the following amounts:

Year 1	$30,000
Year 2	40,000
Year 3 and thereafter	50,000

Variable expenses are expected to rise by the following amounts:

Year 1	$1,000
Year 2	1,200
Year 3 and thereafter	1,500

It is expected that the cost of sales in this department will remain at the same proportion as now. Fixed expenses are expected to remain at the same level.

The fountain's present book value is $10,000. Its present disposal value is $2,000. Its expected useful life is five years, and its expected salvage value is $1,000.

The cost of renovating the store is $18,000. The market value of the new fixtures in five years is estimated at $5,000.

The minimum desired rate of return is 10 percent.

required

Should the proprietor of the Howard Pharmacy go through with his plan? Support your answer by calculations showing the effect of discounted cash flows for the next five years. Use incremental analysis.

13-20. A Study of the Potential Economic Usefulness of an Invention.   A store manager of a large grocery chain has invented a labor-saving machine. It is designed to automatically cut the tops and bottoms from cases of grocery merchandise. These tops and bottoms, with their one and one-half-inch edges, are used as trays to hold 12 and 24 cans each. These filled trays are then stacked directly onto the shelves. Production time is improved as a result of handling 12 or perhaps 24 in one motion as opposed to hand-stacking the same number of cans in from three to six separate motions.

   This "tray-pack" method of shelf stocking and display building is not new to the grocery business. Up until now, however, the trays had to be cut by hand, which is difficult, tedious work that often has unsightly results. The electric tray-cutter is fastened to the roller conveyor in the back room and adjusts itself automatically to any size case. It cuts trays just about as quickly as stock can be pulled by two men in a grocery back room, simply slicing off the trays as the merchandise rolls by on the conveyor.

   Some elementary time-study work was necessary to verify that the machine was indeed a time-saver and to give comparative production figures for the job. The following estimates were made of the annual depreciation and maintenance expenses:

Machine cost	$950.00
Depreciation (annual, straight-line)	200.00
Installation cost	50.00
Annual repair and electricity expense	50.00
Scrap value	00.00

   The weekly savings experienced in an average store, cutting about 600 cases of tray-pack merchandise each week, are as follows:

Manual-cutting rate	2 cases per minute
Machine-cutting rate	12 cases per minute

   The current labor cost is $2.00 per hour plus $.20 in fringe benefits.

   Assume a 20 percent minimum desired rate of return. Also assume that the labor savings are real—that is, that the labor costs under investigation are variable costs.

required

1. Compute payback time, payback reciprocal, and the net present value for the average store.

2. What is the lowest volume of cases per week that could be handled and still make the installation desirable? Show computations.

13-21. Capital Investment in a Baseball Player.   William Voock, president of the Chicago Chartreuse Sox, is currently considering a player deal in which he will acquire Bill Blue, a great gate attraction, from the New York Confederates in exchange for $500,000 cash plus George Bumble, a regular Sox outfielder who is currently receiving a salary of $15,000 a year. Blue is to be Bumble's replacement in the regular outfield. Voock and his fellow executives have assembled the following data:

Estimated useful life of Blue	5 years
Estimated residual value of Blue	$20,000
Estimated useful life of Bumble	5 years
Estimated residual value of Bumble	None
Current cash offer for Bumble received from the Atlanta Carpetbaggers Baseball Club	$50,000
Applicable minimum desired rate of return	10%

Other data:

YEAR	BLUE'S SALARY	ADDITIONAL CLUB GATE RECEIPTS BECAUSE OF BLUE	ADDITIONAL EXPENSES OF HANDLING HIGHER VOLUME
1	$60,000	$330,000	$33,000
2	70,000	300,000	30,000
3	80,000	200,000	20,000
4	80,000	100,000	10,000
5	72,000	40,000	4,000

required   (Ignore income taxes.)

1. Based on the data as given, should the Sox buy Blue? Use the following present value factors for $1 at 10 percent:

	FOR END OF YEAR				
	1	*2*	*3*	*4*	*5*
Factor	.91	.83	.75	.68	.62

2. What other factors should be considered before making the decision? How much confidence do you have in the available data?

13-22. **Purchase of New Furnace: Different Capacities, Different Useful Lives.** The Glen Manufacturing Company is using a single gas-fired furnace at present, but owing to expected increases in output, it is considering the following alternatives:

a. Purchase a new electric furnace with double the capacity of the present furnace, and sell the present furnace.

b. Purchase a new gas furnace similar to the present one, and operate the two gas furnaces.

The following information is available to aid in making the decision:

1. All furnaces are assumed to have a ten-year life with zero salvage value at the end of that time.

2. The old furnace had a cost of $4,000 four years ago. It can be sold outright for $2,400 cash.

3. The price of a new gas furnace is $4,680. This price is expected to increase at a rate of 4 percent compounded annually.

4. Repair and maintenance costs for a gas furnace used regularly during the year are $1,400 per year.

5. The price of the new electric furnace is $22,400; annual repair and maintenance costs are expected to be $1,200.

6. Comparative variable costs per charge (the unit of heating) are:

	GAS	ELECTRIC
Purchased power source	$ 6.80	$12.40
Supplies	2.60	1.20
Labor	10.60	4.40
	$20.00	$18.00

7. Property taxes are estimated to be $150 per gas furnace and $700 per electric furnace per year.
8. Minimum desired rate of return is 6 percent.
9. It is estimated that machine usage over the next ten years will be at the rate of 700 units (charges) per year.

required   To ease computations, round off all factors from the compound-interest tables to two decimal places.

1. The "payout" or "payback" time. The payback reciprocal. What can you conclude from the reciprocal?

2. The net present value of the electric furnace.

3. Indicate for *each* of the following whether the use of the *gas*-furnace system would become more or less desirable. Justify your answer by a *one*-sentence explanation.
   (1) Property tax rates advance.
   (2) New labor contract raises wage rates.
   (3) Interest rates advance.
   (4) Demand for product increases, so that machine usage is increased to 800 units.
   (5) The Federal Power Commission authorizes an increase in natural-gas rates.

13-23. **Compute Minimum Desired Rate of Return.** The Strubel Company has used the net present-value method in making capital-investment decisions. The company rejected an offer of a machinery salesman who had convincing evidence that his $12,500 lifting equipment would save the company $3,000 in cash operating costs per year for ten years. The disposal value of the machine was $2,000 at the end of ten years. In applying the net present-value method, the company computed a negative net present value of $457. What was the minimum desired rate of return? Show computations.

13-24. **When to Cut a Tree.** Del Doller, a wealthy capitalist, bought land and put it in the conservation reserve. He was told that if he planted trees on the land, he would get a yearly check, and the government would not come to inspect for 20 years.

A large industrial firm that needs lumber has approached Del. The firm's employees will plant and care for trees on Del's land. In return for the use of the land, they will pay 10¢ a board foot for the lumber they cut. They will cut at Del's discretion.

The number of board feet of lumber in a tree depends upon the age of the tree in years. Assuming an average growth, the growth function for trees is $f(n) = 300 \sqrt{n} - 900$, where n is years and $f(n)$ is the number of board feet.

required   Del wants to know the most profitable time for cutting the trees. Del uses a 20 percent minimum desired rate of return.

n	$\sqrt{n}$	n	$\sqrt{n}$
10	3.162	16	4.000
11	3.317	17	4.123
12	3.464	18	4.243
13	3.606	19	4.359
14	3.742	20	4.472
15	3.873		

13-25. **Replacement Decision for Railway Equipment.** The Milwaukee Railroad is considering replacement of a Kalamazoo Power Jack Tamper, used in connection with maintenance of track, with a new automatic raising device that can be attached to a production tamper.

The present power jack tamper cost $18,000 five years ago and has an estimated life of twelve years. After the sixth year, the machine will require a major overhaul, estimated to cost $5,000. Its disposal value now is $2,500. There will be no value at the end of twelve years.

The automatic raising attachment has a delivered selling price of $24,000 and an estimated life of twelve years. Because of anticipated future developments in combined maintenance machines, it is felt that the machine should be disposed of at the end of the seventh year to take advantage of newly developed machines. Estimated sale value at the end of seven years is $5,000.

Tests have shown that the automatic raising machine will produce a more uniform surface on the track than the power jack tamper now in use. The new equipment will eliminate one machine operator and one laborer, whose combined annual salary is $9,500.

Track-maintenance work is seasonal, and the equipment normally works from May 1 to October 31 each year. Machine operators and laborers are transferred to other work after October 31, at the same rate of pay.

The salesman claims that the annual normal maintenance of the new machine will run about $1,000 per year. Because the automatic machine is more complicated than the manually operated machine, it is felt that it will require a thorough overhaul at the end of the fourth year, at an estimated cost of $7,000.

Records show the annual normal maintenance of the Kalamazoo machines to be $1,200. Fuel consumption of the two machines is equal.

Should the Milwaukee keep or replace the Kalamazoo Power Jack Tamper? A 10 percent rate of return is desired.

The Milwaukee is not currently paying any income tax.

13-26. **Decision to Sell a Business.** Mr. H. Closet is the sole proprietor of a medium-sized plumbing and heating business. Owing to the increasing amount of government-contract work in his business territory and the fact that the federal government requires that union-scale wages be paid on all government work, Closet is being pressured to unionize his shop.

Sensing Closet's distaste for unions and knowing that he is near the age of retirement, a syndicate promoter, the Ulm Company, has extended a $100,000 cash offer for his business.

Closet, however, sees a large amount of business coming his way if he unionizes and receives the government contracts. He decides that if he does stay in business, he will definitely sell out in eight years. His investment in current assets (cash, inventory, accounts receivable) will be expanded by $24,000 because of the increased volume of business. His equipment will not be in very good condition eight years hence. He therefore expects to sell the business at the end of the eighth year for $40,000.

Closet estimates that the government-contract work will result in a $200,000 increase in yearly sales. Nongovernment sales will remain constant at $400,000 a year. Direct-material costs are proportional to sales. His direct-labor costs are proportional to sales but will increase by 10 percent for all labor because of higher unionized wages. Variable overhead is assumed to vary with sales, and annual fixed overhead will total $60,000. Straight-line depreciation will increase from $8,000 per year to $10,000 per year, because new equipment

KEYSTONE PLUMBING & HEATING WORKS
Income Statement
(*Last Year*)

Sales		$400,000
Cost of goods sold:		
Direct materials	$125,000	
Direct labor	175,000	
Variable overhead	30,000	
Fixed overhead	54,000	384,000
Gross margin		$ 16,000
Selling and administrative expense, fixed		17,000*
Net income (loss)		$ (1,000)

* Includes a $10,000 salary paid to Closet.

must be purchased for $16,000. All fixed assets will be fully depreciated at the end of eight years. Selling and administrative expenses will remain at $17,000. Disregard any tax effects.

required

1. Prepare an income statement, assuming that there will be $200,000 of government-contract work and that all costs will vary as stated above. This statement will be applicable to any of the next eight years.

2. Assume that his minimum desired rate of return is 8 percent and that Closet considers his annual net cash flow as his $10,000 salary plus any cash flow from operations. Should Closet sell his business now, or continue in business for another eight years as a union shop? If he sold out, Closet would retire and not work elsewhere. Assume that all additional investments in the business by Closet will be made immediately.

3. Discuss the limitations of the analysis that influenced your recommendation.

13-27. Three Alternatives, Effects on Inventory Investments.   The Dull Company has a very stable operation that is not marked by detectable variations in production or sales.

The Dull Company has an old machine with a net disposal value of $5,000 now and $1,000 five years from now. A new Rapido machine is offered for $25,000 cash or $20,000 with a trade-in. The new machine promises annual operating cash outflows of $2,000 as compared with the old machine's annual outflow of $10,000. A third machine, the Quicko, is offered for $45,000 cash or $40,000 with a trade-in; it promises annual operating cash outflows of $1,000. The disposal values of the new machines five years hence will be $1,000 each.

Because the new machines will produce output more swiftly, the average investment in inventories will be as follows:

Old machine	$100,000
Rapido	80,000
Quicko	50,000

The minimum desired rate of return is 20 percent. The company uses discounted cash-flow techniques to evaluate decisions.

required

Which of the three alternatives is most desirable? Show calculations. This company uses discounted cash-flow techniques for evaluating decisions. When more than two machines are being considered, the company favors computing the present value of the future costs of each alternative. The most desirable alternative is the one with the least cost.

P.V. of $1 at 20% for 5 years = .40
P.V. of annuity of $1 at 20% for 5 years = 3.00
Amount of $1 at 20% for 5 years = 2.20
Amount of annuity of $1 at 20% for 5 years = 8.00

13-28. **Cost–Volume–Profit Analysis and Discounted Cash Flow.** The Susan Company wants to make doughnuts for its chain of restaurants in Los Angeles. Two machines are proposed for the production of the doughnuts: semiautomatic and automatic. The company now buys doughnuts from an outside supplier at $.04 each. Manufacturing costs would be:

	SEMIAUTOMATIC	AUTOMATIC
Variable costs per doughnut	$.02	$.0125
Fixed costs:		
Annual cash operating outlays	$2,500	$ 3,500
Initial cost of machines	$6,000	$15,000
Useful life of machines in years	4	4
Salvage value at the end of 4 years	—	$ 3,000

required

1. The president wants to know how many doughnuts must be sold in order to have total average annual costs equal to outside purchase costs for the (a) semiautomatic machine and (b) automatic machine.

2. At what annual volume of doughnuts would the total annual costs be the same for both machines? Which machine is preferable if the volume exceeds the volume you computed? Why?

3. Assume that the sales forecast over the next four years is 400,000 doughnuts per year. The minimum desired rate of return is 10 percent. Should the automatic machine be purchased? Why? Show calculations. Ignore income taxes.

P.V. of $1.00 at 10% for 4 periods is   .7
P.V. of annuity of $1.00 at 10% for 4 periods is   3.2

Compare your answer with that in requirement 2. Do the answers differ? How? Why?

Note: Problems 13-29 through 13-33 cover the accounting method, which is discussed in Appendix A of this chapter.

13-29. **Accounting Rate of Return.** Refer to Problem 13-12. Using the data there, compute the accounting rate of return based on (a) average investment, (b) initial investment.

13-30. **Accounting Rate of Return.** Refer to Problem 11-9. Using the data there, compute the accounting rate of return based on (a) initial investment, (b) average investment.

13-31. **Accounting Rate of Return.** Refer to Problem 13-15. Using the data there, compute the accounting rate of return based on (a) average investment, (b) initial investment.

13-32. Accounting Rate of Return. Refer to Problem 11-25. Using the data there, compute the accounting rate of return based on (a) average investment, (b) initial investment.

13-33. Choice of Machines; Comparison of Discounted Cash-Flow and Accounting Methods. The India Manufacturing Company is considering the purchase of a machine for their factory. Two courses are available.

(a) Machine A is being offered at a special price of $50,000 with an estimated life of seven years and a disposal value estimated at $1,000. The cash operating expenses would amount to $30,000 annually. The machine would require major repairs every two years at a cost of $5,000.

(b) Machine B is available for a price of $75,000 with an estimated life of seven years and a disposal value of $5,000. The cash operating expenses with this machine would amount to $26,000 annually. Major repairs cost $3,500 every third year.

Assume the same revenue flow in all years for both alternatives. Assume that the minimum desired rate of return is 10 percent.

required

1. Compute the average annual return on the extra $25,000 needed to buy Machine B, using the accounting method and an "initial" investment base.

2. Using discounted cash flow, compute the present value of all future costs under both alternatives. Also compare the alternatives on an incremental basis.

Answers to exercises in compound interest (Problem 13-8)

The general approach to these problems centers about a key question: Which of the four basic tables am I dealing with? No computations should be made until after this basic question is answered with confidence.

1. $8,954. From Table 1. The $5,000 is a present value. The value ten years hence is an *amount* or *future worth*.

$S = P(1 + r)^n$; the conversion factor, $(1 + r)^n$, is on line 10 of Table 1.

Substituting: $S = 5,000\ (1.7908) = \$8,954$

2. $4,997. From Table 2. The $8,955 is an *amount* or *future worth*. You want the present value of that amount.

$P = S/(1 + r)^n$; the conversion factor, $1/(1 + r)^n$, is on line 10 of Table 2.

Substituting: $P = \$8,955\ (.558) = \$4,997$.

3. $6,590. From Table 3. You are seeking the *amount* or *future worth* of an annuity of $500 per year.

$$S_n = \$500\ F,\ \text{where } F \text{ is the conversion factor}$$
$$S_n = \$500\ (13.1808) = \$6,590$$

4. $679. From Table 3. The $8,955 is a future worth. You are seeking the uniform amount (annuity) to set aside annually.

$$S_n = \text{Annual deposit } (F)$$
$$\$8,955 = \text{Annual deposit } (13.1808)$$
$$\text{Annual deposit} = \frac{\$8,955}{13.1808} = \$679$$

5. $2,717. From Table 4. When you reach age 65, you will get $20,000. This is a present value at that time. You must find the annuity that will just exhaust the invested principal in ten years.

$$P_n = \text{Annual withdrawal } (F)$$
$$\$20,000 = \text{Annual withdrawal } (7.360)$$
$$\text{Annual withdrawal} = \frac{\$20,000}{7.360} = \$2,717$$

6. $20,019. From Table 4. You need to find the present value of an annuity for ten years.

$$P_n = \text{Annual withdrawal } (F)$$
$$P_n = \$2,720 \ (7.360)$$
$$P_n = \$20,019$$

7. Plan B is preferable. Its present value exceeds that of Plan A by $1,038:

YEAR	P.V. FACTORS AT 6% FROM TABLE 2	P.V. OF PLAN A	P.V. OF PLAN B
0	1.000	$ 1,000	$ 5,000
1	.943	1,886	3,772
2	.890	2,670	2,670
3	.840	3,360	1,680
4	.792	3,960	792
		$12,876	$13,914

14

A Closer Look
at Capital Budgeting

This chapter will consider a variety of interrelated problems of capital budgeting, including income tax factors, rationing capital, multiple alternatives, unequal lives, and cost of capital. Some readers may not wish to cover all of these topics. For example, the section on income taxes may be studied alone.

INCOME TAX FACTORS

importance of income taxes As any businessman will be quick to remark, income taxes are major disbursements that often have a tremendous influence on decisions. Even where tax rates and timing are the same for all alternatives, the before-tax differences between alternatives are usually heavily slashed by application of current income tax rates, so that after-tax differences become narrower. This reduction of differences often results in rejection of alternatives that are seemingly attractive on a pre-tax basis. Thus, a 50 percent tax rate reduces the net attractiveness of $100,000 in cash operating savings to $50,000.

The role of taxes in capital budgeting is no different from that of any other cash disbursement. There are two major impacts of income taxes: (a) on the *amount* of cash inflow or outflow, and (b) on the *timing* of cash flows.

The intricacies of the income tax laws are often bewildering. This chapter will concentrate on a few pertinent provisions of the law in order to highlight a general approach to the problem. Our discussion will be confined to corporations rather than partnerships or individuals.

The applicable tax rate to be used in predicting cash flows is dependent on the income tax bracket of the taxpayer and on the type of income in question. For example, the federal rates on ordinary corporate net income in the early 1970's were 22 percent on the first $25,000 and 48 percent on the excess. But most states also levy income taxes, with rates that vary considerably. Thus, the combined tax effect on ordinary income in excess of $25,000 may easily exceed 50 percent.

timing and *Exhibit 14-1 shows the relationship between net income before taxes,*
different income taxes, and depreciation. Assume that a company has a single fixed
depreciation asset, purchased for $90,000 cash, which has a five-year life and zero
methods disposal value. The purchase cost, less any predicted disposal value, is tax-deductible in the form of yearly depreciation. This deduction has been aptly called a *tax shield*, because it protects that amount of income from taxation. As Exhibit 14-2 shows, the cost of the asset represents a valuable

EXHIBIT 14-1

BASIC ANALYSIS OF INCOME STATEMENT,
INCOME TAXES, AND CASH FLOWS

(*Data Assumed*)

TRADITIONAL INCOME STATEMENT		
(S)	Sales	$100,000
(E)	Less: Expenses, excluding depreciation	$ 62,000
(D)	Depreciation (straight-line)	18,000
	Total expenses	$ 80,000
	Income before income taxes	$ 20,000
(T)	Income taxes at 40 percent	8,000
(I)	Net income after income taxes	$ 12,000

Net after-tax cash inflow from operations is either

$$S - E - T = \$100,000 - \$62,000 - \$8,000 = \$30,000$$

or

$$I + D = \$12,000 + \$18,000 \qquad = \$30,000$$

ANALYSIS FOR CAPITAL BUDGETING

	Cash Effects of Operations	
(S − E)	Cash inflow from operations: $100,000 − $62,000 =	$38,000
	Income tax outflow, at 40 percent	15,200*
	After-tax effects of cash inflow from operations	$22,800
	Tax Shield	
(D)	Straight-line depreciation: $90,000 ÷ 5 = $18,000	
	Income tax savings, at 40 percent	7,200*
	Total cash effects	$30,000

*Net cash outflow from income taxes, $15,200 − $7,200 = $8,000.

EXHIBIT 14-2

TAX-SHIELD EFFECTS OF TWO DEPRECIATION METHODS

	10% DISCOUNT FACTOR	PRESENT VALUE AT 10%	SKETCH OF CASH FLOWS YEAR				
			1	2	3	4	5

STRAIGHT-LINE DEPRECIATION

Annual depreciation $90,000 ÷ 5 = $18,000

	10% DISCOUNT FACTOR	PRESENT VALUE AT 10%	1	2	3	4	5
Tax shield: savings in income taxes @ 40% = $7,200	3.791	$27,295	$ 7,200	$7,200	$7,200	$7,200	$7,200

Sum-of-the-Years'-Digits Depreciation

YEAR	MULTIPLIER*	DEDUCTION	INCOME TAX SAVINGS @ 40%	10% DISCOUNT FACTOR	PRESENT VALUE AT 10%	1	2	3	4	5
1	5/15	$30,000	$12,000	.909	$10,908	$12,000				
2	4/15	24,000	9,600	.826	7,930		$9,600			
3	3/15	18,000	7,200	.751	5,407			$7,200		
4	2/15	12,000	4,800	.683	3,278				$4,800	
5	1/15	6,000	2,400	.621	1,490					$2,400
					$29,013					

* The general formula for obtaining the *denominator* of the multiplier under the sum-of-the-digits method is:

$S = n\left(\dfrac{n+1}{2}\right)$ when S = sum of the digits

                 n = numbers of years of estimated useful life

$S = 5\left(\dfrac{5+1}{2}\right) = 5 \times 3 = 15$

future tax deduction of $90,000. The present value of this deduction depends directly on its specific yearly effects on future income tax payments. Therefore, the present value is influenced by the depreciation method selected, the tax rates, and the discount rate.

the best depreciation method The three most widely used depreciation methods are straight-line, sum-of-the-years'-digits, and double-declining-balance. The effects of the first two are shown in Exhibit 14-2. Note that the present value of the tax shield is greater if straight-line depreciation is *not* used. The accelerated depreciation methods will generally maximize present values as compared with the straight-line method. The cumulative dollar tax bills may not change, but the early write-offs defer tax outlays to future periods. The measure of the latter advantage depends on the rate of return that can be gained from funds that otherwise would have been paid as income taxes. The general rule in shrewd income tax planning is: When there is a legal choice, take the deduction sooner rather than later.

effects of income taxes on cash flow The effects of income taxes on cash flow may best be visualized by a step-by-step analysis of a simple example. The following example is similar to those in Chapter 13. However, all income tax effects will now be considered and an after-tax cost of capital is used.

example The Lindo Company is considering replacing an old packaging machine with a new, more efficient machine. The old machine originally cost $22,000. Accumulated straight-line depreciation is $12,000 and the remaining useful life is five years. The old machine can be sold outright now for $4,000. The predicted residual value at the end of five years is $600; however, the company has not used a residual value in allocating depreciation for tax purposes. Annual cash operating costs are $50,000 per year.

Company engineers are convinced that the new machine, which costs $15,000, will have annual cash operating costs of $46,000 per year. The new machine will have a useful life of five years, with an estimated residual value of $700. Sum-of-the-years'-digits depreciation would be useful for tax purposes, with no provision for residual value.

required Assume that the minimum desired rate of return, after taxes, is 10 percent. Using the net present-value technique, demonstrate which action is more profitable with a total-project approach and with an incremental approach. Assume that the zero residual values are acceptable for tax purposes. Assume a 40 percent tax rate.

SOLUTION See Exhibits 14-3 and 14-4 for the complete solution. The following steps are recommended. The pertinent income tax aspects are considered for each step.

Step 1. General Approach. The inclusion of tax considerations does not change the general approach to these decisions. Review Chapter 13.

Step 2. Cash Operating Costs and Depreciation. Cash operating costs and their income tax effects are separated from the depreciation tax shield. These could be combined if preferred. However, the treatment illustrated facilitates comparisons of alternative depreciation effects and allows the use of annuity tables for the cash operating costs if they are equal per year.

In this illustration we assume that any cash flow and the related tax flow occur in the same period. For simplicity, we are neglecting the possibility that some tax payments related to the pre-tax operating cash inflows of year 1 may not actually occur until sometime in year 2. The analysis could be refined to account for any possible lags.

Step 3. Disposal of Equipment. In general, gains and losses on disposal of equipment are taxed in the same way as ordinary gains and losses.[1]

Exhibit 14-3 shows an analysis of the alternative dispositions of the old equipment. Disposal at the end of year 5 results in a taxable gain, the excess of the selling price over book value (zero in this case). The cash effect is the selling price less the 40 percent tax on the gain.

Immediate disposal of the old equipment results in a loss that is fully deductible from current income. The net loss must be computed to isolate its effect on current income tax, but the total cash inflow is the selling price plus the current income tax benefit.

Step 4. Total-Project or Incremental Approach? Exhibits 14-3 and 14-4 demonstrate these approaches. Both result in the same net present value in favor of replacement. Where there are only two alternatives, the incremental approach is faster. However, the incremental approach rapidly becomes unwieldy when there are multiple alternatives or when computations become intricate.

income tax complications The foregoing illustration deliberately excluded many possible complications. Income taxes are affected by many factors, including progressive tax rates, loss carrybacks and carryforwards, many depreciation options, state income taxes, short- and long-term gains, distinctions between capital assets and other assets, offsets of losses against related gains, exchanges of property of like kind, and exempt income. Special tax incentives should also be considered. These come and go, as various legislation is enacted and repealed. For example, most fixed-asset purchases in the 1960's qualified for an "investment credit," which was an immediate income tax credit of 7 percent of the initial cost; furthermore, the full original cost, less the predicted disposal value, was deductible as yearly depreciation.

Managers have a responsibility to avoid income taxes. *Avoidance* is not *evasion.* Avoidance is the use of legal means to minimize tax payments; evasion is the use of illegal means. Because income tax planning is exceedingly complex, professional tax counsel should be sought whenever the slightest doubt exists.

---

[1] In this case, the old equipment was sold outright. Where the old equipment is traded in on new equipment of like kind, no gain or loss can be recognized for tax purposes in the year of the transaction. Rather, the new equipment is capitalized at the book value of the old equipment plus the cash payment. Any gain or loss is then spread over the life of the new equipment through the new depreciation charges.

Before 1962, gains from disposal of equipment were taxed at the capital-gains rate, 25 percent. Since then, the gain on sale of equipment is not considered a capital gain except in special circumstances. This complication frequently results in having part of the gain taxed at ordinary income tax rates and part at capital-gains rates. For simplicity, this chapter does not introduce the latter complication. We assume that gains on disposal are taxed at ordinary rates.

EXHIBIT 14-3

LINDO COMPANY, AFTER-TAX ANALYSIS OF EQUIPMENT REPLACEMENT: TOTAL-PROJECT APPROACH

		PRESENT-VALUE DISCOUNT FACTORS @ 10%	TOTAL PRESENT VALUE	SKETCH OF CASH FLOWS					
				0	1	2	3	4	5
(A) Replace									
Recurring cash operating costs	$46,000								
Income tax savings, @ 40 percent	18,400								
After-tax cash operating costs	$27,600	3.791	($104,631)		($27,600)	($27,600)	($27,600)	($27,600)	($27,600)

Depreciation deductions (sum of digits
$1 + 2 + 3 + 4 + 5 = 15$)

YEAR	MULTIPLIED BY $15,000	DEDUCTION	TAX SHIELD: INCOME TAX SAVINGS, @ 40%		PRESENT-VALUE DISCOUNT FACTORS @ 10%	TOTAL PRESENT VALUE						
1	5/15	$ 5,000	$2,000		.910	1,820		2,000				
2	4/15	4,000	1,600		.830	1,328			1,600			
3	3/15	3,000	1,200		.750	900				1,200		
4	2/15	2,000	800		.680	544					800	
5	1/15	1,000	400		.620	248						400
		$15,000	$6,000									

Residual value, all subject to tax because of book value
will be zero $ 700
Less: 40% tax on gain 280

Net cash inflow	$ 420	.620	260						420
Cost of a new machine:	$15,000	1.000	(15,000)	($15,000)					

Disposal of old equipment:

Book value now	$10,000								
Selling price	4,000								
Net loss	$ 6,000								
Tax savings	× .40								
	2,400								
Net immediate cash effects, including tax savings	$ 6,400	1.000	6,400	6,400					
Total present value of all cash flows			($108,131)						

(B) Keep

				Year 1	Year 2	Year 3	Year 4	Year 5
Recurring cash operating costs	$50,000							
Income tax savings, @ 40%	20,000							
After-tax cash operating costs	$30,000	3.791	($113,730)	($30,000)	($30,000)	($30,000)	($30,000)	($30,000)
Depreciation deductions	$2,000							
Income tax savings, @ 40%	$ 800	3.791	3,033	800	800	800	800	800
Residual value, all subject to tax	$ 600							
Less: 40% tax on gain	240							
Net cash inflow	$ 360	.620	223					360
Total present value of all cash flows			($110,474)					
Difference in favor of replacement			$ 2,343					

EXHIBIT 14-4

LINDO COMPANY, AFTER-TAX ANALYSIS OF EQUIPMENT REPLACEMENT: INCREMENTAL ANALYSIS

	PRESENT-VALUE DISCOUNT FACTORS, @ 10%	TOTAL PRESENT VALUES	SKETCH OF CASH FLOWS					
			0	1	2	3	4	5
Analysis Confined to Differences between (A) and (B) in Exhibit 14-3:								
Recurring operating savings, $50,000 − $46,000 = $4,000								
Income tax, @ 40% 1,600								
After-tax operating savings $2,400	3.791	$9,098		$2,400	$2,400	$2,400	$2,400	$2,400

Differences in depreciation:

YEAR	REPLACE	KEEP	DIFFERENCE	INCOME TAX EFFECT, @ 40%		PRESENT-VALUE DISCOUNT FACTORS	TOTAL PRESENT VALUES	0	1	2	3	4	5
1	$5,000	$2,000	$3,000	$1,200		.910	1,092		1,200				
2	4,000	2,000	2,000	800		.830	664			800			
3	3,000	2,000	1,000	400		.750	300				400		
4	2,000	2,000	—	—		.680	—					—	
5	1,000	2,000	(1,000)	(400)		.620	(248)						(400)

	DISCOUNT FACTOR	TOTAL PRESENT VALUES	0	5
Difference in disposal value, end of Year 5 (see Exhibit 14-3 for details); $420 − $360 = $60	.620	37		60
Incremental initial investment (see Exhibit 14-3 for details): $15,000 − $6,400 = ($8,600)	1.000	(8,600)	($8,600)	
Net present value of replacement		$2,343		

EXHIBIT 14-5

PROJECT	LIFE	ANNUAL NET CASH EARNINGS	INVESTMENT	RANKING BY RATE OF RETURN		RANKING BY NET PRESENT VALUE	NET PRESENT VALUE	
				RATE OF RETURN	RANKING	PRESENT VALUE OF EARNINGS OF 10% MINIMUM DESIRED RATE	AMOUNT	RANK
A	5	$1,000	$2,864	22%	1	$3,791	$ 927	3
B	10	1,000	4,192	20%	2	6,145	1,953	2
C	15	1,000	5,092	18%	3	7,606	2,514	1

NET PRESENT VALUE OR TIME-ADJUSTED RATE OF RETURN?

conflict of
ranking
techniques

Generally, the net present-value and the time-adjusted rate of return techniques lead to the same decisions regarding the relative desirability of competing proposals. However, some crucial differences in the assumptions underlying the methods may occasionally lead to conflicting rankings of mutually exclusive investment proposals. Exhibit 14-5 illustrates this conflict. (Use tables to check the accuracy of the computations in Exhibit 14-5.)

What is the essential difference between these two variations of the discounted cash-flow method? Essentially, differing assumptions are made with respect to the *rate of return on the reinvestment* of the cash proceeds at the end of the shorter investment's life. The two methods make different implicit assumptions as to the reinvestment rate of return.

The rate-of-return approach assumes that the reinvestment rate is equal to the indicated rate of return for the shorter-lived project. The net present-value approach assumes that the funds obtainable from competing projects can be reinvested only at the rate of the company's minimum desired rate of return. Comparison follows:

COMPARISON OF PROJECTS A AND C

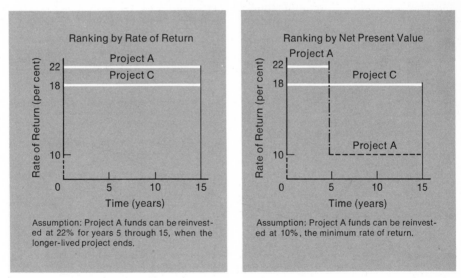

unequal lives
and
reinvestment

As shown in Exhibit 14-5 and in the graphs above, where mutually exclusive projects have unequal lives, the two methods show different rankings.[2] Let us see how these contradictory results occur.

At the end of fifteen years, the original investment in Project A will

---

[2] Also, similar conflicting results can occur when the terminal dates are the same but the sizes of the investment outlays differ (see Exhibit 14-6).

accumulate to more than that in Project C under the rate-of-return method, because it is assumed that the *Project A amount at the end of the fifth year can be reinvested to earn a 22 percent rate of return.* The rate-of-return method assumes the following accumulation of wealth:

> Project A, $1,000 per year for 15 years @ 22%
> will accumulate to $1,000(72.035) $72,035

On the other hand, the net present-value method assumes that the Project A amount at the end of the fifth year can be reinvested to earn only the *10 percent minimum desired rate of return.* The net present-value method assumes the following accumulation of wealth:

> Project A, $1,000 per year for 5 years[3] @ 22% will
> accumulate to 1,000(7.442) $ 7,442
> Then $1,000 for 10 years @ 10% is $1,000 × 15.9376
> (the factor from Table 3)   15,938
> Future accumulation $23,380

As long as projects under consideration promise rates of return in excess of the cutoff rate, the rate-of-return method has a built-in assumption in favor of short-lived projects like Project A, whereas the net present-value method has a built-in minimum rate of return that would favor longer-lived projects. If and when we look upon the minimum desired rate of return as an approximation of the opportunity rate for reinvestment, the net present-value method should be used rather than the time-adjusted rate of return method.

How may we reconcile these two approaches? Ideally, the answer is to reject both assumptions as to the reinvestment rate of return and predict a tailor-made rate of return for the time between the termination of the shorter-lived project and the termination of the longer-lived project. In other words, there is a need for a common terminal date and for explicit assumptions as to the appropriate reinvestment rates of funds. Solomon comments:

1. The valid comparison is not simply between two projects but between two alternative courses of action. The ultimate criterion is the total wealth that the investor can expect from each alternative by the terminal date of the longer-lived project. . . .
2. *If the rate of return* is to be used as an index of profitability, then the relevant rate is the per annum yield promised by each alternative course of action from its inception to a common terminal date in the future (usually the terminal date of the longer-lived project).
3. *If the present value* is to be used as an index of relative profitability, the expected reinvestment rate or set of rates should be used as the discounting factor. These rates will be equal to the company's present cost of capital only by coincidence.[4]

---

[3] The 72.035 in the preceding calculation would be the factor for the 15-period line and the 22-percent column in an expanded Table 3, the amount of an annuity. The 7.442 would be the factor for the 5-period line. These lines and columns for the 22 percent rate are not contained in the table in this book.

[4] Ezra Solomon, "Arithmetic of Capital Budgeting Decisions," *Journal of Business,* XXIX, No. 2, 127.

The practical difficulties of predicting future profitability on *reinvestment* are greater than those of predicting profitability of immediate projects. But reinvestment opportunities should be considered where they may be foreseen and measured.

equipment   Equipment-replacement decisions are often complicated by unequal lives
replacement   of competing equipment. One way of approaching the problem of unequal
lives is to estimate the residual value of the new equipment at the end of the remaining useful life of the old equipment. Then a comparison is made only over the remaining life of the old equipment.

Still another approach is to compare over the longer time span, including a prediction of replacement cost for the old machine at a later date. In essence, this is the approach described by Solomon above.

Of course, the crux of the problem in replacement decisions is the lack of a realistic common terminal date for both proposals. Thus, some estimate of residual value is necessary, whether the comparison is made over the remaining life of old equipment or the useful life of the new equipment. If new equipment is to last eight years and old equipment five years, a decision to retain old equipment implies that replacement will be made in five years. Therefore, if a comparison is to be made over eight years, the future replacement cost (five years hence) of the old equipment has to be predicted and also the terminal value of that replacement at the end of the eight-year span under review. This vicious difficulty goes on and on;[5] the practical answer is to make realistic assumptions regarding residual values at a common terminal date. The common date should be as distant as can be considered with confidence.

reinvestment   Capital-budgeting decisions in one year have chain reactions that may affect
outlook   investment opportunities and availability of capital in future years. Such
diverse factors as price-level changes, technological changes, and future investment choices may strongly influence current capital-spending decisions.

For example, in Exhibit 14-5, if investment opportunities five years hence are expected to return less than 15 percent, Project C, which promises a return of 18 percent for fifteen years, may be preferable to Project A, which promises a return of 22 percent for five years. In contrast, if opportunities to invest at 22 percent or more are anticipated in five years, the shorter-lived Project A might be more desirable than Project C, even if Project A promised only, say a 16 percent rate of return. In the latter case, Project C would require a much bigger investment than would be committed for a prolonged period.

---

[5] Some writers favor handling this problem by assuming an infinitely continuous replacement cycle. Thus, alternatives are compared by using perpetuity formulas. Although this is conceptually most appealing, it is probably too unrealistic to serve as a practical technique.

APPLICATIONS OF NET PRESENT VALUE

Chapter 13 and the preceding section indicated that the attractiveness of a capital project is best measured by discounting at the minimum desired rate of return; *any* project with a positive net present value should be undertaken. This is a general rule. Like all general rules, this is subject to qualifications. We shall now see how this rule is applied in various situations.

rationing capital Many companies specify an overall limit on the total budget for capital spending. There is no conceptual justification for such a budget ceiling.

All projects that enhance long-run profitability should be accepted. This is the only decision rule that makes economic sense. To the extent that capital rationing exists, it should be a "short-run phenomenon, limiting expenditures only to the current year or two."[6]

There are no hard-and-fast rules to be found in practice regarding the selection of an overall constraint. The net present values (or some similar measure, such as time-adjusted rate of return) may strongly influence the overall budget amount. For example, a flock of projects with huge net present values would probably result in a much higher overall budget than would a group of projects that all slightly exceeded zero.

Other interrelated factors that influence the amount of total funds to be committed in a single year include:

1. Top management's philosophy toward capital spending. (Some managements are highly growth-minded, whereas others are very conservative.)
2. The outlook for future investment opportunities that may not be feasible if extensive current commitments are undertaken.
3. The funds provided by current operations less dividends.
4. The feasibility of acquiring additional capital through borrowing or sale of additional stock. Lead times and costs of financial market transactions can influence spending.
5. Period of impending change in management personnel, when the status quo is maintained.

excess present-value index or net present value? The excess present-value index (also sometimes called the profitability index) is the ratio of the total present value of future net cash flows over the initial cash outflow. This index has been proposed by some writers as a means of ranking projects in descending order of attractiveness. If capital rationing does not exist, and if there are no mutually exclusive or indivisible projects, the rankings by index and by net present value will produce the same answers. That is, there is no conflict because all projects will be accepted that have an index of 100 percent or above; these will also have a net present value of zero or above.

[6]H. Martin Weingartner, "The Excess Present Value Index—A Theoretical Basis and Critique," *Journal of Accounting Research*, Vol. 1, No. 2, 214.

However, as we shall now see, conflicts in decisions may be generated if proposals are mutually exclusive, or if certain conditions of capital rationing exist.

mutually Assume that a company is considering two projects that are mutually
exclusive exclusive—that is, where the acceptance of one alternative automatically
alternatives results in the rejection of the other(s). The company can invest in either
and budget special-purpose equipment or general-purpose equipment, as follows:
constraints

	(1) COST	*(2)* *PRESENT VALUE* *AT 10% COST* *OF CAPITAL*	*(2) ÷ (1)* *EXCESS* *PRESENT-VALUE* *INDEX*	*(2) − (1)* *NET* *PRESENT* *VALUE*
GP Equipment	$1,000,000	$1,400,000	140%	$400,000
SP Equipment	3,000,000	3,900,000	130%	900,000

The GP equipment promises a higher return per dollar invested; if all other things, like risk, alternative uses of funds, and the like, were equal, the GP equipment seems an obvious choice. But "all other things" are rarely equal.

Assume that $5,000,000 is the total capital budget for the coming year and that the allocation of resources, using GP equipment for Project A, is as shown under Alternative One in Exhibit 14-6.

EXHIBIT 14-6

ALLOCATION OF CAPITAL BUDGET: COMPARISON OF TWO ALTERNATIVES

				ALLOCATION OF $5,000,000 BUDGET				
	ALTERNATIVE ONE				*ALTERNATIVE TWO*			
PROJECTS[a]	*INVESTMENT* *REQUIRED*	*EXCESS* *PRESENT-* *VALUE* *INDEX*	*TOTAL* *PRESENT* *VALUE* *AT 10%*	*PROJECT*	*INVESTMENT* *REQUIRED*	*EXCESS* *PRESENT-* *VALUE* *INDEX*	*TOTAL* *PRESENT* *VALUE* *AT 10%*
C	$ 600,000	167%	$1,000,000	C	$ 600,000	167%	$1,000,000
A(GP)	1,000,000	140%	1,400,000				
D	400,000	132%	528,000	D	400,000	132%	528,000
				A(SP)	3,000,000	130%	3,900,000
F	1,000,000	115%	1,150,000	F	1,000,000	115%	1,150,000
					$5,000,000[b]		$6,578,000[d]
E	800,000	114%	912,000	E	$ 800,000	114%	Reject
B	1,200,000	112%	1,344,000	B	1,200,000	112%	Reject
	$5,000,000[b]		$6,334,000[c]				
H	$ 550,000	105%	Reject	H	550,000	105%	Reject
G	450,000	101%	Reject	G	450,000	101%	Reject
I	1,000,000	90%	Reject	I	1,000,000	90%	Reject

[a] Each of the specific plans for the projects listed may have been selected from alternative mutually exclusive proposals. For example, Project D may be for new Dodge trucks, selected after considering competing brands. Thus, the capital budget is the crystallization of many "sub-capital-budgeting" decisions.
[b] Total budget constraint.   [c] Net present value, $1,334,000.   [d] Net present value, $1,578,000.

Note that the rationing used in Alternative Two is superior to Alternative One, despite the greater profitability per dollar invested of general-purpose equipment compared with special-purpose equipment. Why? Because the $2,000,000 incremental investment in special-purpose equipment has an incremental present value of $500,000, whereas the $2,000,000 would otherwise be invested in Projects E and B, which have a lower combined incremental present value of $256,000:

	COST	PRESENT VALUE	INCREASE IN NET PRESENT VALUE
SP Equipment	$3,000,000	$3,900,000	
GP Equipment	1,000,000	1,400,000	
Increment	$2,000,000	$2,500,000	$500,000
Project E	$ 800,000	$ 912,000	
Project B	1,200,000	1,344,000	
Total	$2,000,000	$2,256,000	$256,000

The example above illustrates that decisions involving mutually exclusive investments of different sizes cannot be based on the excess present-value index (or the time-adjusted rate of return, for that matter). The net present-value method is the best general guide.

investment indivisibilities In general, any ranking procedure by excess present-value indexes or rates of return or net present value is approximal because of investment indivisibilities. For example, assume that five projects are available, as follows:

(1)	(2)	(3)	(3) ÷ (2)	(3) − (2)
			EXCESS	
		TOTAL	PRESENT-VALUE	NET
PROJECT	COST	PRESENT VALUE	INDEX	PRESENT VALUE
V	$6,000	$8,400	140%	$2,400
W	3,000	4,050	135%	1,050
X	2,000	2,600	130%	600
Y	2,000	2,560	128%	560
Z	1,000	1,000	100%	—

Now, if $10,000 is available for capital spending, there are two likely combinations. The natural tendency would be to select V, W, and Z and reject X and Y. But this would not yield the optimum answer (see top of next page). Given a budget constraint, it may be wisest to accept smaller, even though less attractive, projects to use the limited funds completely in order to maximize total returns. In our example, the optimum solution rejected Projects W and Z,

		ALLOCATION OF $10,000 BUDGET					
		ALTERNATIVE ONE			ALTERNATIVE TWO		
	COST	*COST*	*PRESENT VALUE*	*INDEX*	*COST*	*PRESENT VALUE*	*INDEX*
V	$6,000	$ 6,000	$ 8,400		$ 6,000	$ 8,400	
W	3,000	3,000	4,050				
X	2,000				2,000	2,600	
Y	2,000				2,000	2,560	
Z	1,000	1,000	1,000				
Total available funds	$10,000	$10,000	$13,450	134.5%	$10,000	$13,560	135.6%
Net present value			$ 3,450			$ 3,560	

whose combined excess present-value index and whose combined net present values were less than those of both X and Y.[7]

MULTIPLE ALTERNATIVES

The basic approach to choosing among alternatives is the same, regardless of the number of alternatives available. However, comparisons become more intricate when three or more alternatives are under consideration.

illustration of overall versus incremental approach A retail outlet is considering extending credit to its customers for the first time in its history. A careful study of competitors' experience with a variety of credit plans shows the expected increases in net profits under various plans, as illustrated in Exhibit 14-7. Which choice would you make? Why? Decide before reading on.

incremental approach is best Where multiple alternatives of similar risk are available, the key to the correct decision is the incremental approach. Total investment should be increased, increment by increment (as long as each increment meets the minimum desired rate of return) until the incremental rate of return falls below the cutoff rate (14 percent in this case).

In our example, the incremental approach assumes *that the total $100,000 funds available can be invested in some phase of the business at 14 percent with*

---

[7] Integer programming would be the best attack on these difficulties. See Weingartner, "The Excess Present Value Index," p. 215. Linear programming techniques are also helpful in reaching an optimum solution when there are many variables and many constraints. See Charnes, Cooper, and Miller, "Application of Linear Programming to Financial Budgeting and the Costing of Funds," *Journal of Business,* XXXII, No. 1, 20–46.

EXHIBIT 14-7

MULTIPLE ALTERNATIVE INVESTMENTS

MINIMUM DESIRED RATE OF RETURN—14%

LINE	PLAN	A	B	C	D	E
1	Total investment in receivables	$10,000	$30,000	$50,000	$80,000	$100,000
2	Annual net income	$ 500	$ 4,200	$ 7,800	$12,120	$ 14,320
3	Rate of return	5.0%	14.0%	15.6%	15.2%	14.3%
4	Incremental investment over preceding plan		$20,000	$20,000	$30,000	$ 20,000
5	Incremental net income		$ 3,700	$ 3,600	$ 4,320	$ 2,200
6	Rate of return on incremental investment		18.5%	18.0%	14.4%	11.0%

comparable risk. Our approach would result in choosing Project D, because the incremental rate of return thereafter falls below 14 percent. The desirability of this choice can be proven as follows:

LINE	PLAN	A	B	C	D	E
1	Total funds to invest	$100,000	$100,000	$100,000	$100,000	$100,000
2	Amount invested	10,000	30,000	50,000	80,000	100,000
3	Difference	$ 90,000	$ 70,000	$ 50,000	$ 20,000	$ —
	Return on amount in line 2	$ 500	$ 4,200	$ 7,800	$ 12,120	$ 14,320
	Plus 14% return on investment shown in line 3	12,600	9,800	7,000	2,800	—
		$ 13,100	$ 14,000	$ 14,800	$ 14,920	$ 14,320
	Rate on $100,000	13.1%	14.0%	14.8%	14.92%	14.32%

danger of using overall approach Using overall rates of return as a guide will not yield an optimum choice, no matter what interpretation of overall rate of return is used. Some analysts, interested in maximum overall rate of profitability, would choose Project C (15.6 percent). Such a choice rejects the investment of an additional $30,000 (Project D) at an incremental rate of return of 14.4. The latter is a better rate than the 14 percent available in other phases of the business at comparable risk.

Other analysts, recognizing that the maximum of $100,000 is available for investment, and that the appropriate cutoff rate is 14 percent, would select Project E (14.3 percent). Failure to concentrate on *differences* results in the inclusion of a final $20,000 incremental investment[8] that earns only an 11 percent return.

Any approach based solely on the overall rate of profitability will not necessarily yield an optimum choice. In our example, all alternatives except Project A promise a rate of return in excess of the assumed minimum desired rate of 14 percent.

recapitulation The examples above have demonstrated the weaknesses of adjusted rate of return[9] (see Exhibit 14-5) and the excess present-value index (see Exhibit 14-6, for instance). The net present-value criterion is the best general rule for choosing projects, whether the complexity involves an overall budget limit, different sizes of outlays, different terminal dates, or mutually exclusive investments. This general rule should be used on an increment-by-increment basis and should be modified where there are investment indivisibilities in relation to a fixed overall capital-budget appropriation.[10]

The guides above still do not provide answers to some fundamental questions. How do you consider uncertainty? How do you grapple with changes, over-time, in desired rates of return? How do you decide on the appropriate minimum desired rate of return? These difficulties will be considered in the next section, but do not expect any fully satisfying answers. There are none. These are subjects of controversy.

MINIMUM DESIRED RATE OF RETURN: COST OF CAPITAL

importance Thus far in our study of capital budgeting, a "minimum desired rate of
of concept return" has been somehow given or assumed for use in the analysis of investment proposals. It has been used either as a discount rate under the net present-value method or as a cutoff under the time-adjusted rate of return

---

[8] The incremental approach also assumes that the *previous* increment earned at least the cutoff rate. Otherwise, optimum choices will not be made. To illustrate, using the facts in our example, assume an intervening plan (Plan DD) between D and E:

PLAN	D	DD	E
1. Total investment	$80,000	$90,000	$100,000
2. Annual net income	$12,120	$12,600	$ 14,320
3. Rate of return	15.2%	14.0%	14.3%
4. Incremental investment		$10,000	$ 10,000
5. Incremental net income		$ 480	$ 1,720
6. Rate of return on incremental investment		4.8%	17.2%

Choosing Plan E is unwise because it really means making an investment in DD also, a combined incremental investment of $20,000 showing a combined return of only 11.0 percent (as shown in Exhibit 14-7). For an expanded discussion, see Grant and Ireson, *Principles of Engineering Economy,* 5th ed. (New York: Ronald Press Company, 1970), Chapter 12.

[9] James H. Lorie and Leonard J. Savage, in "Three Problems in Rationing Capital," *Journal of Business,* XXVIII, No. 4, have demonstrated a number of weaknesses of the time-adjusted rate of return. Of special interest is the phenomenon where *two* rates of return can be calculated for *one* project; this can occur when a project, such as an oil well, may entail heavy outlays at termination date.

[10] For a full discussion, see H. Martin Weingartner, *Mathematical Programming and the Analysis of Capital Budgeting Problems* (Englewood Cliffs, N.J.: Prentice-Hall, Inc., 1963).

method. In any event, the minimum desired rate (k) plays a crucial role in determining the acceptability of an investment proposal.

What is k and how should it be measured? Solomon claims that this is "clearly the central question facing financial management." [11] Descriptive terms for k include minimum desired rate of return, cutoff rate, target rate, hurdle rate, financial standard, and cost of capital. The last term is probably used most frequently.

Most theorists in finance agree that the cost of capital is the rate of return on the project that will leave unchanged the market price of the firm's stock. In practice, there is little agreement regarding how to measure this cost. Nevertheless, accountants and managers cannot avoid the problem; they must choose some framework for computing the cost of capital.

***complexity
of measuring*** The measure of the cost of capital is far more complex than the accountant's usual notion; he ordinarily thinks of the cost of capital as being the interest expense that appears on the conventional income statement.

Opinions differ immensely as to what cost of capital should be used for capital-budgeting purposes. A few managers cling to the notion that the cost of capital is the mere out-of-pocket interest and financing charges on any debt arising from an undertaking. This position implies that any ownership funds are cost-free—a dangerous position because it ignores the alternative earnings that could be had from the funds. Thus, a home buyer with a $20,000, 6 percent term mortgage may regard the $1,200 annual interest outlay as his financing charge. But the homeowner with a mortgage-free $20,000 home also bears a real cost of capital, even though no interest outlay is involved. He could sell his home and invest the $20,000 in 6 percent bonds or perhaps reap a bonanza on a mining stock. The sacrifice of these alternative earnings becomes his cost of capital as far as home ownership is concerned.

***computation
of cost of
capital*** There are really two basic approaches to computing the cost of capital. The piecemeal approach considers each financing as a separate problem. The other approach develops an average cost of capital.

The principal objection to the piecemeal approach is the insidious effect of low-cost debt financing on projects over a series of years. To illustrate, the cost of 100 percent financing by 6 percent bonds is only 3 percent after applying a tax rate of 50 percent. If unlimited debt could be arranged in a given year, any project with an after-tax return of over 3 percent would be accepted. Next year, the debt limit for an optimum capital structure may already be reached, and other financing may show a cost as high as 20 percent after taxes. This would mean that any project that could not produce such a high rate would be automatically rejected.

[11] Ezra Solomon, *The Theory of Financial Management* (New York: Columbia University Press, 1963), p. 27.

The reasoning underlying the calculation of a weighted-average cost of capital is complex and subject to disagreement. A thorough treatment is beyond the scope of this text. The following paragraphs summarize the framework advocated by Van Horne.[12] A prime feature of this framework is that *cash dividends are the foundation for valuation of the firm.*

The reasoning underlying the weighted-average cost of capital is that by financing in the proportions specified and accepting proposals that yield more than the average cost, the firm can increase the market price of its stock over the long run. Three influential factors are held constant under this framework. First, the complexion of the business risks of the firm as a whole is unaffected by the acceptance of any investment project or combination of investment projects. Second, the firm intends to maintain a constant dividend-payout ratio. Third, over time, the firm finances in the proportions as specified in the weighting scheme for the capital structure.

debt and preferred stock
To measure the overall cost of capital, the explicit costs of specific sources of funds must first be computed. Although the historical costs of debt and stock may yield insight, we seek to *predict* the costs of new financing in the proportion that the firm intends to use over time.

The cost of debt is essentially an after-tax cost. Therefore, if the before-tax cost is 8 percent, the after-tax cost at a 50 percent income tax rate is 4 percent.

The cost of preferred stock is the stated annual dividend rate. This rate is not adjusted for income taxes because the preferred dividend is paid after taxes.

common stock
The cost of common stock is extremely difficult to measure. In concept, it is defined as the minimum rate of return that the firm must earn on the common-stock-financed portion of an investment project so that the market price of the stock is unaffected.

An example may clarify the fundamental approach. Suppose the required rate of return on common stock was 10 percent after taxes and that the cost of debt was 4 percent after taxes. Suppose all financing was 50 percent debt and 50 percent equity. The minimum desired rate of return on a project would be:

Debt	$.5 \times .04 = .02$
Common stock	$.5 \times .10 = .05$

[12] The approach in James C. Van Horne, *Financial Management and Policy,* 2nd ed. (Englewood Cliffs, N.J.: Prentice-Hall, Inc., 1971), pp. 90–117, is a widely used technique. However, disputes as to the best technique were rampant among specialists in economics and finance in the 1960's and continue to rage in the 1970's. The approach used here is that cost of capital is ultimately determined by the investors in the capital markets, not by the firm itself. Most scholars in the area agree with this concept; but there is a disagreement as to the market effects of leverage (use of debt) on the cost of capital. For a thorough discussion of the issues, see F. Modigliani and M. Miller, "The Cost of Capital Corporation Finance, and the Theory of Investment," *American Economic Review,* XLVIII, 261–97; their "Dividend Policy, Growth, and the Valuation of Shares," *Journal of Business,* XXXIV, No. 4, 411–33; and their "Some Estimates of the Cost of Capital to the Electric Utility Industry, 1954–1957," *American Economic Review,* LVI, 333–91.

Consider a project costing $1,000 with an expected after-tax return of $70 per year forever:

Total return after taxes	$70
Less interest (.04 × $500)	20
Return on common stock	$50

The expected rate of return on common stock is 10 percent ($50 ÷ $500 portion of the total project). This just equals the rate of return required by investors. If the project failed to yield $70 per year, the market price of the stock would decline.

How do you obtain the required rate of return on common stock? The cost of common stock is the rate of discount that equates the present value of the stream of expected future dividends per share, as perceived by investors in the market, with the market price of the stock. In general, it is inappropriate to use the ratio of earnings per share to market price as the cost of common stock. The focus should be on future dividends, which means that a growth rate must be assumed.

For example, suppose a company's expected dividend per share is $2, the current market price is $40, and earnings and dividends are expected to grow about 4 percent per annum. The market valuation model is:

$$P_c = \frac{D_1}{k_c - g}$$

where P_c is the market price of the common stock, D_1 is the dividend per share expected to be paid at the end of period 1, k_c is the market rate of discount (the cost of common stock), and g is the constant rate of growth. Then:

$$P_c(k_c - g) = D_1$$

$$k_c - g = \frac{D_1}{P_c}$$

$$k_c = \frac{D_1}{P_c} + g$$

Consider the example of B Company. If the expected dividend per share at the end of period 1 is $2, the current price is $40, and earnings and dividends per share are expected to grow about 4 percent per annum, the company's cost of common stock is:

$$k_c = \frac{\$ 2}{\$40} + .04 = .09 \text{ or } 9\%$$

Van Horne points out that for k_c to be realistic, expectations in the marketplace must be such that dividends per share are thought to grow in fact at a rate g.

The crucial factor, then, is measuring the growth in dividends per share as perceived by investors. As you might expect, these computations can quickly become complicated.

retained earnings   There are diverse views as to how to compute the cost of retained earnings.[13] The approach favored here has been called the external-yield criterion. It is the opportunity cost as determined by what the firm can obtain on external investment of funds. This return should approximate k_c, assuming equilibrium in the market between expected return and risk.

weighted-average cost of capital   Suppose that the capital structure at the latest statement date is indicative of the proportions of financing that the company intends to use over time:

	AMOUNT*	PROPORTION
Debt	$30	30%
Preferred stock	10	10
Common stock	20	20
Retained earnings	40	40
	$100	100%

* In millions.

These proportions would be applied to the assumed individual explicit after-tax costs below:

	PROPORTION	COST	WEIGHTED COST
Debt	30%	4%	1.2%
Preferred stock	10	8	.8
Common stock	20	9	1.8
Retained earnings	40	9	3.6
Weighted-average cost of capital			7.4%

If measured correctly, a weighted-average cost of capital can lead to optimal capital-budgeting decisions. Van Horne stresses that the cost of capital is only a means to an end: the maximizing of the market price of the common stock. Sometimes this objective is overlooked because of the somewhat mechanical nature of the approach.

---

[13] One controversy is whether the cost should be reduced for a tax effect, because the stockholders would have to pay income taxes if they individually reinvest the retained earnings in question. That is, the company would have to declare a cash dividend in the amount of the retained earnings. In turn, the stockholder would have to pay income taxes on the dividend before the proceeds could be reinvested. See Van Horne, *Financial Management,* pp. 102–3.

degree of The preceding calculation of the cost of capital assumed that the accept-
risk or ance of a project or projects did not change the total risk[14] complexion
uncertainty of the firm as a whole. Capital budgeting would be simplified if all projects
bore the same degree of risk. Then a single cost of capital could be used
for judging all projects. However, different investments bear different degrees
of risk. If the acceptance of an investment proposal(s) alters the risk complexion
of the firm, the investment community may value the company differently before and after the acceptance. The greater the perceived risk, the lower the
valuation.

Because it is very hard to evaluate the overall risk of the firm at the
operating level, the evaluation of risk is often confined to the individual proposal.
Methods for allowing for risk include: adjusting the minimum desired rate of
return; calculation of the certainty equivalent of cash flows; direct analysis of
the probability distributions of possible outcomes; and many others.[15] The most
frequently encountered approach in practice is to boost the minimum required
rate as the risk increases. For example, a petroleum company may use 8 percent
for marketing facilities, 12 percent for refining facilities, and 20 percent for
development facilities. Other practical ways of allowing for risk include the use
of extremely short payback periods or useful lives and the ignoring of potential
salvage values.

Of all the methods for dealing with risk, the direct use of probability
distributions[16] is probably the one that will grow most rapidly in future practice.
This method, which is discussed in Chapter 23, gives management a straightforward way to evaluate the dispersion of possible outcomes for an investment project. This way is better than the use of haphazard techniques such as
employing higher arbitrary minimum desired rates.

A more penetrating analysis of risk will explicitly consider the relationship
of a given investment proposal with existing investments and with other investment proposals. Van Horne points out that if a project is highly correlated with
existing investments, the total risk of the firm will increase more than if a project
is added that has a low degree of correlation with others, all other things being
equal. Management should be aware of the potential benefits of diversifying
investments to obtain the best combination of expected net present value and
risk. In short, a portfolio approach should be used to analyze the trade-off
between the risk and the net present value of the total firm under varying
combinations of investments.

---

[14]Various definitions of *risk* have been offered in the literature. Some writers like to distinguish
between risk (objective) and uncertainty (subjective). As used here, risk is thought of as the probability
of obtaining a future income stream. An investment in United States bonds is risk-free because the
probability of getting the interest income is nearly 100 percent, whereas an investment in a single oil
well is risky because the variability of prospective income is immense.

[15]See Van Horne, *Financial Management,* Chapters 5 and 6, for a discussion analysis of risk for
the single investment and multiple investments.

[16]David B. Hertz, "Risk Analysis in Capital Investment," *Harvard Business Review,* Vol. 42, No.
1, 95–106; and his "Investment Policies That Pay Off," *Harvard Business Review,* Vol. 46, No. 1, 96–108.

summary

The uncertainty about long-run events makes capital budgeting a difficult but challenging area. The imprecision of prediction should overhang any analyst's tendency to split hairs concerning controversial aspects. However, there are a few guideposts that should help toward intelligent decisions. Some are summarized at the end of Chapters 12 and 13. Others were discussed in this chapter.

Income tax factors almost always play an important role in decision making. It is dangerous to assume that income taxes are irrelevant or insignificant.

Decisions on types of production equipment are often only remotely related to cash receipts, if at all. Thus, the decision becomes one of cost minimization. A logical approach, especially if there are income tax complications and several alternative investments available, is to compare all projects, discounting each to the present and choosing the project with the least cost.

Comparisons of projects with unequal lives necessitate predictions of reinvestment of proceeds of shorter-lived projects and a comparison to the terminal date of the longer-lived project.

Two interrelated constraints for rationing capital are overall funds available and a minimum desired cutoff rate(s) of return. Capital rationing has no conceptual justification; that is, all desirable projects should be undertaken and the needed funds acquired if possible. Investment indivisibilities often necessitate juggling project selections to obtain optimum overall results.

Incremental approaches are very useful in checking among multiple alternatives, to be certain that each separable investment is earning the minimum desired rate of return and that overall funds available are earning a maximum amount.

Cost of capital is used for purposes of determining the cutoff rate in the selection of projects. There is no agreement as to how to compute a magic, single-figured cost of capital. But it is agreed that recognition should be given to a "cost" of equity capital as well as debt. In practice, projects are classified by degree of risk, with different minimum cutoff rates being used for different classes of projects. Probabilistic approaches, which formally and explicitly recognize the dispersion in estimated data, have just begun to be used.

suggested readings

Bierman, H., and T. R. Dyckman, *Managerial Cost Accounting*. New York: The Macmillan Company, 1971.

Bierman, H., and S. Smidt, *The Capital Budgeting Decision*, 3rd ed. New York: The Macmillan Company, 1971.

Grant, E. L., and W. G. Ireson, *Principles of Engineering Economy*, 5th ed. New York: Ronald Press Company, 1970.

Hirshleifer, Jack, *Investment, Interest, and Capital.* Englewood Cliffs, N.J.: Prentice-Hall, Inc., 1970.

Morris, William T., *The Capacity Decision System.* Homewood, Ill.: Richard D. Irwin, Inc., 1967.

National Association of Accountants, *Research Report 35, Return on Capital as a Guide to Managerial Decisions.* New York: the Association, 1959.

National Association of Accountants, *Research Report 42, Long-Range Profit Planning.* New York: the Association, 1964.

Quirin, G. David, *The Capital Expenditure Decision.* Homewood, Ill.: Richard D. Irwin, Inc., 1967.

Sharpe, W. F. *Portfolio Analysis and Capital Markets.* New York: McGraw-Hill Book Company, 1970.

Solomon, Ezra, ed., *The Management of Corporate Capital.* New York: The Free Press, 1959.

————, *The Theory of Financial Management.* New York: Columbia Univeristy Press, 1963.

Terborgh, George, *Business Investment Analysis.* Washington, D.C.: Machinery and Allied Products Institute, 1958. This book describes the widely used MAPI formula for equipment-replacement decisions.

Van Horne, J. C., *Financial Management and Policy,* 2nd ed. Englewood Cliffs, N.J.: Prentice-Hall, Inc., 1971.

Weingartner, H. Martin, *Mathematical Programming and the Analysis of Capital Budgeting Problems.* Englewood Cliffs, N.J.: Prentice-Hall, Inc., 1963.

Problems for Self-Study

Review the example on the effects of income taxes on cash flow and the other illustrations.

APPENDIX: THE FINANCIAL LEASE

Leases are frequently classified as operating or financial.[17] An operating lease is one that is cancelable or that terminates before the rental payments have repaid the purchase price. Examples are telephone equipment and monthly rentals of automobiles. For capital-budgeting purposes, the cash flows of operating leases can be analyzed just like ordinary operating cash flows.

The financial lease, according to Vancil, is noncancelable; it obligates the lessee to rentals that in total equal or exceed the purchase price of the asset leased. Examples of assets that are often subject to financial lease arrangements are jet aircraft, sports arenas, office buildings, and grocery stores. We are concerned here with the financial lease only.

example Suppose that it is a tax-free world. A company with a weighted-average cost of capital of 10 percent is contemplating the acquisition of a machine that will save $2,400 in cash operating costs annually over its useful life of four

---

[17] See Richard F. Vancil, "Lease or Borrow—New Method of Analysis," *Harvard Business Review,* Vol. 39, No. 5, 122–33; and Richard S. Bower, Frank C. Herringer, and J. Peter Williamson, "Lease Evaluation," *The Accounting Review,* Vol. XLI, No. 2, 257–65, for thorough examinations of these distinctions and for consideration of income tax factors. For a comparison of a variety of approaches, see Van Horne, *Financial Management,* Chapter 22. Also see the article by Thomas A. Beechy in *The Accounting Review,* XLV, No. 4, 769–73.

years. The machine will have no residual value. The machine may be bought outright for $6,500 cash; it is also available on a four-year, noncancelable lease at $2,000 payable at the end of each year. Should the company buy or lease?

SOLUTION 1   The time-adjusted rate of return of leasing may be calculated as follows:

Net cash operating savings	$2,400
Lease payments	(2,000)
Net increase in cash flow per year	$ 400
Outlay at time zero	0
Time-adjusted rate of return	infinite

Something is wrong here. Intuitively, we know that this proposition does not bear an infinite rate of return.[18]

SOLUTION 2   The lease arrangement is clearly more attractive. The present value of the lease payments at 10 percent is $2,000 × 3.170 (from Table 4 in the appendix at the end of the book), or $6,240, which is less than the $6,500 purchase price. Note that the discounting of lease payments at the lessee's weighted-average cost of capital will lead to leasing rather than buying in all instances where the lessee's cost of capital exceeds the lessor's implicit contractual interest rate.

SOLUTION 3   Perplexing implications arose in the two preceding solutions because of the failure of the prospective lessee to separate the *investment* decision from the *financing* decision. The biggest pitfall is to fail to distinguish these two aspects.

    The financial-lease decision is complicated because each rental payment has two components: the implicit interest charged by the lessor and the amortization of the principal sum. In effect, the lessor is a seller of an asset and a lender of money. The rent must provide him with a recovery of the selling price of the asset plus interest on the money advanced.

I. The financing decision.

    Note that the decision is not whether to buy or lease, despite the fact that advertisements for leasing usually describe the decision in this way. The decision is a twofold one: (a) whether to acquire the asset or not to acquire the asset, and (b) whether to lease or borrow.

    Bierman and Smidt comment on this lease-or-borrow phase as follows:

> Because the lease is presumed to require a contractually predetermined set of payments, it is reasonable to compare the lease with an alternative type of financing available . . . that also requires a contractually predetermined set of payments, i.e., a loan. It follows that the interest rate at which the firm would actually borrow, if it chose to acquire the asset by buying and borrowing, is an appropriate discount rate to use in this analysis. The recommendation holds even if the firm chooses to use some other discount rate for ordinary capital-budgeting decisions.[19]

    The present value of the rentals should be discounted at a relatively low loan rate rather than at the weighted-average cost-of-capital rate. Therefore, the steps necessary for making the financing decision are:

---

[18] See Robert N. Anthony, John Dearden, and Richard F. Vancil, *Management Control Systems* (Homewood, Ill.: Richard D. Irwin, Inc., 1966), pp. 467–74 and 507–16.

[19] Harold Bierman, Jr., and Seymour Smidt, *The Capital Budgeting Decision,* 3rd ed. (New York: The Macmillan Company, 1971), p. 216.

a. Approximate the lowest rate at which cash could be borrowed in an amount equal to the purchase price of the equipment.

b. Discount the rentals at this borrowing rate to obtain the "cash equivalent purchase price" of the equipment. If this "equivalent purchase price" is less than the outright cash purchase cost, then leasing is desirable—provided also that the criterion described below for the overall investment decision is also met. If this equivalent price is greater than the outright purchase cost, then purchasing is desirable—again provided that the criterion below is also met.

Apply these steps to our example:

a. Approximate the company loan rate. Suppose the rate is 6 percent.

b. "Equivalent purchase price" is $2,000 at 6 percent for four years, $2,000 × 3.465 = $6,930, which exceeds the outright purchase price of $6,500. Therefore, purchase is desirable if the criterion below is met.

Note that the lessor may essentially quote two selling prices, one price for a leasing transaction and a different price for an outright sale. He may prefer to lease and thus quote a seemingly ridiculously high outright selling price, as many office equipment manufacturers do. The lessor may have many reasons for his preference for leasing rather than selling outright, including:

1. The ability to earn more in total through the selling and loaning together in the form of a lease. He may be willing to "sell" cheaper via a lease because he is assured of the implicit interest income on the rentals.

2. The lessor may have a different set of income tax considerations, which are frequently important in these cases.

II. The investment decision.

Decide whether to acquire the asset as follows:

a. Discount the operating cash inflows at the minimum desired rate of return (the weighted-average cost of capital, in this example), $2,400 at 10 percent for four years, $2,400 × 3.170 $ 7,608

b. Deduct the lower of the cash outright purchase price ($6,500) or the "cash equivalent purchase price" ($6,930)   (6,500)

c. Net present value $1,108

If the net present value is positive, acquire the asset by the means indicated in Part I. In this instance, the asset would be purchased outright.

The analysis of leases can become vastly more complicated by the introduction of income taxes and residual values. To pursue this topic in more depth, study the readings cited in footnote 17.

questions, problems, and cases

Note: Compound interest tables are at the rear of the book.

14-1. What are the two major aspects of the role of income taxes in decision making?

14-2. "It doesn't matter what depreciation method is used. The total dollar tax bills are the same." Do you agree? Why?

14-3. In general, what is the impact of the income tax on disposals of fixed assets?

14-4. "In the case of mutually exclusive investments, smaller profitability indexes may enhance overall economic returns." How?

14-5. "The crux of the problem in replacement decisions is the lack of a realistic common terminal date for both proposals." Briefly describe two practical approaches to the problem.

14-6. "Cost of capital is the out-of-pocket interest charge on any debt arising from an undertaking." Do you agree? Why?

14-7. The short-run, marginal approach considers each financing as a separate problem. What is the principal objection to the short-run approach?

14-8. Should retained earnings bear a cost of capital? Why?

14-9. "In practice there is no single rate that is used as a guide for sifting among all projects." Why? Explain.

14-10. Tax shield and depreciation methods. A company has just paid $42,000 for some equipment that will have a six-year life and no residual value. The minimum rate of return desired, after taxes, is 10 percent.

The president has attended a management conference luncheon where an accounting professor adamantly stated, "Not using accelerated depreciation for tax purposes is outright financial stupidity." The president has a perpetual fear of rises in income tax rates and has favored straight-line depreciation "to have greater deductions against future income when taxes are higher."

He is having second thoughts now, and has asked you to prepare a financial analysis of the dollar benefits of using sum-of-the-years'-digits depreciation instead of straight-line depreciation under the following assumptions: (a) income tax rates of 60 percent throughout the coming six years; and (b) income tax rates of 60 percent for the first three years and 80 percent for the subsequent three years.

14-11. Tax Impact of Depreciation Policies. The Mays Company estimates that it can save $2,800 a year in cash operating costs for the next ten years if it buys a special-purpose machine at a cost of $11,000. No residual value is expected. Assume that income tax rates average two-sevenths of taxable income, and that the minimum desired after-tax rate of return is 10 percent.

required (Round all computation to the nearest dollar.)

A. Answer all questions below, assuming straight-line depreciation.
1. Payback period
2. Using discounted cash flow:
   a. Time-adjusted rate of return
   b. Net present value
3. Payback reciprocal

B. Answer all questions in Part A, assuming sum-of-the-years'-digits depreciation.

14-12. Approach to Income Taxes and Discounted Cash Flow. The Charles Company is trying to decide whether to launch a new household product. Through the years, the company has found that its products have a useful life of six years, after which the product is dropped and replaced by other new products. Available data follow:
1. The new product will require new special-purpose factory equipment costing $900,000. The useful life of the equipment is six years, with a $140,000 estimated disposal value at that time. However, the Internal Revenue Service will not allow a write-off based on a life shorter than nine years. Therefore, the new equipment would be written off over nine years

for tax purposes, using the sum-of-the-years'-digits depreciation and no salvage value.

2. The new product will be produced in an old plant already owned. The old plant has a book value of $30,000 and is being depreciated on a straight-line basis at $3,000 annually. The plant is currently being leased to another company. This lease has six years remaining at an annual rental of $9,000. The lease contains a cancellation clause whereby the landlord can obtain immediate possession of the premises upon payment of $6,000 cash (fully deductible for tax purposes). The estimated sales value of the building is $80,000; this price should remain stable over the next six years. The plant is likely to be kept for at least ten more years.

3. Certain nonrecurring market-research studies and sales-promotion activities will amount to a cost of $500,000 during year 1. The entire amount is deductible in full for income tax purposes in the year of expenditure.

4. Additions to working capital will require $200,000 at the outset and an additional $200,000 at the end of two years. This total is fully recoverable at the end of six years.

5. Net cash inflow from operations before depreciation and income taxes will be $400,000 in years 1 and 2, $600,000 in years 3 through 5, and $100,000 in year 6.

The company uses discounted cash-flow techniques for evaluating decisions. For example, in this case tabulations of differential cash flows would be made from year 0 through year 6. Yearly cash flows are estimated for all items, including capital outlays or recoveries. An applicable discount rate is used to bring all outlays from year 1 through year 6 back to year 0. If the summation in year 0 is positive, the project is desirable, and vice versa.

The minimum desired after-tax rate of return is 12 percent. Income tax rates are 60 percent for ordinary income.

required   Using an answer sheet, show how you would handle the data listed above for purposes of the decision. Note that you are *not* being asked to apply discount rates. You are being asked for the detailed impact of each of items 1 through 5 on years 0 through 6.

Note, too, that each item is to be considered separately, including its tax ramifications. *Do not combine your answers to cover more than one item.*

Assume that all cash flows take place at the end of each period. Assume that income taxes are due or refundable at the end of the period to which they relate.

SAMPLE ANSWER SHEET FOR PROBLEM 14-12

		NET PRESENT	CASH FLOWS IN YEAR						
ITEM	EXPLANATION	VALUE	0	1	2	3	4	5	6
1.	[Allow ample								
2.	space between								
3.	items]								
4.									
5.									

14-13. Purchase of Computer [SIA, adapted]. A medium-sized manufacturing company is considering the purchase of a small computer in order to reduce the cost of its data-processing operations.

At the present time, the manual bookkeeping system in use involves the following direct cash expenses per month:

Salaries	$7,500
Payroll taxes and fringe benefits	1,700
Forms and supplies	600
	$9,800

Existing furniture and equipment are fully depreciated in the accounts and have no salvage value. The cost of the computer, including alterations, installation and accessory equipment, is $100,000. This entire amount is depreciable for income tax purposes on a double declining basis at the rate of 20 percent per annum.

Estimated annual costs of computerized data processing are as follows:

Supervisory salaries	$15,000
Other salaries	24,000
Payroll taxes and fringe benefits	7,400
Forms and supplies	7,200
	$53,600

The computer is expected to be obsolete in three years, at which time its salvage value is expected to be $20,000. The company follows the practice of treating salvage value as inflow at the time that it is likely to be received. The company owns other assets that are in the same class for tax purposes.

required

1. Compute the savings in annual cash outflow after taxes. Assume a 50 percent tax rate.

2. Decide whether or not to purchase the computer, using the present-value method of discounted cash-flow analysis. Assume a minimum rate of return of 10 percent after taxes. Briefly explain the decision you reach.

14-14. Comparison of Projects with Unequal Lives. The manager of the Robin Hood Company is considering two investment projects, which happen to be mutually exclusive.

The cost of capital to this company is 10 percent, and the anticipated cash flows are as follows:

		CASH FLOWS (INCOME)			
PROJECT NO.	INVESTMENT REQUIRED NOW	YEAR 1	YEAR 2	YEAR 3	YEAR 4
1	$10,000	$12,000	0	0	0
2	$10,000	0	0	0	$17,500

required

1. Calculate the time-adjusted rate of return of both projects.

2. Calculate the net present value of both projects.

3. Comment briefly on the results in 1 and 2. Be specific in your comparisons.

14-15. Ranking Projects. [Adapted from *N.A.A. Research Report No. 35*, pp. 83–85.] Assume that the six projects in the table at the top of the next page have been submitted for inclusion in the coming year's budget for capital expenditures.

required

1. Rates of return (to the nearest half percent) for Projects B, C, and D and a ranking of all projects in descending order. Show computations. What

	YEAR	A	B	C	D	E	F
Investment	0	$(100,000)	$(100,000)	$(200,000)	$(200,000)	$(200,000)	$(50,000)
	1	0	20,000	70,000	0	5,000	23,000
	2	10,000	20,000	70,000	0	15,000	20,000
	3	20,000	20,000	70,000	0	30,000	10,000
	4	20,000	20,000	70,000	0	50,000	10,000
	5	20,000	20,000	70,000	0	50,000	
Per year	6–9	20,000	20,000		200,000	50,000	
	10	20,000	20,000			50,000	
Per year	11–15	20,000					
Time-adjusted rate of return		14%	?	?	?	12.6%	12.0%

approximations of rates of return for Projects B and C do you get by using payback reciprocals?

2. Based on your answer in 1, which projects would you select, assuming a 10 percent cut-off rate:
   a. If $500,000 is the limit to be spent?
   b. If $550,000?
   c. If $650,000?

3. Assuming a 16 percent minimum desired rate of return, and using the net-present-value method, compute the net present values and rank all the projects. Which project is more desirable, C or D? Compare your answer with your ranking in 2. If Projects C and D are mutually exclusive proposals, which would you choose? Why?

4. What factors other than those considered in 1 through 3 would influence your project rankings? Be specific.

14-16. **Effects of Depreciation; Use of Algebra.** [Prepared by David Green, Jr.] The Brogan Company is in the process of acquiring a crane. The model they need is available from the factory at a price of $150,000.

An identical crane was acquired several weeks ago by a competitor. The competitor's requirements have changed and they offer to sell their crane to the Brogan Company.

The Brogan Company uses the sum-of-the-years'-digits method for computing depreciation for tax purposes, wherever the Internal Revenue Code permits. However, the code does not permit any accelerated method for assets acquired secondhand.

For the purposes of this problem, assume:
a. The two cranes are identical.
b. "Money is worth" 8 percent.
c. Income tax payments are made at the end of each year and the year-end will be 12 months removed from acquisition.
d. The cranes have a 5-year life and *no* salvage value.
e. The relevant tax rate is 40 percent for either alternative.

required What is the highest price that Brogan can bid for the secondhand crane? (Support with calculations.)

	1	2	3	4	5
P.V. of 1 at 8%:	.93	.86	.79	.74	.68

14-17. Bargaining Range for Sale of Business.   George Weber controls 100 percent of the stock of a company whose sole business is the operation of a huge apartment building on leased land. The lease will expire, and the building will become fully depreciated, in four years. The building is in excellent condition and fully occupied at favorable rental rates. There has been considerable appreciation in the value of the property. Because depreciation is based on costs of thirty-six years ago—the date of construction of the building—the corporation's taxable income is unusually large. Weber believes that the building and the balance of the leasehold could be sold at a price that would effect a substantial tax advantage to the corporation while still leaving a profitable operation to the buyer for the balance of the four years, when title to the building will revert to the University of Minnesota, the owner of the land. There has been only slight variation in profits for each of the past six years. (Because of a special tax provision, gains on the sale of buildings and leaseholds held more than ten years are subject to income taxes at the capital-gains rate rather than at ordinary income tax rates.)

required   You are to indicate a proper range of bargaining as to price, based on the averages of the income statements, assuming no change in income, expenses, or tax rates. The sale, if made, would be a cash sale. Ignore any possible relationship between buyer and seller and any residual value of furnishings at the expiration of the lease.

AVERAGE OF INCOME STATEMENTS
FOR THE PAST SIX YEARS

Rental revenue		$1,200,000
Expenses		
Operations	$500,000	
Administration	50,000	
Property taxes	133,333	
Depreciation (straight-line)	100,000	783,333
Net income before taxes		$ 416,667
Income taxes at 52%		216,667
Net income after taxes		$ 200,000

1. In this part, ignore interest or discount, alternative uses of the funds by either the buyer or the seller, and any other variables.
   a. What is the most the buyer should pay?
   b. What is the least the seller should take?

2. In this part, assume that the minimum desired rate of return (the cost of capital) for both buyer and seller is 10 percent per annum.
   a. What is the most the buyer should pay?
   b. What is the least the seller should take?

	AT 10%	
PERIODS	P.V. OF $1	P.V. OF ANNUITY OF $1
1	.91	.91
2	.83	1.74
3	.75	2.49
4	.68	3.17

14-18. Trade or Sell for Cash, Use of Algebra.   [Prepared by David Green, Jr.] The Kimbark Company has determined that one of its assets is now obsolete. The asset was acquired three years ago at a cost of $550,000. At acquisition, the expected life was ten years, salvage value was set at zero, and SYD depreciation method has been used. Thus, the book value of the asset now stands at $280,000 [$550,000 − ($100,000 + $90,000 + $80,000)].

The new and successful challenger is offered for sale at a price of $580,000. Its manufacturer, who deals in both new and used machinery of this type throughout the world, has offered $130,000 trade-in allowance. This is a generous and bona fide offer occasioned by the fact that the manufacturer has a foreign order for an asset of this description.

As the controller of Kimbark points out, the loss on disposition of the asset is not deductible under present tax regulations when it is traded in on a new asset. Rather, the unamortized cost of the trade-in plus the additional cash required becomes the tax basis for depreciation of the new asset.

required   What is the immediate lowest cash price that Kimbark can take from some other buyer and not be worse off than by trading in? Assume:
1. The depreciable life of the new asset will be five years. There is zero expected salvage value, and SYD depreciation.
2. The relevant income tax rate is 40 percent.
3. The cost of debt is 8 percent, the cost of equity is 16 percent, and the cost of capital is 12 percent; the following rounded factors for the present value of $1 are to be used as needed.

PERIODS	8%	12%	16%
1	.93	.90	.86
2	.86	.80	.74
3	.80	.71	.64
4	.74	.64	.55
5	.68	.57	.48

4. Provisions for recapture of the investment tax credit are not applicable.
5. All cash flows take place at the end of a period.

14-19. Case Study of Business Flying.   The president of a medium-size Chicago aircraft-supply company is seriously considering the purchase of a five-passenger Beechcraft twin-engine airplane. He and his three top executives travel extensively in representing their products to the base operators at airports all over the country. Since he and two of the other executives have twin-engine and instrument-pilot ratings, he has been tempted to purchase a plane for some time but has been afraid that his business was not large enough to afford plane ownership.

Feeling a burning desire to grasp those twin throttles again, he calls for his secretary to bring in their detailed travel records for the past year. These reveal that the four executives have been flying a total of 400,000 man-miles a year on commercial airlines. They have gone alone 50 percent of the mileage; 25 percent of the mileage has been traveled by two men together; 15 percent of the mileage has been traveled by three men together; and all four men traveling to and from conferences accounted for 10 percent of the total mileage. They have used:

Shuttle service for 50 percent of the mileage at 5.5 cents/mile,
Other service for 40 percent of the mileage at 7.5 cents/mile,
Special service for 10 percent of the mileage at 7.7 cents/mile.

The controller (who is secretly afraid to fly in a small plane) states that it is ridiculous to take anything but a 600-miles-per-hour jet, "as we did most of the time last year." Whereupon the president requests the controller to submit an analysis of the percentage usage of the main types of service and the block-to-block (air-terminal building to air-terminal building) speed that each type of aircraft averages. He finds the following:

PERCENTAGE OF TOTAL MILEAGE TRAVELED	TYPE OF TRIP	BLOCK-TO-BLOCK SPEED
50%	Shuttle	200 m.p.h.
25%	Short	110 m.p.h.
15%	Intermediate	280 m.p.h.
10%	Long	400 m.p.h.

The executive vice-president looks at the above data and exclaims, "Let's be sure to count our time saved by the faster speed on the airlines. Oh, sure, I know it takes longer to go by cab to Midway or O'Hare fields than it does to go to Meigs, where we would moor the new plane if we buy it, but we can count the cost of the extra time against commercial air travel."

All four executives agree that their time savings are worth an average of $10 per hour to the company before company income taxes. That is, each hour saved would add $10 to the company's taxable income.

They also agree that the time wasted on a commercial flight, compared with a flight in their own plane, totals about two hours. The increased distance to the airport accounts for about 45 minutes; they have to be at the airport half an hour before plane time for a commercial flight; they waste another half hour arranging for tickets and picking them up; and they have to wait a quarter of an hour for baggage when they arrive at their destination. In the preceding year, the men made a total of 300 round trips (600 flights).

Average additional cab fares to Midway or O'Hare fields are $2.50. The men have been riding one, two, three, or four in a cab in the same proportions that they travel on airliners. Therefore, the relevant extra cab fare is:

ROUND TRIPS		
150	for one	$ 750
38	for two	190
15	for three	75
7	for four	35
	Total	$1,050

The vice-president in charge of sales states, "I've flown the type of aircraft we are considering buying. It's a 200-m.p.h. honey. Beech figures its block-to-block speed at 185 m.p.h. I believe it would pay, as we take half our mileage traveling in twos to fours. We pay a lot of money each year to travel at the convenience of the airlines.

Purchase cost of the five-seat plane they are considering buying, equipped for night and instrument flight, is $59,165. The company plans to use it for five years, depreciating it in straight-line fashion to a salvage value of $9,165.

Direct operating costs are:

Gasoline: 18 gallons/hour at 35 cents/gallon
Oil (allowing for changes): 37 cents/hour

Indirect operating costs are:

Mooring rental, at home and away: $1,740 per year
Inspections, repairs, parts, and engine overhauls: $4.48 per air-hour
Insurance: $1.00 per air-hour

The controller is overheard remarking as he calculates the depreciation on the private plane, "Now, here is one place where taxation helps us. It will cut the net ownership cost by plenty." The company is subject to a flat 40 percent tax rate.

required

1. Prepare a schedule showing the yearly cost to the company of using commercial airlines and of flying their own plane. Do not consider any costs except those specifically mentioned in the problem. Assume that the mileage and cost figures of the problem will not change in the next five years.

2. Assume a desired after-tax rate of return of 10 percent. Using discounted cash-flow procedures, show whether the plane should be purchased. Assume that yearly expenses are paid at the *start* of the year.

3. What factors other than the ones considered in 1 and 2 should be considered in reaching a decision? This is an important question, so give it more than cursory thought.

14-20. Choosing New Equipment; Complex Considerations. [Prepared by David Green, Jr.] The Playboy Autocar Company has developed a unique engine, which it intends to use in a new model. Two proposals for the necessary manufacturing equipment have been prepared. One, Plan A, considers the use of general-purpose equipment. These machines could be used in the manufacture of other Playboy models or sold on the active "used equipment" market if the new model is not a success. Plan B envisions highly specialized, automated equipment of use only on this prototype. If the new model is not a success, the Plan B equipment will have to be junked.

Costs for each plan (assuming an output of 50,000 units a year) are as follows:

	PLAN A	PLAN B
Machinery costs	$1,850,000	$4,600,000
Annual variable costs:		
Labor	$2,000,000	$ 500,000
Materials	1,500,000	1,350,000
Other	1,000,000	750,000
	$4,500,000	$2,600,000
Annual nonvariable costs:		
Supervision	$ 500,000	$ 600,000
Insurance, taxes, etc.	250,000	500,000
Depreciation on machinery	?	?

Additional Data

1. A conference with representatives of the Internal Revenue Service indicates that the general-purpose machinery (Plan A) is to be depreciated over ten years and the Plan B machinery over five years; for depreciation computations, salvage value is estimated to be $200,000 for Plan A equipment and $100,000 for Plan B. The sum-of-the-years'-digits method of calculating depreciation is to be used.

2. Predicted salvage if the machinery is sold is as follows:

AT END OF YEAR	PLAN A	PLAN B
1	$1,200,000	$300,000
2	1,200,000	300,000
3	1,000,000	250,000
4	1,000,000	200,000
5	800,000	200,000
6	800,000	175,000
7	600,000	150,000
8	400,000	100,000
9	400,000	100,000
10	200,000	100,000

3. A new corporation is to be formed and operated as a wholly owned subsidiary. The new equipment will be purchased by the subsidiary. The engines will be sold, as finished, to the parent company for $125 cash.
4. Income tax rates are assumed to be 50 percent on ordinary income.
5. For purposes of this situation, the factors in the present-value tables may be rounded to two decimal places.

required

1. a. Prepare an analysis that will show which plan is most advantageous, after taxes, assuming that 50,000 units a year will be sold, that the engine will be manufactured for five years, and that the minimum desired rate of return is 10 percent.
   b. What additional information should be supplied to the board of directors to assist them in their decision?

2. One of the directors says, "These new-fangled approaches don't answer the real questions." He asks that you calculate the payback in years for each plan, assuming that 50,000 units a year will be produced and sold.

14-21. Capital Budgeting and Cost of Capital [CPA, adapted]. The Niebuhr Corporation is beginning its first capital-budgeting program and has retained you to assist the budget committee in the evaluation of a project to expand operations, designated as Proposed Expansion Project #12 (PEP #12).
1. The following capital expenditures are under consideration:

Fire sprinkler system	$ 300,000
Landscaping	100,000
Replacement of old machines	600,000
Projects to expand operations (including PEP #12)	800,000
Total	$1,800,000

2. The corporation requires no minimum return on the sprinkler system or the landscaping. However, it expects a minimum return of 6 percent on all investments to replace old machinery. It also expects investments in expansion projects to yield a return that will exceed the average cost of the capital required to finance the sprinkler system and the landscaping in addition to the expansion projects.
3. Under Proposed Expansion Project #12 (PEP #12) a cash investment of $75,000 will be made one year before operations begin. The investment will be depreciated by the sum-of-the-years'-digits method over a three-year

period and is expected to have a salvage value of $15,000. Additional financial data for PEP #12 follow:

TIME PERIOD	REVENUE	VARIABLE COSTS	MAINTENANCE, PROPERTY TAXES, AND INSURANCE
0–1	$80,000	$35,000	$ 8,000
1–2	95,000	41,000	11,000
2–3	60,000	25,000	12,000

The amount of the investment recovered during each of the three years can be reinvested immediately at a rate of return approximating 15 percent. Each year's recovery of investment, then, will have been reinvested at 15 percent for an average of six months at the end of the year.

4. Assume that the corporate income tax rate is 50 percent.

5. The present value of $1 due at the end of each year and discounted at 15 percent is:

END OF YEAR	PRESENT VALUE
2 years before 0	$1.32
1 year before 0	1.15
0	1.00
1 year after 0	.87
2 years after 0	.76
3 years after 0	.66

6. The present values of $1 earned uniformly throughout the year and discounted at 15 percent follow:

YEAR	PRESENT VALUE
0–1	$ .93
1–2	.80
2–3	.69

required

1. Assume that the cutoff rate for considering expansion projects is 15 percent. Prepare a schedule calculating:
   a. Annual cash flows from operations for PEP #12
   b. Present value of the net cash flows for PEP #12

2. a. Assume that the average desired rate of return is 9 percent. Prepare a schedule to compute the minimum return (in dollars) required on expansion projects to cover the desired rate of return for financing the sprinkler system and the landscaping in addition to expansion projects. Assume that it is necessary to replace the old machines.
   b. Assume that the minimum return computed in 2a is $150,000. Calculate the cutoff rate on expansion projects.

14-22. Cost of Capital and Common Stock. Suppose all financing is 40 percent debt and 60 percent equity. Also suppose that the required rate of return on common stock is 10 percent after taxes and that the cost of debt is 6 percent after taxes.

Consider a project costing $10,000, with an expected return that will last forever. What dollar amount must the project yield per year so that the market price of the stock will not change?

14-23. Growth of Rate of Return on Common Stock. Suppose the expected dividend per share at the end of period 1 is $3, the current price is $50, and earnings and dividends are expected to grow about 6 percent per annum. What is the company's cost of common stock?

14-24. Computation of Cost of Capital. Company Y expects the annual return on debt and equity before taxes to be approximately $2 million over the next few years. Annual interest on bonds will be $400,000. The market value of the bonds outstanding is $8 million; of common stock, $12 million. The book value of the bonds is $10 million; of the stock, $10 million. The company intends to finance in a proportion of 40 percent debt and 60 percent common stock.

required   Effective yield on bonds, rate of return on common equity, and overall weighted-average cost of capital. Ignore income taxes.

14-25. After-Tax Cost of Capital. Assume the same facts as in Problem 14-24. The income tax rate is 40 percent.

required   1. After-tax rate of return on common equity. Also compute the weighted-average cost of capital.

2. The company is considering investing $100,000 in a proposed project, which will increase overall return on debt and equity before taxes by $12,000. Should the project be undertaken? Show computations.

14-26. Cost of Capital After Taxes. A company is considering a project costing $100,000. The market value of outstanding bonds is $5 million; of common stock, $5 million; this is indicative of the proportions of financing that the company intends to use over time. The coupon interest on debt is 8 percent. The required after-tax rate on equity is 10 percent. The income tax rate is 50 percent. The project is expected to yield $14,000 annually, before interest and taxes in perpetuity. Ignore depreciation.

required   1. The overall after-tax cost of capital for the company

2. The overall after-tax rate of return on the project

3. The after-tax rate on equity for the project

14-27. The Financial Lease. The Vanthony Company has a weighted-average cost of capital of 12 percent. Its basic loan rate is 6 percent. The financial vice-president is trying to decide whether to buy or lease some machinery. The purchase price is $14,000. A noncancelable lease is also available for six years at $3,000 annually. The useful life of the machine is six years; it will have no residual value. Annual cash operating savings are expected to be $4,000.

The salesman is encouraging the lease. He says, "No matter how you look at it, you can't lose by leasing. You take in $4,000 annually, pay out $3,000 annually, and make no down payment. Your rate of return is infinite."

Should the Vanthony Company buy or lease? Show computations. Ignore income taxes.

14-28. The Financial Lease. An office-equipment company has offered the Dudley Company a four-year, noncancelable lease on a small computer at an annual rental of $3,000, payable at the end of each year. The Dudley Company has a weighted-average cost of capital of 10 percent. Its basic loan rate is 6 percent. The computer is expected to save $3,600 in cash operating costs annually over its useful life of four years. Because of rapid technological change, the computer will have a negligible residual value.

Carl Dudley, the president of the Dudley Company, has read some magazine articles indicating that buying is almost always better than leasing, because the implicit interest rate in the lease is almost always higher than a company's basic loan rate. He asked the salesman, "How much will we have to pay if we buy the equipment outright for cash?" The salesman was reluctant to quote a price. Finally, after checking with his sales manager, he quoted a price of $11,800.

required   Should the Dudley Company buy or lease? Show computations. Ignore income taxes.

15

Inventory Planning, Control, and Valuation

There is an optimum level of investment for any asset, whether it be cash, physical plant, or inventories. For example, even cash balances may be too large or too small. The principal cost of having too much cash is the sacrifice of earnings; idle cash earns nothing. The principal cost of having too little cash may be lost discounts on purchases or harm to one's credit standing. For every asset class, then, there is a conceptual optimum investment that, when considered with optimum levels in other asset classes, helps to maximize long-run profits.

The major goal of "inventory control" is to discover and maintain the optimum level of inventory investment.[1] Two limits must be imposed in controlling inventory levels, because there are two danger points that management usually wants to avoid. The first danger, that of inadequate inventories, disrupts production and may lose sales. The second danger, excessive inventories, introduces unnecessary carrying costs and obsolescence risks. The optimum inventory level lies somewhere between the two danger points. Our major purpose in this chapter will be to see how this optimum inventory level is computed and maintained. We shall also consider the various methods of inventory valuation.

CHARACTERISTICS OF INVENTORIES

need for inventories   If production and delivery of goods were instantaneous, there would be no need for inventories except as a hedge against price changes. Despite

---

[1] Throughout this chapter, the term "inventory control" will refer to both planning inventory investment and implementing the plans.

the marvels of computers, automation, and scientific management, the manufacturing and merchandising processes still do not function quickly enough to avoid the need for having inventories. Inventories must be maintained so that the customer may be serviced immediately, or at least quickly enough so that he does not turn to another source of supply. In turn, production operations cannot flow smoothly without having inventories of work in process, direct materials, finished parts, and supplies.

Inventories are cushions (a) to absorb planning errors and unforeseen fluctuations in supply and demand, and (b) to facilitate smooth production and marketing operations. Further, inventories help isolate or minimize the interdependence of all parts of the organization (for example, departments or functions) so that each may work effectively. For example, many parts and subassemblies may be purchased or manufactured, stored, and used as needed.

inventory records and control Inventory records are only a means to the end of inventory control. A company may have thousands of impressive stores cards whose balances are always in precise agreement with physical counts taken in its immaculate storeroom. The requisition, purchasing, receiving, and material-handling duties may be at peak efficiency. But despite errorless paper shuffling and diligent employees, inventory control may still be inadequate. Management's major duty with respect to inventory control is not clerical accuracy. (In many cases, it is possible to attain excellent inventory control through visual inspection rather than through elaborate perpetual-inventory records.) The major inventory-control problem is to maximize profitability by balancing inventory investment against what is needed to sustain smooth operations.

CONTROL CLASSIFICATIONS: THE ABC METHOD

Sometimes it is difficult to comprehend the enormous number of items that companies must keep in stock—up to 50,000, and often more. An effective inventory-control system will not have all items in the inventory treated in the same manner under the same control techniques. For example, some items are often controlled by the "two-bin" system. Some companies do not bother maintaining perpetual-inventory cards; instead, two bins are kept, and after the first bin is emptied, a withdrawal from the second bin necessitates a reorder. Or physical control is exercised through having a red line painted in a bin at a reorder level. Another example would be keeping reorder quantities in a special package; when this package is finally opened, an attached purchase requisition for replenishment is immediately forwarded to the purchasing department.

Many companies find it useful to divide materials, parts, supplies, and finished goods into subclassifications for purposes of stock control. For example, Exhibit 15-1 shows direct materials, which are subclassified in step-by-step fashion by (a) itemizing total annual purchase cost of each item needed and (b) grouping

EXHIBIT 15-1

ABC ANALYSIS OF MATERIAL INVENTORY

Step 1. Multiply average usage times unit price to obtain total cost:

ITEM	AVERAGE USAGE	UNIT PRICE	TOTAL CONSUMPTION COST (SEE NOTE)
H20	10,000	$10.00	$100,000
H21	1,000	.05	50
H22	10,000	.02	200
H23	11,000	1.00	11,000
H24	110,000	.10	11,000

(and so forth)

Step 2. Group items above in descending order of total consumption cost and then divide into three classes:

	ITEMS		DOLLARS	
CLASS	NUMBER OF ITEMS	PERCENT OF TOTAL	TOTAL COST	PERCENT OF TOTAL
A	5,000	10%	$14,400,000	72%
B	10,000	20%	3,800,000	19%
C	35,000	70%	1,800,000	9%
	50,000	100%	$20,000,000	100%

Note: The total annual cost of raw materials consumed is dependent on two main factors: physical quantity needed and cost per unit. It is the *total* cost rather than the *unit* cost that matters. Thus, 11,000 units @ $1.00 requires the same investment as 110,000 units @ $.10.

in decreasing order of annual consumption cost. This technique is often called the *ABC method*, although it also has other labels.

The final A, B, C classification in Exhibit 15-1 demonstrates that only 10 percent of the items represent 72 percent of the total cost. In general, the greatest degree of continuous control would be exerted over these A items, which account for high annual consumption costs and correspondingly high investment in inventories. This type of control would mean frequent ordering, low safety stocks, and a willingness to incur expediting costs on A items, because the costs of placing and following up orders are relatively low in comparison with costs of carrying excess inventories. At the other extreme, where the total yearly purchase cost is relatively low, there would be less frequent ordering, higher safety stocks, and less paper work (C items).

Type A and B items are ordered according to budget schedules prepared by the production-planning department.[2] Essentially, sales forecasts are the cornerstone for production scheduling.[3] In turn, these production schedules are "exploded" (a commonly used term for giving detailed breakdowns of data) into

[2] The Ford Motor Company uses four inventory classes and keeps two days' supply of A items; five days' supply of B; 10 days' supply of C; and 20 or more days' supply of D items.

[3] An effective production planning and control system is an intricate mechanism. It depends on accurate demand forecasts expressed in units of production capacity, a production budget that establishes inventory levels and production activity, and a control procedure for adjusting inventory levels when errors in the demand forecast cause inventories to exceed or fall below budget.

the various direct-material, parts, and supply components. These explosions result in purchase schedules for major items. The purchase schedules are adjusted for lead times, planned changes in inventories, and normal waste and spoilage. Purchases are made accordingly, and follow-ups are instituted by the purchasing department as needed. In other words, Type A and B items are budgeted almost on a hand-to-mouth basis, because carrying costs are too high to warrant inventories that are sizable in terms of many days' usage.

Stores cards are usually kept for Type A and B items. It is noteworthy that such cards increasingly carry physical-unit balance only. More managements are becoming doubtful that the added clerical costs of carrying actual unit prices on stores cards are worthwhile.

ORDER QUANTITY

associated **The most straightforward approach to computing optimum investment in
costs inventory is to select the inventory level that minimizes total long-run costs.**

Comparisons of total annual costs often serve as a practical guide. Inventories entail two types of associated costs: those of carrying and those of not carrying enough. The optimum solution minimizes the *total* of these two classes of costs:

Cost of Carrying	plus	*Cost of Not Carrying Enough*
1. Risk of obsolescence		1. Foregone quantity discounts°
2. Desired rate of return on investment°		2. Disruptions of production with extra costs of expediting, overtime, setups, hiring, and training
3. Handling and transfer		3. Contribution margins on lost sales°
4. Space for storage		4. Extra costs of uneconomic production runs
5. Personal property taxes		5. Loss of customer goodwill°
6. Insurance		6. Extra purchasing and transportation costs
7. Clerical costs		7. Foregone fortuitous purchases°

° Costs that often do not explicitly appear on formal accounting records.

Note the conflicting behavior of these two classes of costs. For example, if management decides to carry huge inventories, many costs of carrying will soar while many costs of not carrying will fall.

the **Many of the relevant costs influenced by inventory levels usually are not
measurement apparent in the accounting records. For example, ordinary accounting
problem records will not contain opportunity costs such as the desired rate of return
on investment** (which is usually the highest cost of carrying additional inventory), foregone quantity discounts, contribution margins on lost sales, and the like. Then, too, even if the accountant recognizes that such costs are relevant

to inventory policy, some of these costs are extremely difficult to identify and to measure.

relevant costs *for inventory* *decisions*   The size of many relevant costs will differ, depending on the length of time under consideration and the specific alternative uses of resources. For example, if storage space is owned and cannot be used for other profitable purposes, differential space costs are zero. But if the space may be used for other productive activities, or if there is rental cost geared to the space occupied, a pertinent cost of space usage for inventory purposes must be recognized.

To the extent that money is invested in inventories, there is an interest cost of carrying stock. But how is this to be measured? In practice, this rate may be based on current borrowing rates, the long-run average cost of capital, or some "appropriate" rate selected by management. The proper rate should depend on investment opportunities available to management; it may be small or large, depending on specific circumstances.

Other costs that may or may not be relevant in policy decisions include overtime premiums on rush orders that would be unnecessary if bigger inventories were carried, idle time caused by material shortages, emergency expediting, extra transportation costs (for example, air freight), extra physical-count taking, obsolescence risks, and extra moving and handling costs.

As in any policy-making situation, inventory costs that are common to all alternatives are irrelevant and may be ignored. Costs that are often irrelevant because they will not be affected by the inventory decision include salaries of store record clerks, storekeepers, and material handlers, depreciation on building and equipment, and fixed rent.

In practice, however, for purposes of inventory planning most of the wage costs are unitized on a per-order or a per-unit-handled basis. Thus they are regarded as fully variable costs. Whether this is justified depends on specific circumstances. Surely the cost of processing 4,000 orders per period will be strikingly greater than the cost of processing 1,000 orders. The basic question is often whether in the same situation, the cost of processing 3,400 orders will be notably different from the cost of processing 3,000 orders. This is simply another example of the importance of determining what is relevant in any given decision-making situation.

A salient feature of inventory control is that production and inventory decisions are rarely affected by minor variations in cost factors.[4] Sensitivity analysis can be used to test the danger of errors (see Chapter 13). At the same time, the lack of precise cost data does not justify its haphazard use.[5]

---

[4] Note that a total of minor variations may reveal two things: (a) a large total variation, and (b) a trend of costs that may be important.

[5] It is easy to criticize various mathematical approaches to problems of inventory control on the grounds that the relevant costs are impossible to measure. But such criticisms are invalid in nearly all situations. Optimum inventory policies can be achieved without knowledge of "true costs." For an interesting discussion, see D. W. Miller and M. K. Starr, *Executive Decisions and Operations Research,* 2nd ed. (Englewood Cliffs, N.J.; Prentice-Hall, Inc., 1969), pp. 328–36.

There are two central questions that must be faced in designing an inventory control system: (a) How much should we buy (or manufacture) at a time? (b) When should we buy (or manufacture)? Now we turn to the first of these questions.

how much
to order? A key factor in inventory policy is computing the optimum size of either a normal purchase order for raw materials or a shop order for a production run. This optimum size is called the *economic order quantity*, the size that will result in minimum total annual costs of the item in question.

example 1 A refrigerator manufacturer buys certain steel shelving in sets from outside suppliers at $4.00 per set. Total annual needs are 5,000 sets at a rate of 20 sets per working day.

The following cost data are available:

Desired annual return on inventory investment, 10% × $4.00	$.40
Rent, insurance, taxes, per unit per year	.10
Carrying costs per unit per year	$ .50
Costs per purchase order:	
Clerical costs, stationery, postage, telephone, etc.	$10.00
What is the economic order quantity?	

EXHIBIT 15-2

ANNUALIZED COSTS OF VARIOUS STANDARD ORDERS

(250 Working Days)

SYMBOLS					LEAST COST					
E	Order size	50	100	200	400	500	600	800	1,000	5,000
E/2	Average inventory in units*	25	50	100	200	250	300	400	500	2,500
A/*E*	Number of purchase orders**	100	50	25	12.5	10	8.3	6.7	5	1
S(*E*/2)	Annual carrying cost @ $.50	$ 13	$ 25	$ 50	$100	$125	$150	$200	$ 250	$1,250
P(*A*/*E*)	Annual purchase-order cost @ 10.00	1,000	500	250	125	100	83	67	50	10
C	Total annual expenses	$1,013	$525	$300	$225	$225	$233	$267	$ 300	$1,260

E = Order size
A = Annual quantity used in units
S = Annual cost of carrying one unit in stock one year
P = Cost of placing an order
C = Total annual expenses

*Assume that stock is zero when each order arrives. (Even if a certain minimum inventory were assumed, it has no bearing on the choice here as long as the minimum is the same for each alternative.) Therefore, the average inventory relevant to the problem will be one-half the order quantity. For example, if 600 units are purchased, the inventory on arrival will contain 600. It will gradually diminish until no units are on hand. The average inventory would be 300; the storage cost, $.50 × 300 or $150.

**Number to meet the total annual need for 5,000 sets.

SOLUTION   Exhibit 15-2 shows a tabulation of total costs under various alternatives. The column with the least cost will indicate the economic order quantity.

Exhibit 15-2 shows minimum costs at two levels, 400 and 500 units. The next step would be to see if costs are lower somewhere between 400 and 500 units—say, at 450 units:

Average inventory, 225 × $.50   = $113 Carrying costs
Number of orders (5,000/450), 11.1 × $10 =   111 Purchase-order costs
                                                                     $244 Total annual expenses

The dollar differences here are extremely small, but the approach is important. The same approach may be shown in graphic form. See Exhibit 15-3. Note that in this case, total cost is at a minimum where total purchase-order cost and total carrying cost are equal.

order-size   The graphic approach has been expressed in formula form. The total annual
formula   cost (for any case, not just this example) is differentiated with respect to order size. Where this derivative is zero, the minimum annual cost is attained. The widely used formula approach to the order-size problem may be expressed in a variety of ways, one of which follows:[6]

$$E = \sqrt{\frac{2AP}{S}}$$

where E = order size; A = annual quantity used in units; P = cost of placing an order; and S = annual cost of carrying one unit in stock for one year. Substituting:

$$E = \sqrt{\frac{2(5,000)\,(\$10)}{\$.50}} = \sqrt{\frac{\$100,000}{\$.50}} = \sqrt{200,000}$$

$E = 448$, the economic order quantity

As we may expect, the order size gets larger as A or P gets bigger or as S gets smaller.

recapitulation   Note in Exhibit 15-3 that the approach to economic lot size centers on
of economic   locating a minimum-cost *range* rather than a minimum-cost *point*. *The*
order quantity   *total-cost curve tends to flatten between 400 and 800 units.* In practice, there is a definite tendency to (a) find the range, and (b) select a lot size

---

[6]The formula may be derived by expressing the tabular and graphic approaches as follows:

(1) $C = \dfrac{AP}{E} + \dfrac{ES}{2}$ (4) $SE^2 = 2AP$

(2) $\dfrac{dC}{dE} = \dfrac{-AP}{E^2} + \dfrac{S}{2}$ (5) $E^2 = \dfrac{2AP}{S}$

(3) Set $\dfrac{dC}{dE} = 0; \dfrac{S}{2} - \dfrac{AP}{E^2} = 0$ (6) $E = \sqrt{\dfrac{2AP}{S}}$

EXHIBIT 15-3

GRAPHIC SOLUTION OF ECONOMIC LOT SIZE

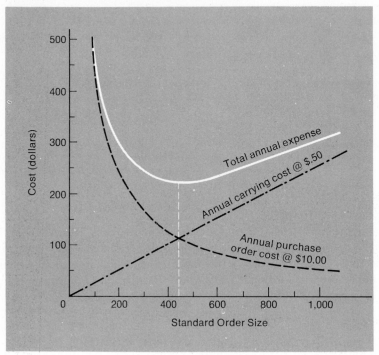

at the lower end of the range. In our example, there would be a tendency to select a lot size of 400 or slightly more.

An analytical approach such as has been outlined here is useful even if cost factors used are approximations. Total annual expenses of inventory control are fairly insensitive to moderate changes in order size. In other words, these tools let us hit the target at least, even if we never score a bull's eye. To illustrate, going back to our data in Exhibit 15-3, assume that the carrying cost is errone-ously estimated at $1 per unit instead of 50¢. Substituting in our formula, we would get

$$\sqrt{\frac{\$100,000}{\$1.00}}, \text{ or } E = 316+ \text{ units.}$$

Now the correct annual cost at 316 units would be:

Carrying cost, 158 × $.50	= $ 79
Purchase-order cost, 5,000/316 or 16 orders × $10 =	160
	$239

Compared with optimum cost of $224, the $15 difference is an error of seven percent, which is certainly not catastrophic.

production
runs

The economic-order-quantity approach may also be applied to production runs. For example, assume the same facts as in our steel-shelving example (Exhibit 15-2), except that the shelving is manufactured rather than purchased. The setup costs (for example, labor costs for adjusting machines) are $50. The same formula may be used; the only difference is substituting a $50 setup cost for the $10 cost of placing an order.

$$E = \sqrt{\frac{2(5,000)\ \$50}{\$.50}} = \sqrt{\frac{\$500,000}{\$.50}}$$

$$E = \sqrt{1,000,000} = 1,000 \text{ units per production run}$$

Incidentally, in various machine shops, the high cost of setup time has historically been a critical factor that tends to boost the size of production runs and the optimal size of inventory. The increasing use of automated machine tools, which are set up and controlled by computer programs, has reduced setup time enormously. It is now much easier to switch from the production of one item to another. This phenomenon has led toward lower production runs and lower optimal inventory sizes.

quantity
discounts

Quantity discounts affect unit prices; in general, the bigger the size of the order, the lower the unit price. The price usually falls between brackets; within each bracket, a uniform unit price prevails.

The basic formula used previously can be adapted to such situations, but its complexities will not be described further here. For our purposes, the following approach will be easiest to understand.

First, compute annual basic expenses in the manner illustrated in Exhibit 15-2. Then merely add the additional expenses of *foregoing* quantity discounts. The economic order quantity will be the one that offers the lowest expenses. See Exhibit 15-4, alternative 1. Or the total yearly delivered cost may be computed, and then added to the annual basic expenses. This method is shown in Exhibit 15-4, alternative 2. Both alternatives are fundamentally the same. The tabulations are usually best made at the break points. Exhibit 15-4 shows such computations at levels of 601 units and the optimal size of 1,001 units.

SAFETY STOCKS

when to order?

Although we have seen how to compute economic order quantity, we have not yet answered another key question: When to order? This question is easy to answer only if we know the *lead time,* the time interval between placing

EXHIBIT 15-4

ANNUAL COSTS OF VARIOUS STANDARD ORDERS

Facts: Carrying costs per unit per year $ .50
Costs per purchase order $10.00

Cost of shelving per set:

In orders of	TOTAL COST	FOREGONE DISCOUNT
400 or less	$4.00	.20
401– 600	3.95	.15
601–1,000	3.90	.10
1,001–5,000	3.80	—

Alternative 1:

Order size	50	100	200	400	500	601	800	1,001	5,000
Annual basic expenses (from Exhibit 15-2)	$ 1,013	$ 525	$ 300	$ 225	$ 225	$ 233	$ 267	$ 300	$ 1,260
Foregone discount per unit × 5,000 annual need	1,000	1,000	1,000	1,000	750	500	500	—	—
Total expenses	$ 2,013	$ 1,525	$ 1,300	$ 1,225	$ 975	$ 733	$ 767	$ 300	$ 1,260

Alternative 2:

	50	100	200	400	500	601	800	1,001	5,000
Yearly delivered cost of inventory (5,000 units)	$20,000	$20,000	$20,000	$20,000	$19,750	$19,500	$19,500	$19,000	$19,000
Annual basic expenses (from Exhibit 15-2)	1,013	525	300	225	225	233	267	300	1,260
Total expenses	$21,013	$20,525	$20,300	$20,225	$19,975	$19,733	$19,767	$19,300	$20,260

Note that the difference in total expenses between alternatives 1 and 2 is a constant $19,000; that is, 5,000 units multiplied by the $3.80 unit cost when there is no foregone discount.

an order and receiving delivery, know the economic order quantity, and are *certain* of demand during lead time. The graph in Exhibit 15-5 will clarify the relationships between the following facts:

Economic order quantity	448 sets of steel shelving
Lead time	2 weeks
Average usage	100 sets per week

Exhibit 15-5, Part A, shows that the *reorder point*—the quantity level that automatically triggers a new order—is dependent on expected usage during lead time; that is, if shelving is being used at a rate of 100 sets per week and the lead time is two weeks, a new order would be placed when the inventory level reaches 200 sets.

EXHIBIT 15-5

DEMAND IN RELATION TO INVENTORY LEVELS

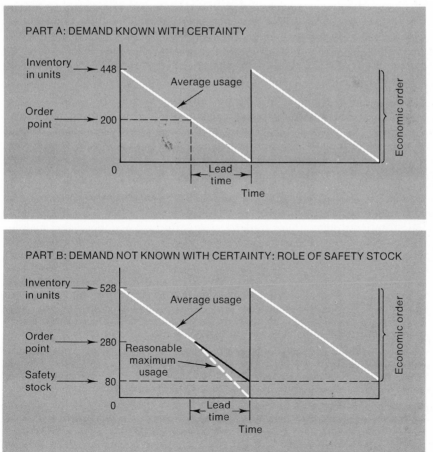

minimum inventory: safety allowance for fluctuations in demand
Our previous example assumed that 100 sets would be used per week—a demand pattern that was known with certainty. Businesses are seldom blessed with such accurate forecasting. Instead, demand may fluctuate from day to day, from week to week, or from month to month. Thus, the company will run out of stock if there are sudden spurts in usage beyond 100 per week, delays in processing orders, or delivery delays. Obviously, then, nearly all companies must provide for some safety stock—some minimum or buffer inventory as a cushion against reasonable expected maximum usage. Part B of Exhibit 15-5 is based on the same facts as Part A, except that reasonable expected maximum usage is 140 sets per week. The safety stock would be 80 sets (excess usage of 40 sets per week $\times$ 2 weeks). The reorder point is commonly computed as safety stock plus the average usage during the lead time.[7]

computation of safety stock
In our example, we used 80 sets as a safety stock. The computation of safety stocks hinges on demand forecasts. The executive will have some notion—usually based on past experience—of the range of daily demand: what percentage of chance (probability) exists for usages of various quantities.

A frequency distribution based on prior daily or weekly changes in demand will offer data for constructing the associated costs of maintaining safety (minimum) stocks. Once again, there are two major costs: the costs of carrying, sometimes called the *costs of overstock*, which are primarily interest on investment, obsolescence write-offs, and space costs; and the costs of not carrying (*stockout costs*), which include expensive expediting, loss of contribution margins, and loss of customer goodwill. The latter costs are difficult to measure, but statisticians and mathematicians have used statistical probability techniques on this problem with some success.[8] The optimum safety-stock level exists where the costs of carrying an extra unit are exactly counterbalanced by the expected costs of not carrying.

The most difficult cost to determine is *stockout cost*, consisting mainly of the foregone present and future contribution to profit from losing an order because of lack of inventory:

> But if there is no demand during the period an item is out of stock, there is no lost profit, and reliable information on unfilled demand is seldom maintained.

[7] This handy but special formula does not apply where the receipt of the standard order fails to increase stocks to the order-point quantity; for example, where the lead time is three months and the standard order is a one-month supply. In these cases, there will be overlapping of orders. The order point will be average usage during lead time plus safety stock minus orders placed but not received. This is really the general formula for computing the reorder point. In most cases, a simplified version is used because the last term in the general formula is zero. For elaboration, see almost any book on inventory systems.

[8] Inventory theory advances the idea that the rational entrepreneur should attempt to vary his inventory levels with the square root of sales rather than with sales. This is based on the relationships expressed in the economic-lot-size formula, discussed earlier, where the optimum lot size increased in proportion to the square root of the annual quantity used. See G. Hadley and T. M. Whitin, *Analysis of Inventory Systems* (Englewood Cliffs, N.J.: Prentice-Hall, Inc., 1963); and M. K. Starr and D. W. Miller, *Inventory Control* (Englewood Cliffs, N.J.: Prentice-Hall, Inc., 1962).

Where there is unfilled demand, but the customer is willing to wait or accept a substitute, there may be no immediate loss of profit. But there may be loss of future business as a result of dissatisfied customers. Because of these difficulties, most of the practical inventory-management systems specify a customer service level (percentage of items in stock) that they wish to meet rather than trying to minimize a total cost that includes stockout cost.[9]

A practical approach to setting levels of safety stock is shown in the following example.

example 2 Suppose that a company has the following distribution of weekly retail sales for one item in a department store for 100 weeks:

NUMBER OF WEEKS	WEEKLY SALES IN UNITS
2	0
7	1
15	2
20	3
18	4 = weighted-average sales
16	5
11	6
6	7
3	8 11% of the time sales > 6 units
1	9 5% of the time sales > 7 units
0	10 2% of the time sales > 8 units
1	11

The lead time for reorder was a constant one week. Average sales were four items per week, and actual sales equaled this average in 18 of the 100 weeks, or 18 percent of the time. Weekly sales exceeded six units in 11 percent of the weeks and exceeded eight units in only 2 percent of the weeks.

The reorder point would be based on a safety stock, plus average sales of four units during the one-week lead time. Because sales of more than eight units occur only 2 percent of the time, a safety stock of four units (eight units minus average sales of four units) should result in weekly potential sales in excess of inventory on hand only 2 percent of the time. A stockout occurs when the safety stock is fully depleted before the inventory is replaced. Stockouts would occur whenever weekly sales exceeded seven units, or about 5 percent of the time. Note that a stockout at a sales level of exactly eight units would do no harm in the sense that the safety stock might be exhausted just as the replenishment arrives. In any event, for an item with a constant lead time, a knowledge of the sales distribution permits a setting of a safety stock that provides a specific level of protection against stockouts.[10]

[9] *N.A.A. Research Report No. 40, Techniques in Inventory Management*, p. 14.

[10] This example was adapted from Joseph Buchan and Ernest Koenigsberg, *Scientific Inventory Management* (Englewood Cliffs, N.J.: Prentice-Hall, Inc., 1963), pp. 7–8. The authors point out, "The tedious process of compiling the distribution of historical sales data for every item in an inventory in order to set buffer levels can often be avoided." They refer to shortcuts that may be taken because many sales distributions are either Poisson, exponential, or normal. The book contains numerous case illustrations of applications of inventory-control systems.

Under the ABC inventory classification, different levels of protection may be specified for different classes, depending on objectives. Thus some firms may specify a 99 percent in-stock condition for the fast-moving A items, 90 percent for B items, and 80 percent for C items. "Other companies that are more concerned with controlling the investment in inventory might set the lowest safety-stock levels, along with the highest frequency of reorders, for the high-cost Class A items and spend less reordering effort, at the cost of proportionately higher safety stocks, for the lowest-cost Class C Items." [11]

constant order-cycle system The foregoing discussion of inventory control revolved around the so-called two-bin or constant order-quantity system: When inventory levels recede to X, then order Y. There is another widely used model in practice, the constant order-cycle system: for example, in Exhibit 15-6, every month review the inventory level on hand and order enough to bring the quantity on hand and on order up to twelve units. The reorder date is fixed, and the quantity ordered depends on the usage since the previous order and the outlook during the lead time. Demand forecasts and seasonal patterns also should be considered in specifying the size of orders during the year.

The minimization of the total associated costs of inventories is still the prime objective, regardless of the system used. A constant order-cycle system may be adopted instead of a constant order-quantity system where (a) the cost of continuous surveillance is too high, or (b) transportation and ordering economies may be gained through regular ordering of several different items from

[11] *N.A.A. Research Report No. 40, op. cit.*, p. 11.

EXHIBIT 15-6

CONSTANT ORDER-CYCLE SYSTEM

Item AB-34

Reorder date: 10th of each month
Reorder quantity: enough to bring the quantity on hand and on order, up to 12 units

DATE	RECEIVED	SHIPPED	ON HAND	ON ORDER	ON HAND AND ON ORDER
6/1	11	3	8		8
6/8		4	4		4
6/10*			4	8	12
6/13	8		12		12
6/20		6	6		6
7/10*			6	6	12
7/11		2	4		10
7/13	6		10		10
7/26		8	2		2
8/10*			2	10	12

*Constant-order date.

the same supplier. The major disadvantage of the constant order-cycle system is that it may require carrying more safety stock to protect against stockouts not only during the replenishment lead time (for example, between the tenth and thirteenth of the month in Exhibit 15-6), but also during the period between the placing of the orders. In contrast, in an order-quantity system, safety stock is needed only to protect against stockouts during the replenishment period.[12]

inventory turnover   Note that the emphasis in this chapter is on the word *optimum*, not *minimum*. Contrast this with the commonly used index of inventory management—inventory turnover, the number of times the average inventory is sold or used in a year. The traditional rule has been, "The higher the turnover, the better the inventory management." Consider the following comments:

> An infinite turnover can be achieved by carrying no inventory whatsoever. But such an inventory policy would not be a good policy because a company with no inventory would be continuously buying, expediting. . . . Turnover is worth improving, yes, but only if there is no substantial increase in ordering cost and only if there is no substantial loss of sales resulting from excessive stockouts.[13]

SUMMARY OF OPTIMUM INVESTMENT IN INVENTORIES

The practical objective of inventory control is to minimize the total associated costs of inventories: the costs of carrying plus the costs of not carrying.

The basic approach described here is applicable to all types of inventories: materials, supplies, parts, work in process, and finished goods. For example, the economic-order-quantity approach may be applied to problems of buying materials or of manufacturing finished units. There are two major subareas for cost analysis: computing economic order quantity (how much to order), and computing optimum safety stocks (when to order). For the "fixed economic-order-quantity system," average inventory quantities will be half the economic order quantity plus the safety stock.

THE MECHANICS OF THE SYSTEM

fixing responsibility   As a business becomes more complex, the interdependent problems of production planning and inventory control become imposing enough to warrant appointing an executive to assume sole responsibility for implementing a coordinated inventory-control policy. The scope of this position varies from company to company. In some firms, he may be a vice-president in charge of production planning and control. In other firms, the planning and control functions may be separated. Duties of purchasing, receiving, and storing may be the responsibility of a single executive, although day-to-day duties may be

[12]*Ibid.*, p. 90.
[13]*Ibid.*, p. 96.

delegated to various officers, such as a purchasing agent, a receiving-room foreman, and a storeroom foreman.

An important aspect of inventory and production control systems is that they may be largely dehumanized. For example, when reorder points, economic order quantities, safety stocks, and other technicalities are calculated, the entire system may be automated with the help of a digital computer. The system can then operate with a minimum dependence on human judgment. That is why inventory-control systems are being increasingly computerized. However, human judgment cannot be eradicated altogether. The ingredients (costs, demand) of the model do frequently change, and a constant surveillance for the sensitivity of the model to such changes is an important, and not too automatic, part of an effective control system.

internal check   Just as in production operations, inventory-control procedures should be systematized in order to promote efficiency and reduce errors, fraud, and waste. Commonly followed internal-control rules[14] should be applied in setting up an inventory system. For example, the stores record clerk should not have access to the physical storeroom, nor should the storeroom employees have access to the formal stores records.

There is a temptation at this point to discuss a typical company system in detail, including descriptions of the routing of multicopies of requisitions, purchase orders, vouchers, invoices, and receiving reports. However, we shall refrain from such a detailed study because (a) such descriptions belong in a book on accounting systems, (b) each system must be tailored to the specific needs of a company, and (c) dwelling on details of paper work often beclouds the important general concepts that need the spotlight.

purchase   The purchasing department is responsible for getting favorable prices,
records   following up irregularities, using approved suppliers, and taking advantage of discounts. Separate, sequential records for each item may be kept by purchase lots, showing dates, source, quantity, unit price, total costs, discounts, and special remarks. Thus, all pertinent data for control are kept on a current basis at the point where control is supposed to be exercised.

The paperwork routine for purchasing and receiving is shown in Exhibit 15-7. Purchasing agents should be free to devote their energies to obtaining optimum prices, investigating sources, and studying market conditions. Their buying should be triggered strictly by purchase requisitions. In general, inventory levels and purchase requisitions are ultimately the responsibility of production planning and control, not of the purchasing department.

---

[14] For a discussion of internal control, see Chapter 20.

EXHIBIT 15-7

SAMPLE ROUTINE FOR PURCHASING MATERIALS

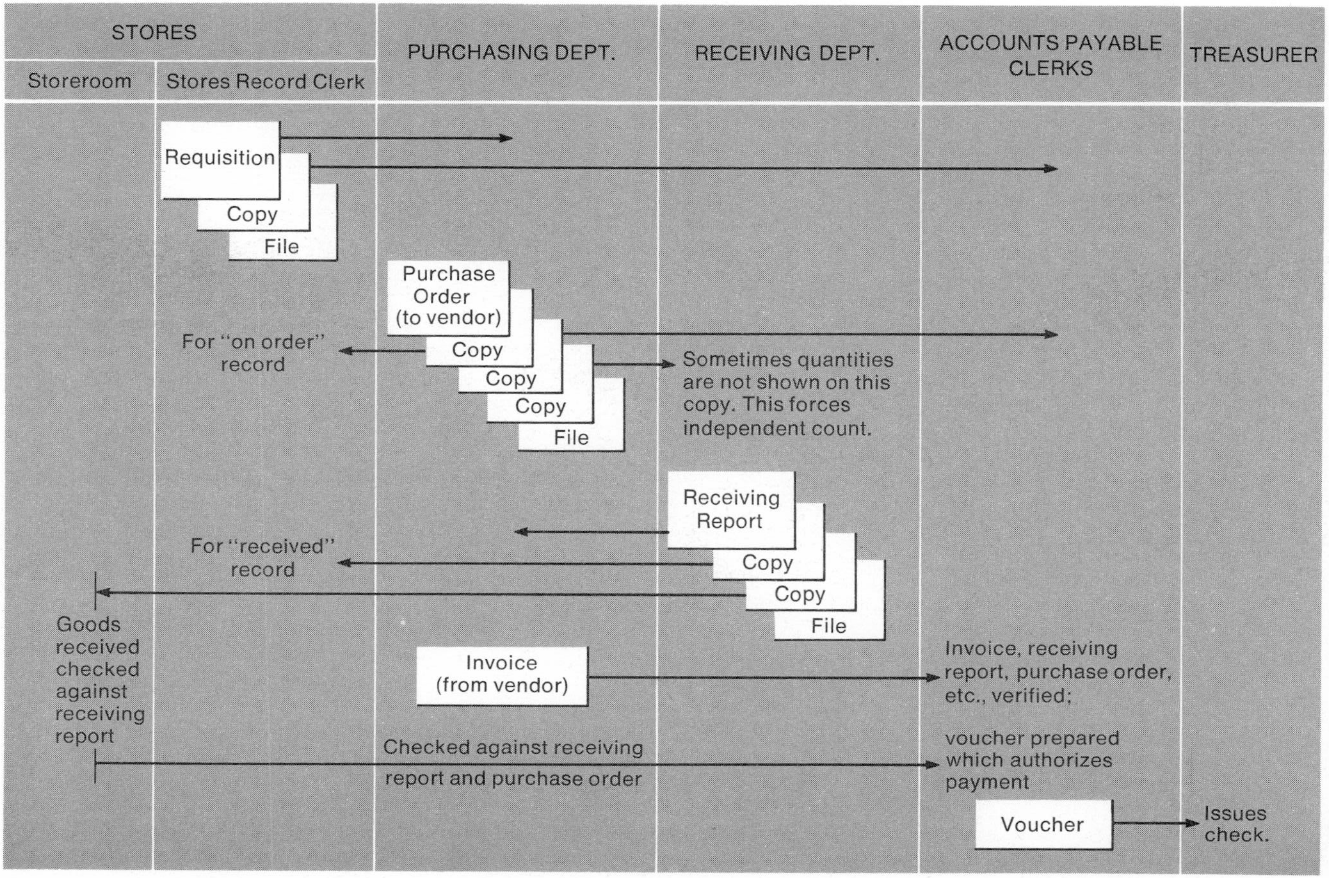

factory usage An effective method of controlling material usage was described in Chapter 8, but we shall summarize it here. Production-planning departments or foremen present standard bills (requisitions) of materials, including allowances for normal spoilage, to the storeroom. If standards are not met, different-colored excess-materials requisitions are used to obtain additional materials. These should be routed to the foreman's superior so that immediate follow-up may be made. Any materials left over are returned to the storeroom by inspectors or foremen.

INVENTORY-VALUATION METHODS

purpose of discussion of inventory methods Management makes policy decisions, at one time or another, regarding methods of inventory valuation. These decisions are important because they directly affect the way income will be computed.

We have already seen how price fluctuations in inventories are accounted for under standard costing. The following discussion surveys alternate approaches to valuation of materials acquired at various prices.[15] The intention here is to demonstrate methodology rather than to dwell on important theoretical issues of inventory valuation that are discussed at length in typical introductory, intermediate, and advanced accounting texts. Also, the influence of income taxes, which is immense, is not discussed at length here.

the question of timing With few exceptions, the differences between inventory methods are merely ones of timing cost releases in relation to income determination.[16] In short, when do inventory costs become expenses? Where it is impractical to identify inventories with specific usage or sales, some assumption is made for transferring certain costs out of inventory. The most commonly used assumption is one of the following three:

1. *First-in, first-out (FIFO)*. The earliest-acquired stock is assumed to be used first; the latest-acquired stock is assumed to be still on hand.

2. *Last-in, first-out (LIFO)*. The earliest-acquired stock is assumed to be still on hand; the latest-acquired stock is assumed to have been used immediately. The LIFO method releases the most recent (or last) inventory costs as cost of goods used or sold. It attempts to match the most current cost of obtaining inventory against sales for a period. As compared to FIFO, the use of LIFO will tend to result in less reported net income during periods of rising prices and more income in periods of falling prices.

3. Some version of an *average-inventory method*. An example would be the *moving-average method*, whereby each purchase is lumped with the former inventory balance so that a new average unit price is used to price subsequent

---

[15] FIFO and weighted-average techniques under process costing are discussed in Chapters 17 and 18.

[16] Certain last-in, first-out inventory situations where base stocks are temporarily depleted call for departures from strict historical costing.

issues of inventory. This method may be used with a perpetual-inventory system. A *weighted-average method* is often used with a periodic-inventory system; this average is computed by dividing the total cost of the beginning inventory plus purchases by the total number of units in those two classes.

example 3 These methods are best understood through illustration.

Try to solve the problem yourself before consulting the answers that follow.

[Adapted from an A.I.C.P.A. examination.] The Saunders Corporation uses raw material A in a manufacturing process. Information as to balances on hand, purchases, and requisitions of material A are given in the table below. You are to answer each question on the basis of this information.

1. If a perpetual-inventory record of material A is operated on a FIFO basis, it will show a *closing inventory* of:
   a. $150
   b. $152
   c. $159
   d. $162
   e. $170
   f. Answer not given

RAW MATERIAL A

| | QUANTITIES | | | | DOLLARS | | |
DATE	RECEIVED	ISSUED	BALANCE	UNIT PRICE	RECEIVED	ISSUED	BALANCE
Jan. 1			100	$1.50			$150
Jan. 24	300		400	1.56	$468		
Feb. 8		80	320				
Mar. 16		140	180				
June 11	150		330	1.60	240		
Aug. 18		130	200				
Sept. 6		110	90				
Oct. 15	150		240	1.70	255		
Dec. 29		140	100				

2. Assume that no perpetual inventory is maintained for material A, and that quantities are obtained by an annual physical count. The accounting records show information as to purchases but not as to issues. On this assumption, the *closing inventory* on a FIFO basis will be:
   a. $150
   b. $156
   c. $159
   d. $160
   e. $170
   f. Answer not given
3. If a perpetual inventory record of material A is operated on a LIFO basis, it will show a *closing inventory* of:
   a. $150
   b. $152
   c. $156
   d. $160
   e. $170
   f. Answer not given

4. Assume that no perpetual inventory is maintained for material A, and that quantities are obtained by an annual physical count. The accounting records show information as to purchases but not as to issues. On this assumption, the *closing inventory* on a LIFO basis will be:
   a. $150
   b. $152
   c. $156
   d. $160
   e. $170
   f. Answer not given
5. If a perpetual-inventory record of material A is operated on a moving-average basis, it will show a *closing inventory* that is:
   a. Lower than on the LIFO basis
   b. Lower than on the FIFO basis
   c. Higher than on the FIFO basis
   d. Answer not given
6. The exact closing inventory in question 5 is $_____.
7. Assume that no perpetual inventory is maintained, and that quantities are obtained by an annual physical count. The accounting records show information as to purchases but not as to issues. On this assumption, the closing inventory on a weighted-average basis will be $_____.

Answers and comments

1. (e) $170. Under FIFO, the ending-inventory valuation may be most easily obtained by first working back from the closing date until the number of units purchased equals the number of units in ending inventory. Then, by applying the appropriate unit purchase costs, the total dollar amount is obtained. In this example, 100 units @ $1.70 is $170.
2. (e) $170. The answer is identical under perpetual and periodic systems. Under a periodic inventory method, files must be combed for recent invoices until 100 units are tallied. In this case, the most recent invoice would suffice. In other cases, more than one invoice may be needed to cover the 100 units in the ending inventory.
3. (b) 90 units @ $1.50 plus 10 units @ $1.70 equals $152. Under LIFO, the ending-inventory valuation may generally be obtained by working forward from the beginning inventory until the total number of units equals the number of units in ending inventory. Then, by applying the appropriate beginning-inventory unit costs and the early current-purchase unit costs, the total dollar amount is obtained.

   However, under a perpetual LIFO method, a temporary reduction (September 6) below the number of units in the beginning inventory calls for the assignment of the base-inventory price to the number of units released from the base inventory.

4. (a) 100 units @ $1.50, or $150. Under a periodic LIFO method, a *temporary* reduction below the number of units in the beginning inventory will have no effect upon the valuation of the ending inventory as long as the number of units in the count of ending inventory for the year as a whole is at least equal to the beginning inventory.
5. (b) FIFO assigns earliest costs to cost of sales and latest costs to inventory. Unit prices have been rising during the period. Therefore, more of the earlier and lower-cost units will be contained in the ending inventory under the moving-average method than under FIFO.

6. $165.125. This technique requires the computation of a new average unit cost after each acquisition; this unit cost is used for all issues until the next purchase is made.

MOVING-AVERAGE
Perpetual Method

DATE	RECEIVED UNITS	RECEIVED PRICE	RECEIVED AMOUNT	ISSUED UNITS	ISSUED PRICE	ISSUED AMOUNT	BALANCE UNITS	BALANCE PRICE	BALANCE AMOUNT
Jan. 1							100	$1.50	$150.00
Jan. 24	300	$1.56	$468				400	1.545	618.00
Feb. 8				80	$1.545	$123.60	320	1.545	494.40
Mar. 16				140	1.545	216.30	180	1.545	278.10
June 11	150	1.60	240				330	1.57	518.10
Aug. 18				130	1.57	204.10	200	1.57	314.00
Sept. 6				110	1.57	172.70	90	1.57	141.30
Oct. 15	150	1.70	255				240	1.65125	396.30
Dec. 29				140	1.65125	231.175	100	1.65125	165.125

Recapitulation

Costs to account for: $150 + $468 + $240 + $255 = $1,113.000
Deduct: Issues   947.875
Ending balance $ 165.125

7. $159. (100 units × $1.59.)

WEIGHTED-AVERAGE
Periodic Method

DATE	UNITS	UNIT PRICE	DOLLARS
Jan. 1	100	$1.50	$ 150
Jan. 24	300	1.56	468
June 11	150	1.60	240
Oct. 15	150	1.70	255
To account for	700		$1,113

Weighted unit cost, $1,113 ÷ 700 = $159
Costs released   600 @ $1.59 $ 954
Costs in ending inventory   100 @ $1.59   159
Costs accounted for $1,113

Note that the assumption of a weighted-average approach is subject to criticism because the October 15 purchase influences the costing of issues throughout the year, even though, strictly speaking, the cost of earlier issues would not have been affected by purchases made later in the year.

**LIFO
versus FIFO**   If unit prices did not fluctuate, all inventory methods would show identical results. Price changes appear in the financial records in different ways, depending on the specific inventory method used. LIFO ordinarily reflects

current purchase prices in current operating results, whereas FIFO delays recognition of price effects. If price changes are volatile, year-to-year reported net incomes may differ dramatically between LIFO and FIFO approaches.

Balance-sheet presentations are also affected by the choice of LIFO or FIFO. LIFO usage tends to result in older and older, and hence less meaningful, prices being shown in inventory if stocks grow through the years, whereas FIFO tends to reflect more nearly current prices on the balance sheet.

If prices are rising, LIFO shows less income than FIFO, and thus it tends to postpone outlays for income taxes. Also, the periodic LIFO method permits immediate influencing of net income by timing of purchases, a feature that has not received the attention it deserves. For example, if prices are rising and a company desires to show less income in a given year because of income tax or other reasons, all that need be done is to buy a large amount of inventory near the end of the year—thus releasing higher costs to expense than ordinarily.

It should also be recognized that neither FIFO or LIFO isolates and measures the effects of price fluctuations as special managerial problems. For example, when prices rise, FIFO buries price gains in the regular income figure, whereas LIFO excludes the effects of price changes from the income statement:

		LIFO			FIFO	
Sales, 5,000 @ 20¢		$1,000			$1,000	
Inventory, beginning	1,000 @ $.10 = $100			$100		
Purchases	5,000 @ $.15 = 750			750		
	$850			$850		
Inventory, ending	1,000 @ $.10 = 100	750	1,000 @ $.15 = 150	700		
Gross margin		$ 250			$ 300	

The $50 price gain (which is attributable to the 1,000 units in ending inventory @ $.05) is submerged in the $300 FIFO gross-margin figure and is ignored in the $250 LIFO gross-margin figure.

Here again we see the benefit of a standard-cost approach. When currently attainable standards are in use, standard costing automatically provides a measure of price "gains" or "losses" that can be reported separately on an income statement. This has two advantages: (a) It prevents price changes from influencing appraisals of efficiency in operations; (b) it spotlights and measures the impact of some price changes on overall company results.

summary

Inventory control is primarily concerned with optimizing inventory balances so that net income is maximized. Record keeping in itself is only one of the important phases of inventory control. Top management's task is to formulate inventory policies that will result in optimum inventory investment, will promote efficiency, and will avoid errors, fraud, and waste.

Associated costs that are affected by various inventory policies are headed by the opportunity cost of interest on investment. Other costs include quantity discounts, contribution margins on lost sales, space costs, overtime premiums, idle time, expediting, transportation, obsolescence, handling, training, learning, setup, order processing, order filling, personal property taxes, insurance, and handling. These costs are often difficult to isolate and measure, especially with regard to their differential behavior between alternatives. However, attempts at sensible measurement at least cast light on a *range* of optimum alternatives.

Different control policies may be applied to different segments of the inventory. Thus, a variety of purchase timing, storing, receiving, and recording techniques may be employed at the same time within the same company.

Modern mathematical methods, especially linear programming, have been applied on a wide front to the problems of production planning and inventory control. The complexity of inventory control is such that many consulting firms specialize in the area to the extent of studying a business's inventory problems and tailor-making a special slide rule for computing economic order quantities.

The subject matter of this chapter again shows how the field of managerial accounting spills over and invades allied fields, such as engineering, modern mathematics, and business policies. The complexities of modern business make it increasingly difficult to construct fences around technical specialties.

First-in, first-out, last-in, first-out, and various average methods of inventory valuation are used to contend with fluctuations in unit prices. However, none of these methods pinpoints a measure of price "gains" or "losses" that can be reported separately. Standard costing, on the other hand, does automatically provide helpful information about price changes.

Problems for Self-Study

PROBLEM 1 Review Example 1 in this chapter. Suppose the annual purchase-order cost was $20 per order instead of $10. What is the economic order quantity?

SOLUTION 1 $$E = \sqrt{\frac{2(5,000)\ \$20}{\$.50}} = \sqrt{\frac{\$200,000}{\$.50}} = \sqrt{400,000} = 633$$

Note that the higher the order cost, the higher the economic order quantity. This problem is an example of sensitivity analysis. The accountant or manager may be unsure about the "true" purchase-order cost, but in this case a doubling of the unit cost will only increase the economic order quantity from 448 to 633 units.

PROBLEM 2 Review Example 2 in this chapter. Suppose management specified that stockouts are acceptable about 11 percent of the time. What safety stock should be provided?

SOLUTION 2 Weekly sales exceeded six units 11 percent of the time and seven units 5 percent of the time. If the safety stock is three units (seven units minus average sales of four units), stockouts will occur whenever weekly sales exceed six units, or about 11 percent of the time.

PROBLEM 3 Review Example 3.

SOLUTION 3 See the solution that follows Example 3.

questions, problems, and cases

15-1. "There are two danger points that management usually wants to avoid in controlling inventories." Explain.

15-2. "Inventory records are only a means to the end of inventory control." Explain.

15-3. Certain costs associated with inventory policies do not appear on formal accounting records. Enumerate at least three.

15-4. "Identical space costs for inventory can be zero during some months and sizable during other months." Explain.

15-5. Define *economic order quantity*.

15-6. "The practical approach to determining economic order quantity is concerned with locating a minimum cost *range* rather than a minimum cost *point*." Explain.

15-7. Define: *lead time, reorder point*.

15-8. What is a *safety stock*? What techniques are used to compute safety stocks?

15-9. Describe a "two-bin" inventory system.

15-10. What are the major responsibilities of the purchasing department?

15-11. Distinguish between the *moving-average* and the *weighted-average* inventory methods.

15-12. "Standard costing is superior to both LIFO and FIFO for isolating and measuring the effects of price fluctuations as special managerial problems." Why?

15-13. **Comparison of LIFO and FIFO.** The Dowell Coal Co. does not maintain a perpetual-inventory system. The inventory of coal on June 30 shows 1,000 tons at $6 per ton. The following purchases were made during July:

July 5	2,000 Tons @ $7 per ton
July 15	500 Tons @ $8 per ton
July 25	600 Tons @ $9 per ton

A physical inventory on July 31 shows a total of 1,200 tons on hand. Revenue from sales of coal for July totals $30,000.

required Compute the inventory value as of July 31, using:

1. LIFO—Last in, first out

2. FIFO—First in, first out

15-14. **Inventory Card, Moving-Average [SIA].** Steel Stores Limited is a dealer in steel products.

The company purchases its steel from various mills. Prices are f.o.b. point of shipment. On January 1, freight costs were $5 per ton; but on January 14, they advanced 10 percent. The steel industry uses the standard 2,000-pound ton.

During the month of January, the following transactions in hot rolled sheets, 60″ long and 36″ wide, took place:

Jan.	1	Inventory	10 tons at $6.00 per 100 lbs.
Jan.	2	Purchased	3 tons at $5.50 per 100 lbs.
Jan.	3	Sold	2 tons
Jan.	5	Purchased	2 tons at $5.60 per 100 lbs.
Jan.	6	Sold	3 tons

Jan. 10	Purchased	8 tons at $5.55 per 100 lbs.
Jan. 12	Sold	8 tons
Jan. 15	Purchased	2 tons at $5.55 per 100 lbs.
Jan. 16	Sold	2 tons
Jan. 30	Purchased	5 tons at $5.60 per 100 lbs.
Jan. 31	Sold	7 tons

Sales prices are determined by applying a markup of 30 percent to laid-down costs at the beginning of each month.

required

1. Show these transactions as they would appear on a perpetual-inventory card, using the moving-average cost method. Calculations should be made to the nearest cent.

2. Calculate the gross profit for the month.

3. Name two methods other than the moving-average cost method that could have been used in pricing the issue transactions above.

15-15. Multiple Choice; Comparison of Inventory Methods [CPA]. The Berg Corporation began business on January 1, 19_4. Information about its inventories under different valuation methods is shown below. Using this information, you are to choose the phrase that best answers each of the following questions. For each question, insert on an answer sheet the letter that identifies the answer you select.

INVENTORY

	LIFO COST	FIFO COST	MARKET	LOWER OF COST OR MARKET
Dec. 31, 19_4	$10,200	$10,000	$ 9,600	$ 8,900
Dec. 31, 19_5	9,100	9,000	8,800	8,500
Dec. 31, 19_6	10,300	11,000	12,000	10,900

1. The inventory basis that would show the *highest net income for 19_4* is:
   a. LIFO cost
   b. FIFO cost
   c. Market
   d. Lower of cost or market
2. The inventory basis that would show the *highest net income for 19_5* is:
   a. LIFO cost
   b. FIFO cost
   c. Market
   d. Lower of cost or market
3. The inventory basis that would show the *lowest net income for the three years combined* is:
   a. LIFO cost
   b. FIFO cost
   c. Market
   d. Lower of cost or market
4. For the year 19_5, how much higher or lower would profits be on the *FIFO cost basis* than on the *lower-of-cost-or-market basis?*
   a. $400 higher   e. $1,000 higher
   b. $400 lower   f. $1,000 lower
   c. $600 higher   g. $1,400 higher
   d. $600 lower   h. $1,400 lower

5. On the basis of the information given, it appears that *the movement of prices* for the items in the inventory was:
   a. Up in 19_4 and down in 19_6
   b. Up in both 19_4 and 19_6
   c. Down in 19_4 and up in 19_6
   d. Down in both 19_4 and 19_6

15-16. **Reconciliation of Inventory Records.** As part of a test of inventory control, you examined the perpetual-inventory records of stockroom M. A full set of records (subsidiary and control) is maintained in the factory, while a controlling account is also kept in the accounting department.

You are required to set up a summarizing schedule in money amounts that simultaneously reflects the flow of materials (starting with initial inventory and ending with final inventory) and reconciles the accounting-department records with those of the factory in regard to opening inventory, receipts, withdrawals of materials, and ending inventory.

The items to be considered in preparing this schedule are as follows:
1. Receipts of materials in stockroom M, entered properly on factory records but treated by the accounting department as stockroom N, $240.
2. Correction made by the accounting department of an error in a prior period. The error was the recording of an $800 withdrawal of materials as $500. The original item had been correctly entered by the factory record clerk.
3. A shortage of item M-143, amounting to $45, which was noted and entered during the period on the factory records but information on which had not been transmitted to the accounting department.
4. An initial inventory, according to factory records, of $11,000 in stockroom M. Receipts were $14,000 and withdrawals were $13,000, according to the records of the accounting department.

15-17. **Prepare Correcting Journal Entries.** Consider each of the following situations separately. Prepare any correcting general-journal entries called for by the following information:
1. During December, raw materials costing $1,000 had been returned to vendors, for which no entry appeared on the books.
2. Freight out of $300 paid on shipments sold f.o.b. destination to customers was charged to Stores.
3. The debit side of the Stores Control account had been overfooted (*overfooted* means "overadded") by $100.
4. A $10,000 shipment of raw materials received from vendors was charged to Selling-Expense Control and credited to Accounts Payable.
5. Some goods returned by customers for credit had been recorded as follows:

dr. Returned sales	$1,000	
cr. Accounts receivable		$1,000
(To credit their accounts at selling price.)		
dr. Stores	$ 700	
cr. Cost of goods sold		$ 700
(To increase our inventory by the factory cost of goods returned.)		

6. On December 28, 19_1, a company clerk discovered that Job #109 (100 units), which was completed and half of which was sold in October, had accumulated $200 of direct-material cost and $300 of direct-labor cost but had not been assigned any overhead. The overhead rate is 50 percent of direct-labor cost. Half the units of Job #109 are still in finished stock.

required   1. Calculate the monthly savings (loss) if the new plan is adopted.

2. Grossman Drug Stores, Inc., expects, and can obtain, a return of 12 percent per annum on invested capital elsewhere. The company policy is to impute a 1 percent per month interest charge on average inventory investment in computing the net monthly saving. What is the monthly saving (or loss)? Would you recommend that the new plan be adopted?

15-24. Make or Buy.   The Gamma Company is considering the feasibility of purchasing from a nearby jobber a component that it now makes. The jobber will furnish the component in the necessary quantities at a unit price of $4.50. Transportation and storage costs would be negligible.

Gamma produces the component from a single raw material. The firm at present orders material in economic lots of 1,000 units at a unit cost of $1; average annual usage is 10,000 units. The yearly storage cost (including rent, taxes, and return on inventory investment) is computed at 50¢ per unit. The minimum inventory is set at 200 units. Direct-labor costs for the component are $3 per unit; fixed manufacturing overhead is applied at a rate of $2 per unit based on a normal annual activity of 10,000 units. In addition to these costs, the machine on which the components are produced is leased at a rate of $100 per month.

Should Gamma make or buy the component?

15-25. Inventory Control and Television Tubes.   The Nemmers Co. assembles private-brand television sets for a retail chain, under a contract requiring delivery of 100 sets per day for each of 250 business days per year. Each set requires a picture tube that Nemmers buys outside, for $20 each. The tubes are loaded on trucks at the supplier's factory door and are then delivered by a trucking service at a charge of $100 per trip, regardless of the size of the shipment. The cost of storing the tubes (including the desired rate of return on investment) is $2 per tube per year. Because production is stable throughout the year, the average inventory is one-half the size of the truck lot. Tabulate the relevant annual cost of various truck-lot sizes at 5, 10, 15, 25, 50, and 250 trips per year. Show your results graphically. (Note that the $20 unit cost of tubes is common to all alternatives and hence may be ignored.)

15-26. Inventory Planning and Control [CPA].   You have been engaged to install an accounting system for the Kaufman Corporation. Among the inventory-control features Kaufman desires as a part of the system are indicators of *how much* to order *when*. The following information is furnished for one item, called a komtronic, which is carried in inventory:

1. Komtronics are sold by the gross (twelve dozen) at a list price of $800 per gross f.o.b. shipper. Kaufman receives a 40 percent trade discount off list price on purchases in gross lots.

2. Freight cost is $20 per gross from the shipping point to Kaufman's plant.

3. Kaufman uses about 5,000 komtronics during a 259-day production year and must purchase a total of 36 gross per year to allow for normal breakage. Minimum and maximum usages are 12 and 28 komtronics per day, respectively.

4. Normal delivery time to receive an order is 20 working days from the date a purchase request is initiated. A rush order in full gross lots can be received by air freight in five working days at an extra cost of $52 per gross. A stockout (complete exhaustion of the inventory) of komtronics would stop production, and Kaufman would purchase komtronics locally at list price rather than shut down.

5. The cost of placing an order is $10; the cost of receiving an order is $20.
6. Space storage cost is $12 per year per gross stored.
7. Insurance and taxes are approximately 12 percent of the net delivered cost of average inventory and Kaufman expects a return of at least 8 percent on its average investment (ignore return on order and carrying cost for simplicity).

required

1. Prepare a schedule computing the total annual cost of komtronics based on uniform order lot sizes of one, two, three, four, five, and six gross of komtronics. (The schedule should show the total annual cost according to each lot size.) Indicate the economic order quantity (economic lot size to order).

2. Prepare a schedule computing the minimum-stock reorder point for komtronics. This is the point below which the komtronics inventory should not fall without reordering so as to guard against a stockout. Factors to be considered include average lead-period usage and safety-stock requirements.

3. Prepare a schedule computing the cost of a stockout of komtronics. Factors to be considered include the excess costs for local purchases and for rush orders.

15-27. **Comprehensive Study of Inventory Planning and Control.** The Ward Company is trying to obtain better means of controlling inventory levels and attendant costs for an expensive part that they have been using for some time. Studies of cost behavior patterns reveal the following information:

Variable costs of placing and following up purchase orders (stationery, postage, telephone, etc.) total $3 per order. Other clerical costs, such as salaries and related office-equipment expenses, have a step cost behavior as follows:

For every additional 200 orders processed per week, there is a $70 increase in purchasing costs, a $60 increase in accounting costs, and an $80 increase in receiving costs.

Insurance and taxes on inventory are 4 percent of average inventory value per year.

The factory is rented at a cost of $60,000 per year. It contains 100,000 square feet of floor space, of which 3,000 square feet is reserved for storing this item. Excess storage space is available in the neighborhood at 75¢ per square foot per year. Extra handling costs for using excess storage space will be 2½¢ per inventory unit in excess storage space per year. The article requires storage space, allowing for aisles, of three square feet each and can be stacked six units high.

Breakage, obsolescence, and deterioration amount to about 2 percent of average inventory per year.

The company's average cost of capital is 10 percent per annum. The company uses this rate for inventory-investment decisions.

The Ward Company works 52 weeks a year, 5 days per week. It uses an average of 100 subassemblies per workday, but usage fluctuates from as low as 50 to as high as 150 per day. Many suppliers are available; but regardless of the source of supply and the size of the order, it will take two weeks from the time a purchase order is placed until delivery. Top management wants to keep an ordinary minimum stock of 1,500 units.

The purchasing agent is anxious to take advantage of savings in unit invoice and freight costs by purchasing in large quantities. Pertinent purchasing data are as follows:

	INVOICE COST		FREIGHT COST	
LOT SIZE	UNIT COST	TOTAL COST	UNIT COST	TOTAL COST
1,000	$55.00	$ 55,000.00	$5.00	$ 5,000.00
2,000	55.00	110,000.00	5.00	10,000.00
4,000	55.00	220,000.00	5.00	20,000.00
5,000	54.00	270,000.00	5.00	25,000.00
6,000	54.00	324,000.00	4.40	26,400.00
8,000	54.00	432,000.00	4.00	32,000.00
10,000	54.00	540,000.00	3.80	38,000.00
13,000	53.50	695,500.00	3.80	49,400.00
26,000	52.00	1,352,000.00	3.50	91,000.00

Special note: Assume that the base stock is already on hand and is therefore irrelevant. The average inventory that is relevant is exclusive of the base. Assume, too, that the maximum inventory to be computed for commitments to excess storage space will be the *absolute* maximum, computed as follows: order point less minimum usage + standard order.

required

1. What order size should the Ward Company use? Support your answer by tabular analysis of the relevant costs for each lot size given above from 1,000 to 26,000.

2. What considerations other than the quantitative data may influence the decision here?

3. Comment on the cost behavior patterns in the situation. Which costs appear to be the most crucial?

15-28. Relevant Costs of Inventory Planning; Sensitivity Analysis. [Prepared by G. A. Feltham] The Super Corporation distributes widgets to the upper delta region of the Sunswop River. The demand for widgets is very constant and Super is able to predict the annual demand with considerable accuracy. The predicted demand for the next couple of years is 200,000 widgets per year.

Super purchases its widgets from a supplier in Calton at a price of $20 per widget. In order to transport the purchases from Calton to the upper delta region, Super must charter a ship. The charter services usually charge $1,000 per trip plus $2 per widget (this includes the cost of loading the ship). The ships have a capacity of 10,000 widgets. The placing of each order, including arranging for the ship, requires about 5 hours of employee time. It takes about a week for an order to arrive at the Super warehouse.

When a ship arrives at the Super warehouse, the widgets can be unloaded at a rate of 25 per hour per employee. The unloading equipment used by each employee is rented from a local supplier at a rate of $5 per hour. Supervisory time for each shipload is about 4 hours.

Super leases a large warehouse for storing the widgets; it has a capacity of 15,000 widgets. The employees working in the warehouse have several tasks:

a. Placing the widgets into storage, after they are unloaded, can be done at the rate of about 40 per hour.

b. Checking, cleaning, etc., of the widgets in inventory requires about one-half hour per widget per year.

c. Removing a widget from inventory and preparing it for shipment to a customer requires about one-eighth hour.

d. Security guards, general maintenance, etc., require about 10,000 hours per year.

The average cost per hour of labor is approximately $10 (including fringe benefits). Super has developed the following prediction equation for its general overhead (excluding shipping materials, fringe benefits, and equipment rental):

Predicted overhead for the year = $1,000,000 + ($8 × Total Labor Hours)

The materials used to ship one widget to a customer cost $1, and the delivery costs average out to about $2 per widget.

The company requires a before-tax rate of return of 20 percent on its investment.

required

1. Super has decided to base its ordering policy on an EOQ model. What amount should they order each time and what should they use as the reorder point? Show all calculations.

2. If the true overhead prediction equation is

$$\$800,000 + (\$12 \times \text{Total Labor Hours})$$

what is the opportunity cost of the prediction error? That is, compare (a) the optimal payoff given the actual magnitude of the parameters with (b) the actual payoff given the order quantity from part 1 and the actual magnitude of the parameters. The difference is the opportunity cost of the prediction error.

16

Joint-Product Costs and By-Product Costs

Nearly every manufacturing operation produces two or more products. But ordinarily, all the manufacturing costs of these multiple products are applied to a single product. For example, as cloth or metal is cut or formed, the excess is regarded as waste or scrap. The minor cost that might be applied to the waste or scrap is usually ignored, and all the production cost is applied to, say, the coat or the lamp that is eventually manufactured.

Whether the accountant applies costs individually among multiple products is dependent on their relative revenue-producing power. When a group of individual products is simultaneously produced, with each product having a significant relative sales value, the outputs are usually called *joint products*. The products are not identifiable as different individual products until a certain stage of production known as the *split-off point*. All costs incurred prior to the split-off point are called *joint-product costs*. The total of these costs is allocated carefully among the members of the product group. A distinguishing characteristic is that no one of the products may be produced without an accompanying appearance of the other products in the joint group, although perhaps in variable proportions. Examples include chemicals, lumber, petroleum products, flour milling, copper mining, meat packing, leather tanning, soap making, gas manufacturing, canneries, and tobacco manufacturing. A meat-packing company cannot kill a pork chop; it has to slaughter a hog, which supplies various cuts of dressed meat, hides, and trimmings.

We shall see that any method of assigning truly joint costs to various units produced is useful only for purposes of inventory costing. *Such assignment is useless for cost-planning and control purposes.*

The term *by-products* is usually confined to those multiple products that have very minor sales values as compared with that of the major or chief product(s).

In this chapter we shall examine (a) the methods of assigning joint costs to products, (b) the impact of joint costs on decision making, and (c) accounting for by-products.

METHODS OF ASSIGNING JOINT COSTS TO PRODUCTS

nature of joint-product cost   Viewed broadly, joint costs plague the accountant throughout his work. The entire problem of allocating the costs of fixed assets to months, years, departments, and products is essentially that of joint costing. Sometimes the term *common cost* is used instead of *joint cost* to describe aspects of joint costing where facilities are shared, such as in computing unit cost of services like bank accounts. Any allocation method is limited in usefulness, because many facilities and services are shared by many revenue-producing activities. Another example of joint-cost problems is the difficulty of reapportioning service-department costs to producing departments. Still another illustration is the application of overhead to job orders. Essentially, factory-overhead items are costs that are jointly shared by all products flowing through the factory. However, we shall confine the term *joint-product* cost to the costs of a single process or series of processes that simultaneously produces two or more products of significant relative sales values. Joint-product costs are total costs incurred up to the point of separation of the different products.

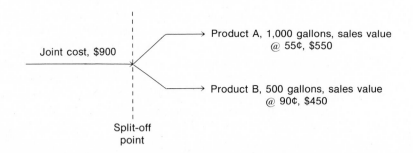

example 1   Example 1 shows the joint costs of a chemical process that produces Products A and B; both become finished goods at the split-off point. How much of the $900 joint cost is assignable to A? How much to B? The $900 cannot be physically identified or traced to either individual product, because the products themselves were not separated before the split-off point. Yet the accountant chooses to select some systematic means of splitting the $900 between the two products so that ending inventories may be costed and income deter-

mined. Two basic approaches are commonly used, although there are many variations of both: (a) physical measures and (b) relative sales values.

physical measures In Example 1, the $900 cost produced 1,500 gallons of product on a physical-quantity basis; therefore, the unit cost is 60¢ per gallon. Costs are assigned as follows: $600 to A, $300 to B. These computations may be shown in a different manner as follows:

	PRODUCTION	WEIGHTING	COSTS ASSIGNED
A	1,000 gal.	1,000/1,500 × $900	$600
B	500 gal.	500/1,500 × $900	300
	1,500 gal.		$900

Assume that one-tenth of the output is unsold at the end of the month. A product-line income statement would appear as follows:

INCOME STATEMENT FOR JOINT PRODUCTS

For the Month Ending _____

	A		B		TOTAL
Sales	900 gals.,	$495	450 gals.,	$405	$900
Joint costs:					
Production costs	1,000 gals.,	$600	500 gals.,	$300	$900
Less inventory	100 gals.,	60	50 gals.,	30	90
Cost of sales	900 gals.,	$540	450 gals.,	$270	$810
Gross margin		($ 45)		$135	$ 90
Gross-margin percentages				33.3%	10%

Note that the use of physical weighting for assignment of joint costs may have no relationship to the revenue-producing power of the individual products. Thus, if the joint cost of a hog were assigned to its various products on the basis of weight,[1] center-cut pork chops would have the same unit cost as pigs' feet, lard, bacon, ham, and so forth. Fabulous profits would be shown for some cuts, although losses would consistently be shown for other cuts.

relative-sales-value approach In the sense that inventory figures should be indicators of sales-generating power, the relative-sales-value approach gives the best practical approximation to the objective of getting a meaningful allocation of joint costs. Traditionally, accountants and managers have felt that costs are incurred with the expectation of recovery at a markup. Therefore, *the relative-sales-value*

---

[1]Sometimes one joint product is a liquid while another is a solid. This situation necessitates converting all physical measures into common terms, such as pounds, gallons, square feet, and the like.

method of joint-cost assignment is most widely used, because it assumes that all end products should show some profit margin under typical marketing conditions. In effect, the relative-sales-value method assigns costs in proportion to a product's ability to absorb the costs. The popularity of the relative-sales-value method may be attributed to the search for a way to assign a cost to each of the final products that is an index of the product's ability to generate revenue:

	PRODUCTION IN TERMS OF SALES VALUE	WEIGHTING	COSTS ASSIGNED
A	$ 550	550/1,000 × $900	$495
B	450	450/1,000 × $900	405
	$1,000		$900

	A	B	TOTAL
Sales	$495.0	$405.0	$900.0
Production costs	$495.0	$405.0	$900.0
Less inventory	49.5	40.5	90.0
Cost of sales	$445.5	$364.5	$810.0
Gross margin	$ 49.5	$ 40.5	$ 90.0
Gross-margin percentage	10%	10%	10%

Compare this income statement with the previous one; note that the gross-margin percentage is the same for both products under the relative-sales-value method. Exhibit 16-1 compares the two methods for assigning joint costs.

costs beyond split-off The relative-sales-value method becomes more intricate when joint products are processed individually beyond the split-off point. A conventional approach to this problem follows (all costs are processing costs):

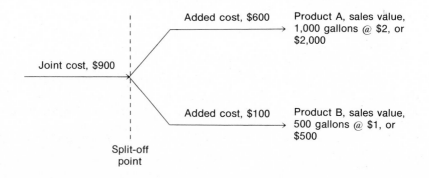

EXHIBIT 16-1

COMPARISON OF TWO METHODS FOR ASSIGNING JOINT COSTS

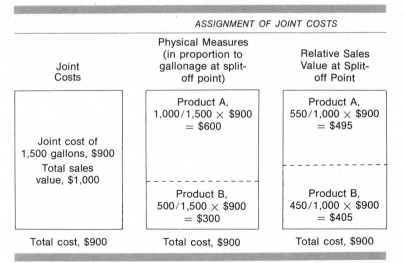

ASSIGNMENT OF JOINT COSTS

Joint Costs	Physical Measures (in proportion to gallonage at split-off point)	Relative Sales Value at Split-off Point
Joint cost of 1,500 gallons, $900 Total sales value, $1,000	Product A, 1,000/1,500 × $900 = $600	Product A, 550/1,000 × $900 = $495
	Product B, 500/1,500 × $900 = $300	Product B, 450/1,000 × $900 = $405
Total cost, $900	Total cost, $900	Total cost, $900

example 2   Although Example 2 is basically the same as Example 1, it assumes that the products are unsalable in their stage of completion at the split-off point. Further processing costs are needed to put them into salable form. *This assumption is important because, when sales-price quotations (or replacement prices) at the split-off point are known or can be determined, they should be used as a basis for splitting joint costs.* That is, the best approach to assigning joint costs is the relative sales values *at the split-off point.* If these values are not explicitly available because there is no market for Products A and B at the split-off point or because the products cannot be purchased from outsiders, the *next best* alternative—for product-costing purposes only—is to take the ultimate relative sales values at the point of sale and work backward to *approximate* (computed) relative sales values at the split-off point. The conventional way of doing this is as follows:

	PRODUCTION IN TERMS OF SALES VALUES	LESS COSTS BEYOND SPLIT-OFF POINT	APPROXIMATE RELATIVE SALES VALUE AT SPLIT-OFF POINT	WEIGHTING	JOINT COSTS ASSIGNED
A (1,000 gallons @ $2.00)	$2,000	$600	$1,400	1,400/1,800 × $900	$700
B (500 gallons @ $1.00)	500	100	400	400/1,800 × $900	200
	$2,500	$700	$1,800		$900

EXHIBIT 16-2

INCOME STATEMENT

For the Month Ending _____

	TOTAL	PRODUCT A	PRODUCT B
Sales	$2,500	$2,000	$500
Cost of goods sold:			
Joint costs	$ 900	$ 700	$200
Separable costs	700	600	100
Total cost of goods sold	$1,600	$1,300	$300
Gross margin	$ 900	$ 700	$200
Gross-margin percentage	36%	35%	40%

Exhibit 16-2 shows a product-line income statement as prepared under this "conventional approximated relative sales value" method,[2] assuming no ending inventories.

If bona fide selling prices are unavailable at the split-off point, as Exhibit 16-2 and footnote 2 assume, the computed (approximated) relative sales values should not be used for further sell-or-process decisions or for judging the performance of either the joint or the separable processes. The relative profitability of joint and separable processes cannot be determined by using artificial market prices, which incorporate shaky assumptions. The latter may be needed for product-costing purposes, but they are useless for planning and control. The relative profitability of joint processing and further separable processing must incorporate an incremental analysis of the level of bona fide selling prices (if

[2] There is another approximated relative-sales-value technique that may be applied in these situations. It entails (a) deducting an *overall profit margin* from the sales values, obtaining the total costs that each product line should bear; and (b) deducting the separable costs from the total costs to obtain the joint-cost assignment. The data from Example 2 and Exhibit 16-2 would yield the following results under this *overall margin* method:

	TOTAL		A		B
Sales value	$2,500	1,000 @ $2.00,	$2,000	500 @ $1.00,	$500
Overall gross-margin percentage (from Exhibit 16-2) (36%)	900	(36%)	720	(36%)	180
Total cost	$1,600		$1,280		$320
Special processing cost	700		600		100
Joint cost	$ 900		$ 680		$220

A favorable aspect of the *overall profit margin* technique is cited by Carl Thomas Devine, in *Cost Accounting and Analysis* (New York: The Macmillan Company, 1950), p. 116, as follows: "Uniform markup on all products is desirable for inventory purposes. Regardless of the composition of finished goods, equal inventory values (costs) will indicate equal sales possibilities."

Once this approach is understood, it is slightly easier to use than the conventional relative-sales-value method. Both techniques rest on arbitrary basic assumptions.

there are none, analysis is impossible) at the split-off point and after separable processing.

costing joint products at realizable values Because the various schemes for joint-cost allocations are subject to so many valid criticisms, many companies refrain from the attempt entirely. Instead, they carry all inventories resulting from joint processing at sales values or at net realizable values (ultimate sales values less estimated separable costs to complete and sell). The meat-packing industry is the primary example, but the canning and mining industries provide other examples. This realizable-value approach ignores joint production costs altogether. It is difficult to criticize this approach when one compares it with the pitfalls of trying to assign joint costs to products.

However, it should be pointed out that accountants ordinarily frown on carrying inventories at sales values, because in this way profit is recognized before sales are made. When compared with generally accepted inventory-costing methods, the realizable-value approach results in higher profits as inventory is increased and lower profits as inventory is decreased. Using selling prices or variations thereof as bases for inventory valuation is more justifiable where differences between costs and selling prices are small and where turnover is high (for example, in the meat-packing and other food-product industries).

Probably the most sensible method is followed by the many companies that carry their inventories at *net realizable values less a normal profit margin* to counteract the criticism that the net realizable-value method recognizes profits before goods are sold.

IRRELEVANCE OF JOINT COSTS IN DECISION MAKING

No technique that is applicable to the problem of joint-product costing should be used for managerial decisions regarding whether a product should be sold or processed further. When a product is an inherent result of a joint process, the decision to process further is not influenced by either the size of the total joint costs or the portion of the joint costs assigned to particular products.

The decision to incur added costs beyond split-off is a matter of comparing the revenue available (if any) at the split-off point with the differential income attainable beyond the split-off point. In Example 2, zero revenue was available at the split-off point, whereas differential revenue for Product B ($500) less differential costs ($100) yields a differential income of $400. In other words, the company is better off by $400, the income that would be foregone if Product B were dumped in the river upon split-off. The amount of joint costs and how they are allocated are completely irrelevant with respect to these decisions.

Many manufacturing companies constantly face the decision of whether to process a joint product further. Meat products may be sold as cut or may be smoked, cured, frozen, canned, and so forth. Petroleum refiners are perpetually trying to adjust to the most profitable product mix. The refining process necessitates separating all products from crude oil, even though only one or two may be desired. The refiner must decide what combination of processes to use to get the most profitable quantities of gasoline, lubricants, kerosene, naphtha, fuel oil, and the like. In addition, at times he may find it profitable to purchase distillates from some other refiner and process them further. Profitability depends on producing the proper product in the proper quantities at the proper time.

In serving management for these decisions, the accountant must concentrate on opportunity costs rather than on how historical joint costs are to be split among various products. The only relevant costs are the additional costs (including the "cost" of capital) as compared with additional revenue. In turn, these must be compared with the revenue foregone by rejecting other alternatives.

To illustrate the importance of the relevant-cost viewpoint, consider another example:

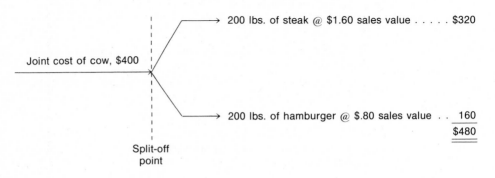

```
                                    ┌───→  200 lbs. of steak @ $1.60 sales value . . . . . $320
                                    │
Joint cost of cow, $400 ────────────┤
                                    │
                                    └───→  200 lbs. of hamburger @ $.80 sales value . .   160
                                                                                          $480
            Split-off
            point
```

example 3 Conventional joint-cost allocations[3] would be:

| | BY WEIGHT | | | BY SALES VALUE | | |
	POUNDS	WEIGHTING	JOINT COST	SALES VALUE	WEIGHTING	JOINT COST
Steak	200	2/4 × $400	$200	$320	32/48 × $400	$267
Hamburger	200	2/4 × $400	200	160	16/48 × $400	133
	400		$400	$480		$400

The packer is faced with the choice of selling the 200 pounds of hamburger at 80¢ ($160) or slicing, freezing, and packaging the hamburger as 200 packages of sandwich steaks. The total additional costs of converting bulk hamburger into sandwich steaks would be $50, while the sales price per package would be $1.20 (total revenue, $240).

Conventional methods of joint-cost allocation are not only irrelevant here, but allowing joint-cost allocations to influence the decision will yield inconsistent

---

[3]As already mentioned, meat packers typically carry inventory at selling prices less costs of disposal rather than use the two approaches here. However, the cow or hog example of a joint cost is useful for illustrative purposes.

results. For example, the weight method would show a loss for sandwich steaks, whereas the relative-sales-value method would show a profit:

	BY WEIGHT		BY RELATIVE SALES VALUE	
Sales, 200 lbs, @ $1.20		$240		$240
Joint cost	$200		$133	
Added cost	50	250	50	183
Profit		$(10)		$ 57

The only approach that will give valid results is to compare the incremental revenue with incremental costs. In this case:

Incremental revenue, 40¢ × 200 pounds	$80
Incremental costs, added processing	50
Additional margin	$30

Another way of looking at the same problem:

Sandwich-steak revenue, 200 lbs. @ $1.20		$240
Costs:		
Added processing	$50	
Opportunity cost, foregoing of hamburger sales (200 × 80¢)	160	210
Difference in favor of added processing		$ 30

The validity of this approach may be proven as follows:

	TOTAL INCOME COMPUTATIONS		
	SELL HAMBURGER	SELL SANDWICH STEAKS	
Sales	$480	($320 + $240)	$560
Total costs	400	($400 + $ 50)	450
Margin	$ 80		$110
Difference in margin	$ 30		

In summary, it is profitable to extend processing or to incur additional distribution costs on a joint product as long as the incremental revenue exceeds the total of incremental explicit costs and incremental opportunity costs of required additional capital.

ACCOUNTING FOR BY-PRODUCTS

problems of definition The distinction among joint products, by-products, and scrap is largely influenced by the relative sales values of the products in question. However, these distinctions are not firm; the variety of terminology and accounting practice is bewildering. For example, valuable brass turnings may be called *scrap* in one company and *by-products* in another. Glycerin, which is ordinarily a *by-product* of soap manufacture, may become at least a *joint product* during wartime production. Many sewage plants that regarded their products as waste have developed the waste into joint-product stature as valuable fertilizer. Kerosene was once a major petroleum product; now it is a by-product.

The Kroehler Company, manufacturer of furniture, provides an example of the impact of technological change on importance of products. Traditionally, there has been 40 percent wastage of wood in a furniture factory. Kroehler now compresses almost all these wood scraps into cultured wood, which is used for bottoms and backs of drawers and other purposes. Previously, two-thirds of the scraps were incinerated at a cost of $2 per ton while the other third was used to fire steam boilers.

By-products are multiple products that have minor sales value as compared with that of the major or chief product(s). Examples are mill ends of cloth and carpets; cotton meal and cotton hulls in processing of cotton oil; tar, naphtha, and kerosene in gasoline production; minor chemicals, gas, and tar from coke manufacture. The distinction between scrap and by-products is often difficult to establish. A view that is sometimes helpful is that by-products (a) have relatively more sales value than scrap, and (b) are often subject to additional costs beyond the split-off point, whereas scrap is usually sold outright. The basic accounting for scrap and for by-products is the same. *The net realizable values of both are best treated as deductions from the cost of the main product.* The rest of this discussion will be confined to accounting for by-products.

accounting methods for by-products There are many methods of accounting for by-products. A comparison of the methods is given in Exhibit 16-3. If the by-product is really a minor product, the differences in results between by-product methods are not significant enough to get excited about.

The following representative methods are illustrated in Exhibit 16-3:

METHOD
ILLUSTRATED

1	By-product income shown as additional revenue
2	By-product income shown as other income
3	By-product income shown as a deduction from cost of sales
4	By-product income shown as a deduction from cost of production
5	Net realizable value of by-products produced shown as a deduction from cost of production
6	Same as 5, except that ending inventory of main product is based on net cost of production rather than on gross cost of production

Conceptually, the best method is probably number 6, where the sales value less costs of disposal is deducted from the total costs of production of the main product. This method eliminates the lag between production and sales and directly matches the cost-reduction power of by-products against the production costs of the main product. The real effect of this approach is to recognize

EXHIBIT 16-3

COMPARISON OF ACCOUNTING METHODS FOR BY-PRODUCTS

DATA FOR ILLUSTRATION

No beginning inventories.

Main product:

Production	10,000 units	Production cost (gross)	$100,000
Sales	9,000 units	Cost of sales (gross)	90,000
Ending inventory	1,000 units	Sales	120,000

By-product:

Production	1,000 units		
Sales	700 units		
Ending inventory	300 units	By-product sales, 700 @ $1.50	$ 1,050
Sales value	$1.50 per unit	Costs of disposal, 700 @ $.30	210
Costs of disposal	$ .30 per unit	Net income from by-product sales	$ 840

INCOME STATEMENTS (IN DOLLARS)

	METHOD (SEE TEXT FOR DESCRIPTION)					
	1	2	3	4	5	6
Sales	120,000	120,000	120,000	120,000	120,000	120,000
Income from by-product sales*	840					
Sales and other income	120,840	120,000	120,000	120,000	120,000	120,000
Cost of sales:						
Production costs, gross	100,000	100,000	100,000	100,000	100,000	100,000
Income from by-product sales*				(840)		
Net realizable value of by-product produced†					(1,200)	(1,200)
Production costs (net) of major product				99,160	98,800	98,800
Ending inventory—main product	(10,000)	(10,000)	(10,000)	(10,000)	(10,000)	(9,880)
Cost of sales (gross)	90,000	90,000	90,000			
Income from by-product sales*			(840)			
Cost of sales (net)			89,160	89,160	88,800	88,920
Gross margin	30,840	30,000	30,840	30,840	31,200	31,080
Other income:						
Income from by-product sales*		840				
Net margin	30,840	30,840	30,840	30,840	31,200	31,080

*By-product sales	$1,050	†Income from by-product sales	$ 840	
Costs of disposal	210	Realizable value of ending inventory,		
Income	$ 840	300 units × ($1.50 − $.30)	360	
		Net realizable value of by-products produced	$1,200	

579

by-product inventory as an asset valued at selling price (or a variation thereof). Furthermore, if the realizable-value method is carried to its logical end, the main-product inventory should be based on the net cost of production and not on the gross cost. Nevertheless, the extra clerical effort involved in the more refined approaches, such as 5 and 6, often results in the practical choice being made among the other methods.

comparison As in so many phases of accounting, the conceptual issue here is one of
of methods timing the recognition of revenue and expenses. Methods 1 through 4 have identical impacts on net margin. It may be helpful to compare these methods with 5 and 6. Assume that the company ceases operations and merely sells its ending inventory in the ensuing period. See Exhibit 16-3, page 579, before examining the following analysis:

INCOME STATEMENT—SECOND PERIOD

| | | METHODS | | |
		1 THROUGH 4	5	6
	Main product:			
	Sales, 10,000 units	$15,000	$15,000	$15,000
	Cost of sales (from ending inventory of prior period—Exh. 16–3)	10,000	10,000	9,880
(a)	Gross margin	$ 5,000	$ 5,000	$ 5,120
	By-product:			
	Sales, 300 units	$ 450	$ 450	$ 450
	Less: Costs of disposal	90	90	90
	Inventory cost	–	360	360
(b)	Income from by-product sales	$ 360	$ 0	$ 0
	Net margin, (a) + (b)	$ 5,360	$ 5,000	$ 5,120
	Net margin for first period	$30,840	$31,200	$31,080
	Net margin for two periods	$36,200	$36,200	$36,200

The two periods taken together show the same income by all methods. The variations in methods raise some provocative theoretical problems concerning matching of revenues and expenses, but expediency usually dictates the method actually used in practice.

The reader who prefers expediency but likes to recognize conceptual niceties will probably prefer either method 3 or method 4. Both of these recognize that by-product margins are somehow reductions of cost of the main product, even though these methods are not very fussy about problems of timing such cost offsets.

Methods 1 and 2 are supported by expediency alone. By-product accounting is an excellent example of how expediency may be the most important criterion in selecting an accounting method. Not much real harm is done if theory is warped in practice, as long as we are confident that the results do not differ significantly between the theoretical method and the practical method. This is the case in by-product accounting, because by definition by-products are minor and thus should be immaterial—their sales values are small in relation to the major product(s).[4]

summary

Joint costs permeate accounting. Costs are joint with respect to time, facilities, and products. Accountants attempt to split joint costs among products having relatively important sales values. Where the joint product is valueless (for example, waste), all costs are applied to the major product. Where the joint product has minor value, it is often called a *by-product;* its net realizable value or income from sales is frequently deducted from the cost of the major product.

No matter what the joint-production situation, any assignment of a joint cost is useless for purposes of managerial decision making. The only use for allocating joint-product costs is for purposes of "reasonable" inventory valuations and income determinations. The *relative-sales-value method* is the technique most frequently used for assigning joint costs to products.

Only opportunity and incremental costs are relevant to the decisions on whether to incur additional separable costs beyond the split-off point. As long as the differential revenue exceeds the differential costs (including the appropriate cost of capital), additional cost incurrence will be warranted.

Problem for Self-Study

PROBLEM   The Alden Oil Company buys crude vegetable oil. The refining of this oil results in four products, A, B, and C, which are liquids, and D, which is a heavy grease. The cost of the oil refined in 19_9 was $27,600, and the refining department had total

---

[4] However, "Determining the Cost of Gasoline," Statement of Tidewater Oil Company before the Federal Trade Commission, May, 1965 (available from Tidewater Oil Company, Los Angeles), describes and favors a linear programming computer method as the standard method for deriving the cost of gasoline in FTC pricing investigations. This method is applied to appropriate marginal or incremental raw materials, product values, and product yields. The linear programming method, in effect, computes total incremental variable costs and subtracts total by-product (such as fuel oil) value; the cost that remains is allocated to gasoline. Note that these results are the same as those obtained by using the by-product method described in this chapter, when applied to the same data. The results are the same because, for a given gasoline volume, the linear programming computer models increase by-product output until profit no longer increases. The models are designed to stop at a level of output at which the by-products literally break even.

For additional economic analysis of the overall problem of costing joint products, see Rene P. Manes and Vernon L. Smith, "Economic Joint Cost Theory and Accounting Practice," *Accounting Review,* January 1965, pp. 31–35. Also see H. Bierman and T. Dyckman, *Managerial Cost Accounting* (New York: The Macmillan Company, 1971), Chapter 8.

processing costs of $70,000. The output and sales for the four products in 19_9 were as follows:

PRODUCT	OUTPUT	SALES	ADDITIONAL PROCESSING COST
A	500,000 gal.	$115,000	$30,000
B	10,000 gal.	10,000	6,000
C	5,000 gal.	4,000	—
D	9,000 gal.	30,000	1,000

required

1. Assume that the conventional approximated relative sales value of allocating joint costs is used. What is the net income for Products A, B, C, and D? Joint costs total $97,600.

2. The company had been tempted to sell at split-off directly to other processors. If that alternative had been selected, sales per gallon would have been: A, 15¢; B, 50¢; C, 80¢; and D, $3. What would the net income have been for each product under this alternative?

3. The company expects to operate at the same level of production and sales in the forthcoming year. Could the company increase net income by altering its processing decisions? If so, what would be the expected overall net income? Which products should be processed further and which should be sold at split-off? Assume that all costs incurred after split-off are variable.

SOLUTION   1.

SELL BEYOND SPLIT-OFF

	(A) SALES VALUE	(B) SEPARABLE COSTS	RELATIVE SALES VALUE AT SPLIT-OFF	(C) ALLOCATION OF JOINT COSTS	A − (B + C) NET PROFIT
A	$115,000	$30,000	$ 85,000	85/122 × $97,600 = $68,000	$17,000
B	10,000	6,000	4,000	4/122 × 97,600 = 3,200	800
C	4,000	—	4,000	4/122 × 97,600 = 3,200	800
D	30,000	1,000	29,000	29/122 × 97,600 = 23,200	5,800
	$159,000	$37,000	$122,000	$97,600	$24,400

2.

SELL AT SPLIT-OFF

	(A) RELATIVE APPROXIMATED SALES VALUE AT SPLIT-OFF	(B) ALLOCATION OF JOINT COSTS	(A) − (B) NET PROFIT
A	500,000 ($ .15) = $ 75,000	75/111 × $97,600 = $65,947	$ 9,053
B	10,000 ($ .50) = 5,000	5/111 × 97,600 = 4,396	604
C	5,000 ($ .80) = 4,000	4/111 × 97,600 = 3,517	483
D	9,000 ($3.00) = 27,000	27/111 × 97,600 = 23,740	3,260
	$111,000	$97,600	$13,400

3. Note that comparing 1 and 2 in the manner computed above is irrelevant. For example, Product C's profit above is $483 or $800, despite the fact that

the same amount is sold at the same price in either case. The only proper way to compare is to use an incremental approach:

	SALES BEYOND SPLIT-OFF	SALES AT SPLIT-OFF	INCREMENTAL SALES	SEPARABLE COSTS BEYOND SPLIT-OFF	INCREMENTAL GAIN OR (LOSS)
A	$115,000	$75,000	$40,000	$30,000	$10,000
B	10,000	5,000	5,000	6,000	(−1,000)
D	30,000	27,000	3,000	1,000	2,000
Increase in profit from further processing					$11,000

Based on the given data, the company income, before considering cost of capital for further processing, could be further improved by $1,000 by selling Product B at the split-off point instead of processing it further.

questions, problems, and cases

Note: When the term "approximated relative sales value" is used, it refers to the conventional method illustrated in Exhibit 16-2.

16-1. "The problem of accounting for depreciation is one of joint costs." Do you agree? Why?

16-2. "Nearly every manufacturing operation produces two or more products." Do you agree? Why?

16-3. List four methods of accounting for by-products.

16-4. What is the main weakness of the relative-sales method of joint-cost allocation?

16-5. Define *net realizable value.*

16-6. "The relative-sales-value method of joint-cost allocation is the best method for managerial decisions regarding whether a product should be sold or processed further." Do you agree? Why?

16-7. Difference Between Joint Products and By-Products [CPA].
1. Explain the basic difference between the method of accounting for joint products and that for by-products.
2. State the conditions under which an item should be treated as a by-product rather than as a joint product.
3. Explain the two principal methods of assigning joint costs to the joint products, and state the circumstances under which each would be appropriate.

16-8. Relative-Sales-Value Method. A company produces two joint products, A and B. The joint cost is $24,000. Added processing costs: A, $30,000; B, $7,500. A sells for $50 per unit; B sells for $25 per unit.

If the company produces 1,000 units of A and 500 units of B, what is the proper amount of joint cost that should be allocated to B, assuming that the approximated relative-sales-value method of allocation of joint costs is used?

16-9. Joint-Product Costs: Ending Inventories. The Darl Company operates a simple chemical process to reduce a single basic material into three separate items, here referred to as X, Y, and Z (all three end products being separated simultaneously at a single split-off point).

Y and Z are ready for sale immediately upon split-off without further processing or any other additional cost. Product X, however, is processed further before being sold.

The selling prices quoted below have not changed for three years, and no future changes are foreseen.

During 19_3, the selling prices of the items and the total number sold were as follows:

X—120 tons sold for $1,600 per ton
Y—340 tons sold for $1,000 per ton
Z—175 tons sold for $800 per ton

There were no beginning inventories whatsoever of X, Y, or Z.

The total joint manufacturing costs for the year were $505,000. An additional $30,000 was spent in order to finish product X.

At the end of the year, the following inventories of completed units were on hand: X, 180 tons; Y, 60 tons; Z, 25 tons. There was no ending work in process.

required Prepare a computation of the "cost" of inventories of X, Y, and Z for balance-sheet purposes as of December 31, 19_3. Include in your presentation a summary of the cost of goods sold by product line. (The Darl Company uses the "approximated relative-sales-value" method of allocating joint costs to end products.)

16-10. **Markups and Allocation of Joint Costs.**

1. Refer to the data and comments about Exhibit 16-2. Suppose that market prices were available at split-off of 70¢ for Product A and 40¢ for Product B. What is the joint cost applicable to A? to B? To what would you attribute the gross margin, the joint process or the separable process?

2. Refer to footnote 2 in the chapter. Suppose that market prices were available at split-off of 68¢ for Product A and 44¢ for Product B. What is the joint cost applicable to A? to B? To what would you attribute the gross margin, the joint process or the separable process? What is the role of bona fide market prices at split-off in management planning and control? Of computed approximate market prices?

16-11. **Introduction to Joint-Costing Techniques.** The Wood Spirits Company produces two products, turpentine and methanol (wood alcohol), by a joint process. Joint costs amount to $12,000 per batch of output. Each batch totals 10,000 gallons, being 25 percent methanol and 75 percent turpentine. Both products are processed further without gain or loss in volume. Added processing costs: methanol, 30¢ per gallon; turpentine, 20¢ per gallon. Methanol sells for $2.10 per gallon; turpentine sells for $1.40 per gallon.

required 1. What joint costs per batch should be assigned to the turpentine and methanol, assuming that joint costs are assigned on a physical-volume basis?

2. If joint costs are to be assigned on an approximated relative-sales-value basis, what amounts of joint cost should be assigned to the turpentine and to the methanol?

3. Prepare product-line income statements per batch for requirements 1 and 2.

4. The company has discovered an additional process by which the methanol

(wood alcohol) can be made consumable and into a pleasant-tasting alcoholic beverage. The new selling price would be $6 a gallon. Additional processing would increase separable costs 90¢ a gallon, and the company would have to pay taxes of 20 percent on the new selling price. Assuming no other changes in cost, what is the joint cost applicable to the wood alcohol? Should the company use the new process?

16-12. **Joint Products and By-Products; Selection of Costing Method.** A and B are joint products. Their cost for the period up to the point of separation was $30,000. There were no costs beyond this point. The production of A was 20,000 units. The production of B was 40,000 units. A's selling price is $5. B's selling price is 20¢.

Use this information in answering the four questions that follow. Each question is independent of all others except as noted. Only the information above is common to all the questions.

1. If there is no ending inventory of A and B (that is, all the units were sold during the period), what allocation of cost would be made to A and B?
2. If the inventory at the end of the period was 10,000 units of A and 20,000 units of B, what valuation figure should be used for the total inventory (that is, A and B together)? Why?
3. If the ending inventory was 10,000 units of A and 10,000 units of B, what would the valuation of A be for balance-sheet purposes? The valuation of B? Use the approximated relative-sales-value method.
4. If B is considered a *by-product* of A, would your answer to 3 have been different? If so, what would the valuation of A now be for balance-sheet presentation? The valuation of B?

16-13. **Christmas Trees; Allocating Joint Costs.** S. Claus is a retired gentleman who has rented a lot in the center of a busy city for the month of December, 19_0, at a cost of $5,000. On this lot he sells Christmas trees and wreaths. He buys his trees by the bundle for $5 each. A bundle is made up of two big trees (average height, seven feet), four regular-sized trees (average height, five feet), and broken branches. The shipper puts in the broken branches merely to make all the bundles of uniform size for shipping advantages. The amount of branches varies from bundle to bundle.

Mr. Claus gets 50¢ a foot for the trees. He takes home the broken branches. He and Mrs. Claus, Donner, Blitzen, and the rest sit about the fire in the evenings and make wreaths, which Mr. Claus sells for $3.50 each. Except for Christmas Eve, these evenings are a time when there is nothing else to do; therefore, their labor is not a cost.

During the course of the season, Mr. Claus buys 1,000 bundles of trees and makes 2,000 wreaths. In addition to the broken branches, the wreaths contain pine cones (100 pounds, total cost $200), twine (4,000 yards @ 5¢ a yard), and miscellaneous items amounting to $600.

In 19_0, Claus sold 1,800 of the seven-foot trees, all the regular-sized ones, and half the wreaths (the local Boy Scouts were also selling wreaths). The department store next door says that they will buy the rest of the wreaths, if Claus will preserve them, for $3 each. The preservative spray costs $2,000 for enough to do the job.

required

1. What unit cost should Claus assign to each of his items?
2. What is the inventory cost on January 1, 19_1, if he doesn't sell to the department store?
3. Should he sell to the department store?

16-14. Joint Costs; Change in Product Mix.   The Laissez Faire Perfume Company processes a secret blend of flower petals into three products. The process works in such a way that the petals are broken down into a high-grade perfume, Charm, and a low-grade flower oil. The flower oil is then processed into a low-grade perfume, Wild Scent, and a cologne, Personally.

The company used 10,000 pounds of petals last month. The costs involved in reducing the petals into Charm and flower oil were:

Direct materials	$150,000
Direct labor	90,000
Indirect costs	60,000
	$300,000

The costs of producing Wild Scent and Personally from the flower oil were:

Direct materials	$15,000
Direct labor	35,000
Indirect costs	20,000
	$70,000

Total production for the month, with no ending work-in-process inventory, was:

Charm	10,000 ounces
Wild Scent	20,000 ounces
Personally	50,000 ounces

The sales price of Charm is $40 an ounce; of Wild Scent, $10 an ounce; and of Personally, $1 an ounce.

Additional costs, entirely separate for each product, of processing and selling are:

Charm	$ 20,000
Wild Scent	160,000
Personally	40,000
	$220,000

required

1. Joint cost of Charm, Wild Scent, and Personally, using the approximated relative-sales-value method.

2. Product-line income statement, assuming no beginning or ending inventories.

3. The management, completely ignorant of cost accounting, is considering the possibility of increasing the quality of Wild Scent, at an increase in final processing cost of $2 per ounce. The selling price would increase to $12 an ounce. This would result in a different product mix of Wild Scent and Personally. Every 10,000 pounds of petals would then result in 10,000 ounces of Charm, 18,000 ounces of Wild Scent and 60,000 ounces of Personally. The separable costs of Personally and Wild Scent are completely variable. All prices and costs not specifically mentioned will remain unchanged. Should this alternative be selected?

16-15. Sell or Process Further.   The Mow Company produced three joint products at a joint cost of $100,000. Two of these products were processed further.

Production and sales were:

	WEIGHT	SALES	ADDITIONAL PROCESSING COSTS
A	300,000 lbs.	$245,000	$200,000
B	100,000 lbs.	30,000	None
C	100,000 lbs.	175,000	100,000

required

1. Assume that the approximated relative value of allocating joint costs is used. What is the net income for Products A, B, and C?

2. The company had been tempted to sell at split-off directly to other processors. If that alternative had been selected, sales would have been: A, $50,000; B, $30,000; and C, $60,000. What would the net income have been for each product under this alternative?

3. The company expects to operate at the same level of production and sales in the forthcoming year. Could the company increase net income by altering its processing decisions? If so, what would be the expected overall net income? Which products should be processed further and which should be sold at split-off? Assume that all costs incurred after split-off are variable.

16-16. Sell or Process Further; Allocation of Fixed Costs. The Space Parts Co. receives cold-worked steel in sheet form from a nearby steel mill. The company has a special patented machine that takes the sheet steel and produces three missile parts simultaneously. Part A is taken from the machine and further processed to make it available for sale at $3.50; the additional processing cost for part A is $495. Parts B and C are run through a vat containing a secret "dip" developed by one of the company engineers to make them heat-resistant. This dip costs 20¢ per cubic foot of product. Part B sells for $5 and part C for $8.25.

ADDITIONAL INFORMATION	
Materials	$ 8,000
Direct labor	1,600
Maintenance and depreciation	1,200
	$10,800 cost of running special machine for month

Month's production and sales (which is the typical product mix):

Part A	600 units
Part B	800 units
Part C	1,000 units

Part B has a volume of 0.50 cu.ft.
Part C has a volume of 0.75 cu. ft.

The vat is being depreciated at the rate of $60 per month, requires three men for its operation at a total salary of $1,500 per month, and necessitates other operating expenses of $165 per month. All these costs are fixed.

required

1. Joint costs assignable to each part for the month's operations. Use the approximated relative-sales-value method.

2. The company has a chance to sell part B undipped at split-off at $4.70 each on a long-run basis. Should the company adopt this alternative?

16-17. **Computation of Breakeven Point for Joint Processes.** [Adapted from a problem prepared by Professor James March.] The March-I Company processes soybeans to obtain oil, meal, and chaff. There are three processes. In the cleaning process, the chaff and foreign materials are separated from the beans. In the pressing process, soybean oil and soybean cake are produced. The oil is stored in tanks and later pumped into tank cars for shipment. In the grinding process, the soybean cake is dried and then ground into meal.

The standard yield from a ton (2,000 lbs.) of beans is 100 pounds of chaff, 800 pounds of meal, and 100 gallons of oil. The following selling prices have been chosen for the purpose of calculations: beans delivered to plant, $120 a ton; chaff, $10 a ton; oil, $1.20 a gallon; and meal, $200 a ton. Budgeted costs of processing are:

	VARIABLE COSTS PER UNIT	FIXED COSTS PER MONTH
Cleaning	10¢ per ton of beans	$ 500
Pressing	$2 per ton of cleaned beans	2,000
Grinding	$2 per ton of meal	1,500

Assume that there are no work-in-process inventories and that selling and administrative expenses are: fixed costs of $1,800 monthly; variable costs of 10 percent of dollar sales in the case of oil sales and meal sales and zero in the case of chaff sales.

required

1. Chart of physical flow.

2. How many tons of beans must be processed monthly in order to break even? Show computations clearly.

16-18. **Comparing Alternatives; Discounted Cash Flow.** Pottsville Process, Inc., processes an ore that yields 60 percent product A, 20 percent product B, and 20 percent complete waste. Willo, Inc., the sole customer and a mere intermediate link in the distribution chain, purchases the entire output of products A and B.

A Pottsville company engineer has developed a process that will produce a 70 percent yield of product A from the ore—a new product A that is in a form that can be sold directly to the prime user. This will eliminate Willo, Inc., as a customer for both products; there is no other available market for product B. The required investment to provide the capital equipment and the necessary expansion is $4,000,000. These new facilities have an estimated life of 20 years, exactly the remaining life of the present equipment. This money can be obtained at a rate of 4 percent. However, the company's average cost of capital is 10 percent.

COMPARATIVE COST DATA

Present

Processed: 1,000,000 tons per year.

Cost data:	PER TON
Variable manufacturing cost	$ 5.00
Fixed manufacturing cost other than depreciation	6.00
Depreciation on equipment (straight-line)	.30
	$11.30

"New Process"

Processed: 1,000,000 tons per year.
Cost data:

Variable manufacturing cost	$10.00
Fixed manufacturing cost other than depreciation	9.00
Depreciation—including new equipment (straight-line)	.50
	$19.50

PRICE DATA

Present:
  Product A—$20.00 per ton
  Product B—$ 3.00 per ton
"New Process":
  "New Product" A—$30.00 per ton

required

1. Prepare comparative annual income statements for the two alternatives.

2. Analyze the alternatives on a discounted cash-flow basis, using the present-value technique.

3. Would your decision in 2 be changed if product B in the amount produced under the present process could also be sold under the new process?

16-19. **Joint Costs and Discounted Cash Flow.** The Faia Company manufactures products A, B, and C. These products all derive from the same basic raw material and are then processed into final products. Current operating data are displayed below:

JOINT COSTS OF PRODUCTION: $200,000 for 100,000 GALLONS

	PER UNIT	
	SELLING PRICE	COST PAST SPLIT-OFF
A	$15	$10
B	10	4
C	6	2

Every 10 gallons of raw material produce 2 gallons of A, 5 gallons of B, and 3 gallons of C.

The Shrewd Co. has offered to lease a patented device to the Faia Company that will increase the yield from the common raw material by 50 percent for an initial fee of $100,000 plus a royalty of 20¢ per gallon of yield. In addition, Shrewd Co. wants an exclusive contract as a term of the license to purchase all of the firm's final output of A at a price of $8 for the next six years. At the end of this time, Shrewd Co. would grant the Faia Company a rebate of $10,000. If the offer were accepted, the Faia Company could scrap existing equipment with a disposal value of $10,000, a remaining useful life of six years, and an expected disposal value of zero at the end of the six years.

The Faia Company expects that it will be able to market all the additional output at existing prices. The sales manager of the Faia Company has indicated that he will turn down the offer, as it involves selling product A to Shrewd Co. at a price below out-of-pocket costs.

The Faia Company's minimum desired rate of return is 10 percent.

required   Ignoring income taxes and using discounted cash flow, prepare data that will aid the president in making a correct decision. Include your recommendations as to the proper course of action.

16-20. Relative-Sales-Value Method; Discounted Cash-Flow Approach to Joint-Process Replacement.

1. The A Company produces two items, X and Y. The items first go through joint processing. Then each receives separable processing. All the production is sold, and no inventories are carried. Annual joint costs are $100,000. What is the gross margin of each product, using the approximated relative-sales-value method?

	X	Y
Yearly sales	$100,000	$300,000
Annual separable costs	50,000	150,000

2. A new joint process has been developed to replace the currently used joint process. It will reduce annual joint costs by 50 percent, but it requires an initial investment of $200,000. Its useful life is five years. Annual additional processing costs of X will be reduced by $15,000, but those of Y will increase by $20,000. Sales will not be affected. Minimum desired rate of return is 10 percent. Should the new method be adopted? (Use discounted cash-flow calculations.) How has the reallocation of joint costs affected the decision?

16.21. Joint Products and By-Products. [Prepared by William F. Crum] Sycamore Company mines an ore, which is crushed and processed in Dept. 1. Out of this process come two major products, Argon and Urgon, and a by-product, Exgon. Exgon is processed in Dept. 4. Argon is further processed in Dept. 2. Urgon is further processed in Dept. 3. The net residual value of Exgon is to be credited against the material cost in Dept. 1, after allowing for a profit of 10 percent on Exgon, in addition to allowing for 25 percent for selling and administrative expenses and $8,000 further costs of operating Dept. 4.

Argon and Urgon are to be treated as joint products, with the net cost of Dept. 1 allocated to them on a relative-sales-value basis.

Cost statistics for the month of January 19_1 are:

Assume no beginning inventories in process.
60,000 lbs. of material costing $90,000 are processed in Dept. 1
Conversion costs of Dept. 1, $20,000
Conversion costs of Dept. 2, $10,000
Conversion costs of Dept. 3, $ 8,000
10,000 lbs. of Argon produced in Dept. 1
20,000 lbs. of Urgon produced in Dept. 1
10,000 lbs. of Exgon produced in Dept. 1
Argon sells for $10 per lb.
Urgon sells for $5 per lb.
Exgon sells for $2 per lb.

required   1. Schedule showing finished cost per lb. of Argon and Urgon.

2. January 31, 19_1, inventory shows 5,000 lbs. of Urgon and 1,000 lbs. of Exgon on hand. Both have been completely processed. At what inventory value would you carry the inventory in the balance sheet?

16-22. Allocating Joint Costs; Sales Decision.

1. The ABC Electronics Company manufactures a line of semiconductor diodes. The diodes are produced in batches, and when they are completed,

several of their electrical parameters are tested. On the basis of these tests, some diodes are scrapped, and the rest are classified according to particular combinations of electrical parameters (the production process cannot be controlled to the extent that the parameters of all the diodes are the same). In a recent batch of 1,000 diodes for which production costs of $3,750 were incurred, 750 of the diodes were estimated to have a net realizable value of $5 apiece (on the basis of their parameters), and the remaining 250, $10 apiece. These estimates were based on competitors' prices for diodes with roughly similar parameters. How should production costs be assigned to the diodes? Show computations. What are the limitations of such a method?

2. The batch described is such that the $10 diodes meet all the electrical specifications of the cheaper $5 diodes. Assume that all the $5 diodes have been sold, but that 100 of the $10 diodes remain in inventory. Should the $10 diodes be sold at a net realizable value of $5 to meet additional demand for the cheaper diodes, given that the production cost assigned to them was $6 apiece? Explain.

16-23. Deciding on a Product Mix. The Barry Company, a major international oil company, refines and markets five petroleum products worldwide. The crude oil can be refined into the following products at these costs:

1. At a joint cost of 75¢ per barrel (which includes the cost of crude), the crude is first refined to yield equal parts of products A and B.
2. Any amount of B can be further processed to yield the same quantity of C at an additional cost of 40¢/bbl.
3. Finally, C can be refined into equal amounts of D and E. Two barrels of C will yield one barrel each of D and E at a cost of 50¢ per barrel of C refined.

required   Ten million barrels of crude are available for the relevant planning period. The following prices per barrel are expected to prevail during that period: A, $1.45; B, $1.05; C, $1.40; D, $1.60; and E, $2.40. How much of which products should the company refine? What is the expected contribution to fixed charges with this mix? Ignore any selling, shipping, and handling costs. Assume that the required refining facilities are available.

16-24. Complex Physical Process; By-Product Accounting [CPA]. The McLean Processing Company produces a chemical compound, Supergro, that is sold for $4.60 per gallon. The manufacturing process is divided into the following departments:

1. *Mixing department.* The raw materials are measured and mixed in this department.
2. *Cooking department.* The mixed materials are cooked for a specified period in this department. In the cooking process there is a 10 percent evaporation loss in materials.
3. *Cooling department.* After the cooked materials are cooled in this department under controlled conditions, the top 80 percent in the cooling tank is syphoned off and pumped to the packing department. The 20 percent residue, which contains impurities, is sold in bulk as a by-product, Groex, for $2 per gallon.
4. *Packing department.* In this department, special one-gallon tin cans costing 60¢ each are filled with Supergro and shipped to customers.

The company's research and development department recently discovered a new use for the by-product if it is further processed in a new boiling department. The new by-product, Fasgro, would sell in bulk for $5 per gallon.

In processing Fasgro, the top 70 percent in the cooling tank would be syphoned off as Supergro. The residue would be pumped to the boiling department, where one-half gallon of raw material, SK, would be added for each gallon of residue. In the boiling department process, there would be a 40 percent evaporation loss. In processing Fasgro, the following additional costs would be incurred:

Material SK	$1.10 per gallon
Boiling department variable processing costs	$1.00 per gallon of input
Boiling department fixed processing costs	$2,000 per month

In recent months, because of heavy demand, the company has shipped Supergro and Groex on the same day that their processing was completed. Fasgro would probably be subject to the same heavy demand.

During the month of July, 19_3, which was considered a typical month, the following raw materials were put into process in the mixing department:

Material FE—10,000 gallons @ $ .90 per gallon
Material QT— 4,000 gallons @ $1.50 per gallon

July processing costs per gallon of departmental input were:

Mixing department	$.40
Cooking department	.50
Cooling department	.30
Packing department	.10

For accounting purposes, the company assigns costs to its by-products equal to their net realizable value.

required Prepare a statement computing total manufacturing costs and gross profit for the month of July that compares (1) actual results for July, and (2) estimated results if Fasgro had been the by-product.

16-25. **Compute Maximum Price to Be Paid for Raw Materials.** The Nerg Fertilizer Company buys special silt and dehydrates, sorts and bales it for sale as powerful fertilizer. The silt is separated into three grades, the separation being dependent upon the relative content of foreign matter. The three grades of fertilizer have the following list prices per ton: (1) $200, (2) $150, and (3) $125. Standards provide for 110 tons to be purchased for every 100 tons yield of baled fertilizer. Processing costs are $40 per ton of baled fertilizer and handling costs are $5 per ton of silt.

Selling and administrative expenses are 15 percent of sales; target income is 10 percent of sales.

The purchasing agent for the Nerg Company has been offered two carloads of silt at a cost of $80 per ton. Tests indicate that this silt will yield 60 percent of grade 1 and 20 percent each of grades 2 and 3; however, waste will be 10 percent higher than present levels. Should the agent accept this offer in light of the target income?

16-26. **Maximum Purchase Price for Ton of Material [CPA, adapted].** The management of the Southern Cottonseed Company has engaged you to assist in the development of information to be used for managerial decisions.

The company has the capacity to process 20,000 tons of cottonseed per year. The yield of a ton of cottonseed is as follows:

PRODUCT	AVERAGE YIELD PER TON OF COTTONSEED	AVERAGE SELLING PRICE PER TRADE UNIT
Oil	300 lbs.	$ .15 per lb.
Meal	600 lbs.	50.00 per ton
Hulls	800 lbs.	20.00 per ton
Lint	100 lbs.	3.00 per cwt.
Waste	200 lbs.	

A special marketing study revealed that the company can expect to sell its entire output for the coming year at the listed average selling prices. You have determined the company's costs to be as follows:

Processing costs
    Variable: $9 per ton of cottonseed put into process
    Fixed: $108,000 per year

Marketing costs
    All variable: $20 per ton sold

Administrative costs
    All fixed: $90,000 per year

From the information above, you prepared and submitted to management a detailed report on the company's breakeven point. In view of conditions in the cottonseed market, management told you that they would also like to know the average maximum amount that the company can afford to pay for a ton of cottonseed.

Management has defined the average maximum amount that the company can afford to pay for a ton of cottonseed as the amount that would result in the company's having losses no greater when operating than when closed down under the existing cost and revenue structure. Management states that you are to assume that the fixed costs shown in your breakeven-point report will continue unchanged even when the operations are shut down.

required

1. Compute the average maximum amount that the company can afford to pay for a ton of cottonseed.

2. You also plan to mention to management the factors, other than the costs that entered into your computation, that they should consider in deciding whether to shut down the plant. Discuss these additional factors.

16-27. Joint Costs and Relevant Costs.   The Curling Chemical Company begins all production in Department A. At the end of processing in Department A, products X and Y appear. Both can be sold immediately, but X can also be processed further in Department B, where products X-1 and X-2 appear at the end of processing. X-1 is then immediately sold; X-2 can be (a) sold in bulk to another processor, (b) packaged and sold as a consumer good, or (c) aged for one year and reintroduced as a raw material, Mysto, in Department A. One unit of aged X-2 is equal to one unit of Mysto.

Production and sales have been stable for the past few years, and the basic demand for all products does not look as though it will change for quite a few more years.

Data for the past year include the following:

Processing costs—Department A:

Variable	$ 75,000
Fixed	45,000

Processing costs—Department B (not including transferred-in costs):

Variable	$ 58,000
Fixed	150,000

Unit data:

	IN UNITS	
	PRODUCTION	ENDING INVENTORIES
X	220,000	20,000
Y	200,000	5,000
X-1	70,000	1,000
X-2	30,000	2,000

Selling prices per unit (unchanged throughout this year):

X (net of separable selling expenses)	$ .20
Y (net of separable selling expenses)	.44
X-1 (after deducting $.10 variable packaging costs)	2.00
X-2 in bulk	4.30
X-2 as consumer good	5.00

Purchase costs:

Mysto: $4.00 per unit

5,500 units of Mysto were needed last year for production operations in Department A.

Selling costs of X-2, all variable, 10% of selling price.

Packaging costs of X-2 for consumer sales, 50¢ per unit.

The company's average cost of capital is 10%.

Packaging costs are considered as manufacturing costs by this company.

Unless otherwise stated, consider each situation below independently. State any special assumptions that you make.

required

1. The company uses "market value at split-off point" as a basis for allocating joint-production costs to products. What are the appropriate total ending-inventory values for products X, Y, X-1 and X-2? Show computations *clearly*. For products X-1 and X-2, show a breakdown in total inventory costs between the Department A portion and the Department B portion.

2. Assume that the outside purchase cost of Mysto is going to rise. Based on the given information, how high will the price of Mysto have to go before the Curling Chemical Company should seriously consider aging X-2 and using it in Department A? Explain.

3. The company is considering adding another material at a cost of $1.00 per unit to product X-1, packaging the resulting product at a variable cost of 42¢ per unit, and selling it through manufacturer's agents at a straight commission of 10 percent of selling price. The prospective selling price will be $3.80 per finished unit. Should the company adopt this plan? Why? Show computations.

4. The company has been offered some new processing equipment for Department A. The salesman says that the new equipment will slash unit costs by 3.5¢. The new equipment will replace old equipment that has a remaining useful life of seven years, has zero disposal value now, and is being depreciated on a straight-line basis at $10,000 per year. The new equipment's straight-line depreciation would be $25,000 per year. It would last seven years and have no disposal value. The salesman pointed out that overall unit costs now are slightly over 28.5¢ per unit of product in Department A, whereas the new equipment is being used by one of Curling's competitors at a unit cost of production of only 25¢ per unit of product, computed as follows:

Variable costs	$ 60,060
Fixed costs	76,440*
Total costs	$136,500
Divide by total units of X and Y produced	546,000
Cost per unit	25¢

* The $76,440 includes $25,000 depreciation on the new equipment in question. Curling's supervisory payroll is $6,000 less than this competitor's.

The salesman went on to point out that a saving of $3\frac{1}{2}$¢ per unit would add $14,700 to Curling's annual profits.

a. Show *specifically* how the salesman made his computations of Department A unit costs.

b. As adviser to Curling's management, evaluate the salesman's contentions and prepare a quantitative summary to support your recommendations for Curling's best course of action.

17

Process Costing: A Type of Product Costing

Process-costing techniques are used for inventory costing when there is continuous mass production of like units, in contrast to the production of tailor-made or unique goods. This chapter will cover the major *product-costing* approaches that may be used in process-cost systems. It will be concerned only incidentally with *planning and control*, because the latter techniques are discussed in other chapters and are applicable to all product-costing systems regardless of whether process costing or job-order costing is used.

GENERAL CHARACTERISTICS OF PROCESS COSTING

all product costing is averaging The most important point is that product costing is an averaging process. The unit cost used for inventory purposes is the result of taking some accumulated cost and dividing it by some measure of production. The basic distinction between job-order costing and process costing is the breadth of the denominator: In job-order costing, it is small; but in process costing, it is large.

The two polar extremes of product costing are usually labeled *job-order costing* and *process costing*. As we saw in Chapter 4, job-order costing is concerned with individual units or batches, each receiving various degrees of attention and skill. In contrast, process costing deals with the mass production of like units that usually pass in continuous fashion through a series of production steps called *operations* or *processes*. Process costing is most often found in such industries as chemicals, oil, textiles, paints, flour, canneries, rubber, steel, glass, food processing, mining, and cement.

If a company mass-produces only one uniform product, the product-costing task at first glance is simple. Obtain a unit cost by dividing the total manufacturing costs by the total units produced. Then use the resultant unit cost to compute the costs of inventories and the cost of goods sold. Indeed, it is simple, provided that there are (a) no work-in-process inventories or no significant changes between the levels of the beginning and ending work-in-process inventories, and (b) no abnormal spoilage, shrinkage, or waste. However, if the foregoing two conditions do not hold, the product-costing task becomes more difficult.

equivalent units: the key

example 1

Consider the following example:

Beginning inventory, in process	0
Units placed in process	40,000
Units finished	38,000
Units in process, end, $\frac{1}{2}$ finished	2,000
Total costs to account for	$39,000

Suppose that the flow of all costs is a continuous and constant stream; that is, materials, labor, and overhead are assumed to be added uniformly as manufacturing progresses.

When average unit cost is computed, the units in process should not be weighted the same as the finished units. The partially completed units have received only half the attention and effort that the finished units have received. Thus, the notion of "equivalent performance" or "equivalent units" is used as a technique for establishing a unit cost within a production process. In substance, the notion of equivalent units is the expression of physical units in terms of *doses* or *charges* of work applied thereto. So a physical unit is viewed by an accountant as a bundle of work charges, as a collection of the factors of production (material and conversion costs). Equivalent units are calculated as follows:

Units finished, charged with full dose of cost	38,000
Units in process, end, each unit is $\frac{1}{2}$ completed:	
$2,000 \times \frac{1}{2}$	1,000
Total equivalent unit performance	39,000
Unit cost, per equivalent unit ($39,000 \div 39,000$)	$ 1.00
Costs to be applied:	
To finished units ($38,000 \times \$1.00$)	$38,000
To work in process ($1,000 \times \$1.00$)	1,000
Total costs accounted for	$39,000

Note that unit cost is *not* calculated on the basis of physical units. It *is* calculated on the basis of equivalent unit performance—that is, on the basis of "charges" or "doses" of cost needed to finish a given unit. Therefore, a finished unit gets a full charge, while a half-finished unit is assigned one-half a charge.

five
basic steps
to solution
Many process-cost situations contain complex production flows. It is essential to understand the production cycle itself before making any calculations; a sketch of the physical flow of units is often helpful. In making computations, concentrate on physical flow and equivalent units at the outset. *Disregard dollar amounts until equivalent units are computed.*

Building in self-checks in a step-by-step solution is an extremely helpful technique. Such self-checks are woven into the five-step uniform approach outlined below. Use caution as you study these steps. There is a real danger in clinging to the five steps as a mechanical technique without understanding *why* nearly all process-cost problems can be solved with the five-step method. The reasoning will be explained as the discussion progresses. If the basic nature of accounting for process costs is understood, the five steps may be developed at any time. Memorization will not be necessary.

As you will see in the examples, most process-cost problems can be solved by a uniform approach as follows:

Step 1. Physical flow.   Trace the physical flow of production. (Where did units come from? Where did they go?) In other words, (a) What are the units to account for? and (b) How are they accounted for? Draw flow charts as a preliminary step, if necessary.

Step 2. Equivalent units.   Convert the physical flow, as accounted for in Step 1(b) above, into equivalent units of production. Thus, if 6,000 physical units are two-thirds complete as to materials and one-half complete as to conversion costs, it means that 4,000 *doses* of material and 3,000 *doses* of conversion costs have been applied. (See Example 2 below.)

Step 3. Total costs to account for.   Summarize, using materials, labor, overhead, and so forth, the *total* costs to be accounted for.

Step 4. Cost per equivalent whole unit.   Divide the data in Step 3 by the equivalent units calculated in Step 2. The result will be the cost per equivalent whole unit.

Step 5. Build the TOTAL cost of production and inventories.   Apply the unit costs obtained in Step 4 to inventories and to goods transferred out. Be sure to *total* these figures to see that they agree with the *grand total* obtained in Step 3.

using the
five steps
The steps above are noted parenthetically by number in the examples that follow.

In the actual presentation of a complete solution, Steps 1 and 2 and Steps 3 and 4 may be combined to make two schedules for the four steps.

This five-step approach is not the only or the fastest way to solve process-cost problems. Nevertheless, it is logical and has self-checks. By applying the five-step approach, you will develop confidence and comprehension. Armed with this approach, you should be able to handle adequately any process-cost situation. Shortcuts should be applied wherever feasible. But it is difficult to generalize on shortcut methods, because they differ depending upon the specific problem and the student's ability to use them.

beginning inventories Calculations become more complicated when beginning inventories exist. There are two commonly used methods of tracing beginning inventory costs: *weighted-average* and *first in, first out* (FIFO). The former will now be presented. The latter is discussed later in this chapter. The data in Example 2 will be used. *For the time being, concentrate on the data for Department A only.*

example 2 A company has two processes. Material is introduced at the *beginning* of the process in Department A, and additional material is added at the *end* of the process in Department B. Conversion costs are applied uniformly throughout both processes. As the process in Department A is completed, goods are immediately transferred to the next department; as goods are completed in Department B, they are transferred to Finished Goods.

Data for the month of March, 19_1, include the following:

	DEPARTMENT A	DEPARTMENT B
Work in process, beginning	10,000 units 2/5 completed,* $7,500 (Materials, $6,000; conversion costs, $1,500)	12,000 units 2/3 completed,* $21,000 (Transferred-in costs, $9,800; conversion costs, $11,200)
Units completed during March	48,000	44,000
Units started during March	40,000	?
Work in process, end	2,000, 1/2 completed*	16,000, 3/8 completed*
Material cost added	$22,000	$13,200
Conversion costs added	$18,000	$63,000

* This means that each unit in process is regarded as being fractionally complete with respect to the conversion costs of the present department only.

required Compute the cost of goods transferred out of each department. Also show journal entries for the transfers. Compute ending-inventory costs for goods remaining in each department. Assume weighted-average costing.

WEIGHTED-AVERAGE METHOD

description As Exhibit 17-1 shows, the weighted-average method treats the beginning work in process as if it were begun and finished during the current period.

EXHIBIT 17-1

DEPARTMENT A
PRODUCTION COST REPORT

Weighted-Average Method
For the Month Ending March 31, 19_1

	(STEP 1)	(STEP 2) EQUIVALENT UNITS	
QUANTITIES	PHYSICAL FLOW	MATERIALS	CONVERSION COSTS
Work in process, beginning	10,000(2/5)*		
Units started	40,000		
To account for	50,000		
Units completed	48,000	48,000	48,000
Work in process, end	2,000(1/2)*	2,000	1,000
	50,000	50,000	49,000

			DETAILS		
COSTS	TOTALS	MATERIALS	CONVERSION COSTS	EQUIVALENT WHOLE UNIT
Work in process, beginning	$ 7,500	$ 6,000	$ 1,500	
Current costs	40,000	22,000	18,000	
(Step 3) Total costs to account for	$47,500	$28,000	$19,500	
Divide by equivalent units		÷50,000	÷49,000	
(Step 4) Cost per equivalent unit		$ .56	$ .398	$ .958
(Step 5) Summary of costs:				
Units completed (48,000)	$45,982†			48,000($.958)
Work in process, end (2,000):				
Materials	$ 1,120	2,000($.56)		
Conversion costs	398		1,000($.398)	
Total cost of work in process	$ 1,518			
Total costs accounted for	$47,500			

* Degree of completion on conversion costs of this department.
† Rounded from 45,984 for decimal discrepancy.

The beginning work-in-process inventory is looked upon as being part and parcel of current production, regardless of the fact that it was begun prior to the current period. Therefore, beginning-inventory costs are mingled with current costs. When equivalent units are calculated, work done in the past is regarded as if it were done currently. Professor William J. Vatter has called the weighted-average method the "roll-back" method because the averaging of cost doses is "rolled back" to include the work carried over from last month.

As you study Exhibit 17-1, note the five steps. First, physical flows are traced. Second, the physical flows are expressed in terms of equivalent units. Third, the costs to account for are delineated. Fourth, the cost per equivalent unit is computed. Fifth, the unit costs are used along with the equivalent units to assign costs to goods completed and goods still in process.

inter-
departmental
transfers   Now examine Department B. Most process-cost situations have two or more departments in the production cycle. Ordinarily, as goods move from department to department, related costs are also transferred. Exhibit 17-2

shows how such a transfer is handled under the weighted-average inventory method.

Transferred-in costs tend to give students much trouble, so special study is needed here. As far as Department B is concerned, units coming in from Department A may be viewed as if they were the raw materials of Department B. Costs transferred from Department A to Department B are similar to the material costs brought into Department A, although they are called *transferred-in costs* (or *previous department costs*), not material costs. That is, one might visualize the situation as if Department B bought the goods from an outside supplier. Thus, Department B's computations must provide for transferred-in costs, for any new material costs added in Department B, and for conversion costs added in Department B.

EXHIBIT 17-2

DEPARTMENT B
PRODUCTION COST REPORT

Weighted-Average Method
For the Month Ending March 31, 19_1

QUANTITIES	(STEP 1) PHYSICAL FLOW	(STEP 2) EQUIVALENT UNITS TRANSFERRED-IN COSTS	MATERIALS	CONVERSION COSTS
Work in process, beginning	12,000(2/3)*			
Units transferred in	48,000			
To account for	60,000			
Units completed	44,000	44,000	44,000	44,000
Work in process, end	16,000(3/8)*	16,000	—	6,000
	60,000	60,000	44,000	50,000

				DETAILS	
COSTS	TOTALS	TRANSFERRED-IN COSTS	MATERIALS	CONVERSION COSTS	EQUIVALENT WHOLE UNIT
Work in process, beginning	$ 21,000	$ 9,800	$ —	$11,200	
Current costs	122,182	45,982	13,200	63,000	
(Step 3) Total costs to account for	$143,182	$55,782	$13,200	$74,200	
Divide by equivalent units		÷60,000	÷44,000	÷50,000	
(Step 4) Cost per equivalent unit		$ .9297	$ .30	$ 1.484	$2.7137
Summary of costs:					
Units completed (44,000)	$119,403				44,000($2.7137)
Work in process, end (16,000):					
Transferred-in costs	$ 14,875	16,000($.9297)			
Materials	—				
Conversion costs	8,904			6,000($1.484)	
Total cost of work in process	$ 23,779				
Total costs accounted for	$143,182				

*Degree of completion on conversion costs of this department.

journal entries The journal entries under the weighted-average method are:
and transfers

Department B—Work-in-process control	45,982	
Department A—Work-in-process control		45,982
To transfer costs from Department A. For detailed computations, see Exhibit 17-1.		
Finished-goods control	119,403	
Department B—Work-in-process control		119,403
To transfer costs of goods finished. See Exhibit 17-2.		

Sometimes a problem requires that the work-in-process account be split into Work in Process—Materials, Work in Process—Labor, and Work in Process—Overhead. In these cases, the journal entries would contain this greater detail, even though the underlying reasoning and techniques would be unaffected.

alternative The format in Exhibit 17-1 attempts to make a step-by-step worksheet also
formats and serve the purpose of a formal production-cost report. However, as proc-
techniques ess-cost situations become more complex, the details become more intricate and unwieldy for jamming into a worksheet that can also serve as a cost report. The point is that a step-by-step, no-shortcut approach to process-costing computations is needed. Therefore, the exhibit is concerned primarily with stressing the logic and the need for built-in checks; the format is of much less importance, principally because production-cost reports vary considerably from company to company anyway.

Professor William F. Crum has suggested a tightly knit format that could serve as a summary production report. For example, consider his format for Department A in Exhibit 17-1:

	WORK IN PROCESS, BEGINNING	CURRENT COSTS	TOTAL COSTS	EQUIVALENT UNITS	AVERAGE UNIT COST
Materials	$6,000	$22,000	$28,000	50,000	$.560
Conversion costs	1,500	18,000	19,500	49,000	.398
	$7,500	$40,000	$47,500		$.958

Goods completed: 48,000 units × $.958	45,982
Work in process, end, 2,000 units	$ 1,518

Note that this summary production report is not as elaborate as that in Exhibit 17-1. For example, the detailed computations of physical flow and equivalent units (Steps 1 and 2 in Exhibit 17-1) need not appear in a formal production report. Note too that the goods completed are simply deducted from the total costs to obtain the cost of the ending work in process.

If the equivalent units are known or computed, this report is also an alternative approach to solving weighted-average process-cost problems. However, if this technique is used, it is advisable to check the accuracy of the cost of ending work in process by the following proof:

Materials (2,000 × $.560)	$1,120
Conversion costs (2,000 × .5 × $.398)	398
	$1,518

FIRST-IN, FIRST-OUT

illustration
of FIFO
The FIFO method regards the beginning inventory as if it were a batch of goods separate and distinct from goods started and finished within the same period. FIFO is really a step in the direction of job-order costing, because it distinguishes batches whereas the weighted-average method does not.

example 3
Study the data in Example 2, page 599. Assume first-in, first-out costing and compute the solution for both departments.

The solution for Department A in Exhibit 17-3 carries costs separately for (a) goods carried over in beginning work in process, and for (b) goods started and finished in the current month. The unit costs differ for each portion (batch) of the total goods completed during the month. As may be seen by comparing computations for Department A in Exhibits 17-1 and 17-3, the weighted-average method is far easier to use than FIFO for process costing.

effect
of transfers:
modification
of FIFO
In a series of interdepartmental transfers, each department is regarded as a distinct accounting entity. All transferred-in costs during a given period are carried at one unit cost, regardless of whether weighted-average or FIFO techniques were used by previous departments.

Thus, although the FIFO method as used by Department A may show batches of goods accumulated and transferred at different unit costs, these goods are typically costed by Department B at *one* average unit cost, as Exhibit 17-4 demonstrates. In other words, a departmental FIFO method may be used, but in practice the strict FIFO method is modified to the extent that subsequent departments use weighted-average methods for cost transferred in during a given period. If this were not done, the attempt to trace costs on a strict FIFO basis throughout a series of processes would become too burdensome and complicated. For example, a four-department process-cost system could have at least eight or more batches, which would need separate costing by the time costs are transferred to and out of the final department. However, as goods are transferred from the last process to Finished Goods, the records of finished stock could be kept on a strict first-in, first-out method if desired. The clerical burden alone is enough to cause most process-cost industries to reject strict FIFO as a costing method. More will be said about the weakness of FIFO in the next chapter concerning spoilage.

EXHIBIT 17-3

DEPARTMENT A
PRODUCTION COST REPORT

First-in, First-out Method
For the Month Ending March 31, 19_1

		(STEP 1)	(STEP 2) EQUIVALENT UNITS	
	QUANTITIES	PHYSICAL FLOW	MATERIALS	CONVERSION COSTS
	Work in process, beginning	10,000(2/5)*		
	Units started	40,000		
	To account for	50,000		
	Units completed:			
	From beginning inventory	10,000	—	6,000
	From current production	38,000	38,000	38,000
	Work in process, end	2,000(1/2)*	2,000	1,000
	Units accounted for	50,000	40,000	45,000

				DETAILS	
	COSTS	TOTALS	MATERIALS	CONVERSION COSTS	EQUIVALENT WHOLE UNIT
	Work in process, beginning	$ 7,500	—	—	
	Current costs	40,000	$22,000	$18,000	
(Step 3)	Total costs to account for	$47,500			
	Divide by equivalent units		÷40,000	÷45,000	
(Step 4)	Cost per equivalent unit		$ .55	$ .40	$ .95
(Step 5)	Summary of costs:				
	Units completed (48,000):				
	From beginning inventory (10,000)	$ 7,500			
	Current costs added:				
	Materials	—			
	Conversion costs	2,400		6,000($.40)	
	Total from beginning inventory	$ 9,900			
	Started and completed (38,000)	36,100			38,000($.95)
	Total costs transferred out	$46,000			
	Work in process, end (2,000):				
	Materials	$ 1,100	2,000($.55)		
	Conversion costs	400		1,000($.40)	
	Total cost of work in process	$ 1,500			
	Total costs accounted for	$47,500			

* Degree of completion on conversion costs of this department.

In summary, although the so-called FIFO method is sometimes used in process-costing situations, only rarely is an application of strict FIFO ever encountered. It should really be called a *modified* or *departmental* FIFO method. FIFO techniques are applied within a department to cost goods transferred *out*, but goods transferred *in* during a given period usually bear a single average unit cost as a matter of convenience.

alternative formats and techniques Professor William F. Crum has suggested a summary production report for Department A in Exhibit 17-3 as follows:

	TOTAL COSTS	EQUIVALENT UNITS	UNIT COSTS
Work in process, beginning	$ 7,500		
Current costs:			
Materials	22,000	40,000	$.55
Conversion costs	18,000	45,000	.40
Total costs to account for	$47,500		$.95
Work in process, end			
Materials (2,000 × $.55)	$1,100		
Conversion costs (2,000 × .5 × $.40)	400	1,500	
Completed and transferred (48,000 × $.95833)		$46,000	

EXHIBIT 17-4

DEPARTMENT B
PRODUCTION COST REPORT
First-in, First-out Method
For the Month Ending March 31, 19_1

QUANTITIES	(STEP 1) PHYSICAL FLOW	(STEP 2) EQUIVALENT UNITS		
		TRANSFERRED-IN COSTS	MATERIALS	CONVERSION COSTS
Work in process, beginning	12,000(2/3)*			
Units transferred in	48,000			
To account for	60,000			
Units completed:				
From beginning inventory	12,000	—	12,000	4,000
From current production	32,000	32,000	32,000	32,000
Work in process, end	16,000(3/8)*	16,000	—	6,000
Units accounted for	60,000	48,000	44,000	42,000

COSTS	TOTALS	TRANSFERRED-IN COSTS	MATERIALS	CONVERSION COSTS	EQUIVALENT WHOLE UNIT
		DETAILS			
Work in process, beginning	$ 21,000	—	—	—	
Current costs	122,200	$46,000	$13,200	$63,000	
(Step 3) Total costs to account for	$143,200				
Divide by equivalent units		÷48,000	÷44,000	÷42,000	
(Step 4) Cost per equivalent unit		$.95833	$ .30	$ 1.50	$2.75833
(Step 5) Summary of costs:					
Units completed (44,000):					
From beginning inventory (12,000)	$ 21,000				
Current costs added:					
Materials	3,600		12,000($.30)		
Conversion costs	6,000			4,000($1.50)	
Total from beginning inventory	$ 30,600				
Started and completed (32,000)	88,267				32,000($2.75833)
Total costs transferred out	$118,867				
Work in process, end (16,000):					
Transferred-in costs	$ 15,333	16,000($.95833)			
Materials	—		—		
Conversion costs	9,000			6,000($1.50)	
Total cost of work in process	$ 24,333				
Total costs accounted for	$143,200				

*Degree of completion on conversion costs in this department.

If the equivalent units are known or computed, this report is also an alternative approach to solving first-in, first-out process-cost problems. Note that in contrast to Professor Crum's approach to the weighted-average method described earlier, under FIFO it is easier and more direct to compute the cost of the ending work in process first and then deduct it from the total costs to obtain the cost of goods transferred. Note too that the unit cost of transfers under FIFO is not the same as the current $.95 cost of producing a whole finished unit. Of course, this is because the cost of the beginning inventory influences the total cost of goods transferred. If this technique is used, it is advisable to check the accuracy of the goods transferred by the following proof:

Work in process, beginning, which is transferred out first	$ 7,500
Additional costs to complete (10,000 × .6 × $.40)	2,400
Cost of 38,000 units started and completed this month (38,000 × $.95)	36,100
Total cost of goods completed and transferred out	$46,000

comparison of weighted-average and FIFO The most apparent cause of any significant difference in results between FIFO and weighted-average methods is the erratic price behavior of raw materials. However, in such cases, the company is likely to rely on some special technique (usually some version of standard or estimated prices) for costing production so as to isolate the influence of price variances on production costs.

Except for raw-material prices, the differences in results between FIFO and weighted-average methods are usually insignificant because of the inherent characteristics of industries using process costing. Process-cost situations usually entail mass production of a continuous nature. Beginning and ending inventory levels are not likely to change radically from month to month. Furthermore, conversion costs per unit are not likely to fluctuate wildly from month to month.

For *cost-control* purposes, FIFO is generally superior to the weighted-average method because current performance should be judged solely on the basis of current cost incurrence. However, neither the FIFO nor the weighted-average method is as effective as standard process costing for purposes of cost control.

Finally, those readers who plan to take the CPA examination should recognize that the FIFO method is frequently required on the examination, even though it is seldom encountered in practice.

pitfalls to avoid in working problems 1. Remember to include transferred-in costs from previous departments in your calculations. Such costs should be treated as if they were another kind of material costs, because each department is treated as a separate entity. In other words, when successive departments are involved, transferred goods from one department become all or a part of the raw materials of the next department, although they are called *transferred-in costs*, not raw materials.

2. Material and conversion costs (labor and overhead) are often not applied at the same rates. Special care should be used, therefore, in expressing work in process in terms of equivalent units. For material doses, the degree of completion may be 100 percent (if all material is added at the beginning of the production cycle) for some materials and 0 percent for materials that will not be added until the end of the process. At the same time, conversion doses may be some other percentage, such as 50 percent or 75 percent.

3. In calculating costs to be transferred on a first-in, first-out basis, do not overlook the costs attached at the beginning of the period to goods that were in process but are now included in the goods transferred.

4. Unit costs may fluctuate between periods. Therefore, transferred goods may contain batches accumulated at different unit costs (see point 3). These goods, when transferred to the next department, are typically valued by that next department at *one* average unit cost.

5. Units may be expressed in terms of pounds in one department and gallons in the next. Consider each department separately. Unit costs would be based on pound measures in the first department and gallons in the second. As goods are received by the second department, they may be converted to the gallon unit of measure.

6. If the problem calls for first-in, first-out calculations, do not use the weighted-average approach, and vice versa.

STANDARD COSTS AND PROCESS COSTS

standards are useful   Previous chapters demonstrated that the use of standard costing is completely general; that is, it can be used in job-order situations or in process-costing situations, and with absorption costing or direct costing. Standard-cost procedures tend to be most effective when they are adapted to process-costing situations. Mass, continuous, and repetitive production conditions lend themselves rather easily to setting meaningful physical standards. Price tags may then be applied to the physical standards to develop standard costs. Such standard costs would allow for normal shrinkage, waste, evaporation, or spoilage.

The intricacies and conflicts between weighted-average and FIFO costing methods are eliminated by using standard costs. Further, weighted-average and FIFO techniques become very complicated when used in industries that produce a variety of products. Standard costing is especially useful where there are various combinations of materials, operations, and product sizes. As Professor James H. March pointed out, a steel-rolling mill uses various steel alloys and produces sheets of various sizes and of various finishes. The items of raw material are not numerous; neither are the operations performed. But used in various combinations, they yield too great a variety of products to permit the averaging procedure of historical process-cost accounting. Elsewhere, similar conditions are frequently found—as, for example, in plants manufacturing rubber goods, textiles, ceramics, paints, and packaged food products.

Standard costing is growing in importance in process-costing industries. Therefore, because of its conceptual and practical appeal, standard costing deserves our study. Because we have already seen how standard costing aids planning and control, we shall concentrate on its product-costing aspects.

computations under standard costing

example 3

The facts are basically the same as those for Department A in Example 2, except that standard costs have been developed for the process as follows:

	PER UNIT
Direct materials, introduced at start of process	$ .53
Conversion costs, incurred uniformly throughout process	.37
Standard cost per unit	$ .90
Work in process, beginning, 10,000 units, 2/5 completed, (materials, $5,300; conversion costs, $1,480)	$ 6,780
Units completed during March	48,000
Units started during March	40,000
Work in process, end	2,000, 1/2 complete

required

1. Compute the standard cost of goods completed and of goods in process at end.

2. If "actual" material costs added during the month were $22,000 and conversion costs were $18,000, show a summary schedule of total material variance and total conversion-cost variance.

The formal solution is shown in Exhibit 17-5. Requirement 2 appears at the bottom of the exhibit. Careful study of Exhibit 17-5 will readily reveal that a standard-cost system greatly simplifies process-cost computations. A standard-cost system not only eliminates the intricacies of weighted-average versus FIFO inventory methods; it also erases the need for burdensome computations of costs per equivalent unit. The standard cost *is* the cost per equivalent unit. In addition, a standard-costing approach facilitates control.

Note that, to obtain a measure of current output, a first-in, first-out physical flow is usually assumed in standard-costing situations. Therefore, as Exhibit 17-5 shows, because all material is added at the beginning of the process, no equivalent units of material are added during the current period for the beginning work in process; similarly, only 6,000 units of conversion costs are added.

Incidentally, the cost-accounting literature often erroneously distinguishes among process costing, job-order costing, and standard costing as if they were mutually exclusive categories of product costing. Standard costing can be used in both process costing and job-order costing. For example, various job-order costs can be compiled using standards for all cost elements; similarly, as Exhibit 17-5 demonstrates, process costs can also be accumulated based on standard costs.

ADDITIONAL ASPECTS OF PROCESS COSTING

estimating degree of completion

This chapter's illustrations plus almost all process-cost problems blithely mention various degrees of completion for inventories in process. The accuracy of these estimates depends on the care and skill of the estimator

EXHIBIT 17-5

DEPARTMENT A
PRODUCTION COST REPORT (AT STANDARD)

Standard Costs in a Process-Cost System
For the Month Ending March 31, 19_1

QUANTITIES	PHYSICAL FLOW	EQUIVALENT UNITS MATERIALS	EQUIVALENT UNITS CONVERSION COSTS
Work in process, beginning	10,000(2/5)*		
Units started	40,000		
To account for	50,000		
Units completed:			
From beginning inventory	10,000(3/5)*	—	6,000
From current production	38,000	38,000	38,000
Work in process, end	2,000(1/2)*	2,000	1,000
Units accounted for	50,000	40,000	45,000

COSTS	TOTALS	DETAILS MATERIALS	DETAILS CONVERSION COSTS	EQUIVALENT WHOLE UNIT
Standard cost per equiv- alent unit (given)		$.53	$.37	$.90
Equivalent units		×40,000	×45,000	
Current standard costs	$37,850	$21,200	$16,650	
Beginning inventory	6,780	$ 5,300	$ 1,480	
	$44,630			
Summary of costs:				
Units completed (48,000)	$43,200			48,000($.90)
Work in process, end (2,000):				
Materials	$ 1,060	2,000($.53)		
Conversion costs	370		1,000($.37)	
Total cost of work in process	$ 1,430			
Total costs accounted for	$44,630			

Summary of variances for current performance:			
Current output in equivalent units		40,000	45,000
Current output at standard costs		$21,200	$16,650
Costs charged to department for the month		$22,000	$18,000
Total variance†		$ 800 U	$ 1,350 U

*Degree of completion on conversion costs of present department.
†These could be broken down further into price, rate, quantity, and efficiency variances, depending upon details that may be available.

and the nature of the process. Estimating the degree of completion is usually easier for materials than for conversion costs. The conversion sequence usually consists of a number of standard operations or a standard number of hours, days, weeks, or months for mixing, heating, cooling, aging, curing, and so forth. Thus, the degree of completion for conversion costs depends on what proportion of the total effort needed to complete one unit or one batch has been devoted to units still in process. In industries where no exact estimate is possible, or, as in textiles, where vast quantities in process prohibit costly physical estimates, all work in process in every department is assumed to be either $\frac{1}{3}$, or $\frac{1}{2}$, or $\frac{2}{3}$ complete. In other cases, continuous processing entails little change of work-in-process levels from month to month. Consequently, work in process is safely ignored and monthly production costs are assigned solely to goods completed.

overhead and   Labor and overhead tend to be lumped together as conversion costs for
predetermined   process-costing purposes. In many process-cost industries, continuous,
rates   uniform production results in little fluctuation of total factory overhead
from month to month. In such cases, there is no need to use predetermined overhead rates. Of course, where overhead costs and production vary from period to period, predetermined overhead rates are used in order to get representative unit costs.

overhead and   The assumption that all conversion costs are incurred uniformly in propor-
cost flow   tion to the degree of product completion is difficult to justify on theoretical
grounds. For example, this implies that a wide variety of overhead-cost incurrence is directly related to labor-cost incurrence. Although such a direct cause-and-effect relationship may not exist, refinements of overhead application beyond this assumption are usually impractical and inexpedient. When more precision is attempted, it is usually confined to developing a predetermined overhead rate to be loaded on material cost to cover such indirect costs as purchasing, receiving, storing, issuing, and transferring materials. In such cases, one overhead rate would be applied along with material costs while a separate overhead rate would be applied along with labor costs.

summary

Process-costing techniques are used for inventory costing when there is continuous, mass production of like units. The key concept in process costing is that of equivalent units, the expression of physical units in terms of doses or charges of work applied thereto.

Five basic steps may be used in solving process-cost problems. Process costing is complicated by uneven flow of cost factors, by the presence of beginning inventories, and by the presence of costs transferred in from prior departments.

Two widely advocated process-costing techniques are known as the *weighted-average* and *first-in, first-out* methods. However, standard costs are the most widely used; they are simpler and more useful than other techniques for both product-costing and control purposes.

Problems for Self-Study

Review each example in this chapter and obtain the solutions on your own. Then check your work against the solutions, which appear in the various exhibits.

questions, problems, and cases

17-1. "Standard-cost procedures are particularly applicable to process-costing situations." Do you agree? Why?

17-2. What are some virtues of standard costs as used in process costing?

17-3. "There is no need for using predetermined overhead rates for product costing in process-cost industries." Do you agree? Why?

17-4. Why should the accountant distinguish between *transferred-in costs* and *new raw-material* costs for a particular department?

17-5. What is the feature of the first two steps of the five-step uniform approach that distinguishes them from the final three steps?

17-6. Introductory Process Costing: Materials Introduced at Start of Process.   A certain process incurred $40,000 of production costs during a month. Materials costing $22,000 were introduced at the start of processing, while conversion costs of $18,000 were incurred at a uniform rate throughout the production cycle. Of the 40,000 units of product started, 38,000 were completed and 2,000 were still in process at the end of the month, averaging one-half complete.

required   In step-by-step fashion, prepare a production-cost report showing cost of goods completed and cost of ending work in process.

17-7. Introductory Process Costs; Single Department.   The following data pertain to the mixing department for July:

UNITS	
Work in process, July 1	0
Units started	50,000
Completed and transferred to finishing department	35,000

COSTS	
Material P	$200,000
Material Q	$ 70,000
Direct labor and overhead	$135,000

Material P is introduced at the start of the process, while Material Q is added when the product reaches a three-fourths stage of completion. Conversion costs are incurred uniformly throughout the process.

required   Cost of goods transferred during July. Cost of work in process as of July 31. Assume that ending work in process is one batch, two-thirds completed.

17-8. Process Costing, Budgeting and Control.   [Prepared by the author and adapted for use in the May 1965 CPA examination.] The Dopern Company uses departmental budgets and performance reports to help plan and control its process-costing operations. Department A has the following budget for January's contemplated production of 1,000 whole units of equivalent performance, which represents a normal month's volume.

VARIABLE AND CONTROLLABLE COSTS	
Direct materials	$20,000
Direct labor	10,000
Indirect labor	2,000
Power	200
Supplies	800
	$33,000

FIXED AND UNCONTROLLABLE COSTS	
Rent	$ 400
Supervision	1,000
Depreciation	500
Other	100
	$ 2,000
Total budgeted costs	$35,000

Direct materials are introduced at the start of the process. All conversion costs are assumed to be incurred uniformly throughout the process. Production fluctuates from month to month, so that the fixed overhead is applied at a rate of $2 per equivalent unit.

There were no beginning inventories. Eleven hundred units were started during the month; 900 were completed, and the 200 still in process at the end of the month were estimated to be three-fourths completed. There is no material shrinkage or spoilage, and no waste of materials.

The following performance report was prepared:

	BUDGET	ACTUAL	VARIANCE
Direct materials	$20,000	$22,550	$2,550 U
Direct labor	10,000	10,500	500 U
Indirect labor	2,000	2,100	100 U
Power	200	210	10 U
Supplies	800	840	40 U
	$33,000	$36,200	$3,200 U

U = Unfavorable

A total of $2,000 of fixed conversion costs were incurred during January.

required

1. Cost of goods completed during January.

2. Cost of ending work in process.

3. Amount of under- or overapplied overhead at January 31.

4. Comment on the performance report in 150 words or less. What *specific* conclusions can you draw from the performance report?

17-9. Comparison of Two Process-Costing Techniques. The following information relates to one department operating under a process-cost system: Work in process, December 1, 19_1, 1,000 units, 40 percent complete, consisting of

$8,703 of materials and $5,036 of conversion costs. Production completed for December, 8,200 units; work in process, December 31, 19_1, 800 units, 20 percent complete.

All materials are introduced at the start of the process, while conversion costs are incurred uniformly throughout the process. Materials added during December were $72,000; conversion costs were $83,580.

required

1. Using weighted averages, show a schedule of equivalent performance, unit costs, and summary of costs. Also prepare a summary entry for the transfer of completed goods to finished stock.

2. Assume standard costs per finished unit as follows: Direct materials, $8.50; Conversion costs, $10.00.
   a. Compute standard costs of goods transferred and still in process.
   b. Give the total variances for current performance on direct materials and conversion costs.

17-10. **Weighted Averages; Standard Costs.** The Dyer Processing Company had work in process at the beginning and end of 19_1 as follows:

	PERCENTAGE OF COMPLETION	
	MATERIALS	CONVERSION COSTS
January 1, 19_1—3,000 units	40%	10%
December 31, 19_1—2,000 units	80%	40%

The company completed 40,000 units of finished goods during 19_1. Manufacturing costs incurred during 19_1 were: materials, $242,600; conversion costs, $445,200. Inventory at January 1, 19_1 was carried at a cost of $10,600 (materials, $7,000; conversion costs, $3,600).

Part One. Assuming weighted average:
1. Compute equivalent production for 19_1 for (a) materials and (b) conversion costs.
2. What is the proper cost of ending goods in process?

Part Two. (Consider independently of requirements in Part One.)
If the standard cost for materials is $5 per finished unit and the standard cost for conversion costs is $10 per finished unit, what would be the total standard cost of work *performed during 19_1?*

17-11. **Weighted-Average Process-Costing Method.** The Bright Paint Co. uses a process-cost system. Materials are added at the beginning of a particular process and conversion costs are incurred uniformly. Work in process at the beginning and end is assumed 50 percent complete. One gallon of material makes one gallon of product.

Data:

Beginning inventory	900 gallons
Materials added	9,900 gallons
Ending inventory	450 gallons
Conversion costs incurred	$18,000
Cost of materials added	$20,000
Conversion costs, beginning inventory	$ 800
Cost of materials, beginning inventory	$ 1,600

Prepare a cost-of-production report for the weighted-average method.

17-12. Weighted-Average Process Costing [CGAA, adapted]. The B Lunder Co. Ltd. manufactures a product that requires processing in three departments. In Department C, materials are added at the very beginning of the Department C processing. Conversion costs are added continuously throughout the process. Manufacturing overhead is applied to units in process in Department C at the rate of 125 percent of direct-labor costs.

The following data pertain to the operations of Department C for the month of July:

In process, July 1: 4,000 units, 60 percent converted costs:

Dept. B costs	$15,340
Dept. C materials	2,273
Dept. C direct labor	2,764
Dept. C applied overhead	?

During the month, 12,000 units were received from Department B at a cost of $45,460.

Costs incurred by Department C during July included:

Direct materials requisitioned	$ 8,975
Direct labor	11,124

On July 31, there were 6,000 units left in process, 40 percent converted. No units were spoiled or lost in processing.

required

Using the weighted-average method of costing, prepare a production-cost report for July.

17-13. Two Departments; Two Months. [Prepared by W. J. Vatter] One of the products of this company is manufactured by passing it through two processes. The materials are started into production at the beginning of Process 1 and are passed directly from Process 1 to Process 2 without inventory between the processes. Operating data for two months are given below:

January

Process 1. No initial work in process. During the month, 800 units were put into process and $8,000 was charged to this account. Operations during the month cost $2,800. Six hundred units were finished and passed on to Process 2. The work in process at January 31 was one-half finished.

Process 2. No work in process on January 1. The work transferred from Process 1 was received and costs of $2,000 were incurred in operations to complete 300 units. At the end of the month, 300 units one-third finished remained in process.

February

Process 1. Six hundred units of material were put into process at a total price of $6,000. Other costs incurred were $2,550. At the end of the month, there were 300 units still within the process, two-thirds finished.

Process 2. Costs charged to operations in this process for February were $2,640. On February 28, there were 300 units still within the process, two-thirds finished.

There is no spoilage or shrinkage in either of the processes; all units unfinished at the beginning of the month are completed within that month.

required   Calculations of production costs for each process for each month on a weighted-average basis.

17-14. Alternative Format and Approach to Weighted-Average Costing. [Prepared by William F. Crum] The Doral Company has the following data for the month of October:

	DEPARTMENT A	DEPARTMENT B
Beginning inventory in process	2,000 units	2,000 units
Prior department cost*	0	$ 4,600
Materials added last month	$ 2,000 (100%)	$ 3,200 (80%)
Conversion costs added last month	$ 900 (60%)	$ 800 (40%)
Units put in process this month	30,000	29,000
Materials added this month	$30,968	$56,580
Conversion costs added this month	$41,800	$29,803
Units completed and transferred	29,000	30,000
Ending inventory in process:	3,000 units	1,000 units
Material content	90%	50%
Conversion costs	50%	30%

*These are transferred-in costs.

required   Using weighted-average costing, prepare a production report for each department. Use the alternative technique described in the chapter. Show the cost of goods completed and transferred and also show the cost of the ending work in process. Include a proof of your answer for the ending work in process.

17-15. Alternative Format and Approach to FIFO Costing. [Prepared by William F. Crum] Refer to Problem 17-14. Using FIFO costing, repeat the requirements. Include a proof of your answer for the cost of goods completed and transferred.

17-16. Process Costing, Weighted Average. [Prepared by William F. Crum] The Hickory Company manufactures a product processed through two departments. The process is lengthy, taking two weeks in Department M and ten days in Department S. Miscellaneous data include:

Dept. S, work in process, Dec. 1, 19_0—6,000 gallons
Dept. M cost in work in process $24,000
Materials added in S in work in process $ 7,500   (100%)
Conversion cost added in S in work in process $12,000   (60%)
Production brought in from Dept. M during month—30,000 gallons, costing—$123,000
Materials added in Dept. S in December—$18,000
Conversion costs added in Dept. S in December—$62,000
Gallons completed and transferred to finished product—32,000
On hand in process in Dept. S at Dec. 31, 19_0—4,000 gallons, with 80% of the material added in S, and 30% of the conversion costs of Dept. S

required   Compute:

1. Unit costs for December, using average-cost method, carrying unit costs to four decimals.

2. December 31, 19_0, inventory of work in process in Department S.

3. Cost of work completed in Department S in December and transferred to finished product.

17-17. **FIFO Computations.** Refer to Problem 17-9. Repeat requirement 1, using the modified first-in, first-out method.

17-18. **FIFO Computations.** Repeat Problem 17-11, using the modified first-in, first-out method.

17-19. **FIFO Computations.** Repeat Problem 17-13, using the modified first-in, first-out method.

17-20. **FIFO Process Costing [CPA, adapted].** The Bisto Corporation manufactures valves and pumps for liquids. On December 1, 19_4, Bisto paid $25,000 to the Poplen Company for the patent for its Watertite Valve. Bisto planned to carry on Poplen's procedure of having the valve casing and parts cast by an independent foundry and doing the grinding and assembling in its own plant.

Bisto also purchased Poplen's inventory of the valves at 80 percent of its cost to Poplen. The purchased inventory was comprised of the following:

	UNITS
Raw materials (unfinished casings and parts)	1,100
Work in process:	
Grinding (25% complete)	800
Assembling (40% complete)	600
Finished valves	900

Poplen's cost-accounting system provided the following unit costs:

	COST PER UNIT
Raw materials (unfinished casings and parts)	$2.00
Grinding costs	1.00
Assembling costs	2.50

Bisto's cost-accounting system accumulated the following costs for the month of December, which do not include cost of the inventory purchased from Poplen:

Raw-material purchases (casings and parts for 5,000 units)	$10,500
Grinding costs	2,430
Assembling costs	5,664

Bisto's inventory of Watertite Valves at December 31, 19_4 follows:

Raw materials (unfinished casings and parts)	2,700
Work in process:	
Grinding (35% complete)	2,000
Assembling (33-$\frac{1}{3}$% complete)	300
Finished valves	2,250

No valves were spoiled or lost during the manufacturing process.

required   Bisto uses the FIFO process-costing method in its accounting system.

Prepare a schedule to compute the equivalent units produced, the costs incurred per unit, and a summary of costs for the month of December, 19_4.

17-21. **Process Costs and Standard Costs [CPA, adapted].** The Kaerwer Corporation operates a machine shop and employs an estimated-cost system. In March 19_8, Kaerwer was low bidder on a contract to deliver 600 kartz by

May 15 at a contract price of $200 each. Kaerwer's estimate of the costs to manufacture each kartz was:

40 pounds of materials at $1.50 per pound	$ 60
20 hours of direct labor at $2.00 per hour	40
Manufacturing overhead (40% variable)	30
Total cost	$130

Inventories on hand at April 1 included 30 completed kartz that had not been transferred to finished-goods inventory, 70 kartz that were 60 percent processed, and 2,000 pounds of materials at a cost of $3,000. Production during March was at estimated costs. During April, 500 kartz were started in production, 450 kartz were completed, and 480 kartz were transferred to finished goods. The work-in-process inventory at April 30 was 10 percent processed. All materials were added when a kartz was started in production. The materials inventory is priced under the FIFO method at actual cost.

The following information is available for the month of April:

POUNDS	AMOUNT
8,000	$12,000
8,000	12,800
4,000	5,600

1. Materials purchased:
2. Materials requisitioned and put into production totaled 21,000 pounds.
3. The direct-labor payroll amounted to $18,648 for 8,880 hours.
4. Manufacturing overhead was applied on the basis of estimated direct-labor hours. Actual manufacturing overhead incurred, including indirect labor, totaled $13,140 and was charged to the Overhead-in-Process account.
5. Accounts employed by Kaerwer include Materials-in-Process, Labor-in-Process, Overhead-in-Process, Work-in-Process Inventory, Finished-Goods Inventory, and Materials Inventory. The first three accounts are closed monthly. Perpetual-inventory systems are maintained for materials and finished-goods inventories.

required

1. Prepare in good form:
   a. A quantity-of-production report that accounts for both actual units in production and equivalent unit production for materials and for labor and overhead for April.
   b. A schedule presenting the computation of the balances (before closing) of the following accounts:
   Materials inventory
   Materials-in-process
   Labor-in-process
   Overhead-in-process
   Work-in-process inventory
   Finished-goods inventory

2. The Kaerwer Corporation would like to install a standard-cost system and requests that you prepare a schedule presenting a computation of an analysis of the material, labor, and overhead variances they could expect from such a system for production during April. Assume that the standard cost of a kartz would have been the same as the estimated cost of a kartz. Assume a denominator activity of 400 kartz per month.

17-22. Process Costs; Standard Costs; Analysis of Variances. The Jammer Company uses standard costs and produces a chemical from a secret formula. Material A is introduced at the start of the single process, while Material B is added when the conversion process is 80 percent completed. Conversion costs are applied uniformly throughout the process.

Standard costs per finished unit:
Materials:

A, five gallons @ 40¢	$ 2.00
B, one pound	10.00
Conversion costs:	
Labor, 2 hours	5.00
Variable overhead*	1.00
Fixed overhead*	4.00
	$22.00

* Applied as a percentage of standard direct-labor cost.

Beginning inventory in process, July 1, 19_1, consisted of 1,000 units, all 30 percent completed. Fifty-two thousand gallons of A were added during July. Twelve thousand pounds of B were added during July. Nine thousand units were completed. Two thousand units were still in process, 90 percent completed, at the end of July.

Actual costs incurred by the production department were as follows:

Material A, $26,000
Material B, $108,000
Direct labor, 22,000 hours @ $2.50 = $55,000
Variable overhead, $10,850
Fixed overhead, $47,800

Normal activity is 12,000 finished units per month.

required Expression of production in terms of equivalent units for:

1. Material A

2. Material B

3. Conversion costs

Give dollar amounts and use *F* or *U* to denote whether the following variances are favorable or unfavorable:

4. Material A price variance (Assume that this company recognizes price variances for materials as they are used rather than as they are purchased.)

5. Material A usage variance

6. Material B price variance

7. Material B usage variance

8. Labor-rate variance

9. Labor-efficiency variance

10. Variable-overhead spending variance

11. Variable-overhead efficiency variance

12. Fixed-overhead spending variance

13. Fixed-overhead volume variance

17-23. **Joint Costs and Process Costs; First-in, First-out; Sell or Process Further.** The Chemo Company manufactures two principal products, known as Gummo and Yummo. The company has three producing departments, A, B, and C. Raw material is started in process in Department A. Upon completion of joint processing in that department, two distinct chemicals are produced. One-fourth of the output goes to Department B, where it is made into Gummo; the other three-fourths goes to Department C, where it becomes Yummo. As Gummo and Yummo are completed, they are immediately transferred to finished stock.

The company assigns Department A costs to Gummo and Yummo in proportion to their net sales values at point of separation, computed by deducting costs to be incurred in subsequent processes from the sales value of the products.

The following information concerns the operations during May 19_1:

INVENTORIES

	APRIL 30		MAY 31
	UNITS	COST	UNITS
Department A	None		None
Department B	500*	$10,000	700†
Department C	1,000*	11,300	700†
Finished goods—Gummo	800	19,200	500
Finished goods—Yummo	600	13,200	800

* Each unit is 1/5 completed.
† Each unit is 3/5 completed.

Twelve thousand units of material were produced in Department A.

COSTS INCURRED IN MAY

	MATERIALS USED	CONVERSION COSTS
Department A	$72,000	$72,000
Department B	—	$15,600
Department C	—	$12.00 per equivalent unit

SALES PRICES

Gummo	$25.00 per unit
Yummo	$22.00 per unit

Prices as of May 31 are unchanged from those in effect during the month. The company uses first-in, first-out to cost out production.

required

1. For May production, conversion cost per equivalent unit in Department B.

2. Conversion cost per equivalent unit in Department A.

3. Total costs transferred to Department B.

4. Costs transferred from Department B to finished stock.

5. The company is considering a chance to sell the product that now goes into Department C at the split-off point, instead of processing it into Yummo. (Gummo would continue to be processed as usual.) If the long-run selling price at split-off point will be $10, should the company close down Department C and sell at split-off? Why? Answer in seventy words or less.

18

Spoilage, Waste, Defective Units, and Scrap

Problems of waste, scrap, or spoilage are found in nearly all manufacturing businesses, regardless of the specific production techniques used. Because there is a general approach to this entire area, this chapter views the problem as a whole before considering the peculiar difficulties in process-costing and job-costing situations.

The conceptual ideas of accounting for spoilage, scrap, and waste center primarily about distinguishing between abnormal and normal spoilage. Abnormal spoilage is often controllable by first-line supervision, whereas normal spoilage is not. Accounting for spoilage, defective units, and the like varies considerably in practice. This chapter will consider these matters from both product-costing and control viewpoints.

TERMINOLOGY

Terminology and accounting in this area are not at all precise or uniform. This chapter distinguishes between the various terms as follows:

Spoilage. Production that does not meet dimensional or quality standards and that is junked and sold for disposal value. Net spoilage cost is the total of the costs accumulated to point of rejection less disposal value (sometimes called *salvage value*).

Defective units. Production that does not meet dimensional or quality standards and that is subsequently reworked and sold through regular channels as firsts or seconds, depending on the characteristics of the product and on available alternatives.

Waste. Material that either is lost, evaporates, or shrinks in a manufacturing process, or is a residue that has no measurable recovery value; for example, gases, dust, smoke, and unsalable residues. Sometimes waste disposal entails additional costs; for example, atomic waste.

Scrap. Material residue from certain manufacturing operations that has measurable but relatively minor recovery value. For example, outlined metal from a stamping operation, shavings, filings, turnings, borings, sawdust, and short lengths from woodworking operations, and sprues and "flash" from foundry and molding processes. Scrap may be either sold or reused.

SPOILAGE IN GENERAL[1]

management implications and factor combination Most production processes generate some bad units along with the good ones, as an unavoidable result of the most economical combination of the factors of production. Although it may be technically possible to eliminate spoilage altogether in many instances, it may be uneconomical to do so, because the costs of lowering spoilage rates are greater than the costs of eliminated spoilage. Thus, beer bottles sometimes explode, defective castings inevitably appear, and impure as well as pure chemicals and food arise. The problem of spoilage is important from many aspects, the most important being that of managerial planning and control. Managers must first select the most economical production method or process. Then they must see that spoilage is controlled within chosen predetermined limits, so that excessive spoilage does not occur.

normal spoilage Working within the selected set of production conditions, management must establish the rate of spoilage that is to be regarded as *normal. Normal spoilage* is what arises under efficient operating conditions; it is an inherent result of the particular process and is thus uncontrollable in the short run. Costs of normal spoilage are typically viewed as a part of the costs of *good* production, because the attaining of good units necessitates the simultaneous appearance of spoiled units. In other words, normal spoilage is planned spoilage, in the sense that the choice of a given combination of factors of production entails a spoilage rate that management is willing to accept.

abnormal spoilage *Abnormal spoilage* is spoilage that is not expected to arise under efficient operating conditions; it is not an inherent part of the selected production process. Most of this spoilage is usually regarded as controllable, in the

[1] The writer acknowledges the helpful suggestions of Dean Samuel Laimon, University of Saskatchewan.

sense that the first-line supervisor can exert influence over inefficiency. Such causes as machinery breakdowns, accidents, and inferior materials are typically regarded as being subject to some manager's influence. Costs of abnormal spoilage are "lost costs," measures of inefficiency that should be written off directly as losses for the period. For the most informative feedback, the Loss from Abnormal Spoilage account should appear on a detailed income statement as a separate loss item and not buried as an indistinguishable part of the cost of goods manufactured.

general | Before discussing debits and credits for spoiled goods, let us try to relate
accounting | spoiled goods to the two major purposes of cost accounting: control and
procedures | product costing. Accounting for control is primarily concerned with charg-
for spoilage | ing responsibility centers for costs as *incurred*. Product costing is concerned

with *applying* to inventory or other appropriate accounts the costs already incurred. Where does costing for spoiled goods fit into this framework? First, it must be made clear that the costs of both normal and abnormal spoiled goods are *product costs*. Thus, product costs can represent either good product or bad product:

	GOOD PRODUCT COSTS—INVENTORIABLE	LOST COSTS— CHARGED OFF AS A LOSS IMMEDIATELY
Cost of spoiled goods—normal	Yes	No
Cost of spoiled goods—abnormal	No	Yes

The existence of spoiled goods does not involve any additional cost beyond the amount already incurred.[2] Therefore, in accounting for spoiled goods:

1. We want to accumulate data to spotlight the cost of spoilage so that management is made aware of its magnitude.
2. We are dealing with cost application and reallocation rather than new cost incurrence.
3. We want to distinguish between costs of normal spoilage (which should be added to the cost of good units) and of abnormal spoilage (which should be written off as a loss).

Depending on the product(s) or departments involved, there is a bewildering mass of treatments in practice, which vary from the inexcusable to the highly informative. This chapter cannot possibly cover all the theoretical and practical ramifications. It will try to contrast conceptual treatments with some methods used in practice.

A study of the conceptual entries in Exhibit 18-1 will show that, when a product is spoiled, some debit must be made to balance the necessary credit to work in process. Further, some means must be found to charge normal spoilage

[2]Where spoilage is not detected until completion of goods, spoiled units require the same effort as good units. In other words, a laborer can be performing with equal efficiency on all goods and yet turn out some spoiled units because of inferior materials, worn cutting tools, and the like. So labor efficiency may be very satisfactory, but spoilage may nevertheless be a major problem. Thus, a workman can efficiently turn out spoiled goods.

EXHIBIT 18-1

GENERAL ACCOUNTING FOR SPOILAGE

Assume: Units worked on		1,100
Good units completed	1,000	
Normal spoilage	30	
Abnormal spoilage	70	1,100

Assume a unit cost of $10, not including any spoilage allowance. Total costs to account for are 1,100 × $10, or $11,000.

CONCEPTUAL TREATMENT			PRACTICAL TREATMENT		
1. Work in process	11,000		1. (Same.)		
Stores, accrued payroll, applied overhead		11,000			
1,100 units worked on.					
2. Cost of spoiled goods	1,000		2,3,4. Finished goods	10,300	
Work in process		1,000	Work in process		10,300
100 units spoiled.			1,000 good units		
3. Finished goods	10,000		completed @ $10		
Work in process		10,000	plus normal spoil-		
1,000 good units completed.			age of 30 units		
4. Finished goods	300		@ $10. Total		
Cost of spoiled goods		300	costs of 1,000		
Normal-spoilage allowance, 30 units.			good units is thus		
			$10,300.		
5. Loss from abnormal spoilage	700		5. Loss from ab-		
Cost of spoiled goods		700	normal spoilage*	700	
Abnormal spoilage, 70 units.			Work in process		700
			Abnormal spoilage, 70 units.		

*In practice, abnormal spoilage is often not isolated at all. Instead, the $700 cost is erroneously lumped with the other costs to show a total cost of $11,000 and a unit cost of $11 for the 1,000 good units produced. The $700 abnormal spoilage should not be concealed as a part of the cost of the good product.

to good inventory and abnormal spoilage to a loss account. The entries in the conceptual treatment use a Cost of Spoiled Goods account to highlight the nature of problem and to stress the notion that the costs applied to work in process are initially product costs that are then transferred either to Finished Goods or to a loss account. In practice, this account is not used, and the second set of entries in Exhibit 18-1 is more likely to be found.

JOB COSTING AND SPOILAGE

spoiled units sold for salvage: treatment in practice
Job-cost accounting for spoilage in practice varies considerably. Where spoiled goods have a disposal value,[3] the net cost of spoilage is computed by deducting disposal value from the costs of the spoiled goods accumulated to the point of rejection.

Where spoilage is considered to be a normal characteristic of a given production cycle, and where causes of spoilage are attributable

[3] In practice, the words *scrap* and *spoilage* are sometimes used indiscriminately. Thus, *spoilage costs* may be thought of as total accumulated cost of spoiled work. Yet the spoiled goods may be "scrapped" (that is, sold for whatever can be recovered—"scrap" value). Thus, *net spoilage cost* is total spoilage cost less scrap recovery.

to work done on all jobs, net spoilage cost is budgeted as a part of overhead, so that the predetermined overhead rate includes a provision for normal spoilage costs. Therefore, spoilage costs are spread, through overhead application, over all jobs rather than being loaded on particular jobs only. The rationale is thus provided for the debit, to the overhead-control account, of the net spoilage cost in the following journal entry made when spoilage is considered to be normal in character: [4]

Stores control (spoiled goods at disposal value)	150	
Department factory overhead control (normal spoilage)	350	
Work in process		500

Assume that 5 pieces out of a lot of 50 were spoiled. Costs accumulated to point where spoilage was detected were $100 per unit. Salvage value is estimated at $30 per unit. Items in parentheses indicate subsidiary postings.

Another method used, where management finds it helpful for control or for pricing, is to credit specific jobs with only the resale value of spoiled units, thus forcing the remaining good units in the job to bear net normal-spoilage costs. Under this method, the predetermined overhead rate would not include a provision for normal-spoilage costs because the spoilage would be viewed as being directly attributable to the nature of particular jobs instead of being attributable to general factory conditions or processes. The journal entry, with the same data as were just used, follows:

Stores control (spoiled goods at disposal value)	150	
Work in process		150

DEFECTIVE UNITS

Defective units are subsequently reworked and transformed into units to be sold as "firsts" or "seconds." Management needs effective control over such actions, because foremen are tempted to rework rather than to junk spoiled units. If control is not exercised, foremen may rework many bad units instead of having

[4] Conceptually, the prevailing treatments just described can be criticized primarily because *product costs* are being charged back to Department Factory Overhead Control, which logically should accumulate only *costs incurred,* rather than both cost incurrence and product costs. If this distinction is not maintained, Department Factory Overhead Control will include duplicate charges for overhead. For example, as both good units and those units which will eventually be spoiled are worked on, the various production costs (including applied overhead) are charged to the departmental work-in-process account. Then, when the normal spoilage is detected, the conventional treatment results in charging back these same product costs (including applied overhead), in an amount equal to the actual net spoilage cost, to the departmental overhead-control account. For an extended criticism of the duplication of charges to Department Factory Overhead Control, see Alfred P. Koch, "A Fallacy in Accounting for Spoiled Goods," *Accounting Review,* XXXV, No. 3, 501–2.

In an unpublished paper, Dean Samuel Laimon evaluates the views expressed by Koch and expands the conceptual treatment described above. Laimon recognizes the existence of two kinds of normal and abnormal spoilage in job-order accounting: spoilage peculiar to the job and spoilage common to all jobs. He suggests the provision of separate normal-spoilage allowances for each of these and, therefore, the use of two special predetermined normal-spoilage application rates. The accounting for spoilage costs is fraught with joint-cost problems and control problems that are among the most difficult in the entire field of cost accounting.

them sold for salvage at a greater economic advantage. Rework should either be authorized by the foreman's superior or be undertaken only in accordance with prescribed operating procedures.

Unless there are special reasons for charging rework to the jobs or batches that contained the bad units, the cost of the extra materials, labor, and so on, are in practice usually charged to overhead.[5] Thus, once again we see that rework is usually spread over all jobs or batches as a part of a predetermined overhead rate. Assume that the five spoiled pieces used in our prior illustration are reworked and sold as firsts through regular channels. Entries follow:

Original cost accumulations:	Work-in-process control	500	
	Stores control		200
	Accrued payroll		200
	Factory overhead applied		100
Rework (Figures assumed):	Departmental factory-overhead control (rework)	190	
	Stores control		40
	Accrued payroll		100
	Factory overhead applied		50
Transfer to finished stock:	Finished-goods control	500	
	Work-in-process control		500

ACCOUNTING FOR SCRAP

Scrap is residue from manufacturing operations that has measurable but relatively minor recovery value. There are two major aspects of accounting for scrap: control and costing. Items like metal chips, turnings, filings, and borings should be quantified by weighing, counting, or some other expedient means. Norms or standards should be determined, because excessive scrap indicates inefficiency. *Scrap tickets* are prepared as source documents for periodic scrap reports that summarize the amount of scrap and compare it with predetermined norms or standards. Scrap should be returned to the storeroom to be held for sale or for reuse. Scrap should be accounted for in some manner, not only from the point of view of efficiency, but because scrap is often a tempting source for embezzlement by workers.

There are many methods of accounting for scrap. Typically, scrap is not assigned any cost; instead, its sales value is regarded as an offset to factory overhead, as follows:

Scrap returned to storeroom:	No journal entry.
	(Memo of quantity received is entered on the perpetual record.)

[5] The criticisms of the practical treatment for spoiled goods are also applicable to the treatment described—but only in the sense that the overhead-incurred and applied accounts may be padded for amounts that in themselves did not necessitate overhead incurrence. In other words, the extra materials, labor, and variable overhead may represent extra cost incurrence, but fixed overhead will not be affected. Also, any accounting entry that simultaneously involves a debit to department overhead and a credit to overhead applied tends to blur the primary purpose of the overhead-control account—that of only accumulating overhead costs *as incurred.*

Sale of scrap:	Cash or Accounts receivable	xx	
	Department factory overhead control		xx
	Posting made to subsidiary record—"Sale of Scrap" column on departmental cost sheet.		

This method is both simple and accurate enough in theory to justify its wide use. A normal amount of scrap is an inevitable result of production operations. Basically, this method does not link scrap with any particular physical product; instead, because of practical difficulties, all products bear regular production costs without any particular credit for scrap sales except in an indirect manner. What really happens in such situations is that sales of scrap are considered when predetermined overhead rates are being set. Thus, the predetermined overhead rate is lower than it would be if no credit for scrap sales were allowed in the overhead budget.

An alternate method in a job-cost situation would be to trace sales of scrap to the jobs that yielded the scrap. This method is used only when it is feasible and economically desirable. For example, there may be agreements between the company and particular customers that provide for charging specific, difficult jobs with all scrap or spoilage costs and crediting such jobs with all scrap sales arising therefrom. Entries follow:

Scrap returned to storeroom:	No journal entry.		
	(Memo of quantity received and related job made on perpetual record.)		
Sale of scrap:	Cash or Accounts receivable	xx	
	Work in process		xx
	Posting made to specific job order.		

The illustrations above assume that no inventory value is assigned to scrap as it is returned to the storeroom. However, when the dollar value is material and there is a significant time lag between storing scrap and selling it, there is justification for inventorying scrap at some conservative estimate of net realizable value so that production costs and related scrap recovery may be recognized in the same period.

Some companies tend to delay sales of scrap until the price is most attractive. Volatile price fluctuations are typical for scrap metal. In these cases, if scrap inventory becomes significant, it should be inventoried at some "reasonable" value—a difficult task in the face of volatile market prices.

COMPARISON OF ACCOUNTING FOR SPOILAGE, DEFECTIVE WORK, AND SCRAP

The basic approach to the accounting for spoilage, defective work, and scrap should distinguish between the normal amount that is common to all jobs, the normal amount that is attributable to specific jobs, and abnormal amounts.

The following entries recapitulate the preceding examples. Note the parallel approach to the three categories:

SPOILAGE COSTS (NET $350)

Normal (common to all jobs)	Stores	150	
	Departmental factory overhead control	350	
	Work in process		500
Normal (peculiar to specific jobs)	Stores	150	
	Work in process		150
Abnormal	Stores	150	
	Special loss account	350	
	Work in process		500

DEFECTIVE WORK COSTS (REWORK COSTS OF $190)

Normal (common to all jobs)	Departmental factory overhead control	190	
	Stores		40
	Accrued payroll		100
	Factory overhead applied		50
Normal (peculiar to specific jobs)	Same as preceding entry, except that the debit of $190 would be to Work in Process		
Abnormal	Same as preceding entry, except that the debit of $190 would be to Special Loss account		

SCRAP VALUE RECOVERED ($100)

Normal (common to all jobs)	Stores or Cash or Accounts receivable	100	
	Department factory overhead control		100
Abnormal (peculiar to specific jobs)	Same as preceding entry except that the credit would be to Work in Process		

SOME APPLICATIONS TO STANDARD COSTS

shrinkage and waste When standard-cost systems are used, allowance is made in the standard product costs for a standard shrinkage. Actual shrinkage is usually computed by working back from product output. Shrinkage in excess of standard is a material usage or quantity variance. Unlike spoilage and scrap, shrinkage cannot be tagged and traced by physical identification.

Examples of waste that are not traced and specifically costed include paint or varnish adhering to the sides of their containers, mill ends, shavings, evaporation, and so forth. Excess material consumption is usually revealed through excess-material requisitions or through standard-yield percentages for such materials as lumber, chemicals, and ores. Thus, where 15,000 gallons of raw chemicals ordinarily produce 12,000 gallons of good finished product, the standard-yield percentage could be expressed as 80 percent of normal input. On the other hand, the waste percentage could be expressed as 20 percent of normal input or as 25 percent of good output.

Note that these percentages provide a physical standard that may be used without worrying about price changes. Further, such a standard is easily understood and can be readily used as a timely index of efficiency—on an hourly or batch basis if desired.

scrap Material-usage standards usually include allowances for scrap. Although the allowance may be computed in various ways, standards are based on a careful study of the operation(s), not on historical data alone or on wild guesses. The standard cost of direct materials thus becomes (a) standard unit price times the standard input per finished unit, less (b) standard scrap price per unit times standard scrap weight loss per finished unit.

To illustrate, assume that the metal rod is fed into an automatic screw machine. About five inches (ten ounces) at the end of each 105-inch rod (210 ounces) are clutched by the chuck and cannot be used. The standard lot size is 1,000 units. The first ten units are scrapped in setting up the run. It takes five ounces of metal to produce a finished unit that weighs four ounces. Standard cost computations follow:

	OUNCES	ASSUMED PRICE PER OUNCE	TOTAL COST
Standard cost per unit:			
Finished piece	4.00		
Turnings	1.00		
Crop loss (10 oz. ÷ 40 units per rod)	0.25		
Scrap piece loss (10 units ÷ 1,000) × 5	.05		
	5.30	$.0300*	$.1590
Less credit for scrap	1.30	.0020†	.0026
Standard cost per finished unit	4.00		$.1564

*Or 48¢ per lb.
†3.2¢ per lb.

Although standards for direct materials are built in this way for each operation, it is usually inexpedient to trace scrap to specific lots or operations. Comparisons are usually limited to monthly, or sometimes weekly, comparisons of standard costs of good work produced with the total "actual" charges to the department.[6]

spoilage In practice, allowances for net spoilage costs and for rework are often incorporated into the flexible budget for overhead. Spoiled units are removed from Work in Process at standard costs and charged to Factory Overhead. Periodic comparisons of budget allowances with actual spoilage provide summary

---

[6]For an extended discussion of spoilage and standard costs, see Stanley B. Henrici, *Standard Costs for Manufacturing* (New York: McGraw-Hill Book Company, 1960), pp. 275–80, 303–8.

information for managerial control. If no spoilage is allowed, the budget provided may be zero. Rework is controlled in a similar manner. Day-to-day control is aided by spoilage tags prepared at the point of inspection. These tags, or a summary thereof, are promptly shown to the foreman and other interested parties.

This procedure really spotlights spoilage and rework as special managerial problems, as opposed to, say, material-quantity variances that are related to good units. For example, the standard cost for a product is as follows:

Direct materials, 1 pound	$ 5.00
Direct labor, 1 hour	3.00
Factory overhead—variable	1.50
Factory overhead—fixed	1.50
Standard cost per unit	$11.00

Assume that no spoilage occurs, but that it takes 1,150 pounds of material to produce 1,000 good units:

Direct materials:	
Actual, 1,150 pounds @ $5.00	$5,750
Standard, 1,000 pounds @ $5.00	5,000
Usage variance	$ 750

Assume, instead, that 1,100 units were produced, but that 100 were spoiled because of careless machine operation. There would be two alternatives for analyzing such a variance. First consider the figures:

	INCURRED COSTS	STANDARD COSTS— GOOD OUTPUT	TOTAL VARIANCE
*Direct materials, 1,150 lbs.	$ 5,750	$ 5,000	$ 750 U
Direct labor, 1,100 hours	3,300	3,000	300 U
Factory overhead—variable	1,650	1,500	150 U
Factory overhead—fixed	1,650	1,500	150 U
	$12,350	$11,000	$1,350 U

* Standard materials allowed for good units	1,000 lbs.
Standard materials allowed for spoiled units, which were spoiled by careless labor	100 lbs.
Excess materials used in producing 1,100 units	50 lbs.
Total	1,150 lbs.

Analysis One. Analyze variances on the basis of good output only. This is the familiar way:

Direct-material quantity variance	$5,750–$5,000	$ 750
Direct-labor efficiency variance	$3,300–$3,000	300
Variable-overhead total variance	$1,650–$1,500	150
Fixed-overhead total variance	$1,650–$1,500	150
Total variance explained		$1,350

Analysis Two. Isolate a separate variance for spoilage, $1,100, consisting of the four elements shown above. This would entail setting up a special Spoilage Variance account in the ledger. This account would represent the standard cost of spoiled work. Thus the other variance accounts would not reflect any spoilage effects:

	SPOILAGE VARIANCE	OTHER VARIANCES		TOTAL VARIANCE EXPLAINED
Direct materials	$ 500	Usage	$250 U	$ 750
Direct labor	300		—	300
Variable overhead	150		—	150
Fixed overhead	150		—	150
	$1,100		$250	$1,350

PROCESS-COST ACCOUNTING PROCEDURES AND SPOILAGE

distinguish between normal and abnormal spoilage

Although this discussion of process costing will emphasize accounting for spoilage, the ideas here are equally applicable to waste (shrinkage, evaporation, or lost units).

Again we must distinguish between control and product costing. For control, most companies use some version of estimated or standard costs that incorporates an allowance for normal spoilage, shrinkage, or waste in the estimate or standard. This section emphasizes product costing in so-called actual process-costing systems. A conceptual framework is stressed because it is needed to judge the many compromises necessary in practice.

As a general rule, it is sensible to trace and build the costs of spoilage separately. Then allocate normal spoilage costs to Finished Goods or Work in Process, depending on where in the production cycle the spoilage is assumed to take place. Spoilage is typically assumed to occur at the stage of completion where inspection occurs, because spoilage is recognized at this point. Normal spoilage need not be allocated to units that have not yet reached this point in the production process, because the spoiled units are related solely to the units that have passed inspection.

Many writers on process costing advocate ignoring the computation of equivalent units for spoilage, shrinkage, or waste. The reason cited in favor of this shortcut technique is that it automatically spreads normal-spoilage costs over good units through the use of higher equivalent unit costs. However, the results of this shortcut are inaccurate unless (a) no work-in-process inventories exist, or (b) material, conversion, *and* spoilage costs are all incurred uniformly throughout the production cycle. To illustrate, assume that a department has no beginning inventory. It starts 1,000 units; 500 are completed, 400 are in process, half-completed, and 100 are spoiled. The 100 units represent normal spoilage. Spoilage is detected upon completion. Material costs are $1,800 and conversion costs are $1,400. All material is introduced at the start of the process.

EXHIBIT 18-2

COMPARISON OF ACCOUNTING FOR SPOILAGE

UNITS	ACCURATE METHOD: COUNT SPOILAGE EQUIVALENT PERFORMANCE PHYSICAL FLOW	MATERIALS	CONVERSION COSTS	LESS ACCURATE METHOD: IGNORE SPOILAGE EQUIVALENT PERFORMANCE PHYSICAL FLOW	MATERIALS	CONVERSION COSTS
Completed	500	500	500	500	500	500
Normal spoilage	100	100	100	100	—	—
In process, end (½)	400	400	200	400	400	200
Accounted for	1,000	1,000	800	1,000	900	700

COSTS	TOTALS	DETAILS MATERIALS	CONVERSION COSTS	TOTALS	DETAILS MATERIALS	CONVERSION COSTS
Current costs	$3,200	$1,800	$1,400	$3,200	$1,800	$1,400
Divide by equivalent units		1,000	800		900	700
Cost per equivalent unit		$1.80	$1.75		$2.00	$2.00

SUMMARY OF COSTS

Units completed (500):						
Costs before spoilage	$1,775	500 ($1.80)	500 ($1.75)			
Add normal spoilage	355	100 ($1.80)	100 ($1.75)			
Total costs transferred out	$2,130			$2,000	500 ($2.00)	500 ($2.00)
Work in process, end (400):						
Materials	$ 720	400 ($1.80)		$ 800	400 ($2.00)	
Conversion costs	350		200 ($1.75)	400		200 ($2.00)
Total cost of work in process	$1,070			$1,200		
Total costs accounted for	$3,200			$3,200		

The solution in Exhibit 18-2 shows that ignoring spoilage lowers total equivalent performance; when the latter is divided into the production costs, a higher *unit cost* results. The effective result is to load higher unit costs on work in process that has not reached the inspection stage of completion. At the same time, total charges to completed units are too low. Therefore, ending work in process contains costs of spoilage ($130 in this example) that do not pertain to such units and that properly should be charged to completed goods. Further, ending work in process that has not reached inspection undoubtedly contains some units that will not properly be recognized as spoiled until a subsequent period. Thus, work in process is being loaded now with spoilage ($130) that should instead be charged to goods later as they are completed. In effect, work in process is being doubly charged, because it is being charged with spoilage both now and also later when inspection occurs.

In summary, when spoilage occurs, trace the units spoiled as well as the units finished and in process. Compute both normal and abnormal spoiled units. Build separate costs of spoiled units. Then reallocate normal-spoilage costs to good units produced; charge off abnormal-spoilage costs as a loss. Even if no abnormal spoilage exists, it is helpful to compute normal-spoilage costs separately before reallocation. In this way, management will be constantly reminded of the normal-spoilage costs of a given process.

base for computing normal spoilage   Normal spoilage should be computed from the good output, or from the *normal* input—not from the total input. Total input includes the abnormal as well as the normal spoilage and is therefore irrational as a basis for computing normal spoilage. For example, if the normal rate of spoilage of polio vaccine is sloppily stated as 5 percent, an input of 100,000 cubic centimeters would be expected to produce 5,000 cubic centimeters of spoilage. Now, if 85,500 cubic centimeters of good units are produced, normal spoilage is not 5,000 cubic centimeters (5 percent of 100,000), because it should have taken only 90,000 cubic centimeters of input to get 85,500 cubic centimeters of good vaccine. If normal spoilage is expressed as 5 percent of input, then good output should be 95 percent of normal input. In this case, abnormal spoilage would be 10,000 cubic centimeters and normal spoilage would be 4,500 cubic centimeters. These relationships may be clarified by the following:

			RELATIONSHIPS
Input	100,000 c.c.		
Output:			
Good units	85,500 c.c.		95%
Normal spoilage	4,500 c.c.	90,000 c.c.*	5% 100%
Abnormal spoilage		10,000 c.c.	
		100,000 c.c.	

*Normal input.

Thus, we could express the normal-spoilage rate more accurately either as 5 percent of *normal input* or as $\frac{5}{95}$ of good output.

weighted- average process costing and spoilage   The costs of producing one of the B Company's products are accumulated on a process-cost basis. Materials for this product are put in at the beginning of the cycle of operations; labor and indirect costs are assumed to flow evenly over the cycle. Some units of this product are spoiled as a result of defects not ascertainable before inspection of finished units. Normally the spoiled units are one-tenth of the good output.

example 1   At January 1, the inventory of work in process on this product was $29,600, representing 2,000 pounds of material ($15,000) and conversion cost of $14,600 representing four-fifths completion. During January, 8,000 pounds of material ($61,000) were put into production. Direct labor of $40,200 was charged to the process. Indirect costs are assigned at the rate of 100 percent of direct-labor cost. The inventory at January 31 consisted of 1,500 pounds, two-thirds finished. Seventy-two hundred pounds of good product were transferred to finished-goods stock after inspection.

required   Using the weighted-average technique, show calculations of:

1. The dollar and unit amount of the abnormal spoilage during January.

2. Total product costs transferred to finished stock.

3. The work-in-process inventory at January 31.

4. Journal entries for transfers out of work-in-process inventory.

Example 1 illustrates a spoilage situation in process-cost accounting.[7] Exhibit 18-3 employs the weighted-average techniques. The requested journal entries follow:

Finished goods	139,392	
Processing department—Work in process		139,392
To transfer good units completed in January.		
Loss from abnormal spoilage	10,208	
Processing department—Work in process		10,208
To recognize abnormal spoilage in January.		

FIFO PROCESS COSTING AND SPOILAGE

Reexamine Example 1 and Exhibit 18-3. Try to solve the problem using the first-in, first-out technique.

A comparison of the methods used in Exhibits 18-3 and 18-4 will show that the FIFO method necessitates an arbitrary assumption in order to split normal-spoilage costs between those goods completed from current production during a given period and those completed from beginning work in process. The most widely used assumption is to load spoilage on all good units at current unit costs. But to do this is inconsistent with the FIFO assumption; examine the footnote to Exhibit 18-4 for an illustration of the inconsistencies that arise.

In contrast, the weighted-average method does not necessitate splitting normal-spoilage costs between two batches of good units completed, because the initial inventory is merged with the current costs to determine unit costs. The more one examines process costing, the more one becomes convinced that weighted-average costing is generally superior to first-in, first-out costing for *product-costing* purposes. Moreover, standard costing is superior to either weighted-average costing or first-in, first-out costing for *control* purposes.

---

[7] This illustration assumes inspection upon completion. In contrast, inspection may take place at some other stage—say, at the halfway point in the production cycle. In such a case, normal-spoilage costs would be reallocated to completed goods and to the units in process that are more than half completed.

EXHIBIT 18-3

B COMPANY
PRODUCTION COST REPORT

Weighted-Average Method
For the Month Ending January 31, 19_1

	(STEP 1)	(STEP 2) EQUIVALENT UNITS	
QUANTITIES	PHYSICAL FLOW	MATERIALS	CONVERSION COSTS
Work in process, beginning	2,000(4/5)		
Units started	8,000		
To account for	10,000		
Abnormal spoilage	580	580	580
Normal spoilage	720	720	720
Good units completed	7,200	7,200	7,200
Work in process, end	1,500(2/3)	1,500	1,000
Accounted for	10,000	10,000	9,500

	COSTS	TOTALS	MATERIALS	CONVERSION COSTS (DETAILS)	EQUIVALENT WHOLE UNIT
	Work in process, beginning	$ 29,600	$15,000	$14,600	
	Current costs	141,400	61,000	80,400	
(Step 3)	Total costs to account for	$171,000	$76,000	$95,000	
	Divide by equivalent units		÷10,000	÷9,500	
(Step 4)	Cost per equivalent unit		$7.60	$10.00	$17.60
(Step 5)	SUMMARY OF COSTS				
	Abnormal spoilage (580)	$ 10,208			580 ($17.60)
	Units completed (7,200):				
	Costs before adding spoilage	$126,720			7,200 ($17.60)
	Normal spoilage	12,672			720 ($17.60)
	Total cost transferred out	$139,392			
	Work in process, end (1,500):				
	Materials	$ 11,400	1,500 ($7.60)		
	Conversion costs	10,000		1,000 ($10.00)	
	Total cost of work in process	$ 21,400			
	Total costs accounted for	$171,000			

interim fluctuations in spoilage rates There is a tendency among accountants to seize a single figure or a single rate as the standard or index of normal efficiency, when in reality the standard or norm is in the middle of a range. Thus, normal spoilage may average 10 percent of good output, but random influences may cause deviations from the 10 percent norm in a range of, say, 6 percent to 14 percent. Over an extended period—say, a year—the rate should center around 10 percent.

This situation, as shown in Example 2, calls for using a predetermined 10 percent normal-spoilage cost rate for charging spoilage costs to good units produced throughout the year, regardless of actual month-to-month fluctuations within the normal range. The differences between normal-spoilage costs charged to production and those actually incurred within the normal range would rest in a temporary general-ledger account called Spoilage Random Fluctuations. It

634

should have a zero balance by the end of a year. If a balance tends to build up, it would indicate that an erroneous normal rate of spoilage was being used.

example 2   Let us assume that a single department process produces 1,000 good units per month, but that spoilage fluctuates. Normal spoilage averages 10 percent of good output, with the normal range considered to be from 6 percent to 14 percent of good output. The company's cost behavior is such that all units are produced at an equivalent unit cost of $10. All spoilage is detected upon completion. The company uses a Spoilage Random Fluctuations account and costs completed units as if they were all accompanied by a 10 percent normal-spoilage factor. Possible situations and general-ledger entries are shown below:

	CASE			
	1	2	3	4
Total units completed	1,100	1,130	1,170	1,060
Good units completed	1,000	1,000	1,000	1,000
Actual spoilage	100	130	170	60
Normal spoilage	100	100	100	100
General-ledger entries:				
Finished goods	$11,000 dr.	$11,000 dr.	$11,000 dr.	$11,000 dr.
Spoilage random fluctuations	—	300 dr.	400 dr.	400 cr.
Loss from abnormal spoilage	—	—	300 dr.	—
Department—work in process	11,000 cr.	11,300 cr.	11,700 cr.	10,600 cr.

If a Spoilage Random Fluctuations account were used, abnormal spoilage would usually be recognized only when actual spoilage exceeded the top of the normal range (14 percent in this example; see Case 3 in Example 2).

The handling of subnormal spoilage is shown in Case 4 of Example 2.

SPOILAGE RANDOM FLUCTUATIONS

(2)	300	(4)	400
(3)	400		

This account should balance out to zero over a period of, say, 12 months. If it does not, the process may not be performing in accordance with expectations.

summary

Nearly every manufacturing company has some problems of waste, scrap, or spoilage as a consequence of management's choice of those factors of production that will render the most economic benefit. Hence, some waste, scrap, or

EXHIBIT 18-4

B COMPANY
PRODUCTION–COST REPORT

FIFO Method
For the Month Ending January 31, 19_1

QUANTITIES	(STEP 1) PHYSICAL FLOW	(STEP 2) EQUIVALENT UNITS MATERIALS	CONVERSION COSTS
Work in process, beginning	2,000(4/5)		
Units started	8,000		
To account for	10,000		
Abnormal spoilage	580	580	580
Normal spoilage	720	720	720
Good units completed:			
From beginning inventory	2,000	—	400
Started and completed	5,200	5,200	5,200
Work in process, end	1,500(2/3)	1,500	1,000
Accounted for	10,000	8,000	7,900

		DETAILS		
COSTS	TOTALS	MATERIALS	CONVERSION COSTS	EQUIVALENT WHOLE UNIT
Work in process, beginning	$ 29,600			
Current costs	141,400	$61,000	$80,400	
(Step 3) Total costs to account for	$171,000			
(Step 4) Divide by equivalent units		÷8,000	÷7,900	
(Step 5) Cost per equivalent unit		$7.625	$10.1772	$17.8022
SUMMARY OF COSTS				
(A) Abnormal spoilage (580)	$ 10,325.28			580 ($17.8022)
Units completed (7,200):				
From beginning inventory (2,000):				
Current costs added	$ 29,600.00			
	$ 4,070.88		400 ($10.1772)	
Total cost from beginning inventory before spoilage	$ 33,670.88			
Started and completed before spoilage (5,200)	92,571.56			5,200 ($17.8022)
Normal spoilage*	12,817.58			720 ($17.8022)
(B) Total costs transferred out	$139,060.02			
Work in process, end (1,500):				
Materials	$ 11,437.50	1,500 ($7.625)		
Conversion costs	10,177.20		1,000 ($10.1772)	
(C) Total cost of work in process	$ 21,614.70			
(A) + (B) + (C) Total costs accounted for	$171,000.00			

*Note that normal spoilage should really be split between the two batches of good units completed if FIFO is to be followed thoroughly. But to split spoilage costs on a pro rata basis implies that all spoilage traceable to beginning inventory is costed on the basis of full *current* costs, not past costs. This is inconsistent with the FIFO assumption, which states that past costs should be kept separate from current costs. In effect, using current costs for attaching normal-spoilage costs to beginning inventory assumes that all spoilage traceable thereto was begun and completed during the current period—an obvious contradiction of the FIFO concept.

Special Note: For a computer application to solving this process-cost problem, see Werner Frank, "A Computer Application to Process Cost Accounting," *Accounting Review*, October 1965, pp. 854–62.

spoilage is a normal result of efficient production. Yet there is a need to distinguish between, for example, normal and abnormal spoilage. Standards or norms must be computed so that performance may be judged and costs properly accounted for. Normal spoilage, then, is spoilage that is unavoidable under a given set of efficient production conditions; abnormal spoilage is spoilage that is not expected to arise under efficient conditions. Laxity in setting careful standards often results in too liberal allowances for normal spoilage.

Abnormal spoilage is often controllable by first-line supervision, whereas normal spoilage is controllable only by those managers who determine the nature of products and processes.

Managerial cost accounting must distinguish between normal and abnormal spoilage, primarily for keeping management informed, but also for proper product costing.

Accounting for spoilage, defective units, and the like varies considerably. Practically, most of these net costs are allowed for in predetermined overhead rates; or, where standard costs are employed, scrap and spoilage allowances are often incorporated in the standard costs for direct materials, direct labor, and overhead.

Conceptually, some practical treatments are faulty because they muddle the distinction between product costs and costs for control by charging product costs back to Department Factory Overhead Control.[8]

Problems for Self-Study

Review each example in this chapter and obtain the solutions on your own. Then check your work against the solutions, which appear in the text.

questions, problems, and cases

18-1. "Management has two major planning and control problems regarding spoilage." What are the two problems?

18-2. "Normal spoilage is planned spoilage." Discuss.

18-3. "Costs of abnormal spoilage are lost costs." Explain.

18-4. "In accounting for spoiled goods, we are dealing with cost application and reallocation rather than cost incurrence." Explain.

18-5. "Total input includes the abnormal as well as the normal spoilage and is therefore irrational as a basis for computing normal spoilage." Do you agree? Why?

18-6. Explain the operation of a Spoilage Random Fluctuations account.

18-7. "The practical treatments of spoilage in job-order costing can be criticized on conceptual grounds." What is the major criticism?

[8] Werner Frank, in "A Computer Application in Process Cost Accounting," *Accounting Review*, October 1965, pp. 854–62, shows how the approach in this chapter can be applied on a computer.

18-8. Describe the general accounting for scrap where no inventory value is assigned to scrap.

18-9. How is scrap usually accounted for under standard costing?

18-10. Two Ways of Accounting for Spoilage [CPA].   In manufacturing activities, a portion of the units placed in process is sometimes spoiled and becomes practically worthless. Discuss two ways in which the cost of such spoiled units could be treated in the accounts, and describe the circumstances under which each method might be used.

18-11. Process Costing and Spoilage.   The Alston Company operates under a process-cost system. It has two departments, Cleaning and Milling. For both departments, conversion costs are applied in proportion to the stage of completion. But materials are applied at the *beginning* of the process in the cleaning department, and additional materials are added at the *end* of the milling process. Following are the costs and unit production statistics for May. All unfinished work at the *end* of May is one-fourth completed. All beginning inventories (May 1) were four-fifths completed as of May 1. All completed work is transferred to the next department.

Beginning inventories:	CLEANING	MILLING
Cleaning: $1,000 materials, $800 conv. costs	$1,800	
Milling: $6,450 previous dept. cost (trans-ferred-in cost) and $2,450 conv. costs		$8,900
Current costs		
Materials	$9,000	$ 640
Conversion costs	$8,000	$4,950
Units in beginning inventory	1,000	3,000
Units *started* this month	9,000	7,400
Total units finished and transferred	7,400	6,000
Normal spoilage	500	400
Abnormal spoilage	500	0

Additional Factors

1. Spoilage is assumed to occur at the *end* of *each* of the two processes, when the units are inspected.
2. Assume that there is no other waste, shrinkage, evaporation, or abnormal spoilage than that indicated in the tabulation above.
3. Carry unit-cost calculations to three decimal places where necessary. Calculate final totals to the nearest dollar.

required   Using the weighted-average method, show for *each* department:

1. Analysis of physical flows and an analysis of equivalent performance.
2. Calculations of *unit* costs.
3. *Detailed* presentation of the *total* values assigned to goods transferred out and the total values assigned to ending work in process.

   Be certain that your solution is presented in step-by-step fashion so that your reasoning can be followed easily.

18-12. Allocating Spoilage.   The ABC Company operates under a process-cost system for one of its products. During the period in question for this product,

3,850 units were put into production. During the period, 3,000 finished units were turned out. Inspection of this product occurs at the halfway point in the process. Normally, rejects amount to 10 percent of the good units passed. The inspection department informs us that the process did in fact function normally during this period. The department foreman estimates that units still in process are on the average two-thirds complete. All, however, are at least one-half done.

Costs for the period were:

Materials	$38,500—Applied at the beginning of the process
Conversion cost	35,080—Applied uniformly during the process
	$73,580

required   Determine the cost of goods completed and the cost of the ending inventory of work in process. Assume that there were no beginning inventories.

18-13. Multiple Choice; Weighted-Average Method; Spoilage.   The data that follow are to be used in answering questions 1–9, inclusive. Support your answers with a statement of production costs.

The manufacture of product XT-123 is begun in Department No. 1. From there it goes to Department No. 2, where the product is completed. Upon completion, it is sent to finished-goods storage in the warehouse. At the end of processing in each department, the units of products are inspected; only those that pass inspection are sent to Department No. 2 and to finished-goods storage, respectively. The spoiled units (both normal and abnormal spoilage) cannot be salvaged, have no scrap value, and are thrown away.

Below are listed the pertinent data regarding the production of XT-123 for the month of December 19_3:

	DEPARTMENT NO. 1	DEPARTMENT NO. 2
Costs applied to product:		
Materials	At the beginning of processing in the department	At 50% completion of processing in the department
Other costs	Evenly throughout entire period of processing	Evenly throughout entire period of processing
Work in process, December 1, 19_3:		
Number of units	600 units	2,000 units
Percent complete	66⅔%	25%
Accumulated cost:		
Department No. 1 materials	$ 2,844 ⎫	
Department No. 1 other cost	$ 3,120 ⎭	$30,280
Department No. 2 materials		None
Department No. 2 other cost		$ 6,200
Work in process, December 31, 19_3:		
Number of units	1,400 units	800 units
Percent complete	50%	75%
Normal spoilage (detected by inspection of product upon completion of processing in each department)	140 units	40 units

Abnormal spoilage:		
Number of units	60 units	None
Percent complete	100%	
Units of finished product transferred to finished-goods warehouse	—	3,960 units
December cost applied to product (exclusive of accumulated cost of work in process at December 1, 19_3):		
Materials	$19,800	$15,140
Other costs	34,260	52,860

Indicate your answer by letter.

1. The actual number of units transferred to Department No. 2 from Department No. 1 during the month was:
   a. 3,000; b. 2,760; c. 3,960; d. 2,800; e. 2,860.
2. The actual number of units begun in Department No. 1 during the month was:
   a. 4,400; b. 3,620; c. 3,520; d. 3,760; e. 3,800.

Note: Questions 3–9, inclusive, refer to answers you would secure using the weighted-average method. (Round off unit costs to the nearest cent.)

3. In Department No. 1, the total equivalent performance for "other costs" was:
   a. 3,000; b. 3,700; c. 4,400; d. 2,800; e. 4,200.
4. In Department No. 1, the equivalent unit cost for materials was:
   a. $7.71; b. $8.09; c. $5.15; d. $5.39; e. $5.22.
5. In Department No. 1, the cost of work in process at December 31, 19_3, was:
   a. $14,280; b. $18,396; c. $17,864; d. $14,616; e. $14,378.
6. The cost of goods transferred from Department No. 1 to Department No. 2 during the month of December was:
   a. $42,700; b. $43,615; c. $44,100; d. $42,010; e. $44,835.
7. In Department No. 2, the total equivalent performance for materials (only those materials *added* by Department No. 2) was:
   a. 4,800; b. 4,000; c. 5,000; d. 4,400; e. 4,600.
8. In Department No. 2, the equivalent unit cost for "other costs" (only those "other costs" *added* by Department No. 2) was:
   a. $14.91; b. $12.84; c. $12.30; d. $13.42; e. $12.95
9. In Department No. 2, the total cost of units transferred to the finished-goods warehouse was:
   a. $125,294; b. $63,960; c. $63,310; d. $145,544; e. $126,560.

18-14. Process Costs; Weighted Average [CGAA]. The H Co. Ltd. manufactures a single product that is processed in three departments. The process-cost procedure in use bases inventory values on the weighted-average cost method. The following cost and production data are available for Department 2 for the month of April:

Opening work-in-process inventory—1,500 units:	
Cost from preceding department	$12,000
Dept. 2 material (added at the beginning of the process)	2,041
Dept. 2 labor and applied overhead	4,168
(These units were 40% complete as to conversion costs.)	

Transferred in during April from Dept. 1:	
6,000 units	46,800
Department 2 costs for April:	
Materials	8,459
Labor and applied overhead	41,727

Production Data: 5,900 units were completed and transferred to Dept. 3; 1,000 units were still in process (20 percent complete) at the end of April; the balance were spoiled units, detected at the end of the Dept. 2 processing. One-half the spoilage is abnormal in nature and is to be charged to an Abnormal Spoilage Loss Account.

required   Prepare a cost-of-production report for April.

18-15. **Different Ways of Accounting for Spoilage [CPA].** The D. Hayes Cramer Company manufactures product C, whose cost per unit is $1 of materials, $2 of labor, and $3 of overhead costs. During the month of May, 1,000 units of product C were spoiled. These units could be sold for 60¢ each.

The accountant said that the entry to be made for these 1,000 lost or spoiled units could be one of the following four:

ENTRY NO. 1

Spoiled goods	$ 600	
Work in process—Materials		$ 100
Work in process—Labor		200
Work in process—Overhead		300

ENTRY NO. 2

Spoiled goods	$ 600	
Manufacturing expenses	5,400	
Work in process—Materials		$1,000
Work in process—Labor		2,000
Work in process—Overhead		3,000

ENTRY NO. 3

Spoiled goods	$ 600	
Loss on spoiled goods	5,400	
Work in process—Materials		$1,000
Work in process—Labor		2,000
Work in process—Overhead		3,000

ENTRY NO. 4

Spoiled goods	$ 600	
Receivable	5,400	
Work in process—Materials		$1,000
Work in process—Labor		2,000
Work in process—Overhead		3,000

required   Indicate the circumstance under which each of the four solutions above would be appropriate.

18-16. **Spoilage; Two Departments [CPA, adapted].** The Mantis Manufacturing Company manufactures a single product that passes through two departments:

extruding and finishing–packing. The product is shipped at the end of the day on which it is packed. The production in the extruding and finishing–packing departments does not increase the number of units started.

The cost and production data for the month of January are as follows:

COST DATA	EXTRUDING DEPARTMENT	FINISHING–PACKING DEPARTMENT
Work in process, January 1:		
Cost from preceding department	—	$60,200
Materials	$ 5,900	—
Labor	1,900	1,500
Overhead	1,400	2,000
Costs added during January:		
Materials	20,100	4,400
Labor	10,700	7,720
Overhead	8,680	11,830
Percentage of completion of work in process:		
January 1:		
Materials	70%	0%
Labor	50	30
Overhead	50	30
January 31:		
Materials	50	0
Labor	40	35
Overhead	40	35
JANUARY PRODUCTION STATISTICS		
Units in process, January 1	10,000	29,000
Units in process, January 31	8,000	6,000
Units started or received from preceding department	20,000	22,000
Units completed and transferred or shipped	22,000	44,000

In the extruding department, materials are added at various phases of the process. All lost units occur at the end of the process when the inspection operation takes place.

In the finishing–packing department, the materials added consist only of packing supplies. These materials are added at the midpoint of the process, when the packing operation begins. Cost studies have disclosed that one-half the labor and overhead costs apply to the finishing operation and one-half to the packing operation. All lost units occur at the end of the finishing operation when the product is inspected. All the work in process in this department at January 1 and 31 was in the finishing-operation phase of the manufacturing process.

(The company uses the average-costing method in its accounting system.)

required

1. Compute the units lost, if any, for each department during January.

2. Compute the equivalent units for the calculation of unit costs for each department by January.

3. Prepare a cost-of-production report for both departments for January. The report should disclose the departmental total cost and cost per unit (for

materials, labor, and overhead) of the units (a) transferred to the finishing–packing department and (b) shipped. Assume that January production and costs were normal. (Submit all supporting computations in good form.)

18-17. **Normal and Abnormal Spoilage.**   The Van Brocklin Company manufactures one style of long, tapered wax candle, which is used on festive occasions. Each candle requires a two-foot-long wick and one pound of a specially prepared wax. Wick and melted wax are placed in molds and allowed to harden for twenty-four hours. Upon removal from the molds, the candles are immediately dipped in a special coloring mixture that gives them a glossy lacquer finish. Dried candles are inspected, and all defective ones are pulled out. Because the coloring mixture penetrates into the wax itself, the defective candles cannot be salvaged for reuse. They are destroyed in an incinerator. Normal spoilage is reckoned as 3 percent of the number of candles that pass inspection.

Cost and production statistics for a certain week were as follows:

Raw materials requisitioned (including wicks and wax)	$3,340.00
Direct labor and indirect costs (applied at a constant rate during the hardening process)	1,219.50
Total cost incurred	$4,559.50

During the week, 7,800 candles were completed; 7,500 passed inspection, and the remainder were defective. At the end of the week, 550 candles were still in the molds; they were considered 60 percent complete. There was no beginning inventory. Show computations.

1. Which of the following is the normal cost of the 7,500 candles that passed inspection?
   a. $4,333.73
   b. $4,125.00
   c. $4,217.85
   d. $4,248.75
   e. $4,290.00
2. Which of the following is the normal cost of the candles still in the molds at the end of the week?
   a. $393.25
   b. $185.13
   c. $269.50
   d. $274.72
   e. $300.30

18-18. **Process Costs; Abnormal Spoilage [SIA].**   The Quebec Manufacturing Company produces a single product. There are two producing departments, Departments 1 and 2, and the product passes through the plant in that order.

There were no work-in-process inventories at the beginning of the year.

In January, materials for 1,000 units were issued to production in Department 1 at a cost of $5,000. Direct-labor and factory-overhead costs for the month were $2,700. During the month, 800 units were completed and transferred to Department 2. The work-in-process inventory at the end of the month contained 200 units, complete in materials and one-half complete in labor and overhead.

Direct labor and factory overhead in Department 2 amounted to $6,250 in January. During the month, 500 units were completed and transferred to finished stock. At the end of the month, 200 units remained in process, one-quarter complete. Ordinarily, in Department 2, spoilage is recognized upon inspection at the end of the process, but in January there was an abnormal loss of 50 units when one-half complete. The effect of abnormal loss is not to be included in inventory.

required Prepare a detailed cost-of-production report for the month of January.

18-19. **Standard Process Costing; Spoilage.** [Prepared by Samuel Laimon] The Sharbill Company uses standard process costing in accounting for its costs of production. One product only is manufactured, with standard costs *per thousand units* as follows:

Material A	15 lbs. @ 80¢		$12.00
Material B	4 lbs. @ $2.25		9.00
Direct labor	5 hours @ $3.60		18.00
Variable overhead	5 hours @ $2.00		10.00
Fixed overhead	5 hours @ $1.60		8.00
Normal spoilage	10% of Material A	$1.20	
	5% of Conversion costs	1.80	3.00
Total standard cost per 1,000 units			$60.00

The standards for materials and conversion costs are exclusive of spoilage costs. The latter costs are allowed for separately in the standard. Material A is added at the beginning of the process. Labor and overhead are added evenly throughout the process. Inspection at the 50 percent stage of completion removes all spoiled units. Normal spoilage amounts to 10 percent of all *good* units passing the inspection point. Immediately after the removal of spoiled units, Material B is added to the remaining good units, and the processing of these units is then completed.

Production data for April, 19_1, were as follows:

Beginning work-in-process inventory	400,000 units—40% complete	
Put into process during April	500,000	
Transferred to finished goods	600,000	
Spoiled units	100,000	
Ending work-in-process inventory	200,000	—60% complete

Cost Data

1. Materials: All price variances on materials are recognized at the time of purchase.
   a. Material A: Beginning inventory, 2,000 pounds
      Purchased, 10,000 lbs. @ 84¢ = $8,400
      Issued to production, 8,000 pounds
   b. Material B: Beginning inventory, 1,000 pounds
      Purchased, 4,000 lbs. @ $2.00 = $8,000
      Issued to production, 3,100 pounds
2. Direct-labor payroll: 3,100 hours @ $3.50 = $10,850.
3. Overhead costs incurred:
   a. Variable, $6,500
   b. Fixed, $5,610
4. Budget data: Planned production for the month was 675,000 units.
5. Variance disposition: All variances are charged to the period of their incurrence.

required   1. Presentation at standard cost of:
       a. Abnormal spoilage
       b. Units transferred
       c. Ending work in process

2. Summary analysis of all variances, including detailed breakdown of direct-labor and overhead variances.

18-20. Redo Problem 18-11, using FIFO.

18-21. First-in, First-out Process Costing; Multiple Choice. The Meara Company uses a process-cost system (first-in, first-out) in costing its sole product. Materials for the product are added at the beginning of the operating cycle; conversion costs are assumed to accrue evenly over the cycle. Spoilage is detected by inspection upon completion of the product. Normally the spoiled units are equal to one-tenth of the good output.

At January 1, the inventory of work in process was 2,000 units of product, representing an average of three-fourths complete. The cost of these units was $32,200, being $17,000 for raw materials and $15,200 for conversion cost (direct labor and indirect cost). During January, 8,000 additional units of product were begun. During January, material cost of $64,000 was requisitioned from stores and charged to operations. Direct-labor costs for the month were $38,000. Indirect costs are assigned at the rate of 100 percent of direct-labor cost.

At January 31, the work in process consisted of 1,500 units of product, two-thirds complete. During the month, 7,200 units of good product were transferred to finished-goods stock after inspection.

Select the answer that correctly completes each of the following statements (identify your answer by letter). Support your overall answer with a production-cost report.

1. Units of normal spoilage amounted to:
    a. 580; b. 1,000; c. 950; d. 800; e. 720.
2. Units of abnormal spoilage amounted to:
    a. 950; b. 580; c. 1,000; d. 720; e. 800.
3. The total equivalent performance for material cost was:
    a. 10,000; b. 8,500; c. 9,500; d. 9,000; e. 8,000.
4. The total equivalent performance for conversion costs was:
    a. 8,000; b. 9,000; c. 8,500; d. 7,000; e. 7,500.
5. The equivalent unit cost for materials was:
    a. $8.00; b. $8.50; c. $6.40; d. $8.10; e. $8.25.
6. The cost of products transferred to finished goods was:
    a. $140,184; b. $138,550; c. $127,950; d. $108,350; e. $140, 550.

18-22. FIFO Process Costs; Lost Units [CPA]. The Biltimar Company manufactures gewgaws in three steps or departments. The finishing department is the third and last step before the product is transferred to finished-goods inventory.

All materials needed to complete the gewgaws are added at the beginning of the process in the finishing department, and lost units, if any, occur only at this point. The company uses the FIFO cost method in its accounting system and has accumulated the following data for July for the finishing department:

1. Production of gewgaws (in units):

In process, July 1 (labor and manufacturing expense three-fourths complete)	10,000
Transferred from preceding departments during July	40,000

Finished and transferred to finished-goods inventory during July	35,000
In process, July 31 (labor and manufacturing expense one-half complete)	10,000

2. Cost of work-in-process inventory, July 1:

Cost from preceding departments	$ 38,000
Costs added in finishing department prior to July 1:	
Materials	21,500
Labor	39,000
Manufacturing expense	42,000
Cost of work in process inventory, July 1	$140,500

3. Gewgaws transferred to the finishing department during July had costs of $140,000 assigned from preceding departments.

4. During July, the finishing department incurred the following production costs:

Materials	$ 70,000
Labor	162,500
Manufacturing expense	130,000
Total	$362,500

required

1. The cost of the gewgaws lost in production during July.

2. The cost of the gewgaws transferred to finished-goods inventory in July.

3. The cost of the work-in-process inventory at July 31.

18-23. Process Costs; Spoilage; FIFO and Weighted Average [CPA].   The King Process Company manufactures one product, processing it through two processes—No. 1 and No. 2.

For each unit of Process No. 1 output, 2 units of raw material X are put in *at the start* of the processing. For each unit of Process No. 2 output, 3 cans of raw material Y are put in *at the end* of processing. Two pounds of Process No. 1 output are placed in at the start of Process No. 2 for each unit of finished goods started.

Spoilage generally occurs in Process No. 2 when processing is approximately 50 percent complete.

In-process accounts are maintained for raw materials, conversion costs, and prior department costs.

The company uses FIFO basis for inventory valuation for Process No. 1 and finished goods, and average cost for inventory valuation for Process No. 2.

Data for March:

1. Units transferred: From Process No. 1 to Process No. 2   2,200 lbs.
                 From Process No. 2 to finished goods   900 gallons
                 From finished goods to cost of goods sold   600 gallons

2. Units spoiled in Process No. 2—100 gallons

3. Raw-material unit costs: X—$1.51 per unit; Y—$2.00 per can

4. Conversion costs: Process No. 1—$3,344; Process No. 2—$4,010

5. Spoilage recovery: $100 (treated as cost reduction)

6. Inventory data:

	PROCESS NO. 1		PROCESS NO. 2		FINISHED GOODS	
	INITIAL	FINAL	INITIAL	FINAL	INITIAL	FINAL
Units	200	300	200	300	700	1,000
Fraction complete conversion costs	½	⅓	½	⅔		
Valuation:					$13,300	
Materials	$560		0			
Conversion costs	$108		$ 390			
Prior-department costs			$2,200			

required   Journalize March entries to record the transfer of costs from Process No. 1 to Process No. 2, from Process No. 2 to finished goods, and from finished goods to cost of goods sold. Prepare schedules of computations to support your entries. Regard spoilage as normal spoilage.

18-24. **Process Costing, FIFO, Two Departments [CPA].**   The Crews Company produces a chemical agent for commercial use. The company accounts for production in two cost centers: (1) cooking and (2) mix–pack. In the first cost center, liquid substances are combined in large cookers and boiled; the boiling causes a normal decrease in volume from evaporation. After the "batch" is cooked, it is transferred to mix–pack, the second cost center. The "batch" then has a quantity of alcohol added equal to the liquid measure of the "batch," is mixed, and is bottled in one-gallon containers.

Material is added at the beginning of production in each cost center, and labor is added equally during production in each cost center. Overhead is applied on the basis of 80 percent of labor cost. The method of neglect is used in accounting for lost units (that is, all costs are allocated only to equivalent good units); the process is "in control" so long as the yield ratio for the first department is not less than 78 percent.

The FIFO method is used to cost work-in-process inventories, and transfers are at an average unit cost; that is, the total cost transferred divided by the total number of units transferred.

The following information is available for the month of October 19_7:

COST INFORMATION	COOKING	MIX–PACK
Work in process, October 1, 19_7		
Materials	$ 990	$ 120
Labor	100	60
Prior-department cost		426
Month of October		
Materials	39,600	15,276
Labor	10,050	16,000

Inventory and production records show that Cooking had 1,000 gallons 40 percent processed on October 1 and 800 gallons 50 percent processed on October 31; Mix–Pack had 600 gallons 50 percent processed on October 1 and 1,000 gallons 30 percent processed on October 31.

Production reports for October show that Cooking started 50,000 gallons into production and completed and transferred 40,200 gallons to Mix–Pack, and Mix–Pack completed and transferred 80,000 one-gallon containers of the finished product to the distribution warehouse.

required

1. Prepare in good form a quantity report for the cooking cost center and for the mix–pack cost center that accounts for both actual units and equivalent unit production.

2. Prepare in good form a production-cost report for each of the two cost centers that computes total cost and cost per unit for each element of cost in inventories and October production. Total cost and cost per unit for transfers should also be computed.

3. Compute the yield ratio for Cooking and state whether or not the process was "in control" during October.

19

Accounting
for Payroll

The tasks of accounting for payrolls are complicated by the necessity for withholding specified amounts from employee earnings, measuring costs of employment fringe benefits, and meeting the government requirements for taxation and regulation. There are three major problems: (a) distributing labor costs to functions, departments, and products; (b) accurately computing and promptly paying individual employees; and (c) computing and remitting withholdings and fringe benefits. Many of the aspects of classifying and controlling labor costs—point (a) above—have been covered previously (Chapters 4 and 8). This chapter will concentrate on other facets of payroll.

Individuals who are responsible for payroll accounting agree that, from the viewpoint of employees at least, promptness of payment and pinpoint accuracy are the foremost criteria for judging the merits of any payroll system. Whatever their educational level, be it twenty years of schooling or two, employees are excellent auditors of their own paychecks. Employees demand prompt and accurate payment, and they voice their dissatisfaction with vigor.

GOVERNMENT IMPACT

complexity of payroll accounting
Many years ago, an employee who earned $60 per week received $60 in cash on payday. The bookkeeping problems for payroll were relatively simple. Only two parties (employer and employee) were involved.

Nowadays, the data-processing problems of accounting for payroll are staggering, and the clerical expenses for payroll accounting have soared accordingly. The rash of withholdings, fringe benefits, and incentive pay schemes requires an intricate network of accounts and supporting documents. Accounting for payroll has become so voluminous that new machine or computer installations invariably handle payroll as one of their first routine tasks.

Government requirements regarding payroll records play a big role in systems and forms design. Exhibits 19-1 and 19-2 show some of the government's impact on payroll accounting. The government has at least two major influences: (a) it requires the employer to be its collecting agent for income taxes from employees and (b) it levies special payroll taxes on the employer.

withholding taxes
The employer must withhold ordinary income taxes plus a special income tax, commonly called the *Social Security tax*. Other terms for the Social Security tax are *federal insurance contributions act tax* (F.I.C.A. tax) and *federal old-age benefits tax* (F.O.A.B. tax). The timing of these tax payments to the government is shown in Exhibits 19-1 and 19-2. The basic journal-entry pattern is as follows:

Work-in-process control	120,000	
Factory-overhead control	30,000	
Selling-expense control	40,000	
Administrative-expense control	10,000	
Accrued payroll (gross)		200,000
Accrued payroll	35,000	
Withheld income taxes payable		29,000
Withheld F.I.C.A. taxes payable		6,000
Withheld income taxes payable	29,000	
Withheld F.I.C.A. taxes payable	6,000	
Cash (or some similar credit that has this ultimate effect on cash)		35,000

The entries above show that the *gross* payroll cost is the measure of the various basic labor costs incurred by the employer. The taxes *on employees* are withheld and remitted (usually monthly) to the government. Somehow this practice tends to make the pain of the tax bite seem less severe to the employee. Thus, the employer does not regard withheld taxes as an employer tax; instead, the employer performs a collection-agent service for the government.[1]

---

[1] Employees who have held jobs with two or more employers during a single year are entitled to a refund if excess F.I.C.A. taxes were withheld. For example, if the F.I.C.A. withholding rate is 6 percent and an employee earned $12,000 from one employer and $4,000 from another, each employer would legally have to withhold 6 percent of the first $9,000 paid. Therefore, this employee would be entitled to a refund as follows:

Employer 1	$.06 \times \$9,000 =$	$540
Employer 2	$.06 \times \$4,000 =$	240
Total withheld		$780
Taxable limit for individual:	$.06 \times \$9,000 =$	540
Excess F.I.C.A. tax withheld		$240

His claim would be filed on his own individual income tax return. His W-2 forms would be evidence in support of his claim.

The employer is not entitled to any refund.

EXHIBIT 19-1

U.S.A. PAYROLLS AND TAXES

TAX	RATE	BASIS FOR COMPUTATION	DATE OF FILING FORM	PERIOD COVERED
Federal income tax on employees	Depends on gross earnings and dependents	Gross earnings paid	On or before end of month following close of calendar quarter	Calendar quarters supplemented by a reconciliation at year-end
F.I.C.A. tax on employees	1972: 5.2% 1973–1975: 5.4%	First $9,000 of gross earnings paid to each employee	Same as above— Form 941	Calendar quarters
F.I.C.A. tax on employers	Same as above	First $9,000 of gross earnings paid to each employee	Same as above— Form 941	Calendar quarters
State unemployment insurance tax on employers*	Generally 2.7%, but may vary from .2% to 4%, depending on various state merit-rating systems for employer's labor turnover experience	First $3,000 of gross earnings paid to each employee†	Same as above— Special state form	Calendar quarters
Federal unemployment insurance tax on employers	Generally, effective rate is .4% (3.1% nominal rate less 2.7% rate credit for state unemployment tax payments)	Same as above†	January 31—Form 940	Previous calendar year
State workmen's compensation insurance (or tax) on employers	Varies for different occupational classifications	Gross earnings paid	If insured by private company, annual premium is usually paid in advance. If taxed by state, same due-date provisions apply as for state unemployment tax.	

*A few states also have an employee unemployment tax.
†Employers are not subject to tax unless they have four or more employees for at least one day a week for 20 weeks in a calendar year.

other withholdings A flock of other withholdings from employees also exists. Withholdings as such are not employer costs. They are merely slices of the employee's gross earnings that are being funneled via the employer to third parties, primarily for the employee's convenience. Examples include employee contributions to group life insurance plans, hospitalization insurance, pension funds, employee savings plans, donations, and union dues.

FRINGE BENEFITS

large size of fringe benefits The gross earnings of employees are only nominal measures of the payroll costs really borne. The employer must not only pay payroll taxes like old-age and unemployment levies; he must also incur many more fringe costs. The following breakdown of payroll costs illustrates the general pattern:

Gross earnings of employee (Assume $9,000.)	100.00%
Federal old-age tax on employers (Rate based on average employee earnings of $9,000. Tax would be, say, 5.2%.)	5.20
Federal unemployment tax (.4% of $3,000, or $12. Divide $12 by $9,000.)	.13
State unemployment tax (2.7% of $3,000, or $81. Divide $81 by $9,000.)	.90
Workmen's compensation tax (Rates vary with hazards; average rate shown.)	1.50
Vacations and paid holidays (10 days' vacation and 7 holidays. Divide 17 by 260 days' pay.)	6.20
Minimum total for most employers	113.93%
Add:	
Employer contributions to pension funds (average rate)	5.00
Employer contributions to health, life, and other insurance, etc. (average rate)	3.00
Employer contributions to guaranteed annual wage funds (average rate)	2.50
Total cost incurred by many employers	124.43%

These figures demonstrate that fringe costs are no longer a little dribble; their waterfall proportions have caused an increasing number of companies to recast their account classifications. Instead of treating all fringe costs as overhead, some companies add an average (that is, "equalized" or "leveled") fringe rate to the basic direct-labor rate to bring into focus a better measure of direct-labor costs. This leveled rate is computed as shown in the table above. However, perhaps because of inertia, most companies continue to treat fringe costs as a part of overhead.

timing of cost recognition As in many other phases of accounting, there is often a time lag between incurrence and payment of various payroll fringe costs. For example, the liability for vacation payments really accrues from week to week as each

EXHIBIT 19-2

CALENDAR OF EMPLOYER'S OBLIGATIONS UNDER U.S.A. FEDERAL LAW

	FORM NUMBER
WHEN HIRING	
Get withholding exemption certificate.	W-4
Get Social Security number. If employee has no account number, he should file application on	SS-5
WHEN PAYING	
Withhold both income taxes and F.I.C.A. taxes.	
By end of April, July, October, and January:	
File combined return for all F.I.C.A. taxes and withheld income taxes covering the quarter ending with the prior month. For example, the first calendar quarter's return must be filed by April 30.	941
By January 31 and at termination of employment:	
Give each employee a withholding statement in duplicate showing F.I.C.A. earnings and withholdings, total earnings subject to income tax withholdings, and income tax withheld.	W-2
By January 31:	
File reconciliation of quarterly returns	W-3
—plus collector's copy of all individual W-2's given to employees for prior year	W-2a
File annual return and pay unemployment tax	940

employee accumulates his claim to vacation pay. Thus, many companies use an estimate to spread total vacation costs over a year instead of recognizing such costs as payments are made:

Work-in-process control (direct labor)	19,000	
Factory-overhead control (indirect labor plus $1,000 vacation pay)	7,000	
Estimated liability for vacation pay		1,000
Accrued payroll		25,000

To accrue vacation pay throughout the year because it is related to work done throughout the year.

Leveled rate is 4% of Accrued Payroll. Entry here is, say, for January:

Accrued payroll	25,000	
Estimated liability for vacation pay	300	
Cash		22,000
Withholdings payable (various)		3,300

The accrued vacation pay is debited as vacation payments are made.

Similar treatment can be given to bonus plans, holiday pay, contributions to pension funds, and contributions to guaranteed annual wage funds. The decision to adopt such leveling arrangements in accounting for fringe costs largely depends on the significance of the amounts involved and on the distortion of month-to-month costs that may arise from failure to spread charges over the year.

EMPLOYER PAYROLL TAXES: THEORY AND PRACTICE

At this writing, employers must pay old-age taxes on the first $9,000, and unemployment taxes on the first $3,000, paid to each employee every calendar year. In most cases, this means that heavier tax outlays will be made in the earlier months of the calendar year than in the later months, because the employer liability diminishes as wage payments to an increasing number of employees gradually reach and pass the yearly statutory taxable-wage limit.

The problem of timing charges for employer payroll taxes raises some special theoretical questions. The employer's legal liability is ordinarily a function of wages *paid* rather than of wages *accrued*. Yet in practice, employer payroll taxes are usually accrued as wages are *earned*. Furthermore, such payroll tax accrual diminishes as months pass because more and more employees' earnings gradually surpass the maximum taxable limit.[2]

To illustrate, assume that a company has a gross payroll of $25,000 per month, $16,000 of which is direct labor. Assume that the tax rate on employers is .4 percent for federal unemployment, 2.7 percent for state unemployment, and 5.9 percent for old-age benefits, a total payroll tax rate of 9 percent.

Early months: Work-in-process control	16,000	
Factory-overhead control ($9,000 plus $2,250)	11,250	
Accrued payroll		25,000
Employer's payroll taxes payable		2,250
Payroll tax is .09 × $25,000 = $2,250.		
Late months: Work-in-process control	16,000	
Factory-overhead control	9,000	
Accrued payroll		25,000
Payroll is not subject to payroll tax because every employee's salary has passed the maximum taxable limits.		

In theory, employer payroll taxes (a) should be accrued as wages are earned (this practice is widely followed), and (b) should be spread over the year, using a leveled rate. Thus, payroll taxes would be handled in a fashion similar to the previous illustration on vacation pay. The reasoning in support of spreading payroll taxes over the year is that, for a going concern, the commitment to hire employees is made for a year; the payroll tax is an annual tax that is related to the year as a whole. Because it benefits the entire year's operations, such a tax should not be loaded on the early months of the calendar year. In practice, the additional clerical costs and complications often outweigh any informational advantages of this more refined approach. Therefore, early months bear the brunt of payroll tax charges.

ILLUSTRATION OF PAYROLL ACCOUNTING

example   The Stengal Company has a gross payroll of $1,000 per day, based on a five-day, forty-hour, Monday-through-Friday workweek. Withholdings for income taxes

---

[2]Conceivably, in some companies, if no new workers are hired in November or December, the employer may show no payroll tax costs for these months.

amount to $100 per day. Payrolls for each week are paid on the following Tuesday.

Gross payrolls consist of $600 direct labor, $200 indirect labor, $140 selling expense, and $60 administrative expenses each day. The general-ledger entry to record the total of the payroll cost incurred (including accrued employer payroll fringe costs) is made on the last day of each month. Fringe costs borne by the employer are:

	PERCENT OF GROSS PAYROLL
Vacation pay	4.0%
F.I.C.A. tax	5.9%
Federal unemployment tax	0.4%
State unemployment tax	2.7%
	13.0%

For our purposes, assume that the company starts business on March 3.

MARCH						
S	M	T	W	T	F	S
						1
2	3	4	5	6	7	8
9	10	11	12	13	14	15
16	17	18	19	20	21	22
23	24	25	26	27	28	29
30	31					

APRIL						
S	M	T	W	T	F	S
		1	2	3	4	5
6	7	8	9	10	11	12
13	14	15	16	17	18	19
20	21	22	23	24	25	26
27	28	29	30			

Try to solve by yourself before examining the solution. (Exhibit 19-1 contains some helpful information.)

required

1. All general-journal payroll entries for March 11, 18, 25, and 31, April 1, 8, 15, 22, 29, and 30.

2. All postings to Accrued payroll, Employees' income taxes payable, Employees' F.I.C.A. taxes payable, and Employer's F.I.C.A. taxes payable.

SOLUTION 1. Journal entries follow:

March 11	Accrued payroll (5 × $1,000)	5,000.00	
	Cash		4,205.00
	Employees' income taxes payable (assume 5 × $100)		500.00
	Employees' F.I.C.A. taxes payable (.059 × $5,000)		295.00
	To pay payroll.		

The identical entry would be repeated every Tuesday, March 18 through April 29. Note that payroll settlements are made every *payday*, regardless of when payroll costs are recognized as being incurred.

March 31	Work-in-process control (21 days × $600)	12,600.00	
	Factory-overhead control (21 × $200) + .13(21 × $200) + .13($12,600)	6,384.00	
	Selling-expense control (21 × $140) + .13(21 × $140)	3,322.20	
	Administrative-expense control (21 × $60) + .13(21 × $60)	1,423.80	
	Accrued payroll (21 days × $1,000)		21,000.00
	Estimated liability for vacation pay (.04 × $21,000)		840.00
	Employer's F.I.C.A. taxes payable (.059 × $21,000)		1,239.00
	Federal unemployment taxes payable (.004 × $21,000)		84.00
	State unemployment taxes payable (.027 × $21,000)		567.00

Such an entry is usually made and posted monthly. If desired, it could be made weekly, biweekly, or at any other interval. As contrasted with the previous entry, this entry recognizes cost incurrence rather than payment. Its measurements depend on the number of work days in a calendar month.

(Note that the entries on *paydays* are the same for April as for March.)

April 30	Work-in-process control (22 × $600)	13,200.00	
	Factory-overhead control (22 × $200) + .13(22 × $200) + .13($13,200)	6,688.00	
	Selling-expense control (22 × $140) + .13(22 × $140)	3,480.40	
	Administrative-expense control (22 × $60) + .13(22 × $60)	1,491.60	
	Accrued payroll (22 × $1,000)		22,000.00
	Estimated liability for vacation pay (.04 × $22,000)		880.00
	Employer's F.I.C.A. taxes payable (.059 × $22,000)		1,298.00
	Federal unemployment taxes payable (.004 × $22,000)		88.00
	State unemployment taxes payable (.027 × $22,000)		594.00

The entry above is based on 22 days of work done in April.

April 30	Employees' income taxes payable (3 paydays × $500)	1,500.00	
	Employees' F.I.C.A. taxes payable (3 × $295)	885.00	
	Employer's F.I.C.A. taxes payable (3 × $295)	885.00	
	Cash		3,270.00
	Payment of taxes withheld on *paydays* in March plus employer's matching of F.I.C.A. taxes withheld.		

These taxes are detailed on Form 941, a quarterly return. Legal liability arises as payroll is paid during a calendar quarter rather than as payroll is accrued. Compare, for example, the employer's F.I.C.A. taxes accrued as of March 31 ($1,239) with the amount remitted with this return ($885). This difference represents six days' cost in March ($59 per day × 6 days) that was not paid with this quarterly return. It will be paid during a subsequent period.

April 30   State unemployment taxes payable
   (.027 × $5,000 × 3 paydays in March)   405.00
         Cash   405.00
   Payment to state for legal liability for
   first calendar quarter.

2. Postings to certain accounts for March and April follow:

ACCRUED PAYROLL

March 11	5,000		
March 18	5,000		
March 25	5,000		
To balance	6,000	March 31	21,000
		March 31 balance, six days' gross earnings	6,000
April 1	5,000		
April 8	5,000		
April 15	5,000		
April 22	5,000		
April 29	5,000	April 30	22,000
To balance	3,000		
		April 30 balance, three days' gross earnings	3,000

Employees' Income Taxes Payable				Employees' F.I.C.A. Taxes Payable			
		March 11,18,25	1,500			March 11,18,25	885
April 30	1,500	April 22,29	2,500	April 30	885	April 1,8, 15,22,29	1,475

Employer's F.I.C.A. Taxes Payable			
		March 31	1,239
		April 30	1,298
April 30	885		

A study of the T-accounts above shows the following:

(1) The Accrued Payroll balance at the close of business on March 31 represents the unpaid amount of *gross* earnings of employees applicable to the last six days worked in March.

(2) The timing of recognition of liability for employees' and employer's F.I.C.A. taxes differs. Legally, both liabilities arise when payroll is paid. But the employer accrues his liability when he recognizes regular labor-cost incurrence, because such payroll taxes are basically related to time of *earnings* rather than to time of *payout*.

INCENTIVE PLANS

objective of incentives Most employees are paid a flat salary or a flat rate per hour, but wage incentive systems are widespread. Incentive plans provide extra compensation for performance that is superior to some predetermined goal or standard. The wide variety of factory incentive systems has a common objective: minimization of total costs for a given volume of production. In other words, the sweetening of the pay envelope must at least be balanced by reductions in other cost factors or by reductions in labor cost per unit. For example, assume that a worker is paid $2.00 an hour and produces 10 units in that time. He is placed on a strict piece-rate system at a rate of 18¢ per piece. His productivity may increase to 12 units per hour. His earnings would then be $2.16 per hour (12 × 18¢)—higher pay per worker and yet less cost per unit for the employer. A piece rate of 21¢ or more may even be desirable for the employer, if savings in other costs like materials, power, repairs, or other variable-overhead items can offset increased labor costs.

Incentive plans are not panaceas for problems of cost control. They add to clerical costs and may tend to increase spoilage costs and lessen quality. Yet many companies have been pleased with overall results. In any event, no incentive plan can substitute for adequate management as the most effective means of controlling labor costs.

accounting for incentive plans Incentive plans vary widely in their details and application. The Gantt Task and Bonus Plan awards a higher piece rate, or bonus, for all production in excess of standard. The Taylor Differential Piece-Rate System applies a higher piece rate for *all* production per hour or day as long as the hourly or daily production standard is met. Incentive plans may be arranged to reward individual performance, group performance, assembly-line performance, and even plant-wide performance.

A common incentive plan is piecework coupled with a guaranteed minimum hourly rate. Thus, if the standard number of pieces per hour is not produced, pay is provided to "make up" the difference between the guaranteed rate and the piecework earnings. An example of computations follows:

DAILY EARNINGS SUMMARY*

CLOCK NUMBER	NAME	DEPARTMENT	OPERATION	UNITS PRODUCED	PIECE RATE	PIECEWORK EARNINGS	MAKEUP	TOTAL EARNINGS
414	Atwood	4	1004	500	$.04	$20.00	$—	$20.00
445	Barnes	4	1004	330	.04	13.20	2.80	16.00
446	Charnes	4	1004	400	.04	16.00	—	16.00

* Guaranteed rate is $2.00 per hour or $16.00 per day.

Makeup pay would be charged to the department as an overhead item and would be part of the department's overhead budget. The standard labor cost for the operation would be 4¢ per unit.

PAYROLL BANK ACCOUNT

Companies with many employees usually use a separate checking account to keep payroll checks apart from checks for other disbursements. This facilitates control, preparation, and reconciliation of vast numbers of payroll checks. The general working of a payroll bank account is as follows:

Accrued payroll	10,000	
Withholdings payable		1,500
Cash (in regular checking account)		8,500

A single $8,500 check is drawn against the company's general bank account to cover the net payroll. The bank would transfer $8,500 from the general-deposit account to a special payroll account. Assume that there are 100 employees. One hundred payroll checks totaling $8,500 would be prepared and issued. The size, color, and numerical sequence of these checks would differ from those of the general checks. Note that, as far as this company is concerned, its payroll bank account should always have a zero balance. Any balance in the payroll account as shown by the bank represents outstanding payroll checks.[3]

summary

Payroll accounting is overwhelmed with detail, much of which is kept because of legal requirements rather than because of managerial needs.

The data-processing function is often divided between cost distribution and payouts to employees. Although electronic data processing increasingly accomplishes these objectives simultaneously, most companies distribute costs on one time basis (for example, monthly in the general ledger, daily in subsidiary records) and account for payouts on another time basis (for example, weekly).

Problem for Self-Study

Review the problem used as an illustration in the chapter.

questions, problems, and cases

19-1. "Accounting for payroll embraces plenty of big problems." Name three.

19-2. "The need for accuracy in payroll accounting is paramount." Explain.

[3]The use of special bank accounts is not confined to payrolls. They can also be used for dividends, commissions, royalties, and so forth.

19-3. "The government has at least two major influences on payroll accounting." What are they?

19-4. Name the major taxes associated with payrolls.

19-5. George Ripon worked for three employers during a year. His gross earnings were $1,000, $7,800, and $1,500—a total of $10,300.
a. How much of the earnings should each employer regard as subject to F.I.C.A. taxes?
b. How much of Ripon's earnings should he regard as subject to F.I.C.A. taxes?

19-6. "The Federal Unemployment Insurance Tax rate is 0.4%." Do you agree? Why?

19-7. Identify the following forms: W-4, 941, W-2, W-3, 940.

19-8. "Withheld taxes are taxes on employers." Do you agree? Why?

19-9. Name four common withholdings other than taxes.

19-10. "Payroll fringe costs are large enough these days to justify adding an average fringe rate to the basic direct-labor rate." Do you agree? Why?

19-11. "Leveling or averaging of vacation costs and holiday pay is used to relate them to work done throughout the year." What criteria should affect the decision to adopt such leveling arrangements?

19-12. "Conceivably, in some companies an employer may show no payroll tax costs for the last quarter of the year." Why? Explain.

19-13. Contrast the theoretical and practical accounting treatments of employer payroll taxes.

19-14. If all bookkeeping is up to date, what does the balance in Accrued Payroll represent?

19-15. "The timing of recognition of liability for employees' and employer's F.I.C.A. taxes differs." Explain.

19-16. What are incentive plans? What is their objective?

19-17. What is "makeup"? How is it accounted for?

19-18. A company uses a separate payroll bank account. Weekly wage payments are $10,000. A $1,000 minimum balance is kept to provide for salary advances, separation payments, and so forth. What cash balance should ordinarily be shown on the company balance sheets?

19-19. Briefly describe how EDP can affect conventional payroll procedures.

19-20. Unemployment Compensation Taxes [CPA]. The cost of unemployment compensation taxes to an employer is sometimes reduced as a result of a "good" experience rating. A manufacturer negotiated with the federal government a contract that necessitated the construction of a specific plant and related facilities for the sole purpose of producing the goods called for in the contract. Because the goods were required to meet emergency needs of the government, it was possible that after the plant facilities were constructed, the employees hired, and work on the order begun, the contract would be cancelled. The ensuing termination of services of employees hired for this specific job would make the employer's experience rating worse, which in turn would increase the cost of his unemployment compensation taxes. This "possible" cost was recognized as a cost in negotiating the contract.

Describe in order of preference three alternate methods of recording in accounts and/or disclosing on the financial statements the "possible" cost during the course of operations of this emergency plant under the contract. State your reasons.

19-21. **Accounting for Idle Time.**   [Prepared by James H. March] The labor distribution of the Dunne Desk Company is made from its payroll, all the wages of its twenty shop employees, except the foreman's, being treated as direct labor. The company pays for idle time of workmen caused by material shortages, and this amounts to a substantial portion of the payroll.

For the year 19_1, the direct labor, according to the ledger, was $20,000 and the overhead $16,000. Accordingly, an overhead rate of 80 percent was used in 19_2 for the purpose of estimating costs of new products. The manager thinks that the estimates are wrong, for his income statement shows a gross margin of only $1 a desk, whereas his selling prices are at least $5 a desk above the estimated costs. He suspects that the idle-time factor is not being included in the cost estimates, and he asks you to investigate the situation.

1. How would you proceed to determine whether the manager's suspicions are correct?

2. Recompute the overhead rate for 19_1 on the assumption that $2,000 was paid for idle time that should be treated as overhead instead of as direct labor.

3. Suggest a change in the method of labor-cost allocation that would result in a more accurate accounting for idle time.

19-22. **Group Incentives [SIA, adapted].**   The Smart Company of Hong Kong operates with five direct workers in its stamping department. All work is done on a job-order basis. During the week of August 15, each man worked a full 40-hour week, with output as follows:

NAME	GUARANTEED HOURLY MINIMUM	UNITS PRODUCED
Brackett, S. J.	$1.50	1,840
Emery, P. L.	1.60	1,900
Evans, E. C.	1.50	1,960
Forest, T. A.	1.70	2,050
Simmons, F.	1.50	1,650

required

1. Compute the gross earnings of each worker, assuming that a group incentive plan is in operation and that the standard output of the department is 7,200 units per week. Each member of the group receives the guaranteed hourly minimum if production is equal to or less than the standard output. The hourly rate for each worker is increased 1 percent for each 200 units per week in excess of standard production.

2. What effect does excess of "normal" or "standard" output have on the unit cost of production? Explain.

3. Assess the effectiveness of this incentive system for the Smart Company, giving reasons for your answer.

19-23. **Incentive Wage Plans [CPA, adapted].**   During your audit of the accounts of the Gelard Manufacturing Corporation, your assistant tells you that he has found errors in the computation of the wages of factory workers and he wants you to verify his work.

Your assistant has extracted from the union contract the following description of the systems for computing wages in various departments of the company. The contract provides that the minimum wage for a worker is his base rate, which is also paid for any "downtime"—time when the worker's machine is under repair or he is without work. The standard workweek is 40 hours. The union contract also provides that workers be paid 150 percent of base rates for overtime production. The company is engaged in interstate commerce.

1. *Straight piecework.* The worker is paid at the rate of $.20 per piece produced.
2. *Percentage bonus plan.* Standard quantities of production per hour are established by the engineering department. The worker's average hourly production, determined from his total hours worked and his production, is divided by the standard quantity of production to determine his efficiency ratio. The efficiency ratio is then applied to his base rate to determine his hourly earnings for the period.
3. *Emerson Efficiency System.* A minimum wage is paid for production up to $66\frac{2}{3}$ percent of standard output or "efficiency." When the worker's production exceeds $66\frac{2}{3}$ percent of the standard output, he is paid at a bonus rate. The bonus rate is determined from the following table:

EFFICIENCY	BONUS
Up to 66⅔%	0%
66⅔–79%	10%
80–99%	20%
100–125%	45%

Your assistant has prepared the following schedule of information pertaining to certain workers for a weekly payroll selected for examination:

WORKER	WAGE INCENTIVE PLAN	TOTAL HOURS	DOWN-TIME HOURS	UNITS PRODUCED	STANDARD UNITS	BASE RATE	GROSS WAGES PER BOOKS
Long	Straight piecework	40	5	400	—	$1.80	$ 82.00
Loro	Straight piecework	46	—	455[a]	—	1.80	91.00
Huck	Straight piecework	44	4	420[b]	—	1.80	84.00
Nini	Percentage bonus plan	40	—	250	200	2.20	120.00
Boro	Percentage bonus plan	40	—	180	200	1.90	67.00
Wiss	Emerson	40	—	240	300	2.10	92.00
Alan	Emerson	40	2	590	600[c]	2.00	118.00

[a] Includes 45 pieces produced during the 6 overtime hours.
[b] Includes 50 pieces produced during the 4 overtime hours. The overtime, which was brought about by the "downtime," was necessary to meet a production deadline.
[c] Standard units for 40 hours' production.

required Prepare a schedule comparing each individual's gross wages per books and his gross wages per your calculation. Computations of workers' wages should be in good form and labeled with the workers' names.

19-24. Journal Entries for Payroll. The Stable Company operates the year around with a gross payroll of $500 a day. Withholdings for Social Security taxes and federal income taxes amount to $100 a day. The concern works five days a week, and the payroll period covers Monday to Friday, both inclusive. Payrolls for the week are paid on the following Tuesday.

Gross payrolls consist of $300 direct labor, $100 indirect labor, $70 selling expense, and $30 general and administrative expense each day. The general-ledger entry to record the total of the payroll cost incurred each month is made on the last day of the month. These totals are obtained by summarizing the Payroll Cost Recapitulation sheets. This firm uses a "leveled" percentage of 4 percent to estimate its own contribution to Social Security.

required

Using the calendar above as a guide, answer the following questions:

APRIL

S	M	TU	W	TH	F	SAT
		1	2	3	4	5
6	7	8	9	10	11	12
13	14	15	16	17	18	19
20	21	22	23	24	25	26
27	28	29	30			

1. What is the balance in Accrued Payroll as of the close of business on March 31?

What journal entries should be made on:

2. April 1?

3. April 29?

4. April 30?

5. What is the ending balance in Accrued Payroll as of the close of business on April 30?

19-25. **Journal Entries for Payroll.** [Prepared by James H. March] The balance of the Accrued Wages of Kem Industries, Inc., was $12,120 on October 31, 19_1. The company has a job-order cost system. The cost accounts are in the general ledger. Time tickets for pay periods falling wholly or partly in November are summarized as follows:

PAY PERIOD	DIRECT LABOR	FACTORY OVERHEAD	TOTAL
Nov. 1–7	$8,250	$4,510	$12,760
Nov. 8–14	8,450	4,490	12,940
Nov. 15–21	8,570	4,570	13,140
Nov. 22–28	7,920	4,060	11,980
Nov. 29–Dec. 5	8,430	4,470	12,900

Of the wages earned in the pay period ending December 5, one-third is applicable to November.

Payrolls for pay periods ending in November are summarized as follows:

| PAY PERIOD ENDING | GROSS EARNINGS | DEDUCTIONS | | NET PAY |
		F.I.C.A.	INCOME TAX	
Oct. 31	$12,120	$110	$1,200	$10,810
Nov. 7	12,760	108	1,250	11,402
Nov. 14	12,940	112	1,280	11,548
Nov. 21	13,140	102	1,300	11,738
Nov. 28	11,980	95	1,200	10,685

The payroll for the period ending November 28 was paid December 2.

required

1. Journal entry for labor-cost allocation.
2. Journal entry for payrolls paid in November.
3. Postings in the Accrued Wages account.
4. Journal entry for accrual of employers' payroll taxes for the month of November at a leveled rate of 5 percent of gross earnings.
5. Answer the following questions:
   a. Theoretically, should the accrual of employers' payroll taxes be based on wages earned or on wages paid during the month?
   b. Why is the amount of F.I.C.A. deductions less than 1 percent of the gross earnings?
   c. What does the balance of Accrued Wages represent?

Journal explanations in all cases should state clearly how you arrived at your amounts.

20

Accounting Systems and Internal Control

This book has already emphasized many planning and control features of accounting systems. This chapter will concentrate on some features not previously covered, such as internal control and the impact of computers.

The accounting system is intertwined with operating management. Accounting records are kept not only because they are needed to tally performance for later appraisal and for income determination, but also because business operations would be a hopeless tangle without the paperwork that is so often regarded with disdain. For example, receivables and payables must be recorded, and cash receipts and disbursements must be traced to these and other accounts, or else confusion would ensue. The act of recording events has become as much a part of operating activities as the act of selling or buying. Even the simplest of businesses must have a minimum of records, a semblance of routine. As businesses become more complex, managers find themselves increasingly dependent on the systematic compilation of records for keeping informed and for help with planning and control.

The size of the physical handling of records is often staggering. For example, in 1972 a major oil company processed 15 million pieces of paper monthly just to handle its credit-card business. This illustrates one overwhelming feature of a total system: the voluminous data-processing procedures that tend to require a minimum of human judgment and that lend themselves to routine procedures. Other examples are check handling, payroll accounting, production scheduling, inventory control, and automated manufacturing. The accountant's role in these routine situations is largely one of scorekeeping.

Recent revolutionary changes in processing business data have been so extensive that a specific system is likely to be outdated by the time its description is off the press. That is why this chapter describes the general features of an internal control system that have wide applicability to a variety of organizations, regardless of their specific systems. The aim here is not to develop skills in auditing. Rather, it is to create an awareness on the part of the manager and the management accountant of the importance of the problem and of some general approaches to its solution. The prime responsibility for internal control rests with the managers themselves, not their accountants.

INTERNAL CONTROL: DEFINITION

Previous chapters have covered numerous features of an accounting system, such as the need for the following: timely data; competent accounting personnel who encourage the respect, confidence, cooperation, and cost-consciousness of operating managers; and constant search for improvement of the accounting system. The feature of *internal control* has not yet received direct attention.

Internal control is defined by the American Institute of Certified Public Accountants as follows:

> Internal control comprises the plan of organization and all of the coordinate methods and measures adopted within a business to safeguard its assets, check the accuracy and reliability of its accounting data, promote operational efficiency, and encourage adherence to prescribed managerial policies.[1]

The most important phrase in this definition is "promote operational efficiency." Internal control may be visualized as being much more inclusive than *internal check*,[2] which is confined to checking "the accuracy and reliability of its accounting data." Accounting is an essential instrument in maintaining and enhancing internal control. Still, internal control is a management function, not an accounting function. Another look at the definition will show it to be merely an elaboration of a broad objective of managerial *control:* attaining adherence to plans.

This book has already described the features of systems and procedures that promote effectiveness and efficiency (budgets, standards, responsibility accounting, and so forth). *In its broadest sense, internal control embraces all these accounting techniques.* This chapter will highlight those aspects of internal control that minimize errors, fraud, and waste.

All good systems of internal control have certain features in common. These features may be termed a checklist of internal control, which may be used to appraise any procedure for cash, purchases, sales, payroll, and the like. This checklist may sometimes be called *principles* or *rules.*

---

[1] Committee on Auditing Procedure, *Auditing Standards and Procedures* (New York: American Institute of Certified Public Accountants, 1963), p. 27.

[2] In practice, however, the words *internal control* and *internal check* are often used interchangeably, so that many accountants regard internal control narrowly as being those characteristics of an accounting system that are designed to minimize errors, fraud, and waste.

CHECKLIST FOR INTERNAL CONTROL

No framework for internal control is perfect in the sense that it can prevent some shrewd individual from "beating the system" either by outright embezzlement or by producing inaccurate records. The task is not total prevention of fraud, nor is it implementation of operating perfection; rather, the task is the designing of a tool that will help achieve efficient operations and reduce temptation. Also, the most streamlined accounting system is deficient if its prescribed procedures are not being conscientiously followed.

A checklist for a good internal control system[3] includes:

1. Reliable personnel. Individuals obviously should be given duties and responsibilities commensurate with their abilities, interests, experience, and reliability. Yet many employers use low-cost talent that may prove exceedingly expensive in the long run, not only from the point of view of fraud but also from the point of view of productivity. The accounting system, no matter how elaborate, is only as good as the individuals who implement it.

2. Separation of powers. Record keeping and physical handling of assets should not be in the hands of one person. For example, the bookkeeper should not handle cash, and the cashier should not have access to ledger accounts such as subsidiary receivable records. The general-ledger bookkeeper should not have access to subsidiary records. The entire accounting function should be divorced from operating departments, so that objective, independent records may be kept, either by other operating people (for example, inspectors, not machine operators, should count good pieces) or by accounting clerks (for example, stores record clerks, not storekeepers, should keep perpetual inventory counts). This point not only better insures accurate compilation of data; it also necessitates collusion of two or more persons to perpetrate a fraud.

3. Supervision. The typical organization chart illustrates this point. Everyone has a boss who oversees and appraises performance.

4. Responsibility. This means tracking actions as far down in the organization as is feasible, so that results may be related to individuals. It means having salesclerks sign sales slips, inspectors initial packing slips, and workmen sign time cards and requisitions. The psychological impact of fixing responsibility promotes care and efficiency; it keeps people on their toes. Individuals tend to perform better when they must answer for inefficiencies.

The accumulation of costs by department would be impossible without some means of fixing responsibility for cost incurrence.

5. Routine and automatic checks. In a phrase, this means doing things "by the numbers." Just as manufacturing activities tend to be made more efficient by the division and specialization of repetitive activities, so can record-keeping

[3] Also see William J. Vatter, *Managerial Accounting* (Englewood Cliffs, N.J.: Prentice-Hall, Inc., 1950), Chapter 11, for his ten principles of internal control, most of which are described here.

activities be made less costly and more accurate. Repetitive procedures may be prescribed for nonmanufacturing activities such as order taking, order filling, collating, and inspecting. The use of general routines permits specialization of effort, division of duties, and automatic checks on previous steps in the routine.

For example, disbursement-voucher systems are widely used in industry. The essential feature of such a system is that no checks may be signed without a disbursement voucher that so authorizes. In turn, the voucher will not be prepared unless all supporting documents, such as pertinent requisitions, purchase orders, invoices, receiving reports, and freight documents, have been reviewed. Each step in the review serves as a check on previous steps.

Forms are designed so that the absence or incorrectness of key information is automatically uncovered and corrected on the spot. For example, the absence of a receiving clerk's signature on a receiving report would halt preparation of a disbursement voucher, and the omission of a foreman's signature prevents payments of overtime pay.

6. Document control. This means immediate recording, complete recording, and tamper-proof recording. This point is especially important for handling cash sales. Devices used to insure immediate recording include cash registers with loud bells and compiling tapes, private detectives, guaranteeing "rewards" to customers if they are not offered a receipt at the time of sale, and forcing clerks to make change by pricing items at $1.99, $2.99, and $3.99 rather than at $2, $3, and $4.[4]

Complete and tamper-proof recording is encouraged by having all source documents prenumbered and accounted for, by using devices such as cash registers and locked compartments in invoice-writing machines, and by designing forms for ease of recording.

7. Bonding, vacations, and rotation of duties. Key people may be subject to excessive temptation; top executives, branch managers, and individuals who handle cash or inventories should be bonded, have understudies, and be forced to take vacations.

A facet of this idea is also illustrated by the common practice of having receivables and payables clerks periodically rotated in duties. Thus, a receivables clerk may handle accounts from A to C for three months and then be rotated to accounts M to P for three months, and so forth.

8. Independent check. All phases of the system should be subjected to periodic review by outsiders (for example, by independent public accountants) and by internal auditors who do not ordinarily have contact with the operation under review.

The idea of independent check extends beyond the work performed by professional auditors. For example, bank statements should be reconciled with book balances. The bank provides an independent record of cash. Furthermore,

---

[4]Historically, such pricing was originally adopted to force clerks to make change as well as for its psychological impact on potential customers.

the monthly bank reconciliations should be conducted by some clerk other than the cash, receivables, or payables clerk. Other examples of independent checks include monthly statements sent to credit customers and physical counts of inventory to check against perpetual records.

One of the main jobs of internal auditors and outside auditors is to appraise the effectiveness of internal control; such appraisal affects the extent of the sampling of transactions needed to test validity of account balances.

9. Physical safeguards.   Obviously, losses of cash, inventories, and records are minimized by safes, locks, watchmen, and limited access.

10. Cost feasibility.   The complexity and costs of an internal control system must be compared with its benefits. Highly complex systems tend to strangle people in red tape, so that the system impedes rather than promotes efficiency. Besides, there is "a cost of keeping the costs" that sometimes gets out of hand. Investments in more costly systems must be judged in the light of expected benefits. Unfortunately, such benefits are difficult to measure. It is much easier to relate new lathes or production methods to cost savings in manufacturing than a new computer to cost savings in the form of facilitating new attacks on problems of inventory control, production scheduling, and research. Yet hard-headed efforts, as are used in making other business decisions, must be made to measure alternative costs of various accounting systems.

Although many companies implement more complex procedures to improve internal control, a few have taken a reverse course. They have decided that the increased costs of additional scrutiny are not worth the expected savings from catching mistakes or crooks. For example, an aerospace manufacturer routinely pays the invoice amounts without checking supporting documentation except on a random-sampling basis. An aluminum company sends out a blank check with its purchase orders, and then the supplier fills out the check and deposits it.

ILLUSTRATIONS

McKesson & Robbins fraud: the limitations of systems   A fraud case that had a big and lasting impact on auditing procedures was the infamous McKesson & Robbins embezzlement of the 1930's. The president engineered a complicated fraud in collusion with the assistant treasurer, the head of shipping, receiving, and warehousing, and an outside party who managed dummy companies with whom McKesson purportedly conducted business. It so happened that the partners in crime were the president's brothers. The four men did not use their real names.[5]

Essentially, the fraud involved setting up an entirely fictitious Canadian

---

[5] For fascinating accounts of the president's exploits, see the *New Yorker,* October 22, 1955, and October 29, 1955, or the *Saturday Evening Post,* February 28, 1953.

crude drug division. Pretended purchases were made from a number of Canadian vendors, who supposedly retained the merchandise in their own warehouses for the account of McKesson. Pretended sales were made by a fictitious W. W. Smith and Company, as agent for McKesson; goods were shipped directly to customers. Payment for goods purchased and collections from customers were pretended to have been made by the Montreal banking firm of Manning & Company—also for the account of McKesson. The actual cash embezzlement from the central headquarters of McKesson took the form of commissions paid to W. W. Smith and Company. All these transactions were supported by proper-looking but false invoices, contracts, Dun and Bradstreet credit reports, and the like.

The vastness of the fraud framework can be seen from McKesson's certified balance sheet as of December 31, 1937; it showed $87 million in assets, $20 million of which were fictitious, consisting of $10 million in receivables and $10 million in inventories, and $75,000 of cash on deposit with "Manning & Company."

The fraud, which had been conducted over a period of twelve years, was finally uncovered by Julian Thompson, controller and treasurer, when he went to Montreal to check on inventories and found none.

The president killed himself, McKesson & Robbins was taken over by a trustee in bankruptcy, and the public accounting firms were placed in a state of shock—sending their men scurrying all over the world to make sure that their clients' inventories really existed. One major change in auditing procedure that all auditing firms adopted as an outgrowth of this case was the physical testing of inventories instead of reliance on the client's word.

The Securities and Exchange Commission launched a detailed investigation of the matter. A thorough investigation of the fraud was hampered by the president's suicide, but some of the figures involved are worth repeating:

1. The costs of investigation totaled $3 million.
2. The public accounting firm that investigated the fraud had 300 accountants work a total of 146,000 man-hours. They found 91 bank accounts, 57 brokerage accounts, and 10 loan accounts that the president had used in the course of his twelve years at the helm of McKesson & Robbins. Ultimately, they found that the actual cash stolen was about $3,200,000.

The moral of this story for both managers and accountants may be best expressed by the sentence that the president underlined in a book (Morrill Goddard's *What Interests People and Why*) he had been reading shortly before committing suicide:

> The truth, which the public has never been told, is that no practical system has ever been devised by which the complicated finances of a large institution can be thoroughly checked so that every transaction is verified, except at prohibitive time and cost.

using the
checklist   The next illustration will show how the checklist for internal control may be used as a starting point in judging a system.

example[6]   The Y Company has come to you with the following problem.
        It has three clerical employees who must perform the following functions:
        a. Maintain general ledger
        b. Maintain accounts-payable ledger
        c. Maintain accounts-receivable ledger
        d. Prepare checks for signature
        e. Maintain disbursements journal
        f. Issue credits on returns and allowances
        g. Reconcile the bank account
        h. Handle and deposit cash receipts
        Assuming that there is no problem as to the ability of any of the employees, the company requests that you assign the functions above to the three employees in such a manner as to achieve the highest degree of internal control. It may be assumed that these employees will perform no other accounting functions than the ones listed and that any accounting functions not listed will be performed by persons other than these three employees.
        1. State how you would distribute the functions among the three employees. Assume that, with the exception of the nominal jobs of the bank reconciliation and the issuance of credits on returns and allowances, all functions require an equal amount of time.
        2. List four possible unsatisfactory combinations of the listed functions.
        Try to answer the questions before consulting the following solution.

SOLUTION   1. Assignment of functions:
        Employee No. 1:
        a. Maintain general ledger
        b. Reconcile bank account
        c. Issue credits on returns and allowances
        Employee No. 2:
        a. Prepare checks for signature
        b. Handle and deposit cash receipts
        c. Maintain disbursements journal
        Employee No. 3:
        a. Maintain accounts-payable ledger
        b. Maintain accounts-receivable ledger
        2. Undesirable combinations are as follows:
        a. Cash receipts and accounts receivable
        b. Cash receipts and credits on returns and allowances
        c. Cash disbursements and accounts payable
        d. Cash receipts and bank reconciliation
        e. General ledger and cash receipts
        f. Accounts receivable and credits on returns and allowances

        The major feature of the suggested division of duties is the separation of powers so that *one individual does not have sole control over all record keeping and physical handling for any single transaction.* Not only does this limit the chances for fraud, but—probably more important—it provides for automatic checks on efficiency and accuracy.

inventory   Retail merchants must contend with a major operating problem that is often
shrinkage   called inventory shrinkage, a polite term for shoplifting by customers and

[6]Adapted from a CPA examination.

embezzling by employees. The National Retail Merchandise Association reported that in 1970, shrinkage amounted to 2.7 percent of all general merchandise sales, up from 2.0 percent in 1965. Buffums, a chain of California department stores, reported an annual growth in shoplifting losses of 25 percent per year in 1969 and 1970, compared to 5 percent annual increases in 1965 and 1966. In 1970, the FBI described retail inventory losses as the "fastest-growing larceny in the nation." Some department stores suffered shrinkage losses of 4 to 5 percent of their sales volume; compare this to the typical net-profit margin of 5 to 6 percent.

In 1970, a management consultant firm demonstrated how widespread shoplifting has become. The firm concentrated on a midtown New York department store. Five hundred shoppers, picked at random, were followed from the moment they entered the store to the time they departed. Forty-two shoppers, or one out of every twelve, took something. They stole $300 worth of merchandise, an average of $7.15 each. Similar experiments were conducted in Boston (1 of 20 shoplifted), Philadelphia (1 of 10), and again in New York (1 of 12).

The experts on controlling inventory shrinkage generally agree that the best deterrent is an alert employee at the point of sale. But other means are also used. Retail stores have gone so far as to use tiny sensitized tags on merchandise; if not detached or neutralized by a sales clerk, these miniature transmitters trip an alarm as the culprit begins to leave the store. Macy's in New York has continuous surveillance with over fifty television cameras. Retailers must scrutinize their own personnel, because they account for 30 to 40 percent of inventory shortages.

The imposing magnitude of retail inventory shrinkage demonstrates how management objectives may differ among industries. For example, consider the grocery business, where the net income percentage on sales hovers around 1 percent. You can readily see why a prime responsibility of the store manager is to control inventory shrinkage rather than boost gross sales volume. The trade-off is clear: If the operating profit on sales is 2 percent, to offset a $1,000 increase in shrinkage requires a $50,000 boost in gross sales.

retail method of inventory control A widely used inventory method, known as the *retail method*, is utilized as a control device as well as for obtaining an inventory valuation for financial-statement purposes. The wide variety, low unit value, and high volume of most retail merchandise prevent any economical use of a perpetual-inventory system as commonly conceived. The following is a general version of how food stores use the retail method to control grocery inventories at the store level. All merchandise is accounted for at retail prices[7] as follows:

---

[7] Of course, an inventory measured at retail prices can be restated in terms of an average cost for financial-statement purposes by applying an average-cost ratio. For example, if the average gross profit is 20 percent of sales price, the $11,100 inventory would be shown at a cost of .8 × $11,100, or $8,880.

			RETAIL PRICES
	Inventory, January 5 (by surprise count by branch auditors)		$ 15,000
	Purchases (shipments to store from branch warehouse)		101,000
	Additional retail price changes:		
	Markups		2,000
	Markdowns		(5,000)
(1)	Total merchandise to account for		$113,000
	Sales (per cash-register records)		$100,000
	Allowable shrinkage (shoplifting, breakage, etc.— usually a predetermined percentage of sales)		1,000
(2)	Total deductions		$101,000
(1) – (2)	Inventory, February 11, should be		$ 12,000
	Inventory, February 11, by physical count		$ 11,100
	Inventory shortage		$ 900

If the inventory shortage is not within predetermined limits, the manager usually bears prime responsibility. There are worrisome behavioral implications here. For utmost accuracy, the retail method requires the prompt application of the directed changes in retail prices that are ordered by the branch managers. For example, to help insure a good performance regarding his control of shrinkage, the store manager will be inclined to delay the entering of markdowns on price tags and will be inclined to overstate the retail prices of merchandise if possible. The branch manager typically relies on other means, such as surprise spot checks, to insure that markup and markdown directives are being followed.

effects of computers on internal check The use of computers has both positive and negative effects on the possibilities of errors, fraud, and waste. New types of errors arise when data must be manually punched into cards or paper tape. Each step that places data into a different form boosts the probability of error. Common blunders include using the wrong magnetic tape, using an obsolete or erroneous program, processing the same data twice, and skipping a batch of data.

Computer systems also are less flexible than manual systems. Humans regularly interpret, adjust, and act upon imperfect documents that are unacceptable under the tight discipline of computer programs. The computer correction system is necessarily more complicated, more formal, and tends to be concentrated on the first run of the data.

Despite frequent horror stories to the contrary, the computer itself has very high reliability. Data are processed in strict accordance with the program, and both manual and programmed internal checks can enhance that reliability.

Although computers have generally tended to increase the efficiency and effectiveness of information systems, they sometimes have an unwarranted constraining effect on overall systems design. The attitude to avoid is "Oh, we can't do that. It won't fit on our card!"

The checklist of internal control applies to both computer and manual systems. For example, consider the separation of powers. Programmers should not be allowed to operate the computers physically. A computer consultant commented that he had immense stealing opportunities when he ran computer operations for a large bank: "I alone designed the dividend-payment operation, wrote the program for it, and ran the job on the machine. The operation was so big that it had a mistake tolerance of nearly $100,000. I could have paid at least half that much to myself, in small checks, and the money wouldn't even have been missed."

Another example of separation of powers is the necessity to keep the check-writing process out of reach of computer operators. Unless he has some way to convert his tampered machine records onto checks, he cannot operate successfully.

The rotation of duties is another characteristic of good internal check. Companies should shift operators and programmers unpredictably from machine to machine and project to project. If a tempted individual cannot depend on making substitutions in punched cards or adjusting the program for one machine, he is not likely to begin stealing.

Reliability of personnel is a check that applies to all employees, including computer personnel. It is surprising how often embezzlements are repeated by individuals who move from employer to employer. It is also surprising how often employers fail to investigate the backgrounds of newly hired personnel.

summary

The following general characteristics form a checklist that may be used as a starting point for judging the effectiveness of internal control:

1. Reliable personnel	6. Document control
2. Separation of powers	7. Bonding, vacations, and
3. Supervision	rotation of duties
4. Responsibility	8. Independent check
5. Routine and automatic	9. Physical safeguards
checks	10. Costs and feasibility

This checklist is equally applicable to both computer and manual systems.

The blizzard of paperwork continues to intensify in most organizations. Too frequently, systems and forms and reports tend to "just grow." Periodic appraisals of systems are needed to see whether they are indeed optimal under new conditions. Occasionally, managers overreact to an overwhelming number of reports and documents by deleting them entirely. The key question involves the cost and value of information: "What are the costs and benefits of alternate systems?"

Managers at all levels have a major responsibility for the success of a given system. If they do not insist on accurate documents, separation of duties, and so on, trouble is inevitable.

Problem for Self-Study[8]

PROBLEM   As a member of the controller's department, you have been asked to review the company's payroll system and procedures where all payrolls are paid in currency.
    a. State what questions you would ask in your review of the system of internal control and procedures relative to payrolls.
    b. Give your reasons for asking the questions, including an explanation of how you would use the questions in deciding on the effectiveness of the control over payrolls.
Formulate your own answer before examining the solution that follows.

SOLUTION   a.   1. *Reliable personnel:* Who prepares payrolls? Have their past employment references been checked? What is their performance record as far as efficiency is concerned?
    2. *Separation of powers:* Are hiring and firing properly authorized and reported? Are pay rates and changes properly authorized and reported? Is payroll preparation divided among employees?
    3. *Supervision:* Who supervises payments? Are time records approved by a timekeeper or foreman?
    4. *Responsibility:* Who is in charge of each step in the payroll process? Do overtime hours require special approval? By whom?
    5. *Routine and automatic checks:* Are receipts submitted by employees? How do employees identify themselves? How is validity of signatures checked? What procedures are used for review, approval, and reconciliation of payroll charges to various accounts?
    6. *Document control:* Who has control over unclaimed pay envelopes? How are envelopes claimed after regular pay dates? Are time clocks used? Are time records properly prepared and controlled?
    7. *Bonding and vacations:* Are key payroll employees bonded? Is there rotation of payroll duties?
    8. *Independent check:* Are payroll calculations independently checked before payment? Do auditors witness or perform a distribution of payroll, including control of unclaimed envelopes? Are receipts compared with payroll by somebody not engaged in payroll preparation?
    9. *Physical safeguards:* Are there physical safeguards, like alarm systems, police, safes, and the like?
    10. *Costs and feasibility:* Is the overall system working efficiently and smoothly? Are there any glaring weaknesses? Is there any unnecessary routine or duplication of effort?

    b. These questions were asked to determine that hiring and separation, accumulation of periodic payroll time and rate records, and payouts were handled with a minimum chance of error, fraud, and waste. The questions above are designed to discover whether duties are separated, whether adequate personnel and payroll records are kept, and whether proper authority and supervision are exercised at every step affecting payroll. The controller wants satisfactory cross-checks, physical safeguards, rotation of duties, step-by-step routines, and constant review and supervision.

[8] Adapted from a CPA examination.

APPENDIX: FACTORY LEDGERS

In this appendix, we study an example of some specialized techniques for accumulating accounting data. The purpose here is not to dwell on the intricacies of a specific system. Rather, it is to offer an overview of the immense task of effective systems design. Persons without accounting experience often find it difficult to visualize the avalanche of paper work that most companies face. It should be recognized that routine data collection and classification is the most time-consuming task of the controller's department. That is why the expenditure of time, care, and money on planning and shaping an accounting system is nearly always a worthwhile investment.

classification and coding   Any sizable company finds it convenient to classify accounts in detail and to number or otherwise code the accounts accordingly. Although an outsider may not know what the code means, accounting employees become so familiar with the code that they think, talk, and write in terms of account numbers instead of account names. Thus, if Cash is account No. 1000 and Accounts Payable is account No. 7000, an outside auditor may find payments to creditors journalized as follows:

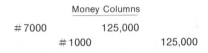

A company usually has a chart of accounts that classifies all accounts in the entire company by name and code number. Codes differ from company to company. Each coding system is usually some variation on the following example:

GEOGRAPHIC LOCATION	GENERAL-LEDGER ACCOUNT	DEPARTMENT	SUBSIDIARY CLASSIFICATION
0	00	000	000

This classification may be used by a multiplant company with far-flung operations. It would be too cumbersome for many companies and not detailed enough for giant companies.

Assume that a company has a central plant in Chicago and branch plants in Dallas, Pittsburgh, and San Francisco. Debits for various transactions could be coded as shown in Exhibit 20-1.

The numbers used to code debits and credits are obtained from the company chart of accounts. These numbers are originally entered or keypunched on the source documents (requisitions, vouchers, work tickets) that are the basis for ledger entries and other analyses. For example, Chicago is coded as 1, Factory Overhead Control as 91, a machining department as 011, and supplies used as 112. What would be the complete account number for indirect-labor cost incurred by the finishing department in Chicago? The answer is 1-91-015-202.

EXHIBIT 20-1

CODING OF ACCOUNTS

TRANSACTION	GENERAL-LEDGER ENTRY	POSSIBLE NUMBER CODE FOR DEBIT			
		GEOGRAPHIC LOCATION	GENERAL-LEDGER ACCOUNT	DEPARTMENT	SUBSIDIARY CLASSIFICATION
1. Requisition of supplies by a machining department in Chicago	Factory-overhead control Stores	1	91	011	112
2. Requisition of supplies by a finishing department in Dallas	Factory-overhead control Stores	2	91	015	112
3. Indirect labor incurred by machining department in San Francisco	Factory-overhead control Stores	4	91	011	202
4. President's salary	Administrative-expenses control Accrued payroll	1	98	060	801

factory ledger   Many companies have branch plants sprawled all over the country and the world. Cost accumulation and analysis are most often conducted at the various geographic locations, whereas records of receivables, payables, and similar accounts may be centralized in the home office. The division of accounting between central headquarters and a branch plant calls for splitting the accounts between the two locations. At the same time, some technique must be used to ensure the dovetailing of all company accounts so that duplications, omissions, and other errors are minimized. Generally, two reciprocal accounts are introduced, one in the home office and one at the factory.

example   The central offices of the Homeware Company are in Chicago, but the manufacturing operations are located in Richmond, Indiana. The company uses a separate factory ledger that is maintained at Richmond for the benefit of the plant management. The factory is given credit for finished goods at cost when the goods are shipped to the central warehouses. All goods are shipped to customers from the warehouses.

The chart of general-ledger accounts for the company is as follows:

CODE	HOME-OFFICE ACCOUNTS	CODE	FACTORY ACCOUNTS
1	Cash in bank	A	Stores control
2	Accounts-receivable control	B	Work-in-process control
3	Finished-goods control	C	Factory overhead applied
4	Plant and equipment control	D	Factory-overhead control
5	Allowance for depreciation	E	Home-office-ledger control
6	Accounts payable		
7	Accrued payroll		
8	Common stock		
9	Retained earnings		
10	Factory-ledger control		
11	Sales		
12	Cost of goods sold		
13	Selling-cost control		
14	Administrative-cost control		

required   Below is a summary of some transactions for one month.

Indicate the accounts debited and credited in the factory ledger and in the home office ledger. Show postings and ending balances in Factory-Ledger Control and Home-Office-Ledger Control. Try to solve this problem yourself before looking at the solution.

PARTIAL LIST OF TRANSACTIONS

1. Materials purchased on credit	$200,000
2. Direct materials requisitioned	150,000
3. Factory payroll accrued (direct labor, $130,000; other $70,000)	200,000
4. Miscellaneous factory overhead incurred*	68,000
5. Factory overhead applied	65,000
6. Cost of goods shipped to warehouse	325,000
7. Cost of goods sold	300,000
8. Sales (on credit)	450,000
9. Cash collected on account	340,000

* Credit Accounts Payable, except for $5,000 depreciation.

EXHIBIT 20-2

SAMPLE JOURNAL ENTRIES FOR BRANCH ACCOUNTING

TRANSACTION	HOME-OFFICE LEDGER		FACTORY LEDGER		ENTRIES THAT WOULD BE MADE IN A REGULAR, UNIFIED LEDGER	
1. Material purchases	Factory-ledger control	200,000	Stores control	200,000	Stores control	200,000
	Accounts payable	200,000	Home-office-ledger control	200,000	Accounts payable	200,000
2. Requisitions	None		Work-in-process control	150,000	Work-in-process control	150,000
			Stores control	150,000	Stores control	150,000
3. Factory payroll	Factory-ledger control	200,000	Work-in-process control	130,000	Work-in-process control	130,000
	Accrued payroll	200,000	Factory-overhead control	70,000	Factory-overhead control	70,000
			Home-office-ledger control	200,000	Accrued payroll	200,000
4. Miscellaneous overhead	Factory-ledger control	68,000	Factory-overhead control	68,000	Factory-overhead control	68,000
	Allowance for depreciation	5,000	Home-office-ledger control	68,000	Allowance for depreciation	5,000
	Accounts payable	63,000			Accounts payable	63,000
5. Overhead application	None		Work-in-process control	65,000	Work-in-process control	65,000
			Factory overhead applied	65,000	Factory overhead applied	65,000
6. Shipments to warehouse	Finished-goods control	325,000	Home-office-ledger control	325,000	Finished-goods control	325,000
	Factory-ledger control	325,000	Work-in-process control	325,000	Work-in-process control	325,000
7. Cost of goods sold	Cost of goods sold	300,000	None		Cost of goods sold	300,000
	Finished-goods control	300,000			Finished-goods control	300,000
8. Sales	Accounts-receivable control	450,000	None		Accounts-receivable control	450,000
	Sales	450,000			Sales	450,000
9. Collections	Cash	340,000	None		Cash	340,000
	Accounts-receivable control	340,000			Accounts-receivable control	340,000

Postings:

Factory-Ledger Control

(1)	200,000	(6)	325,000
(3)	200,000		
(4)	68,000		
		To bal.	143,000
Bal.	143,000		

Home-Office-Ledger Control

(6)	325,000	(1)	200,000
		(3)	200,000
		(4)	68,000
To bal.	143,000		
		Bal.	143,000

SOLUTION Remember that this is only an example. The solution is shown in Exhibit 20-2. A general ledger may be split into two or more parts in any manner whatsoever, depending on practical needs. Thus, the ledger in our example could have been designed so that accounts for plant and equipment could be kept at the factory instead of at the home office. If this were done, what journal entry or entries would be changed?

Difficulties in factory-ledger accounting center around lagging or otherwise faulty communications, which result in disagreement in the balances of the reciprocal accounts. Common causes for discrepancies include transfers of inventories and cash that are in transit at the trial-balance cutoff date and failure to recognize nonroutine payments for factory costs by the office on behalf of the branch.

questions, problems, and cases

20-1. "Business operations would be a hopeless tangle without the paper work that is often regarded with disdain." Explain.

20-2. Define *internal control*. Distinguish it from *internal check*.

20-3. "There are ten check points that I always use as a framework for judging the effectiveness of an internal-control system." Name nine of the ten.

20-4. "The words *internal control* are commonly misunderstood. They are thought to refer to those facets of the accounting system that are supposed to help prevent embezzling." Do you agree? Why?

20-5. "Internal-control systems have both negative and positive objectives." Do you agree? Explain.

20-6. Briefly describe how a bottler of soda water might compile data regarding control of finished product at the plant, where normal breakage can be expected.

20-7. The branch manager of a national retail grocery chain has stated, "My managers are judged more heavily on the basis of their merchandise-shrinkage control than on their overall sales volume." Why? Explain.

20-8. Internal Control Over Cash and Payroll [CPA].
1. In what ways can the use of cash registers contribute to the effectiveness of internal control over receipts from cash sales? Explain.
2. The general ledger of the XY Manufacturing Company contains a Payroll-clearing account. Debits to the account originate in the payroll section of the factory accounting office. Credits to the account originate in the payroll section of the factory accounting office. Credits to the account originate in the cost-distribution section. The company does not use standard or estimated costs. On the assumption that there is effective internal control over payrolls, you are to:
   a. State the information needed by the payroll section and indicate the source of this information.
   b. State the information needed by the cost-distribution section and the source of the information.
   c. State the principal controls over the payroll in the system as you have described it.

20-9. Appraisal of Payroll System [CPA]. The Generous Loan Company has 100 branch loan offices. Each office has a manager and four or five subordinates who are employed by the manager. Branch managers prepare the weekly payroll, including their own salaries, and pay their employees from cash on hand. The employee signs the payroll sheet, signifying receipt of his salary. Hours worked by hourly personnel are inserted in the payroll sheet from time cards prepared by the employees and approved by the manager.

The weekly payroll sheets are sent to the home office along with other accounting statements and reports. The home office compiles employee earnings records and prepares all federal and state salary reports from the weekly payroll sheets.

Salaries are established by home-office job-evaluation schedules. Salary adjustments, promotions, and transfers of full-time employees are approved by a home-office salary committee, based upon the recommendations of branch managers and area supervisors. Branch managers advise the salary committee of new full-time employees and of terminations. Part-time and temporary employees are hired without referral to the salary committee.

required Based upon your review of the payroll system, how might payroll funds be diverted?

20-10. Retail Method and Internal Control. The following figures pertain to the Zenith Gift Store for the two-month period, November and December, 19_8.

Sales	$170,000	Purchases (at sales price)	$ 80,000
Additional markups	10,000	Inventory at November 1, 19_8:	
Markdowns	25,000	At cost price	105,000
Purchases (at cost price)	52,000	At selling price	160,000

required 1. What should the inventory amount to at December 31, 19_8, at retail price using the conventional retail inventory method?
2. Suppose the allowable shrinkage is 2 percent of sales. The physical inventory at December 31 amounts to $50,000. What is the inventory shortage?

20-11. Appraisal of Internal Control System. From the *San Francisco Chronicle*, April 3, 1971:

The flap over missing ferry fares was peacefully—and openly—resolved at a meeting of the Golden Gate Bridge District finance committee yesterday.

Only a week ago, the subject was a matter of furious dispute in which bridge manager Dale W. Luehring was twice called a liar and there were prospects of a closed meeting on personnel matters.

But yesterday, after a week of investigation, the meeting turned out to be public after all, and attorney Thomas M. Jenkins revealed the full total of stolen ferry tickets equaled $26.20.

The controversy began when auditor Gordon Dahlgren complained that there was an auditing "problem" and that he had not been informed when four children swiped $13.75 worth of tickets February 28. Committee chairman Ben K. Lerer, of San Francisco, ordered a full investigation.

Jenkins said the situation was complicated because children under 5 have been allowed to ride the ferry without a ticket, but after May 1 everyone will have to have a ticket, allowing for a closer audit.

Secondly, Jenkins explained, the "vault" in which tickets are deposited was proved insecure (resulting in two thefts totaling $26.20 worth of tickets) but has been replaced.

In the future, it was decided, all thefts of cash or tickets must be reported immediately to the California Highway Patrol or the local police, the bridge lieutenant on duty, the general manager, the security officer, the auditor-controller, and the transit manager.

In addition, employees must make a full written report within 24 hours to the president of the district board, the chairman of the finance-auditing committee, the auditor controller, the attorney, the bus transit manager, the water transit manager, the toll captain, and the chief of administration and security.

required What is your reaction to the new system? Explain, giving particular attention to applicable criteria for appraising an internal-control system.

20-12. **Use of Credit Card.** A business-school student used a Bank Americard for a variety of purchases. When checking his monthly bill, he compared his original copy with a duplicate copy for a gasoline purchase made at a local discount-store shopping center. The original copy showed a purchase of $4.25; the duplicate was raised to $6.25.

required Who obtained the extra $2.00? How? How can the system be improved to prevent such thievery?

20-13. **Multiple Choice; Discovering Irregularities.** In questions 1 through 7, you are given a well-recognized procedure of internal control. You are to identify the irregularity *that will be discovered or prevented by each procedure.* Write the numbers 1 through 7 on your answer sheet. Then place the letter of your chosen answer next to your numbers.

1. The general-ledger-control account and the subsidiary ledger of accounts receivable are reconciled monthly. The two bookkeepers are independent.
    a. The accounts-receivable subsidiary-ledger bookkeeper charges a customer with $72 instead of $74, the correct amount. The error is due to misreading the sales slip. The credit-sales summary for the day has the correct amount of $74.
    b. The accounts-receivable subsidiary-ledger bookkeeper charges a sale to Mr. Smith instead of Mr. Smithe (that is, the wrong customer). The error is due to misreading the sales slip.
    c. The employee opening mail abstracts funds without making a record of their receipt. Customer accounts are not credited with their payments.
    d. The general-ledger bookkeeper takes funds and covers the loss by charging "Miscellaneous General Expenses."
    e. When friends purchase merchandise, the salesclerk allows them an employee discount by using an employee name on the sales slip and deducting the discount on the slip. This is against company policy.
2. The voucher system requires that invoices be compared with receiving reports and express bills before a voucher is prepared and approved for payment.
    a. Unrecorded checks appear in the bank statement.
    b. The treasurer takes funds by preparing a fictitious voucher charging "Miscellaneous General Expenses."
    c. An employee in the purchasing department sends through fictitious invoices and receives payment.
    d. A cash shortage is covered by underfooting outstanding checks on the bank reconciliation.
    e. A cash shortage is covered by omitting some of the outstanding checks from the bank reconciliation.
3. Both cash and credit customers are educated to expect a sales ticket. Tickets are serially numbered. All numbers are accounted for daily.

a. Customers complain that their monthly bills contain items that have been paid.

b. Some customers have the correct change for the merchandise purchased. They pay and do not wait for a sales ticket.

c. Customers complain that they are billed for goods they did not purchase.

d. Customers complain that goods ordered are not received.

e. Salesclerks destroy duplicate sales tickets for the amount of cash stolen.

4. The storekeeper should sign a receipt for goods received from the receiving and inspection room, and no payment should be made without his signature.

a. Invoices are paid twice.

b. Employees send through fictitious invoices and receive payment.

c. Materials are withdrawn from the storeroom for personal use rather than for business purposes.

d. Employees send through purchase requisitions for materials for personal use. After the materials are received and receiving reports are issued, employees take the merchandise for personal use.

e. The storekeeper takes materials and charges them to company use.

5. At a movie-theatre box office, all tickets are prenumbered. At the end of each day, the beginning ticket number is subtracted from the ending number to give the number of tickets sold. Cash is counted and compared with the number of tickets sold.

a. The box office gives too much change.

b. The ticket taker admits his friends without a ticket.

c. The manager gives theatre passes for personal expenses. This is against company policy.

d. A test check of customers entering the theatre does not reconcile with ticket sales.

e. Tickets from a previous day are discovered in the ticket taker's stub box despite the fact that tickets are stamped "Good on Date of Purchase Only."

6. In Hutchinson Commons Cafeteria, the customers enter at an *IN* door and choose their meals. Before leaving the serving rail, they are billed by a biller for the food taken. After they eat, they present their bills and make payments to a cashier. At the end of the day, cash receipts are reconciled with billings.

a. A friend of the biller and the cashier moves through the lines and takes a free meal without being billed or paying.

b. A customer who has been billed goes out the *IN* entrance without paying.

c. Meat is stolen by an employee.

d. The biller makes an error by billing a meal at $1.15 instead of the correct amount, $1.35.

e. A customer sneaks under the serving rail, takes an extra cup of coffee, sneaks back under the rail, and returns to his table.

7. The duties of cashier and accounts-receivable bookkeeper should be separated.

a. There are two cashiers. At the end of a certain day, there is a sizable cash shortage. Each cashier blames the other. It is impossible to fix responsibility.

b. A cash shortage is covered by overfooting (overadding) cash in transit on the bank reconciliation.

c. A cash shortage is covered by charging it to "Miscellaneous General Expenses."

d. Customers who paid their accounts in cash complain that they still receive statements of balances due.

e. The accounts-receivable bookkeeper charges off the accounts of friends to "Allowance for Bad Debts."

20-14. Refer to Exhibit 20-1. State the debit number code for: (a) requisition of supplies by a finishing department in San Francisco; (b) indirect labor incurred by a machining department in Dallas.

20-15. Factory-Ledger Fundamentals. Refer to the chart of general-ledger accounts used in the factory-ledger illustration in this chapter. Indicate the proper journal entries for the following transactions. Set up your solution in a form similar to the one illustrated in Exhibit 20-2.

1. Payments made to creditors on open account	$ 50,000
2. Cash sales	3,000
3. Depreciation on factory equipment	15,000
4. Declaration of dividend	24,000
5. Payment of payroll	105,000
6. Return of materials to vendors	2,000
7. Direct materials requisitioned	40,000
8. Factory overhead applied	30,000
9. Cost of goods shipped to warehouse	50,000
10. Cost of goods sold	25,000

20-16. Factory Ledger [SIA]. The DEF Company uses both a factory ledger, which includes all transactions up to Cost of Sales, and a general ledger. It records its cost under a job-cost plan.

The following transactions took place during the month of March:

1. Materials purchased and delivered directly to production order No. 305—$200.
2. Depreciation on factory buildings and equipment—$5,000.
3. Finished goods returned for credit—$2,000.
4. Cost of finished goods returned—$1,200.
5. The raw-material book inventory at the end of the month amounted to $354,348. A physical inventory taken at that time showed a value of $354,148.

required   Prepare the journal entries necessary to record this information in the general and factory ledgers.

20-17. Factory Ledger; Journal Entries. The home offices of the Splitpea Company are in Chicago, but the manufacturing operations are located in Gary. The company uses a separate factory ledger, which is maintained at Gary for the benefit of the plant management. The factory is given credit for finished goods when the goods are shipped to the central warehouses. All goods are shipped to customers from the warehouses.

Some transactions for the month of March 19_6 are summarized below:

1. Miscellaneous manufacturing expenses incurred—$10,000. The invoices for $10,000 were received.
2. Materials received by the factory (proper invoice received)—$75,000.
3. Sales to customers billed during March—$90,000.
4. Factory cost of goods sold—$70,000.
5. Direct materials placed into production—$50,000.

Questions 6–8 refer to certain discrepancies that were found upon auditing the reconciliation accounts. You are to select the entry (or entries) that *would correct* the general-ledger accounts involved.

6. Salesmen's salaries of $2,000 were incorrectly charged to Manufacturing-Expense Control.
7. Machinery of $1,200 purchased by the home office for the branch was taken up in the branch books as a Stores item.

8. The machinery in 7 had been ignored in computing depreciation for one month (rate, 1 percent per month).

CODE	HOME OFFICE ACCOUNTS	CODE	FACTORY ACCOUNTS
1	Cash in bank	A	Material-stores control
2	Accounts receivable	B	Work-in-process control
3	Finished goods	C	Manufacturing-expense control
4	Accounts payable	D	Manufacturing expense applied
5	Accrued payroll	E	Home-office-ledger control
6	Common stock	F	Direct-labor control
7	Retained earnings		
8	Factory-ledger control		
9	Sales		
10	Factory cost of goods sold		
11	Selling-cost control		
12	Administrative-cost control		
13	Plant and equipment control		
14	Allowance for depreciation		

required   For each of the eight transactions, indicate by code the accounts debited and credited in the factory ledger and the home ledger. Use the account codes given. More than one account may be debited or credited for each entry.

Note: The following two problems are from *Case Problems in Internal Auditing and Control* (Prentice-Hall, Inc.).

20-18. **Internal Audit of Inventory Differences.**   Superfine Supermarkets is the operator of a chain of ninety-five supermarket grocery stores. The individual stores are the familiar supermarket type, located in community shopping centers in the outskirts of a number of large cities in the Middle West. The company makes careful studies of potential locations before establishing a unit, and in general will not give consideration to any location in which the potential first-year volume is under $500,000. The result of this policy is that each of the units is a sizable operation, with volume running from $500,000 to $1,200,000 per year.

Control of packaged grocery items follows the customary pattern of retail inventory value. The majority of products handled in the stores are ordered by the store managers from the central warehouse, where accounting control over the stores is maintained. At the time of shipment, the store inventory account is charged with the retail sales value of the shipment. Perishable products, such as dairy items, are delivered directly to stores by suppliers. These direct deliveries are reported to the warehouse on the store report, where they are compared with billing by suppliers. On the basis of this billing, the store inventory account is charged at selling price.

When a price change is made, the store reports inventory of the products affected by the change to the warehouse, and corresponding adjustment is made in the retail inventory control value.

Fruits and vegetables are handled by a separate produce supervisor, who has authority to order according to his own judgment. Highly perishable items may be purchased locally, while semiperishables, such as potatoes and oranges, are ordered from the warehouse. In this department, the maintenance of a strict monetary control based upon units is not feasible, because much of the product is supplied in bulk for repackaging and there is considerable loss because of waste and spoilage. Consequently, inventory control over the produce department is effected by changing the produce department at cost for all shipments from the warehouse or direct purchases.

The meat department is handled on a basis similar to the produce department. The reason for this is that the large meat items, such as a side of beef, are delivered at a single overall price per pound. The butchers in the meat department then cut the meat, with the value of the final cut depending on the desirability of the meat. There is also considerable waste in bones, fat, and similar unsalable items.

To a considerable degree, the profit of the meat and produce departments will depend on the skill of the managers. The expertness of the butchering will be a most important factor in the meat department, while skill in purchasing and anticipating requirements will be a governing factor in the profitability of the produce operations. Consequently, supervisory control over produce and meat departments is through a watch of gross margin realized from sales.

So far we have been concerned with the charges to inventory controls. To summarize, packaged groceries are charged at retail, while produce and meat are charged at cost. For purposes of this problem, we will assume that all credits will come through sales (disregarding minor adjusting items such as breakage, returnable containers, and the like). Sales credits are developed when customers pass by the checking counters. The cashier-checkers, in operating their cash registers, develop separate totals for the three departments. Thus, total sales are developed separately for packaged groceries, produce, and meat. Register totals are taken each day by the store manager and recorded on the daily report to the warehouse accounting office. Entry of these sales in the accounting records has the following results:

1. In the case of packaged groceries, total reported sales should offset original charge at retail selling price.
2. In the case of produce and meats, sales in comparison with cost will result in development of separate gross-margin figures for each of these departments.

Under company policy, internal auditors take inventories of stores every three months. Packaged-grocery inventories are taken at selling prices, so that there should be no difference if all transactions were perfectly handled, and if there had been no losses from theft by customers or for other reasons. Naturally, perfect operation does not exist, and it is usual to develop a shortage, which is written off at the time of inventory. In the produce and meat departments, the physical inventory by auditors is used to adjust the book value, which is arrived at through applying an estimated percentage of markdown to reported sales for each accounting period.

Below are shown final figures developed as the result of three inventories of the Springfield store. In the case of the packaged grocery department, a percentage of loss (shrinkage) in relation to sales for the period is shown; in the case of produce and meat, the percentage of gross margin on sales developed as a result of the inventories is the figure given.

	PACKAGED GROCERIES (SHRINKAGE)	PRODUCE MARGIN	MEAT MARGIN
January	2/3%	20%	23%
April	3% over	10%	32%
July	4% short	15%	24%

One of the control records that is maintained is a comparative record of packaged grocery inventory shrinkage and produce- and meat-department margins at all stores. In checking the January inventory, you find that all the Springfield store figures are comparable with other stores and may therefore be assumed to be correct. A further factor in considering the answer to the questions is the quantity of the average inventory. In packaged groceries, it is three weeks' sales; in produce, two days; and in meat, one week.

required

1. In the April inventory, what items merit immediate attention and follow-up? What are the possible explanations for the apparent abnormalities?

2. In the July inventory, which items appear to be out of line? What would be possible explanations?

20-19.   **Analysis of Production and Shipping Control.**   The Cucaracha Coffee Company is a large producer of coffee for the retail market. Each day, 300,000 pounds of green coffee are roasted; this results in finished-goods production of somewhat more than 250,000 pounds, as there is a loss in roasting of from 14 to 15 percent of the original weight of the green coffee. This loss is known as "shrinkage." About one-half the production is in the most expensive coffee, Cuca Special, which is packed in vacuum cans. The remainder is in a cheaper blend that is packed in paper bags.

From the roasting plant, shipment is made by truck to fifty distributing branches, from which sale and delivery is made to 100,000 retail grocery stores.

part I

From an anonymous source, a report comes to the company that the most expensive grade of coffee—the vacuum pack—is being stolen from the roasting plant and sold to retail stores. Original investigation of this report is assigned to the sales branch in the territory from which the report comes. They find that the company's Cuca brand is being offered for sale in several small stores in poorer neighborhoods at a price that is considerably lower than the usual retail price and that is even somewhat lower than the company's selling price to its smaller outlets. The branch has no record of sales to these stores, so it seems quite possible that the report of stealing is true.

As internal auditor, you are then assigned to checking the entire control plan for finished products at the roasting plant, to the end of finding out where the possibility of leakage exists and who may be responsible. As has been previously mentioned, the production is over 250,000 pounds per day, packed in shipping cases of 24 pounds; this means that over ten thousand cases clear through the production and shipping cycle each day.

You begin by observing the whole production operation, which starts with the dumping of green coffee from the bags in which it is received into mixers. Various grades and types are combined according to formulas prescribed by the coffee blenders, with a total of twenty bags being combined and mixed in a single batch. After mixing, the coffee is stored in hoppers from which it is fed to the roasters. The roasting is done in batches of about 600 pounds; after roasting, the coffee is cooled and conveyed to grinders, and then the ground coffee is fed into hoppers that feed the scales on the automatic packing lines.

The vacuum-can packing lines on which Cuca Special is produced are highly automatic and operate at a speed of about 150 cans per minute for each line. The employees on the line are principally concerned with watching for cans that may not be completely filled, damaged or defective cans, or anything else that may be wrong in the finished product or that may interrupt the operation of the line. At the end of the lines, cans are accumulated in lots of 24, which are put into corrugated cases that run through a machine that seals the cases on top and bottom. The finished cases are then stacked upon platform skids in lots of sixty cases to each skid.

The packing lines for the cheaper grade of coffee, which is packed in bags, are less automatic, because the paper bags cannot be handled in the packing equipment. On these lines, the empty bags are unfolded by hand by a girl who holds them under a scale that is set to "dump" 25 pounds a minute. This speed sets the pace for the line. After filling, the bags move on a conveyor belt past girls who fold over and seal the tops. At the end of the line, bags are packed in cases of 24 pounds each; these cases are sealed in a case sealer and then stacked on skids, also in lots of sixty cases.

To the point that the cases leave the packing line, your observation is that there is no opportunity for abstraction of finished goods. The entire flow is mechanical, down through the filling operation. Once the coffee is in containers, it is under observation by a number of employees until it is packed in cases and the cases are sealed and placed on skids.

Separate packing foremen supervise the vacuum and bag lines. As skids are loaded, the number of skids loaded is tallied before they are moved to the shipping floor. This tally is forwarded to the factory accounting department and serves to establish the original charge to the finished-goods inventory. When skids are moved to the shipping floor, the shipping clerk acknowledges the quantities received, and subsequently accounts for these quantities as shipments to branches or as stock on hand.

Shipping-floor stocks are checked by physical inventory taken by the plant accounting department every few days, and quantities reported shipped (which are the credits to inventory) are reported to the central-office accounting department where they are checked with quantities acknowledged by sales branches. You examine all the reports of production, inventory, and acknowledgement and can find only inconsequential differences for the several months that you check.

Despite the seeming indication that all is in order, you are faced with the fact that the sales-department reports indicate very definitely that coffee is being stolen. You then conclude that the only possibility is collusion within the plant. Again reviewing the established controls, you narrow the field. Your final conclusion is determined to some extent by the fact that the tally sheet of skid loads delivered to the shipping floor is a check sheet, prepared in pencil, that could readily be altered.

What would be your analysis of the situation and of the employees who must be in on any collusion? Pause and formulate your own answer before proceeding to Part II.

part II   Based on your analysis of the employees who may be involved, other plant employees and outside detectives have "broken" the case, with the result that the accounting department employee who handles the production records has confessed to altering the tally sheets by one skid load (1,440 pounds) each day, and a shipping clerk has confessed to giving this extra skid load to one of the regular truckers, who in turn sold it to outside sources for about one-half the regular selling price.

Your next concern is consideration of further controls to guard against a repetition. You decide that one or two of the following four possibilities would provide greater protective control. (In your recommendation, you are concerned with the cost to the company, with the value to management, and with the capabilities of the employees who must prepare the reports.)

1. To have an additional tally sheet prepared by the operator of the lift truck who moves the filled skids from the packing lines to the shipping floor.
2. To install a cumulative, nonresettable counter on the case-sealing machine and to provide for daily counter readings, which must balance with inventory controls over production.
3. To balance the consumption of vacuum cans with production on a monthly basis, when physical inventory of cans on hand is taken. This would require the keeping of a count of cans spoiled and discarded in packing lines—which has not previously been taken.
4. To check carefully each month and inquire into any unusual variations in "shrinkage" between the weight of green coffee put into process and the weight of roasted coffee produced. As previously mentioned, this figure may vary between 14 and 15 percent normally.

required   Two of these plans you discard, and two you recommend. In recommending one of them, a factor in your recommendation is the value that the control figures will have for the plant management.

Tell which plans are discarded and why, and the reasons for recommendation of the remaining two.

21

Decentralization and Measurement of Performance

We have previously seen how responsibility accounting helps measure the performance of managers of cost centers by focusing on the cost items subject to an individual's control. The basic ideas of responsibility accounting have been extended beyond cost centers to profit centers and investment centers. Now we will examine the nature of these centers and the major accounting problems that occur in the measurement of performance. We will be especially concerned with a widely used measure: rate of return on investment (hereafter often referred to as ROI).

COST CENTERS, PROFIT CENTERS, AND INVESTMENT CENTERS

A *cost center* is the smallest segment of activity or area of responsibility for which costs are accumulated. Typically, cost centers are departments, but in some instances a department may contain several cost centers. For example, although an assembly department may be supervised by one foreman, it may contain several assembly lines. Sometimes each assembly line is regarded as a separate cost center with its own assistant foreman.

A *profit center* is a segment of a business, often called a division, that is responsible for both revenue and expenses. An *investment center* goes a step further; its success is measured not only by its income but also by relating that income to its invested capital. In practice, the term *investment center* is not widely used. Instead, *profit center* is used indiscriminately to describe segments that are always assigned responsibility for revenue and expenses but may or may not be assigned responsibility for the related invested capital.

NATURE OF DECENTRALIZATION

freedom to make decisions: the substance of decentralization

As organizations grow, top managers face two continuing problems: (a) how to divide activities and responsibilities, and (b) how to coordinate subunits. Inevitably, the power to make decisions is distributed among various managers. *The essence of decentralization is the freedom to make decisions.* Decentralization is a matter of degree. Total decentralization means minimum constraints and maximum freedom for managers to make decisions, even at the lowest levels. At the other extreme of the continuum, total centralization means maximum constraints and minimum freedom.

In practice, organizations are seldom totally centralized or decentralized. Full centralization is not economic in most instances, because of the impossibility of administering the unavoidable massive volume of decisions at the top-management level. On the other hand, full decentralization implies a collection of completely separate businesses. Solomons[1] has pointed out that subunits should be more than investments. They should contribute not only to the success of the corporation but to the success of each other. They may use a common raw material, and therefore permit its purchase more cheaply in bulk. They may provide complementary products (like phonographs and records), so that each division's products help to create a demand for the others'. They may share technical information about manufacturing processes or market information about various channels of distribution.

profit centers: the form of decentralization

Normally, the profit center is the major organizational device used to maximize decentralization. Nevertheless, decentralization and creation of profit centers are not necessarily synonymous terms. Although profit centers typically accompany decentralization, their existence does not necessarily mean that heavy decentralization exists. A company may have many divisions called profit centers, but their managers may have little leeway in making decisions. A manager may be unable to buy or sell outside his company, he may have to obtain approval from corporate headquarters for every capital expenditure over $200, and he may be forced to accept central-staff "advice." In another company, which has only cost centers, managers may have great latitude on capital outlays and on where to purchase materials and services. In short, the labels of *profit center* and *cost center* are sometimes deceptive as clues to the degree of decentralization.

---

[1] David Solomons, *Divisional Performance: Measurement and Control* (Homewood, Ill.: Richard D. Irwin, Inc., 1968), p. 10. His Chapter 1 is a good summary of the organization of divisionalized businesses.

Moreover, the size or the number of profit centers is no criterion for judging whether decentralization exists or is desirable. A huge company with many profit centers may indeed be heavily centralized, and a small company with few profit centers may be effectively decentralized. An example of the latter would be the departments in a retail department store or a medical center. It is superficial reasoning to say that decentralization is not applicable to small organizations.

benefits of How should top managers decide on how much decentralization is optimal?
decentral- The optimal amount of decentralization is the amount that attains top
ization management's overall objectives most efficiently and effectively. These objectives are often expressed as the maximization of short-run profits, of long-run profits, of rate of return, of net present value, or as some other measure.

Conceptually, top managers try to choose a degree of decentralization that maximizes the excess of benefits over costs. Practically, top managers cannot quantify either the benefits or the costs. Nevertheless, this cost–benefit approach helps us identify the central issues.

The claimed benefits of decentralization include the following:

1. More optimum decisions are likely, because the manager of the subunit is in a better position to react to information about local conditions in a timely way.

2. The burden of decision making is distributed, so that the managers' collective decisions are optimized. Top managers are also likely to have more time for strategic planning than if they had to control day-to-day operations.

3. Greater freedom heightens the managers' incentives, because they have more control over the factors that affect the measures of their performance.

4. Greater freedom induces managers to check outside markets for both raw materials and finished goods more frequently. Intracompany transfers are often based on these market prices. Where market-based prices are used as a part of the information system, there is a routine check on market forces that is otherwise not available. This built-in check on market prices often focuses on uneconomic activities that would not be as readily detected in a centralized system.

5. More decision making on a wide spectrum provides better training for managers as they rise in the organization.

6. Decentralization is often accompanied by the use of profit or investment centers. The managership of a profit center is somehow viewed as a higher-status position than that of a cost center, and therefore may provide the psychological benefits of first-class citizenship. In other words, the profit-center structure has a more desirable motivational effect.

All these claimed advantages are "benefits" because they are supposed to result in larger gross increases in profits than would occur with a more heavily centralized organization.

costs of decentralization The largest cost of decentralization is probably dysfunctional decision making—that is, decision making where the benefit to one subunit is more than offset by the costs or loss of benefit to other subunits. This may be caused by (a) a lack of harmony or congruence between the overall organizational goals and the individual goals of the decision maker, and (b) a lack of information for guiding the individual manager concerning the effects of his decisions on other parts of the organization. Moreover, the costs of gathering and processing information often increase, since decentralization is usually accompanied by more elaborate information systems. A formal information system becomes more important to top managers because it provides the principal means of obtaining goal congruence and of monitoring a collection of more independent managers. In addition, some central corporate services and administrative talent tend to be duplicated.

Transfer pricing is an example of the comparative information-gathering costs of centralization and decentralization. A centralized system might impose a transfer price based on, say, standard costs, and might require all purchases or sales of a particular item to be made internally. In contrast, a decentralized system might let the managers of the selling and buying divisions negotiate a price and might allow the managers discretion to buy or sell the item in outside markets—in which case, there will probably be additional costs of management time in negotiations, of friction, and perhaps of extra information gathering for making these individual decisions.

Dysfunctional decision making is most likely where the subunits in the organization are highly interdependent—that is, where the decisions affecting one part of the organization influence the decisions and performance of another part. If interdependence is great, coordination is needed to obtain optimum decisions for the organization as a whole. Subunits can rarely be completely autonomous or self-contained, so interdependence is the biggest inhibiting factor in decentralization. There are countless examples of interdependence where the performance of the receiving unit depends on the quality of the work done by the supplying unit. For instance, parts and raw materials must meet schedules and specifications; two segments of the organization may share or compete for computer services, management skills, or raw materials; they may sell in a common market (for example, Buick and Oldsmobile) in such a way that an action beneficial to one subunit may be harmful to another and to the corporation as a whole.

comparison of benefits and costs The foregoing benefits and costs must be compared by top managers, often on a function-by-function basis. For example, the controller's function may be heavily decentralized for many attention-directing and problem-solving purposes (such as operating budgets and performance reports), but heavily centralized for other purposes (such as accounts-receivable processing and income tax planning).

The patterns of benefits and costs of decentralization are shown in Exhibit

EXHIBIT 21-1

BENEFITS AND COSTS OF DECENTRALIZATION

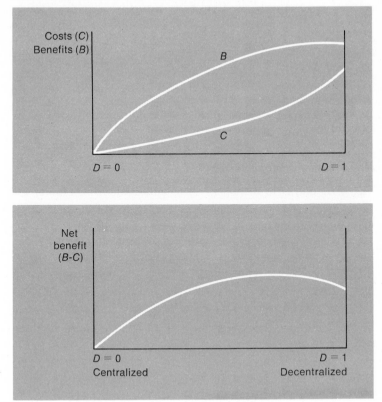

21-1. The first graph hypothesizes that the benefits (B) of decentralization will increase at a decreasing rate and that the costs (C) will increase slowly at lower degrees of decentralization but then start to soar.[2]

The degree of decentralization (D) varies from zero to one. D is essentially a gauge of the freedom to make decisions. For example, it could be measured by the percentage of acquisition decisions that a division manager can make without needing top-management consent. Various attempts have been made to obtain a measure of D that might be used for comparing various organizations.[3]

Decentralization is likely to be most beneficial and least costly when the

[2]In correspondence with the author, Professor Joshua Ronen has commented that while it is plausible to hypothesize this particular shape of the curves, there is no evident reason why B should be concave and C should be convex, except in some regions. For example, it is not unreasonable to expect the cost curve to start off being concave, owing to decreasing marginal cost of decentralization, and to become convex later on. (In fact, it should probably start being concave at the point D = 0 until it reaches some positive degree of decentralization.) Conversely, the benefits curve will probably start at D = 0 being convex, and it would start becoming concave at some positive point of decentralization.

[3]See T. L. Whisler, H. Meyer, B. H. Baum, and P. F. Sorenson, "Centralization of Organization Control: An Empirical Study of Its Meaning and Measurement," *Journal of Business,* Vol. 40, No. 1, 10–26. They develop a Gini ratio of concentration, which is applied to the distribution of individual compensation within each department studied. Their rationale assumes that the way in which executive compensation is distributed reflects rather closely the way in which responsibility and control are distributed.

organizational units are independent. Then there is minimal likelihood of dysfunctional decisions. In general, a subunit is independent (self-contained) to the extent that it

1. Does not compete with other subunits for the use of limited resources within the organization, such as capital, research services, or management skill
2. Does not compete in the same market or buy from the same sources as other subdivisions
3. Does not provide goods to other subunits or depend upon them for its own inputs
4. Can make decisions and obtain goal congruence without coordination with other subunits and without explicitly considering the objectives of the other subunits or of the organization[4]

Of course, B, C, and D in Exhibit 21-1 are impossible to determine with precision. There are indications that top managers perceive the optimum decentralization in practice as somewhere in the middle. The extent of decentralization in a particular organization is obviously affected by numerous factors. As I mentioned previously, heavy decentralization may be appropriate for small as well as large companies. However, caution is needed, because decentralization is a relative matter. For example, a decentralized division of General Electric may be as large as or larger than most other companies in its industry.[5] This point has been cited as evidence against breaking a smaller company up into decentralized divisions; after all, the mammoth corporations do not think it desirable to break these large divisions into smaller decentralized subunits.

There is a tendency to jump to fallacious conclusions about the extent of decentralization in a particular company. For example, the *number* of profit centers is not a valid index of decentralization. Consider General Electric, which has over 160 subdivision managers with profit responsibility. Some of these subunits have annual sales of over $300 million. Is GE a heavily decentralized company? The answer depends on whether these individual subunits are, in turn, managed on a decentralized basis. A $300-million subdivision that is subject to autocratic rule by the general manager is surely less decentralized than a $200-million outside competitor in the same product lines that has several nearly independent subunits. Taken as a whole, General Electric may appear decentralized; however, each division may be heavily centralized when compared to its outside competitors.

SYSTEMS DESIGN AND DECENTRALIZATION

three We explored the meaning of decentralization because accounting systems
criteria should primarily aim at facilitating the objectives of management. For
example, top management's foremost objective may be the optimal acquisition

---

[4]See William T. Morris, *Decentralization in Management Systems* (Columbus, O.: Ohio State University Press, 1968), p. 15.

[5]David Solomons, *Divisional Performance*, p. 13. See also John Dearden, "Mirage of Profit Decentralization," *Harvard Business Review*, Vol. 40, No. 6, 140–54.

and allocation of resources to maximize profit or payoff (whether defined in a short-run or long-run sense). In turn, management may decide that heavy decentralization is the best way to obtain that objective. Accordingly, an accounting system for prediction and control should provide information that facilitates the decisions that lead to optimum payoffs for the organization as a whole.

In the light of this objective, how do you judge whether an accounting system can be improved? Keep in mind that an organization is a group of individuals seeking to achieve some common goals, or, in different language, to maximize an objective function. Each member has objectives of his own, often not coinciding with those of the organization. Each member has a range of decisions to make, within limits set partly by the environment and partly by the decisions of other members. The challenge is to keep the organization's members in step with each other to maximize the objective function.[6]

Three criteria are helpful for designing or judging a particular accounting system in a decentralized setting: (a) goal congruence, (b) performance evaluation, and (c) autonomy.[7] As you know, goal congruence focuses on the harmonizing of the interests of the managers with the interests of the organization as a whole. Evaluation of performance (feedback) is needed to help make predictions for future decisions, to appraise the abilities of the *manager,* and to assess the profitability of the capital invested in the organizational *subunit* as an economic investment. Moreover, the choice of various performance measures will have different influential effects on manager behavior. Finally, if top management wants to preserve a given decentralized structure, it must respect the subunits as decentralized entities.

Note that the common thread of these criteria is motivation. The aim is to get a system that will point the managers toward the top-management goals. But pointing them in the right direction is only the first step. In addition, incentives must be provided that will spur managers toward those goals.

how much
information
is enough?

The accounting systems and techniques that we shall discuss fall short of meeting all the objectives just specified. In practice, however, the fact that measures of return on investment (ROI) or transfer prices are not conceptually perfect may be unimportant. It depends on the sensitivity of these crude techniques in various decision settings. Often they are better than even cruder techniques because they are the best feasible means of prompting the desired attitudes and decisions. Again and again, we find that in complex organizations the key question is not what combination of information and decision techniques leads to the optimum solution—because the optimum decision is almost always unknown. Instead, the key question is: Given the available techniques, the human and inanimate resources, and our limited knowledge, what combination will lead to the best perceived solution?

[6] Kenneth J. Arrow, "Control in Large Organizations," *Management Science,* Vol. 10, No. 3, 398.

[7] Joshua Ronen and George McKinney, "Transfer Pricing for Divisional Autonomy," *Journal of Accounting Research,* Spring 1970, pp. 100–101.

Consider the steps that must be taken by the control-system designer, who may be an accountant, a manager, or both. First, he must choose a measure of accomplishment that represents top-management objectives. This provides a conceptual structure. Should it be net income, rate of return on investment, contribution margin, sales, or some other measure? Second, whatever measure is chosen, the designer must then choose how to define such items as income or investment. Should income be based on variable or absorption costing? Should central corporate costs be allocated? Should investment consist of assets, or assets minus liabilities, or some other collection? Third, how should items be measured? Historical cost? Replacement cost? Realizable value? Fourth, what standards should be applied; should all divisions be required to earn the same rate of return on all their investments? Fifth, what timing of feedback is needed? Quarterly? Annually? Should feedback on the performance of managers be timed differently from feedback on the performance of divisions as economic investments?

These five steps are not necessarily taken sequentially. Instead, the answers to these questions are interdependent. Taken together, they produce a particular control system that is supposed to be optimal for the specific organization as a whole.

We will explore these questions in subsequent sections. However, the answers are not uniform. They depend on the particular needs of specific managers in a particular organization. The basic job of control systems is to supply information. Information is gathered at a cost. The manager (and the accountant) must decide whether to seek (buy) more information. Numbers are routinely provided as clues regarding whether to buy more or "better" information. For instance, the weaknesses of historical costs as a basis for making economic decisions are well known. However, most managers apparently have decided that a historical-cost system is good enough for the *routine* evaluation of managers—for providing feedback that will have the desired motivational effects and that will give clues to whether to invest or disinvest in a particular division. The investment decision is not made in a routine manner; therefore, it may be uneconomical to gather information on replacement costs or realizable value except as special needs arise. In other words, a system may be designed to help in the routine evaluation of managers, but the information that will provide for the evaluation of subunits as economic investments may be too expensive to collect repetitively.

MEASURE THAT REPRESENTS TOP-MANAGEMENT OBJECTIVES

*role of
investment*   What quantitative measure best represents top-management objectives? Income? Rate of return? Some other measure? Many managers are preoccupied with the measures of dollar sales, dollar profits, and profit margins (the ratio of profits to dollar sales). However, the ultimate test of profitability is not the absolute amount of profit or the relationship of profit to sales. The critical test is the relationship of profit to invested capital. The most popular

way of expressing this relationship is by means of a rate of return on investment (ROI). The ROI approach has been used for centuries by financiers and others. Still, this technique did not become widespread in industry for judging operating performance until the early 1960's. Conceptually, ROI has innate appeal because it blends in one number all the major ingredients of profitability. The ROI statistic by itself can be compared with opportunities elsewhere, inside or outside the company. Practically, ROI is an imperfect measurement that should be used with skepticism and in conjunction with other performance measurements.

The major advantage of the rate-of-return technique is its focus on an often-neglected phase of management responsibility—the required investment in assets. For a given company at a given time, there is an optimum level of investment in any asset—whether it be cash, receivables, physical plant, or inventories. Cash balances, for example, may be too large or too small. The principal cost of having too much cash is the sacrifice of possible earnings; idle cash earns nothing. The principal cost of having too little cash may be lost discounts on purchases or harm to one's credit standing. For every class of asset, then, there is an optimum level of investment that, along with optimum levels of investment in other assets, helps to maximize long-run profits.

Companies take different approaches to the problem of measuring return on investment, differing mostly with respect to the appropriate measure of invested capital, but also differing in the measure of income.

A useful approach to the problem may be outlined by using the following relationships:

$$\frac{\text{Sales}}{\text{Invested capital}} \times \frac{\text{Net income}}{\text{Sales}} = \frac{\text{Net income}}{\text{Invested capital}}$$

or

Capital turnover $\times$ Margin percentage on sales $=$ Return on investment

Consider the components of the relationships. One may make the following obvious generalizations: Any action is beneficial that (a) boosts sales, (b) reduces invested capital, or (c) reduces costs—while holding the other two factors constant. Put another way, there are two basic ingredients in profit making: turnover and margin percentages. An improvement in either without changing the other will enhance return on invested capital.

ROI as a tool for management Assume that top management decides that a 20 percent return on invested capital is a profit target that will yield adequate rewards and yet not invite entry into the market by new competitors. How can this return be attained? Present performance (in millions of dollars) follows:

	$\dfrac{\text{Sales}}{\text{Invested capital}}$		$\times$	$\dfrac{\text{Net income}}{\text{Sales}}$	$=$	$\dfrac{\text{Net income}}{\text{Invested capital}}$
Present	$\dfrac{100}{50}$		$\times$	$\dfrac{9}{100}$	$=$	9/50, or 18%

Alternatives:

A. Increase margin by lowering expenses	$\dfrac{100}{50}$	$\times$	$\dfrac{10}{100}$	$=$	10/50, or 20%
B. Decrease assets	$\dfrac{100}{45}$	$\times$	$\dfrac{9}{100}$	$=$	9/45, or 20%

Alternative A demonstrates a popular way of improving performance. Margins may be increased by reducing expenses, as in this case, or by boosting selling prices, or by increasing sales volume relative to a given amount of fixed expenses.

Alternative B shows that changes of investments in assets may also improve performance. Management has always been very conscious of the need for increasing sales and for controlling costs so that good profit margins may be attained. But control of investment has not always received conscientious managerial attention. Too often, asset balances rise without justification. Not only do operating costs have to be controlled, but investment in cash, inventory, receivables, and fixed assets must be kept to the minimum that is consistent with effective performance. This means investing idle cash, determining proper inventory levels, managing credit judiciously, and spending carefully on fixed assets. In other words, increasing asset turnover means getting the maximum mileage in sales out of every dollar invested in business resources. For example, having too much inventory is sometimes worse than having too little. Turnover decreases and goods deteriorate or become obsolete, thus dragging the rate of return downward.

ROI or residual income?   Earlier we saw that the ultimate test of profitability is the relationship of profit to invested capital. Until this point, our examples implied that the desired objective of management is the maximization of the rate of return on investment. But an investment center may be judged on what has been labeled *residual income* instead of on its rate of return. Residual income is the operating income of an investment center, less the "imputed" interest on the assets used by the center. The choice of whether to use ROI or residual income as a management objective will induce different decisions.

Compare the calculations for two identical divisions:

		DIVISION A	DIVISION B
(1)	Operating income	$ 25,000	$ 25,000
(2)	Imputed interest at 16% of assets		16,000
(3)	Operating assets	100,000	100,000
	ROI [(1) ÷ (3)]	25%	
	Residual income [(1) − (2)]		9,000

The objective of maximizing residual income assumes that as long as the division earns a rate in excess of the charge for invested capital, the division should expand. The manager of Division B would expand as long as his incremental opportunities earned 16 percent or more on his incremental assets.

General Electric favors this approach because managers will concentrate on maximizing a number (dollars of residual income) rather than a percentage (rate of return).[8] The objective of maximizing ROI may induce managers of highly profitable divisions to reject projects that, from the viewpoint of the corporation as a whole, should be accepted. For example, the manager of Division A would be reluctant to accept a new project with a 20 percent rate even though top management regards 16 percent as a minimum desired rate of return. In such a case, the residual-income approach would charge him 16 percent and he would be inclined to accept all projects that exceed that rate.

There is a parallel between the discounted cash-flow methods in capital budgeting and the comparison of ROI and residual income. In Chapter 14, comparisons were made between the time-adjusted rate of return and the net present-value methods. The time-adjusted rate of return method is similar to the ROI method, and the net present-value method is similar to the residual-income method. Residual income changes the goal from "maximize ROI" to "maximize dollar return in excess of minimum desired ROI."

DISTINCTION BETWEEN MANAGERS AND INVESTMENTS

A distinction should be made between the performance of the division manager and the performance of the division as an investment by the corporation. The manager should be evaluated on the basis of his controllable performance (in many cases some controllable contribution in relation to controllable investment). For other decisions, "such as new investment or a withdrawal of funds from the division, the important thing is the success or failure of the divisional venture, not of the men who run it."[9]

The most skillful division manager is often put in charge of the sickest division in an attempt to change its fortunes. Such an attempt may take years, not months. Furthermore, it may result in merely bringing the division up to a minimum acceptable rate of return. The division may continue to be a poor profit performer in comparison to other divisions. If top management relied solely on the absolute rate of return to judge management, the skillful manager would be foolhardy to accept such trouble-shooting assignments.

This distinction helps clarify some vexing difficulties. For example, top management may want to use an investment base to gauge the economic performance of a retail store, but the *manager* may be best judged by focusing on income and forgetting about any investment allocations. If investment is assigned to the manager, the aim should be to assign controllable investment only. Controllability[10] depends on what *decisions* managers can make regarding the size of the investment base. In a highly decentralized company, for instance, the manager can influence the size of all his assets and can exercise judgment

---

[8] See Robert W. Lewis, *Planning, Managing, and Measuring the Business* (New York: Financial Executives Research Foundation, 1955), p. 32.

[9] David Solomons, *Divisional Performance,* p. 84.

[10] See Chapter 6 for an expanded discussion of controllability.

regarding the appropriate amount of short-term credit and perhaps some long-term credit.

DEFINITIONS OF INCOME

contribution
approach
The selection of performance measures requires some concept or definition of income. A contribution approach (see also Chapter 12) can help distinguish between the performance of the division and the performance of the manager. Exhibit 21-2 shows a sample format of the contribution approach

EXHIBIT 21-2

FORMAT FOR DIVISIONAL INCOME STATEMENT

	DOLLARS	DOLLARS
Sales to outside customers	xxx	
Transfers to other divisions at market value	xxx	
Transfers to other divisions at other than market value	xxx	
Total revenue		xxx
Deduct:		
Variable cost of goods sold and transferred	xxx	
Variable divisional expenses	xxx	xxx
Contribution margin		xxx
Add (deduct):		
Fixed costs allocated to other divisions for transfers made at other than market value[a]		xxx
Contribution margin plus other revenue		xxx
Deduct:		
Controllable discretionary and committed costs:[b]		
Division overhead	xxx	
Depreciation, property taxes, and insurance on controllable plant assets	xxx	xxx
Controllable operating income		xxx
Deduct: imputed and explicit interest		xxx
Controllable residual income before income taxes		xxx
Deduct:		
Uncontrollable division costs	xxx	
Uncontrollable central expenses	xxx	
Interest on uncontrollable investment	xxx	xxx
Residual income before taxes		xxx
Income taxes		xxx
Net residual income (after taxes)		xxx

[a] This line might be included above with the other revenue items.
[b] Chapter 12 explains that the line between discretionary and committed expenses must be drawn on a company-by-company basis. Getting agreement as to these classifications is not an insurmountable task.

Source: Adapted from David Solomons, *Divisional Performance: Measurement and Control* (New York: Financial Executives Research Foundation, 1965), p. 82. Reprinted in paperback form by Richard D. Irwin, Inc., 1968.

coupled with residual income. If an ROI approach were used instead, imputed interest would be excluded and two ROI figures would be presented:

$$\text{Controllable ROI} = \text{Controllable income} \div \text{Controllable investment}$$

$$\text{Net ROI} = \text{Net income after taxes} \div \text{Total investment}$$

Note that income taxes are deducted for purposes of measuring the performance of the unit as an investment but not ordinarily for purposes of measuring the manager's performance per se. Of course, how income taxes are accounted for is highly dependent on who has the responsibility for income tax planning.

allocating costs and assets to divisions   Chapter 12 concentrated on the problems of cost allocation. The points made there apply also to the problems of asset allocation. Again, the aim is to allocate in a manner that will be goal-congruent, will provide incentive, and will recognize autonomy insofar as possible. Incidentally, as long as the managers feel that they are being treated uniformly, they tend to be more tolerant about the imperfections of the allocation. For example, should cash be included under controllable investment if the balances are strictly controlled by corporate headquarters? Arguments can be made for both sides, but the manager is usually regarded as being responsible for the volume of business generated by the division. In turn, this volume is likely to have a direct effect on the overall cash needs of the corporation.

A common criterion for allocation should be avoidability. That is, the amount allocable to any given segment for the purpose of evaluating the division's performance is the amount that the corporation as a whole could avoid by not having that segment. Commonly used bases for allocation, when assets are not directly identifiable with a specific division, include:

ASSET CLASS	POSSIBLE ALLOCATION BASE
Corporate cash	Budgeted cash needs
Receivables	Sales weighted by payment terms
Inventories	Budgeted sales or usage
Plant and equipment	Usage of services in terms of long-run forecasts of demand or area occupied

Where the allocation of an asset (such as central corporate facilities) would indeed be arbitrary, many managers feel that it is better not to allocate.

DEFINITIONS OF INVESTMENT

possible investment bases   The base that is used for measuring invested capital may appropriately differ between companies and within segments of the same company. The alternative bases that may be used include:

1. *Total assets available.* This base includes all business assets, regardless of their individual purpose.

2. *Total assets employed.* This base excludes excess or idle assets, such as vacant land or construction in progress.

3. *Net working capital plus other assets.* This base is really the same as 1, except that current liabilities are deducted from the total assets available. In a sense, this represents an exclusion of that portion of current assets that is supplied by short-term creditors. The main justification for this base is that the manager often does have direct influence over the amount of short-term credit that he utilizes. An able manager should maximize the use of such credit, within some overall constraints to prevent endangering the company's credit standing.

4. *Stockholders' equity.* This base centers attention on the rate of return that will be earned by the business owners.

comparison of asset and equity bases Stockholders' equity, as a possible investment base, is important to the owners, but it is not so significant to the operating manager. He is usually concerned with the management of assets, not with the long-term sources of assets. There are two major management functions: operating and financing. To the extent possible, the measurement of operating decisions (the acquisition and utilization of assets) should not be influenced by financing decisions (what long-term sources of assets were chosen).

For example, consider the following companies:

	(1)	(2)	(3)	(4)	(5)	(6)	(4) + (1)	(6) + (3)
		EQUITIES					RETURN ON INVESTMENT	
	ASSETS	LIABILITIES	STOCK-HOLDERS' EQUITY	INCOME BEFORE INTEREST	8% INTEREST	NET INCOME	ASSETS	STOCK-HOLDERS' EQUITY
Co. A	$1,000,000	$500,000	$ 500,000	$200,000	$40,000	$160,000	20%	32%
Co. B	1,000,000	—	1,000,000	200,000	—	200,000	20%	20%

It would be invalid to use stockholders' equity as a basis for comparing the operating performance of the managers of Company A and Company B. The 32 percent rate of return does not distinguish between the operating and the financing decisions. Company A in effect has paid 8 percent for the use of $500,000, which in turn has earned a return on assets of 20 percent. This is an example of risk-taking that is often called *trading on the equity* or *using financial leverage.* It is a financing decision that results in borrowing money at a fixed interest rate with the expectation of earning a higher rate on such funds. Trading on the equity should be viewed as a separate decision and should not affect the measurement of operating performance.

For measuring the performance of division managers, one of the three other asset bases listed above is almost always superior to stockholders' equity. If the division manager's mission is to utilize all assets as best he can without regard to their financing, then base 1 is best. If top-management directives force him to carry extra assets that are not currently productive, then 2 is best. If he has direct control over the amount of the division's short-term trade credit and bank loans, then 3 is best. In practice, 1 is used most often, although 3 is not far behind.[11]

MEASUREMENT ALTERNATIVES

why historical cost? How should we measure the assets that are included in the investment base? Should assets be valued at net book value, replacement cost, realizable value, or some other value? There is a propensity to have one investment measure serve many masters. Therefore, net book value[12] predominates, but its prevalence does not mean that it is necessarily correct. Of course, the correct but unsatisfying answer is: The relevant value depends on the decisions being affected and evaluated. These decisions often concern the evaluation of performance. They are decisions about the wisdom of past decisions; they require a follow-up of the historical cost and the predictions that were related thereto.

Given the frequently cited infirmities of historical cost, why do organizations continue to use it for evaluating performance? There are several reasons. Some seem unjustifiable, while others make sense. Ignorance and inertia have been cited as two likely reasons. However, the routine use of some alternative investment measure that may have more appeal to many, such as replacement cost, is an extra cost of compiling data. As mentioned earlier, the central manager wants *routine* data essentially as clues for deciding whether to seek (buy) more information. Routine scorekeeping and attention-directing data are used to promote goal congruence and evaluate performance. Historical costs may be regarded as good enough for such purposes. The decisions to invest or disinvest, which we will consider below, are not routine decisions. From the viewpoint of the systems designer, it may be more economical to get replacement and disposal values by conducting special studies when the need is perceived rather than by routine recording.

disposal or continuance Let us consider the problem of measuring assets for a few classes of decisions. First, we examine the disposal or continuance decision. As Chapters 13 and 14 demonstrated, the discounted cash-flow (DCF) model needs two values for the disposal or continuance decision: economic value and disposal (exit) value in the best alternative use. Historical cost is irrelevant except as a basis for prediction. For example, suppose there is a world of perfect certainty and there is old equipment that is expected to produce $20,000 in operating cash inflows during each of the next five years. Also suppose the disposal value today

---

[11] John J. Mauriel and Robert N. Anthony, in "Misevaluation of Investment Center Performance," *Harvard Business Review,* Vol. 44, No. 2, 98–105, summarize the practice of 2,658 companies. Sixty percent, or 1,603, used investment centers. Of these, 40 percent deducted short-term external payables in arriving at the investment base.

[12] Mauriel and Anthony, *op. cit.,* report that 73 percent of the companies used net book value as their valuation measure and 18 percent used gross book value. Only 3 percent of the companies used some measure that departs from cost, such as insurance value or appraisal value.

is $38,000 and five years hence is zero. The opportunity cost of capital is 10 percent. The analysis follows:

> Economic value, the total present value of
> the alternative to continue operations,
> $20,000 × 3.791 (P.V. of $1.00 at
> 10 percent for 5 years) $65,820
>
> Disposal value, the total present value of
> the alternative to sell today $38,000

The analysis favors retention of the asset. The relevant data consisted of *both* the economic value and the current disposal value[13] in the best alternative use.

The very act of continuance implies that, as a minimum, the continuance or disposal decision has been made. Often, continuance occurs automatically, simply because disposal is so obviously economically unattractive that formal analysis is unnecessary. The decision is made unconsciously. However, the economic recession of 1968–71 in the United States induced many managers to pause and explicitly analyze some activities. These analyses led to decisions to disinvest. Managers found that disposal values were higher than the economic values of continuance in use. This illustrates the need for a periodic monitoring of both economic values and disposal values, a monitoring that is not ordinarily incorporated in existing management control systems.

disposal or continuance or expansion   The manager often considers three basic alternatives simultaneously: disposal, continuance, or expansion. Expansion will be desirable if the alternative is more attractive than other investment opportunities. The general decision rule for adding new investments is a familiar one: Invest if the economic value (total present value) exceeds the required investment so that the net present value is positive. For example, suppose additional equipment can be obtained for $50,000 that will produce an expected annual operating cash flow of $20,000 for five years:

> Economic value at 10%, $20,000 × 3.791 $65,820
> Required investment   50,000
> Net present value $15,820

The analysis favors buying the asset. The relevant data consisted of both the economic value and the required investment to obtain that stream of cash inflows. Of course, this required investment at time zero is the acquisition cost.

---

[13] The terms *current value* and *market value* are often used to describe disposal or sales or exit value. These terms are avoided here because they are ambiguous in the literature and in discussions. Sometimes *current value* is used to represent economic value. At other times it is used to represent replacement cost. At still other times, it is used to represent market value. Similarly, *market value* is sometimes used to describe disposal value, but at other times it means replacement cost. The two values are needed because they must be compared before an intelligent decision can be made. If the disposal value exceeds the economic value, the asset should be sold, and vice versa.

The relevant data are again two values: the economic value and the required investment (acquisition cost).

To recapitulate, if the manager examines an existing investment, he often considers three decision alternatives that may be likened to investments in securities. The required data are:

DISPOSAL (SELL)	CONTINUANCE (HOLD)	EXPANSION (BUY MORE)
Economic Value compared to Disposal Value	Economic Value compared to Disposal Value	Economic Value compared to Required Investment

Note that economic value depends on a deliberate subjective assessment of expected future cash inflows. Disposal value and required-investment values may be identical for highly marketable securities[14] (ignoring brokerage fees, markups, and income tax aspects), but they may be quite different for investments in highly specialized assets with no market values. For example, a company may invest $50,000 in new special equipment. An instant after acquisition, the replacement cost is $50,000 but the disposal value in the next best use may be only $38,000 or less. Note especially that economic value is always needed for these decisions, whether the alternative is to contract, continue, or expand.

need for consistency between models Ideally, the decision model used to make a capital-investment decision and the model used to judge subsequent performance would be consistent. However, in practice we often find DCF models being used for investment decisions and the accrual-accounting models being used for performance evaluation.

This conflict of models may lead to dysfunctional decisions. Managers are sometimes reluctant to make capital outlays that are justified by DCF methods but that lead to poor performance records in the first year or two after the outlay. This is especially likely if the outlay is subject to immediate write-off (for instance, product advertising, engineering development, and process improvement costs) or to accelerated-depreciation methods.

compound interest and compatibility How can compatibility be achieved? As explained in Chapter 13, DCF methods assume a capital-recovery factor that is related to funds in use. Suppose a company is considering investing in a project with a two-year life and no salvage value. Cash inflow will be equal payments of $4,000 at the end of each of the two years. If the company paid $7,132 for the project, present-value tables would reveal its time-adjusted rate of return as 8 per-

[14]Both would be measured by quoted market prices. That is why "market value" is cited as being the relevant number for sell, hold, or buy decisions in managing a security portfolio. Historical cost is irrelevant for these decisions except as it bears on the determination of income tax aspects.

cent. Each cash payment consists of "interest" (rate of return) plus recovery of principal.

YEAR	INVESTMENT AT BEGINNING OF YEAR	OPERATING CASH INFLOW	(INTEREST) RETURN, @ 8% PER YEAR	(DEPRECIATION) AMOUNT OF INVESTMENT RECEIVED AT END OF YEAR	(NET BOOK VALUE) UNRECOVERED INVESTMENT AT END OF YEAR
1	$7,132	$4,000	.08 × $7,132 = $571	$4,000 − $571 = $3,429	$7,132 − $3,429 = $3,703
2	3,703	4,000	.08 × $3,703 = $297	$4,000 − $297 = $3,703	$3,703 − $3,703 = 0

If subsequent performance were the same as had been forecast, the income statement based on the DCF model would be as shown in the first two columns below. For comparison, the results of using other depreciation methods are also shown:

	METHOD OF DEPRECIATION					
	COMPOUND-INTEREST		STRAIGHT-LINE		SUM-OF-YEARS'-DIGITS	
Year	1	2	1	2	1	2
Cash operating income	$4,000	$4,000	$4,000	$4,000	$4,000	$4,000
Depreciation	3,429[a]	3,703[a]	3,566[b]	3,566[b]	4,755[c]	2,377[c]
Net income	$ 571	$ 297	$ 434	$ 434	$ (755)	$1,623
Investment base— beginning balance	$7,132	$3,703	$7,132	$3,566	$7,132	$2,377
Rate of return on beginning balance	8%	8%	6%	12%	−11%	68%

[a] See preceding table for computations.
[b] $7,132 ÷ 2 = $3,566 per year.
[c] Sum of digits = 1 + 2 = 3. Therefore, ⅔ × $7,132 = $4,755 for first year and ⅓ × $7,132 = $2,377 for second year.

The compound-interest method results in an increasing charge for depreciation over the useful life of the asset. But it does provide for a rate of return that dovetails with the assumptions in the DCF model. The comparison above shows how the commonly used depreciation models of accrual accounting produce varying rates of return that have no relation to the DCF planning models.[15]

A residual-income approach to the compound-interest method would show:

	YEAR			
	1		2	
Cash operating income		$4,000		$4,000
Depreciation (based on original expectations)	$3,429		$3,703	
Imputed interest (at minimum desired rate)	571	4,000	297	4,000
		$ 0		$ 0

This example assumes that the 8 percent rate of return on this project is equal to the minimum desired rate that would be used in charging the division for

[15] For an elaboration of the differences, see Ezra Solomon, "Alternative Rate of Return Concepts and Their Implications for Utility Regulation," *The Bell Journal of Economics and Management Science,* Vol. 1, No. 1 (Spring 1970), 65–81.

its capital and in the computing of depreciation. Any cash flow that increased the rate of return would result in positive residual income. Assume that the cash flow was $4,500 and $3,800, respectively:

	YEAR			
	1		2	
Cash operating income		$4,500		$3,800
Depreciation (based on original expectations)	$3,429		$3,703	
Imputed interest	571	4,000	297	4,000
Residual income		$ 500		$−200

Industry has rejected the compound-interest method of depreciation primarily because:

1. It usually produces an increasing charge over the useful life of an asset. Intuitively, however, managers do not see the justification for an increasing charge for depreciation if cash flows remain constant or decline.

2. The compound-interest method works clearly if projected annual operating cash flows are reasonably equal, but the implicit principal-recovery pattern is more difficult to compute and explain if projected cash flows differ markedly through the years.

3. The market values of particular assets do not coincide with the book values, particularly in the early years of use.

Until formal attempts are made to reconcile DCF models for planning with accrual-accounting models for control,[16] follow-up of investment decisions must rely on the sampling of projects or on a dual planning scheme. In sampling, DCF decisions would be audited by gathering data, year by year, to see whether the specific cash-flow predictions proved accurate. In dual planning, the DCF decision would simultaneously be cast in the form of an accrual-accounting rate-of-return prediction; then the follow-up would be based on the accrual-accounting model.

evaluation of performance   As we have seen, the evaluation of performance entails a follow-up of past decisions with the hope that such an appraisal will improve incentive and future decision making. But "evaluation of performance" is a catchall term that needs subdivision before choosing the relevant investment base. For the purpose of assessing the wisdom of past investment decisions, decision by decision, using historical costs as an investment measure and compound-interest depreciation will provide a comparison that is consistent with the predictions made and the DCF decision model used.

The evaluation of performance is also needed for making *comparisons* of

---

[16] For examples see H. Bierman, Jr., and T. R. Dyckman, *Managerial Cost Accounting* (New York: The Macmillan Company, 1971), pp. 365–81, and Alfred Rappaport, ed., *Information for Decision Making* (Englewood Cliffs, N. J.: Prentice-Hall, Inc., 1970).

executives as managers and of divisions as economic investments for a given time period and over a number of time periods. A fundamental rule for making comparisons of the productivity of assets is that their measurement basis be uniform. That is, you would expect assets that produce the same net cash inflows with the same risk to have the same value. For example, it would be nonsense to judge either manager performance or economic productivity on the holding of 100 shares of General Motors common stock for one year by comparing the increase in the market value of that stock (plus cash dividends) with its historical cost. If one portfolio manager bought the stock in 19_1, another in 19_4, and another on December 31, 19_6, the comparisons of performance for holding the hundred shares during 19_7 would surely not be related to the historical costs of investments. Instead, they would be related to what the 100 shares would have cost on December 31, 19_6. In short, the relevant investment measure for the routine evaluation of performance is replacement cost, because it provides a common denominator representing the equivalent of what would have been the required investment at the beginning of any given period.

Consider another example. If one manager acquired plant and equipment in 19_1, and another manager acquired *identical* plant and equipment on December 31, 19_6 (identical in every way: appearance, technology, and expected cash-inflow productivity), the value of the investment measure for judging 19_7 performance should be identical. In a sense, every manager and every economic unit starts a new year afresh;[17] all existing assets are viewed as if they were acquired on New Year's Eve. Thus, replacement value is used as a common denominator to compare current productivity and to help predict the potential for competitive entry.

When assets are already in use, approximations of replacement market prices often do not exist. Note that the task of approximation is *not* to obtain a price of a new asset that would in fact be used to replace an existing asset. Instead, the aim is to approximate how much it would cost to obtain similar assets that would produce the *same* expected operating cash inflows as the existing asset. The essence of the asset is its expected cash flow, not its physical or technological features. Managers rarely replace assets exactly in kind with new assets having identical operating and economic characteristics.

Approximating a replacement cost for the 1972 delivery truck in 1976 may not be too difficult, because active markets exist. But the hunt would be for prices for 1972 models in equivalent condition, not for a new 1976 model—even though in fact a 1976 model would actually be purchased if replacement occurred in 1976.

As equipment gets more highly specialized and subject to obsolescence, the task of approximating replacement cost becomes trickier. If no market exists, either specific price indexes for similar classes of equipment or appraisal might be used. The use of indexes provides more objectivity but perhaps less relevance, because they may not be exactly applicable to the particular assets in question.

---

[17] Also see Yaaqov Goldschmidt, *Information for Management Decisions* (Ithaca, N. Y., and London: Cornell University Press, 1970), p. 64.

On the other hand, if appraisals are used, subjectivity heightens. In many instances, the appraisal value is often obtained by discounting the expected operating cash inflows. In such cases, economic value and replacement cost may be indistinguishable. That is, the economic value is assumed to be the best surrogate for replacement cost in the absence of an active replacement market. But the distinction, at least in concept, should be kept in mind. Economic value is a subjective appraisal of expected cash inflows, whereas replacement cost is an approximation of what investment would currently be required to obtain that expected stream.

economic value as a measure Many advocates cite economic value as the ideal investment measure for the evaluation of performance. Of course, the use of such a measure requires a concept of income (an income model) that differs from the conventional accounting model. Annual income is defined as the difference between economic values at the beginning and at the end of a year (assuming no cash dividends or additional investments). This requires an annual computation of a new economic value—that is, the present value of the expected cash inflows. The resulting income would be affected by more than just current operating activities. Because it is dependent on a measurement of economic value at the end of the year, it would also be affected by other events and by explicit predictions of future events.

The economic-value approach to measuring performance has overwhelming practical limitations because of its high degree of subjectivity. It necessitates predictions of cash flows that are uncertain and that are often interdependent with the cash flows of other assets. It also requires choosing a discount rate and perhaps changing that rate through the years. For these reasons, the use of economic values for routine judging of performance of managers is rarely feasible. However, periodic attempts should be made to approximate economic values in judging the desirability of assets as investments. Otherwise, managers will overlook obsolescence and investment opportunities.

Incidentally, many advocates of replacement cost favor it as an investment measure for routine evaluation of performance because, even though as a concept it is distinct from economic value, it provides answers that are reasonably objective approximations of what would be obtained under an economic-value approach. In short, replacement cost is a practical surrogate for the "ideal" economic value in the sense that it serves, at least usually, as a somewhat objective approximation of a *minimum* economic value.

example of approximation of replacement cost If an old asset provides a service that is comparable to a new asset's service (or vice versa), the value of the assets should be based on these services. Suppose a new warehouse will cost $100,000 and will provide the same services as an existing warehouse, which yields net rents of $10,000 per year, a return of 10 percent. The old asset should be valued at $100,000—the replacement cost of an asset that will provide similar services.

But suppose the old warehouse requires maintenance costs that are $2,000 higher than those of the new warehouse. The net services provided would be $10,000 − $2,000 = $8,000. Therefore, the value of the old warehouse would be $8,000 ÷ .10 = $80,000. All other things being equal, management would be indifferent as to buying a new warehouse for $100,000, paying $10,000 in interest charges, and selling it after a year for $100,000; or buying an old warehouse for $80,000, paying $8,000 in interest and $2,000 for maintenance, and selling it for $80,000 after a year.[18]

Suppose the old warehouse had a net book value of $6,000 and the new warehouse a book value of $100,000. As a manager, which warehouse would you prefer to supervise? You can readily see why in practice managers often prefer to manage the old assets if ROI computations are based on net book values. In most cases, replacement costs (even if crudely approximated) would probably be regarded as providing a more "equitable" or "fair" basis for performance evaluation.

Note too that in this example there is no readily obtainable market price for the old asset per se. The $80,000 approximation of replacement cost is based on a subjective appraisal of the value of expected future cash inflows—economic value. In a practical setting, economic value is often used as an approximation of replacement cost where no market prices are available. This illustrates how economic value and replacement-cost values can get blurred together even though they are essentially different concepts.

plant and equipment: gross or net? Because historical-cost investment measures are used most often in practice, there has been much discussion[19] about the relative merits of using undepreciated cost (gross value) or net book value. Those who favor using gross assets claim that it facilitates comparisons among plants and divisions.

If income decreases as a plant ages, the decline in earning power will be made evident, while the constantly decreasing net book value will reflect a possibly deceptive higher rate of return in later years. For this reason, du Pont and Monsanto use gross book value as a measure of their fixed assets when they compute rate of return. Eighteen percent of the companies surveyed[20] use gross book value.

One reason often cited for using undepreciated cost is that it partially compensates for the impact of the changing price level on historical cost. However, if a company desires to use replacement cost as a base, it should face the problem squarely by using appraisal values or specific price indexes. Reliance on gross book value is an unreliable means of approximating replacement value.

---

[18] Adapted from an example in Yaaqov Goldschmidt, *Information for Management Decisions*, p. 74.

[19] *Return on Capital as a Guide to Managerial Decisions*, National Association of Accountants, Research Report No. 35, and David Solomons, *Divisional Performance*, pp. 134–42.

[20] Mauriel and Anthony, "Misevaluation," p. 101.

Solomons comments on the gross versus net book value debate:

> There is something inherently strange about the view that it is right to include fixed assets in a balance sheet at their depreciated value, but wrong to include them in a computation of capital at that value. The only reason for holding such a view is the irrational behavior of ROI when fixed assets are taken at book value rather than at cost. The proper remedy is to be found in the use of a compound interest method of depreciation, not in the abandonment of book value as a basis for valuing investment. If depreciation were handled in a theoretically correct manner (i.e., by the compound interest method), the decline in the book value of depreciating assets would not of itself disturb the stability of ROI.[21]

The proponents of using net book value as a measure maintain that it is less confusing because (a) it is consistent with the total assets shown on the conventional balance sheet, and (b) it is consistent with net-income computations, which include deductions for depreciation. The major criticism of net book value is not peculiar to its use for ROI purposes. The critics say that historical cost does not represent a current economic sacrifice and is useless for making decisions about allocations of resources. On the other hand, as previously explained, if net book value is used in a manner that is consistent with the planning model, it can be useful for auditing past decisions and it might suffice for incentive purposes.

CHOOSING DESIRED RATES OF RETURN

Whatever their merits, neither the ROI nor the residual-income method avoids the question of cost of capital. The critical questions are (a) what minimum rates to specify; (b) when and by how much minimum rates should be altered; and (c) whether the same minimum rates should be used in each segment of the organization. If a uniform rate is used and many divisions are currently earning different rates, the use of a very low rate will surely drive ROI down toward such a rate. Moreover, frequent changes in the rate may be demoralizing as well as nonoptimal. It might lead to acceptance of, say, an 11 percent prospective return when the minimum rate is 11 percent, and rejection of a 15 percent prospective rate when the minimum rate is 16 percent.

Modern financial theory supports the use of different rates for different divisions.[22] Portfolio theory provides the analytical framework for the investment decision under uncertainty. The firm would be viewed as a collection of different classes of assets whose income streams bear different risks. The minimum desired rates of return are functions of risk. Various divisions face different risks. Therefore, a different minimum desired rate should be used for each division, based on the relative investment risks of each.

[21] David Solomons, *Divisional Performance,* p. 135. He discusses these issues at length on pp. 134–42.

[22] For a presentation of modern financial theory as it relates to accounting, see Ray Ball and Phillip Brown, "Portfolio Theory and Accounting," *Journal of Accounting Research,* Vol. 7, No. 2 (Autumn 1969), 300–323. They state (p. 313), "Thus there is some foundation to the practice of requiring different rates of return from different divisions, and similar rates from within each division."

The use of different required rates for different divisions is apparently not widespread. The most extensive survey of practice in this area indicated an overwhelming tendency to use the same required rate for all divisions and for all classes of assets.[23] The use of uniform rates is probably attributable to the attitude that managers must be treated fairly (or uniformly unfairly). In this context, fairness means that the same required rate should apply to all divisions. Moreover, even the uniform use of different rates for different classes of assets (that is, one rate for investments in current assets and another rate for plant assets) may be perceived as unfair if divisions have different compositions of such assets.

The foregoing was a description of a central problem in guiding decisions and evaluating performance. Unfortunately, there is no pat solution. Researchers in economics and finance continue to quarrel about these issues. For our purposes, we explore the design of accounting systems given minimum required rates of return, however determined.

ALTERNATIVES OF TIMING

Accounting textbooks, including this one, do not discuss at length the problem of timing. However, timing is an important factor to consider when an information system is designed. For instance, the costs of gathering and processing information and the need for frequent feedback for controlling current operations may lead to using historical-cost measures rather than replacement costs. The need for replacement costs, realizable values, and economic values tends to be less frequent, so the systems are not designed for providing such information routinely.

Admittedly, this point was made earlier in the chapter. Nevertheless, it is repeated here because it is a likely explanation of why actual practice seems to differ so markedly from what alternative theory may prefer. The essence of the matter is that management seems unwilling to pay for more elegant information because its extra costs exceed its prospective benefits.

PITFALLS IN CURRENT PRACTICE

In all cases, the limitations of ROI techniques should temper the zeal of managers who are inclined to overplay the significance of one or two measures. ROI techniques are usually used in complex organizations having complex problems. There are no simple answers where objectives and decisions are manifold and interdependent.

harmony between goals Motivation is the overriding consideration that should guide management in deciding (a) how assets should be allocated, and (b) how the investment base should be measured. That is, the system should be designed so that

---

[23] Mauriel and Anthony, in "Misevaluation," report that only 7 percent of the 258 respondents to this question used different rates.

the division managers will be inclined toward action that will be in harmony with overall company goals.

For example, the use of *net* assets as an investment base may encourage incorrect decisions by divisional management. If assets are replaced or scrapped before they are fully depreciated, the division may have to show a loss. Even though, as Chapter 11 explains, such a loss is irrelevant to replacement decisions (except for its impact on timing of income tax outlays), it does affect the division's immediate profit and could influence the division manager's decision.[24]

company accounting policies The use of traditional historical-cost-based accounting measurements is subject to all the criticisms usually leveled at such practices, including the overemphasis on short-run results and the ignoring of general and specific price-level changes.

Company accounting policies will have a telling impact on the amount of assets included in the investment base. For example, the variety of methods of accounting for inventories, leased assets, research, depreciation, patents, secret processes, trademarks, and advertising will have an important influence on the asset base.

the time period and managerial performance As Chapter 6 stressed, an executive's performance should contribute to the maximization of profits, not for one quarter or for one year, but over the long run. The focus should be on long-run earning power, not on short-run profits. Yet managers switch from one executive position to another over the years; they are typically appraised in terms of those short-run factors that tend to maximize long-run earnings potential. Managers are evaluated in terms of quantifiable performance and also performance that is difficult to measure (such as public relations or employee morale).

Rate of return wraps the quantifiable factors in one convenient package. Yet short-run maximization of rate of return may not provide the best measure of managerial performance in many cases. For example, profitability in one year may have a direct relationship to profitability in the long run, but not necessarily. A division may increase sales by reducing quality in one period and cause a harmful effect on the corporate image. (Some observers felt that Buick made this mistake in 1955, resulting in disastrous sales in 1958–59. Demand in 1955 resulted in record-breaking output, which was marked by poor quality control.) In these cases, the manager may deserve a low ranking, despite the division's high rate of return.

Thus, rate of return should be studied in relation to budgets, standards, conformity to company policies, maintenance of quality, employee relations,

[24] For an interesting discussion of various investment bases and depreciation methods plus several examples of how division managers' interest can conflict with the interests of the company as a whole, see John Dearden, "Problem in Decentralized Profit Responsibility," *Harvard Business Review,* Vol. 38, No. 3, 79–86. He concludes (p. 86), "It is my belief that the only completely satisfactory method for assigning values to divisional facilities is one that uses replacement values and is not tied directly into the books of account."

customer relations, development of subordinates, and other factors. Numerical weights are sometimes assigned to various factors and a scorecard is kept for each executive.

In summary, rate of return as a measure of performance cannot stand alone. Short-run profitability is only one of the factors that contribute to a company's long-run objectives. Rate of return is a short-run concept, dealing only with the past quarter or year, whereas managerial performance must include future results that can be expected because of present actions.[25]

Other measures commonly used to judge managerial performance include plant efficiency, share of the market, employee turnover, sales volume, discovery of new products, and public relations.

emphasis on changes, not absolute amounts　The imprecision of the rate-of-return tool has not necessarily resulted in its rejection. Companies often limit its use to broad areas of the business where problems of allocation of assets and expenses are not overwhelming. For example, a rate of return may be easily computed for a division or a plant, but not for individual products within a product line or individual departments within a factory. Furthermore, companies tend to emphasize change in rates of return rather than absolute percentages. Thus, changes may be budgeted, actual performance may be appraised, and variances may be investigated. There are two major classes of variances: turnover and profit margins. These may be analyzed in detail to discover underlying causal factors.

Each division's performance may be compared with its own performance in a prior period, but comparisons with other divisions inside or outside the company are likely to be invalid. The point is that, given our existing state of knowledge, routine reports of performance are quite crude. ROI or residual-income tools raise questions and provide clues; by themselves, they do not provide answers.

summary

As organizations grow, decentralization of some management functions becomes desirable. Decentralization immediately raises problems of obtaining decisions that are coordinated with the objectives of the organization as a whole. Ideally, planning and control systems should provide information that (a) aims managers toward decisions that are goal-congruent, (b) provides feedback (evaluation of performance) that improves incentive and future decisions, and (c) preserves autonomy. Note that the common thread of these criteria is motivation.

Many techniques like ROI or residual income fall far short of the ideal

---

[25]For an expanded discussion of the limitations of rate of return, see William J. Vatter, "Does Rate of Return Measure Business Efficiency?" *N.A.A. Bulletin*, XLI, No. 4.

goals stipulated above. Nevertheless, in practice their conceptual shortcomings may be unimportant; often they are the best techniques available for obtaining the perceived top-management goals.

Performance reports should distinguish between the performance of the division manager and the performance of the divisional unit as an economic investment.

Although in practice the book values of assets tend to be used for ROI and residual-income purposes, many accountants believe that replacement value is a preferable multipurpose basis. If net book value is used, the compound-interest method of depreciation will be more likely to provide a basis for performance evaluation that is consistent with the past decisions being evaluated.

Despite the theoretical attractiveness of various alternative accounting methods, most managements have apparently decided that a historical-cost system is good enough for the *routine* evaluation of managers. Evidently, this crude approach provides the desired motivational effects and gives clues as to whether to invest or disinvest in a particular division. The investment decision is evidently not routine enough to justify gathering information regarding replacement costs or realizable values except as special needs arise.

A basic decision that management must face is whether the maximization of ROI or of residual income should be specified as a fundamental management goal. In practice, the ROI idea dominates; but capital-budgeting theory lends support to the maximization of residual income as being a better goal. Finance theory also points toward using different minimum desired rates of return for different divisions having different risks.

ROI techniques tend to have been oversold in the business literature. Practically, they are fraught with limitations and should be used in conjunction with other measures such as budgets and standards, market shares, employee turnover, and the like. The relative change in these measures is often more significant than their absolute size.

suggested readings

Anthony, R. N., J. Dearden, and R. F. Vancil, *Management Control Systems: Cases and Readings*. Homewood, Ill.: Richard D. Irwin, Inc., 1965.

Goldschmidt, Yaaqov, *Information for Management Decisions*. Ithaca, N.Y., and London: Cornell University Press, 1970.

Morris, William T., *Decentralization in Management Systems*. Columbus, O.: Ohio State University Press, 1968.

N. A. A. Research Reports Nos. 30 and *35* and *Practice Report No. 14* should be enlightening.

Solomons, David, *Divisional Performance: Measurement and Control*. New York: Financial Executives Research Foundation, 1965.

Also see the Suggested Readings at the end of Chapter 22.

Problems for Self-Study

PROBLEM 1 Suppose that a division's budgeted data are as follows:

Average available assets:	
Receivables	$300,000
Inventories	200,000
Fixed assets, net	500,000
	$1,000,000
Fixed overhead	$225,000
Variable costs	$5 per unit
Desired rate of return	
on average available assets	27.5%
Expected volume	200,000 units

a. What average unit sales price is needed to obtain the desired rate of return on average available assets?

b. What would be the expected turnover of assets?

c. What would be the net-income percentage on dollar sales?

d. What rate of return would be earned on assets available if sales volume is 300,000 units, assuming no changes in prices or variable costs per unit?

SOLUTION 1　a. 27.5% of $1,000,000 = $275,000 target net income

Let X = unit sales price

Dollar sales = Variable costs + Fixed costs + Net Income

$$200,000\ X = 200,000\ (\$5) + \$225,000 + \$275,000$$
$$X = \$1,500,000 \div 200,000$$
$$X = \$7.50$$

b. Expected asset turnover $= \dfrac{200,000 \times \$7.50}{\$1,000,000} = \dfrac{\$1,500,000}{\$1,000,000} = 1.5$

c. Net income as a percentage of dollar sales $= \dfrac{\$275,000}{\$1,500,000} = 18.33\%$

d. At a volume of 300,000 units:

Sales @ $7.50	$2,250,000
Variable costs @ $5.00	1,500,000
Contribution margin	$ 750,000
Fixed expense	225,000
Net income	$ 525,000
Rate of return on $1,000,000 assets	52.5%

Note that an increase of 50 percent in unit volume almost doubles net income. This is so because fixed costs do not increase as volume increases.

PROBLEM 2　A division has assets of $200,000 and operating income of $60,000.

a. What is the division's ROI?

b. If interest is imputed at 14 percent, what is the residual income?

c. What effects on management behavior can be expected if ROI is used to gauge performance?

d. What effects on management behavior can be expected if residual income is used to gauge performance?

SOLUTION 2   a. $60,000 \div $200,000 = 30\%$
b. $60,000 - .14($200,000) = $32,000$
c. If ROI is used, the manager is prone to reject projects that do not earn an ROI of at least 30 percent. From the viewpoint of the organization as a whole, this may be undesirable because its best investment opportunities may lie in that division at a rate of, say, 22 percent. If a division is enjoying a high ROI, it is less likely to expand if it is judged via ROI than if it is judged via residual income.
d. If residual income is used, the manager is inclined to accept all projects whose expected ROI exceeds the minimum desired rate. His division is more likely to expand, because his goal is to maximize a dollar amount rather than a rate.

PROBLEM 3   Using DCF analysis, the Ezra Company invested $100,000 in plant and equipment having a useful life of six years and generating $22,961 in operating cash inflows each year. At the end of six years, the assets are scrapped at zero salvage value.
a. What is the time-adjusted rate of return?
b. Suppose straight-line depreciation is used as a basis for performance evaluation. What is the ROI for the first, fourth, and sixth years if ROI is based on the initial balance (gross investment base)? On net book value?
c. How closely do the answers in part b approximate the time-adjusted rate of return? Why do they differ?

SOLUTION 3   a. The DCF factor in Table 4 in Appendix B of this book is $100,000 \div $22,961 = 4.355$. Line 6 shows that the time-adjusted rate is 10 percent.

b.
Operating cash inflows per year	$22,961
Depreciation	16,667
Operating income	$ 6,294

	YEAR		
	1	4	6
ROI on initial balance (gross investment base):			
$6,294 \div $100,000 =	6.3%	6.3%	6.3%
ROI on net book value:			
$6,294 \div $100,000 =	6.3		
$6,294 \div $ 50,000 =		12.6	
$6,294 \div $ 16,667 =			37.8

c. The answers in b vary considerably from the time-adjusted rate used to guide the original investment decision. The answers differ because the DCF model was used to justify the investment and the accrual-accounting model was used to evaluate performance.

questions, problems, and cases

21-1. "Net income divided by sales is the most important single measure of business success." Do you agree? Why?

21-2. List four possible bases for computing the cost of invested capital.

21-3. "The stockholder's-equity base is the best investment base for appraising operating management." Do you agree? Why?

21-4. "The use of undepreciated cost of fixed assets as part of the investment base compensates for the impact of the changing price level on historical cost." Do you agree? Why?

21-5. Under what circumstances does the gross-asset base make most sense?

21-6. Proponents of net book value as an investment base usually cite two major reasons for their position. What are these reasons?

21-7. How should interest expense and nonrecurring expenses be considered in computing incomes that are related to investment bases?

21-8. "In recent years there has been a tendency toward corporate decentralization, accompanied by a setting of individual rate-of-return targets for corporate segments. This provides incentive because managers can operate their segments as if they were separate companies of their own." Do you agree? Why?

21-9. What income concept is likely to be most realistic for measuring performance of various corporate segments?

21-10. "The rate-of-return tool is so hampered by limitations that we might as well forget it." Do you agree? Why?

21-11. What measures besides rate of return are commonly used to judge managerial performance?

21-12. "Too much stress on rate of return can hurt the corporation." How?

21-13. **Government Contracts and Profit Margins.** Spokesmen for many companies that are heavily involved in government-contract work often complain that defense work is not very profitable. They cite low-percentage profit margins as evidence.

Are such contentions justified? Why, or why not?

21-14. **Analysis of Return on Capital; Comparison of Three Companies.** [Adapted from *N.A.A. Research Report No. 35*, pp. 34–35.]
1. Rate of return on capital is often expressed as follows:

$$\frac{\text{Income}}{\text{Capital}} = \frac{\text{Income}}{\text{Sales}} \times \frac{\text{Sales}}{\text{Capital}}$$

What advantages can you see in the breakdown of the computation into two separate components?
2. Fill in the blanks:

	COMPANIES IN SAME INDUSTRY		
	A	B	C
Sales	$1,000,000	$500,000	$ —
Income	100,000	50,000	—
Capital	500,000	—	5,000,000
Income as a percent of sales	—	—	0.5%
Turnover of capital	—	—	2
Return on investment	—	1%	—

After filling in the blanks, comment on the relative performance of these companies as thoroughly as the data permit.

21-15. **Pricing, Rate of Return, and Measuring Efficiency.** A large automobile company follows a pricing policy whereby "normal" or "standard" activity is used as a base for pricing. That is, prices are set on the basis of long-run annual-volume predictions. They are then rarely changed, except for notable changes in wage rates or material prices.

You are given the following data:

Materials, wages, and other variable costs	$1,320 per unit
Fixed overhead	$300,000,000 per year
Desired rate of return on invested capital	20%
Normal volume	1,000,000 units
Invested capital	$900,000,000

required

1. What net-income percentage based on dollar sales is needed to attain the desired rate of return?

2. What rate of return on invested capital will be earned at sales volumes of 1,500,000 and 500,000 units, respectively?

3. The company has a sizable management bonus plan based on yearly divisional performance. Assume that the volume was 1,000,000, 1,500,000, and 500,000 units, respectively, in three successive years. Each of three men has served as division manager for one year before being killed in an automobile accident. As the major heir of the third manager, comment on the bonus plan.

21-16. Using Gross or Net Book Value of Fixed Assets.   Assume that a particular plant acquires $400,000 of fixed assets with a useful life of four years and no residual value. Straight-line depreciation will be used. The plant manager is judged on income in relation to these fixed assets. Annual net income, after deducting depreciation, is $40,000.

Assume that sales, and expenses except depreciation, are on a cash basis. Dividends equal net income. Thus, cash in the amount of the depreciation charge will accumulate each year. The plant manager's performance is judged in relation to fixed assets because all current assets, including cash, are considered under central company control.

1. Prepare a comparative tabulation of the plant's rate of return and the company's overall company rate of return based on:
   a. Gross (i.e., original cost) assets.
   b. Net book value of assets. Assume (unrealistically) that any cash accumulated remains idle.

2. Evaluate the relative merits of gross assets and net book value of assets as investment bases.

21-17. The General Electric Approach to Measuring Divisional Profitability. [Adapted from David Solomons, *Divisional Performance: Measurement and Control* (New York: Financial Executives Research Foundation, Inc., 1965).] Consider the following:

	(000'S OMITTED)	
	DIVISION A	DIVISION B
Total assets	$1,000	$5,000
Net annual earnings	$ 200	$ 750
Rate of return on total assets	20%	15%

required

1. Which is the most successful division? Why?

2. General Electric Company has chosen "residual income," the excess of net earnings over the cost of capital, as the measure of management success—the

quantity a manager should try to maximize. The cost of capital is deducted from the net annual earnings to obtain residual income. Using this criterion, what is the residual income for each division if the cost of capital is: (a) 12 percent, (b) 14 percent, (c) $17\frac{1}{2}$ percent? Which division is more successful under each of these rates?

21-18. Various Measures of Profitability. When the Coronet Company formed three divisions a year ago, the president told the division managers that a bonus would be paid to the most profitable division. However, absolute profit as conventionally computed would not be used. Instead, the ranking would be affected by the relative investments in the three divisions. Each manager has now written a memorandum claiming that he is entitled to the bonus. The following data are available:

DIVISION	GROSS BOOK VALUE AT START OF YEAR	NET INCOME AS COMPUTED FOR CONVENTIONAL EXTERNAL ANNUAL REPORT COMPILATION
X	$400,000	$47,500
Y	380,000	46,000
Z	250,000	30,800

All the assets are fixed assets that were purchased ten years ago and have ten years of usefulness remaining. The Coronet cost of capital is 10 percent. All computations of current return should be based on a balance at the start of the year.

required

Which method for computing profitability did each manager choose? Make your description specific and brief. Show supporting computations. Where applicable, assume straight-line depreciation.

21-19. Influence of Profitability Measure on Decisions. Suppose that the Solomons Company has the following relationships between net income and investment:

TOTAL INVESTMENT LEVEL	NET INCOME	
	CASE A	CASE B
$ 1,000,000	$ 10,000	$ 10,000
2,000,000	50,000	50,000
3,000,000	120,000	200,000
4,000,000	220,000	350,000
5,000,000	370,000	500,000
6,000,000	520,000	650,000
7,000,000	680,000	760,000
8,000,000	830,000	860,000
9,000,000	980,000	950,000
10,000,000	1,110,000	1,010,000
11,000,000	1,150,000	1,050,000
12,000,000	1,180,000	1,070,000

The minimum desired rate of return is 6 percent.

required

1. For *each* level of investment for Cases A and B:
   a. Compute the overall rate of return as measured by net income divided by investment (ROI).

b. Compute the residual income as measured by net income less a capital charge of 6 percent on investment. Prepare your answer as a comparative table, showing for each level:

		CASE A		CASE B	
TOTAL INVESTMENT LEVEL	6% RETURN	ROI	RESIDUAL INCOME	ROI	RESIDUAL INCOME

2. Explain any difference in potential effects on a manager's investment decisions that you detect between Case A and Case B. That is, will ROI and residual income lead to the same decisions? What is the essential conceptual difference between the maximization of ROI and the maximization of residual income as management goals?

21-20. Discounted Cash Flow and Evaluation of Performance. John Castleman, the general manager of a division of a huge, highly diversified company, recently attended an executive training program. He learned about discounted cash-flow analysis, and he became convinced that it was the best available guide for making long-range investment decisions.

However, upon returning to his company, he became frustrated. He wanted to use the discounted cash-flow technique, but top management had a long-standing policy of evaluating divisional management performance largely on the basis of its rate of return as calculated by dividing divisional net income by the net book value of total divisional assets. Therefore, in his own best interests and in accordance with the specifications of his superiors, he had to make decisions that he felt were not really the most desirable in terms of maximizing what he considered to be the "true" rate of return (that is, the discounted cash-flow rate).

required

1. Suppose Mr. Castleman had an opportunity to invest $30,000 cash in some automated machinery with a useful life of three years and a scrap value of zero. The expected cash savings per year were $12,060. Compute the time-adjusted rate of return. Ignore income tax effects.

2. Show the effect on net income for each of the three years, assuming straight-line depreciation. Also show the rate of return based on the beginning balance of the net book value of the fixed asset for each year.

3. Repeat requirement 2, assuming sum-of-the-years'-digits depreciation.

4. Top management has indicated a minimum desired rate of return of 10 percent. After examining the results above, Mr. Castleman was more baffled than ever. He just could not see why he should invest in the machinery if his net income in the first year would not be at least 10 percent of the investment base. He discussed the matter with a professor at a nearby business school.

The professor reacted: "The basic trouble is not confined to your company. Many companies now insist that their managers use discounted cash-flow techniques for appraising investment opportunities, but they use conventional accounting techniques for judging operating performance. In short, one model is supposed to be used for planning, but another model is used for control.

"A possible solution is to use the compound-interest method of depreciation for evaluating subsequent performance. The compound-interest method is based on the same model as the discounted cash-flow technique. That is, each receipt ($12,060 in this case) consists of interest on the beginning investment balance plus the recovery of principal. For example, the $12,060 cash savings during the first year would be analyzed as consisting of 'interest' of 10 percent of $30,000, or $3,000, plus a recovery of principal ('depreciation') of $9,060."

Repeat requirement 2, assuming the compound-interest method of depreciation.

5. Contrast the pattern of depreciation in requirement 4 with the other methods. Why is industry reluctant to use the compound-interest method of depreciation? What other means might be used to reconcile the two models described in requirement 4?

21-21. Conflict of Accrual and DCF Models.

1. The Marples Company, a small job shop, has landed a three-year exclusive contract for 10,000 proprietary widgets per year at $2.50 each. Total variable costs, including overhead but exclusive of the machinery required, are estimated at $1.00 per unit. John Marples, the president, is considering some proposals for tooling up to meet this demand.

One of the alternatives is the purchase of a new special-purpose machine. This would cost about $30,000 including installation and setup, and maintenance requirements would be about $310 yearly.

Marples will introduce an entirely new line of widgets in three years. The machine is not adaptable to the new manufacturing process, and the expected salvage value at that time will barely cover removal costs. The company depreciates its tools and equipment investments on a straight-line basis, and uses 20 percent as its minimum desired rate of return on new investments.

Ignoring income taxes, compute the time-adjusted rate of return on the initial investment. Do you recommend its purchase?

2. Marples invests in the new machine, and conducts a project review at the end of one year. He evaluates product profitability on the basis of ROI on the beginning investment for the year. He uses straight-line depreciation. He finds a significant difference between the observed rate and the projected rate of return, despite the fact that all costs were kept to budgeted figures. He asks you to explain the difference, and to recommend a simple system that will eliminate this problem.

What will you tell him?

3. After Marples digests the implications of the compound-interest method of depreciation, he asks another question: "Last week I had an offer of $21,000 for the machinery and the contract. I wanted to accept it, since I thought I could realize a gain of $1,000 over book value. Also, I could earn 30 percent if I used the proceeds to shift this manufacturing space to a new product. Now with this compound-interest method, it seems the value of my machine is about $22,000. I guess I should not sell, should I?"

How do you answer Marples' question?

21-22. Various Investment Bases. Lookabill Co. is a small manufacturer whose primary product is a one- or two-person snow vehicle, called a snowauto. The snowauto is primarily used as a winter recreation vehicle, although a substantial number are also used as a primary means of transportation during the winter.

Lookabill Co. started making snowautos about ten years ago, when they purchased a company that made small gasoline engines. The plant where the engines were produced was about ten years old at that time. The company purchased most of the parts other than the engines from outside suppliers. They also contracted with other firms for the assembly of the snowautos, until six years ago, when they built an assembly plant. The assembly plant also produces a few nonstandard parts (such as skids) for the snowauto.

For the first few years, Lookabill Co. had little competition. Because of steadily increasing demand, sales and profits soared. However, during the last three to four years, there has been an influx of competition, and the trend will probably continue. Thus Lookabill's share of the total market has been steadily declining over this period. Sales have continued to increase, but at a much slower rate.

In addition, Lookabill has had to cut its sales price on snowautos to meet competition; this caused an absolute decline in net income last year. Management is very much concerned about this decline and attributes much of the problem to excessive manufacturing costs. Lookabill's cost per snowauto has always been somewhat high. Rapid expansion and strict attention to quality have not been accompanied by attentive control of costs. Now management feels that to increase profit, something must be done about the cost of production. Both plants are currently operating at near practical capacity.

The company considers each plant to be a profit center. Transfers from the engine-manufacturing plant to the assembly plant are on the basis of market value of the engines, a figure that is readily ascertainable. Neither of the plant managers has ever objected to this system.

The two plant managers are evaluated and their bonuses calculated on the basis of return on investment (ROI), using net book value of assets as the investment base. The plant managers have wide latitude with respect to operating decisions and acquisition of assets. The only decisions that require central management's approval are major expansion programs. The two managers set production levels by joint agreement based upon projected demand.

The ROI in the engine-manufacturing plant is much higher than the firm's estimated cost of capital, which is about 10 percent. Management attributed the high returns and also the high variable costs of production to the fact that the plant manager did not tend to replace old equipment or purchase new equipment, even though he had almost complete freedom to do so. Consequently, much of the equipment in the engine-manufacturing plant is nearly obsolete.

Management is now trying to determine how to motivate the plant managers to replace obsolete equipment and cut costs so as to accomplish the company's goal of constantly increasing profit. They are considering two performance-evaluation methods and ask your advice as to which one would be better to use in this situation. The two methods are ROI (the system they now use) and residual income. They also want to know the probable effect, if any, on the plant managers' behavior if they use gross assets as an investment base rather than net assets.

The income and asset figures for each of the two plants are given at the top of the next page.

required Compute the ROI and residual income for each plant for each of the two years, using both *average* net book value and gross book value as investment bases.

1. Which of the two proposed investment bases would be better for motivating the plant managers to work toward the company's goals under each of the evaluation methods? Use the figures you computed above to explain your choice of investment base in each instance.

2. Using the figures you computed above, describe the advantages and disadvantages of each of the methods of performance evaluation. How will each

	19_8	19_7	19_6
Engine Manufacturing Plant (age 20 years) (Depreciable life 15 years from date of purchase)			
Gross assets, December 31	$5,000,000	$5,000,000	$5,000,000
Net assets, December 31	1,666,667	2,000,000	2,333,333
Average net book value of assets	1,833,333	2,166,667	
Income before nonallocated general expenses	529,000	532,000	530,000
Assembly Plant (age 6 years) (Depreciable life 20 years)			
Gross assets, December 31	4,000,000	4,000,000	4,000,000
Net assets, December 31	2,800,000	3,000,000	3,200,000
Average net book value of assets	2,900,000	3,100,000	
Income before nonallocated general expenses	420,000	425,000	422,000

method affect the plant managers' behavior with respect to the company's goal?

21-23. **Soviet Approach to Return on Investment.** The Soviet System is a management control and evaluation system (bonus system) that is used in much of the Soviet economy. It is used to evaluate managers and determine their bonuses, and thus (it is hoped) to motivate the individual managers to cut costs and work toward the country's goals as specified by the central planning agency. One of these goals is to modernize the country's production facilities. The stated purpose was to increase the material interest of the management and employees in the economic results of the enterprise. The new management control system was a part of sweeping economy reforms that took effect in January 1966. As stated in Bertrand Horwitz, *Accounting Controls and the Soviet Economic Reforms of 1966* (Sarasota, Fla.: American Accounting Association, 1970), p. 23:

> Prior to January 1966, when the reforms first took effect, the director of a Soviet enterprise was confronted with the requirement of satisfying numerous physical and accounting goals. The enterprise was essentially a cell in a tautly administered system which allowed the director little room for independent action because the number of physical and accounting indexes by which he could be judged highly constrained his economic actions.

The new bonus system was based on the enterprise's increase in profits and the rate of return on assets employed in the enterprise. The exact formula used to compute the total bonuses to be distributed to the enterprise's employees is as follows:

$$(1) \qquad \lambda_t = \alpha \frac{(P_t - P_{t-1})}{P_{t-1}} + \beta \frac{(P_t)}{K_t}$$

and the total amount of the bonus for the enterprise is:

$$(2) \qquad TB_t = W_t \lambda_t$$

Where W_t = the wage fund for time period t, centrally determined
  P_t = profit in period t that is net of explicit charges for the use of current and fixed gross assets at original cost
  TB_t = total amount of enterprise bonus for period t

K_t = total average gross assets in t at original cost

α, β = coefficients that are centrally assigned norms; both are less than one and are nonnegative

The first term of equation (1) is the rate of increase in earnings over the previous year. The second term is the ROI for the enterprise based on its gross assets. The sum of these two terms gives a factor (λ_t) that, when multiplied by the enterprise's wage fund, determines the total bonus for the enterprise. Thus, the total bonus for the enterprise depends on the enterprise's increase in profit over the previous year and its ROI.

The wage fund (W_t) for the enterprise in a period is centrally determined and therefore is a given amount for purposes of computation of the bonus. The accounting profit (P_t) is the enterprise's net profit before capital charges, minus (a) charges at the rate of 6 percent of gross assets, for the use of fixed assets and normal or planned working capital; (b) fixed (rent) payments; and (c) interest on bank credit. The charge of 6 percent is essentially the enterprise's cost of capital, because the enterprise gets its fixed assets from the government. The charge is also based on gross assets. The rent payments are designed to eliminate the differences between different enterprises because of natural operating conditions. Thus, a firm with very favorable conditions would have to make rent payments, while one operating under less favorable conditions would not. The interest is for short-term loans from the central bank.

Average gross assets (K_t) is used as the investment base in order to motivate managers to replace their older, less efficient assets. The purpose is to get managers to modernize their equipment.

The coefficients α and β are centrally assigned and are set so that the resulting bonuses will be reasonable in light of the enterprise's operating conditions. This is essentially another way of equalizing the natural operating conditions of the various enterprises in the economy.

Assume that the enterprise did not have to make any rent payments and had no short-term loans from the central bank. Suppose the enterprise had the following profit before deductions, gross assets, and wage fund, in thousands of rubles:

$$P_t = 3,000 \qquad K_t = 20,000$$
$$P_{t-1} = 2,800 \qquad W_t = 4,000$$

Also, suppose that the central planners had assigned the firm an $\alpha = .5$ and $\beta = .25$.

required

1. Compute the total bonus.

2. Compare the probable motivational effects of the Soviet method with those of ROI and residual income.

21-24. Soviet Approach to Return on Investment.   Refer to problem 21-22. Using the Soviet method, compute λ_{19_8} and λ_{19_7} for the engine-manufacturing plant, using both net assets and gross assets as the investment base. Using these figures plus the ROI and residual-income figures you computed in problem 21-22, compare the Soviet approach to your answers in that problem. Assume that: (1) the cost of capital is 10 percent, (2) $\alpha = .5$ and $\beta = .25$. The income and asset figures for the engine-manufacturing plant for 19_5 are given below:

Gross assets, December 31	$5,000,000
Net assets, December 31	2,666,667
Net income before nonallocated general expenses	526,000

21-25. Investment Bases in an Oil Company.   An oil company is having trouble in deciding whether to continue to use its old gasoline stations and in evaluating the performance of these stations in terms of return on investment. Top management has explored various ways of establishing a value for such stations. Book value, market value, and replacement value are the three alternatives now under consideration.

required

1. Which of the three bases is applicable to deciding whether to dispose of an old station? Why?

2. Which of the three bases is applicable for judging the performance of the station and its manager? Why? Why is your answer the same as or different from your answer in requirement 1?

21-26. What Investment Bases Should Be Used?   The president of a giant corporation has attended miscellaneous management education programs during the past few years. He has a persistent desire to keep abreast of the latest thinking regarding information for decisions and performance measurement. He greets you, a new graduate from a school of management, with the following comments and questions:

"As I read more and more on this subject and as I listen to more and more discussions, I become increasingly bewildered by the nomenclature and the concepts. Oh, I am aware of the infirmities of historical costs. What I am concerned about are such terms and concepts as market value, current value, replacement value, economic value, present value, opportunity value, disposal value, entry value, exit value, and countless similar terms.

"Consider our new processing equipment in Division A. It cost $10 million. We could sell it for perhaps $7 million. How should it be valued for measuring performance in year 1? In year 5? In year 10?

"I am not asking you to pick from the existing practices of valuation. I am asking a normative question. That is, first tell me how these assets *should* be valued to assist decisions and to evaluate performance—without regard to the practical difficulties of implementation. After you answer the question on a normative basis, then answer it again on the basis of what might be accomplished now in our organization to implement what is conceptually most desirable."

required

Prepare a memorandum in response to the president's requirements. Include definitions of the various cost terms he mentioned. You may wish to use an example to clarify your points.

22

Decentralization and Transfer Pricing

Goods and services are often exchanged between various departments and divisions of a company. What values (prices) should be assigned to these exchanges or transfers? Historical cost? Market price? Some version of either? The transfer-pricing question is often the most troublesome aspect of a control system. As with other techniques, transfer pricing should be viewed in the perspective of the total system.

Transfer pricing is most often viewed in the context of one profit center's supplying a product or service to another profit center. For example, a foundry may supply castings for an assembly division; it may also sell castings to outsiders. If the foundry and the assembly division are separate profit centers, the transfer price will have an important bearing on the reported profits of each. More fundamentally, transfer-price information affects many critical decisions concerning the acquisition and allocation of an organization's resources, just as prices in the entire economy affect decisions concerning the allocation of a nation's resources. Ideally, transfer prices should guide each manager to choose his inputs and outputs in coordination with other subunits so as to maximize the profits of the organization as a whole.

Of course, transfer pricing is not confined to accounting for profit centers. It takes many forms. For example, the allocation of service-department costs to production departments is essentially a form of transfer pricing, because it is a measure of the services rendered to and received from another subunit of the organization.

OBJECTIVES OF TRANSFER PRICING

facilitating
decentralized
decision
making

Many organizations are decentralized through profit centers, because a vast variety of decisions is processed more efficiently and effectively at local levels. From the viewpoint of the total system, a given level of decentralization is justified, since the day-in, day-out benefits of local decision making offset the occasional blunders that hurt the overall organization. Transfer pricing is a requirement that arises from interactions between decentralized subunits. Its fundamental objective is to facilitate optimal decision making in a decentralized organization. Optimality is defined here as the best conceivable decision given top-management objectives. For example, if the objective is to maximize the present value of the expected future cash flows of the firm, the optimal decision is the choice that results in such maximization.

criteria
for judging
transfer prices

How do you judge whether a given transfer-pricing scheme can be improved? Transfer prices induce certain decisions and thus affect behavior. The section on systems design and decentralization in the previous chapter mentioned three criteria that are also applicable to the issues of transfer pricing: (a) goal congruence, (b) performance evaluation, and (c) autonomy.[1] The aim is to design a transfer-pricing scheme that will point subunit managers toward the top-management goals and that will provide incentive to reach those goals. Again we face the unending task of increasing the managers' motivation toward making optimal economic decisions.

In subsequent sections, we will apply these criteria to various possible transfer-pricing schemes. As you might expect, each of these criteria may conflict with the others. For instance, there is a pervasive temptation to direct a manager from above in order to assure optimal decisions; but such direction undercuts the freedom of individual managers.

MARKET PRICES

the appeal of
market prices

For day-in, day-out use where the intermediate market is competitive and where interdependencies of subunits are minimal, market price is the most desirable transfer price because it generally leads to optimal decisions. There are no inherent conflicts in fulfilling all three criteria (goal congruence, performance evaluation, and autonomy). The guidelines are these: (a) A market or negotiated market price should be used; (b) the seller should have the option of not selling internally;[2] and (c) an arbitration procedure should be available for settling disputes.[3] These guidelines assume that the managers of the divisions

---

[1] Joshua Ronen and George McKinney, "Transfer Pricing for Divisional Autonomy," *Journal of Accounting Research,* Vol. 8, No. 1 (Spring 1970), 100–101.

[2] The reason for this option is that the seller might have more profitable alternative opportunities for using his facilities to sell *other products.*

[3] R. N. Anthony, J. Dearden, and R. F. Vancil, *Management Control Systems* (Homewood, Ill.: Richard D. Irwin, Inc., 1965), p. 259.

have access to outside markets. Where market prices are relevant for making economic decisions, and if the costs of maintaining such a system are justifiable, they are also relevant for performance evaluation and preserving subunit autonomy.

When the market-price approach is used, the attempt is to transfer goods at a price no higher than that prevailing in an outside market at the time of transfer—that is, at the price that the receiving division would have to pay outsiders. Put another way, the market-price approach is an attempt to approximate an arm's-length, bargained, open-market price.

In most cases, internal procurement is expected where the selling division's products and services are equal to those of outsiders in quality and price. The buying division often obtains benefits such as better quality, assurance of supply, and dependable delivery.

The usefulness of a market-price method is contingent on the availability of dependable market-price quotations of other manufacturers. It is these prices that would be taken into account by parties dealing at arm's length as they establish the competitive price levels.

In sum, if a company's participation in a market has no effect on price, market prices typically establish the ceiling for transfer pricing. In many instances, a lower price may easily be justified, particularly when large purchases are made, when selling costs are less, or when an advantage is obtained through an exclusive supplier contract or through a cost-plus arrangement assuring profits in all cases. These situations lead to the notion of negotiated market prices, whereby the cost savings to the firm as a whole are split between the selling and buying divisions through bargaining.

Arbitrating or umpiring is sometimes necessary. However, its frequent use indicates a step toward centralization, because it usually elevates the decision to a representative of the organization as a whole. Consequently, too much reliance on arbitration indicates the inability of the division managers to operate smoothly on a decentralized basis.

When market prices and manager options are not available as a foundation for negotiations, the resultant transfer prices are artificial to a point that severely limits the significance of measures of performance. The whole idea of decentralization and of profit centers is based on the manager's freedom and independence. Unless he has alternatives, unless he can resort to buying and selling outside the company, his profit center is not as decentralized as it might seem at first glance.

pitfalls in market prices   The use of market prices wherever possible has innate appeal for purposes of both decision making and performance evaluation. Without routine checks on market prices, managers often obtain critical information only in a haphazard or tardy fashion. A frequently cited advantage of profit centers is that they compel an approximation of what revenue might be if a division were operated as a completely independent entity; in this way, the managers become more sensitive to market conditions than otherwise.

The trouble with the use of market price is either that few markets are perfectly competitive or that no intermediate market exists for the exact product or service in question. A quoted price for a product is strictly comparable only if the credit terms, grade, quality, delivery terms, and auxiliary services are precisely the same. Moreover, isolated price quotations are sometimes temporary distress or dumping prices. Such prices can seldom be used as a basis for long-range planning, although they may be appropriate for monitoring short-term performance. In nearly all cases, however, temporary market prices are not applicable for repetitive, high-volume transactions, and they hurt the credibility of the so-called market transfer prices.

What transfer-pricing scheme should be used for judging performance if distress prices prevail? Some companies use these distress transfer prices, but others use long-run average or "normal" market prices. The decision as to which transfer-pricing basis is preferable depends on subjective judgments regarding the costs and benefits of each alternative.

If distress pricing is used, in the short-run the manager of the supplier division will meet the price as long as it exceeds his additional cost. In the long-run, he must decide whether contraction is desirable by predicting its effect on price. The danger is that managers may not take the long-range, global view and may constrict facilities to boost a short-run divisional rate of return. The resulting cut in the total industry supply may lead to higher outside future prices that may be disadvantageous to the company as a whole in the long run.

On the other hand, transfers may be based on the long-run average price. But this has the weakness of not incorporating current market prices in the information system; to the extent that transfers are forced at above-current-market prices, the short-run performance of the buying division will be hurt and that manager will be unhappy about both his performance measure and his partial loss of autonomy. However, unless the selling division's additional costs exceed the market price, the company as a whole would benefit by an internal transfer.

If the danger of precipitous disposal of facilities is not overlooked when analysis is conducted, the use of current market prices (even distress prices) is generally preferable to the use of some long-run average price. In this way, two evaluations are made. The first is a comparison of long-run predictions and current prices; this gives insights on past capital-budgeting decisions. The second entails assessing the current performance of both the buying and supplying divisions in relation to existing opportunities in the form of current prices.

Many product parts are unique, a situation that causes considerable costs for preparing bids. If an outside supplier prepares a few bids and discovers that the internal supplier division always wins, the so-called resulting market prices either will not be forthcoming in the future or will be unreliable (and perhaps artificially high; after all, the bidder may submit a high price with little effort). Some companies deliberately purchase from outside suppliers to maintain alternate sources of supply and to provide a valid check on market prices.

market prices Suppose that there is no outside market for the intermediate product, or
not always that the market is affected by the pricing decisions of the subunit managers.
applicable For example, consider a full cost-pricing scheme where there is no intermediate market and whereby a foundry division may boost its transfer prices
if its costs increase. The resulting increase in the succeeding assembly costs may
affect the pricing policies of the assembly division and reduce its market and
profits, so that the company as a whole suffers a decrease in profits. There is
an interdependency here that may call for a decision by top managers to insure
the desired goal congruence. However, there is a clash between the criteria,
because as soon as top managers interfere, subunit autonomy may be diminished.
The need is for the two divisions to act like one so as to maximize their joint
profit. Where interdependence is significant, decentralization may be an organizational design that is too costly.

How do you devise, in these messy situations, a transfer-pricing scheme
that will work in accordance with the three criteria? It is not easy. In practice,
managers tend to resort to uncomplicated approaches. Rigid adherence to pat,
simple rules for transfer pricing, whether they be some version of cost or some
version of market price, will inevitably lead to dysfunctional decision making.
Management must make a trade-off between the perceived benefits from decentralization and the costs of relatively simple schemes for transfer pricing. If
the rules for transfer pricing become complex and more constraining, they
represent a move toward more centralization. This move is an attempt to find
some intermediate point on the graph (Exhibit 21-1 in the preceding chapter)
that may decrease some benefits of decentralization (those arising from giving
a manager more freedom of action), but that it is hoped will decrease to a greater
extent some costs of dysfunctional decisions until some optimal point is reached.

GENERAL RULE FOR TRANSFER PRICING?

The preceding section demonstrated that market price was not a cure-all
answer to the problem of setting transfer prices. The most obvious example is
the nonexistence of an intermediate market for a highly specialized product
component.

Is there an all-pervasive rule for transfer pricing that will lead toward
optimal economic decisions? The answer is negative, because the three criteria
of goal congruence, performance evaluation, and autonomy must all be considered simultaneously. If an optimal economic decision is wanted in a particular
situation, the following general rule serves as a helpful first step in the analysis.
The transfer price should be (a) *the additional outlay costs incurred to the point
of transfer* (*sometimes approximated by variable costs*), *plus* (b) *opportunity costs
for the firm as a whole.*

The term *outlay cost* in this context represents the cash outflows that are
directly associated with the production and transfer of the goods or services.
Of course, these cash outflows do not necessarily have to be made at a particular

instant, but the action of production and transfer will result sooner or later in some cash outflows that will be termed outlay costs.[4] Opportunity costs are defined here as the maximum contribution to profits foregone by the firm as a whole if the goods are transferred internally. These may be foregone contribution margins in some instances and even foregone net proceeds from the sale of facilities in other instances.

The distinction between outlay and opportunity costs is made here because the accounting records ordinarily record the outlay costs of the alternative selected but fail to record the opportunity costs of the best of the rejected alternatives.[5] If a perfect intermediate market exists, the opportunity cost is market price less outlay cost. For example, if the outlay cost is $1 and the market price is $4, the transfer price is $1 + ($4 − $1) = $4, which happens to be the market price. However, if no market exists for the intermediate product or alternative products that might utilize the same supplying division's facilities, the opportunity cost may be zero. In the latter case, outlay cost (perhaps approximated by variable cost) may be the correct transfer price.

The problems in transfer pricing would be trivial if the intermediate market price were widely applicable. But too often the intermediate markets are nonexistent, ill-structured, or imperfect. Therefore, market price is a special case rather than a universal guide. The key computation is the (b) part of the general rule above. It is easy to say, "Measure the foregone contribution from rejecting the next best alternative." However, it is not easy to do this. For example, consider a supplier division with idle capacity and an imperfect demand in the intermediate market. Is its opportunity cost zero? Probably not. One alternative may be to cut price so as to increase demand and hope to increase overall

---

[4] Other terms, including *incremental costs, additional costs, direct costs,* and *variable costs,* were rejected as not being as sharply descriptive as is the term *outlay cost.*

[5] The jungle of terminology in this area is too dense to dwell on at length here. The "general rule" has been expressed here with the hope that it will ease the understanding of those who are more comfortable with the terminology of accountants than with that of economists. For example, some economists would examine this general rule and say that *both* (a) and (b) together are opportunity cost. That is, the outlay cost is also an opportunity cost because it measures what the firm would have saved had the outlay *not* been incurred. For an excellent discussion of cost as it is used in economics, see George Stigler, *Theory of Price,* 3rd ed. (New York: The Macmillan Company, 1966).

Other economists would say that both (a) and (b) together are the *marginal cost,* because transfer prices are usually expressed on a per-unit basis. The term *marginal cost* is avoided here because it is ambiguous in the literature. That is, some economists in some situations will use it, at any given point of production, to embrace both (a) and (b) for the last unit produced. In other situations, they will use it to represent (a) only. For example, the loss of external profits is not included in the usual economic description of marginal costs, but it must be included in one way or another for marginal cost to be appropriate as a transfer price for the cases of demand or cost dependencies. Moreover, many accountants will use *variable cost* and *marginal cost* as if they were synonymous terms.

The economist would be inclined to express the general rule slightly differently. David Solomons, in *Divisional Performance: Measurement and Control* (Homewood, Ill.: Richard D. Irwin, 1968), p. 181, points out: "Transfer prices should be set equal to the marginal cost of supply, not at just any output, but at one particular equilibrium output." This requires the matching of the outlay costs of the supplying division at different levels of output with the summation of quantities demanded at each level of additional revenue for all demands. Therefore, a general, unchanging transfer price may be appropriate only in the case of a perfect intermediate market or in the case of constant marginal costs. Instead, the transfer price must be determined in relation to constantly changing levels of supply and demand. There is not a transfer price; rather, there is a schedule of transfer prices (a transfer-price function) for various quantities.

revenue. But measuring the probable effect is difficult, so measuring the opportunity cost is also difficult.

Above all, transfer prices must be judged by using the three criteria simultaneously rather than one at a time. The answers are not ordinarily generated by economic analysis alone as it applies to a particular decision situation. For example, economic analysis can demonstrate that if no intermediate market exists, the correct transfer price is marginal cost. But division managers of supplying divisions are not gleeful about transferring at marginal cost because it does not enhance their measure of divisional performance and it impinges on their autonomy. The point is that forced transfers at a perceived economic-optimum transfer price may hurt the credibility of the overall decentralized system and may impede the obtaining of other wanted benefits.

As soon as alternate uses for capacity are considered, the transfer-pricing mechanism gets complicated. In practice, simple rules tend to be used (market, negotiated market, standard cost plus some markup) and unusual cases are negotiated. Whether such simplicity is optimal depends on the existence of profit opportunities and interdependencies among the segments of the company. The more opportunities and interdependencies, the more likely is the need for centralized control.

PERSPECTIVE OF FIRM AS A WHOLE

Transfer pricing becomes a fascinating analytical problem when many interdependencies exist among divisions and markets. The central question is whether decisions will be made that are optimal from the viewpoint of the organization as a whole. Market prices often fail to provide optimal guidance when divisions are highly interdependent—even if no transfers are contemplated. For example, consider Divisions A, B, and H of Company X, which has more than 100 divisions.

Suppose that Division A needs a part as a component of its final product. Two outside bids have been received, one for $200 and one for $212. Acting in his own best interest, the Division A manager would choose the $200 bid. However, top management knows that the supplier who bid $212 will, in turn, buy some raw materials for $30 from Division H that will increase its contribution to profits by $20. The supplier who bids $200 will not buy any raw materials from Company X. The cash flows are diagrammed (see the top of page 736) for both alternatives:

(1) Buy at $200
(2) Buy at $212

This case illustrates how external market prices may not automatically lead to optimal decisions for the company as a whole, even in a non-transfer-pricing context. In this example, there is a net advantage of $8 if the $212 price is accepted:

	(1) BUY AT $200	(2) BUY AT $212
Cash outflow for firm as a whole	$200	$212 − ($30 − $10) = $192

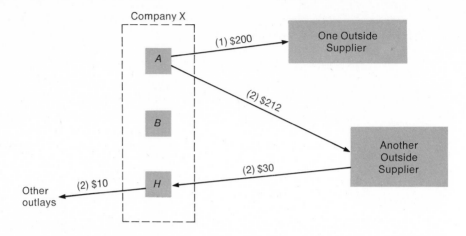

Note the conflicts among our three criteria of decentralization. The firm as a whole will benefit if A pays $12 more for its goods. H will also benefit. But poor A will suffer because A would be better off paying $200 rather than $212. Goal congruence says that A should be instructed or induced to pay $212. However, if the system is not designed to give A some credit for its self-sacrifice, the criteria of performance evaluation and autonomy will be undermined. This dilemma is also applicable to the next example.

A modification of this case demonstrates again why market transfer prices fail to induce optimal decisions. Suppose Division B is working at full capacity and can provide the needed part to A or to an outside buyer at the same price of $212. (For convenience, we now assume that $212 is the uniform market price.) If market price were the rule, B would have to meet the $212 bid. Assume that the outlay costs to B of filling the order were $150. Finally, assume that B, unlike the outside supplier, does not buy from H because this conglomerate organization is so large and communications are so bad that the B manager is unaware of this alternative. Then the decision to transfer at $212 would have been wrong. The cash flows are diagrammed for both alternatives:

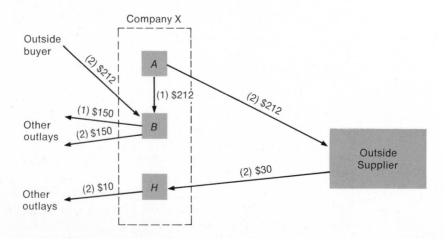

(1) Buy inside
(2) Buy outside

NET EFFECTS ON CASH FLOWS

	(1) BUY INSIDE @ $212		(2) BUY OUTSIDE @ $212
Outflow of B	−$150	Outflow of A	−$212
		Contributions:	
		B($212 − $150) = +$62	
		H($ 30 − $ 10) = + 20	+ 82
Cash outflow for firm as a whole	−$150	Cash outflow for firm as a whole	−$130

Only the general rule will work correctly. The transfer price should be:

Outlay cost to point of transfer + Opportunity cost for firm as a whole

$$\$150 + [(\$212 - \$150) + (\$30 - \$10)] = \$232$$

Note that the opportunity cost is influenced not only by the opportunity that B has to sell outside ($212 − $150) but also by the opportunity that H has to sell outside ($30 − $10). A price of $232 will lead to the correct decision because it will force A to go outside. No transfers will be made, and that is the desired behavior. Clearly, the $232 price is optimal only if the $20 contribution from H is available. If this contribution decreases to zero, then the transfer price will revert to $212.

As companies become more diverse and operations become more decentralized, there is a heightened possibility of having subunits operating knowingly or unknowingly at cross-purposes. Occasional dysfunctional decisions are the costs of decentralization. As the president of a huge company remarked in a private conversation, "We use market prices as transfer prices as much as possible because this harmonizes with our policy of heavy decentralization. Occasionally we encounter some resultant costly blunders, but we swallow hard and view these incongruent decisions as part of the price we pay for other benefits from decentralization." The trouble is that the benefits are hard to quantify, so management must feel its way. Frequently, interdependencies are overwhelming, and occasional mistakes become routine debacles. Then the extent of decentralization must be reduced via additional constraints that remove some decision-making power from the division managers.

By now it should be clear that the general rule, whether it is expressed in the manner illustrated in this chapter or in the terminology of the economist, may serve as a good starting point, because it underscores the importance of viewing the transfer-pricing problem in the perspective of the firm as a whole. However, the opportunity-cost portion is hard to pinpoint and measure in practice. Opportunity cost is dependent on the degree of competition in the intermediate markets, the presence or absence of idle capacity, the materiality of the number of units transferred, the disposal value of idle facilities, and the interdependence of the units regarding demands and costs.

Moreover, because of performance evaluation and autonomy factors, the price produced by the general rule may not be the best price to use to induce the manager to make a decision that is congruent with top-management goals. Therefore, the general rule may be a good starting point for determining a transfer price that would be used by top management for the benefit of the firm as a whole. However, the analysis is incomplete until the long-run ramifications of the price on the evaluation of performance and autonomy are also considered.

ALTERNATIVES TO USING MARKET PRICES

Sometimes market prices are either unavailable, inappropriate, or too costly to be used for transfer pricing. Let us explore other ways to set transfer prices. Nearly every version of a transfer price has some drawbacks.

no intermediate market   Sometimes, specialized product components are not readily salable to or available from intermediate markets. The general rule advocated earlier applies here. However, the act of internal transfer does not result in foregoing any opportunities to sell goods in intermediate markets, so at least in the short run, the opportunity cost of internal transfers is zero because no contributions to profit are foregone. In these cases, the economic interests of the organization as a whole are best served by transfers at the additional outlay costs of bringing the units to the point of transfer. In the short run, this is frequently approximated by so-called variable or marginal costs. The first example in the appendix to this chapter shows the economic analysis.

Marginal or variable cost is frequently cited as being the relevant transfer price when there is no intermediate market. However, the applicability of marginal cost is not widespread. The assumption of "no intermediate market" is a strong one and is indeed rare; conceivably, there is almost always the possibility of getting a part made to order on the outside. Moreover, even when there are idle facilities, there is almost always the alternative of using the facilities for making some other product. Still, let us examine the problem, because managers often perceive their situations as those of having no intermediate market, and they act accordingly.

An example may clarify the issue. Suppose Supplier Division A is a profit center that sells a variety of products inside and outside the company. Suppose further that there is idle capacity and that Product X is a component of a finished product made by Division B. There is no intermediate market for Product X. Finally, suppose the variable cost of X is $1, its absorption cost is $1.50, and Division A has an average markup on all its products of 60 percent of absorption cost.

Note the dilemma here. To benefit the organization as a whole, the supplying division should transfer the intermediate good at variable cost, because variable cost is the information needed for deciding on how many finished units should be produced. As the manager of the supplying division, how would you feel about such a rule? Unless you were totally generous, you probably would not be willing to transfer at a price of $1. After all, the production of this part is essential to the overall company profit, so you are entitled to a share of that profit. In short, the transfer price of $1 may seemingly be goal-congruent for the organization as a whole, but it may not lead to the wanted decisions because it fails to meet the other two criteria of performance evaluation and autonomy.

dual pricing   The dilemma may be met in various ways. The interdependence of the two divisions regarding this product may be overtly recognized by making a centralized decision and imposing the $1 transfer price. In effect, this approach jettisons decentralization, at least for transactions in this product. Because most organizations are hybrids of centralization and decentralization anyway, this approach deserves serious consideration where such transfers are significant.

Alternatively, the seeming harshness of the foregoing authoritarian approach can be modified if organizations recognize that there is no necessity to have a *single* transfer price. The profit center concept can be preserved more easily if one transfer price is used for one purpose (making the economic decision) and another for a second purpose (evaluation of performance). In our example, such a dual-pricing scheme could result in the transfer price to Division B being $1, while Division A is given credit for a synthetic market price of perhaps $2.40 ($1.50 plus 60 percent). Under this scheme, each division's performance would be enhanced by the transfer, and the $1 transfer price to Division B would induce the Division B manager to make the correct economic decisions from the viewpoint of the organization as a whole. Note that this dual-pricing plan essentially gives Division A a corporate subsidy. The profit for the company as a whole will be less than the sum of the divisional profits. Suppose that 100,000 units are transferred:

DIVISION A			DIVISION B		
Sales to B @ $2.40	$240,000		Sales of finished product @ $5		$500,000
Variable costs @ $1.00	100,000		Variable costs:		
Contribution	$140,000		Division A @ $1	$100,000	
			Division B @ $3	300,000	400,000
			Contribution		$100,000

Note that the contribution to the corporation as a whole is $100,000.

prorating the overall contribution   If a dual transfer-pricing plan is unattractive because of its strangeness or for some other reason, another possibility is to impose a variable-cost transfer price but credit each division for a prorated share of the overall contribution to corporate profit. Suppose that 100,000 units were in question:

Sales of finished product @ $5		$500,000
Division A @ $1	$100,000	
Division B @ $3	300,000	400,000
Contribution to corporate profit		$100,000

The proration would probably be negotiated in any number of ways. Suppose that it were in proportion to the standard variable costs incurred by each division. Then Division A would get credited for $25,000 and Division B for $75,000. In this way, Division A would be willing to transfer at $1, knowing that the transfers would somehow improve its showing as a profit center. Essentially, this is a standard-variable-cost-plus transfer-pricing system; the "plus" is a function of the overall contribution to corporate profit.

imperfect markets   *Imperfect competition* exists when one seller or buyer, *acting alone*, can exert an influence on the market price. If the intermediate market is imperfectly competitive, additional volume can be obtained only if selling prices are lowered. This means that the existing market price at a particular volume level is no longer applicable for the decision regarding how much to produce and sell. The additions to revenue will be less than the sales of the additional units at the new selling price because the new lower price will apply to the entire volume. For example, suppose the current selling price is $1 per unit and 80,000 units are being sold. The revenue is $80,000. A cut in price from $1 to $.90 may increase unit sales to 90,000. The increase in revenue is (10,000 × $.90) minus (80,000 × $.10, the loss in revenue on the 80,000 units), or $1,000. In these situations, the analyses can become exceedingly complex. The optimal transfer price from the viewpoint of the corporation as a whole is different for each situation, depending on the existence of cost interdependencies and demand interdependencies. Some of these complexities are explored in the appendix to this chapter. An example of a cost interdependency is the case where the price of a certain raw material may be dependent on the total purchases by two or more divisions. An example of a demand interdependency is any vertically integrated operation where there is no intermediate market for a unique component part of a finished product. Then the total number of finished products sold is dependent on the total number of components available, and vice versa.

The general rule mentioned earlier still applies to these situations. The interests of the corporation as a whole are paramount, and where interdependencies are large, decentralization may be a nonoptimal form of organization.

full-cost bases   There are no recent surveys of actual practices in transfer pricing. However, the use of full cost-plus is widespread. The intermediate transfers of products on the basis of accumulated cost typically mean that the supplying divisions are really cost centers rather than profit centers. If the transfers are based on actual costs, the performance of the receiving divisions would bear the accumulated efficiencies or inefficiencies of other divisions not subject to their control. Transfer prices that insure recovery of actual costs often fail to provide an incentive to control costs; therefore, some version of standard or budgeted costs is better than actual costs because it gives incentive to control costs.

Full or normal standard costs may minimize the problem of inefficiency, but may lead to suboptimal decisions. For example, Division A may supply parts to Division B at a standard cost of $5, including a charge of $3 for fixed costs based on some normal activity level. (There may also be some "plus" added in a cost-plus transfer-pricing system.) Suppose A and B have idle capacity and B has additional processing and selling costs of $4 per unit. B can obtain additional revenue of $8 per unit. B would refuse, because its performance would worsen at the rate of $1 per unit:

		DIVISION B PERFORMANCE
Additional revenue		$8
Additional costs:		
Transfer price from A	$5	
Additional costs in B	4	9
Additional loss		− $1

But the entity as a whole would benefit:

		ENTIRE ENTITY
Additional revenue		$8
Additional costs:		
A	$2	
B	4	6
Additional profit		$2

This is a clear example of goal incongruence that is induced by a transfer price based on so-called full or average total costs. The transfer-pricing scheme has led B to regard the fixed costs in A as variable costs. From the viewpoint of the firm as a whole, this may lead to dysfunctional decisions.

cost-plus as a synthetic market price   Despite the obvious limitations of the approach, transfer prices based on full cost, or on full cost plus some markup, are in common use. A major reason for the wide use of cost-based transfer pricing is its clarity and convenience. Moreover, the transferred product or service in question is often slightly different in quality or other characteristics from that available from outside sources. As a result, cost-plus pricing is often viewed as yielding a "satisfactory" approximation of an outside market price. Therefore, the resulting synthetic market price is regarded as a good practical substitute that is acceptable for both economic decisions and performance evaluation. The alternative—getting "real" market prices—is perceived as being too costly for incorporating into a routine control system.

variable cost plus lump sum   Top management often wants the buyer-division manager to make month-to-month purchasing decisions based on the variable costs of the supplier division. Otherwise, as the example in the preceding section showed, the buyer division may be led toward the wrong decision. One way to satisfy the needs of the two divisions and the company as a whole is to transfer at a standard variable cost. A separate predetermined lump-sum charge is made for fixed costs plus a lump-sum profit; this charge may be made annually or monthly. It is based on an annual expectation, not on actual purchases. In any event, the buyer's month-to-month decisions are not influenced by the supplier's fixed costs or the supplier's profit. Note that except for the profit, this was the approach recommended in Chapter 12 for the reallocation of service-department costs to operating departments.

THE NEED FOR MANY TRANSFER PRICES

Previous sections have already pointed out that there is seldom a single transfer price that will meet the three criteria that will induce the desired decisions. The "correct" transfer price depends on the economic and legal circumstances and the decision at hand. We may want one transfer price for motivation and a second for evaluation. Furthermore, the optimal price for either may differ from that employed for tax reporting or for other external needs.

Income taxes, property taxes, and tariffs often influence the setting of transfer prices so that the firm as a whole will benefit, even though the performance of a subunit may suffer under this set of prices. To minimize tariffs and domestic income taxes, a company may want to set an unusually low selling price for a domestic division that ships goods to foreign subsidiaries in countries where the prevailing tax rates are lower. To maximize tax deductions for percentage depletion allowances, which are based on revenue, a petroleum company may want to transfer crude oil to other subunits at as high a price as possible. As somebody in the oil industry once said, "Only fools and subsidiaries pay posted prices."

Transfer pricing is also influenced in some situations because of state fair-trade laws and national antitrust acts. Because of the differences in national tax structures around the world or because of the differences in the incomes of various divisions and subsidiaries, the firm may wish to shift profits and "dump" goods, if legally possible. These considerations are additional illustrations of the limits of decentralization where heavy interdependencies exist and of why the same company may use different transfer prices for different purposes.

THE TOTAL SYSTEM APPROACH

Exhibit 21-1 in the previous chapter demonstrated how management attempts to find some intermediate point between total centralization and total decentralization that will maximize the organization's profits (or other objectives). Transfer prices may be viewed as constraints on decentralization because they are designed to link at least two divisions or subsystems, whereas by definition all subsystems in a totally decentralized system should act as though they were independent.

At its extreme, decentralization means complete freedom to make local decisions in the best interests of a subunit as if the unit were independent. The major cost of such decentralization is dysfunctional decision making; an example would be buying outside when purchases should be made inside. To reduce the likelihood of such a decision and thus increase profit, a transfer-pricing scheme can help bring the system to an intermediate point between total centralization and total decentralization. This attempt to reach an intermediate point may decrease some of the benefits gained by decentralization, but it is intended to decrease the costs even further.

Two basic situations occur. A market for an intermediate product either exists or does not exist. If a market exists, and there are no demand or cost dependencies, a market-based price will preserve independence and will lead to the maximization of both divisional and company profits. The buying division will not be forced to accept a transfer that lowers the profit of the division and the company. Moreover, the buying division will buy in the open market if the outlay cost of making the intermediate product is greater than the market price. The selling division can sell in the open market, so it will not be forced to make a transfer that will decrease its profit.

The use of a market price is likely to minimize dysfunctional decision making and maximize divisional and overall profits. Furthermore, it adds no constraints, is simple in concept, and provides a credible basis for the evaluation of divisional performance.

If market prices are not applicable, special analyses are usually necessary to lead to what are apparently optimal decisions. However, the implementation of such pricing schemes, geared to special computations of opportunities or marginal revenues and marginal costs, often entails moving toward centralized management. The desirability of such a movement depends on whether the additional profits resulting from apparently better decisions are not exceeded by any perceived loss in benefits from reducing decentralization. From a systems viewpoint, when reliable market prices do not exist, the conceptual questions are:

1. What would be gained by reducing dysfunctional decisions under various sets of transfer prices?
2. For each set, what is the loss in benefits from reducing decentralization?

The optimal transfer price will maximize the excess of the gain over the loss. The trouble with economic analysis is that it often considers only the first question and produces some mathematical decision rules that ignore the second. As the chapter appendix indicates, economic analysis of transfer pricing often calls for elaborate processing of a vast amount of data by a central decision maker, who may then either impose a transfer price or induce goal-congruent decisions by a system of subsidies and taxes for division managers. Subsidies and taxes can be calculated mathematically, often using decomposition procedures so that an optimal solution can be reached.[6] One method that has been suggested favors

[6] Jack Hirshleifer, "Economics of Divisionalized Firm," *Journal of Business*, Vol. XXX, No. 2.

crediting the supplying division with one price (usually market) and charging the buying division with a different price (usually variable cost). Another method provides for each division's getting credit for the standard cost of its work on the product, plus the entire incremental corporate profit upon the sale of the finished item. In this way, divisional profits will reflect divisional contribution to corporate profits—the amount by which the corporation's profits will be diminished in the short run if the division is abandoned.[7]

Even if the economic analysis were economically feasible in a practical setting (and this is very doubtful), the models neglect the reduction in benefits that may be suffered from the necessary loss of decentralization that must occur through the use of total models, decomposition procedures, and the like. To facilitate transfer-pricing decisions, top management usually needs detailed information regarding the operations of each division.[8] This tends to detract from divisional managers' impression of managing an independent business. The slow acceptance of the use of large-scale models to set transfer prices is probably attributable to their current lack of economic feasibility, and perhaps also to inertia; the reductions in costs from preventing dysfunctional decisions do not exceed the added costs of constructing and operating a more complex system.

In addition, there seems to be an uneasy feeling on the part of many managers about complex control systems that either (a) add constraints on divisional actions or (b) burden the division with providing profuse, detailed information to the central authorities. Such systems are movements away from decentralization, accompanied by decreases in the benefits of decentralization. Therefore, top management is basically confronted with a decision regarding the cost and value of information. What are the relative costs and benefits, given the particular circumstances of the specific firm that is considering the elaborate transfer-pricing model? An elaborate model may be useful for one firm but not for another, depending on the quantification of the benefits from eliminating dysfunctional decisions relative to the particular, though unquantifiable, costs of complexity.[9]

WHY PROFIT CENTERS?

At this point, after studying all the weaknesses of profit centers and transfer prices, students often jump to the conclusion that organizations should stay heavily centralized and use nothing fancier than flexible budgets. Early in Chapter 21, the point was stressed that accounting systems and techniques fall short of meeting the goal of optimally acquiring and utilizing resources for the organ-

---

[7] Ronen and McKinney, "Transfer Pricing," p. 111.

[8] But see Ronen and McKinney, *op. cit.,* p. 112.

[9] See Kenneth J. Arrow, "Control in Large Organizations," *Management Science,* Vol. 10, No. 3, 397–408, for a sweeping view of decentralization, and on pp. 405–6, for an assessment of the difficulties in applying a price system to the control of an organization. He sees these difficulties as four mutually interacting types: (a) the choice of enforcement rules, (b) the complexity of the operating rules, (c) the limits on the theoretical validity of the price system, and (d) the presence of uncertainty.

ization as a whole. However, we must still choose among various models and systems so that we may point and spur managers toward that goal. Therefore, the conceptual perfection of a particular transfer price or profit center may be unimportant. Given our objectives, we seek the best feasible system in a specific organization.

Again and again, organizations have found flexible budgets and cost centers insufficient. These systems are a good first step, but profit centers and cost-plus transfer pricing have evolved in response to a need for more incentive toward top-management goals. For example, some top managers have found that cost-center managers aim at meeting a budget and keeping costs under control, and nothing more. When the cost centers are changed into profit centers, perhaps transferring goods at merely cost-plus prices, subunit managers continue to worry about costs, but they start worrying also about boosting production and about possible marketing needs. In these situations, nobody pretends that the "profit center" is an independent unit, but top managers often obtain the wanted goal congruence through profit centers more readily than through cost centers.

ACCOUNTING ENTRIES FOR TRANSFERS

Transfer pricing is governed by managerial objectives, including measuring divisional performance, minimizing taxes, and controlling the rate of return. These objectives often lead to transfers at prices in excess of the conventional inventory costs used for external reporting.

Accounting for market-based transfer prices provides another illustration of how current accounting systems are being designed primarily to aid managerial planning and control rather than to serve the need for external financial reports. After all, from the viewpoint of the consolidated enterprise, any goods or services transferred within the enterprise and not yet sold to outsiders should be carried at cost. Thus, although intracompany transfers may be accounted for and reported in any manner that helps achieve managerial objectives, intracompany margins must be eliminated periodically when consolidated financial statements are prepared.

The basic approach may be illustrated as follows:

Whole Company has two divisions, A and B. Goods having a manufacturing cost of $100 are transferred from A to B at a price of $135. Entries follow:

ON BOOKS OF SUPPLIER DIVISION A		
Accounts receivable—Division B	135	
Sales to Division B		135
Cost of goods sold (transferred)	100	
Inventory—Division A		100

ON BOOKS OF RECEIVING DIVISION B		
Inventory—Division B	135	
Accounts payable—Division A		135

An examination of the entries above shows that essentially the two divisions operate as separate companies. However, if the Whole Company had to prepare consolidated financial statements immediately after the transaction, the following eliminating entries would be needed:

Accounts payable—Division A	135	
Accounts receivable—Division B		135
To eliminate intracompany receivable and payable.		
Sales to Division B	135	
Cost of goods sold (transferred)		100
Intracompany gross profit—A		35
To close and recognize Division A's intracompany gross profit.		
Intracompany gross profit—A	35	
Inventory—Division B		35
To eliminate intracompany gross profit.		

summary

Transfer-pricing systems are needed if decentralization is to be established in companies whose divisions exchange goods and services. A transfer-pricing system must be judged in relation to its impact on (a) economic analysis and decisions, (b) evaluation of performance, and (c) subunit autonomy. Some version of market price as a transfer price will usually best motivate managers toward optimal economic decisions; moreover, the evaluation of performance will then be consistent with the ideas of decentralization.

There is rarely a single transfer price that will serve all needs. Instead, there may be one transfer price for making a particular production decision, another for evaluating performance, and another for minimizing tariffs or income taxes.

Economic analysis can demonstrate that market price is not always the best guide to optimal decisions. In such instances, some centralization of control is needed to prevent dysfunctional decisions. If so, serious thought should be given to whether profit centers and decentralization provide the optimum organizational design. Above all, the perceived costs and benefits at alternative levels of decentralization should be explicitly considered when choosing a transfer-pricing scheme.

suggested readings

Arrow, Kenneth J., "Control in Large Organizations," *Management Science*, Vol. 10, No. 3, 397–408.

Baumol, William, and Tibor Fabian, "Decomposition, Pricing for Decentralization and External Economies," *Management Science*, Vol. 11, No. 1, 1–32.

Dearden, John, "Interdivisional Pricing," *Harvard Business Review,* Vol. 38, No. 1.

Dopuch, Nicholas, and David Drake, "Accounting Implications of a Mathematical Programming Approach to the Transfer Price Problem," *Journal of Accounting Research,* Vol. 2, No. 1, 15–21.

Gould, J. R., "Internal Pricing in Firms When There Are Costs of Using an Outside Market," *The Journal of Business,* Vol. XXXVII, No. 1, 61–67.

Hass, Jerome E., "Transfer Pricing in a Decentralized Firm," *Management Science: Application,* Vol. 14, No. 6, B-310 through B-331.

Hirshleifer, Jack, "Internal Pricing and Decentralized Decisions," in *Management Controls: New Directions in Basic Research,* eds. C. Bonini, R. Jaedicke, and H. Wagner, p. 30. New York: McGraw-Hill Book Company, 1964.

Ronen, Joshua, and George McKinney, "Transfer Pricing for Divisional Autonomy," *Journal of Accounting Research,* Vol. 8, No. 1 (Spring 1970), p. 103.

Whinston, Andrew, "Pricing Guides in Decentralized Organizations," in *New Perspective in Organizational Research,* eds. W. W. Cooper, H. J. Leavitt, and M. W. Shelly. New York: John Wiley & Sons, Inc. 1964.

Also see N.A.A. *Research Report No. 30* and the other suggested readings in the preceding chapter. The Solomons book is particularly strong in transfer pricing.

Problem for Self-Study

PROBLEM 1   A transportation equipment manufacturer, the Pillercat Corporation, is heavily decentralized. Each division head has full authority on all decisions regarding sales to internal or external customers. Division P has always acquired a certain equipment component from Division S. However, when informed that Division S was increasing its unit price to $220, Division P's management decided to purchase the component from outside suppliers at a price of $200.

Division S had recently acquired some specialized equipment that was used primarily to make this component. The manager cited the resulting high depreciation charges as the justification for the price boost. He asked the president of the company to instruct Division P to buy from S at the $220 price. He supplied the following information:

P's annual purchases of component, in units	2,000
S's variable costs per unit	$ 190
S's fixed costs per unit	20

required
1. Suppose there are no alternative uses for the S facilities. Will the company as a whole benefit if P buys from the outside suppliers for $200 per unit? Show computations.

2. Suppose internal facilities of S would not otherwise be idle. The equipment and other facilities would be assigned to other production operations and would result in annual cash operating savings of $29,000. Should P purchase from outsiders?

3. Suppose there are no alternative uses for S's internal facilities and that the selling price of outsiders drops $15. Should P purchase from outsiders?

4. As the president, how would you respond to the request of the manager of S? Would your response differ according to the specific situations described in parts 1–3 above? Why?

5. What rule would you favor for setting transfer prices in the Pillercat Corporation?

SOLUTION   1. Assume that fixed costs are unaffected. The company as a whole will not benefit if P buys on the outside:

Purchase costs from outsider, 2,000 units @ $200	$400,000
Less: Savings in variable costs by reducing S output, 2,000 @ $190	380,000
Disadvantage to company as a whole	$ 20,000

2. The company will benefit if P buys on the outside:

Purchase costs from outsider, 2,000 units @ $200		$400,000
Less: Savings in variable costs as above	$380,000	
Savings related to other production operations	29,000	409,000
Advantage to company as a whole		$ 9,000

3. The company will benefit if P buys on the outside:

Purchase costs from outsider, 2,000 units @ $185	$370,000
Less: Savings in variable costs as above	380,000
Advantage to company as a whole	$ 10,000

4. As president, I probably would not want to become immersed in these disputes. If arbitration is necessary, it should probably be conducted by some other officer on the corporate staff. One possibility is to have the immediate line boss of the two managers make a decision.

    If decentralization is to be strictly adhered to, the arbitrator should probably do nothing under any of the conditions described. If no forced transfer were made, P would go outside, resulting in an optimal decision for the overall company in parts 2 and 3 but not in part 1.

    Of course, in part 1, if the manager of S understood cost–volume–profit relationships, and if he wanted to maximize his short-run net income, he would probably accept a price of $200. This would bring a contribution to the divisional profit of $2,000 \times (\$200 - \$190)$, or $20,000.

    Suppose, however, that he refuses to meet the price of $200. This would mean that the company will be $20,000 poorer in the short run. Should top management interfere and force a transfer at $200? This would undercut the philosophy of decentralization. Many managers would not interfere because they would view the $20,000 as the price that has to be paid for mistakes made under decentralization. But how high must this price go before the temptation to interfere would be irresistible? $30,000? $40,000? How much?

    In sum, the point of this question is that any superstructure that interferes with lower-level decision making weakens decentralization. Of course, such interference may occasionally be necessary to prevent horrendous blunders. But recurring interference and constraints simply transform a decentralized organization into a centralized organization.

5. The information given indicates that the best rule would be a market price with the seller having the option to refuse to sell internally. This would have led to the correct decision from the viewpoint of both the divisions and the company as a whole.

    In situation 1, S would obtain a contribution of $200 - $190, or $10 per unit. In 2, S would lose a contribution of $10 per unit, or $20,000; but its $29,000 cost saving on other work would lead to a net saving of $9,000, or $4.50 per unit. In 3, S would lose $5 per unit, or $10,000, if the business were kept inside.

	EFFECT ON CONTRIBUTION TO INCOME		
DESIRED ACTION	WHOLE COMPANY	S	P
1. P buys inside	+20,000	+20,000	—
2. P buys outside	+ 9,000	+ 9,000	—
3. P buys outside	+10,000	+10,000	—

APPENDIX: ECONOMIC ANALYSIS OF TRANSFER PRICING

two examples of inter-dependencies Transfer pricing is analyzed in depth in the literature of economics and management science. Some of these readings are contained in the list on page 746. A long series of individual situations may be analyzed, including various combinations of intermediate and final markets, availabilities of capacity, and interdependencies of costs and demands. This appendix will limit the discussion to two situations as examples of the analysis.

In the first example, suppose a firm has a vertically integrated operation with two divisions, manufacturing and distribution. Assume further that the two divisions are cost-independent, so that the operations of either have no effect on the cost functions of the other. Also assume that there is no market whatsoever for the intermediate product.

In this case, to optimize overall firm profits, the first division and the second division must operate at the same level of output. The optimal output and price will be where firm marginal cost (MC) equals marginal revenue, as Exhibit 22-1 demonstrates.

MC is the sum of the marginal manufacturing cost (mmc) and the marginal

EXHIBIT 22-1

BEST JOINT LEVEL OF OUTPUT

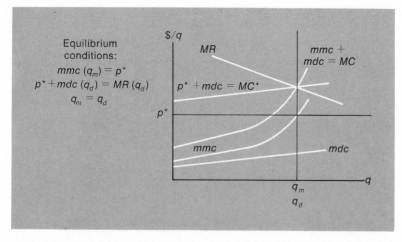

Source: This and the next exhibit are from Jack Hirshleifer, "Internal Pricing and Decentralized Decisions," in C. Bonini, R. Jaedicke, and H. Wagner, eds., *Management Controls: New Directions in Basic Research* (New York: McGraw-Hill Book Company, 1964), pp. 31, 33.

distribution cost (mdc). If the transfer price is p^*, the second-division manager will choose an output level of q_d, so that $MR = p^* + mdc = MC^*$. In turn, the first-division manager would independently choose an output level of q_m, so that $mmc = p^*$. The transfer price p^* should, therefore, be set so that $q_d = q_m$; that is, so the two divisions operate at the same level.

Hirshleifer comments:

> There are a variety of ways in which the optimum solution might be arrived at operationally. Some device like a neutral umpire might be employed to set an initial trial p^*—after which the divisions would respond by declaring tentative outputs q_m and q_d. If q_m exceeds q_d, the p^* should be adjusted downward by the umpire, and the reverse if q_d exceeds q_m—until a p^* is found such that the planned outputs are coordinated.[10]

But coordination cannot be assured by counting on the independent decisions of the division managers. Each is in a monopolistic position. The first division is inclined to limit supply and generate more profit for itself at the expense of the overall firm. The second division is inclined to behave in the opposite way, but with a similar impact on overall profits.

Note that gamesmanship is likely. Either party may give inaccurate responses to a neutral umpire with the hope of attaining a more favorable price. The forcing of transfers at marginal cost will not be welcomed by the manager of the first division. There is an obvious conflict between the notion of what ordinarily constitutes revenue for profit centers and of what transfer price leads to optimal economic decisions. In this situation, the first division would operate at a loss at all times. Systems of subsidies or taxes have been suggested as remedies for this weakness.

In the second example, assume that there is an imperfectly competitive external market for the intermediate product, so that the marginal cost of division 1, mmc, is less than the prevailing market price, p. Therefore, division 1 is a monopoly. Assume further that there is demand independence; that is, that additional internal sales do not affect external demands. To illustrate, in some cases a refinery selling unbranded gasoline to an independent distributor does not expect an adverse effect on the final demand for its branded gasoline.

As Exhibit 22-2 shows, the overall profits of the firm are optimized by having the prices for internal intermediate transfers differ from sales prices in the external intermediate markets. The equilibrium value for mmc (p^*) is found by equating mmc with Σmr (which is the sum of mr and nMR). This value is then set equal to nMR (which is $MR - mdc$) to give q_d, and also equal to mr to give q_s and p (quantity and price in the imperfect intermediate market).

The correct transfer price p^* again equals mmc, but note that the external

---

[10] Jack Hirshleifer, "Internal Pricing and Decentralized Decisions," in C. Bonini, R. Jaedicke, and H. Wagner, eds., *Management Controls: New Directions in Basic Research* (New York: McGraw-Hill Book Company, 1964), p. 30. Hirshleifer's work is the basis for the presentation here. Joshua Ronen and George McKinney, in "Transfer Pricing for Divisional Autonomy," *Journal of Accounting Research,* Vol. 8, No. 1 (Spring 1970), 103, suggest an alternative method of supplying information, which might be less restrictive than the Hirshleifer method. Also recommended is David Solomons, *Divisional Performance: Measurement and Control* (Homewood, Ill.: Richard D. Irwin, Inc., 1968), pp. 160–232.

EXHIBIT 22-2

IMPERFECTLY COMPETITIVE MARKET FOR INTERMEDIATE PRODUCT

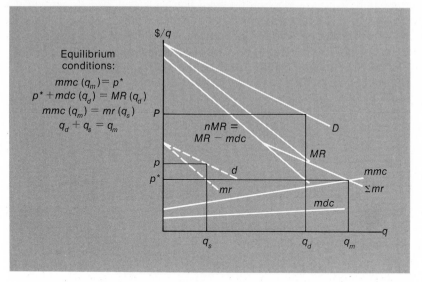

Equilibrium
conditions:

$$mmc\,(q_m) = p^*$$
$$p^* + mdc\,(q_d) = MR\,(q_d)$$
$$mmc\,(q_m) = mr\,(q_s)$$
$$q_d + q_s = q_m$$

price p for the intermediate commodity exceeds p^*. Also, external intermediate revenue mr = internal price p^* = mmc. A neutral umpire would set p^* so that $q_m = q_s + q_d$.

By setting the transfer price p^* at the marginal cost of the internal supplier division, the firm exploits its monopoly power on intermediate and final external customers. However, no internal exploitation is permitted. The correct level of p^* for the umpire to set is summarized by Hirshleifer:

> . . . in the case where outputs must be coordinated, by the coordination requirement; in the competitive intermediate market case, by the competitive external price; and in the monopolistic intermediate market case, by the condition that transfer price p^* to the internal customer should equal marginal revenue mr from the external customers for the intermediate product.[11]

management science approaches to transfer pricing   How can we have decentralization and also minimize dysfunctional decisions from the entire company's point of view? There are a number of approaches that attempt to develop systems whereby each division manager acting in his own self-interests also optimizes the company's allocation of resources. Two such approaches are described below.

Linear programming.   Linear programming is an applicable technique when capacity constraints exist in the divisions making intermediate products. The format of linear programming is well known and will not be discussed here. The

[11]Hirshleifer, "Internal Pricing," p. 34. In discussing the case of interdependent demands for the intermediate and final products, he stresses that internal transfers at marginal cost now entail loss of profitable sales at full price. "So the rule of marginal-cost pricing to internal customers no longer applies—unless marginal cost is redefined to include the loss of external profit."

primal solution gives a production program that makes the best (least costly or most profitable) use of the division's limited capacity. Of particular interest is the by-product of the primal solution—that is, the shadow prices given by the dual solution. Shadow prices are the amount by which total profit could be increased (or the cost reduced) if the scarce resource could be increased by one unit. It is not difficult to derive transfer prices for products, using shadow prices as a base. The major problem with using shadow prices to derive transfer prices is that, depending on the situation, either the supplying or the consuming division obtains the full increase in profit because of a transfer. Thus, division evaluation is a problem. Linear programming also has other limitations as a technique:

1. The objective function must, of course, be linear. This implies that the company must be a perfect competitor. That is, the company can sell all its outputs, and its actions have no effect on input or output prices.
2. Because the constraints are linear, only constant returns to scale are permitted.

Linear programming leads to maximizing corporate profits, but only by reducing decentralization. In general, profit centers are turned into cost centers.

An elaborate procedure called decomposition[12] has been proposed to optimize corporate resource allocation and in addition retain a considerable degree of decentralized authority.

Decomposition procedures.   The claimed benefits of decomposition include (a) maintenance of the favorable effects of decentralization on the divisional managers' motivation, and (b) reduction of the cost of dysfunctional decisions.

The decomposition procedure views the problem as follows:

$$\textbf{Max } P = \textbf{Corporate Profit}$$

subject to

(	Kc		)	≤	(Rc)
(K1)				≤	(R1)
	(K2)			≤	(R2)
		(K3)		≤	(R3)

$$\text{(K}n\text{)}\quad \le \quad \text{(R}n\text{)}$$

where

(Kc) = Corporate constraints	(= matrix)
(Ki) = Constraints of division #i	(= matrix)
(Rc) = Corporate resources	(= matrix)
(Ri) = Resources of division #i	(= matrix)

The following steps are taken:

---

[12] See W. J. Baumol and Tibor Fabian, "Decomposition, Pricing for Decentralization and External Economics," *Management Science,* Vol. 11, No. 1, 1–32; and Jerome E. Hass, "Transfer Pricing in a Decentralized Firm," *Management Science: Application,* Vol. 14, No. 6, B-310 through B-331.

1. Every division is asked by top management to submit an optimal plan of operations based on a unit profit figure assigned by the company for each product and on this division's constraints (K_i), resources (R_i), and objective.

2. Top management calculates the impact of each division's activities on the other divisions' profit, in terms of how much benefit (external economy) or cost (external diseconomy) the activities of division #i create for all other $n - 1$ divisions.

3. Top management adds to each division's unit profit (a) a subsidy, for those activities leading to external economies, or (b) a tax, for those activities leading to external diseconomies. These subsidies and taxes are based on each division's initial plans.

4. In view of these new inputs to their income statements, divisions submit new plans, based on the objective of increasing their own divisional profit.

5. The entire process is repeated a number of times, until the solution reached is the same optimum solution that would have been reached by solving the decomposed problem as one big linear programming problem (by using the simplex algorithm once only).

The role of the subsidies and taxes at every stage is of course crucial. Subsidies and taxes can be calculated mathematically for every stage, so that an overall optimum solution can be reached with certainty after a finite number of iterations. In case of nonlinearities, the same general method can be applied.

A highlight of decomposition is that every time top management maximizes the corporate-profit function, it takes into account only the corporate constraints, not the divisional constraints. Consequently, top management need know nothing about what technically happens inside a division.

There are variations of decomposition that are designed to minimize the undesirable behavioral effects that may evolve from having top management manipulate unit profits to induce congruent decisions. For example, writers have suggested crediting each division with its contribution to the profits of the firm as a whole.[13]

The decomposition procedure cannot work without exhaustive information about the revenue and cost functions of many divisions being processed at either the corporate or divisional level. Such knowledge may be unobtainable or obtainable only at prohibitive cost. Moreover, if top management has such information, perhaps the firm should be centralized. For decomposition to be attractive in a cost–benefit sense, there must be imperfect competition and heavy interdependencies of costs or demands among divisions. All these conditions lead to the conclusion that a centralized organization structure may result in more net benefits than an elaborate scheme of decomposition that preserves a myth of decentralization.

---

[13] See Hass, "Transfer Pricing in a Decentralized Firm," p. B-329; and Ronen and McKinney, "Transfer Pricing for Divisional Autonomy," p. 103.

questions, problems, and cases

22-1. Why are intracompany transfer prices often necessary?

22-2. What are two major bases for pricing intracompany transfers?

22-3. What is the major limitation to transfer prices based on cost?

22-4. "Company transfer-pricing policies must satisfy dual objectives." What are the objectives?

22-5. Where reliable market prices cannot be ascertained for transfer pricing, what is the impact on divisional-performance measurement?

22-6. What is the most common example in transfer pricing of a clash between divisional action and overall company profitability?

22-7. If an optimal economic decision is wanted in a particular situation, what is a general rule for transfer pricing?

22-8. What is outlay cost in the context of transfer pricing?

22-9. Why is market price as a basis for transfer pricing a special case rather than a universal guide?

22-10. What three criteria on systems design are also applicable to transfer pricing?

22-11. "Transfer pricing is confined to profit centers." Do you agree? Why?

22-12. When does imperfect competition exist?

22-13. Profit Centers and Transfer Pricing in an Automobile Dealership.   A large automobile dealership is installing a responsibility-accounting system and three profit centers: parts and service; new vehicles; and used vehicles. Each department manager has been told to run his shop as if he were in business for himself. However, there are interdepartmental dealings. For example:
a. The parts and service department prepares new cars for final delivery and repairs used cars prior to resale.
b. The used car department's major source of inventory has been cars traded in in part payment for new cars.

The owner of the dealership has asked you to draft a company policy statement on transfer pricing, together with specific rules to be applied to the examples cited. He has told you that clarity is of paramount importance because your statement will be relied upon for settling transfer-pricing disputes.

22-14. Variable Cost as a Transfer Price.   A product's variable cost is $1 and its market value is $2 at a transfer point from Division S to Division P. Division P's variable cost of processing the product further is $1.25, and the selling price of the final product is $2.75.

required

1. Prepare a tabulation of the contribution margin per unit for Division P performance and overall performance under the two alternatives of (a) processing further and (b) selling to outsiders at the transfer point.

2. As Division P manager, which alternative would you choose? Explain.

22-15. Transfer Pricing.   The Plastics Company has a separate division that produces a special molding powder. For the past three years, about two-thirds of the output has been sold to another division within the company. The remainder has been sold to outsiders. Last year's operating data follow:

	TO OTHER DIVISION		TO OUTSIDERS	
Sales	10,000 T. @ $70*	$700,000	5,000 T. @ $100	$500,000
Variable costs @ $50		$500,000		$250,000
Fixed costs		150,000		75,000
Total costs		$650,000		$325,000
Gross margin		$ 50,000		$175,000

*The $70 price is ordinarily determined by the outside sales price less selling and administrative expenses wholly applicable to outside business.

The buying-division manager has a chance to get a firm contract with an outside supplier at $65 for the ensuing year.

required Assume that the molding-powder division manager says that he cannot sell at $65, because no margin can be earned. As the buying-division manager, write a short reply. Assume that the 10,000 tons cannot be sold by the molding-powder division to other customers.

22-16. Transfer-Pricing Dispute. Allison-Chambers Corp., manufacturer of tractors and other heavy farm equipment, is organized along decentralized lines, with each manufacturing division operating as a separate profit center. Each division head has been delegated full authority on all decisions involving the sale of his division's output both to outsiders and to other divisions of Allison-Chambers. Division C has in the past always purchased its requirement of a particular tractor-engine component from Division A. However, when informed that Division A was increasing its price to $150, Division C's management decided to purchase the engine component from outside suppliers.

The component can be purchased by C for $135 on the open market. Division A insists that owing to the recent installation of some highly specialized equipment and the resulting high depreciation charges, A would not be able to make an adequate profit on its investment unless it raised its price. A's management appealed to top management of Allison-Chambers for support in its dispute with C and supplied the following operating data:

C's annual purchases of tractor-engine component	1,000
A's variable costs per unit of tractor-engine component	$120
A's fixed costs per unit of tractor-engine component	$ 20

required 1. Assume that there are no alternative uses for internal facilities. Determine whether the company as a whole will benefit if Division C purchases the component from outside suppliers for $135 per unit.

2. Assume that internal facilities of A would not otherwise be idle. By not producing the 1,000 units for C, A's equipment and other facilities would be assigned to other production operations, and would result in annual cash operating savings of $18,000. Should C purchase from outsiders?

3. Assume that there are no alternative uses for A's internal facilities and that the price of outsiders drops $20. Should C purchase from outsiders?

22-17. Transfer-Pricing Problem. Assume in the Allison-Chambers Corp. problem that Division A could sell the 1,000 units to other customers at $155 per unit with variable selling costs of $5 per unit. If this were the case, determine whether Allison-Chambers would benefit if C purchased the 1,000 components from outsiders at $135 per unit.

22-18. **Evaluation of Transfer-Pricing Policy.** The Altos Chemical Company has recently been decentralized. Several profit centers have been formed. The transfer-pricing system stipulates that average market prices should govern the intracompany sales; however, discounts from such prices should be made for any expenses that do not pertain to intracompany sales. Examples would be certain selling, shipping, and credit expenses.

The Fox Division, a large intracompany supplier of more than 100 products, tried to develop a workable method for quoting intracompany prices. The task was complicated by the presence of many selling and manufacturing costs that were common to a number of products. The Fox Division finally proposed a flat markup above variable manufacturing cost as a feasible approximation of market price:

Sales to outsiders	$11,000,000
Less:	
Selling, shipping, credit, and customer service expenses not applicable to intracompany sales	1,000,000
Adjusted sales	$10,000,000
Variable manufacturing costs	6,000,000
Markup	$ 4,000,000

Markup formula: $10,000,000 ÷ $6,000,000 = 167% of variable manufacturing costs. This formula would be reviewed and adjusted every 120 days.

required   What are the strengths and weaknesses of the proposed markup formula? Does the formula adhere to the company policy on transfer pricing?

22-19. **Conflict of Interests of Profit Centers and Company as a Whole.** [Adapted from David Solomons, *Divisional Performance: Measurement and Control* (New York: Financial Executives Research Foundation, 1965), pp. 167–72.] Division A of a company is the only source of supply for an intermediate product that is converted by Division B into a salable final product. Most of A's costs are fixed. For any output up to 1,000 units a day, its total costs are $500 a day. Total costs increase by $100 a day for every additional thousand units made. Division A judges that its own results will be optimized if it sets its price at 40¢ a unit, and it acts accordingly.

Division B incurs additional costs in converting the intermediate product supplied by A into a finished product. These costs are $1,250 for any output up to 1,000 units, and $250 per thousand for outputs in excess of 1,000. On the revenue side, B can increase its revenue only by spending more on sales promotion and by reducing selling prices. Its sales forecast is:

SALES IN UNITS	NET REVENUE PER THOUSAND UNITS
1,000	$1,750.00
2,000	1,325.00
3,000	1,100.00
4,000	925.00
5,000	800.00
6,000	666.67

required   1. Prepare a schedule comparing B's costs, including its purchases from A, revenues, and net income at various levels of output.

2. What is B's maximum net income? At that level, what is A's net income? At that level, what is the corporation's aggregate net income?

3. Suppose the company abandons its divisionalized structure. Instead of being two profit centers, A and B are combined into a single profit center with responsibility for the complete production and marketing of the product. Prepare a schedule similar to that in requirement 1. What volume level will provide the most net income?

4. Evaluate the results in 3. Why did the circumstances in requirement 1 lead to less net income than in requirement 3? How would you adjust the transfer-pricing policy to assure that overall company net income will be maximized where separate profit centers A and B are maintained?

22-20. Evaluation of Transfer-Pricing Policy. The Sunnyvale Corporation is a mammoth enterprise with more than forty profit centers. A company-wide transfer-pricing rule states that a selling division must always sell to a buying division at bona fide market prices.

The S Division was asked to quote prices on 10,000 standard parts (representing 10 percent of the S Division's practical capacity) that the B Division has ordered from time to time in past years. The S Division quoted a price of $20 each, which would bring S a $60,000 total contribution margin for the 10,000 parts. However, an outside supplier quoted a price of $16, and the S Division was forced by company policy to fill the order at that price.

required

1. How much total contribution margin will the S Division earn at the $16 price? By how much is the net income of the Sunnyvale Corporation affected by keeping the business inside at the $16 price rather than going outside at that price?

2. The practical capacity of the S Division is 100,000 machine-hours. Suppose that it takes one machine-hour to make one of the standard parts. Suppose further that the order is indivisible; that is, the S Division must make all 10,000 parts or none—it cannot accept a third or a half of the order. Suppose, finally, that only 10,000 machine-hours of capacity were available for this production.

The S Division manager had also planned to submit a bid to an outside company for making 4,000 special parts at a selling price of $40 each, which would bring S a total contribution margin of $80,000 for the 4,000 parts. The manager felt virtually certain that he would get the order. It takes two machine-hours to make one special part. However, he could not handle both orders, and so he delayed submitting his bid because of the B Division's need for the standard parts. In view of these circumstances, how were the S Division's and the Sunnyvale Corporation's net income affected by the decision to keep the standard-parts order inside? How would you modify the transfer-pricing rule?

22-21. Transfer Prices in an Imperfect Market. [Adapted from David Solomons, *Divisional Performance: Management and Control* (New York: Financial Executives Research Foundation, 1965), pp. 178–79.] Division A is the supplier division and Divisions B and C are the consumer divisions of a large company. After Division B deducts its own processing costs, the total net revenue and the marginal net revenue it derives from various quantities of intermediate product are:

DIVISION B

QUANTITY OF INTERMEDIATE PROCESSED, IN POUNDS	TOTAL NET REVENUE	MARGINAL NET REVENUE
1,000	$ 600	$600
2,000	900	300
3,000	1,100	200
4,000	1,200	100

Similarly, for Division C we have:

DIVISION C

QUANTITY OF INTERMEDIATE PROCESSED, IN POUNDS	TOTAL NET REVENUE	MARGINAL NET REVENUE
2,000	$1,200	$—
3,000	1,800	600
4,000	2,100	300
5,000	2,300	200
6,000	2,400	100

Division A, the producing division, faces the following cost conditions:

DIVISION A

QUANTITY OF INTERMEDIATE PRODUCED, IN POUNDS	TOTAL COST	MARGINAL COST
4,000	$2,000	$—
5,000	2,100	100
6,000	2,250	150
7,000	2,425	175
8,000	2,625	200
9,000	2,925	300
10,000	3,325	400

What transfer price should be set for A's output? Why?

22-22. **Transfer Pricing of Monopolist Division.** Company XYZ has two divisions. Division A has developed and patented a special substance, Fixitall, which has no competitive substitutes. Division A has sold this substance in market X and has effectively acted as a monopolist. The division manager of A noted that he sold 10,000 tons of Fixitall at an average price of $35 per ton in 19_6 as compared with 5,000 tons at an average price of $42.50 in 19_5. In this no-fixed-cost division, profits had been $150,000 in 19_6 and $112,500 in 19_5. Looking at 19_6, the manager concluded that he had optimized profit in 19_6 but not in 19_5. In reaching this conclusion, he believed the marketplace demand curve for his product had not changed between 19_5 and 19_6, nor had his unit variable costs changed.

Division B made one product. For this product, which sold in a competitive market Y at $40 per ton, it used materials costing $30 per ton. Other direct costs of production were $5 per ton.

The manager of Division B was intrigued with the possibilities of using Fixitall as the material input for his product, rather than that presently used.

If Fixitall were used, he felt, his selling price structure could be maintained and sales volume could easily increase because of product improvement.

Both division managers knew that their performance evaluation was dependent on their division ROI's. The managers had been advised that if interdivisional transfers were to take place, market price (if it existed) should be the basis of the transfer price. If this were so, then the managers should be able to act independently to maximize their individual ROI's and the total company's ROI at the same time.

When both managers met to discuss the possibilities of Division B's using Fixitall as a material input for the B Division product, the manager of A concluded by saying, "Well, you know, I get $35 per ton in the marketplace for Fixitall. How could I possibly transfer it to you for anything less? At $35 for materials and $5 for other direct costs, how could you justify the change?"

required

1. Is manager A using a rule that will optimize company profits? If not, why not?

2. What do you consider to be the correct transfer price or range of transfer prices for Fixitall?

3. If Division B begins to use Fixitall, what is the effect on total company profits when Division B sells 6,000 tons per year? Assume A has sufficient capacity.
   (Hint: Make some assumption about A's revenue and cost structure.)

22-23. **The Pertinent Transfer Price.** The XYZ Company has two divisions, A and B. For one of the company's products, Division A produces a major subassembly and Division B incorporates this subassembly into the final product. There is a market for both the subassembly and the final product, and the divisions have been delegated profit responsibility. The transfer price for the subassembly has been set at long-run average market price.

The following data are available to each division:

Estimated selling price for final product	$300
Long-run average selling price for intermediate product	200
Variable cost for completion in Division B	150
Variable cost in Division A	120

The manager of Division B has made the following calculation:

Selling price—final product		$300
Transferred-in cost (market)	$200	
Variable cost for completion	150	350
Contribution (loss) on product		$(50)

required

1. Should transfers be made to Division B if there is no excess capacity in Division A? Is market price the correct transfer price?

2. Assume that Division A's maximum capacity for this product is 1,000 units per month and sales to the intermediate market are presently 800 units. Should 200 units be transferred to Division B? At what relevant transfer price?

22-24. **Pricing and Lack of Information.** Suppose that Division B of the Y Company, a huge conglomerate company, can buy its needs for component #109 either within the company from Division S or outside the company from X

Company, which will meet S's market selling price of $300 per unit. X Company happens to buy all of certain subpart requirements for component #109 from Division L of the Y Company at $210 per unit; the incremental costs to Division L of supplying such subparts is $80 per unit.

In filling B's order for #109, S would incur incremental costs of $180 per unit that would go outside the company. S, unlike the outside supplier, does not buy goods from L because this huge company is so large and communications are so bad that the S manager is unaware of this alternative.

required   What transfer price should be used to guide the managers of Divisions B and S so as to maximize overall company net income for the current period? Why?

Ignore the issue of performance evaluation of individual managers, and assume, for the purposes of your analysis, that all prices and costs are valid and are not subject to alteration.

22-25. Transfer Pricing in Different Situations.   The Neumann Company, Ltd., adopted a philosophy of decentralization several years ago. All the company's autonomous manufacturing divisions are located in Great Britain, where the company manufactures a wide range of electronic controls and automated machine tools. Nominally, all divisions of the company are conducted as separate enterprises, which must negotiate all orders independently with prospective purchasers. Each division is then responsible for its own profitability and return on investment. However, all divisions are required to consider purchasing from other Neumann divisions whenever possible.

The machine-products division (MPD), situated in London, manufactures small precision components that can be integrated with other Neumann components in a variety of automated systems. Both the components and the entire systems are generally quite profitable and in high demand by other Neumann divisions, as well as by independent purchasers. The machine-products division is the only Neumann plant with the facilities to produce a very essential component, magnesium balance wheels. The market price for these items is £100, both in Great Britain and in the United States. However, an import duty of 10 percent (of the selling price without the duty) is charged on the import of this type of product into the United States. The MPD income statement for the last twelve months is as follows (in thousands of pounds):

Net sales		£1,100
Direct labor	£250	
Direct materials	300	
Manufacturing overhead	250	800
Gross margin		300
Fixed selling expenses	100	
Fixed administrative expenses	80	180
Divisional profit		120

The cost of a batch of balance wheels has been calculated in the following manner:

Direct labor	£25
Direct materials	30
Manufacturing overhead*	25
Total cost	£80

*100% of direct labor.

When the company was decentralized, several assembly and marketing divisions were opened in new areas to expand the size of the markets for existing manufacturing divisions. These divisions were expected to be less profitable than other Neumann divisions, especially where import duties might necessitate more burdensome costs. One of these new marketing and assembly divisions (Middle Continental) was headquartered in Chicago under Mr. Gorot. Gorot had previously worked in London under the divisional manager for MPD, Mr. Miller, who was a 35-year veteran of the company. Even though Gorot had been a highly successful department head while in London, Miller had surreptitiously instigated a transfer for Gorot because of a personality conflict. Needless to say, Miller was quite unhappy to hear of Gorot's recent successes as head of Middle Continental while he himself was struggling to eliminate unfavorable capacity variances in the MPD.

Miller has been reluctant in the past to sell MPD components to other divisions at less than the domestic price; he sees no reason why he should make less profit than if he sold them in Great Britain. Furthermore, he has stated categorically, "I will not hurt my own profits to help that upstart in Chicago.!"

One of the most important systems sold by Middle Continental requires the use of magnesium balance wheels. In the past, Gorot has been under some pressure to purchase balance wheels from MPD at a base price of £100 plus £10 import duty. This practice has unduly affected his profit performance, and he is necessarily eager to obtain permission to purchase these components from local suppliers.

required

1. As the divisional controller at MPD, you are asked by Miller for advice in response to a memorandum from Gorot that he has obtained permission to purchase balance wheels in the United States unless MPD lowers its price. What would you advise Miller to do? Why? For this and the next part, assume that the manufacturing overhead is totally variable.

2. After you have given your advice to Miller, he receives a cablegram from Gorot indicating that several manufacturers in the United States have reduced their price on balance wheels to £85. How would you change your advice, if at all? Why?

3. Several days later, you determine that half the manufacturing overhead is fixed cost. Would this cause you to alter any of your previous decisions? In what way?

4. About a year later, MPD is operating at practical capacity. Gorot sends MPD another order for balance wheels at the previously negotiated price in part 1. Would you now recommend that this price be accepted? Why?

5. If the Neumann Company were to eliminate its divisions, what company guidelines should be established for transfers of goods between segments of the company?

6. Two years later, you are promoted to the controller's office of the entire Neumann Company. You are then asked to advise your new superior on whether some firm guidelines should be established for the determination of transfer prices between divisions as they were organized in 1–4 above. What would you recommend? Why?

22-26. Transfer Pricing in Banks. The Jackson Stone National Bank is a two-branch bank servicing retail and wholesale customers in the greater Big City metropolitan area. The head-office staff consists of the president and the controller. With minor exceptions, the branch managers are permitted to conduct their affairs like the heads of two independent banks. The planning and control system centers around branch income statements prepared by the controller.

The Big City branch, located in the growing downtown area, serves primarily commercial customers. The manager, Mr. Jones, has found in recent years that while he faces a number of vigorous competitors, the principal constraint on his ability to generate new loan business is a lack of supporting deposits, which are dollar deposits held in a bank outside the United States. The *only* alternative source of lendable funds is the purchase of Eurodollars. This option is considered less than acceptable by Jones, as the 11 percent interest he would have to pay for such funds is higher than the rate he is able to charge loan customers, currently 10 percent.

The new Sun City branch, on the other hand, is located outside of town in a large and growing retirement community and is primarily a retail branch. Mr. Smith, the manager, is in his first year with the Stone Bank. In his attempts to sell the bank's services to the Sun City residents, he has found that his only success is in the area of savings deposits. Loan business, on the other hand, is both competitive and scarce. The interest rate he can charge is constrained by the fact that the manager of the local branch of the Behemoth Bank, while not actively soliciting loan business, is apparently charging rates below the prevailing Big City prime rate. Additionally, there seems to be a fundamental resistance on the part of the Sun City residents to the idea of borrowing, even at the 6 percent rates Smith has been offering. In spite of his frequent lectures on the merits of leverage, the best Smith has been able to do is to generate a few golf-cart installment and Social Security check receivable loans. As a result, he finds himself with substantial excess savings deposits on which he is paying 5 percent interest but earning nothing. Aside from the deposits, which he has to keep in the vault to satisfy the government's 20 percent (of deposits) reserve requirement, the vault additionally contains excess lendable funds equal to almost 70 percent of total savings deposits. The controller has suggested that he lend these funds to Jones at the Big City branch. This was acceptable to both managers, although some disagreement arose as to the interest rate appropriate for such a loan. The argument was finally settled by the controller, who indicated that the theoretically correct rate was the rate Smith was paying on savings deposits, 5 percent. It has been further agreed that if Smith could find additional loans, any or all of the funds lent to Jones would be returned.

required   1. Evaluate the 5 percent interbranch loan rate, and suggest appropriate changes, in relation to the following criteria:
   a. Motivating managers to act in a manner consistent with the best interests of the bank as a whole.
   b. Evaluating the performance of individual *branches*.

2. Would your answer change if the Sun City loan rate were to rise to 7 percent, while all other rates, as well as the level of loan demand at Sun City, remained the same?

3. Would your answer change if all rates were the same as in part 1, except that the cost of Eurodollars dropped to 9 percent?

4. Based on your answers to the questions above, what general statements can you make about the interbranch loan rate appropriate for evaluating individual *managers*?

22-27. Design of Management Control System; Review of Chapters 21 and 22.

Firm History

Western Pants, Inc., is one of America's oldest clothing firms. Founded in the mid-nineteenth century, the firm weathered lean years and depression largely as the result of the market durability of its dominant, and at times only, product—blue denim jeans. Until as recently as 1950, the firm had never seriously marketed other products or even additional types of trousers. A significant change in marketing strategy in the 1950's altered that course, which had been revered for 100 years by Western's management. Aggressive new management decided at that time that Western's well-established name could and should be used to market other lines of pants. Initial offerings in a men's casual trouser were well received. Production in different patterns of this basic style continued, and stylish, tailored variations of the same casual motif were introduced almost yearly.

Alert planning in the early 1960's enabled Western to become the first pants manufacturer to establish itself in the revolutionary "wash and wear" field. Further refinement of this process broadened the weave and fabric types that could be tailored into fashionable trousers and still survive enough machine washings and dryings to satisfy Western's rigid quality-control standards.

With the advent of "mod" clothing and the generally casual yet stylish garb that became acceptable attire at semiformal affairs, pants became fashion items, rather than the mere clothing staples they had been in years past. Western quickly gained a foothold in the bell-bottom and flare market, and from there grew with the "leg look" to its present position as the free world's largest clothing manufacturer.

Today Western, in addition to its still remarkably popular blue denim jeans, offers a complete line of casual trousers, an extensive array of "dress and fashion jeans" for both men and boys, and a complete line of pants for women. Last year the firm sold approximately 30 million pairs of pants.

Production

For the last twenty years, Western Pants has been in a somewhat unusual and enviable market position. In each of those years it has sold virtually all its production and often had to begin rationing its wares to established customers or refusing orders from new customers as early as six months prior to the close of the production year. Whereas most business ventures face limited demand and, in the long run, excess production, Western, whose sales have doubled each five years during that twenty-year period, has had to face excess and growing demand with limited—although rapidly growing—production.

The firm has developed 25 plants in its 150-year history. These production units vary somewhat in output capacity, but the average is roughly 20,000 pairs of trousers per week. With the exception of two or three plants that usually produce only the blue denim jeans during the entire production year, Western's plants produce various pants types for all of Western's departments.

The firm has for some years augmented its own productive capacity by contractual agreements with independent manufacturers of pants. At the present time, there are nearly 20 such contractors producing all lines of Western's pants (including the blue jeans). Last year contractors produced about one-third of the total volume in units sold by Western.

Tom Wicks, the Western vice-president for production and operations, commented on the firm's use of contractors. "The majority of these outfits have been with us for some time—five years or more. Five or ten of them have served Western efficiently and reliably for over 30 years. There are, of course, a lot of recent additions. We've been trying to beef up our output, because sales have been growing so rapidly. It's tough to tell a store like Macy's halfway through the year that you can't fill all their orders. In our eagerness to get the pants made, we understandably hook up with some independents who don't know what they're doing and are forced to fold their operations after a year or so because their costs are too high. Usually we can tell from an independent's experience and per-unit contract price whether or not he's going to be able to make it in pants production.

"Contract agreements with independents are made by me and my staff. The word has been around for some years that we need more production, so we haven't found it necessary to solicit contractors. Negotiations usually start either when an interested independent comes to us, or when a salesman or product manager interests an independent and brings him in. These product managers are always looking for ways to increase production! Negotiations don't necessarily take very long. There are some incidentals that have to be worked out, but the real issue is the price per unit the independent requires us to pay him. The ceiling we are willing to pay for each type of pants is pretty well established by now. If a contractor impresses us as both reliable and capable of turning out quality pants, we will pay him that ceiling. If we aren't sure, we might bid a little below that ceiling for the first year or two, until he has proven himself. Nonetheless, I'm only talking here about a few cents at most. We don't want to squeeze a new contractor's margins so much that we are responsible for forcing him out of business. It is most definitely to our advantage if the independent continues to turn out quality pants for us indefinitely. Initial contracts are for two years. The time spans lengthen as our relationship with the independent matures."

Mr. Wicks noted that the start-up time for a new contractor can often be as short as one year. The failure rate of the tailoring industry is quite high; hence, new entrepreneurs can often walk in and assume control of existing facilities.

The Control System

"We treat all our plants pretty much as cost centers [See Exhibit 22-3]," Mr. Wicks continued. "Of course, we exercise no control whatever over the contractors. We just pay them the agreed price per pair of pants. Our own operations at each plant have been examined thoroughly by industrial engineers. You know, time-motion studies and all. We've updated this information consistently for over ten years. I'm quite proud of the way we've been able to tie our standard hours down. We've even been able over the years to develop learning curves that tell us how long it will take production of a given type of pants to reach the standard allowed hours per unit after initial start-up or a product switchover. We even know the rate at which total production time per unit reaches standard for every basic style of pants that Western makes!

"We use this information for budgeting a plant's costs. The marketing boys figure out how many pants of each type they want produced each year and pass that information onto us. We divvy the total production up among plants pretty much by eyeballing the total amounts for each type of pants. We like to put one plant to work for a whole year on one type of pants, if that's possible. It saves time losses from start-ups and changeovers. We can sell all we make, you know, so we like to keep plants working at peak efficiency. Unfortunately, marketing always manages to come up with a lot of midyear changes, so this objective winds up like a lot of other good intentions in life. You know what they say about the road to Hell! Anyhow, it's still a game plan we like to stick to, and two or three plants making the basic blue jeans accomplish it every year.

The budgeting operation begins with me and my staff determining what a plant's quota for each month should be for one year ahead of time. We do this mostly by looking at what past performance at a plant has been. Of course,

EXHIBIT 22-3

ORGANIZATION CHART
WESTERN PANTS INC.

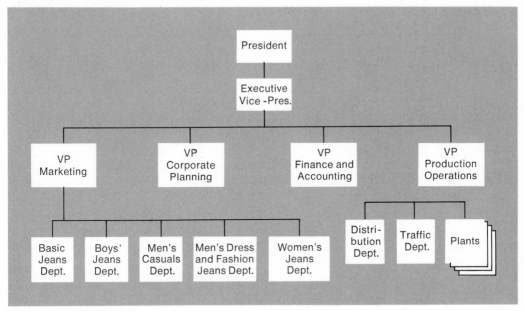

we add a little to this. We expect people to improve around here. These yearly budgets are updated at the end of each month in the light of the previous month's production. Budget figures, incidentally, are in units of production. If a plant manager beats this budget figure, we feel he's done well. If he can't meet the quota, his people haven't been working at what the engineers feel is a very reasonable level of speed and efficiency. Or possibly absenteeism, a big problem in all our plants, has been excessively high. Or turnover, another big problem, has been unacceptably high. At any rate, when the quota hasn't been made, we want to know why, and we want to get the problem corrected as quickly as possible.

"Given the number of pants that a plant actually produces in a month, we can determine, by using the standards I was boasting about earlier, the number of labor hours each operation should have accumulated during the month. We measure this figure against the hours we actually paid for to determine how a plant performed as a cost center. As you might guess, we don't like to see unfavorable variances here any more than in a plant manager's performance against quota.

"We watch the plant performance figures monthly. If a plant manager meets his quota and his cost variances are OK, we let him know that we are pleased. I almost always call them myself and relay my satisfaction, or, if they haven't done well, my concern. I think this kind of prompt feedback is important.

"We also look for other things in evaluating a plant manager. Have his community relations been good? Are his people happy? The family that owns almost all of Western's stock is very concerned about that."

A Christmas bonus constitutes the meat of Western's reward system. Mr. Wicks and his two chief assistants subjectively rate a plant manager's performance for the year on a one-to-five scale. Western's top management at the close of each year determines a bonus base by evaluating the firm's overall performance and profits for the year. That bonus base has recently been as high as $3,000. The performance rating for each member of Western's management cadre is multiplied by this bonus base to determine a given manager's bonus.

Western's management group includes many finance and marketing specialists. The casewriter noted that these personnel, who are located at the corporate headquarters, were consistently awarded higher ratings by their supervisors than were plant managers. This difference consistently approached a full point. Last year the average rating in the corporate headquarters was 3.85; the average for plant managers was 2.92.

Evaluation Of The System

Mia Packard, a recent valedictorian of a business school, gave some informed opinions regarding Western's production operation and its management control procedures.

"Mr. Wicks is one of the nicest men I've ever met, and a very intelligent businessman. But I really don't think that the system he uses to evaluate his plant managers is good for the firm as a whole. I made a plant visit not long ago as part of my company orientation program, and I accidently discovered that the plant manager "hoarded" some of the pants produced over quota in good months to protect himself against future production deficiencies. That plant manager was really upset that I stumbled onto his storehouse. He insisted that all the other managers did the same thing and begged me not to tell Mr. Wicks. This seems like precisely the wrong kind of behavior in a firm that usually has to turn away orders! Yet I believe the quota system that is one of Western's tools for evaluating plant performance encourages this type of behavior. I don't think I could prove this, but I suspect that most plant managers aren't really pushing for maximum production. If they do increase output, their quotas are going to go up, and yet they won't receive any immediate monetary rewards to compensate for the increase in their responsibilities or requirements. If I were a plant manager, I wouldn't want my production exceeding quota until the end of the year.

"Also, Mr. Wicks came up to the vice-presidency through the ranks. He was a plant manager himself once—a very good plant manager. But he has a tendency to feel that everyone should run a plant the way he did. For example, in Mr. Wicks' plant there were eleven workers for every supervisor or member of the office and administrative staff. Since then, Mr. Wicks has elevated this supervision ratio of 11:1 to some sort of sacred index of leadership efficiency. All plant managers shoot for it, and as a result, usually understaff their offices. As a result, we can't get timely and accurate reports from plants. There simply aren't enough people in the offices out there to generate the information we desperately need *when we need it!*

"Another thing—some of the plants have been built in the last five years or so and have much newer equipment, yet there's no difference in the standard hours determined in these plants than the older ones. This puts the managers of older plants at a terrific disadvantage. Their sewing machines break down more often, require maintenance, and probably aren't as easy to work with.

"The essence of my criticism is that I am not sure it is in the best interests of Western for the plants to operate as cost centers. This is a very difficult issue, and I haven't really thought it through yet. But my intuition tells me that the designation of plants as profit centers would lead plant managers to make decisions more in keeping with the interests of the firm as a whole."

Miss Packard continued with an embarrassing admission. "If Mr. Wicks were to decide tomorrow to make plants profit centers, I wouldn't be able to tell him what to use as the appropriate transfer price. The firm has established accurate standards, so the units could be transferred at their standard costs. I am not sure, though, whether full standard or variable standard costs should be used in this case. Another possibility, of course, would be to transfer them at their actual per-unit cost. Finally, I remember from one of my accounting courses at school that market price is often the best transfer price. I don't see how we could use that at Western, though. Plants can't sell directly to customers, and the only established market prices are those for the final product."

required
Evaluate the management control system used for Western's plants. Do you agree with Miss Packard's intuition? If plants were to be regarded as profit centers, what transfer price should be used? Defend your choice. Consider Western's present methods for assigning production commitments to its plants. Would the establishment of a meaningful transfer price lead you to change this system? What system would you use?

22-28. Design of Management Control System; Review of Chapters 21 and 22. [This case, Empire Glass Company (A), EA-C, was prepared by Professor David F. Hawkins of the Harvard University Graduate School of Business Administration as the basis for class discussion rather than to illustrate either effective or ineffective administration. It also appears in *Management Control Systems* by Robert N. Anthony, John Dearden, and Richard F. Vancil, published by Richard D. Irwin, Inc., in 1965. Copyright © 1964 by the President and Fellows of Harvard College. Used by specific permission.]

Organization

Empire Glass Company was a diversified company organized into several major product divisions, one of which was the glass products division. This division was responsible for manufacturing and selling glass food and beverage bottles. Each division was headed by a divisional vice-president who reported directly to the company's executive vice-president, Landon McGregor.

Mr. McGregor's corporate staff included three men in the financial area—the controller, the chief accountant, and the treasurer. The controller's department consisted of only two men—Mr. Walker and the assistant controller, Allen Newell. The market research and labor relations departments also reported in a staff capacity to Mr. McGregor.

All the product divisions were organized along similar lines. Reporting to each product division vice-president were several staff members in the customer service and product research areas. Reporting in a line capacity to each individual vice-president were also a general manager of manufacturing and a general manager of marketing. The general manager of manufacturing was responsible for all the division's manufacturing activities. Similarly, the general manager of marketing was responsible for all the division's marketing activities. Both these executives were assisted by a small staff of specialists. Exhibit 1 presents an organization chart of the glass product division's top-management group. All the corporate and divisional management groups were located in British City, Canada. Exhibit 2 shows the typical organization structure of a plant within the glass products division.

Products and Technology

The glass products division operated a number of plants in Canada producing glass food and beverage bottles. Of these products, food jars constituted the largest group, including jars for products like tomato catsup, mayonnaise, jams and jellies, honey, and soluble coffee. Milk bottles and beer and soft drink

EXHIBIT 1

EMPIRE GLASS COMPANY

Glass Products Division Top Management and Staff

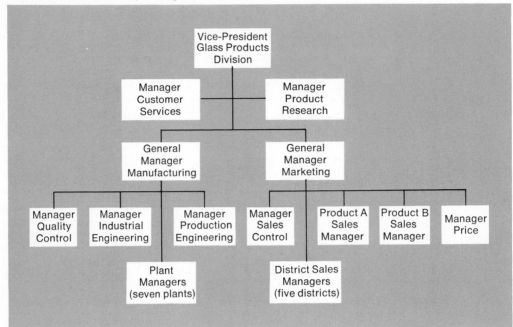

EXHIBIT 2

EMPIRE GLASS COMPANY

Typical Plant Organization—Glass Products Division

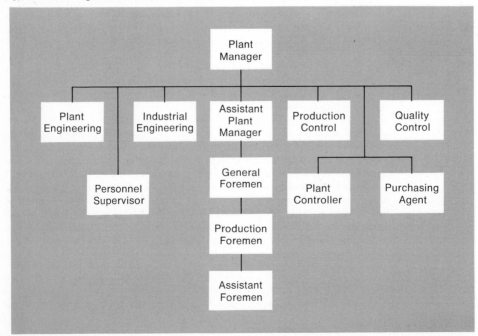

bottles were also produced in large quantities. A great variety of shapes and sizes of containers for wines, liquors, drugs, cosmetics, and chemicals were produced in smaller quantities.

Most of the thousands of different products, varying in size, shape, color, and decoration were produced to order. According to British City executives, during 1963 the typical lead time between the customer's order and shipment from the plant was between two and three weeks.

The principal raw materials for container glass were sand, soda ash, and lime. The first step in the manufacturing process was to melt batches of these materials in furnaces or "tanks." The molten mass was then passed into automatic or semiautomatic machines, which filled molds with the molten glass and blew the glass into the desired shape. The ware then went through an automatic annealing oven or lehr, where it was cooled slowly under carefully controlled conditions. If the glass was to be coated on the exterior to increase its resistance to abrasion and scratches, this coating—often a silicone film—was applied at the lehr. Any decorating (such as a trademark of other design) was then added, the product inspected again, and the finished goods packed in corrugated containers (or wooden cases for some bottles).

Quality inspection was critical in the manufacturing process. If the melt in the furnace was not completely free from bubbles and stones (unmelted ingredients or pieces of refinery material), or if the fabricating machinery was slightly out of adjustment, or molds were worn, the rejection rate was very high. Although a number of machines were used in the inspection process, including electric eyes, much of the inspection was still visual.

Although glassmaking was one of the oldest arts, and bottles and jars had been machine molded at relatively high speed for over half a century, the glass products division had spent substantial sums each year to modernize its equipment. These improvements had greatly increased the speed of operations and had substantially reduced the visual inspection and manual handling of glassware.

Most of the jobs were relatively unskilled and highly repetitive, and gave the worker little control over work methods or pace. The moldmakers who made and repaired the molds, the machine repairmen, and those who made the equipment setup changes between different products were considered to be the highest classes of skilled workers. Wages were relatively high in the glass industry. Production employees belonged to two national unions, and for many years bargaining had been conducted on a national basis. Output standards were established for all jobs, but no bonus was paid to hourly plant workers for exceeding standard.

Marketing

Over the years, the sales of the glass products divisions had grown at a slightly faster rate than had the total market for glass containers. Until the late 1950's, the division had charged a premium for most of its products, primarily because they were of better quality than competitive products. In recent years, however, the quality of the competitive products had improved to the point where they now matched the division's quality level. In the meantime, the division's competitors had retained their former price structure. Consequently, the glass products division had been forced to lower its prices to meet its competitor's lower market prices. According to one division executive:

"Currently, price competition is not severe, particularly among the two or three larger companies that dominate the glass bottle industry. Most of our competition is with respect to product quality and customer service. . . . In fact, our biggest competitive threat is from containers other than glass. . . ."

Each of the division's various plants shipped its products throughout Canada to some extent, although transportation costs limited each plant's market primarily to its immediate vicinity. While some of the customers were large and bought in huge quantities, many were relatively small.

Budgetary Control System

In the fall of 1963, James Walker, Empire Glass Company controller, described the company's budgetary control system to a casewriter. Mr. Walker had been controller for some fifteen years. Excerpts from that interview are reproduced below.

"To understand the role of the budgetary control system, you must first understand our management philosophy. Fundamentally, we have a divisional organization based on broad product categories. These divisional activities are coordinated by the company's executive vice-president, while the head office group provides a policy and review function for him. Within the broad policy limits, we operate on a decentralized basis; each of the decentralized divisions performs the full management job that normally would be inherent in any independent company. The only exceptions to this philosophy are the head office group's sole responsibilities for sources of funds and labor relations with those bargaining units that cross division lines.

"Given this form of organization, the budget is the principal management tool used by head office to direct the efforts of the various segments of the company toward a common goal. Certainly, in our case, the budget is much more than a narrow statistical accounting device."

Sales Budget. "As early as May 15 of the year preceding the budget year, top management of the company asks the various product division vice-presidents to submit preliminary reports stating what they think their division's capital requirements and outlook in terms of sales and income will be during the next budget year. In addition, corporate top management also wants an expression of the division vice-president's general feelings toward the trends in these particular items over the two years following the upcoming budget year. At this stage, head office is not interested in too much detail. Since all divisions plan their capital requirements five years in advance and had made predictions of the forthcoming budget year's market when the budget estimates were prepared last year, these rough estimates of next year's conditions and requirements are far from wild guesses.

"After the opinions of the divisional vice-presidents are in, the market research staff goes to work. They develop a formal statement of the marketing climate in detail for the forthcoming budget year and in general terms for the subsequent two years. Once these general factors have been assessed, a sales forecast is constructed for the company and for each division. Consideration is given to the relationship of the general economic climate to our customers' needs and Empire's share of each market. Explicitly stated are basic assumptions as to price, weather conditions, introduction of new products, gains or losses in particular accounts, forward buying, new manufacturing plants, industry growth trends, packaging trends, inventory carry-overs, and the development of alternative packages to or from glass. This review of all the relevant factors is followed for each of our product lines, regardless of its size and importance. The completed forecasts of the market research group are then forwarded to the appropriate divisions for review, criticism, and adjustments.

"The primary goal of the head office group in developing these sales forecasts is to assure uniformity among the divisions with respect to the basic assumptions on business conditions, pricing, and the treatment of possible emergencies. Also, we provide a yardstick so as to assure us that the company's overall sales forecast will be reasonable and obtainable.

"The product division top management then asks each district manager what he expects to do in the way of sales during the budget year. Head office and the divisional staffs will give the district sales managers as much guidance as they request, but it is the sole responsibility of each district sales manager to come up with his particular forecast.

"After the district sales managers' forecasts are received by the divisional top management, the forecasts are consolidated and reviewed by the division's general manager of marketing. Let me emphasize, however, that nothing is changed in the district sales manager's budget unless the district manager agrees. Then, once the budget is approved, nobody is relieved of his responsibility without top-management approval. Also, no arbitrary changes are made in the approved budgets without the concurrence of all the people responsible for the budget.

"Next, we go through the same process at the division and headquarters levels. We continue to repeat the process until everyone agrees that the sales budgets are sound. Then, each level of management takes responsibility for its particular portion of the budget. These sales budgets then become fixed objectives."

Manufacturing Budgets. "Once the vice-presidents, executive vice-president, and company president have given final approval to the sales budgets, we make a sales budget for each plant by breaking down the division sales budgets according to the plants from which the finished goods will be shipped. These plant sales budgets are then further broken down on a monthly basis by price, volume, and end use. With this information available, the plants then budget their gross profit, fixed expenses, and income before taxes.

"The plant manager's primary responsibility extends to profits. The budgeted plant profit is the difference between the fixed sales-dollar budget and the sum of the budgeted variable costs at standard and the fixed-overhead budget. It is the plant manager's responsibility to meet this budget profit figure, even if actual dollar sales drop below the budgeted level.

"Given his sales budget, it is up to the plant manager to determine the fixed overhead and variable costs—at standard—that he will need to incur so as to meet the demands of the sales budget. In my opinion, requiring the plant managers to make their own plans is one of the most valuable things associated with the budget system. Each plant manager divides the preparation of the overall plant budget among his plant's various departments. First, the departments spell out the programs in terms of the physical requirements, such as tons of raw material, and then the plans are priced at standard cost.

"The plant industrial engineering department is assigned responsibility for developing engineered cost standards and reduced costs. Consequently, the phase of budget preparation covered by the industrial engineers, includes budget standards of performance for each operation, cost center, and department within the plant. This phase of the budget also includes budgeted cost reductions, budgeted unfavorable variances from standards, and certain budgeted programmed fixed costs in the manufacturing area, such as service labor. The industrial engineer prepares this phase of the budget in conjunction with departmental line supervision.

"Before each plant sends its budget into British City, a group of us from head office goes out to visit each plant. For example, in the case of the glass products division, Allen Newell, assistant controller, and I, along with representatives of the glass products division manufacturing staffs visit each of the division's plants. Let me stress this point: We do not go on these trips to pass judgment on the plant's proposed budget. Rather, we go with two purposes in mind. First, we wish to acquaint ourselves with the thinking behind the figures that each plant manager will send in to British City. This is helpful, because when we come to review these budgets with the top management—that is, management above our level—we will have to answer questions about the budgets, and we will know the answers. Second, the review is a way of giving guidance to the plant managers in determining whether or not they are in line with what the company needs to make in the way of profits.

"Of course, when we make our field reviews we do not know about what each of the other plants is doing. Therefore, we explain to the plant managers that while their budget may look good now, when we put all the plants together in a consolidated budget, the plant managers may have to make some changes because the projected profit is not high enough. When this happens, we must tell the plant managers that it is not their programs that are unsound. The problem is that the company cannot afford the programs. I think it is very important that each plant manager has a chance to tell his story. Also, it gives them the feeling that we at headquarters are not living in an ivory tower.

"These plant visits are spread over a three-week period, and we spend an average of half a day at each plant. The plant manager is free to bring to these meetings any of his supervisors he wishes. We ask him not to bring in anybody below the supervisory level. Then, of course, you get into organized labor. During the half day we spend at each plant, we discuss the budget primarily. However, if I have time, I like to wander through the plant and see how things are going. Also, I go over in great detail the property replacement and maintenance budget with the plant manager.

"About September 1, the plant budgets come into British City, and the accounting department consolidates them. Then, the product division vice-presidents review their respective divisional budgets to see if the division budget is reasonable in terms of what the vice-president thinks the corporate management wants. If he is not satisfied with the consolidated plant budgets, he will ask the various plants within the division to trim their budget figures.

"When the division vice-presidents and the executive vice-president are happy, they will send their budgets to the company president. He may accept the division budgets at this point. If he doesn't, he will specify the areas to be reexamined by division and, if necessary, by plant management. The final budget is approved at our December board of directors meeting."

Comparison of Actual and Standard Performance. "At the end of the sixth business day after the close of the month, each plant wires to the head office certain operating variances, which we put together on what we call the variance analysis sheet. Within a half-hour after the last plant report comes through, variance analysis sheets for the divisions and plants are compiled. On the morning of the seventh business day after the end of the month, these reports are usually on the desks of the interested top management. The variance analysis sheet highlights the variances in what we consider to be critical areas. Receiving this report as soon as we do helps us at head office to take timely action. Let me emphasize, however, we do not accept the excuse that the plant manager has to go to the end of the month to know what happened during the month. He has to be on top of these particular items daily.

"When the actual results come into the head office, we go over them on the basis of exception; that is, we look only at those figures that are in excess of the budgeted amounts. We believe this has a good effect on morale. The plant managers don't have to explain everything they do. They have to explain only where they go off base. In particular, we pay close attention to the net sales, gross margin, and the plant's ability to meet its standard manufacturing cost. Incidentally, when analyzing the gross sales, we look closely at the price and mix changes.

"All this information is summarized on a form known as the Profit Planning and Control Report No. 1 [see Exhibit 3]. This document is backed up by a number of supporting documents [see Exhibit 4]. The plant PPCR No. 1 and the month-end trial balance showing both actual and budget figures are received in British City at the close of the eighth business day after the end of the month. These two very important reports, along with the supporting reports (PPCR No. 2, PPCR No. 11) are then consolidated by the accounting department on PPCR-type forms to show the results of operations by division and company. The consolidated reports are distributed the next day.

"In connection with the fixed-cost items, we want to know whether or not the plants carried out the programs they said they would carry out. If they have not, we want to know why they have not. Here, we are looking for sound reasons. Also, we want to know if they have carried out their projected programs at the cost they said they would.

"In addition to these reports, at the beginning of each month the plant managers prepare current estimates for the upcoming month and quarter on forms similar to the variance analysis sheets. Since our budget is based on known programs, the value of this current estimate is that it gets the plant people to look at their programs. We hope they will realize that they cannot run their plants on a day-to-day basis.

"If we see a sore spot coming up, or if the plant manager draws our attention to a potential trouble area, we may ask that daily reports concerning this item be sent to the particular division top management involved. In addition, the division top management may send a division staff specialist—say, a quality control expert if it is a quality problem—to the plant concerned. The division staff members can make recommendations, but it is up to the plant manager to accept or reject these recommendations. Of course, it is well known throughout the company that we expect the plant managers to accept gracefully the help of the head office and division staffs."

Sales–Manufacturing Relations.   "If a sales decline occurs during the early part of the year, and if the plant managers can convince us that the change is permanent, we may revise the plant budgets to reflect these new circumstances. However, if toward the end of the year the actual sales volume suddenly drops below the predicted sales volume, we don't have much time to change the budget plans. What we do is ask the plant managers to go back over their budgets with their staffs and see where reduction of expense programs will do the least harm. Specifically, we ask them to consider what they may be able to eliminate this year or delay until next year.

"I believe it was Confucius who said, 'We make plans so we have plans to discard.' Nevertheless, I think it is wise to make plans, even if you have to discard them. Having plans makes it a lot easier to figure out what to do when sales fall off from the budgeted level. The understanding of operations that comes from preparing the budget removes a lot of the potential chaos and confusion that might arise if we were under pressure to meet a stated profit goal and sales declined quickly and unexpectedly at year-end, just as they did last year. In these circumstances, we don't try to ram anything down the plant managers' throats. We ask them to tell us where they can reasonably expect to cut costs below the budgeted level.

"Whenever a problem arises at a plant between sales and production, the local people are supposed to solve the problem themselves. For example, a

EXHIBIT 3

EMPIRE GLASS COMPANY

Profit Planning and Control Report No. 1

	MONTH		Ref.		YEAR TO DATE		
Income Gain (+) or Loss (−) From		**Actual**			**Actual**	**Income Gain (+) or Loss (−) From**	
Prev. Year	Budget					Budget	Prev. Year
			1	Gross Sales to Customers			
			2	Discounts & Allowances			
			3	Net Sales to Customers			
%	%	//////	4	% Gain (+)/Loss (−)	//////	%	%
				DOLLAR VOLUME GAIN (+)/ LOSS (−) DUE TO:			
		//////	5	Sales Price	//////		
		//////	6	Sales Volume	//////		
			6(a)	Trade Mix	//////		
			7	Variable Cost of Sales			
			8	Profit Margin			
				PROFIT MARGIN GAIN (+)/ LOSS (−) DUE TO:			
		//////	9	Profit Volume Ratio (P/V)	//////		
		//////	10	Dollar Volume	//////		
%	%	%	11	Profit Volume Ratio (P/V)	%	%	%
		Income Addition (+)			Income Addition (+)		
			12	Total Fixed Manufacturing Cost			
			13	Fixed Manufacturing Cost−Transfers			
			14	Plant Income (Standard)			
%	%	%	15	% of Net Sales	%	%	%
		Income Addition (+) Income Reduction (−)			Income Addition (+) Income Reduction (−)		
%	%	%	16	% Performance	%	%	%
			17	Manufacturing Efficiency			
		Income Addition (+)			Income Addition (+)		
			18	Methods Improvements			
			19	Other Revisions of Standards			
			20	Material Price Changes			
			21	Division Special Projects			
			22	Company Special Projects			
			23	New Plant Expense			
			24	Other Plant Expenses			
			25	Income on Seconds			
			26				
			27				
			28	Plant Income (Actual)			
%	%	//////	29	% Gain (+)/Loss (−)	//////	%	%
%	%	%	30	% of Net Sales	%	%	%
			36A				
Increase (+) or Decrease (−)				EMPLOYED CAPITAL		**Increase (+) or Decrease (−)**	
			37	Total Employed Capital			
%	%	%	38	% Return	%	%	%
			39	Turnover Rate			

_____ _____ _____ 19____

Plant Division Month

774

EXHIBIT 4

EMPIRE GLASS COMPANY

Brief Description of PPCR No. 2–PPCR No. 11

INDIVIDUAL PLANT REPORTS

REPORT	DESCRIPTION
PPCR No. 2	Manufacturing expense: Plant materials, labor, and variable overhead consumed. Detail of actual figures compared with budget and previous year's figures for year to date and current month.
PPCR No. 3	Plant expense: Plant fixed expenses incurred. Details of actual figures compared with budget and previous year's figures for year to date and current month.
PPCR No. 4	Analysis of sales and income: Plant operating gains and losses due to changes in sales revenue, profit margins, and other sources of income. Details of actual figures compared with budget and previous year's figures for year to date and current month.
PPCR No. 5	Plant control statement: Analysis of plant raw material gains and losses, spoilage costs, and cost reduction programs. Actual figures compared with budget figures for current month and year to date.
PPCR No. 6	Comparison of sales by principal and product groups: Plant sales dollars, profit margin, and P/V ratios broken down by end-product use (i.e., soft drinks, beer). Compares actual figures with budgeted figures for year to date and current month.

DIVISION SUMMARY REPORTS

REPORT	DESCRIPTION
PPCR No. 7	Comparative plant performance, sales, and income: Gross sales and income figures by plants. Actual figures compared with budget figures for year to date and current month.
PPCR No. 8	Comparative plant performance, total plant expenses: Profit margin, total fixed costs, manufacturing efficiency, other plant expenses, and P/V ratios by plants. Actual figures compared with budgeted and previous year's figures for current month and year to date.
PPCR No. 9	Manufacturing efficiency: Analysis of gains and losses by plant in areas of materials, spoilage, supplies, and labor. Current month and year to date actuals reported in total dollars and as a percentage of budget.
PPCR No. 10	Inventory: Comparison of actual and budget inventory figures by major inventory accounts and plants.
PPCR No. 11	Status of capital expenditures: Analysis of the status of capital expenditures by plants, months, and relative to budget.

customer's purchasing agent may insist he wants an immediate delivery, and this delivery will disrupt the production department's plans. The production group can make recommendations as to alternative ways to take care of the problem, but it's the sales manager's responsibility to get the product to the customer. The salesmen are supposed to know their customers well enough to judge whether or not the customer really needs the product. If the sales manager says the customer needs the product, that ends the matter. As far as we are concerned, the customer's wants are primary; our company is a case where sales wags the rest of the dog.

"Of course, if the change in the sales program involves a major plant expense that is out of line with the budget, then the matter is passed up to division for decision.

"As I said earlier, the sales department has the sole responsibility for the product price, sales mix, and delivery schedules. They do not have direct responsibility for plant operations or profit. That's the plant management's responsibility. However, it is understood that sales group will cooperate with the plant people wherever possible."

Motivation. "There are various ways in which we motivate the plant managers to meet their profit goals. First of all, we promote only capable people. Also, a monetary incentive program has been established that stimulates their efforts to achieve their profit goals. In addition, each month we put together a bar chart that shows, by division and plant, the ranking of the various manufacturing units with respect to manufacturing efficiency.* We feel the plant managers are 100 percent responsible for variable manufacturing costs. I believe this is true, since all manufacturing standards have to be approved by plant managers. Most of the plant managers give wide publicity to these bar charts. The efficiency bar chart and efficiency measure itself is perhaps a little unfair in some respects when you are comparing one plant with another. Different kinds of products are run through different plants. These require different setups, etc., which have an important impact on a position of the plant. However, in general, the efficiency rating is a good indication of the quality of the plant manager and his supervisory staff.

"Also, a number of plants run competitions within the plants, which reward department heads or foremen, based on their relative standing with respect to a certain cost item. The plant managers, their staffs, and employees have great pride in their plants.

"The number one item now stressed at the plant level is *quality*. The market situation is such that in order to make sales you have to meet the market price and exceed the market quality. By quality I mean not only the physical characteristics of the product but also such things as delivery schedules. As I read the company employee publications, their message is that if the company is to be profitable, it must produce high-quality items at a reasonable cost. This is necessary so that the plants can meet their obligation to produce the maximum profits for the company in the prevailing circumstances."

The Future. "An essential part of the budgetary control system is planning. We have developed a philosophy that we must begin our plans where the work is done—in the line organization and out in the field. Perhaps, in the future, we can avoid or cut back some of the budget preparation steps and start putting together our sales budget later than May 15. However, I doubt if we will change the basic philosophy.

"Frankly, I doubt if the line operators would want any major change in the system; they are very jealous of the management prerogatives the system gives to them.

"It is very important that we manage the budget. We have to be continually on guard against its managing us. Sometimes the plants lose sight of this fact. We have to be made conscious daily of the necessity of having the sales volume to make a profit. And when sales fall off and their plant programs are reduced, they do not always appear to see the justification for budget cuts—although I do suspect that they see more of the justification for these cuts than they will admit. It is this human side of the budget to which we have to pay more attention in the future."

required   Comment on the strong points and the weak points in the management control system of the Empire Glass Company. What changes, if any, would you suggest?

$$^*\text{Manufacturing efficiency} = \frac{\text{Total actual variable manufacturing costs}}{\text{Total standard variable manufacturing costs}} \times 100\%$$

23

Decision Models, Uncertainty, and the Accountant

The first part of Chapter 11 concentrated on the nature of the decision process and the role information plays in it (See Exhibit 11-1). The accountant needs to be familiar with the entire decision process if he is going to design the best possible accounting information system. He must be concerned with decision objectives, prediction methods, decision methods or models, and net payoffs (outcomes). Essentially, he must (a) predict the set of signals that will be generated by alternative information systems; (b) predict the actions that will be induced by each alternative set of signals; (c) predict the net payoff associated with each set of actions; and (d) pick the information system that will maximize the net payoff. Net payoff is also affected by the cost of accumulating the information.

This chapter will explore the nature of formal decision models, the effects of model choice, and the role of uncertainty. Before proceeding, you may find it helpful to review the first part of Chapter 11.

FORMAL DECISION MODELS

Decision models are often expressed in mathematical form. However, the role of these powerful mathematical models must be kept in perspective. A mathematical decision model may indicate a choice that is nevertheless declined by management because of legal, political, behavioral, or other considerations not incorporated in the specific model. In these cases, the output of the mathematical model is only one input into a more complicated, ill-defined decision model that includes qualitative as well as quantitative considerations.[1]

Whether the decision maker uses a well-defined mathematical model or some very informal decision model will not affect our conclusions. For example, a manager may buy a particular machine or raw material because the salesman sends him an annual Christmas gift. However, we do not isolate and analyze such models; they are neither explicit nor widely applicable. Therefore, most applications of decision theory concentrate on well-defined mathematical models.

The careful use of mathematical models supplements hunches and implicit rules of thumb with explicit assumptions and criteria. If the decision can be portrayed by a mathematical model that includes the critical factors bearing on it, the resulting choice is likely to be more consistent with an organization's objectives.

Mathematical-model building has been criticized because the process of abstraction may oversimplify the problem and ignore important underlying factors. This danger is always present. Still, many examples of successful applications can be cited. For instance, inventory and linear-programming models are widely used. The test of success is not whether mathematical models are the perfect answer to the manager's needs, but whether such models provide better answers than would have been achieved via alternative techniques.

In this regard, consider budgets in general, which are mathematical models of sorts. Budgets are imperfect instruments for decision making. Yet, because these techniques are often the best available for many purposes, few managers are willing to abandon their use.

Most mathematical decision models have the following characteristics:

1. An organizational objective that can be quantified. This objective can take many forms. Most often, it is expressed as a maximization (or minimization) of some form of profit (or cost). This quantification is often called a *choice criterion* or an *objective function*. This objective function is used to evaluate the courses of action and to provide a basis for choosing the best alternative.

2. A set of the alternative courses of action under explicit consideration. This set of *actions* should be collectively exhaustive and mutually exclusive.

3. A set of all the relevant events or *states*, or states of nature, that can occur. This set should also be collectively exhaustive and mutually exclusive. Therefore, only one of the states will actually occur.

4. A set of *probabilities* that describes the possibilities of the various states' occurrence.

5. A set of *payoffs* that describes the consequences of the various possible outcomes evaluated in terms of the objective function. These are conditionally dependent on a specific course of action and a specific state.

An example may clarify the essential ingredients of a formal model, even though the illustration may seem too contrived. Suppose a decision maker has

---

[1] Report of the Committee on Managerial Decision Models, American Accounting Association, *The Accounting Review,* Supplement to Vol. XLIV, pp. 44ff. Also see the Supplement to Vol. XLVI for three more reports on related topics.

two mutually exclusive and exhaustive alternative courses of action regarding the quality-control aspects of his project: accept or reject. He also predicts that two mutually exclusive and exhaustive states of nature will affect his payoffs. Either the product conforms to the quality standards, or it does not. The combinations of actions and states and their conditional payoffs can be presented in a *payoff table:*

ALTERNATIVE ACTIONS	ALTERNATIVE STATES OF NATURE	
	CONFORM	NONCONFORM
Accept	$12[1]	$2[2]
Reject	$ 7[3]	$7[4]

Note: The superior figures in the table above relate to the corresponding numbers in the list which follows.

The conditional payoffs are assumed to take the pattern shown because:

1. Acceptance and conformance should bring the normal "contribution" to profit.
2. Acceptance and nonconformance eventually results in expensive rework after the product is processed through later stages.
3. Rejection and conformance results in unnecessary rework that reduces the normal contribution.
4. Rejection and nonconformance results in immediate necessary rework.

The payoff table includes three of the five ingredients of the formal model: actions, states, and payoffs. The other two ingredients are the probabilities and the choice criterion. Assume that the probability of conform is 0.6 and that of nonconform is 0.4. Assume also that the choice criterion is to maximize the expected value of the dollar payoff. Given this model, the decision maker would always accept the product, because the expected payoff $\overline{A}$ for each action is[2]

If Accept, $\overline{A} = \$12\ (0.6) + \$2\ (0.4) = \$8$

If Reject, $\overline{A} = \$7\ (0.6) + \$7\ (0.4) = \$7$

The accountant often provides much of the data that are included in these decision models. His understanding of the nature of decision models should have a direct effect on how he designs a formal information system.[3]

[2] An expected value is an arithmetic mean, a weighted average using the probabilities as weights. The formula is

$$\overline{A} = \sum_{x=1}^{n} A_x P_x$$

where A_x is the payoff or outcome or cost or cash flow for the *x*th possible state of nature, P_x is the probability of occurrence of that payoff, and $\overline{A}$ is the expected value of the payoff.

[3] For a more rigorous approach to this topic, see G. Feltham and J. Demski, "The Use of Models in Information Evaluation," *The Accounting Review,* Vol. XIV, No. 4 (October 1970). The systematic analysis portrayed in the example illustrates the central feature of rational choice under uncertainty. That is, given a set of basic assumptions, it can be formally proved that the entire problem of choice can be reduced to a problem of computation. The decision maker's preferences are reflected in the payoff measure, and his likelihood assessments are reflected in the probability measure in such a manner that selection of the maximum *expected* payoff alternative always results in selection of the decision maker's preferred set of outcomes. For further discussion, see William J. Baumol, *Economic Theory and Operations Analysis,* 2nd ed. (Englewood Cliffs, N.J.: Prentice-Hall, Inc., 1965), Ch. 24; and Howard Raiffa, *Decision Analysis: Introductory Lectures on Choices Under Uncertainty* (Reading, Mass.: Addison-Wesley Publishing Co., Inc., 1968).

MODEL SELECTION

The decision maker faces a fundamental problem of model selection. In any given decision situation, there is probably a variety of models that can be used. This problem has two levels, and each is important.

First, the choice criterion or objective chosen by the decision maker has a direct impact on the selection of a decision model. For example, consider two very simple decision models. A manager might use either a discounted cash-flow model or an accrual-accounting model to make capital-budgeting decisions. The discounted cash-flow model maximizes net present value as its choice criterion or objective function. The accrual-accounting model maximizes net income, earnings per share, or some rate of return based on book values.

The choice of a particular objective will indeed affect the choice of a decision model, and this in turn will affect the information choices. For example, the book loss on the disposal of a product line or equipment may be irrelevant data if the discounted cash-flow model is being used, but relevant data if the earnings-per-share model is being used. Moreover, if the real objective were to maximize the market price of the shares, the choice of the best model may be far from obvious.[4]

Second, ideally the model should be complex in the sense that it incorporates all the possible niceties, interdependencies, and uncertainties of the real-world situation that the model portrays. But the complexity of the model that is finally used is directly dependent on its operational and economic feasibility.

The decision model must be operational. For example, in a choice of the mix of products (such as in an integrated oil company), it may be possible to state all alternatives. However, without an efficient computer-based solution model, it is not possible to evaluate the various alternatives in terms of their impact on company profit (which is one possible choice criterion). In such a situation, the decision model is not feasible operationally.

Economic feasibility may be measured by using cost and value of information models, the least developed but most universally important models for making decisions about the design of information systems. The potential benefits from adopting a more complex, "realistic" model must exceed the costs if a prospective change in a model is to be justified on economic grounds. For example, in some organizations there may be justification for the use of elaborate simulation models that explicitly provide for uncertainties under a wide variety of product combinations, demands, and cost configurations. In other organizations, simple predictions of a few possible revenue and cost figures may be satisfactory, because the decisions about how much to buy and what products to produce would not be significantly affected by the availability of outputs from a more complicated model.

---

[4]R. H. Litzenberger and A. P. Budel, "Corporate Investment Criteria and the Valuation of Risk Assets," *Journal of Financial and Quantitative Analysis,* December 1970.

ROLE OF COST INFORMATION IN DECISIONS

dependence
on decision
model selected
As we said earlier, cost information is compiled for use in decision making. *Information* has a variety of meanings in both the popular and technical literature. For our purposes, information is that subset of data that is likely to alter a decision maker's prediction. The following illustration will help stress (a) that the information required is dependent on the decision model selected, and (b) that prediction methods have a role in the decision-making process.

example
The H Company has a special molding machine, with a net book value of $81,000, for producing a unique product. The product and the machine have an expected useful life of three years. The expected disposal value of the machine at the end of year 3 is zero; its current disposal value is $16,000. The cash operating costs are $60,000 annually.

A technically superior machine is offered for $51,000. It is expected to save $35,000 per year in cash operating costs, although it too will have no disposal value at the end of three years.

The manager is trying to decide whether to buy the new machine.

An analysis of the figures is given in Exhibit 23-1. For simplicity, we ignore income taxes momentarily. We also assume perfect certainty, so that the

EXHIBIT 23-1

COMPARISON OF ALTERNATIVES

	(1) CASH FLOWS (IN THOUSANDS OF DOLLARS)						
	KEEP		BUY NEW MACHINE				CUMULATIVE ADVANTAGE OF BUYING
	YEARS 1, 2, 3	TOGETHER	YEAR 1	YEAR 2	YEAR 3	TOGETHER	
Cash operating costs	60	180	25	25	25	75	
Purchase of new machine			51			51	
Sale of old machine			(16)			(16)	
Net effects on cash outflows	60	180	60	25	25	110	70

	(2) INCOME STATEMENT EFFECTS (IN THOUSANDS OF DOLLARS)						
	KEEP		BUY NEW MACHINE				CUMULATIVE ADVANTAGE OF BUYING
	YEARS 1, 2, 3	TOGETHER	YEAR 1	YEAR 2	YEAR 3	TOGETHER	
Cash operating costs	60	180	25	25	25	75	
Depreciation—old machine	27	81	—	—	—	—	
Depreciation—new machine	—	—	17	17	17	51	
Loss on disposal:							
Proceeds			(16)			(16)	
Book value			81			81	
Net effects on income	87	261	107	42	42	191	70

complications of probabilities do not dilute the major point of this section. Straight-line depreciation is assumed.

Before answering the question of what data qualify as information, the accountant must know the decision model that the manager has chosen. Of course, many types of models might be deemed appropriate. Let us consider (1) a cumulative-cash-flow (CCF) model, whereby the decision maker wants to choose the course of action that will maximize the H Company's total asset balance at the end of year 3; and (2) an earnings-per-share (EPS) model, whereby the decision maker wants to maximize earnings per share for year 1 only.

Exhibits 23-1 and 23-2 show how the decision itself, as well as the information required, depends on the decision model selected. If the CCF model is chosen, the decision model would favor buying the new machine. In contrast, the EPS model would favor keeping the old machine.

EXHIBIT 23-2

DECISION PROCESS AND ROLE OF INFORMATION

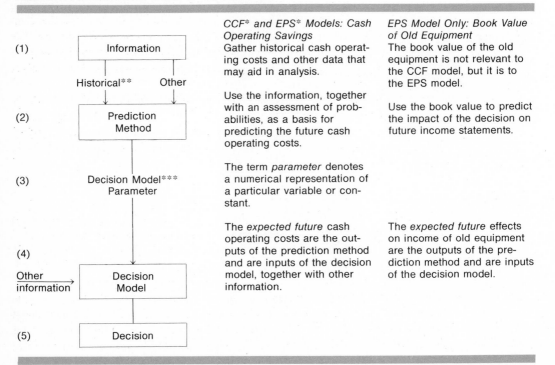

CCF* and EPS* Models: Cash Operating Savings
Gather historical cash operating costs and other data that may aid in analysis.

Use the information, together with an assessment of probabilities, as a basis for predicting the future cash operating costs.

The term *parameter* denotes a numerical representation of a particular variable or constant.

The *expected future* cash operating costs are the outputs of the prediction method and are inputs of the decision model, together with other information.

EPS Model Only: Book Value of Old Equipment
The book value of the old equipment is not relevant to the CCF model, but it is to the EPS model.

Use the book value to predict the impact of the decision on future income statements.

The *expected future* effects on income of old equipment are the outputs of the prediction method and are inputs of the decision model.

* CCF = Cumulative-cash-flow model   EPS = Earnings-per-share model
** Note that historical data may be information for prediction methods.
*** Historical data are never information for decision models. Only expected future data that are different are relevant.

The decision model will require specific predictions. Information is usually sought to help make these predictions. The three actual steps in choosing information are in the reverse order of those shown in Exhibit 23-2: (3) identify the decision-model parameter to be predicted (for instance, future cash operating costs), (2) select a method to use for the prediction process, and (1) collect and report the information needed as inputs to the prediction method.

expected future costs Both the CCF and EPS models require predictions of the expected future cash operating costs of operating the old machine. In all likelihood, the historical cash operating costs would aid in making this prediction and would be "information" to the *prediction method* (2). Strictly speaking, however, as Chapter 11 stressed, such historical costs would not be "information" to the *decision model* (4). (Of course, historical costs can be regarded as being relevant to the decision process viewed in its totality.)

How much data concerning the historical cash operating costs would be sought? This depends on what prediction method is being used. The decision maker may want the cash operating costs for only the immediately preceding year, or for two or three or more years. He may want to know the fluctuations in such costs from month to month or over a range of production volume. The type and amount of information that he needs depend on the prediction method chosen; this selection is similar to his problem of what decision model to choose.

Note that the expected future cash operating costs in Exhibit 23-1 may have been the result of elaborate studies of operating characteristics, past experience, and the various probabilities of production volumes ensuing. At this point, we are skipping the role of probability distributions in these prediction methods, except to stress that they are often essential.

role of book values In the CCF model, the $16,000 disposal value of the old equipment is information, but the $81,000 book value is not. The book value is irrelevant in this case because it is a past cash outlay that will be unaffected by the decision. Therefore, it may be ignored entirely.

However, the $81,000 book value is critical information to the EPS model. The replacement of the equipment will result in having the full $81,000 written off in one year as a part of the computation of a loss on disposal, instead of its being allocated over three years as depreciation of $27,000 annually. This has a devastating effect on next year's income and will impel the decision maker to keep the old machine if he relies exclusively on the EPS model.

If income tax effects at a rate of 50 percent are considered, the role of book value of the old equipment in the CCF model would be:

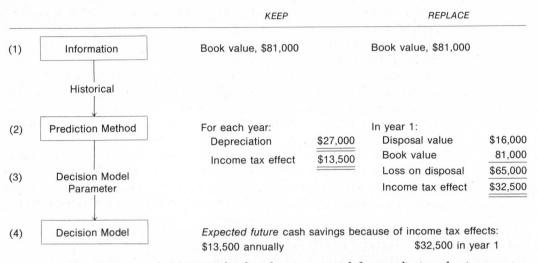

		KEEP	REPLACE
(1)	Information	Book value, $81,000	Book value, $81,000
	Historical		

(2)	Prediction Method	For each year:
		  Depreciation $27,000
		  Income tax effect $13,500
			In year 1:
			  Disposal value $16,000
			  Book value 81,000
			  Loss on disposal $65,000
			  Income tax effect $32,500

(3)	Decision Model Parameter		
(4)	Decision Model	*Expected future* cash savings because of income tax effects: $13,500 annually $32,500 in year 1	

Note that the $81,000 book value is essential for predicting the income tax cash-flow effects.

summary of role of information

To recapitulate:

1. A choice of the decision model and the prediction method must be made. Ways must be devised for helping the decision maker select the best model and the best method, or at least satisfactory ones.

2. The cost information sought is dependent on the decision model and the prediction method selected.

3. Historical data may be useful as inputs to prediction methods, but only predictions (expected future data) are inputs to decision models.

ROLE OF UNCERTAINTY

decisions under certainty

Decisions are frequently classified as those made under certainty and those under uncertainty. Certainty exists when there is absolutely no doubt about which state of nature will occur and when there is a single payoff for each possible action. The payoff table would appear as follows (data assumed):

ACTION	STATE
Buy A	− $1,000
Buy B	− 1,400
Buy C	− 1,900
Buy D	− 800

Note that there is only one column in the payoff table because there is only one possible state of nature. The decision obviously consists of choosing the action that will produce the greatest payoff (least cost). However, decisions under certainty are not *always* obvious. There are often countless alternative actions, each of which may offer certain payoffs. The problem is then finding the best one. For example, the problem of allocating twenty different job orders to twenty different machines, any one of which could do the job, can involve literally *billions* of different combinations. Each way of assigning these jobs is another possible action. This decision's payoff table would have only one *column*, because the costs of production using the various machines are assumed as known; however, it would have $2\frac{1}{2}$ quintillion *rows*. This demonstrates that decision making under certainty can be more than just a trivial problem.[5]

When a payoff is certain, the prediction is a single point with no dispersion on either side. There is a 100 percent chance of occurrence; in other words, the probability is 1.0. For example, the expected cash inflow on a federal Treasury note might be, say, $4,000 for next year. This might be graphed as follows:

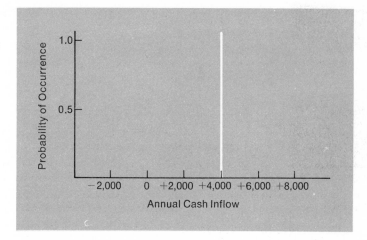

decisions Of course, the decision maker must frequently contend with uncertainty
under risk rather than certainty; he faces a number of possible states of nature. The
or uncertainty distinction among various degrees of uncertainty centers on the degree of
objectivity by which probabilities are assigned. The probabilities may be assigned with a high degree of objectivity.[6] That is, if the decision maker knows the probability of occurrence of each of a number of states of nature, his assignment of probabilities is "objective," because of mathematical proofs or the compilation of historical evidence. For example, the probability of obtaining a head in the toss of a symmetrical coin is 0.5; that of drawing a particular playing card from a well-shuffled deck, $\frac{1}{52}$. In a business, the probability of having a

---

[5] See D. W. Miller and M. K. Starr, *Executive Decisions and Operations Research*, 2nd ed. (Englewood Cliffs, N.J.: Prentice-Hall, Inc., 1969), pp. 104–5. Their distinctions among certainty, risk, and uncertainty are used here.

[6] This is sometimes called decision making under risk, as distinguished from decision making under uncertainty. See Miller and Starr, *op. cit.,* p. 105. The distinction between risk and uncertainty in the current literature and in practice is so blurred that the terms are used interchangeably here.

specified percentage of spoiled units may be assigned with great confidence, which is based on production experience with thousands of units.

If the decision maker has no basis in past experience or in mathematical proofs for assigning the probabilities of occurrence of the various states of nature, he must resort to the subjective assignment of probabilities. For example, the probability of the success or failure of a new product may have to be assessed without the help of any related experience. This assignment is subjective, because no two individuals assessing a situation will necessarily assign the same probabilities. Executives may be virtually certain about the *range* of possible states of nature or possible payoffs, but they may differ about the likelihoods of various possibilities within that range.

The concept of uncertainty can be illustrated by considering two investment proposals on new projects.[7] The manager has carefully considered the risks. He has the following discrete probability distribution of expected cash flows for the next year (assume that the useful life of the project is one year):

PROPOSAL A		PROPOSAL B	
PROBABILITY	CASH INFLOW	PROBABILITY	CASH INFLOW
0.10	$3,000	0.10	$2,000
0.20	3,500	0.25	3,000
0.40	4,000	0.30	4,000
0.20	4,500	0.25	5,000
0.10	5,000	0.10	6,000

expected value and standard deviation

Exhibit 23-3 shows a graphical comparison of the probability distributions. The usual approach to this problem is to compute an expected value for each probability distribution.

The expected value of the cash inflow in Proposal A is

$$\bar{A} = 0.1(3,000) + 0.2(3,500) + 0.4(4,000) + 0.2(4,500) + 0.1(5,000) = \$4,000$$

The expected value for the cash inflow in Proposal B is also $4,000:

$$\bar{A} = 0.1(2,000) + 0.25(3,000) + 0.3(4,000) + 0.25(5,000) + 0.1(6,000) = \$4,000$$

Incidentally, the expected value of the cash inflow in the federal Treasury note is also $4,000:

$$\bar{A} = 1.0(4,000) = \$4,000$$

Note that mere comparison of these $4,000 expected values is an oversimplification. These three single figures are not strictly comparable; one represents certainty, whereas the other two represent the expected values within their respective ranges. The decision maker must explicitly or implicitly (by "feel" or hunch) recognize that he is comparing figures that are really representations

[7] James C. Van Horne, *Financial Management and Policy,* 2nd ed. (Englewood Cliffs, N.J.: Prentice-Hall, Inc., 1971), pp. 124–25.

EXHIBIT 23-3

COMPARISON OF PROBABILITY DISTRIBUTIONS

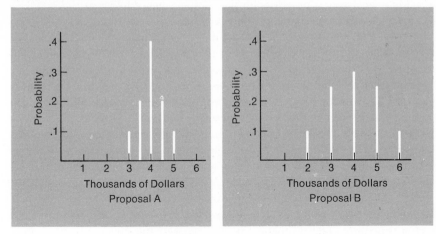

of probability distributions; otherwise the reporting of the expected value alone may mislead him.[8]

To give the decision maker more information, the accountant could provide the complete probability distribution for each proposal. However, often that course means flooding the manager with too much data for his comprehension. Therefore, a middle ground is often used. A summary measure of the underlying dispersion is supplied. The conventional measure of the dispersion of a probability distribution for a single variable is the standard deviation. The standard deviation is the square root of the mean of the squared deviations from the expected value:

$$\sigma = \sqrt{\sum_{x=1}^{n} (A_x - \bar{A})^2 P_x}$$

The standard deviation for Proposal A is smaller than that for Proposal B:

For A: $\sigma = [0.1(3,000 - 4,000)^2 + 0.2(3,500 - 4,000)^2 + 0.4(4,000 - 4,000)^2$
$+ 0.2(4,500 - 4,000)^2 + 0.1(5,000 - 4,000)^2]^{1/2}$
$= [300,000]^{1/2} = \$548$

For B: $\sigma = [0.1(2,000 - 4,000)^2 + 0.25(3,000 - 4,000)^2 + 0.3(4,000$
$- 4,000)^2 + 0.25(5,000 - 4,000)^2 + 0.1(6,000 - 4,000)^2]^{1/2}$
$= [1,300,000]^{1/2} = \$1,140$

For the Treasury note: $\sigma = \sqrt{1.0(4,000 - 4,000)^2} = 0$

A measure of relative dispersion is the coefficient of variation, which is the standard deviation divided by expected value. The coefficient for Proposal B is $1,140 \div 4,000 = 0.29$; for A it is $548 \div 4,000 = 0.14$; and for the Treasury note it is $0 \div 4,000 = 0$. Therefore, because the coefficient is a relative measure of risk or uncertainty, B is said to have a greater degree of risk.

[8]For example, how would you feel about choosing between the following two investments? First, invest \$10 today with a probability of 1.0 of obtaining \$11 in two days. Second, invest \$10 today with a probability of 0.5 of obtaining \$22 in two days and 0.5 of obtaining \$0. The expected value is \$11 in both cases. Also see the final section of this chapter on expected monetary value and utility.

the accountant
and
uncertainty Many accounting practitioners and businessmen shudder at the notion of using subjective probabilities to quantify things that are supposedly "intangible" or "unmeasurable" or "qualitative" or "unquantifiable." However, their position is weak, simply because decisions *do* have to be made. The attempts by statisticians, mathematicians, and modern accountants to measure the unmeasurable is an old and natural chore that scientists have performed for centuries. The use of subjective probabilities merely formalizes the intuitive judgments and hunches that businessmen so often use.[9] It forces the decision maker to expose and evaluate what he may have done unconsciously for years.

We should distinguish between *cost estimation,* which is an attempt to measure historical costs, and *cost prediction,* which is an attempt to measure expected future costs. Almost all accounting data are subject to uncertainty, whether the data are predictions or are historical. Too often, managers and accountants regard historical accumulations as precise calibrations rather than as approximations. The estimates (the measures of the effects of past events) should be marked by less uncertainty than are the predictions. Still, we must recognize that the accounting process deals with the real world, a world marked by uncertain predictions and uncertain estimates about what really happened.

Many statisticians and accountants favor presenting the entire probability distribution directly to the decision maker. Others first divide the information into a threefold classification of optimistic, middle, and pessimistic categories. Still others provide summary measures of dispersion, such as the standard deviation or the coefficient of variation. In any event, we are likely to see the accountant's formal recognition of uncertainty and probability distributions in his reporting. In this way, the information will portray underlying phenomena in a more straightforward fashion instead of as if there were only a world of certainty.

illustration
of general
approach to
uncertainty An example of the general approach to dealing with uncertainty may clarify some of the preceding ideas.

PROBLEM Once a day, a retailer stocks bunches of fresh-cut flowers, each of which costs 40¢ and sells for $1. The retailer never cuts his price; leftovers are given to a nearby church. He estimates demand characteristics as follows:

DEMAND	PROBABILITY
0	0.05
1	0.20
2	0.40
3	0.25
4	0.10
5 or more	0.00
	1.00

[9] Moreover, the approach rests on a defensible axiomatic base. See L. J. Savage, *The Foundations of Statistical Inference* (New York: John Wiley & Sons, Inc., 1962).

He wants to know how many units he should stock in order to maximize profits. Try to solve before consulting the solution that follows.

SOLUTION   The profit, per unit sold, is 60¢; the loss, per unit unsold, is 40¢. All the alternatives may be assessed in the following *payoff table.*

State of nature: Demand of	0	1	2	3	4	EXPECTED VALUE (PAYOFF)
Probability of state:	0.05	0.20	0.40	0.25	0.10	
Actions, units purchased:						
0	$ 0	$ 0	$0	$0	$0	$0
1	− .40	.60	.60	.60	.60	.55
2	− .80	.20	1.20	1.20	1.20	.90
3	−1.20	−.20	.80	1.80	1.80	.85
4	−1.60	−.60	.40*	1.40	2.40	.55

* Example of computation: (2 × $1.00) − (4 × $.40) = $.40

As was shown in an earlier section, the computation of expected value $(\overline{A})$ for each action is affected by the probability weights and the conditional payoff associated with each combination of actions and states.

$$\overline{A} \text{ (Stock 1)} = 0.05(-.40) + 0.20(.60) + 0.40(.60) + 0.25(.60) + 0.10(.60) = \$.55$$

$$\overline{A} \text{ (Stock 2)} = 0.05(-.80) + 0.20(.20) + 0.40(1.20) + 0.25(1.20) + 0.10(1.20) = \$.90$$

and so on.

To maximize expected payoff, the retailer should stock two units $(\overline{A} = \$.90)$.

obtaining
additional
information

Sometimes the executive is hesitant about making a decision. He would like to obtain more information before making a final choice. Some additional information is nearly always obtainable—at a price. Schlaifer[10] describes a technique for computing the maximum amount that should be paid for such additional information. The general idea is to compute the expected value under ideal circumstances—that is, circumstances that would permit the retailer to predict, with absolute certainty, the number of units to be sold on any given day. A payoff table *with perfect information* would appear as follows:

States of nature: Demand of	0	1	2	3	4	EXPECTED VALUE (PAYOFF)
Probability of state:	0.05	0.20	0.40	0.25	0.10	
Actions, units purchased:						
0	$0					$0
1		$ .60				.12
2			$1.20			.48
3				$1.80		.45
4					$2.40	.24
Total expected value						$1.29

[10] Robert Schlaifer, *Analysis of Decisions Under Uncertainty* (New York: McGraw-Hill Book Company, 1969), pp. 585–88.

The total expected value with perfect information is computed as follows:

$$\bar{A} \text{ (Perfect Information)} = 0.05(0) + 0.20(.60) + 0.40(1.20) + 0.25(1.80) \\ + 0.10(2.40) = \$1.29$$

In this table, it is assumed that the retailer will never err in his forecasts and that demand will fluctuate from zero to four exactly as indicated by the probabilities. The maximum day-in, day-out profit is $1.29. Consequently, the most he should be willing to pay for perfect advance information would be the difference between the expected value with perfect information and the expected value with existing information—$1.29 minus the $.90 E.V. computed in the previous example, or 39¢ Schlaifer calls the latter the expected value of perfect information, the top price the retailer should pay for additional knowledge.

In the real world, of course, the retailer would not pay 39¢, because no amount of additional information is likely to provide perfect knowledge. But businesses often obtain additional knowledge through sampling, and sampling costs money. The executive needs a method, such as the one described at length by Schlaifer, (a) of assessing the probable benefits, in relation to its cost, of additional information from sampling; and (b) of determining the best sample size. In the present example, no sampling technique would be attractive if its cost, allocated to each day's operations, exceeded 39¢.[11]

expected In most business cases, expected monetary value is a useful guide to action;
monetary that is, the manager chooses the act that he expects will bring the greatest
value and financial advantage. However, there are instances where expected monetary
utility profit will not be governing. For psychological reasons—perhaps fear of
bankruptcy—managers may have *personal* evaluations that do not coincide with monetary evaluations.

For example, suppose that two businessmen both have an opportunity to prepare a proposal at a cost of $10,000. There is a 50–50 chance that the proposal will be accepted, in which case a $25,000 net profit is sure. The payoff table and the computation of an expected monetary value of $7,500 for making the proposal follow:

State:	Get contract	Do not get
Probability:	0.5	0.5
Action:		
Make proposal	$25,000	−$10,000
No proposal	-0-	-0-

$$\bar{A} \text{ (Make proposal)} = 0.5(25,000) + 0.5(-10,000) = \$7,500$$

$$\bar{A} \text{ (No proposal)} \quad = 0$$

[11] Note that the basic decision here is whether to purchase advance revelation without knowing what the revelation will be. That is, should the retailer hire a fortune-teller who can foretell the future with absolute precision? The 39¢ represents an upper limit on the fee that should be paid to the prophet if one is hired.

But the two men may have very different attitudes toward the situation. The attractiveness of the proposal to each man may depend on his own financial position. As Schlaifer and others have emphasized, one of the men may be easily bankrupted by the loss of $10,000; he may decide to forego this opportunity. The other man may have adequate working capital and may make the proposal. What must be decided is simply whether it is worth taking a 50 percent risk of losing $10,000 in order to have an even chance of a $25,000 profit. This decision depends on a direct expression of personal preference.

Thus, where the amounts at stake are large, a dollar may not be worth a dollar to the businessman; that is, a dollar may have a *utility value* of only 70 cents (a direct expression of personal preference). Strict money value then will not be a valid guide to action. The approach to the decision will be the same; but in these special cases, *dollar values* will no longer coincide with *utility values,* and so the latter will replace dollar values in the evaluation.[12]

summary

The accountant must be acquainted with the entire decision process if he is going to maximize his service to management. He must focus on decision objectives, prediction methods, decision models, and alternative payoffs.

Formal decision models are used increasingly, because they replace or supplement hunches and implicit rules with explicit assumptions and criteria. The decision maker must choose the decision model to use. Both the choice criterion or objective function and the complexities of the decision situation affect the choice of model. What information is to be compiled depends on the chosen prediction method and the decision model.

Managers and accountants are often prone to regard quantification as precise just because numbers are somehow supposed to be accurate. However, almost all data, whether they depict the past or the future, are subject to uncertainty. Accounting reports for decision making are aimed increasingly toward the formal, explicit recognition of uncertainty. Cognizance of probability distributions is often essential to providing information for decisions.

suggested readings

American Accounting Association, "Report of the Committee on Managerial Decision Models," *Accounting Review* (Supplement), Vol. XLIV, 1969. Also see the three reports of other committees on related topics in the *Accounting Review* (Supplement) Vol. XLVI, 1971.

[12] Throughout this chapter, we have implied that expected monetary values represent the general case. However, decision theory regards the use of expected monetary values as a special application of the general approach, which uses utility values.

Anton, H., and P. Firmin, *Contemporary Issues in Cost Accounting.* Boston: Houghton Mifflin Company, 1966.

Ball, R., and P. Brown, "Portfolio Theory and Accounting," *Journal of Accounting Research,* Autumn 1969.

Beer, S., *Decision and Control.* New York: John Wiley & Sons, Inc., 1966.

Benston, G. J., ed., *Contemporary Cost Accounting and Control.* Encino, Calif.: Dickenson Pub. Co., Inc., 1970.

Demski, J. S., "Decision-Performance Control," *Accounting Review,* October 1969.

——, *Information Analysis.* Reading, Mass.: Addison-Wesley Publishing Co., Inc., 1972.

Dopuch, N., and J. Birnberg, *Cost Accounting.* New York: Harcourt Brace Jovanovich, Inc., 1969.

Feltham, G. A., *Information Evaluation.* Evanston, Ill.: American Accounting Association, 1972.

——, "The Value of Information," *Accounting Review,* October 1968.

Feltham, G. A., and J. S. Demski, "The Use of Models in Information Evaluation," *Accounting Review,* October 1970.

Hertz, D. B., "Investment Policies that Pay Off," *Harvard Business Review,* January–February 1968.

——, "Risk Analysis in Capital Investment," *Harvard Business Review,* January–February 1964.

Miller, D. W., and M. K. Starr, *Executive Decisions and Operations Research* (2nd ed.). Englewood Cliffs, N.J.: Prentice-Hall, Inc., 1969. This contains a highly readable introduction to decision theory.

Morris, W. T., *Management Science: A Bayesian Introduction.* Englewood Cliffs, N.J.: Prentice-Hall, 1968.

Raiffa, H., *Decision Analysis: Introductory Lectures on Choices Under Uncertainty.* Reading, Mass.: Addison-Wesley Publishing Co., Inc., 1968.

Rappaport, A., ed., *Information for Decision Making.* Englewood Cliffs, N.J.: Prentice-Hall, Inc., 1970.

Rosen L., ed., *Topics in Managerial Accounting.* Toronto: McGraw-Hill Company of Canada, Ltd., 1970.

Schlaifer, Robert, *Analysis of Decisions Under Uncertainty.* New York: McGraw-Hill Book Company, 1969.

Problems for Self-Study

Review the examples by trying to compute your own solutions, particularly for the examples on standard deviation and the expected value of perfect information.

questions, problems, and cases

23-1. Define *decision making.*

23-2. "Determining the problem is the key to successful decision making." Comment.

23-3. A fire has destroyed a factory. As the company manager, list as many alternative actions as you can formulate.

23-4. "Taking no action must always be listed among alternative courses of action." Discuss.

23-5. "The management consultant is happy when he finds that his client has wholeheartedly accepted a beautiful decision program that is the consultant's brainchild and the product of weeks of analysis." Later, the consultant's joy often becomes sadness when he finds that the decisions were never transformed into action. What is the probable reason for the apparent failure of the consultant's plans?

23-6. "The wisdom of a decision can never really be measured until the future becomes the past." What are the merits and weaknesses of a postdecision audit?

23-7. Distinguish among *risk, certainty,* and *uncertainty.*

23-8. Define *expected value.*

23-9. What steps should be taken in computing expected value?

23-10. Many businessmen refuse to accept marginal business at cut prices under any circumstances. They say that acceptance of such orders will hurt the industry price structure and thus boomerang to the detriment of "unmeasurable" future profits. Does the businessman base such decisions on qualitative tangible factors? Explain.

23-11. What is the major benefit of using subjective probabilities in forecasting?

23-12. What is *utility value?*

23-13. Assessment of Subjective Probabilities. Both Sears, Roebuck and Montgomery Ward faced the same general economic conditions in the decade after World War II. Ward's policy was to keep a relatively large proportion of its assets in liquid form, whereas Sears invested heavily in expansion of operations.

required   Comment on the influence of subjective probabilities on the chief executives.

23-14. Role of Uncertainty in Forecasts. Refer to Problem 11-9. The forecast of $150,000 of sales per year was arrived at by the owner and his brother-in-law, who runs a car wash on the opposite side of town. They had made a thorough study of the market potential and had arrived at the following estimates:

SALES	PROBABILITY
$100,000	0.1
130,000	0.2
160,000	0.5
180,000	0.2
	1.0

required   Show how the $150,000 forecast was decided upon.

23-15. Choosing a Selling Price [CPA, adapted].   Management wants to determine the best sales price for a new appliance, which has a variable cost of $4 per unit. The sales manager has estimated probabilities of achieving annual sales levels for various selling prices as shown in the following chart:

SALES LEVEL (UNITS)	SELLING PRICE			
	$4	$5	$6	$7
20,000	—	—	20%	80%
30,000	—	10%	40%	20%
40,000	50%	50%	20%	—
50,000	50%	40%	20%	—

required   Prepare a schedule computing the expected incremental income for each of the sales prices proposed for the new product. The schedule should include the expected sales levels in units (weighted according to the sales manager's estimated probabilities), the expected total monetary sales, the expected variable costs, and the expected incremental income. Which price should be chosen?

23-16. Fundamentals of Computing Expected Value. The figures used in many examples in previous chapters were subject to uncertainty. For simplicity, however, the future dollar amounts of sales, direct materials, direct labor, and other operating costs were given as if they represented errorless predictions. Consider a new vending machine that "promises annual operating income of $1,600 before depreciation." Suppose the most likely payoff is $1,500 with a probability of 0.5 and that the worst payoff is $1,100 with a 0.2 probability. If the $1,600 represents the expected value, what was the optimistic payoff?

23-17. Competitive Bidding. A road-building company gets contracts by competitive bidding. It has estimated that its costs on a particular project will be $100,000. Based on past experience, the president anticipates the following probabilities of bids:

BID*	PROBABILITY OF BID
$ 90,000	0.05
100,000	0.10
110,000	0.20
120,000	0.30
130,000	0.25
140,000	0.10
150,000	0.00
	1.00

* For simplicity, assume that bids must be in $10,000 units.

required   The company's objective is to maximize expected profit. What bid should be made? Show computations.

23-18. Inspection or Maintenance. [Adapted from an example in Robert Schlaifer, *Analysis of Decisions Under Uncertainty* (New York: McGraw-Hill Book Company, 1969).] An automatic machine has just been readjusted by an operator. A production run of 500 parts has been scheduled. For simplicity, only four events are assumed possible:

EVENT	PROBABILITY
5 rejects	0.7
25 rejects	0.1
75 rejects	0.1
125 rejects	0.1
	1.0

The incremental cost of reworking a defective part is 40¢. An expert mechanic can check the setting; he can, without fail, bring the rejects down to 5. The use of the mechanic costs $6 per setting. Should the setting be checked?

23-19. **Selection of Production Plan.** [Adapted from Malcom Pye, "Reasons, Probabilities, and Accounting Principles," *Accounting Review*, Vol. XXXV, No. 3, 440–41.] Assume that the XYZ Company manufactures the Gadget, in which a Gismo is installed. The Gismo costs $10, but when a Gadget is returned because of a defective Gismo, the replacement cost of the Gismo will be $25 because of special handling and the necessary dismantling of the Gadget. Prior to the installation of the Gismo, these alternatives are available to management:

1. If the Gismos are tested by random sampling, quality can be controlled so that only 3 percent of the installed Gismos will be defective. The average cost of such sampling, per Gadget, is $.10.
2. All Gismos can be tested and no replacements will be necessary. The average cost is $1.50.
3. The manufacturer of the Gismo will guarantee that 92 percent will be good. The cost of replacing Gismos in excess of this 8 percent level will be borne by that manufacturer. However, the price per Gismo will be $10.25.

required   Assume that annual production is 100,000 units. Select an alternative. Show computations.

23-20. **Marketing a New Product; Selection of Equipment.** The Ardo Company makes specialty items that are sold through novelty stores. The demand for specific items is difficult to predict. Yet long experience is helpful in predicting the probable range of sales volumes for most items.

The president must decide on whether to manufacture and market a new item that will sell for $2 per unit. If the item is produced, one of the following types of special equipment will be used. The equipment will be scrapped after the selling season is over.

	SPECIAL EQUIPMENT	
	A	B
Cost of equipment	$50,000	$100,000
Variable production cost per unit	$1.39	$.90

No matter which equipment is chosen, batches of production may be closely geared to demand so that no unsold units will be left after the season is over.

The president and other executives have assigned the following probabilities to the range of anticipated sales volumes:

SALES VOLUME IN UNITS	PROBABILITY
50,000	0.30
100,000	0.40
150,000	0.20
200,000	0.10
	1.00

required   (Show computations.)

1. Assuming that profit maximization is the sole objective, which course of action should be taken?
2. What sales volume in units would show identical profits regardless of the choice of machine?

23-21. **Buying Equipment.** The board of directors is faced with a decision on buying special equipment for a new product. The wisdom of the decision is ultimately dependent on total sales volume. Labor and associated variable costs per unit will be much less with the more elaborate equipment. Assume zero disposal values for the equipment:

EQUIPMENT	TOTAL ORIGINAL COST	VARIABLE COSTS PER UNIT OF PRODUCT
M-1	$40,000	$4
M-2	95,000	3

Marketing executives believe that this highly specialized product will be salable only over the next year. They are very uncertain about sales prospects, but their best judgment of sales potential at $5 per unit is as follows:

TOTAL UNITS	TOTAL SALES	PROBABILITY
30,000	$150,000	0.2
50,000	250,000	0.4
60,000	300,000	0.2
70,000	350,000	0.2

required   Prepare an analysis to guide the board's action.

23-22. Evaluation of Degree of Risk: Standard Deviation and Coefficient of Variation.   Suppose that you are the manager of a bottling company. You are trying to choose between two types of equipment, F and G. The proposals had the following discrete probability distributions of cash flows in each of the next four years:

PROPOSAL F		PROPOSAL G	
PROBABILITY	NET CASH INFLOW	PROBABILITY	NET CASH INFLOW
0.10	$3,000	0.10	$1,000
0.25	4,000	0.25	2,000
0.30	5,000	0.30	3,000
0.25	6,000	0.25	4,000
0.10	7,000	0.10	5,000

required   1. For each proposal, compute (a) the expected value of the cash inflows in each of the next three years, (b) the standard deviation, and (c) the coefficient of variation.

2. Which proposal has the greater degree of risk? Why?

23-23. Expected Value, Standard Deviation, and Risk.   Suppose the Van Horne Company is planning to invest in a common stock for one year. An investigation of the expected dividends and expected market price has been conducted. The probability distribution of expected returns for the year, as a percent, is:

PROBABILITY OF OCCURRENCE	POSSIBLE RETURN
0.05	.284
0.10	.224
0.20	.160
0.30	.100
0.20	.040
0.10	−.024
0.05	−.084

required

1. Compute the expected value of possible returns, the standard deviation of the probability distribution, and the coefficient of variation.

2. Van Horne could also earn 6 percent for certain on federal bonds. What is the standard deviation and coefficient of variation of such an investment?

3. Relate the computations in part 1 with those in part 2. That is, what role does the coefficient of variation play in determining the relative attractiveness of various investments?

23-24. Standard Deviation and Comparisons. Freund, a salesman of industrial chemicals, made sales of $15,000 in April; Williams, a salesman of office supplies, made sales of $6,250. Sales in April by salesmen of industrial chemicals and of office supplies had, respectively, means of $13,000 and $5,000 and standard deviations of $2,000 and $500.

required

1. How many standard deviations above the mean were the sales of Freund and Williams? Who rated higher in their respective groups?

2. Which group of sales had higher dispersion?

23-25. Effects of Variability on Decisions to Analyze Operations. A plant manager is trying to determine when to analyze operations. He does not have a standard-cost system, but he has accumulated a great deal of data. He finds that the cost of Process A per week per thousand units is $76,000 with a standard deviation of $22,000. Last week the cost was $109,000. Process B has a cost per week per thousand units of $26,000 with a standard deviation of $4,000. Last week the cost was $38,000.

required

Suppose the costs of investigation are identical for each process, and the plant manager has decided to investigate only one of the two processes. Which process should be investigated? Which process is more variable?

23-26. Setting Prices and Uncertainty. Assume that the unit cost of a product is known with certainty to be $1.60. The top executives are trying to decide whether to set a selling price of $2.00 or of $2.20. The top price has been $2.00 for the past 30 months. Average monthly sales are forecast as follows:

AT A PRICE OF $2.00	
UNITS	PROBABILITY
1,050	0.05
1,000	0.90
950	0.05

AT A PRICE OF $2.20	
UNITS	PROBABILITY
800	0.10
750	0.60
700	0.30

required

Which is the optimal price? Show computations.

23-27. Measuring Dispersion. Refer to Problem 23-26. Compute, for the two alternative prices, the expected monthly sales in units, their standard deviation, and their coefficient of variation.

23-28. Weather Predictions and Profitability [CPA]. Food Products, Inc., posed the following problem and requested guidelines that can be applied in the future to obtain the largest net income.

A Food Products plant on the coast produces a food product and ships its production of 10,000 units per day by air in an airplane owned by Food Products. The area is sometimes fogbound, and shipment can then be made only by rail. The plant does not operate unless shipments are made. Extra costs of preparation for rail shipment reduce the marginal contribution of this product from 40¢ per unit to 18¢ per unit, and there is an additional fixed cost of $3,100 for modification of packaging facilities to convert to rail shipment (incurred only once per conversion).

The fog may last for several days; Food Products normally starts shipping by rail only after rail shipments become necessary to meet commitments to customers.

A meteorological report reveals that during the past ten years, the area has been fogbound 250 times for one day, and that fog continued 100 times for a second consecutive day, 40 times for a third consecutive day, 20 times for a fourth consecutive day and 10 times for a fifth consecutive day. Occasions and length of fog were both random. Fog never continued more than five days and there were never two separate occurrences of fog in any six-day period.

required

1. Prepare a schedule presenting the computation of the daily marginal contribution (ignoring fixed conversion cost)
   a. When there is no fog and shipment is made by air.
   b. When there is fog and shipment is made by rail.

2. Prepare a schedule presenting the computation of the probabilities of the possible combinations of foggy and clear weather on the days following a fogbound day. Your schedule should show the probability that, if fog first occurs on a particular day,
   a. The next four days will be foggy.
   b. The next three days will be foggy and day 5 will be clear.
   c. The next two days will be foggy and days 4 and 5 will be clear.
   d. The next day will be foggy and days 3, 4, and 5 will be clear.
   e. The next four days will be clear.

3. Assume you determine it is probable that it would be unprofitable to start shipping by rail on either the fourth or fifth consecutive foggy day. Prepare a schedule presenting the computation of the probable marginal income or loss that should be expected from rail shipments if they were started on the third consecutive foggy day, and the probability that the next two days will be foggy is 0.25; the probability that the next day will be foggy and day 5 will be clear is 0.25; and the probability that the next two days will be clear is 0.50.

23-29. Uncertainty and Sales Orders [CPA, adapted].   The Commercial Products Corporation requested your assistance in determining the potential loss on a binding purchase contract that will be in effect at the end of the corporation's fiscal year. The corporation produces a chemical compound, which deteriorates and must be discarded if it is not sold by the end of the month during which it is produced.

The total variable cost of the manufactured compound is $25 per unit, and it is sold for $40 per unit. The compound can be purchased from a vertically integrated competitor at $40 per unit plus $5 freight per unit. It is estimated that failure to fill orders would result in the complete loss of eight out of ten customers placing orders for the compound.

The corporation has sold the compound for the past 30 months. Demand has been irregular and there is no sales trend. During this period, sales per month have been:

UNITS SOLD PER MONTH	NUMBER OF MONTHS*
4,000	6
5,000	15
6,000	9

*Occurred in random sequence.

required

1. For each of the following, prepare a schedule (with supporting computations in good form):
   a. Probability of sales of 4,000, 5,000, or 6,000 units in any month.
   b. Marginal income—i.e., contribution margin—if sales of 4,000, 5,000, or 6,000 units are made in one month and 4,000, 5,000, or 6,000 units are manufactured for sale in the same month. Assume all sales orders are filled.
   c. Average monthly marginal income the corporation should expect over the long run if 5,000 units are manufactured every month and all sales orders are filled.

2. The cost of the primary ingredient used to manufacture the compound is $12 per unit of compound. It is predicted that there is a 60 percent chance that the primary-ingredient supplier's plant may be shut down by a strike for an indefinite period. A substitute ingredient is available at $18 per unit of compound, but the corporation must contract immediately to purchase the substitute or it will be unavailable when needed. A firm purchase contract for either the primary or the substitute ingredient must now be made with one of the suppliers for production next month. If an order were placed for the primary ingredient and a strike should occur, the corporation would be released from the contract and management would purchase the compound from the competitor.

   Assume that 5,000 units are to be manufactured and all sales orders are to be filled.
   a. Compute the monthly marginal income from sales of 4,000, 5,000, and 6,000 units if the substitute ingredient is ordered.
   b. Prepare a schedule computing the average monthly marginal income the corporation should expect if the primary ingredient is ordered with the existing probability of a strike at the supplier's plant. Assume that the expected average monthly marginal income from manufacturing will be $65,000 using the primary ingredient or $35,000 using the substitute, and the expected average monthly loss from purchasing from the competitor will be $25,000.
   c. Should management order the primary or substitute ingredient during the anticipated strike period (under the assumptions stated in 2b above)? Why?
   d. Should management purchase the compound from the competitor to fill sales orders when the orders cannot otherwise be filled? Why?

23-30. Probabilities and a New Product. James Doyle is trying to assess the profit potential for a new novelty product, a Batman toy auto. Doyle is experienced in the novelty market and is well qualified to assess the auto's chances for success. He is certain that sales will not be less than 25,000 units. Plant capacity limits total sales to a maximum of 80,000 units during the auto's brief life.

Doyle thinks that there are two chances in five for a sales volume of 50,000 units. The probability that sales will exceed 50,000 units is four times the probability that they will be less than 50,000. If sales are less than 50,000, he feels quite certain that they will be 25,000 units. If sales exceed 50,000, unit volumes of 60,000 and 80,000 are equally likely. A 70,000-unit volume is four times as likely as either.

Variable production costs are $3 per unit, selling price is $5, and the special manufacturing equipment (which has no salvage value or alternate use) and promotional outlays will cost $125,000. Assume, for simplicity, that the only possible sales volumes are those given above.

Should the Batman toy auto be produced? Show detailed computations.

23-31. Uncertainty and Cost–Volume–Profit Analysis. [This and the next problem are adapted from Robert K. Jaedicke and Alexander A. Robichek, "Cost-Volume-Profit Analysis under Conditions of Uncertainty," *The Accounting Review*, Vol. XXXIX, No. 4, 917–26.] The Jaedicke and Robichek Company is considering two new products to introduce. Either can be produced by using present facilities. Each product requires an increase in annual fixed expenses of $400,000. The products have the same selling price and the same variable cost per unit—$10 and $8, respectively.

Management, after studying past experience with similar products, has prepared the following subjective probability distribution:

EVENTS (UNITS DEMANDED)	PROBABILITY— PRODUCT A	PROBABILITY— PRODUCT B
50,000	—	0.1
100,000	0.1	0.1
200,000	0.2	0.1
300,000	0.4	0.2
400,000	0.2	0.4
500,000	0.1	0.1
	1.00	1.00

required

1. What is the breakeven point for each product?

2. Which product should be chosen? Why? Show computations.

3. Suppose management was absolutely certain that 300,000 units of Product B would be sold. Which product should be chosen? Why? What benefits are available to management from the provision of the complete probability distribution instead of just a lone expected value?

23-32. Uncertainty, Choice of Product, and Cost–Volume–Profit Analysis. You are a division manager of the K Company. You have conducted a study of the profit potential of three products:

	PRODUCTS		
	1	2	3
Expected profit	$450,000	$450,000	$ 450,000
Standard deviation of profit	$500,000	$681,500	$1,253,000
The probability of:			
At least breaking even	0.816	0.745	0.641
Profit at least $250,000	0.655	0.615	0.564
Profit at least $600,000	0.382	0.413	0.456
Loss greater than $300,000	0.067	0.136	0.274

The expected contribution per unit for each product is $1,250, and the expected fixed expenses per year are $5,800,000, so each product has the same breakeven quantity, 4,640 units.

required   Which product would you choose? Explain fully, including comparisons of the relative riskiness of the three products.

23-33. Expected-Value Tables. As an appliance dealer, you are deciding how to service your one-year warranty on the 1,000 color television sets you have just sold to a large local hotel. You have three alternatives:

1. A reputable service firm has offered to service the sets, including all parts and labor, for a flat fee of $18,000.

2. For $15,000, another reputable service firm would furnish all necessary parts and provide up to 1,000 service calls at no charge. Service calls in excess of that number would be $4 each. The number of calls is likely to be:

EVENT	CHANCE OF OCCURRENCE	PROBABILITY OF OCCURRENCE	TOTAL COST
1,000 calls or less	50%	0.5	$15,000
1,500 calls	20	0.2	17,000
2,000 calls	20	0.2	19,000
2,500 calls	10	0.1	21,000
	100%	1.0	

3. You can hire your own labor and buy your own parts. Your past experience with similar work has helped you to formulate the following probabilities and costs:

EVENT	CHANCE OF OCCURRENCE	PROBABILITY OF OCCURRENCE	TOTAL COST
Little trouble	10%	0.1	$ 8,000
Medium trouble	70	0.7	10,000
Much trouble	20	0.2	30,000
	100%	1.0	

required   Using expected-value tables, compare the three alternatives. Which plan do you favor? Why?

23-34. Standard Deviation and Coefficient of Variation. Refer to Problem 23-33. For each alternative, compute the standard deviation and the coefficient of variation. Which alternative is most risky?

23-35. Inventory Levels and Sales Forecasting. The owner of a small bakery must decide on how many dozens of a new kind of sweet roll to bake each day. He estimates it will cost him 15¢ per dozen to bake the new rolls, which can then be sold the same day for 35¢ per dozen. And any rolls not sold during the day on which they are baked, the baker is certain, can be sold the next day for 10¢ per dozen. Although he has never sold this type of roll before, his experience leads him to assess probable demand as follows:

FIRST MONTH

DEMAND (DOZENS PER DAY)	PROBABILITY
Less than 3	0.00
3	0.10
4	0.25
5	0.45
6	0.20
7 or more	0.00

SECOND MONTH AND THEREAFTER

DEMAND (DOZENS PER DAY)	PROBABILITY
Less than 3	0.00
3	0.00
4	0.15
5	0.35
6	0.40
7	0.10
8 or more	0.00

required How many dozen rolls should he bake each day for the first month? The second month?

23-36. Value of Perfect Information. In the previous problem, assume that the local witch goes into a trance every night and forecasts the exact demand for sweet rolls for the next day. What would be the baker's expected profit per day? How much would the baker be willing to pay the witch for this information? Answer for both time periods referred to above.

23-37. Cost and Value of Information; Using Decision Trees. [Adapted from "Report of Committee on Managerial Decision Models," *Accounting Review,*

EXHIBIT 23-4

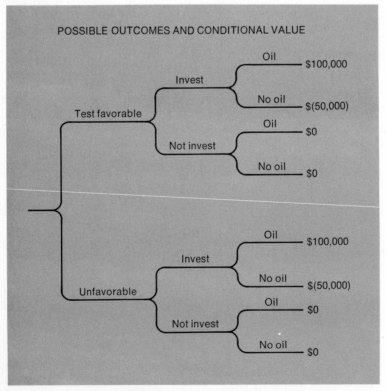

POSSIBLE OUTCOMES AND CONDITIONAL VALUE

Test favorable

Invest — Oil — $100,000

No oil — $(50,000)

Not invest — Oil — $0

No oil — $0

Unfavorable

Invest — Oil — $100,000

No oil — $(50,000)

Not invest — Oil — $0

No oil — $0

Supplement to Vol. XLIV.] An oil well driller, George Davis, is thinking of investing $50,000 in an oil well lease. He estimates the probability of finding a producing well as 0.4. Such a discovery would result in a net gain of $100,000 ($150,000 revenue − $50,000 cost). There is a 0.6 probability of not getting any oil, resulting in the complete loss of the $50,000.

required

1. What is the net expected value of investing?

2. Mr. Davis desires more information because of the vast uncertainty and the large costs of making a wrong decision. There would be an unrecoverable $50,000 outlay if no oil is found; there would be a $100,000 opportunity cost if he does not invest and the oil is really there. What is the most he should be willing to pay for perfect information regarding the presence or absence of oil? Explain.

3. Although perfect information is seldom obtainable, some additional information is usually available at some price. Mr. Davis might consider a geological test of the subsurface. His decision tree would then appear as in Exhibit 23-4.

   The geological testing company might advise the wildcatter that if there is oil on the land, the test results will be favorable (positive) three-quarters of the time and unfavorable (negative) one-quarter of the time. In other words, the test is not perfect. Similarly, if there is no oil, the test will give unfavorable results two-thirds of the time but will be (falsely) favorable one-third of the time. (These probabilities will be referred to as conditional probabilities.)

   The wildcatter wants to know the probability of finding oil, given the result of the test. These revised conditional probabilities are found by weighing the prior subjective probabilities by the appropriate likelihoods:

PROBABILITIES OF STATES, GIVEN A FAVORABLE OR UNFAVORABLE TEST RESULT

EVENT (E)	(1) PRIOR P (E)	(2) CONDITIONAL PROBABILITIES OF FAVORABLE TEST	(1) × (2) PROBABILITIES OF TEST OUTCOME AND EVENT	PROBABILITIES OF EVENTS GIVEN THE TEST OUTCOMES
If the test is favorable:				
Oil	0.4	¾	0.3	0.3 ÷ 0.5 = 0.6
No oil	0.6	⅓	0.2	0.2 ÷ 0.5 = 0.4
Probability of favorable test			0.5	1.0
If the test is unfavorable:				
Oil	0.4	¼	0.1	0.1 ÷ 0.5 = 0.2
No oil	0.6	⅔	0.4	0.4 ÷ 0.5 = 0.8
Probability of unfavorable test			0.5	1.0

The computations of conditional probabilities show that the probability of finding oil is 0.6, given a *favorable* test. However, if the test is *unfavorable*, the probability of finding oil is only 0.2. With this knowledge, construct a payoff table for Mr. Davis. How much should he be willing to pay for the test? Explain.

23-38. Uncertainty and Capital Investment [CPA, adapted]. Vernon Enterprises designs and manufactures toys. Past experience indicates that the product life cycle of a toy is three years. Promotional advertising produces large sales in the early years, but there is a substantial sales decline in the final year of a toy's life.

Consumer demand for new toys placed on the market tends to fall into three classes. About 30 percent of the new toys sell well above expectations, 60 percent sell as anticipated, and 10 percent have poor consumer acceptance.

A new toy has been developed. The following sales projections were made by carefully evaluating consumer demand for the new toy:

CONSUMER DEMAND FOR NEW TOY	CHANCE OF OCCURRING	ESTIMATED SALES IN		
		YEAR 1	YEAR 2	YEAR 3
Above average	30%	$1,200,000	$2,500,000	$600,000
Average	60	700,000	1,700,000	400,000
Below average	10	200,000	900,000	150,000

Variable costs are estimated at 30 percent of the selling price. Special machinery must be purchased at a cost of $860,000 and will be installed in an unused portion of the factory that Vernon has unsuccessfully been trying to rent to someone for several years at $80,000 per year and that has no prospects for future utilization. Fixed expenses (excluding depreciation) of a cash-flow nature are predicted at $50,000 per year on the new toy. The new machinery will be depreciated by the sum-of-the-years'-digits method with a predicted salvage value of $110,000 and will be sold at the beginning of the fourth year. Advertising and promotional expenses will be incurred uniformly and will total $100,000 the first year, $150,000 the second year, and $50,000 the third year. These expenses will be deducted as incurred for income tax reporting.

Vernon believes that state and federal income taxes will total 60 percent of income in the foreseeable future and may be assumed to be paid uniformly over the year income is earned.

required

1. Prepare a schedule computing the probable sales of this new toy in each of the three years, taking into account the probability of above-average, average, and below-average sales occurring.

2. Assume that the probable sales computed in part 1 are $900,000 in the first year, $1,800,000 in the second year, and $410,000 in the third year. Prepare a schedule computing the probable net income for the new toy in each of the three years of its life.

3. Prepare a schedule of net cash flows from sales of the new toy for each of the years involved and from disposition of the machinery purchased. Use the sales data given in part 2.

4. Assuming a minimum desired rate of return of 10 percent, prepare a schedule of the present value of the net cash flows calculated in 3. The following data are relevant:

YEAR	PRESENT VALUE OF $1 DUE AT THE END OF EACH YEAR DISCOUNTED AT 10 PERCENT	PRESENT VALUE OF $1 EARNED UNIFORMLY THROUGHOUT THE YEAR DISCOUNTED AT 10 PERCENT
1	.91	.95
2	.83	.86
3	.75	.78

23-39. **Judging Risk of Investment.**   Refer to Problem 23-38. Suppose the project is abandoned if the sales at the end of the first year are below average.
1. Compute the total loss if the salvage value at the end of the first year is $385,000.
2. Compute the total loss if the project is abandoned at the end of the second year because the sales continue to be below average throughout the two years. Assume that the salvage value at the end of the second year is $235,000.
3. When should the project be abandoned? Why?
4. In your view, is the project very risky? Why?

23-40. **Relevant Costs, Probabilities, Discounted Cash Flow, and Pricing.**   The Vang Construction Company is bidding on a construction contract. If the bid is accepted, work will begin in a few days, on January 1, 19_1. Ten thousand units of material X will be needed at that date. The company currently has 10,000 units of this material in stock, originally costing a total of $10,000. The current purchase cost of material X is $1.20 per unit. The company could sell material X now for $.80 per unit after all selling costs.

If this current contract is not landed, material X could be used on another job to begin in one year, on January 1, 19_2. Then the company would not need to buy a substitute material at $1.02 per unit.

If it is not used in either of these ways, material X would be of no use to the company and would be sold a year hence, probably for $.80 per unit, net. The president estimates that the probability of using material X on the other job is 0.7.

The president of the construction company is puzzled about the appropriate total cost of material X to be used in bidding on the current contract. He has assembled the following data:

	TOTAL COSTS
Miscellaneous materials	$ 40,000
Material X, 10,000 units	?
Direct labor	60,000
Relevant overhead	30,000
	$xxx,xxx

Competition is intense and markups are thin. He asks you to suggest the appropriate total-cost figure for material X. Show all computations, carefully labeled, and state all assumptions made. The minimum desired rate of return is 10 percent per annum; assume that the present value at 10 percent of $1 to be received one year hence is .900.

24

Determination of Cost Behavior Patterns

How do costs fluctuate? What is the relationship between various actions and the level of costs? We have seen again and again throughout this book that various predictions of costs under assorted alternatives can have a significant influence on decisions—decisions such as these: What products should we manufacture or sell? When? How much? What inputs should be used? How? When should the inputs be acquired? In what quantities?

A knowledge of how costs behave under a variety of influences is essential to intelligent predictions, decision making, and performance evaluation. This chapter will explore the complex problem of how to determine cost behavior patterns (cost functions) so that predictions are as accurate as is feasible.

COST ESTIMATION AND COST PREDICTION

The term *cost estimation* is often used to describe the measurement of historical costs for the ultimate purpose of facilitating the prediction of expected costs for decision purposes. Many people are inclined to regard historical costs as "actual" or "true" costs, even though the accounting measures of costs are permeated by many assumptions, including those of the ubiquitous average. Consequently, some accountants and statisticians distinguish between *cost estimation,* which in their minds is an attempt to measure historical costs, and *cost prediction.* This distinction is not universal; many often use *estimated cost* and *cost estimation* to describe forecasts or predictions. Consequently, be wary when you encounter the term. Make sure of its meaning in a specific situation.

OBJECTIVES PROVIDE THE FRAMEWORK

The subject of determining cost functions should be viewed from the perspective of the sensitivity of the results to the decision. Ideally, the decision maker wants to know the "true" or "exact" impact of a variety of actions and states (such as events) on costs. In the vast majority of instances, that impact cannot be known with certainty. Instead, the statistician or accountant provides some cost function (for example, $y = bx$) that is a simplification of the underlying relationships.

The central question is whether the resulting approximation, which is nearly always a linear function, is good enough for the purpose at hand. The answer to that question is often difficult to establish with much confidence. Nevertheless, it is a cost-and-value-of-information question that cannot be avoided. By the very act of using the cost function, the manager has made an information decision. He may have faced the decision squarely and explicitly by saying, "Yes, I can use this cost function for my prediction rather than a simpler or more complicated cost function." Or he may have reached the same conclusion implicitly, by proceeding with the given function with no questions asked. For example, when a manager uses an overhead rate of $2 per direct-labor hour as a part of the accumulation of costs for a pricing decision—even though he knows that overhead is affected by labor-hours, machine-hours, weight of materials, dimensions of materials, and weather conditions—he has made an information decision. He has decided that the simple $2 cost function is good enough for his purpose. In his mind, his pricing decision would not be sufficiently affected by a more complicated cost function to justify its added cost.

Two common simplifications are widely used in the determination of cost functions. First, a common assumption is that cost behavior can be sufficiently explained by one independent variable (such as labor-hours) rather than by more than one (for instance, labor-hours, machine-hours, and dimensions of materials). Second, linear approximations to cost functions are "good enough," even though nonlinear behavior is more likely. We will investigate these two simplifications later in this chapter. Of course, whether these simplifications provide sufficiently accurate approximations of underlying relationships is a question that can be answered only in actual situations on a case-by-case basis.

LINEARITY AND COST FUNCTIONS

Almost without exception, accountants and managers use linear cost functions to approximate the relationships of total costs to a given range of inputs or outputs. There are several assumptions that are sufficient conditions for linearity to exist when total costs are related to output:

1. The technological relationships between inputs and outputs must be linear; for example, each unit of finished product must contain the same amount of raw materials.

2. The inputs acquired must equal the inputs used; for example, each worker hired must be fully utilized.

3. The cost of acquiring each input must be a linear function of the quantity acquired; for example, the unit price of raw materials must be identical regardless of the amount purchased.

The relevant range of output under consideration may permit a linearity assumption within specified limits of output. Beyond that point, the cost of production may increase much faster or slower than the assumed linear rate.

NONLINEARITY AND COST FUNCTIONS

Nonlinear cost behavior can be caused by a variety of circumstances. For example, suppliers may offer quantity discounts on some inputs; other inputs may require higher prices in order to bid scarce resources away from competitors; some inputs (like most workers) may not be obtainable in fractional quantities, even though they may be used in fractional quantities; there may be economies or diseconomies of scale; and so forth.

For example, consider the step-cost function:

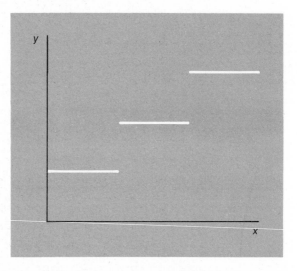

The cost of an input is a step-function cost if the cost of the input is constant over various ranges of output, but it increases by discrete amounts as activity moves from one range to the next. This step-like behavior occurs when the input is acquired in discrete quantities but is used in fractional quantities. For example, employees may be hired for the week, but the firm may need them for some fraction of that week.

Another example of a nonlinear function is the upward-sloping supply curve for a raw material:

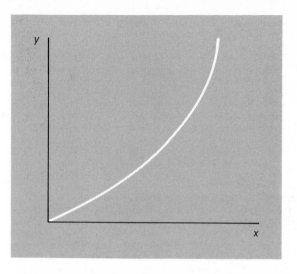

The purchase price soars as the desired quantity increases.
Another example is the availability of quantity discounts:

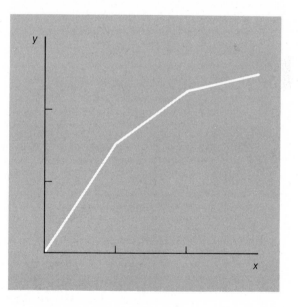

INDUSTRIAL-ENGINEERING APPROACH

Although the industrial-engineering approach to determining cost functions usually gets little attention in books on accounting and statistics, its importance should not be overlooked. It is a frontal assault on the problem of cost prediction, because it takes a normative—what costs *should* be—stance. As Chapter 8 explained, the engineering approach systematically attempts to find the most efficient means of achieving the wanted output. The approach looks forward rather than backward, so it provides a good philosophical approach as well as a practical approach in operational settings that are marked by frequent changes in workers, skills, materials, machines, processes, and products. The watchword is to avoid placing too much weight on what has happened, as if it were almost the only basis for prediction. Estimates of historical cost functions are usually just a part of the information needed for predicting future costs.

Engineering approaches are particularly suitable for determining the technical relationships for materials, supplies, many labor operations, and many machine-related inputs. Any input–output relationship that is physically observable is an obvious candidate for this approach. However, the engineering approach of time and motion studies of labor and physical measurements of material falters when costs cannot be directly traced to inputs or outputs. As Chapter 12 stressed, many indirect costs may indeed be affected by an action that produces, say, 100 more units of service or products. Among these indirect costs are those of such service departments as personnel, engineering, maintenance, power, and accounting. In these instances, other cost-prediction tools, such as regression analysis, may be desirable.

The engineering approach has been used increasingly in more and more departments in many organizations in recent years. For example, clerical, shipping, warehousing, order filling, and stocking have become subject to formal work measurement. (For a discussion, see Chapter 8.) Even though the work-measurement approach is expensive at first glance, its growth in nonmanufacturing as well as in manufacturing activities is evidence that in many places its perceived benefits exceed its costs.

Subsequent sections of this chapter will discuss other means of approximating cost functions: (a) account analysis, (b) high–low points, (c) representative incremental cost, (d) visual fit, (e) simple regression, and (f) multiple regression. The engineering method may be used in conjunction with one or more of these other means, each serving as a check on the other. For example, the individual engineer may use multiple regression as an integral part of his techniques. The point is that each of these six techniques is insufficient by itself; they are only first steps to solving the problem of cost prediction. In contrast, the engineering approach, appropriately applied, is the most complete attack on the problem because it draws on all available tools.

GENERAL APPROACH TO APPROXIMATING COST FUNCTIONS

To approximate cost functions, *relationships* are sought between the actions and the costs incurred. The preferable cost function is one that facilitates the prediction of changes in costs, that accurately depicts persistent relationships, regardless of whether particular causes or effects can be established with assurance.

Physical observation probably provides the best evidence of a relationship. That is why the distinction between direct and indirect costs is important. Direct costs are the obvious effects of the choice of a particular action; the indirect costs are not so obviously affected. For example, the production of more auto-mobiles will have an obvious impact on the total costs of tires utilized. Not many troubles arise in cost analysis under such circumstances. The troubles arise where there is no convincing relationship, or where the association is indirect and unclear, or where the relationship is joint or multiple, or, worse still, where a relationship is nearly impossible to detect or measure. Examples include advertising, research, sales promotion, and public relations.

If the decision maker cannot resort to physical identification to establish a basis for prediction, he may use regression analysis to help identify a reliable relationship. But first he uses his prior knowledge of operations to choose a particular relationship that may be so intuitively satisfying that formal regression is unnecessary (as in allocating power on the basis of related machine-hours). Of course, where it is applicable and feasible, such intuition should be buttressed by regression analysis.

Note that knowledge of operations and cost accounting is needed for intelligent regression analysis. For example:

> . . . repairs to equipment in a machine shop is a cost-causing activity that often is not specified because of the quantification difficulties. However, these repairs may be made when output is low because the machines can be taken out of service at these times. Thus repair costs will be negatively correlated with output. If these costs are not separated from other costs, the estimated coefficient of output will be biased downward, so that the true extent of variables of cost with output will be masked.[1]

The point is that qualitative correlation, which is in our minds and discerns causality in a logical sense, should ideally be coupled with quantitative correlation, which uses formal statistical means to determine the extent to which a change in one factor was accompanied by a change in another factor. Regression analysis is a valuable tool, but it must be used skillfully and cautiously. The clumsy use of regression analysis may produce deceptive results.

In summary, the following guides should help obtain approximations of cost functions that reflect underlying relationships as closely as possible:

1. To the extent that physical relationships are observable, use them.

2. To the extent that relationships can be implicitly established via logic and knowledge of operations, use them—preferably in conjunction with number 3.

3. To the extent that relationships can be explicitly established by appropriate statistical techniques such as regression analysis, use them. The use of 3 is a check on 2.

CHOOSING THE INDEPENDENT VARIABLE AND RELEVANT RANGE

The manager must make three basic decisions when he tries to determine cost behavior patterns. First, he must choose the cost to be predicted, which

---

[1] George J. Benston, "Multiple Regression Analysis of Cost Behavior," *Accounting Review,* Vol. XLI, No. 4, 668.

is the *dependent* variable, usually called *y*. Second, he must choose an *independent* variable, usually called *x*. The latter is sometimes termed the *controllable* or *decision* variable, because the choice—for example, to travel a particular number of miles—is within the specific influence of the decision maker. The dependent variable—say, cost of gasoline—may be expressed as a function of the independent variable—that is, $y = f(x)$. Third, he must choose a relevant range of activity, the range where the relationship expressed by the cost function is valid.

The function may be either linear or nonlinear. The general formula for a straight line is $y = a + bx$, where y is the computed value of y for any specified value of x. The constant a is the value of y when x is zero; b is the amount of increase in y for each unit increase in x. In other words, the value of b represents the slope of the line. The values of a and b are each called *coefficients*.

Which of the possible independent variables should be chosen? Should it be units of product, direct-labor hours, machine-hours, weight of materials, season of the year? And should only one of these, or more than one, be chosen? Very often—perhaps too often—the analyst chooses only one independent variable. He tries to pick the one that is likely to have the most influence on cost incurrence.

When the independent variable is chosen and a decision is made to employ a simple linear equation ($y = a + bx$), the remaining tasks are the determinations of the appropriate slope (b) and intercept coefficients.

ANALYSIS OF ACCOUNTS

a necessary first step The analysis of accounts, which facilitates cost estimation (for example, compiling the costs of jobs in process at the end of the year) and cost prediction (for example, establishing a predetermined overhead rate for the coming year), is the first of six methods of linear approximation of cost functions that will be described. These six methods may be viewed as increasingly complex ways of determining cost functions. The first method may be good enough in simple situations. However, in many organizations each of these six methods is used in succession over the years as the need for more accurate approximations becomes evident.

One way to approximate cost functions is to pick the independent variable(s) and the relevant range. Then the cost analyst proceeds through the accounts, one by one, and classifies each into one of three categories: variable, fixed, and mixed (often called semivariable). In so doing, he may use his past experience intuitively and nothing else. However, many analysts will at least study how total costs behave over a few periods before making judgments.

An examination of the accounts is obviously a necessary first step, no matter whether cost functions are approximated via simple inspection of the accounts or via multiple regression. Familiarity with the data is needed to avoid analytical pitfalls. The study of the accounts should alert the analyst to how closely the cost records comply with some technical requirements for the determination of cost functions by means of statistical tools. Let us look at some of these requirements.

length of   The time periods should be long enough to permit the recording procedures
time periods   to link output produced with the cost incurred because of that production.
For example, allowance should be made for lags in recording costs.[2] The recording of production in one period and related costs such as supplies or indirect labor in another will obscure the true underlying relationships.

The time periods should be short enough to avoid the averaging of fluctuations in production within a period. Averages also tend to hide the true relationship between cost and output. For example, month-to-month comparisons may overlook some important week-to-week changes in production within particular months.

separate   All factors that influence costs should be identified separately as far as is
specification   feasible. Other factors besides output that influence costs include changes
of factors   in technology, periods of adjustment to new processes or products (learning time), seasonal differences, and unusual events. These factors must often be separately specified as independent variables.

errors in   In addition to detecting clerical errors, the analyst must be on guard against
measurement   the tendency to allocate fixed costs as if they were variable. For example, such costs as depreciation, insurance, or rent may be allocated on a per-unit-of-output basis. The danger is to regard these costs as variable rather than fixed. They may seem to be variable because of the accounting methods used; however, they are not variable, owing to the underlying economic relationships. There is no point in including these costs in the dependent variable; they really do not vary with the independent variables.

As we said previously, the account-analysis method, which implies that mere inspection of the accounts will be sufficient for determining cost functions, is merely a first step in any serious attempt to determine costs.

HIGH–LOW METHOD

A major disadvantage of the account-classification method is its inherent subjectivity. The high–low method is a slightly less subjective method, in that it at least employs a series of samples and relies on two of their results.

The high–low method is described in Chapter 8, so an extensive description will not be repeated here. This method necessitates the plotting of two points,

---

[2]Benston, "Multiple Regression Analysis," p. 663.

representing the highest cost and the lowest cost, respectively, over the *contemplated relevant range*. The slope of the line that connects the two points is regarded as the variable cost per unit of volume. Whether the resulting line is an acceptable approximation of the cost function depends on the behavior of that function over the entire relevant range. The high–low method may provide a poor approximation, as the following diagram indicates:

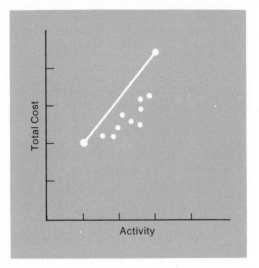

The graph illustrates the need to plot the data and not rely on picking the highest and lowest cost. Note in this case that the high–low method overstates the variable-cost component of the total cost function. Because of the obvious danger of relying on extreme points, which often represent abnormal rather than normal situations, the high–low method is not recommended.[3]

REPRESENTATIVE MARGINAL OR INCREMENTAL COST

Another approach is to choose, within the relevant range, an activity level that is perceived to have a marginal or incremental cost representative of that range. If the actual cost function is continuous and differentiable in the region of the representative activity level, then differential calculus can be used to compute the marginal cost.[4] Again, this method depends on the judgment of the analyst and so is regarded as too subjective for widespread use. Either method, of course, relies on one or two sample points, disregarding all others. A more inclusive procedure would recognize all sample points.

---

[3] Professor Joel Demski has suggested, "If you don't want to use the high–low method, you may want to use the next-high, next-low method or the next-next-high, next-next-low method."

[4] The marginal cost is an estimate at any given *point* of activity and only at that point. If differential calculus is applicable, the incremental cost over a *range* of activity may be approximated by expanding the function into a Taylor series around the nominal marginal cost.

VISUAL FIT

An advantage of the next three methods—visual fit, simple regression, and multiple regression—is that all sample points are used in determining the cost function. To avoid the use of more formal procedures, sometimes a visual fit is applied by drawing a straight line through the points on a scatter diagram. This procedure may provide more accurate estimates than the previous methods described. Nevertheless, there are no objective tests to assure that the line is the most accurate representation of the underlying data. Moreover, visual fit ignores information that may be valuable about the quality of the fit.

Regression analysis, which will be described in the next section, is a more systematic approach to cost estimation. Under certain assumptions, it has measures of probable error and it can be applied when there are several independent variables instead of just one.

SIMPLE REGRESSION

The term "regression analysis" refers to the measurement of the average amount of change in one variable that is associated with unit increases in the amounts of one or more other variables. When only two variables are studied, the analysis is called *simple regression;* when more than two variables are studied, it is called *multiple regression.*

scatter diagrams   The first step in simple regression is to select the independent variable and plot the data on a scatter chart. Perhaps the points are widely dispersed, as follows:

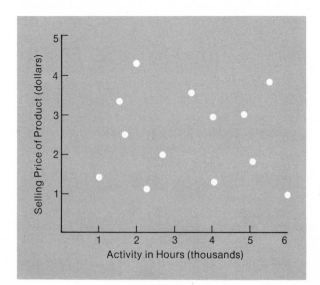

There is apparently no relationship between the selling price of the product and the activity in hours. These variables are described as being *uncorrelated*.

On the other hand, the points may be closely related:

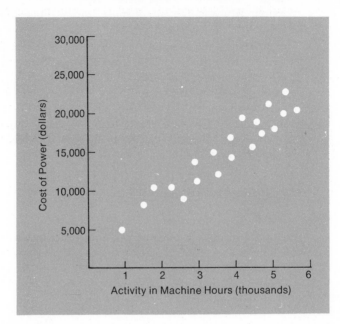

The chart clearly indicates a high degree of *correlation* between activity in hours and cost of power. Moreover, the points generally follow a straight line, so there is a *linear* correlation. Sometimes the points indicate a *curvilinear* correlation, because a nonlinear curve follows the dots more closely than a (linear) straight line.

objective of regression analysis   The major purpose of regression analysis is not to establish relationships for their own sake; rather, it is to assist the task of prediction, decision making, and feedback. The manager can use one of the variables in simple regression analysis to predict the value of the other variable and the probable error in his prediction. For example, if he knows how many miles are going to be traveled, he can use the relationships revealed by regression analysis to predict the cost of gasoline. He can also calibrate his chances of being wrong by any given magnitude.

least squares   Although an experienced statistician can visually fit a straight line to a scatter diagram with remarkable accuracy, the surest, most exact fit is obtained by two major steps. First, inspect the scatter chart to detect any unusual features that warrant further investigation. For example, one or two dots may be obviously awry. Investigation may reveal clerical errors that need correction. Perhaps an unusual situation (such as a strike or a storm that disrupted the usual relationships between, say, machine-hours and direct-labor costs) may justify removing isolated or extreme cases from the data.

Second, apply the mathematical method of least squares. This assures an objective, precise fit, and it can be easily performed with widely available, inexpensive standardized computer programs.

To illustrate regression analysis,[5] suppose that a manufacturer is troubled by fluctuations in labor productivity and wants to determine how direct-labor costs are related to the various sizes of batches of output. The workers in question set up their own jobs on complex machinery. The following data show the results of a random sample of ten batches of a given kind:

BATCH SIZE x	DIRECT-LABOR COSTS y
15	$180
12	140
20	230
17	190
12	160
25	300
22	270
9	110
18	240
30	320

Note that the data are paired. For example, the next-to-last sample consists of a batch size (independent variable) of 18 with an *associated* direct-labor cost (dependent variable) of $240.

The scatter diagram of these ten points in Exhibit 24-1 indicates that a straight line should provide a reasonable approximation of the relationship between labor costs and size of batch that prevailed during the sample history. The least-squares criterion is the most widely used means of judging whether a line drawn through the points provides the best possible fit. That is, the sum of the squares of the vertical deviations (distances) from the points to the line must be smaller than they would be from any other straight line. Note especially that, as the graph in Exhibit 24-2 shows, the deviations are measured vertically. The deviations are not perpendicular to the regression line.

The object is to find the values of a and b in the predicting equation $y' = a + bx$, where y' is the calculated value as distinguished from the observed value y. We wish to find the numerical values of the constants a and b for which

---

[5] This illustration and analysis is adapted from John E. Freund and Frank J. Williams, *Elementary Business Statistics: The Modern Approach* (Englewood Cliffs, N.J.: Prentice-Hall, Inc., 1964), pp. 299ff.

EXHIBIT 24-1

SCATTER DIAGRAM AND POSSIBLE LINEARITY

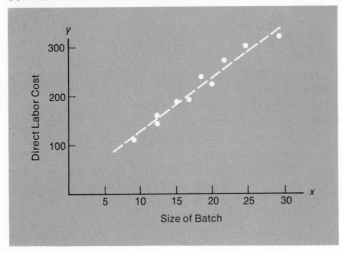

$\Sigma(y - y')^2$ is minimized. This is accomplished by using two equations, usually called *normal equations:*[6]

$$\Sigma y = na + b(\Sigma x)$$
$$\Sigma xy = a(\Sigma x) + b(\Sigma x^2)$$

where n is the number of pairs of observations, Σx and Σy are, respectively, the sums of the given x's and y's, Σx^2 is the sum of the squares of the x's, and Σxy is the sum of the products obtained by multiplying each of the given x's by the corresponding observed value of y.

Using our numerical illustration, we obtain the ingredients of our normal equations from the table in Exhibit 24-3.

---

[6] These normal equations can be derived through elementary calculus. Let

$$q = \sum_{i=1}^{n} (y_i - a - bx_i)^2$$

where n is the number of paired observations in the sample.

The objective of least squares requires the estimates of a and b to minimize q. Therefore, a and b should be values that make

$$\frac{\partial q}{\partial a} = 0 \quad \text{and} \quad \frac{\partial q}{\partial b} = 0$$

These partial derivatives are

$$\frac{\partial q}{\partial a} = -2 \sum_{i=1}^{n} (y_i - a - bx_i)$$

$$\frac{\partial q}{\partial b} = -2 \sum_{i=1}^{n} x_i(y_i - a - bx_i)$$

The normal equations are then obtained by setting the partial derivatives equal to zero and performing the indicated summations. (The discerning student would check second-order conditions here to insure that a minimum is being attained.)

EXHIBIT 24-2

LEAST-SQUARES CRITERION

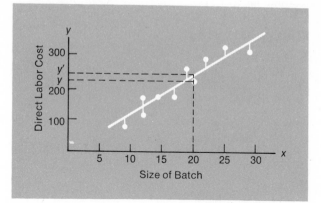

Substituting into the two simultaneous linear equations, we obtain:

$$2,140 = 10a + 180b$$
$$42,480 = 180a + 3,616b$$

The solution is $a = 24.43$ and $b = 10.53$, which can be obtained by direct substitution if the normal equations are reexpressed symbolically as follows:

$$a = \frac{(\Sigma y)(\Sigma x^2) - (\Sigma x)(\Sigma xy)}{n(\Sigma x^2) - (\Sigma x)^2}$$

$$b = \frac{n(\Sigma xy) - (\Sigma x)(\Sigma y)}{n(\Sigma x^2) - (\Sigma x)^2}$$

EXHIBIT 24-3

COMPUTATIONS FOR LEAST SQUARES

BATCH SIZE	DIRECT-LABOR COSTS		
x	y	x^2	xy
15	$ 180	225	$ 2,700
12	140	144	1,680
20	230	400	4,600
17	190	289	3,230
12	160	144	1,920
25	300	625	7,500
22	270	484	5,940
9	110	81	990
18	240	324	4,320
30	320	900	9,600
180	$2,140	3,616	$42,480

and for our illustration we now have[7]

$$a = \frac{(2{,}140)(3{,}616) - (180)(42{,}480)}{10(3{,}616) - (180)^2} = \frac{91{,}840}{3{,}760} = 24.43$$

$$b = \frac{10(42{,}480) - (180)(2{,}140)}{10(3{,}616) - (180)^2} = \frac{39{,}600}{3{,}760} = 10.53$$

Placing the amounts for a and b in the equation of the least-squares line, we have:

$$y' = 24.43 + 10.53x$$

where y' is the predicted labor cost for any given batch size. A prime is placed on the y to distinguish between the value of y that was actually observed for

[7]Another way of obtaining the values is often used. First, b is calculated as above. Then its value is substituted into the first of the two normal equations to obtain a:

$$2{,}140 = 10a + 180(10.53)$$
$$a = 24.46$$

EXHIBIT 24-4

ENLARGED VIEW OF EXHIBIT 24-2

The following is an enlarged version of the graph in Exhibit 24-2 at a batch size of 20:

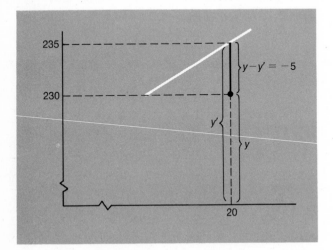

Example, batch size of 20:
$$y' = 24.43 + 10.53 \,(20) = \$235$$
$$y = 230$$
$$y - y' = -5$$

a specified value of x and the corresponding value obtained with the use of the equation of the line.

If we apply the equation, we would predict, for example, that a lot size of 20 would have labor costs on average of $24.43 + 10.53(20) = \$235$. See Exhibit 24-4, an enlarged version of the graph in Exhibit 24-2, for the graph at this lot size.

Because the points in Exhibit 24-1 are somewhat dispersed, we know that our predictions for any given lot size x will be subject to error. The regression line represents an *average* relationship; it is an estimation of the average values of y for different batch sizes.

ASSUMPTIONS AND REGRESSION ANALYSIS

Although regression analysis can be a helpful tool for predictions and decisions, it can be easily misused. There is no shortcut or substitute for the scrutiny of a particular situation to assure that the assumptions of regression analysis are applicable to the data. Too often, regression is conducted mechanically, using canned computer programs and invalid assumptions about the pertinence of the statistical tools to the data being analyzed. The reading of one chapter on regression does not qualify a person to apply regression analysis in practice. Professional help from statisticians is vital for any successful application.

Probably the most important limitation of regression analysis is the assumption that the relationships will persist—that there is an ongoing, stable relationship between cost and the independent variable or variables used to estimate the cost. That is why regression analysis is usually confined to repetitive operations.

fundamental *assumptions* *for making* *inferences* To make valid inferences from sample data about population relationships, four assumptions must be satisfied.[8]

First, linearity must exist between x and y in the population. The underlying expected relation, $E(y)$, has the form

$$E(y) = A + Bx$$

where A and B are the true (but unknown) parameters of the regression line. The deviation of the *actual* value of y from the true regression line is called the *disturbance term u*, which is defined as $y - y'$. The average or expected value of u is zero.

Second, the standard deviation and variance of the u's is constant.[9] It is the same for all values of x. This indicates that there is a uniform scatter or

---

[8] William A. Spurr and Charles P. Bonini, *Statistical Analysis for Business Decisions* (Homewood, Ill.: Richard D. Irwin, Inc., 1967), pp. 564–65.

[9] Constant variance is known as *homoscedasticity* (but let us refer to it as constant variance).

dispersion of points about the regression line. This assumption is valid for the first chart, but not the second, of the following:

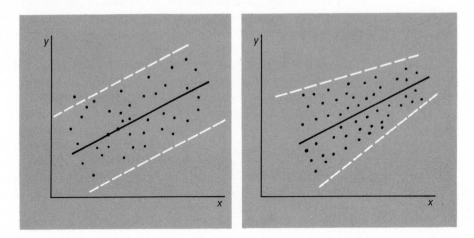

Third, the u's are independent of each other. That is, the deviation of one point about the line (its u value, where $u = y - y'$) is unrelated to the deviation of any other point. If the u's are not independent, the problem of serial correlation is present. (This is discussed in a later section.)

Fourth, the points around the regression line are normally distributed. That is, the u values are normally distributed.

Note that such assumptions as linearity and constant variance can be checked most easily by studying the data on a scatter diagram. That obvious step is frequently skipped. As a result, inappropriate relations are often unjustifiably assumed.

The inherent appeal of regression is that computer programs usually have tests that may be systematically applied to see whether these and other assumptions hold. These tests are often referred to as *specification analysis*. When these four assumptions are satisfied, the sample values a and b are the best available estimates of the population values A and B.

cause and effect Does a high correlation between two variables mean that either is a cause of the other? Correlation, by itself, cannot answer that question; x may cause y, y may cause x, x and y may interact on one another, both may be affected by z, or the correlation may be due to chance. High correlation merely indicates that the two variables move together. No conclusions about cause and effect are warranted. For example: "Church attendance and beer consumption correlate over the years, but this does not mean that attending church makes one thirsty or that drinking beer incites piety; they both simply increased with population growth."[10]

[10] Spurr and Bonini, *Statistical Analysis*, p. 580.

relevant range The concept of a relevant range was discussed in Chapter 2 and elsewhere. In the present context, the relevant range should be perceived as the span of activity that encompasses the observed relationships. A cost function that is estimated for a mixed (semivariable) cost may yield a good approximation to the actual cost function over the relevant range. However, that relevant range rarely includes zero activity. Therefore, rather than thinking of the intercept (the fixed component) as a fixed cost, it is probably better to think of it as merely the intercept at $x = 0$. For example, see Exhibit 24-5. Note that a would be a valid estimate of fixed cost if the actual observation included the point where activity was zero and the relationship between activity and output was linear. If more observations were available, perhaps the dashed curve would be a better approximation and a would be zero. Therefore, the value of the constant term, a, is not the expected cost at zero activity; it is only the value that is computed as a result of the regression line calculated from the available data. Too often, cost analysts unjustifiably extrapolate beyond the range of the data upon which the regression equation was estimated.

EXHIBIT 24-5

DEMONSTRATION OF RELEVANT RANGE

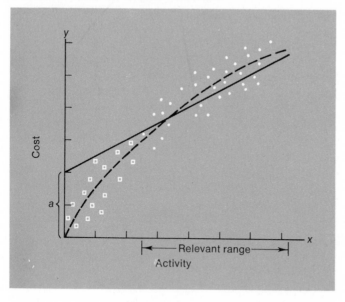

a is the y intercept at $x = 0$
Actual observations ● ● ●
Regression line ━━━━━━
Additional observations □ □ □
Newly fitted curve ━ ━ ━ ━

Source: Adapted from George J. Benston, "Multiple Regression Analysis of Cost Behavior," *The Accounting Review*, XLI, No. 4, p. 662.

CORRELATION

How much of the total variation of the y's can be attributed to chance? How much can be attributed to the relationship between the two variables x and y? The coefficient of correlation (r) is a measure of the extent to which the independent variable accounts for the variability in the dependent variable. Note in Exhibit 24-6 that the total deviation of the dependent variable y from its mean $\bar{y}$ (that is $y - \bar{y}$) can be divided into two parts: first, the deviation of the value on the line (y') from the mean $\bar{y}$, or ($y' - \bar{y}$), which is explained by the given value of x; and second, the deviation of y from the regression line ($y - y'$), which is not explained by x.

The measure of the closeness of fit of a regression line is made by comparing $\Sigma(y - y')^2$ with the sum of the squares of the deviations of y's from their mean $\Sigma(y - \bar{y})^2$. Using our illustration from Exhibit 24-3, $\Sigma y = 2,140$ and $\bar{y} = 2,140 \div 10 = 214$. Therefore,

$$\Sigma(y - \bar{y})^2 = (180 - 214)^2 + (140 - 214)^2$$
$$+ \cdots + (240 - 214)^2 + (320 - 214)^2 = 43,640$$

Chance variation is measured by the deviations of the points from the regression line, by the quantity $\Sigma(y - y')^2$. If all the points actually fell on a straight line, $\Sigma(y - y')^2$ would equal zero. To compute this quantity for our illustration, the predicted values y' must be calculated by substituting the given values of x into the least-squares equation

$$y' = 24.43 + 10.53x$$

EXHIBIT 24-6

FUNDAMENTAL MEASURE OF VARIATION

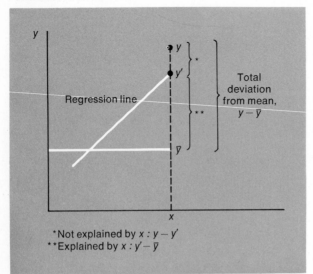

*Not explained by x : $y - y'$
**Explained by x : $y' - \bar{y}$

Therefore, we obtain $y' = 24.43 + 10.53(15) = 182.38$ for the first batch, $y' = 24.43 + 10.53(12) = 150.79$ for the second batch, and so on. Substituting these values and the observed y's into $\Sigma(y - y')^2$, we get

$$\Sigma(y - y')^2 = (180 - 182.38)^2 + (140 - 150.79)^2$$
$$+ \cdots + (320 - 340.33)^2 = 1{,}934$$

Therefore,

$$\frac{\Sigma(y - y')^2}{\Sigma(y - \bar{y})^2} = \frac{1{,}934}{43{,}640} = .0443 = 4.43\%$$

of the variation in the cost of the batches can be attributed to random variation (chance) and the effect of other variables not explicitly incorporated in the model. The remaining 95.57 ($100 - 4.43$) percent of the variation in the costs is accounted for by differences in the size of the batch.

The coefficient of determination is often called r-square (r^2). It indicates the proportion of the variance, $(y - \bar{y})^2$, that is explained by the independent variable x. The coefficient of determination is also more informatively expressed as 1 minus the proportion of total variance that is not explained:

$$r^2 = 1 - \frac{\Sigma(y - y')^2}{\Sigma(y - \bar{y})^2} = 1 - \frac{\text{Unexplained variance}}{\text{Total variance}}$$

$$= 1 - \frac{1{,}934}{43{,}640} = 1 - .0443 = 0.9557$$

The square root of the proportion 0.9557 (that is, the proportion of the total variation in costs that is accounted for by differences in the size of the batches) is called the coefficient of correlation, r:

$$r = \pm \sqrt{1 - \frac{\Sigma(y - y')^2}{\Sigma(y - \bar{y})^2}}$$

The sign attached to r is the sign of b in the predicting equation:

$$r^2 = 0.9557$$

$$r = +\sqrt{0.9557} = 0.978$$

In this illustration, the least-squares line provides an excellent fit, so there is indication of a strong relationship between the costs of the labor and the size of the batch. The coefficient of correlation is a relative measure of the relationship between two variables, varying from zero (no correlation) to ± 1 (perfect correlation).

Note that the coefficient of correlation may indicate a higher degree of explanation than is warranted. For instance, if 60 percent of the variance in y is explained by x, $r^2 = .60$, but $r = \sqrt{0.60} = 0.775$.

STANDARD ERROR OF ESTIMATE

How accurate is the regression line as a basis for prediction? We are using a sample of historical events. Obviously, if we duplicated that sample using different data, we would not expect to obtain the same line. The values for a and b would be different for each sample taken. What we really want to know is the true regression line of the entire population,

$$y = A + Bx$$

where A and B are the true coefficients. The values of a and b are estimates based on samples. Therefore, they are subject to chance variation like all sample statistics.

In Chapter 23, we saw that data are often expressed as averages. A standard deviation and a coefficient of variation were computed to help indicate the relative degree of dispersion about the mean. Similarly, the line we obtained with the method of least squares, $y' = 24.43 + 10.53x$, is only an *estimate* of the true regression line.

To judge the accuracy of the regression line, we examine the dispersion of the observed values of y around the regression line. A measure of this dispersion will assist us in judging the probable accuracy of a prediction of the average labor cost of a batch of, say, 20 units. The measure of the scatter of the actual observations about the regression line is termed the *standard error of estimate*. The standard error of estimate for the population may be calculated from a sample in linear regression, as follows:

$$s_e = \sqrt{\frac{\Sigma(y - y')^2}{n - 2}}$$

where n is the size of the sample.[11]

As will be demonstrated in more detail later, the sum of the squared deviations, $\Sigma(y - y')^2$, is that portion of the total variation in y's that can be attributed to chance.

When a linear regression has been fitted by least squares, a simpler computation is

$$s_e = \sqrt{\frac{\Sigma y^2 - a\Sigma y - b\Sigma xy}{n - 2}}$$

Consider our illustration. All the data are from Exhibit 24-3, except for Σy^2, which happens to be 501,600.

$$s_e = \sqrt{\frac{501,600 - 24.43(2,140) - 10.53(42,480)}{10 - 2}}$$

$$s_e = 15.8$$

[11]The standard error of the estimate for the sample itself is $\sqrt{\Sigma(y - y')^2/n}$. The use of $n - 2$ represents the degrees of freedom around the regression line. It is $n - 2$ because two constants, a and b, had to be computed first on the basis of the original data.

If the four assumptions underlying regression analysis (linearity, independence, constant variance, and normality) are satisfied, we can use the standard error to help gauge our confidence in our predictions. For instance, if no sampling error exists, then approximately two-thirds of the points should lie within the band measured by $y' \pm 15.8$. Therefore, management can predict that a batch size of 20 would result in costs of $\$235 \pm \$15.80$, or between $\$219.20$ and $\$250.80$, with two chances out of three of being correct.

SAMPLING ERRORS AND REGRESSION COEFFICIENTS

testing for significance of a relationship   Does a significant explanatory relationship exist between x and y? For example, the regression coefficient for x of 10.53 implies a change in cost of $\$10.53$ for each additional unit in a batch. The regression coefficient 10.53 is an estimate of a population parameter. A particular sample may indicate a relationship, even when none exists, by pure chance. If there is no relationship, then the slope B of the true regression line would be zero. A hypothesis can be set up that $B = 0$. If the sample value b is significantly different from zero, we would reject the hypothesis and assert that there is a definite relationship between the variables.

To test this hypothesis, we need to calculate the standard error of the b regression coefficient:

$$s_b = \frac{s_e}{\sqrt{\Sigma(x - \bar{x})^2}}$$

It may also be expressed as:

$$s_b = \frac{s_e}{\sqrt{\Sigma x^2 - \bar{x}\Sigma x}}$$

where s_e is the sample standard error of the estimate, and the denominator describes the dispersion of x values around their mean. The value s_b is a measure of the amount of sampling error in b. The s_b for our example is

$$s_b = \frac{15.8}{\sqrt{3,616 - 18(180)}} = \frac{15.8}{\sqrt{3,616 - 3,240}} = \frac{15.8}{\sqrt{376}} = \frac{15.8}{19.4} = .81$$

The procedure[12] for deciding whether a positive relationship exists between batch size and labor costs is this:

Null hypothesis: $B = 0$ (no relationship)
Alternative hypothesis: $B \neq 0$ (labor costs increase as batch sizes increase)

The value of b is 10.53. If the null hypothesis is true, $B = 0$, and b is 10.53 units from B. In terms of its standard error, this is $10.53 \div .81 = 13.0$. Therefore, b is 13 standard errors from $B = 0$. A deviation of more than two standard errors

[12] Spurr and Bonini, *Statistical Analysis*, pp. 566–68.

is usually regarded as significant. Therefore, the chance is infinitesimal that a deviation as large as 13 standard errors could occur by chance. Consequently, we reject the null hypothesis and accept the alternative hypothesis that there is a significant relationship between the variables.

The amount of 13.0 standard errors just computed is called the *t-value* of the regression coefficient:

$$t\text{-value} = \frac{\text{Coefficient}}{\text{Standard error of}} = \frac{10.53}{.81} = 13.0$$
$$\text{the coefficient}$$

High *t*-values enhance confidence in the value of the coefficient as a predictor. Low *t*-values (as a rule of thumb, under 2.00) are indications of low reliability of the predictive power of that coefficient.

confidence intervals and t-values   The standard error of the regression coefficient and the *t*-value permit us to assess a probability that the "true" B is between specified limits. These limits are usually called confidence intervals. The 95 percent confidence interval is computed with the use of the appropriate *t*-value from the table in Exhibit 24-7.

For instance, with a sample size of 10, we find the row in Exhibit 24-7 with $n - 2 = 8$ degrees of freedom and the column $t_{.025}$ (for one-tail) to find the confidence interval:

$$b \pm t_{.025}(s_b)$$

This is

$$10.53 \pm 2.306(.81)$$

$$= 10.53 \pm 1.87$$

If all the pertinent assumptions hold, the accountant could assess a probability of 0.95 that the "true" marginal cost (B) is between \$8.66 and \$12.40. Similarly, he could assess a probability of 0.80 that the interval is between \$9.40 and \$11.66. The latter is computed by using $t_{.100}$ instead of $t_{.025}$: $10.53 \pm 1.397(.81) = 10.53 \pm 1.13$.

practical approaches to analysis of results   The equation of the least-squares line is often presented as follows:

$$y' = 24.43 + 10.53x$$
$$(15.70) \quad (.81)$$
$$r^2 = .9557$$

where the numbers in parentheses are the standard errors of the regression coefficients. The *t*-values may or may not be presented.

EXHIBIT 24-7

VALUES OF t

d.f.	$t_{.100}$	$t_{.050}$	$t_{.025}$	$t_{.010}$	$t_{.005}$	d.f.
1	3.078	6.314	12.706	31.821	63.657	1
2	1.886	2.920	4.303	6.965	9.925	2
3	1.638	2.353	3.182	4.541	5.841	3
4	1.533	2.132	2.776	3.747	4.604	4
5	1.476	2.015	2.571	3.365	4.032	5
6	1.440	1.943	2.447	3.143	3.707	6
7	1.415	1.895	2.365	2.998	3.499	7
8	1.397	1.860	2.306	2.896	3.355	8
9	1.383	1.833	2.262	2.821	3.250	9
10	1.372	1.812	2.228	2.764	3.169	10
11	1.363	1.796	2.201	2.718	3.106	11
12	1.356	1.782	2.179	2.681	3.055	12
13	1.350	1.771	2.160	2.650	3.012	13
14	1.345	1.761	2.145	2.624	2.977	14
15	1.341	1.753	2.131	2.602	2.947	15
16	1.337	1.746	2.120	2.583	2.921	16
17	1.333	1.740	2.110	2.567	2.898	17
18	1.330	1.734	2.101	2.552	2.878	18
19	1.328	1.729	2.093	2.539	2.861	19
20	1.325	1.725	2.086	2.528	2.845	20
21	1.323	1.721	2.080	2.518	2.831	21
22	1.321	1.717	2.074	2.508	2.819	22
23	1.319	1.714	2.069	2.500	2.807	23
24	1.318	1.711	2.064	2.492	2.797	24
25	1.316	1.708	2.060	2.485	2.787	25
26	1.315	1.706	2.056	2.479	2.779	26
27	1.314	1.703	2.052	2.473	2.771	27
28	1.313	1.701	2.048	2.467	2.763	28
29	1.311	1.699	2.045	2.462	2.756	29
inf.	1.282	1.645	1.960	2.326	2.576	inf.

The t-value describes the sampling distribution of a deviation from a population value divided by the standard error.

Degrees of freedom ($d.f.$) are in the first column. The probabilities indicated as subvalues of t in the heading refer to the sum of a one-tailed area under the curve that lies outside the point t.

For example, in the distribution of the means of samples of size $n = 10$, $d.f. = n - 2 = 8$; then .025 of the area under the curve falls in one tail outside the interval $t \pm 2.306$.

Alternatively, a digital computer will often present the results of regression analysis in the following format:

VARIABLE	COEFFICIENT	STANDARD ERROR	T-VALUE
INTERCEPT	24.43		
2	10.53	.81	13.00
VALUE OF R-SQUARE IS			.9557

Often the accountant or the manager is confronted with a choice among various possible regressions that use different independent variables or combinations thereof. For example, one regression may use direct-labor hours as the independent variable, another may use machine-hours, and another some combination thereof. How does the decision maker pick from among these alternatives? My colleague, Joel Demski, has suggested that for regression to be helpful at all, the following four criteria should be met:

1. The regression should make sense intuitively to both the accountant and the operating manager.
2. The r^2 (coefficient of determination) should be "high."
3. The t-values (the regression coefficient of each independent variable divided by its standard error) should be "respectable"—say, at least 2.0.[13]
4. Specification analysis should be conducted so that various statistical pitfalls are guarded against or allowed for. This analysis includes tests of the basic

---

[13] The t-value for a is not important, because regression is rarely concerned with ascertaining the value at the y-intercept. Instead, the major objective is to predict how costs behave as activity changes over a relevant range of activity, which seldom encompasses zero activity. The standard error of a is computed as follows:

$$s_a = s_e \sqrt{\frac{1}{n} + \frac{\overline{x}^2}{\Sigma(x - \overline{x})^2}}$$

$$s_a = 15.8 \sqrt{\frac{1}{10} + \frac{324}{376}} = 15.8 \sqrt{.962}$$

$$s_a = 15.8(.981) = 15.70$$
$$t\text{-value}_a = 24.43 \div 15.70 = 1.56$$

An example may clarify why the t-value of a is unimportant. Suppose a company had the following nonlinear cost function but used a linear approximation over the relevant range of activity:

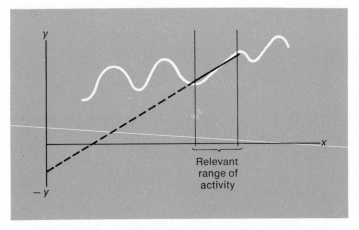

Note: Assume that the intercept is $-48,000 and that its t-value is 12.
Assume also that the t-value for b, the slope within the relevant range, is 25.

Notice that a has a high t-value, but a is negative! The cost analyst should be unconcerned, because he wants a reliable basis for prediction within the relevant range; the t-value for b is critical for this purpose. Its extremely high value of 25 indicates that great confidence can be placed in b as a predictor *within the relevant range*.

assumptions underlying regression analysis. Digital computer programs are widely available for the routine performance of these tests.

If the accountant decides that regression analysis is indeed appropriate, he may then use the results to pick one or more independent variables. For instance, in choosing between direct-labor hours and machine-hours as a base for overhead application, he would ordinarily run three regressions using (a) labor-hours, (b) machine-hours, and (c) labor-hours *and* machine-hours 'as independent variables. He would then pick the regression equation having the highest r^2, assuming that the *t*-values of the coefficients were sufficiently high, that both independent variables were logically defensible, and that no specification difficulties were apparent.

When all its assumptions are met, and when *analysis* rather than just mechanical curve fitting is conducted, regression is a powerful technique. When the assumptions hold, regression analysis is superior to other techniques because it has measures of probable error. Moreover, specification analysis can be performed to test the assumptions, and regression can be applied where there are several independent variables instead of just one.

MULTIPLE REGRESSION

improving *accuracy*   In many cases, satisfactory predictions of a cost may be based on only one variable, such as labor-hours. Nevertheless, there are instances where accuracy can be substantially improved by basing the prediction on more than one independent variable. The most widely used equations to express relationships among more than two variables are linear equations of the form[14]

$$y = a + bx_1 + cx_2 + dx_3 + \cdots u$$

where y is the variable to be predicted, x_1, x_2, and x_3 are the independent variables on which the prediction is to be based; a, b, c, and d are unknown constants; and u is the "disturbance term" that includes the net effect of other factors. For cost predictions, there may be two, three, or more independent variables such as labor-hours, labor cost, machine-hours, weight, dimensions, temperature, types of machines, types of labor skill, and so forth. For example, the weekly cost of labor in a shipping room may be more accurately predicted by the equation

$$y = \$180 + \$.80 \text{ (units shipped)} + \$.30 \text{ (weight of units shipped)}$$

[14] These equations may be expressed in many alternate forms. For instance:

$$y = b_0 + b_1x_1 + b_2x_2 + b_3x_3 + \cdots$$

A general form is:

$$Y_i = A_0 + \sum_{j=1}^{m} X_{ij}A_j + u_i \qquad i = 1, \ldots, n$$

where the Y_i are the independent variables, the x_{ij} are the independent variables, and the u_i are the residual (error) terms. The u_i is the sum of the unspecified factors, the disturbances, that are assumed to be normally distributed with a zero mean and constant variance.

than by basing the prediction on either units shipped or weight of units shipped alone.

The terms b, c, d . . . are the *net regression coefficients*. Each measures the change in y per unit change in the particular independent variable while holding the other independent variables constant. In the example above, the 80¢ rate per unit shipped indicated how much cost will rise for units of the same weight.

The major difficulty in fitting a linear equation having more than two unknowns to a given set of data is that of finding the constants a, b, c, d, . . . , so that the resulting equation will yield the best possible predictions. As in the two-variable case described in a previous section, this problem is generally solved by using the method of least squares.

Fundamentally, the problem of finding predicting equations of the form $y = a + bx_1 + cx_2 + dx_3 + \cdots$ does not differ from that of fitting lines of the form $y = a + bx$. Moreover, the widespread availability of suitable computer programs makes the use of multiple regression feasible. Least-squares equations having 25 or more variables can be solved in a matter of seconds on a fast digital computer.

illustration of technique   The details of multiple regression are beyond the scope of this text. However, the following example will show how regression may be used for cost analysis.[15] Suppose a firm manufactures electronic circuit boards and other products in which the services of several departments are used. In the assembly department, two types of circuit boards are produced, *nenex* and *denex*. The nenex are assembled in batches, but the denex are assembled singly. Weekly observations on cost and output are taken and punched on cards. Graphs are prepared, and it appears that a linear relationship is present. Furthermore, the cost of producing nenex is not believed to be a function of the production of denex or other explanatory variables. Therefore, the following regression is computed:

$$y = \underset{(40.8)}{110.3} + \underset{(.53)}{8.21n} - \underset{(1.69)}{7.83b} + \underset{(2.10)}{12.32d} + \underset{(100)}{235s} + \underset{(204)}{523w} - \underset{(154)}{136a}$$

$$r^2 = .892 \text{ (the coefficient of multiple determination)}$$

where the number of observations is 156 and

  $y =$ expected cost
  $n =$ number of nenex
  $b =$ average number of nenex in a batch
  $d =$ number of denex
  $s =$ summer dummy variable, where $s = 1$ for summer, 0 for other seasons
  $w =$ winter dummy variable, where $w = 1$ for winter, 0 for other seasons
  $a =$ autumn dummy variable, where $a = 1$ for autumn, 0 for other seasons

[15] Adapted from Benston, "Multiple Regression Analysis," pp. 670–71.

As before, the numbers in parentheses beneath the coefficients are the standard errors of the regression coefficients. For example, the regression coefficient for n is 8.21 with the other factors affecting costs "held constant" or "accounted for." The regression coefficient 8.21 is an estimate of the population parameter. The sampling error associated with this estimate is called the *standard error of the regression coefficient*. If the underlying assumptions of regression are satisfied, the standard error of the coefficient, .53, permits us to assess a probability of 0.67 that the "true" marginal cost is between 7.68 and 8.74 (8.21 ± .53) and of 0.95 that it is between 7.15 and 9.27 (8.21 ± 1.06).

Moreover, we can use the t-value to test whether the presence of the independent variable contributes significantly toward explanation of the movements in the dependent variable. For example, the t-value of n is 8.21 ÷ .53 = 15.68. Such a high t-value enhances confidence in the value of the coefficient as a predictor.

The regression might be used for flexible budgeting and the analysis of performance. For example, suppose the following for one week: $n = 532; b = 20$, $d = 321$; and $s =$ summer $= 1$. If this week is like an average of the experience for past weeks, total costs would be

$$110.3 + 8.21(532) - 7.83(20) + 12.32(321) + 235.3(1) = 8501$$

With the help of a computer program, the standard error of the estimate can be computed so that the budget can provide a range of $8501 ± the standard error. The actual costs can then be compared to this expected amount. With these figures, management can judge how unusual the actual production costs are in the light of past experience.

TROUBLESOME ASPECTS OF REGRESSION ANALYSIS

An earlier section pointed out the need to satisfy some fundamental assumptions[16] in the use of regression analysis. These apply to both simple regression and multiple regression. Two special problems of specification analysis will now be discussed. The first problem, multicollinearity, is present in multiple regression, not simple regression. However, the problem of serial correlation exists for both simple and multiple regression.

multi-collinearity   A condition called multicollinearity is an imposing difficulty of multiple regression. When the independent variables are highly correlated with each other, the net regression coefficients may be unreliable. For example, when marginal costs are computed, we would prefer to estimate the marginal cost of each class of product manufactured in a multiproduct firm. Consider the manufacturer of major home appliances. If the demand for all appliances is highly correlated, the number of refrigerators, dishwashers, and clothes dryers produced

---

[16]See Benston, *op. cit.;* and Robert Jensen, "Multiple Regression Models for Cost Control—Assumptions and Limitations," *Accounting Review,* Vol. XLI, No. 4, 265–72.

will move together. Then it is impossible to use multiple regression to disentangle the marginal cost of making refrigerators from the marginal cost of making dishwashers and clothes dryers. However, the computed regression can provide accurate predictions of total costs if the past relationships of production among the different outputs are maintained.

serial correlation An important pitfall in least squares is the presence of serial correlation of the disturbance term, u. This means that when observations are taken in successive time periods, the disturbances that arose in a period t are not independent from those that arose in previous periods $t - 1$, $t - 2$, and so on. One cause of serial correlation is the tendency of costs to be sticky. That is, costs may rise in response to increases in volume over time. However, those costs may not decline in the same way as volume declines.

When serial correlation exists, (a) the standard errors of the regression coefficients are seriously underestimated, (b) the sampling variances of the coefficients will be very large, and (c) the predictions of cost made from the regression equations will be more variable than is ordinarily anticipated from least-squares estimation.[17] Fortunately, computer programs usually have tests for serial correlation (and also for multicollinearity and for the lack of constant variance).

summary

Predictions of how costs will behave in response to various actions usually have an important bearing on a wide number of decisions. The cost function used to make these predictions is usually a simplification of underlying relationships. The choice of a cost function is a decision concerning the cost and value of information.

Two common assumptions are widely used in cost analysis. First, cost behavior can be sufficiently explained by one independent variable. Second, linear approximations to cost functions are "good enough" for most purposes.

The engineering approach, which concentrates directly on the future, is recommended as the best practical and philosophical approach to approximating cost functions. This approach may encompass all kinds of techniques, from time and motion studies to multiple regression. However, in all cases the techniques should serve as checks on one another. The following guides for cost estimation and prediction should be used:

1. To the extent that physical relationships are observable, use them.
2. To the extent that relationships can be implicitly established via logic and knowledge of operations, use them—preferably in conjunction with 3.

[17] Benston, *op. cit.*, p. 668.

3. To the extent that relationships can be explicitly established via regression analysis, use them. The use of 3 is a check on 2. This step should never be taken before step 2 is performed.

Regression analysis is the most systematic approach to cost estimation. Unlike other approaches, it has measures of probable error and it can be applied when there are several independent variables instead of one. Nevertheless, regression has many assumptions and pitfalls, so professional help should be sought when it is applied.

suggested readings

Association of American Railroads, *A Guide to Railroad Cost Analysis.* Washington D.C.: Bureau of Railway Economics, The Association, 1964.

Benston, George, "Multiple Regression Analysis of Cost Behavior," *Accounting Review,* Vol. XLI, No. 4, 657–72.

Jensen, Robert, "Multiple Regression Models for Cost Control—Assumptions and Limitations," *Accounting Review,* Vol. XLII, No. 2, 265–72.

Johnston, J., *Econometric Methods.* New York: McGraw-Hill Book Company, 1963.

————, *Statistical Cost Analysis.* New York: McGraw-Hill Book Company, 1960.

Perles, Benjamin, and Charles Sullivan, *Freund and Williams' Modern Business Statistics.* Englewood Cliffs, N.J.: Prentice-Hall, Inc., 1969.

Peters, William S., and George W. Summers, *Statistical Analysis for Business Decisions.* Englewood Cliffs, N.J.: Prentice-Hall, Inc., 1968.

Spurr, William A., and Charles P. Bonini, *Statistical Analysis for Business Decisions.* Homewood, Ill.: Richard D. Irwin, Inc., 1967.

Problems for Self-Study

PROBLEM 1   Review the example on simple regression in the chapter. Suppose the standard error of the estimate were 19.4 instead of 15.8. If all other data were unchanged (admittedly an unlikely event), what would be the standard error of the b coefficient? Would your confidence in the value of b as a predictor be higher or lower? Why? Suppose you wanted to assess a probability of 0.95 that the true marginal cost B is within an upper or lower limit. What would the range be?

SOLUTION 1   As computed in the chapter:

$$s_b = \frac{15.8}{19.4} = .81$$

Therefore, if s_e is now 19.4 instead of 15.8,

$$s_b = \frac{19.4}{19.4} = 1.00$$

My confidence in the value of b would be lower, because its t-value is now $10.53 \div 1.00 = 10.53$ instead of 13.00.

If I were to assess a probability of 0.95 that the true value is between certain limits, I would use the *t*-distribution to compute

$$b \pm t_{.025}(s_b)$$

This is

$$10.53 \pm 2.306 \ (1.000)$$

$$= 10.53 \pm 2.31$$

The range would be $8.22 to $12.84.

PROBLEM 2   You are trying to predict the cost of overhead. You have decided to choose one of the following independent variables: labor-hours or machine-hours. A computer program has been used to analyze the past behavior of overhead over eighteen months in relation to each independent variable:

VARIABLE	COEFFICIENT	STANDARD ERROR	T-VALUE	R-SQUARE
INTERCEPT	30,000	5,000	6.00	
2 (Labor-hours)	1.50	.30	5.00	
				.907
INTERCEPT	10,000	4,000	2.50	
3 (Machine-hours)	.50	.15	3.33	
				.658

Which base should be used to predict overhead cost incurrence? Why?

SOLUTION 2   Labor-hours would be chosen as the basis for the application of overhead, because they explain a higher percentage of the past variations in overhead than did machine-hours (r^2 of .907 versus .658). The *t*-values are significant in both cases; the higher *t*-value for labor-hours reinforces the choice of labor-hours in preference to machine-hours.

questions, problems, and cases

Note: Also see Problems 8-22, 8-24, 8-25, and 8-26.

24-1. Distinguish between *cost estimation* and *cost prediction*.

24-2. What two common simplifications are used in determining cost functions?

24-3. Describe three assumptions that are sufficient conditions for linearity.

24-4. To make valid inferences from sample data about population relationships, what four assumptions must be satisfied?

24-5. "High correlation between two variables means that one is the cause and the other is the effect." Do you agree? Why?

24-6. Why does regression analysis offer a means of cost estimation that other methods do not?

24-7. High–Low Method.   Examine Exhibit 24-3. Compute the cost equation using the high–low method. How does your answer compare with the equation produced by the method of least squares? Does this comparison enhance or detract from your confidence in the high–low method as a means of estimating cost behavior? Why?

24-8. Least Squares [CPA]. Labor-hours and production costs for a company for the last four months of 19_9, which you believe are representative for the year, were as follows:

MONTH	LABOR-HOURS	TOTAL PRODUCTION COSTS
September	2,500	$ 20,000
October	3,500	25,000
November	4,500	30,000
December	3,500	25,000
	14,000	$100,000

Based upon the information above and using the least-squares method of computation with the letters listed below, select the best answer for each of questions 1 through 5.

Let a = Fixed production costs per month
b = Variable production costs per labor-hour
n = Number of months
x = Labor-hours per month
y = Total monthly production costs
Σ = Summation

1. The equation(s) required for applying the least-squares method of computation of fixed and variable production costs could be expressed
   a. $\Sigma xy = a\Sigma x + b\Sigma x^2$
   b. $\Sigma y = na + b\Sigma x$
   c. $y = a + bx^2$
      $\Sigma y = na + b\Sigma x$
   d. $\Sigma xy = a\Sigma x + b\Sigma x^2$
      $\Sigma y = na + b\Sigma x$
2. The cost function derived by the least-squares method
   a. Would be linear
   b. Must be tested for minima and maxima
   c. Would be parabolic
   d. Would indicate maximum costs at the point of the function's point of inflection
3. Monthly production costs could be expressed
   a. $y = ax + b$
   b. $y = a + bx$
   c. $y = b + ax$
   d. $y = \Sigma a + bx$
4. Using the least-squares method of computation, the fixed monthly production cost is approximately
   a. $10,000
   b. $9,500
   c. $7,500
   d. $5,000
5. Using the least-squares method of computation, the variable production cost per labor-hour is
   a. $6.00
   b. $5.00
   c. $3.00
   d. $2.00

24-9. Fundamentals of Least Squares. [Adapted from *Separating and Using Costs As Fixed and Variable, N.A.A. Bulletin,* Accounting Practice Report No. 10] Assume that nine monthly observations of power costs are to be used as a basis for developing a budget formula. A scatter diagram indicates a mixed cost behavior in the form $y = a + bx$. The observations are:

MONTH	MACHINE HOURS	TOTAL MIXED COST
1	22	$ 23
2	23	25
3	19	20
4	12	20
5	12	20
6	9	15
7	7	14
8	11	14
9	14	16
	129	$167

required   Using least squares, compute the equation for the budget formula.

24-10. Rudiments of Least-Squares Analysis. [Adapted from an analysis prepared by Robert Keyes] Assume that train-miles y traveled (and costs) are a function of the gross ton-miles x (tons times miles) of work to be performed. The records show:

DATE	(x) GROSS TON-MILES (THOUSANDS)	(y) TRAIN-MILES
10-1	800	350
10-2	1,200	350
10-3	400	150
10-4	1,600	550

This example is used only to illustrate the methods that can be used for determining similar information. If, as in this instance, the number of observations is small, additional analysis should be performed to determine whether the results are reliable.

required   1. Draw a scatter diagram.

2. Use simple regression to fit a line to the data. What is the equation of the line? Plot the line.

3. Compute the coefficient of determination, the r^2.

24-11. Simple Regression. [Adapted from an illustration in Benjamin Perles and Charles Sullivan, *Freund and Williams' Modern Business Statistics* (Englewood Cliffs, N.J.: Prentice-Hall, Inc., 1969), pp. 288ff.] A random sample of various batch sizes and of recorded direct-labor costs is shown top of page 839:

required   1. Prepare a scatter diagram.

2. Using least-squares analysis, compute the equation of the line.

3. Compute the coefficient of determination.

4. What is the level of fixed costs at zero activity? Explain fully.

SIZE OF BATCH	DIRECT-LABOR COST
48	$312
32	164
40	280
34	196
30	200
50	288
26	146
50	361
22	149
43	252

24-12. Simple Least Squares [SIA]. The annual sales of the Major Department Store, Limited, are being analyzed for sales-forecasting purposes.
Results for the past six years are:

	$ MILLIONS
19_4	8
19_5	11
19_6	9
19_7	10
19_8	11
19_9	12

required   Estimate the sales expected in 19_0 by the least-squares method.

24-13. Perform Least-Squares Analysis [SIA, adapted]. The GH Manufacturing Company makes a product called Z. Some of the manufacturing expenses are easily identified as fixed or directly variable with production. The cost accountant of the company is confronted with the problem of preparing a flexible budget for the coming year and wishes to determine the fixed and variable elements of the semivariable manufacturing expenses.
The following details are provided for the first ten months of the past year:

MONTH	NUMBER OF UNITS PRODUCED	SEMIVARIABLE MANUFACTURING OVERHEAD
1	1,500	$ 800
2	2,000	1,000
3	3,000	1,350
4	2,500	1,250
5	3,000	1,300
6	2,500	1,200
7	3,500	1,400
8	3,000	1,250
9	2,500	1,150
10	1,500	800

required   Determine by simple regression the fixed and variable elements of the semivariable manufacturing overhead based on the first ten months of the past year.

24-14. **Least-Squares Estimate of Sales [SIA, adapted].** Sales of the Popular Manufacturing Co., Ltd., for the past 11 years have been:

	SALES (IN THOUSANDS OF DOLLARS)
19m8	30
19m9	40
19n0	60
19n1	70
19n2	70
19n3	90
19n4	100
19n5	110
19n6	120
19n7	140
19n8	140

required   By the method of least squares, determine the annual trend equation of sales for the company.

Hint: Let the origin be the midpoint in time, 19n3. Then 19n2 is -1 and 19n4 is $+1$, and so on. The values of x in the first half of the series offset the positive values in the second half. In this way, the normal equations to be solved become

$$\Sigma y = na \quad \text{and} \quad \Sigma xy = bx^2$$

24-15. **Forecasting Sales at Different Locations [SIA, adapted].** Sellman Department Stores Ltd. have 40 retail outlets across Canada. Studies covering stores in cities with a population of 10,000 to 400,000 show a definite relationship between sales and population.

The following data have been developed:

1. Y (annual sales) $= \$200,000 + 5X$, where X is the population
2. $s_e = \$20,000$
3. $r = .85$

Market surveys have been made in two cities in which the company does not have stores, and you have been asked to forecast potential sales for each of the proposed locations. The population in City A is 200,000; in City B, 500,000.

required   1. What sales would you anticipate in City A with 95 percent confidence in your results?

2. Forecast the sales for City B and state what degree of reliability you would put in these results.

24-16. **Prepare Scatter Diagram to Determine Cost Behavior.** [Adapted from a problem prepared by Professor James H. March.] You are the factory accountant of Rex Products, Inc., Hong Kong, and you are a member of the plant budget committee. The other members are the works manager, the methods and standards engineer, and the plant superintendent. The committee is engaged in establishing departmental budget allowances for the coming year. One of the problems of the committee is to establish budget standards for in-plant trucking. Formerly the cost of this service was borne by the various processing departments, but in the future it will be charged to a newly formed department, to be called the Internal Transportation Department. You have volunteered to make a study of the labor cost, which has in the past been charged to the natural classification Trucking Labor, and you have tabulated plant totals of this cost and of direct hours and direct-labor cost, as shown in the accompanying table.

		TRUCKING LABOR	DIRECT MAN-HOURS	DIRECT-LABOR COST
19_1	Nov.	$ 9,600	200,000	$320,000
	Dec.	10,000	200,000	320,000
19_2	Jan.	10,000	210,000	336,000
	Feb.	9,600	190,000	304,000
	Mar.	9,800	210,000	336,000
	Apr.	10,000	220,000	352,000
	May	10,400	220,000	352,000
	June	11,000	230,000	368,000
	July	11,000	240,000	384,000
	Aug.	10,800	230,000	368,000
	Sept.	11,000	200,000	320,000
	Oct.	11,200	210,000	378,000
	Nov.	10,000	190,000	342,000
	Dec.	9,000	150,000	270:000
19_3	Jan.	9,200	160,000	288,000
	Feb.	8,400	140,000	252,000
	Mar.	8,600	150,000	270,000
	Apr.	8,200	140,000	252,000
	May	8,800	150,000	270,000
	June	8,400	150,000	270,000
	July	6,400	100,000	180,000
	Aug.	7,600	130,000	234,000
	Sept.	7,600	120,000	216,000
	Oct.	7,800	120,000	240,000
	Nov.	7,600	110,000	220,000
	Dec.	7,400	100,000	200,000
19_4	Jan.	8,200	120,000	240,000
	Feb.	8,000	120,000	240,000
	Mar.	8,400	130,000	262,000
	Apr.	8,600	130,000	262,000
	May	9,000	140,000	282,000
	June	9,200	140,000	282,000
	July	7,200	100,000	200,000
	Aug.	8,400	120,000	242,000
	Sept.	8,800	130,000	262,000
	Oct.	8,600	140,000	284,000

required

1. Prepare a scatter diagram to show the relationship of in-plant trucking labor and direct man-hours.

2. Prepare a scatter diagram to show the relationship of in-plant trucking labor and direct-labor cost.

3. Inspect the two scatter diagrams and select the one that comes closer to a straight-line pattern. By inspection, fit a straight line to the plotted points on the scatter diagram that you have selected. Determine the equation of the line.

4. Answer the following questions:
   a. When wage rates have been subject to marked fluctuation, would you expect the monthly variations in trucking-labor cost to conform more closely to variations in direct hours or to variations in direct-labor dollars?
   b. Which of the two variables (direct hours or direct-labor cost) would be a better measure of the physical volume of internal trucking?
   c. What adjustment should be made in the budgets of the processing departments owing to the establishment of the Internal Transportation Department?
   d. In your opinion, is it an accounting function to determine the budget allowances? Discuss.

24-17. Least-Squares Method of Determining Cost Behavior.   By the method of least squares, compute the equation of linear relationship between the trucking cost and the direct-labor cost of Rex Products, Inc., on the basis of the data given in Problem 24-16. Compare.

24-18. Interpretation of Regression Coefficient.   A manager learned about linear regression techniques at an evening college course. He decided to apply regression in his study of repair costs in his plant. He plotted 24 points for the past 24 months and fitted a least-squares line, where

$$\text{Total repair cost per month} = \$80{,}000 - \$.50x$$

where x = number of machine hours worked
   He was baffled because the result was nonsense. Apparently, the more the machines were run, the less the repair costs. He decided that regression was a useless technique.

required   Why was the puzzling regression coefficient negative? Do you agree with the manager's conclusion regarding regression? Explain.

24-19. Account Analysis and Cause and Effect.   The costs of maintenance of way and structures (M of W & S) are incurred by a railroad to continue in usable condition the fixed facilities employed in the carrier's railway operations. These costs are usually very material in relation to revenue and net income. A substantial portion of M of W & S costs is incurred on a cyclical program. For example, the costs are influenced by the tonnage that moves over the road for periods of up to or more than ten years. The costs are also influenced by management policy decisions and other nontraffic factors.

required   1. What are likely to be heavy influences (the influential independent variables) on the M of W & S costs for any given year? Be as specific as possible.

   2. If M of W & S costs were estimated by simple regression using a measure of traffic (such as train-miles or gross ton-miles) as the independent variable, will the variable-cost portion (the b-coefficient) tend to be too high or too low? Why?

24-20. Explaining a Multiple-Regression Equation.   [Adapted from an example prepared by George Benston] Assume that a cost recorded in a week is a function of such specified factors as x_1 = units of output, x_2 = number of units in a batch, and x_3 = the ratio of the number of luxury units to total units produced. The expected cost for any given week is $C = 100 + 30x_1 - 20x_2 + 500x_3$.

required   1. What is the marginal cost of producing an additional unit of output?

2. The coefficient for x_2 is negative. Why? Explain fully.

24-21. Coefficient of Determination.   Consider the following data:

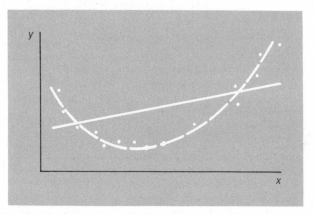

required   If you computed r^2, the coefficient of determination, would you expect it to be high or low? Why?

24-22. Nonlinear Cost Behavior.   Assume that total overhead cost depends on only one variable, direct-labor hours. The actual cost behavior pattern is the nonlinear function represented by curve (N) in the graph. Through statistical analysis or historical experience, we have the four points A, B, C, and D. If we use linear regression or visual fit, we are likely to obtain a linear relationship. Our budgeted overhead curve will be the line (L).

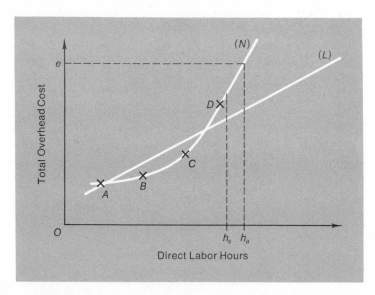

Suppose foreman Smith controls direct labor, manager Jones controls overhead, and manager Johnson controls the whole plant. At the end of the period, actual hours are $0h_a$, actual overhead is $0e$, and the standard hours allowed for the work done are $0h_s$.

required

1. Suppose the budget were based on line (L). Use the graph to measure the amount of the spending variance (call it ge), the efficiency variance (call it hg), and the budget variance (he).

2. Suppose the budget were based on line (N). Would your answers to requirement 1 be different? How? Be specific.

3. Compare your answers to those of requirements 1 and 2. What are the likely effects on the attitudes of the three managers if line (L) is used as the basis for budgeting?

24-23. **Two Independent Variables.** Suppose the cost behavior pattern of overhead is linear but two-dimensional. That is, cost incurrence depends on two independent variables, direct-labor hours, x_1, and machine-hours, x_2. For example, there may be two subdepartments, one heavily automated and one extremely labor-intensive. Therefore, the actual cost behavior pattern is:

$$\text{Total overhead} = a + bx_1 + cx_2$$

where a = fixed costs, b = rate per direct-labor hour, and c = rate per machine-hour.

Using the traditional approach, the controller has examined the cost behavior of total overhead in relation to x_1 and x_2. He has decided to compute a budgeted-overhead function that is based on direct-labor hours:

$$\text{Budgeted total overhead} = a + bx$$

The results for the most recent reporting period appear on the following graph:

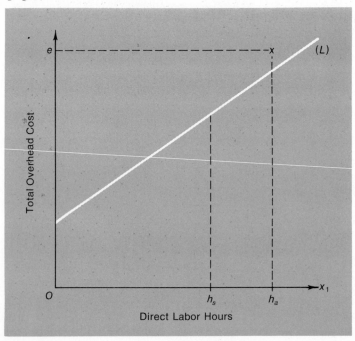

The budget is based on line (L). At the end of the period, actual hours are $0h_a$, the standard hours allowed for the work done are $0h_s$, and actual overhead is $0e$. Smith controls direct labor, James controls machine-hours, and Johnson is responsible for total overhead.

required

1. Use the graph to measure the amount of the spending variance (call it *ge*), the efficiency variance (call it *gh*), and the budget variance (*he*). Which of the three managers is ordinarily held responsible for each variance?

2. What are the likely effects on the attitudes of the three managers if line (L) is used as a basis for budgeting?

24-24. **Selecting an Order.** [Prepared by Joel Demski] Z Company has excess production capacity. The manager is trying to decide between two orders, one for 300 units of Product G at $38 each and the second for 200 units of Product H at $54 each. The cost predictions per unit are:

	DIRECT MATERIALS	DIRECT LABOR	FACTORY OVERHEAD	TOTAL
G	$20	$ 6	$12	$38
H	30	8	16	54

Five hundred machine-hours of capacity are going to be idle next year, so they could be utilized for producing one of these products. Factory overhead is applied at a rate of $8 per machine-hour. Nonmanufacturing costs will not be allocated to either order. Freight costs will be borne by the purchaser.

Further examination of the accounting indicates that the $8 per machine-hour is a firm-wide rate that reflects allocations of central management overhead. Listed below are data relating to actual overhead expenditures for the particular producing facilities concerned. The underlying relationships and levels of expenditures are expected to remain essentially the same during the coming period.

TOTAL FACTORY OVERHEAD EXPENDITURES	PRODUCTION OF G	PRODUCTION OF H	MACHINE-HOURS
$12,935	169 units	41 units	1,279 hrs.
25,918	306 units	366 units	4,559 hrs.
31,821	371 units	453 units	5,947 hrs.
26,367	270 units	480 units	5,045 hrs.
20,513	375 units	166 units	3,486 hrs.
31,736	258 units	513 units	5,737 hrs.

required Which order should be accepted? Explain, showing computations.

24-25. **Special Order and Breakeven Analysis.** [Prepared by Gerald Feltham] The Holman Company manufactures a synthetic fiber that can be sold in its raw state or chemically impregnated and manufactured into cloth. The demand for the cloth has been spotty in the past, but Holman's prime customer (and usually the only one) has offered to sign a contract for 9,000 bolts per month at a price of $160 per bolt. This would be a 12-month contract, and if Holman does not accept it, the customer will go elsewhere. The Holman Company must decide whether to accept this contract and has accumulated the following information:

a. The demand for fiber has been weak during the past year, but the marketing manager believes that the company can sell 20,000 units per month at $80 per unit during the coming year. (A unit of fiber is the amount required to produce one bolt of cloth.)

b. The company has two production facilities, and each has a 10,000 unit capacity. The standard cost of a unit of fiber in each of these facilities is given below:

	A	B
Materials	$20	$20
Labor	10	12
Overhead (300% of labor)	30	36
Total	$60	$68

c. Facility B may be used to produce cloth instead of fiber. If B is used to produce cloth, the capacity is 10,000 bolts and the standard cost of a bolt of cloth is:

Cost of fiber produced in Facility A	$ 60
Additional materials	10
Additional direct labor	15
Overhead	45
Total	$130

Facility B will be used to produce either fiber or cloth, but not both.

d. The overhead rate is based on the labor costs and overhead incurred during the previous year. The monthly data plus the total production (units of fiber plus bolts of cloth) are given below:

MONTH	TOTAL OVERHEAD (THOUSANDS)	TOTAL PRODUCTION (THOUSANDS)	LABOR COST (THOUSANDS)
1	$ 585	19	$ 208
2	515	13	160
3	535	15	166
4	590	18	225
5	570	17	215
6	545	14	150
7	585	20	220
8	530	16	200
9	540	16	178
10	495	10	125
11	505	13	138
12	565	17	205
Total	$6,560	188	$2,190

required

1. Will acceptance or rejection of the contract yield the highest profits? Present the analysis that supports your answer.

2. What level of sales is required to break even if only fiber can be sold?

3. What level of sales is required to break even if only cloth can be sold?

24-26. Analysis of Results of Regression. [Prepared by Gerald Feltham] The Davidge Company produces two products, known as A and B. The following predictions have been made for the coming year:

	PRODUCT	
	A	B
Selling price per unit sold	$60	$50
Direct-material cost per unit of production	$10	$12
Direct-labor hours per unit of production	3.0	1.5
Machine-hours per unit of production:		
Type 1 machines	.2	.5
Type 2 machines	.3	.1
Total sales in units	9,000	22,000
Total production in units	10,000	20,000
Direct-labor cost per hour	$8.00	

No predictions have yet been made for overhead or for selling and administrative costs, but the company intends to base these predictions on 24 months of observations of the following:

1. Overhead
2. Selling and administrative costs
3. Direct-labor hours
4. Type 1 machine hours
5. Type 2 machine hours
6. Sales of A in dollars
7. Sales of B in dollars

A computer program has been used to analyze these data; the results of this analysis are summarized below:

DEPENDENT VARIABLE	INDEPENDENT VARIABLE	COEFFICIENT	STD. ERROR	T-VALUE	R^2
1	INTERCEPT	10000	500.	20.0	
	3	4.000	1.00	4.00	
					.751
1	INTERCEPT	9000.	3.60	2.50	
	4	13.00	3.25	4.00	
	5	20.00	4.00	5.00	
					.872
2	INTERCEPT	4100.	410.	10.0	
	6	.0800	.025	3.20	
	7	.0600	.025	2.40	
					.744

required Predict the total overhead and the total selling and administrative costs for the coming year. Show all calculations and state why you selected the prediction equations you used in these calculations.

24-27. **Predicting How Costs Will Vary.** [Prepared by Joel Demski] You are to determine a set of equations that will be useful for predicting the manner in which certain costs will vary. Listed below are three costs—production overhead, direct production, and marketing—along with five possible independent variables. Determine a "satisfactory" prediction model for each of the three costs. Determine each one separately, and defend your selection. (Note that labor quantity and production quantity are highly correlated; also, marketing is totally separate from production.)

	(1)	(2)	(3)	(4)	(5)	(6)	(7)	(8)
				DIRECT-LABOR INPUT	PRODUCTION QUANTITY	SALES QUANTITY	PRODUCTION LESS PRODUCTION LAST PERIOD	PRODUCTION LESS PRODUCTION LAST PERIOD, THE QUANTITY SQUARED
	OVERHEAD	DIRECT	MARKETING					
1	$11,719	$1,035	$604	81.9	76	100	−24	576
2	11,190	1,071	582	85.5	79	95	3	9
3	11,860	871	565	65.1	70	70	−9	81
4	19,225	1,756	735	132.3	136	136	66	4,356
5	12,876	1,618	591	127.9	125	109	−11	121
6	11,922	1,725	387	130.3	128	91	3	9
7	12,261	1,698	622	124.9	125	105	−3	9
8	11,747	1,804	355	143.8	133	83	8	64
9	11,747	1,725	696	135.1	124	122	−9	81
10	12,057	1,699	609	126.6	129	113	5	25
11	12,771	1,477	636	120.1	115	94	−14	196
12	12,575	1,060	748	83.1	84	104	−31	961
13	11,034	1,088	666	90.9	84	92	0	0
14	14,316	1,597	551	122.4	122	91	38	1,444
15	13,380	1,148	537	89.1	90	100	−32	1,024

24-28. Choosing from Among Independent Variables. [Prepared by Joel Demski] Data relating overhead cost to possible independent variables have been collected for the ten most recent periods and are presented below. Determine an equation that you feel would be useful in predicting the dependent variable (overhead cost) for the coming period. Your answer should contain the equation and the reason you feel it is the most appropriate alternative.

PERIOD	OVERHEAD COST	PRODUCTION (UNITS OF A)	PRODUCTION (UNITS OF B)	PRODUCTION (UNITS OF C)
1	$7792	8	67	45
2	1514	0	16	45
3	1189	12	11	57
4	6670	5	70	64
5	3912	12	37	31
6	3313	12	30	44
7	7857	5	98	65
8	1810	6	20	66
9	8435	1	76	76
10	2671	13	24	53

24-29. Choosing a Product Mix. [Prepared by Gerald Feltham] Early in January 19_1, the president of the Salow Company called together his management team for a special meeting to establish the product mix for 19_1. Mr. Thurow, the controller, provided the following information:

1. Salow has a production facility that can be used to produce four products in any combination. Approximately 100,000 machine hours are available for 19_1.

2. Standard cost information for 19_1:

	PRODUCTS			
	A	B	C	D
Material cost	$3	$6	$1	$4
Direct labor	6	5	2	4
Overhead assigned	5	20	5	10
Total cost	$14	$31	$8	$18

3. Overhead is assigned to products at the rate of $5 per machine-hour. The $5 rate was determined by dividing total overhead costs by total machine-hours for the preceding year.
4. Analysis of the overhead and production data for the previous twelve months yielded the following information:

MONTH	UNITS PRODUCED				TOTAL MACHINE-HOURS	TOTAL DIRECT-LABOR COST	OVERHEAD
	A	B	C	D			
1	2,000	—	3,000	1,000	7,100	$ 22,000	$ 34,100
2	3,000	500	1,800	750	8,300	27,000	38,000
3	3,500	—	1,400	1,000	6,850	27,750	35,200
4	4,000	700	1,500	—	8,250	30,600	39,000
5	3,500	500	2,100	250	8,100	28,750	37,900
6	4,000	500	2,000	100	8,250	30,900	39,100
7	3,000	500	2,000	400	7,600	26,200	36,400
8	3,500	400	1,500	900	7,600	29,600	37,400
9	3,500	—	2,000	1,100	7,800	29,300	37,400
10	4,000	300	2,500	200	8,050	31,400	38,800
11	2,000	500	4,100	100	8,350	23,000	36,900
12	4,000	—	2,000	600	7,100	30,300	36,600
Total	40,000	3,900	25,900	6,400	89,350	$306,800	$446,800

The controller felt that the overhead varied, in part, with the mix of products produced. This variation largely depended on the machine-hours used, but some elements of the overhead probably depended more on the labor used.

5. The 19_1 demand and prices for the four products are predicted to be:

PRODUCT	DEMAND	PRICE
A	40,000	$15.00
B	8,000	30.00
C	30,000	8.50
D	20,000	21.00

The demand need not be met, and the prices will hold for whatever sales are made.

6. The selling and administrative expenses are entirely fixed and are expected to be $100,000.

required   What is the optimal product mix and what is the predicted profit associated with that mix? Show all calculations.

25

Cost Control
and the Analysis
of Variances

Chapters 7 and 8 introduced standard costs and budgets as the principal accounting tools for aiding decision making and implementation. Throughout those chapters, variances were used to illustrate how accounting reports can provide feedback, an essential part of any control system, and direct the attention of managers toward areas that warrant investigation. Variances, by themselves, are useful only if they lead to improved actions. This chapter will explore the approaches to answering a complex question: Given feedback in the form of cost variances, when should managers investigate a process?

Investigation usually takes the form of search followed by whatever corrective action, if any, seems appropriate. Consequently, control decisions are typically based on data relating to the recent history of the process. These data are usually provided by routine performance reports. As usual, the decisions are based on layers of simplifications, assumptions, and incomplete knowledge about relative costs and benefits.

OVERALL DECISION PROCESS AND ACCOUNTING CONTROL

facilitating
and
motivating

Control has two major purposes for the decision maker: facilitating and motivating.[1] For example, feedback in the form of performance reports may facilitate because the decision maker is provided with data that will lead to corrective action. In addition, the mere collection of such data may

---

[1] The ideas in this section and in the subsequent section on the dimensions of the investigation decision are heavily influenced by Joel S. Demski, *Information Analysis* (Reading, Mass.: Addison-Wesley Publishing Co., Inc., 1972), Chapter 6.

have a desired motivational impact regardless of whether particular numbers are used for specific decisions. The motivational aspects of feedback are discussed elsewhere in this book (for instance, see Chapters 6, 21, and 22), so this chapter will concentrate on the facilitating purpose.

dimensions of the investigation decision   Exhibit 1-1 (page 6) showed the relationship of accounting information and the decision process. Control is shown there as the implementation of a decision model and the use of feedback so that objectives are optimally obtained. Feedback reveals variances that may lead to investigation or no investigation. In turn, investigation may prompt correction or no correction.

Suppose feedback—such as a cost variance—prompts a decision maker to investigate the process. One or more of five separate deviations (that is, sources of variances) might have contributed to this variance between actual and predicted costs: implementation, prediction, measurement, model, and random. These types of deviations are discussed in sequence. Note that each may call for different corrective actions.

1. An *implementation* deviation is a human or mechanical failure to achieve a specific obtainable action. For example, consider the economic-lot-size inventory model, which was discussed in Chapter 15. Perhaps because of improper motivation or instruction, a clerk or worker may order the wrong quantity or produce the wrong size of batch. The economic lot size is assumed to be obtainable, given whatever events that may have occurred. Consequently, there is a strong likelihood that the deviation can be immediately suppressed once its existence is determined.

The optimal correction requires that we compare the cost of suppression (which is likely to be minimal) with the resultant saving (benefit). If no other deviations are present, this net saving indicates the expected amount of net benefit (per future period, if this deviation is likely to persist) that will be saved by correction.

2. A *prediction* deviation is an error in predicting a parameter value in the decision model. For example, in an economic-lot-size model, the cost of storage, the cost of a setup, or the total amount of production or materials required in a time period may be incorrectly predicted. (Another example is a discounted cash-flow model for capital budgeting, where perhaps the useful life or the annual cash inflows may be incorrectly predicted.)

Optimal correction in the economic-lot-size model again requires that we compare the cost of adjusting the optimal lot size with the resultant cost saving per period. Sensitivity analysis, which is described in Chapters 13 and 15, will help the manager to decide the potential payoff for maintaining a routine monitoring of possible prediction deviations.

3. A *measurement* deviation is an error in measuring the actual cost of operating a process. For example, a worker may incorrectly count the ending inventory, resulting in an erroneous measure of total costs. Note the distinction made here between the prediction of a future cost and the measurement of a

past cost. Improper classification, counting, or recording produces such measurement deviations.

Optimal correction usually centers on the problems of obtaining accurate documentation by individual employees as a part of their everyday work habits. As Chapter 6 points out, this is an especially troublesome problem of systems design and motivation that permeates all types of organizations. For example, employees are sometimes encouraged to falsify time records so that the true variances from standards on particular operations are masked.

4. A *model* deviation is an erroneous functional representation or formulation in the decision model. That is, the objective function, variables, or constraints may be incorrectly identified. For example, the failure to include a constraint for maximum storage space may be an error in the formulation of an inventory model. Another example would be the failure to provide for salvage value or interest in a capital-budgeting model.

Note that a model error is not the same as a prediction error. The former pertains to an incorrect functional relationship, while the latter pertains to an incorrect parameter prediction.

Deciding to correct a model error usually necessitates a comparison of the cost of correction with the benefits over many future time periods. In contrast, the decision to correct a parameter prediction involves a similar analysis but typically relates to a shorter time period, because these predictions are updated more frequently.

5. A *random* deviation is a divergence between actual cost and (statistically) expected cost arising from the stochastic operation of some correctly specified random parameter. For example, the raw materials per unit of output in a chemical process may be subject to fluctuation because of random variations beyond management's influence. By definition, a random deviation per se calls for no corrective action affecting the existing process. However, as we shall see in later sections, to distinguish random deviations from other types is a helpful step in deciding whether and when to investigate any deviations.

The distinctions among the five deviations above formalize and make explicit the complexities that decision makers face. The manager should be alert for these five sources of variances because they focus on his assumptions about his prediction methods, his decision models, and his implementation. In contrast, the traditional view of a cost variance tends to focus almost wholly on implementation deviations.

THE DECISION TO INVESTIGATE

difficulties
in analysis
of variances
Ideally, managers would like to have an information system that pinpoints the deviations just described into five mutually exclusive categories and that indicates a sequence of investigation that will maximize net payoff, the excess of benefit over cost. Unfortunately, the state of the world is

complex and the state of the accountant's and the mathematician's art in this area is primitive and simple. The overall problems can be delineated, sometimes with rigor.[2] However, the interdependences are manifold and the difficulties of measuring the costs and benefits of investigation are imposing. For example, the five sources of variances described above may not be independent. The time needed for investigation of each source may also not be independent. Furthermore, the net payoff associated with each alternative of when, how, and where to investigate a deviation will depend on the state of each process subject to investigation. Neither the processes, investigations, nor time periods are necessarily independent.

When a manager is deciding whether to investigate a deviation, he must consider the nature of the search. For instance, the time needed for investigation will differ for each form of deviation. An implementation-deviation search may require interviewing a specific worker or his supervisor. A model-deviation search may focus on discussions with the appropriate engineer or mathematician. Of course, the expected costs of these investigations must be compared with their expected benefits before investigation is launched.

comparison of costs and benefits The essential nature of the decision to investigate is best illustrated by a simple example. Consider the two-state, two-action situation depicted in Exhibit 25–1.[3] Examine the exhibit carefully so that the facts are clear.

[2] See Demski, *Information Analysis*, Chapter 6; T. R. Dyckman, "The Investigation of Cost Variances," *Journal of Accounting Research*, Vol. 7, No. 2, 215–44; and H. Bierman, Jr., and T. R. Dyckman, *Managerial Cost Accounting* (New York: The Macmillan Company, 1971), Chapter 2.

[3] The example is based on one in Bierman and Dyckman, *op. cit.*, pp. 36–40. As they point out (p. 35), there are several implicit assumptions, including the following: The decision maker is willing to act on the basis of expected values; incurred costs are reported on a periodic basis, so a do-not-investigate action implies that an activity is continued at least until the next cost observation is available; and an investigation always detects the cause of an out-of-control situation that can and will be immediately corrected.

EXHIBIT 25-1

COST PAYOFF TABLE

ACTIONS: a_i	STATES: θ_j	
	θ_1: IN CONTROL	θ_2: OUT OF CONTROL
a_1: investigate	$C = \$2,000$	$C + M = \$\ 5,000$
a_2: do not investigate	0^*	$L = \$15,000$

where

$C = \$2,000$, the cost of investigation; $M = \$3,000$, the cost of correction if an out-of-control process is discovered; $L = \$15,000$, the present value of the cost savings over the planning horizon, which may be either the time until the process is expected to go out of control again or the time until a routine intervention is scheduled.

* All other amounts in this table are incremental in relation to this action and state.

Suppose the probability of the process being in control (θ_1) is .82 and the probability of its being out of control (θ_2) is 0.18. Then the expected costs (E) are:

If investigate,

$$E(a_1) = C(1 - p_{\theta_2}) + (C + M)p_{\theta_2}$$
$$E(a_1) = \$2,000(.82) + \$5,000(.18) = \$2,540$$

If do not investigate,

$$E(a_2) = \qquad\qquad Lp_{\theta_2}$$
$$E(a_2) = \$0 \qquad\qquad + \$15,000(.18) = \$2,700$$

Therefore, investigation is the optimal action because the expected costs are $160 less than the alternative of no investigation.

role of probabilities The foregoing computation illustrates the critical role of the assessment of probabilities in the decision of whether or not to investigate. A low probability, say 0.10, of the process being out of control will change the desirability of conducting an investigation:

If investigate,

$$E = \$2,000(.90) + \$\ 5,000(.10) = \$2,300$$

If do not investigate,

$$E = \$0 \qquad\qquad + \$15,000(.10) = \$1,500$$

Of course, the level of the critical probability will depend on the relative costs and benefits in a particular situation. In our example, it can be computed as follows. The point of indifference (sometimes called the breakeven point) is where the expected costs of each action are the same:

Let p_{θ_2} = level of probability where E_{a_1} and E_{a_2} are equal

$$E_{a_1} = E_{a_2}$$

Substituting:

$$C(1 - p_{\theta_2}) + (C + M)p_{\theta_2} = Lp_{\theta_2}$$
$$C - Cp_{\theta_2} + Cp_{\theta_2} + Mp_{\theta_2} = Lp_{\theta_2}$$
$$C + Mp_{\theta_2} = Lp_{\theta_2}$$
$$C = Lp_{\theta_2} - Mp_{\theta_2}$$
$$p_{\theta_2} = \frac{C}{L - M}$$
$$p_{\theta_2} = \frac{\$2,000}{\$15,000 - \$3,000} = .17$$

Therefore, in this example, investigation is desirable only if the probability of being out of control exceeds 0.17.[4]

Note especially that variances provide the information for assessing these critical probabilities. However, the measurements of the costs and benefits are unlikely to be provided by the variances. For example, the table in Exhibit 25-1 does not contain the cost variance itself, but the size of the cost variance may be crucial in assessing the probabilities of 0.82 and 0.18.

practical
approach
Again and again we have seen that managers use simple decision models in complex situations. In the area of variance analysis, they use judgments that generally grow from the experience and know-how of the executives involved. For some items, any tiny variance from budget or standard may spark scrutiny. For other items, 5, 10, or 25 percent variances from standard may be necessary to spur follow-ups. Rules of thumb are frequently developed that focus either on the absolute size of the variance or on some percentage obtained by dividing the cost variance by the budgeted or standard cost.

Of course, when rules of thumb or intuition are used to decide whether to investigate, the manager has at least implicitly proceeded through the decision process illustrated in our example. He has combined costs, benefits, and probabilities in such a way that the rules of thumb are equivalent to go/no-go points of indifference.

STATISTICAL QUALITY CONTROL AND STANDARD COSTS

The first section of this chapter distinguished among five types of deviations as sources of variances. However, in practice, the variance is often a simple signal that does not neatly trace back to one of these five categories. Instead, a variance usually provides a measure of a deviation and little more. Nevertheless, because the expected costs and benefits of investigation differ, depending on the deviation, managers are faced with the problem of at least implicitly classifying the likely deviations. As a first step in deciding whether to investigate variances, managers frequently attempt to distinguish random deviations from all other types. This section will describe the general approach to pinpointing random variances. This approach relies on classical statistics.

standard as a
band rather
than a single
measure
The standard-cost accounting system is built upon a set of standards. Standards, in their purest sense, are measures of performance expressed in physical terms—gallons, pounds, labor time taken, dimensions, color, hardness. The "right" standard is generally defined as very efficient performance under a given set of operating methods, working conditions, and

---

[4] Prior probabilities, based on past performance, are subject to revision by means of current sample evidence and Bayes' Theorem to provide posterior probabilities for use in revising expected costs. See Dyckman, "Investigation of Cost Variances," pp. 222ff.

skills. The conversion of physical standards into dollar standards is achieved by applying appropriate price tags to the operation under review. Note especially that the accountant's system views a standard as a *single* acceptable measure.

Practically, the accountant (and everybody else) realizes that the standard is a *band* or *range* of possible acceptable outcomes. In other words, the performance (and costs) ought to be generated by a well-behaved underlying process. If the process is not behaving, it may be economical to intervene to make it behave better. For example, a foreman may expect a machine operator to produce an average of 100 bearing brackets per hour. If he notices that 105 are being turned out the first hour, 98 the second, 103 the third, and 95 the fourth, he may consider such a variation in performance to be *normal*. However, if the performance falls to 85 and then jumps to 120, he may consider the performance *abnormal* and worth investigating. Statistical quality control offers one practical set of techniques for formally distinguishing between normal and abnormal variances.

purpose of The statistical control chart has been developed in the field of statistical
control charts quality control (SQC). The problems attacked by quality-control procedures are broader than the word *quality* suggests. For example, SQC techniques may deal with the time per labor operation or the quantity of material used in a product.

Control charts use samples as a way of isolating operating situations that need managerial investigation. These charts help sharpen managerial control by disclosing current situations—not situations too old for fruitful scrutiny. The programmed taking of samples detects variances that otherwise go unnoticed.

A control chart is illustrated in Exhibit 25-2. Assume that average performance for assembling a finished unit is 10.5 minutes, that the upper control limit is 13 minutes, and that the lower control limit is 8 minutes.

The accountant and manager who use a statistical approach to variance analysis think along the following lines:

> Measured quality of manufactured product is always subject to a certain amount of variation as a result of chance. Some stable "system of chance causes" is inherent in any particular scheme of production and inspection. Variation within this stable pattern is inevitable. The reasons for variation outside this stable pattern may be discovered and corrected.[5]

The control chart helps distinguish chance variances (also called *random causes*) from variances that need investigation (often called *assignable causes*). The analysis of the latter helps to obtain improvements in products and processes. The identification of chance variances avoids unnecessary investigations of variances and eliminates frequent changes (for example, machine settings) that may tend to increase rather than to decrease the variability of the process.

Statistical control charts are applicable to any repetitive manufacturing

[5] Eugene Grant, *Statistical Quality Control,* 3rd ed. (New York: McGraw-Hill Book Company, 1964), p. 3. This is a lucid book-length treatment of the entire field.

EXHIBIT 25-2

CONTROL CHART

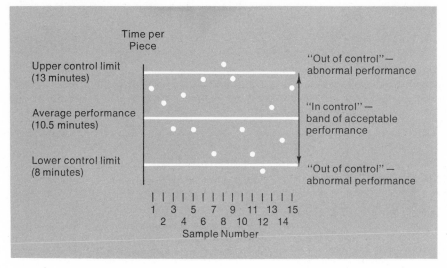

Time per Piece

Upper control limit (13 minutes)

"Out of control"— abnormal performance

Average performance (10.5 minutes)

"In control" — band of acceptable performance

Lower control limit (8 minutes)

"Out of control" — abnormal performance

1 3 5 7 9 11 13 15
2 4 6 8 10 12 14

Sample Number

or nonmanufacturing operation. Examples include billing, filling containers, boring, turning, stamping, using materials and supplies, printing, customer complaints, sales returns, orders received, travel expenses, and the like.

Note that the control chart is very crude. The chart suggests that the manager do either something or nothing. It does not tell the manager what to do about or how to investigate the nonrandom variances.

state of statistical control The control chart helps to decide whether a process (operation) is in a *state of statistical control. A process is said to be in a state of statistical control if the variation is such as would occur in random sampling from some stable population.* If this is the case, the variation among the items is attributable to chance—it is inherent in the nature of the process. There is no point in seeking special causes for individual cases, because random variations are beyond management's ability to regulate or eliminate. With a given process and a given state of knowledge about the process, this chance variation is either impossible or impracticable to reduce. If the performance of a process is considered to be unsatisfactory even though it is statistically in control, the only remedy is some change in the process.

The probability is small that a point will fall outside the control limits from chance causes alone; so it is concluded that the process is out of control when this occurs. When the process is out of control, it is often possible to locate specific causes for the variation. As the first section of this chapter stated, removal of these causes improves the future performance of the process.

Wallis and Roberts point out:

When the process is in control, one may predict future performance on the basis of past performance. Note that statistical control does not judge whether the process (operation) is satisfactory; it only judges whether it is in a state of statistical control and hence predictable.[6]

ILLUSTRATION OF CONTROL CHART

the basic data

Assume that a sample study is made of hand-assembly operation on a transistor radio. Samples of the time spent to assemble one unit are taken twice a day, in mid-morning and mid-afternoon. Four units are included in each sample.

example

Observations are continued for two weeks, so that 20 samples are collected. The results are shown in Exhibit 25-3. Each figure in a sample is the actual time taken to assemble one unit.

Two key figures are computed for each sample, the arithmetic mean ($\bar{X}$, called "X bar") and the range (R). The calculations for Sample 1 are as follows:

$$\bar{X} = 12 + 11 + 10 + 9 \text{ divided by } 4$$
$$\bar{X} = 42 \div 4 = 10.50$$
$$R = \text{largest figure in sample minus smallest figure}$$
$$R = 12 - 9 = 3$$

[6]W. Allen Wallis and Harry V. Roberts, *Statistics: A New Approach* (New York: The Free Press, 1956), p. 496.

EXHIBIT 25-3

MEASUREMENT OF TIME SPENT PER UNIT

Two Samples Taken Daily for 10 Days

SAMPLE NUMBER	TIME SPENT ON EACH OF FOUR ITEMS WITHIN SAMPLES				ARITHMETIC MEAN $\bar{X}$	RANGE R
1	12	11	10	9	10.50	3
2	10	10	9	11	10.00	2
3	13	11	10	9	10.75	4
4	10	9	8	11	9.50	3
5	12	11	10	10	10.75	2
6	11	11	14	9	11.25	5
7	10	9	12	10	10.25	3
8	11	12	10	11	11.00	2
9	13	9	10	10	10.50	4
10	11	9	10	10	10.00	2
11	11	11	11	10	10.75	1
12	8	14	10	10	10.50	6
13	10	11	9	11	10.25	2
14	12	10	9	10	10.25	3
15	8	10	10	12	10.00	4
16	11	10	10	9	10.00	2
17	13	10	9	11	10.75	4
18	11	8	10	13	10.50	5
19	10	9	13	12	11.00	4
20	13	12	8	13	11.50	5
				Totals	210.00	66
			Grand arithmetic mean		10.50($\bar{\bar{X}}$)	3.3($\bar{R}$)

Similar calculations are made for each of the 20 samples.

The next steps are (a) to average the averages—that is, to obtain the grand mean ($\bar{\bar{X}}$) of the means ($\bar{X}$); and (b) to obtain the average ($\bar{R}$) of the ranges. These calculations follow:

$$\bar{\bar{X}} = \text{Sum of } \bar{X}\text{'s divided by number of samples}$$

$$\bar{\bar{X}} = 210.00 \div 20 = 10.50$$

$$\bar{R} = \text{Sum of } R\text{'s divided by number of samples}$$

$$\bar{R} = 66 \div 20 = 3.3$$

standard deviation and control limits In practice, the means (averages) of small samples—samples of four are widely used—are plotted successively on a control chart. These means will approach a normal (bell-shaped) distribution. Statistical tables of the normal distribution will show what proportions of the observations ($\bar{X}$) will be within a given distance of $\bar{\bar{X}}$, measuring the distance of multiples of sigma (σ_X), the standard deviation. To be specific, 68.27 percent of the observations will be in the interval $\bar{\bar{X}} \pm 1$ sigma, 95.45 percent in the interval $\bar{\bar{X}} \pm 2$ sigmas, and 99.73 percent in the interval $\bar{\bar{X}} \pm 3$ sigmas.

As is shown in Exhibit 25-4, the control chart often uses $\bar{\bar{X}} \pm 3$ sigmas as *upper and lower control limits.* Each successive $\bar{X}$ is plotted, and, if they are normally distributed, only about three in a thousand will fall outside the control limits as long as the universe does not change.

Statistical tables are available for setting control limits when $\bar{\bar{X}}$, $\bar{R}$, and the sample size are known. If 3-sigma limits are desired, the detailed work is really finished, because we need not bother calculating the standard deviation.

EXHIBIT 25-4

RELATIONSHIP BETWEEN NORMAL DISTRIBUTION AND CONTROL CHART

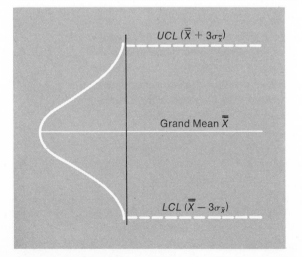

EXHIBIT 25-5

FACTORS FOR DETERMINING FROM $\bar{R}$ THE
3-SIGMA CONTROL LIMITS FOR $\bar{X}$ AND $\bar{R}$ CHARTS

NUMBER OF OBSERVATIONS IN SUBGROUP n	FACTOR FOR $\bar{X}$ CHART A_2	FACTORS FOR R CHART	
		LOWER CONTROL LIMIT D_3	UPPER CONTROL LIMIT D_4
2	1.88	0	3.27
3	1.02	0	2.57
4	0.73	0	2.28
5	0.58	0	2.11
6	0.48	0	2.00
7	0.42	0.08	1.92
8	0.37	0.14	1.86
9	0.34	0.18	1.82
10	0.31	0.22	1.78
11	0.29	0.26	1.74
12	0.27	0.28	1.72
13	0.25	0.31	1.69
14	0.24	0.33	1.67
15	0.22	0.35	1.65
16	0.21	0.36	1.64
17	0.20	0.38	1.62
18	0.19	0.39	1.61
19	0.19	0.40	1.60
20	0.18	0.41	1.59

Source: Eugene Grant, *Statistical Quality Control*, 3rd ed. (New York: McGraw-Hill Book Company, 1964), p. 563.

The table to be used is in Exhibit 25-5. Find the line for $n = 4$ as you study the following computations of control limits:

For $\bar{X}$:

$$\text{Control limits} = \bar{\bar{X}} \pm A_2\bar{R}$$
$$= 10.5 \pm .73(3.3)$$
$$= 10.50 \pm 2.41$$

Upper control limit, $UCL_{\bar{X}} = 12.91$
Lower control limit, $LCL_{\bar{X}} = 8.09$

For R:

$$\text{Upper control limit} = D_4\bar{R}$$
$$UCL_r = 2.28(3.3)$$
$$UCL_r = 7.524$$
$$\text{Lower control limit} = D_3\bar{R}$$
$$LCL_r = 0(3.3)$$
$$LCL_r = 0$$

Note that factors A_2, D_3, and D_4 are contained in the statistical table of Exhibit 25-5. They are based on the concept of standard deviation. Such tables are widely used in practice

$$\text{Upper control limit for } \bar{X} = UCL_{\bar{X}} = \bar{\bar{X}} + A_2\bar{R}$$
$$\text{Lower control limit for } \bar{X} = LCL_{\bar{X}} = \bar{\bar{X}} - A_2\bar{R}$$

(If aimed-at or standard value $\bar{X}'$ is used rather than $\bar{\bar{X}}$ as the central line on the control chart, $\bar{X}'$ should be substituted for $\bar{\bar{X}}$ in the preceding formulas.)

$$\text{Upper control limit for } R = UCL_R = D_4\bar{R}$$
$$\text{Lower control limit for } R = LCL_R = D_3\bar{R}$$

All factors above are based on the normal distribution.

plotting All the data are now ready for preparation of a control chart. The $\bar{X}$ chart is shown in Exhibit 25-6. Sample numbers appear on the horizontal scale, while the $\bar{X}$'s are measured on the vertical scale. First, lines for $\bar{\bar{X}}$ and the control limits are plotted. Then $\bar{X}$ for each sample is plotted. No observations are outside the control limits, so the process is apparently in control as far as the sample means are concerned. If any observations were outside the control limits, they would signal the need for investigation.

The R chart is shown in Exhibit 25-7. Sample numbers appear on the horizontal scale, while R's of each sample are measured on the vertical scale. The process also seems to be in control as far as the range is concerned.

Caution is needed here. Given certain men, materials, machines, and methods, the process or operation may be statistically in control. However, this does not mean that the process or operation is beyond change or improvement.

EXHIBIT 25-6

CONTROL CHART FOR $\bar{X}$

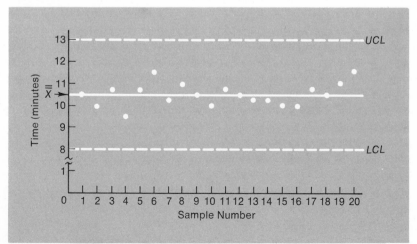

EXHIBIT 25-7

CONTROL CHART FOR *R*

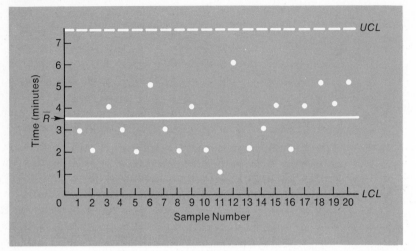

All it means is that variations from an average or standard have been measured and that these variations are apparently due to random causes.

observations A sample mean that falls outside the control limits or a "run" of observa-
out of control tions that fall on one side of $\overline{\overline{X}}$ is a signal for managerial investigation.
Samples may be taken hourly, daily, upon completion of a run, or at any other suitable time. Consider the following samples that are out of control (plot them on their respective charts to see for yourself):

SAMPLE NUMBER	TIME SPENT ON EACH OF FOUR ITEMS WITHIN SAMPLES				ARITHMETIC MEAN $\overline{X}$	RANGE R
21	13	15	12	15	13.75	3
22	7	10	15	11	10.75	8

Sample 21 indicates a marked upward shift in average time spent per unit, although the range is in control. There may be several reasons for this. Perhaps the sample was taken very late on a Friday afternoon or very early on a Monday morning, or the weather was oppressive, or the worker was just learning. Remedial action would be taken as soon as causes for the out-of-control situation were discovered. The conventional accounting system may easily bury such information in a mass of other detail, or the information may be found too late for management either to discover the cause or to take corrective action. The chief drawback of many accounting systems is their failure to produce key numbers that require quick action.

Sample 22 has a mean in control but a range that is out of control. The investigation of such a marked dispersion in performance often finds new and better ways of doing things—methods, motions, machine settings, and the like.

STATISTICAL MEAN AND STANDARDS

How can the managerial notion of standards be reconciled with the statistical mean used on control charts? There are two situations. The first is the setting of tight standards as incentives, a situation in which management normally expects unfavorable variances. In these cases, the statistical mean and the standard will not coincide.

In the second situation, where management desires the standard to be currently attainable, the control-chart mean and the standard may coincide. Properly used, the control chart helps in the setting of currently attainable standards and in the signalling that either the standards are unrealistic or that the operation is no longer in control *in terms of its physical "natural" standard.*

The control chart can be helpful in setting standards because it indicates the random variability of the results and gives an indication of how tight an attainable standard may be. In other words, well-conceived attainable standards will automatically consider average (statistical-mean) performance, either explicitly or implicitly. This performance is based on observations of an efficient operation. Thus, the control-chart mean and the physical standard go hand in hand; ideally, the control-chart mean *is* the standard, where the standard is supposed to be currently attainable.

All manufacturing processes have some natural variability, depending on the characteristics of elements of the process—machines, men, materials, and methods. The control chart helps determine the amount of this random variability and thus helps determine the reasonableness of the standards. Thus, if standard labor time for performing a drilling operation is four minutes, and control charts reveal a large random variability so that many drill operations are outside the standard time limits, at least one of two things may happen. If the source of the deviation is a prediction error, the standards may be revised. If the source of the deviation is an implementation error, the operation itself may be studied for possible carelessness of the operators or faulty machine settings.

ENGINEERING TOLERANCE LIMITS

It is often fruitful to compare the statistical-control patterns of a process against the specification limits as determined by engineers or draftsmen as "engineered standards or tolerances."[7]

example   The diameter of a special aircraft part had specifications of .250 $\pm$ .002 inches. There was much production trouble in attaining this tolerance and a high rejection rate upon inspection. The foreman insisted that a $\pm$.002-inch tolerance could not be attained with existing equipment. The experienced engineer who had specified the tolerance insisted that it could be attained.

To resolve the dispute, painstaking statistical sample studies were made on a typical week's production. Both foreman and engineer agreed that the equipment, tools, jigs, and other requirements were satisfactory.

---

[7] See Grant, *Statistical Quality Control,* for a discussion, comparison, and many examples.

The pattern of results is shown in Exhibit 25-8. The "natural" statistical control limits were ±.005 inches, so all agreed that the ±.002-inch tolerance could not normally be met with the existing process.

Four alternatives are usually available in these situations:

1. Widen the tolerance. This is often feasible and an obvious solution.
2. Buy new equipment.
3. Continue to produce the parts to this tolerance using existing equipment and expecting a high rate of rejects. This solution is frequently the one found where better productive equipment is unavailable and where narrow tolerances are absolutely necessary because of safety requirements or the economic importance of the final finished product. Examples would be aircraft parts or missile components.
4. Completely reexamine and redesign the process. This involves reviewing such aspects as materials, skills, machines, specifications, and methods.

This case showed that control charts may reveal performance within statistical control but well outside the engineering tolerance limits. This would give the production manager or foreman valid evidence of the unreasonableness of the tolerance limits. In this case, chance variation was the reason for inability to meet tolerances. So again, control charts often tell management what *not* to do; it would be fruitless to exert managerial pressure for improvement in performance under the given conditions.

On the other hand, control charts may reveal processes that perform well within the tolerance limits. In these cases, lower-cost alternatives may not be available. But perhaps either full advantage is not being taken of the precision

EXHIBIT 25-8

CHART OF RELATIONSHIPS BETWEEN SPECIFICATION LIMITS AND
STATISTICAL-CONTROL LIMITS

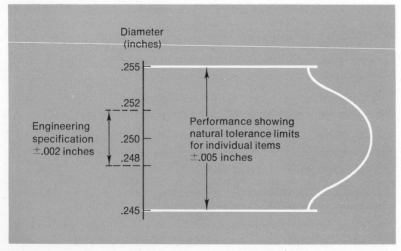

or capabilities of process facilities, or the men, materials, or equipment being used cost too much in relation to the product needs.

SETTING CONTROL LIMITS

Statistical-control limits, as usually calculated, are based on the proven concept that a population of means of repeated random samples from a fixed universe will vary in a foreseeable manner (the normal curve). The control chart implements carefully developed, tested principles. It circumvents the arbitrary, inconsistent features of fitful analysis of variances.

Control limits should ideally be set in accordance with the cost–benefit analysis described earlier in the example on whether to investigate variances. The analysis of Exhibit 25-1 showed that a control limit (the decision rule to investigate) should be set by using the probabilities, the costs, and the benefits to compute net expected costs or payoffs for the alternative actions.[8]

In practice, control limits at $\overline{X} \pm 2$ sigmas or $\overline{\overline{X}} \pm 3$ sigmas are often used.[9] A decision rule of ± 2 sigmas says that the probability of observing a nonrandom deviation from an in-control state is only 0.05. Therefore, only a variance outside that control limit is worth investigating. This implies (see the earlier section on the "Role of Probabilities") that $C/(L - M) = .05$.

summary

Feedback is essential for control. It often takes the form of performance reports containing cost variances from budgets or standards. Variances may lead to investigation or no investigation. In turn, investigation may prompt correction or no correction.

There are five separate types of deviations that cause variances: implementation, prediction, measurement, model, and random. Each may call for different corrective actions.

The decision to investigate is essentially one of minimizing expected costs (maximizing payoff). It requires consideration of the probable states of the process, the costs of investigation and correction, and the present value of the net savings.

In practice, statistical quality-control techniques are often used to distinguish between random and other types of deviations. Decisions to investigate variances are frequently based on 2- or 3-sigma control limits rather than on a formal analysis of expected costs.

[8] F. S. Luh, in "Controlled Cost: An Operational Concept and Statistical Approach to Standard Costing," *Accounting Review*, Vol. XLIII, No. 1, 123–32, objects to the notion of standard cost as a range of cost with firm upper and lower bounds, because such a definition fails to reflect the pattern of variation within the range and does not identify occasional variations falling outside the range because of chance causes.

[9] The justification for using three sigmas has often been hunch or feel: "Two sigmas are too tight, and four sigmas are too loose, so we use three."

suggested readings

Bierman, H., and T. R. Dyckman, *Managerial Cost Accounting*, Chapter 2. New York: The Macmillan Company, 1971.

Demski, Joel S., *Information Analysis*, Chapter 6. Reading, Mass.: Addison-Wesley Publishing Co., Inc., 1972.

Duvall, R. M., "Rules for Investigating Cost Variances," *Management Science*, Vol. 13, No. 10, 631–41.

Lev, B., "An Information Theory Analysis of Budget Variances," *Accounting Review*, Vol. XLIV, No. 4, 704–10.

Luh, F. S., "Controlled Cost: An Operational Concept and Statistical Approach to Standard Costing," *Accounting Review*, Vol. XLIII, No. 1, 123–32.

Ozan, T., and T. R. Dyckman, "A Normative Model for Investigation Decisions Involving Multi-Origin Cost Variances," *Journal of Accounting Research*, Vol. 9, No. 1.

Ronen, Joshua, "Nonaggregation versus Disaggregation of Variances," *Journal of Accounting Research*, Vol. 9, No. 1.

Problem for Self-Study

PROBLEM Refer to the example in Exhibit 25-1. Suppose that C, the expected cost of investigation, were $4,000 instead of $2,000, with the probability of being in control unchanged. What would be the expected costs of investigation and of no investigation? What level of probability would exist of the process's being out of control where the expected costs of each action would be the same?

SOLUTION If investigate, $E = \$4,000(.82) + \$\ 7,000(.18) = \$4,540$
If do not investigate, $E = \$0 \qquad + \$15,000(.18) = \$2,700$

Therefore, do not investigate. The level of probability of being out of control where the expected costs would be the same is

$$p_{\theta_2} = \frac{\$4,000}{\$15,000 - \$3,000} = .33$$

PROOF: If investigate, $E = \$4,000(.67) + \$\ 7,000(.33) = \$5,000 \text{ (rounded)}$
If do not investigate, $E = \$0 \qquad + \$15,000(.33) = \$5,000$

questions, problems, and cases

Note: Also see Problem 23-25.

25-1. Define a *sample*. Is sampling more accurate than a 100 percent count? Why?

25-2. Name five statistical applications to business situations.

25-3. What are some common difficulties in the analysis of variances?

25-4. Contrast the accountant's and the statistician's concept of the word *standard*.

25-5. Describe the basic approach of statistical quality control.

25-6. What does the word *quality* mean as it is used in *statistical quality control?*

25-7. What is the *state of statistical control?*

25-8. "When a process is in control, it is beyond change or improvement." Comment.

25-9. Can the managerial notion of standards be reconciled with the statistical mean used on control charts?

25-10. "If statistical-control patterns do not coincide with engineering tolerances, you may as well alter the latter or else buy new equipment." Do you agree? Why?

25-11. What is the appropriate basis for setting control limits in a given case?

25-12. Why are 3-sigma control limits used most widely in practice?

25-13. "This statistics stuff is O.K., I guess, but my company has a separate SQC department; so, as the company controller, I don't have to worry about it." Comment.

25-14. "The procedure included isolating the important areas of better-than-budget and worse-than-budget performance. By mutual agreement, it had been decided previously that any variance over $2,000 should be disclosed, as well as any excess cost of 2 percent or more." Comment.

25-15. Some critics of conventional SQC techniques maintain that all the original data in a sample should be plotted, rather than just the $\bar{X}$. Why?

25-16. **SQC and Investigation of Variances.** Dick Cleaver is an observant cost accountant for a large tool manufacturer. One month he noted that the cost for a particular machined part had increased to 13.5¢ from about 11¢, where it had been running in recent months. Cleaver investigated the cost distribution for the part and found that it had a material cost of 1¢ and that the rest was direct labor and overhead, which was applied at the rate of $6 per hour. He checked the time cards and found that a new man had been put on the job, but he did not believe that a new operator should increase costs that much.

A time-study engineer unobtrusively observed the worker twice a day for ten successive days and checked with a stopwatch the time required to make six parts. The times were as follows:

TIME PER PIECE (MINUTES)

TRIAL	1	2	3	4	5	6	$\bar{X}$	R
1	1.2	1.1	1.3	1.1	1.0	1.1	1.13	.3
2	.8	.9	.8	.7	.8	.7	.78	.2
3	.7	.9	1.0	.9	.8	.9	.87	.3
4	1.0	1.1	.9	1.0	.9	.9	.97	.2
5	.7	1.0	1.3	1.0	.9	1.1	.83	.6
6	1.3	1.2	1.5	1.3	1.1	1.2	1.27	.4
7	1.1	1.2	1.1	1.4	1.0	.9	1.12	.5
8	1.7	1.5	1.5	1.4	1.3	1.5	1.48	.3
9	1.0	1.1	1.1	.9	.9	.8	.97	.3
10	1.1	1.3	1.1	1.0	1.1	1.0	1.10	.3
11	.9	.9	.8	.7	.8	1.0	.85	.3
12	.8	.7	.7	.7	.8	.9	.77	.2
13	1.0	1.2	1.3	1.1	1.1	1.0	1.12	.3
14	1.1	1.3	.9	.9	.9	.9	1.00	.4
15	1.2	1.1	1.1	1.0	.9	.8	1.18	.4
16	.9	.9	1.0	1.1	1.0	.9	.97	.2
17	.8	.9	1.0	1.0	1.1	1.2	1.00	.4
18	1.3	1.2	1.2	1.1	1.3	1.5	1.26	.4
19	.7	.8	.8	.9	1.0	1.1	.88	.4
20	1.1	1.0	1.2	1.3	1.1	1.0	1.12	.3
						Totals	20.67	6.7

required 1. Assuming that the material cost was 1¢ per unit and that the total of conversion costs was applied at $6 per hour, compute $\bar{\bar{X}}$, $\bar{R}$, and the upper and lower control limits for each in dollars and cents.

2. Draw a control chart for $\bar{X}$ and R, with the centers on $\bar{\bar{X}}$ and $\bar{R}$, respectively. Show the control limits and the twenty values for $\bar{X}$ and R.

3. On the basis of your analysis of Cleaver's data, do you think the operator has been loafing?

25-17. Samples versus Individual Measurements as a Basis for Control. An SQC program is being used to help control material usage on a stamping operation. Samples of four units each are taken hourly. The following three samples are typical of a pattern that has been in effect for quite some time:

SAMPLE NUMBER	COST FOR EACH OF FOUR ITEMS WITHIN SAMPLES				ARITHMETIC MEAN
1	$94	$87	$85	$94	$90
2	82	94	94	78	87
3	94	90	94	86	91

The control limits for $\bar{X}$ are $88 \pm $6.

required 1. Prepare two control charts, using the control limits designated. First, prepare an $\bar{X}$ chart for the three samples. Second, on another chart plot the individual measurements.

2. Comment on the charts. Does the second chart reveal anything that the first chart did not?

25-18. Case Study of Statistical Quality Control. [Adapted from Eugene L. Grant, *Statistical Quality Control*, 3rd ed. (New York: McGraw-Hill Book Company, Inc., 1964), pp. 14–15.] In the kit of tools provided by statistical quality control, the most potent tool for the diagnosis of production problems is the control chart for variables. A course in statistical quality control often starts with a brief introduction to this control chart. This chart was the topic for discussion in the third two-hour lecture in an evening course given in the subject.

One of the members of the class was a production foreman in a small department in a plant that had never before used any statistical quality-control methods. After hearing the two-hour lecture, this foreman, in order to familiarize himself with the control chart, made an experimental application to one of the operations in his department.

This operation consisted in thread-grinding a fitting for an aircraft hydraulic system. The pitch diameter of the threads was specified as 0.4037 ± 0.0013 inches. All these fittings were later subject to inspection of this dimension by go and no-go thread-ring gauges. This inspection usually took place several days after production. In order to minimize gauge wear in this inspection operation, it was the practice of the production department to aim at an average value a little below the nominal dimension of 0.4037 inches.

To make actual measurements of pitch diameter to the nearest ten-thousandth of an inch, the foreman borrowed a visual comparator that had been used for other purposes. Approximately once every hour he measured the pitch diameter of five fittings that had just been produced. For each sample of five, he computed the average and the range (largest value in sample minus smallest value). The figures he obtained are shown in Exhibit 25-9.

required 1. Prepare an $\bar{X}$ chart based on the average value of the observations.

2. Prepare an R chart.

3. What conclusions do you derive from studying the charts?

EXHIBIT 25-9

MEASUREMENTS OF PITCH DIAMETER OF THREADS ON AIRCRAFT FITTINGS

(Values Are Expressed in Units of 0.0001 In. in Excess of 0.4000 In. Dimension Is Specified as 0.4037 ± 0.0013 In.)

SAMPLE NUMBER	MEASUREMENT ON EACH ITEM OF FIVE ITEMS PER HOUR					AVERAGE $\bar{X}$	RANGE R
1	36	35	34	33	32	34.0	4
2	31	31	34	32	30	31.6	4
3	30	30	32	30	32	30.8	2
4	32	33	33	32	35	33.0	3
5	32	34	37	37	35	35.0	5
6	32	32	31	33	33	32.2	2
7	33	33	36	32	31	33.0	5
8	23	33	36	35	36	32.6	13
9	43	36	35	24	31	33.8	19
10	36	35	36	41	41	37.8	6
11	34	38	35	34	38	35.8	4
12	36	38	39	39	40	38.4	4
13	36	40	35	26	33	34.0	14
14	36	35	37	34	33	35.0	4
15	30	37	33	34	35	33.8	7
16	28	31	33	33	33	31.6	5
17	33	30	34	33	35	33.0	5
18	27	28	29	27	30	28.2	3
19	35	36	29	27	32	31.8	9
20	33	35	35	39	36	35.6	6
Totals						671.0	124

25-19. Types of Deviations. The chapter described five possible kinds of deviations as sources of a variance between actual and predicted costs: (a) implementation, (b) prediction, (c) measurement, (d) model, and (e) random. Below are listed some examples of deviations. Use one of the letters (a) through (e) to identify the most likely type of deviation being described.

1. A foreman gets a year-end bonus that is really attributable to overtime that he worked seven months previously. The bonus is charged to overhead at year-end.
2. Costs of supplies are charged to overhead as acquired rather than as used.
3. Costs of setting up printing jobs are consistently pegged too low when bids are made.
4. The salvage value of scrap from production is forecast incorrectly.
5. Normal spoilage in a food-processing plant amounts to 5 percent of good output.

6. The salvage value of scrap from production is ignored completely.

7. A worker is inefficient because of daydreaming.

8. A worker is inefficient because he is new at his job and is just learning how to do the work.

25-20. Decision to Investigate a Variance. A semiautomated process is rarely out of control. The cost of investigation is $300. If a process is discovered to be out of control, its cost of correction is $1,000, and gross savings are the equivalent of $2,500 received at the end of each year for three years.

required

1. Suppose the minimum desired rate of return is 12 percent per annum. The manager has examined a cost variance that makes him assess a probability of 0.05 that the process is out of control. Should the process be investigated? Show computations.

2. At what level of probability will the manager be indifferent about whether to investigate?

25-21. Decision to Investigate a Variance. When a process is investigated in an automated department, the costs of investigation are $1,000. If an out-of-control process is discovered, the cost of correction is $1,500. The manager is always indifferent about conducting an investigation when there is a probability of 0.60 that the process is in control.

required

How large must the present value of the cost savings be to warrant an investigation?

25-22. Statistical-Control Limits and Investigation Decision. Traditionally, control limits, using the techniques of statistical quality control, have been set a ± 2 sigmas in British countries and ± 3 sigmas in the United States. Consider the 2-sigma limits, which imply that the probability is 0.05 of observing a nonrandom deviation when the dollar amount of the variance is within the 2-sigma limits.

required

1. Suppose C is $100, M is $800, and L is $5,800. Would you investigate deviations that lie within the 2-sigma limits? Why?

2. In the decision of whether to investigate, what is the role of the size of the variance in relation to the standard cost? In relation to the potential savings?

25-23. Decision to Investigate a Variance. You are the manager of a manufacturing process. A variance of $10,000 in excess material usage has been reported for the past week's operations. You are trying to decide whether to investigate. You feel that if you do not investigate and the process is out of control, the present value of the cost savings (L) over the planning horizon is $3,800. The cost to investigate is $500. The cost to correct the process if you discover that it is out of control is $1,000. You assess the probability that the process is out of control at 0.30.

required

1. Should the process be investigated? What are the expected costs of investigation and of no investigation?

2. What level of probability that the process is out of control would exist where the expected costs of each action would be the same?

3. If the cost variance is $10,000, why is L only $3,800?

26

Sales Mix and Production Mix and Yield Variances

Most companies produce more than one finished product. Therefore, overall sales plans usually assume some combination (mix) of products to be sold. Analysis of subsequent results should ordinarily focus on any significant deviations from original expectations. We are already familiar with the cost variances for price and quantity. Now we concentrate on the complications that arise when mix factors differ from original plans. The fundamental approach is to hold two of the three major factors (price, quantity, and mix) constant when calculating the third factor. The basic problem is how to analyze a total contribution margin variance as measured by the difference between the total budgeted contribution margin and the total actual contribution margin. Of course, the total variance does not change, regardless of how it is analyzed.

PURPOSE OF THE THREE VARIANCES

The primary purpose of measuring these variances is to (a) identify the impact of controllable and noncontrollable variables on the contribution margin, and (b) pinpoint possible reasons for the variance. Specifically, the approach is:

1. Isolate price and unit cost changes. These are similar to the familiar "price" variances.
2. Remainder is either a quantity variance, a mix variance, or both.

Variances often affect a superior's judgment of performance. The quantity and mix variances should be analyzed in conjunction with each other because the manager is often responsible for both. Where multiple products exist, differences between actual performance and budgeted performance are due to one or more of the following:

1. Changes in unit price and cost, here summarized as a contribution-margin-per-unit variance.
2. Changes in the physical volume of each product sold. This is the quantity variance.
3. Changes in the physical volume of the more profitable or less profitable items. This is the mix variance. *It has economic meaning only if the products in question are interchangeable; that is, if they may be substituted for one another.* For example, a customer ordinarily buys either a luxury model of a given product or a plainer model, not both.

example 1   Suppose that the Arlen Company has the following budget:

	PRODUCT X			PRODUCT Y			TOTAL		
	UNITS	*PRICE*	*TOTAL*	*UNITS*	*PRICE*	*TOTAL*	*UNITS*	*PRICE*	*TOTAL*
Sales	1,000	$10.00	$10,000	9,000	$2.50	$22,500	10,000	$3.25	$32,500
Variable costs	1,000	6.00	6,000	9,000	2.00	18,000	10,000	2.40	24,000
Contribution margin	1,000	$ 4.00	$ 4,000	9,000	$ .50	$ 4,500	10,000	$ .85	$ 8,500
Contribution margin percentage		40%			20%			26.15%	

	PRODUCT X			PRODUCT Y			TOTAL		
	UNITS	*PRICE*	*TOTAL*	*UNITS*	*PRICE*	*TOTAL*	*UNITS*	*PRICE*	*TOTAL*
Sales	3,000	$10.00	$30,000	7,000	$3.00	$21,000	10,000	$5.10	$51,000
Variable costs	3,000	6.00	18,000	7,000	2.00	14,000	10,000	3.20	32,000
Contribution margin	3,000	$ 4.00	$12,000	7,000	$1.00	$ 7,000	10,000	$1.90	$19,000
Contribution margin percentage		40%			33.33%			37.26%	

Suppose the price of Y were changed to $3.00 and 10,000 units were actually sold—3,000 of X and 7,000 of Y:

1. Contribution-margin-per-unit[1] variance = Difference in contribution margin per unit × Actual product quantity

For X: = ($4.00 − $4.00) × 3,000 = $ 0

For Y: = ($1.00 − $0.50) × 7,000 = 3,500 F

Total $3,500 F

The remaining variance is divided into quantity and mix components, using *budgeted* unit contribution margins:

[1] This example has focused on the contribution margin. A more detailed breakdown can be easily formulated for the unit sales price and cost of each product. Then these detailed variances can be dovetailed precisely with the further breakdowns that occur in detailed variance analysis concerning price and efficiency factors. See James B. Hobbs, "Volume-Mix-Price/Cost Budget Variance Analysis: A Proper Approach," *Accounting Review*, Vol. XXXIX, No. 4, 905–13. Also see N. Chumachenko, "Once Again: The Volume-Mix-Price/Cost Budget Variance Analysis," *Accounting Review*, Vol. XLIII, No. 4, 753–62.

2. Quantity variance   = Difference in units × Budgeted average contribution margin per unit

    For X: = (3,000 − 1,000) × $.85 = $1,700 F

    For Y: = (7,000 − 9,000) × $.85 = 1,700 U

    Total $ 0

3. Mix variance   = Difference in units × (Budgeted product contribution margin per unit − Budgeted average contribution margin per unit)

    For X: = (3,000) − 1,000) × ($4.00 − $.85) = $6,300 F

    For Y: = (7,000 − 9,000) × ($0.50 − $.85) =   700 F

    Total $7,000 F

As the appendix to this chapter demonstrates, there are many different ways to compute quantity and mix variances. The method above is recommended because a particular manager's quantity performance on a specific product is not affected by the performance of another product. If the quantity of X rises and that of Y is unchanged, then the quantity variance of X changes but that of Y does not. If products are interdependent (substitutes for one another), the lowest profit center should be at the level where the product combination (mix) decision is made.

Although several theorists have stressed that the sales of each product should be evaluated by using three variances, problems arise when the mix variance is attributed to individual products. Clearly, the manager of an individual product has little control over the selling mix of the firm as a whole, particularly if he is competing for sales with similar products of the same firm. A product manager may have some influence over unit selling prices and unit costs, and thus he can control his unit contribution margins. He may also have some control over promotional and advertising efforts, and thus he can influence his quantity variance. However, he can have little influence over his overall mix. When mix variances are assigned to products, it is solely for the analytical benefit of the manager who oversees all the products that are being evaluated.

For quantity-variance purposes, this method weights all physical units at a single overall weighted-average budgeted contribution margin per unit. For a given change in physical volume, the total contribution margin would be expected to change at the rate of the average unit margin ($.85 per unit in the example).

For mix-variance purposes, this method measures the impact of the deviation from the budgeted average contribution margin per unit associated with a change in the quantity of a particular product. The actual mix produced a weighted-average unit contribution of $1.55:

	UNITS SOLD	BUDGETED UNIT CONTRIBUTION MARGIN	ACTUAL CONTRIBUTION AT BUDGETED MARGINS
X	3,000	$4.00	$12,000
Y	7,000	.50	3,500
			$15,500

Weighted average = $15,500 ÷ 10,000 = $1.55

Therefore, the unit margins attained were $.70 higher than the unit budgeted margin of $.85. This produced a mix variance of $7,000, which could be computed by multiplying 10,000 units by $.70.

A mix variance has no practical meaning if there are no capacity limitations or market characteristics[2] that lead the manager to think that one product is a substitute for the other. In these cases, a simple physical-volume variance will suffice:

Physical-volume variance = Difference in units × Budgeted product contribution per unit
For X: = (3,000 − 1,000) × $4.00 = $8,000 F
For Y: = (7,000 − 9,000) × $.50 = $1,000 U
                                            $7,000 F

The straightforward variance attributes the change in total contribution to the selling of more units of X than expected and fewer units of Y than expected.

DECISION MAKING FROM VARIANCE ANALYSIS

The method for computing mix, quantity, and price variances considers them as independent variables—but surely they are mutually dependent. For example, sales mix is a function of the quantity sold and the sales prices charged, so that if prices change, mix will also change, causing additional changes in quantities sold, and so on. The variances as computed do not directly consider this interdependence.

There are five distinct variables that can cause actual performance to differ from budgeted performance:

1. Direct substitution of products
2. Actual product quantity different from budgeted product quantity
3. Actual total quantity different from budgeted total quantity
4. Difference between actual and budgeted unit cost
5. Difference between actual and budgeted unit sales price

For example:

1 and 2 can occur without 3
1 and 2 can occur with 3
2 and 3 can occur without 1

Each represents a different decision situation for the manager. In addition, 4 and 5 may not be independent of 1 through 3.

The variances attributable to changes in unit costs and selling prices must be examined in conjunction with mix and quantity variances. For example, decreases in selling prices coupled with a favorable product-quantity variance may help assess the price elasticity of demand; increases in unit costs coupled with unfavorable mix variances may lead to lower production of a particular product in relation to other products.

---

[2]When there are capacity limitations or market limitations, the optimal mix is the one obtained through the solution of a linear-programming model.

In sum, none of the variables 1 through 5 will, standing alone, lead to correct operating decisions. In choosing an approach to variance analysis, the manager should stress not only the isolation of the controllable variables, but also their interaction.

CHANGES IN MATERIAL MIX AND YIELD

Manufacturing processes often entail the combination of a number of different materials to obtain a unit of finished product. Chemicals, plastics, lumber, fruit, vegetables, rubber, and fabrics, for example, can sometimes be combined in various ways without affecting the specified quality characteristics of a finished product. Yield is the quantity of finished product manufactured from a given combination and amount of materials. Sometimes trade-offs between the mix of materials and the quantity (yield) of finished product are made. That is, a favorable mix variance may more than offset an unfavorable yield variance, and vice versa. For instance, a shoe manufacturer may try some variations in the grades of leather if the potential savings exceed the potential excessive waste or rejects.

Mix variances will arise when deliberate changes in input are attempted or where humidity, temperature, molecular structure, or other physical characteristics result in various combinations of raw materials to produce a given output.

As the following example shows, there is basically no difference between the analysis of a change in sales mix and the analysis of a change in material mix:

example 2   Suppose a company has the following standards:

5 gallons of Material F at $ .70 = $3.50
3 gallons of Material G at 1.00 = 3.00
2 gallons of Material H at   .80 = 1.60
10                                   $8.10 for 10 gallons of standard mix, which should produce 9 gallons of finished product at a standard cost of $.90 ($8.10 ÷ 9) a gallon.

Suppose, for simplicity, that no inventories of raw materials are kept. Purchases are made as needed, so that all price variances relate to materials used. Actual results show that 100,000 gallons were used during a certain period:

45,000 gallons of F at actual cost of $ .80 = $36,000
33,000 gallons of G at actual cost of $1.05 = 34,650
22,000 gallons of H at actual cost of $ .85 = 18,700
100,000 $89,350

Good output was 92,070 gallons at
  standard cost of $.90   82,863
Total material variance to be explained $ 6,487 U

The price variances are computed in the usual manner:

Price variance = Difference in unit price × Actual product quantity
For F: = ($ .70 − $ .80) × 45,000 = $4,500 U
For G: = ($1.00 − $1.05) × 33,000 =   1,650 U
For H: = ($ .80 − $ .85) × 22,000 =   1,100 U
                                            $7,250 U

The usage variances may also be computed in the usual manner. The differences in inputs are:

MATERIAL	DETAILED COMPUTATIONS FOR COLUMN (1)	(1) BUDGETED OR STANDARD QUANTITY OF INPUTS ALLOWED	(2) ACTUAL QUANTITY OF INPUTS USED	(1) − (2) DIFFERENCE
F	(.5 × 102,300)	51,150	45,000	+6,150
G	(.3 × 102,300)	30,690	33,000	−2,310
H	(.2 × 102,300)	20,460	22,000	−1,540
Total	(10/9 × 92,070)	102,300*	100,000	2,300

*Note that the budgeted input must be that normally needed to produce 92,070 gallons, or 92,070 ÷ .9, or 102,300 gallons. Material F's budgeted share would be .5 × 102,300, or 51,150 gallons; G's, .3 × 102,300, or 30,690; and so on.

The dollar amounts are:

Usage variance = Difference in inputs × Standard price
For F: = +6,150 × $ .70 = $4,305 F
For G: = −2,310 × $1.00 =   2,310 U
For H: = −1,540 × $ .80 =   1,232 U
                                    $ 763 F

Using the framework of Chapter 8, we see that the total material variance is analyzed by this twofold distinction.

MATERIAL	ACTUAL USAGE × ACTUAL RATE	ACTUAL USAGE × STANDARD RATE	STANDARD USAGE ALLOWED × STANDARD RATE
F	45,000 × $ .80 = $36,000	45,000 × $ .70 = $31,500	51,150 × $ .70 = $35,805
G	33,000 × $1.05 = 34,650	33,000 × $1.00 = 33,000	30,690 × $1.00 = 30,690
H	22,000 × $ .85 = 18,700	22,000 × $ .80 = 17,600	20,460 × $ .80 = 16,368
Total	$89,350	$82,100	$82,863

Price variance, $7,250 U   Usage variance, $763 F

Total variance, $6,487 U

The analysis above may suffice in those instances where managers control each input on a material-by-material basis and where no discretion is allowed regarding the physical mix of inputs. That is, there may be a predetermined mix of inputs needed for the scheduled production. Suppose that all deviations from the engineered input/output relationships are deemed to be attributable to efficiency. Then any unusual efficiency in usage results in quantities of output that are greater than normally expected, which is usually a favorable phenomenon. To the extent that inefficiency exists, an unfavorable variance would be generated, because output would be less than normally expected.

Of course, the operating efficiency subject to the control of a manager (perhaps a different manager for each raw material) is only one possible explanation for the variance. Other explanations might include random causes or uncontrollable quality characteristics of each raw material. The point is that in these cases the price-quantity analysis on a material-by-material basis may provide all that is needed for decisions and follow-up by managers because no deliberate substitutions among inputs are possible or allowable.

There may be instances where the subdivision of a usage variance into yield and mix components may give managers better insights for decisions. As in the case of the sales-mix variances, the justification for a material-mix variance must be some sort of substitutability between the materials. There is always some minimum technical relationship that is absolutely essential for the production of a desired amount of finished output. However, there are often trade-offs that fall within relatively narrow ranges, and these trade-offs may be subject to deliberate decisions. If so, an information system should help pinpoint the results of such substitutions.

A distinction must be drawn between complete substitutability of materials and constrained or partial substitutability. For example, shirts may be made of 100 percent cotton or 100 percent dacron or some combination thereof. If the manager has discretion regarding complete substitution, no mix variance is necessary. He should pick the material that results in the product with the lowest overall cost. (We are assuming, perhaps foolishly in this example, that the quality of the product is unaffected by this substitution decision.) Where there is complete substitution, there is no mix problem. Only one input should be used. There should be no mix variance because there should be no mix.[3]

In Example 2, suppose the materials may be blended differently—within limits—without affecting the required quality of the given output. The usage variance of $763 can be subdivided into yield and mix components:

Yield variance = Difference in units of input × Budgeted average price per unit

For F:	= +6,150 × $.81 =	$4,981.50 F
For G:	= −2,310 × $.81 =	1,871.10 U
For H:	= −1,540 × $.81 =	1,247.40 U
Total	= +2,300 × $.81 =	$1,863.00 F[4]

[3] J. L. Livingstone, ed., *Management Planning and Control: Mathematical Models* (New York: McGraw-Hill Book Company, 1970), p. 190.

[4] Another way of computing this variance is to compute the difference between the standard cost of the output and the standard cost of input:

Output:	92,070 gallons at $.90 =	$82,863
Input:	100,000 gallons at $.81 =	81,000
Yield variance		$ 1,863

Still another way is to compute the standard yield from 100,000 gallons of input, which is 90,000 gallons. The actual production exceeded the standard yield of the input by 2,070 gallons (92,070 − 90,000). At a standard material cost of $.90 per gallon, the favorable yield variance is $1,863.

Mix variance = Difference in units of input × (Budgeted product price per unit − Budgeted average price per unit)

For F: = +6,150 × ($ .70 − $.81) = $ 676.50 U
For G: = −2,310 × ($1.00 − $.81) = 438.90 U
For H: = −1,540 × ($ .80 − $.81) = 15.40 F
Total $1,100.00 U

This subdivision of the usage variance shows that if the proportion of ingredients were held constant and 2,300 units less input were used, the savings would have been $1,863, solely because of improved yield of a given mix of inputs. In effect, the yield variance holds average unit price constant and views all units of input as if they were alike. The mix variance shows that heavier usage of more expensive ingredients and lighter usage of less expensive ingredients caused higher costs. In short, there was a trade-off among ingredients that boosted yield but caused average unit costs of the overall inputs to be higher than expected. The trade-off resulted in a net favorable variance of $763.[5]

DIRECT LABOR AND VARIABLE OVERHEAD VARIANCES

Refinements in the usual direct-labor and variable-overhead usage variances may be computed when actual product yields vary from standard expectations:

example 3   Suppose that in Example 2, the following direct-labor and variable-overhead factors prevailed:

	Direct Labor	Variable Overhead
(1) Standard rate per hour	$ 4.00	$ 1.00
(2) Standard rate per gallon of output at 10 gallons per hour	$ .40	$ .10
(3) Standard cost of 92,070 gallons of output	$36,828	$ 9,207
(4) Normal input for 92,070 gallons would be 92,070 ÷ .9 = 102,300 gallons		
Standard cost of normal input (same as 3)	$36,828	$ 9,207
(5) Total actual costs	$41,000	$10,500
(6) Actual hours	10,000	10,000
(7) Actual rate per hour—averaged	$ 4.10	$ 1.05
(8) Standard hours allowed for 92,070 gallons of output	9,207	9,207
(9) Standard hours allowed for normal input would be the same	9,207	9,207
(10) Actual input of 100,000 gallons has a standard yield of 90,000 gallons, which should have required 9,000 standard hours	9,000	9,000

First, let us analyze our usual approach to direct-labor variance analysis. Two variances, rate and usage, are computed:

[5]An alternate mix variance for individual materials is widely used, but it seems more difficult to interpret. The reasoning closely follows that of the physical-quantity method for sales-mix variances described in the appendix to this chapter. Problem 26-10 describes the method in detail, using the data from Example 2 above.

INPUT:	INPUT:	OUTPUT:
ACTUAL × ACTUAL	ACTUAL HOURS × STANDARD RATE	STANDARD × STANDARD
(10,000 × $4.10)	(10,000 × $4.00)	(9,207 × $4.00)
$41,000	$40,000	$36,828

↑ Rate Variance ↑ Usage* Variance ↑

10,000 × $.10 = $1,000 U   793 × $4.00 = $3,172 U

*Previously, this variance has been called an efficiency variance, which is the most commonly encountered terminology.

The usage variance can be further divided into a yield variance and an efficiency variance:

INPUT:	STANDARD YIELD OF INPUT:	OUTPUT:
ACTUAL HOURS × STANDARD RATE	SEE ITEM (10) FOR EXPLANATION	STANDARD × STANDARD
(10,000 × $4.00)	(9,000 × $4.00)	(9,207 × $4.00)
$40,000	$36,000	$36,828

↑ Efficiency Variance ↑ Yield Variance ↑

1,000 × $4.00 = $4,000 U   207 × $4.00 = $828 F

The standard yield from 100,000 gallons of input should be 90,000 gallons (100,000 × .9). The actual production of 92,070 gallons exceeded the standard yield by 2,070 gallons and produced a favorable material-quantity (yield) variance of $1,863 (2,070 × $.90).

At $.40 per gallon, the favorable labor-yield variance is $828 (2,070 gallons × $.40, or 207 hours × $4. In other words, the yield variance represents the labor cost that should have been saved because the material yield exceeded normal by 2,070 gallons. However, the typical usage variance, as initially computed above, revealed an unfavorable variance of $3,172 and failed to disclose the favorable yield variance. The 100,000 gallons of input should have taken 9,000 hours to process into 90,000 gallons of standard yield. The actual time was 10,000 hours, so that 1,000 hours more than standard were devoted to the quantity processed. At $4 per hour, these 1,000 excessive hours represent a $4,000 unfavorable efficiency variance. In summary:

DIRECT LABOR	
Efficiency variance	$4,000 U
Yield variance	828 F
Usage variance	$3,172 U

This variance analysis, like all others, is merely a first step toward directing attention to possible areas that need investigation. Many explanations are possible for these results. In many cases, the failure to subdivide a usage variance into its efficiency and yield components would cloud important information. For instance, horrible inefficiency can sometimes be more than offset by an unusually favorable yield variance. Yet in our example, the $4,000 unfavorable efficiency variance was too great to be offset by the $828 yield variance. Other explanations are possible. The unfavorable efficiency variance could also have arisen because of the nature of the material, or faulty equipment, or a combination of circumstances. Moreover, the favorable yield could have been attributable to special care on the part of labor, better-quality materials, or especially efficient equipment.

The analysis of variable overhead would be similar to that used for direct labor:

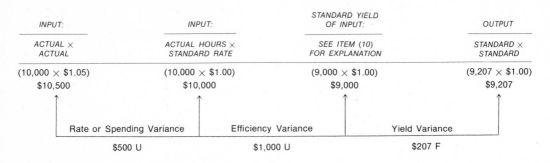

INPUT:	INPUT:	STANDARD YIELD OF INPUT:	OUTPUT
ACTUAL × ACTUAL	ACTUAL HOURS × STANDARD RATE	SEE ITEM (10) FOR EXPLANATION	STANDARD × STANDARD
(10,000 × $1.05)	(10,000 × $1.00)	(9,000 × $1.00)	(9,207 × $1.00)
$10,500	$10,000	$9,000	$9,207

Rate or Spending Variance	Efficiency Variance	Yield Variance
$500 U	$1,000 U	$207 F

Because fixed overhead incurred in the short run is unaffected by efficiency or yield factors, such variances are not calculated for fixed costs.

summary

The previous chapter stressed that various aspects of the analysis of variances basically entail cost and value of information decisions. For example, the size of the variance may influence the decision about whether to investigate. When several products are produced, a basic question that must be faced is whether a mix variance should be calculated at all. A mix variance has economic meaning only if the products in question may be substituted for one another. Moreover, the mix and quantity variances are essentially interdependent, even though insights may be obtained by calculating them as separate variances. Therefore, they should always be analyzed together so that their interactions are not overlooked.

Computations of mix variances are similar for sales-mix and material-mix situations. The objective is to hold price–cost and quantity (yield) factors constant when computing mix variances. Similarly, mix and price–cost factors are held constant when quantity (yield) variances are computed.

When yield variances exist, direct-labor and variable-overhead variances are separated into three major components (rate, efficiency, and yield) instead of the more typical two components (rate and usage).

There are many alternative ways to compute sales mix and other variances. Choosing among these alternatives forces the accountant and the manager to grapple with the basic question of why these variances are computed. The aim is to (a) identify the impact of controllable and noncontrollable variables on the contribution margin, and (b) pinpoint possible reasons for the variance. In this way, the decision processes can be facilitated and improved.

suggested readings

Chumachenko, Nikolai G., "Once Again: The Volume-Mix-Price/Cost Budget Variance Analysis," *The Accounting Review*, Vol. XLIII, No. 4, 753–62. This is an exhaustive article by a Soviet author on the alternative ways of analyzing sales-mix variances.

Hasseldine, C. R., "Mix and Yield Variances," *The Accounting Review*, Vol. XLII, No. 3, 497–515. This article concentrates on alternative ways of analyzing mix and yield of various combinations of direct materials in a production context.

Hobbs, James R., "Volume-Mix-Price/Cost Budget Variance Analysis: A Proper Approach," *The Accounting Review*, Vol. XXXIX, No. 4, 905–13.

Manes, Rene P., "In a Seminar on Budget Mix Variances," *The Accounting Review*, Vol. XLIII, No. 4, 784–87.

Problem for Self-Study

PROBLEM The following budget is the same as the original budget in Example 1:

	PRODUCT X			PRODUCT Y			TOTAL		
	UNITS	PRICE	TOTAL	UNITS	PRICE	TOTAL	UNITS	PRICE	TOTAL
Sales	1,000	$10.00	$10,000	9,000	$2.50	$22,500	10,000	$3.25	$32,500
Variable costs	1,000	6.00	6,000	9,000	2.00	18,000	10,000	2.40	24,000
Contribution margin	1,000	$ 4.00	$ 4,000	9,000	$ .50	$ 4,500	10,000	$ .85	$ 8,500
Contribution margin percentage		40%			20%			26.15%	

Suppose that 7,000 units were actually sold—2,000 of X and 5,000 of Y:

	PRODUCT X			PRODUCT Y			TOTAL		
	UNITS	PRICE	TOTAL	UNITS	PRICE	TOTAL	UNITS	PRICE	TOTAL
Sales	2,000	$10.25	$20,500	5,000	$2.50	$12,500	7,000	$4.71+	$33,000
Variable costs	2,000	6.00	12,000	5,000	2.00	10,000	7,000	3.14+	22,000
Contribution margin	2,000	$ 4.25	$ 8,500	5,000	$ .50	$ 2,500	7,000	$1.57+	$11,000
Contribution margin percentage		41.46%			20%			33.33%	

Prepare a complete explanation of why the contribution margin is $2,500 more than originally budgeted. Include a detailed variance analysis of contribution margin per unit, changes in quantities, and changes in mix.

SOLUTION For X, the quantity sold exceeded expectations; therefore, the quantity variance was favorable. The mix variance was also favorable, because more high-margin goods were sold than had been anticipated.

For Y, the quantity sold was less than expected; therefore, the quantity variance was unfavorable. However, the mix variance was favorable, because fewer of the low-margin goods were sold than had been anticipated.

				SUBDIVISION OF VARIANCES		
	BUDGET	ACTUAL	TOTAL VARIANCE	CONTRIBUTION MARGIN PER UNIT	QUANTITY	MIX
Total contribution margin	$8,500	$11,000	$2,500 F	$500 F	$2,550 U	$4,550 F

Contribution-margin = Difference in contribution margin
per-unit variance   per unit x Actual product quantity

For X: = ($4.25 − $4.00) × 2,000 = $500 F
For Y: = ($ .50 − $ .50) × 5,000 =   0
Total $500 F

Quantity variance   = Difference in units × Budgeted average
contribution margin per unit

For X: = (2,000 − 1,000) × $.85 = $ 850 F
For Y: = (5,000 − 9,000) × $.85 =   3,400 U
Total $2,550 U

Mix variance   = Difference in units × (Budgeted product
contribution margin per unit—Budgeted
average contribution margin per unit)

For X: = (2,000 − 1,000) × ($4.00 − $.85) = $3,150 F
For Y: = (5,000 − 9,000) × ($ .50 − $.85) =   1,400 F
Total $4,550 F

APPENDIX: ALTERNATIVE WAYS OF COMPUTING QUANTITY AND MIX VARIANCES

There is no general agreement concerning how to calculate quantity and mix variances. This appendix will compare the method advocated in the chapter with two more popular methods. In any event, there is no single right or wrong method for variance analysis. The basic guide is to choose the method that is most likely to guide managers toward optimal decisions.

Example 1 from the chapter will also be used here to illustrate the characteristics of the other means of analyzing variances. The basic data are reproduced as follows:

The Arlen Company has the following budget:

	PRODUCT X			PRODUCT Y			TOTAL		
	UNITS	PRICE	TOTAL	UNITS	PRICE	TOTAL	UNITS	PRICE	TOTAL
Sales	1,000	$10.00	$10,000	9,000	$2.50	$22,500	10,000	$3.25	$32,500
Variable costs	1,000	6.00	6,000	9,000	2.00	18,000	10,000	2.40	24,000
Contribution margin	1,000	$ 4.00	$ 4,000	9,000	$ .50	$ 4,500	10,000	$ .85	$ 8,500
Contribution margin percentage		40%			20%			26.15%	

Suppose that 10,000 units were actually sold—3,000 of X and 7,000 of Y:

	PRODUCT X			PRODUCT Y			TOTAL		
	UNITS	PRICE	TOTAL	UNITS	PRICE	TOTAL	UNITS	PRICE	TOTAL
Sales	3,000	$10.00	$30,000	7,000	$3.00	$21,000	10,000	$5.10	$51,000
Variable costs	3,000	6.00	18,000	7,000	2.00	14,000	10,000	3.20	32,000
Contribution margin	3,000	$ 4.00	$12,000	7,000	$1.00	$ 7,000	10,000	$1.90	$19,000
Contribution margin percentage		40%			33.33%			37.26%	

The two popular methods described here essentially differ in how to measure quantities. The physical-quantity method adheres to measuring volume in terms of units only, without regard to the sales value of the units. In contrast, the sales-dollar method[6] advocates the use of total sales in dollars as the best measure of quantity or volume; this really results in a volume measure that gives more weight to physical quantities bearing high sales values.

The method explained in the chapter is also a physical-quantity method, so there are two versions of the physical-quantity method. For convenience, they will be labeled the *chapter method* and the *appendix method*. Their differences will be pointed out after the calculations are made.

Exhibit 26-1 contains an abbreviation key that may help you see the similarities and differences of the methods.

the appendix
physical-
quantity
method

The contribution-margin-per-unit variance is computed in the same manner for all methods discussed:

$$\text{Contribution-margin per unit variance} = \text{Difference in contribution margin per unit} \times \text{Actual product quantity}$$

or

$$\text{PCMUV} = (\text{APM} - \text{BPM}) \times \text{APQ}$$

For X:	$= (\$4.00 - \$4.00) \times 3{,}000 =$	\$ 0
For Y:	$= (\$1.00 - \$ .50) \times 7{,}000 =$	3,500 F
Total		$\overline{\underline{\$3{,}500 \text{ F}}}$

[6]Incidentally, this is the method followed in the Soviet Union. See Chumachenko, "Once Again," p. 754.

EXHIBIT 26-1

ABBREVIATION KEY

APDSB	Actual *product* dollar sales at budgeted price
APM	Actual *product* contribution margin per unit
APQ	Actual *product* quantity
ATDSB	Actual *total* dollar sales at budgeted prices
ATQ	Actual *total* quantity
BACMP	Budgeted average contribution margin percentage
BAM	Budgeted average contribution margin per unit
BMPDS	Budgeted mix percentage of budgeted *total* dollar sales
BPCMP	Budgeted *product* contribution margin percentage
BPDSB	Budgeted *product* dollar sales at budgeted price
BPM	Budgeted *product* contribution margin per unit
BPP	Budgeted *product* percentage of budgeted total quantity
BPQ	Budgeted *product* quantity
PCMUV	Product contribution-margin-per-unit variance
PMV	Product-mix variance
PQV	Product-quantity variance

The quantity variance for each product is calculated in a way quite different from that in the chapter:

Quantity variance = [(Budgeted mix percentage × Actual total quantity) − Budgeted product quantity] × Budgeted contribution margin per unit

or

$$PQV = [(BPP \times ATQ) - BPQ] \times BPM$$

For X: = [(1,000/10,000 × 10,000) − 1,000] × $4.00

            = (1,000 − 1,000) × $4.00 = $0

For Y: also   0

Total $0

Note that there is no quantity variance if the *total* units budgeted equal the *total* units actually sold.

Mix variance = [Actual product quantity − (Budgeted mix percentage × Actual total quantity)] × Budgeted contribution margin per unit

or

$$PMV = [APQ - (BPP \times ATQ)] \times BPM$$

For X: = [3,000 − (.10 × 10,000)] × $4.00

            = 2,000 × $4.00 = $8,000 F

For Y: = [7,000 − (.90 × 10,000)] × $.50

            = −2,000 × $.50 =   1,000 U

Total $7,000 F

sales-dollar method   All quantities are measured in terms of sales dollars. Some essential calculations include the budgeted mix percentage of total dollar sales:

	BUDGETED SALES	BUDGETED MIX PERCENTAGE
X	$10,000	30.8%
Y	22,500	69.2%
	$32,500	100.0%

Computations of variances follow:

Contribution-margin-per-unit variances, same as other methods $3,500 F

Quantity variance = [(Budgeted mix percentage of budgeted total dollar sales × Actual total dollar sales at budgeted prices) − Budgeted product dollar sales at budgeted price] × Budgeted product contribution margin percentage

or

$$PQV = [(BMPDS \times ATDSB) - BPDSB] \times BPCMP$$

For X: = [(.308 × $47,500[7]) − $10,000] × .40

            = ($14,630 − $10,000) × .40

            = $4,630 × .40 = $1,852 F

[7](3,000 units × $10.00) + (7,000 units × $2.50) = $30,000 + $17,500 = $47,500.

For Y: $= [(.692 \times \$47,500) - \$22,500] \times .20$
                       $= (\$32,870 - \$22,500) \times .20$
                       $= \$10,370 \times .20 =$ 2,074 F

Total $\overline{\$3,926\ F}$

Mix variance   = [(Budgeted mix percentage of budgeted total dollar sales $\times$ Actual total
                       dollar sales at budgeted prices) $-$ Actual product dollar sales at
                       budgeted price] $\times$ (Budgeted average contribution margin percent-
                       age $-$ Budgeted product contribution margin percentage)

          or

                       $PMV = [(BMPDS \times ATDSB) - APDSB] \times (BACMP - BPCMP)$

For X: $= [(.308 \times \$47,500) - \$30,000] \times (.2615 - .40)$
                       $= (14,630 - \$30,000) \times -.1385$
                       $= -\$15,370 \times -.1385 =$ $\$2,129\ F$

For Y: $= [(.692 \times \$47,500) - \$17,500] \times (.2615 - .20)$
                       $= (\$32,870 - \$17,500) \times .0615$
                       $= \$15,370 \times .0615 =$ 945 F

Total $\overline{\$3,074\ F}$

comparison   A comparison of the results of the three methods is shown in Exhibit 26-2.
of methods

The appendix physical-quantity method (middle column of Exhibit 26-2)
tells the manager:

1. You have produced the total number of units budgeted, so there is no
quantity variance. This variance holds the other variables—prices and mix—

EXHIBIT 26-2

COMPARISON OF ANALYSIS OF VARIANCES

| | TYPE OF METHOD | | |
| | PHYSICAL QUANTITY | | |
	IN CHAPTER	IN APPENDIX	SALES DOLLAR
Type of variance:			
Contribution margin per unit			
X	$ 0	$ 0	$ 0
Y	3,500 F	3,500 F	3,500 F
Quantity			
X	1,700 F	0	1,852 F
Y	1,700 U	0	2,074 F
Mix			
X	6,300 F	8,000 F	2,129 F
Y	700 F	1,000 U	945 F
Total difference in contribution margin	$10,500 F	$10,500 F	$10,500 F

constant; it concentrates solely on the effects of physical volume, as if the mix percentage in physical units had not changed at all.

2. This mix variance holds the other variables—prices and quantities—constant; it concentrates solely on the effects of changes in mix percentage on the actual quantity attained, without worrying about whether the actual quantities agreed with the budget. The move to increase the sales of X by 2,000 units was more favorable than the move to decrease Y by 2,000 units is unfavorable. You did not sell more units, but of those units you did sell, you had a higher percentage represented by high unit-margin goods. This produced a favorable variance for X. But you sold a lower percentage of low unit-margin goods than anticipated. This produced an unfavorable variance for Y. Under this method, the signs (favorable or unfavorable) will always be offsetting; however, the absolute dollar amounts will not generally be offsetting, as the example shows.

In contrast, the sales-dollar method tells him:

1. You augmented your quantity as measured by sales dollars, which is favorable. Doing so at a constant mix would have given more advantage to Y than to X in absolute terms. You generated more revenue, and because mix is held constant for this computation, both products have favorable quantity variances.

2. You changed your mix. To increase X is favorable. To decrease Y is favorable too, because you decreased the product that yields the lower margin per dollar of sales in favor of the product that yields the higher margin. Of the total revenue, you had a higher proportion of high-percentage-margin goods than expected and a lower proportion of low-percentage-margin goods.

The chapter physical-quantity method seems more informative than either of the preceding two methods. It tells the decision maker all that is contained in the other two methods, and perhaps more clearly:

1. You changed your mix. All sets tell you that, but the appendix physical-quantity method (see middle column in Exhibit 26-2) shows an unfavorable mix variance for Y. This may not be as intuitively appealing, because Y is a low-margin product. Intuitively, to sell less of lower-margin items should generate a favorable mix variance.

2. You augmented the quantity of X, and that was favorable. The middle method (Exhibit 26-2) does not tell you that, but the other methods do.

3. You decreased the quantity of Y. Taken alone, this is unfavorable because your share of Y's market may be declining. Only the chapter method (first column of Exhibit 26-2) tells you that clearly. The appendix method (middle column of Exhibit 26-2) says nothing. The sales-dollar method produces an intuitively unappealing answer, because it shows a favorable quantity variance for Y even though the sales of Y were lower than budgeted.

The primary advantage of the physical-quantity method advocated in the chapter is that *no* variance in Y would be affected by the performance of X, and vice versa. In the appendix physical-quantity method (middle column in

Exhibit 26-2), the quantity variance of X is dependent not only on X but on Y. For instance, suppose sales of Y fell to 5,000 units instead of the 7,000 units obtained. The quantity variance for X would be:

$$[(.10 \times 8,000) - 1,000] \times \$4.00 = \$800 \text{ U}$$

Therefore, an unfavorable quantity variance would appear for X despite the fact that its sales of 3,000 units were 2,000 more than budgeted!

Similarly, in the sales-dollar method both the quantity and the mix variances for X are dependent not only on the performance of X but also on the performance of Y. This is because the actual *total* dollar sales at budgeted prices is a basic part of the calculation of both the quantity and the mix variances.

Finally, the chapter physical-quantity method produces both quantity and mix variances that are intuitively appealing. For any product, if units sold exceed budget, the quantity variance is favorable. Also, if fewer low-unit-margin goods are sold than budgeted, the mix variance is favorable. In addition, as you have undoubtedly observed by now, the chapter method is simpler to use and probably easier to understand than the two alternatives described in this appendix.

questions, problems, and cases

26-1. Define *sales mix.*

26-2. Define *sales-mix variance.*

26-3. Define *material-yield variance.*

26-4. "Material-mix variances and material-yield variances always tend to offset one another." Do you agree? Why?

26-5. Why does the sales-mix variance have economic meaning only if the products in question are interchangeable?

26-6. What are the five distinct variables that can cause actual performance to differ from budgeted performance?

26-7. Material Yield and Mix.   A company has the following standards for producing a special gasoline additive:

50 gallons of petroleum concentrate G-101 @ $.10 =	$ 5.00
50 gallons of petroleum concentrate G-177 @ $.30 =	15.00
100 gallons of standard mix @ $.20	= $20.00

Every 100 gallons of input should yield 80 gallons of PST, the finished product.

The production manager is supposed to make the largest possible amount of finished product for the least cost. He has some leeway to alter the combination of materials within certain wide limits, as long as the finished product meets specified quality standards.

Actual results showed that 400,000 gallons of PST were produced during the previous week. The raw materials used in this production were 280,000 gallons of G-101 and 240,000 gallons of G-177.

No price variances were experienced during the period.

required   Comment on the performance of the manager. Include a presentation of yield and mix variances.

26-8. Material-Mix and -Yield Variances   A company has the following standards:

```
 50 pounds of Material C at  $1.40 = $ 70.00
 30 pounds of Material D at   2.00 =   60.00
 20 pounds of Material E at   1.60 =   32.00
100 pounds of standard mix at 1.62 = $162.00 should produce 90 pounds of
                                              finished product at a standard
                                              cost of $1.80 per pound
                                              ($162.00 ÷ 90).
```

No inventories of raw materials are kept. Purchases are made as needed, so that all price variances relate to materials used. Actual results showed that 50,000 pounds were used during a period.

```
26,000 pounds of C at actual cost of $1.20 = $31,200
16,000 pounds of D at actual cost of  2.10 =  33,600
 8,000 pounds of E at actual cost of  1.90 =  15,200
50,000                                       $80,000
```

Good output was

```
40,000 pounds at standard cost of $1.80   =  72,000
Total material variance to be explained   = $ 8,000 U
```

What are the mix, yield, and price variances?

26-9. Conversion-Cost-Rate, Efficiency, and Yield Variances.   Suppose that in Problem 26-8, the following direct-labor and variable-overhead factors were combined in a single conversion-cost analysis:

1. Standard rate per hour	= $ 7.20
2. The conversion of 10 pounds of raw materials into 9 pounds of finished product should take 30 minutes, so that the standard rate per pound of output should be $7.20 ÷ 18 pounds per hour	= $ .40
3. Standard cost of 40,000 pounds of output	= $16,000
4. Actual rate per hour (averaged)	= $ 7.50
5. Total actual costs	= $18,000
6. Actual hours	= 2,400
7. Standard hours allowed for 40,000 pounds of output (40,000 ÷ 18)	= 2,222

What are the conversion-cost-rate, efficiency, and yield variances?

26-10. Material-Mix and -Yield Variances.   The Azure Chemical Division has the following standards:

```
5 gallons of Material X at $ .70 = $3.50
3 gallons of Material Y at $1.00 =  3.00
2 gallons of Material Z at $ .80 =  1.60
                                   $8.10 for 10 gallons of standard mix, which
                                         should produce 9 gallons of finished
                                         product at a standard cost of $.90
                                         ($8.10 ÷ 9) a gallon.
```

No price variances were experienced during the period. Actual results showed that 100,000 gallons were used:

```
45,000 gallons of X at actual cost of $ .70 = $31,500
33,000 gallons of Y at actual cost of  1.00 =  33,000
22,000 gallons of Z at actual cost of   .80 =  17,600
100,000                                      $82,100
```

```
Good output was 92,070 gallons at
   standard cost of $.90            =  82,863
Material usage variance            = $   763 F
```

The differences in quantities were:

MATERIAL	DETAILED COMPUTATIONS FOR COLUMN (1)	(1) BUDGETED OR STANDARD QUANTITY ALLOWED	(2) ACTUAL QUANTITY USED	(1) − (2) DIFFERENCE
X	(.5 × 102,300)	51,150	45,000	+6,150
Y	(.3 × 102,300)	30,690	33,000	−2,310
Z	(.2 × 102,300)	20,460	22,000	−1,540
Total	(10/9 × 92,070)	102,300	100,000	+2,300

Some discretion in the blending of X, Y, and Z is possible without harming the quality of the finished product.

The general manager of the division is puzzled by two alternative ways of subdividing the usage variance:

METHOD ONE

Yield variance	= Difference in units of input × Budgeted average price per unit
For x:	= +6,150 × $.81 = $4,981.50 F
For y:	= −2,310 × $.81 = 1,871.10 U
For z:	= −1,540 × $.81 = 1,247.40 U
Total	= +2,300 × $.81 = $1,863.00 F

Mix variance	= Difference in units of input × (Budgeted product price per unit − Budgeted average price per unit)
For x:	= +6,150 × ($ .70 − $.81) = $ 676.50 U
For y:	= −2,310 × ($1.00 − $.81) = 438.90 U
For z:	= −1,540 × ($ .80 − $.81) = 15.40 F
Total	$1,100.00 U

METHOD TWO

Yield variance	= [(Budgeted mix percentage × Actual total quantity) − Budgeted product quantity] × Standard price
For x:	= [(.50 × 100,000) − 51,150] × $ .70 = $ 805 F
For y:	= [(.30 × 100,000) − 30,690] × $1.00 = 690 F
For z:	= [(.20 × 100,000) − 20,460] × $ .80 = 368 F
Total	$1,863 F

Mix variance	= [(Budgeted mix percentage × Actual total quantity) − Actual product quantity] × Standard price
For x:	= (50,000 − 45,000) × $ .70 = $3,500 F
For y:	= (30,000 − 33,000) × $1.00 = 3,000 U
For z:	= (20,000 − 22,000) × $ .80 = 1,600 U
Total	$1,100 U

The general manager had been hired only recently. He had plenty of manufacturing experience but had never encountered any yield or mix variances. He was used to analyzing variances in general via the latter analytical framework, but he had trouble fitting the Method One approach into such a framework.

required As a consultant on management control systems, write a short memorandum to the general manager advising him as to whether he should use Method One or Method Two for the routine analysis of yield and mix variances for raw materials.

26-11. Sales-Mix, Quantity, and Unit-Contribution Variances. Suppose that a company has the following budget:

	PRODUCT X			PRODUCT Y			TOTAL		
	UNITS	PRICE	TOTAL	UNITS	PRICE	TOTAL	UNITS	PRICE*	TOTAL
Sales	1,000	$3.00	$3,000	3,000	$2.00	$6,000	4,000	$2.25	$9,000
Variable costs	1,000	1.20	1,200	3,000	1.00	3,000	4,000	1.05	4,200
Contribution margin	1,000	$1.80	$1,800	3,000	$1.00	$3,000	4,000	$1.20	$4,800
Contribution margin percentage		60%			50%			53.3%	

* Weighted average obtained by dividing total sales or costs by total units.

Suppose that 6,000 units were actually sold—3,000 of X and 3,000 of Y. However, all unit prices differed from the budget:

	PRODUCT X			PRODUCT Y			TOTAL		
	UNITS	PRICE	TOTAL	UNITS	PRICE	TOTAL	UNITS	PRICE	TOTAL
Sales	3,000	$2.80	$8,400	3,000	$2.10	$6,300	6,000	$2.45	$14,700
Variable costs	3,000	1.10	3,300	3,000	1.20	3,600	6,000	1.15	6,900
Contribution margin	3,000	$1.70	$5,100	3,000	$ .90	$2,700	6,000	$1.30	$ 7,800
Contribution margin percentage		60.7%			52.9%			53.1%	

required For each product, compute a contribution-margin-per-unit variance, a quantity variance, and a mix variance. Comment on the meaning of the variances.

26-12. Sales-Mix, Quantity, and Unit-Contribution Variances. Refer to the original budget in Problem 26-11. Suppose that actual results show the following:

	PRODUCT X			PRODUCT Y			TOTAL		
	UNITS	PRICE	TOTAL	UNITS	PRICE	TOTAL	UNITS	PRICE	TOTAL
Sales	600	$4.00	$2,400	2,400	$1.70	$4,080	3,000	$2.16	$6,480
Variable costs	600	1.50	900	2,400	.90	2,160	3,000	1.02	3,060
Contribution margin	600	$2.50	$1,500	2,400	$ .80	$1,920	3,000	$1.14	$3,420

required Prepare a complete explanation of why the contribution margin is $1,380 less than originally budgeted. Include a detailed mix, quantity, and contribution-per-unit variance analysis for each product.

26-13. Sales-Mix Variances for Automobile Dealer. Suppose an automobile dealer planned on selling only two models, Fairlanes and Thunderbirds. He expected to sell the following during a given year:

	FAIRLANES			THUNDERBIRDS			TOTAL		
	UNITS	PRICE	TOTAL	UNITS	PRICE	TOTAL	UNITS	PRICE	TOTAL
Sales	4,000	$4,000	$16,000,000	1,000	$6,000	$6,000,000	5,000	$4,400	$22,000,000
Variable costs	4,000	3,200	12,800,000	1,000	4,500	4,500,000	5,000	3,460	17,300,000
Contribution margin	4,000	$ 800	$ 3,200,000	1,000	$1,500	$1,500,000	5,000	$ 940	$ 4,700,000

Suppose that 5,100 units were actually sold:

	FAIRLANES			THUNDERBIRDS			TOTAL		
	UNITS	PRICE	TOTAL	UNITS	PRICE	TOTAL	UNITS	PRICE	TOTAL
Sales	3,700	$4,000	$14,800,000	1,400	$6,000	$8,400,000	5,100	$4,550	$23,200,000
Variable costs	3,700	3,200	11,840,000	1,400	4,500	6,300,000	5,100	3,558	18,140,000
Contribution margin	3,700	$ 800	$ 2,960,000	1,400	$1,500	$2,100,000	5,100	$ 992	$ 5,060,000

The dealer is astounded to learn that he reached his target unit selling prices, unit costs, and unit contribution margins. He realizes that his unit sales were not on target, and he has asked you to analyze the figures in more depth so that he may get more insight into his problems.

required

1. Prepare an explanation of why the actual total contribution margin differed from the budgeted margin, using (a) only a physical-volume variance, and (b) a quantity variance and a mix variance.

2. Which of the two variances in part 1 did you prefer? Explain fully.

26-14. Alternative Ways of Analyzing Sales-Mix and Quantity Variances. Refer to the Problem for Self-Study at the end of the chapter. Compute variances using the three methods described in the appendix. Explain to the manager who must use the analysis why one method is better than the other two.

26-15. Alternative Methods of Computing Variances. A Soviet accountant, Nikolai G. Chumachenko, wrote an article in the *Accounting Review* (Vol. XLIII, No. 4, 753–62) that strongly advocated the sales-dollar method for computing mix variances. He used the following data:

TABLE I

X CORPORATION: SUMMARY BUDGET OF THE SALES FOR THE YEAR
ENDED DECEMBER 31, 19_7

PRODUCT	SALES			VARIABLE COSTS		MARGINAL CONTRIBUTION	
	UNITS	PRICE	AMOUNT	PRICE	AMOUNT	PRICE	AMOUNT
A	1,000	$ 5.00	$ 5,000	$2.80	$ 2,800	$2.20	$ 2,200
B	3,000	10.00	30,000	6.50	19,500	3.50	10,500
C	1,000	8.00	8,000	4.00	4,000	4.00	4,000
Total	5,000	$ 8.60	$43,000	$5.26	$26,300	$3.34	$16,700

TABLE II

X CORPORATION: STATEMENT OF ACTUAL MARGINAL CONTRIBUTION
FOR THE YEAR ENDED DECEMBER 31, 19_7

| PRODUCT | SALES | | | VARIABLE COSTS | | MARGINAL CONTRIBUTION | |
	UNITS	PRICE	AMOUNT	PRICE	AMOUNT	PRICE	AMOUNT
A	2,500	$ 5.50	$13,750	$2.50	$ 6,250	$3.00	$ 7,500
B	2,500	11.00	27,500	6.50	16,250	4.50	11,250
C	500	7.50	3,750	4.50	2,250	3.00	1,500
Total	5,500	$ 8.18	$45,000	$4.50	$24,750	$3.68	$20,250

TABLE III

X CORPORATION: ACTUAL SALES AT BUDGET PRICES

| PRODUCT | SALES | | | VARIABLE COSTS | | MARGINAL CONTRIBUTION | |
	UNITS	PRICE	AMOUNT	PRICE	AMOUNT	PRICE	AMOUNT
A	2,500	$ 5.00	$12,500	$2.80	$ 7,000	$2.20	$ 5,500
B	2,500	10.00	25,000	6.50	16,250	3.50	8,750
C	500	8.00	4,000	4.00	2,000	4.00	2,000
Total	5,500	$ 7.54	$41,500	$4.59	$25,250	$2.95+	$16,250

Chumachenko's approach resulted in the following analysis of variances:

Quantity		$ 580 U
Sales price		3,500 F
Unit cost		500 F
Mix:		
A	400 F	
B	150 F	
C	420 U	
Total		130 F
Total change in contribution margin		$3,550 F

required Using the data supplied by Chumachenko, prepare a detailed comparative analysis of three methods of analyzing the variances. Include a product-by-product analysis. Three methods, including Chumachenko's, are illustrated in the appendix to this chapter. Which method do you prefer? Why?

26-16. Comparison of Alternative Ways of Analyzing Sales-Mix and Quantity Variances. Mac's Marina is a retail company that sells boats and other water-sport equipment during the summer months. Until recently, the winters have been almost totally nonproductive. But three years ago, the proprietor of Mac's Marina, Mr. McSundem, started selling snowmobiles. Sales have climbed steadily; last year they comprised 40 percent of the total sales. Being unfamiliar with the snowmobile business, Mr. McSundem has some problems along with his success.

The snowmobile sales season is short; 95 percent of the sales take place in November, December, and January. During the season, the sales effort takes all Mr. McSundem's time, so none is left for planning. Because of this, an overall plan for snowmobile sales is formulated during October. This plan is then compared with the actual results in February. From this comparison, Mr. McSundem hopes to improve his plan for next year's sales.

Mac's Marina sells only Snomoco brand snowmobiles, with two models, the Bobcat and the Wolverine. Before the recently completed snowmobile season, he developed the following budget:

	BOBCAT			WOLVERINE			TOTAL		
	UNITS	PRICE	TOTAL	UNITS	PRICE	TOTAL	UNITS	PRICE	TOTAL
Sales	25	$900	$22,500	225	$500	$112,500	250	$540	$135,000
Variable costs	25	540	13,500	225	400	90,000	250	414	103,500
Contribution margin	25	$360	$ 9,000	225	$100	$ 22,500	250	$126	$ 31,500
Contribution margin percentage		40%*			20%			23.33%	
Sales-dollar percentage			16.67%**			83.33%			100%
Physical-volume percentage	10%			90%			100%		

* $360 ÷ $900 = 40%
** $22,500 ÷ $135,000 = 16.67%

When the results were analyzed in February, Mr. McSundem found that he had sold exactly the 250 snowmobiles that he had planned. But other than that, the results were quite different than planned, as shown below:

	BOBCAT			WOLVERINE			TOTAL		
	UNITS	PRICE	TOTAL	UNITS	PRICE	TOTAL	UNITS	PRICE	TOTAL
Sales	75	$875	$65,625	175	$500	$87,500	250	$612	$153,125
Variable costs	75	540	40,500	175	400	70,000	250	442	110,500
Contribution margin	75	$335	$25,125	175	$100	$17,500	250	$170	$ 42,625
Contribution margin percentage		38.29%			20%			27.78%	
Sales-dollar percentage			42%			58%			100%
Physical-volume percentage	30%			70%			100%		

Mr. McSundem remembered from a management course that there was a method for analyzing variances when multiple products were sold. So he bought the latest book on cost accounting. From this he learned that there are at least three ways to divide the total variance in contribution margin. An abbreviation key (Exhibit 26-1 in the chapter) was developed to facilitate comparisons among the three methods.

I. Physical-Quantity Method One (note that this is the so-called appendix method):

A. Contribution-margin-per-unit-variance $=$ Difference in contribution margin per unit × Actual product quantity

or

$$PCMUV = (APM - BPM) \times APQ$$

Bobcat: $PCMUV = (\$335 - \$360) \times 75$

$PCMUV = -\$25 \times 75 = \$1,875 \text{ U}$

Wolverine: None

B. Quantity variance   = [(Budgeted mix percentage × Actual total quantity) − Budgeted product quantity] × Budgeted contribution margin per unit

or

$$PQV = [(BPP \times ATQ) - BPQ] \times BPM$$
Bobcat: $PQV = [(.10 \times 250) - 25] \times \$360$
            $PQV = (25 - 25) \times \$360 = 0$
Wolverine: Also zero

Note that there is no quantity variance if the *total* units budgeted equal the *total* units actually sold.

C. Mix variance   = [Actual product quantity − (Budgeted mix percentage × Actual total quantity)] × Budgeted contribution margin per unit

or

$$PMV = [APQ - (BPP \times ATQ)] \times BPM$$
Bobcat: $PMV = [75 - (.10 \times 250)] \times \$360$
            $PMV = 50 \times \$360 = \$18,000$ F

Wolverine: $PMV = [175 - (.90 \times 250)] \times \$100$
            $PMV = -50 \times \$100 = \$5,000$ U

II. Physical-Quantity Method Two (note that this is the chapter method):

A. Contribution-margin-per-unit variance   = Same as Method One = $1,875 U

B. Quantity variance   = Difference in units × Budgeted average contribution margin per unit

or

$$PQV = (APQ - BPQ) \times BAM$$
Bobcat: $PQV = (75 - 25) \times \$126 \quad = \$6,300$ F
Wolverine: $PQV = (175 - 225) \times \$126 = \quad 6,300$ U
                                        $\overline{\$ \quad 0}$

C. Mix variance   = Difference in units × (Budgeted product contribution margin per unit − Budgeted average contribution margin per unit)

or

$$PMV = (APQ - BPQ) \times (BPM - BAM)$$
Bobcat: $PMV = (75 - 25) \times (\$360 - \$126) \quad = \$11,700$ F
Wolverine: $PMV = (175 - 225) \times (\$100 - \$126) = \quad 1,300$ F
Total $\overline{\$13,000 \text{ F}}$

III. Sales-Dollar Method

A. Contribution-margin-per-unit variance = Same as other methods = $1,875 U

B. Quantity variance = [(Budgeted mix percentage of budgeted total dollar sales × Actual total dollar sales at budgeted prices) − Budgeted product dollar sales at budgeted price] × Budgeted product contribution margin percentage

or

PQV = [(BMPDS × ATDSB) − BPDSB] × BPCMP

Bobcat: PQV = [(.1667 × $155,000) − $22,500] × .40
PQV = ($25,833 − $22,500) × .40 = $1,333 F

Wolverine: PQV = [(.8333 × $155,000) − $112,500] × .20
PQV = ($129,167 − $112,500) × .20 = $3,333 F

C. Mix variance = [(Budgeted mix percentage of budgeted total dollar sales × Actual total dollar sales at budgeted prices) − Actual product dollar sales at budgeted price] × (Budgeted average contribution margin percentage − Budgeted product contribution margin percentage)

or

PMV = [(BMPDS × ATDSB) − APDSB] × (BACMP − BPCMP)

Bobcat: PMV = [(.1667 × $155,000) − $67,500] × (.2333 − .40)
PMV = −$41,667 × (.2333 − .40)
PMV = −$41,667 × −.1667 = $6,945 F

Wolverine: PMV = [(.8333 × $155,00) − $87,500] × (.2333 − .20)
PMV = $41,667 × (.2333 − .20)
PMV = $41,667 × .0333 = $1,389 F

A comparison of the results of the three methods follows:

	METHOD		
	PHYSICAL QUANTITY		
	METHOD ONE	METHOD TWO	SALES DOLLAR
Type of variance:			
Contribution margin per unit			
Bobcat	$ 1,875 U	$ 1,875 U	$ 1,875 U
Wolverine	0	0	0
Quantity			
Bobcat	0	6,300 F	1,333 F
Wolverine	0	6,300 U	3,333 F
Mix			
Bobcat	18,000 F	11,700 F	6,945 F
Wolverine	5,000 U	1,300 F	1,389 F
Total difference in contribution margin	$11,125 F	$11,125 F	$11,125 F

Mr. McSundem was very confused by the different figures produced by the three methods. He has asked you to help him use these figures correctly.

required   Prepare a report for Mr. McSunden explaining the essential differences among these three methods. Also explain which figures will be the most useful in analyzing this year's results and planning for next year. Convince Mr. McSundem that the method you choose is indeed better than the other two.

27

Cost Accounting and Mathematics

We shall now briefly reexamine modern cost accounting, particularly as it relates to mathematics, and with special attention to the field of operations research. This chapter is in the nature of a survey; technical competence in mathematics can be achieved only by specialized study.

The problems at the end of the chapter are divided into two main categories. The first set is suitable for students who have studied this book and who have minimal training in mathematics; the second is a variety of cost-accounting material, some of which requires a knowledge of mathematics not covered in this text.

MODERN COST ACCOUNTING

Cost accounting provides information for several purposes. These purposes were discussed in detail in Chapters 1 and 6, so they will not be explored in depth here. A major role of the management accountant is to design and improve information systems for executive decision making and implementation. In order to do this, the accountant must be aware that accounting-systems design has a vital interrelationship with other areas, such as engineering, statistics, mathematics, economics, organization theory, decision theory, and social psychology. This awareness does not imply that the cost accountant must be a master in all fields. But it does mean he should be broad-minded enough to recognize that other fields contain approaches and techniques that may be pertinent to some of his problems.

Earlier chapters offered examples of interrelationships among business fields: industrial engineering and setting standards; analysis of variances and statistical quality control; budgets, motivation, and psychology; theory of probability and predicting future data; controllership and operating management. Some accountants rigidly maintain that these interrelationships are "not accounting" and therefore are of little concern to the cost accountant. This unrealistic view implies that accounting is an art that should be practiced for its own sake and that business operations are heavily compartmentalized with practically no interaction between functions. However, the cost accountant is most effective when he is highly conscious of these interrelationships. Whether he becomes aware of them through management books, accounting books, engineering books, or on-the-job training does not really matter.

Chapter 23 discussed the role of mathematical models and decision theory. As management decisions are more closely studied, they become subject to more sophisticated models that tend to employ more mathematics. Examples are discounted cash-flow models for capital budgeting and multiple-regression models for the estimating of cost functions. The accountant must obviously be able to cope with the models and the related accounting system. In fact, decision theory provides a useful framework for the accountant as he makes his judgments about the *what, where, when, whom,* and *how* questions concerning the accounting system.

The remainder of this chapter will discuss *operations research* in relation to cost accounting.

OPERATIONS RESEARCH

definition   *Operations research* (abbreviated hereafter as OR) is a diffused collection of mathematical and statistical models that are applied to decision making.[1] It is anchored to decision theory; has an overall approach; uses mixed teams of engineers, statisticians, mathematicians, and, to a lesser extent, accountants; and uses mathematical and statistical models as a framework for analysis. OR is primarily a tool for *planning* rather than *controlling;* that is, it is a rigorous means for discovering feasible alternatives, evaluating them, and choosing the best alternative.

OR techniques   Mathematical and statistical techniques are the principal tools used by OR men for constructing and testing their models. These techniques include

---

[1] Operations research is sometimes referred to as *management science.* The distinction between the two is fuzzy. Management science is a broader concept, in the sense that it embraces computer technology as a science, in addition to operations research. For example, the management-science division of one large public accounting firm has two major departments: "Operations Research" and "Computers," Operations-research techniques were developed initially in England during World War II. Groups of physicists, chemists, statisticians, mathematicians, and military commanders combined their talents to solve complex problems. Examples include problems of optimal bombing-group sizes, convoy sizes and patterns, and schedules for repairing aircraft engines.

linear programming, correlation, and an extensive batch of *probabilistic models.* Linear programming is the most widely used OR technique; it is discussed in a later section of this chapter. Correlation techniques are used to discover and evaluate possible cause-and-effect relationships. These techniques have been used most widely in trying to solve problems of utilizing advertising and selling efforts. In many cases, arbitrary methods of setting advertising and sales-promotion budgets as fixed percentages of sales are being replaced by tested formulas based on mathematical equations containing many variables.

Most of the analytical techniques used in OR make heavy use of statistical probability theory to deal explicitly with the uncertainty that plagues management. The models so developed are often called *probabilistic models.* Applications include the inventory-control and statistical quality-control problems that were discussed in Chapters 15, 23, and 25. For example, complex problems of how much inventory to stock, where to stock, and when to stock have been successfully solved by OR specialists.

Another example of probabilistic models is *waiting-line* or *queuing theory,* which deals with the problem of supplying sufficient facilities to meet the needs of things or individuals that demand service in uneven spurts: cars at a toll booth, boats at landing docks, machines awaiting a limited number of repairmen. There are a vast number of variables in these problems, each combination of which requires separate mathematical analysis. These variables include different probability distributions for arrivals and for service times, number of facilities, servicing order, priorities, and so on.

One of the ingredients of the decision is computation of the waiting-time costs. Although the cost of operating extra facilities (having an extra repairman or bank teller) may be obtainable from regular accounting data, the cost of waiting may not be so easy to obtain. Measuring the dollar loss if prospective customers leave or never appear is difficult and often nearly impossible. OR men maintain that waiting-line analysis will be more likely to yield optimum results than mere haphazard selection of required facilities.

PERT (Program Evaluation and Review Technique) is a formal, probabilistic diagram of the interrelationships of a complex time series of activities. Its objective is to discover potential bottlenecks and to chart progress. PERT was initially used in missile research and development, where time estimates are considered crucial. Many military contracts now specify that PERT must be used. PERT is also very popular in the construction industry. When PERT is combined with costs to determine optimum trade-offs between time and costs, it is called PERT-COST.

Simulation is the formulation of a detailed model of a system or process. It is valuable because it permits experimentation with different alternatives before a final course of action is selected.

Normal and Poisson distributions are widely used in model building by statisticians. The data may then be tested repeatedly on a digital computer and average expected results obtained.

However, because normal and Poisson distributions often do not adequately describe the distribution of demand met in practice, a simulation is not necessarily repeated over and over and then averaged. In inventory-control models, for example, a company's historical demand data may be fed into a simulation; the ingredients (combinations of various stock levels, purchase-order sizes, and sales) of the model may then be manipulated until the best (optimal) set is discovered. The solution can then be tested on a separate set of historical demand data, preferably from a different year.

Dynamic programming is a technique for optimizing the overall effect of a time sequence of interrelated decisions, basically by working backward from the last point to the first point in a complex network of decisions.

the accountant and OR   The modern cost accountant has many traits of the OR practitioner. He recognizes that different costs are applicable for different purposes, that probability theory and statistical tools may be helpful with certain problems, and that an overall, formalized, "scientific" approach to business problems is extremely helpful. In other words, the modern managerial accountant already has the OR approach and, in fact, may hold the key to OR's ultimate success or failure. Why? Because OR models and solutions, despite awesome matrices, equations, inequations, payoff tables, and utility measures, are dependent on the reliability of the data used. Much of this information is furnished by the accountant. In cases where the accounting system cannot be the cornerstone for supplying data, the OR specialist will often be constructing a less reliable and hence less useful model.

LINEAR PROGRAMMING

definition   Linear programming is a powerful mathematical method for selecting an optimum plan; it is an efficient search procedure for computing the best solution to certain business problems that contain many interacting variables and that essentially involve selecting the combination of resources that maximizes profits or minimizes costs.[2] In many cases of linear programming, the goal is to maximize the total profit for a given total of scarce resources. There are nearly always scarce resources that are constraints (also called *restraints* or *restrictions*) on available alternatives. Examples of linear-programming applications include determination of optimal product mixes, material mixes, machine and manpower combinations; utilization of storage or shipping facilities; and, in general, combining of manpower, materials, and facilities to best advantage when all the relationships are approximately linear and many combinations are possible. More specifically, practical applications have been successfully applied in designing transformers, scheduling flight crews, blending gasoline, formulating shipping schedules, routing production, and selecting transportation routes.

[2] The desired objective in a specific case may be one of a number of possibilities: sales maximization, minimization of idle time, maximum utilization of a particular machine, and so on.

In practical situations, most linear-programming problems are solved by digital computers, because the number of variables is vastly greater than that used in the example we shall consider.

the techniques, the accountant, and the manager   All of us are more or less familiar with linear equations (for example, $X + 3 = 9$). We also know that simultaneous linear equations become progressively more difficult to solve with pencil and paper as the number of unknowns increases. Linear programming essentially involves: (a) constructing a set of simultaneous linear equations, which represent the model of the problem and which include many variables; and (b) solving the equations with the help of the digital computer.

The formulation of the equations—that is, the building of the model—is far more challenging than the mechanics of the solution. The model must be a valid and accurate portrayal of the problem. Computer programmers can then take the equations and process the solution.

As a minimum, accountants and executives should be able to recognize the types of problems in their organizations that are most susceptible to analysis by linear programming. They should also be able to help in the construction of the model—that is, in specifying the objectives, the constraints, and the variables. Ideally, they should understand the mathematics and should be able to talk comfortably with the operations researchers who are attempting to express their problem mathematically. However, the position taken here is that the accountant and the manager should concentrate on the formulation of the model and not worry too much about the technical intricacies of the solution. The latter may be delegated to the mathematicians; the ability to delegate the former is highly doubtful.

example   Consider a company that has two departments, machining and finishing. This plant makes two products, each of which requires processing in each of the two departments. Relevant data are summarized as follows:

	CAPACITIES (PER DAY) IN UNITS		CONTRIBUTION MARGIN PER UNIT
PRODUCTS	DEPT. 1 MACHINING	DEPT. 2 FINISHING	
A	200	120	$2.00
or			
B	100	200	$2.50

Severe material shortages for Product B will limit its production to a maximum of 90 per day. How many units of each product should be produced to obtain the maximum profit?

Two underlying assumptions are necessary for using linear-programming techniques. First, all relationships between capacity and the amounts produced are linear; that is, these relationships can be demonstrated graphically by straight lines rather than by curves. Second, all factors and relationships are stated with certainty; in other words, all ingredients of the situation are assumed to be certain rather than uncertain or probable.[3]

The linear-programming approach has the following basic pattern, although variations and short cuts are available in unique situations:

1. Determine objectives. Usually this takes some form of either maximization of profit or minimization of cost. Technically, this objective is called an *objective function*, a figure of merit, or a measure of effectiveness.
2. Determine basic relationships in the situation, especially the constraints.
3. Determine available *feasible* alternatives.
4. Compute the optimum solution. Techniques may vary here. In uncomplicated situations, the graphic approach is easiest to see. However, algebraic approaches are more widely used in practice.

Using our example, let's apply these steps.

1. *Determine objectives.* The objective here will be to find the product combination that maximizes *total* contribution margin. This can be expressed in equation form as follows: $2.00A + $2.50B = Total contribution margin. We want to maximize this objective function.
2. *Determine basic relationships.* The relationships here can be depicted by inequalities as follows:

Department 1:	$A + 2B \leq 200$
Department 2:	$A + .6B \leq 120$
Material shortage for Product B:	$B \leq 90$
Because negative production is impossible,	$B \geq 0$ and $A \geq 0$

The three solid lines on the graph in Exhibit 27-1 will aid visualization of the existing constraints for Departments 1 and 2 and of the material shortage.

3. *Determine available feasible alternatives.* The feasible alternatives are those that are technically possible. We do not want to bother with useless computations for impossible alternatives. The shaded area in Exhibit 27-1 shows the boundaries of those product combinations that are feasible.
4. *Compute optimum solution.* In steps 2 and 3 we have concentrated on physical relationships alone. Now we return to the economic relationships expressed as the objective in step 1. We test various feasible product combinations to see which one maximizes the total contribution margin.

In the graphic solution, we are fortunate because the optimum solution must lie on one of the corners of the "Area of feasible product combinations." Methods exist for moving from one corner to another to see if the total contribution is improved. This procedure is continued until the optimum solution is found. In this case, the optimum corner shows that the best combination is 86 units of A plus 57 units of B.

The same result can be accomplished algebraically, usually by working with the corners of the polygon. The steps are simple:

a. Start with a possible combination.
b. Compute the profit.
c. Move to another possible combination to see if it will improve the result

---

[3]However, probabilities may be used to forecast the specific data used in the construction of the linear-programming model.

EXHIBIT 27-1

LINEAR PROGRAMMING—GRAPHIC SOLUTION

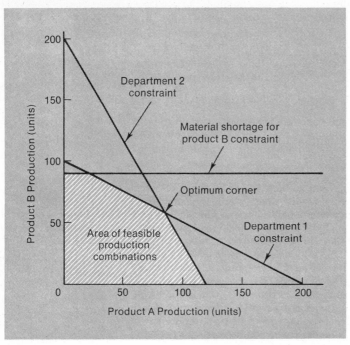

in b. Keep moving from corner to corner until no further improvement is possible.[4]

These computations, corner by corner, are summarized as follows:

		COMBINATION				
TRIAL	CORNER	PRODUCT A	PRODUCT B	TOTAL CONTRIBUTION MARGIN		
1	0,0	0	0	$2.00 (0)	+ $2.50 (0)	= $ 0
2	0,90	0	90	2.00 (0)	+ 2.50 (90)	= 225.00
3	20,90	20	90	2.00 (20)	+ 2.50 (90)	= 265.00
4	86,57	86	57	2.00 (86)	+ 2.50 (57)	= 314.50*
5	120,0	120	0	2.00 (120)	+ 2.50 (0)	= 240.00

* Optimum.

Why must the best solution lie on a corner? Consider all possible combinations that will produce a total contribution margin of $1 ($2.00 A + $2.50 B = $1). This is a straight line through (.5,0) and (0,.4). Other total contribution margins are represented by lines parallel to this one. Their associated total contribution margins increase as the lines get further from the origin. The optimum line is the one furthest from the origin that has a feasible point on it; intuitively, we know that this happens at a corner (86,57). Furthermore, if you put a ruler on the graph and move it parallel with the $1 line, the optimum corner will become apparent.

At the outset of this example, the reader may have jumped to the conclusion that production of Product B, which promises the most margin *per unit*, should

[4]This is a simplified version of the *simplex* method, which is described later in this section.

be maximized. Then any remaining productive capacity should be devoted to Product A. This is fallacious reasoning, because the scarce factor is productive capacity. The key to the optimum solution rests in the relative rates of substitution and profitability per unit (hour or day) of *productive capacity*. This point becomes clearer if we examine the graph. Moving from corner (20,90) to corner (86,57) implies that the company is transferring the scarce resource (productive capacity) between the products. In Department 1, each productive hour devoted to one unit of Product B may be given (sacrificed or traded) for two units of Product A. Will this exchange add to profitability? Yes, as shown below:

Total contribution margin at corner (20,90)		$265.00
Added contribution margin from Product A:		
66 units @ $2.00	$132.00	
Lost contribution margin, Product B:		
33 units @ $2.50	82.50	
Net additional contribution		49.50
Total contribution margin at corner (86,57)		$314.50

As we move from corner (86,57) to corner (120,0), we face the Department 2 constraint rather than the Department 1 constraint. The rate of substitution may be stated as follows: Each productive hour devoted to one unit of Product B may be devoted to .6 of a unit of Product A. This would entail giving up $2.50 contribution margin in exchange for .6($2.00) or $1.20 contribution margin, a decrease of the total contribution margin of $1.30 for each unit of Product B given up. Therefore, corner (86,57) is the optimum solution.

Note that the heart of the substitutions discussed above is a matter of swapping a given contribution margin per unit of scarce resource for some other contribution margin per unit of scarce resource; it is not simply a matter of comparing margins per unit of *product*.

simplex method The fundamental problem of linear programming is to discover the specific set of variables that satisfies all constraints and maximizes (or minimizes) the objective sought. Although graphical methods aid visualization and are useful for two or possibly three variables, they are impractical where many variables exist. The *simplex method*, a general technique for solving any linear-programming problem, is an iterative, step-by-step process that is very effective, especially when a digital computer performs the calculations. Although it is much too detailed to be described here, the simplex method essentially starts with a specific feasible alternative and algebraically tests it by substitution to see if the solution can be improved. These substitutions continue until no further improvement is possible, and thus the optimum solution is produced.

reliability of cost data Cost accountants who are skeptical of linear programming because imprecise data may be used should consider:

. . . even if the cost figures are not really reliable, the linear programming procedure will still be based on the same data that management would use if it selected a strategy by some other means. Therefore, the use of linear programming will at least ensure the selection of the optimal strategy on the basis of the data management would use anyhow.[5]

summary

The main point of this chapter is that the alert cost accountant should seize those contributions of allied fields that will strengthen and enrich his role as the major advisor to operating management. After all, few companies can afford the full-time services of a mathematician, a statistician, or some variation thereof. The accountant will undoubtedly remain entrenched as the top figure man in most organizations. However, this position will be endangered if the accountant does not broaden his horizons to recognize the contributions of decision theory and mathematics.

suggested readings

Bierman, Harold, and Thomas R. Dyckman, *Managerial Cost Accounting*. New York: The Macmillan Company, 1971.

Bowman, Edward H., and Robert B. Fetter, *Analysis for Production and Operations Management*, 3rd ed. Homewood, Ill.: Richard D. Irwin, Inc., 1967.

Demski, Joel S., *Information Analysis*. Reading, Mass.: Addison-Wesley Publishing Co., Inc., 1972.

Feltham, Gerald A., *Information Evaluation*. Evanston, Ill.: American Accounting Association, 1972.

Goetz, Billy E., *Quantitative Methods: A Survey and Guide for Managers*. New York: McGraw-Hill Book Company, 1965.

Livingstone, John Leslie, ed., *Management Planning and Control: Mathematical Models*. New York: McGraw-Hill Book Company, 1970.

Miller, D. W., and M. K. Starr, *Executive Decisions and Operations Research*, 2nd ed. Englewood Cliffs, N.J.: Prentice-Hall, Inc., 1969.

Morris, William T., *Management Science: A Bayesian Introduction*. Englewood Cliffs, N.J.: Prentice-Hall, Inc., 1968.

Rappaport, Alfred, ed., *Information for Decision Making*. Englewood Cliffs, N.J.: Prentice-Hall, Inc., 1970.

Stockton, R. Stansbury, *Introduction to Linear Programming*. Homewood, Ill.: Richard D. Irwin, Inc., 1971.

Wagner, Harvey M., *Principles of Operations Research with Applications to Managerial Decisions*. Englewood Cliffs, N.J.: Prentice-Hall, Inc., 1969.

[5] David W. Miller and Martin K. Starr, *Executive Decisions and Operations Research,* 2nd ed. (Englewood Cliffs, N.J.: Prentice-Hall, Inc., 1969), p. 551.

Problem for Self-Study

Review the example of linear programming. In particular, express the objectives and constraints in mathematical form. Superimpose a ruler on the graph as directed in the text's explanation of why the best solution must lie on a corner.

questions, problems, and cases

Note: As the introduction to the chapter pointed out, this assignment material is divided into two sets. The first set (Problems 27-1 through 27-19) can be solved with the background of this and other chapters in this book. The second set includes some problems that require a knowledge of mathematics not explicitly covered in this book.

27-1. Define *operations research.* What are its two most prominent characteristics?

27-2. What is another name for *queuing theory?*

27-3. Briefly define PERT.

27-4. Name and briefly describe some OR techniques.

27-5. Compare and contrast the work of the modern cost accountant with that of the operations researcher.

27-6. Define *linear programming.*

27-7. Give five examples of business applications of linear programming.

27-8. Define *dynamic programming.*

27-9. What is an *objective function?* A *feasible* alternative?

27-10. What are the four basic steps in linear programming?

27-11. Linear Programming; Graphic Solution. [Adapted from Robert K. Jaedicke, "Improving B-E Analysis by Linear Programming Technique," *N.A.A. Bulletin,* XLII, No. 7, 5–12.] A firm produces and sells two products, A and B. Selling price and cost data are as follows:

	PRODUCT A	PRODUCT B
Selling price	$10	$8
Variable costs of production and selling	5	6
Hours of production time per unit	4	1
Total fixed costs, $200,000.		

The maximum number of units of B that can be sold is 300,000. The total production hours available is 400,000.

required Express the basic relationships in mathematical form. Graph the relationships. Which product combination is optimal?

27-12. Allocation of Machine Time. Machine 1 has 24 hours available time and Machine 2 has 20 hours for processing of two products. Product X yields a contribution margin of $2 per unit; Product Y, $1 per unit. These products must be sold in proportions such that the quantity of X will be equal to or less than the quantity of Y. X requires 6 hours' time on Machine 1 and 10 hours' time on Machine 2. Product Y requires 4 hours' time on Machine 1 only.

required   Using graphic techniques, determine which product combination will maximize profit. Express the relationships in mathematical form.

27-13. Finding Optimal Mixture for Box of Chocolates. [Adapted from Miller and Starr, *Executive Decisions and Operations Research*, pp. 217–22.] A candy manufacturer is attempting to find the optimal mixture for a box of chocolates. There are two kinds of candy that he wants in the box, C_1 and C_2. The following are the characteristics of the candy and the box:

	C_1	C_2	BOX
Number of pieces	*x*	*y*	35 or greater
Weight per piece (oz.)	1.6	0.8	32 or more
Space per piece (sq. in.)	2.0	1.0	65*
Cost per piece	$0.02	$0.01	$0.60 maximum

*Maximum. By the use of fillers, the box can range from 40 square inches to 65 square inches.

required   Find the optimal mixture by graphic means.

27-14. Adding Another Constraint. Assume the same facts and requirements as in 27-13 except that at least 10 pieces of C_1 must be in the mixture.

27-15. Linear Programming and Minimum Cost. The local agricultural center has advised Sam Bowers to spread at least 4,800 pounds of a special nitrogen fertilizer ingredient and at least 5,000 pounds of a special phosphate fertilizer ingredient in order to increase his crops. Neither ingredient is available in pure form.

A dealer has offered 100-pound bags of VIM at $1 each. VIM contains the equivalent of 20 pounds of nitrogen and 80 pounds of phosphate. VOOM is also available in 100-pound bags, at $3 each; it contains the equivalent of 75 pounds of nitrogen and 25 pounds of phosphate.

Express the relationships as inequalities. How many bags of VIM and VOOM should Bowers buy in order to obtain the required fertilizer at minimum cost? Solve graphically.

27-16. Formulate Equations for LP [SIA]. A small manufacturing company produces two products, X and Y. Although selling the units produced is not a problem, management is concerned that the production mix maximize the total contribution to overhead and profit within the constraint of existing facilities. You are provided with the following data:

	PRODUCT X	PRODUCT Y
Selling price per unit	$60	$45
Variable cost per unit	30	24
Per-unit contribution to overhead and profit	$30	$21
Machine hours needed to produce one unit:		
On machine M	10 hours	6 hours
On machine N	5 hours	4 hours
Total machine hours available:		
On machine M	10,000 hours	
On machine N	6,000 hours	

required   Management knows that product-combination problems can be stated in linear-programming terminology by way of equations. On the basis of the data above, you have been asked to provide management with the following equations:

1. The objective function
2. The basic relationships and constraints

27-17. Choice of Product Mix. A firm has an assured market for any quantities of two products, which are processed on one machine and then finished by hand. The products are not complementary and may be produced independently in varying quantities. Planned output is 600 units per week of each product, a combination chosen because it fully utilizes machine and labor capacities. Maximum utilization is the rule-of-thumb strategy recommended by an OR consultant as most likely to yield maximum profit.

Machine capacity is 1,200 units per week of either product or a combination of the two; no time is lost in changing over from one product to the other. Machine operators' wages are included in fixed overhead. Finishing-labor supply is limited to 2,400 direct hours per week. Finishing labor is a fixed cost in the short run, as no other work is available if machine output is delayed for any reason. Standard product costs are as follows:

	A	B
Materials	2	2
Finishing labor @ $3 per hour	9	3
Fixed overhead @ ⅓ labor cost	3	1
Standard cost	$14	$6
Standard profit	2	2
Selling price	$16	$8

Last week the factory manager scheduled production of only 500 units of each product, as he wanted to overhaul the machine, reducing available machine capacity to 1,000 units. As a result, the finishing staff was idle for most of one day while the operators carried out the overhaul.

required

1. Calculate the contribution per unit of each limiting factor.
2. How many units of each product should have been scheduled to keep the finishing staff occupied (as well as utilizing the available machine capacity) and, on this basis, how much should the overhaul have cost in terms of lower profit?
3. How much profit was lost by the wrong production decision? Check your answer with the appropriate factor contribution in requirement 1.

27-18. Automobile Profit Analysis. [Prepared by David Green, Jr., and Gibbes Miller] The *Wall Street Journal* reported in February 1970 on the Chrysler Corporation's performance for the year 1969. Among other items, the story pointed out that Chrysler had boosted its market share from 10 percent in 1962 to 18 percent in 1968. In 1969, however, countermeasures by Ford and General Motors plus a 10 percent decline (that is, 1 million units) in total industry sales created severe problems for Chrysler. In its (unsuccessful) efforts to maintain its market share and protect its profitability, Chrysler cut prices and increased advertising allowances, which reduced contribution by an average of $100 per unit compared to 1968. Working toward internal economies, cutbacks in technical and administrative staff permitted a 20 percent reduction in fixed costs for 1969 relative to 1968. Nonetheless, 1969 pre-tax profits were only $80 million on sales of 1.4 million units, whereas 1968 pre-tax profit was $300 million.

required   From these fragments, answer the following questions. *Notice:* It is not hard to solve this by trial and error.

1. What was the fixed cost in 1968?
2. What was the fixed cost in 1969?
3. What was per-unit contribution in 1968?
4. What was per-unit contribution in 1969?
5. List major assumptions you have made and discuss them briefly.

27-19. **Choosing a Product Mix.**   Brian Jones has just received a university degree in management. He has taken the position of assistant to the president of a fairly small company in South Africa that manufactures tungsten carbide drill steels for the gold-mining industry.

Two types of drill steels are manufactured. One has a steel rod of $\frac{3}{4}$-inch diameter and the other a diameter of 1 inch. The manufacturing takes place in three departments. In the tip-fabricating department, tungsten carbide tips are manufactured from powdered wolfram. In the steel-forging department, the steel rods are slotted and prepared for the insertion of the tips. The assembly department puts the tips and steel rods together in a brazing process.

Each department has severe capacity limits. The first constraint prohibits further capital expenditure because of a very weak liquid position arising from past losses; the second is the labor situation in South Africa, which makes the hiring of more labor or the working of overtime virtually impossible. The capacity of each department is as follows:

Tip fabricating (Dept. A)	240,000 hours
Steel forging (Dept. B)	180,000 hours
Assembly (Dept. C)	180,000 hours

The treasurer has just completed the budget for the forthcoming year. Because of the renewed confidence in gold, the company is expected to produce at full capacity.

The treasurer has produced the following profit analysis of the two products, on which a major production decision was based:

	$\frac{3}{4}''$	$1''$
Selling price	$5.00	$6.00
Direct materials		
Tungsten carbide	$ .75	$1.00
Steel	1.45	2.05
	$2.20	$3.05
Direct labor		
Department A	$ .60	$ .30
Department B	.20	.30
Department C	.20	.15
	$1.00	$ .75
Prime costs (from above)	$3.20	$3.80
Factory overhead	.80	.60
Selling and administration	.50	.60
Total costs	$4.50	$5.00
Profit	$ .50	$1.00

The market survey performed by the sales manager showed that the company could sell as many of either type of rod as it could produce. However, the sales manager urged that the needs of three of the big gold mines must be satisfied in full, even though this meant producing a large number of the $\frac{3}{4}$-inch rods that had only half the profit of the 1-inch rods. The quantities required by these three gold mines amounted to 270,000 $\frac{3}{4}$-inch rods and 540,000 1-inch rods.

As the 1-inch rods have twice the profit of the $\frac{3}{4}$-inch rods, the treasurer suggested that the remaining capacity be used to produce two 1-inch rods for every $\frac{3}{4}$-inch rod. This would mean producing an additional 135,000 $\frac{3}{4}$-inch rods and 270,000 1-inch rods. Department B would then be working at full capacity and would be the constraint on any further production.

The treasurer then produced the following budgeted income statement for the forthcoming year. Sales are expected to occur evenly throughout the year.

	¾″	1″
Sales (in units)	405,000	810,000
Sales (in dollars)	$2,025,000	$4,860,000
Direct materials	891,000	2,470,500
Direct labor	405,000	607,500
Factory overhead	324,000	486,000
Selling and administration	202,500	486,000
Total costs	$1,822,500	$4,050,000
Profit	$ 202,500	$ 810,000

Jones, as his first assignment, is asked by the president to comment on the budgeted income statement. Specifically, the president feels that capacity might be better utilized with a different sales mix. He wants to know just how much it is costing the company in lost profits by supplying the full needs of the three big gold-mining customers. He feels it might be more profitable to produce only the 1-inch rods.

Jones gathers the following additional information before making his recommendations:

Wolfram is purchased at $10 per kilogram (1,000 grams). The $\frac{3}{4}$-inch tips use an average of 75 grams and the 1-inch tips 100 grams. The special alloy steel costs $2,000 per 2,000 pounds. The $\frac{3}{4}$-inch rods use 1.45 pounds and the 1-inch rods 2.05 pounds.

Direct-labor costs per hour follow:

Department A	$2.40
Department B	1.80
Department C	1.50

Tip fabricating (Department A) is a skilled process. The smaller tips require twice as much detailed work. Owing to the nature of the work, most of the labor is considered fixed because it would be difficult to replace. Approximately 200,000 hours per annum in Department A are considered fixed. In the steel-forging process, the bigger rods require more time because of the handling difficulties. In the assembly department, the smaller rods again take more time because of the intricacies of the operations. However, this is not skilled work.

Factory overhead in the budgeted income statement is considered 50 percent fixed. It has been allocated to the products on the basis of direct labor.

Selling and administrative expenses have been allocated on the basis of selling price. Variable selling expenses are predicted to be 10¢ per unit sold of either size.

required   If you were Jones, what would be your recommendations to the president?

supplementary problems for chapter 27

Note that Problems 27-20 through 27-22 are taken verbatim from CPA examinations, which have begun to include subject matter on quantitative methods. Some parts of these problems can be solved with the background provided by this book. Examples are most of the questions in 27-20, part C of Problem 27-21, and part A of Problem 27-22.

Note also that much of this material relates to previous chapters. Part A of Problem 27-20 relates to Chapter 15; Part B of Problem 27-21 to Chapter 12; Part C of Problem 27-21 to Chapter 3; and Part A of Problem 27-22 to Chapter 7.

Problem 27-23 is a comprehensive problem that includes linear programming and the regression analysis that was discussed in Chapter 24. Access to a computer is necessary for its solution.

27-20. Economic Lot Size; Linear Programming [CPA]. Choose the best answer for each item.
  A. A manufacturer expects to produce 200,000 widgets during the fiscal year ending June 30, 19_2, to supply a demand that is uniform throughout the year. The setup cost for each production run of widgets is $144, and the variable cost of producing each widget is $5. The cost of carrying one widget in inventory is $.20 per year. After a batch of widgets is produced and placed in inventory, it is sold at a uniform rate, and inventory is exhausted when the next batch of widgets is completed.

  Management wishes an equation to describe this situation and determine the optimal quantity of widgets to produce in each run in order to minimize total production and inventory carrying costs.

Let c = total annual cost of producing and carrying widgets in inventory
  X = number of widgets to be produced in each production run

1. The number of production runs to be made in fiscal year 19_2 could be expressed as
   a. 200,000 + 144X
   b. 200,000 + X   d. $\dfrac{200,000}{X}$ e. $\dfrac{X}{200,000}$
   c. 200,000

2. Total setup costs for fiscal year 19_2 could be expressed as
   a. $144\left(\dfrac{200,000}{X}\right)$ c. $144X$ e. $\dfrac{\$144}{200,000} + \$X$
   b. $\dfrac{\$200,000}{X}$ d. $\dfrac{\$144X}{200,000}$

3. Total cost of carrying inventory during fiscal year 19_2 could be expressed as
   a. $.20($144X)
   b. $.20X   d. $.20\left(\dfrac{X}{2}\right)$ e. $.20\left(\dfrac{\$144X}{200,000}\right)$
   c. $.20\left(\dfrac{200,000}{X}\right)$

4. The derivative, dc/dx, of the equation to determine the optimal quantity of widgets that should be produced during each production run in fiscal year 19_2 is

    a. $-28,800,000X^{-2} + \dfrac{.20}{2}$

    b. $-144(200,000)X^{-1} + \dfrac{.20}{2}$

    c. $-28,800,000X^{2} + 1,000,000 + \dfrac{.20}{2}$

    d. $-28,800,000X + \dfrac{.20}{2}$

    e. $-28,800,000X$

5. The quantity of widgets (to the nearest whole number) that should be produced in each run in fiscal year 19_2 to minimize total costs is
    a. 19,000; b. 17,000; c. 16,000; d. 12,480; e. 12,000.

B. A company markets two products, Alpha and Gamma. The marginal contributions per gallon are $5 for Alpha and $4 for Gamma. Both products consist of two ingredients, D and K. Alpha contains 80 percent D and 20 percent K, while the proportions of the same ingredients in Gamma are 40 percent and 60 percent respectively. The current inventory is 16,000 gallons of D and 6,000 gallons of K. The only company producing D and K is on strike and will neither deliver nor produce them in the foreseeable future. The company wishes to know the numbers of gallons of Alpha and Gamma that it should produce with its present stock of raw materials in order to maximize its total revenue.

6. The objective function for this problem could be expressed as
    a. $f_{max} = 0X_1 + 0X_2 + 5X_3 + 5X_4$
    b. $f_{min} = 5X_1 + 4X_2 + 0X_3 + 0X_4$
    c. $f_{max} = 5X_1 + 4X_2 + 0X_3 + 0X_4$
    d. $f_{max} = X_1 + X_2 + 5X_3 + 4X_4$
    e. $f_{max} = 4X_1 + 5X_2 + X_3 + X_4$

7. The constraint imposed by the quantity of D on hand could be expressed as
    a. $X_1 + X_2 \geq 16,000$
    b. $X_1 + X_2 \leq 16,000$
    c. $.4X_1 + .6X_2 \leq 16,000$
    d. $.8X_1 + .4X_2 \geq 16,000$
    e. $.8X_1 + .4X_2 \leq 16,000$

8. The constraint imposed by the quantity of K on hand could be expressed as
    a. $X_1 + X_2 \geq 6,000$
    b. $X_1 + X_2 \leq 6,000$
    c. $.8X_1 + .2X_2 \leq 6,000$
    d. $.8X_1 + .2X_2 \geq 6,000$
    e. $.2X_1 + .6X_2 \leq 6,000$

9. To maximize total revenue, the company should produce and market
    a. 106,000 gallons of Alpha only
    b. 90,000 gallons of Alpha and 16,000 gallons of Gamma
    c. 16,000 gallons of Alpha and 90,000 gallons of Gamma
    d. 18,000 gallons of Alpha and 4,000 gallons of Gamma
    e. 4,000 gallons of Alpha and 18,000 gallons of Gamma

10. Assuming that the marginal contributions per gallon are $7 for Alpha and $9 for Gamma, the company should produce and market

a. 106,000 gallons of Alpha only

b. 90,000 gallons of Alpha and 16,000 gallons of Gamma

c. 16,000 gallons of Alpha and 90,000 gallons of Gamma

d. 18,000 gallons of Alpha and 4,000 gallons of Gamma

e. 4,000 gallons of Alpha and 18,000 gallons of Gamma

27-21. Simplex Method; Matrix Algebra and Overhead Allocation; Breakeven Analysis for Two Products [CPA]. Select the best answer choice for each of the following items, which relate to applications of quantitative methods to accounting.

A. Beekley, Inc., manufactures widgets, gadgets, and trinkets and has asked for advice in determining the best production mix for its three products. Demand for the company's products is excellent, and management finds that it is unable to meet potential sales with existing plant capacity.

Each product goes through three operations: milling, grinding, and painting. The effective weekly departmental capacities in minutes are: milling, 10,000; grinding, 14,000; and painting, 10,000.

The following data are available on the three products:

	SELLING PRICE PER UNIT	VARIABLE COST PER UNIT	PER-UNIT PRODUCTION TIME (IN MINUTES)		
			MILLING	GRINDING	PAINTING
Widgets	$5.25	$4.45	4	8	4
Gadgets	5.00	3.90	10	4	2
Trinkets	4.50	3.30	4	8	2

1. The quantitative technique most useful in determining the best product mix would be
   a. Least-squares analysis
   b. Queuing theory
   c. Linear regression
   d. Linear programming

2. The objective function for this problem using the simplex method might be expressed
   a. $f_{min} = 4.45X_1 + 3.90X_2 + 3.30X_3 + 0X_4 + 0X_5 + 0X_6$
   b. $f_{max} = 5.25X_1 + 5.00X_2 + 4.50X_3 + X_4 + X_5 + X_6$
   c. $f_{max} = .80X_1 + 1.10X_2 + 1.20X_3 + X_4 + X_5 + X_6$
   d. $f_{max} = .80X_1 + 1.10X_2 + 1.20X_3 + 0X_4 + 0X_5 + 0X_6$

3. The requirement that total production time in the painting department may not exceed 10,000 minutes per week might be expressed
   a. $4X_1 + 2X_2 + 2X_3 \geq 10,000$
   b. $4X_1 + 2X_2 + 2X_3 > 10,000$
   c. $4X_1 + 2X_2 + 2X_3 \leq 10,000$
   d. $4X_1 + 2X_2 + 2X_3 < 10,000$

4. The variables X_4, X_5, and X_6 included in the answers to item 2 are referred to as
   a. Artificial variables
   b. Primary variables
   c. Stochastic variables
   d. Slack variables

5. The variables X_1, X_2, and X_3 included in the answers to item 2 are referred to as
   a. Artificial variables
   b. Primary variables

    c. Stochastic variables

    d. Slack variables

6. The coefficients for X_1, X_2, and X_3 included in the answers to item 2 are

    a. The coefficients of the objective function in the problem

    b. The coefficients of the artificial variables in the problem

    c. The coefficients of the constraints in the problem and represent the contribution margin for each project

    d. The shadow prices of the stochastic variables in the problem

7. If Beekley were willing to pay $.12 for every minute of additional grinding time that might be made available, this may be called

    a. A primal restraint

    b. A slack variable

    c. A shadow price

    d. An artificial variable

8. A significant advantage of applying the simplex method to certain problems having four or more variables of a single class is that solutions may be arrived at quickly using

    a. Graphic analysis

    b. Electronic computer routines

    c. Simple algebraic methods

    d. Set theory

B. A manufacturer's plant has two service departments (designated below as S_1 and S_2) and three production departments (designated below as P_1, P_2, and P_3) and wishes to allocate all factory overhead to production departments. A primary distribution of overhead to all departments has already been made and is indicated below. The company makes the secondary distribution of overhead from service departments to production departments on a reciprocal basis, recognizing the fact that services of one service department are utilized by another. Data regarding costs and allocation percentages are as follows:

SERVICE-DEPARTMENT OVERHEAD COST ALLOCATION

SERVICE DEPARTMENT	PERCENTAGES TO BE ALLOCATED TO DEPARTMENTS				
	S_1	S_2	P_1	P_2	P_3
S_1	0%	10%	20%	40%	30%
S_2	20	0	50	10	20

		PRIMARY OVERHEAD TO BE ALLOCATED		
$98,000	$117,600	$1,400,000	$2,100,000	$640,000

    Matrix algebra is to be used in the secondary allocation process. The amount of overhead to be allocated to the service departments you express in two simultaneous equations as:

$$S_1 = 98{,}000 + .20S_2 \quad \text{or} \quad S_1 - .20S_2 = \$\ 98{,}000$$
$$S_2 = 117{,}600 + .10S_1 \quad \text{or} \quad S_2 - .10S_1 = \$117{,}600$$

9. The system of simultaneous equations above may be stated in matrix form as

    a.   A   S   b

$$\begin{bmatrix} 1 & -.20 \\ -.10 & 1 \end{bmatrix} \begin{bmatrix} S_1 \\ S_2 \end{bmatrix} = \begin{bmatrix} \$\ 98{,}000 \\ \$117{,}600 \end{bmatrix}$$

b.
$$
\begin{bmatrix} 1 & \$\,98{,}000 & 1 \\ -.20 & \$117{,}600 & -.10 \end{bmatrix}
\begin{bmatrix} S_1 \\ S_2 \end{bmatrix} =
\begin{bmatrix} \$\,98{,}000 \\ \$117{,}600 \end{bmatrix}
$$
A   S   b

c.
$$
\begin{bmatrix} 1 & S_1 & 1 \\ -.20 & S_2 & -.10 \end{bmatrix}
\begin{bmatrix} S_1 \\ S_2 \end{bmatrix} =
\begin{bmatrix} \$\,98{,}000 \\ \$117{,}600 \end{bmatrix}
$$
A   S   b

d.
$$
\begin{bmatrix} 1 & 1 & S_1 \\ -.20 & -.10 & S_2 \end{bmatrix}
\begin{bmatrix} S_1 \\ S_2 \end{bmatrix} =
\begin{bmatrix} \$\,98{,}000 \\ \$117{,}600 \end{bmatrix}
$$
A   S   b

10. For the correct matrix A in item 9, there exists a unique inverse matrix A^{-1}. Multiplication of the matrix A^{-1} by the matrix A will produce
   a. The matrix A
   b. Another inverse matrix
   c. The correct solution to the system
   d. An identity matrix

11. Without prejudice to your previous answers, assume that the correct matrix form in item 9 was

$$
\begin{bmatrix} 1 & -.20 \\ -.10 & 1 \end{bmatrix}
\begin{bmatrix} S_1 \\ S_2 \end{bmatrix} =
\begin{bmatrix} \$\,98{,}000 \\ \$117{,}600 \end{bmatrix}
$$
A   S   b

Then the correct inverse matrix A^{-1} is

a.
$$
\begin{bmatrix} \dfrac{1}{.98} & \dfrac{.20}{.98} \\ \dfrac{.10}{.98} & \dfrac{1}{.98} \end{bmatrix}
$$
   c.
$$
\begin{bmatrix} \dfrac{1}{.30} & \dfrac{.20}{.30} \\ \dfrac{.10}{.30} & \dfrac{1}{.30} \end{bmatrix}
$$

b.
$$
\begin{bmatrix} \dfrac{1}{.98} & \dfrac{1}{.98} \\ \dfrac{.20}{.98} & \dfrac{.10}{.98} \end{bmatrix}
$$
   d.
$$
\begin{bmatrix} \dfrac{1}{.98} & -\dfrac{1}{.98} \\ -\dfrac{.20}{.98} & \dfrac{.10}{.98} \end{bmatrix}
$$

12. The total amount of overhead allocated to department S_1 after receiving the allocation from department S_2 is
   a. \$141,779; b. \$124,000; c. \$121,520; d. \$117,600.

13. The total amount of overhead allocated to department S_2 after receiving the allocation from department S_1 is
   a. \$392,000; b. \$220,000; c. \$130,000; d. \$127,400.

14. Without prejudice to your previous answers, assume that the answer to item 12 is \$100,000 and to item 13 is \$150,000; then the total amount of overhead allocated to production department P_1 would be
   a. \$1,508,104; b. \$1,495,000; c. \$1,489,800; d. \$108,104.

C. The Dooley Co. manufactures two products, baubles and trinkets. The following are projections for the coming year:

	BAUBLES		TRINKETS		
	UNITS	AMOUNT	UNITS	AMOUNT	TOTALS
Sales	10,000	\$10,000	7,500	\$10,000	\$20,000
Costs:					
Fixed		\$ 2,000		\$ 5,600	\$ 7,600
Variable		6,000		3,000	9,000
		\$ 8,000		\$ 8,600	\$16,600
Income before taxes		\$ 2,000		\$ 1,400	\$ 3,400

15. Assuming that the facilities are not jointly used, the breakeven output (in units) for baubles would be
    a. 8,000; b. 7,000; c. 6,000; d. 5,000.
16. The breakeven volume (dollars) for trinkets would be
    a. $8,000; b. $7,000; c. $6,000; d. $5,000.
17. Assuming that consumers purchase composite units of four baubles and three trinkets, the composite unit contribution margin would be
    a. $4,40; b. $4.00; c. $1.33; d. $1.10.
18. If consumers purchase composite units of four baubles and three trinkets, the breakeven output for the two products would be
    a. 6,909 baubles; 6,909 trinkets
    b. 6,909 baubles; 5,182 trinkets
    c. 5,000 baubles; 8,000 trinkets
    d. 5,000 baubles; 6,000 trinkets
19. If baubles and trinkets become one-to-one complements and there is no change in the Dooley Co.'s cost function, the breakeven volume would be
    a. $22,500; b. $15,750; c. $13,300; d. $10,858.
20. If a composite unit is defined as one bauble and one trinket, the composite contribution margin ratio would be
    a. 7/10; b. 4/7; c. 2/5; d. 19/50.

27-22. Learning Curve; Calculus; Waiting-Line Theory [CPA]. Select the best answer for each item.

A. The average number of minutes required to assemble trivets is predictable, based upon an 80 percent learning curve. That is, whenever cumulative production doubles, cumulative average time per unit becomes 80 percent of what it was at the previous doubling point. The trivets are produced in lots of 300 units, and 60 minutes of labor are required to assemble each first lot.

Using the concept of the learning curve and the letters listed below, select the best answer for each of questions 6 through 10.

Let MT = marginal time for the xth lot
M = marginal time for the first lot
X = lots produced
b = exponent expressing the improvement; b has the range $-1 < b \leq 0$

1. A normal graph—that is, not a log or log-log graph—of average minutes per lot of production where cumulative lots are represented by the x-axis and average minutes per lot are represented by the y-axis, would produce a
   a. Linear function sloping downward to the right
   b. Linear function sloping upward to the right
   c. Curvilinear function sloping upward to the right at an increasing rate
   d. Curvilinear function sloping downward to the right at a decreasing rate
2. A log-log graph of average minutes per lot of production, where cumulative lots are represented by the x-axis and average minutes per lot are represented by the y-axis, would produce a
   a. Linear function sloping downward to the right
   b. Linear function sloping upward to the right
   c. Curvilinear function sloping upward to the right at a decreasing rate
   d. Curvilinear function sloping downward to the right at a decreasing rate

3. The average number of minutes required per lot to complete four lots is approximately
   a. 60.0; b. 48.5; c. 38.4; d. 30.7.

4. Average time to produce X lots of trivets could be expressed
   a. MX^{b+1}; b. MX^{b}; c. MT^{b+1}; d. MX^{b-1}.

5. Assuming that $b = -.322$, the average number of minutes required to produce X lots of trivets could be expressed
   a. $40.08X^{.678}$; b. $40.08X$; c. $60X^{-.322}$; d. $60X^{1.322}$.

B. MacKenzie Park sells its trivets for $.25 per unit and during 19_9 reported net sales of $500,000 and net income of $35,000. Production capacity is limited to 15,000 trivets per day, and trivets are produced 300 days each year. Variable costs are $.10 per trivet.

The company does not maintain an inspection system but has an agreement to reimburse the wholesaler $.50 for each defective unit the wholesaler finds. The wholesaler uses a method of inspection that detects all defective units. The number of defective units in each lot of 300 units is equal to the daily unit production rate divided by 200.

Letting X = daily production in units, select the best answer for each of questions 6 through 10.

6. The number of defective units per day could be expressed

   a. $\dfrac{X}{60,000}$ c. $\dfrac{X}{500}$

   b. $\left(\dfrac{200}{X}\right)\left(\dfrac{X}{300}\right)$ d. $\dfrac{X^2}{60,000}$

7. The equation to compute the maximum daily contribution to profit, including the reimbursement to the wholesaler for defective units, could be expressed

   a. $.25X - .10X - .50\left(\dfrac{X}{60,000}\right)$

   b. $.25X - .10X - .50\left(\dfrac{X^2}{60,000}\right)$

   c. $.25X - .10X - \dfrac{X^2}{60,000} - \dfrac{125,000}{300}$

   d. $.25X - .10X - \dfrac{X}{60,000} - 125,000$

8. The first derivative of the equation to determine the number of units to maximize daily profits could be expressed

   a. $.25 - .10 - \dfrac{X}{60,000}$ c. $\dfrac{X^2}{60,000}$

   b. $.10 - .25 - \dfrac{X^2}{60,000}$ d. $\dfrac{X}{(200)\,(300)}$

9. The second derivative of the equation to determine the number of units to be produced daily to maximize profits would be

   a. $\dfrac{1}{(200)\,(300)}$ c. $\dfrac{\$125,000}{60,000}$

   b. $\$.25 - \$.10 - \dfrac{1}{60,000} - \$125,000$ d. $-\dfrac{1}{60,000}$

10. To maximize profits, the results of the equation to determine the daily contribution margin of MacKenzie Park Co. should yield
    a. A negative first derivative and a positive second derivative

   b. A positive first derivative and a negative second derivative
   c. Negative first and second derivatives
   d. Positive first and second derivatives
C. MacKenzie Park has recently experienced costly production slowdowns due to maintenance problems in its assembly department. There are four machines in the department and one repairman to service them. Experience indicates that the repairman can service ten machines in one eight-hour day if necessary, and that two machines generally require his services during any one day.

   Management is considering the employment of a second repairman for the department and has asked for your advice. It has been decided that the company will hire the second repairman if it is found that the average time a machine lies idle waiting to be serviced exceeds one hour.

   Use the letters and formulas below and select the best answer for each of questions 11 through 15.

   Let A = Average number of machines needing repairs during a day
         S = Average number of machines that can be repaired in a unit of time, assuming machines are available for repair
         m = Total number of machines
         k = Number of machines operating
         p_m = Probability of all machines being down and either waiting or being serviced
         p_0 = Probability of no machines being down
         $E(t)$ = Average time a machine spends waiting

   And $p_m = \left\{ 1 + \dfrac{1}{1}\left(\dfrac{S}{A}\right)^1 + \cdots + \dfrac{1}{m!}\left(\dfrac{S}{A}\right)^m \right\}^{-1}$

   $p_{m-k} = \dfrac{1}{k!}\left(\dfrac{S}{A}\right)^k p_m$

   $E(t) = \dfrac{1}{S}\left(\dfrac{m}{1 - p_0} - \dfrac{1 + \dfrac{A}{S}}{\dfrac{A}{S}} \right)$

11. As evidenced by the formulas shown above, the quantitative technique being used here is known as
    a. Linear programming
    b. Game theory
    c. The transportation model
    d. Queueing theory
12. The probability of all machines being down and either waiting or being serviced (after rounding the denominator to the nearest whole number) is
    a. $\dfrac{1}{5}$; b. $\dfrac{1}{13}$; c. $\dfrac{1}{39}$; d. $\dfrac{1}{65}$.

13. The probability of no machines being down (after rounding the denominator to the nearest whole number) is
    a. $\dfrac{4}{5}$; b. $\dfrac{125}{312}$; c. $\dfrac{25}{78}$; d. $\dfrac{1}{65}$.

14. The average portion of a day that a machine spends waiting (after rounding) is
    a. .47; b. .25; c. .15; d. .07.

15. On the basis of your computations and the criterion specified by management, you should advise MacKenzie Park
   a. That the decision is a borderline one because there is a difference of only ±2 minutes between the average time a machine spends waiting and management's one-hour limitation
   b. Not to hire the additional repairman
   c. To hire the additional repairman
   d. To eliminate the existing repairman position

27-23. **Comprehensive Review; Product-Mix Decision; Simplex Method; Regression Analysis.** ["Report of Committee on Measurement Methods," *Accounting Review*, Supplement to Vol. XLVI, 229–31. Access to a computer is necessary.] In November 19_9, the Bayview Manufacturing Company was in the process of preparing its budget for the next year. As the first step, it prepared a pro forma income statement for 19_9 based on the first ten months' operations and revised plans for the last two months. This income statement, in condensed form, was as follows:

Sales		$3,000,000
Materials	$1,182,000	
Labor	310,000	
Factory overhead	775,000	
Selling and administrative	450,000	2,717,000
Net income before taxes		$ 283,000

These results were better than had been expected and operations were close to capacity, but Bayview's management was not convinced that demand would remain at present levels and hence had not planned any increase in plant capacity. Its equipment was specialized and made to its order; more than a year's lead time was necessary on all plant additions.

Bayview produces three products; sales have been broken down by product as follows:

100,000 of Product A @ $20	$2,000,000
40,000 of Product B @ 10	400,000
20,000 of Product C @ 30	600,000
	$3,000,000

Management has ordered a profit analysis for each product and has available the following information:

	A	B	C
Materials	$ 7.00	$ 3.75	$16.60
Labor	2.00	1.00	3.50
Factory overhead	5.00	2.50	8.75
Selling and administrative	3.00	1.50	4.50
Total costs	$17.00	$ 8.75	$33.35
Selling price	20.00	10.00	30.00
Profit	$ 3.00	$ 1.25	(−$3.35)

Factory overhead has been applied on the basis of direct-labor cost at a rate of 250 percent; and management asserts that approximately 20 percent of the overhead is variable and does vary with labor costs. Selling and administrative costs have been allocated on the basis of sales at the rate of 15 percent;

approximately one-half of this is variable and does vary with sales in dollars. All the labor expense is considered to be variable.

As the first step in the planning process, the sales department has been asked to make estimates of what it could sell; these estimates have been reviewed by the firm's consulting economist and by top management. They are as follows:

A	130,000 units
B	50,000 units
C	50,000 units

Production of these quantities was immediately recognized as being impossible. Estimated cost data for the three products, each of which requires activity of both departments, were based on the following production rates:

	PRODUCT		
	A	*B*	*C*
Department 1	2 per hour	4 per hour	3 per hour
Department 2	4 per hour	8 per hour	4/3 per hour

Practical capacity in Department 1 is 67,000 hours and in Department 2, 63,000 hours; and the industrial-engineering department has concluded that this cannot be increased without the purchase of additional equipment. Thus, while last year Department 1 operated at 99 percent of its capacity and Department 2 at 71 percent of capacity, anticipated sales would require operating both departments at more than 100 percent capacity.

These solutions to the limited-production problem have been rejected: (a) Subcontracting the production out to other firms is considered to be unprofitable because of problems of maintaining quality; (b) operating a second shift is impossible because of shortage of labor; (c) operating overtime would create problems because a large number of employees are "moonlighting" and would therefore refuse to work more than the normal 40-hour week. Price increases have also been rejected; although they would result in higher profits this year, the long-run competitive position of the firm would be weakened, resulting in lower profits in the future.

The treasurer then suggested that Product C has been carried at a loss too long and that now was the time to eliminate it from the product line. If all facilities are used to produce A and B, profits would be increased.

The sales manager objected to this solution because of the need to carry a full line. In addition, he maintains that there is a group of customers who have provided and will continue to provide a solid base for the firm's activities, and these customers' needs must be met. He furnished a list of these customers and their estimated purchases (in units), which total as follows:

A	80,000
B	32,000
C	12,000

It was impossible to verify these contentions, but they appeared to be reasonable and they served to narrow the bounds of the problem, so that the president concurred.

The treasurer reluctantly acquiesced, but he maintained that the remaining capacity should be used to produce A and B. Because A produced 2.4 times as much profit as B, he suggested that the production of A (in excess of the

80,000 minimum set by the sales manager) be 2.4 times that of B (in excess of the 32,000 minimum set by the sales manager).

The production manager made some quick calculations and said that this would result in budgeted production and sales of:

A	104,828
B	42,344
C	12,000

The treasurer then made a calculation of what profits would be, as follows:

A	104,828 @ $3.00	$314,484
B	42,344 @ $1.25	52,930
C	12,000 @ (−$3.35)	(−40,200)
		$327,214

As this would represent an increase of almost 15 percent over the current year, there was a general feeling of satisfaction. Before final approval was given, however, the president said that he would like to have his new assistant check over the figures. Somewhat piqued, the treasurer agreed, and at that point the group adjourned.

required

The next day the information above was submitted to you as your first assignment on your new job as the president's assistant. Prepare an analysis showing the president what he should do.

Exhibits 27-2 and 27-3 contain information that you are able to obtain from the accounting system.

EXHIBIT 27-2

YEAR	DIRECT-LABOR EXPENSE			OVERHEAD EXPENSE			SELLING AND ADMINISTRATIVE EXPENSE
	(in thousands) DEPT. 1	DEPT. 2	TOTAL	(in thousands) DEPT. 1	DEPT. 2	TOTAL	(in thousands)
19_9	$140	$170	$310	$341	$434	$775	$450
19_8	135	150	285	340	421	762*	445
19_7	140	160	300	342	428	770	445
19_6	130	150	280	339	422	761	438
19_5	130	155	285	338	425	763	433
19_4	125	140	265	337	414	751	437
19_3	120	150	270	335	420	755	438
19_2	115	140	255	334	413	747	434
19_1	120	140	260	336	414	750	430
19_0	115	135	250	335	410	745	425

* Rounding error.

EXHIBIT 27-3

SALES (in thousands)

YEAR	PROD. A	PROD. B	PROD. C	TOTAL
19_9	$2,000	$400	$600	$3,000
19_8	1,940	430	610	2,980
19_7	1,950	380	630	2,960
19_6	1,860	460	620	2,940
19_5	1,820	390	640	2,850
19_4	1,860	440	580	2,880
19_3	1,880	420	570	2,870
19_2	1,850	380	580	2,810
19_1	1,810	390	580	2,780
19_0	1,770	290	610	2,670

28

Cost Accounting in the CPA Examination

Many readers may eventually take the Certified Public Accountant examination. This chapter will discuss how to prepare for the cost-accounting topics in the examination. It will also consider some major alternative approaches in general-ledger treatments, standard costs, and spoilage. This book includes numerous questions and problems extracted from past CPA examinations.[1]

Cost accounting and income taxes are the two most important topics in the Practice section of the examination. Of special note is the increasing emphasis in recent years on the management decision-making purposes of cost accounting rather than the inventory and income-determination purposes. Topics covered include standard costs, flexible budgets, analysis of variances, cost–volume–profit analysis, direct costing, relevant costs for special decisions, and discounted cash-flow analysis. Each recent examination has included quantitative methods and techniques, including mathematics, statistics, and probability analysis (see Chapters 23, 24, and the supplementary problems in Chapter 27 for examples). Problems on product costing emphasize process costs, including spoilage, and joint costs.

---

[1] These are designated in this book as "[CPA]." The Society of Industrial Accountants of Canada administers a set of annual examinations on accounting. There are various sections with graduated levels of difficulty. The problems designated "[SIA]" in this book have been taken with permission from the society's examinations. Some of these problems have been adapted, to bring out particular points in the chapter for which they were chosen. Several additional problems have been taken from the examinations of the Certified General Accountants Association of Canada (CGAA). For an analysis of the coverage of cost accounting topics in CPA exams, see Milton F. Usry, "Cost Accounting in the CPA Examination—Updated," *Accounting Review*, XLVI, No. 4, 791–96.

CPA REVIEW

The CPA candidate faces an imposing task of review. In addition to preparing for probable cost-accounting topics, he must recognize two special characteristics of a national examination. First, accounting terminology is not uniform. Second, alternative solutions are possible for many accounting problems.

divergent terminology   Variations in terminology will inevitably appear in a national examination that is drawn from many sources. Likely questions and problems are contributed by individual accounting practitioners, public accountants, accounting teachers, and employees of the A.I.C.P.A. (American Institute of Certified Public Accountants). They are stockpiled by the A.I.C.P.A. and used as needed.

Thus, the candidate should be familiar with the variety and interchangeability of many cost terms.[2] For example, *factory overhead* is usually interchangeable with the following terms: *indirect manufacturing costs, manufacturing expenses, factory burden,* and *manufacturing overhead. Cost of goods sold* is often called *cost of sales.*

alternative solutions   Alternative solutions can arise because (a) there are slight variations in practical accounting procedures or techniques, and (b) there are different schools of thought on certain cost matters, such as ledger designs, analysis of variances, and accounting for spoilage. Thus, the candidate must anticipate problem situations that do not exactly coincide with either the text treatments that he knows or the cases that he has encountered in practice.

The American Institute of Certified Public Accountants takes elaborate steps to insure equitable grading of CPA examinations. The A.I.C.P.A. graders recognize and give full credit to all alternative solutions that are reasonable. Therefore, the CPA candidate should not be discouraged if in the course of his review he finds published CPA solutions[3] that do not precisely agree with his favorite approach or the approach that he learned when he took a cost-accounting course. The A.I.C.P.A. has found it impracticable to publish a large collection of alternative solutions, so it usually confines its "unofficial answers" to one widely accepted approach.

CPA problems are designed to be straightforward. Requirements should be taken at face value. Special assumptions are rarely necessary. Sometimes a candidate still feels that an assumption must be made. If so, the assumption should be stated, together with the reasons therefor. *Such reasons should include a statement as to why a possible alternate assumption is being rejected.*

---

[2] Eric Kohler, *Dictionary for Accountants,* 4th ed. (Englewood Cliffs, N.J.: Prentice-Hall, Inc., 1970) is a helpful reference.

[3] Divergences in practice and terminology creep not only into the examination but also into the "unofficial answers" that are published by the A.I.C.P.A. subsequent to the examination dates. These published answers are neither official nor necessarily the only acceptable solutions. Yet many students and teachers have the mistaken belief that the A.I.C.P.A. published solutions are *the* only acceptable answers.

In summary, although the candidate does not have to worry about the acceptability of alternate solutions to a given CPA problem, he should have an awareness of divergencies in accounting practice and terminology. As a minimum, his terminology should coincide with that given in the problem. He should also know what areas of cost accounting tend to have alternative treatments. In these areas especially, he should take particular pains with his answer so that it will be clear to all graders.[4] We shall examine these areas in the remainder of this chapter.

ALTERNATE GENERAL-LEDGER TREATMENTS

The text has generally shown one technique for cost accumulation in the general ledger. Obviously, there are alternative methods, some of which have been briefly described (Chapters 4 and 7). Comparisons of a few alternative techniques are shown in Exhibit 28-1. The first and third columns show the methods used throughout this book; the second and fourth columns show alternate techniques that are preferred by many accountants for reasons of convenience or feasibility. For example, consider the problem of when to isolate a material-usage variance. In concept, it should be isolated as quickly as possible for control purposes (see column 3). Yet often the usage variance is impossible to calculate until the work is completed. Consequently, in these cases, the method shown in the fourth column is used.

STANDARD COSTS

Standard costs may be integrated into the general ledger in a number of ways, depending on the preferences of the person who is setting up the standard-cost system. The candidate should be familiar with alternative methods, because the ledger procedure described in a given problem will influence a solution. No computations or entries should be prepared until the given general-ledger procedure (and specific types of variance analysis called for, if any) is fully comprehended. Problems on standard costs usually emphasize general-ledger entries and variance analysis. A key account, Work in Process, could appear in any one of three alternative ways, depending upon the system employed:

(*ALTERNATIVE 1*)	WORK IN PROCESS	
Actual quantities × Actual prices	Standard quantities × Standard prices

(*ALTERNATIVE 2*)	WORK IN PROCESS	
Actual quantities × Standard prices	Standard quantities × Standard prices

(*ALTERNATIVE 3*)	WORK IN PROCESS	
Standard quantities × Standard prices	Standard quantities × Standard prices

[4] The candidate can be confident that the *proper* use of the specific techniques he has learned will be given full credit. However, in some instances, he can strengthen his solution by pointing out important aspects that might receive alternative treatment.

EXHIBIT 28-1
ALTERNATIVE GENERAL-LEDGER DESIGNS

TRANSACTION	NONSTANDARD COST ACCOUNTING		STANDARD COST ACCOUNTING	
	COL. 1	COL. 2	COL. 3	COL. 4
Direct-material usage	Work in process xx Stores xx	Direct materials used xx Stores xx Work in process xx Direct materials used xx	Work in process xx Usage variance xx Stores xx	Work in process xx Stores xx Finished goods xx Usage variance xx Work in process xx
Payroll accounting	Work in process xx Department overhead xx Accrued payroll xx	Direct labor xx Department overhead xx Accrued payroll xx Work in process xx Direct labor xx	Work in process xx Direct-labor rate variance xx Direct-labor efficiency variance xx Department overhead xx Accrued payroll xx	Direct labor xx Department overhead xx Direct-labor rate variance xx Accrued payroll xx Work in process xx Direct labor xx Finished goods xx Direct-labor efficiency variance xx Work in process xx
Overhead accounting	Department overhead xx Various accounts xx or (a) Depreciation xx Repairs xx Supplies used xx Various accounts xx (b) Department overhead xx Depreciation xx Repairs xx Supplies used xx	(Similar methods to those shown at the left.)		

As explained in Chapter 7, the timing of the isolation of material, labor, and overhead variances will be influenced by the specific system employed.

Although the computations of material and labor variances are usually the same regardless of the standard-cost system used, the computations of overhead variances are by no means uniform in practice. The methodology described in Chapter 9 is generally superior to other methods, but published solutions to CPA problems have shown a number of alternative approaches. Moreover, a single overhead application rate, composed of both variable and fixed elements as described in the appendix to Chapter 9, is often used. These alternative solutions are described below, using the following basic data:

Budget formula for monthly overhead: $100,000 fixed overhead
+ ($1.00 × direct-labor hours)
Denominator volume, which is more often called normal or standard volume: 400,000 hours
Combined-overhead rate for product costing:

$$\frac{\$100,000 + (400,000 \times \$1.00)}{400,000} = \$1.25$$

Month of August:

Actual direct hours	450,000
Standard direct hours allowed for work done	430,000
Actual overhead, including $103,000 of fixed costs	$570,000
Applied overhead, 430,000 × $1.25	$537,500
Total variance, $570,000 less $537,500	$ 32,500

Alternative 1. The recommended approach as described in Chapter 9. Budget based on standard hours allowed.

	ACTUAL	BUDGET—ACTUAL HOURS	BUDGET— STANDARD HOURS	APPLIED
		$100,000 + $1(450,000)	$100,000 + $1(430,000)	
V	$467,000	$450,000	$430,000	$430,000
F	103,000	100,000	100,000	107,500
	$570,000	$550,000	$530,000	$537,500

Spending Variance, $20,000 U

Efficiency Variance, $20,000 U ($1.00 × 20,000 hours)

Volume Variance, $7,500 F ($.25 × 30,000 hours)

Budget Variance, $40,000 U

Alternative 2. The pertinent budget level for measuring volume variance is considered to be actual hours rather than standard hours as in Alternative 1. Also, fixed factory overhead shows an efficiency variance (sometimes called an *effectiveness variance*), measured like other efficiency variances. This supposedly gives a measure of the efficient or inefficient utilization of facilities.

	ACTUAL	BUDGET—ACTUAL HOURS	ACTUAL HOURS × OVERHEAD RATE	APPLIED
V	$467,000	$450,000	$450,000	$430,000
F	103,000	100,000	112,500	107,500
	$570,000	$550,000	$562,500	$537,500

Budget Variance, $20,000 U

Volume Variance, $12,500 F
(450,000 − 400,000)
× $.25

Efficiency Variance:
Variable $20,000 U
Fixed   5,000 U
          $25,000 U

Comparison of alternatives 1 and 2: Efficiency variance for fixed overhead? Note that the efficiency variance is a subpart of the budget variance under Alternative 1, whereas it could be considered a subpart of the volume variance under Alternative 2. Let us compare these two alternatives more closely.

Alternative 1: Budget variance consists of both spending and efficiency variance.
Alternative 2: Budget variance is the same as the "spending" variance under Alternative 1.

The efficiency variance for variable overhead is the same under both alternatives.

Under Alternative 2, the fixed-overhead analysis differs considerably from that in Alternative 1. Basically, however, all that is done is to take the volume variance of $7,500 computed in Alternative 1 and subdivide it further as follows:

Volume variance in Alternative 1		$7,500 F
Breakdown in Alternative 2:		
Fixed-overhead efficiency variance, $.25 × 20,000 hours	$ 5,000 U	
True "volume" variance (actual hours worked minus denominator hours) × rate (50,000 hours × $.25)	12,500 F	7,500 F

The efficiency variance for fixed overhead is a misnomer; it would be better to call it an effectiveness variance. It should be distinguished sharply from the efficiency variances for materials, labor, and variable overhead, because efficient usage of these three factors can affect actual cost incurrence, whereas short-run fixed-overhead cost incurrence is not affected by efficiency. Thus, a better label for the fixed-overhead "efficiency" variance would be "effectiveness" variance, a sort of rough-and-ready measure that may have some psychological value as a reminder to the department head that his efficiency has an impact on effective utilization of facilities.

This writer sees little merit in this computation except where ineffective utilization of facilities means a loss of sales. For instance, if maximum capacity is 500,000 standard hours, and the sales department can obtain orders in excess of 500,000-hour capacity, the inefficient use of facilities involves an opportunity cost that is properly chargeable to the foreman. The best measure of this cost would often be the lost contribution margins on the orders not filled. In lieu of this measure, the use of the effectiveness variance could be a crude attempt to quantify the foreman's performance. Hence, if an efficiency or effectiveness variance is employed, its weakness should be recognized.

Thus, the volume variance in Alternative 1 would be chargeable to someone other than the foreman. It might be traceable to the sales manager, to the head of production control, or to random outside influences. Under Alternative 1, the foreman would not ordinarily be considered explicitly responsible for efficient use of facilities.

Alternative 3. This is a hybrid of Alternatives 1 and 2. It demonstrates that overhead-variance analysis can be conducted in a great number of ways. Here the budget is based on standard hours allowed, but the efficiency variance is computed by using a combined $1.25 rate rather than attributing efficiency to variable-overhead control only.

ACTUAL	BUDGET—STANDARD HOURS ALLOWED	APPLIED
$570,000	$530,000	$537,500

Budget Variance, $40,000 U   Volume Variance, $7,500 F

Subdivide the budget variance as follows:

Efficiency variance is $1.25 × 20,000 hours	$25,000 U
Remainder is spending variance	15,000 U
Budget variance	$40,000 U

Alternative 4. This is the most miserable alternative of all, because the flexible-budget concept is not employed. Instead, the appropriate budget is considered to be the one based on the planned activity level used to set the overhead rate for product costing (normal or standard volume), regardless of the actual level of activity that ensues. The resulting variance analysis seems more confusing than it is worth; yet it is shown here because several CPA solutions through the years have presented this approach.

ACTUAL	BUDGET—DENOMINATOR ACTIVITY	ACTUAL HOURS × OVERHEAD RATE	APPLIED
$570,000	$500,000	$562,500	$537,500

*Budget Variance,   †Volume Variance,   Efficiency Variance,
$70,000 U $62,500 F $25,000 U

* Note that this compares actual cost incurrence with a budget based on activity entirely different from the actual activity level.

† The volume variance's main weakness is the use of a combined rate rather than the fixed-overhead rate, which is pertinent to the measure of a volume variance.

SPOILAGE

The alternate ways of accounting for spoilage in process costing were discussed in Chapter 18. Many published CPA solutions ignore the computations of equivalent units for spoilage, shrinkage, or waste. The reason cited in favor of this shortcut technique is that it automatically spreads spoilage costs over good units through the use of higher equivalent unit costs. However, the results of this shortcut are questionable in many cases, as was shown in Chapter 18. If the candidate faces a spoilage problem, he should solve it in the conceptually correct manner but make a special note to describe his approach and to state that alternative approaches ignore computations of equivalent units for spoilage, shrinkage, and waste.

summary

The CPA candidate needs to be aware of which cost-accounting topics are most likely to appear on the CPA examination. An analysis of the five to ten most recent examinations provides the best clues.

He also should have a general knowledge of what areas in cost accounting are marked by divergent accounting terminology and techniques. These include general-ledger design, analysis of overhead variances, and accounting for spoilage.

Careful study of appropriate topics in this book will fortify the CPA candidate with sufficient background for success in the cost-accounting phases of the CPA examination. Chapters 7–13 and 16–18 should be particularly helpful.

suggested readings

Horngren, Charles T., and J. Arthur Leer, *CPA Problems and Approaches to Solutions,* 3rd ed. Englewood Cliffs, N.J.: Prentice-Hall, Inc., 1969.

Miller, Herbert E., and George Mead, eds., *CPA Review Manual,* 4th ed. Englewood Cliffs, N.J.: Prentice-Hall, Inc., 1972.

questions, problems, and cases

28-1. What are two special characteristics of the national CPA examination that the candidate must recognize?

28-2. "We should be careful to review the A.I.C.P.A. solutions to past CPA questions so that we learn the official answers." Do you agree? Why?

28-3. Four Methods of Analyzing Overhead Variances.   The Signe Company uses a combined-overhead rate of $4.00 per hour for product costing under a standard-cost system. Denominator activity is 10,000 hours, or 5,000 finished units. At that level the overhead budget is: variable, $30,000; fixed, $10,000.

Actual level of activity: 8,700 hours and 4,400 units produced
Actual overhead incurred: variable, $28,000; fixed, $9,700

required   Show at least four different methods of analyzing overhead variances. Include one method in which the appropriate budget is considered to be one based on denominator activity regardless of the actual activity that ensues; that is, assume that the flexible-budget concept is not employed.

28-4. Standard Costs, Alternate Analysis of Variances [CPA]. The Dearborn Company manufactures Product X in standard batches of 100 units. A standard-cost system is in use. The standard costs for a batch are as follows:

Raw materials	60 lbs. @ $ .45 per lb.	$ 27.00
Direct labor	36 hrs. @ $2.15 per hr.	77.40
Overhead	36 hrs. @ $2.75 per hr.	99.00
		$203.40

Production for April 19_0 amounted to 210 batches. The relevant statistics follow:

Denominator output per month	24,000 units
Raw materials used	13,000 lbs.
Cost of raw materials used	$ 6,110.00
Direct-labor cost	$16,790.40
Overhead cost	$20,592.00
Average overhead rate per hour	$2.60

The management has noted that actual costs per batch deviate somewhat from standard costs per batch.

required   Prepare a statement that will contain a detailed explanation of the difference between actual costs and standard costs.

SECTION FOUR

APPENDIXES

List of N.A.A.
Research Publications

The following articles are from research publications of the National Association of Accountants, 505 Park Avenue, New York City. For many years, these were issued as separate third sections of the association's monthly *N.A.A. Bulletin*, now called *Management Accounting*. That is why volume numbers are shown for many of the items in this listing. Also of interest is Walter B. McFarland, *Concepts for Management Accounting* (New York: National Association of Accountants, 1966). The aim of this book is "to unify the association's research findings from previous studies into ordered patterns."

ACCOUNTING RESEARCH REPORTS

No.

11–15 (Combined).
       "How Standards Costs Are Being Used Currently."
16–18 (Combined).
       "The Analysis of Cost-Volume-Profit Relationships."
19–21 (Combined).
       "The Analysis of Non-Manufacturing Costs for Managerial Decisions."
22.   "The Analysis of Manufacturing Cost Variances." XXXIII, No. 12.
23.   "Direct Costing." XXXIV, No. 8.
24.   "Product Costs for Pricing Purposes." XXXIV, No. 12.
25–27 (Combined).
       "Cost Control for Marketing Operations."
28.   "Presenting Accounting Information to Management." XXXVI, No. 4.
29.   "Accounting for Research and Development Costs." XXXVI, No. 10.
30.   "Accounting for Intra-Company Transfers." XXXVII, No. 10.
31.   "Costing Joint Products." XXXVIII, No. 8.

32. "Accounting for Labor Costs and Labor-Related Costs." XXXIX, No. 3.
33. "Current Practice in Accounting for Depreciation." XXXIX, No. 8.
34. "Classification and Coding Techniques to Facilitate Accounting Operations." XLV, No. 8.
35. "Return on Capital as a Guide to Managerial Decisions."
36. "Management Accounting Problems in Foreign Operations."
37. "Current Applications of Direct Costing."
38. "Cash Flow Analysis for Managerial Control."
39. "Accounting for Costs of Capacity."
40. "Techniques in Inventory Management."
41. "Control of Maintenance Cost."
42. "Long-Range Profit Planning."

ACCOUNTING PRACTICE REPORTS

No.
1. "Controlling and Accounting for Supplies." XXXVI, No. 10.
2. "Planning, Controlling, and Accounting for Maintenance." XXXVII, No. 3.
3. "Modifying the Calendar to Meet Business Needs." XXXVII, No. 10.
4. "Accounting for Returnable Containers." XXXVIII, No. 5.
5. "Speeding Up Interim Closings and Reports." XXXVIII, No. 7.
6. "Serving Sales Through Planning of Production and Inventory." XXXIX, No. 5.
7. "The Capital Expenditure Control Program." XXXIX, No. 7.
8. "Cost Improvement for Profit Improvement." XLI, No. 2.
9. "Reports Which Managements Find Most Useful." XLI, No. 6.
10. "Separating and Using Costs as Fixed and Variable." XLI, No. 10.
11. "Applying Accruals and Deferrals to Interim Closings." XLII, No. 8.
12. "Cost Control of Spoiled Work." XLII, No. 10.
13. "Use of Graphs in Internal Reporting." XLIII, No. 2.
14. "Experience with Return on Capital to Appraise Management Performance." XLIII, No. 6.
15. "Development and Reporting of Variances." XLIII, No. 11.
16. "Departures in Communicating Accounting Data to Foremen." XLIV, No. 5.

B

Notes on Compound Interest and Interest Tables

INTEREST

Interest is the cost of using money. It is the rental charge for funds, just as rental charges are made for the use of buildings and equipment. Whenever a time span is involved, it is necessary to recognize interest as a cost of using invested funds. This applies even if the funds in use represent ownership capital and if the interest does not entail an outlay of cash. The reason why interest must be considered is that the selection of one alternative automatically commits a given amount of invested funds that otherwise could be invested in some other opportunity. The measure of the interest in such cases is the return foregone by rejecting the alternative use.

Interest is often unimportant when short-term projects are under consideration, but it looms large when long-run plans are being considered. Because of this, the rate of interest in question is of telling import. The rate used will often influence the ultimate decision. For example, $100,000 invested now and compounded annually for ten years at 3 percent will accumulate to $134,392; at 7 percent, to $196,715.

INTEREST TABLES

Four basic tables are used for computations involving interest. Tables 2 and 4 are the most pertinent for our purposes.

table 1—
amount of $1

Table 1 shows how much $1 invested now will accumulate to in a given number of periods at a given compounded interest rate per period. The future proceeds of an investment of $1,000 for three years at 8 percent compound interest could be sketched as follows:

Accumulate

$1,000 × (1.08)^3 or $1,000 × 1.2597 (from Table 1) = $1,259.70

| 0 | 1 | 2 | 3 |

Present Value ← — Amount

Discount

TABULAR CALCULATION

YEAR	INTEREST PER YEAR	CUMULATIVE INTEREST, CALLED COMPOUND INTEREST	TOTAL AT END OF PERIOD
0	$ —	$ —	$1,000.00
1	80.00	80.00	1,080.00
2	86.40	166.40	1,166.40
3	93.30	259.70	1,259.70

Note that what is really being done in the tabular presentation is a series of computations that could appear as follows:

$$S_1 = 1,000(1.08)$$
$$S_2 = 1,000(1.08)^2$$
$$S_3 = 1,000(1.08)^3$$

The formula for the "amount of 1," often called the "future value of 1," can be written:

$$S = P(1 + r)^n$$
$$S = 1,000(1 + .08)^3 = \$1,259.70$$

S is the *amount*, the future worth; P is the present value, $1,000 in this case; r is the rate of return; n is the number of periods.

Fortunately, tables make key computations readily available, so that a facility in selecting the *proper* table will minimize computations. Check the accuracy of the answer above against Table 1, page 939.

table 2—
present value
of $1

In the previous example, if $1,000 compounded at 8 percent per annum will accumulate to $1,259.70 in three years, then $1,000 must be the present value of $1,259.70 due at the end of three years. The formula for the present value can be derived by reversing the process of *accumulation* (getting the amount) that we just finished. Look at the earlier sketch to see the relationship between accumulating and discounting.

If
$$S = P(1 + r)^n$$

then
$$P = \frac{S}{(1 + r)^n}$$

$$P = \frac{\$1,259.70}{(1.08)^3} = \$1,000$$

Use Table 2, page 940, to check this calculation.

When accumulating, we advance or roll forward in time. The difference between our original amount and our accumulated amount is called *compound interest*. When discounting, we retreat or roll back in time. The difference between the future amount and the present value is called *compound discount*. Note the following formulas:

$$\text{Compound interest} = (1 + r)^n - 1 = \$259.70$$

$$\text{Compound discount} = 1 - \frac{1}{(1 + r)^n} = \$259.70$$

table 3—
amount of
annuity of $1

An (ordinary) *annuity* is a series of equal payments (receipts) to be paid (or received) at the *end* of successive periods of equal length. Assume that $1,000 is invested at the end of each of three years at 8 percent:

0		1		2		3	

			AMOUNT
1st payment	$1,000.00	$1,080.00	$1,166.40
2nd payment		$1,000.00	1,080.00
3rd payment			1,000.00
Accumulation (Amount)			$3,246.40

The arithmetic shown above may be expressed algebraically as the amount of an ordinary annuity of $1,000 for three years = $1,000(1 + r)^2 + $1,000(1 + r)^1 + $1,000.

We can develop the general formula for S_n, the amount of an ordinary annuity of $1, by using the example above as a basis:

(1) $\qquad\qquad\qquad S_n = 1 + (1 + r)^1 + (1 + r)^2$

(2) Substitute: $\qquad\quad S_n = 1 + (1.08) + (1.08)^2$

(3) Multiply (2) by $(1 + r)$: $\quad (1.08)S_n = 1.08 + (1.08)^2 + (1.08)^3$

(4) Subtract (2) from (3): $\quad 1.08S_n - S_n = (1.08)^3 - 1$

Note that all terms on right-hand side are removed except $(1.08)^3$ in equation (3) and 1 in equation (2).

(5) Factor (4): $\qquad$ $S_n(1.08 - 1) = (1.08)^3 - 1$

(6) Divide (5) by $(1.08 - 1)$: $\quad S_n = \dfrac{(1.08)^3 - 1}{1.08 - 1} = \dfrac{(1.08)^3 - 1}{.08}$

(7) The general formula for the amount of an ordinary annuity of \$1 becomes:

$$S_n = \frac{(1 + r)^n - 1}{r} \quad \text{or} \quad \frac{\text{Compound Interest}}{\text{Rate}}$$

This formula is the basis for Table 3, page 941. Look at Table 3 or use the formula itself to check the calculations.

table 4—
present value
of an ordinary
annuity of \$1

Using the same example as for Table 3, we can show how the formula of P_n, the present value of an ordinary annuity, is developed.

```
 |_____|_____|_____|
 0       1       2       3
```

PRESENT VALUE

1st payment: $\dfrac{1{,}000}{1.08} = \$\ \ 926.14 \qquad \$1{,}000$

2nd payment: $\dfrac{1{,}000}{(1.08)^2} = \$\ \ 857.52 \qquad\qquad\qquad \$1{,}000$

3rd payment: $\dfrac{1{,}000}{(1.08)^3} = \dfrac{\$\ \ 794.00}{\$2{,}577.66} \qquad\qquad\qquad\qquad\qquad \$1{,}000$

For the general case, the present value of an ordinary annuity of \$1 may be expressed:

(1) $\qquad P_n = \dfrac{1}{1 + r} + \dfrac{1}{(1 + r)^2} + \dfrac{1}{(1 + r)^3}$

(2) Substituting, $\qquad P_n = \dfrac{1}{1.08} + \dfrac{1}{(1.08)^2} + \dfrac{1}{(1.08)^3}$

(3) Multiply by $\dfrac{1}{1.08}$: $\qquad P_n \dfrac{1}{1.08} = \dfrac{1}{(1.08)^2} + \dfrac{1}{(1.08)^3} + \dfrac{1}{(1.08)^4}$

(4) Subtract (3) from (2): $\qquad P_n - P_n \dfrac{1}{1.08} = \dfrac{1}{1.08} - \dfrac{1}{(1.08)^4}$

(5) Factor: $\qquad P_n \left(1 - \dfrac{1}{1.08}\right) = \dfrac{1}{1.08}\left[1 - \dfrac{1}{(1.08)^3}\right]$

(6) or $\qquad P_n \left(\dfrac{.08}{1.08}\right) = \dfrac{1}{1.08}\left[1 - \dfrac{1}{(1.08)^3}\right]$

(7) Divide by $\dfrac{.08}{1.08}$: $\qquad P_n = \dfrac{1}{.08}\left[1 - \dfrac{1}{(1.08)^3}\right]$

The general formula for the present worth of an annuity is:

$$P_n = \frac{1}{r}\left(1 - \frac{1}{(1 + r)^n}\right) = \frac{\text{Compound Discount}}{\text{Rate}}$$

Solving,

$$P_n = \frac{.2062}{.08} = 2.577$$

This formula is the basis for Table 4, page 942. Check the answer in the table. The present value tables, Tables 2 and 4, are used most frequently in capital budgeting.

Note that the tables for annuities are not really essential. That is, with Tables 1 and 2, compound interest and compound discount can be readily computed. Then it is simply a matter of dividing either of these by the rate to get values equivalent to those shown in Tables 3 and 4.

TABLE 1

AMOUNT OF $1.00

$S = P(1 + r)^n$

PERIODS	2%	4%	5%	6%	8%	10%
1	1.0200	1.0400	1.0500	1.0600	1.0800	1.1000
2	1.0404	1.0816	1.1025	1.1236	1.1664	1.2100
3	1.0612	1.1249	1.1576	1.1910	1.2597	1.3310
4	1.0824	1.1699	1.2155	1.2625	1.3605	1.4641
5	1.1041	1.2167	1.2763	1.3382	1.4693	1.6105
6	1.1262	1.2653	1.3401	1.4185	1.5869	1.7716
7	1.1487	1.3159	1.4071	1.5036	1.7138	1.9488
8	1.1717	1.3686	1.4775	1.5938	1.8509	2.1436
9	1.1951	1.4233	1.5513	1.6895	1.9990	2.3589
10	1.2190	1.4802	1.6289	1.7908	2.1589	2.5938
11	1.2434	1.5395	1.7103	1.8983	2.3316	2.8532
12	1.2682	1.6010	1.7959	2.0122	2.5182	3.1385
13	1.2936	1.6651	1.8856	2.1329	2.7196	3.4524
14	1.3195	1.7317	1.9799	2.2609	2.9372	3.7976
15	1.3459	1.8009	2.0709	2.3966	3.1722	4.1774
16	1.3728	1.8730	2.1829	2.5404	3.4259	4.5951
17	1.4002	1.9479	2.2920	2.6928	3.7000	5.0545
18	1.4282	2.0258	2.4066	2.8543	3.9960	5.5600
19	1.4568	2.1068	2.5270	3.0256	4.3157	6.1160
20	1.4859	2.1911	2.6533	3.2071	4.6610	6.7276
30	1.8114	3.2434	4.3219	5.7435	10.0627	17.4495
40	2.2080	4.8010	7.0400	10.2857	21.7245	45.2597

TABLE 2

PRESENT VALUE OF $1.00

$$P = \frac{S}{(1 + r)^n}$$

PERIODS	4%	6%	8%	10%	12%	14%	16%	18%	20%	22%	24%	26%	28%	30%	40%
1	0.962	0.943	0.926	0.909	0.893	0.877	0.862	0.847	0.833	0.820	0.806	0.794	0.781	0.769	0.714
2	0.925	0.890	0.857	0.826	0.797	0.769	0.743	0.718	0.694	0.672	0.650	0.630	0.610	0.592	0.510
3	0.889	0.840	0.794	0.751	0.712	0.675	0.641	0.609	0.579	0.551	0.524	0.500	0.477	0.455	0.364
4	0.855	0.792	0.735	0.683	0.636	0.592	0.552	0.516	0.482	0.451	0.423	0.397	0.373	0.350	0.260
5	0.822	0.747	0.681	0.621	0.567	0.519	0.476	0.437	0.402	0.370	0.341	0.315	0.291	0.269	0.186
6	0.790	0.705	0.630	0.564	0.507	0.456	0.410	0.370	0.335	0.303	0.275	0.250	0.227	0.207	0.133
7	0.760	0.665	0.583	0.513	0.452	0.400	0.354	0.314	0.279	0.249	0.222	0.198	0.178	0.159	0.095
8	0.731	0.627	0.540	0.467	0.404	0.351	0.305	0.266	0.233	0.204	0.179	0.157	0.139	0.123	0.068
9	0.703	0.592	0.500	0.424	0.361	0.308	0.263	0.225	0.194	0.167	0.144	0.125	0.108	0.094	0.048
10	0.676	0.558	0.463	0.386	0.322	0.270	0.227	0.191	0.162	0.137	0.116	0.099	0.085	0.073	0.035
11	0.650	0.527	0.429	0.350	0.287	0.237	0.195	0.162	0.135	0.112	0.094	0.079	0.066	0.056	0.025
12	0.625	0.497	0.397	0.319	0.257	0.208	0.168	0.137	0.112	0.092	0.076	0.062	0.052	0.043	0.018
13	0.601	0.469	0.368	0.290	0.229	0.182	0.145	0.116	0.093	0.075	0.061	0.050	0.040	0.033	0.013
14	0.577	0.442	0.340	0.263	0.205	0.160	0.125	0.099	0.078	0.062	0.049	0.039	0.032	0.025	0.009
15	0.555	0.417	0.315	0.239	0.183	0.140	0.108	0.084	0.065	0.051	0.040	0.031	0.025	0.020	0.006
16	0.534	0.394	0.292	0.218	0.163	0.123	0.093	0.071	0.054	0.042	0.032	0.025	0.019	0.015	0.005
17	0.513	0.371	0.270	0.198	0.146	0.108	0.080	0.060	0.045	0.034	0.026	0.020	0.015	0.012	0.003
18	0.494	0.350	0.250	0.180	0.130	0.095	0.069	0.051	0.038	0.028	0.021	0.016	0.012	0.009	0.002
19	0.475	0.331	0.232	0.164	0.116	0.083	0.060	0.043	0.031	0.023	0.017	0.012	0.009	0.007	0.002
20	0.456	0.312	0.215	0.149	0.104	0.073	0.051	0.037	0.026	0.019	0.014	0.010	0.007	0.005	0.001
21	0.439	0.294	0.199	0.135	0.093	0.064	0.044	0.031	0.022	0.015	0.011	0.008	0.006	0.004	0.001
22	0.422	0.278	0.184	0.123	0.083	0.056	0.038	0.026	0.018	0.013	0.009	0.006	0.004	0.003	0.001
23	0.406	0.262	0.170	0.112	0.074	0.049	0.033	0.022	0.015	0.010	0.007	0.005	0.003	0.002	
24	0.390	0.247	0.158	0.102	0.066	0.043	0.028	0.019	0.013	0.008	0.006	0.004	0.003	0.002	
25	0.375	0.233	0.146	0.092	0.059	0.038	0.024	0.016	0.010	0.007	0.005	0.003	0.002	0.001	
26	0.361	0.220	0.135	0.084	0.053	0.033	0.021	0.014	0.009	0.006	0.004	0.002	0.002	0.001	
27	0.347	0.207	0.125	0.076	0.047	0.029	0.018	0.011	0.007	0.005	0.003	0.002	0.001	0.001	
28	0.333	0.196	0.116	0.069	0.042	0.026	0.016	0.010	0.006	0.004	0.002	0.002	0.001	0.001	
29	0.321	0.185	0.107	0.063	0.037	0.022	0.014	0.008	0.005	0.003	0.002	0.001	0.001	0.001	
30	0.308	0.174	0.099	0.057	0.033	0.020	0.012	0.007	0.004	0.003	0.002	0.001	0.001	0.001	
40	0.208	0.097	0.046	0.022	0.011	0.005	0.003	0.001	0.001						

TABLE 3

AMOUNT OF ANNUITY OF $1.00 IN ARREARS

$$S_n = \frac{(1 + r)^n - 1}{r}$$

PERIODS	2%	4%	5%	6%	8%	10%
1	1.0000	1.0000	1.0000	1.0000	1.0000	1.0000
2	2.0200	2.0400	2.0500	2.0600	2.0800	2.1000
3	3.0604	3.1216	3.1525	3.1836	3.2464	3.3100
4	4.1216	4.2465	4.3101	4.3746	4.5061	4.6410
5	5.2040	5.4163	5.5256	5.6371	5.8666	6.1051
6	6.3081	6.6330	6.8019	6.9753	7.3359	7.7156
7	7.4343	7.8983	8.1420	8.3938	8.9228	9.4872
8	8.5830	9.2142	9.5491	9.8975	10.6366	11.4360
9	9.7546	10.5828	11.0266	11.4913	12.4876	13.5796
10	10.9497	12.0061	12.5779	13.1808	14.4866	15.9376
11	12.1687	13.4864	14.2068	14.9716	16.6455	18.5314
12	13.4121	15.0258	15.9171	16.8699	18.9771	21.3846
13	14.6803	16.6268	17.7130	18.8821	21.4953	24.5231
14	15.9739	18.2919	19.5986	21.0151	24.2149	27.9755
15	17.2934	20.0236	21.5786	23.2760	27.1521	31.7731
16	18.6393	21.8245	23.6575	25.6725	30.3243	35.9503
17	20.0121	23.6975	25.8404	28.2129	33.7502	40.5456
18	21.4123	25.6454	28.1324	30.9057	37.4502	45.6001
19	22.8406	27.6712	30.5390	33.7600	41.4463	51.1601
20	24.2974	29.7781	33.0660	36.7856	45.7620	57.2761
30	40.5681	56.0849	66.4388	79.0582	113.2832	164.4962
40	60.4020	95.0255	120.7998	154.7620	259.0565	442.5974

TABLE 4

PRESENT VALUE OF ANNUITY OF $1.00 IN ARREARS

$$P_n = \frac{1}{r}\left[1 - \frac{1}{(1+r)^n}\right]$$

PERIODS	4%	6%	8%	10%	12%	14%	16%	18%	20%	22%	24%	25%	26%	28%	30%	40%
1	0.962	0.943	0.926	0.909	0.893	0.877	0.862	0.847	0.833	0.820						
2	1.886	1.833	1.783	1.736	1.690	1.647	1.6051	1.566	1.528	1.492						
3	2.775	2.673	2.577	2.487	2.402	2.322	2.246	2.174	2.106	2.042						
4	3.630	3.465	3.312	3.170	3.037	2.914	2.798	2.690	2.589	2.494						
5	4.452	4.212	3.993	3.791	3.605	3.433	3.274	3.127	2.991	2.864						
6	5.242	4.917	4.623	4.355	4.111	3.889	3.685	3.498	3.326	3.167						
7	6.002	5.582	5.206	4.868	4.564	4.288	4.039	3.812	3.605	3.416						
8	6.733	6.210	5.747	5.335	4.968	4.639	4.344	4.078	3.837	3.619						
9	7.435	6.802	6.247	5.759	5.328	4.946	4.607	4.303	4.031	3.786						
10	8.111	7.360	6.710	6.145	5.650	5.216	4.833	4.494	4.192	3.923						
11	8.760	7.887	7.139	6.495	5.988	5.453	5.029	4.656	4.327	4.035				3.335	3.147	2.438
12	9.385	8.384	7.536	6.814	6.194	5.660	5.197	4.793	4.439	4.127		3.725	3.606	3.387	3.190	2.456
13	9.986	8.853	7.904	7.103	6.424	5.842	5.342	4.910	4.533	4.203	3.912	3.780	3.656	3.427	3.223	2.468
14	10.563	9.295	8.244	7.367	6.628	6.002	5.468	5.008	4.611	4.265	3.962	3.824	3.695	3.459	3.249	2.477
15	11.118	9.712	8.559	7.606	6.811	6.142	5.575	5.092	4.675	4.315	4.001	3.859	3.726	3.483	3.268	2.484
16	11.652	10.106	8.851	7.824	6.974	6.265	5.669	5.162	4.730	4.357	4.033	3.887	3.751	3.503	3.283	2.489
17	12.166	10.477	9.122	8.022	7.120	6.373	5.749	5.222	4.775	4.391	4.059	3.910	3.771	3.518	3.295	2.492
18	12.659	10.828	9.372	8.201	7.250	6.467	5.818	5.273	4.812	4.419	4.080	3.928	3.786	3.529	3.304	2.494
19	13.134	11.158	9.604	8.365	7.366	6.550	5.877	5.316	4.844	4.442	4.097	3.942	3.799	3.539	3.311	2.496
20	13.590	11.470	9.818	8.514	7.469	6.623	5.929	5.353	4.870	4.460	4.110	3.954	3.808	3.546	3.316	2.497
21	14.029	11.764	10.017	8.649	7.562	6.687	5.973	5.384	4.891	4.476	4.121	3.963	3.816	3.551	3.320	2.498
22	14.451	12.042	10.201	8.772	7.645	6.743	6.011	5.410	4.909	4.488	4.130	3.970	3.822	3.556	3.323	2.498
23	14.857	12.303	10.371	8.883	7.718	6.792	6.044	5.432	4.925	4.499	4.137	3.976	3.827	3.559	3.325	2.499
24	15.247	12.550	10.529	8.985	7.784	6.835	6.073	5.451	4.937	4.507	4.143	3.981	3.831	3.562	3.327	2.499
25	15.622	12.783	10.675	9.077	7.843	6.873	6.097	5.467	4.948	4.514	4.147	3.985	3.834	3.564	3.329	2.499
26	15.983	13.003	10.810	9.161	7.896	6.906	6.118	5.480	4.956	4.520	4.151	3.988	3.837	3.566	3.330	2.500
27	16.330	13.211	10.935	9.237	7.943	6.935	6.136	5.492	4.964	4.525	4.154	3.990	3.839	3.567	3.331	2.500
28	16.663	13.406	11.051	9.307	7.984	6.961	6.152	5.502	4.970	4.528	4.157	3.992	3.840	3.568	3.331	2.500
29	16.984	13.591	11.158	9.370	8.022	6.983	6.166	5.510	4.975	4.531	4.159	3.994	3.841	3.569	3.332	2.500
30	17.292	13.765	11.258	9.427	8.055	7.003	6.177	5.517	4.979	4.534	4.160	3.995	3.842	3.569	3.332	2.500
40	19.793	15.046	11.925	9.779	8.244	7.105	6.234	5.548	4.997	4.544	4.166	3.999	3.846	3.571	3.333	2.500

Glossary

ABNORMAL SPOILAGE. Spoilage that should not arise under efficient operating conditions.

ABSORPTION COSTING. That type of product costing which assigns fixed manufacturing overhead to the units produced as a product cost. Contrasts with direct costing.

ACCOUNTING METHOD. *See* Unadjusted rate of return.

ACCOUNTING SYSTEM. A formal communications network that supplies relevant information for planning, control, decision making, and evaluation. Accounting systems are judged by how they help promote and impel personnel toward organizational goals.

ACTIVITY ACCOUNTING. *See* Responsibility accounting.

ALLOCATION. Assigning one or more items of cost or revenue to one or more segments of an organization according to benefits received, responsibilities, or other logical measures of use.

APPROPRIATION. An authorization to spend up to a specified dollar amount.

ASSET TURNOVER. The ratio of sales to total assets available.

ATTENTION DIRECTING. That function of the accountant's information-supplying task which focuses problems in the operation of the firm or which points out imperfections or inefficiencies in certain areas of the firm's operation.

BILL OF MATERIALS. A specification of the quantities of direct materials allowed for manufacturing a given quantity of output.

BOOK VALUE METHOD.   *See* Unadjusted rate of return.

BREAKEVEN POINT.   That level of operations where total expenses equal total revenue.

BUDGET.   A plan of action expressed in figures.

BUDGET VARIANCE.   The difference between the actual amount incurred and the budget figure.

BY-PRODUCTS.   Joint products that have minor sales value as compared with that of the major or chief product(s).

CAPACITY COSTS.   An alternate term for *fixed costs*, emphasizing the fact that fixed costs are needed to provide operating facilities and an organization ready to produce and sell at a planned volume of activity.

CAPITAL BUDGETING.   Long-term planning for proposed capital outlays and their financing.

CASH BUDGET.   A schedule of expected cash receipts and disbursements.

CASH FLOW.   The net effect of cash receipts and disbursements for a specified period.

COMMITTED COSTS.   Those fixed costs arising from the possession of plant and equipment and a basic organization and, thus, affected primarily by long-run decisions as to the desired level of capacity.

COMMON COST.   *See* Joint cost.

COMPTROLLER.   *See* Controller.

CONTINUOUS BUDGET.   A budget which perpetually adds a month or quarter in the future as the month or quarter just ended is dropped.

CONTRIBUTION APPROACH.   A method of preparing income statements which separates variable costs from fixed costs in order to emphasize the importance of cost behavior patterns for purposes of planning and control.

CONTRIBUTION MARGIN.   Excess of sales price over variable expenses. Also called *marginal income*. May be expressed as a total, a ratio, or on a per-unit basis.

CONTROL CHART.   A scatter diagram that helps to distinguish chance variances from variances that need investigation. Used in statistical quality control situations.

CONTROLLABLE COST.   A cost which may be directly regulated at a given level of managerial authority, either in the short run or in the long run.

CONTROLLER.   The chief management accounting executive. Also spelled *comptroller.*

CONTROLLING.   Obtaining conformity to plans through action and evaluation.

CONVERSION COST.   The sum of direct labor and all factory overhead.

COST ACCOUNTING.   A quantitative method that accumulates, classifies, summarizes, and interprets information for three major purposes: (1) operational planning and control, (2) special decisions, and (3) product costing.

COST CENTER. The smallest unit of activity or area of responsibility for which costs are accumulated.

COST OF GOODS SOLD. Inventoriable costs released to the current period (an expense) as a result of the sale of goods.

COSTS OF CARRYING. The unavoidable costs of carrying inventory. They are primarily interest on investment, obsolescence write-offs, and space costs. Overstocking may raise these costs to dangerous levels.

COSTS OF NOT CARRYING. These include expensive expediting, loss of sales, and loss of customer goodwill associated with carrying too little inventory. They are more difficult to measure than costs of carrying, and they are potentially more harmful.

CURRENTLY ATTAINABLE STANDARDS. Standards expressing a level of economic efficiency which can be reached with skilled, diligent, superior effort.

DATA PROCESSING. The accumulation, classification, analysis, and reporting of large quantities of information. Mechanical equipment rather than human beings are the major processors of this information.

DECISION MAKING. Choosing between alternate courses of action.

DENOMINATOR VOLUME. That level of activity that is divided into total budgeted fixed manufacturing costs in order to obtain a unit cost for product costing purposes.

DIFFERENTIAL COST. *See* Incremental cost.

DIRECT COSTING. That type of product costing which charges fixed manufacturing overhead immediately against the revenue of the period in which it was incurred, without assigning it to specific units produced. Also called *variable costing* and *marginal costing.*

DIRECT LABOR. All labor which is obviously related and specifically and conveniently traceable to specific products.

DIRECT MATERIAL. All raw material which becomes an integral part of the finished good and which can be conveniently assigned to specific physical units.

DISCRETIONARY COSTS. Those fixed costs that arise from periodic, usually yearly, appropriation decisions that directly reflect top-management policies. Also called *managed costs* and *programmed costs.*

DISTRIBUTION COSTS. Nonmanufacturing costs of marketing, shipping, warehousing, billing, financing, and so forth.

ECONOMIC ORDER QUANTITY. The amount of inventory which should be ordered at one time in order to minimize the associated annual costs of the inventory.

EFFICIENCY VARIANCE. Quantity variance applied to labor and variable overhead.

EQUIVALENT UNITS. The number of full doses of work applied to units of product. For example, if 1,000 units are $\frac{3}{4}$ complete in terms of direct labor, then 750 equivalent units of direct labor exist.

EXCESS MATERIAL REQUISITIONS. A form to be filled out by the production staff to secure any materials needed in excess of the standard amount allotted for output.

EXPECTED ANNUAL ACTIVITY. A widely used basis for determining a fixed overhead rate for product costing.

EXPECTED VALUE. A weighted average of all the conditional values of an act. Each conditional value is weighted by its probability.

EXPIRED COST. A cost that should be released to the current period as an expense or loss.

FACTORY BURDEN. *See* Factory overhead.

FACTORY OVERHEAD. All factory costs other than direct labor and direct material. Also called *factory burden, indirect manufacturing costs, manufacturing overhead,* and *manufacturing expense* (the latter is a misnomer).

FEEDBACK. The data (performance reports and cost analyses) supplied by an accounting system for purposes of investigation, evaluation, and follow-up.

FINISHED GOODS INVENTORY. The cost of a manufacturer's completed product that is being held for sale.

FIXED COST. A cost which, for a given period of time and range of activity called the relevant range, does not change in *total* but becomes progressively smaller on a *per-unit* basis as volume increases.

FLEXIBLE BUDGET. A budget, usually referring to overhead costs only, which is prepared for a range, rather than for a single level of activity; one which can be automatically geared to changes in the level of volume. Also called *variable budget.* Direct materials and direct labor are sometimes included in the flexible budget.

FORECAST. In budgeting, a projection of what costs and revenues should be.

FUNCTIONAL AUTHORITY. The right to command action laterally and downward with regard to a specific function or specialty.

FUNCTIONAL COSTING. Classifying costs by allocating them to the various functions performed, such as warehousing, delivery, billing, and so forth.

HISTORICAL COST. *See* Sunk cost.

IDEAL CAPACITY. The absolute maximum number of units that could be produced in a given operating situation, with no allowance for work stoppages or repairs. Also called *theoretical capacity.*

IDLE TIME. A classification of indirect labor which constitutes wages paid for unproductive time due to circumstances beyond the worker's control.

IMPUTED COST. A cost that does not appear in conventional accounting records and does not entail dollar outlays. A common example is the inclusion of "interest" on ownership equity as a part of operating expenses.

INCREMENTAL APPROACH. In capital budgeting, a method of determining which of two alternative courses of action is preferable by calculating the present value of the difference in net cash inflow between one alternative and the other.

INCREMENTAL COST. The difference in total cost between two alternatives. Also called *differential cost* and *relevant cost.*

INDIRECT LABOR. All labor which is not specifically associated with or cannot be practically traced to specific units of output.

INDIRECT MANUFACTURING COSTS. *See* Factory overhead.

INTERNAL CHECK. The coordinated methods and measures in an organization designed to check the accuracy and validity of organization data and to safeguard assets. This definition represents parts (c) and (d) of the definition of *internal control,* a more inclusive concept.

INTERNAL CONTROL. The coordinated methods and measures in an organization designed to: (a) promote efficiency; (b) encourage adherence to prescribed management plans and policies; (c) check the accuracy and validity of organization data; and (d) safeguard assets.

INVENTORIABLE COST. A cost associated with units produced; a cost which may be looked upon as "attaching" or "clinging" to units produced.

JOB COST SHEET. *See* Job order.

JOB ORDER. The basic record for the accumulation of job costs. Also called *job cost sheet.*

JOB ORDER COSTING. A system of applying manufacturing costs to specific jobs or batches of specialized or unique production in proportion to the amounts of materials, attention, and effort used to produce each unit or group of units.

JOINT COST. A cost which is common to all the segments in question and which is not clearly or practically allocable except by some questionable allocation base. Also called *common cost.*

JOINT PRODUCT COSTS. Costs of two or more manufactured goods, of significant sales values, that are produced by a single process and that are not identifiable as individual products up to a certain stage of production known as the *split-off point.*

LEAD TIME. The time interval between placing an order and receiving delivery.

LINEAR PROGRAMMING. A mathematical approach to a group of business problems which contain many interacting variables and which basically involve combining limited resources to maximize profits or minimize costs.

LINE AUTHORITY. Authority which is exerted downward over subordinates.

MANAGED COSTS. *See* Discretionary costs.

MANAGEMENT BY EXCEPTION. The practice, by the executive, of focusing his attention mainly on significant deviations from expected results. It might also be called *management by variance.*

MANAGEMENT SCIENCE. The formulation of mathematical and statistical models applied to decision making and the practical application of these models through the use of digital computers.

MANUFACTURING EXPENSES.   *See* Factory overhead.

MANUFACTURING OVERHEAD.   *See* Factory overhead.

MARGINAL COSTING.   *See* Direct costing.

MARGINAL INCOME.   *See* Contribution margin.

MARGIN ON SALES.   The ratio of net income to sales.

MASTER BUDGET.   The budget which consolidates the organization's overall plans.

MERCHANDISE INVENTORY.   The inventory held by a retailer or wholesaler which is intended solely for resale.

MIXED COST.   A cost that has both fixed and variable elements.

NEGOTIATED MARKET PRICE.   A transfer price negotiated by the buying and selling segments when there is no market mechanism to fix a price clearly relevant to the situation.

NET PRESENT VALUE METHOD.   A method of calculating the expected utility of a given project by discounting all expected future cash flows to the present, using some predetermined minimum desired rate of return.

NORMAL ACTIVITY (NORMAL VOLUME, STANDARD VOLUME, OR STANDARD ACTIVITY).   The level of production that will satisfy average consumer demand over a span of time which includes seasonal, cyclical, and trend factors.

NORMAL CAPACITY.   *See* Normal activity.

NORMAL COSTING.   A type of product costing which applies to units produced, as costs of production, the actual direct materials consumed, the actual direct labor used, and an estimated, predetermined portion of overhead calculated on the basis of a normal or average schedule of production.

NORMAL SPOILAGE.   Spoilage expected during a production run under efficient operating conditions.

ON-LINE, REAL-TIME.   Computer compilation of information as events occur (on-line) and supplying the relevant information rapidly enough so that interested managers may exert needed control (real-time).

OPERATIONS RESEARCH (OR).   A diffused collection of mathematical and statistical models applied to decision making.

OPPORTUNITY COST.   The maximum alternative earning that might have been obtained if the productive good, service, or capacity had been applied to some alternative use.

ORDER-FILLING COST.   A marketing cost incurred in the storing, packing, shipping, billing, credit and collection, and other similar aspects of selling merchandise.

ORDER-GETTING COST.   A marketing cost incurred in the effort to attain a desired sales volume and mix.

ORDER POINT. That level of inventory which should trigger a reorder of goods. It is usually measured by the safety stock plus average usage during lead time.

ORGANIZATION CHART. A drawing of the lines of authority and responsibility in an organization.

OUT-OF-POCKET COSTS. Costs which entail current or near-future outlays for the decision at hand.

OVERABSORBED OVERHEAD. *See* Overapplied overhead.

OVERAPPLIED OVERHEAD. The excess of amount of overhead cost applied to product over the amount of overhead cost incurred. Also called *overabsorbed overhead.*

OVERTIME PREMIUM. A classification of *indirect labor costs*, consisting of the extra wages paid to *all* factory workers for overtime work.

PAYBACK. The measure of the time needed to recoup, in the form of cash inflow from operations, the initial dollars invested. Also called *payout* and *payoff.*

PAYBACK RECIPROCAL. This approximates the true rate of return when the life of the project is at least twice the payback period and when cash inflows are uniform.

PAYOFF TABLE. A convenient technique for showing the total expected value of each of a number of contemplated acts in the light of the varying probabilities of the possible events or states of nature and the varying values of each act under each of the states.

PAYOUT. *See* Payback.

PERFORMANCE REPORT. The comparison of actual results with budgeted allowances.

PERIOD COST. *See* Expired cost.

PERIODIC INVENTORY METHOD. An inventory accounting system that requires a physical count of inventory to determine the ending amounts of raw materials, work in process, and finished goods, and hence also the cost of goods sold.

PERPETUAL INVENTORY METHOD. An inventory accounting system whereby a continuous record is kept which tracks raw materials, work in process, finished goods, and cost of goods sold on a day-to-day basis.

PERT. (Program Evaluation and Review Technique). A formal probabilistic diagram of the temporal interrelationships of a complex series of activities.

PLANNING. Selecting objectives and the means for their attainment.

POPULATION (universe). A group of items or individuals from which a sample is drawn.

PRACTICAL ATTAINABLE CAPACITY. *See* Practical capacity.

PRACTICAL CAPACITY. The maximum level at which the plant or department can realistically operate most efficiently, that is, ideal capacity less allowances for unavoidable operating interruptions. Also called *practical attainable capacity.*

PRICE VARIANCE.   The difference between the actual price and the standard price, multiplied by the total number of items acquired. The term "price variance" is usually linked with direct materials; the term "rate variance," which is conceptually similar to the price variance, is usually linked with direct labor.

PRIME COST.   The sum of direct material and direct labor.

PROBLEM SOLVING.   That function of the accountant's information-supplying task which expresses in concise, quantified terms the relative advantages and disadvantages to the firm of pursuing a possible future course of action, or the relative advantages of any one of several alternative methods of operation.

PROCESS COSTING.   A method of costing products with average costs computed on the basis of total costs divided by equivalent units of work performed. Usually used in high-volume, similar-product situations.

PRODUCT COST.   *See* Inventoriable cost.

PROFITABILITY ACCOUNTING.   *See* Responsibility accounting.

PROFIT CENTER.   A segment of a business that is responsible for both revenue and expense.

PRO-FORMA STATEMENTS.   Forecasted financial statements.

PROGRAM.   A list of instructions which indicates to a computer the nature and sequence of operations it is to perform.

PROGRAMMED COSTS.   *See* Discretionary costs.

PROJECT SELECTION.   *See* Capital budgeting.

QUALITATIVE FACTOR.   A factor which is of consequence but which cannot be measured precisely and easily in dollars.

QUALITY CONTROL.   A statistical sampling application which spotlights controllable variances.

QUANTITY DISCOUNT.   A reduction in unit price inversely proportional to the size of the order. Usually constrained by the Robinson-Patman Act.

QUANTITY VARIANCE.   The standard price for a given resource, multiplied by the difference between the actual quantity used and the total standard quantity allowed for the number of good units produced.

QUOTE SHEET.   An analysis of costs used as a basis for determining selling prices.

RATE VARIANCE.   The difference between actual wage rate paid and the standard wage rate, multiplied by the total actual hours of direct labor used. *See* Price variance.

REALLOCATION (REAPPORTIONMENT). Allocation of the costs of operating the service departments to the various production departments in proportion to the relative benefits or services received by each production department.

RELATIVE SALES VALUE METHOD. A method of joint-cost assignment which assigns costs in proportion to a product's ability to generate revenue.

RELEVANT COST. *See* Incremental cost.

RELEVANT DATA FOR DECISION MAKING. Expected future data which will differ as between alternatives.

RELEVANT RANGE. The band of activity in which budgeted sales and expense relationships will be valid.

RESPONSIBILITY ACCOUNTING. A system of accounting that recognizes various responsibility centers throughout the organization and that reflects the plans and actions of each of these centers by allocating particular revenues and costs to the one having the pertinent responsibility. Also called *profitability accounting* and *activity accounting*.

RETURN ON INVESTMENT (rate of return). The most widely used single measure of a firm's operating efficiency. It is the ratio of net income to invested capital or asset turnover times margin on sales.

SAFETY STOCK. A minimum inventory that provides a cushion against reasonably expected maximum demand and against variations in lead time.

SALES MIX. The relative combination of the quantities of a variety of company products that compose total sales.

SAMPLE. A portion of a group (population or universe) chosen to estimate some characteristic of the entire group without complete examination of all the items constituting the group.

SCORE KEEPING. That data-accumulation function of the accountant's information-supplying task which enables both internal and external parties to evaluate the financial performance of the firm.

SCRAP. Residue from manufacturing operations that has measurable but relatively minor recovery value.

SEGMENT. Any line of activity or part of an organization for which separate determination of costs and/or sales is wanted.

SEGMENT CONTRIBUTION. The contribution margin for each segment less all separable fixed costs, both discretionary and committed. A measure of long-run profitability.

SEPARABLE COST. A cost directly identifiable with a particular segment.

SERVICE DEPARTMENTS. Those departments that exist solely to aid the production departments by rendering specialized assistance with certain phases of the work.

SHORT-RUN PERFORMANCE MARGIN. The contribution margin for each segment, less separable discretionary costs.

SHUTDOWN COST.   A fixed cost which continues to be incurred even when there is no activity (production).

SOURCE DOCUMENT.   The original record of any transaction, internal or external, which occurs in the firm's operation.

SPENDING VARIANCE.   Basically, a price variance applied to variable overhead. However, other factors besides prices may influence the amount of the variance.

SPLIT-OFF POINT.   That point in a production process where goods with joint costs are separated.

STAFF AUTHORITY.   The authority to *advise* but not to command; may be exerted laterally or upward.

STANDARD ABSORPTION COSTING.   That type of product costing in which the cost of the finished unit is calculated as the sum of the standard manufacturing costs, *including* fixed overhead, without reference to the costs actually incurred.

STANDARD COST.   A carefully predetermined cost that should be attained. Usually expressed per unit.

STANDARD DIRECT COSTING.   That type of product costing in which the cost of the finished unit is calculated as the sum of the costs of the *standard allowances* for the factors of production, *excluding* fixed factory overhead, which is treated as a period cost, and without reference to the costs actually incurred.

STANDARD HOURS ALLOWED (earned or worked).   The number of standard hours that are chargeable to production for the actual goods produced.

STATIC BUDGET.   A budget prepared for only one level of activity and, consequently, one which does not adjust automatically to changes in the level of volume.

STEP-VARIABLE COSTS.   Those variable costs which change abruptly at intervals of activity because their acquisition comes in indivisible chunks.

SUNK COST.   A cost which has already been incurred and which, therefore, is irrelevant to the decision-making process. Also called *historical cost*.

TAX SHIELD.   The amount of depreciation charged against income, thus protecting that amount from tax.

THEORETICAL CAPACITY.   *See* Ideal capacity.

TIME-ADJUSTED RATE OF RETURN.   The rate of interest at which the present value of expected cash inflow from a particular project equals the present value of expected cash outflow of that same project.

TOTAL PROJECT APPROACH.   A method of comparing two or more alternative courses of action by computing the total expected cash inflows and outflows of each alternative and then converting these flows to their present value by applying some predetermined minimum rate of return.

TRANSFER PRICE.   The price charged by one segment of an organization for a product or service which it supplies to another segment of the same organization.

UNADJUSTED RATE OF RETURN.   An expression of the utility of a given project as the ratio of the increase in future average annual net income to the initial increase in required investment. Also called *book value method* and *accounting method.*

UNDERABSORBED OVERHEAD.   *See* Underapplied overhead.

UNDERAPPLIED OVERHEAD.   The excess of the amount of overhead cost incurred over the amount of overhead cost applied. Also called *underabsorbed overhead.*

UNEXPIRED COST.   A cost which may be properly carried forward to future periods as an asset measure.

UNIT COST.   A total cost divided by some related base, such as labor hours, machine-hours, or units of product.

USAGE VARIANCE.   *See* Quantity variance.

VARIABLE BUDGET.   *See* Flexible budget.

VARIABLE COST.   A cost which is uniform *per unit,* but which fluctuates *in total* in direct proportion to changes in the related total activity or volume.

VARIABLE COSTING.   *See* Direct costing.

VARIANCE.   The deviation of actual results from the expected or budgeted result.

WORK IN PROCESS INVENTORY.   The cost of uncompleted goods still on the production line.

Index

Note: See also the glossary, pages 943–953